CONCRETE 2000

Economic and durable construction through excellence

VOLUME TWO
INFRASTRUCTURE, RESEARCH,
NEW APPLICATIONS

Other Books on Materials and Structures from E & FN Spon

Alternative Materials for the Reinforcement and Prestressing of Concrete
Edited by J.L. Clarke

Calcium Aluminate Cements
Edited by R.G. Mangabhai

Corrosion of Steel in Concrete
Edited by P. Schiessl

Design of Prestressed Concrete
R.I. Gilbert and N.C. Mickelborough

Durability of Building Materials and Components
Edited by J.M. Baker, P.J. Nixon, A.J. Majumdar and H. Davies

Durability of Concrete Structures: Investigation, Repair and Protection
Edited by G.C. Mays

Fibre Reinforced Cement and Concrete
Edited by R.N. Swamy

High Performance Concrete: From Material to Structure
Edited by Y. Malier

Hydration and Setting of Cements
Edited by A. Nonat and J-C. Mutin

Manual of Ready-Mixed Concrete
J. D. Dewar and R. Anderson

Monitoring Building Structures
Edited by J.F.A. Moore

Properties of Concrete
Edited by H.J. Wierig

Protection of Concrete
Edited by R.K. Dhir and J.W. Green

Recycling of Demolished Concrete and Masonry
Edited by T.C. Hansen

Reinforced Concrete: Design Theory and Examples
T.J. MacGinley and B.S. Choo

Rheology of Fresh Cement and Concrete
Edited by P.F.G. Banfill

Structural Grouts
Edited by P.L.J. Domone and S.A. Jefferis

Testing During Concrete Construction
Edited by H.W. Reinhardt

Test Quality for Construction, Materials and Structures
Edited by M. Fickelson

The Design Life of Structures
Edited by G. Somerville

Workability and Quality Control of Concrete
G.H. Tattersall

For details of these and other titles, contact the Promotions Department, E & FN Spon, 2–6 Boundary Row, London SE1 8HN, Tel: 071-865 0066

CONCRETE 2000

Economic and durable construction through excellence

Proceedings of the International Conference
held at the University of Dundee, Scotland, UK
on 7–9 September 1993

Edited by

Ravindra K. Dhir
Director, Concrete Technology Unit,
University of Dundee

and

M. Roderick Jones
Lecturer in Concrete Technology,
University of Dundee

VOLUME TWO
INFRASTRUCTURE, RESEARCH,
NEW APPLICATIONS

E & FN SPON
An Imprint of Chapman & Hall
London · Glasgow · New York · Tokyo · Melbourne · Madras

Published by E & FN Spon, an imprint of Chapman & Hall,
2–6 Boundary Row, London SE1 8HN

Chapman & Hall, 2–6 Boundary Row, London SE1 8HN, UK

Blackie Academic & Professional, Wester Cleddens Road, Bishopbriggs,
Glasgow G64 2NZ, UK

Chapman & Hall Inc., 29 West 35th Street, New York NY10001, USA

Chapman & Hall Japan, Thomson Publishing Japan, Hirakawacho
Nemoto Building, 6F, 1-7-11 Hirakawa-cho, Chiyoda-ku, Tokyo 102,
Japan

Chapman & Hall Australia, Thomas Nelson Australia, 102 Dodds Street,
South Melbourne, Victoria 3205, Australia

Chapman & Hall India, R. Seshadri, 32 Second Main Road, CIT East,
Madras 600 035, India

First edition 1993

© 1993 Chapman & Hall

Printed in Great Britain at the University Press, Cambridge

ISBN 0 419 19000 7   0 419 18120 2 (set)

A catalogue record for this book is available from the British Library

Library of Congress Cataloging-in-Publication data available

∞

Printed on acid-free text paper, manufactured in accordance
with ANSI/NISO Z 39.48-1992 and ANSI Z 39.48-1984
(Permanence of Paper)

Publisher's Note

This book has been compiled from camera ready copy provided by the
individual contributors. This method of production has allowed us to supply
finished copies to the delegates at the Conference.

PREFACE

As the year 2000 approaches, it could be said that concrete has served well, but not without problems. Much is changing in the perception of concrete and the understanding of material performance and construction methods. At the same time, ever greater demands are being placed on concrete, which must be met without cost penalty. It could be argued that revolution rather than evolution will be necessary to achieve excellence in the 21st century, exploiting the full potential of materials and methods.

The Concrete Technology Unit (CTU) of the University of Dundee has organised this 3 day International Conference, following the Protection of Concrete held in 1990, as part of its continuing commitment to excellence in concrete construction. The main objective was to provide a unique opportunity to discuss and present methods of achieving the highest quality of concrete construction technology and practice for the coming century; whilst achieving economy and durability together.

In total, 161 papers were presented from over 40 countries worldwide. The Conference Proceedings were organised in six Themes covering a wide subject area, including research and development of new and traditional materials, trends in design and specification, novel construction techniques, infrastructure and new applications.

The Opening Addresses were given by the Rt. Hon. Ian Lang MP, the Secretary of State for Scotland and Professor Michael Hamlin, Principal and Vice-Chancellor of the University of Dundee, who introduced the Conference and welcomed the delegates. The Keynote Paper was presented by Professor Peter Hewlett, Director of the British Board of Agrément. The closing address was given by Dr Tom Harrison, Technical Director of the British Ready Mixed Concrete Association.

A Conference of this size and scope was a considerable undertaking. It benefitted from having excellent International Advisory and Technical Committees, who advised on the selection and review of the papers. Seven major institutions supported the Conference together with twenty Sponsors and fifty Exhibitors, highlighting the need to look forward to the challenges of the next century and the close cooperation between the CTU and industry.

The Organisers would like to acknowledge the efforts of the Authors and Chairmen of the various Technical Sessions and, in particular, those who travelled from afar to come to Dundee. The Organisers also wish to thank all the CTU staff and research students and the University's supporting services for their sterling efforts.

It was gratifying to have so many papers on this important subject and editing the two volumes of these Proceedings has been a enormous task. The Editors would like to make special mention of the help of Mr Steven Scott. The Proceedings have been prepared from the manuscripts provided by the Authors and whilst every effort has been made to remove any errors or inaccuracies the Editors apologise for any which may have been inadvertently overlooked.

Dundee   Ravindra K Dhir
September 1993   M Roderick Jones

ORGANISING COMMITTEE

Professor Ravindra K Dhir (Chairman)
Unit Director

Dr Michael J McCarthy (Secretary)
Manager, CPD Courses

Professor Peter C Hewlett
Visiting Industrial Professor

Dr Frederick H Hubbard
Senior Lecturer

Dr M Roderick Jones
Lecturer

Dr Ewan A Byars
Lecturer

Mr Jasbir S Lota
Research Fellow

Mr Steven R Scott
Unit Assistant

Mrs Ann Robertson
Mrs Karen Evans
Unit Secretaries

Concrete Technology Unit
Department of Civil Engineering
University of Dundee

INTERNATIONAL ADVISORY COMMITTEE

TECHNICAL COMMITTEE
(from United Kingdom)

Mr Bev V Brown
Divisional Technical Executive, RMC Technical Services Ltd

Dr Roger D Browne
Assistant Managing Director, Taywood Engineering Ltd

Mr Michael A Courtney
Director, Ove Arup & Partners

Mr Peter M Deason
Managing Director, Trafalgar House Technology

Professor Ravindra K Dhir (Chairman)
Director, Concrete Technology Unit, University of Dundee

Professor Peter C Hewlett
Director, British Board of Agrément

Dr M Roderick Jones
Lecturer in Concrete Technology, University of Dundee

Dr Michael J McCarthy (Secretary)
Research/Teaching Fellow, University of Dundee

Mr Laurence H McCurrich
Technical Director, Fosroc International Ltd

Dr John F A Moore
Head, Construction Technology Division, Department of the Environment

Dr Derek J Pollock
Director, Sir William Halcrow & Partners

Dr David C Spooner
Director, Materials and Standards, British Cement Association

Dr Howard P J Taylor
Technical Director, Costain Building Products

SUPPORTING BODIES

American Concrete Institute

British Board of Agrément

Concrete Society

Institution of Civil Engineers

Institute of Concrete Technology

Institution of Structural Engineers

Royal Institute of British Architects

SPONSORING ORGANISATIONS

Allied Bar Coaters

AMEC Civil Engineering

Blue Circle Cement

British Board of Agrément

British Cement Association

Cormix Construction Chemicals Ltd

Feb Ltd

Fosroc International Ltd

Frodingham Cement Company Ltd

JMP Consultants Ltd

Lafarge Special Cements

G Maunsell and Partners

National Ash, National Power plc

Pozament Ltd

Pozzolanic Lytag Ltd

Ready Mixed Concrete (UK) Ltd

Rugby Cement

Scottish Power plc - Ash Sales

Scottish Pozament Ltd

Trafalgar House Construction

EXHIBITORS

Advantage Precast
Allied Bar Coaters
AMEC Civil Engineering
Ash Resources Ltd
W S Atkins Engineering Software
Babtie Group
David Ball Group plc
Blue Circle Cement
Britflex Ltd
British Board of Agrément
British Cement Association
Building Research Establishment
Castle Cement Ltd
Cem-FIL International Ltd
CIS Construction Products Ltd
Civil & Marine Slag Cement Ltd
Colebrand Ltd
Cormix Construction Chemicals Ltd
ECC International Ltd
Elkem Materials Ltd
W A Fairhurst and Partners
Feb Ltd
Fosroc Expandite Ltd
Frodingham Cement Company Ltd

EXHIBITORS (Continued)

Haswell Consulting Engineers

International Composites Ltd

JMP Consultants Ltd

Lafarge Special Cements

G Maunsell and Partners

McCalls Special Products

McKenzie Construction Ltd

National Ash, National Power plc

Pozament Ltd

Pozzolanic Lytag Ltd

The Quality Scheme for Ready Mixed Concrete

RBR Scotland Ltd

Ready Mixed Concrete (UK) Ltd

Research Engineers (Europe) Ltd

Rugby Cement

Scottish Power plc - Ash Sales (3 stands)

Scottish Pozament Ltd

Seament UK

E & FN Spon

STATS Group of Companies

Tarmac Topmix Ltd

Trafalgar House Construction

Transport Research Laboratory (2 stands)

CONTENTS

OPENING ADDRESSES

Chairman   Professor R K Dhir, University of Dundee, United Kingdom

Opening of the Conference
Rt. Hon. Ian Lang MP, Secretary of State for Scotland

Welcoming the Delegates to the University
Professor Michael J Hamlin, Principal and Vice-Chancellor, University of Dundee

VOLUME ONE:
DESIGN, MATERIALS, CONSTRUCTION

THEME 1   NEW TRENDS IN SPECIFICATION AND DESIGN

Chairmen   Professor C Bob, Technical University, Timisoara, Romania
              Professor G Fagurlund, University of Lund, Sweden
              Professor R H Mills, University of Toronto, Canada
              Dr D C Spooner, British Cement Association, United Kingdom
              Dr H P J Taylor, Costain Building Products Ltd, United Kingdom
              Mr E Walter, Hilti Aktiengesellschaft, Liechtenstein

THEME 2 EFFICIENT CONCRETE PRODUCTION
AND NEW MATERIALS

Chairmen   Dr K van Breugel, Delft University of Technology, The Netherlands
Dr M R Jones, University of Dundee, United Kingdom
Professor P V Krivenko, Civil Engineering Institute, Ukraine
Professor G F Loedolff, University of Stellenbosch, South Africa
Dr K Tuutti, Cementa AB, Sweden
Professor F H Wittmann, Institute for Buidling Materials, Switzerland

THEME 3 CONSTRUCTION TECHIQUES

Chairmen Professor C Andradé, Institute of Construction Sciences, Spain
Mr W B Butler, Rocla Construction Materials, Australia
Professor P C Hewlett, British Board of Agrément, United Kingdom
Professor P G Lowe, University of Auckland, New Zealand
Dr D J Pollock, Sir William Halcrow & Partners Ltd, United Kingdom
Professor Z Rusin, Kielce University of Technology, Poland

xix

VOLUME TWO:
INFRASTRUCTURE, RESEARCH, NEW APPLICATIONS

THEME 4   INFRASTRUCTURE

Chairmen   Mr B V Brown, Ready Mixed Concrete (UK) Ltd, United Kingdom
Professor H G Meyer, Institut für Bautechnik, Germany
Mr L H McCurrich, Fosroc International Ltd, United Kingdom
Professor T S Nagaraj, Indian Institute of Science, India
Dr A Ogawa, Ohmotogumi Co Ltd, Japan
Professor A Samarin, Boral Resources Pty Ltd, Australia

THEME 5 RESEARCH, DEVELOPMENT AND EDUCATION

Chairmen Mr G S Adam, Chairman, The Concrete Society, Scotland
Dr R D Browne, Taywood Engineering Ltd, United Kingdom
Dr H C Chan, University of Hong Kong, Hong Kong
Mr J F Lamond, Joseph F Lamond P.E., United States of America
Professor D M F Orr, University College, Eire
Professor H B Sun, Zhejiang University of Technology, China

THEME 6   NEW APPLICATIONS - THE FUTURE

Chairmen   Dr D H Bager, Aalborg Portland A/S, Denmark
Dr W J Harvey, University of Dundee, United Kingdom
Professor M Kawamura, Kanazawa University, Japan
Professor A A Sagüés, University of South Florida, USA
Professor P Spinelli, University of Florence, Italy
Mr M Wiig, AAS-JAKOBSEN A.S., Norway

ADDITIONAL PAPERS

CLOSING ADDRESS

Chairman	Professor P C Hewlett, Director
	British Board of Agrément, United Kingdom
Presented by	*Dr Tom A Harrison, Technical Director*
	British Ready Mixed Concrete Association

INFRASTRUCTURE

Chairmen   **Mr B V Brown**
Ready Mixed Concrete (UK) Ltd, United Kingdom

Professor H G Meyer
Institut für Bautechnik, Germany

Mr L H McCurrich
Fosroc International Ltd, United Kingdom

Professor T S Nagaraj
Indian Institute of Science, India

Dr A Ogawa
Ohmotogumi Co Ltd, Japan

Professor A Samarin
Boral Resources Pty Ltd, Australia

THE QUEEN ELIZABETH II BRIDGE

P M Deason

Trafalgar House Technology

M Miller

A Nicklinson

Trafalgar House Construction

United Kingdom

ABSTRACT. When opened in October 1992 the Queen Elizabeth II Bridge was the longest Cable Stayed Bridge in Europe. Although utilising steel for the composite decks the project nonetheless required 165000m³ of concrete, all of which used low heat Portland cement, with up to 70% ground granulated blastfurnace slag. After describing the background and salient features of the project the paper looks at the application of Quality Management to the design and construct process. The paper concludes by describing the concrete mix specifications and designs, their use in a variety of construction elements, and the control of their quality. The project demonstrates that concrete and the benefits a Quality Management System can deliver a quality product which is easy to construct and cost effective. The project was Highly Commended in the 1992 Concrete Society Awards.

Keywords: Quality Management, low heat Portland cement (LHPC), ground granulated blastfurnace slag (GGBS), Durability, Design and Construct.

Mr Peter M Deason is Managing Director of Trafalgar House Technology, and was project Director for the substructure design of the Queen Elizabeth II Bridge. He has significant experience of Design and Construct Projects, and specialises in solving soil–structure interaction problems. He is chairman of Trafalgar House Construction Working Party on Design & Build.

Mr Michael Miller CEng MICE FIQA, is Quality Systems Manager for Trafalgar House Construction (MP). He became involved in the implementation of quality management systems, particularly in the construction industry, after gaining broad experience of civil engineering design and construction with both Consulting Engineers and Civil Engineering Contractors.

Mr Tony Nicklinson I.Eng AMICE MICT, is Company Materials Engineer for Trafalgar House Construction (MP). His work over the last twenty years has embraced most aspects of heavy civil engineering, both in the UK and overseas. He has extensive experience managing site laboratories for materials testing within a quality assured environment.

Concrete 2000. Edited by Ravindra K. Dhir and M. Roderick Jones.
© 1993 Published by E & FN Spon. ISBN 0 419 18120 2.

INTRODUCTION

On 30 October 1991, the Queen Elizabeth II Bridge spanning the River Thames between Thurrock and Dartford was opened by Her Majesty The Queen.

The project included approximately 165000m³ of reinforced and un-reinforced concrete. This was the responsibility of THC under a D&C contract. The entire process, including the design by Trafalgar House Technology, was conducted within a quality assurance environment.

A large part of the success of the project is due to the speed of construction afforded by concrete, and the benefits of a Quality Management System.

THE PROJECT

The crossing is an 812m long cable-stayed bridge, comprising a 450m long main span, 118m backspans and approach viaducts of 1051m and 1008m. The viaduct and bridge decks are of composite steel and concrete construction, and the sub-structure is a mixture of structural reinforced concrete and mass concrete for the main pier foundations.

Queen Elizabeth II Bridge

Each main pier comprised a cellular reinforced concrete caisson which was slipformed, floated into place and sunk onto a prepared rock blanket. Unreinforced concrete was tremied into place to provide the necessary mass to resist ship impact, after which a reinforced concrete cap was constructed to enable the twin pier legs to be slipformed.

The other marine foundations were formed within cofferdams plugged with unreinforced concrete, but employed similar structural caps and hollow piers. Landside pier foundations utilised 750mm diameter continuous flight auger piles with a working capacity of 300 tonnes, incorporated into reinforced concrete pile caps. The hollow section viaduct piers were cast in 5m lifts, and the reinforcement and formwork for the crosshead were fabricated on the ground and placed in a single 50 tonne lift ready to receive concrete.

QUALITY MANAGEMENT

The contract required the project to be constructed under an ISO 9000 Quality Management System. The Contractor embraced this requirement enthusiastically, and used it as a proactive management tool for both the design and construction phases. This resulted in cost savings through fewer errors, a much reduced Client inspection team, and a 'build it once' attitude by all engaged on the project.

Design Control

The Designer's Quality Plan was in two parts. The first set out the design brief, the lines of communication and responsibility, and the administrative and document control procedures. The second set out the technical plan against which the technical quality was controlled. The Contract required the preparation of a Preliminary Design Statement. This formed the basis of the technical plan and followed the Department of Transport TA1 – "Technical Approval in Principle" – format. It included a list of all design standards, set out the overall geometry and leading dimensions of the project, the loading requirements, the proposed methods of analysis and salient design parameters. The systems were kept simple. The requirement for a Category 3 design check by an independent Consulting Engineer was deemed to provide significant assurance regarding the adequacy of the design and compliance with the required standards. Both the designer and checker were required to sign Design Certificates confirming compliance with the requirements of the preliminary design statement. The design activities were subject to quality audits both internally and by the Contractor.

Construction Control

The Construction phase was also controlled through a Quality Plan, which set out the policy on quality, detailed the project organization, defined the responsibilities of the different levels of management, outlined the quality systems relevant to each of the applicable ISO criteria and listed the procedures applicable to the project. The procedures for each site activity , supported by Method Statements, were prepared by the Manager responsible and detailed "who" was responsible for "what" and "how", "where" and "when". A section in each procedure included examples of the records, which when completed during implementation, provided the objective evidence of compliance.

All work items were checked by a member of the construction team who was independent of the work to be checked.

All suppliers and subcontractors were assessed to ensure they operated acceptable quality systems. Those companies not implementing a quality system were either required to comply with the Contractor's system or were helped to establish their own. Where a supplier could demonstrate he had a Certificate of Approval from a recognised Certification body, this was accepted as evidence that he was implementing an acceptable quality system, and no assessment of that supplier's quality system was undertaken. All suppliers and subcontractors, however, were subject to audit during their production of materials or work for the contract.

Control Of Concrete Construction

Prior to concrete placement each pour was subject to a pre–concreting inspection. The batch plant was not permitted to batch concrete for a pour until a copy of the relevant completed "Pre–concreting Inspection Checklist" had been received.

Concrete delivered to a pour was subject to routine inspection and test, in accordance with the requirements of the Specification and was documented by laboratory staff on an "In–process Concreting Checklist".

Each completed concrete pour was subject to a post–concreting inspection, which was recorded. When any defect in workmanship was identified, it was marked and a "Nonconformance Report" raised. Designers' approval was sought and recorded for any solution to the problem that affected a change to the specified product or tolerances.

Monitoring The Construction Quality Management System

Work activities were subject to surveillances were documented and copied to project senior management. This assisted in all functions understanding procedural requirements, and was an effective means of determining compliance with the requirements of procedures and method statements.

All procedures were audited at least once and were re–audited at least annually. Some procedures were audited more frequently, especially when deficiencies had been identified during a previous audit. The formal reporting of audits to senior management ensured that they could be involved in appropriate corrective action when necessary.

Design & Construction Planning

The Design and Build approach permitted a close integration of the Design and Construction. A Project team manager was appointed by the Contractor at the outset, and he and his team worked with the Designer, and with specialist subcontractors, to ensure the design was harmonised with the most effective construction methods.

Examples of the influence of this close liaison were numerous. Pylon heights and caisson founding depths were designed to suit the limits of the proposed construction plant. Caissons were detailed to suit the available dry dock and construction methods. The pier legs were designed to suit the jump shutter modules or slipforming methods as appropriate. Where necessary, trials were conducted to check the viability or optimise the chosen solutions.

The result was a design which was constructed at a remarkable speed by any measure and yet maintained high quality standards.

Concrete Specifications

The Specifications, based upon the Department of Transport's Specification for Road and Bridge Works 1976, and particularly those for concrete materials, were considered at a very early stage by the Designer and the Contractor.

With a design life of 120 years, the durability of the concrete was of prime concern. The decision was taken to specify low heat Portland blastfurnace cement for all concrete because of its superior properties compared to Portland cement concrete. These properties included reduced risk of early age thermal cracking, reduced permeability, reduced susceptibility to the ingress of chlorides and sulphates, superior long–term strength gain over the equivalent all–PC grade, and enhanced appearance.

The use of 70% ground granulated blastfurnace slag was checked for its influence on the construction process, as it was considered by some to be potentially disadvantageous. This was found not to be the case, and two significant advantages were identified. First, a reduction in crack control reinforcement was possible with attendant cost savings, and second, the basic price of concrete was reduced.

The Specifications and mix designs for the concrete materials used are given in Tables 1, 2 and 3.

Table 1 – Material Specifications

Material	Standard	Title
Aggregates	BS 882	Aggregate for concrete from natural sources
Cementitious Materials	BS 12	Ordinary Portland Cement
	BS 6699	Specification for ground granulated blastfurnace slag for use with Portland Cement
Admixture	BS 5075	Concrete admixtures

Table 2 – Principal Concrete Mixes

Mix Ref.	Grade	Design Slump(mm)	Purpose	Test Rate (m³)
M4	C20	175	Underwater concrete for foundations with 12–24 hours' retardation	200
M6	C20*	150	Mass infill to caissons, above water	200
M7	C20*	175	Mass infill to caissons, underwater	200
R2	C30	75	Landside piers and crossheads	10
R4	C40	75	Landside pile caps	100
R13	C40	75	Marine pier foundation bases	100
R16	C40	75	Marine piers and crossheads	10
R16S	C40	**	Marine piers for slipforming	10
R17	C45	75	Deck parapet	10
R20	C40	75	Viaduct deck	20
C35+P4	C35	175	CFA piles to Class 3 sulphates	5

Notes :   *   indicates compliance at 90 days
          ** indicates that workability was adjusted to suit the slipforming

Table 3 – Nominal Mix Designs

Mix Ref.	Mass per m³ of oven–dry materials						Free W/C
	PC	GGBS	20mm	10mm	Sand	Admixture	
M4	120	280	690	300	806	1.120	0.50
M6	86	199	709	304	852	0.800	0.65
M7	90	210	712	305	837	0.840	0.60
R2	99	231	729	318	816	0.920	0.53
R4	126	294	735	316	725	1.180	0.42
R13	123	287	727	312	723	1.120	0.58
R16	114	266	735	316	765	1.060	0.44
R16S	114	266	735	316	765	1.060	0.46
R17	220	220	729	312	692	1.230	0.40
R20	114	266	733	316	765	1.060	0.46
C35+P4	126	294	638	312	841	1.176	0.42

CONCRETE CONSTRUCTION TECHNIQUES

The construction employed a mixture of traditional techniques and innovative processes and developments. These processes included CFA piling, Large volume pours, Underwater concreting, Conventional reinforced concreting, Slipformed concrete, and grouting under water.

The CFA Piling was conventional in that the specialist subcontractor, Cementation Piling and Foundations Limited, undertakes this type of piling as a matter of routine. It was however the first use of CFA piles on a Department of Transport project, and the full depth reinforcement cages were the longest so far used in this pile type. Further considerations in the selection of the concrete mix were the presence of sulphates and the poor ground. Grade C35 concrete was chosen using 70% GGBS to resist Class 3 sulphates in accordance with BRE Digest 363. The workability was high at 175mm slump, and the reinforcement cages were specially designed to facilitate their insertion. To demonstrate that satisfactory piles could be constructed using this technique, two test piles were extracted from the ground. Inspection revealed that they were satisfactory, with the specified cover maintained to the reinforcement. The piling rigs were fully instrumented to measure concrete flows and pressures and to control the rate of auger extraction. All piles were integrity tested, and horizontal and vertical load tests conducted on selected piles.

Large Volume Pours were a feature of the Project, and ranged from 500m³ for pile caps for the viaduct to some 2500m³ for the marine pier S2.   The potential for early–age thermal cracking was of greatest concern for the smaller pile cap pours, so the early pours were monitored by multi–channel data loggers to record the temperature histories.ʼ This enabled the duration of curing to to be determined, and provided the necessary documentary evidence that the Specification limit of 20°C difference between the maximum and minimum concrete temperatures, applicable to the flint aggregate used was met.   Figure 1 illustrates the temperature history of a 150m³ pile cap using mix R13 it will be seen that the maximum temperature difference, which occurred a little under three days after casting, was maintained within the 20°C limit.

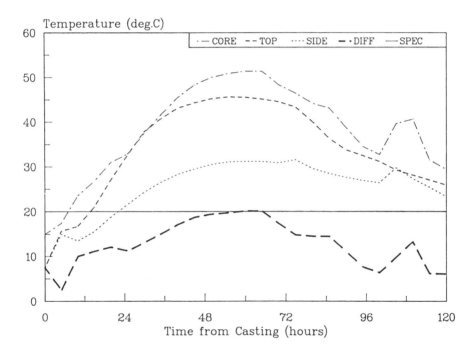

Figure 1 Temperature History of Pile Cap, 150m³ 70% GGBS

Underwater Concreting was of great importance for both foundation construction within the cofferdams, and infilling the main pier caissons.   The technique for the caissons was straightforward tremie placement of a high workability mix, but for the cofferdams, a more innovative technique was used.   The large plan area of the cofferdams required that a mix be designed to flow without segregation for up to 50m, be self–compacting and retarded for a minimum of 12 hours.   Extensive laboratory and field trials were conducted by the Site Laboratory prior to construction.   The Hop Dobber technique was selected and proved to work very well.

Full depth cores of 7m were taken from the first pour, and examination showed an excellent concrete had been produced, with uniform distribution of aggregate and no evidence of either mortar loss or silt infiltration.

Conventional reinforced concrete was used for the viaduct pier lifts and crossheads. The programme, however, required a concreting cycle for the pier lifts of 48 hours, and the concrete was required to have an in-situ strength of at least 7.5N/mm² before the proprietary timber formwork could be cantilevered from the top of the previous lift. It was therefore necessary to have objective evidence that this strength had been attained before the formwork could be struck and re-positioned. The Site Laboratory devised a maturity-based procedure for estimating the in-situ strength which proved very successful, and has since been further refined by the THC and applied to other contracts. The procedure required a number of test cubes to be cast and cured in the laboratory at a range of temperatures embracing those anticipated on Site. The maturity of each cube, using Sadgrove's Function, was calculated at the time of test, and the resultant strength-maturity relationship plotted. The data was analysed by linear regression over a narrow range of strength, and a high correlation was obtained, illustrated by Figure 2 for mix R20. This procedure gave results which compared favourably with TMC, and was instrumental in achieving the planned 48 hour cycle.

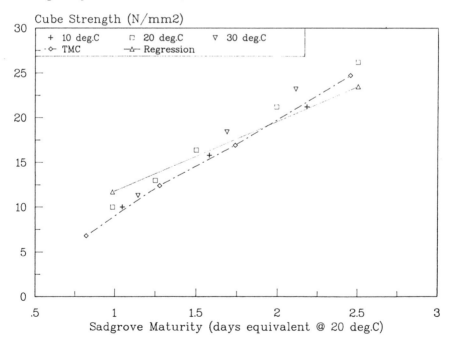

**Figure 2 Strength – Maturity Relationship Compared
Temperature Matched Curing, 50% GGBS**

Slipformed Concrete was used for constructing the eight marine piers, the first starting in February 1989 on Pier S4.   It is understood that this was the first time that a 70% GGBS mix had been used for slipforming, and there was natural concern that the required rate of climb of the shutter would not be met in winter.   This was found not to be the case.   Aided by protective skirts to the underside of the formwork and intensive temperature monitoring the programmed rate of climb was achieved.   Close control of the workability and admixture dosage was required, and specific procedures were developed for the necessary control.   On one occasion, the procedures were not adhered to resulting in an admixture overdose.   The control procedures were immediately reviewed and the necessary amendments made to prevent a recurrence of the problem.

Grouting was an integral part of the caisson installation.   The caissons were sunk onto a granular bed prepared to a tolerance of -100mm to $+0$mm.   The design required filling the gap between the bed and underside of the caisson with grout to provide a shear key to resist ship impact.   The caisson itself was designed with a grooved downstand around and across the perimeter of the base.

A circular canvas tube hung from these grooves and when filled with a cementitious grout under pressure, expanded and provided a continuous seal between the concrete above and the granular bed below.   Once this seal was effected, further grouting took place through access pipes cast into the base to expel the entrapped water.

Following laboratory trials by the inhouse Research and Development Centre a large mock-up was constructed at the Site Laboratory to prove the grout mix. As a result of extensive trials, the mix was refined and techniques perfected prior to the permanent work commencing.   Although some further modifications to the techniques developed at the trial were necessary, the caissons were securely grouted to the river bed.

APPLICATION OF QUALITY CONTROL

The Contractor was responsible for all compliance testing, and a fully-equipped Site Laboratory was established to undertake basic soil, aggregate and concrete testing.   The laboratory was managed by a Materials Engineer reporting directly to the Project Chief Engineer under the functional responsibility of the Company Materials Engineer at the Head Office.

It was recognised at an early stage in the planning of the Project that gaining the confidence of the companies whose materials were to be tested was crucial if the laboratory was to be seen as impartial.   To this end suppliers were often brought to the laboratory to observe and in some instances participate in the testing.

In addition to THC trials and the specified compliance testing, the Laboratory also undertook additional quality control testing.   Examples included exercises to examine the relationship between water/cement ratio and slump as part of the approval process, and extensive sampling and testing of aggregates and quarry materials for uses such as scour protection.

The sampling and testing of concrete for compliance was based on BS 5328:1981, and each pour was attended by an experienced technician, who assessed whether to test for workability more frequently than the specified rate. All concrete, a significant proportion of which was batched on site, was produced under QSRMC Technical Regulations.

A computer system developed previously for the Materials Department was installed in the Site Laboratory. This enabled the majority of test results including calculations to be reported in a standard format, and archived in electronic rather than hard copy form. The software also enabled statistical analysis of data and the printing of comprehensive summaries of concrete sampling and testing, which was an important element of the control exercised over concreting operations.

In addition to checking results for compliance with BS 5328, all compliance cubes from the principal mixes were analysed for trends by plotting the mean strength and target mean strength, based on the standard deviation of these data on a moving average of 40 results. The laboratory's approach, based on single mixes with many more results available, was found to be more sensitive to changes in strength than the suppliers' "cusum" control. For example, results in the summer of 1990 indicated that the R17 mix was going out of control as illustrated by Figure 3.

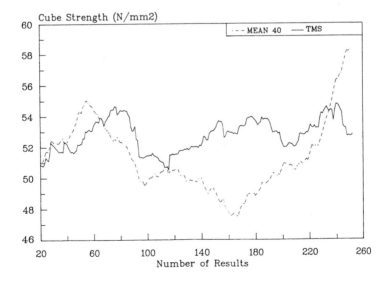

**Figure 3 Analysis of Compliance Cubes
for Trends, Mix R17/C45S**

To correct the situation, the initial action was to increase the total cementitious content by 20kg/m³, (at result number 100) and then to change the GGBS content from 70% to 50% and increase the plasticiser content by some 40% (at result number 190).

This situation lasted from mid–June to the end of September, and a number of BS 5328 failures were recorded, as had been predicted by the Site Laboratory. One of the reasons for the length of time taken to correct the mix was that the suppliers' 'cusums' did not indicate the same trend.   They were therefore reluctant to incur increased costs until satisfied that this course of action was necessary.   Amendments to the QSRMC Technical Regulations to improve the supplier's control have now made this situation less likely.

An important aspect of the applied quality control was the ability to analyse easily concrete data from individual conrete plants. The north and south of the river were river were served by their own plants, but it frequently occurred that pours included concrete from both plants. It was intended that all plants used common mix designs, but it was discovered that the southern plant, using aggregates from a different supplier, needed to use a higher cementitious content than the northern plants, even though the cement source was common to both.

The regime applied analysed each principal mix, irrespective of plant source. It a trend occured which showed a significant deviation of the mean from the TMS, the data was re–analysed on a plant by plant basis to determine the relative effect of each. For illustration of this point, Figures 4 and 5 show the performance of the R17 mix described above over the same time period.   It will be seen that the southern plants were not only lower in strength than the north side, but contributed far more to the problem identified by the overall analysis.

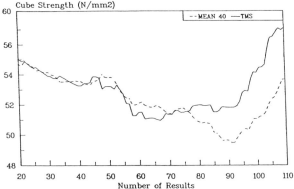

**Figure 4 Analysis of Compliance Cubes
for Mix R17/C45, North Side Plants**

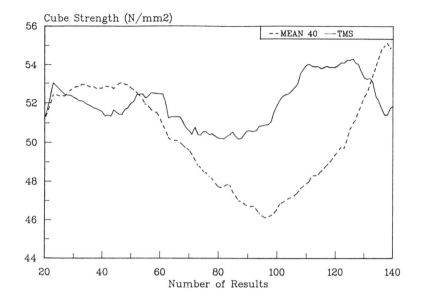

**Figure 5 Analysis of Compliance Cubes
for Mix R17/C45, South Side Plants**

CONCLUSIONS

The Project has been highly successful, receiving a number of prestigious construction awards. The combination of concrete and the benefits of a Quality Management System has been shown to deliver a quality product which is easy to construct and cost effective.

The Design and Construction procurement route has many critics, but the success of this project demonstrates clearly that with the right skills and attitude it can offer the Client a number of advantages in terms of time and cost, while maintaining high quality standards.

The 165,000m³ of concrete, including the complex marine foundations, were placed in 17 months and the whole of construction was completed in 38 months.

Key factors in achieving this success were:

o The close working relationship between Designer and Contractor throughout the Contract
o The pro-active use of the Quality Management Systems
o The close attention to detail paid to the Specification, placing and testing of the concrete from the outset
o The careful planning of the construction methods, with pre-construction trials where appropriate and the calculated use of new techniques

NEW BRIDGES FOR HIGH-SPEED TRAINS

G König
R Grimm
M Zink
Technical University Darmstadt

Germany

ABSTRACT. Building new bridges for high-speed trains will be an important task for structural engineering in the next years. The bridges of the new German lines built in the eighties still leave room for improvements. The appearence of the single-cell box girders is determined by the slenderness ratio of length / height = 11. By starting the design with the minimum stiffness, an optimum in girder height is achieved and aesthetics is improved. A new type of composite structures emanating from France offers a chance to obtain a significant decrease in dead load. Corrugated steel webs are used to carry shear. Using high-strength concrete for the top and bottom slabs, the depth of the girder can be decreased to less than 75 % compared to the current girders. High-strength concrete has to carry the increased stresses in the slabs due to the decreased girder height and improves the durability of the whole structure. Concrete with a strength up to 85 MPa (12,300 psi) is suitable for the box girders.

Keywords: High-strength concrete (HSC), Bridges for High-Speed tracks, Corrugated steel webs

Prof. Dr.-Ing. Dr.-Ing. h. c. G. König was a partner in the consulting office BGS in Frankfurt/Main from 1970 to 1975. In 1975, he became professor for the faculty of civil engineering at the Technical University Darmstadt. Since 1976 he owns a partnership in the consulting office *König und Heunisch* in Frankfurt/Main. He published several contributions, for example to the construction of high rise buildings, safety theory for r.c. and p.c. structures and durability. He serves in several national and international commitees, for example in ACI, ASCE, IABSE, CEB-FIP and CIB.

Dipl.-Ing. Rainer Grimm studied Structural Engineering at the Technical University Darmstadt, Germany. He is now working as a research engineer at the Technical University Darmstadt in the field of HSC. Tests and models for tensile strength, shear behaviour and fracture energy are his main research topics. He is a member of both code commitees working for the Code of HSC in Germany.

Dipl.-Ing. Martin Zink studied Structural Engineering at the Technical University Darmstadt, Germany. During that time he was engaged in the research group for HSC. He is now working at the engineering office *König und Heunisch* in Frankfurt/Main. His main interests are bridges and other engineering facilities for high-speed tracks.

Concrete 2000. Edited by Ravindra K. Dhir and M. Roderick Jones.
© 1993 Published by E & FN Spon. ISBN 0 419 18120 2.

INTRODUCTION

The development of an European high-speed network is a necessity to solve the problems caused by the enormous increase in transportation. On the other hand, building railway bridges has been a main task of structural engineering since it's beginning in the late 19th century. Many bridges have reached an age of 80 years or more. Due to this fact, the rehabilitation and maintenance of old bridges is another reason to stress the importance of the topic.

Requirements as for new high-speed railway lines have never been known up to now. A route selection compatible to the topography of the highlands is excluded by the design speed of 300 km/h, which requires a maximum grade of 40.0 °/oo and a standard radius of 7,000 m. About 9 % of the two new lines in Germany are bridges. To be able to build so many bridges with equal demands in a high quality, the German Federal Railway published the General Design, the so-called 'Rahmenplanung'.

The General Design introduces two different distances of pier-axis, 44.00 m and 58.00 m. The corresponding construction heights are 4.00 m and 5.00 m for the single-span superstructures. Examples are shown in Fig. 1 to Fig. 3. There are two main reasons to choose this kind of standard system. A track structure without any rail expansion joint is possible. With continuously welded rails there is no difference between bridge and open track, and problems caused by the expansion joints are avoided. Another advantage is the possibility of easy lateral shifting. Generally, the renewal of superstructures is facilitated by a limited length. Using any temporary structures to carry track is unthinkable due to the design criterea, the high share of tunnels and an average bridge length of about 1,000 m. However, the break-down of traffic during interchange of girders is limited to only one night.

The feasibility of a new type of bridge has to be verified at the two standard systems, the 44.00 m and the 58.00 m single-span girder. The results may be transferred to any related structure, for example continuous girder bridges or bridges with special systems for the longitudinal loads.

Figure 1   Leinach Valley-Bridge near Würzburg - 44.00 m Single-span Girder

Figure 2   Bartelsgraben Valley Bridge
58.00 m Continuous Girder

Figure 3   Rombach Valley Bridge
near Fulda

Figure 4   Rail Expansion Joint

DESIGN

The basic idea is to start the design with a girder which fulfills the demands of minimum stiffness. This girder will be light and must withstand higher stresses. To overcome these stresses high-strength concrete (HSC) is used. Using improved materials, as for instance HSC and steel in a composite structure, is the second approach.

Deformation Limits

The deformation limits are taken from the German standard for bridges with a design speed of 250 km/h. The new European standard including tracks for 300 km/h is still in preparation.

The minimum stiffness of the girder is determined by the deformation limit, which is the starting point for the improvement of the superstucture. The midspan deformation limit for the girder is length divided by 2700 for bridges with more than one span. For bridges with a ballast track structure, the deformation is caused only by live load and temperature variations. Due to the German requirements the minimum moment of inertia *min I* for the 58.00 m single-spann girder is determined by the following equation:

$$I(E_c,h) \geq \frac{12,012.552 \ MNm^2}{E_c \cdot \left(\dfrac{56.0}{2,700} - \dfrac{0.0196m}{h} \right)}$$

Shear deformation has been neglected in this study. Its share is smaller than 20 % of total deformation if shear stiffness is only calculated from the web area. The stiffness of the edge caps has been neglected also. Additional research on this topic is necessary regarding the durability of bond between the edge caps and the cantilevering plates.

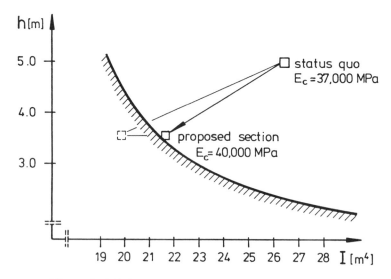

Figure 5   Minimum stiffness / graph for $E_c = 37,000$ MPa

Requirements

The main task for the valley bridges is to provide maximum railway transportation. The classical principale 'form follows function' has to be realized. Some important aspects are:

- durability
- convenient equipment
- maintenance
- aesthetics
- economical efficiency
- simplicity of construction

Some main features of the new bridges are taken from the General Design:

- Distances of pier-axis are 44.00 and 58.00 m.
- Elements and structure of carriageway; the track ballast is increased by 0.10 m for the new design speed of 300 km/h. There are no slab tracks used.
- Section of edge caps with standard equipment adjusted to the modified track ballast.
- System of single-cell box girder superstructures with two tracks and possibility of access.
- Piers and abutments; pier heads may be improved by use of high-strength concrete.

Cross Section of the Box Girder

A new composite structure mixed with improved materials is used for the superstructure. It is a composite bridge with corrugated steel webs and concrete slabs for the top and bottom. In the report of the IABSE Symposium Brussels 1990 [1] the main features of this new type of bridges are listed.

Compared to the current girders of new high-speed tracks in Germany, the advantages of corrugated steel webs are:

- Self-weight is decreased in the webs.
- Structural functions are divided among webs, top and bottom slab.
- The concrete slabs build up stiffness. They are principally under axial load.
- Steel is used to carry shear.
- The inner lever arm is nearly increased up to the total girder height.
- Difficulties linked with the casting of the 4.00 to 5.00 m deep concrete webs are avoided. Serious problems like screening of aggregate by reinforcing steel and tendons occurred at many bridges.
- Web stiffeners, as used for conventional steel webs are avoided.
- Buckling is no critical criterion for the webs because they are only used to carry shear.
- Prestressing forces are not dissipated by the steel webs.
- The webs may be used as scaffolding.

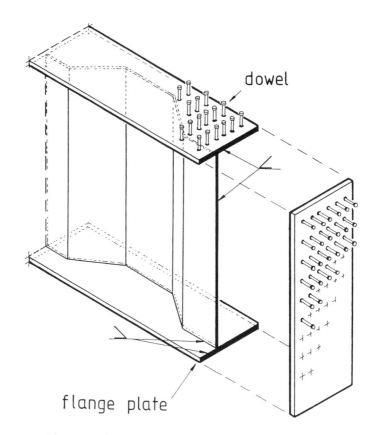

Figure 6   Corrugated Steel Webs (Sketch)

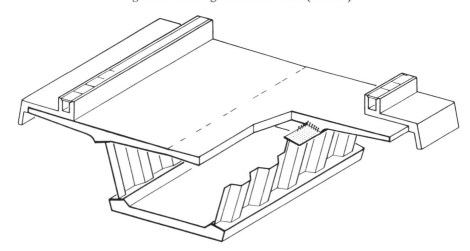

Figure 7   Box Girder with Corrugated Steel Webs

Improved Materials

- **Steel ST 52**

The target of this design study was to decrease the girder depth to a minimum. To be able to carry shear with the decreased web height and a maximum web thickness of 30 mm, including a sufficient safety against fatigue, it was necessary to use steel ST 52 with a 520 MPa ultimate yield point.

If the girder height is not the criterion to choose this new type of composite structure, the conventional steel ST 37 is sufficient. Problems with welding (for instance preheating) can be avoided.

- **High-strength concrete**

As a result of the extensive research on this topic in the last years, the developement of the new European standards including concrete up to a compressive strength of 115 MPa has come to a final state. Since 1990 high-strength concrete up to $f_c = 85$ MPa is used in different projects in Germany. Table 1 shows a typical mix design used in a current project for columns in a 8 to 10-story printing plant. The tested strength after 28 days was $f_c = 108$ MPa.

The use of high-strength concrete in heavily prestressed slabs requires an improved reinforcement at the point of application of prestressing forces. Due to the reasons mentioned below, the bond between tendons and concrete is much better than in structures with normal-strength concrete, for instance with $f_c = 45$ MPa.

- Tensile and shear strength of h.s.c. is increased [7]:

$$f_{ct} = 2.12 \cdot ln \, (\, 1 + f_c / 10 \, MPa \,)$$

- Modulus of elasticity E_c is improved.

The conventional models for the load application will fail. The inclination of compressive strains is increased. The total prestressing force has to be spread over the whole bottom slab in a shorter distance from the anchor plate. Due to the increased inclination of the compressive strains there is a significant increase in the tensile forces of the transverse reinforcement around the tendon heads.

Table 1   Mix design for a 85 MPa concrete

materials			content		remarks
cement PZ 45		c	450	kg / m³	
microsilica fume (dry)		s	35	kg / m³	
aggregate	35 % 0 - 2 mm		613	kg / m³	
	22 % 2 - 8 mm		385	kg / m³	
	43 % 8 -16 mm		753	kg / m³	
		Σ	2236	kg / m³	
water		w	150.00	1/ m³	
retarder VZ 4 Add.		r	1.56	1/ m³	0.4 % of c
super plasticizer FM 93 Add.		p	9.78	1/ m³	2.5 % of c

44.00 M SINGLE-SPAN GIRDER

The 44.00 m distance of pier axis is the standard case for bridges on the new German lines. The following specific results are achieved when using corrugated steel webs:

- Girder height is reduced from 4.00 m to 3.20 m. A further reduction to 3.00 m is possible.

- Corrugated steel webs have a thickness of 27 mm. To guarantee a sufficient safety against fatigue, steel ST 52 with an ultimate yield point of 520 MPa is used.

- High-strength concrete B 75 with a compressive strength of 75 MPa is used

- Longitudinal prestressing of the bottom slab with a force of 57.970 MN - 30 cables of SUSPA 0.6"-15 wire system with 1.932 MN/cable are used.

The limit for the reduction in girder height is set by the shear area of steel webs and the requirement of an accessable girder. In the calculated example a profiled underside view is proposed to improve aesthetics. Without this detail a further decrease of girder height of 0.2 m is possible without reaching the deformation limits.

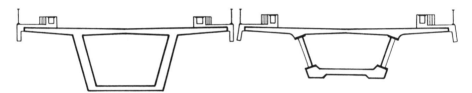

Figure 8   General Design Section   **Figure 9   Proposed Section**

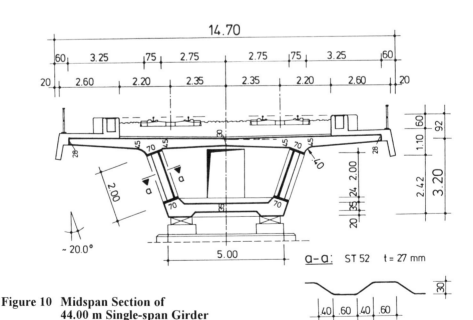

Figure 10   Midspan Section of 44.00 m Single-span Girder

58.00 M SINGLE-SPAN GIRDER

The 58.00 m distance of pier axis is the system for high bridges crossing valleys without rivers. The following specific results are achieved when using corrugated steel webs:

- Girder height is reduced from 5.00 m to 3.50 m

- Deformation limits are met exactly

- Corrugated steel webs have a thickness of 27 mm. To guarantee a sufficient safety against fatigue, steel ST 52 with an ultimate yield point of 520 MPa is used.

- High-strength concrete B 85 with a compressive strength of 85 MPa is used

- Longitudinal prestressing of the bottom slab with a force of 83.944 MN - 28 cables of SUSPA 0.6"-22 wire system with 2.998 MN/cable are used.

The limit for the reduction in girder height is set by the deformation requirements and the possible number of prestressing cables in the bottom slab. The shear stresses in the dowelled composite joint are also at a high level.

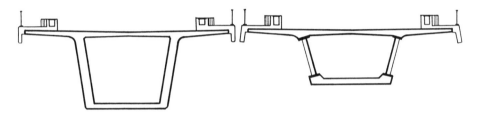

Figure 11   General Design Section   **Figure 12   Proposed Section**

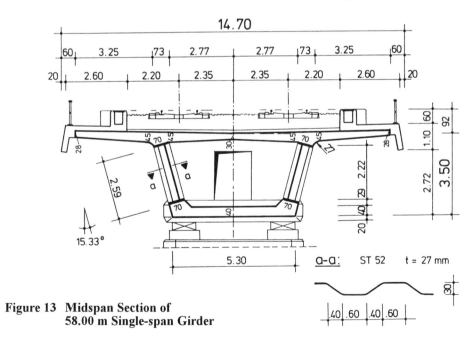

Figure 13   Midspan Section of
58.00 m Single-span Girder

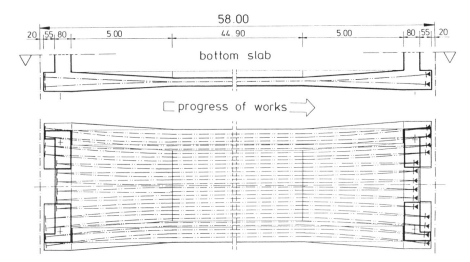

Figure 14   Longitudinal Prestressing of 58.00 m Girder

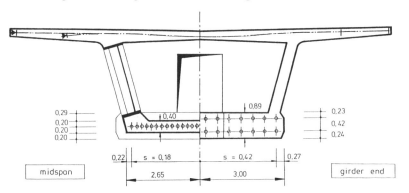

Figure 15   Tendons of 58.00 m Girder in Section

PROSPECT

The study has now been proposed to the German Federal Railway. Some German construction companies have already signed interest in this new type of bridge. The construction costs of the corrugated web structures should be compared to the costs of the conventional bridges at one of the new bridges for high-speed tracks in Germany. The high costs for the improved materials and the economization using simple construction methods have to be examined.

The use of high-strength concrete in beam-shaped bridges demands for high-performance tendons with an extremely high tensile strength and a small section compared to usual tendons. Fatigue problems have to be taken under consideration.

Figure 16   Train passing the bridge

Figure 17   Corrugated Web Structure

Figure 18   Web Structure From Below

CONCLUSIONS

The use of improved materials, like high-strength concrete and steel mixed with the new corrugated web structure, enables a significant reduction in girder depth. As the study shows, the chosen system is able to meet the requirements of the German General Design. No important technical problems prevent the testing of such a structure in full-size. To improve the durability of bridges and to economize their construction by using the advantages of composite structures leads to a promising way into the 21. century. Finally, one may assume that the classic engineering topic railway bridge has not lost its fascination today. To use new techniques and materials is a challenge for the age of high-speed traffic.

REFERENCES

1. CHEYREZY M. and COMBAULT J., Composite Bridges with Corrugated Steel Webs - Achievements and Prospects, Proceedings of IABSE SYMPOSIUM BRUSSELS 1990, International Association for Bridge and Structural Engineering.

2. GERMAN FEDERAL RAILWAY, DS 804, Standard for railway bridges and other engineering structures.

3. GERMAN FEDERAL RAILWAY, DS 899/59, Special Requirements for Bridges of New High-Speed Lines, BZA Munich, 01/01/85.

4. GERMAN FEDERAL RAILWAY, General Design, Series 1a, Valley Bridges, Box Girder, two Tracks, single Cell, P.C., state of 1991

5. KÖNIG G. AND REMMEL G., Zum Zugtragverhalten hochfester Betone (High-strenth concrete under tensile load), Darmstadt Concrete Seminar 6, Technical University Darmstadt 1991.

6. PROMMERSBERGER G., DB Neubaustrecke Mannheim-Stuttgart / Talbrücken Engineering Structures ibw Nr. 4, Elite Trust Reg. Vaduz, 03/1987.

7. REMMEL G., Schubtragverhalten von Bauteilen aus hochfestem Beton ohne Schubbewehrung (Behaviour of structural members without shear reinforcement under shear load), Darmstadt Concrete Seminar 6, Technical University Darmstadt 1991.

8. REMMEL G., Zum Zugtragverhalten hochfester Betone und seinem Einfluß auf die Querkrafttragfähigkeit von schlanken Bauteilen ohne Schubbewehrung (Contribution to tensile behaviour of high-strength concrete and its impact on shear strength of slender members without shear reinforcement), doctor thesis, Technical University Darmstadt / Philipp Holzmann AG, Neu-Isenburg, 12/1992

9. SIEBKE H. AND SCHACKNIES O., Bedarfgerechte Eisenbahnbrücken - ein Beitrag zum wirtschaftlichen Schienenverkehr (Railway Bridges due to Request - Contribution to Economic Railroading), Die Bundesbahn (magazine), Vol. 6/1987.

Pictures are taken from the high-speed track bridges in Germany and from an 1:87 scale model of the new 58.00 m bridge structure in spring 1992.

EVALUATION, PROTECTION, REPAIR AND REHABILITATION OF CHLORIDE-INDUCED CORROSION IN EXISTING BRIDGES

J F Lamond

Strategic Highway Research Program

United States of America

ABSTRACT. The corrosion of reinforcing steel in concrete bridges is one of the most expensive problems facing highway agencies. The number of bridges needing repair or rehabilitation is backlogging and will extend well into the 21th century. New and more cost-effective techniques are needed to be developed. The Strategic Highway Research Program (SHRP) is a five-year, $150 million dollar program to cost effectively solve highway research needs. The Structures program was totally related to chloride-induced corrosion. The total funding was $10 million dollar. The research developed new and improved methods for condition evaluation, protection systems, and rehabilitation techniques. The combined results of the four projects completed in 1993 are presented with the guidelines on diagnostic evaluation and selection and application of the most life cycle cost effect protection, repair or rehabilitation technique.

KEYWORDS: Corrosion, Chloride, Concrete, Evaluation, Bridges, Rehabilitation, Protection, Repair, Research.

Mr. Joseph F. Lamond is a Senior Staff Engineer with the Strategic Highway Research Program in Washington, DC and a Consulting Engineer in Springfield, Virginia. He is past Director, a Fellow, Chairman of two committees, a member of four other committees of the American Concrete Institute. He serves on the ASTM Concrete and Cement committees and Concrete committee of the Transportation Research Board. He is a member of the International Association of Concrete Repair Specialists and a Professional Engineer. He retired from the U. S. Army, Corps of Engineers, Washington, DC in May 1989.

Concrete 2000. Edited by Ravindra K. Dhir and M. Roderick Jones.
© 1993 Published by E & FN Spon. ISBN 0 419 18120 2.

INTRODUCTION

The STRATEGIC HIGHWAY RESEARCH PROGRAM (SHRP) is one of the most compressive highway research programs undertaken in the United States. SHRP is a five-year program with funding of $150 million US dollars. The US Congress authorized SHRP under the 1987 highway act in response to recommendations formulated by state highway officials, industry representatives, and researchers. SHRP is administered as a unit of the non-profit National Research Council through an agreement among the National Research Council, the Federal Highway Administration, and the American Association of State Highway and Transportation Officials. The National Research Council is the principal operating agency of the National Academy of Sciences and the National Academy of Engineering.

SHRP is a strategic program because it is concentrating on a short list of high-payoff activities, where even modest progress will yield savings many times in excess of research costs. The targeted research areas are asphalt, pavement performance, concrete and structures, and highway operations.

Concrete and Structures Program

The concrete materials research is developing improved test methods and procedures to improve concrete durability in highway applications. Also, the research will develop quality control and quality assurance procedures and better concrete materials engineering criteria.

The structures program is developing cost-effective solutions for controlling chloride-induced corrosion distress in existing concrete bridges. Corrosion of reinforcing steel in concrete is the number 1 concrete durability problem needing a solution in the 21th century. Presently corrosion repairs are being accomplished many times during the life of the structure and is not cost effective. This problem is not only confined to concrete bridges but is prevalent in parking structures and building in a marine environment.

The SHRP Structures program was divided into four phases as follows: condition evaluation, electrochemical techniques, nonelectrochemical techniques, and decision criteria guidelines.

The first phase was a project at Pennsylvania State University to provide guidelines for inspecting and evaluating the condition of a concrete bridge and its components.

Second is multi-phased project at Eltech Research Corporation studying removal of chlorides by electrochemical methods. Also in the second phase are projects at Eltech Research Corporation, Construction Technology Laboratories, Inc., Corrpro Companies Inc., and Kenneth C. Clear, Inc. doing research on cathodic protection.

The third phase is a project at Virginia Polytechnic Institute providing cost-effective methods for concrete removal and replacement with various protective and corrective procedures.

The fourth and final phase is a project at Wilbur Smith Associates to take the results from the first three phases and develop easily applied guidelines and decision criteria for use in protective and corrective actions on life-cycle cost basis.

The total research cost is approximately $10 million US dollars.

Chloride-Induced Corrosion

To the motorist on the nation's highway system, the poor riding quality of a bridge deck and the delays and detours which inevitably occur during reconstruction are major problems. Chloride-induced corrosion is caused by the use of salt in winter to maintain the road open to the public or seawater exposure of structures in a marine environment.

The bond between the concrete and steel and the highly alkalinity of the concrete provides protection from corrosion. Chlorides penetrate the concrete and the protective layer at the reinforcing steel surface can be destroyed. As the steel corrodes, it expands and develops stresses which eventually induce cracking, delamination, and spalling of the concrete.

Thousands of concrete bridges constructed from 1950 through mid-1970 have chloride-induced corrosion distress. Very few of these bridges were built with high-quality concrete, adequate cover over the reinforcing steel, or other methods of corrosion protection. Recent estimates place the cost for repairing, rehabilitating, or replacing these bridges at $20 billion in the United States alone, and predictions are that this figure will increase by more than $500 million each year.

The SHRP Structures program addresses many of the problems associated with corrosion of existing concrete bridges. While the program will have a significant impact within its defined scope, it would be a mistake to assume it will take care of all the research needs concerning the performance of highway bridges. Those subject areas relating to durability of highway bridges which are not included are as follows: steel or timber bridge components; design of concrete components; concrete bridges with epoxy-coated reinforcing steel; and prestressed concrete components.

CONDITION EVALUATION

The research at Pennsylvania State University was based on integration of current practices with new methods. Data has to be obtained on the condition of each bridge component. Condition evaluation data is needed to either select a protective or corrective strategy or identify additional information needed to complete an evaluation. Any bridge in an environment that will be subjected to chloride-induced corrosion should have a condition evaluation. Reports for this project were published in eight volumes [1-8]. Volume 1 is "State of the Art of Existing Methods" [1]. Volumes 2 -7 are the new test methods and the research on these methods is summarized below. Volume 8 is the "Procedure Manual" [8] and is discussed in the four steps for condition evaluation.

Data Analysis

The first step in condition evaluation is to review the pertinent data on the bridge. To understand the current condition of a concrete bridge, it is imperative to consider how the design, construction, operation, and maintenance have interacted since the bridge was designed and constructed. Sources of engineering data are plans and specifications, construction reports, as-built drawings, concrete records, operations and maintenance records, and any previous inspection reports. Information on other concrete durability and structural problems related to the bridge is mandatory. These problems could include freeze-thaw, alkali reactivity, carbonation, abrasion, low compressive strength, and inadequate load-carrying capacity.

Visual Inspection

The second step in a condition evaluation is a visual inspection. The exposed concrete of each bridge element should be inspected in a systematic and consistent order. The overall condition of each element is recorded and all defects detailed and photographed. The inspection comprises eyeballing all the accessible parts of the bridge at a distance of not greater than 200 mm by an experienced inspector. The surface should be sounded with a hammer to detect delaminated concrete. Any evidence of previously applied protective or corrective actions should also be recorded and photographed.

Routine Condition Survey

The third step in a condition evaluation is a routine condition survey. Any bridge in an environment exposed to chloride-induced corrosion should have a routine condition survey. The frequency of the survey is dependent on the condition of the structure and the severity of the environmental exposure. This inspection should include the following: 1) sounding for delaminations on the exposed concrete deck using ASTM D 4580; 2) sounding with a hammer on the other elements; 3) measuring the concrete cover over the reinforcing steel using a pachometer; 4) measuring the percentage of spalling related to corrosion 5) determining the chloride content at the reinforcing steel level using AASHTO T 260 or SHRP revised field test method which is discussed later.

Detailed Condition Survey

The fourth and final step in a condition evaluation is a detailed condition survey. The detailed condition survey should include all other testing needed to complete the condition evaluation and provide the information to make the rational decisions for preventative or corrective strategies for protection, repair, rehabilitation, or replacement of the bridge element. The estimation of the electrical half-cell potential of uncoated reinforcing steel using ASTM C 876 should be performed when there is evidence of active corrosion. The chloride content at the surface level using AASHTO T 260 or the SHRP revised field method should be performed when the chloride level at the reinforcing steel level is less than 0.84 kg per cubic meter. This information will be used to predict the rate of corrosion distress. The rate of corrosion testing may be considered when long-term rate of corrosion information is desired. Many bridges have asphalt-covered decks some with membranes between the asphalt and the concrete. Ground penetrating radar and pulse velocity may be used to evaluated the concrete in the deck and the effectiveness of the membrane. The permeability of the concrete near the surface is important to corrosion evaluation. An indication of the surface permeability may be obtained using a SHRP developed test method which is discussed below. Some surfaces are sealed with a penetrating sealer. Two test methods were developed by SHRP research to determine the effectiveness of sealers.

Chloride Content Test

A laboratory evaluation of four procedures was performed. Those procedures used the specific ion probe, spectrophometer, digital titrator, and Quantab titrator strips. All procedures require drilled power samples as does the current standard AASHTO T 260, a potentiometric titration procedure. The specific ion probe was selected as the best alternative, based on cost, speed, and ease of field operation.

It was field validated in three states which represented a wide range of chloride environmental conditions. The results indicated the field procedure worked well, producing chloride content results that correlated with AASHTO T 260.

The sampling procedure consists of drilling concrete, using a rotary impact drill with a 29 mm diameter Heller bit, this diameter was considered sufficiently large to minimize the influences that the coarse aggregate has on the test. The Heller bit is designed to allow the drill cuttings to be removed from the drilling surface by a vacuum system. A drillstop with 6 mm division marks controls the drilling depth. The sample collection system consists of a 2.25 horsepower wet and dry vacuum cleaner fitted with a Plexiglass sample collection chamber, coffee filters, and plastic tubing connected to the Heller bit assembly.

A 3.0 gram drilled power concrete sample is digested in a 20 ml of digestion solution. This is stabilized by the addition of 80 ml of stabilizer solution. A stable millivolt reading is taken of the stabilizer solution using the chloride specific ion electrode probe. The millivolt results are mathematically converted into equivalent total percent chloride content or chloride content in pounds per cubic yard.

Corrosion Rate Devices

Three commercially developed prototype corrosion rate devices discussed in the literature were chosen to be evaluated. They were provided by Nippon Steel Corporation, K. C. Clear, Inc., and Geocisa Geotechnical and Cement, S.A. Laboratory.

The Nippon Steel Corporation device is a portable corrosion monitor. It is operated automatically using a galvanosatic double pulse. Two currents of different frequencies are superimposed. The difference between the two frequencies provides polarization resistance from which the corrosion current and corrosion rate are calculated.

The K.C. Clear, Inc. device is model 3LP. It uses a three linear polarization technique. The operation is manual and it takes 3 minutes to obtain one polarization reading.

The Geocisa device is model LG-ECM-03. The device operates automatically and effectively confines the current to an area directly below the central electrode, permitting calculation of the true polarization resistance. The device stores data for up to 3500 tests.

Asphalt-Covered Deck Evaluation

Short-pulse, ground-penetrating radar was selected for investigation because of its noncontacting ability to penetrate asphalt overlays. The system has automated data acquisition and processing. The results of the radar survey shows the delaminated areas and other deteriorated concrete cracking locations on a bridge. The system consists of one to three ground-penetrating radars operating in parallel on a truck traveling up to 40 kilometers per hour. The radar data is processed in the truck on an 80486-based computer system, a master control unit, distance measurement equipment, and custom software.

Membrane Effectiveness

The integrity and effectiveness of preformed membranes overlaid with asphalt were investigated using infrared technology, pulsed radar, and ultrasonic pulse velocity. The ultrasonic pulse velocity system showed repeatable and consistent results in the laboratory evaluation and was selected to field-validate the method on 15 different bridges. ASTM C 567 ultrasonic pulse velocity test method is used with the sending and receiving transducers placed 89 mm apart on the asphalt surface. The test may be used to assess the membrane integrity for debonding between the membrane and the concrete slab or the asphalt overlay, perforations or deterioration of the membrane, or a combination of these. The transmitted time of the ultrasonic pulse is used to estimate the relative condition of the membrane system in terms of a condition rating scheme.

Penetrating Sealer Effectiveness

A penetrating sealer as a surface treatment is sometimes used to prolong the life of reinforced concrete bridges. A sealer is used because they are inexpensive and easy to use. The sealer penetrate the concrete surface to some degree and problems have been reported in the application. Two test methods were developed to determine the effectiveness of sealers. One test method is based on surface absorptivity, and the other on the electrical response of the concrete surface layer. The water absorptivity test has a water reservoir with a graduated water column affixed to the concrete surface. The water column drop, as a function of time, is monitored over 10 minutes. The greater the water drop the poorer the effectiveness of the sealer. In the other method, the electrical resistance is measured between two narrowly spaced strips of conductive paint. The gage area is wetted, dried and an AC resistance reading is taken after 4 minutes. The lower the resistance reading the more ineffective the sealer.

Field Permeability Testing

The permeability of the concrete over the reinforcing steel is not easily measured or known. A rapid field concrete permeability test was developed and it was qualitatively correlated with existing laboratory methods. It was recognized that any rapid, nondestructive field test would not yield a true permeability value. The test apparatus is a portable and self-contained device that may be used on horizontal, vertical and overhead concrete surfaces. A vacuum plate fitted with a soft rubber gasket is held in contact with the concrete surface and a vacuum is applied. The rate of air flow is measured using a gas flowmeter. The rate of air flow in milliliters per minute is compared with typical values, and the relative permeability is expressed in a qualitative manner as low, medium, or high.

PREVENTATIVE AND CORRECTIVE STRATEGIES

Several strategies have been developed to combat corrosion of reinforcing steel in concrete. Preventative strategies are protection systems, membranes, thin overlays, and chloride removal. These strategies prevent corrosion before concrete deteriorates. Corrective strategies are repair, rehabilitation, or replacement of a deteriorated element of a bridge. The corrective strategy involves concrete removal, patching, overlays, impregnation, corrosion inhibitor concrete, and cathodic protection. Some strategies may be both preventive and corrective.

Preventative strategies usually involve systems and techniques that require periodic actions to prevent or delay damage or deterioration to the bridge. For example, repairing by patching with various materials may restore the bridge element to a serviceable condition but does not remove the cause of deterioration the chlorides.

SHRP research did not address the corrective action of replacement. Current practices, such as low water-cement ratio high-quality concrete, adequate cover over the reinforcing steel, and other preventive measures, are taken during replacement of an element of a bridge. Replacement also may occur when the bridge is functionally obsolete or structurally inadequate and these actions may be unrelated to any chloride-induced corrosion damage.

CHLORIDE REMOVAL

Chloride removal research was performed at Eltech Research Corporation. This research is to develop methods of preventing deterioration of chloride contaminated concrete bridge components. The feasibility of electrochemically removing chlorides from bridge elements was determined in the laboratory. These studies investigated the effect of total charge passed on reinforcement bond, hydrogen embrittlement, changes in concrete permeability, changes in the reinforcing steel concrete interface, chloride removal rates, and gas generation. This engineering study defined the equipment needed and procedures for chloride removal. The chloride removal process has been field validated on three bridges. Criteria, equipment, procedures, and non-proprietary specifications will be in an implementation package.

The condition evaluation, including the chloride content, has to be evaluated to determine the feasibility of using the chloride removal process. This is required on each component of the bridge. The process can be used on both horizontal and vertical surfaces. When used, an anode material is installed. The reinforcing steel, the cathode, and the anode material are connected to a rectifier to provide an electrical circuit. An electrolyte is circulated. The electrolyte needs to be circulated in a porous medium on a vertical surface. The chloride ion has a negative charge and is attracted to the anode. The electric current used during chloride removal process is about 3.2 amps per square meter of concrete surface area. For safety reasons the voltage is limited to 50 volts. A removal time of 3 to 6 week is typical. The total removal time varies according to the condition of the bridge. The report on this research will be published by SHRP in 1993.

CATHODIC PROTECTION

Electrochemical methods such as cathodic protection can be used as a corrective or protective strategy to control corrosion. Cathodic protection reduces the corrosion rate of reinforcing steel to acceptable levels. If properly maintained, it will perform for the service life of the bridge. The research is being performed by Eltech Research Corporation, with data on various aspects of the research being performed for SHRP by Construction Technology Laboratories, Inc., Corrpro Companies,Inc., and Kenneth C. Clear, Inc.

The research will consolidate the background information in a state of the art report. The guideline manual will be the most comprehensive publication ever put together on the subject of cathodic protection. The manual will contain the fundamentals of cathodic protection, step by step approach to system selection, estimating costs, design, construction, commissioning, and maintenance. Also to be included are draft specifications for both bridge deck and substructure installations. The third phase of this research will be operational criteria. Corrosion rate experiments, mathematical modeling, and concentration profiles are being studied for optimizing long-term operation of a system and to minimize long-term effects such as damage to the concrete due to excessive current levels. The reports on this research will be published by SHRP in 1993.

PROTECTION AND REHABILITATION BY
OTHER THAN ELECTROCHEMICAL METHODS

This project is evaluating existing and new techniques for concrete removal and surface preparation. It is also exploring new techniques using corrosion inhibitors and polymers. Existing overlay techniques using low slump high performance concretes are being studied. Methods of rapidly rehabilitating bridge decks are being addressed. Each technique will be described, with its limitations, estimated service life, estimated construction cost, construction procedure and specifications. This research, phase three of the SHRP Structures Program, is being performed by Virginia Polytechnic Institute and State University.

Concrete Removal and Surface Preparation

There are a number of methods for concrete removal. The removal of chloride contaminated concrete to or around the reinforcing steel is necessary. This research identified the characteristics, productivity, costs, and advantages and disadvantages of three dominant methods used in bridge repair or rehabilitation.

Pneumatic breakers are extremely flexible in terms of size and depth of removal, but are the most expensive.

Milling was the lowest cost on a unit area basis, but inflexible as it can only remove concrete above the reinforcing steel on large horizontal surfaces.

Hydrodemolition is relatively inexpensive, it is flexible with regard to depth of removal but limited to large horizontal surfaces.

Removal of surface contaminants and concrete up to a depth of 13 mm can be accomplished with scrabbling, planing, sandblasting, and shotblasting.

Sandblasting, wire brushing, and hydrodemolition were identified as the most feasible methods for bar cleaning.

SHRP has published a report on removal and bar cleaning. [9]

Concrete Rehabilitations with Overlays

High performance concrete overlays are placed on decks to reduce the infiltration of water and chlorides and to improve the ride quality and skid resistance. Corrective strategies using latex-modified, silica fume, low-slump dense, special blended cements, and high-early strength concretes are being studied. SHRP will publish a report on rapid deck rehabilitation in 1993.

Corrective strategies using concrete replacement,and shotcrete are being studied for substructure elements. Applications, limitations, specifications, costs, and service lives will be presented for each technique.

Patching Materials

A number of patching materials may be used to repair concrete. Most patching is performed to restore the damaged element to a serviceable condition. Some of the repairs being studied are crack repair and sealing, bituminous concrete patching, portland cement concrete patching, polymer concrete patching, steel plate over concrete, and specialized cements patching. These repairs are neither preventive or corrective strategies and are usually temporary until a permanent solution is available.

Protection Systems

Most protection systems are used as a preventive strategies. These include penetrating sealers, coatings, polymer impregnation, and liquid and preformed membranes with bituminous overlays. Applications, limitations, specifications, costs, and service lives will be presented for each technique.

Corrosion Inhibitors

Extensive research was performed on the use of corrosion inhibitors. The results indicated they are effective as concrete admixtures and ponding on existing chloride contaminated concrete.

The ponding procedure involves the removal of chloride contaminated concrete to the depth of the reinforcing steel, dry the surface, pond with a corrosion inhibitor and overlay with corrosion inhibited concrete on decks.

For substructure rehabilitations, expose the reinforcing steel, paint the concrete and reinforcing steel with a corrosion inhibitor, and apply either a shotcrete or patching concrete with a corrosion inhibitor admixture. These techniques will be field validated in five states.

Guidance Manual

The report on "Concrete Bridge Protection and Rehabilitation: Physical and Chemical Techniques" will be published by SHRP in 1993. This will be a guidance manual providing a description, limitations, estimated construction costs, estimated service life, construction procedures, and construction specifications for new and existing techniques outlined above.

METHODOLOGY FOR PROTECTION AND
REHABILITATION OF EXISTING BRIDGES

This is the fourth and final phase of the SHRP Structures Program. The project is being performed by Wilbur Smith Associates. A decision model is being developed which will ensure a rational cost-effective approach to the protection or rehabilitation of an existing concrete bridge.

The research results from the other SHRP Structures Program projects and other information will be used. Data from a bridge evaluation provides the information necessary to determine its condition. The procedure manual of the first phase project is being used. The preventive and corrective strategies for the protection, repair or rehabilitation systems will be from techniques developed in phases two and three.

The goal of this project is to develop a manual and computer program that can be used at the project level, and which will select the most cost-effective method for any specific bridge. To do this, two items must be know: 1) the condition of the bridge, and 2) the cost, service life, and technical viability of a range of techniques from which a selection can be made.

Either a manual or computer program will be used to enable the user to predict future corrosion-related distress, the life expectancy of specific bridge elements, and the life-cycle cost benefits of many options for protecting or rehabilitating bridges of various ages, types of design and materials, and level of distress. Guidelines and decision criteria are provided to assess the corrosion-related condition of the concrete and the reinforcing steel. A model will predict future distress and functional life of the existing structure with and without preventive or corrective action.

A simplified optimization approach will be used to get the most cost-effective methods for protection and rehabilitation using life-cycle basis. The model is significant because it integrates the engineering, economic, technological, analytical, and computer system requirements to provide solutions based on information about various procedures and site-specific types of constraints.

Any bridge will deteriorate with time after construction. Normal maintenance will keep the bridge functionally operational. Environmental conditions may accelerate deterioration even with normal maintenance. When corrosion-induced distress becomes evident, the actual life of the structure may be less than the theoretical design life.

If the corrosion distress is detected prior to active corrosion of the reinforcing steel, a preventive strategy using protection systems is a viable solution to the problem. Many protection systems may need many applications during the life of the bridge.

The chloride threshold for active corrosion is about 0.84 kg per cubic meter of concrete. When active corrosion is detected, a corrective strategy using repair or rehabilitation systems are viable solutions to the problem. If a repair system is used, the corrosion distress will continue at the same rate or an accelerated rate. If a rehabilitation system is used, the corrosion rate may decrease with time or stop but increase as chlorides in the future diffuse back to the reinforcing steel. Therefore, some rehabilitation systems may be needed more than once during the life of the bridge.

The selection of a preventive or corrective strategy can only be accomplished on a life cycle basis. The life cycle cost approach to structuring decisions on which systems are best to apply, and at what time for an existing bridge in a given condition. The analytic approach identifies the minimum cost of each system and its optimal time of application. This approach considers both estimated agency costs and user cost for three distinct time periods: 1) prior to; 2) during the project; and 3) after the application of the selected system.

The manual will include appropriate flow charts, figures, tables, nomographs, equations, and other aids with explanatory text to identify the most appropriate action for specific bridge elements and situations. The PC-Based computer program designed for deck analysis will incorporate the same data bases and analytical relationships as the manual. The program facility for on-line interaction with the user makes it possible to quickly explore the benefits of various systems. The user may alter the input parameters by using a selection menu or enter more specific information on the costs, lives, and benefits of the various systems, as dictated by the user's locality. The program will provide the capability of printing a variety of reports and ranking systems that have been evaluated. The manual and computer program will be available from SHRP in 1993.

SUMMARY

The SHRP is a five-year, $150 million research program. Ten million is devoted to the Structures Program on chloride-induced corrosion in existing concrete highway bridges. This program was divided into four phases which started in 1987 and completed in 1993. It is unusual in that it deals only with strategies for existing concrete bridges. This is important because implementation of the results requires only that the existing practices be modified rather than the introduction of entirely new activities.

The research at Pennsylvania State University developed a procedure manual for condition evaluation assessment of a bridge. It is based on a rational integration of thirteen applicable, presently used test methods with seven newly developed methods. While the primary emphasis is on distress associated with chloride-induced corrosion, all aspects of concrete durability are addressed. The procedure is designed to be flexible and amenable tailored to suit the needs of the individual highway agency.

The research at Eltech Research Corporation studied the technique of electrochemical removal of chlorides from concrete. An electrical field will be used to remove chlorides from concrete, thus preventing corrosion related deterioration. The project involved laboratory studies, field trials, and an implementation package for use by highway engineers.

The research at Eltech Research Corporation, Construction Technology Laboratories, Inc., Corrpro Companies, Inc., and Kenneth C. Clear, Inc. will document the effectiveness and limitations of cathodic protection. Guidelines for design, installation, operation, and maintenance of cathodic protection systems will be developed. This will include a state of the art report, data collection on existing and newly installed systems, estimated costs and benefits, and manuals and specifications for various cathodic protection systems.

The research at Virginia Polytechnic Institute and State University studied the nonelectrochemical techniques and removal methods for various preventive and corrective strategies. This includes a field survey of existing techniques, feasibility studies on new techniques, evaluation of methods of removing chloride contaminated concrete, rapid rehabilitation techniques for bridge decks, and field validation of the most viable and cost effective techniques. The results will produce a guidance manual with description, limitations, estimated service life, estimated cost, construction procedures, and specifications for each technique.

Wilbur Smith Associates are compiling the research results for the other SHRP Structures Program projects and other sources. A manual and computer program is being developed that will enable the user to develop a preventive or corrective strategy for cost-effective protecting, repairing, or rehabilitating existing concrete highway bridges.

The SHRP research will be implemented by the United States Department of Transportation, Federal Highway Administration. SHRP reports will be available through Transportation Research Board and National Technical Information Service.

REFERENCES

1. Gannon, E.F. and Cady, P.D., "Condition Evaluation of Concrete Bridges Relative to Reinforcement Corrosion, Volume 1: "State of the Art of Existing Methods," SHRP-S-323, Strategic Highway Research Program, 1992

2. Flis, J., Sehgal, A., Li, D., Kho, Y., Sabol, S., and Cady, P.D., "Condition Evaluation of Concrete Bridges Relative to Reinforcement Corrosion, Volume 2: Method for Measuring the Corrosion Rate of Reinforcing Steel," SHRP-S-324, Strategic Highway Research Program, 1992

3. Alongi, A.J., Clemena, G.G., and Cady, P.D., "Condition Evaluation of Concrete Bridges Relative to Reinforcement Corrosion, Volume 3: Methods for Evaluating the Condition of Asphalt-Covered Decks," SHRP-S-325, Strategic Highway Research Program, 1992

4. Al-Qadi, I.L., Weyers, R.E., Galagedera, N.L., and Cady, P.D., "Condition Evaluation of Concrete Bridges Relative to Reinforcement Corrosion, Volume 4: Deck Membrane Effectiveness and a Method for Evaluating Membrane Integrity," SHRP-S-326, Strategic Highway Research Program, 1992

5. Whiting, D., Ost, B., Nagi, M., and Cady, P.D., "Condition Evaluation of Concrete Bridges Relative to Reinforcement Corrosion, Volume 5: Methods for Evaluating the Effectiveness of Penetrating Sealers," SHRP-S-327, Strategic Highway Research Program, 1992

6. Herald, S.E., Henry, M. Al-Qadi, I.L., Weyers, R.E., Feeney, M.A., Howlum, S.F., and Cady, P.D., "Condition Evaluation of Concrete Bridges Relative to Reinforcement Corrosion, Volume 6: Method for Field Determination of Total Chloride Content," SHRP-S-328, Strategic Highway Research Program, 1992

7. Whiting, D., and Cady, P.D., "Condition Evaluation of Concrete Bridges Relative to Reinforcement Corrosion, Volume 7: Method for Field Measurement of Concrete Permeability," SHRP-S-329, Strategic Highway Research Program, 1992

8. Cady, P.D., and Gannon, E.J., "Condition Evaluation of Concrete Bridges Relative to Reinforcement Corrosion, Volume 8: Procedure Manual," SHRP-S-330, Strategic Highway Research Program, 1992

9. Vorster, M.C., Merrigan, J.P., Lewis, R.W., and Weyers, R.E., "Techniques for Concrete Removal and Bar Cleaning on Bridge Rehabilitation Projects," SHRP-S-336, Strategic Highway Research Program, 1993

CONCRETE AND CONCRETE BRIDGES

S F Popa

The Institute for Research and Technological Design

Romania

ABSTRACT. As known as the concrete is, from time to time a synthesis is welcome, to point out important topics and to identify future directions for research; this paper tries to offer not only a view over the execution technics for concrete bridges, but some considerations of the aesthetics of concrete bridges and also future trends. As an introduction to the role of this material as a building material in the future, some ideas about concrete and its behaviour in a few different circumstances are included; a special view is perhaps concrete for bridges where its behaviour is much improved using steel. But in spite of the part the steel has, it can be noticed that for economic and functional highway bridges the future is concrete.

Keywords: Concrete, Class, Cyclic loading, Prestress, Reinforcement, Stress, Strain, Transfer, Transom, Prefabrication.

Eng. Sanda Florentina Popa is a scientific researcher at the Institute for Research and Technological Design in Transport of Bucharest, Romania. She specialises in the durability of roads and in bridge behaviour under dynamic load, and is interested in data processing systems. Eng. Sanda Florentina Popa is a member of the Civil Engineers' Association of Romania (1990), the Technical Committee for Roads and Bridges, and the Engineers' General Association of Romania (1990). She has participated in some scientific meetings and has a few papers published in their proceedings and in the journals of the organizations she belongs to. She is candidate for the doctor's degree at the Civil Engineering Institute of Bucharest, where she graduated in the Faculty of Railways, Roads and Bridges (1987).

Concrete 2000. Edited by Ravindra K. Dhir and M. Roderick Jones.
© 1993 Published by E & FN Spon. ISBN 0 419 18120 2.

INTRODUCTION

Concrete

The last necessities called for changes in the concepts used for concrete, replacing for instance the name of 'mark of concrete' with the one of 'class of concrete'. Table 1 shows the equivalence based on design strengths and on the cement consumption, as can be found in specifications and in (1).

The elastic modulus appears in specifications according to the class of concrete and varies by different percentages for concrete with coarse aggregates and for the light concrete with granulite, in accordance with the verifications which are made. It is also recommended to use a certain concrete class according to the type of the building element (class Bc22.5 at least for prefabrication and class Bc30 at least for other elements) the concrete having a compressive strength and a tensile resistance for each class.

Under prolonged static load concrete has lower resistance, this reduction being compensated by an increasing produced by ageing. The concrete behaves under cyclic loading according to the amplitude of the load oscillation. The usual stress-strain diagram for concrete under cyclic compression loading (2) is shown in Figure 1.

If the characteristics presented until now were induced by a wide range of factors, it must be mentioned that the next specific phenomena: shrinkage, bulking, creep, are strongly impressed by characteristics of the concrete composition, and they have a certain part in the prestress concrete analysis.

For the materials which cannot resist tension, the performance curve is established by compression tests. It is also the situation of the concrete, when the samples

Table 1 Changes in the classification of the concrete

Class of concrete	Mark of concrete
Bc15	B200
Bc20	B250
Bc22.5	B300
Bc30	B400
Bc35	B450
Bc40	B500
Bc50	B600
Bc60	B700

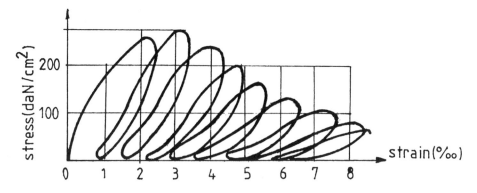

Figure 1   Stress-strain diagram of concrete
under cyclic compression loading

have another shape. Tests are made on cubes or cylindrical prisms with a height twice the diameter, to eliminate the buckling effects which come with the compression.

To prepare the concrete it is important to adopt a good proportioning of the mixture and it is possible that studies are made to obtain an acceptable workability, a suitable durability, resistance and economy of the hardened product. It seems that no property is as critical for the quality of the concrete as the water/cement ratio, and the use of chemical or puzzolanic admixtures influences the behaviour of the concrete (hardened or not).

Concrete for Bridges

In contrast with the situations where the concrete is compressed under displacements which cause shortening of the element, for bridge girders (as for other building elements), it is convenient to choose to introduce into the structure tensioned steel reinforcements so that they work in conjunction with the concrete.

The necessity of reducing metal consumption imposed researches concerning the prestressed concrete structures using it for very large spans, comparable to highway bridges with the only metallic solutions. Studies begun at Stuttgart (C. V. Bach, O. Graf) about prestressing raised the question of shrinkage; it was noticed that after a period of time the effect of the prestressing was lost. But in time this problem became entirely mastered, being performed even a partial prestressing of the element and recognizing it nowadays as more economic and functional for many situations than the total one.

Special attention is given to prestressing, to its technology, the post-tensioned reinforcement systems generalized and for this purpose different types of setting the reinforcements are studied. In the world, more prestress systems have been developed: Freyssinet, BBR, Coignet, Stronghold, Dywidag, Morandi, INCERC. They differ in the following aspects:

- the anchor device (location at the extremities of the girder, construction characteristics, anchoring, etc)
- reinforcements (material and size)
- the jacket of the reinforcement (material and size)
- the values of the characteristic stress of the anchor device/initial stress, fracture stress, permanent tension

The achievements with prestressed concrete do not cease here. The researches will tackle the problem of the tension losses and of the prestress transfer zones from the reinforcements to the concrete. Recently the favourable use of passive reinforcements with the pre-tensioned ones has been evident (3) (Figure 2: a, b, c- mixed reinforcement, and on another side the external prestress).

The passive reinforcements are preferred in fact at wires of PC52, PC60 type which fulfil a resistance function too.

- at transfer: by locating them so as to contribute to the reduction of the unitary tensile stresses from the dead load (Figure 2a):
- during lifting: by locating them in the zones where stresses can appear (Figure 2b);
- under exploitation loading (Figure 2c).

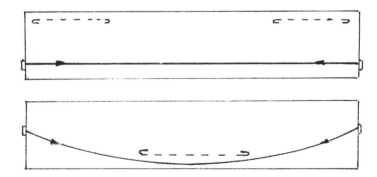

Figure 2a   Passive reinforcement necessary at transfer for rectilinear and parabolic lay-out (of the prestressed reinforcement).

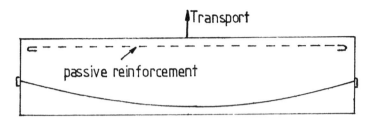

Figure 2b   Passive reinforcement necessary at the transport.

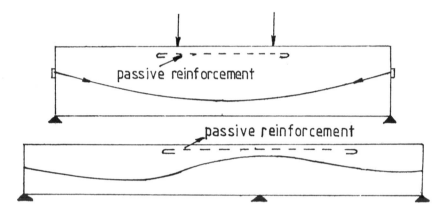

Figure 2c   Passive reinforcement to reinforce the prestressed concrete in exploitation at different types of girders.

In the cross-section the passive reinforcement is:

* as cross-ties, so as to take over the main tensile stresses and the shear stresses, where the prestress stressed longitudinal reinforcement changes its direction
* as special cross-ties, around the canal of the post-tensioned reinforcements, to take over the tensile stress.

To get some special results it was necessary to make researches about:
- the design characteristics of the concrete and of the reinforcement
- the ultimate cracking state
- rigidities and deflections
- structure

CONCRETE BRIDGES

The practice proved the lack of an execution technology to be applied everywhere and the many peculiarities of such a succession of construction stages of bridges. But a simple classification in large groups can be done.

Modern Execution Techniques

A present classification of the main construction means for bridges (4, 5) which in Romania corresponds to those existing in the rest of the world, is:

- prefabricated girders - mounted with different types of cranes, with metallic launching girder or metallic inclined planes, etc. Used for entirely prefabricated beams some of these equipments can be used at prefabricated transoms, too
- construction by displacement: the 'cast-push' method, the rotation, the translation (transversal and even vertical)
- construction by launching
- 'cantilever' construction - very new even for some of the developed countries, and certain to be used for its simplicity in the next century.

Modern execution techniques with prefabricated elements apply nowadays for arch bridges, too. At the usual structures is noticed the evanescence of the slabs (compact or with voids because of the inadequate execution technology, both economic and functional, so that they are replaced by the prefabricated girders. On another side, prefabrication opens an advantageous way for the structures of transoms and for the standard type ones, so that in well-known situations to choose a classic execution solution, with corresponding execution speed. Because of the method with transoms, prestressed structures are advantageous for large bridge spans, too. An example is a bridge structure built recently (1990) over a canal at Calarasi in Romania of twin box continuous girders with three spans (Figure 3a) (6).

This technique allowed the survey of the execution too, establishing with the mechanical tensometer the strain at the underside surface of the boxes, in sections and points previously fixed and at each stage of the work schedule. A very simple calculation program called 'DIF' (S. F. Popa) allowed some data processing where one of the necessary results can be for instance the variation of the strain at a point with time (Figure 3b), a type of analysis of the day.

The execution of the prefabricated girders, isostatic, wholly cast or with transoms, assembled before placing, did not develop too much. These types of structures are used in specific conditions, and they are considered to be economic; the most indicated sections are for the box type ones (for all the values of the span).

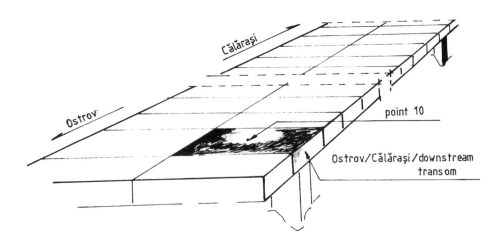

Figure 3a   Bridge over a canal at Calarasi, Romania

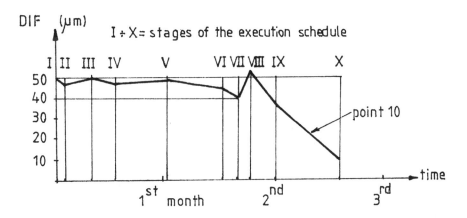

Figure 3b   Variation of strain with time for one point at the bridge over the canal at Calarasi

For cable-stayed bridges on cables it is economic to be foreseen with a prestressed concrete deck which is possible for very large spans, to a metallic deck resorting of resistance or aesthetic reasons; the solution is applied less as mixed decks. A mixed structure, with concrete (aluminium and light concrete slabs) was tried recently for the suspended bridges.

There are of course some new methods of rehabilitation instead of demolition and rebuilding, and of strengthening too, which are able to proceed above live traffic, and in order to add much time for the life of bridges. They have the advantage of being fast and economic, so they certainly belong to the next century. And, as it is already begun, even the reshaping of a structure is going to be assisted by calculations run on computer models.

Aesthetics

To design a bridge together with an architect became a primordial problem, the mental condition of the individual depending on the quality of the environmental aesthetics. Almost ideal because of low cost, box girders are extremely aesthetic, especially the ones with inclined walls which offer to the deck a slender aspect.

At the girder bridges (7) with haunches, the stress goes to the bearings, so that an economy of material is achieved in the central area in comparison with the girders of equal height along the span. Linear or parabolic haunches will be used in accordance with the shape of the longitudinal profile (straight line or curved).

At the arches (7) the impression of stability appears from the conformation of piers and the aspect is special when as a building material, brick or stone is chosen. Stone, very expensive, is still used because of its known durability. Arches of prestressed concrete or steel for small and medium spans became rare because of economic reasons. A variety of frame structures have inclined piers too, some of them are derived from the arch bridges - and there are also standard type frame structures, prefabricated, for very small spans. For larger spans the concrete frame structures are less used.

Cable-stayed bridges come from the suspended ones and they are much more used than the last ones. Triangular pylons are considered to be both aesthetic and economic. More stay cables spaced closely (French studies, 1978) simplify not only the execution, but also the structure itself, and they allow thin decks. At the inferior side, the setting system of the stay cables is aesthetic to be realized at the inside of the cross section.

The resistance and the simplicity in execution impose more and more bridges with a compact slab deck, continuous and of a constant height, made of reinforced or prestressed concrete where the solution of lateral spans instead of the abutments with front wall is more aesthetic and more economic.

CONCLUSIONS

1.   Behaviour. In the situation of mixed reinforcement, passive reinforcement has the possibility to reduce creep more. The behaviour of prestressed concrete differentiated with time not only in accordance with the

reinforcement method, but with the prestressing degree, too.   The difference between the degrees of prestressing may be made with a ratio K (1) between the moment produced by the prestressing stress and the moment of the total exploitation load as against a same limit of the central kernel.   Highway bridges are well adapted to the use of limited prestressing.

2.   Trends. The trends of the future development of concrete as a building material in the world and in the country impose to the research some directions:

- studies regarding the determination of the effect of creep
- studies to realize:
- reinforced concrete with glass fibres, carbonic fibres or synthetic materials
- lightweight concrete with high strength or partially prestressed
- concrete with dispersed reinforcement
- polymer concrete
- new compositions of concrete aiming the reaction cement-granules and corrosion
- studies on models concerning the behaviour of composite concrete in highway bridges
- the behaviour of concrete under cyclic loads
- the exterior prestress (as an execution technique too)
- the prestressing of curved elements where the condition of the limit pin cannot be applied and trying to consider than unbalanced values of the exterior loads to be as small as possible (5).

3.   Aesthetics. The integration in the landscape will imply:
- to avoid a harsh structure (heavy girders at long spans, in gentle vales with little houses)
- to choose the facade (materials, surface texture, colour)
- the feature of the structure: comfort, purpose, safety
- a relation between complexity and order
- to consider the special situations (for instance to build a new bridge near an old one)
- the use of coloured concrete

4.   Execution. The classical methods stand some changes aiming to reduce the stresses which appear in the structure at the execution, the stayed cables bridges being suitable for instance at an erection method by rotation. The difficult use of centring and scaffolds remains actually to be applied less and less.

REFERENCES

1.   DUMITRESCU, D, POPAESCU, A.   Beton precomprimat, Edit. Academiei, Bucuresti, 1987, 186 pp.

2.   NICULA, I, ONET, TR.   Beton armat, Edit. didactica si pedagogica, Bucuresti, 1982, 327 pp.

3.   TERTEA, I.   Betonul precomprimat, Edit. tehnica, 1981, 416 pp.

4.   RADU, PI, NEGOESCU, E, IONESCU, P.   Poduri din beton armat, Edit. didactica si pedagogica, Bucuresti, 1981, 591 pp.

5.   CAPATU, C.   Poduri din beton precomprimat, Editura tehnica, 1983, 468 pp.

6.   POPA, SF.   Masurari în timpul executiei podului pe grinzi casetate gemene continue cu trei deschideri la Calarasi, Materialele schimbului de experienta (IX) al Comisiei A.I.C.R. Comportarea in situ a constructiilor - Sovata, 1-3 octombrie 1992, INCERC, vol.2, pp. 283-288.

7.   POPA, SF. Podurile de sosea si mediul inconjurator, Simpozion Suceava, 7-8 iunie 1991, AICR, INCERC, GDEB, IJCC, pp. 61-68.

8.   RUSU, M. Podurile de-a lungul timpului, Edit. tehnica, 1988, 98 pp.

DESIGN OF CONCRETE BRIDGES
IN HOSTILE ENVIRONMENTS

K R Wilson

S H R Sham

G Maunsell & Partners

United Kingdom

ABSTRACT. This paper examines some of the critical factors which should be taken into consideration when designing concrete bridges in hostile environments, such as estuarial and sea crossings. The salient points discussed are illustrated by reference to the specified requirements for the Second Severn Crossing. The paper contends that a study on the problem can be instigated from a system reliability standpoint. It describes how the application of a reliability approach, coupled with advancements in design, detailing, specification, material quality and workmanship, will improve the performance of concrete bridges in hostile environments. The strategic importance of the crossing and the consequences of any failure are discussed in the context of setting an acceptable level of reliability. The effects of the length of a structure, the number of spans, bearings and movement joints, together with structural determinacy are examined in the light of their implications on the overall reliability of a long bridge crossing. The paper expands the subject of bridge design in hostile environments to address the important issue of the protection of users. Special reference is made to the advantages which are derived from provision of wind shielding.

Keywords: Bearings, Bridge, Concrete, Durability, Hostile, Probability, Reliability, Wind-shielding.

Mr Keith R Wilson is a Technical Director of G Maunsell and Partners with special responsibility for prestressed concrete structures. He has extensive experience in designing bridges in many parts of the world. Mr Wilson has served on many technical committees dealing with the design and detailing of reinforced and prestressed concrete structures and has contributed to publications on both British and European codes.

Dr S H Robin Sham is a Senior Engineer with G. Maunsell & Partners. He has gained varied experience in the design and construction of major bridgeworks in prestressed concrete, steel and structural plastics. He received his doctorate from Imperial College for work on artificial intelligence in bridge design, which led to his receiving the McNaughton Award and a sponsorship by the Royal Academy of Engineering to visit research centres in the United States. He now specialises in long-span, cable-supported structures.

Concrete 2000. Edited by Ravindra K. Dhir and M. Roderick Jones.
© 1993 Published by E & FN Spon. ISBN 0 419 18120 2.

INTRODUCTION

The last decade has been an era in which most forms of bridge structure, particularly those constructed in hostile environments, have been found to have shortcomings in their performance. The fundamental reason is that the whole undertaking of bridge design and construction was conceived within objectives that were too narrow.

Historically, concrete bridge design has concentrated on providing structural adequacy based on either a working stress or ultimate capacity approach. Efforts were channelled towards perfecting the behaviour of the structure in isolation, to the exclusion of any concerted study on the performance of a bridge system in its environment. It was often assumed at the design stage that the durability of concrete bridges was unrivalled and that only token maintenance would be necessary to ensure satisfactory performance. Recent studies [1] have revealed that, contrary to past optimism, many concrete bridges are exhibiting signs of deterioration. If the performance of many concrete structures in normal conditions is shown to be impaired, a fundamental but urgent re-assessment must be launched for the design of concrete bridges in hostile environments.

This paper suggests that serious attempts to study this problem can be instigated from a systems reliability standpoint. The bridge system under consideration is not merely the structure in isolation, but comprises the structure as it exists in the transport infrastructure, the users and the maintenance team [2, 3].   It is only after the comparative reliabilities of the components in such a bridge system are known that the correct emphasis or weighting can be assigned to each in order to achieve the best overall reliability. This paper endeavours to illustrate, by special reference to major bridge crossings,   how a better understanding of a reliability approach coupled with advancements in design, detailing, specification, material quality and workmanship [4], can lead to fundamental improvements in the performance of concrete bridges in hostile environments.

RELIABILITY OF LONG CROSSINGS

Basic Theory of Structural Reliability

Conceptually the reliability of a structure is its ability to fulfil its design purpose for some specified reference period, which is commonly referred to as its design life. Implementation of this concept requires the determination of a probability of failure, which combines both engineering and statistical principles.   Failure occurs when a structure attains a specified limit state, or a number of limit states, during its design life. The reliability of a structure, R, and the probability of failure of that structure, P_f, are complementary and related by the expression:

$$R = 1 - P_f$$

When considering the ultimate limit state of collapse, a reliability analysis examines the probability that the applied load effects will exceed the ultimate resistance of the structure. Application of the theory to the serviceability limit state follows a similar logic, once the criterion for a failure in service has been defined. The analysis requires assessments of the potential modes of failure of the structure, in the context of collapse or malfunction in service, and the corresponding probabilities of the structure attaining these modes. A systems approach can then be used to establish the overall reliability of the structure taking into account variability and correlation both in loading and in material properties.

Strategic Importance and Length of Structure

If structures are to be designed to ensure reliability, some measure of this concept is required. Given that major crossings in hostile environments tend to be of much greater strategic importance in the transport infrastructure than bridges on minor roads, such a measure should be able to reflect the difference in reliability demanded by these different situations.

A common measure for structural reliability is the 'target reliability'. Current thinking on the assignment of target reliability is largely influenced by the method outlined in a report by the Construction Industry Research and Information Association (CIRIA) [5]. CIRIA proposes two approaches, one based on social, the other on economic, criteria.

Using social criteria as the basis, the target probability of failure of a structure due to any cause in its design life, P_{ft}, is given by:

$$P_{ft} = \frac{10^{-4}}{n_r} K_s n_d$$

where 10^{-4} is a basic risk calculated from the 1973 fatalities statistics in the United Kingdom,

K_s is a social criterion factor based on the type of structure used,

n_d is the design life of the structure in years,

n_r is the average number of people within or near to the structure during the period of the risk.

The public's aversion to structural failure underpins the justification for target reliabilities based on social criteria. The collapse of a strategic bridge crossing in a hostile environment would have serious economic, social and political consequences. The delays and disruptions which result from traffic restrictions or closure of the bridge for maintenance and repair would also tend to cause public outcry. It therefore follows that the public would expect a higher degree of reliability to be intrinsic in an important structure. This criterion is also appropriate in requiring a greater reliability for longer structures as, in such cases, a greater number of people would be affected.

The social criterion factor, K_s, however does not differentiate between different classes of bridges; the strategic and functional values of a structure are therefore not properly treated in this approach. Recognition of the shortcomings of this approach led to the adoption of economic criteria.

Methods for evaluating target reliability using economic criteria exist in many forms. They attempt, at different levels of sophistication and completeness, to examine the potential costs involved in satisfying safety requirements. The merit of this approach lies in its ability to incorporate in the assessment the importance of a structure in the overall transport infrastructure. It can also explore the costs related to traffic disruptions caused by future inspection and maintenance and therefore it integrates neatly into the modern framework of bridge economics which is founded on whole-life costing [6].

In this approach, the importance of a bridge crossing may be measured by the volume of traffic which the crossing serves, and the lengths of the diversion routes which in turn are partly governed by the length of the crossing. These factors contribute to the lifetime costing and therefore the required reliability of the structure. Costs incurred by traffic delays and disruptions can be derived using the Department of Transport's program QUADRO which takes account of alternative routes for diversion and the anticipated growth of traffic.

On the existing Severn Bridge, the diversion route for traffic would be an extra 50 miles if the crossing were closed for maintenance. It is therefore important to ensure that the second crossing is able to remain in service even in the most hostile weather conditions. This implies that the reliability expected of the second crossing is higher than that of a comparable crossing where the penalties of closure are readily accepted. The provision of hard-shoulders and wind-shielding barriers was therefore specified for the Second Severn Crossing, after comparative studies on alternatives routes using cost-benefit analysis supplemented by considerations of operational and safety aspects had been carried out [3].

Number of Spans

The reliability of a long crossing is affected by the number of spans and the articulation of the structure. Consider a statically determinate system constructed of simply-supported spans (Figure 1a). There are n number of structural elements (spans) and it

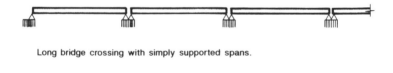

Long bridge crossing with simply supported spans.

Typical collapse mechanism.

(a)   Bridge crossing.

Series system model.

(b)   System reliability model

Figure 1   Bridge crossing with simply-supported spans

is assumed that each span has only one failure element (plastic hinge). The total number of failure elements is also n. In this form of construction, the total length of crossing fails as soon as any span fails. Hence,

R_{system} = P (system has required reliability)
= P (all spans have required reliability)
= P (span 1 has required reliability) x
  P (span 2 has required reliability | span 1 has required reliability)
      x x
  P (span n has required reliability | span 1 ... span n-1 has required reliability)

where P(A)   is the probability that event A occurs,
        P(A|B) is the probability that event A will occur given that event B occurs.

This formulation allows for dependence of one span on another. In the limit, if independence is assumed between spans, the equation simplifies to:

R_{system} = P (span 1 has required reliability) x
  P (span 2 has required reliability) x x
  P (span n has required reliability)
= R_1 x R_2 x .... x R_n

The implication of the derivation is that the reliability of a bridge crossing with simply-supported spans, in the form of a series system (Figure 1b) is that less than that of the individual spans. For simplification, if the spans are assumed to be identical in all respect, then for a chosen value of reliability, r, the overall reliability of the structural system is given by:

$$R_{\text{system}} = r^n$$

From another perspective, the probability of failure of the system is given by:

$$P_{f_{\text{system}}} = 1 - R_{\text{system}}$$
$$= 1 - \{(1 - P_{f1})(1 - P_{f2}) \ldots (1 - P_{fn})\}$$
$$= 1 - \{1 + (-1)\sum_{i=1}^{n} P_{fi} + (-1)^2 \sum_{i \neq j}^{n} P_{fi}P_{fj}$$
$$+ (-1)^3 \sum_{i \neq j \neq k}^{n} P_{fi}P_{fj}P_{fk} + \ldots + (-1)^n \prod_{i=1}^{n} P_{fi}\}$$

If individual spans have equal probability of failure, P_f, then, ignoring terms of second and higher order,

$$P_{\text{system}} = n \times P_f$$

The significance of this derivation is that the probability of failure of the simply-supported configuration for the bridge crossing is approximately proportional to the number of spans. As the number of spans increases in a long estuarial or sea crossing, the failure probability will become unacceptably high.

For a long crossing consisting of continuous spans to reach total failure (Figure 2a), it is necessary that a mechanism is formed. Each failure mode is governed by the formation of sufficient plastic hinges, namely two hinges in an end span or three in an internal span. Although a group of hinges which together form a mechanism is

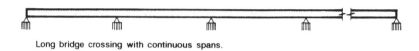

Long bridge crossing with continuous spans.

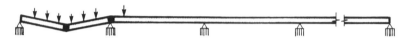

Typical collapse mechanism in end span.

Typical collapse mechanism in an internal span.

(a)   Bridge crossing.

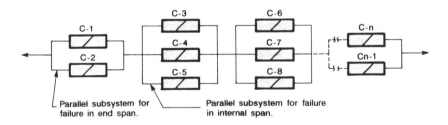

Parallel subsystem for failure in end span.

Parallel subsystem for failure in internal span.

(b)   System reliability model.

Figure 2   Bridge crossing with continuous spans

perceived as a parallel system, the failure modes for each span are combined in a series system (Figure 2b). The total number of mechanisms in a real structure tends to be too high to be included in the combined series-parallel system. Consequently, only the most predominant mechanisms, in terms of probability of occurrence, are included in practice. While it can be proved, either by a simple analysis or by intuitive reasoning, that a pure parallel system has an intrinsically higher reliability than a series system, the assessment of a combined series-parallel system may warrant some caution.

Assuming ductile behaviour, the lower bound reliability for the mixed series and parallel system in Figure 2b is given by:

$$R_{lower} = \{1 - (1 - r_1)(1 - r_2)\} \times \{1 - (1 - r_3)(1 - r_4)(1 - r_5)\} \times$$
$$\{1 - (1 - r_6)(1 - r_7)(1 - r_8)\} \times ... \times \{1 - (1 - r_{n-1})(1 - r_n)\}$$

A qualitative understanding of the reliability of the continuous bridge crossing can be derived by manipulation of the expression for R_{lower} and comparing it with the reliability equation given for simply-supported spans. If some simplifying assumptions are made, such that all component reliabilities are identical, both in the simply-supported and the continuous structures ($r_1 = r_2 = r_3 = r$), then a parametric study using typical values for r enables the following observations to be made. As the number spans in the crossing increases, the system reliability of a continuous structure will be raised above that of the simply-supported structure. At the same time, the system reliability derived from continuity will escalate and approach that of a single span simply-supported bridge. To quantify the absolute levels of reliability, a detailed examination of load distribution and the ductility or brittleness of the spans must be carried out.

Bearings and Movement Joints

A bridge crossing exposed to a hostile environment would render its bearings and movement joints susceptible to accelerated deterioration. If structural reliability is focused on the serviceability limit state, a criterion for failure may be defined as one in which road closure is required for maintenance and repair. The larger the number of elements in the articulation, the smaller the reliability will be. If the crossing is constructed of simply-supported spans, then by virtue of the increased number of bearings and joints, compared with that of a continuous structure, the articulation is far more vulnerable to serviceability failure. If provisions are made in the design to facilitate inspection and replacement of these key elements, then the probability of failure, in the context of disruption to users, will be reduced.

The conceptual design of the articulation further draws on reliability theory. In a long structure, collapse of a span or a pier could provoke progressive collapse of the entire structure. In the tender documents for the Second Severn Crossing, the Second Severn Crossing Group (SSCG) (Maunsell/Atkins) specified a design which would confine any potential progressive collapse of structural members to regions between movement joints. At the same time a maximum allowable number of joints was stipulated to ensure reliability was not impaired by the introduction of an excessive number of simply-supported spans.

A Reliability Approach in Design

In the preparation of the tender documents, The SSCG carried out a Level II reliability assessment [5] on a number of viable designs in both concrete and steel, taking full consideration of moment redistribution and live load distribution, as well as the variability and correlations in material properties and in applied load. Amongst other important conclusions, the SSCG work verified that, if simply-supported spans with a single box girder were used throughout the length of the structure, the probability of failure would escalate in proportion to the number of spans, rendering the system reliability alarmingly low. The work further proved that if deck continuity was achieved, with any span containing halving joints designed to preclude progressive collapse, then the system reliability would be comparable to that of a single, simply-supported bridge span. To safeguard this reliability, bridge decks with twin girders would have to be connected through the deck [3].

Further Applications of a Reliability Approach

The durability problems associated with grouted tendons in precast concrete segmental construction has been under scrutiny for some time. In segmental concrete construction, concern often arises regarding the watertightness of the joints between segments. Precast segmental construction using match-cast deck segments joined by epoxy glue to achieve structural continuity has been in use since the 1960s. To avoid potential hazards with epoxy glue and to achieve economy, dry joints are often used in climatic regions where freeze-thaw cycles do not occur and de-icing agents are not used. Dry joints however are relatively prone to leakage and, if conventional grouted tendons are used, grouting may be hampered and corrosion protection impaired. For these reasons, the use of unbonded, external prestressing became attractive in precast segmental construction using dry joints.

A logical step towards enhancing durability would be to adopt inspectable, replaceable and properly protected external prestressing in precast segmental construction with any form of jointing. This can be verified by the use of a sensitivity analysis which would demonstrate that the probability of failure in prestressed concrete structures is disproportionately dependent on the loss in the area of the tendons. Therefore, overall reliability can most effectively be achieved by proper protection of the prestressing steel against corrosion.

The use of inspectable and replaceable unbonded tendons in precast segmental construction for the Second Severn Crossing was the result of a comparative reliability study. The investigation examined the relative reliabilities inherent in all forms of construction likely to be used for the crossing. Part of the findings was that, as the length of unbonded tendons increases in proportion to the span, the overall reliability diminishes. Structural reliability arising from the use of long lengths of unbonded tendons was also found to be inferior to that of a similar structure with bonded tendons; parity being achieved when the permissible length of unbonded tendon was curtailed. Short lengths of unbonded tendons however, would pose detailing difficulties caused by congestion of anchorages; they also aggravate construction problems and lead to unduly high costs. After these implications had been assessed, a tendon length of 0.4 of the span was selected. This criterion was specific to the structures considered for the Second Severn Crossing; it was to be used in conjunction with a conservative design approach which only permitted the prestress after all losses to be used in an ultimate flexural analysis.

CONCRETE DURABILITY

Improved durability and the minimising of the costs for future inspection and maintenance should be the prime objectives in the development of bridge designs. The exposure of a long bridge crossing to salinity and unrelenting wind increases the vulnerability of such structures to deterioration, results in an accelerated rate of corrosion and compound problems in inspection and repair. In the preparation of the tender specifications and drawings for the Second Severn Crossing, extensive studies were conducted to review the different potential risks and effective means of prevention.

In addition to the allowance made in the capital costs for the use of materials and structural details which had a proven record of durability in marine environments, provisions were also made for the future inspection and maintenance of all parts of the structures. In terms of structural details, permanently protected access was incorporated in the design, with special attention paid to vulnerable elements such as bearings, movement joints and drainage which would require frequent inspection. In the main cable-supported structure, the cable system was designed to provide multiple load paths and to allow unhindered access to the anchorages, thereby permitting removal of individual stay cables for future maintenance while enabling the crossing to remain operational.

The durability of concrete elements in the crossing was ensured by careful consideration to structural detail and methods of construction. In general the critical details included structural configuration, concrete constituents, cover to reinforcement and drainage, together with the provision of waterproof membranes and other protective coatings.

Structural configurations for the bridge decks and substructures were developed to minimise the surface area of concrete which would be exposed to the estuarial environment. Allowance was made in the costing for increased cover to reinforcement, the use of air-entrainment to protect concrete elements from the action of freezing and thawing, and the use of surface coatings on particularly vulnerable members.

Although significant improvements on durability could be achieved by specification, much would depend on the quality of workmanship in construction. The emphasis was therefore to build into the design forms and details which would simplify construction to ensure better workmanship. In this respect, concrete mix design, site control, the curing regime, as well as concrete placing and attainment of sufficient cover were very much objectives by which the design was driven.

PROTECTION TO USERS

The operational characteristics of estuarial or sea crossings must be considered if the performance of a bridge system is to be judged in respect of its role in the transport infrastructure and the level of service it provides. One of the most critical, but often neglected, operational aspects of high-level crossings is the destabilising effects of hostile winds on vehicles. The provision of effective wind-shielding barriers to allow all vehicles to use a crossing in safety, without compromising on the criteria for aerodynamic stability of the superstructure, was a recent development in this field [2].

The benefits of wind shielding can readily be identified if the performance of long crossings in high winds is examined. Traffic using the existing Severn Bridge is exposed to high cross-winds. To help prevent overturning of vehicles and other wind-induced accidents, lane and speed restrictions are imposed. At times when very high cross-winds occur, the passage of high-sided and light vehicles is prohibited. These restriction are imposed, on average, for 150 hours per year. A cost-benefit analysis using QUADRO was used to ascertain the extent and hence the costs incurred by traffic delays and disruptions resulting from hostile winds. The study concluded that the extent to which the cost penalties would be eliminated by a second crossing of the Severn Estuary would depend on the degree of flexibility with which traffic could be assigned between the existing and the new crossing. The flexibility in traffic diversion would only be possible if the performance of the Second Severn Crossing would be unimpaired by the wind-instigated restrictions implemented on the existing bridge.

Concepts for wind shielding were therefore developed [2]. The feasibility of providing full-length wind shielding was examined in conjunction with the aerodynamic stability of the structure. The overall external shape of the crossing was developed through aerodynamic stability studies supported by wind tunnel investigations. A porous barrier in a vertical plane was judged to be viable; it would allow airflow to dissipate energy, eliminate potential risk of blockage, which would aggravate the wind drag, and facilitate future maintenance.

Different combinations of barrier heights and porosities were tested at model scale. This was followed by full scale testing, conducted at the Motor Industry Research Association test track, of vehicles in wind, using controlled cross-winds generated by jet-engines. It was found that a 3-metre high barrier with 45 percent porosity should reduce the forces and overturning moments to at least 50 percent of their values on bridges without wind shielding. With the installation of wind-shielding barriers, the driver would perceive the effects of cross-winds as no worse than those experienced on roads at ground level notwithstanding the severe exposure at the bridge site.

CONCLUSION

This paper presents a unified approach to the design of concrete bridges in hostile environments. Through the use of system reliability analysis, the performance of a concrete bridge in the overall transport infrastructure can be examined. The merits of this approach are manifold. The concept properly addresses the interactions between the bridge structure, the users and the maintenance teams; it can therefore cope with the demands of modern bridge economics which are founded on whole-life costing. The ability to substantiate the comparative reliability of the components in a bridge system will also enable the correct emphasis or weighting to be ascribed to the constituents in order to achieve the best overall reliability. The importance of design, detailing, specification, material quality and workmanship, which are reviewed in this paper by special reference to experience gained from the design of long crossings, now emerge more logically and distinctively when juxtaposed in the framework of the proposed unified approach. The design principles can be further extended to incorporate the subject of user protection. The specific illustrations given in the paper exemplify the innovations which have been achieved in improving the performance of bridges in hostile environments.

REFERENCES

1.   WALLBANK, E.J., The Performance of Concrete in Bridges, A Survey of 200 Highway Bridges, H.M.S.O., London, 1989, 96pp.

2.   RICHMOND, B., Cable-stayed bridges: developments related to wind effects on vehicles, Proc. Int. Conf. Cable-stayed Bridges, Bangkok, 1987, pp 1061-1070.

3.   HEAD, P.R., The performance of bridge 'systems': the next frontier for design and assessment, The Structural Engineer, 1991, Vol. 69, No. 17, pp 310-316.

4.   WILSON, K.R.,AND WALLBANK, E.J., Design for Durability, Proc. Int. Conf. Concrete 2000, Dundee, 1993.

5.   CONSTRUCTION INDUSTRY RESEARCH AND INFORMATION ASSOCIATION, Rationalisation of Safety and Serviceability Factors in Structural Codes, Report 63, London, 1977.

6.   DEPARTMENT OF TRANSPORT, Evaluation of Maintenance Costs in Preparing Alternative Designs for Highway Structures, Departmental Standard BD 36/88, London, 1988.

DURABILITY TEST AND NEW LONG LIFE DESIGN
CONCEPT OF CONCRETE STRUCTURES

K Katawaki

H Sakamoto

I Nishizaki

Public Works Research Institute

Japan

ABSTRACT.
This paper presents the state of durability tests on concrete bridge protection and its life design concept. Many road bridges that constructed on coastal areas are affected by sea salt and so concrete bridge protection techniques are particularly important in Japan.
We use heavy duty coating systems on the concrete surface, epoxy resin powder coated steel, salt resistant steel, plastic sheaths and epoxy resin coated steel stands for pre-stressed concrete.
These protection techniques are used in severely corrosive environments such as along shorelines in order to evaluate the long term performance of these concrete protection systems and the materials. New protection materials and techniques will continue to be investigated and improve life design concept of concrete structures.

Keywords: Corrosion, Protection, Concrete, Maritime structure, Epoxy, Coating, Polymer impregnated, Cathodic protection, Carbon fiber composite

Dr. Kiyoshi KATAWAKI is the director of Chemistry Division, Public Works Research Institute, Ministry of Construction, where he has been most active in concrete technology for 18 years by performing researches, committee members, and managing research activities. His current research work includes: protection of concrete structure, maintenance and diagnosis of structure, hi-tech materials, and computer aided designing.
Mr. Hiroyuki SAKAMOTO is a senior research engineer of Chemistry Division, PWRI MOC. He studies concrete protection techniques and pavement materials.
Mr. Itaru NISHIZAKI is a research staff of Chemistry Division, PWRI, MOC. He is a research chemist, and his current research work includes: concrete protection techniques, hi-tech materials and its application techniques for the construction field and durability of polymers for public structure.

Concrete 2000. Edited by Ravindra K. Dhir and M. Roderick Jones.
© 1993 Published by E & FN Spon. ISBN 0 419 18120 2.

INTRODUCTION

Japan is surrounded by the sea. Typhoons often hit the country in succession from summer to autumn, and Japan is exposed to strong seasonal winds in winter, especially on the Japan sea side. Therefore, many coastal areas are affected by sea salt, and techniques for protecting concrete structures are important. Areas particularly affected by sea salt and the strong seasonal winds in winter include Okinawa, the southern tropical islands, and the coast facing the Japan sea from Hokuriku to Hokkaido. In the 1980s, the corrosion of the steel of concrete structures by sea salt has become a big problem. Many main lines with many concrete bridges have been constructed on the Japan sea coast since 1970. These areas are exposed to strong seasonal winds in winter, and the bridges are adversely affected by the sea salt.

However, the bridges were constructed using traditional techniques which did not offer corrosion protection. As a result, many bridges have been damaged as the sea salt corrodes the steel in the concrete after about ten years. This has forced the development of concrete protection and restoration techniques.

Past we have not effective countermesure for protection except concrete quarity and coverdepth. Nowadays we can select appropriate protection techniques according to the design concept of concrete structure using newly developed protection systems.

DETERIORATION PROCESS

The deterioration process involves many phenomena: chloride penetration (Fig.1), chloride accumulation, start of steel corrosion,,crack initiation and crack propagation. The deterioration process due to corrosion is shown in Fig. 2.

Although crack propagation seems to be the most influential factor causing a structure to fail, chloride penetration is the first stage of the chain reaction of events.

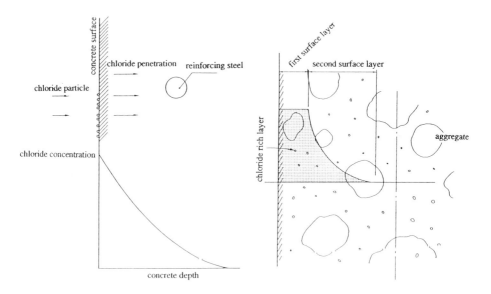

Fig.1 Chloride concentration in concrete

LONG LIFE DESIGN CONCEPT

Concrete structures such as bridges must last a minimum of 50 years without requiring major restoration. The prematuredeterioration of concrete by chloride corrosion shortens the lifespan of the structure and is a severe problem. In the long life design concept, corrosion protection plays a major role.

In Fig. 2 the simple chain reaction occurs particularly under severe atmospheric conditions: chloride penetration - chloride accumulation - corrosion of steel-crack initiation -- crack propagation.

The faster these reactions can be stopped, the more effective is the protection. Even once the reaction has started, the deterioration process can be stopped by using different protective techniques. It is most effective to combine some of the effective protection techniques to extend the life and hence reduce the cost of concrete structures.

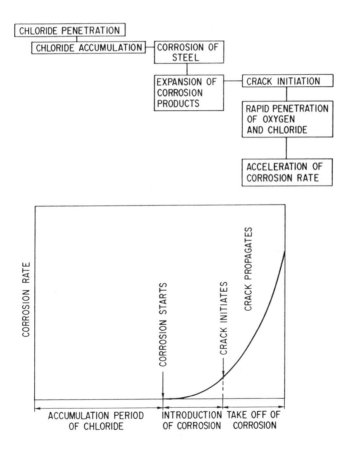

Fig. 2 Deterioration process in deterioration mechanism

Typical examples are as follows:

Surface coating	+15 years
Silica fume concrete	+20 years
Epoxy coated	+15 years
Total	50 years longer

Even under severe atmospheric conditions, the life of a concrete structure can be extended by more than 50 years without major repair.

A tentative guideline of countermeasures for road bridges in coastal areas to prevent corrosion was published by the Japan Road Association. The contents of that guideline are briefly outlined as follows:

Japan is divided into three areas according to the severity of the environment and countermeasures are classified into three types according to the area and the distance from the coast.

Three protection methods are detailed in the guideline: increasing the cover depth on reinforcement, using epoxy coated reinforcement, and coating the concrete.

If the minimum cover depth given in the classification cannot be used, an epoxy coated reinforcement or concrete coating should be chosen.

When an epoxy coated reinforcement is used, the allowable design bond stress is 80% of normal, and it must have sufficient workability and durability in situ, sufficient bonding strength to the concrete, and must be alkali-resistant.

When a concrete coating is used, the coating material should be chosen from one of the following:

A. Epoxy and polyurethane
B. Soft type epoxy or soft type polyurethane
C. High build type epoxy or glass-flake polyester

A is applied to prestressed concrete structures, B is applied to reinforced concrete and C is applied to important concrete structures or ones which are difficult to repair. Concrete surface coatings are easy to acquire and offer good workability.

Soft coating materials are recommended for RC structures, and relatively hard coating materials for PC structures. The life of coats of this type is thought to be at least fifteen years, somewhat longer than first expected.

Table-1 Mechanism and protection technique

Mechanism	Protection technique
Chloride penetration	Heavy duty coating
Chloride accumulation	Silica hume concrete
	Very dense concrete
Corrosion	Epoxy coated steel
	Epoxy coated tendons
	Cathodic protection
	Carbon composite

We have a plan to revise this tentative guideline from durability tests results and long-term evaluation that describes later.

NEWLY DEVELOPED PROTECTION SYSTEMS

Some examples of relatively new concrete protection techniques are introduced.

Heavy Duty Coating Systems for Concrete Protection

Coating the surface of new concrete used not to be a common technique, but recently a protection system using a heavy duty coating has been established and used in severely corrosive environments such as on shorelines. The technique is detailed in a manual, and is now used very commonly; we are making the final evaluation and improvement of these materials.

Former studies have shown that coating concrete surfaces is effective for protecting reinforced steel concrete We researched various coating systems to determine the effective and suitable ones for concrete, and the results are included in the "Manual for protecting road bridges from sea salt". The heavy duty coating systems are summarized below:

Table-2 Heavy Duty Coating Systems

	A	B	C
Applied for	pre-stressed concrete members	reinforced concrete members	when repainting is difficult or severe corrosion is expected
Primer	epoxy resin	epoxy resin or polyurethane resin	epoxy resin or polyurethane resin
Putty	epoxy resin	epoxy resin	epoxy resin or vinyl ester resin
Midcoat	epoxy resin 60μm	epoxy resin or polyurethane resin resin (pliable type) 60μm	epoxy resin or vinyl ester 350μm (thick type)
Top coat	polyurethane resin 30μm	polyurethane resin (pliable type) 30μm	polyurethane resin 30μm

The coatings are classified into three groups as follows. Group 1 is for prestressed concrete members, and the coating membrane is not required, thus giving a high crack 'followability' (1% or more). Group 2 is for reinforced concrete members, and the membrane requires a crack followability of 4% or more. Group 3 is for long term corrosion preventive coatings intended for use on concrete structures in particularly corrosive environments. Testing will be carried out for these three groups for 15 types of coating.

The protective effect of the coating materials was tested for four years in coastal areas affected directly by splashing sea water. The tests confirmed that these high performance coating materials do intercept chloride and are waterproof. The weathering protection of almost all of them will continue for a long time to come.

Concrete beam coated with epoxy
(precast beam fabricated)

Concrete beam applied with cathodic protection
(under construction)

High Durability Coating Materials

Techniques of applying high durability coating materials, which use fluorine resin paint
or silicone resin paint as the top coat, for concrete structures are being developed. The
purpose is not only to improve the protective ability but also to add new functions such
as preserving beautiful colors over time, or providing resistance to dirt. These
techniques will be published in a new manual in autumn 1993.

Cathodic Protection

We performed various experiments on disused bridges. One of the experiments used a
T-beam reinforced concrete bridge built in 1935, located about 60 meters from the coast
of the Japan sea. The following protection systems were tested:

Table-3 Cathodic protection system

	A	B
Wire electrode	conductive resin electrode 7.87mm (dia) 3 wires	titanium wire plated by platinum 1.5mm (dia) 3 wires
Coating electrode	conductive mortar 15mm(thickness)	conductive paint 300um(thickness)
Top coat lining	polyurethane resin 200μm	acrylurethane resin 50μm
Power supply	DC18V, 1A	DC18V, 1A
Reference electrode	16s lead electrodes 18mm(dia) 100mm	16s steel probes 13mm(dia) 100mm

Cathodic Protection Technique for PC Bridge Members

Cathodic protection may be used for severely damaged concrete members in order to ensure there is no more damage. We experimented with many methods and materials using disused bridges, and derived valuable data. We used this data as the basis for a manual on using cathodic protection techniques for concrete members. In Japan, there are approximately 30 operational bridges which are protected by cathodic protection techniques. The evaluation experiments are still continuing.

Application of Cathodic Protection to Bridges

Cathodic protection techniques are now being used to protect actual bridges, and are showing excellent performance.
We will continue to monitor the long term protective performance.

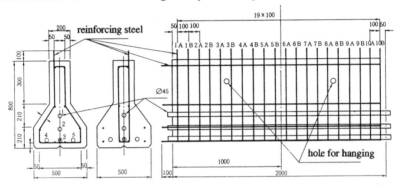

Fig. 3 Typical concrete specimen for durability test (unit: cm)

We conducted field tests on large structures and collected basic data. The applicability and the effects of cathodic protection were tested on a bridge which has been in use for 50 years or more.
Since a number of cracks were detected on the surface of the concrete due to corrosion of the reinforcement, the surface concrete was partially chipped, and the surfaces of the reinforcing bars were polished with sand. Then, the chipped sections were repaired with non-shrinkable mortar.
A cathodic protection method called the external power supply method was used. This approach uses a combination of a linear electrode (directly connected to the power supply) and a covered electrode (for better distribution of the current). For cathodic protection, two systems were used: one was a combination of a conductive resin linear electrode and conductive mortar (system A), and the other was a combination of platinum plated titanium linear electrode and conductive paint (system B). In order to identify the protective effects, lead reference electrodes and reinforcement probes were embedded into the concrete to monitor the reinforcement potential and the current, respectively.
The test results show that this procedure is relatively easy and the cathodic protection test results agree with the predicted values. The maintenance cost of the protection was also shown to be reasonable, and a guideline for cathodic protection design was therefore proposed by PWRI.

New Materials of Concrete Protection Materials

Recently, many new-performance matererials are being developed, and ways of using these materials for public structures are still being researched.
The main protection materials are epoxy resin coated steels, salt resistant steel, plastic sheaths, and epoxy resin coated steel strands for pre-stressed concrete. We performed loading and grouting tests, using full-scale beam models with a polyethylene sheath.
A plastic sheath appears to offer sufficient performance to be used in actual structures.
Fiber-reinforced plastics for pre-stressed concrete tendons offer promising possibilities for protecting concrete. In Japan, several bridges have been already constructed with carbon fiber reinforced plastic or aramid fiber reinforced plastic tendons. The main technical key points are anchorage, the sheath, and long term durability. PWRI is now researching these items using many physical tests, long term exposure tests, loading tests using full-scale models, and will publish the results in a manual.

Concrete bridge first applied with CFRP

To prevent chloride ions penetrating into the concrete members, the concrete members were made fine by adding an internal sealing mixture. Silica fume is a possible mixture, and this was used in the test.

DURABLITY TEST

Evaluation of Protective System for Bridge Members

We conducted many experiments on epoxy power coated steel, salt resistance steel, plastic sheaths, and epoxy resin coated steel strands for pre-stressed concrete, and are evaluating the protection performance of these materials.

Long Term Evaluation in Marine Environment

We are conducting exposure tests in a severely corrosive environment such as on shorelines in order to evaluate the long term performance of the concrete protection systems and materials. For these tests, we selected several typical exposed sites, which are located in Suruga bay, the sea coast of Okinawa, and the coast facing the Japan sea.

Exposure Test at the Suruga Marine Test Station

To improve the durability of steel materials and reinforced concrete used for marine structures, a comprehensive test is being conducted to study the development of corrosion protection technologies. The research station constructed off Oimachi in Shizuoka-ken is being used for the test.

This test station was constructed using the special research fund for the utilization of marine space by coastal and offshore structures, under the supervision of the Science and Technology Agency. The test site is located in Suruga bay in Shizuoka prefecture, central Japan. Suruga bay is the deepest sea around the Sea coast of Japan, and was formed by sand brought down the Oi river.

The dimensions of the test station are as follows:

First deck (top floor)	10.5m x 18m
Second deck	15m x 15m
Third deck	7.5m x 7.5m
Observation tower and house	

The exposure test has just started and the period of the study is scheduled for ten years at present.

Concrete test beams exposed at the Suruga Test Station

The test objects were set up in the Ministry of Construction's Oigawa Research Station installed near the river Oi in Suruga bay; the exposure tests have already started.

This study mainly consists of especially long term exposure tests in the splash zone exposed to the air on April 1984, and a total of 264 cylinders (150 x 300) were also prepared as auxiliaries.

CONCLUSION

This paper briefly describes the state of development of new techniques for concrete structures in a marine environment. We have established a tentative guideline from the recent results of experiments on concrete durability.

This guideline includes a new design concept that incorporates modern protection techniques for a variety of different geographical regions. The protection techniques have been developed, and they must now be evaluated. For this purpose, the long term exposure test in an actual environment is the most reliable and useful for improving the materials and refining the techniques. The current exposure test at the Suruga Marine Test Station is a typical example of an evaluation test.

Protective measures against corrosion urgently need to be established, but this depends on the progress of materials technology and engineering. We intend to accelerate the development of protection engineering for concrete structures which will prove useful for improving the durability of marine structures.

REFERENCES

1. Japan Road Association : 'Manual for road bridge protection from sea salt'
2. Ministry of Construction : 'Development of concrete durability improvement techniques,' 1988 ("A manual for restoring concrete structures which are damaged by sea salt" is included in this document.)
3. K. KATAWAKI, H. SAKAMOTO,et. al.: 'Cooperative investigation on cathodic protection of reinforcing steel in concrete structures,' Aug. 1988
4. K. KATAWAKI, H. SAKAMOTO, et. al.: 'Development of cathodic protection for deteriorated concrete structures,' Second Canmet/ACI International Conference on Durability of Concrete, Montreal, 1991
5. K. KATAWAKI : 'Research on epoxy coated reinforcing steel, materials test of epoxy for reinforcing barp,' Technical Report of PWRI, 1986
6. K. KATAWAKI, S. KOBAYASHI : 'Research on epoxy coated reinforcing steel, performance of reinforced concrete in marine environments,' Technical Report of PWRI, 1986
7. K. KATAWAKI, M. FUKUSHIMA, T. TSUJI, S. HASHIMOTO : 'Research on concrete surface coating, materials performance,' Technical Report of PWRI, 1986
8. K. KATAWAKI, H. SAKAMOTO, J. TOMURA, K. SHIMIZU : 'Research on cathodic protection for concrete structures, protection design of cathodic protection,' Technical Report of PWRI, 1986
9. K. KATAWAKI, H. SAKAMOTO : 'Research on cathodic protection for concrete structures, a guideline of cathodic protection design,' Technical Report of PWRI, 1986
10. Large scale exposure tests for improving the protection technology of maritime structures,' The Science and Technology Agency, 1988
11. K. KATAWAKI, I. NISHIZAKI : 'Research on polymer impregnated concrete, treatment techniques of PIC,' Technical Report of PWRI, 1986
12. K. KATAWAKI : 'Research on polymer impregnated concrete, corrosion resistance of PIC,' Technical Report of PWRI, 1986

TOWARDS AN EARLY-AGE INDEX
FOR THE DURABILITY OF CONCRETE

Y Ballim

University of Witwatersrand

South Africa

ABSTRACT. This paper discusses the correlations between the 28-day oxygen permeability and water sorptivity of concretes (as index tests) and the corresponding 10 month depths of carbonation measured (as a durability process). In the test programme, OPC, OPC/fly ash and OPC/blastfurnace slag concretes of varying strength grades were manufactured and exposed in the normal laboratory environment during drying and carbonation. Samples were exposed to a range of moist curing periods before being exposed to the drying conditions. Oxygen permeability and water absorption measurements were obtained at 28 days and the depths of carbonation were determined at 10 months after casting using the phenolphthalein test. The results show that a significant correlation is obtained between the 28-day permeability and water absorption of the concrete and its rate of carbonation. While this is only one of the many forms of concrete deterioration, the results are positive from the point of view of the development of a general durability index for concrete.

Keywords: Durability, Testing, Permeability, Sorptivity, Curing, Carbonation, Blastfurnace slag, Fly ash.

Mr. Yunus Ballim is presently a lecturer in Construction Materials in the Department of Civil Engineering at the University of the Witwatersrand, Johannesburg, South Africa. He is also registered as a PhD candidate at this university. His main research interests are in the areas of concrete durability, curing, construction practice, deterioration mechanisms, rehabilitation and movement properties of concrete.

Concrete 2000. Edited by Ravindra K. Dhir and M. Roderick Jones.
© 1993 Published by E & FN Spon. ISBN 0 419 18120 2.

INTRODUCTION

The past few decades have seen major advances in the effectiveness with which concrete is used as a construction material. Improved design procedures, better and more consistent quality of cement and a greater understanding of the engineering performance of the material has led to increased strength-to-weight ratios of structural elements. Added to this, construction techniques are developing to allow concrete structures to be completed in increasingly shorter time periods. Waste materials, such as fly ash (FA), ground granulated blastfurnace slag (GGBS) and silica fume have become commonplace in concrete applications. The general use of "workability-enhancing" admixtures have also caused reductions in the cement content required to achieve target strengths.

These developments are all to be encouraged as they are aimed at optimising the use of resources which we have come to recognised as not being inexhaustible. Current developments in this area of concrete technology means that we will increase the effectiveness with which we use the material in future.

However, these developments also mean that concrete structures are more susceptible to deterioration by aggressive agents and hence, require that greater attention be paid to durability aspects. The main factors accounting for this problem are:
-    Reduced OPC contents [1] caused by the use of plasticisers and blends of cement extenders, means that there is less active material to resist deterioration forms such as carbonation and chloride ingress. In these examples, a shorter time will be required to de-passivate the reinforcing steel.
-    The use of thin structural members means that a greater proportion of the member is affected by early drying, which causes the hydration process to be interrupted.
-    Reduced cement contents required to achieve target strengths mean that there is less "spare capacity" to ensure an acceptable quality of surface concrete despite the hydration process being interrupted.
-    The slower rate of hydration of FA and GGBS blended with OPC, makes these materials more sensitive to abuse, especially during the early stages after casting.

If we are to maximise the benefits of these developments in concrete materials and construction technology, designers of reinforced concrete structures and the specifications which are meant to guide them must adequately responded to the new durability challenges. This paper argues for the development and adoption of an early-age index test of the concrete surface quality which can be related to long-term durability performance. Such a test will allow designers to specify and control the surface quality of their concretes during the construction phase and hence, ensure long-term durability with a greater degree of confidence.

As a contribution to the development of such a test, this paper presents the results of a laboratory test programme aimed at relating oxygen permeability and water sorptivity of surface concrete (index tests) to depth of carbonation (durability performance). In this test programme, concretes with a range of binder types and strength grades were exposed to different curing regimes and then subjected to the index tests. These values were then compared with the depths of carbonation after 10 months of indoor exposure.

The discussion in this paper is mainly concerned with reinforced concrete elements and the term "durability" is associated with deterioration of concrete due to the ingress of aggressive agents from the surrounding environment. Deterioration due to actions such as AAR are not considered here.

THE NEED FOR A DURABILITY INDEX TEST

In the absence of an acceptable index or performance test of the surface quality of concrete members during the early period after casting, most specifications have resorted to "method specifications". With this approach, the contractor is given a set of instructions as to the method of construction to ensure long-term durability. For example, the method of curing is specified and the selection of the particular method is usually based on past experience and/or convenience of application. The problems associated with this method of specification are:
- it is often difficult to ensure that the prescribed procedure is being adhered to in practice;
- even with rigid policing procedures, the designer is unable to establish if the desired surface quality has been achieved, since different concretes may respond differently to the same curing method;
- because of the uncertainty associated with this approach, there is a tendency towards over-specification and concretes exposed to innocuous environments are often required to be treated in the same way as concretes exposed to aggressive environments;

To illustrate a further problem, the South African code of practice on concrete curing [2] allows the contractor to choose from a range of curing methods which may be used on site. These methods include steam curing, water ponding for a minimum of 7 days, application of curing compounds and plastic covering. In so doing, the code makes a statement about the equivalence of curing effectiveness of these different methods. However, Ballim et al [3] have shown that a local curing compound which gave results five times better than the requirement set by ASTM C309 [4], when applied at the supplier's recommended dosage, was equivalent to approximately 3 days of water curing in terms of surface oxygen permeability and water sorptivity.

These problems would largely be overcome if an acceptable index test could be developed which would measure the quality of the in situ surface concrete. The contractor would then be requested to achieve a certain index test level and the method of achieving this need not be specified. Like the compressive strength test as a quality control indicator, the index test would be used as an acceptance criterion for the durability of the structure.

THE DEVELOPMENT OF AN INDEX TEST

Oberholzer [5] and Mehta [1] correctly argue that clear definitions of the concrete and the environment of exposure needs to established in order to develop a reliable method for predicting durability. Most researchers in this field have accepted that the resistance of concrete to the ingress of aggressive fluids is best characterised by a fluid transport parameter of the material. These include gas permeability [6], water permeability [7] and water sorptivity [8].

While there are a number of problems [9] which have yet to be addressed before a standard test method can be adopted, the relationship between the index tests and the extent of deterioration due to given aggressive environments needs to be quantified. A database of such information will assist in the adoption of a test method, on the basis of its reliability in predicting the durability of concrete. The results presented in this paper are intended as a contribution to that development.

LABORATORY TEST PROCEDURE

Materials and Mixes

Concretes were prepared using three binder types as follows:
  (a) plain OPC;
  (b) 50% OPC and 50% GGBS;
  (c) 70% OPC and 30% FA.

Table 1 Mix proportions (kg/m³) and properties of the various concretes tested

Binder Type	Water	FA	OPC	GGBS	Coarse Agg.	Sand	Slump (mm)	Strength at 28 days (MPa)
100%	205	-	308	-	800	1033	30	39.6
OPC	210	-	378	-	800	976	40	47.7
	210	-	441	-	800	923	40	59.4
70/30	190	117	273	-	780	1003	45	45.3
OPC/FA	188	135	316	-	780	951	45	58.6
50/50	205	-	164	164	780	1047	60	37.1
OPC/	202	-	197	197	790	989	50	39.4
GGBS	200	-	230	230	790	937	40	53.2

Three strength grades of concrete were prepared using each of binders (a) and (b) and two strength grades of binder type (c). Water/binder (w/b) ratios were selected to give equivalent 28-day strengths. These values were obtained from curves presented in Fulton [10]. A crushed silica was used as coarse and fine aggregate for all the concretes. The coarse aggregate consisted of a nominal 19 mm stone while the fine aggregate had a fineness modulus of 3.6. All mixes were designed to have slumps ranging between 30 and 60 mm. Table 1 shows the mix proportions, slumps and 28-day standard cured compressive strengths of each of the concretes tested.

Sample Preparation and Storage

Sufficient 100 mm cubes of each of the concretes listed in Table 1 were cast in the standard manner. After de-moulding, equal numbers of samples were exposed to the following curing conditions:
(a)   in air at 23 °C and 65% RH for a further 27 days;
(b)   immersed in water for 2 days followed by exposure as for (a) for a further 25 days;
(c)   immersed in water for 6 days followed by exposure as for (a) for a further 21 days;
(d)   immersed in water for 27 days.
Samples were water cured by being immersed in a curing tank where the temperature was held constant at 22 ± 1 °C.

At the time that samples were to be exposed to air drying, two coats of a water-based epoxy were applied to four contiguous surfaces which included the top surface of the cube, as cast. This allowed uni-directional drying through two opposite, moulded faces. When the epoxy coating had dried, the samples were placed on shelves which allowed free air movement around the two exposure surfaces.

At 28 days after casting, a 68 mm diameter central core was drilled from each cube perpendicular to the two exposed surfaces. Three consecutive disks, approximately 14 mm thick, were cut from one end of the core. The disks therefore represented nominal depths of 0 to 15 mm, 15 to 30 mm and 30 to 45 mm from the drying surface of the sample. The method of coring and cutting the samples to obtain the disks is described by Ballim [11]. A number of cubes were left on the drying shelves to be tested at later ages for carbonation.

Immediately after the disks were obtained, they were transferred to an air ventilated oven, controlled at a temperature of 48 ± 2 °C. All disk samples were dried in this manner for 7 days before testing.

Test Methods

Oxygen permeability and water sorptivity

After the disk samples were oven dried, they were tested for the coefficient of oxygen permeability and water sorptivity as indexes of the concrete surface qualities. The oxygen permeability test involves the use of a falling head permeameter. A 68 mm concrete sample is fixed in the permeameter and a reservoir on the upstream side of the sample is pressurised with oxygen. Oxygen then passes through the sample and the rate of pressure decay in the reservoir is monitored with time. This gives a direct measure of the Darcy coefficient of permeability.

In the water sorptivity test, the top of the sample (after the permeability test) is exposed to a free water surface. The rate of water absorption is then monitored by weighing the sample at regular intervals. Both the permeability and sorptivity test methods are described in more detail by Ballim [11],[12].

Depth of carbonation

At 10 months after casting, the samples which had been left on the shelves in the temperature and relative humidity controlled room, were split perpendicular to the drying faces. The depth of carbonation was then determined by spraying the broken surface with a 1% phenolphthalein in alcohol solution and measuring the depth of the uncoloured zone.

RESULTS AND DISCUSSION

As expected, the samples tested showed a gradation of permeability and sorptivity values with depth from the drying surface. However, for the purposes of relating the 28-day durability index test results to the 10 month depths of carbonation, only the results of the 0-15 mm disks are presented here. This decision was based on the fact that, in the majority of samples, the carbonation depth was restricted to this layer of concrete.

Figure 1 shows a plot of the 28-day oxygen permeability against the corresponding 10 month depth of carbonation. The points plotted on this graph are distinguished according to binder type and a regression line for each binder type is also shown.

Figure 1 shows a clear trend of increasing depth of carbonation with increasing surface permeability. The following points are noted with regard to the regression lines shown:
-      The FA line is approximately parallel to and shifted above the OPC line. This indicates that, for the same value of permeability, FA concretes carbonate faster than OPC concretes. This phenomenon can be ascribed to the lower calcium hydroxide content of the FA concrete presenting less "resistance" to the advance of the carbonation front.
-      The GGBS line is rotated with respect to the OPC line indicating that, for concretes in the high permeability range, GGBS concretes carbonate faster than OPC concretes and vice versa.
It should be noted, however, that while the trends discussed above are evident, all the regression lines lie within the range of scatter of the data points.

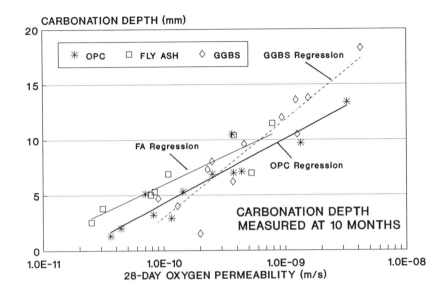

Figure 1   Relationship between 28-day coefficient of permeability and 10-month depth of carbonation

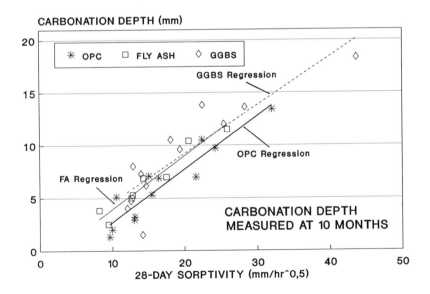

Figure 2   Relationship between 28-day sorptivity and 10-month depth of carbonation

Figure 2 shows the relationship between 28-day sorptivity and 10 month carbonation. These results are presented in the same manner as Figure 1 above.

Figure 2 also shows a good correlation between 28-day sorptivity and the depth of carbonation. Here again, the regression line of the FA results is approximately parallel to and shifted above the OPC line. The GGBS line is rotated with respect to the OPC line but not as markedly as for the oxygen permeability relationship.

Table 2 shows the correlation coefficients obtained for the regression lines shown in Figures 1 and 2. A power regression was used for the oxygen permeability relationship and a linear regression was used for sorptivity relationship.

Table 2   Correlation coefficients of the regression curves shown in Figures 1 and 2

Binder type	Correlation coefficient for the relationship based on:	
	Oxygen permeability	Water Sorptivity
100% OPC	0.940	0.938
70/30 OPC/FA	0.938	0.965
50/50 OPC/GGBS	0.954	0.924

Table 2 shows that approximately equal correlation coefficients were obtained for the relationships between water sorptivity and carbonation depth and between oxygen permeability and carbonation depth. The implication is that both these parameters are good indicators of long-term durability. These correlation coefficients could possibly have been improved if thicker samples were used in this investigation, thereby reducing variability, especially with the oxygen permeability results [9].

General discussion

The results presented in Figures 1 and 2 above indicate a potential problem in the use of early age index tests to ensure long-term durability of concrete. It is clear that, for a given index value, concrete with different binder types respond differently in terms of durability performance. Hence, if the surface quality of concrete was to be specified on the basis of an early index test, in order to limit long term deterioration, the binder type will have to be accounted for in such a specification. It would be difficult to account for all possible combinations of binder type in such a specification.

However, if designed to achieve similar 28-day strengths as plain OPC concretes, concretes with cement extenders will usually require lower w/b ratios. If these concretes are adequately cured, they generally result in improved surface impermeability. Hence, the problem stated above is overcome if the specification is based on appropriate limits for an early age index test in combination with a minimum strength requirement.

CONCLUSIONS

1. Good correlation exists between 28-day oxygen permeability and water sorptivity, as concrete surface quality index tests, and 10-month depths of carbonation, as a deterioration process. This indicates that such index tests may be used to specify the quality of surface concrete required to ensure a particular level of durability.

2. The relationship between the index test and the durability performance is dependent on the binder type of the concrete. From the point of view of specification, this problem may be resolved by combining an index test specification with a minimum strength requirement.

3. Water sorptivity and oxygen permeability appear to be reliable early-age index tests for predicting long-term durability. Further research is necessary to confirm the measured correlation coefficients.

4. For given values of surface oxygen permeability and water sorptivity at 28 days, FA concretes carbonate faster than OPC concretes. This is ascribed to the lower calcium hydroxide content of the FA concretes.

5. In the range tested, GGBS concretes carbonate faster than OPC concretes with the same 28-day sorptivity values. This effect was not noted as clearly in the relationship between 28-day oxygen permeability and carbonation depth.

REFERENCES

1. MEHTA, P.K. Durability of concrete - Fifty years of progress? Second Int. Conference on the Durability of concrete, Montreal, Canada. 1991. ACI SP126. pp. 1-30.

2. SOUTH AFRICAN BUREAU OF STANDARDS. Code of practice : The structural use of concrete. Part 2: Materials and execution of work. SABS 0100:1992.

3. BALLIM, Y, TAYLOR, P AND MACDONALD, H.K. A preliminary assessment of the effectiveness of a liquid membrane-forming curing compound. Concrete/Beton, Jnl. of the Concrete Society of Southern Africa. No. 66, Jan. 1993. pp. 25-26.

4. AMERICAN SOCIETY FOR TESTING MATERIALS. Specification for liquid membrane-forming compounds for curing concrete. ASTM C309-81.

5. OBERHOLZER, R.E. "Pore structure, permeability and diffusivity as related to durability". Proc. of 8th Int. Congress on the Chem. of Cement, Rio de Janeiro, 1986. pp 321-335.

6.   DHIR, R.K, HEWLETT, P.C AND CHAN, Y.N. Near surface characteristics of concrete: Intrinsic permeability". Mag. of Conc. Res. Vol. 41, No. 147. June 1989. pp 87-97.

7.   VAN DER MEULEN, G.J.R AND VAN DIJK, J. A permeability testing apparatus for concrete. Mag. of Concr. Res. Vol. 21, No. 67. June 1969. pp. 121-123.

8.   HALL, C. Water sorptivity of mortars and concretes: A review. Mag. of Conc. Res. Vol. 41, No. 147. June 1989. pp 51-61.

9.   HOOTON, R.D. Problems inherent in permeability measurement. Engineering Foundation Conference: Advances in Cement Manufacture and Use. Potosi, Missouri. Aug. 1988. pp 143 - 154.

10.   ADDIS, B.J. (Ed.) Fulton's concrete technology. Sixth edition. Portland Cement Institute. Midrand, South Africa. 1986.

11.   BALLIM, Y. Curing and the durability of OPC, fly ash and blastfurnace slag concretes. Awaiting publication in the RILEM Journal: Materials and Structures.

12.   BALLIM, Y. A low cost, falling head permeameter for measuring concrete gas permeability. Concrete/Beton, Jnl. of the Concrete Society of Southern Africa. No. 61, Nov. 1991. pp 13-18.

CONSTRUCTIVE CHEMICALLY RESISTANT CONCRETE

V P Kirilishin

Building Institute

Ukraine

ABSTRACT. In present paper synthesis conditions of new binding substance of tridymite-cristobalite mineralogical content (TC) for concretes, received by roasting at temperature of 1320 ± 20 °C of natural quartz sands or industrial quartz waste with additives of oxides alkaline metals as mineralizator in low - alkaline part of $SiO_2^- R_2O$ system are examined. Recommended chemical composition of sodium-alkaline TC is to correspond to the content of Na_2O from 0.5...1.0 to 4..5 wt.pct. for the most favourable hardening in homogeneous mixture with fine milled quartz sand in autoclave treatment conditions under pressure of saturated water steam of 12 B due to crystallization mechanism with complete TC dissolution and its crystallization into cryptocrystalline quartz on microparticles of milled sand, having the role of prepared crystallisation centers. TC is to be applied in corns forms of size up to 0,5 - 0,6 mm, and quartz sand is to be milled up to fine milling of rapid hardening cements. Received on TC base silica concrete (SC) with cement connective from synthetic microcrystalline quartz, with quartz sand as a fine aggregate and with quartzite crushed stone inherits the properties of natural guartzose sandstones and quartzite breccia, related to the most long-lived natural rocks. Taking into account studied building-technical properties of SC rational range of its application in building engineering is recommended.

KEYWORDS. Inorganic binder, SiO_2-R_2O system , Durability, Quartz, Tridymite, Cristobalite, High-strength concrete, Chemically resistant materials and articles, Anti-corrosion protection, Silica concrete.

Professor Vsevolod Petrovich Kirilishin is the Chief of the Research Laboratory 'Silica Concrete' and simultaneously he is engaged in teacher's activity at the department of Building materials of the Odessa Civil Engineering Institute. He specializes in the field of development, investigation and using of new materials and articles on the base of silica raw materials in SiO_2- R_2O system.

Concrete 2000. Edited by Ravindra K. Dhir and M. Roderick Jones.
© 1993 Published by E & FN Spon. ISBN 0 419 18120 2.

INTRODUCTION

In modern conditions of social production intensification, the most increasing role of industrial and agricultural chemistryzation, of ecological problems of surroundings pollution, become stronger the processes   of chemical corrosion and premature destructions of building constructions of edifices,building and technological equipment, provoking progressive increase of expenses for repair-restoring works, often bound up with additional losses because of industrial stoppage. That's why raising the durability of building constructions exploitation, increase of interrepair periods may be significant reserve of releasing additional material, fuel-energetical and labour resources for increase the effectiveness of capital investment and cutting of production costs.

One of the ways of the most radical decision of this important scientific-technical problem is   the organization of manufacture and using new construction building materials and articles with special consumers gualities,which   are not   inherent in traditional materials conformably   to concrete conditions of their exploitation in building constructions.

Thus,for a long time the attention of the investigators has been attracted by exclusively high physical stability and chemical inertness of extensive mineral family of silica group [1], forming the eighth part of Earth crust mass.But binding properties of free silica are realized in practice only on the base of amorphous hydrated gel SiO_2, educed by chemical way from water solutions of sodium or potassium hydrosilicates for acid and fireresistant compositions.

By the author's investigations of this publication, in 1964 has been discovered the unknown earlier,so called "effect of crystallizationed hardening of glassed silica" in hydrothermal conditions [2,3] for artificial stone materials synthesis of natural guartzose sandstones and guartzite breccia type,where guartz has the role not only of inert fine and coarse aggregate, but also of cementing substance.

At the same time it is known, that besides amorphous varieties SiO_2 of hightened solubility in water-alkaline solutions in relation to guartz, which is necessary as an obligatory condition of crystallizationed hardening of synthetic quartz newformation, tridymite and cristobalite have the identic properties [4]. Receiving tridymite and cristobalite by solid phase transformation of quartz in the presence of only $0,05-0,1\%$ admixture of alkaline ions as mineralizators [5,6] at temperatures of $1200...1400$ °C creates preconditions of significant power capacitance shortening of industrial production process of initial ingredient for silica concrete, of expensive alkaline component diminution and expansion of using new binder.

Present paper,which is a fragment of author's thesis for a Doctor's dissertation, is devoted to the low-alkaline part   phase   diagram of SiO_2-R_2O system investigation, with the aim of optimization of chemical, mineralogical and grain composition of tridymite-cristobalite (TC) binder for constructive chemically   resistant   silica concrete of "the second generation"(SC-II [7-8]) and its varieties with specific properties.

EXPERIMENTAL DETAILS, RESULTS AND DISCUSSION

TRIDYMITE-CRISTOBALITE BINDER

Materials

Natural guartz sand, containing $99,47\%$ of SiO_2 and of primary corn size of $0,15 ...0,30$ mm. As alkaline additive - mineralizator in experiments soda ash "pure for analyses" is used for laboratory investigations and soda of technical purity (not less than 97% of Na_2CO_3)by prefabrication of TC optimum composition.

Apparatus and technigue of phases identification

For studying polymorphous guartz transformations into cristobalite and tridymite at high-temperature roasting of guartz sand and products of autoclave hardening of TC, gualitative express-analysis was made by light microscopy in immersion oils and in microsections by the help of polarization microscope MIN-8, and selectively-with the use of differential thermometry on derivatograph Q-1500D of system by F.Paulik, J.Paulik, L.Erdey. The guantative analysises were performed by X-ray difractometry method Shvite-Shtolenverk [9]. Complete chemical tests analysis was made by common methods, real content of Na_2O was defined with the use of flame photometry.

Optimization of mineralogical and chemical composition

In order to ascertain, which from active modifications of SiO_2 will be primary by hydrothermal hardening of their mixture with milled guartz sand on crystallization mechanizm, first of all were carried out experiment on receiving active silica of monomineral composition.For presezvation of known in technology SC -I conditions of binding mixture qualitative hardening content of Na_2O in all new types binder samples remained equal to 9% for comparing technical properties of quartz stone on alkaline - crystalline forms of active silica with being hardened binder on the base of high-silica alkaline glass.

Tridymite was received by thermal treatment of glass by regime, recommended in vitroceramic manufacture identic chemical composition in system SiO_2 - Na_2O [10]-4hours of time delay at 720°C and 2 hours of heating at 900°C.

For receiving cristobalite with 9% of Na_2O and minimal guantity of tridymite impurity quartz was roasted at temperature of 1250°C in finely milled form.

All three binder types were crushed to working fraction of 0,315...1,25 mm, which was mixed, each separately, with milled quartz sand (Sm) in relationship 1:1,5 by weight,water was added and groups of 6 standart prisms of 4x4x16 sm of each mixture were formed. Formed by usual methods with the use of vibration, testing specimens were loaded into laboratory autoclave by 600 l capacitance and after hydrothermal processing by regime of 3+21+6 hours at P = 12 B were put to the strength test by flexural,and prism halfs by compression in dry and water - saturated state byhastening technigue of boiling process in the water.

From analysis of tests results (Table I) the significant difference in mechanical strength is not seen, so one can't give preference to any of three modifications of SiO_2.

Table I. Test findings of being hardened alkaline-silica binder

Type of binder	Strength, N/mm^2			
	in dry state		in water-saturated state	
	flexural	compressive	flexural	compressive
Cristobalite	16,6	58,3	8,6	23,6
Tridymite	14,4	56,4	8,0	22,2
Glassed silica	14,4	52,2	7,5	21,1

Basing on received test findings one can make a conclusion, that mineralogical composition of silica active forms in binding mixture doesn't influence on the guality of crystallisation structure of quartz newformations. However, taking into account the fact of quartz inversion by roasting into final steady at temperatures up to $1470\,°C$ tridymite phase in the presence of mineralizators is carried out due to the scheme: quartz → intermediate (X-ray amorphous) phase → cristobalite → intermediate phase → tridymite [9,11],for power expenses shortening to new production is more useful to carry out the roasting process not later, than to finish cristobalitization of alkali-guartz raw mixture.

As in real conditions of soda-sand mixtures roasting in laboratory shaft or chamber electric furnaces because of inevitable temperatures gradient by reaction mass volume, broad range on alkalinity of accepted charge compounds (from 2 to 8 wt.% of Na_2O) and roasting duration at different temperatures (from 1100 to $1300\,°C$) is difficult to receive monocrystalline material out of tridymite,TC chemical composition optimization was made on roasting products of natural mineralogical composition with different relationship between cristobalite, tridymite and disregulated silica phase, containing impurity of not more,than 5 % residual quartz. From cooled up to room temperature, after unloading TC from furnace, necessary graines fraction less then 0,63 mm size was isolated by screening.

For binding mixture preparation its second component-quartz sand - was milled in laboratory ball mill up to particles fineness of high-hardening portland cement.

Relationship of TC: milled sand (Sm) was taken stable in all cases- 1:1,5 pts. wt. with W/Sm=0,30. Simultaneously mixtures SC-II were prepared with the use of natural guartz sand (S), as a fine aggregate in wt.pts.: TC: Sm: S=1:1:2,8 and W/Sm=0,56.

The most favourable conditions of cementing substance guality, forming from synthetic microcrystalline guartz stone with changing guantity of sodium oxide in TC,were stated by absolute and relative measurements of shength by flexural and by compressive of being hardened of microcrystalline quartz binder (microsilica concrete) and of fine-grain SC-II after their autoclave treatement.

Table 2. Properties of optimized compositions TC by alkalinity

Calculated content of Na_2O ,wt. %	Strength N/mm^2			
	in air-dry state		in water-saturated state	
	flexural	compressive	flexural	compressive
I. Microsilica concrete				
8,0	14,4	46,8	6,1	19,8
6,5	19,4	68,5	9,0	31,0
4,0	19,1	65,7	17,6	29,0
3,0	11,2	35,6	8,7	26,0
II. Fine-grain silica concrete				
6,5	13,8	46,0	7,5	28,8
5,5	12,7	44,3	9,7	35,4
5,0	13,3	43,9	11,5	39,0
4,0	12,0	41,0	10,1	32,0
3,0	7,1	32,8	6,2	25,1

The results obtained from series of test specimens showed (Table 2), that the most high strenght and the best water - resistance has been achieved by content of Na_2O 4...5 wt. %. Quantity hightening of alkaline metal oxide up to 6,5...8% leads to abrupt lowering of strength in water. Additions decreasing of Na_2O up to the level lower then 4% impendes completed dissolution and crystallization of TC in cryptocrystalline quartz, what become apparent in stregth and water-resistance shortening, presence of remained unsoluted TC grains in circled macropores, and by 2% of Na_2O - specimens of sand SC-II are broken by hands.

On the other side, increase of additions-mineralizators quantity in the system of SiO_2- Na_2O over 5 mol% doesn't practically influence on the acceleration process of quartz polymorphous transformations in range temperature stability of tridymite (870...1470°C) [12].

In halfindustrial and industrial rotary kiln, as factory experiments have shown, it is enough for material being in roasting zone only 5..10 minutes to receive binder, preferably of cristobalite content with 4..5% of Na_2O. At the same time it is known, that for the production of alite portland cement clinker, are required temperatures not lower than 1400° C with time of raw mixture being in rotary kiln 20 ... 35 min.

X-ray phase analysis of TC and Sm, taken separately and in their mixture according to accepted proportion 1: 1,5 by wt. before and after autoclave treatement with calculated content of Na_2O 0,5 % in TC, shows complete transformation of tridymite and cristobalite into quartz after hydrothermal hardening. Judging by Fig.I, one can say, that even traces of residual crystalline modifications on peaks phone, presented only to low quartz, are absent. In microsection specimen of being hardened microsilica concrete on common phone of cementing quartz newformations on milled guartz sand particles are distinctly marked out dark macrohollows, exactly repeating the outlines of previous graines of crushed TC, without indissoluting substance remainders (Fig.2).

SILICA CONCRETE

Raw components

TC low-alkaline (TCL) of factory roasting at 1320±20°C of mixture from natural guartz sand and technical soda ash in cement rotary kiln of 1,25x16m with chemical content, % :

SiO_2	Na_2O	K_2O	Al_2O_3	Fe_2O_3	CaO	SO_3	Ignition loss
98,04	0,44	0,05	0,09	0,13	0,95	0,32	0,16

Mineralogical content: metastable cristobalite with tridymite impurity of not more than 5...10% and disorder intermediate phase (having by A.C.D. CHAKLADER and A.L. ROBERTS [13] glassed nature with 2,30±0,005 g/sm³density and taking intermediate position between quartz glass and metastable cristobalite). The second component of binding mixture was quartz sand, milled in laboratory ball mill up to specific surface by air-penetrability of 4800 sm²/g. Natural sand was used as a fine aggregate and as acoarse aggregate (CA) was used acid resistant breakstone of 5-20 mm fraction from crushed natural guartzite. For accelerated hardening of modified SC-II with minimum of $R_2O=0,5$% in TC binder [7], solid components of silica concrete was mixed with aqueous solution NaOH of 12,5% concentration.

Mixing proportion

Relationship of SC-II ingredients was defined by special methods of concrete design, optimal by concrete placeability, technical and economical indicators, taking into account specificity of concretely taken inindustrial manufacture articles of initial raw components. Calculated content of silica concrete

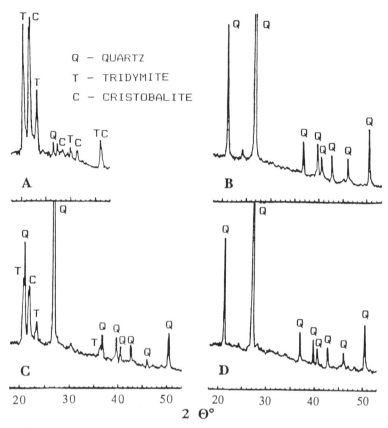

Figure I.Diffractogram of tridymite-cristobalite binding (A), milled quartz sand (B), mixture of A:B=1:1,5 wt.pts. before autoclave treatment (C) and after it (D).

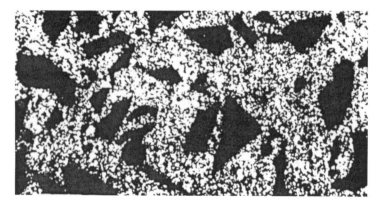

Figure 2. Microstructure of synthetic quatz stone (x 50, polarized light)

mixture with stiffness by technical viscosimeter up to 40...45 sec for it's placement by usual vibration   on   used   basic   materiales   turned   out to be the following, kg/m^3 :   TCL=340, Sm=370, S=300, CA=1230, W=150.

Manufacturing of test specimens

Being measured components for 30 liter SC-II   were mixed   in usual   concrete   mixer during 2-3 minutes. The specimens in steel moulds were formed from prepared mixture on laboratory vibrating table and them were loaded into autoclave for thermal-damp treatment during 16 hours at P=12 B. The specimens quantity for each tests type and methods of carrying them out correspondend to common standarts. Nonstandart tests are set forth below.

Properties SC-II

Volume weight, kg/m^3.. 2250
Compression strength, N/mm^2 :
-of cubic...114,0
-of prism.. 104,9
Tensile strength, N/mm^2.. 7,2
Modul of elasticity, N/mm.^{2}... 4,8x10^4
Cohesion with steell reinforcement, N/mm^2... 24
Acid-resistance (at weight waste during 1 hour boiling in sulphuric acide), % 99,51
Coefficient of chemical resistance in acids (at degree of strength decrease)...................... 0,9-1,0
Water -resistant coefficient... 0,84
Calculated porosity, %... 15,5
Water-absorption, wt. %...1,4
Water-proof, Bar.. not less than 16
Freezing-resistance, cycles.., not less than 1500
Abrasion-resistance, g/sm^2...about 0,1
Mohs' hardness.. 7
Shock resistance : summary height of 2 kg hammer blows, sm...... 52
               specific work of destruction, kNm/sm^3... 32,1
Thermal Shock resistance " 350°C -water ", cycles... 28
Thermal conductivity coefficient , wt/m°C.. 1,85
Coefficient of linear thermal expansion.. 10,06x10^{-6}
Solidification contraction.. absent
Toxicity.. absent

Analysis of compression diagram by instantaneous load of 10x10x40 sm and 7x7x30 sm prisms and of hollow cylinders with 11,5 sm external   diameter,50 sm height and 3,5 sm   wall thickness corroborates practical linear dependence "stress-deformation" up to breaking load, in consequenceof crystalline structure of cementing quartz.

Creep of SC-II to 185 days tests of prism specimens with loading levels from 0.3 to 0.85 of breaking load acquired damping character and limited relatjve deformation for load level 0,8 didn't exceed 40x10^{-5} by absolute value. Creep measure was 0,8x10^{-6} 1/N/mm and long-term strenth silica concrete are in interval 0,7... 0,8 from momentary strength [14].

Influence of water saturation on deformativeness and strength of SC-II by durable loading (191 days) were studied on hollows cylindrical specimens, filled of water. Deformations of cylinders in water-saturated state to the tests ending increased on 19 and 23% by 0,3 and 0,5 loading levels relatively from limited level respectively in comparison with dry specimens. By results of additional loading under momentary load tested cylinders there are no specific differences in strength indices of water-saturated and air-dry specimens.

Long tests on forcible stand of beams with section of 8x17 sm, reinforced by steel frames with ratio of reinforecement 0,0227 and loaded by two single forces at distance of 53,5 sm from suppors by span of 137 sm, after 185 days of precuring under exploitation level load with the following discharge and breakage under the press also confirmed the fact of specific differences absence in rapidness of deformations development of being pressed beams zone, tensiled reinforcement and deflections,also in the character of fracture from momentary tests of beams-twins.

Silica concrete strength and deformative properties don't change also at high temperatures. Plastic deformations in loading state almost don't develop and by middle level of stresses,typical for temperature sums,that's why creeps can't be taken into account [15].

Water-inpenetrability of silica concrete as constructive chemically resistant material for pressure pipes production in land-improvement and agricultural building, besides standart tests on cylinders of 150 mm diameter and height, was defined also on the models of pipes specimens with internal diameter of 280... 300 mm, with wall thickness accordingly 65 ... 55 mm and with length of 840 mm. All specimens stood the tests on hydraulic stand by internal water pressure of 30 B without signs of its percolation on the surface.

Durable corrosion resistance and protective properties of silica concrete in relation to steel reinforcement in solutions of 5 and 30% concentration sulphuric acid were studied on specimens - cubes of 10x10x10 sm with plates, put into them by forming, from usual steel to the depth of protective coating from SC-I of 20 and 50 mm and cubes without plates. Being completely loaded into acids solutions specimens stood the tests in exsiccator 800 days.In intermediates the storage intervals the specimens were weighed and after final testing they were splitted according to crosses of steel plates with depth determination of acid penetration by phenolphtaleine action on freshnaked surface and of signs presence of steel corrosion in silica concrete, and specimens without plates were tested by compession.

Tests findings by kinetics of acid-saturation testify the fact,that process absorption of both concentrations acid lasts up to 180...200 days.Then it becomes stable and reaches 2...2,3 wt.% for 5% solution H_2SO_4 and 1,3...1,35 wt.% - for 30% solution.

High impenetrability and alkaline medium in volume of silica concrete secures also reliable safety of usual steel reinforcement at sufficient thickness of 20 mm coating. Depth of acid penetration into specimens-cubes from the side theirs lower moulding surface after 800 days time delay in H_2SO_4 solutions and in contact with 30 % sulphuric acidsolution by capillary inflow of SC-II study for this period didn't exceed 3-5 mm.

RATIONAL SPHERE OF APPLICATION

Realised scientific investigations permit to set up production line on pilot-industrial manufacture of alkaline-silica binders in quantity up to 5 th.t.a year with one rotary kiln of 1,25x16 m at the Pilot cement plant of Institute "Juzhgiprocement" (city of Kharkov in Ukraine). By industrial production line plan of 100 th.t.year output with the use of one expanded clay rotary kiln of 2,5x40 m, the 1t production of TC needs according to calculations in 2 times less of equivalent fuel quantity for roasting, electric energy waste lowers in 2,5 times, specific investments decrease in 3 times in comparison with M-400 portland cement production at the cement plant with two rotary kiln of 5x185 m and annual efficiency of 1200 th.t

Constructive chemical resistant silica concrete was used for the first time in formerly USSR by reinforced concrete chimney stack building of height up to 330m with inside suspended flue from reinforced by usual steel 2,5x10 m panels instead lining from of acidproof brick at modern thermoelectric power stations.Economical and technical effectiveness of new progressive solution is characterized by waste reduction of acid resistant materials for one chimney stack of $H=320m$ in 10 times, by decrease of labour input in 2 times and by reduction of building periods in 4 times [3]. The first from built chimneys has been exploited during 21 years without running repairs of silica concrete suspended flue.

Taking into consideration the unique combination of SC-II building, technical and economic indications there exists an opportunity to realize not only its gualities, as high strength corrosion resistant material for production of building constructions with chemically aggressive exploitation mediums,but as a constructive material in bridge building, tunnel building instead of cast-iron tubbings,pressure pipes of big diameters, in road and sea hydrotechnical building, in production of nonfired refractories [16] etc., and also as a decorative material,which substitute not only broadly applied natural facing materials of marble and granite type, but also such rare varieties of natural semi-precious stone as jasper, hephrite, lazurite, rhodonite in the form of piece plate articles with the best properties and with cost in 10-s times less,than theirs natural analogues,or in the form of decorative coating on facing surface of wall panel size articles from reinforced   heat isolation-consructive light or cell silica concrete [17].

Broad perspectives in sphere production and further expansion application of different building materials on silica base are opened by author's last scientific developments also using instead of tridymite- cristobalite binder unlimited stores of natural raw materials in active form of amorphous SiO_2 ,requiring no preliminary roasting for autoclave hardening of silica concrete "third generation" and its of "fourth generation" without autoclave method of articles and constructions manufacture .

CONCLUSION

New binding substance of tridymite-cristobalite mineralogical content, received in low-alkaline part of SiO_2 - R_2O system on the base of guartz raw mixture and of mining industry waste with the opportunity of alkaline containing by-products application, f. e.,of sodium carbonate in manufacture of caprolactam,caustic soda out of disinfectants, etc.,is an additional reserve of perspective development of building industry of 2000 y., of producing durability building materials, articles and constructions of broad nomenclature, where well-known materials application is less effective. By combine of technical,technological and economical indices SC-II does not have analogues amongst constructive materials application of common and special nomination.

ACKNOWLEDGEMENTS

Author expresses his thanks to sponsor - Holland firm "Biemans Groep B.V." in the person of Mr. M.M.F.M. Biemans and Mr. B.V. van Rhee for attention and financial supporting of research laboratory "Silica concrete" in development of investigations on SC-III and SC-IV and their industrial realization in Western Eropean countries.

REFERENCES

1. H.W.FAIRBAIRN. Synthetic quartzite —Am. Miner., vol. 35, 1950,pp. 735

2. V.P.KIRILISHIN, N.I.KHITAROV. Preparation of chemically resistant concrete. —Pat. G.B. № 1277154, 1972, 4pp.

3. В.П.Кирилишин.   Кремнебетон. — Изд. 'Будiвельник', Киев, 1975, 110 с.

4.В.А.АВАКОВ. Сравнительная растворимость некоторых модификаций кремнезема. - Строительные материалы, № 11, 1972.

5. Н.Н.СИНЕЛЬНИКОВ. О кристабалите и его превращении в тридимит. - ДАН СССР. т.110, № 4. 1956, с. 651-654.

6. O.W.FLORKE. A discussion of the tridymite-cristobalite problem. - Sil. Ind., 1960, pp. 415-417.

7. V.P.KIRILISHIN. Binder for chemically resistant concrete and process for producing binder. - Pat.G.B. № 2057408B, 1983, 15pp

8. В.П.КИРИЛИШИН, А.А.ПОБОКИН, Ю.Н.КОЛОТ. Новый эффективный бетон для химически стойких строительных элементов и конструкций. -Сб."Коррозия бетона и повышение долговечности железобетонных конструкций". Изд. Ростовского университета, 1985, с.42-46.

9.E.H.SCHWIETE,H.STOLLENWERK. Beitrag zur Quartz-cristobalit Umwandlung. - Archiv fur das Eisen-huttenwesen, H-1, 1957, S. 17-30.

10.А.И.БЕРЕЖНОЙ. Ситаллы и фотоситалы."Изд. Машиностроение", М., 1966, 348 С.

11. S.MITRA. Influence of some inorganic Additives of the phase Transformations of Silica - Trans. Indian Ceram. Soc., vol XXXV (1), 1967, pp. 16-24.

12. W.L. DE KEYSER, R. CYPRES. Constribution a l'etude de la formation de la tridimite:Action combinee de la chaux et des oxydes alcalins. - Sil. Ind., vol. 25, 1960, pp. 109-137.

13. A.C.D. CHAKLADER, A.L.ROBERTS. Transformation of Quartz to Cristobalite. - j.Amer. Cer. Soc.,vol. 44, 1961,pp. 35-42

14. В.П.КИРИЛИШИН,В.И.ПОЛОВЕЦ, Б.С.ГАПШЕНКО. Деформативность и длительное сопротивление кремнебетона при близких к разрушающим нагрузках. - Межвузовский сб. "Работоспособность строительных материалов на основе и с применением местного сырья и отходов промышленности. КИСИ, Казань, 1991, с.79-83.

15. Ф.П.ДУЖИХ,Ю.В.МАТВЕЕВ,А.А.КОНОВАЛОВ. Исследование работы дымовых труб в маневренных режимах. - Теплоэнергетика, № 5, 1983, с.34-37.

16. Ю.А.СЕЛИВАНОВ, В.П.КИРИЛИШИН, И.А.ЛИХАЧЕВА, Л.А.ИВАНОВА. Исследование стабилизированного кремнезема для безобжиговых футеровок. - Известия вузов. Черная металлургия, №6, 1989, с.116-121.

17. В.П.КИРИЛИШИН, Э.Н.РЕПЬЕВ, С.И.СЛАНЕВСКИЙ, В.И.МАРТЫНОВ. Бетонная смесь. - Авт.свид. СССР № 1520054, С 04 В 38/02, И. № 41, 1989, 2 с.

CATHODIC PROTECTION OF REBARS
IN CONCRETE WITH DIFFERENT AGGREGATES

G Batis

A Aidini

National Technical University

Greece

ABSTRACT. The influence of different parameters of steel corrosion in concrete is studied after exposion in 3.5% NaCl solution. The effectivity of cathodic protection in the same corrosion medium is examined in combination with different types of aggregates (English sand, Quarry sand and pumice) and different cover thickness of the rebars. In order to study the influence of these parameters it is measured the weight loss of rebars and the Cl⁻ content of mortar. Finally, the different types of specimens are giving different corrosion which is compared.

Keywords: Corrosion, Chloride, Mortar, Ordinary Portland Cement (OPC), Aggregate, Cathodic Protection.

George Batis is Assistant Professor in National Technical Univercity of Athens, Department of Chemical Engineer, Section of Materials Sience and Engineering. His main research interest include Corrosion of Metals and Protection by anticorrosive paints with or without Cathodic Protection.

Athina Aidini is Chemical Engineer, Senior Student in National Technical University of Athens, Department of Chemical Engineer, Section of Materials Science and Engineering. Her main research interest is Corrosion of Rebars in Concrete and Cathodic Protection.

Concrete 2000. Edited by Ravindra K. Dhir and M. Roderick Jones.
© 1993 Published by E & FN Spon. ISBN 0 419 18120 2.

INTRODUCTION

Cathodic protection is an already recognised method used to prevent the corrosion of metals, especially when they are exposed in strong corrosive environment as sea water (1).

In the case of rebars in concrete many esseys have shown that cathodic protection finally cost less than any other method used to repairing concrete already destroyed from the diffusion of corrosion products and protect rebars from further corrosion (2).

Parameters as thickness of rebars covering and type of aggregates are also influencing the corrosion (3).

This work is studying the effectiveness of cathodic protection in rebars' corrosion of mortars exposed in NaCl solution (3.5 % wt), in combination with other parameters as types of aggregates and the thickness of the cover of the rebars.

EXPERIMENTAL DETAILS

MATERIALS

Specimens are made using ordinary portlant cement (OPC), and a Greec cement type K35 (table 1). There are also used different types of aggregates (Engish sand, Quarry sand and Pumice).In all cases the rebars are of the type Stahl 1.

TABLE 1   Cement composition

	SiO_2	Al_2O_3	Fe_2O_3	CaO	MgO	K_2O
OPC	20.5	5.02	3.20	63.56	2.7	0.37
K35	22.36	6.62	4.08	56.55	3.52	0.72

	Na_2O	SO_3	CaOF	LOI	AU	TiO_2
OPC	0.29	2.52	2.14			—
K35	0.53	2.44	1.99	2.59	1.27	0.37

MIX PROPORTION

All cases except from the pumice specimens, the aggregates/cement ratio (a/c) is 3/1 and water/cement ratio (w/c) is 0.5/1. For the specimens with fine pumice (gradation 0-8 mm) a/c is 3/1 and w/c is 0.7/1.

SPECIMENS DESIGN

Two types of specimens are made: cylindrical ones (6, 7) and specimens with square profile and four embedded steel bars, with different thickness of cover of the rebars (figure 1).

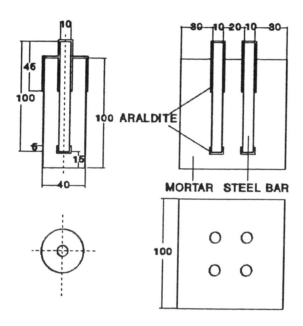

Figure 1: Specimens dimensions

CORROSIVE ENVIRONMENT

All speciments are exposed in NaCl solution (3.5 %).

CATHODIC PROTECTION

In order to impose cathodic protection, as the anode connected to the (+) of potentiostat, is used graphite. In the case of cubic specimens, a graphite bar is embedded in the middle of the specimen. Steel bars are connected to the minus pole (−) of the potentiostat. Calomel electrode (SCE) is used as an external reference electrode, in most cases. For the pumice specimens an embeddable reference electrode is used, which is made from $MnO_2/Ca(OH)_2$ (figure 2). The applied potential is equal to −840 mV versus SCE.

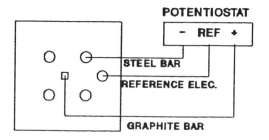

Figure 2: Cathodic Protection

METHODS

WEIGHT LOSS

The weight loss of rebars is measured after their removal from the NaCl solution. The weight loss is the difference of the weight of the rebar before its embeddance to the mortar, to the weight of the extracted rebar from the specimen which was in the corrosive environment. Corrosion products are cleaned according to ISO/DIS 8407

CHLORIDE CONTENT DETERMINATION

For the study of the chloride penetration in mortar, a Cl^- selective electrode connected to pH/mV measurment system is used. For the determination of soluble Cl^- the mortar powder is dilluted in absolut ethanol (9). For the total Cl^- determination, the mortar powder is disolved in 1N HNO_3 heated solution, and the CL$^-$ are measured by the pH/mV system (8, 9).

X-RAY DEFFRACTION ANALYSIS

For the X-Ray Deffraction analysis (XRD), the mortar powder prepared from the pieces of the exposed specimens is used.

RESULTS AND DISCUSSION

CATHODIC PROTECTION IN CYLINDRICAL SPECIMENS

Cathodic protection is effective enough to prevent rebars corrosion. Comparison of weight loss versus time for cylindrical specimens with and without Cathodic Protection indicated that (fig. 3). According to these measurements is obvious that the difference in the weight loss between the two types of specimens increases versus time and the effectivity of the cathodic protection becomes more important.

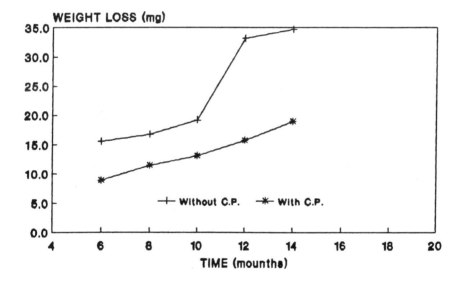

Figure 3: Weight Loss versus time for cylindrical specimens with and without Cathodic Protection.

The determination of Cl^- content indicated that specimens with Cathodic Protection have a lower soluble Cl^- level. This is attributed either to the chloride electrodeposition (5),or to the formation of aluminates because of the OH^- concetration increment (fig. 4).

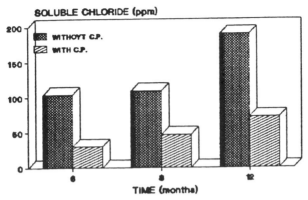

Figure 4: Soluble Chloride content for cylindrical specimens with and without Cathodic Protection.

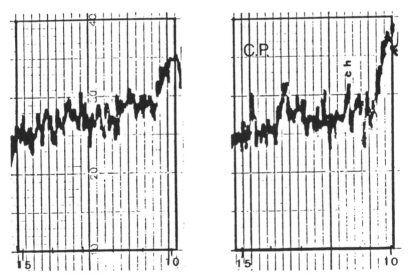

Figure 5: X-Ray diagrams showing the chloroaluminates peaks of cylindrical specimens with and without C. P.

XRD examination in cylindrical specimens with and without cathodic protection indicates the formation of chloroaluminates in the case of cathodic protection. This confirms the above mentioned supposition which comes out from the lower soluble Cl- content of the corresponding specimens (fig. 5).

CATHODIC PROTECTION IN CUBIC SPECIMENS WITH DIFFERENT TYPES OF AGGREGATES

CUBIC SPECIMENS WITH QUARRY SAND

The weight loss versus time for cubic specimens with and without cathodic protection is performed in figure 6. The absolut values of the weight loss are obviously decreased compared with the previous ones of the cylindrical specimens. This is expected because of the encrease of the cover thickness of the rebars from 15mm (cylindrical specimens) to 30mm (cubic specimens).

Cathodic protection seems to be able to delay rebars corrosion. Specimens with cathodic protection which are exposed for 13 months are almost as much corroded as specimens without cathodic protection exposed for 7 months in the corrosive environment.

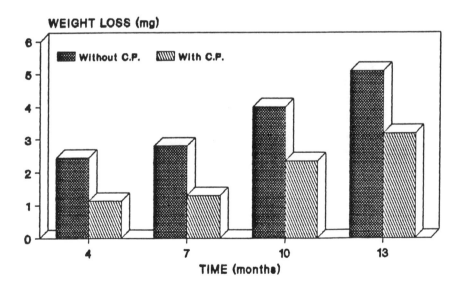

Figure 6: Weight Loss versus time for cubic specimens with quarry sand, with and without Cathodic Protection.

CATHODIC PROTECTION IN CUBIC SPECIMENS WITH FINE PUMICE

Pumice specimens are exposed in the corrosive environment
for 2 and 4 months (fig. 7). These specimens are much more
corroded than the conversional cubic ones with quarry sand.
It is impotant that after 2 months exposure in the
corrosive environment, their corrosion is equal to the
corrosion of specimens with quarry sand, after
approximetely 10 months exposure in the NaCl solution. This
is expected because of their porosity.

The specimens with cathodic protection resist better
against corrosion. In this case the results of the
imposition of the cathodic protection are absolutly
satisfactory. The weight loss of the specimens with
cathodic protection which are exposed for 4 months in the
corrosive environment remains in the same level as it was
after 2 months exposure in the NaCl solution (10).

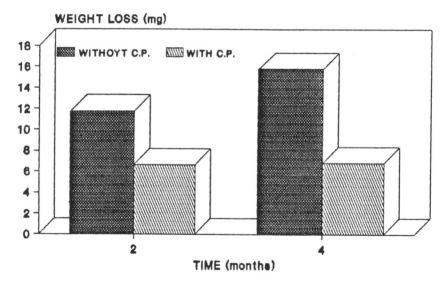

Figure 7: Weight Loss for specimens with fine pumice, with
and without Cathodic Protection exposed for 2 and 4 months.

The determination of the chloride content confirms the
above conclusion. The results of this measurement compared
with these of the weight loss, indicate that specimens with
lower level in Cl- content are finally less corroded (fig.
8). Also, XRD examination indicates that C. P. promotes the
formation of chloroaluminates (fig. 9).

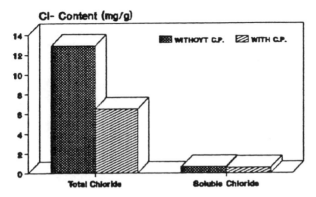

Figure 8: Total and Soluble Cl- for specimens with fine pumice, with and without C.P. exposed for 4 months.

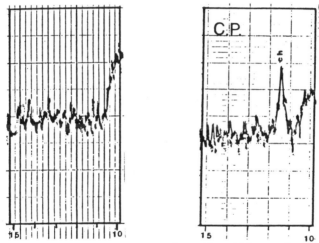

Figure 9: X-Ray Diagrams showing the Chloroaluminate peaks of pumice specimens with and without Cathodic Protection.

CONCLUSIONS

- In all cases, Cathodic Protection seems to prevent rebars corrosion.
- The combination of Cathodic Protection and thickness increment of rebars cover gives best results.
- The Cathodic Protection possibly promotes the formation of aluminates because of the high concetration level of OH⁻, and need extensive future research.
- Porous materials increase corrosion. Porosity has to be deminised by different methods to avoid corrosion. Cathodic Protection resulted best protection to the specimens.

REFERENCES

1. GJOTV, OE AND VENNESLAND, O. Diffusion of Chloride   Ions from Sea Water into Concrete, Cement and Concrete   Reseach, 1979, Vol. 9, p.p. 229-238.

2. MARTIN, BL AND   KOVATCH,   WA.   Cathodic   Protection   for Viaduct,Concrete International, 1989, p.p. 50-53.

3. ARUP, H. Embeddable   References   Electrode   for   use   in Concrete, Nordic Concrete Research 40, 1991.

4. GOTO, N, MATSUOKA, K, KIHIRA, H AND   ITO,   S.   Corrosion Monitoring for Reinforcing Bars in   Concrete,   EVAMALT   89, Tokyo 1989, p.p. 629-636.

5. KUMADA, M, SASAKI, H, YOKOTA, M AND UKITA, K.   Corrosion Protection and Repair   of   Marine   Concrete   Structures   by Electrodeposition Method,   EVALMAT   89,   Tokyo   1989,p.p. 543-548.

6.   SKOYLIKIDIS,   TH,   SAROPOULOS,   K,   BATIS,   G, THEODOROPOULOS,   D,   ANDROULAKIS,   M   AND   KALOGYROY,   J. Corrosion Marine-Fouling, 1976, Vol.1, p.p. 1-25.

7. SKOYLIKIDIS, TH, BATIS, G, KALOGYROY, J, KASSELIMIS,   I, AND THEODOROPOYLOS, D. Corrosion Marine-Fouling, 1976,   Vol 1, p.p. 26-35.

8. TRITTHART, J. Chloride Binding in   Cement,   Cement   and Concrete Research, 1989, Vol. 19, p.p. 683-691.

9. YONESAWA, T, ASHWORTH, V AND PROCTER, RP. Pore   Solution Composition and Chloride Effects on the Corrosion of   Stell in   Concrete,   Corrosion   Engineering,   1988,   Vol.7,   p.p. 489-499 .

10. CHERRY, BW AND KASHMIRIAN, AS. Cathodic   Protection   of Steel   Embedded   in   Porous   Concrete,   British   Corrosion Journal, 1983, Vol. 18, p.p. 194-199.

CHEMICAL ADMIXTURES FOR
INHIBITION OF ASR IN CONCRETE

E K Attiogbe

Institute of Scientific Research

Kuwait

S A Farrington

Master Builders Inc

United States of America

ABSTRACT Alkali-aggregate reaction is a phenomenon that occurs worldwide, causing abnormal expansion and cracking of concrete in service. The most prevalent type of reaction is the alkali-silica reaction (ASR), which results from interaction between reactive silica in the aggregate and alkalis from the cement paste to form an alkali-silica gel. This gel can swell with the uptake of water to cause expansion and cracking of both the paste and the aggregate. Research in the 1950's showed that lithium compounds can be effective in inhibiting ASR. Such compounds have yet to be included in commercial chemical admixtures for concrete. The present study presents lithium-containing water-reducing admixtures for concrete that are effective in reducing the expansion caused by ASR. This effectiveness is verified by performance results in various types of accelerated expansion tests. The effects of these admixtures on the plastic and hardened properties of concrete are also presented.

Keywords: Alkali-Aggregate Reaction (AAR), Alkali-Silica Reaction (ASR), Expansion, High-Range Water Reducer, Lithium Compounds, Normal-Range Water Reducer

Dr. Emmanuel K. Attiogbe is a Research Scientist in the Civil and Building Dept. of the Kuwait Institute for Scientific Research. He was formerly a Senior Research Engineer with Master Builders.

Stephen A. Farrington is a Senior Research Engineer at Master Builders, Inc., Cleveland, Ohio, USA. His research interests include portland cement and pozzolan chemistry and the performance of cement-based materials.

Concrete 2000. Edited by Ravindra K. Dhir and M. Roderick Jones.
© 1993 Published by E & FN Spon. ISBN 0 419 18120 2.

INTRODUCTION

Alkali-aggregate reaction (AAR) can cause expansion in concrete from the swelling of gels that are formed when minerals in the coarse and/or fine aggregate react with soluble alkalis in the cement paste. The alkali-silica reaction (ASR) occurs in concrete fabricated with aggregates containing reactive forms of silica, and is the most prevalent form of AAR worldwide. The reaction can result in expansion and cracking of both the cement paste and aggregate, and the subsequent loss of structural integrity within concrete structures. ASR occurs when alkalis attack reactive silica in the aggregates to form an alkali-silica gel by the following generalized reaction:

$$SiO_2 \quad + \quad (Na,K)OH \quad ---> \quad (Na,K)_xSi_y(OH)_z$$

Silica in Aggregate   Pore Fluid   Alkali-Silica Gel

The rate of this reaction is controlled by many factors, including the amount of reactive silica in the aggregate, amount of available alkali, and the presence of moisture.

Previous research on the inhibition of ASR has involved the evaluation of the effects of various salts, such as those of lithium and barium on test specimen expansion (1,2). On the basis of the suggested mechanism by which the salts reduce expansion due to ASR, an insoluble, non-swelling lithium silicate gel is formed by the following generalized reaction:

$$SiO_2 \quad + \quad (Na,K)OH \quad ---> \quad Li_xSi_y(OH)_z$$

Silica in aggregate   Pore fluid   Lithium Silicate Gel

Early research (1) included expansion testing with mortars containing alkali-silica reactive glass as aggregate. It was found that additions of 1% by weight of cement of lithium compounds (e.g. LiF and LiCO3) reduced expansion by greater than 90% in an eight week period.

The present study concerns the effects of addition of lithium compounds and water-reducing chemical admixtures containing lithium salts into mortar and concrete. Expansion due to ASR was measured in testing that was performed by a short-term accelerated test method, and current and proposed American Society for Testing and Materials (ASTM) methods for ASR. In addition to testing for expansion, typical concrete properties were measured.

EXPERIMENTAL DETAILS

Materials

All evaluations, with the exception of the mortar bar test, used a known reactive aggregate from the Spratt quarry in Ontario, Canada as the coarse aggregate fraction of the concrete mix. Extensive research has shown that Spratt aggregate is a representative alkali-silica reactive aggregate (3). The Spratt aggregate gradation met that of #78 stone (4). The cement met the requirements of ASTM C 150 (5) for a Type I or Type III portland cement. The cements had an average alkali content of 0.6%.

Test Methods

Short-Term Accelerated Expansion Test

This method is effective as a relatively quick test for screening of potentially reactive aggregates and inhibitors of AAR. The test requires fabrication of concrete prisms with dimensions of 7.6 cm square cross-section by 30.5 cm. A cement factor of 304 kg/m^3 is used in all concrete mixes. Following a curing period of seven days at 21°C and 100% relative humidity, prismatic test specimens of 1.9 cm square cross-section and 5.1 cm length are cut from the concrete beams. These smaller test specimens are conditioned in a one-molar sodium hydroxide solution at a temperature of 80°C for 24 hours prior to measurement of the initial length. The specimens are stored in this hot alkaline solution for the duration of the test. For the evaluations that have been reported, the test duration was 35 days.

Concrete Prism Accelerated Expansion Test

This is a non-standard test method for ASR in which the conditions of testing are less severe than those of the short-term test described in the previous section. The test requires fabrication of concrete prisms with dimensions of 7.6 cm square cross-section by 30.5 cm. For this evaluation, the concrete mix design is adjusted by the addition of alkali to reflect a cement alkali content of 1.25%. The cement factor for this evaluation is also set at 304 kg/m^3. Following a 24-hour curing period at 21°C and 100% relative humidity and measurement of the initial length, the specimens are stored at 38°C under conditions of 100% relative humidity.

Expansion measurements are performed for a minimum duration of one year and may be carried out until destruction of the reference concrete occurs.

Proposed ASTM Standard Test for Length Change of Concrete Due to ASR (6).

This proposed test method is based on current ASTM and Canadian Standards Association (CSA) methods. The method is similar to the non-standard concrete prism test described previously, with the exception of the cement content requirement in the concrete that is much higher at 420 kg/m^3, to increase the alkali level and cause the reaction to occur at a faster rate.

ASTM C 441 Standard Test Method for Effectiveness of Mineral Admixtures or Ground Blast-furnace Slag in Preventing Excessive Expansion Due to the Alkali-Silica Reaction (7).

This test method is used to screen mineral admixtures such as fly ashes and slags for use in concrete that will be exposed to ASR conditions. It uses ground glass as aggregate in a mortar, and results are calculated in 14 days. The test seems to be suitable for evaluation of chemical admixtures as well.

EXPERIMENTAL PROGRAM

Initial investigations were undertaken to confirm the earlier results that had been reported for the use of lithium salts in slowing the effects of ASR (1). It was confirmed that concrete expansion was reduced by the addition of the compounds lithium carbonate and lithium fluoride at 0.25% and 1% by weight of cement. The setting time of the concrete, however, was extended upon the addition of either of these materials.

Research Phase

The first phase of this experimental program focused on the performance of concrete containing a sampling of different lithium compounds with regard to ASR expansion. Two evaluations were performed in this phase.

The first expansion evaluation involved the addition of four distinct compounds to concrete. Performance was measured in the short-term accelerated test.

The four compounds represented an inorganic lithium salt, an organic lithium salt, a lithium-containing high-range water reducing polymer (#1), and a lithium-containing water-reducing polymer (#1). Both the inorganic and organic salts were added at a dosage rate of 1% by weight of cement, while the polymers were added at a rate of 0.82% and 0.31% by weight of cement, respectively.

The reduction in ASR expansion of concrete containing these compounds relative to an untreated reference concrete follows in Figure 1. The inorganic salt had the greatest effect in reducing expansion due to ASR, while the water-reducing polymer (#1) had the least effect in this regard.

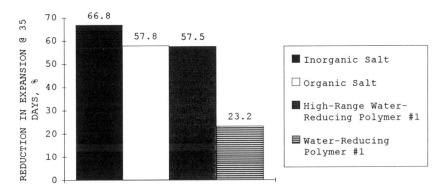

Figure 1: Reduction in ASR Expansion of Concretes Containing Lithium Materials in the Short-Term Accelerated Test

The second evaluation involved the addition of three lithium-based materials for performance in the concrete prism accelerated expansion test. The compounds consisted of the inorganic salt examined in the first evaluation, and two lithium-containing high-range water-reducing polymers (#2 and #3), each at a dosage rate of 1.82%. The reduction in ASR expansion of concrete prisms containing these compounds relative to an untreated reference concrete (3) is shown in Figure 2. Significant levels of reduction in expansion were obtained for the three lithium-based materials. Based on recent accounts, the test age of the specimens is well into the area of expansion for concrete prisms containing Spratt aggregate under the storage conditions (8).

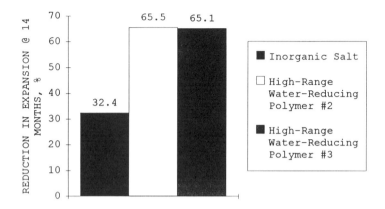

Figure 2: Reduction in ASR Expansion of Concretes
Containing Lithium Materials in Concrete Prism
Accelerated Test

The performance of the materials that was reported in the
two evaluations in the research phase formed the basis
for the admixture development program that followed.

Admixture Evaluation Phase

The next phase of the experimental program focused on the
development of admixture formulations containing lithium
compounds. Two formulations were developed at this stage,
which consisted of a water-reducing polymer admixture
(#2) and a high-range water-reducing polymer admixture
(#4).   Results of an expansion evaluation that is in
progress with concrete containing these two admixtures,
using the proposed ASTM Standard Test (with higher cement
content) are shown in Figure 3.

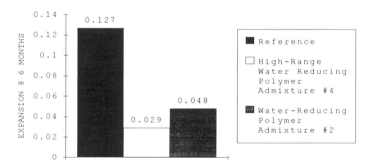

Figure 3: ASR Expansion of Concretes in the Proposed ASTM
Standard Test

At this testing age, both admixtures have significantly reduced expansion relative to the reference concrete. It must be noted that this test is designed to be run for a minimum duration of one year, and an expansion limit of 0.04% has been proposed for non-reactive aggregates in this test. As evidenced by the results, when reactive aggregates are utilized in this method, the 0.04% value is achieved in a short period of time (which was more three months in the case of the reference concrete, and slightly longer than five months in the case of the concrete containing water-reducing admixture #2).

Concrete mixes containing each of the admixtures that were evaluated in the previous expansion evaluation, which were similar in all aspects except lower cement contents, were fabricated for measurement of fresh and hardened properties. Performance data for these concretes is presented in Tables 1 and 2.

The evaluation attempted to compare concretes of similar consistency and air content. The fresh properties of the concretes reflect a water reduction of 15% in the case of the high-range water-reducing admixture (#4), and 7% in the case of the water-reducing admixture (#2). Both values are considered acceptable as these admixtures are defined.

Table 1: Mix Proportions and Properties of Concrete

	ADMIXTURE DOSAGE*	CEMENT FACTOR	WATER: CEMENT RATIO	SLUMP	AIR
REFERENCE CONCRETE	——	305 kg/m^3	0.50	15.2 cm	6.5%
CONCRETE WITH HIGH-RANGE WATER-REDUCING POLYMER #4	0.49%	305 kg/m^3	0.42	14.6 cm	6.0%
CONCRETE WITH WATER-REDUCING POLYMER #2	0.35%	305 kg/m^3	0.47	14.0 cm	6.8%

* % by weight of cement, equivalent to 9.75 ml/kg of cement

Table 2: Strength Development of Concrete

	COMPRESSIVE STRENGTH		
	@7 Days	@28 Days	@56 Days
REFERENCE CONCRETE	22.1 MPa	28.7 MPa	31.0 MPa
CONCRETE WITH HIGH-RANGE WATER-REDUCING POLYMER #4	27.8 MPa	34.3 MPa	38.1 MPa
CONCRETE WITH WATER-REDUCING POLYMER #2	29.2 MPa	35.7 MPa	37.7 MPa

Additionally, a mortar bar test was performed using the method described in ASTM C 441. This method utilizes Pyrex glass as an alkali-silica reactive aggregate. A mortar containing the normal-range water-reducing admixture (#2) was evaluated against an untreated reference mortar.

Typically, a reduction of greater than 50% expansion is considered acceptable. Figure 4 shows that the admixture treatment reduced expansion in the mortar by 75% as compared to the reference mortar.

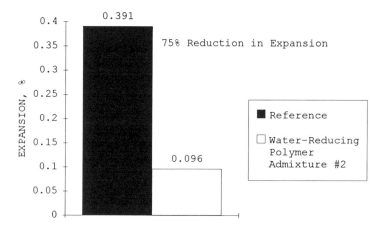

Figure 4: ASR Expansion of Mortars in ASTM C 441 Test

CONCLUSIONS

1. Two types of lithium-based chemical admixtures have been developed and are effective in reducing the expansion due to alkali-silica reaction (ASR). The effectiveness was measured using various accelerated test methods.

2. The two types of ASR-inhibiting admixtures are suitable for use in applications where normal-range water-reduction and high-range water-reduction are required.

3. At the dosage rate of 9.75 ml/kg of cement, water reductions of 7% and 15% are obtained for the water-reducing and high-range water-reducing formulations, respectively.

4. The lithium-based admixtures have shown no deleterious effects on the plastic properties of the concrete, nor on the compressive strength development.

REFERENCES

1. McCoy, W.J. and Caldwell, A.G., New Approach to Inhibiting Alkali-Aggregate Expansion, ACI Journal, May 1951, V.22, No.9, pp.993-706.

2. Hansen, W.C., Inhibiting Alkali-Aggregate Reactions with Barium Salts, ACI Journal, March 1960, V.31, No.9, pp.881-883.

3. Rogers, C.A., General Information on Standard Alkali-Reactive Aggregates from Ontario, Canada, Engineering Materials Office, Ministry of Transportation, Ontario, Canada, 1st Edition, June, 1988.

4. AMERICAN SOCIETY FOR TESTING AND MATERIALS: Concrete and Aggregates, V.4.02, D 448-86, 1992, pp.642-643.

5. AMERICAN SOCIETY FOR TESTING AND MATERIALS: Cement; Lime; Gypsum, V.4.01, C 150-92, 1992, pp.121-125.

6. AMERICAN SOCIETY FOR TESTING AND MATERIALS, Subcommittee C09.02.02 Draft, 1992.

7. AMERICAN SOCIETY FOR TESTING AND MATERIALS: Concrete and Aggregates, V.4.02, C 441-89, 1992, pp.229-231.

8. Alasali, M.M., Malhotra, V.M., and Soles, J.A., Performance of Various Test Methods for Determining the Potential Alkali Reactivity of Some Canadian Aggregates, ACI Materials Journal, November-December 1991, V.88, No.6, pp.613-619.

DEVELOPMENT OF CONCRETE FOR A PRECAST QUAY WALL SYSTEM

B Y Hughes

Newfoundland Geosciences Limited

W S Langley

Jacques, Whitford and Associates Ltd

Canada

ABSTRACT. The development of the Hibernia Oil Field off the East Coast of Canada, has necessitated the construction of a dry dock and two quays as part of the infrastructure. Conventional quay construction in eastern Canada have included reinforced concrete caissons, rockfilled timber cribwork and piling. Information is provided on the development of a concrete mixture for a novel precast "Hollow Block Quay Wall" system, the first of its kind in Canada. Laboratory studies included concrete mixtures with varying cement contents, the fabrication of test blocks cast in wood and metal forms and instrumentation of test cylinders and blocks for maturity measurements. Field studies included monitoring maturity and strength development in full size units. In order to meet the construction schedule, a 24 hour production cycle was used.

Keywords: Marine Environment, Durability, Quay wall, Maturity concept, Non-destructive tests, Concrete mixtures, Electrical curing, Thermocouples, Compressive strength.

Yvette Hughes is a Concrete Engineer with Newfoundland Geosciences Limited, St. John's, Newfoundland, Canada. She received her B. Eng. from Memorial University of Newfoundland and her M.A.Sc. from the University of Windsor, Ontario. She is presently Supervising Engineer for the materials testing laboratory at the Hibernia GBS construction site in Newfoundland. She is a member of ACI and serves on the ASTM sub-committee for Testing High Strength Concrete.

Wilbert S Langley, FACI, is Senior Materials Specialist with the Jacques Whitford Group of Companies. He is a member of several Canadian Standard Association committees. He has been involved in research in alkali aggregate reactivity, supplementary cementing materials and high strength concrete. He has authored numerous papers on concrete related subjects.

Concrete 2000. Edited by Ravindra K. Dhir and M. Roderick Jones.
© 1993 Published by E & FN Spon. ISBN 0 419 18120 2.

INTRODUCTION

Marine environments pose a relentless and severe exposure condition for concrete structures. The durability and service life of a marine structure is dependent on the adequacy of design and a judicious choice of material components of the concrete. To ensure that the intent of the design is fulfilled, that materials are proportioned accurately and that the construction specifications are followed, requires that a strict quality control and quality assurance program be implemented.

The search for oil and gas off the east coast of Canada has been ongoing for nearly two decades. The first oil field identified for development, the Hibernia oil field, is located some 315 km southeast of the Newfoundland coast. The development of this field was initiated by Mobil Oil Canada, Ltd. in partnership with the Canadian Federal government and three other partners at a cost of five billion in 1984 Canadian dollars. A concrete gravity base structure (GBS) was selected for the production platform. The construction of such a platform requires a drydock for initial casting of the GBS and a deep water site for completion of the platform.

Construction of the Hibernia GBS development site was carried out during the period 1991-1992. The development required the construction of two marginal wharves, using the quay wall principle consisting of a rock filled retaining structure, to accommodate the existing topography and to provide the required area for off-loading and storage of cargo. Conventional quay wall construction in eastern Canada consists of concrete caissons, piling or a combination of caissons, piling and rock fill.

The method of design selected for the Hibernia development site is known as the "Hollow Block Quay Wall" which is a proprietary system using precast reinforced concrete blocks developed by Guillaume-Dumez of France. The quays were designed by Dumez Construction & Direction Technique (France) and constructed by Atlas Construction Maritimes Limited, Canada. The significant advantages of the precast method of construction are reduced environmental impact on the work site, better quality control of concrete and reinforcement placement and better production tolerance.

The contractor required a 24 hour casting cycle to maximize production with a minimum of formwork since space at the site was limited. In a 24 hour cycle, the concrete would be placed and initially cured, forms stripped, the concrete block removed and placed into the quay wall structure, and the forms prepared for the next cycle.

In order to meet the construction schedule, the concrete in the precast block had to achieve a compressive strength of 10 MPa at 15-16 hours so as to accommodate lifting stresses. The blocks at this age were to be placed directly into the quay wall in seawater at a temperature of 0°C to 5°C.

The concrete mixture suitable for this particular application must have early strength development for early lifting of the block, while at the same time minimizing the heat development such that high temperature differentials would not exist between the interior and surface of the concrete block, as well as between the surface of the block and the seawater. The development of the mixture design for this application involved laboratory trial mixtures, monitoring of test block sections in both wood and steel forms, and the instrumentation of a full-scale quay wall test block. Non-destructive test methods were used in the laboratory studies to provide a database for field production. A QA/QC program meeting Canadian Standards Association Z299.3 [1] and CAN3 A23.1 [2] was used throughout production.

This paper presents the work undertaken to develop a suitable concrete mixture to meet the demands of the project and also presents data on an economical method for the construction of a continuous berthing structure using the "Hollow Block Quay Wall" system. The versatility of concrete as a construction material is exemplified, as in this situation, which often occurs when several opposing criteria must be satisfied.

"Hollow Block Quay Wall" System

The purpose of selecting this design was to utilize the advantages of the traditional block quay wall construction to provide a continuous berthing structure, which supports relatively high loadings while minimizing foundation soil stresses, and to reduce construction time and cost of materials.

The design consists of a series of vertical jointing piers without interlocking. Each pier is made of several hollow concrete blocks assembled as shown in Figure 1. The blocks

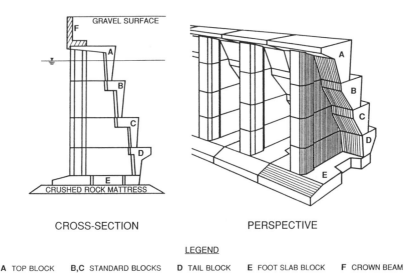

| CROSS-SECTION | PERSPECTIVE |

LEGEND

A TOP BLOCK   B,C STANDARD BLOCKS   D TAIL BLOCK   E FOOT SLAB BLOCK   F CROWN BEAM

Figure 1 Section and perspective views of quay wall

are supported by a foot-slab. The number of blocks varies according to the height of the structure. Following completion of construction of the piers, a reinforced crown beam and cope wall are cast-in-place to distribute the berthing stresses and additional concentrated loads such as wharf cranes to a module of three or more stacks.

The hollow blocks have a "T-shaped" horizontal section as shown in Figure 2 and range in weight up to 70 tonnes. The block is comprised of a front 'pillar' with a 0.7 m diameter well, a back 'tail' or screen wall approximately 6 m wide and an intermediate 'web' which permits the proper transmission of the stresses between the pillar and tail. The length and height of the blocks vary according to design requirements. The wells are filled with concrete to ensure the monolithic behaviour of each pillar and also to ensure the stability of the blocks.

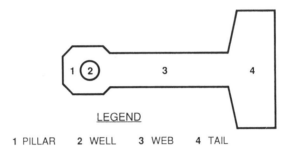

LEGEND

1 PILLAR   2 WELL   3 WEB   4 TAIL

Figure 2 Horizontal section of hollow block

Concrete Mixture Requirements

The "Hollow Block Quay" system requires that the formwork be cycled on a 24 hour basis, from time of casting the concrete to time of lifting the block in place. A minimum compressive strength of 10 MPa is required to accommodate lifting stresses and to ensure that damage does not occur at the edge of the block during form removal. To maintain this cycle, the compressive strength of 10 MPa must be achieved in approximately 15 hours.

The current requirements of the Canadian Standards Association CAN3 A23.1-M90 [2], for concrete in a marine exposure condition would require that concrete in the tidal zone have a minimum compressive strength of 35 MPa and a maximum water-cement ratio of 0.42. Since it was clearly desirable to maintain thermal gradients and temperature rise to a minimum (low cement contents desirable) and since the structure was not designed as a "permanent" structure, permission was obtained to use a 28 day strength of 30 MPa, with a maximum water-cement ratio of 0.45. In the event that concrete mixtures were unable to meet the early strength criteria of 10 MPa, the system was designed to use an integral electric heat curing system which would be embedded at the outer layer of reinforcing steel to accelerate early strength gain. Any system of dry heat for strength acceleration may not be desirable for concrete exposed to severe environmental conditions, due to an adverse effect on the surface concrete.

EXPERIMENTAL WORK

Materials

Normal Portland cement Type 10, with a long history of use in marine structures is produced locally in western Newfoundland. This cement has good early strength potential which makes it particularly well suited for this purpose. It does, however, have a relatively high alkali content which is not desirable. Since the structure is deemed not "permanent," alkali-aggregate reactivity was not considered to be a particular problem. A typical cement test report is shown in Table 1.

The coarse and fine aggregate was a crushed granite produced commercially for the concrete industry. Studies using the CSA prism test method for alkali-silica reaction, showed the aggregate to be non-reactive.

Admixtures used included an air-entraining admixture, water reducing agent and superplasticizer.

Table 1 Cement test report

Chemical		Physical	
LOI	1.35	Blaine (m²/kg)	419
SO_3	3.86	Fineness (45 micron)	96.3
C_3A	5.93	Autoclave	0.32
SiO_2	21.16	Sulphate Expansion	0.004
Fe_2O_3	3.37	Setting Time - Initial (min)	140
Al_2O_3	4.39		
MgO	3.98	Compressive Strength	
Total CaO	59.97	1 day	15.9 MPa
Free CaO	0.70	3 day	24.1 MPa
Insoluble Residue	0.33	7 day	27.0 MPa
Na_2O equiv.	1.10	28 day	35.4 MPa

Laboratory Test Program

The laboratory test program consisted of three trial concrete mixtures with cement contents of 310 kg/m³, 330 kg/m³ and 350 kg/m³ cured at 5°C, and two trial concrete mixtures with cement contents 330 kg/m³ and 350 kg/m³ cured at 15°C. Four concrete test blocks were also cast at cement contents of 330 kg/m³ and 350 kg/m³.

Standard cylindrical compression test specimens of 150 mm x 300 mm were cast from each mixture and were standard moist cured for 3, 7 and 28 days to evaluate the potential compressive strength of the concrete. A number of cylinders were also air cured at 5°C and 15°C to establish a strength-maturity relationship under actual field conditions. Test blocks, constructed as 1.0 x 1.0 x 0.6 m prisms, were cast to simulate the thicker sections in the precast quay blocks. The two cement contents were used in

Table 2 Summary of laboratory test program

MIXTURE ID	CEMENT CONTENT kg/m³	FRESH CONCRETE TEMPERATURE °C	CURING TEMPERATURE °C	TYPE OF FORM
Trial Mixtures				
A-N10-310-5	310	16	5	-
A-N10-330-5	330	18	5	-
A-N10-350-5	350	17	5	-
A-N10-330-15	330	15	15	-
A-N10-350-15	350	18	15	-
Trial Blocks				
A-Block-330	330	16	5	Wood
A-Block-350-1	350	16	5	Wood
A-Block-350-2	350	10	*	Metal
A-Block-350-3	350	15	5	Metal

* 5°C for 16 hours then 15°C after 16 hours.

each of wood and steel forms. The test blocks were instrumented with thermocouples to monitor temperature rise and maturity during initial curing. The test blocks were cored at regular intervals to determine compressive strength. The test program is summarized in Table 2.

Field Test Program

Full-scale quay wall test block

A full-scale quay wall test block was cast at the site to monitor temperature gradients within the block both in air and in seawater and to provide an opportunity for visual inspection of the block after immersion in seawater for signs of cracking. The full-scale quay wall test block was instrumented with thermocouples to monitor temperature gradients and maturity of the concrete. Cores were obtained to determine actual strength gain.

Electrical heat curing system

Previous application of the hollow block quay wall design by the system developer required an integral electric heat curing system at the outer layer of reinforcing steel so as to enhance autogenous curing within the concrete block for early strength gain. Based on the results of the laboratory test program, the early compressive strengths achieved for the concrete mixture designs were sufficient for the production schedule, therefore the electric curing system was not recommended in this application. To confirm these findings in the field, two test blocks, 0.65 x 1.6 x 1.0 m, and a full-scale quay wall test block were cast. One test block and the full-scale quay wall test block were equipped with the electric curing system. The temperature environment within the electric heat cured test block was monitored by control leads embedded in the block and connected to a regulating device which created the same temperature environment for test cylinders via heating hoods. The temperature regulated cylinder curing system is called the Cipec system. Temperature rise and maturity gain were monitored in both test blocks and the full-scale quay wall test block. Test cylinders were autogenously cured and cured by the Cipec method.

TEST RESULTS

Trial Mixtures

The compressive strength test results for the standard moist cured cylinders are included in Table 3. The compressive strength tests in the first 24 hours for cylinders air cured at 5°C and 15°C are included in Table 4. Maximum temperature rise in the air cured cylinders were 27°C and 17°C for the A-N10-350-15 and A-N10-350-5 trial mixtures, respectively. The designation 15 and 5 indicate the temperature in °C at which the test cylinders were cured. The strength-maturity data recorded for the air cured cylinders is presented in Table 5.

Table 3 shows that a compressive strength of 30 MPa at 28 days was achieved by all concrete mixtures.

Table 4 indicates that cylinders cured at a temperature of 5°C did not achieve the required 10 MPa at 15 hours. The concrete mixture containing 350 kg/m^3 of cement and cured at 15°C did achieve the required 10 MPa at 15 hours.

Table 5 indicates that for a curing temperature of 15°C a maturity of 500°C-h would be required for a compressive strength of 10 MPa with the 350 kg/m^3 cement content.

Table 3 Compressive strength test results for moist cured cylinders

TRIAL MIXTURE	COMPRESSIVE STRENGTH (MPa)		
	3 d	7 d	28 d
A-N10-310-5	21.9	25.6	33.9
A-N10-330-5	24.0	28.8	37.2
A-N10-350-5	23.2	27.1	35.8
A-N10-330-15	22.6	28.0	37.0
A-N10-350-15	22.5	28.3	37.4
A-Block-330	22.0	28.5	37.0
A-Block-350-1	21.4	26.0	33.5
A-Block-350-2	-	24.4	34.1
A-Block-350-3	-	29.0	38.2

Trial Blocks

The results of compressive strength tests for moist cured cylinders are included in Table 3. The temperature rise and maturity of the concrete in the test blocks were monitored at the locations shown in Figure 3. The recorded temperatures are presented in Figure 4. The maturity readings are presented in Table 6.

Table 4 Compressive strength test results for test cylinders cured in air

CURING TIME (h)	A-N10-310-5	A-N10-330-5	A-N10-350-5	A-N10-330-15	A-N10-350-15
12	0.4	0.4	0.5	2.6	8.2
14	0.6	1.0	0.9	4.7	9.6
16	2.1	2.2	2.5	8.3	11.5
18	2.8	3.3	2.1	10.6	13.2
20	2.4	3.7	4.5	12.8	13.8
22	3.5	6.0	4.2	13.3	13.8
24	3.8	6.0	5.6	13.4	14.1
42	-	-	15.3	-	-
43	-	13.3	-	-	-
44	13.3	-	-	-	-

Table 5 Cylinder Compressive Strength - Maturity Test Results

A-N10-310-5		A-N10-330-5		A-N10-350-5		A-N10-330-15		A-N10-350-15	
MPa	°C-Hr	MPa	°C-Hr	MPa	°C-Hr	MPa	°C-Hr	MPa	°C-Hr
0.4	269	0.4	271	0.5	261	2.6	325	8.2	368
0.6	309	1.0	310	0.9	301	4.7	389	9.6	439
2.1	349	2.2	340	2.5	343	8.3	458	11.5	506
2.8	389	3.3	381	2.1	385	10.6	526	13.2	569
2.4	429	3.7	423	4.5	429	12.8	590	13.8	628
3.5	469	6.0	467	4.2	474	13.3	651	13.8	685
3.8	509	6.0	511	5.6	519	13.4	709	14.1	739
						21.7	1868	21.3	1848

Figure 4 indicates that for A-Block-330 (wood form) a peak temperature of 41°C was reached at 16 hours while cured at an ambient temperature of 5°C. A-Block 350-1 (wood form) cured at an average temperature of 7°C, reached approximately 41°C at 15 hours and remained at this temperature for 10 hours before heat dissipation was observed. A-Block 350-2 (steel form) cured at a temperature increasing from 5°C at 5 hours to 12°C at 22 hours, reached a peak temperature of 27°C at 22 hours. A low initial temperature of 10°C for the fresh concrete contributed to the lower temperature rise. A-Block 350-3 (steel form) cured at an average temperature of 7°C reached a peak temperature of 37°C at 19 hours.

Maturity results presented in Table 6 show the required maturity of 500°C-h could be obtained within 16 to 18 hours at a low ambient curing temperature of 7°C.

Cores (94 x 188 mm) were extracted from the test blocks to determine early strength gain with time. The core compressive strengths are presented in Table 7. Each test result is the average of two cores; one from the outer 190 mm and one from 190 to 380 mm within the test block. The results of the core tests generally indicate that a compressive strength of 10 MPa was achievable in 16 hours.

Field Test Results

Full-scale quay wall test block

The full-scale quay wall test block was cast in a metal form and instrumented with thermocouples for monitoring temperature and maturity. The location of the thermocouples are shown in Figure 5. The ambient air temperature during the initial 24 hours of curing dropped from 9°C to 0°C. A wind shelter around the form maintained

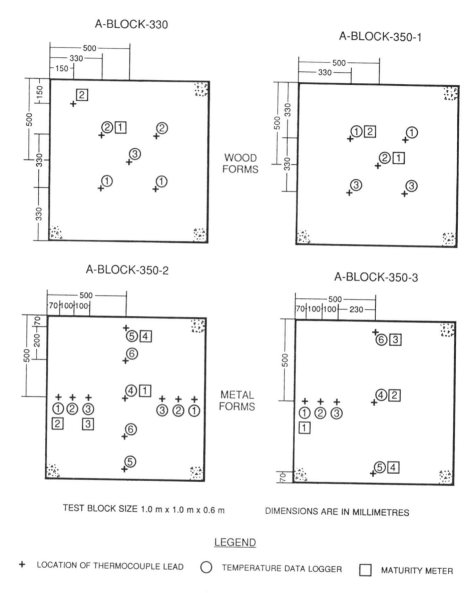

Figure 3   Location of thermocouples in laboratory test blocks

an ambient temperature of 5°C towards the base of the unit, however, the top of the unit was exposed to lower temperatures. An insulated tarpaulin placed over the top of the form provided some degree of heat retention during the early curing stages. The full -scale quay wall test block was immersed in seawater at 22 hours after casting. The recorded temperatures in the full-scale quay wall test block are shown in Figure 6. A

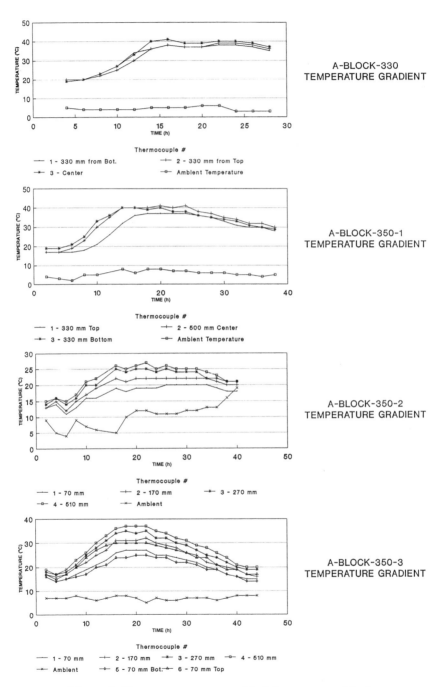

Figure 4 Temperatures measured in laboratory test blocks

Table 6 Maturity for concrete test blocks

TIME (h)	A-BLOCK-330		A-BLOCK-350-1		A-BLOCK-350-2				A-BLOCK-350-3			
					Location in Block							
	1	2	1	2	1	2	3	4	1	2	3	4
10	-	-	289	303	-	-	-	-	260	287	260	242
12	445	351	375	350	310	240	273	267	322	364	330	300
14	543	429	471	450	372	290	333	327	387	448	407	361
16	642	510	571	550	435	342	394	388	454	539	490	424
18	715	592	671	600	501	396	458	450	524	629	578	490
20	-	-	-	-	570	450	524	510	598	725	660	558
22	-	-	-	-	640	506	591	573	672	820	742	626
24	-	-	-	-	692	564	659	637	745	912	821	694
26	-	-	-	-	780	622	727	703	815	1001	989	762
28	-	-	-	-	850	680	795	767	883	1087	973	829
30	-	-	-	-	919	733	862	831	949	1170	1045	895
32	-	-	-	-	987	796	928	895	1012	1250	1114	958
34	-	-	-	-	1054	864	993	957	1073	1328	1181	1018
36	-	-	-	-	1119	911	1055	1019	1131	1399	1241	1075

Maturity expressed in °C-h.

maturity of 550°C-h was achieved in the center of the test block 16 hours after placement. Lower maturity readings were measured at the top of the block due to exposure to low temperatures.

Electrical heat curing system

The effect of the electrical heat curing system was investigated using two test blocks, Block A and Block B, 0.65 x 1.6 x 1.0 m, and a full-scale quay wall test block. The electrical heat curing system was installed in test Block A and was activated on for the time period 2.5 hours to 5.5 hours after completion of casting, while Block B was autogenously cured. Block A and Block B were placed in the water 19 hours after casting. Maturity and temperature were monitored. The maturity of the concrete at the

Table 7 Core compressive strengths

BLOCK ID	COMPRESSIVE STRENGTH (MPa)									
	Time (h)									
	15.0	15.5	16.5	17.5	18.0	19.0	19.5	20.0	25.0	43.0
A-Block-330	8.6	9.4	-	12.0	15.3	-	16.3	14.8	-	-
A-Block-350-1	-	-	13.5	-	-	13.3	-	-	-	-
A-Block-350-2	-	-	-	-	-	-	-	-	10.0	17.9
A-Block-350-3	7.3	-	-	11.2	-	-	-	-	-	-

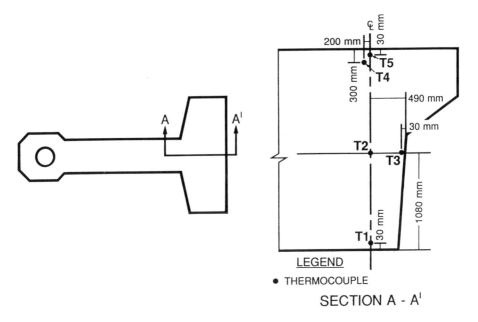

Figure 5   Location of thermocouples in the full-scale quay wall test block

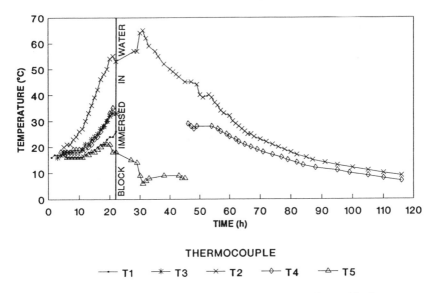

Figure 6   Temperature rise in full-scale quay wall test block

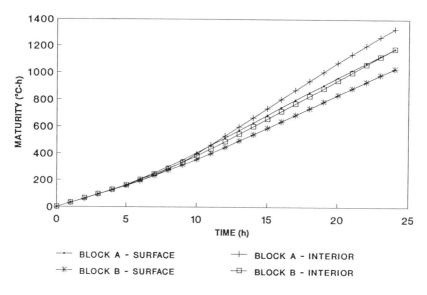

Figure 7   Maturity in Block A and Block B

surface and interior of Block A and Block B is shown graphically in Figure 7.   The maximum temperature of the core in Block A (heat cured) reached 61°C at 11 hours. The maximum temperature of the core in Block B (autogenously cured) reached 50°C.

The same electrical heat curing procedure was carried out for the full-scale quay wall test block.   The locations of the thermocouples are shown in Figure 5.   The temperatures recorded are shown in Figure 8.   Test cylinders were cured by autogenous curing and by the Cipec system.   The cylinder compressive strengths are shown in Table 8.

Table 8   Comparison of cylinder compressive strengths for autogenous cylinders and Cipec cylinders

SPECIMEN	AGE (h)	DATE TESTED	COMPRESSIVE STRENGTH (MPa)
Autogenous Cylinders	14.0	July 17	19.6
Cipec Cylinders - Core	19.5	July 17	19.2
Cipec Cylinders - Skin	19.5	July 17	19.8

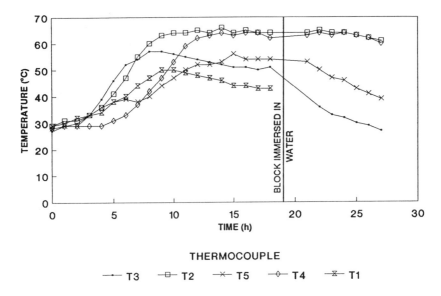

Figure 8 Temperature rise in full-scale quay wall test block (heat cured)

DISCUSSION OF RESULTS

Compressive strength test results included in Table 4 show a compressive strength gain of 10 MPa at 18 hours for a cement content of 330 kg/m³ and at 15 hours for a cement content of 350 kg/m³, for cylinders cured at 15°C. As shown in Table 7, cores removed from A-Block-330, cast in a wood form, reached a compressive strength of 10 MPa in approximately 16 hours. Trial block A-Block-350-3, which was cast in a metal form, reached a compressive strength of 10 MPa in 16 to 17 hours. The test results illustrate the difference in early strength gain of the concrete when cast in wood or metal forms and at low ambient temperatures.

Temperature rise within the test blocks in the laboratory varied with cement content and the type of form used. The most significant test was A-Block-350-3 which was cast at a temperature of 15°C with a 350 kg/m³ cement content and in metal formwork. This test block reached a peak temperature of approximately 38°C in 20 hours with a temperature gradient of 14°C. The ambient temperature was 5°C to 8°C.

The test results presented in Table 5 for cylinders air cured at 15°C indicate a maturity of 500°C-h must be attained to achieve a compressive strength of 10 MPa. To maintain a factor of safety in the field a maturity of 550°C-h was specified before removal of the quay wall block could commence.

The initial concrete placing temperature of 15°C appeared to be significant with respect to controlling peak temperatures, thermal gradient and maturity. Lower placing temperatures significantly decrease early strength gain as shown by A-Block-350-2, in Table 7, while a high initial concrete temperature increased peak temperature during initial curing.

The maturity of the concrete in the full-scale quay wall test block indicated that a maturity of 550°C-h was reached in the center of the unit at 16 to 17 hours after placement. However, due to the lower ambient temperatures at the top of the form, the maturity of the concrete 70 mm from the top surface of the block reached 400°C-h at 23.5 hours from start of placement. To alleviate the problem of low ambient temperatures at the top of the blocks, better heating was providing during winter production.

Figure 6 shows the temperature rise in the full-scale quay wall test block. The block was immersed in seawater at 22 hours. At the time of immersion the temperature of the concrete at the center of the block was approximately 60°C. The temperature of the concrete 30 mm from the face of the unit ranged from 17°C at the top of the unit (T5) to 34°C at mid-height of the unit (T3). The concrete reached a maximum temperature of 66°C at the center of the unit after immersion. At this time the temperature 70 mm from the face of the unit ranged from 8°C to 15°C producing a temperature gradient of 48°C over a distance of approximately 1.0 m.

The full-scale quay wall test block was visually inspected at 48 hours and 115 hours from the start of the test program. At 48 hours the temperature at the center of the block ranged from 38°C to 45°C. During the first visual inspection a slight hairline crack was observed at the intersection of the top and leg of the T shaped unit. When visually examined at the end of the test program the crack was not apparent.

The laboratory and field results of the test blocks and full-scale quay wall test block indicated that the electrical heat curing system was not required to maintain the short production schedule proposed. This was confirmed when additional test blocks were cast in the field and a second full-scale quay wall test block with the electrical heat curing system was cast. The maturity values shown in Figure 7 for the heated and unheated test blocks indicate no significant difference between the two blocks. However, when the heating system was applied to the full-scale quay wall block the effect was to cause an excessively high temperature rise in the concrete during the initial 10 hours of curing resulting in a temperature difference of approximately 30°C between the surface of the concrete block and the seawater at time of immersion, 19 hours after casting, as shown in Figure 8. The temperature of the seawater was 12°C. The high temperature differential resulted in thermal cracking in the block. As a result, it was confirmed that the internal electrical heat curing system was not required for the production of the quay wall blocks and would in fact be a detriment to the durability and structural integrity of the quay structure.

The compressive strength test results of cylinders cured by the Cipec method and the more conventional autogenous method showed good predictability of the strength of the in-situ concrete using autogenous curing. As a result autogenous curing was used for field cylinders throughout the production of the hollow block quay units to supplement the prediction of in-situ strength by maturity.

CONCLUSION

The "Hollow Block Quay Wall" system is a unique and beneficial method of constructing marine quays. An adequate program for concrete mixture development prior to construction and a QA/QC program during construction can ensure adequate performance to meet the system's requirements of casting and placing the blocks in final position within a 24 hour cycle. With a judicious choice of materials, and carefully planned temperature for placing concrete and subsequent curing, a 24 hour cycle can be accommodated without the likelihood of thermal cracking in the concrete block.

ACKNOWLEDGEMENT

The research carried out for the project described in this paper was funded by Atlas Construction Maritimes Limited, Fredericton, New Brunswick, Canada and Dumez Construction, Paris, France. The authors are greatly appreciative for permission to use the data developed and the information provided by these companies.

REFERENCES

1. Canadian Standards Association, CAN3-Z299-85, Quality Assurance Program Standards, Rexdale, Ontario, Canada, 1986.

2. Canadian Standards Association, CAN/CSA-A23.1-M90, Concrete Materials and Methods of Concrete Construction, Rexdale, Ontario, Canada, 1990.

3. American Concrete Institute, ACI 224R, Control of Cracking in Concrete Structures, Detroit, Michigan, USA.

POLYMETHYL METHACRYLATE CONCRETE
FOR UNDERWATER CONSTRUCTION

M R Bhutta

Y Ohama

K Demura

Nihon University

Japan

ABSTRACT. A basic investigation of the mix proportions and properties of fresh and hardened polymethyl methacrylate (PMMA) concretes for underwater placement is described. PMMA concretes using methyl methacrylate monomer are prepared with various binder formulations and mix proportions. The effects of the binder formulations and mix proportions on the working lives of PMMA binders and concretes and on their workability, strength and adhesion (to PMMA concrete substrates) are discussed from an underwater construction point of view. As a result, the appropriate mix proportions of PMMA concretes are recommended for underwater concreting.

Keywords: Polymethyl methacrylate concrete, Binder, Silane coupling agent, Underwater strength properties, Underwater concreting.

Mohammad Aamer Rafique Bhutta is a graduate student at the College of Engineering, Nihon University, Koriyama, Japan. He received his MS degree from Nihon University, Japan in 1992. He is currently working for his Ph.D. degree at the College of Engineering, Nihon University, Japan.

Dr. Yoshihiko Ohama is a professor of architecture at the College of Engineering, Nihon University, Koriyama, Japan. He has actively been involved in the research and development of concrete-polymer composites for over 30 years. He is vice-president of ICPIC and a member of RILEM, ACI, ASTM, Architectural Institute of Japan, Japan Technology Transfer Association, Society of Materials Science, Japan, and Japan Concrete Institute committees.

Dr. Katsunori Demura is a lecturer of architecture at the College of Engineering, Nihon University, Koriyama, Japan. He has been involved with research work on concrete-polymer composites, fiber reinforced concrete and superdurable concrete for about 14 years.

Concrete 2000. Edited by Ravindra K. Dhir and M. Roderick Jones.
© 1993 Published by E & FN Spon. ISBN 0 419 18120 2.

INTRODUCTION

At present, polymethyl methacrylate (PMMA) concretes having good workability, low-temperature curability, high early strength development, watertightness, chemical resistance and abrasion resistance are popularly employed for field applications and precast products. Until recently, the use of PMMA concretes has been limited to almost dry surroundings. The authors have already found that PMMA mortars can be used for underwater placement if their suitable binder formulations are selected [1,2,3].

The present paper deals with a basic investigation of the mix proportions and properties of PMMA concretes for underwater placement. PMMA concretes using methyl methacrylate monomer are prepared with various binder formulations and mix proportions for the objective of underwater construction work, which has gained popularity in recent years. The effects of the binder formulations and mix proportions on the properties of fresh and hardened PMMA concretes are discussed from an underwater construction point of view. The effect of a silane coupling agent on their underwater strength properties is also described.

MATERIALS

Materials for Binders

Binders for PMMA concretes were based on methyl methacrylate (MMA) monomer, together with trimethylolpropane trimethacrylate (TMPTMA) as a crosslinking agent, unsaturated polyester resin (UP) and polyisobutyl methacrylate (PIBMA) as shrinkage-reducing agents, benzoyl peroxide (BPO) as an initiator, N,N-dimethyl-p-toluidine (DMT) as a promoter, and γ-methacryloxypropyltrimethoxy silane (Silane) as a coupling agent.

Filler and Aggregates

Commercially available ground calcium carbonate ($CaCO_3$) (size; 2.5 μm or finer) was used as a filler. Crushed andesite (sizes; 10-20mm and 5-10mm) and river sands (sizes; 1.2-5mm and 1.2mm or finer) were used as aggregates. The water contents of the filler and aggregates were controlled to be less than 0.1% by heat drying.

TESTING PROCEDURES

Preparation of PMMA Concretes

PMMA concretes were mixed with the binder formulations and mix proportions as given in Tables 1 and 2 respectively in accordance with JIS A 1181 (Method of Making Polyester Resin Concrete Specimens).

Table 1 Formulations of Binders for PMMA Concretes

Formulations by Weight					
%				phr*	
MMA	TMPTMA	UP	PIBMA	BPO	DMT
				1.00	0.50
				1.50	0.50
					0.25
67.00	1.80	22.90	8.30		0.50
				2.00	0.75
					1.00

Note, *: Parts per hundred parts of resin (MMA+TMPTMA+UP+PIBMA).

Table 2 Mix Proportions of PMMA Concretes

			Mix Proportions by Weight, %				
Mix No.	Binder	Filler, CaCO$_3$	Aggregate				Binder-Filler Ratio, B/F
			Crushed Andesite		River Sand		
			10-20mm	5-10mm	1.2-5mm	>1.2mm	
1	9.50	7.60	15.59	15.59	10.28	41.44	1.25
2		9.50	15.23	15.23	10.04	40.50	1.00
3		12.67	14.63	14.63	9.65	38.92	0.75
4	10.00	8.00	15.42	15.42	10.17	40.99	1.25
5		10.00	15.04	15.04	9.92	40.01	1.00
6		13.34	14.41	14.41	9.51	38.33	0.75
7	10.50	8.40	15.25	15.25	10.06	40.54	1.25
8		10.50	14.85	14.85	9.80	39.50	1.00
9		14.00	14.19	14.19	9.36	37.76	0.75

Working Lives of Binders and PMMA Concretes

The working life of binders with the formulations given in Table 1 for PMMA concretes was measured underwater and in air according to JIS K 6833 (General Testing Methods for Adhesives). The working life of PMMA concretes with the binder formulations shown in Table 1 and the mix proportions of Mix No.5 (binder content, 10.00%; binder-filler ratio, 1.00) in Table 2 was determined underwater and in air by the Finger-Touching Method specified in JIS A 1186 (Measuring Method for Working Life of Polyester Resin Concrete).

Figure 1 represents the effects of BPO and DMT contents on the working lives of the binders and fresh PMMA concretes placed underwater and in air. As a matter of course, the working lives of the binders and fresh PMMA concretes shorten rapidly with increasing BPO and DMT contents regardless of the placing conditions. A difference in the working life between the binders and fresh PMMA concretes becomes smaller with raising BPO and DMT contents. The working lives of the binders and fresh PMMA concretes underwater are almost the same as those of the binders and fresh PMMA concretes in air irrespective of BPO and DMT contents. It is concluded from these data that the working life of the fresh PMMA concretes placed underwater can be controlled like that of the fresh PMMA concretes placed in air. Furthermore, in consideration of the working conditions from the above working life results, the working life of the fresh PMMA concretes is decided to be about 30 minutes for the tests of the fresh and hardened PMMA concretes, and BPO and DMT contents for the working life are 2.00 phr and 0.50 phr respectively.

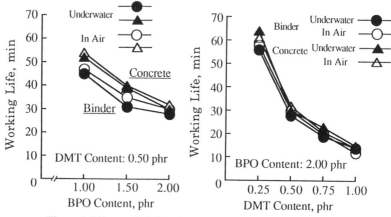

Figure 1 Effects of BPO and DMT Contents on Working Lives of PMMA Binders and Concretes Placed Underwater and in Air.

Slump and Slump-Flow Tests

The slump of fresh PMMA concretes was measured in accordance with JIS A 1101

(Method of Test for Slump of Concrete), and then the average base diameter of the fresh PMMA concrete mass on the plate glass was measured as a slump-flow in air according to Interim JSCE (Japan Society of Civil Engineers) Standard (Method of Test for Slump-Flow of Concrete).

Antiwashoutability Test

According to Interim JSCE Standard (Quality Requirements for Antiwashout Admixtures for Underwater Concrete) Appendix 2 (Method of Test for Antiwashoutability of Antiwashout Underwater Concrete), the antiwashoutability of fresh PMMA concretes was tested by freely dropping the concrete in water in a 1000-ml measuring cylinder. The antiwashoutability of the fresh PMMA concretes was evaluated by checking the suspensoids in water in the measuring cylinder.

Compactability Test

For the preparation of specimens for compaction test, fresh PMMA concretes were placed into molds 6x6x24cm underwater at 20°C and in air at 20°C and 50%R.H., and then cured for 1 day in the molds kept underwater and in air. The weight of the specimens was measured in air and in clean water at 20°C, and the bulk specific gravity of the specimens was calculated by the following equation:

$$\text{Bulk specific gravity} = Wa/(Wa-Ww)$$

where Wa and Ww are the weights (g) of the specimens in air and in water respectively. In addition, the compaction index was calculated by the following equation:

$$\text{Compaction Index (\%)} = (Gw/Ga) \times 100$$

where Gw and Ga are the bulk specific gravities of the specimens placed underwater and in air respectively.

Strength and Adhesion Tests

Specimens 6x6x24cm for flexural and compressive strength tests, specimens 7.5x15cm for tensile strength test and beams 6x6x12cm as substrates for adhesion test were molded with fresh PMMA concretes at 20°C and 50%R.H., and then cured for 1 day in the molds kept underwater and in air. Specimens for adhesion test in flexure were prepared by bonding the fresh PMMA concretes to PMMA concrete substrates 6x6x12cm in the molds 6x6x24cm underwater at 20°C and in air at 20°C and 50%R.H., and then cured for 1 day in the molds kept underwater and in air. According to JIS A 1184 (Method of Test for Flexural Strength of Polyester Resin Concretes), the flexural strength test and adhesion test in flexure of cured specimens were conducted by use of the Amsler-type universal testing machine. After adhesion test, the failed crosssections of the specimens were observed for failure modes, which were classified into the following three types:

A: Adhesive failure (failure at the interface)
M: Cohesive failure in the bonded PMMA concrete
S: Cohesive failure in PMMA concrete substrate

The total area of the bonded surfaces was supposed to be 10, and the respective approximate rates of A, M and S areas on the failed crosssections were expressed as suffixes for A, M and S. After flexural strength test, the broken portions of the specimens were tested for compressive strength by using the same testing machine according to JIS A 1183 (Method of Test for Compressive Strength of Polyester Resin Concrete Using Portions of Beams Broken in Flexure). The tensile strength test of cured specimens were performed by use of the same testing machine according to JIS A 1185 (Method of Test for Splitting Tensile Strength of Polyester Resin Concrete).

TEST RESULTS AND DISCUSSION

Properties of Fresh PMMA Concretes

Table 3 gives the properties of fresh PMMA concretes.

Table 3 Properties of Fresh PMMA Concretes

Binder Content, %	Binder-Filler Ratio, B/F	Slump, cm	Slump-Flow, cm	Antiwashout-ability	Compaction Index, %
9.50	1.25	-*	-*	No Washout	97
	1.00	0	20.0	No Washout	96
	0.75	0	20.0	No Washout	98
10.00	1.25	0	20.0	No Washout	97
	1.00	0	20.0	No Washout	98
	0.75	3.0	20.0	No Washout	99
10.50	1.25	0	20.0	No Washout	97
	1.00	0.5	20.0	No Washout	98
	0.75	4.0	21.5	No Washout	98

Note, *: Unable to measure.

Figure 2 illustrates the effects of binder content and binder-filler ratio on the slump and slump-flow of fresh PMMA concretes respectively. The slump of the fresh PMMA concretes tends to increase with an increase in the binder content. On the other hand, the slump-flow of the fresh PMMA concretes hardly changes with increasing binder content. From Table 3, the fresh PMMA concretes with any binder contents and binder-filler ratios show completely no washout. Because MMA monomer in the binders is almost insoluble in water at 20°C, and the binders provide protective coverings for the aggregates and filler to prevent segregation. It can also be observed from Table 3 that the compaction index of the fresh PMMA concretes with any binder contents and binder-filler ratios is 96% or more. This means that the compaction of the fresh PMMA concretes underwater is possible in the same degree as that of the fresh PMMA concretes in air.

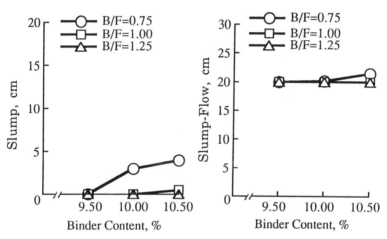

Figure 2 Binder Content vs. Slump and Slump-Flow of PMMA
Concretes for Underwater Placement.

Properties of Hardened PMMA Concretes

Figure 3 shows the effect of binder content on the flexural and compressive strengths of PMMA concretes placed underwater and in air. Regardless of binder-filler ratio and placing conditions, the flexural and compressive strengths of PMMA concretes tend to increase with an increase in the binder content, and to become nearly constant or reach a maximum at a binder content of 10.00%. The reason for such a strength increase is because the aggregates and filler are well enveloped by the sufficient binders at higher binder content. However, the flexural and compressive strengths of PMMA concretes placed underwater are about one-half to two-thirds of those of PMMA concretes placed in air at the respective binder contents and binder-filler ratios.

Figure 4 represents the binder-filler ratio vs. flexural and compressive strengths of

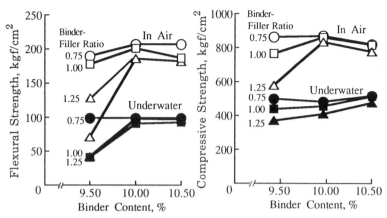

Figure 3 Effect of Binder Content on Flexural and Compressive Strengths
of PMMA Concretes Placed Underwater and in Air

PMMA concretes placed underwater and in air. Except for a few cases, the flexural and compressive strengths tend to decrease with increasing binder-filler ratio irrespective of binder content and placing conditions. In particular, this phenomenon is clearly observed for the flexural strength at a binder content of 9.50%, and attributed to a reduction in the binder content necessary to bind the aggregates due to the increased binder-filler ratio, i.e., the decreased filler content.

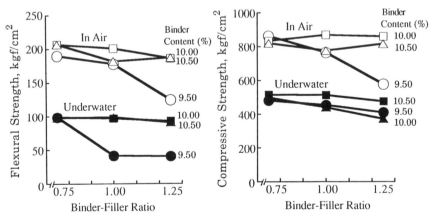

Figure 4 Binder-Filler Ratio vs. Flexural and Compressive Strengths
of PMMA Concretes Placed Underwater and in Air

Figure 5 exhibits the effect of Silane addition on the compressive, tensile and flexural strengths, and adhesion in flexure (to PMMA concrete substrates) of PMMA concretes placed or bonded underwater and in air. From these figures, it is evident that the Silane addition to their binders causes an increase in the compressive, tensile and flexural strengths, and adhesion in flexure of PMMA concretes regardless of the placing and bonding conditions.The addition of Silane to the binders for PMMA concretes helps to improve the bond between the binders and aggregates or filler.

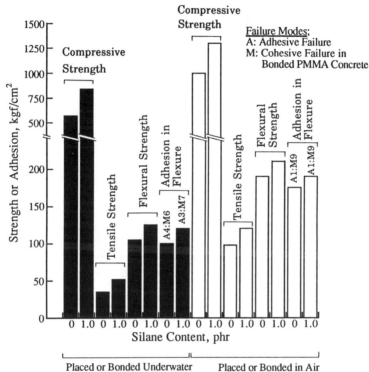

Figure 5 Effects of Silane Content on Strength and Adhesion of
PMMA Concretes Placed or Bonded Underwater and in Air.

CONCLUSIONS

1. The slump and slump-flow of fresh PMMA concretes are found to increase with increasing binder content. In the binder content and binder-filler ratio ranges of 9.50 to 10.50 and 0.75 to 1.25 respectively, the fresh PMMA concretes show completely no washout in their underwater placement, and can be compacted underwater like their placement in air. In addition, the working life of the fresh PMMA concretes placed underwater can be controlled like that of the fresh PMMA concretes placed in air.

2.. In general, the flexural and compressive strengths of PMMA concretes tend to decrease with an increase in the binder-filler ratio. However, the strengths increase with raising binder content, and become nearly constant or reach a maximum at a binder content of 10.00%. Therefore, a binder content of 10.00% can be recommended for the mix proportions of PMMA concretes for underwater placement. The flexural and compressive strengths of PMMA concretes placed underwater are generally about one-half to two-thirds of those of PMMA concretes placed in air.

3. The compressive, tensile and flexural strengths, and adhesion in flexure (to PMMA concrete substrates) of PMMA concretes placed or bonded underwater and in air are somewhat improved by the addition of a silane coupling agent, γ-methacryloxypropyltrimethoxy silane to their binders.

REFERENCES

1. OHAMA, Y., DEMURA, K., PAREEK, S.N. and RAFIQUE, M.A.,"Underwater Adhesion of Polymethyl Methacrylate Mortars", Presented at the Technical Session on the Application of Polymer Concrete in the Precast Industry - Part II, ACI Fall Convention, Philadelphia, Nov. 1990, in press.

2. OHAMA, Y., DEMURA, K., and BHUTTA, M. A. R.,"Techniques for Improving Adhesion and Strength Properties of Polymethyl Methacrylate (PMMA) Mortars Placed and Bonded Underwater", Proceedings of the Thirty-Fifth Japan Congress on Materials Research, Japan, The Society of Materials Science, Japan, Kyoto, Mar. 1992, pp.119-123.

3. OHAMA, Y., DEMURA, K., and BHUTTA, M.A.R.,"Polymer Mortars for Underwater Concreting", Proceedings of the 7th International Congress on Polymer in Concrete, Betecom, Moscow, Sept. 1992, pp.86-97.

DEVELOPMENTS IN THE DESIGN AND CONSTRUCTION OF ESTUARINE STRUCTURES

M W Pinkney

Rendel Palmer & Tritton

United Kingdom

ABSTRACT: Design and construction techniques for estuary structures are reviewed. Starting with the techniques used for the Thames barrier and port structures built during the 1970s the paper discusses how these methods have been developed during feasibility studies, which have just been completed, for the proposed Mersey Tidal Power Barrage. Future developments in construction and materials technology applicable to concrete estuary structures are discussed, using example from this study and other similar schemes; a floating berth, a floating bridge and a wave energy device.

The paper identifies the use of higher strength concrete, the scope for reduction in weight by employing lightweight concrete, the improved durability offered by non ferrous tendons, opportunities for and limitations in the use of offshore plant and the possible use of Roller Compacted Concrete in an estuarine environment as being most relevant to future developments in estuarine and marine structures.

Keywords: Estuary, Barrage, Diaphragm Wall, Caissons, High Strength Concrete, Lightweight, Floating Bridge, Wave Energy.

Michael Pinkney, born 1951, read Engineering Science at Oxford and obtained MSc in Concrete Structures and Technology at Imperial College. Now assistant director with consultants Rendel Palmer and Tritton, London, he specialies in the design of marine structures and has worked on feasibility studies for floating bridges, wave energy devices, barrages and ports.

Concrete 2000. Edited by Ravindra K. Dhir and M. Roderick Jones.
© 1993 Published by E & FN Spon. ISBN 0 419 18120 2.

INTRODUCTION

In 1837 the modern day use of concrete was in its infancy and a future President of the Institution of Civil Engineers was asked to report on the practicability of solving the problems of flooding and siltation at the mouth of Looe River in the southwest of England. This was preventing navigation which had in Tudor times been possible as far as Helston.   The Consultant, James Meadows Rendel made a number of proposals to overcome the difficulty including construction of two piers to prevent longshore drift, and control structures to increase the backwater flushing effect. He proposed to use concrete for the structures and, in an appendix, gave the history of its use to date.   He pointed out that Telford had successfully used the material when building St. Katherines Docks in London more than a decade earlier.

Although modern concrete is a very different material from that used in the early nineteenth century, it is perhaps worth remembering that its use in the construction of estuary structures has a long and distinguished history and that, in developing new uses for new materials and new methods of construction, we should not forget the lessons of the past.   The structures proposed by Rendel in 1837 were not dissimilar in function to the Thames Barrier, constructed over a century later or the structures which have recently been proposed to generate electricity from the tides in the UK, notably on the Severn and the Mersey Estuaries.

This paper commences with a review of various forms of estuary structure using examples of structures designed in recent years by Rendel Palmer & Tritton.   It continues with a more detailed analysis of a specific example of a project carried out by Rendel Parkman (a joint venture between Rendel Palmer and Tritton and Parkman Consulting Engineers) to investigate economical methods of construction for the proposed tidal power barrage on the River Mersey which culminated in the Stage III report submitted to the Mersey Barrage Company in 1992. A scheme for a floating bridge which makes use of high strength lightweight concrete and a design for a floating concrete wave energy converter are also described.

REVIEW OF CONSTRUCTION TECHNIQUES

Earth Cofferdams

Historically estuary structures have most commonly been constructed in-situ behind temporary cofferdams.   This allows access for inspection of the foundations and thus gives additional confidence in the finished structure.   It also allows the design of the permanent works to be based solely on the permanent loadings and allows construction of lightly reinforced massive concrete sections which helps ensure durability.

Many of the ports which were developed in the UK during the 19th century were constructed in this way behind earth dams using continuous pumping to remove water from the excavation. The difficulty with this form of construction is the space required for temporary works which increases rapidly as the depth of excavation increases.

Sheet Piled Cofferdam

The width of the cofferdams can be reduced significantly by using a cut off within the earth dam but for optimum space efficiency it is necessary to dispense with the earth dam altogether and use a strutted sheet pile cofferdam. This was the solution adopted for the Thames barrier where the largest cofferdams were up to 29m deep and required a tremie concrete plug 5m thick with pressure relief wells to seal the bottom against water ingress (1). Once tremie concrete is needed the inspection of the foundation can only be undertaken by divers and most of the advantage is lost.

Open Caisson

Where complex fitting out underwater is required such as on the Thames Barrier, the cofferdam remains an effective solution, but where it is only required to provide a deep marine foundation for a bridge or other structure the open caisson method of construction was developed. It is believed that the open caissons constructed to found the supports of the first electrical interconnector crossing of the Jamuna River in Bangladesh in the 1970s remain the deepest ever constructed at a depth of up to 110m below mean water level (2). This crossing was in a seismically active zone and the piers, founded in a braided river, where the maximum scour depth is predicted to be 40m were constructed on sand islands by controlled sinking of open bottomed concrete cylinders constructed in-situ. This method of construction avoids the need for a cofferdam and dewatering and allows construction of the permanent works in the dry without expensive temporary works. But it is limited in its applicability to bridge foundations and other relatively simple structures such as wharfs where the caissons are normally called monoliths.

Where geological conditions are not suitable it may be necessary to excavate the caisson by hand under compressed air as was used for the foundations of Dolsan Bridge, in Korea, also designed by RPT.

Diaphragm Walls

An alternative to the open caisson method of construction was developed for marginal estuary structures in the 1960's. This was the use of diaphragm walls.

A diaphragm wall is a vertical panel constructed below ground in a trench excavated under bentonite slurry. The bentonite slurry stabilises the sides of the trench. Subsequently the slurry is displaced by concrete fed into the trench through a 'tremie' pipe. Steel reinforcement cages may be inserted prior to placing the concrete. A series of panels up to 6m long in plan and typically 0.6m to 1.4m thick can be made to form a continuous wall. Wall depths in excess of 50m below ground level are achievable.

In the UK several marine projects using diaphragm walls upto 40m deep constructed through fill material have been designed by Rendel Palmer & Tritton including Seaforth Dock - Liverpool (3), Royal Port Lock - Bristol (4) and the Iron Ore Terminal - Redcar (5).

This method of construction has similar limitations to those of the open caisson. However, although it is more adaptable to different ground conditions it is difficult to provide structural continuity between panels and again this limits the type of structure for which it is suitable.

Floating Caissons

With the advent of heavy lift equipment and much more powerful tugs and winches it has become more usual to use floating caisson construction. In this method the structure is constructed offsite and floated into its final position either partially or completely finished.

Immersed Tube Tunnels

Immersed tube tunnels are another type of structure in which concrete has been used extensively in estuary situations and in which large prefabricated units are constructed in casting basins and installed on prepared foundations. Techniques for producing watertight structures and for control of weight and installation forces have been developed for immersed tube tunnels and must also be adopted for floating caisson construction techniques.

Floating Structures

An application which is being developed in Norway and elsewhere for the use of concrete in estuary structures is in buoyant pontoon supports for floating bridges in deep water. RPT have developed a tender design and contract documents for a floating bridge across the Gulf of Corinth between Rion and Antirion which permit either normal weight or lightweight aggregate concrete pontoons (Figure 1). The site is not as favourable for a floating bridge as at the Bergsoysundet in Norway where a floating crossing is being constructed as this paper is being written but no doubt the lessons learned in Norway will be put to good use in the next century in suitably sheltered sites.

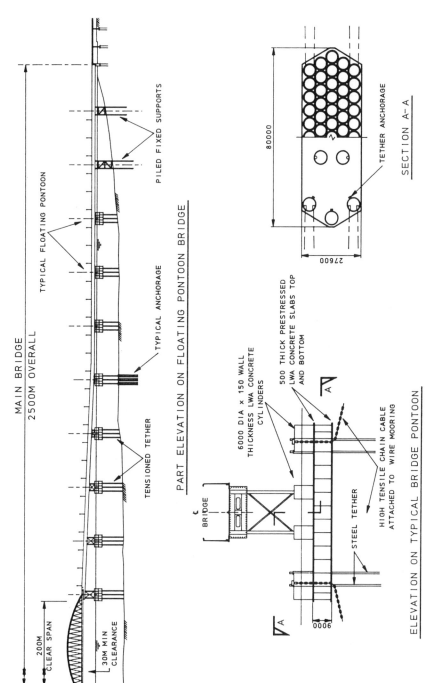

MAIN BRIDGE
2500M OVERALL

200M
CLEAR SPAN

30M MIN
CLEARANCE

TENSIONED TETHER

TYPICAL FLOATING PONTOON

TYPICAL ANCHORAGE

PILED FIXED SUPPORTS

PART ELEVATION ON FLOATING PONTOON BRIDGE

BRIDGE ℄

6000 DIA x 150 WALL
THICKNESS LWA CONCRETE
CYLINDERS

500 THICK PRESTRESSED
LWA CONCRETE SLABS TOP
AND BOTTOM

STEEL TETHER

HIGH TENSILE CHAIN CABLE
ATTACHED TO WIRE MOORING

A

A

9000

ELEVATION ON TYPICAL BRIDGE PONTOON

80000

27600

TETHER ANCHORAGE

SECTION A-A

Figure 1 Proposed Floating Bridge Scheme for the Rion-Antirion Crossing

Techniques for producing economical designs of floating concrete structures are being developed rapidly, making use of the experience being gained in the North Sea and elsewhere. RPT have just designed a large floating berth in prestressed normal weight concrete which is currently being fitted out. The structure measures 200m long by 80m wide, displaces 85,000 tonnes – 18,000 tonnes greater than the QE2, and is the largest floating concrete dock completed to Lloyds Register Class, in the world. Details of this structure will be reported elsewhere. The experience gained has already been used in barrage and bridge projects undertaken by the firm.

Further into the future it is possible that floating wave energy converters will be constructed in concrete. A recent study of alternative methods of construction for the CLAM device (Figure 2) by RPT for Lanchester Polytechnic (now University) demonstrated the inherent superiority of concrete over steel for these fatigue sensitive structures and where concrete's additional weight was not a disadvantage (6).

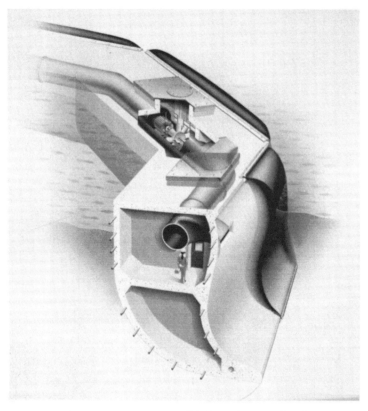

Figure 2 Concrete CLAM Wave Energy Device

DESIGN CONSIDERATIONS

Looking towards the twenty first century it is apparent that protection of the estuarial and marine environment will be one of the major considerations in planning any development along our coast. This will present engineers with problems both in planning and in designing structures which will be solved by developing construction techniques to minimise the interference with the natural coastal processes. This may demand new structural forms or developments of existing forms to reduce the size or weight of structures, or perhaps more rapid construction techniques. The challenge to the engineer is to develop forms of structure that can be economically constructed within the environmental constraints imposed by society.

Whichever method of construction is used economy and durability will always be principal requirements. All estuary structures are subject to severe environmental conditions which affect both durability and ease of construction and maintenance. The splash zone experiences regular wetting and drying with salt laden spray; the intertidal zone is subject to similar conditions but also has the risk of damage; the submerged zone can be subjected to erosion where large sediment loads are carried by the water; and buried structures may need to be chloride or sulphate resistant. Because of the difficulty of obtaining access for maintenance within a tidal estuary, concrete is normally the construction material of choice to provide a long lasting structure with minimum maintenance.

SCHEMES FOR A TIDAL POWER BARRAGE

Constraints

When schemes were being developed to extract tidal power from the Mersey by constructing a Barrage during the mid and late 1980's we had the advantage of having access to the experience gained from previous work on La Rance Barrage and the studies which were then underway for the Severn Barrage. The main constraints were seen to be environmental (7) and economic. There was a requirement to maintain the existing environmental conditions as long as possible during construction and to avoid the complete closure of the estuary as had been found necessary at La Rance. There was also great pressure to find a more economical solution than was then being considered for the Severn. A further constraint was that shipping access to upriver ports must be maintained at all times.

The layout of the scheme finally selected consisted of twenty eight 8m diameter turbines, forty six channel sluices and two locks as shown in Figure 3. By planning the installation of the sluices first and the judicious use of dredging it is theoretically possible to maintain the existing tidal prism (the total volume of water passing a given section between low and high tides) well into the construction phase. The aim thereafter is that the tidal prism should be gradually reduced as construction progresses to that of the operational barrage.

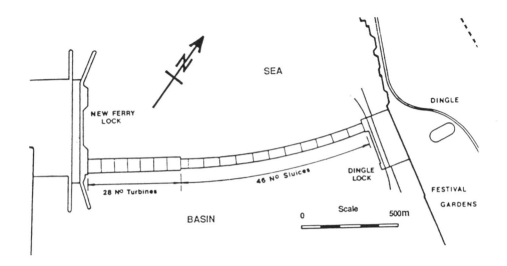

Figure 3 - Mersey Barrage Layout

Two methods of construction were considered. The first proposal was for in-situ construction in approximately five stages excluding the locks.   The   aim   was   to achieve economy of construction by incorporating part of the temporary works into the permanent works. The second proposal was to use large floating caissons. Both steel and concrete caissons were considered but it was generally considered that concrete offered a more conventional solution for such massive structures and would prove to be more economical. This scheme was therefore worked up in some detail.

In-Situ Construction

The construction of barrages in deep tidal water with depths of up to 30 metres poses significant problems. The solution adopted in most projects to date, including La Rance, has been to use an enclosure to allow construction in the dry. The conventional method of doing this would be to use a polder or sand cofferdams which, almost inevitably, involves closing the estuary and can lead to severe environmental problems.   Another solution, which was the subject of study in phases 1 and 2 of the Mersey Barrage project involves the construction of diaphragm wall cofferdams through sand filled embankments (Figure 4).   This method allows subsequent construction or fitting out to proceed in the dry and, by incorporating part of the cofferdam into the permanent works, gives an economical construction method. Since the sand-filled embankment does not itself form the enclosure it can have a much reduced crest length and, by phasing the construction, estuaries of limited width do not have to be completely blocked at any time during the construction period.

The technique of forming the diaphragm wall cells itself is not new and has been used world-wide for a variety of structures including some sited in estuarial condition.

The extension of the technique to embrace barrage construction involves the development of methods of constructing and protecting temporary sand embankments in deep tidal water. As far as is known there is no direct precedent for this although there is a certain degree of similarity between aspects of this type of structure and schemes for man made islands and for the sea protection works in Holland.

The cell walls constructed parallel to the principal current direction were to be incorporated into the permanent works (Fig 4) but the walls across the ends of the cells had to be removed to open up the water passages.

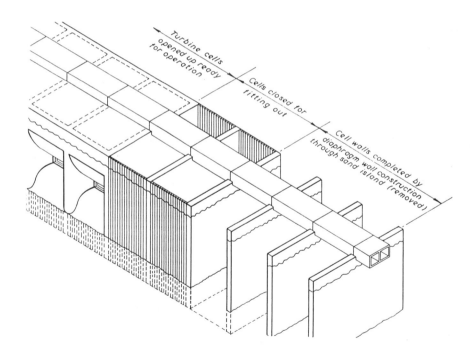

Figure 4 Diaphragm Wall Construction Method
for the Mersey Barrage

Several different forms of construction were considered for these walls including:

(a)   diaphragm wall arch closures

(b)   strutted heavy sheet pile walls

(c)   steel caisson closures.

The results of the studies indicated that in-situ construction using diaphragm wall cofferdams was practicable and could be economical in certain circumstances where the estuary was wide enough to allow multiple re-use of the temporary works required to form the sand islands and where construction could proceed continuously from one or both banks thus simplifying access.

Although these conditions were satisfied on the Mersey, severe programme constraints were identified. These were caused by the need to maintain permeability throughout the construction sequence. Thus although the estuary could be closed within the target period of five years it was found that first power could not be produced for another eighteen months.

Caisson Construction

In order to improve the financial projections power had to be produced as soon as possible. In Phase three of the project we examined alternative methods of construction using the following principles.

(a)   Maximise use of prefabricated elements, incorporating civil, mechanical and electrical components, to shorten the construction programme.

(b)   Use of floating caissons wherever possible.

(c)   Maximise use of existing construction facilities around the estuary, whether of a permanent or temporary nature.

(d)   Minimise disposal of dredged material outside the estuary, in order to reduce vessel movements within the estuary and to provide land areas for temporary construction yards and barrage operational support facilities.

(e)   Use, wherever possible, of proven construction techniques, in order to limit any potential design and construction risk.

These principles formed the basis of the design development and construction planning phases of the civil engineering studies (8).

A variety of forms of construction were proposed for different barrage elements including one in-situ tied sheet pile lock one roller compacted concrete (RCC) lock and eight turbine cells constructed within a dewatered cofferdam as well as reinforced concrete caissons used for the remainder of the turbines (Figure 5) and the sluices (Figure 6). Each structure was designed for economy within the programme constraints. Thus the sheet piled lock had to be completed in advance of the installation of the first concrete caisson structures for navigational reasons. However, the second lock could be constructed in the dry and mass roller compacted concrete proved to be the most economical form of construction and had the advantage of simplifying the logistical demands on an already congested site.

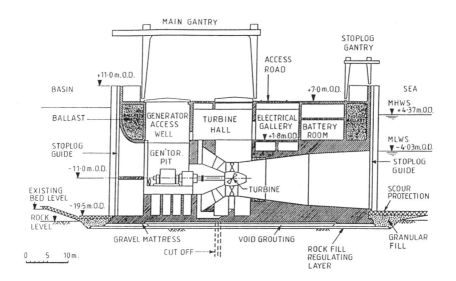

Figure 5 Mersey Barrage Turbine Generator Caisson

The greatest design effort had to be expended on the turbine caissons each measuring approximately 69m x 62m x 32m high, containing four turbines and weighing some 78,000 tonnes at float-out. The draft at floatout was critical from the point of view of both the installation method and the depth of the construction basin.

Because of the time required to deballast and remove a caisson from the basin they had to float at all states of a neap tide cycle in the basin. The lighter the caisson could be made the less excavation would be required and the cheaper the cofferdam would become. On the other hand the bed level at the barrage line was determined by the permanent foundation level.   The caissons had to be made to float freely at low tide with this bed level for installation but had to be capable of being ballasted down with sufficient preponderance to prevent flotation at high tide when operational.

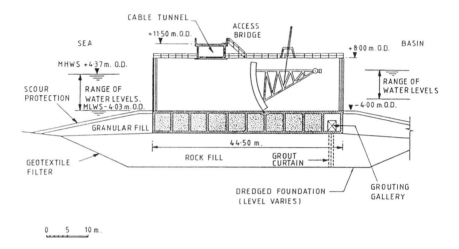

Figure 6 Mersey Barrage Sluice Caisson

In order to economise on temporary works the cofferdam forming the casting basin in which were constructed the large turbine caissons also enclosed one of the locks and the insitu turbines.   The sluice caissons were constructed in two batches within an adjacent cofferdam.   Space in both casting basins was at a premium.

In order to achieve the intended overall construction programme of five years the turbine structures would have to be completed within a two year period with an average production rate of about 9000m^3 of heavily reinforced concrete per month and with peak rates at least double this.   As this was all to take place side by side with lock construction which required a maximum of 27,000 m^3 per month of mass concrete the maximum use of system formwork precasting, and slipforming was essential, together with low heat cements for large pours.

DEVELOPMENTS IN CONCRETE DESIGN AND CONSTRUCTION TECHNOLOGY

During the course of the studies into the Mersey Barrage the CLAM Wave Energy device and the Rion-Antirion Floating Bridge state of the art construction techniques were discussed with a range of contractors and designers. This included a review of current Dutch practice in relation to the Delta Works and of Norwegian experience of slipforming and the use of lightweight concrete for offshore structures and, more recently, floating bridges. Ideas for development of techniques and for extrapolations from current practice were discussed in relation to the schemes with experts from a range of companies. One of the most important features which was identified by all those consulted was to ensure the constructability of new techniques. Some of the areas where developments are considered to be most likely to emerge in future years are listed below.

Diaphragm Wall Technology

Diaphragm wall technology has developed rapidly since first being used in the 1950's. The use of modern "milling" machines with closed circuit bentonite treatment can achieve extremely rapid construction through sandy soils - or in this case - sand islands. The restrictions on the use of the technique for the Mersey Barrage were due to the difficulty of opening the water passages and providing structural continuity.

A number of developments in diaphragm wall technology were proposed to allow the removal of temporary diaphragm wall arch cofferdam closures (an idea used in 1972 for Portbury Lock) by means of diamond wire sawing techniques in conjunction with cast-in conduits. A number of ideas were also developed to provide continuity between diaphragm wall panels. This was done at Redcar Ore Terminal in the 1970's and is currently being done in France and Japan - generally using proprietary systems.

High Strength Lightweight Concrete

More uses will be found for high strength and lightweight concretes in specific circumstances and particularly in the estuarial and marine environment. In Norway, for example, very large scale marine structures are currently being constructed using C75 normal weight concrete and C50 lightweight concrete. Our studies for the Mersey Barrage demonstrated that there are circumstances where the cost of saving 5 to 10% of the weight could be recouped many times over from consequential savings in other project costs such as rock excavation for casting basins or dredging and installation equipment costs.

The use of C50 lightweight concrete with a density of around 2000kg/m^3 will allow the use of concrete to replace steel construction for buoyancy elements for tension leg structures for bridges, buoyant immersed tunnels or floating structures.

Roller Compacted Concrete

The Mersey studies showed that, where in-situ mass concrete construction was practicable in the marine environment, roller compacted concrete (RCC) could be a very economical structural material. However, more research may have to be performed to derive the optimum material mix for RCC in the estuarine environment since a range of opinions appears to exist as to the minimum cement content which should be required.

Heavier Plant

Increases in the capacity of lifting, winching and towing equipment for offshore construction will undoubtedly lead to greater use of prefabrication for all marine and estuary structures. The 85000 tonne floating dock at Coulport was successfully towed 20 miles into position using methods normally employed for offshore structures. The turbine caissons for the Mersey Barrage which would have a similar displacement were designed to be winched into position using pre-programmed winch barges which have been demonstrated to be able to achieve pin point accuracy in other situations.

Prestressing Techniques

Prestressing technology develops to keep pace with structural innovations but, as concrete strengths increase and consequently wall thicknesses are reduced, it will become necessary to provide greater density of prestressing strand; and, for floating structures at least, "external" prestressing will become standard practice. Unfortunately, unlike bridge structures where access for regular inspections of external tendons can be provided easily this is not generally the case for estuary structures. Where it is necessary to use prestressing it is likely that grouted tendons will remain standard practice for most structures for some time to come - perhaps until confidence has been gained in the use of non ferrous tendons in the marine environment.

In the case of the floating wave energy converter, the CLAM both internal and external prestressing was considered. It was found that the wall thickness was governed by the required cover to the centrally placed stressing tendon if a fully grouted tendon was used whereas "external" tendons (protected from the marine environment by being inside the cellular device) allowed more flexibility in the structural design.

CONCLUSIONS

It has been demonstrated that many innovational structural designs for estuarial structures from tidal power barrages to floating bridges are ready for suitable opportunities to arise.

However, environmental considerations will dictate that construction techniques used only a few years ago will have to be re-assessed to minimise the effect on the estuary. Our recent studies have shown that there is scope for much more general use of new materials, heavier plant and new techniques in concrete construction in the estuarial environment in the next century.

In order to make full use of developments in materials or technology will require a more rational design approach and a re-appraisal of traditional "factors of safety" will be necessary.

REFERENCES

1.   GRICE, J.R. and HEPPLEWHITE, E.A. Design and construction of the Thames Barrier Cofferdams, Proc Instn Civ Engs Part 1, 1983, 74 February pp191-223.

2.   HINCH, L.W., McDOWELL D.M and ROWE, P.W. Jamuna River 230 kV crossing Bangladesh I Design of foundations. Proc Instn Civ Engs Part 1, 1984,76,Nov, pp927-949.

3.   AGAR, M. and IRWIN-CHILDS, F, Seaforth Dock, Liverpool planning and design, Proc Instn Civ Engs Part 1, 1973, 54, May, pp255-274.

4.   IRWIN-CHILDS, F. et al, The Royal Portbury Dock, Bristol, Proc Instn Civil Eng, Part 1, 1978,64,Feb, pp63-82.

5.   IRWIN-CHILDS, F. et al, Redcar Ore Terminal. Proc Instn Civ Eng, 1975,58,May, pp125-146.

6.   LOCKETT, F.P., The CLAM wave energy converter, Wave Energy, I.Mech E, 28/11/91, 60 pages.

7.   PINKNEY M.W. and WILSON E.A. Tidal Power and the Environment on the River Mersey. The Interaction between Major Engineering Structures and the Environment. Proceedings of the IABSE Colloquium, Nyborg, 1991.

8.   JONES, B.I. et al. The Mersey Barrage - civil engineering aspects. Proc. ICE Conference Tidal Power: Trends and Developments, Thomas Telford, 1992.

CONCRETE ARMOUR BLOCKS IN THE CONSTRUCTION OF COASTAL STRUCTURES

S S L Hettiarachchi

University of Moratuwa

Sri Lanka

ABSTRACT. The need to construct breakwaters in deep water exposed to very severe conditions imposed limitations on the use of rock as primary armour in the design of coastal structures. This led to the development of artificial armour units of various shapes designed to obtain a high degree of hydraulic stability at a relatively small block weight. An increased number of breakwater failures in the early part of the last decade made it necessary to consider in detail the structural integrity of armour units together with other design factors. This paper reviews the development of different types of armour units used in coastal structures and breakwaters, highlighting their advantages and disadvantages. Reference is made to several failures which have occurred due to poor structural design. A review is also made of experimental, computational and field investigations which have been undertaken to understand the structural behaviour of concrete armour units.

Keywords: Concrete armour Units, Coastal Structures, Breakwaters

Dr. S.S.L. Hettiarachchi is a Senior Lecturer in Civil Engineering at the University of Moratuwa, Sri Lanka. He specialises in the field of hydraulic performance of coastal structures and breakwaters.

Concrete 2000. Edited by Ravindra K. Dhir and M. Roderick Jones.
© 1993 Published by E & FN Spon. ISBN 0 419 18120 2.

INTRODUCTION

Although breakwaters have been used for hundreds of years it has been only in the last two decades that the design of these structures has developed on a more systematic basis. This has led to a better understanding of the wave mechanics principles related to the design and construction of breakwaters and in the case of rubble mound structures, greater emphasis being given to the functions and performance of primary armour, secondary armour and the core.

The need to construct breakwaters in deep water exposed to more severe conditions imposed limitations in the use of rock as the primary armour. Often the size of rock needed for the protection against large waves is impossible to obtain in the quantities required. This led to the development of artificial concrete armour units. There are also situations where rock is not available at a reasonable price under which circumstances the use of concrete armour is a preferred option.

During the last four decades various shapes of artificial armour units have been developed by breakwater designers in order to obtain a high degree of hydraulic stability at a relatively small block weight. It was expected that these armour units would withstand the design wave height without significant damage to individual armour units or to the breakwater as a whole.

The increased number of breakwater failures in the early part of the last decade made it necessary to consider in detail the structural integrity of armour units together with other design factors. Until this stage the designs were based primarily on hydraulic stability tests for which the strength of armour units was not scaled. This led to the development and the use of comparatively large armour units which had interlocking characteristics. On most occasions these large concrete armour units have been used without reinforcement materials.

Recent failures clearly indicate that the limits of applicability of these units have been exceeded mainly because due conisderation was not given to other aspects, particularly the hydro-geotechnical effects, influence of dynamic forces, structural design and the overall capability of armour units to withstand such loads in a hostile marine environment. Because of the large number of structures armoured with concrete units of various geometrical shapes used all over the world this resulted in a strong demand to investigate the concrete technology of armour units. Failure of one type of armour unit at a particular location naturally causes considerable alarm at almost all sites where such armour units have been used and hence the global demand for research and development work.

The objective of this paper is to review the development of concrete armour units used in coastal structures and breakwaters. Primarily attention will be focused on the development of different types of armour units highlighting their advantages and disadvantages in coastal engineering practice. Secondly reference will be made to several major failures which occurred in the last decade. Thirdly a review will be made of the lessons learnt from these failures, discussion of important issues and developments in research in specific areas of interest.

TYPES OF ARMOUR UNITS

The different types of artificial armour units used in practice can be broadly classified into three types.

    (1) Bulky
    (2) Slender, interlocking
and   (3) Hollow Block

The bulky type of armour units rely mainly on their weight for stability and are usually placed in two layers at random. However, there have been cases in which solid cubes were placed in a predetermined manner resulting in a structure similar to a sloping wall.

The slender interlocking type of units have the advantage of greater hydraulic stability due to interlocking effects. However, armour units of this type develop greater static and dynamic forces under wave action. These armour units which have a relatively reduced block weight are normally placed in two layers at random. However, there are instances when these units have been placed in a predetermined layout.

It is important to note that in the case of both bulky and slender interlocking type of units the voids which contribute to the dissipation of wave energy are generated between the armour units in a random manner. For all practical purposes, this is even valid when slender interlocking type of armour units are placed in a predetermined form.

The hollow block type of armour units which are of more recent origin, are somewhat different to the other two types in that the voids are built into the individual units in the required form. Armour units belonging to this type are always placed in a predetermined manner using a

TABLE 1 - CLASSIFICATION OF BREAKWATER ARMOUR UNITS

ARMOUR UNITS	METHOD OF PLACING	VOID STRUCTURE OF THE PRIMARY ARMOUR LAYER
Natural rock	– at random	voids are created between the armour units in a random manner
Artifical armour		
1) Bulky type	– normally at random sometimes in a regular pattern	voids are created between the armour units in a random manner
2) Slender interlocking type	– normally at random sometimes in a regular pattern	
3) Hollow block type	– in a regular pattern	
	a) without lateral porosity	voids are created within the armour in a pre-determined manner.
	b) with lateral porosity	
	c) with lateral porosity and placed in sets of two or more units.	

single layer and thus the resulting voids matrix of the
primary armour is geometrically well-defined, in contrast
to those belonging to the other two types for which the
voids matrices are generated randomly by irregular voids
between the armour units.

It is evident that the stability of breakwaters consisting
of single layer hollow block armour units does not depend
on the degree of interlocking between the units and as a
result the weight of the individual armour units can be
reduced considerably. The characteristic feature of a hollow block unit is the presence of a large volume of void
in the unit relative to the volume of solid material.
These armour units are designed to have the minimum volume
of solid material and surface area which in practice would
give the largest overall armour block size, minimising
cost provided stability requirements are satisfied. Hollow
block armour units have been produced in various external
shapes of which the cubic form has been more popular in
relation to placing of units.

Hollow block armour units can be broadly classified into
three types, as given below, based on the presence of
lateral porosity and the method of placing

     (1)   Armour units without lateral porosity
     (2)   Armour units with lateral porosity
     (3)   Armour units with lateral porosity and placed
          in sets of two or more units.

In the case of the first group when the armour units are
placed in the prescribed manner on the breakwater slope,
the resulting voids matrix is not interconnected laterally
although individual armour units have a void in the direction normal to the slope.

In contrast to the first group, units belonging to the
second group generate a laterally interconnected voids
matrix. By adopting a method of placement in which alternate rows are staggered by a length of half an armour unit
it is possible to generate a voids matrix of equal
porosity but with increased tortuosity.

Armour units categorised into the third group are very
similar to those belonging to the second group but are
placed in sets of two or more armour units. They have been
designed on the basis that three-dimensional symmetry of
individual units is not an essential requirement in relation to the top surface of the armour layer and that
having parallel edges of adjacent blocks is uneconomical
with regard to material usage. It has been also pointed
out that the latter generates long narrow spaces in which
wave pressure can concentrate, resulting in abrasion. It

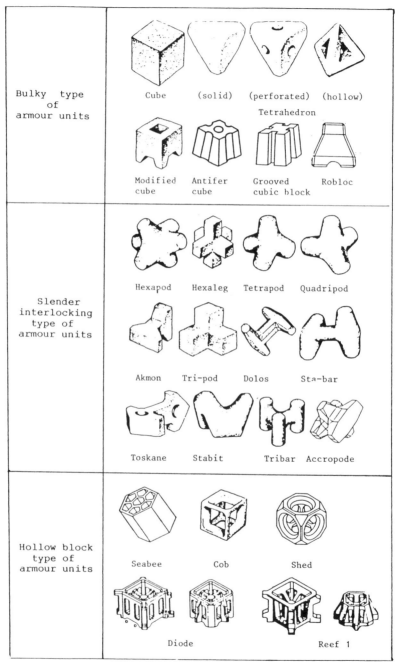

Bulky type of armour units	Cube (solid) (perforated) (hollow) Tetrahedron Modified cube Antifer cube Grooved cubic block Robloc
Slender interlocking type of armour units	Hexapod Hexaleg Tetrapod Quadripod Akmon Tri-pod Dolos Sta-bar Toskane Stabit Tribar Accropode
Hollow block type of armour units	Seabee Cob Shed Diode Reef 1

FIGURE 1 - DIFFERENT TYPES OF ARMOUR UNITS

is evident that the armour units belonging to this group will have a rather complex geometry in contrast to those belonging to the first and second groups. Care has to be exercised when placing hollow block armour units to a given overall layout pattern to ensure proper and close alignment.

Table 1 summarises the classification of armour units used for breakwater construction. Figure 1 illustrates typical examples from different types of armour units.

It is important to note that the voids matrix of the primary armour layer has a significant influence on the energy dissipating characteristics of the breakwater. This was highlighted by Whillock (1) who pointed out that the stability increased with the porosity of the armour layer. In improving the design of armour units it is important to understand the mechanism by which wave energy is dissipated and the characteristics of the resulting force domain which has to resisted by the system.

In comparing the performance of different types of armour units it is observed that water entering a hollow block unit having lateral porosity spills in four directions within the unit and out into the adjacent units where it encounters water moving, generally, in opposite directions. Wave energy is thus dissipated in turbulence within the block as opposed to between blocks in the case of other types of units. Since hollow block armour units are placed in a single layer close to each other forces of appreciable magnitude do not act to force apart adjoining blocks and this is assisted by the relatively small surface area of the blocks. (4,5,6).

The above discussion identifies some of the fundamantal aspects relating to the conceptual design of concrete armour units. The overall geometry the porosity and the method of placement of the units as well as the overall voids matrix of the primary armour layer have a significant influence on the energy dissipation characteristics of a breakwater. However due consideraton should be given to the structural design of the individual armour unit and the assembly as a whole. An armour assembly which is hydraulically very efficient may not be structurally stable or easily produced. It may also create durability problems in the long term.

REVIEW OF MAJOR FAILURES

A series of major breakwater failures which took the coastal engineering profession by surprise occurred in the late seventies and the early eighties. Of these, Port

TABLE 2 - RELEVANT DETAILS OF THE BREAKWATERS

	Maximum water depth (m)	Length (km)	Construction	Major storm damage	Significant storm wave height (m)	Principal armour	Typical section
Port Sines. Portugal	50	2	1974-1978	Feb 1978	11-12	42 t Dolosse	
San Ciprian Harbour Spain	20	1	1977-1979	Jan, March 1980	8-9 estimated	50 t Dolosse	
Port d'Arzew El Djedid Algeria	25	2	1976-1979	Dec 1980	6-10 hindcast	48 t Tetrapod	
Tripoli Harbour Libya	9	4.7	1973-1980	Jan 1981	8-9 hindcast	18 t Tetrapod	

Sines, Portugal, San Ciprian Harbour, Spain, Port d'Arzew
El Djedid, Algeria and Tripoli Harbour, Libya were considered four major failures. Investigations into these
failures revealed that the failures were not due to one
particular reason and that several different factors contributed to these disasters. However, it was widely accepted that breakwater designers have been engaged in excessive extrapolation beyond experience without recognising the limits of the existing state of the art of the
traditional breakwater design. The relevant details of the
four breakwaters are summarised in Table 2 (2). There have
been several publications relating to these failures. Burcharth (3) presented some of the important aspects and
identified the general trends of these failures. Some of
the key observations are summarised in the following sections.

At Sines the main armour was 42 t unreinforced Dolosse of
waist ratio 0.35 and mass density 2.35 t/m^3. A heavy superstructure with the crest made of reinforced concrete
was located approximatley + 19 m above MWL. The breakwater
was subjected to severe storm attacks in February 1978,
December 1978 and in February 1979. The estimated significant wave heights (H_s) were in the range 8 - 9 m and
the peak periods (T_p) were in the range 16 -20 secs. The
first storm destroyed the major part of the 10,000 Dolosse
and the resulting erosion of the seaward breakwater
profile caused the superstructure to be undermined and
destroyed. The last two storms destroyed most of the 5000
Dolosse including some which had light steel bar reinforcement placed as a refurbishment measure after the
first storm. According to the design criteria such storms
should not have caused significant damage.

The resulting investigations highlighted three major
issues. It was primarily observed that the storm wave
climate including the effects of nearshore wave processes
had been underestimated with respect to both wave heights
and wave periods. Secondly the limitations of the mechanical strength of the large armour unit had not been considered. Thirdly the hydraulic stability against displacements of the Dolosse armour units had been overestimated.

This failure highlighted the vulnerability of large interlocking armour units with respect to both hydraulic and
structural considerations. The structural limitations of
adapting large armour units having interlocking characteristics and their response towards dynamic as well as
static loading was fully exposed. From a hydraulic point
of view, it was evident that wave period might not have
been given due consideration.

For the provisional repair a decision was taken to use 90

t grooved cubes (antifer type) as the main armour placed
in a wide horizontal berm and on a rather flat slope in
front of the still intact wave wall at the inner part of
the breakwater. The grooved cube has a relatively good
mechanical strength and reasonably good hydrauilc
stability.

At San Ciprian the main armour was 50 t Dolosse. The newly
built breakwater showed failure of the main armour layer
after two winter seasons 1979 and 1980. Damage was in the
form of loss of integrity of the Dolosse layer on outer
200 m of the northern breakwater resulting in erosion of
underlying rocks. Rest of the dolos layer was damaged
around water level and some Dolosse damage on outer end of
the southern breakwater. It is believed that long period
waves appear to have been the main cause of damage contributing to failure around 3 m below the significant
height of the design wave. In the short term the breakwater was refurbished with similar size but heavily reinforced units. Some of these were also subjected to damage.
Here again the vulnerability of large interlocking type of
armour units was exposed.

At Arzew El Djedid, the main armour consisted of 48 t
Tetrapods. The breakwater was severely damaged during a
storm in December 1980. Major portion of the trunk was
severly destroyed with most Tetrapods damaged and washed
down the slope and subsequent undermining and damage of
the concrete superstructure. Along other parts of the
trunk the profile seemed almost intact with large settle-
ments in the armour layer and a substantial percentage of
broken Tetrapods. It is believed that the failure of the
breakwater was due to breakage of the large Tetrapods and
not due to hydraulic stability considerations. This indicates that interblock forces and moments generated by
dynamic wave induced loads and by settlement and compaction during wave action contributed to the breakage of a
major part of the tetrapods. It is important to note that
a large settlement of the very steep armour layer was also
noticed in the model tests. Short term repairs in the form
of construction of a new berm of 1 t - 5 t rocks added 5 m
below mean sea level with two layers of 24 t antifer cube
(grooved cubic) blocks placed above at 1:1.33 slope and 5
m thick crest formed with 12 t cubes were undertaken.

At Tripoli, the main armour was 19 t Tetrapods supported
by a berm of 5-8 t rocks. A concrete capping wall with the
crest at approximately 9 m above MWL was placed directly
on the filter layer stones of 2-4 t and the sand used as
reclamation material was separated from the coarse core
material of 0.025 - 2 t quarry run by a geotextile and a
filter layer. The reclaimed land was used for a double
carriage roadway.

During the period of construction problems relating to overtopping and venting under the superstructure had been observed. The breakwater was severely damaged in January 1981. It was evident that the wave climte had been underestimated. The damage included the collapse of 550 m parapet wall accompanied by movement and cracking of the base slab. Tetrapods were displaced and broken above sea level, the toe was also damaged in places. The reclaimed area was subjected to excessive erosion and damage.

Investigations revealed that many design parameters had been underestimated and the model tests had not monitored the effect of pressure build up below and behind the parapet base slab. As a refurbishment measure a 2 m high sheet pile flood wall was built behind the breached parapet wall and the broken tetrapods were replaced.

FACTORS CONTRIBUTING TO FAILURES

Investigations of major breakwater failures have identified certain important issues which need to be considered in detail. These include the following.

1) Under estimation of the design wave climate.
2) Limitations of adopting standard hydraulic model investigations for the total design.
3) Poor assessment of wave induced loads and resulting force domain.
4) Limited relative strength of large unreinforced interlocking types of armour units.
5) Factors leading to the sudden collapse of steep slopes armoured with artificial units.
6) Durability of concrete in the marine environment.
7) Need to understand the interrelationship among different failure modes (i.e. clear understanding of the fault tree).

The above factors, perhaps with the exception of the first, are very important in relation to the structural design and the concrete technology of armour units. There are several other factors which relate to the hydraulic and geotechnical design of the breakwater.

DISCUSSION OF IMPORTANT ISSUES

A review of the major failures and some of the contributing factors were discussed in the preceeding sections. Some of the important issues arising from this discussion will be identified in detail in this section.

Hydraulic Model Investigations

One of the major drawbacks of the design of armour units relates to the fact that the overall design was dependent purely on the hydraulic design based primarily on hydraulic model tests. These tests are conducted to determine the hydraulic stability and the modelling procedure does to usually permit the strength of armour units to be scaled. Hence it is not surprising to observe the development of large interlocking type of armour units which performs satisfactorily in model tests using model units made of a material having a greater strength than that of the prototype at the corresponding reduced scale. Extrapolation from this deceptive stability exhibited in model tests have on many occasions resulted in the usage of large concrete armour units without any reinforcements.

Loading on armour units

For a given armour unit there are three important phases that can be identified in relation to its overall performance.

(1) Manufacture and transport for storage
(2) Transport to site and placing
(3) Service

The load conditions corresponding to the first and second phases are reasonably well defined and are mainly influenced by the static weight of the unit. Thermal stresses due to temperature differences during the hardening process may also be present. Adequate support should be provided during handling, transport and placing. Sufficient precautions should be exercised when placing one unit beside another because a certain amount of abrasion and impact may occur when doing so. This is of particular relevance for hollow block armour units which have to be placed to a predetermined layout. The load conditions corresponding to the service state are complex and demand closer examination. The types of loads encountered in this phase include static, dynamic, abrasive, thermal and chemical loads.

Dynamic hydraulic loads acting on armour units are essentially of two types. The first are oscillatory forces which are gradually varying or quasi-static loads due to wave action on the slope. These oscillatory forces are usually exerted during uprush and downrush of waves. The second type of dynamic hydraulic loads are impact forces due to direct wave impact. The presence of these forces and their magnitude will be very much dependent on the type of wave profile at the point of wave impact. Impact forces due to direct wave action influence the armour unit in two ways. Firstly, they impose hyraulic impact loads of high mangitude acting over a very short time interval. This is of particular relevance to armour units placed in the vicinity of the still water level. Secondly, they cause the movement of a given unit which in turn will strike neighbouring armour units, thus imparting structural impact loads. Rocking, rolling and collisions between armour units and parts of one broken unit striking another unit are some of the main effects of this type of load. Reference is made to Table 3 which outlines the types of loads and their origin.

Assessment of Wave Induced Loads and Structural Integrity

Static and dynamic loads acting on armour units can be asessed by theoretical and experimental methods which consider wave action on prototype and model units. Indirect methods where wave action has been simulated by other means have also been used very effectively in experimental investigations.

A theoretical assessment can be made by adopting analytical approaches. The difficulties related to a purely theoretical approach arise from the complex characteristics of flow associated with wave action on armour units. Theoretical models have to be developed based on simplifying assumptions which are necessary in the absence of quantitative expressions which identify and describe some of the complex interactions between wave motion and coastal structures (7).

The loads can be determined experimentally by incorporating instrumentation in the model or prototype units. In model investigations the following methods have been adopted.

(1) Monitoring the movement by photographic techniques or by means of accelerometer gauges placed in the units (8).
(2) Use of strength scaled armour units (9).
(3) Use of strain gauges mounted on model units as a stress measuring device (10).

Comparatively few investigations have been performed on prototype armour units at site. At present two projects are in progress where Dolos units (11) and Cob units (12) have been extensively instrumented to monitor dynamic loads acting on them.

Indirect methods of load evaluation have also been used effetively by researchers. Of these the Dynamic Similarity Method introduced by Burcharth (13) has proved to be very

TABLE 3 - TYPES OF LOADS ACTING ON ARMOUR UNITS

For a given armour unit there are <u>three important phases</u> that can be identified in relation to its overall performance.

1) Manufacture and transport for storage
2) Transport to site and placing
3) In service

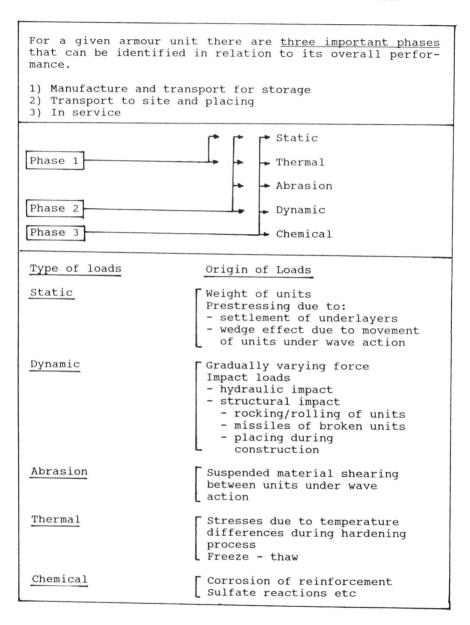

Type of loads	Origin of Loads
<u>Static</u>	Weight of units Prestressing due to: - settlement of underlayers - wedge effect due to movement of units under wave action

<u>Dynamic</u>	Gradually varying force
	Impact loads
	- hydraulic impact
	- structural impact
	  - rocking/rolling of units
	  - missiles of broken units
	  - placing during construction

<u>Abrasion</u>	Suspended material shearing between units under wave action
<u>Thermal</u>	Stresses due to temperature differences during hardening process Freeze - thaw
<u>Chemical</u>	Corrosion of reinforcement Sulfate reactions etc

successful in providing design information for interlocking type of armour units. This method of testing has been widely used by many researchers.

Numerical stress modelling has also been used to determine the structural integrity of armour units (14, 17). These studies have provided very useful design information which have contributed towards improved structural design. In particular attention has been focused on the ability of armour units to withstand dynamic load with acceptable levels of damage in a hostile marine environment.

Material Characteristics

Concrete and rock stones are the two principal materials used for the construction of breakwaters. With respect to the use of concrete in coastal structures due attention should be focused on fatigue, thermal stresses and durability in the marine environment. This subejct has been investigated recently by many researchers and the most notable contribution has been made by Burcharth (15).

As identified earlier waves cause gradually varying loads and impact loads to act on armour units. Since armour units are exposed to repeated loads and also because concrete exhibit significant fatigue this effect must be incorporated in the design process. Using reinforcement in concrete is a way of imporving the strength properties. Both conventional steel bar reinforcement and fibre reinforcement have been used. Burcharth (15) conducted detailed impact fatigue flexural stress tests using 200 kg Dolosse units. Both unreinforced and steel fibre reinforced concrete were subjected to investigation.

It was observed that the fatigue effect is smaller in the fibre reinforced units. The fatigue life of the steel fibre reinforced concrete was the better of the two except for small number of impacts. However, the difference is considerably smaller and probably much smaller than usually cited in literature. It is often quoted that fibres increase the energy absorbtion at failure many times, compared to plain concrete. Burcharth also observed that the effect of steel fibres on the fatigue life and on the impact strength of slender armour units seemed to be small and was certainly much smaller than the effect of similar quantities of steel in a conventional bar reinforcement. Results from full scale static tests and dynamic drop tests with Dolosse units in the range of 1.5 t to 30 t have showed that conventional reinforcement is superior to steel fibres of equal quantity. Burcharth has pointed that fibre is beneficial only in very slender, flexible structural members and not in relatively stiff elements. Hence their applicability in units such as

Dolosse and Tetrapods may not be very effective. On the other hand chopped polypropylene fibres can be beneficial in preventing the occurrence of shrinkage cracking. Although small shrinkage cracks may not have a significant influence on the strength, the presence of such cracks may have adverse effects with respect to long term durability. In the production of Cob and Shed units, considerable use has been made of chopped polypropylene fibre as reinforcement in the proportion of 0.2% by weight to improve impact and handling stress resistance. Investigations from numerical stress modelling (17, 18) have identified the relevance of the use of such fibre in that proportion.

During the curing process the heat of hydration contributes to an increase in the temperature. Burcharth (16) points out that due to low conductivity of concrete and because of the relatively poor insulation of the formwork, higher temperatures will be reached in the central parts of the armour unit than that at the surfaces. The temperature differences will create different thermal expansion and with the restriction of movement due to formwork thermal stresses are generated. Stresses will be higher at points at a greater distance from the surface and also a high cement content will increase stresses. It has been identified that it is not desirable to lower the cement content (usually in the range 300 - 400 kg/m^3) because of the requirement of effective long term durability and also because of the need of fast development of strength to facilitate the removal and re-use of relatively expensive formwork. The importance of the geometry of the armour unit is also a relevant factor in controlling thermal stresses. For example, the positioning of a central hole in a cube will reduce the thermal stresses and also increase the hydraulic efficiency.

Due to its low tensile strength, concrete is a very brittle and it is this characteristic which plays a critical role in the design of armour units. Apart from basic findings from concrete technology, Burcharth (16) identified two important observations from full scale tests of armour units. The first is that a very low water cement ratio (<0.4) obtainable by the use of super-plasticizers and the use of puzzolan cement seemed favourable on dynamic and static strength. The second is that high - strength concretes exhibit only a marginally larger impact strength than normal concretes. This has been attributed to the fact that high-strength concretes are relatively more brittle.

CONCLUDING REMARKS

This paper has reviewed the development of different types of concrete armour units which have been used in practice. Some of the important aspects relating to major failures which occurred in the early eighties have been presented. Factors which contributed to these failures have also been identified. It was evident that breakwater designers have engaged in excessive extrapolation beyond experience without recognising the limits of existing state of the art. A brief review of hydraulic model investigations, wave induced loads material characteristics and structural integrity of armour units are presented.

REFERENCES

1. WHILLOCK, A.F.   An appraisal of rubble mound break-waters. The Dock and Harbour Authority, Vol. 62, pp 186 - 189, 1981.

2. NEW CIVIL ENGINEER, Magazine of the Institution of Civil Engineers, pp 27-30, 5th May 1983.

3. BURCHARTH, H.F.   The lessons from recent breakwater failures. Developments in Breakwater Design. World Federation of Engineering Organizations Technical Congress, Vancouver, May 1987.

4. STICKLAND, I.W. COB units - Report on hydraulic model research. Wimpey Laboratory. Ref. No. H/334, 1969.

5. WILKINSON, A.R. and ALLSOP, N.W.H. Hollow block armour units. Proc. ASCE Conf. on Coastal Structures 83. Virginia, U.S.A. 1983, pp 208-221.

6. HYDRAULICS RESEARCH STATION. The SHED breakwater armour unit, model tests on random waves. Report EX 124, 1983.

7. McDOUGAL, W.G., MELBY, J.A. and TEDESCO, J.W. Wave forces on concrete armour units. Jr. of Waterway, Port, Coastal and Ocean Engineering ASCE, Volume 114, No. 5 September 1988.

8. LIGTERINGEN, H. and HEYDRA, G. Recent progress in breakwater design. The Dock and Harbour Authority. July 84, pp 47 -50.

9. TIMCO, G. and MANSARD, E.P.D. Improvements in modelling rubble-mound breakwaters. Int. Conf. on Coastal Engineering, Cape Town, 1982, Chapter 22, pp 2047 - 2061.

10. PAAPE, A. and LIGTERINGEN, H. Model investigations as a part of the design of rubble-mound breakwaters. Delft Hydraulics Laboratory Publication No. 246, 1980.

11. HOWELL, G. A system for the measurement of the structural response of Dolos armour units in the prototype. Proc. Int. Conf. on Measuring Techniques of Hydraulic Phenomena in Offshore, Coastal and Inland Waters. BHRA, April 86, pp 177-188.

12. TONER, W.L. WALDRON, P. and FLOYD, J.A. Structural behaviour of single layer concrete breakwater armour units. Proc. Seminar on Developments in Coastal Engineering. Organised by the University of Bristol, Bristol. 1991.

13. BURCHARTH, H.F. Full scale dynamic testing of Dolosse to destruction. Journal of Coastal Engineering, 1981, Vol. 4 pp 229-251.

14. SCOTT, D., TURCKE, D. and BAIRD, W.F. Structural Modelling of Dolos Armour Units. Jr. of Waterway, Port, Coastal and Ocean Engineering ASCE, Vol. 116, No. 1 Jan. 1990.

15. BURCHARTH, H.F. Fatigue in breakwater concrete armour units. Report of University of Aalborg, Denmark, October 1984.

16. BURCHARTH, H.F. Material, Structural Design of Armour Units. Seminar on Rubble Mound Breakwaters, Stockholm, Sweden, 1983.

17. FRANCO, L. MATERAZZI, A. NOLI, A and RADOGNA, E. Impact response of fibre-reinforced concrete elements in the marine environment. Proc. 2nd AIOM Congress, Nov. 89.

18. HETTIARACHCHI, S. FRANCO, L. and MATERAZZI, A. Wave induced loads on single layer hollow block armour units. The Dock and Harbour Authority. Vol. LXXII No. 830, July/August 1991.

FACTORS INFLUENCING CHLORIDE INGRESS INTO MARINE STRUCTURES

P B Bamforth

W F Price

Taywood Engineering Ltd

United Kingdom

ABSTRACT The paper provides quantitative information on two parameters, essential in the prediction of chloride ingress into concrete, namely the surface chloride level and the chloride diffusion coefficient. Factors which affect these two parameters are discussed, including location, mix type, curing surface treatment and the use of controlled permeability formwork. The relative benefits have been estimated and guidance is given on appropriate mix designs for durable reinforced concrete in a marine environment. The most significant benefits are achieved using blended cements, comprising ground granulated blastfurnace slag (GGBS), pulverised fuel ash (PFA) or silica fume (SF) in combination with OPC, which can potentially extend the time to activation of reinforcement by as much as ten times.

Keywords: Chloride, Surface Level, Diffusion, Durability, Pulverised Fuel Ash (PFA), Ground Granulated Blastfurnace Slag (GGBS), Silica Fume (SF), Controlled Permeability Formwork (CPF).

Dr Phillip B Bamforth is the Technical Manager of the Research Laboratory for Taywood Engineering. He has been involved in concrete technology for over 20 years, through research work and site support. He has published papers on many aspects of concrete behaviour, but has a special interest in durability and blended cements.

Dr Bill Price is the Manager of the Concrete Technology Group within Taywood Engineering. He has extensive experience in concrete technology both in the laboratory and on sites worldwide. Research interests include concrete surface properties, durability and high strength concrete.

Concrete 2000. Edited by Ravindra K. Dhir and M. Roderick Jones.
© 1993 Published by E & FN Spon. ISBN 0 419 18120 2.

INTRODUCTION

The major cause of deterioration in marine reinforced concrete structures is corrosion of the embedded reinforcement, resulting from penetration of chlorides through the cover concrete to the steel. The migration of chlorides into concrete may be conveniently expressed in terms of a diffusion process and as such it may be described by Ficks second diffusion law[1], a solution to which is given by:

$$C_x = C_s \left[1 - \mathrm{erf} \frac{x}{2\sqrt{D_c t}} \right] \qquad - (1)$$

where C_s is the surface chloride level, C_x is the chloride level at depth x and time t, D_c is the chloride diffusion coefficient and erf is the error function (from tables). Whilst, the diffusion coefficient is a convenient single parameter for describing resistance to chloride penetration, the build up of chlorides at depth is governed both by D_c and by C_s, which determines the initial chloride concentration gradient within the cover zone. As the understanding of chloride induced corrosion increases, and quantitative design lives are being included in National Standards[2], project specifications are beginning to adopt performance limits on the chloride diffusion coefficient[3], but the significance of the surface chloride level is usually overlooked.

This paper examines the factors which control both the surface chloride level and the chloride diffusion coefficient of concrete in marine structures, in an effort to identify the optimum combination of materials, curing and formwork type for minimising the rate of chloride ingress.

SURFACE CHLORIDE LEVELS

Location

The level of chloride which builds up on the surface of concrete is determined to a large degree by the location of the structure, the orientation of the surface, the degree of exposure to salt and the general exposure conditions with regard to prevailing winds and rainfall. For coastal and marine structures the proximity to seawater is obviously a primary factor. Unfortunately, there has been little comprehensive research on the effects of location, but some limited available data[4-7] are shown in Figure 1. This demonstrates quantitatively what is now generally accepted, namely that the splash zone is the most severe with regard to the accumulation of surface chlorides. This is due to the wetting and drying cycles which result in a progressive build up of chloride by a process of wetting with seawater, evaporation and salt cyrstallization.

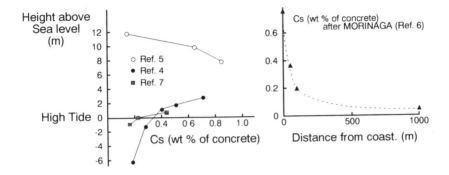

Figure 1 - Effect of Location on Surface Chloride Levels

While the data in Figure 1 are by no means comprehensive, they demonstrate the widely varying values of C_S which may occur and the need to accommodate relatively high values of C_S in the most extreme locations.

Mix Design and Curing

In a recent study[8] involving reinforced concrete test blocks exposed to salt spray on the South Coast of England, chloride profiles were measured after exposure for 6, 12, 24 and 36 months. The study was designed, principally, to investigate the effect of concrete mix constituents and the degree of curing on chloride penetration and to achieve this, grade 30 mixes were used throughout. Values of C_S, were estimated by deriving a best fit curve through the incremental chloride levels (Table 1). No consistent change in C_S was observed between 6 months and 3 years and the average values have been calculated, therefore, using measurements from the four periods of exposure.

Two effects are immediately apparent. Firstly, the blended cement mixes consistently exhibited higher surface chloride levels than the OPC concretes. And secondly, higher surface levels were achieved by the better (W) cured concretes. The difference between values for OPC and blended cement concretes has been attributed to the higher sorptivities of the latter when first exposed to salt spray at 28 days[9,10]. This is illustrated in Figure 2 which also shows the effect of curing.

The authors had assumed, prior to obtaining these results, that curing would reduce sorptivity to the extent that C_S would be reduced also. However, there appears to be an additional effect of curing which more than offsets the benefit of reduced sorptivity. It is postulated that this additional effect may be related to the

Table 1 - Values of Cs and D from Exposure Blocks, and Standard Cell

MIX TYPE	CURING	SURFACE CHLORIDES Cs(%)	Dce x 10^{-12}M²/SEC AT AGE (MONTHS)				AVE	Dc (Cell) x 10^{-12}M²/SEC
			6	12	24	36		
OPC	W	0.48	7.91	3.24	5.06	6.53	5.69	2.31
	E	0.44	10.12	2.89	13.68	4.55	7.81	1.53
	M	0.46	10.78	2.97	5.46	5.59	6.20	2.38
AVERAGE		0.46	9.60	3.03	8.07	5.56	6.57	2.07
30% PFA	W	0.63	2.29	1.66	1.28	0.89	1.53	0.04
	E	0.47	4.55	1.22	3.34	1.29	2.60	0.04
	M	0.50	5.77	2.06	1.10	1.00	2.48	0.04
AVERAGE		0.53	4.20	1.65	1.91	1.06	2.20	0.04
OPC/PLAST	W	0.45	4.71	2.23	4.56	4.27	3.94	1.47
	E	0.51	5.60	2.60	5.13	4.66	4.50	2.01
	M	0.42	5.06	3.13	6.76	5.78	5.18	1.00
AVERAGE		0.46	5.12	2.65	5.48	4.90	4.54	1.49
70% GGBS	W	0.64	5.68	2.72	1.13	0.76	2.57	0.02
	E	0.51	9.34	3.24	2.57	1.18	4.08	0.02
	M	0.56	7.21	2.68	2.00	1.07	3.24	0.02
AVERAGE		0.57	7.41	2.88	1.90	1.00	3.30	0.02
WATER- PROOFED	W	0.48	3.36	2.12	2.07	2.43	2.50	1.62
	E	0.32	2.78	2.34	4.53	3.04	3.17	1.83
	M	0.43	5.95	0.80	5.74	2.04	3.63	1.85
AVERAGE		0.41	4.03	1.75	4.11	2.50	3.10	1.77
8% SF	W	0.69	5.15	0.92	4.79	3.98	3.71	0.31
	E	0.50	8.04	2.00	4.67	2.89	4.42	2.05
	M	0.52	3.49	2.39	5.55	4.96	4.10	0.27
AVERAGE		0.57	5.56	1.77	5.00	3.94	4.08	0.88

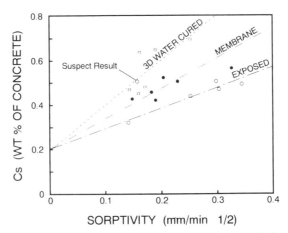

Figure 2 - Relationship between Cs, Sorptivity and Curing

increased amount of cement hydrate in well cured concrete, which leads to an increased ability to bind chlorides to the surface, probably by adsorption. This being the case, it would be expected that concrete with a higher cement content would also have a tendency for higher surface chloride level, even though higher cement content mixes would generally have lower w/c ratios and thus lower sorptivities.

Figure 3 shows the relationship between C_s and cement content, derived using the authors' results and published data[4,11-14]. While the results are scattered a trend for increasing C_s with higher cement content is apparent, supporting the hypothesis. This presents a serious dilemma as current good practice, which includes prolonged curing to improve durability, has been shown to increase C_s, which, in turn, will result in a higher concentration gradient and more rapid chloride ingress. Further research in this area is needed, however, before considering changes in current curing practice.

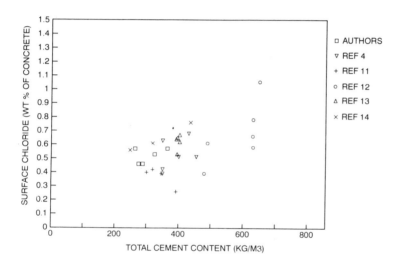

Figure 3 - Influence of Cement Content on Cs

Controlled Permeability Formwork

The relationship between C_s and the cement content at the surface has been further demonstrated in tests using controlled permeability formwork (CPF), which markedly reduces the w/c ratio in the near surface zone with an associated increase in cement content[15]. Table 2 gives results using an accelerated chloride penetration test[16] for concretes cast against both CPF and polyurethane

Table 2 - Effect of CPF on Activation Time for Reinforcement at 75mm Cover

Mix Type	Mean 28 day Strength (MPa)	Formwork Type	Cure	Cs (% Conc)	Dce at 28 days (m²/s x 10⁻¹²)	Relative Activation Time
100% OPC	41.5	Imp	3 Wet	0.16	2.50	1.03
		Imp	None	0.18	2.22	1.00
		CPF	3 Wet	0.28	0.76	1.91
		CPF	None	0.27	0.76	1.97
30% PFA	47.0	Imp	3 Wet	0.16	2.50	1.03
		Imp	None	0.24	1.40	1.18
		CPF	3 Wet	0.18	0.51	4.32
		CPF	None	0.15	1.00	2.76
50% GGBS	36.0	Imp	3 Wet	0.19	2.64	0.79
		Imp	None	0.20	2.01	0.97
		CPF	3 Wet	0.11	0.44	10.62
		CPF	None	0.12	0.62	6.38
70% GGBS	40.0	Imp	3 Wet	0.18	1.26	1.76
		Imp	None	0.24	1.40	1.18
		CPF	3 Wet	0.11	0.46	10.14
		CPF	None	0.11	0.45	10.38

coated plywood formwork. The C_S levels indicate that, for an OPC concrete, CPF does increase the level of surface chlorides. However, when OPC is blended with either PFA or GGBS the CPF causes C_S to diminish. As CPF has been shown to increase the near surface cement content of blended cement concretes as well as OPC concretes[17], it could be inferred either that surface chloride levels may be determined primarily by the amount of OPC in the near surface zone, or that the relative reduction of surface sorptivity by using CPF is greater for blended cements than for OPC. Results obtained from studies by Thomas et al[11] support the former hypothesis, but this behaviour is not consistent.

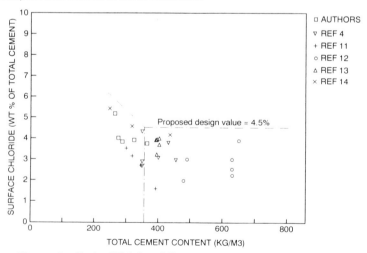

Figure 4 - Cs, by Weight of Cement, vs Total Cement Content

Cs by Weight of Cement

The results given in Figure 3 have been replotted in Figure 4, showing the relationship between C_s by weight of cement and the total cement content of each mix. For mixes with cement contents in excess of about 350kg/m^3 (ie typical structural concrete) C_s is proportional to the cement content with an upper value of about 4.5%. At cement contents lower than 350kg/m^3 C_s increases in relation to cement content, but this would be expected at lower cement contents as the sorptivity becomes more influential, and due to the fact that the curve must approach infinity as the cement content approaches zero. For predictive purposes, however, a value of 4.5% by weight of cement is proposed for marine grade structural concrete, unless specific data are available from which to derive a more reliable value.

Means for Reducing Cs

While the relationship between, C_s, sorptivity, cement content and curing is undoubtedly complex, the results do, however, demonstrate means by which C_s can be minimised. Avoiding the contentious issue of curing, low C_s is associated with low sorptivity and low cement content. The effect of cement content is not normally relevant, however, when considering the overriding objective, namely, prevention of corrosion of reinforcement. As the activation of steel is determined by the ratio of chloride to hydroxyl ions (normally expressed as percent chloride by weight of cement) the lower value of C_s in a lower cement content mix will be directly offset by the reduced level of hydroxyl ions at the steel and hence the increased Cl$^-$/OH ratio, provided the cement content is greater than 350kg/m^3.

The most effective way to reduce C_s and its consequences is therefore to use concrete with a low surface sorptivity. This can be achieved using either integral waterproofing admixtures, or treatment to the surface. The test mix including a calcium stearate waterproofing admixture exhibited the lowest value of C_s, (Table 1) being about 10% lower than the OPC control mix. Higher performance water reducers are available which can reduce sorptivity by as much as 75%, and in laboratory tests[17] the effect of an ammonium stearate waterproofer was to reduce Cs by about 20%.

Surface treatments can also be used to achieve low surface sorptivity and hence low values of C_s. Extensive research in the US[18] has demonstrated that silanes in particular can potentially reduce chloride levels significantly and the UK Department of Transport now specify surface treatments of this type for bridges which are exposed to deicing salts. Results from the South Coast exposure site indicate significant benefits with the use of silanes on grade 30 concrete, with C_s being reduced by 60%.

CHLORIDE DIFFUSION COEFFICIENT

The chloride diffusion coefficient D defines the rate at which the chloride migrates from the surface to the steel. In Concrete Society Report No. 31 published in 1987[19] typical values of chloride diffusion coefficient in concrete were defined in the range 5 x 10^{-12}m²/sec to 5 x 10^{-11}m²/sec. At that time there was limited published data and that which was available had not been analysed in relation to the design and performance of structures. Since then, the importance of this property has been recognised with a progressive increase in the amount of published data.

Cement Type

Results obtained by analysis of the chloride profiles for the exposure blocks are given in Table 1. These are not true diffusion coefficients, D_c, and are referred to as effective diffusion coefficients, D_{ce}, as part of the chloride ingress has resulted from absorption[9] and steady state conditions have not been achieved[20]. Values of D_c, measured using the standard diffusion cell[9] are, however, also given in Table 1. It is clear that the most significant effect has resulted from changing the cementing materials. For OPC concretes, with or without admixtures, the variations were relatively small. However, by replacing OPC with either GGBS, PFA or SF, substantial reductions in both D_c and D_{ce} were achieved. It is interesting to note that the differences in D_{ce} from mix to mix were relatively small, due to the increasing relative contribution to D_{ce} of early chloride penetration by absorption. A review of published results[11-13,20-30], showing the relative effects of PFA, GGBS and SF is illustrated in Figure 5.

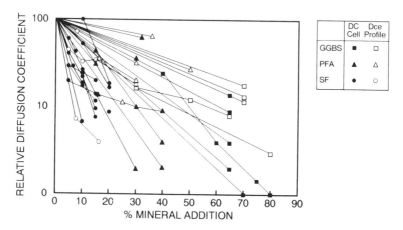

**Figure 5 - The Effects of PFA, GGBS and SF on Dc (or Dce) using the Authors'
Results with Data from Refs 11-13 and 20-30**

In each case, Dc (and Dce) reduces as the proportion of PFA, GGBS or SF is increased, with maximum reductions of up to two orders of magnitude. For each mix type there was significant scatter of results due to variations in the materials used and, more importantly, the test methods employed. This highlights the need for a standardised test method and compliance criteria which can be used to predict performance in-situ, if the enhanced performance of concretes containing blended cements is to be taken advantage of in the design of r.c. structures.

Curing

Both Dhir et al[20], using standard tests, and Thomas et al[11], by measurement of chloride profiles under marine exposure, have shown that increasing the length of water curing reduces the chloride diffusion of OPC and PFA concrete. These data, shown in Figure 6 with the authors' results, indicate that extending a typical 'site' curing period of 3 days, even to 28 days, has a significant, but relatively modest effect compared with changes resulting from the use of blended cements.

CPF

The effect of CPF, measured either as an 'effective' diffusion coefficient based on chloride profiles (Table 2) or as a true ionic diffusion coefficient[15] is consistently beneficial, reflecting the substantially lower water/cement ratio in the surface zone. Although the effect of casting concrete against CPF has been shown to be limited to the outer 10-20mm[15], it is this zone which provides the first line of defence against chloride penetration.

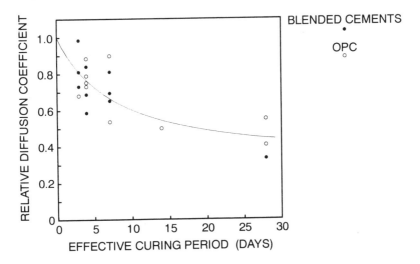

Figure 6 - The Relative Effect of Curing on Dc

COMBINED EFFECTS

It is clear that significant changes in either Cs or Dc can be affected by appropriate selection of materials, or surface treatments.   However, assessment of the improvements (or otherwise) in the marine durability of reinforced concrete must be based on the combined effect of Cs and Dc. Calculations have been carried out using typical values Dc (Table 1) to estimate the time for the chloride level at 25, 50, 75 and 100mm depth to achieve a value of 0.4% by weight of cement (Table 3). The results demonstrate that where there is scope for major changes in chloride diffusion coefficients, by use of blended cements, changing Cs will have relatively little influence. However, for concretes limited to the use of Portland cements, for which Dc is unlikely to fall much below 10^{-12}m²/sec, reducing Cs can have a much greater influence.

Table 3 - Estimated Times to Activation

MIX TYPE	Dc (10^{-12}m²/sec)	TIME (IN YEARS) TO ACTIVATION FOR COVER (IN mm) OF			
		25	50	75	100
OPC GRADE 45	2.0	<2	7	15	28
30% PFA 10% SF	0.4	9	35	78	138
70% GGBS	0.2	17	69	155	275

Considering the effects of CPF on both Cs and Dce, early age chloride penetration profiles for an OPC concrete cast against different formworks, (Figure 7) illustrate the reduced chloride build up at depth. The activation time for reinforcement at a cover depth of 75mm has been estimated (Table 2) relative to an OPC concrete with no curing after formwork removal at 24 hours. CPF is more effective than 3 day wet cure, and, for these early life tests, than changing the cement type. CPF appears to be particularly beneficial (3-10 times better) when used in conjunction with concrete containing PFA or GGBS as it causes reductions in both Cs and Dc.   For OPC concretes, CPF reduces Dc, but not Cs and the subsequent increase in activation time is, therefore, relatively small (less than 2 times).

It is interesting to note that, while early life tests often indicate that blended cement concretes are both sensitive to curing and prone to rapid early chloride penetration, the early age resistance of blended cement concretes to chloride ingress was significantly enhanced by the use of CPF.

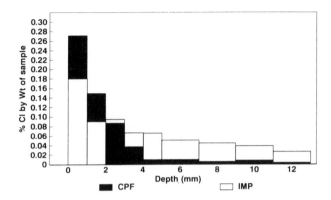

Figure 7 - Chloride Profiles with and without CPF

CONCLUSIONS

It has been shown that benefits in terms of increased service life (defined as time to activation of steel corrosion based on a chloride diffusion model) can be achieved by various means including selection of cements, the use of an integral waterproofer, or surface treatments, including the use of CPF. The greatest benefits can be achieved by those options which have a significant effect on Dc. For concretes where significant reduction in Dc are precluded by limitations on the characteristics of the cement, measures to reduce Cs are also relatively effective.

Cement type has been shown to have the dominant influence on Dc, with blended cement mixes using high proportions of GGBS (70%) yielding values of Dc up to two order of magnitude lower than equal grade OPC concretes, and mixes using PFA (30%) and SF (15%) also providing substantial benefits.

The benefits achieved by the use of CPF are also significant and cement dependent, with potential increases in service life from 2 to 10 times.

The study indicates that to achieve a long service life in a marine environment, blended cements, using PFA, GGBS and SF are essential. The high early chloride ingress in the near surface zone when using slow growth mixes with high early sorptivity, can be offset by the use of an integral waterproofer, or improvements in the surface zone using a hydrophobic treatment or CPF.

REFERENCES

1.   CRANK, J. The Mathematics of Diffusion. Oxford University Press. 1975, 2nd Edition.

2.   BRITISH STANDARDS INSTITUTION. Durability of Buildings and Building Elements, Products and Components, BS 7543, BSI London, 1992.

3.   KJAER, U. Concrete for the fixed link across the Great Belt - Storebaelt. Dansk Beton No. 2, 1990, 77-80.

4.   TAYLOR WOODROW RESEARCH LABORATORIES, Concrete with Oceans - Marine durability of the Tongue Sand Tower, CIRIA UEG Technical Report No. 5.

5.   BIJEN, J.M.J.M. Durability aspects of the King Fahd Causeway, Concrete in Hot Climates, Ed, M J Walker, RILEM, Published by E & F Spon, London, 1992, pp231-245.

6.   MORINAGA, S. Life prediction of reinforced concrete structures in hot and salt-laden environments, Concrete in Hot Climates, Ed. M J Walker, RILEM, Published by E&F Spon, London, 1992, pp155-164.

7.   LIAM, K.C., ROY, S.K. and NORTHWOOD, D.D.,   Chloride ingress measurements and corrosion potential mapping study of a 24 year old reinforced concrete jetty in a tropical marine environment.   Magazine of Concrete Research, Vol 44, No. 160, Sept. 1992, pp 205-215.

8.   POCOCK, D.C. and BAMFORTH, P.B. Cost effective cures for reinforcement corrosion - Collaboration research brings new developments.   Concrete Maintenance and Repair, v.5, No.6, 1991, 7-10.

9.   BAMFORTH, P.B. and POCOCK, D.C. Minimising the risk of chloride induced reinforcement by selection of concreting materials. Proc. 3rd Int. Symp. "Corrosion of Reinforcement in Concrete Construction" SCI, 21-24 May 1990, 119-131.

10.   THOMAS, M.D.A. Marine Performance of PFA Concrete, Magazine of Concrete Research, v.43, No.156, 1991, 171-185.

11.   THOMAS, M.D.A., MATTHEWS, J.D., and HAYNES, C.A.   Chloride diffusion and reinforcement corrosion in marine exposed concretes containing pulverised fuel ash.   Proc. 3rd Int. Symp. "Corrosion of Reinforcement in Concrete Construction" SCI May 21-24, 1990, 198-212.

12. GJORV, O.E. and VENNESLAND, O.   Diffusion of Chloride ions from Seawater into Concrete. Cement and Concrete Research, v.9, 1979, 229-238.

13. MARUSIN, S.L.   Chloride ion penetration in conventional concrete and concrete containing condensed silica fume. Proceedings of 2nd Int. Conf. of Fly Ash, Silica Fume, Slag and Natural Pozzolans in Concrete, Madrid, 1986, ACI SP-91, Vol 2, pp 1119-1133.

14. MAKITA, M., MORI, Y., and KATAWAKI, K.   Marine corrosion behaviour of reinforced concrete at Tokyo Bay. American Concrete Institute, SP65, pp 271-289.

15. PRICE, W.F. and WIDDOWS, S.J. The effects of permeable formwork on the surface properties of concrete. Magazine of Concrete Research, v.43, No.155, 1991, 93-104.

16. PRICE, W.F. and WIDDOWS, S.J.   Durability of concrete in hot climates: benefits from permeable formwork. Proc. 3rd Int. RILEM Conf. "Concrete in Hot Climates" Torquay, Sept. 21-25, 1992, 207-220.

17. PRICE, W.F. A comparison of heat cured PFA concretes, with and without the Everdure Caltite System, TEL Report 014H/88/3705, 1988.

18. PFEIFER, D.W., Landgren, J.R. and Zoob, A.   Protective Systems for new prestressed and substructure concrete.   FHWA Report FHWA/RD-86/193, 1987.

19. CONCRETE SOCIETY. Permeability testing of site concrete. Conc. Soc. Tech. Rep. 31, 1987.

20. DHIR, R.K., JONES, M.R. and AHMED, H.E.H.   Concrete durability: estimation of chloride concentration during design life. Magazine of Concrete Research, v.43, No.154, 1991, 37-44.

21. SMOLCZYK, H.G.   State of knowledge on chloride diffusion in concrete Betonwerk Fertigteil - Technik, Heft 12, 1984, pp 837-843.

22. BYFORS, K. Influence of Silica Fume and Flyash on chloride diffusion and pH values in cement paste. Cement and Concrete Research, Vol. 17, 1987, pp 115-130.

23. PAGE, C.L., SHORT, N.R. and El TARRAS, A. Diffusion of chloride ions in hardened cement pastes. Cement and Concrete Research, Vol. II, 1981, pp 395-406.

24.   GAUTEFALL, O. Effect of condensed silica fume on the diffusion of chlorides through hardened cement paste. American Concrete Institution. SP92, pp 991-997, 1986.

25.   ROY, D.M., KUMAR, A. and RHODES, J.P. Diffusion of chloride and cesium ions in Portland cement pastes and mortars containing blastfurnace slag and flyash. American Concrete Institute, SP91, pp 1423-1444, 1986.

26.   KUMAR, A., KOMARNEWI, S. and ROY, D.M. Diffusion of Cs^+ and Cl^- through sealing materials. Cement and Concrete Research, Vol 17, 153-160. 1987.

27.   FISCHER, K.P., BRYHN, O. and AAGAARD, P. Corrosion of steel in concrete, some fundamental aspects of concrete with added silica. Norwegian Geotechnical Institute Report 51304-06, 1982.

28.   THOMAS, M.D.A. A comparison of the properties of OPC and PFA concrete in 30 year old mass concrete structures. Proc. of 5th int. Conf. on Durability of Building Materials and Components, Brighton, Nov. 1990.

29.   ROSE, J. The effect of cementitious blastfurnace slag on chloride permeability of concrete. ACI SP-102, Corrosion, Concrete and Chlorides - Steel Corrosion in Concrete, Causes and Restraints. American Concrete Institute, 1987, pp107-126.

30.   TUUTTI, K. Corrosion of steel in concrete, Swedish Cement and Concrete Research Institute. Report No. Fo. 4, 1982.

DEGRADATION OF CEMENT MORTAR LINING IN WATER PIPES

R S Ravindrarajah

University of Technology

G R Oven

Sydney Water Board

Australia

ABSTRACT. Performance of the mortar lining for iron pipes when the pipes contain soft and poorly buffered water creates some concern to the water authorities. In such cases the quality of drinking water may not satisfy the recommended standard specifications This paper reports the results of both field and laboratory studies on the problems associated with the quality of water due to degradation of mortar lining. The degree of degradation of cement-rich mortar lining is influenced by the hardness of water in the pipe, the detention time and the pipe diameter. Application of bituminous coating was found to be effective in reducing the extent of degradation of mortar lining. The results also showed that the mortar lining is in an active state even after a long period of 54 years. Lime leaching from the uncoated mortar lining from the early age was identified.

Keywords: Pipeline materials, Cement mortar, Degradation of mortar, Water quality, Coatings, Soft water, Drinking water, Serviceability of pipes

Dr Rasiah Sri Ravindrarajah is a member of the teaching staff of the School of Civil Engineering, University of Technology, Sydney, Australia. His current research interest include use of waste materials in concrete, high-strength concrete, lightweight concrete, ferrocement, in-situ concrete testing and durability of concrete. Dr Sri Ravindrarajah has published widely in many international journals and conferences and served on many Technical Committees.

Gavin R Oven is a civil engineer with the Sydney Water Board, Australia and graduated from the University of Technology, Sydney, Australia.

Concrete 2000. Edited by Ravindra K. Dhir and M. Roderick Jones.
© 1993 Published by E & FN Spon. ISBN 0 419 18120 2.

INTRODUCTION

Clean water is the man's the most precious commodity for survival. For many years, man has gone to great lengths to ensure that water is at his disposal. Over hundreds of years, the pipes have been used as the transport medium which has allowed the water to travel vast distance and to bring it within almost everyone's reach. In the ancient times the pipes were made from bamboo by the Chinese, earthenware by the Greeks and Middle Eastern civilisations, wood and lead by the Romans and cast-iron by the French. Asbestos cement, reinforced concrete and prestressed concrete and thermoplastic are used as pipeline materials. Klien and Rancome [1] reviewed the performance of these materials in service. Ductile-iron pipes with cement mortar lining are the most commonly used by the water authorities in Australia. The mortar lining provides physical barrier for the iron from water as well as passivates the iron from corroding due to its high alkalinity (pH >12.5). However, there exist some problems in service with the mortar-lined pipes and this paper discusses the results of the field and laboratory studies carried out with ductile-iron pipes.

Hydration of Portland cement liberates calcium silicate hydrates and crystalline calcium hydroxide. The water soluble calcium hydroxide, which takes up approximately 25% of the solid volume [2], gradually leaches out when the mortar is in contact with aggressive water. This process increases the alkalinity of the water and roughen the lining surface, resulting the hydraulic head losses [3]. The leaching rate depends on the water quality and the permeability of mortar. The extent of degradation of lining can be related to the amount of leaching occurred.

Some substance in water can be detected by taste, principally the salts of calcium, copper, iron, magnesium, manganese, sodium and zinc and some organic compounds. Since the individuals have different sensitivities to, and perceptions of odours and tastes it may not be surprising to note few complaints from some consumers. However, majority of the consumers may not aware of the problem. Recommended quality for drinking water indicates that the pH of the water should be within the range of 6.5 to 8.5. Where asbestos cement or cement mortar lined pipes are used, the upper limit for pH of 9.2 may be tolerated [4].

CEMENT MORTAR LINING

The mortar used for lining the ductile iron pipes was produced with ordinary Portland cement, washed beach sand, river sand and warm water (about 40oC). The physical properties of the sands are given in Table 1. The river sand and the beach sand were used in equal weight proportion to obtain continuous grading. The materials were mixed in a paddle mixer and the combined weight of sand and cement used was 17tonne/h. The weight ratios of sand/cement and water/cement were 1.83 and 0.51, respectively.

Table 1: Properties of mortar sands

Properties	Units	River sand	Beach sand
Bulk density - loose	kg/cu m	1450	1405
Bulk density - compacted	kg/cu m	1890	1720
Particle density - SSD	kg/cu m	2615	2625
Particle density - Oven-dry	kg/cu m	2580	2600
Void content - loose	%	43.8	46.0
Void content - compacted	%	26.7	33.8
Water absorption	%	1.40	0.80
Passing 600 μm sieve	%	50.0	99.5

The mortar was pumped through a pipeline to the pipe lining section and the mortar was injected into a spinning pipe from a moving lance. Immediately after placing the mortar, the pipe was subjected to a high speed spinning to improve the quality of lining by removing the excess air and water from the mortar. The duration of spinning depends on the pipe diameter and 70s was used for the 100mm pipe. The specified thickness of lining ranged from 7 to 13mm for the ductile iron pipe for the pipe diameter ranging from 100 to 750mm. The specified tolerance limit for lining thickness was ± 2 to 3mm.

Properties of mortar

The consistency of mortar was determined with a sand flow cone apparatus by measuring the time taken for a fixed volume of mortar to flow out through a 14mm diameter opening at the bottom of a funnel. Tests on 20 random samples, over a period of 4 weeks, showed that the mean flow time was 34.5s with a coefficient of variation of 27%. A total of 6 fresh mortar random samples were taken over a period of 4 weeks and nine 75mm mortar cubes were cast in steel moulds from each sample. The cubes were demoulded after 2 days and cured in water at 20ºC until testing. The compressive strength was monitored with 18 cubes at each age of testing.

Table 2: Compositions of mortar lining layers

Pipe No.	Layer type	Cement kg/cu m	Sand kg/cu m	Water kg/cu m	W/C	S/C
1	Laitance	1590	295	330	0.20	0.19
	Mortar	485	1775	85	0.18	3.65
	Total	1040	1035	415	0.20	1.00
2	Laitance	1385	530	390	0.28	0.38
	Mortar	455	1715	150	0.34	3.77
	Total	920	1125	270	0.29	1.22

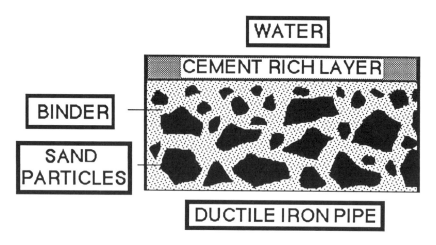

Figure 1: Structure of cement mortar lining

The mean compressive strengths of mortar were 21.5, 39.7 and 44.5 MPa with the coefficient of variation of 11.5, 13.4 and 9.3 % after 2, 7 and 14 days from casting, respectively. The high degree of variability for the quality of fresh and hardened mortar are mainly due to the variation in the water content of the mixes. The density of water saturated hardened mortar was varied between 2140 to 2260kg/cu m.

Composition and structure of mortar lining

A close examination of the cross-section of the mortar lining indicated the presence of a cement rich layer, known as laitance layer, at the surface. Thickness of the laitance layer varied between 2 to 3mm depending upon the fluidity and bleeding capacity of the mortar mix. The mortar samples across the cross-section of the lining were taken in a 100mm diameter pipe for the determination of mix compositions.

Table 3: Alkalinity of water in watermain carrying soft water

pH range	No. of locations	% of results
6.5 - 7.5	1	1.5
7.5 - 8.5	4	5.0
8.5 - 9.5	41	52.5
9.5 - 10.5	30	39.0
> 10.5	2	2.5

The results shown in Table 2 indicated that the cement content of the laitance layer is more than three times of that for the mortar layer below the surface. The surface layer is, therefore, rich in soluble lime.and the structure water pipes, lined with centrifuged cement mortar, can be schematically represented by Fig. 1.

QUALITY OF WATER IN WATERMAIN

Alkalinity of water in watermain

The alkalinity test on water samples from several locations in the watermain indicated that the pH of water was not affected significantly when it flows through a large diameter pipe with high rate of flow. However, the rise in pH is confined to the smaller diameter pipe in the reticulation network. The maximum pH observed at 78 sampling points are summarised in Table 3. The pH value of as high as 11.3 was recorded at a location with a 18 years old pipe. Therefore, the leaching of lime in cement mortar lined pipes is an active process continuing for a very long period of time.

This study indicates that the rise in the pH of pipe water increases as a result of the following: (a) low rate of water flow as it increases the detention time; (b) age of the pipes as a new pipe has larger thickness of cement rich lining; (c) smaller diameter pipes have large surface area to volume ratio; and (d) increased distance of water travelled to reach its final destination.

Alkalinity of drinking water

Investigation into the quality of water from several sources in Sydney area indicated that the hardness of water expressed in terms of calcium carbonate equivalent ranged from 10 to 47mg/l. Calcium content and pH of water ranged from 1.4 to 9.3mg/l and from 6.2 to 7.4, respectively. Areas where the soft water is in distribution were selected for the detail study on the quality of pipe water and the degradation of mortar lining. Tap water samples were collected from 340 sites over a 18-month period and the results of the pH values obtained are summarised in Table 4. The pH of the water in more than half of the selected locations is significantly more than the specification limit of 8.5 for the drinking water, although the pH of water in the reservoir was between 6.0 and 7.0.

Alkalinity of flowing water in watermain

In order to establish the leaching effect on the alkalinity of water, the pH test was performed on water samples passing through an unbranched 1.2km length of 300mm diameter ductile iron pipe.

Table 4: Alkalinity of pipe water when soft water distributed

Sampling period	12 months	5 months
No. of samples	831	206
pH range	6.8 - 10.3	6.7 - 10.0
No. of samples with pH >8.5	384	132
% of samples with pH > 8.5	46%	64%

The results showed that the pH of water flowing in the pipe over a distance of 1.2km experienced an increase in pH from 7.0 at the first sampling point to 8.3 at the second sampling point. A further pH increase to 9.77 was recorded at the third sampling point about 1km away from the second sampling point.

Alkalinity of water in static watermain

The static test was carried out to study the effect of water stagnation on the pH of water. The watermain was shut down so that a section of water in 300mm diameter pipe was isolated between the shut off point and the sampling point. The distance between these two points was 800m. The water samples were take at 5 minutes intervals for pH testing and the results are shown in Fig. 2. It can be noted that the pH of stagnant water fluctuated with time and no definite trend.

Alkalinity of water in a flowing watermain

The same 300mm diameter watermain was used to study the effect of flow rate on the alkalinity of water when it was flowing over a distance of 1.75km. The results, given in Table 5, showed that pH of water increased for the flow rates of 1200 and 3700l/min. The pH rise of 0.50 was noted for the water at the high flow rate condition. The slower rate of water flow had not produced more change in pH as expected than that for the faster rate of water flow.

Alkalinity of water in newly laid watermain with mortar lining

A sampling point which was originally fed by the watermain had a 200m section of 100mm diameter galvanised iron pipe mixed in with a 100mm diameter cement mortar lined cast-iron pipe. Due to low flow rate and reduced pressure the galvanised iron pipe was replaced with ductile-iron pipe. This replacement brought new complaints from the water users in relation to the taste of tap water. The water samples were taken at 3 points along the pipe length and tested for the pH and the results are given in Table 6. The results show that there is a definite pH rise resulting from the new section of watermain with cement mortar lining being in service.

Table 5: Effect of flow rate on pH of water in watermain

Test No.	Flow rate l/min	Water travel time (min.)	Initial pH	Final pH	Change in pH
1	1200	109	7.70	7.90	0.20
2	3700	35	7.30	7.80	0.50

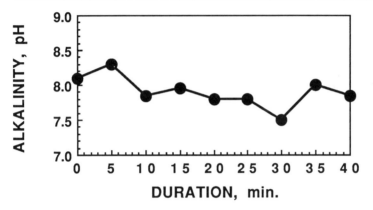

Figure 2: Variation in pH of stagnant water in a watermain

DURABILITY OF MORTAR LINING - FILED STUDY

Staining method for lime content

Degradation testing was carried out on the sections of 100mm diameter pipes which have been exhumed, after the service ages between 3 and 54 years, from an area that was supplied with soft water. Degradation in the mortar lining was determined using a staining technique which highlighted the lime content of mortar across the cross-sections. Sample preparation involved cleaning of the cross-section and oven-drying at 105ºC to allow better absorption of the stains. The staining material used consisted of a mixture of pH indicators ranging from 1 to 14. Table 7 shows the relationships among colour, pH, lime content and degradation of mortar lining. The lime content of new mortar is between 62 and 65%.

Table 6: pH of water in newly laid mortar lined watermain

Sample location	pH before flushing	pH after flushing
1	7.4	7.4
2	9.3	8.9
3	10.0	9.0

Table 7: Degradation of cement mortar lining indicators

Colour	pH	% Lime content	Degradation	Condition rating
Red	3 to 5	2 to 10	Mortar susceptible to erosion	Very poor
Orange	5 to 6	5 to 20	Marginal adherence of sand particles	Poor
Green	7 to 8	15 to 45	Moderate adherence of mortar components	Fair
Blue	9 to 10	40 to 55	Good adherence of mortar components	Good
Purple	10 to 12	55 to 65	Mortar unaffected by leaching	Very good

Results and discussion

54 years old pipe: The mortar lining in this pipe was 7mm in thickness with a 4mm red zone of lime leached mortar and a 3mm blue/green base strata, showing early stages of lime migration to the mortar surface. The mortar surface was coated with a bituminous material except for small areas where the coating was flaked off with some parts of the mortar. Considering the age of the pipe it is most common to find a bituminous coating and mortar lining so well in tact. The mortar lining is in fair to good condition even after 54 years of service.

42 years old pipe: The mortar lining thickness in this pipe varied between 3 and 5mm. The staining test revealed a red zone of poorly adhering mortar of 1 to 3mm in thickness. The mortar surface contained patches of a loosely adhering the bituminous material. Some areas showed signs of mortar flaking. The lining suffered varying degree of degradation and the areas where the bituminous coating was in tact showed minimum degradation. The general condition of the mortar lining is fair to poor.

24 years old pipe: The pipe had a uniform mortar lining of 4mm in thickness with a fairly in tact bituminous coating along one hemisphere of the pipe length. The other hemisphere had patchy areas of coating still remaining suggesting erosion from the water flow. This area had less than 15% lime component remaining in the mortar as indicated by the red/orange staining and can be regarded as in poor condition. The other hemisphere which showed blue/green staining was in fair to good condition. The mortar lining can be considered as in poor condition.

8 years old pipe: The mortar lining was a uniform 7mm in thickness with no bituminous coating. The thickness of the laitance surface was about 1mm. Staining test indicated a red zone into 1mm thick laitance layer continuing into 1.5mm thick blue zone indicating of leaching in mortar below the laitance layer. The mortar lining is generally in very good condition.

DURABILITY OF MORTAR LINING - LABORATORY STUDY

Effect of age of the pipes on degradation of mortar lining

In this study, the 100mm diameter watermain which was in service for varying ages were used to store soft water. The chosen pipe length was 330mm with one end sealed. The water was stirred for 30s prior to sampling and the samples were analysed at varying time intervals for pH, conductivity, calcium and magnesium contents. Figs. 3 and 4 show the variation in the pH and conductivity with elapsed time, for the water stored in the 54 yrs and 3 yrs old pipes, respectively. Figs. 5 to 8 show the effects of the pipe age on the pH, conductivity, calcium content and magnesium content of water after 10 days of storage.

The results clearly showed that the old pipes are still active in exchanging hydroxyl, calcium and magnesium ions with the water in contact with the mortar. There was no clear trend was notice on the degree of degradation with the age of the pipe. This may be due to the varying surface conditions of the mortar lining. The factors which influence the degradation rates are the permeability of mortar, effectiveness of the coating, thickness of the laitance layer, previous service history and softness of the water.

Effect of hardness of water on degradation of mortar lining

In order to study the effect of hardness of on the degradation of mortar lining, 330mm long sections of unused new 100mm diameter cement mortar lined pipes were used. The pH, conductivity, calcium content and magnesium content of the stored water were determined at varying time intervals. Two natural water types with the calcium carbonate content of 10.4 and 40.9mg/l were used together with distil water. The pH of the distil, soft and hard waters was 5.26, 6.60 and 7.26, respectively.

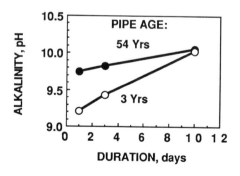
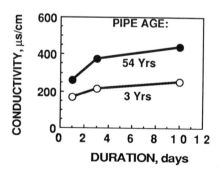

Figures 3 and 4: Development of alkalinity and conductivity
with time in stored water with 3 and 54 years pipes

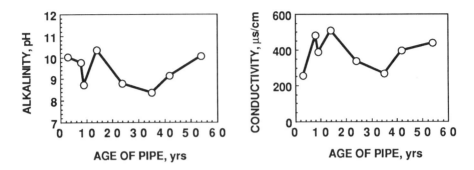

Figures 5 and 6: Effect of the age of pipe on the pH and
conductivity of stored water after 10 days

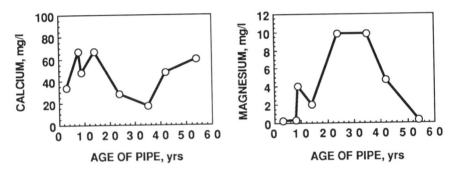

Figures 7 and 8: Effect of the age of pipe on the calcium and
magnesium contents of stored water after 10 days

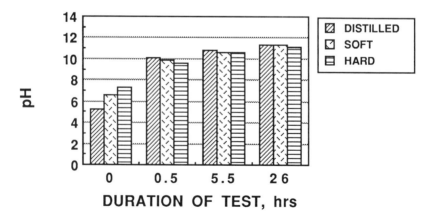

Figure 9: Effect of hardness of water on alkalinity of stored water

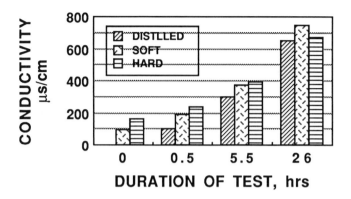

Figure 10: Effect of hardness of water on conductivity of stored water

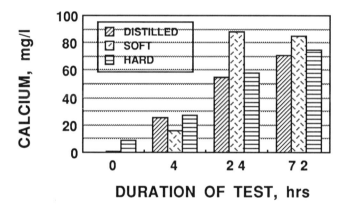

Figure 11: Effect of hardness of water on calcium content of stored water

Figs. 9 to 11 show the variations of pH, conductivity, calcium content and magnesium content with time for the water stored in new pipes. The pH of water increased sharply within the first 30 minutes and the differences in pH were not significant among the water types used. After the 26 hrs, the pH of the water was 11.2. The conductivity, indicating the ions concentration, increased considerable within the first 30 minutes and continued to increase at a significant rate over the test period. After the 28 hrs, the conductivity was 648, 654 and 514μs/cm for the distil, soft and hard waters, respectively. These results indicated that the distil and the soft waters are highly aggressive to the mortar lining.

CONCLUSIONS

1. The cement mortar used for lining the ductile iron pipes are varied in quality in fresh and hardened states. The spinning action during lining operation produced 2 to 3 mm thick cement rich laitance layer.

2. The pH of tap water is influenced by several factors such as, rate of water flow, age of the pipe, diameter of the pipe and distance of water travelled to reach its final destination.

3. Bituminous coating on the mortar lining is efficient in controlling the degradation lining for a very long period of time.

4. The cement mortar lining without any coating showed early signs of degradation in the laitance layer due to leaching of lime.

5. Even after 54 years of service, the mortar lining showed continuing degradation due to leaching of lime.

6. Significant rate of degradation of mortar lining in soft water was observed from this study.

ACKNOWLEDEMENT

The authors wish to thank the Sydney Water Board for the research support provided during this investigation.

REFERENCES

1. KLEIN, RL. AND RANCOMBE, AJ. Performance of water pipeline materials. Chemistry and Industry, 3 June 1985, pp 353-358.

2. MEHTA, PK. Concrete, Structures, Properties and Materials. Prentice-Hall, Eaglewood Cliffs, New Jersey, USA, 1986.

3. MASON, PJ. The effects of aggressive water on dam concrete. Construction & Building Materials, 1990, Vol. 4, No. 3, pp. 115-118.

4. AUSTRALIAN WATER RESOURCES COUNCIL.AND NATIONAL HEALTH AND MEDICAL RESEARCH COUNCIL Desirable quality of drinking water in Australia, Department of Health, Australia, 1980.

FRM FOR CONCRETE WATER PIPELINES
AND INTERCEPTING SEWERS RENOVATION

L Hebda

Kielce University of Technology

W Glodkowska

Koszalin University of Technology

Poland

ABSTRACT. Concrete interceptors were deteriorated with the time. It is the result of the chemical and physical corrosion. The renovation is much more cheaper then new interceptors pipe-laying, particularly in towns. Fibre reinforcement mortars are very attractive material for concrete intercepting sewers renovation: quite cheap (cheaper then f.en. epoxy resin lining), quite good properties in tensile and bending stress, satisfactory resistance to physical corrosion. The paper present the original method which enable the choice of the fibre reinforcement mortars lining thickness. It is the first publication of this method and authors treat this paper like the initial and they continue the investigation.

Keywords: Corrosion, Concrete Interceptors, Fibre Reinforcement Mortar (FRM), Thickness of Renovation Layer.

Dr Lesław Hebda, c.eng., is assistant professor, Kielce University of Technology, Poland, Division of Civil Engineering. He is specialises in concrete technology and fibre reinforcement composite materials with concrete matrix, especially in water permeability, durability. He is author or co-author more than 30 papers.

Eng. Wiesława Głodkowska, M.Sc., civil engineer, is assistant, Koszalin University of Technology, Poland, Division of Civil and Sanitary Engineering. She is interesting in modeling of cooperation between old concrete and renovation materials like resinous concretes.

Concrete 2000. Edited by Ravindra K. Dhir and M. Roderick Jones.
© 1993 Published by E & FN Spon. ISBN 0 419 18120 2.

INTRODUCTION

The decision about the concrete sewer renovation it is the result of the the technical condition assessment of this sewer. It is well known a lot of sewer renovation methods. One of the most simple and cheap technology is the spraying or coating the cement mortar or composite materials with cement matrix like the fibre reinforcement mortars for example [1]. This method is particularly useful in pipelines where the physical type of corrosion is the predominant [2]. In this technology, the thickness of FRM lining is one of the most important data. It is depend on the level of deterioration of concrete pipe, properties of FRM and condition of concrete base. The proper choice of FRM thickness secures good cooperation between concrete base and new FRM layer.

Basing on data of concrete base and repairing material (class of the material, tensile and flexural strength, thickness of concrete pipe wall after refining, the level of roughness, Young Modulus, deformability) it is possible to design the depth of renovation layer according to criteria of good cooperation between this two materials. Authors made an analysis of the most simple case, where the old concrete pipe was before cracking process, but the margin of safety of sewer construction was spent and the influence of chemical type of corrosion was on typicall level for municipal wastes. Special computer program was prepared by Miss Głodkowska to solve the problem of new layer depth. The construction of this program is open and it is possible to find the thickness of renovation layer in different cases. This paper presents first, very simple example of calculation and shows the assumption of the method.

CALCULATIONS

Theoretical assumptions

The calculations of fibre reinforcement mortars lining thickness were carried out with assumptions of good cooperation between old beding concrete and new renovation surface of FRM and following others rules:
- the concrete pipe works under the load in range of Hook law,
- in the wall of the pipe is the biaxial state of the stresses and deformations,
- the statical load involves the bending in the pipe,
- Bernoullie hypothesis holds good (flatness of deformations),
- the deformations are small,
- the concrete base is rough (coefficient $\alpha_t = 0.5$).

The solution of the problem was carried out basing on rules of the classical theory of elasticity.
Using the follow equations of:
1) geometry (resulting from the Bernoullie hypothesis of flatness of deformations)

$$\frac{\Delta\varepsilon_f}{d_f} = \frac{\Delta\varepsilon_c}{d_c} \qquad (1)$$

where: $\Delta\varepsilon_i$ the deformation gain of the old concrete layer (c) or new FRM
          -   renovation layer (f);
          d_i the depth of the old concrete pipe wall after refining (c) or
          -   FRM layer (f);

2) geometry (resulting from principle of inseparability of deformation in contact zone between concrete and FRM)
$$\varepsilon_o = \varepsilon_c + \varepsilon_f \qquad (2)$$

where:

$$\varepsilon_c = \frac{(1-\nu_c)\,\sigma_c}{E_c} ; \qquad \varepsilon_f = \frac{(1-\nu_f)\,\sigma_f}{E_f}$$

and: ε_i -   the deformation of the old concrete layer (c) or FRM layer (f);
         σ_i -   the stress in the concrete layer (c) or in the FRM layer (f);

         ν_i -   Poisson ratio of the old concrete (c) or FRM (f);

         E_i -   Young Modulus in tensile of the old concrete (c) or FRM (f).

3) equilibrium of forces in flexural cross-section
$$P_f + P_c = 0 \qquad (3)$$
where: P_i -   the force in the old concrete layer (c) or FRM layer (f)
and assuming that
$$\sigma_c = R_{tc}^c \quad \text{lub} \quad \sigma_f = R_{tc}^f$$

where: R_{tc}^i -   characteristic tensile strength of concrete (c) or FRM (f),
authors found the relation which define the thickness of fibre reinforcement mortar renovation layer. This relation is as follows:

$$^1d_f \le d_c \left[\frac{2R_{tc}^c\,\alpha_t}{R_{tc}^f} + \frac{(1-\nu_f)\,E_c}{(1-\nu_c)\,E_f} \right] \qquad (4)$$

The magnitude ^1d_f from (4) is defined basing on mechanical properties of concrete and fibre reinforcement mortar. The concrete in the interceptors and the same renovation layer of FRM are worked under constant chemical attack in normal situation. This factor has influence on d definition similar like mechanical properties of components materials.

The influence of chemical corrosion on d magnitude can be describe by following relation [3], [4]:

$$^2d_f \geq \Pi\sqrt{D\,t} \qquad\qquad (5)$$

where: D -   coefficient of ions diffusion through the d_f thickness FRM layer;
normal range of D is on level from 1.0 to $7.0 * 10^{-5}\,m^2$/sec

t -   ions diffusion time (sec)

Intersection of ^1d_f and ^2d_f is the definition of FRM renovation layer thickness when the good connection between old concrete and FRM is ensured similar like durability of material.

Basing on the above relation authors prepared exemply calculation of d_f magnitude taking into account following material properties.

Materials properties

a) Concrete
concrete class: B 25, compressive strength $R_c^c = 18.62$ N/mm^2, $R_{tc}^c = 1.55$ N/mm^2,
$E_c = 19.518$ N/mm^2, $v_c = \dfrac{1}{6}$, $d_c = 100$ mm (after refining)

b) Fibre reinforcement mortar
kind of fibres: steel, compressive strength $R_c^f = 32 - 42$ N/mm^2,
$R_{tc}^f = 3.8 - 5.0$ N/mm^2, $E_f = 14000 - 19000$ N/mm^2, $v_f = 0.15 - 0.20$,
$\varepsilon_f = 3.2 - 4.8 * 10^{-3}$

RESULTS

The results are presented in Figure 1. The solution of the FRM renovation layer thickness problem make the space limited by the domain of experiment on lateral surface and by ^2d_f surface on bottom side (the minimum thickness of FRM layer) and by ^1d_f surface on top side (the maximum thickness of FRM layer).

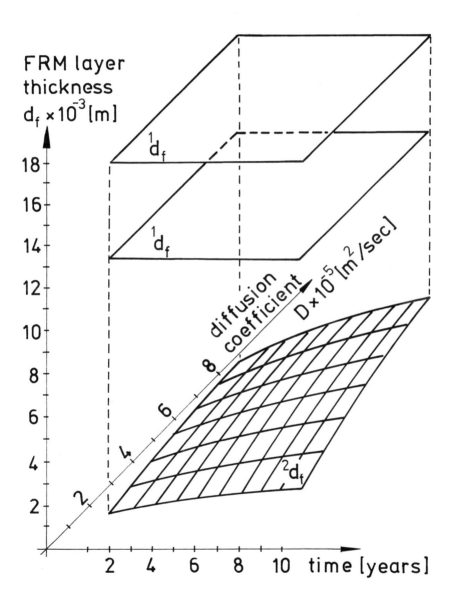

Fig. 1. The range of the solution of the FRM renovation layer thickness problem

DISCUSSION

The minimum thickness of FRM layer is dependent on structural properties of FRM and action time of corrosion medium. The description of FRM durability on chemical attack by the diffusion coefficient is a kind of simplification. The kinetic of FRM destruction under chemical attack is dependent not only on speed of diffusion but on concentration of chemical substances, on mineral composition of cement and on kind of aggregate in matrix too.

However, the authors consider that the diffusion coefficient of FRM is quite good approximation of FRM durability description on first level of solving the problem.

The maximum thickness of FRM layer is dependent on mechanical properties of this material. The FRM layer is thinner when the strength and Young Modulus of this material are higher. The definition of top limit which was taken into account in this paper gives impression of quite precise.

The equation (4) and (5) together with domain of experiment describe a kind of space of answers on question of FRM layer thickness.

From engineering practice point of view, the exact data for FRM layer thickness is most necessary.

The special computer program, prepared by Miss. Glodkowska, make the optimal, precise estimation of FRM depth possible in one number form. Taking into account, that magnitude of R_{tc}^f is changed from 3.8 to 5.0 N/mm^2 , and E_f from 14.000 to 19.000 N/mm^2 in this experiment, the following magnitudes of d are estimated dependly on D and t value:

D $[*10^{-5} m^2/sec]$	t [sec]	d_f [mm]
1.0	$1.000 * 10^7$	1.5
1.6	$13.636 * 10^7$	60.0
1.6	$18.964 * 10^7$	60.0

It is interesting that the optimal d_f magnitudes are defined in such way that they are enough for different values of diffusion coefficient and time of action.

The steel fibres are 60 - 70% of total cost of FRM in Polish price structure and taking into account the cost criterion, the FRM renovation layer should be the most thin as possible. The ordinary portland cement mortar is about three times cheaper than FRM, but minimal addition of fibres improve significantly the mechanical properties of this material like tensile strength, abrasion resistance, impact load resistance etc. [5]. It is the reason why the FRM are used in renovation of water aqueducts, of the wearing surface on dam spillways, of the runway key joints, highway pavements, tunnel decks etc. [6]. The renovation of concrete water pipelines and intercepting sewers is the area, where FRM should be successfully used.

CONCLUSIONS

* the definition of optimal FRM renovation layer depth is very important problem in concrete interceptors renovation; too thin layer is not durable on chemical attack and too thick layer loose the good cooperation with old concrete
* the description of FRM destructive kinetic under chemical attack need more precise from than coefficient of diffusion
* the special computer program afford quite versatile data of d_f ; when FRM diffusion coefficient is changed from 1.6 to 4.6 $*$ 10^{-5} m^2/sec and time of aggressive medium action is in range 4.3 to 6.0 years, the 60 mm FRM renovation layer is quite enough.

REFERENCES

1. Multi-author work., Wasser Versorgungs und Abwasser Technik., Vulkan-Verlag., Essen 1989. (in German).

2. Michael J., Theoretische und versuchstechnische Ermittlung des Abriebs in Freispiegelleitungen und ihre praktische Anwendung auf Abwasserleitungen., Dissertation A., Technische Hochsule Leipzig, 1988. (in German).

3. Paturojev V.M., Technologija polimerobietonov., Stroizdat., Moskov 1977. (in Russian).

4. Czarnecki L., Betony żywiczne., Arkady., Warsaw 1982. (in Polish).

5. Barr B.I.G., Fibre reinforced concrete - where do we go from here?, Proceedings of the Fourth RILEM International Symposium "Fibre Reinforced Cement and Concrete" Sheffield 1992, E & FN SPON, London 1992, pp.3-11.

6. Lankard D.R., Fibre concrete applications, Proceedings of the RILLEM Symposium 1975 "Fibre Reinforced Cement and Concrete", Sheffield 1975, The Construction Press Ltd, pp.3-19.

STRENGTH DEVELOPMENT OF CONCRETE MIXES ON SITE

T Chmielewski

Technical University of Opole

Poland

E Konopka

Fachhochschule für Technik

Germany

ABSTRACT. The paper deals with the investigations of two classes of high strength concrete C35 and C45 applied on construction sites in Baden-Württemberg state of Germany in years 1990 - 1992. The concrete strength is treated as a random variable. A concrete mix was always elaborated on laboratory test for any construction site and for any transport condition. The choice of materials components were based on the help of computer aided design of concrete programs. The concrete mixing plants have worked automatically with attested equipment. Samples of concrete were taken for any construction site and the first 7 days were under water and next up to 28 days in air conditions. Than they were tested. Some histograms and their statistical characteristics for both concrete classes are shown in the paper. The results have confirmed assumed classes of concrete. Their characteristic strength in some cases is largely exceeded. From that point of view it is not economic.

Keywords: Concrete classes, Characteristic strength, High strength concrete, Random variable, Construction sites, Histogram, Statistical characteristics.

Professor Tadeusz Chmielewski is Dean of the Faculty of Civil Engineering, Technical University of Opole, Poland. He specializes in the application of the probability theory and stochastic processes in civil engineering, especially in wind and earthquake engineering and reliability of structures. Professor Chmielewski has published widely and was an active participant of many scientific conferences and symposia in Poland and abroad.

Dipl.Eng.Eduard Konopka has been appointed some years ago as Research Assistant in Building Materials Laboratory, Fachhochschule für Technik, Stuttgart, Federal Republik of Germany. His main research include Quality control of concrete and Quality Assurance on construction sites.

Concrete 2000. Edited by Ravindra K. Dhir and M. Roderick Jones.
© 1993 Published by E & FN Spon. ISBN 0 419 18120 2.

INTRODUCTION

The modern concrete technology, which has been developed during last twenty years, make possible an application of high strength concretes on construction sites. But the Quality Assurance in such conditions plays an important role.

The Standard DIN 1045, [1], considers two groups of concrete classes:
   1) CI - for which characteristic strength ≤ 25 MPa,
   2) CII -for which characteristic strength ≥ 35 MPa;
this group includes also concretes with special requirements. The second group is called the high strength concretes.

The paper deals with the investigations of the high strength concretes applied on construction sites in Baden-Württemberg state of Germany. On the basis of these investigations the authors study more carefully the future effective management of concreting work and Quality Assurance problems on construction sites. The regulation of German and Polish standards in these matters are taken into account.

CONCRETE STRENGTH AS A RANDOM VARIABLE

It is now well recognized that measurements of a strength of concrete (on a cube or a cylinder) is a physical random phenomenon. It is due to that the concrete strength is influenced by so many parameters as: cement,aggregates, water/cement ratio, additives, mixture ratio, material is not perfectly homogeneous, etc. It is only possible for man to govern them to some extent.

Suppose, that we are interested in the concrete strength of a high rise building. For quality assurance we are taking n concrete samples for each floor. Let us have m floors, so we have $n \times m$ samples. Since not all samples so manufactured are identical, before one sample is picked from this set and tested, it is not possible to predict its exact strength. One can only expect the value from the certain range. Uncertainties of the concrete strength are not small, so the probabilistic description of this concrete feature is more realistic and has been applied in national and international codes, e.g.[1,2,3].

Let X is the continuous random variable which prescribe the concrete strength as the random phenomenon. Full probabilistic description of X is given by the probability distribution function $F_X(x)$ or by the probability density function $f_X(x)$, where $f_X(x) = \frac{dF_x(x)}{dx}$. There is a question in this engineering problem: how one of these functions can be determined? Unfortunately, nature is generally reluctant to reveal the exact probabilistic of a physical phenomenon, and man has to exercise his best judgment based upon some available clues, i.e. for engineers upon experiments.

To estimate $F_X(x)$ or $f_X(x)$ many tests are required in research program. But practically on construction sites we are able to prepare only some concrete samples. That is why it is much easier to estimate only the two moments of X: the mean value x_s (the first moment) and variance of X (the second moment) or its square root - the standard deviation of X, denoted by s.

In domestic and international standards concrete classes are determined, and for each class its characteristic value f_{ck} (defined as 5% fractile of X) is known. Relation among x_s, s and f_{ck} for any random variable X is as follows

$$f_{ck} = x_s - \lambda s, \tag{1}$$

where λ is the coefficient which depends upon the probability distribution of X.

One have to remember that if N classes of concrete are fixed (e.g. C15, C20, ..., CN) it means that for each class the new random variable $X_i (i = 1, 2..., N)$ is formulated. In construction site conditions the situation presented in Fig. 1 can happen.

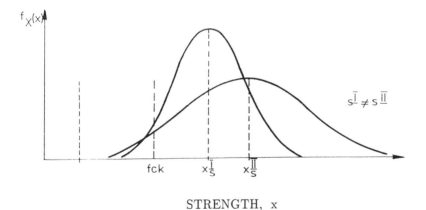

STRENGTH, x

Figure 1 Probability density function of concrete strength

TEST DESCRIPTION

Concrete Mix And Its Materials

The following materials have been used for the production ready - mixed concrete.
Cement. Portland cements PZ35 and PZ45 were mostly applied. For structures with big capacity and for concretes with special requirements alumina cement

HOZ 35 was also applied. All cement was taken from 4 nearest plant cements in the region and fulfilled quality requirements according standard DIN 1164, [4], i.e. had attests.

Water - was taken from public pipes.
Aggregate - was used mainly as valley gravel (from Ren river) plus mixture sand-gravel, fractions from 0 to 32 mm (mainly).
Additives. One additive was mostly applied - flue dust.
Admixtures. The following admixtures were mostly used: concrete workability and concrete retarder.

According to the standard DIN 1045 concrete mix for a high strength concrete was always elaborated on laboratory tests for any construction site and for any transport condition. The choice of materials components were based on the help of computer aided design of concrete programs.

The concrete mixing plants have worked automatically with attested equipments. The changes of aggregates humidity was continuously taken into account and water/cement ratio was corrected.

Test Materials

The two classes of high strength concrete C35 and C45 applied on construction sites in Baden-Württemberg state of Germany in years 1990 - 1992 have been chosen for investigations. All concrete was produced in concrete - mixing plants and than was transported by means of trucks concrete mixer. On construction sites the following features of fresh concrete have been tested:
 a) consistency,
 b) concrete temperature,
 c) air temperature,
 d) density volume.
Next minimum 6 samples,cubes 200x200x200 mm or 150x150x150 mm, for strength test were taken according the rules as follows:
 - for each $500m^3$ concrete volume,
 - for each floor in high building,
 - for 7 days of concreting work.
The condition given bigger quantity was taken into account. The samples were under water during the first 7 days and next up to 28 days were in air conditions in temperature range from 15^oC to 22^oC.

Tested Features of Concrete

After 28 days all samples were tested in laboratories - according to the standard DIN 1048, [5]. The following quantities were measured:

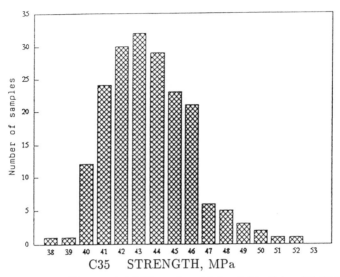

n=191, x_s=43.6 MPa, s=2.4 MPa, f_{ck}=43.6 − 1.64 · 2.4 = 39.66 MPa

Figure 2 Histogram of concrete strength for building in Stuttgart (5 storey)

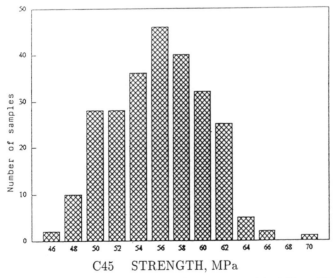

n=240, x_s=54.40 MPa, s=4.26 MPa, f_{ck}=54.4 − 1.64 · 4.26 = 47.41 MPa

Figure 3 Histogram of concrete strength for bridge in Stuttgart

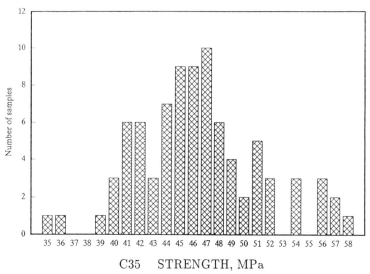

C35   STRENGTH, MPa

n=85, x_s=46.5 MPa, s=4.73 MPa, f_{ck}=46.5 − 1.64 · 4.73 = 38.7 MPa

Figure 4 Histogram of concrete strength for hospital in Reutlingen

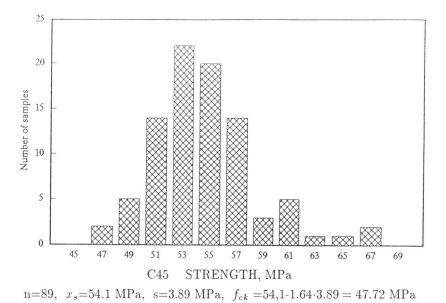

C45   STRENGTH, MPa

n=89, x_s=54.1 MPa, s=3.89 MPa, f_{ck} =54,1-1.64·3.89 = 47.72 MPa

Figure 5 Histogram of concrete strength for bridge in Hausach

- dimensions of samples,
- weight,
- concrete strength (with test error 1 N/mm^2).

RESULTS

The concrete strength for two concrete classes C35 and C45 was treated as the random variable. All data which have been obtained during the investigations were treated as statistical data. Four histograms and their statistical characteristics are shown in Figure 2, Figure 3, Figure 4 and Figure 5.

CONCLUSIONS

1. The class of the concrete C35 or C45 has been always confirmed.
2. The characteristic strength in some cases is largely exceeded. From that point of view it is not economic.
3. The standard deviation has values in the range from 2.4 MPa to 4.73 MPa. There are small and concretes, which were investigated, are considered as good or very good.

REFERENCES

1. DIN 1045 BETON UND STAHLBETONBAU, Bemessung und Ausführung 1977, pp. 83.
2. PN-88/B-06250 BETON ZWYKŁY (Concrete) pp. 16.
3. PN-84/B-03264 KONSTRUKCJE BETONOWE, ŻELBETOWE i SPRĘŻONE. Obliczenia statyczne i projektowane (Concrete, reinforced concrete and prestressed concrete design rules) pp. 68.
4. DIN 1164 PORTLAND-, EISENPORTLAND-, HOCHOFEN - und TRAßZEMENT, Begriffe, Bestandteile, Anforderungen, Lieferund (Portland-, blast-furnace-, pozzolanic cement: definitions, components, requirements, delivery), 1986, pp. 31.
5. DIN 1048 PRÜFVERFAHREN FÜR BETON, Frischbeton, Festbeton gesondert hergestellter Probekörper (Testing methods for concrete; fresh - mixed concrete, concrete of freshly moulded specimens), 1978, pp. 41.

EVALUATION OF INSITU TEST DATA
FROM EXISTING CONCRETE STRUCTURES

W F Wong

S P Chiew

Nanyang Technical University

N Y Ho

M/s L&M Structural Systems Pte Ltd

Singapore

ABSTRACT This paper discusses on two main issues. Firstly, it focuses on some of the practical aspects in the assessment of in-situ concrete strength and its use in the structural appraisal program. Secondly, this paper discusses on some findings of the carbonation study of some existing reinforced concrete building structures. The research data was derived from a database of field test data obtained as a result of non-destructive concrete strength testing of 33 existing concrete building structures in Singapore and Malaysia from 1986 to 1990. The discussion reveals that some finer thoughts on concrete strength assessment should be considered. On the durability aspect, the carbonation analysis seems to indicate that for more adequate protection of buildings in the local humid tropical environment, a specified minimum Grade 35 concrete strength would be more appropriate.

Keywords: Carbonation, Durability, Estimated in-situ concrete cube strength, Permeability constant, Structural appraisal.

Wai-Fan Wong is currently Senior Lecturer in the School of Civil and Structural Engineering, Nanyang Technological University, Singapore. Mr Wong has assumed various senior positions in consulting and construction companies in the industry before joining the University in 1986. He specialises in construction management and has been involved in various outside consulting works.

Sing-Ping Chiew is currently Senior Lecturer in the School of Civil and Structural Engineering, Nanyang Technological University, Singapore.

Nyok-Yong Ho is currently General Manager of M/s L&M Structural Systems Pte Ltd, Singapore.

Concrete 2000. Edited by Ravindra K. Dhir and M. Roderick Jones.
© 1993 Published by E & FN Spon. ISBN 0 419 18120 2.

INTRODUCTION

A building structure is designed under the premises that it has to be functionable, aesthetical and durable.   As existing building stock increases rapidly, building appraisals are becoming more important, particularly in this part of the world due to the building booms in the 1970s.

Structural appraisal program serves not only to identify structural adequacy or otherwise of the existing building structures, the data collected from the exercise usually contains some revealing information that some improvements may be made on the design standard and philosophy of which the design of existing structures were originally based on. Our study made on structural appraisal and the existing database on non-destructive field testing reveals the following findings:

(i)   On the in-situ concrete strength appraisal, the determination of concrete strength based on present practice may be devoted with more thoughts to reflect the reality of dealing with an existing structure;

(ii)   On durability aspect, data on carbonation collected suggests that the average carbonation depth could exceed what has been normally expected from BS design code. The BS code provision of concrete cover for certain grade of concrete may not seem to be quite adequate in this respect for buildings in tropical environment.

SOME PRACTICAL ASPECTS IN STRUCTURAL APPRAISAL

Overall Procedure of Structural Appraisal

Non-destructive in-place tests such as Ultrasonic Pulse Velocity Test (UPV) and Windsor Probe Test (WP) together with core test are most commonly performed in appraisal program. In order to obtain a reliable interpretation from the data collected and be able to predict the estimated in-situ concrete cube strength for the structure, the results of insitu concrete strength obtained from core tests are correlated with the corresponding in-place tests results. These correlated curves would then be used to determine an estimated in-situ cube strength for the rest of the structure. This value of estimated in-situ cube strength will then be used by the appraising engineer in his structural analysis and investigation.

The Estimated In-situ Cube Strength

The estimated in-situ cube strength of r.c. structures varies from areas to areas even to the extent of within the same particular structural member. For example, an in-place test results taken near support and at mid-span of a same beam would possibly give two different test values and hence two different inferred values of estimated in-situ cube strength from the correlation curve.

BS 6089 recommends that the mean value of in-place test on the selected critical locations be used to obtain an estimated in-situ cube strength by identifying the critical design section and/or the location of weakest concrete.

While this can be done and considered sufficient for the purpose of evaluating the strength adequacy or otherwise of the particular member, it can hardly be possible to extend it for the subsequent structural analysis. This is due to the fact that in analysis, a single representative value of estimated in-situ cube strength of the group is to be used to check on each individual group of structures. Therefore, in a four storey building structure, we need to obtain a value of estimated in-situ cube strength each for say first storey beams, second storey beams and so on from the in-place test data with the use of the corresponding correlation curve of each group. Inevitably, a problem arises in the need of deciding whether a mean value or other confidence level of in-place test value to be used in order to obtain an estimated in-situ cube strength from the correlation curve.

The present practice seems to adopt the following procedure:

For a particular group of structure in a building, say the second storey beams, the distribution of in-place test data X taken from the building structure, is assumed to be normally distributed, and the lower fifth percentile (or equivalent 95% confidence of the group) value is obtained by using the equation (1):

$$X_{0.05} \quad = \quad X_m - 1.64 \, S_x \qquad\qquad \ldots (1)$$

where X_m is the mean value and S_x, the standard deviation of X. This value of $X_{0.05}$ is then used to determine a value of estimated in-situ characteristic cube strength from the corresponding correlation curve and the equivalent design characteristic concrete cube strength f_{cu} to be used for detailed structural checking and analysis is subsequently obtained as in equation (2):

$$\text{Equivalent } f_{cu} = (1.5/1.2) \times (\text{Est. in-situ characteristic cube strength}) \quad \ldots (2)$$

The above outlined approach has in fact adopted a value $X_{0.05}$ allowing only five percent of in place test value to fall below $X_{0.05}$. The central issue is whether this is in fact too low a value of in-place test used that the subsequent investigation does not reflect the true nature and extent of rectification needed.

The above procedure follows closely to the philosophy for a new design in which a design characteristic cube strength f_{cu} is chosen allowing only 5% of cube test result to fall below the value. However, the significance in using $X_{0.05}$ or X_m in an existing structure should deserve a closer look:

(i)   If $X_{0.05}$ is used to obtain the estimated in-situ concrete strength, it means that only 5% of X values of the particular group is allowed to fall below $X_{0.05}$, it would also mean that there may be 95% of the group's estimated in-situ cube strength are in fact under-estimated; and

(ii)   On the other hand, using a mean value X_m would infer that you may risk to have 50% of estimated in-situ cube strength over-estimated.

The practical implication of the above is very significant when we translate this into the extent of rectification needed. If $X_{0.05}$ is used, it could possibly mean that a large percentage of identified area of rectification may in fact be unnecessary due to the effect of underestimating the in-situ cube strength of the existing structures. On the other hand, using a mean value X_m could lead to insufficient area of rectification actually required for the existing structure.

In order to get some indication on the effect of adopting a different confidence level in X, we studied the impact of using two slightly different values of X in one appraisal project and the results is presented in Table 1 for comparison. In our study, a normal practice of $X_{0.05}$ (95% confidence level) and a $X_{0.10}$ (90% confidence level) is used. From Table 1, we can clearly see that a slight reduction of only 5% of the confidence level in X's value can result in a difference in estimated in-situ characteristic strength value of up to 1.3 N/mm^2. In this particular case and the required rectification area can be reduced substantially by as much as 30%.

Table 1: Case Study On the Effect of X Value on Rectification Need

STRUCTURAL GROUP	EST. IN-SITU MEAN STRENGTH (N/mm^2)	CONFIDENCE LEVEL OF IN-PLACE TEST X (%)	EST. IN-SITU CHARAC-TERISTIC STRENGTH (N/mm^2)	NO. OF BEAMS NEED RECTIFI-CATION
1st storey beams	19.0	95%	13.7	13
		90%	15.0	8
2nd storey beams	15.0	95%	10.0	48
		90%	11.2	34

As can be seen from the above simple case study, the impact of selection of confidence level in X's value is very substantial in terms of rectification need and cost. The question to ask is what value of X is more practical and acceptable in order to deliver a meaningful appraisal of an existing structure; should we adopt a value of $X_{0.05}$ which follows closely the practice of new design or should a very liberal value be used to reflect the reality of existing structure. The authors' view on this issue is that there may be no consensus on which is the best value to use, a possible approach is that we may actually assign different confidence levels to categories of building corresponds to the level of importance of buildings. A typical example could be illustrated by Table 2 where a building if classified as more important, is assigned with a higher level of confidence level in X value. However, the authors are not in favour of using a X value with confidence level of less than 75%.

Table 2: Model of Confidence Level vs Importance of Building

CATEGORY OF BUILDING	LEVEL OF IMPORTANCE OF BUILDING	CONFIDENCE LEVEL OF IN-PLACE TEST (%)
I	Very important	95%
II	Important	85%
III	Ordinary	75%

The importance of building can be tight to its usage, for example, a public commercial building will be categorised as very important. However, Table 2 is meant to serve only as an idea of possible approach. The authors' opinion on this matter is basically to highlight that the present practice in the determination of in-situ strength may not be very appropriate when it is applied to an existing structure. In the case of a new design, a stringent value of concrete cube strength need to be set with the aim of achieving that in the construction. Whereas in the case of existing structure, a more practical standard recognising the reality of the existing structure would appear to be more appropriate and meaningful.

Recognising the Relative Importance of Members

While all areas of inadequacy shall be treated properly, an engineer should also be aware of the fact that the structural performance of a structure is both a result of interaction on structural members as well as relying on the performance of individual key members. The real implication and significance of inadequacy should be well understood by an appraising engineer.

There are areas of inadequacy that may not cause any major structural failure and the effect of damage is generally localised; on the other hand, there are some areas of inadequacy that if not checked and rectified may lead to a major and sudden failure of the building structure without much pre-warning. A case where a floor beam which is found to be slightly deficient in moment resistance would not be a matter of great concern. However, if a main beam that is substantially short in shear or a column short in compressive strength would certainly deserve to be closely examined.

Therefore, in summarizing the appraisal result, an engineer need to focus on what areas need to be emphasised and ask a typical question like "If it is not rectified, what would be the likely consequence". In this way, the major areas that repair most needed would not be over-looked. In any case, key structural members such as columns, main beams and shear walls etc. should be accorded with a higher level of attention.

CARBONATION STUDIES ON EXISTING BUILDING STRUCTURES

How durable would be a building structure depends on many factors, the main factors that would determine the durability aspects of building structures are environmental factors, design provisions and quality of material used. For concrete structures, carbonation depth is one of the most direct measurement made that can closely relate to the durability of the structures.

Carbonation is the effect that carbon dioxide from the atmosphere makes on the concrete. Concrete, having variable degrees of permeability, will permit carbon dioxide to penetrate and diffuse inwards from the concrete surface. With moisture, carbon dioxide will react with the constituents of concrete, particularly calcium hydroxide to form calcium carbonate, thus depassivating the concrete layer and lowering its pH values from approximately 12.6 for non-carbonated concrete to 8.3 for carbonated concrete. If the carbonation advance through the cover to reinforcement during the service life of a structure, corrosion of reinforcement may take place due to the loss of protection by the passive environment, thus making the structure less durable.

For a given set of environmental factors such as weather, humidity and pollution, the depth of carbonation would therefore depends on the age of exposure and the permeability of concrete. Currie R.J. (1986) suggested that the relationship to be given as:

$$d = k \sqrt{t} \qquad \qquad \dots (3)$$

where
d = depth of carbonation;
k = permeability constant; and
t = age of concrete.

This equation supports the common observation that carbonation rates decreases with time. As permeability is related to concrete strength; it is therefore possible to assign on average permeability constant to concrete that is having a fixed range of concrete strength.

Carbonation Analysis

Based on the field test data collected from 1986 to 1990 covering 33 reinforced concrete buildings in Singapore and Malaysia, data on carbonation depth, age and type of buildings, in-place test of UPV and Windsor Probe are available in our data-base. Carbonation analysis can be performed on these existing building stocks to find out the adequacy or otherwise on the design provision of concrete cover specified in BS Standard under the tropical environment. Table 3 contains all the relevant field data used in this carbonation analysis.

The equivalent characteristic strengths can be obtained from the estimated insitu cube strengths from UPV (or Windsor Probe) with the use of correlation curves developed under the recommendations of BS 6089. With the age of structures known and the measured carbonation depth from cores, the permeability constants corresponds to various characteristic strengths can be obtained from Equation (3). These characteristic strengths can then be plotted against the permeability constants on chart. Various equations could then be tried out to obtain a best fit curve using regression analysis. Upon adopting a best fit equation, this curve could then be located on the same chart and readings could then be read off from this curve.

In order to simulate the similar exposure environment of the existing buildings, we have classified the building stocks in four different categories, namely All types, Institutional & Residential, Industrial and Commercial. The above described procedure was then carried out for these four categories of buildings with the resulting curves shown in Figure 1, 2, 3 and 4.

Summary of Results

Based on the above study, we have summarised the results on average permeability constants for different concrete strength and different category of buildings in Table 4. In this Table, the magnitude of permeability constant, K, was observed to increase in the order from Institutional & Residential, Industrial and to Commercial indicating a consistently increase on severity of exposure environment.

TABLE 3 – SUMMARY OF BUILDING STRUCTURES USED FOR CARBONATION STUDY

USAGE OF BUILDING	BUILDING REPORT NO	AGE OF BUILDING (year)	NUMBER OF CORES INVESTIGATED	AVERAGE ESTIMATED INSITU CUBE STRENGTH OF CORES (N/mm^2)	AVERAGE PERMEABILITY CONSTANT k (mm/year$^{0.5}$)	AVERAGE CARBONATION DEPTH (mm)	STANDARD DEVIATION ESTIMATED INSITU CUBE STRENGTH OF CORES (N/mm^2)	STANDARD DEVIATION PERMEABILITY CONSTANT k (mm/year$^{0.5}$)
Institutional	1	25	9	19.9	4.2	21	6.5	3.2
Industrial	4	5	3	24.3	6.3	14	3.2	2.4
Residential	11	5	2	12.0	4.9	11	0.7	0.0
Institutional	19	8	20	10.6	9.4	27	4.8	3.6
Institutional	21	8	12	13.6	9.0	25	4.0	3.4
Commercial	26	15	29	11.4	14.4	56	2.6	4.6
Residential	27	5	3	12.9	11.2	25	2.7	3.2
Commercial	29	10	7	21.9	8.6	27	11.0	4.5
Institutional	41	15	5	17.2	8.8	34	5.9	2.7
Industrial	42	12	4	13.1	7.6	26	1.9	4.0
Institutional	44	15	14	15.7	6.4	25	4.8	3.9
Commercial	45	12	24	28.9	3.3	11	5.9	1.4
Institutional	46	15	8	14.6	4.4	17	3.6	1.7
Residential	47	10	4	17.9	10.2	32	1.4	2.0
Residential	48	10	4	16.0	4.1	13	2.1	2.3
Institutional	49	50	5	29.0	7.5	53	7.4	3.9
Residential	56	25	10	10.6	5.3	27	2.1	2.7
Commercial	57	15	9	26.1	5.1	20	5.0	1.0
Industrial	59	10	25	16.8	8.0	25	7.3	3.4
Commercial	72	20	5	28.2	3.1	14	2.5	0.3
Institutional	73	90	21	34.7	2.5	23	10.7	1.1
Institutional	74	13	55	14.0	9.9	36	5.1	3.1
Institutional	75	25	48	14.3	13.2	66	3.3	5.7
Industrial	76	5	5	11.3	17.2	38	4.9	2.6
Institutional	77	13	27	11.9	10.9	39	4.2	4.8
Industrial	80	25	2	27.5	4.1	21	3.5	1.6
Residential	81	14	37	13.9	6.1	23	2.8	2.9
Commercial	83	20	27	16.0	10.0	45	3.1	5.6
Commercial	85	15	4	13.5	7.5	29	6.1	5.7
Commercial	87	20	3	36.8	2.4	11	10.7	1.2
Institutional	90	67	19	20.7	6.6	54	4.3	2.1
Residential	96	27	30	14.0	3.3	17	3.0	3.0
Commercial	97	21	33	20.4	5.5	25	9.1	2.4

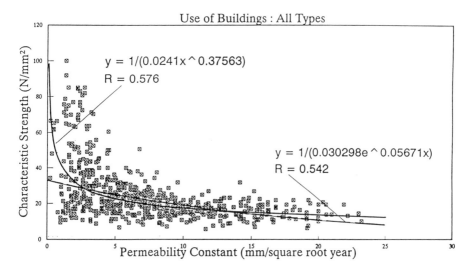

Figure 1   Characteristic Strength vs Permeability Constant for All Types of Building

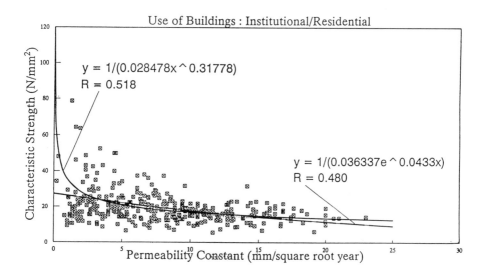

Figure 2   Characteristic Strength vs Permeability Constant for Institutional / Residential Building

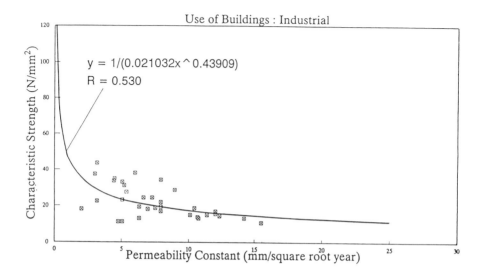

Figure 3   Characteristic Strength vs Permeability Constant for Industrial Building

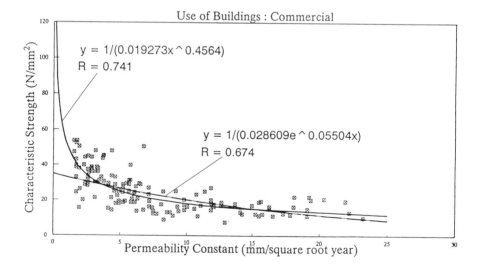

Figure 4   Characteristic Strength vs Permeability Constant for Commercial Building

In general, our study on carbonation rates on existing structures seems to indicate the followings:

Concrete Characteristics Strength (N/mm²)	Average Permeability Constant K(m/year^(1/2))
20	6.0 - 8.1
30 - 40	1.8 - 3.4
Above 40	1.8[a]

Note a: The k value indicate here is the maximum average value of all category of buildings.

Table 4 - Average Permeability Constant for Various Concrete Strengths and Building Category

CONCRETE CHARACTERISTICS STRENGTH, f_{cu} (N/mm²)	AVERAGE PERMEABILITY CONSTANT, K (mm/year^(1/2))			
	ALL TYPES OF BUILDING	INSTITUTIONAL AND RESIDENTIAL	INDUSTRIAL	COMMERCIAL
20	7.0	5.9	7.2	8.1
30	2.4	1.7	2.9	3.2
35	1.6	1.0	2.1	2.4
40	1.1	0.7	1.5	1.8
45	0.81	0.5	1.2	1.4
50	0.61	0.3	0.9	1.1

These results compare quite well with that of M.G. Richardson (1988) who classified permeability constant K value in terms of strength and the exposure condition as follows:

Low Strength   ($<$ 20 N/mm²)   Outdoors K = 6 , Indoor K = 10
Middle Strength (20 - 40 N/mm²) Outdoors K = 2 , Indoor K = 5

Comparison of Results

From the results of permeability constants presented in Table 4, we can predict the carbonation depth for different time span of building structure. If we take a service life span of 99 years as reference, then the design provision of concrete cover must be at least equal to that of the predicted carbonation depth. Using this as a common datum, we can produce the general comparison on recommended concrete cover as follows:

Concrete Grade	BS 8110	Euro Code EC2	Richardson's	Authors'
20 - 40	20 - 40	25 - 35	25 - 40	18 - 80
35	20 - 35	-	-	10 - 24
45 - 50	20 - 45	-	15 - 20	14

A more specific comparison with BS 8110 can be carried out and this is presented in Table 5.

Table 5 - Comparison of Recommended Concrete Cover with Result of Study

CONCRETE GRADE	BS 8110*	AUTHORS'**
30	25	17 - 34
35	20 - 35	10 - 24
40	20 - 40	7 - 18
45	20 - 30	5 - 14
50	20 - 30	3 - 11

*   For exposure conditions covering mild, moderate and severe environment
**   For practical purpose, a minimum concrete cover of 20 mm should be used

From the results presented in Table 5, it is noted that for Grade 30 concrete, the variability of predicted concrete cover from our study exceeds that specified by the BS Code. Cross checking the details from Table 4, it also shows that for grade 30 concrete, except for the Institutional & Residential category, the other two categories of buildings namely Industrial and Commercial would have their carbonation depths exceed those specified by BS code. On the other hand, with concrete strength of Grade 35 and above, our predicted concrete cover fall within the range specified by the BS Code. This analysis results, albeit could be limited by the number of available data, seems to indicate that in order to design our building to have at least 99 years of service life, a minimum concrete strength of grade 35 may be preferable under the tropical environment.

CONCLUSIONS

1. The current common practice that used to determine a value of estimated in-situ concrete cube strength for an existing concrete structure follows basically on design practice used for a new building. While this should produce a very safe rectification proposal, at times may tend to over-estimate the extent of necessary rectification. A possible alternative approach would be to suggest a different value of the in-place test to recognise the reality of the existence as well as the importance of the existing building structures.

2. The carbonation study carried out from the field test data in tropical environment indicates that for the thickness of concrete cover specified in BS code, for grade 30 and below, the average carbonation depth would likely exceed the designed concrete cover. The result from this study seems to indicate that a minimum concrete strength of Grade 35 would need to be used.

REFERENCES

1. BS 8110: Part 1: 1985, "Structural Use of Concrete - Code of Practice for Design and Construction", British Standard Institute, London, 1985.

2. BS 6089: 1981: "Guide to Assessment of Concrete Strength in Existing Structures", British Standard Institution, London, 1981.

3. Chong, Y.K. and Phua, H.C., "Assessment of In-situ Strength of Concrete using Non-destructive Test Methods". Nanyang Technological University, Final Year Research Report, Singapore 1991.

4. Currie, R.J., "Carbonation Depths in Structural Quality Concrete", Building Research Establishment, UK, 1986.

5. Hindo, K.R. and Bergstrom, W.R., "Statistical Evaluation of In-place Compressive Strength of Concrete". Concrete International, February 1985, pp 44-48.

6. Richardson, M.G., "Carbonation of Reinforced Concrete". Citis Ltd, New York, 1988.

INTERLOCKING CONCRETE BLOCK PAVEMENTS FOR ROADS

A N S Beaty

Royal Military College

Canada

ABSTRACT: Although concrete has some advantages over asphalt as a road construction material, concrete pavements account for a relatively small proportion of total road network kilometres in industrialised countries. The relative advantages and disadvantages of bituminous and concrete pavements are presented. Interlocking concrete block pavements are introduced and the essential details of their constituents outlined. The advantages of this form of paving for roads are indicated and a number of design methods are briefly reviewed. Potential sources of failure are identified and the uses of concrete block pavements for various categories of road are discussed. It is concluded that by using concrete blocks for road pavements the traditional advantages of concrete as a material are obtained while the disadvantages associated with conventional concrete road slabs are avoided. Interlocking concrete block pavements will permit economic and durable construction of concrete roads into the twenty–first century.

Keywords: Concrete, Pavements, Roads, Interlocking Blocks, Design, Construction

Dr. Anthony N.S. Beaty is a graduate of the University of Nottingham where he also obtained a Ph.D. for work on the behaviour of road subgrades under repeated loading. Following a number of years of varied experience in engineering practice, he was appointed to a lectureship at the University of Dundee, with responsibility for highway and transportation engineering. Since 1978 he has been a professor at the Royal Military College of Canada. He specialises in road–making materials and pavement design and is currently concentrating on interlocking concrete block pavements.

Concrete 2000. Edited by Ravindra K. Dhir and M. Roderick Jones.
© 1993 Published by E & FN Spon. ISBN 0 419 18120 2.

INTRODUCTION

Paved roads are usually surfaced with either concrete slabs or bituminous materials. Although concrete offers a number of advantages, concrete pavements account for a relatively small proportion of total road network kilometres in industrialised countries. There are a number of reasons why flexible road construction has been preferred over concrete and these will be reviewed. In a number of countries, notably Holland and Germany, concrete is used as a road surfacing in the form of pavers similar in size to a brick. It is argued that the use of interlocking concrete blocks, or pavers, as a road surface, offers the advantages of concrete as a material while avoiding the difficulties associated with roads constructed of concrete slabs. In the form of interlocking blocks whose high quality is assured by computer controlled manufacture, economic and durable concrete construction can be developed and applied to the building of roads appropriate to the needs of the twenty−first century.

CONCRETE OR ASPHALT FOR ROADS?

Generally in countries which have an extensive network of paved roads, bituminous materials predominate over the use of concrete slabs. The reasons for this are complex and often political rather than technical. Ideally, a range of road structure designs employing various materials and each capable of satisfying the technical requirements will be developed for a road project. From these, the design meeting the technical requirements at the lowest cost will normally be implemented. It is in the approach to costs that concrete pavements are often at a disadvantage. It is desirable that the basis for a cost comparison should be discounted whole−life costs over the design life of the pavement. As the life of a concrete pavement is often taken to be forty years the whole−life cost analysis raises many difficulties and the result is sensitive to the discount rate used. Furthermore, politicians are primarily concerned with the costs and benefits during one term of office. In practice, therefore, road structure selection is usually strongly influenced by initial construction costs.

Some of the disadvantages associated with concrete pavements are:

- higher initial cost
- minimum slab thickness is excessively strong for lightly loaded pavements
- adequate skid−resistance is difficult to achieve and maintain
- access to buried services is difficult and is costly both to carry out and to reinstate
- dimensional changes due to varying temperature and moisture content necessitate joints between slabs
- joints between slabs can be sources of structural weakness, mud−pumping and poor riding quality
- cracking

On higher speed roads in particular, road users strongly object to the effect of joints on riding quality. The major advantages of concrete road slabs are:

- their flexural rigidity permits them to bridge areas of weak subgrade support
- they distribute applied wheel loads effectively with negligible surface deformation
- concrete slabs have a long life with low maintenance costs

Bituminous mixtures can be laid in thin layers permitting them to be tailored to traffic requirements. They offer smooth, quiet running surfaces, with good skid – resistance. They protect the road structure and soil subgrade against ingress of water. The major negative factors associated with bituminous mixtures are:

- their strength and deformation are temperature and time dependant
- they consume finite petroleum resources
- petroleum products raise environmental concerns

In the form of block paving, the strength, durability and longevity of concrete are obtained without the problems associated with concrete road slabs. In addition, the initial construction cost of a concrete block pavement is often competitive with that of a bituminous surfaced alternative. This is not, however, currently the case in North America where asphalt enjoys a significant price advantage.

INTERLOCKING CONCRETE BLOCK PAVING

An interlocking concrete block pavement is a pavement in which the surfacing consists of concrete pavers laid to a prescribed pattern on a thin layer of bedding sand. The pavement structure below the surfacing is similar to that provided beneath bituminous surfacing. The pavement is designed and constructed generally as a conventional flexible pavement in which the pavers and their laying course take the place of the bituminous surfacing. It is widely accepted that an 80mm thick paver on 30mm (after compaction) of bedding sand is equal, in load – bearing capacity, to the same thickness (110mm) of hot rolled asphalt [1]. The general arrangement of a concrete block road pavement, is shown in Figure 1, in which the key elements are also identified. These are:

- pavers
- bedding sand
- joints
- jointing sand
- edge restraint
- laying pattern

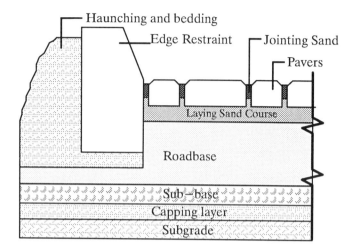

Figure 1   Typical concrete block pavement cross−section

As in any flexible road pavement, the required thickness and material properties of the roadbase and sub−base (if included) depend on the strength of the underlying subgrade soil and on the anticipated traffic loading.

Limitations

Concrete block pavements are considered appropriate for traffic speeds up to 70 km/h. Longitudinal evenness does not currently meet the standards established for bituminous surfaced roads having higher design speeds. However on many roads paved with concrete blocks, particularly in Holland and Germany, traffic speeds considerably in excess of 70km/h can be observed. Concrete block paving is widely accepted for residential roads, for rural roads and also for renewal of urban streets. To date, experience with concrete block pavements on primary routes has been limited.

Advantages

Many advantages of concrete block paving have been identified. These have been reviewed by Shackel [2] and include the following:

- concrete pavers may be mass−produced in highly automated factory conditions leading to low unit cost, consistent high strength and good dimensional tolerances
- concrete block pavements, when properly constructed, are very durable; they have a long life which depends on the performance of the sub−base and subgrade, rather than on the blocks themselves
- compared to roads constructed of rigid concrete slabs, interlocking block pavements can tolerate larger deflections and thus make better use of concrete

- concrete block pavements use the strength of concrete without the problems of joints between slabs which occur in conventional concrete slab pavements
- unlike pavements using either concrete slabs or bituminous surfacings, a concrete block pavement may be opened to traffic immediately on completion
- interlocking pavements are usually laid by hand using relatively unskilled labour and simple, inexpensive equipment
- if machine laying is desired, for example on very large areas, this can be achieved with machines which are much simpler and less expensive than paving trains
- in the event of any localised defects such as settlement, only the affected area needs to be repaired, the blocks can be lifted and re−used; this leads to very low maintenance costs
- openings in concrete block pavements can be readily made for access to buried services, the pavers lifted for access can be cleaned and relaid, thus recycling the concrete, and when trenches are reinstated, the restored pavement shows no unsightly patches
- block pavements can be lifted by hand without the use of jackhammers thus greatly reducing the noise pollution normally associated with roadworks in urban or residential areas
- concrete block paving has very low life−cycle costs resulting from its durability and the high salvage value of reusable pavers
- concrete block pavements have a high resistance to fuel and oil spillage
- block pavements make no use of bitumen or other expensive, oil−based products and are environmentally neutral
- through the use of different coloured blocks, traffic markings such as lane lines, pedestrian crossings or route guidance can be permanently built into the pavement, thus eliminating the need for frequent re−marking with paint or thermo−plastic
- available in a wide range of colours and shapes, pavers offer unique aesthetic advantages in their ability to be integrated harmoniously into the built environment
- a well−constructed block pavement is highly resistant to both punching loads and horizontal shear forces caused by braking, accelerating or slewing of heavy vehicles such as container handling equipment

CONSTITUENTS

Subgrade

The strength of the subgrade is a key factor in the design of all flexible pavements. In general, the weaker the subgrade, the greater the thickness of pavement required. The method most widely used to characterise the bearing capacity of subgrade soils is the California Bearing Ratio (CBR) test, which can be carried out in situ or in the laboratory, depending on requirements. It is important to minimise disturbance of weak subgrades. On soils having a CBR value of five or less, the subgrade must be protected from weakening by weathering and construction traffic [3].

Capping Layer

Immediately after the topsoil has been removed, exposed subgrade having a CBR value less than five is covered with a layer of low−cost, unbound granular material. This protects the weak subgrade against loss of strength and provides a working platform for construction and compaction of the road structure. The thickness of this layer should be 600mm for subgrade CBR values less that two percent and 350mm for CBR values of two to five percent.

Sub−base

A sub−base layer may be included in a flexible pavement where the thickness of roadbase required would otherwise be excessive. The sub−base usually consists of an unbound granular layer, although cement−bound materials are sometimes used. Being lower down in the pavement structure, the sub−base is subjected to lower stresses than those in the roadbase; in consequence a lesser quality, lower cost material is used. The usual materials are crushed rock or naturally occurring sands and gravels. Suitable materials are specified, for example, by the U.K. Department of Transport [4], however, Knapton [5] has indicated that DTp Type 2 materials, which can have a plasticity index up to 6, should not be used. The quality specified depends on the severity of the traffic loading. When compacted in place, sub−base materials should have a minimum CBR value of 30% and should not contain plastic fines. The aim is to have a material which is non−moisture−susceptible. In U.K. practice, where the subgrade is frost−susceptible, a total thickness of 450mm of pavement is required above it. Where this requirement would not otherwise be met, the thickness of sub−base may be increased. The sub−base thickness will ordinarily be between 150mm and 225mm.

Roadbase

The roadbase is the main structural element in a flexible pavement. For an interlocking concrete block pavement the roadbase will normally consist of either a good quality crushed rock or a cement−stabilised material such as a soil−cement or lean concrete. The surface of the roadbase is shaped to the required finished profile of the road surface, including a minimum crossfall of 2½%. A minimum longitudinal fall of 1¼% is also recommended [6]. The tolerance on the finished surface of the roadbase should be ±15mm.

Laying Course

The laying course is placed on the surface of the finished roadbase and consists of a clean, angular, washed sand, typical of that used to make concrete. Where an unbound granular roadbase is used it may be necessary to place a suitable geotextile above it, to prevent loss of the bedding sand. Acceptable gradings specified by the Australian Cement and Concrete Association and in British Standard 6717 [6] are shown in Figure 2. However, it is considered that in conditions where frost action can occur the amount passing the 75 micron sieve should be limited to 3%. Recently it has been suggested [7] that, for the laying course of concrete block paving subjected to traffic or industrial loading, only naturally occurring silica sands should be used and that the amount passing the 75 micron sieve should not exceed 3%. This is in contrast to more general experience with granular materials where angular (crushed or naturally occurring) particles are considered essential. In the most demanding applications of channelised flow, material finer than 75 microns should be avoided altogether, this being expressed as a practical limit of 0.1% finer than 75 microns.

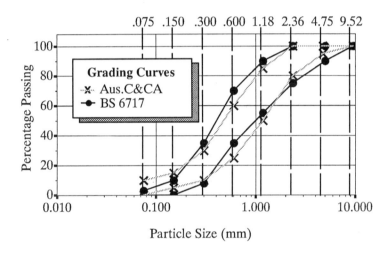

Figure 2 Bedding Sand Grading Envelopes

It is essential that the sand particles should interlock and not break down under repeated loading. Particle shape and mineral hardness contribute to this; flaky or elongated particles are fragile and should be avoided. It is useful to subject the sands to a degradation test such as that proposed by Lilley and Dowson [8] in order to avoid fragile sand particles. A small number of failures of concrete block paving under heavy, channelised loading, have been attributed to loss of bedding sand fines in suspension following particle degradation under repeated loading [8]. The bedding sand at placement should have a uniform moisture content and should be screeded, without compaction, to a loose thickness of 40 to 45mm. The laying course sand compacts when the pavers are vibrated and should have a finished compacted thickness of not be less than 25mm.

Pavers

Pavers are concrete blocks, typically the size of a house brick. Pavers may be rectangular, approximately 200x100mm in plan, or may be one of more than two hundred proprietary shapes. Paving blocks are structural elements designed to be placed together with the block to block joints filled so as to develop frictional interlock.

Three categories of paver shape have been recognized [9], examples are shown in Figure 3. Category A comprises dentated blocks which key into each other on all four faces and which, by their plan geometry, when keyed together, resist the spread of joints parallel to both the longitudinal and transverse axes of the joints. Category B comprises dentated blocks which key into one another on two faces only and which, when keyed together, resist the spread of joints parallel to the longitudinal axis of the units but which rely on the dimensional accuracy of laying to interlock on the other faces. Category C comprises non−dentated blocks which do not key together geometrically but which rely on the accuracy of their dimensions, and on that of laying, to develop interlock.

Category A
Dentated in
2 axes

Category B
Dentated in
1 axis

Category C
Undentated

Figure 3   Block shape categories

In Canada, pavers are governed by a CSA Standard [10]. The average compressive strength of cube specimens cut from pavers is to be not less than 50MPa after 28 days with no individual test value less than 45MPa. Pavers should lose no more than 1% of their initial dry weight when subjected to fifty freeze−thaw cycles while totally immersed in a 3% saline solution. Permissible dimensional tolerances are: length ±1.6mm, width ±1.6mm, and thickness ±3.2mm. In the U.K. pavers are governed by BS6717:Part 1 [11], which specifies an average crushing strength of 49MPa and a minimum value for any individual paver of 40MPa. U.K. dimensional tolerances are length and width ±2mm; thickness ±3mm. For architectural applications a paver thickness of 60mm is used, whereas for pavements supporting traffic, a thickness of 80mm is required. In exceptional applications pavers 100mm or 120mm in thickness may be used, but this is generally not necessary. Pavers are factory produced by a dry pressing process using a combination of vibration and pressure to achieve compaction. Batching and pressing are computer controlled and the high degree of automation of the plant ensures a uniform high strength and good control of dimensions.

PAVER PLACEMENT

The majority of pavers are placed by hand, working from the existing paving. Machine laying has been developed and both hand operated and motorised lifting clamps are in use. The choice is an economic one and depends on many factors including labour rates, productivity, job size and laying pattern. Once the blocks have been placed, a vibrating plate compactor is run over their surface. This achieves an even surface, forces some of the bedding sand up into the lower part of the joints between the blocks and compacts the laying course. The use of too light a compactor should be avoided. The plate should have an area of not less than $0.25m^2$ and should transmit an effective force of not less than $75kN/m^2$ of plate at a frequency of vibration in the range 75Hz to 100Hz [6].

LAYING PATTERN

The laying pattern chosen for interlocking concrete block road pavements should be resistant to horizontal creep. The integrity of the pattern should not be affected by traffic stresses as this can lead to separation of the bond lines with consequent loss of interlock. In practice it has been found that herringbone bond performs best and should always be used on pavements subjected to traffic. As shown in Figure 4, herringbone bond can have three orientations relative to the direction of traffic. It

Herringbone bond   Stretcher bond   Basketweave bond

Figure 4   Typical bond patterns

should be laid at 45° to the traffic direction; of the two 45° orientations, that marked A is slightly preferable. Herringbone bond can be maintained through bends in the road or at junctions. The 45° orientation necessitates cutting the blocks at the pavement edge, but this can be largely eliminated by the use of special edge blocks called Bishop's mitre blocks which are shown in Figure 5. Other laying patterns, particularly stretcher bond laid parallel to the traffic direction, incorporate potential shear planes and have little ability to resist traffic stresses.

EDGE RESTRAINT

An essential feature of an interlocking block pavement is edge restraint which resists lateral movement of the blocks and prevents loss of sand from the laying course. For

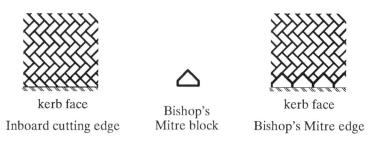

kerb face

Inboard cutting edge

Bishop's
Mitre block

kerb face

Bishop's Mitre edge

Figure 5   Bishop's Mitre edge detail

block pavements supporting traffic, the edge restraint should be a concrete kerb or combined kerb and gutter, extending well below the laying course and bedded and haunched in concrete to prevent movement. This detail is shown in Figure 1. If effective edge restraint is not provided, lateral movement of the blocks occurs due to traffic stresses, resulting in loss of structural interlock and failure of the pavement.

JOINT WIDTHS

Sand filled joints are an integral part of a concrete block pavement. They permit the block surface course to behave flexibly by allowing some articulation of individual blocks and they provide the structural interlock necessary for stresses to be distributed among adjacent blocks. Joints need to be sufficiently wide to permit entry of the jointing and bedding sand, but not so wide as to permit excessive movement of the blocks. In practice, 3mm is the optimum joint width, joints wider than 5mm should not be accepted. Joints smaller than 2mm in width do not get properly filled and allow both movement of the blocks and free entry of rain water. 2mm wide spacer ribs cast integrally on the vertical faces of the blocks assist in rapid laying while ensuring a minimum joint width.   They need to be well designed to avoid excessive stress concentration.

JOINTING SAND

A fine, dry, washed, sand such as that used for cement mortar is required for joint filling.   Suitable gradings have been specified in BS 6717 and by the Australian Cement and Concrete Association. These are shown in Figure 6, but it is considered that in climates subject to frost action, the amount passing the 75 micron sieve should be less than 3%. The jointing sand should be dry when applied. It is spread over the surface of the pavers and further passes of a plate vibrator are made so that the sand enters and progressively fills the joints. Spreading of sand and vibration continue as necessary until the joints are full. Surplus sand is removed by brushing; care being taken not to remove sand from the joints. This filling of the joints provides both translational and rotational interlock and also greatly reduces the ingress of water through the joints. Incorrect specification or application of jointing sand can be a source of poor pavement performance. Difficulties which have occurred include: use of too coarse a sand which cannot enter the joints, attempting to wash the sand into the joints, this does not fill the joints, but can saturate the laying course and the base. Loss of jointing sand in service can contribute to pavement failure by permitting water to enter the underlying layers of the structure and the subgrade. If the subgrade is fine−grained, the resulting increase in its moisture content will be accompanied by a loss of bearing capacity, giving rise to rutting of the pavement and, in extreme cases, to failure.

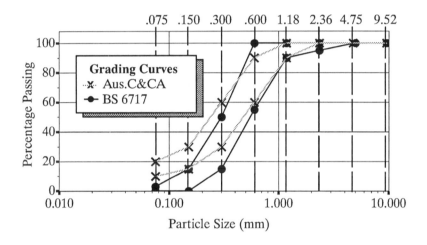

Figure 6   Jointing Sand Grading Envelopes

JOINT SEALING

In most road applications, joint sealing is not considered necessary. It has been shown [12] that well−constructed concrete block pavements, built with normal crossfalls, are substantially waterproof and that there is a significant improvement in the waterproof characteristics after an initial settling−in period. In special cases, a sealant should be applied to stabilise the sand in the joints of newly constructed concrete block road pavements, these have been discussed by Emery [13] and include:

- heavy channelised load locations, such as bus stops where degradation and liquifaction of laying course sand may occur due to ingress of water through the joints.

- areas where vacuum sweeping or high pressure cleaning equipment may be used.
- cold climates where de−icing and snow removal operations are frequent.
- areas where turbulent flow may occur across the pavement, e.g. around gullies and on steep slopes

DRAINAGE

Effective surface and sub−surface drainage is essential to the satisfactory performance of all pavements. A minimum crossfall of 2½% and a minimum longitudinal fall of 1¼% should be provided [6]. The water collected should be properly disposed of in such a way that it cannot enter the pavement structure or the supporting subgrade. After an initial period of traffic, equivalent to some ten thousand standard axles, interlock should be fully developed, the pavement should have stiffened and the joints should have become relatively impervious. Nevertheless, where drainage is inadequate subgrade softening and deformation will occur with the risk of eventual subgrade failure by excessive settlement. Sub−surface drainage should keep the water table at least 1.5m below the road surface wherever possible.

DESIGN METHODS

The general approach to the design of an interlocking concrete block road pavement is to use an accepted method for the design of a bituminous surfaced road and substitute an 80mm thick paver on 30mm (after compaction) of bedding sand for an equivalent thickness (110mm) of hot rolled asphalt. Design guides have been published in a number of countries [14][15][16].

In the United Kingdom method, subgrade strength is characterised by the CBR, which is obtained either by direct measurement or indirectly from a measurement of plasticity index. Soaked values are only used where it is expected that the subgrade will be saturated in service. Traffic loading is represented by the cumulative equivalent standard 8.2t axle loads over the design life (usually twenty years). Multipliers are used for channelised traffic (x 3) and for dynamic loading (x 2) for traffic speeds in excess of 50km/h. The method is summarised in Figure 7 which has been adapted from a flow chart given in the design standard. Material conversion factors are included to permit the selection of thicknesses of different materials on the basis of equal load−spreading ability. The method makes no distinction between block shapes

The method used in Australia is similar in principle to the U.K. method, but with the following significant differences:

- block shape is a factor, category A shape is stated to be superior in resisting the development of rutting and longitudinal creep

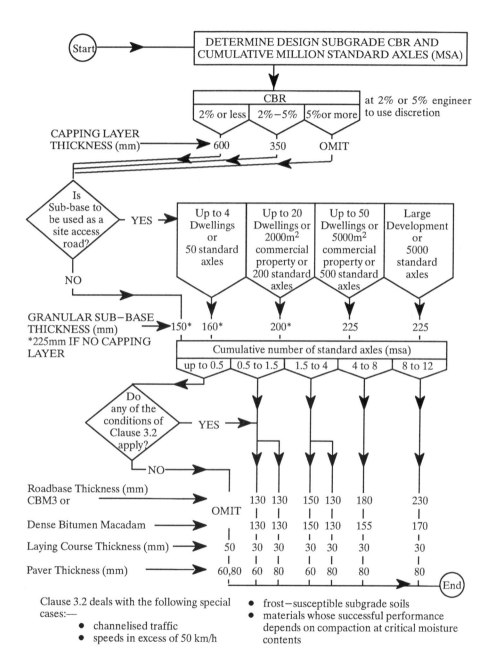

Figure 7   Concrete block pavement design procedure
simplified from BS 7533

- traffic is defined as the cumulative number of commercial vehicles in excess of three tonnes gross mass rather than in terms of equivalent standard axles
- the CBR value used to characterise the subgrade soil is specified as the laboratory soaked value rather than that corresponding to estimated equilibrium moisture content
- concrete block paving on an unbound roadbase develops an interlocked condition beyond which neither the wheel load nor the number of load applications has any significant influence on the pavement performance. Hence, the design must ensure that the permanent deformation (rutting) which occurs during the development of interlock remains within acceptable limits

Design charts are provided for bound and unbound roadbases. Design criteria are— for an unbound roadbase: allowable cumulative pavement deformation (rutting) and for a bound roadbase: limiting deflections to prevent cracking and loss of stiffness.

Recommended structures for optimum economy are:

- granular roadbase over subgrade having a CBR>30%
- granular roadbase on cement−stabilised sub−base over subgrade having 30%>CBR>10%
- cement−stabilised roadbase on cement−stabilised sub−base over subgrade having CBR<10%

CAUSES OF FAILURE

Notwithstanding the inherent advantages of concrete block pavements to support road traffic, failures do occur. Where emphasis is placed on the aesthetic use of pavers, there is a risk that engineering factors may not be properly taken into account. Potential sources of failure include:

- use of an inappropriate laying pattern; 45° Herringbone bond should be used.
- use of unsuitable bedding sands
- incorrect joint width
- use of unsuitable jointing sand or incorrect joint filling method
- inadequate edge restraint allowing lateral movement and loss of bond
- mixing block sizes and shapes
- inadequate drainage
- absence of transition zones

ROAD APPLICATIONS

In countries where modern block paving has been introduced during the last twenty years, early use was largely in areas where it was chosen for its aesthetic appeal, such as pedestrian malls. As confidence in its use has developed and as appreciation of potential uses has grown, concrete block paving has spread to all types of road except motorways and high−speed rural roads.   In the last five years it has appeared on sections of the British primary route network in towns, notably in Kent on the A26 and A275 [17]

In the Netherlands there is a long tradition of small element paving for city streets. Since the 1950's, concrete pavers have progressively replaced clay bricks because of their lower cost and smaller dimensional tolerances. Concrete block paving has also been adopted for urban street construction and renewal in many other countries. Particular advantages in this application include:

- ability to support heavy, slow−moving traffic
- ease of access to buried services and reinstatement of pavement
- aesthetic appearances
- use of colour to build crossings and markings

Residential roads are typically less liable to changing use or increased traffic than urban streets. Conventional concrete slab road construction to a minimum thickness of 150mm and a design life of forty years has often been considered appropriate in view of this stability. More recently concrete blocks have been effectively used to pave residential roads, where the sensitive use of shape and colour and their human scale have proved advantageous. This application is quite widespread in Australia and New Zealand.   As concrete block paving can be opened to heavy traffic immediately after construction without need for curing or hardening, the road can be installed prior to building the houses.   This guarantees all−weather access for construction materials and equipment.   Access on a finished road of pleasing appearance also favours sales of building plots and houses. As blocks only 80mm, or possibly only 60mm, in thickness are required, a block pavement will have a lower unit cost than a comparable concrete slab pavement.

Concrete block pavements are widely used for rural roads in Germany, the Netherlands and Central America. Shackel [18] has reported a particular application on steep gradients in the mountains of Bavaria, where the use of paving machines is impractical due to the steep slope and where conventional surfacings are prone to creep under traffic.

Bus loadings are among the most severe applied to road pavements. They are also highly channelised, particularly at stops. In addition, leakage of oil is damaging to bituminous pavement surfacings. Concrete block paving has proved outstandingly successful for bus terminal roads, well−known examples being at Euston Station and at Heathrow airport.

CONCLUSIONS

1. Interlocking concrete block pavements have become established for all classes of road except motorways and high—speed roads.

2. Concrete block pavements offer the advantages of concrete as a material, while avoiding the difficulties associated with roads constructed of concrete slabs.

3. Economic and durable concrete roads, appropriate to the needs of the twenty—first century, can be constructed using interlocking block paving.

REFERENCES

1. KNAPTON J., Structural design of pavements with concrete blocks or clay pavers. *Seminar on the Economics and Engineering of Concrete Pavements*, Canadian Portland Cement Association, University of New Brunswick, 1989

2. SHACKEL B., A review of the technology of interlocking concrete block paving for roads and industrial pavements. National Institute for Transport and Road Research RP/8/80, CSIR, Pretoria, 1980

3. POWELL W.D. et al, The structural design of bituminous roads. Transport and Road Research Laboratory, LR 1132, 1984

4. DEPARTMENT OF TRANSPORT, Specification for highway works. HMSO, London, 1986

5. KNAPTON J., Structural design for concrete block roads. Highways, March, 1988, pp. 20—25

6. BRITISH STANDARDS INSTITUTION, Precast concrete paving blocks: Code of practice for laying. BS 6717, Part 3, 1989

7. COOK I.D., and KNAPTON J., Bedding course sands. Proc. 4th. Int. Conf. on Concrete Block Paving, Vol. 2, 1992, pp. 285—294

8. LILLEY A.A. and DOWSON A.J., Laying course sand for concrete block paving. Proc. 3rd. Int. Conf. on Concrete Block Paving, 1988, pp. 457—462

9. MORRISH C.F., Interlocking concrete paving — the state of the art in Australia. Proc. 1st. Int. Conf. on Concrete Block Paving, 1980, pp. 85—92

10. CANADIAN STANDARDS ASSOCIATION, Precast concrete pavers. Standard CAN3—A321.2—M85, 1985

11. BRITISH STANDARDS INSTITUTION, Precast concrete paving blocks. Specification for paving blocks. BS 6717, Part 1, 1986

12. CLIFFORD J.M., Segmental block paving in southern Africa: a review and structural design guide. National Institute for Transport and Road Research, RP/27 CSIR, Pretoria, 1986

13. EMERY J.A., Erosion of jointing sand from concrete block paving. Proc. 4th. Int. Conf. on Concrete Block Paving, Vol. 2, 1992, pp. 295–299

14. BRITISH STANDARDS INSTITUTION, Guide for structural design of pavements constructed with clay or concrete block pavers. BS 7533, 1992

15. CEMENT AND CONCRETE ASSOCIATION OF AUSTRALIA, Interlocking concrete road pavements— a guide to design and construction. Publication T35, 1986

16. CEMENT AND CONCRETE ASSOCIATION OF NEW ZEALAND, Interlocking concrete block road pavements: a guide to design and construction. Publication IB 67, 1988

17. ANON, Kent 'first' in primary route block paving. Highways, July, 1989, p. 17

18. SHACKEL B., Design and construction of interlocking concrete block pavements. Elsevier Applied Science, London, 1990

ABRASION RESISTANCE OF CONCRETE ROAD SURFACINGS

B Shackel

University of New South Wales

Australia

ABSTRACT. This paper describes the evaluation of abrasion tests for concrete paving based on ASTM test C779 and British Standard 5395. Comparisons are made between the tests and it is shown that the test derived from the British Standard is more consistent and reproducible than that derived from the ASTM procedure. However, the two tests do not, in general, correlate with one another. Overall, neither test is clearly superior to the other but the result of the modified ASTM procedure appears to be more consistent with end-user assessments of paver performance than those from the modified BS 5395 test. Inter-alia, the paper summarises studies of the factors affecting abrasion resistance of concrete. These include the cement content, the water-cement ratio, the type of cement and/or pigment and the curing regime.

Keywords: Abrasion, Aggregate, Curing, Durability, Ordinary Portland Cement (OPC), Pigment, Water-Cement Ratio.

Dr Brian Shackel is Associate Professor in Civil Engineering and Head of the Department of Geotechnical Engineering in the School of Civil Engineering at the University of New South Wales, Sydney, Australia. His main research interest is pavement engineering with recent emphasis on concrete pavements. He has published widely in that field and is the author of the first book published on the design and construction of concrete block paving (recently republished in Japan).

Concrete 2000. Edited by Ravindra K. Dhir and M. Roderick Jones.
© 1993 Published by E & FN Spon. ISBN 0 419 18120 2.

INTRODUCTION

During the last 15 years there has been increasing use of concrete segmental paving in urban areas in Australia. Whilst the structural performance of such pavements has generally been satisfactory a significant number of pavements have exhibited surface wear during the first few years of service. For this reason, both manufacturers and users of concrete paving have developed a variety of tests to assess abrasion wear. Generally, these have been modifications or adaptations of overseas tests. The earliest procedure, developed by Perth City Council, represented a modified version of ASTM Test C779-82. This was incorporated into the MA20 Concrete Paver Specification published in 1986 by the Concrete Masonry Association of Australia. More recently, two developments of the procedure given in British Standard BS 5395: 1977 have emerged as alternatives to the MA20 test. The first of these is known as the South Sydney City Council, (SCC) test. This was later adopted in a modified form by the Brick Development Research Institute (3). Both of these procedures comprise rattler tests in which steel balls are tumbled against the paver surface. Abrasion wear is expressed as the volume of material knocked from the surface. Considerable and so far unresolved argument surrounds the relative merits of the MA20 and SCC procedures. This paper reports a comparative evaluation of both these tests. In the course of this evaluation several of the factors affecting abrasion wear were identified and studied.

ABRASION TESTS

MA20 Abrasion Test

Details of the MA20 abrasion test have been given elsewhere (4). Essentially, a vertically mounted electric drill drives a hollow shaft bearing on a ball race running on the paver surface. Water is run through the drive shaft whilst the equipment is running. The abrasion resistance is measured in terms of the penetration of the ball race into the paver surface for a given number of revolutions (1). An Abrasion Index, I_a, has been defined as

$$I_a = \frac{\sqrt{N}}{p} \tag{1}$$

where N is the number of ball race revolutions (thousands) and p is the penetration (mm). The interim MA20 Specification for Concrete Pavers recommended the limiting values of I_a given in Table 1. Here $I_{a\ min}$ represents the smallest (worst case) value obtained in tests of 5 pavers (1).

The SCC Abrasion Test

The SCC abrasion test is similar to that described in British Standard BS 368-56 except that abrasion is induced by the impact of 600 chrome balls during 3600 revolutions at

60 ±2 rpm (2). Eight specimens representing a single batch of concrete are tested at one time. The mass loss of each sample is measured and is converted to an "abraded volume loss" by dividing the mass loss by the density of the samples. Current SCC requirements for concrete pavers carrying heavy pedestrian traffic are that the Abrasion Loss should not exceed 3 cm³ for any specimen in a group of eight.

The objectives of the research described herein were:

1)   To evaluate the MA20 abrasion resistance equipment and procedures in tests involving up to 4 independent laboratories.
2)   To compare the MA20 and SCC tests
3)   To investigate factors affecting the abrasion resistance of concrete pavers.
4)   To establish minimum in-service criteria for abrasion test results.

Table 1   Interim abrasion limits

Pavement Use	Minimum 28 Day Abrasion Index, I_a
Heavy Pedestrian use	2.0
Road and Industrial traffic	1.5
Footpaths with light pedestrian traffic	1.2
Car parks	1.2

Evaluation of the MA20 Abrasion Test

An evaluation of the MA20 test has been published elsewhere (4) and only a summary of those points relevant to the drafting of abrasion specifications are given here. Initially, tests involving 4 independent laboratories indicated that the procedures set out in the MA20 specification were insufficient to ensure consistent results between laboratories. Tests were then conducted to examine whether the test procedures could be improved.

Overall it was concluded that much of the variability evident in comparative testing was intrinsic to the test procedure and was not readily amenable to reduction by refinement of the testing techniques. Despite this, it was found that the reproducibility of the MA20 test was better than that reported for the ASTM C779 test from which it evolved. In this respect the average coefficients of variation for I_a in equation 1 were 11.79% and 11.54% at 2,000 and 5,000 revolutions respectively. By contrast, ASTM procedure C779 reports a coefficient of variation of 17.74%.

Tests to evaluate the inherent variability of the MA20 procedure were conducted using 100 mm cubes cast from a single batch of zero-slump concrete. This allowed up to 4 independent tests on the vertical faces of each sample. From such tests it was possible to relate the number of tests needed to achieve any given confidence interval. This is shown in Figure 1. This figure shows that, for a single test, the confidence interval for I_a is approximately ±0.85 at the 95% confidence interval. This value does not provide the discrimination required by Table 1. Nor does the mean of five test results.

It may be concluded that the use of either a single worst-case value or the mean of 5 abrasion values is inadequate to delineate the abrasion resistance. The best way to improve the MA20 abrasion test is to increase the number of samples and to base the acceptance criteria on statistics such as the mean or characteristic Abrasion Indices. As shown in Figure 1, increase in the number of tests beyond 10 determinations yields only limited improvements in the confidence intervals for the Abrasion Index, I_a. Accordingly, the use of a sample of 10 abrasion test specimens is recommended as the basis for any abrasion standard based on the MA20 test.

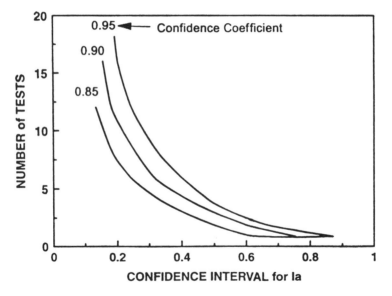

Figure 1.   Confidence Limits for Abrasion Index, I_a

COMPARISON OF THE MA20 AND SCC ABRASION TESTS

As in the evaluation of the MA20 test, 100 mm cubical samples were used in studying the SCC test. This enabled both the MA20 and SCC tests to be conducted on the same specimens.

As shown in Table 2 the samples were manufactured in two phases. Depending on the curing conditions set out in Table 2 the samples were continuously moist or air cured between manufacture and testing. Mix details are given in Table 2. Each mix contained 40 ml of a water reducing admixture (Eucobet 777) and 4 ml of an air-entraining agent (Darex). Twelve cubes and three cylinders were manufactured from each mix.

Table 2   Mix and experiment details

Phase	Variable	Levels
1	Cement Content by vol.	9.14% 10.16% 11.17%
	Type of Aggregate	Crushed Aggregate, River Gravel
	Water/Cement Ratio	0.47 0.49 0.52 0.54
2	Pigment Type	Black, Brown
	Pigment Content	0 5%
	Cement Type	ASCE A, Off-white
	Curing conditions	air-cured, moist-cured

Table 3   Test results on phase 1 samples

Cement Content % by Vol.	Agg Type	No of Specs	Comp. Strength MPa	MA20 Abrasion Index, Ia				SCC Abrasion Loss cm^3	
				28 days		600 + days			
				Mean	Std dev	Mean	Std dev	Mean	Std Dev
10.16	Crushed	12	47.9	2.74	0.40	3.88	0.18	2.156	0.242
10.16	Crushed	12	39.8	2.69	0.26	3.55	0.54	1.892	0.189
10.6	Gravel	12	35.9	2.66	0.30	2.92	0.45	2.428	0.337
9.14	Crushed	12	31.3	2.54	0.24	2.67	0.46	2.199	0.212
9.14	Gravel	12	30.2	2.32	0.28	2.71	0.54	2.298	0.290
11.17	Crushed	12	50.4	3.12	0.68	4.83	1.16	1.783	0.205
11.17	Gravel	12	43.7	3.32	0.44	4.28	0.81	1.643	0.221

The results of the tests are summarised in Tables 3 and 4. From these results the following conclusions can be drawn:

Test Variability

a)   The SCC test generally showed much smaller variability within each group of specimens tested (expressed as the standard deviation relative to the mean value) than the MA20 test.

b)   The SCC test showed a more consistent variability (expressed as the standard deviation of the Abrasion Volume) between test batches than was shown by the MA20 test expressed in terms of the standard deviation of Ia.

Table 4   Test results on phase 2 samples

Pigment Type	Pigment Content %	Curing Condition Air/Moist	No. of Specimens	Comp. Strength (MPa)	MA 20 Ia		SCC Abrasion Loss cm^3	
					Mean	Std dev	Mean	Std dev
Brown	5	A	12	39.8	4.32	0.90	2.230	0.275
Black	5	A	12	43.7	3.68	0.61	1.932	0.529
None	0	A	12	39.5	3.78	0.62	2.072	0.160
Brown	5	M	12	56.3	4.63	0.55	2.716	0.289
Black	5	M	12	52.0	3.87	0.63	3.055	0.264
None	0	M	12	30.4	4.57	0.71	2.869	0.286

Sensitivity to Mix Variables

The ranking of the effects of the experimental variables listed in Tables 2 to 4 was generally similar for both the MA20 and SCC tests except for two important differences. In the case of air-cured specimens, the SCC test indicated *better* abrasion performance in terms of Abrasion Loss than for moist cured specimens. In other words, the SCC test yielded an unexpected result. Moreover, the SCC test gave a different ranking of the effects of pigment type than the MA20 test. These effects are believed to be associated with carbonation of the outer surface of the specimen.

Correlation between the SCC and MA20 Tests

For moist cured samples it was possible to establish a strong correlation between the SCC test and the MA20 test. This appeared to be independent of such mix variables as the type of aggregate, type or amount of pigment or cement content but was highly dependent on the age of the specimens at the time of test. In this respect it was not possible to combine the results of the Phase 1 and Phase 2 tests even though in both instances, the SCC and MA20 tests were performed at least 100 days after the specimens had been cast.

The relationship between the Abrasion Loss (AL) data given by the SCC test and the Ia values determined using the MA20 test together with the corresponding correlation coefficients, r, were found to be

for Phase 1 samples:

$$AL = 3.0285 - 0.276 \, Ia \tag{2}$$
$$\text{(with } r = 0.79, \, n = 7)$$

for Phase 2 samples:

$$AL = 4.5118 - 0.3738 \, Ia \tag{3}$$
$$\text{(with } r = 0.93, \, n = 3)$$

In the case of the Phase 1 samples, the Ia values obtained at the time of the SCC tests were substantially higher than those measured 28 days after casting the specimens. In other words, the abrasion resistance of moist cured specimens continued to increase well beyond 28 days.

The relationships given in equations 2 and 3 apply to moist cured specimens only. For air-cured specimens it was not possible to establish any relationship between the results of the SCC and MA20 tests.

FACTORS AFFECTING ABRASION RESISTANCE

To explore the major factors affecting abrasion resistance a series of tests were conducted (5, 6, 7). From these studies the following conclusions can be drawn.

a)   The abrasion index, Ia, increased with increase in the cement content of the mix.

b)   Increasing the water content or water/cement ratio to improve the workability of the mix led to a reduction in the abrasion index, Ia.

c)   Moist curing yielded higher abrasion resistance and compressive strength than air curing of specimens. Curing conditions affected abrasion more than strength.

d)   Some pigments significantly increased the abrasion resistance of moist-cured specimens manufactured using ASCE cement type A.

e)   For pavers manufactured from off-white cements, the addition of up to 7% of pigment produced no significant change in abrasion resistance.

f)   For moist-cured samples, it proved possible to obtain weak correlations between abrasion resistance and the compression strength of the concrete. These correlations were not, however, sufficient to permit the use of strength data as reliable indicators of abrasion resistance.

IN-SERVICE ABRASION CRITERIA

In this phase of the investigation the objective was to determine how the results of the abrasion tests would relate to of the wear performance of pavements in service. This work was done with the assistance of the Department of Works, Brisbane City Council, which supplied pavers whose performance was considered to range from acceptable through partially acceptable to unacceptable. These pavers were taken from pedestrian areas because experience indicated that more severe abrasion wear occurs under pedestrians than under vehicles. Four groups of pavers were supplied (see Table 5). In the case of the concrete pavers deemed unacceptable, substantial wear was evident to the naked eye.

Table 5   Abrasion test data on Brisbane pavers

Rating	No of	MA20, Abrasion Index Ia				SCC, Abraded Vol cm^3			
	Specs	min	max	mean	std dev	min	max	mean	std dev
acceptable	10	2.80	7.99	4.55	1.79	1.494	1.919	1.657	0.131
	8	-	-	-	-	1.494	1.726	1.613	0.094
acceptable	8	-	-	-	-	3.728	5.984	4.909	0.872
	9	1.49	7.71	4.05	2.57	-	-	-	-
partially	10	6.58	11.18	9.06	1.86	2.194	3.799	3.080	0.459
acceptable	8	-	-	-	-	2.614	3.799	3.196	0.378
unacceptable	10	1.35	4.22	2.75	0.95	4.614	7.740	5.755	1.169
	8	-	-	-	-	4.614	7.740	5.486	1.103

The results of the MA20 and SCC abrasion tests on these pavers are given in Table 5. It should be noted that, where more than 8 specimens were tested using the SCC procedure, it was necessary to combine two test runs. From Table 5 it may be seen that, as in the case of the laboratory prepared samples, the variability in the SCC test, expressed as the relationship of the standard deviations to the mean abrasion values, was better than for the MA20 test.   However, unlike the tests on the cubical concrete samples, there was no acceptable correlation between the MA20 and SCC results in terms of individual data points for each group of pavers or for the whole group of test results. Similar comments apply to the relationship between the mean values of abrasion resistance. On the basis of these limited data it was concluded that there was no useful correlation between the results of the MA20 and SCC abrasion tests for actual pavers chosen from a variety of projects.   Moreover, the rankings of abrasion wear were different for the two test procedures (see Table 5).

Overall, it must be concluded that on the basis of the limited data presented in Table 5, it is not possible to set limits for either test procedure. Nor does it appear that the two tests provide similar discrimination amongst different levels of abrasion performance. However, it would appear reasonable for heavily trafficked pedestrian areas to require the mean value of the Abrasion Index to exceed 3.0 and the Abrasion Loss not to exceed 3 cm^3.

CONCLUSIONS

The principal conclusions that can be drawn from the data summarised herein are:

1.   The SCC test derived from BS 5395 was more consistent and reproducible than the MA20 test derived from ASTM C779. However, the MA20 test exceeded the ASTM requirements for the coefficient of variation of the test results.

2.   With some significant exceptions the MA20 AND SCC tests responded in similar ways to change in mix variables for specimens prepared under laboratory conditions. However, the SCC test appeared to be sensitive to shallow surface effects such as those produced by air-curing.

3.   For moist-cured laboratory samples there were weak negative correlations between the results of the MA20 and the SCC tests. These correlations were highly dependent on the age of the test specimens. It was not possible to establish similar relationships for air-cured specimens prepared in the laboratory or for the pavers supplied by the Department of Works, Brisbane. Overall, it must be concluded that there was no intrinsic or unique relationship between the results of the MA20 and SCC abrasion tests. In other words, results or standards established in terms of one test cannot be easily or reliably translated into the values given by the other procedure.

4.   On the basis of the very limited data available for actual pavers it is not possible to set firm levels of the Abrasion Index, Ia, necessary to ensure an acceptable level of performance. However, a mean value of Ia exceeding 3.0 or an Abraded Volume Loss of less than about 3 cm^3 would appear desirable for heavily trafficked pedestrian areas. Much more research is needed in this respect.

5.   The principal mix variables affecting abrasion resistance have been shown to be cement content, water/cement ratio and the curing regime. Factors such as the type of cement or the type and amount of pigment are of much lesser importance.

ACKNOWLEDGEMENTS

The work described in this paper was funded in part by the Concrete Masonry Association of Australia. The assistance of Mr E. Jones of Brisbane City Council in supplying samples of paving and Mr T Gabrawy and the Council of the City of South Sydney in conducting SCC abrasion tests is gratefully acknowledged.

REFERENCES

1. CONCRETE MASONRY ASSN OF AUST., (1986), Specification for Concrete Segmental Paving Units, MA20 CMAA.

2. GABRAWY, T., (1986), The Sydney City Council Abrasion Test for Paving, SCC.

3. ZSEMBERY, S., VUCKO, J. AND SHARPE, K., (1989), Interim Report, Evaluation of the Paver Abrasion Testing Machine Proposed by the Sydney City Council, Research Paper 13, Clay Brick and Paver Inst.

4. SHACKEL, B. AND SHI, X., (1992), The Abrasion Testing of Concrete Pavers, Proc. 4th Int. Conf. on Conc. Block Paving, Auckland, Vol 1 pp 229-238; 1992,

5. SYAHMANSYAH,   An experimental study of the abrasion resistance of concrete pavement surfaces. M.Eng.Sc Report, Univ. NSW; Dec; 1990. - unpublished.

6. LARIBA, C.C., (1990), Abrasion Resistance of Concrete, M.Eng.Sc. Report, Univ. NSW, Aug, 1991 - unpublished.

7. HON, W.,   An Experimental Study of the Factors Affecting the Abrasion Resistance of Concrete. Project Rpt, School of Civil Engg, Univ. NSW, - 1991 - unpublished.

A GRAPHICAL OBJECT-ORIENTED SYSTEM
FOR MAINTENANCE OF CONCRETE PAVEMENTS

S H C Foo

G Akhras

Royal Military College

Canada

ABSTRACT. Maintenance of concrete pavements involves inspection, damage assessment and recording and managing inspection/repair data. It requires appropriate expertise to recognize and correct problems at hand. Very few engineers have an in-depth expertise of the whole maintenance process. At times, methods of rehabilitation appear to be more practically available than competent engineers. The spread of such expert knowledge by means of knowledge-based expert systems to a wider group of engineers is needed. Economic and durable concrete pavements through an effective maintenance program can be achieved in the 21st century by exploiting the full potential of expert system technology. This paper presents the development of a graphical object-oriented system for the maintenance of concrete pavements, using expert system technology, relational database models and hypertext paradigm.

Keywords : Computer, Expert systems, Knowledge-based, Maintenance, Pavement.

Dr. Simon H C Foo is a Research Engineer of Civil Engineering at the Royal Military College of Canada, Kingston, Ontario. His research interests include applications of expert systems in civil engineering, dynamic behaviour of reinforced concrete structures and rehabilitation of timber truss structures.

Dr. Georges Akhras is an Associate Professor of Civil Engineering at the Royal Military College of Canada, Kingston, Ontario. For 10 years, he was a project manager for computer applications and numerical analysis in government and industry, before joining RMC in 1987. His current interests include expert systems, numerical modelling and composite materials.

Concrete 2000. Edited by Ravindra K. Dhir and M. Roderick Jones.
© 1993 Published by E & FN Spon. ISBN 0 419 18120 2.

INTRODUCTION

Pavement management systems consist of planning, design, construction, maintenance and evaluation. With well organized planning, proper analysis and design tools, and consistent and reliable construction practice, economic and durable pavement construction can be assured under normal circumstances. However, due to changing environmental, service and other conditions, condition of pavements also changes. Consequently, evaluation and maintenance of a pavement play vital roles in an effective and successful pavement management.

Pavement evaluation process can be considered in terms of four categories : namely structural capacity, condition, roughness and safety. Condition survey can be defined as the process of examining the exposed concrete to identify the areas of distress, including riding quality and distress manifestations. Pavement condition surveys can be used to evaluate the ability of the pavement to continue to provide required service and to plan maintenance and rehabilitation programs if necessary. Pavement evaluation is needed at regular intervals so that management is aware of changing conditions and can plan maintenance and rehabilitation programs.

Condition surveys require appropriate expertise to recognize and correct existing or expected pavement problems. Decisions made by the inspectors during a condition survey can have significant effects on the performance and durability of the pavement. At times, paving inspectors may not have enough experience to decide when there is a deficiency, nor do they know the correct remedial actions for a particular deficiency with different degrees of severity and extent. The world-wide trend of government spending restraints puts additional pressure on the well being of our road systems.

A method of transferring knowledge from the pavement inspection experts to less experienced or local inspection personnel is required. An expert system, also known as knowledge-based expert system (KBES), is a computer program which captures human knowledge and decision making processes. Fully developed KBESs are capable of accepting facts from the user, processing these facts against the knowledge base, and on the basis of these facts and knowledge, delivering solutions which are close to the solutions by a human expert.

Primary benefits of using a KBES include reliability (increased possibility of correct and consistent decisions) and productivity (improved efficiency). KBESs can also be used as training and education tools for both practising engineers and university students.

MAINTENANCE OF CONCRETE PAVEMENTS

Background

It is apparent, at least in Canada, that fewer and fewer new roads and streets are being built each year while there is a huge and growing inventory of aging roadways. The province of Ontario has one of the best road systems in the world. In recent years, because of shrinking budgets and rising cost, the emphasis has been shifting from developing new construction and upgrading of standards to preserving existing road systems. As such, maintenance of these aging road systems are becoming more and more important. The province emphasizes preservation of its highway system by carrying out both corrective and preventive maintenance activities.

In corrective maintenance process, pavement deficiencies are identified and corrective actions are taken in accordance with the type and severity of the problems as well as cost effectiveness. The corrective action is carried out to maintain and ensure the safe operation of the pavement system. To prolong the life of the pavement, preventive maintenance is carried out to retard the occurrence or progression of deficiencies.

A systematic strategy for pavement maintenance has been developed in Ontario [1]. A set of guidelines has been developed to assist maintenance staff in identifying the pavement distress problem and in choosing consistently, from among the available alternatives, the most cost-effective treatment method for that particular distress problem. The guide contains four essential elements, namely, distress identification and classification on the basis of condition survey, corresponding treatment selection, performance standard of treatment, and cost estimation. Figure 1 summarizes the various steps in the maintenance decision procedure as outlined in the guidelines.

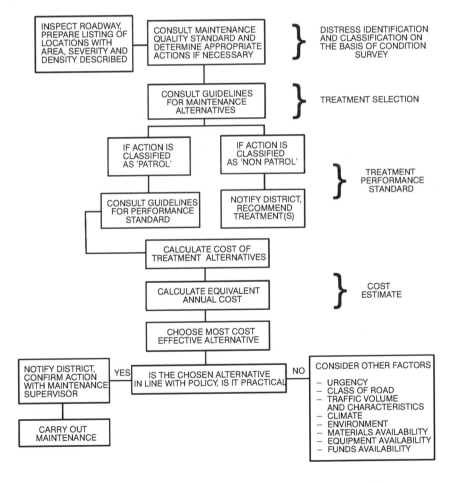

Figure 1 Maintenance decision procedures for Ontario [1]

Knowledge-based approach

Evaluation of pavement condition is a key part of pavement management system. On one hand, there is a large number of aging roads in need of rehabilitation and maintenance. On the other hand, there are usually only a limited number of inspection experts who have to travel to many different sites to evaluate the pavement conditions. More often than not, condition surveys are being performed by inspectors who have limited or little experience with the evaluation process. A good maintenance system is one that is based upon reliable, consistent and cost-effective decisions. There is a need for tools capable of not only disseminating expert knowledge but also assisting the experts themselves in carrying out a condition survey in a more reliable and efficient approach.

During the past five years, there has been a steadily increasing interest in the development of KBESs for civil engineering and transportation-related problems. Response to a recent questionnaire [2] indicated that there were a total of 90 expert systems of which a majority were either operational or developed and under evaluation. These systems can be classified by function as traffic management and control, traffic impact and safety, highway design and planning, and highway management, and by category as diagnosis/monitoring, interpretation/classification, prediction/forecasting, and design/planning.

One important note from this survey is that there was an increasing number of operational expert systems, which is indicative of a gradual acceptance of expert systems by the end user work force. Another point of interest is that there were a total of 23 systems, a quarter of all 90 systems, which belonged to the category of diagnosis and monitoring. Of the systems reported, 80 % were personal computer based, 5 % were for mainframes and the remaining 15 % for workstations.

The potential for the application of KBESs in the highway engineering field is great. These systems can perform certain tasks, such as decision support, design aids, and training, more effectively and consistently than is possible with current tools and engineering aids. An expert system is an intelligent assistant and a training aid as much as a problem solver. Fully integrated decision support/training systems are both possible and practical by combining KBESs with interactive videodisc training systems and other conventional media.

OBJECT-ORIENTED SYSTEMS WITH GRAPHICS

An expert system has basic components : a knowledge base and an inference engine which is also the control structure of the system. The knowledge base comprises of expert knowledge specific to the domain of the problem being addressed. The inference engine interprets and applies the knowledge base and attempts to make decisions to problems that would ordinarily require a human expert.

The heart of any expert systems is the knowledge base, which is usually a collection of rules, typically in the form of 'IF...AND..OR...THEN...AND..ELSE..'. If the antecedent of a rule (IF...AND..OR...) is found to be true, the inference engine fires the rule, inferring the 'THEN...AND...' statement(s). There are other components which the knowledge base may be constructed of, such as frames, nets, and more recently object-oriented approach. Because of its modularity, data abstraction and inheritance characteristics, object-oriented programming or OOP, will likely subsume other approaches in the very near future.

There is no shortage of literature on OOP [3,4,5]. The term OOP was first used to describe the Smalltalk programming environment developed at Xerox, who did much of the early work in applying object concepts [6]. The fundamental concept of object-orientation is that the real world can be modeled more accurately in information system through the representation of objects. Objects provide an excellent mechanism for information representation and manipulation. The five key words in OOP are object, class, instance, method and message.

Objects represent the properties of a data structure and the operations permitted and performed on the structure. In other words, an object is the sum of its data and procedures and performs operations on itself. A class describes the structure and behaviour of an object within an application and is defined by a collection of characteristics called attributes. An instance is a specific occurrence of an object. Methods are procedures associated with an attribute that can determine the attribute's value or execute a series of procedures when the attribute's value changes. Message is used to invoke operations of an object or among objects. Figure 2 shows the tree structure of an object used by Level5 Object [7], which is one of the many commercially available software for object-oriented expert system development.

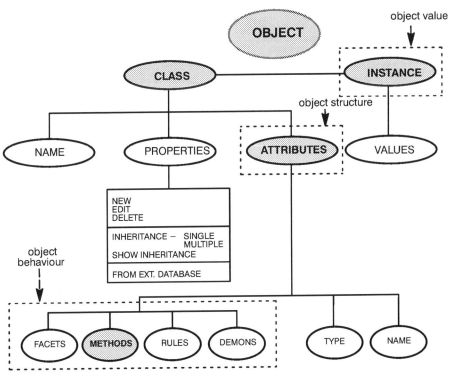

Figure 2 Tree structure of an object

The object orientation is particular evident in a new class of programming environments that are based on graphical objects rather than text listings. For example, the key feature of the typical information-handling problem encountered during an inspection is the correct interpretation of visual images. To reduce the dependency on subjective judgement and to improve the consistency in decision making, a diagnostic KBES with graphical representation of knowledge is very useful.

An object-oriented system can display implicit knowledge by means of real graphic images as shown in Figure 3. Figure 3a illustrates an example of meandering crack while Figure 3b depicts a typical edge crescent crack. Inspector in the field can learn from these photo images that the former represents cracks which wander like a serpent across the traffic lane and that the later represents arc cracks extending from transverse joint or transverse crack to the pavement edge.

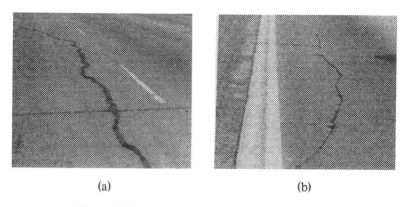

(a)   (b)

Figure 3 Graphical representation of knowledge

INSPECTION OF CONCRETE PAVEMENTS

Pavement evaluation process can be considered in terms of a number of categories, one of which is condition survey of distress manifestation. In practice, the term 'condition' is used to refer to pavement surface distress. Condition survey measures various types and degrees of distress. The purpose of condition survey is to locate, identify and classify the distresses on the highway that require treatment.

Different agencies adapt different methods for conducting condition surveys. Close examination of several survey guidelines [8,9,10] reveals that there is a great degree of commonality about the types of distresses to be considered in condition survey. There are basically five general classes of distresses : surface defects, surface deformation, joint deficiencies, cracking, and miscellaneous.

During a condition survey, each type of distress is evaluated in terms of its severity and density. The Ontario maintenance system contains a comprehensive set of photographic examples and detailed descriptions of all types of distress manifestations. Description, possible causes, severity, density and example are given for each type of distress. An extract from [9] on the example, severity and density of "D" cracks are illustrated in Figure 4, Table 1 and Table 2 respectively.

class 2 slight (3 mm - 13 mm)

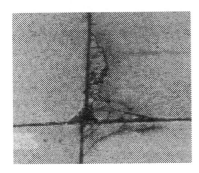

class 4 severe (19 mm - 25 mm)

Figure 4 Photographs of various degrees of severity of "D" cracks

Table 1 Guide for describing severity of "D" cracks

CLASS	UNIFORM DESCRIPTION	GUIDELINES *
1	Very slight	< 3 mm
2	Slight	3 mm - 13 mm
3	Moderate	13 mm - 19 mm
4	Severe	19 mm - 25 mm (with spalling and faulting developed)
5	Very severe	> 25 mm (with spalling and faulting developed)

*   Based on crack width and its condition

User help screens are important for both the acceptance and efficient use of KBESs by the user community. They also enhance the use of the system as a training tool. The system has an efficient explanatory component to make the comprehension and checking of how a solution is reached possible and effective. The explanatory facility of the system can be used as an aid for novice engineers to learn, with or without the manuals, more about the inspection process.

User interface plays a major role in the acceptance of any system by its end users. Since the system has graphical user interface with explanatory facilities, little or no programming knowledge and experience is required to use the system. Users simply point and click his/her way through the inspection process to appreciate the dynamic behaviour of the system.

Example

Figures 5a and 5b illustrate the typical screen images from a sample session when conducting an inspection of a particular pavement section. Half of Figure 5a is devoted to information display and to available database function keys. Pavement identification is drawn from a database. The user can use the database function keys to delete, replace, clear or insert the current record, or to edit the first (<<), previous (<), next (>) or the last (>>) record of the database.

A list of 24 possible distress manifestations is also given in Figure 5a in a checkbox form. Clicking on "Explain" pushbutton in Figure 5a directs the user to an explanatory section as shown in Figure 5b. The user can learn more about any particular type of distress, with the aid of photographic images, by selecting the appropriate button in Figure 5b. Inspection of pavement is completed after the user has selected the appropriate checkbox(s) and pressed 'replace' or 'insert' database function key in Figure 5a.

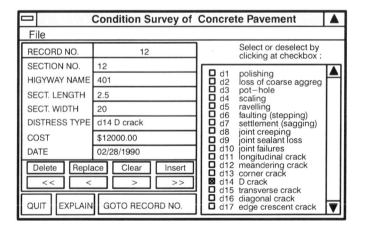

(a)

Figure 5 Typical screen displays of inspection system

Table 2 Guide for describing density of "D" cracks

CLASS	UNIFORM DESCRIPTION	GUIDELINES *
1	Few	< 10%
2	Intermittent	10 - 20 %
3	Frequent	20 - 50 %
4	Extensive	50 - 80 %
5	Throughout	80 - 100 %

* Based on percent of total pavement surface area in the pavement section affected by defect

Recommended procedure for surface condition evaluation of pavements as outlined in [9] are as follows :
1. Drive slowly over or walk along the road to visibly inspect the overall surface condition of the pavement.
2. Divide the road into appropriate sections with distinctive difference in uniformity and appearance.
3. Inspect each section to examine type, density and severity of distress.
4. Use the pavement distress manifestation classifications and the evaluation terminology, in accordance with the descriptive guidelines and illustrative photographs.
5. Complete the pavement condition rating form, which includes the evaluation of riding quality of the pavement surface.

AN OBJECT-ORIENTED SYSTEM FOR PAVEMENT INSPECTION

System description

A KBES is being developed at the Royal Military College of Canada, Kingston, to aid in the condition survey of concrete pavements. The goal of the expert system is to provide advice to inspectors concerning how to identify deficiencies in the condition evaluation process. Initial use of the system will be as a tutorial for inexperienced paving inspectors.

The expert system is being developed using information taken from current Pavement Maintenance Manuals [1,9]. The knowledge base is being developed on an IBM-compatible personal computer, using an object-oriented shell program [7] in a windowing environment.

The system being developed is highly user friendly with many graphics-oriented interface features such as interactive graphics, window management, explanation expansion and graphical representation of knowledge base by mapping graphic displays to and from conclusions.

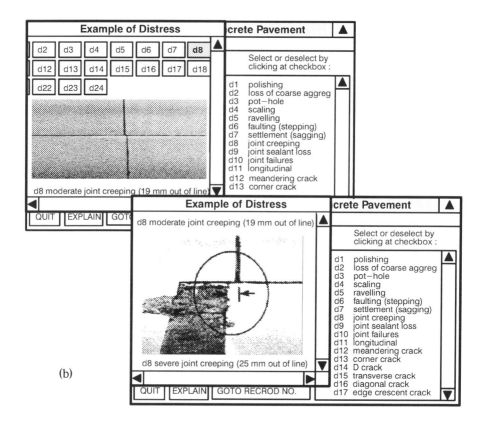

Figure 5 Typical screen displays of inspection system (cont.)

AN OBJECT-ORIENTED SYSTEM FOR DATA MANAGEMENT

System description

To maintain a huge network of highways, historic data as well as data to be collected from future inspection projects needs to be stored and managed properly and effectively. A system is being developed for database management. The system allows direct communication with external programs and databases, using a management system that integrates and controls the interaction between the knowledge base and the databases. Direct database access enables the system to read and write to files directly from within the knowledge base.

In an object-oriented database management system, data and procedures are coupled. The system views these database entities as objects, which are referenced and manipulated with standard Production Rule Language grammar. Each object combines attributes of procedures and data. The attributes of a class and their attribute types correspond to fields and field types in the external database. Instance of an attribute represents the records in a database.

Example

Figures 6a and 6b represent the typical screen images during a consultation session with the database management system. Figure 6a is the selection display which controls the display and search functions of the system. Depending on the selection option chosen by the user, the system can display data for all records one at time, search and display any record as specified by the user, search and display records related to a particular distress problem, or conduct a relational search. User can specify up to three criteria for the relational search (Figure 6a). The search (Figure 6b) was based on highway name and date of the inspection.

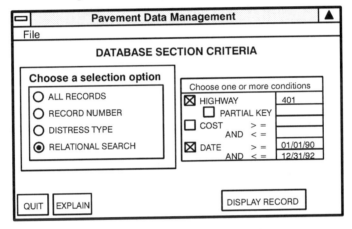

(a)

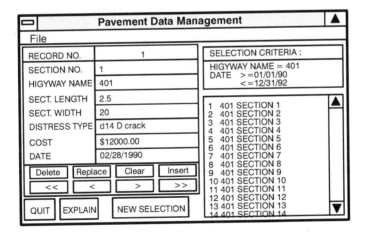

(b)

Figure 6 Typical screen displays for data management system

CONCLUSIONS

Economic and durable concrete pavements through an effective maintenance program can be achieved by exploiting the full potential of expert system technology. Fully developed knowledge-based expert systems can perform certain tasks, such as decision support, design aids and training more effectively and consistently than is possible with current tools and engineering aids.

The development of an object-oriented expert system for the condition survey of concrete pavements is described. The proposed system integrates the concepts of expert systems, object-oriented programming, relational database and graphics. The system is being developed on and for personal computers. The portable system can be used in the field by inspectors and in the office by management personnel.

REFERENCES

1.   CHONG, G J, JEWER, F and MACEY, K. Pavement Maintenance Guidelines: Distresses, Maintenance Alternatives, Performance Standards. Report SP-001, Ontario Ministry of Transportation and Communications, Downsview, 1982.

2.   WENTWORTH, J A. Overview of Expert Systems Activities in OECD Countries. Proceedings of the Second International OECD Workshop on Knowledge-Based Expert Systems in Transportation, Montreal, 1992.

3.   COX, B. Object-Oriented Programming : An Evolutionary Approach. Addison-Wesley Publishing Co., Menlo Park, California, 1988.

4.   PASCOE, G A. Elements of Object-Oriented Programming. Byte, Mc-Graw Hill, Inc., New York, 1986, pp 139-144.

5.   TESLER, L. Programming Experiences. Byte, Mc-Graw Hill, Inc., New York, 1986, pp 195-210.

6.   GOLDBERG, A and ROBSON, D. Smalltalk-80 : The Language and Its Implementation. Addison-Wesley Publishing Co., Menlo Park, California, 1985.

7.   INFORMATION BUILDERS INC. Level5 Object : User's Guide. New York, 1990.

8.   ACI COMMITTEE 201. Guide for Making a Condition Survey of Concrete Pavements (ACI 201.3R-86). American Concrete Institute, Detroit, 1986.

9.   CHONG, G J, PHANG, W A and WRONG G A. Manual for Condition Rate of Rigid Pavements : Distress Manifestations. Report SP-005, Ontario Ministry of Transportation and Communications, Downsview, 1982.

10.   STRATEGIC HIGHWAY RESEARCH PROGRAM. Distress Identification Manual for the Long-Term Pavement Performance Studies. National Research Council, Washington, D.C., 1990.

RECYCLING OF CONCRETE PAVEMENTS

W Wilk

Swiss Federal Institute of Technology

Switzerland

G Tsohos

Thessaloniki University.

Greece

Abstract The paper deals with the laboratory and in situ investigation of using recycled concrete material of old pavements as aggregate for the rehabilitation of concrete pavements. The test admixtures were designed with Ordinary Portland Cement (OPC) and recycled concrete material 66, 87 and 100 % of the whole aggregate. The concrete has been tested in Laboratory for flexural and compressive strength, air entrainment, frost resistance. In situ it has been tested additionally the skid resistance. The results have shown that the use of 100 % of recycled materials is possible. The concrete has been tested after 1 and 2 years to verify its strength. It has been examined in laboratory conditions (specimens, which have been kept in humidity conditions) and in situ conditions (cores). The results of strength resistance were satisfactory. It is obvious that the recycled concrete gives an attractive alternative to pavement rehabilitation, having the advantage to be friendly to environment.

Keywords, Concrete, recycling, aggregate, Ordinary Portland Cement (OPC), pavement, strength resistance.

Prof. Willy Wilk is a titular Professor at the Swiss Federal Institute of Technology, Zurich and Executive Vice President of the Research and Consulting Institute (TFB) of the Swiss Cement Industry. He has published many articles on the field of Cement and Concret Technology. He is member of various international and national scientific societies.

Dr. Georgios Tsohos, is Professor of Highway Engineering at the Thessaloniki University, Greece. His activities cover various subfects both on theoretical and laboratory domain. He has written 3 books and he has published more than 50 articles.

Concrete 2000. Edited by Ravindra K. Dhir and M. Roderick Jones.
© 1993 Published by E & FN Spon. ISBN 0 419 18120 2.

INTRODUCTION

The need to reuse or recycle existing pavement materials for the reconstruction and rehabilitation of portland cement concrete pavements is of increasing importance as it offers several advantages over the use of conventional materials and techniques. Among the major benefits are conservation of aggregates and energy as well as preservation of the environment and existing highway geometrics.

The recycling concept appears to be an attractive alternativ for pavement rehabilitation and maintenance, so it has been proposed and it has been accepted to rehabilitate a part of the National Highway N13 in Switzerland using the recyling technique. The construction has been executed during 1990 and 1991

Because of the existing pavement conditions, it has been decided to use the Cold Mix Process [1]. The mixture design covers 3 different mix proportions using 66 %, 87 % and 100 % of recycled material.

The recycled concrete, has been tested for compressive and flexural strength (in 3, 7 and 28 days), air entrainment, frost-thaw durability. In 1992 the compressive and flexural strength has been checked on specimens (kept in Laboratory from the construction phase) and on cores taken from the pavement.

In both cases the results, even with 100 % recycled material, were very satisfactory.

LABORATORY   RESEARCH

Materials
The recycled material, has been taken from the existing concrete pavement on National Motorway N13 (Oberriet-Haag). Its grading curve was according to Swiss specifications (SIA 162). An Ordinary Portland Cement (OPC) of on a mount 375 kg/m^3 complying with swiss specification SIA 215 was used.

Mix Proportions-fresh concrete
The used mix proportions are summarised in Table 1. Their gradings were according swiss specification SIA 162.

Table 1   Concrete admixtures

	Admixture				
Factor	1a (1990)	1b (1990)	2a (1990)	1c (1991)	2b (1991)
Aggregate	100 % recycled material (RM) (0-32 mm)	100 % RM (0-32 mm)	100 % natural sand (0-4 mm) 100 % RM (4-16 mm)	100 % RM 0-32 mm	40 % natural sand + 60 % RM (0-4 mm) and 100 % RM 4-32 mm
Admixtures: -air entrainment -plastifyer	Fro V5 – 0.8 % Plastiment FN – 0.8 %	Fro V5 – 0.8 % Sikacrete-PP1 2.4 %	Fro V5 – 0.8 % Sikacrete-PP1 2.4 %	Fro V5 – 1.3 % Sikament 10 0.71 % Sikafume-HR 4.75 %	Fro V5 1.3 % Sikament 10 0.71 % Sikafume-HR 4.75 %
W/C ratio	0.45	0.53	0.41	0.53	0.47
Compacting factor	1.34	1.38	1.33	1.20	1.28
Air content	6.2	5.7	6.4	5.5	5.0
Portion of re-cycled material in admixture (%)	100	100	66	100	87

Source [2]

From table 1 it can be remarked that:

a. the w/c-ratios are greater in comparison with conventional concrete, due to the greater water absorption of the cementious aggregates.

b. admixture 1c presents a low compacting factor, corresponding to a very good workability

c. the air content, with the exception of 1a and 2a is also good. That means sufficient frost resistance.

It has been also determined the chloride concentration (0.24 kg/m^3), which is very satisfactory. The Polished Stone Value (PSV) was equal to 50 (just the lowest permitted).

The comparison between our tests and the corresponding values given in bibliography, has been summarized in Tabel 2.

Table 2   Tests values of air content, w/c ratio, skid resistance and corresponding values from bibliography

	Authors' values	Bibliography values
Air content (%)	5.0 - 6.4	5.3 - 6.9
w/c-ratio	0.41 - 0.53	0.41 - 0.81
skid resistance (pendulum)	73 - 77	47 - 60

Source [3], [4], [5], [6], [7]

Hardened concrete properties

The following properties are of great importance for concrete pavements, namely frost durability, compressive and flexural strength. The measured frost resistance (Laboratory) is given in Table 3, while the compressive and flexural stresses are given in Figures 1 and 2 respectively.

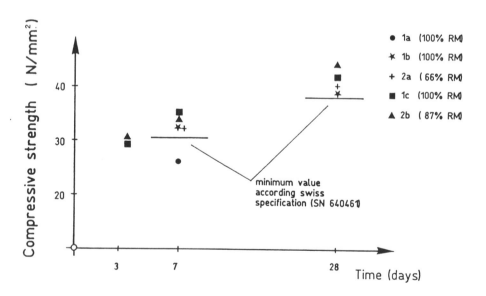

Fig. 1   Compressive strength (mean values) as function of concrete age

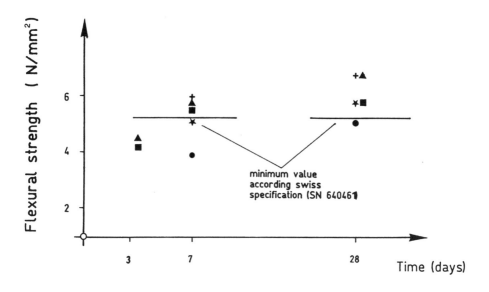

Fig. 2   Flexural strength (mean values) as function of concrete age

Table 3 Frost resistance of various concrete admixtures

Mixe	1a	1b	2a	1c	2b
Frost resistance (%)	50 - 80	50 - 80	> 80	50 - 80	> 80

Frost resistance (%)		
	> 80	good
	50 - 80	medium
	< 50	poor

Source [2]

CONTROL DURING CONSTRUCTION

During the construction it has been tested the strength of concrete (on cylindrical specimens of 28 days), the frost resistance and it has been also measured the skid resistance, using the Pendulum device (Table 4).

Table 4 Concrete properties during construction

| Property | Admixture | | | | | |
	1a	1b	2a	1c	2b	min. value according swiss norms
Compressive strength (N/mm^2)	32.4	38.3	39.7	42.2	44.3	38.0
Flexural strength (N/mm^2)	5.04	5.74	6.70	5.66	6.61	5.20
Frost resistance (%)	50 - 80	50 - 80	> 80	50 - 80	50 - 80	> 50
Skid resistance	77	74	78	73	76	> 50

LONG TERM BEHAVIOUR

Specimens of the placed concrete have been taken and they have been stored (in 18 °C temperature and 40 % moisture). In July 1992 new specimens were bored and the existing-compressive and flexural strength on all specimens has been measured. The results are given in Table 5.

Table 5 Strength development of recycled concrete

| Admixture | % recycled material | Compressive strength (N/mm^2) | | | | | |
| | | 28 days | | 1 year | | 2 years | |
		L	S	L	S	L	S
1a	100 %	38.8 ± ?	32.4±0.2	---	---	39.1±0.1	41±2.9
1b	100 %	45.8 ± ?	38.3±1.6	---	---	39.3±1.0	39.9±2.7
2a	66 %	(?)	39.7±2.6	---	---	32.5±1.6	40.5±3
1c	100 %	38.2±2.3	42.2±2.5	47.1±2.3	45.8±0.8	---	---
2b	87 %	46.1±3.6	44.3±3.8	46.4±3.7	45.9±1.0	---	---

| Admixture | % recycled material | Flexural strength (N/mm^2) | | | | | |
| | | 28 days | | 1 year | | 2 years | |
		L	S	L	S	L	S
1a	100 %	5.5 ± ?	5±0.4	---	---	3.6±0	4.1±0.1
1b	100 %	7.0 ± ?	5.7±0.15	---	---	3.8±0.1	4.4±0
2a	66 %	(?)	6.7±0.4	---	---	2.8±0.1	3.7±0
1c	100 %	5.6±0.6	5.7±0.7	9.4±0.7	8.5±0.5	---	---
2b	87 %	5.7±0.8	6.6±0.25	8.4±0.3	7.2±0.2	---	---

L = specimens in laboratorium the flexural strength has been determined of split tests
S = specimens in situ
?: not statistical sufficient values

The main remark regarding Table 5 is that the strength of a concrete with 100 % recycled material is not less than any other of the examined proportions (87 % and 67 %).

COMPARISON WITH THE INTERNATIONAL EXPERIENCE

The strength comparison between various concrete types made with recycled materials appears many difficulties, as the strength depends on factors like w/c ratio, cement type, mix design, curing etc. In Figures 3 and 4 are given the results of, such a comparison based on bibliography [3], [7], [8], [9], [10].

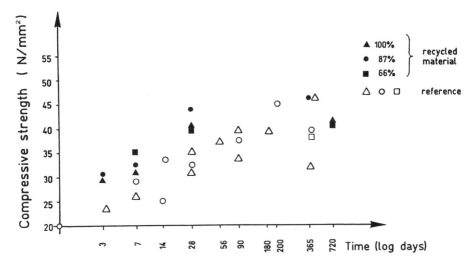

Fig. 3   Compressive strength as function of the time (authors' and references results).

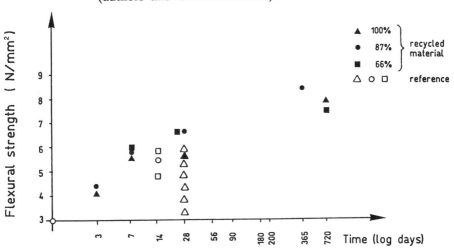

Fig. 4   Flexural strength as function of the time (authors' and references results).

CONCLUSIONS

The research concludes:

a.   The use of recycled concrete as aggregate can be used up to 100 %, without any disadvantages, as its strength is similar to those of concrete with recycled material 87 % or 67 %.

b.   The w/c ratio has to be kept higher than the conventional one, because of the greater water absorption of the cimentious aggregates. The higher w/c ratio has no influence on concrete strength.

c.   The long term behariour is satisfactory

d.   It has to be payed great attention, during the mix design phase, for receiving a frost durable concrete. It is clear that more research work has to be undertaken

e.   The comparison of strength to other research works has shown that both compressive and flexural strength is generally better.

f.   The long time development of the strength is not the expected one. In any case it is also sufficient.

The recycled concret for pavements will gain importance in the next 20 years as it is an alternativ of many advantages as energy and natural resources saving, satisfactory technical behaviour, minimization of enviromental pollution. The main problem is to be recognised, especially from the public authorities, its advantages. This task is our responsibility.

ACKNOWLEDGEMENTS

The authors would like to express their appreciation to all collaborators at the TFB (Technical Research and Consulting office) of the swiss cement industry, for their help to realize this research project. They also thank the VSS (Swiss Union of Highway Engineers) for its financial support.

REFERENCES

1. TRANSPORTATION RESEARCH BOARD. Guidelines for Recycling Pavement Materials. National Cooperative Highway Research Program Report 224, TRB, September 1980, pp. 36-37.

2. WILK W., TSOHOS G., WERNER R. Neue Betondecken aus Betonrecyclingmaterial, Zwischenbericht 1991, Wildegg, Switzerland 1991 pp. 19-23.

3. NIXON P. J. Recycled concrete as an aggregate for concrete-a review. RILEM, Matériaux et constructions, no 65, 1978 pp 372, 374

4. VAN MATRE F. R. - SCHUTZBACH A. M. Illinois experience with recycled concrete inlay. Proceedings 4th International Conference on Concrete Pavement Design and Rehabilitation, Purdue University, USA 1989 pp. 663.

5. DE PAUW C. Beton recyclé CSTC-Revue, No 2, Juin 1980 pp. 9-10.

6. FRONDISTOU-YANNAS S. Waste Concrete as Aggregate for new concrete. ACI Journal, August 1977 pp. 375.

7. YRJANSON W. A. Recycling Portland Cement Concrete. Proceedings, 2nd International Conference on Concrete Pavement Design and Rehabilitation, Purdue University USA 1981, pp 433

8. HANSEN T. C. Recycling of demolished concrete and masonry. Report of Technical Committee 37 - DRC Demolition and Reuse of Concrete, RILEM, E and FN SPON, London 1992 pp. 61

9. BUCK A. D. Recycled Concrete as a Source of Aggregate. ACI Journal, May 1977, pp. 217

10. BAIRAGI M.K. - VIDYADHARA H. S. - RAVANDE K. Mix design procedure for recycled aggregate concrete, Construction and Building Materials, Vol. 4, No. 4, 1990 pp. 192

A MECHANISTIC METHOD FOR ESTIMATION
OF CONCRETE PAVEMENT PARAMETERS

A A Sha'at

Dundee Institute of Technology

United Kingdom

ABSTRACT. Current methods of evaluating the structural adequacy of highway and airport pavements are principally based on a subjective interpretation of the defects which are visible on the road surface. This approach may be satisfactory for determining the present serviceability of the road but not for predicting the future life or for determining the degree of strengthening required to extend the pavement life.

A description is given of a mechanistic method has been developed to estimate the dynamic Young's moduli of the main pavement structural layers from a deflection bowl measured by nondestructive deflection testing equipment. These moduli are used as input to a finite element mechanistic model for further analysis allowing computation of the critical stresses and strains, and the remaining life of the pavement based on fatigue and deformation mechanisms. The use of this methodology will provide the maintenance engineer with reliable estimate of the damage caused by the past traffic and the requirements for future traffic loading in order to minimise cost, manpower and time. This translates to substantial economic benefits for highway and airport authorities and for taxpayers and road users.

Keywords: NDT, Falling Weight Deflectometer, Deflection, Elastic Modulus, Concrete Pavement, Evaluation.

Dr. Ali Shaat obtained his BSc in Civil Engineering from Egypt in 1982. He worked in civil engineering design and construction in the Arabian Gulf for three years before joining the Queen's University in Belfast for his postgraduate studies. He obtained an MSc in 1986 and a PhD in 1989 in Highway and Airport Pavement Engineering. From 1989 to 1992, he worked at the Queen's University as a research fellow and P/T lecturer in concrete and pavement technology. Currently, he is a lecturer in Highway and Material Engineering at Dundee Institute of Technology. He has published 25 technical papers in pavement technology and has been involved in several major research and consultancy activities in the UK and overseas.

Concrete 2000. Edited by Ravindra K. Dhir and M. Roderick Jones.
© 1993 Published by E & FN Spon. ISBN 0 419 18120 2.

INTRODUCTION

In the mechanistic design and evaluation of pavement structure there are two major aspects of material properties which have to be considered. Firstly, the stress-strain characteristics of the material used in the various layers of the pavement structure need to be known so that analysis of stress and displacement of the deformable medium due to external environmental and loading conditions, can be performed. Traditionally, highway engineers express the stress-strain characteristics of a material using Young's modulus of elasticity (E) and Poisson's ratio (μ).   Secondly, it is essential to define the mechanisms which lead to loss of serviceability and eventual pavement failure.   Each distress mechanism must be expressed in terms of stresses, strains or deflections, so that it can be incorporated into an analytical model.

Component Approach

The current test methodologies used for collecting data on pavement material properties which used in evaluating the structural condition of a pavement are either destructive or nondestructive. The difference between them is normally dependent on physical disturbance of the pavement materials. The destructive test approach for obtaining critical concrete pavement evaluation data depend on extensive field sampling and laboratory testing. This is denoted as component approach which is not only expensive and time consuming but also lacks the consideration of materials loading and environmental condition variabilities.   Also, it is difficult to select a laboratory test procedure which models exactly the field stress, moisture and temperature gradient conditions, primarily because these are not known with certainty.   In addition, field destructive tests will severely impact the traffic operations in highways and commercial airfields.

System Approach

Fortunately, in recent years great strides have been made in the development of equipment that can rapidly and nondestructively collect data on which an estimate of the pavement material properties can be made with a reasonable degree of accuracy. Of particular importance in evaluating the structural condition of concrete pavements was the development of the Falling Weight Deflectometer (FWD) and the Deflectograph. These devices measure the surface deflection shape (bowl) produced from a stationary impulsive load or from a creep rolling wheel load, respectively. In the late 1980s, the author developed an evaluation methodology based on simplified layered elastic model and limiting stress/strain criteria [1]. From this work, it was determined that the deflection bowl produced by applying an NDT load to the pavement gives input parameters to an elastic layered system analysis that can be used to derive the strength parameters of the pavement layers. This is denoted as system approach which has a number of advantages over the component approach. The most significant advantage is that the system approach is an NDT full-scale testing of the pavement which realistically represents the actual traffic loading and the real interactions between any two layers in the system. This makes the system approach presented here, using in situ NDT, an economic, rapid and versatile method for determining the structural capacity of a pavement system.   The analogies and differences between the system approach and the component approach are illustrated in Figure 1.

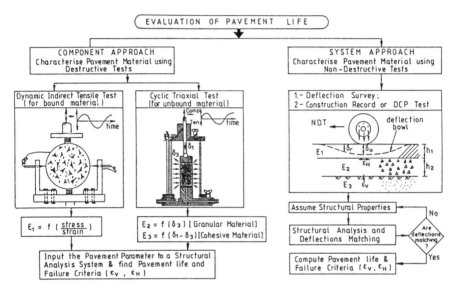

Figure 1 Approaches for evaluation of concrete pavement life.

NDT EQUIPMENT

The current deflection measuring equipment using NDT techniques are classified under three groups: (a) Rolling Wheel, (b) Stationary Transient Load; and (c) Wave Propagation. The procedure for concrete pavement structural evaluation presented herein is based on the measurement of deflection using a stationary or fixed transient load technique well known as the Falling Weight Deflectometer (FWD).   The principle of the FWD, schematically shown in Figure 2, is that a mass with a given weight drops from a certain height on a number of parallel rubber buffers, which act as springs, on a 300mm diameter rigid circular footplate. A properly designed mass configuration and springs are very important to achieving the desired peak stress, shape, and duration of the FWD force signal. This produces an impact load of 25-30 milliseconds duration, and a peak force of up to 250 KN, corresponding to the load on one wheel of a fully loaded Boeing 747.

The resulting pavement deflections are measured by means of seven velocity transducers (geophones) mounted on a beam which is lowered automatically with the loading plate during testing. The beam places one geophone at the centre of the loading plate and the other geophones at six different distances (up to 2100mm) from the plate. This is very important for capturing deflection bowl shape adequately for analysis purposes. Because geophones measure the velocity of the pavement surface, no reference point (or support as in the case of the Deflectograph) is needed. The deflection is obtained by integrating the velocity signal once.

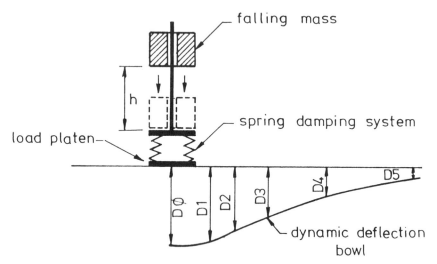

Figure 2 Schematic of Falling Weight Deflectometer and deflection bowl.

The high accuracy of the FWD is needed for the calculation of the layer elastic moduli. The deflections at some distance from the loading plate are used to evaluate the subgrade modulus. These deflections are often very small, they may be as small as 10-30 mm. If these deflections are not measured accurately, the modulus calculated for the subgrade will be incorrect. This will have some very important implications for the moduli calculated for the concrete layers in the pavement system. The subgrade usually contributes more than 60% of the total centre deflections. A small error in the determination of the subgrade modulus will, therefore, lead to very large errors in the moduli of the other pavement layers.

For the same reason it is essential to consider any non-linearity of the subgrade or a stiff layer within shallow depth. Most subgrades have moduli that increase with decreasing stress level. This means that the subgrade modulus may be considerably higher at some distance from the load than at the centre line. A similar effect can be caused by a stiff layer at some depth. The mechanistic model used in this paper is capable of considering non-linearity of subgrade as well as the depth to a rigid layer, if it is assumed that such a layer is present.

The deflection and load information from the geophones and load cell are fed into a PC computer which records them on A4 papers and 3.5 inch desk. The PC also controls the complete operation, including lowering the plate and deflection sensors to the pavement surface, raising the mass to predetermined drop heights, releasing the mass, recording the results, raising the loading plate and sensors, and signalling the operator at completion of the test. Results can be processed and stored in either metric or British units. The entire operation can be controlled by one person from the front seat of a tow vehicle and typically requires 45 seconds to complete an entire test sequence.

PAVEMENT DEFLECTIONS

When any type of load is placed on a rigid pavement slab, whether it be an aircraft gear or a bicycle, the slab will deflect nearly vertically to form a bowl shape. The deflection shape of the basin is a function of several variables, which can be categorised in two groups: (I) pavement characteristics and (II) environmental factors. Pavement characteristics include the thickness and elastic modulus (stiffness) of the slab, the stiffness of the underlying materials, the magnitude and duration of the applied load, presence of voids beneath the slab and joints and other discontinuities. For example, a strong concrete slab with a high elastic modulus on a weak subgrade material will produce the flat deflected shape of structure 2 in Figure 3. On the other hand, a weak concrete slab on a strong foundation will deflect as seen in structure 1 of Figure 3. This interaction between the elastic moduli of subgrade foundation and the concrete slab (E1 & E2) results in a characteristic deflection bowl for a given magnitude and duration of load and thickness of concrete.

Environmental factors such as temperature, season, and moisture condition. The vertical temperature differential TD (the algebraic difference between the temperatures of the top and bottom of a concrete slab) has a strong influence on the slab curl and vertical movement, with more pronounced effects on edges and corner deflections when compared with the effect of the horizontal movements on deflections due to a change in the average slab deflection. From the results of an extensive seasonal effects study carried out by the author it is recommended to perform FWD testing on concrete pavements during early morning hours to avoid high variation in TD values when evaluating load transfer at joints. Nevertheless, it should be mentioned that FWD testing at the middle of the slab, for stiffness calculations, does not vary with TD variations. Seasonal and moisture effects are found to be more significant for the foundation than for the concrete slab. During the spring thaw season, deflections are generally higher than other seasons. Therefore different moduli will be calculated for the deflection bowls measured in different seasons.

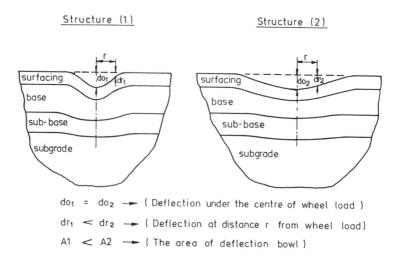

Figure 3 The characteristic shape of weak and strong deflected slabs.

Another set of pavement related factors affecting deflection measurements and hence backcalculated layer moduli are pavement discontinuities. The presence of pavement discontinuities such as cracks and/or joints, and subsurface conditions such as voids beneath concrete pavements will lead to higher deflection readings and hence lower moduli for all other factors being the same. The magnitude of the deflection increase is, however, dependent on the degree and severity of cracking and/or the joint opening. In addition to pavement discontinuities, deflection measurements are also affected by the presence of a rigid (rock) layer at some finite depth. The measured deflections decrease as the depth to rigid layer decreases. Ignoring rigid bottom considerations in the analysis can lead to substantial errors in the calculated layer moduli, particularly the subgrade.

CALCULATION OF ELASTIC MODULI

The determination of in-situ pavement elastic moduli based on measured performance parameters such as the deflection bowl is a field of growing interest for civil engineers since it involves NDT techniques of multilayer systems. However, there is no direct closed-form theoretical solution exists giving the elastic moduli of the pavement layers from measured deflection bowls using NDT. Such a procedure has to be an inverse technique that opposite to conventional approach which calculates the deflection bowl from given layer moduli. The inverse procedure is necessarily an iterative or trial and error process which will be denoted in this paper as 'backcalculation'.

The extensive findings of a parametric study and sensitivity analysis of 300 typical pavement structures resulted in the formation of an automatic iterative methodology for determining a set of layer elastic moduli based on the best fit technique using least squares theory [2] . This backcalculation methodology relies on generating theoretical deflection bowl using finite element method. The initial values of assumed moduli are then changed using a procedure of successive correction in order to obtain a best fit to the deflection bowl measured by the FWD. This involved choosing a set of initial modulus values, and computing the resulting absolute deflection bowl from these moduli. The computed deflections are compared to measured FWD deflections, and the initial user-supplied moduli are adjusted as a function of the magnitude of the difference in deflections. Then a set of moduli are interpolated which agrees with the measured deflections. This process is entirely repeated until the computed deflection bowl matches the measured FWD deflection bowl within the specified tolerance.

Structural Response Model

The selection of theoretical model to use in pavement design and evaluation depends in large part on the degree of sophistication and accuracy required, on the materials and other input properties available or required, on the responses to be analysed or backcalculated, and the cost of analysis involved.

The Finite Element Method (FEM) is one of the most advanced techniques in analysing complex structures. In this study the FEM program DEFPAV has been selected for further development and refinements to achieve the objective of pavement evaluation. The program was originally developed to solve problems of axi-symmetrical stress distribution in layered systems and named as DYNASTCO. This original form was then modified to calculate the permanent surface deformation (rutting), and the program was renamed as DEFPAV [3].

The basic assumption of the analysis is that the total deformation of a pavement is composed of a small recoverable component superimposed on cumulative permanent strains where the contribution to permanent set per wheel pass is infinitesimal. The elastic analysis, linear or non-linear, in this model employs the successive over relaxation technique to obtain the stress distribution. The first step in the analysis is to reduce the continuum to a system of discrete bodies. This is done by dividing the continuous structure into an assemblage of axi-symmetric 'discrete' or 'finite' elements.   These elements are interconnected at the circumferential joints and represent the structure by a number of ring elements, with rectangular sections as illustrated in Figure 4. Since the number of elements must be finite, the pavement structure is limited in the horizontal and vertical directions by a number of bearings at the nodal points. Element dimensions must be refined in the areas where stress gradients are expected to be large. The computer program, automatically generates the finite element mesh, so the amount of data introduced for running the program is nearly the same as for any of the traditional elastic layer computer programs used in pavement design and analysis [2].

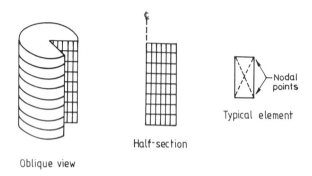

Oblique view

Half-section

—Nodal points

Typical element

(a) Finite Element Idealization of a Cylinder

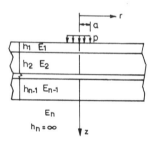

(b) Layered System

Fig. 4   TYPICAL LAYERED SYSTEM AND FINITE ELEMENT
IDEALIZATION

The concrete pavement is modelled as a system of horizontal layers of continuous, isotropic and homogenous materials, with constant thickness. Although pavement and subgrade materials are generally known to exhibit non-linear behaviour, in the present model, they are considered to be linear-elastic. This simplification is generally overcome by the fact that stress levels induced by the FWD loading are close to the ones induced by the actual traffic. Therefore, material characteristics that must be input for the use of the program for concrete pavements are: elastic moduli, Poisson's ratios and the material thicknesses.

New Model for Boundary Conditions

The main drawback of the described version of DEFPAV is that the program is limited to solve finite domain problems in both the vertical and horizontal directions. Therefore, the infinite depth of the foundation is neglected and hence the computed surface deflection is less than the real one. For this reason, the author is applying a considerable effort in re-writing the FEM code to consider the infinite thickness of the subgrade using a new infinite element boundary conditions. The new FEM model consider the concrete slab and 3 metres of the subgrade soil supported by an elastic foundation. The elastic foundation (infinite elements) are idealised into a finite number of dependent vertical large elements, each element is analogous to a massless elastic column of low stiffness in relation to the subgrade stiffness. In practice, such concept is exhibited by a dense liquid supporting a thick floating body. In the new model, the foundation stiffness matrix is diagonal, its non-zero elements being associated with only one displacement at each node (deflections). Thus the overall size of the structure stiffness matrix size is not really affected and hence the computational time is practically the same.

Mechanistic Model

The new FEM model was incorporated into an iterative computer program DEFBAC which backcalculate the elastic moduli of the concrete pavement from a measured FWD deflection bowl. DEFBAC is developed to determine a set of modulus values that provide the best fit between a measured deflection bowl and a computed deflection bowl. A set of simplified assumptions is used to validate the application of FEM for the backcalculation program DEFBAC.

1. Assumption inherent in the use of FEM elastic linear program to calculate concrete pavement response as described earlier are used. These are related to material properties, thickness information, boundary conditions, etc.

2. The peak dynamic force of the FWD is assumed to be equal to a pseudostatic load uniformly distributed on a circular area represented by the loading plate.

3. Thickness and flexural strength of the concrete slab is assumed to be known and exact (from as-built drawings and construction records).

4. Unbound road base/subbase and subgrade are combined into one foundation layer and characterised by an effective value of elastic modulus.

5.   The backcalculated moduli of concrete and subgrade are "dynamic" or time dependent in nature because they are derived from rapid FWD impulse loadings as opposed to static plate loadings.

The mechanistic model DEFBAC computes pavement elastic moduli, fatigue life, and remaining life. The initial set of moduli required to commence the backcalculation procedure is automatically provided by a set of predictive equations. These moduli predictive equations are functions of measured deflection bowl parameters from numerous FEM solutions for a wide range of structures and conditions. The convergence of the iterative procedure in DEFBAC will be more rapid and if the predicted initial moduli are close to the actual values. The backcalculated moduli, layer thicknesses and loading information are then input in the FEM structural response subroutine to compute the maximum tensile stress at the bottom of concrete layer and compressive strain in the subgrade. These parameters are then used to compute the concrete pavement fatigue life (N_f) and remaining life (N_r) in terms of number of standard axle loads to failure.

Fatigue and Remaining Life of Concrete Pavement

Concrete pavements are subject to fatigue under repeated loading, in the sense that they may crack under repeated applications of stress less than the modulus of rupture. As with most brittle materials there is a linear relation between the applied tensile stress and the logarithm of the number of applications of that stress which will cause cracking and failure. In DEFBAC mechanistic model, the load applications to failure are determined based upon the ratio of the maximum tensile stress to static flexural strength (referred to as the stress ratio) in the pavement concrete layer. It should be noted that the static flexural strength is equal to the modulus of rupture. Several relationships have been presented in the literature for the stress ratio versus load applications to failure[2]. The lower bound of these relationships showed that the concrete layer is capable of sustaining an infinite number of load applications if the stress ratio is less than 0.50. Analysis of the full-scale AASHTO concrete road test data has established the following relationship as used in DEFBAC:

$$N_f = 225,000(MR/\sigma_t)^4 \qquad (1)$$

where, σ_t = the tensile concrete stress (psi)
       MR = the concrete Modulus of Rupture (psi)

The modulus of rupture for the in-service concrete pavement layer is estimated from average modulus value backcalculated from the FWD deflection data on the same pavement. The following relationships are used to determine the modulus of rupture (MR) of the concrete layer:

$$MR = K(f_c)^{0.5} \qquad (2)$$

where, k = coefficient, range from 8 to 10, and

$$(f_c)^{0.5} = E/[33(\rho)^{1.5}] \tag{3}$$

E = concrete backcalculated elastic modulus (psi), and
ρ = density of concrete (pcf)

For DEFBAC mechanistic analysis, the density (ρ) of the concrete pavements is assumed to be 140 pcf and k is 9, so that

$$MR = E/6074 \tag{4}$$

The evaluation of fatigue life generally take place in two stages:

1. Tensile stress at the bottom of the concrete layer (σ_t), computed and expressed as a stress ratio (MR/σ_t) is used in equation (1) to obtain the fatigue life due to concrete cracking.

2. Maximum vertical compressive strain in the subgrade (ε) is computed to deal with permanent deformation (rutting) criterion. This is achieved using the following equation [4]:

$$N_f = (1.07 \times 10^{15})/\varepsilon^{3.57} \tag{5}$$

To account for the intermittent primary cracks, stresses and strains calculated from DEFBAC analysis are increased by a shift factor proposed [5], as follows: Tensile stresses in concrete layer are multiplied by 1.25 and compressive strain in subgrade by 2.5. The adjusted values are then used in assessing the fatigue lives from equations 1 and 5, and the lower value is taken as the design fatigue life.

The prediction of remaining life N_r (expressed in load repetitions) in a pavement must begin with an estimate of the past accumulated traffic Np (expressed in load repetitions). That is,

$$N_r = N_f - Np \tag{6}$$

If the remaining life (N_r) is less than the required extension, then the tensile stress at the bottom of the original concrete layer for an assumed overlay thickness is calculated using DEFBAC and new fatigue and remaining life are calculated as before. This step is repeated by increasing the overlay thickness until the required life extension is achieved.

SUMMARY

The DEFBAC finite backcalculation mechanistic computer program, which uses least squares deflection fitting technique, was developed as a convenient tool for estimation of concrete pavement parameters from FWD data. Use of finite elements model provides a rational approach to evaluating the structural integrity of in-service concrete pavements. The NDT procedure has the added advantages of being less costly, presenting less interference to normal highway and airfield functions, and providing the maintenance engineer with much more data for decision-making. In addition to their utility for arriving at structural pavement remaining lives and overlay thickness requirements, the values from NDT are useful for qualitative comparisons between one pavement area and another and for locating areas that may show early distress and that may warrant further investigation.

REFERENCES

1. SHAAT, AA, and FAROUKI, OT. Development of an analytical method for assessing the bearing capacity of roads and airfields. Proceedings of the 3rd International Conference on Bearing Capacity of Roads and Airfields, Vol. II, Norway, 1990. pp517-530.

2. SHAAT, A A. Evaluation of highway and airport pavement life based on non-destructive structural assessment techniques. PhD Thesis, The Queen's University of Belfast, UK, 1989.

3. KIRWAN, RW, SNAITH, MS, and GLYNN, TE. A computer based sub-system for the prediction of pavement deformation. Proceedings of the 4th International Conference on the Structural Design of Asphalt Pavements, Vol. I, USA, 1977. pp509-518.

4. BROWN, S F. Design of pavements with lean-concrete base. Transportation Research Board Record, Vol. 725, Washington, D.C., USA, 1979. pp12-18.

5. WALKER, RN, PATERSON, WDO, FREEME, CR, and MARAILS, CP. The South African mechanistic pavement design procedure. Proceedings of the 4th International Conference on the Structural Design of Asphalt Pavements, Vol. II, USA, 1977. pp363-415.

EVALUATION OF CORROSION INHIBITORS
FOR THE REHABILITATION OF RC STRUCTURES

B D Prowell

R E Weyers

I L Al-Qadi

Virginia Polytechnic Institute and State University

United States of America

ABSTRACT. In 1991, five corrosion inhibitors, surface applied   liquids and concrete admixtures, were identified as promising for the repair of reinforced concrete structures subject to chloride induced corrosion.

Small scale (1 ft.^{2}) reinforced concrete specimens were cast to evaluate the inhibitors effectiveness. A treatment matrix was established to evaluate the inhibitors performance on three ranges of corrosion activity and evaluate the effect of application time and drying. Corrosion rate measurements taken with a linear polarization device were used to monitor the inhibitors effectiveness.

The effect of the admixtures on the concrete properties, and the effect of the surface applied inhibitors on the overlay bond strength were evaluated. Rapid freeze-thaw tests were conducted to estimate the durability of the inhibitor modified concrete.

Three combinations of inhibitors were identified for large scale testing after ten months of accelerated chloride exposure. The larger specimens, removed from an actual bridge deck, were treated to test the effectiveness of the inhibitor field application techniques.

Keywords: Corrosion Inhibitors, Linear Polarization, Bond Strength, Freeze-Thaw Durability Post-Treatment, Reinforced Concrete.

Mr. Brian D. Prowell is an Instructor of Civil Engineering at the Virginia Polytechnic Institute and State University, Blacksburg, VA, USA. His current research includes: corrosion abatement measures and freeze-thaw durability of modified concretes.

Dr. Richard E. Weyers is a Professor of Civil Engineering at the Virginia Polytechnic Institute and State University, Blacksburg, VA, USA. He is Director of the Center for Infrastructure Assessment and Management. His current research includes: maintenance and rehabilitation of concrete bridge components, and service life prediction of reinforced concrete structures.

Dr. Imad L. Al-Qadi is an Assistant Professor of Civil Engineering at the Virginia Polytechnic Institute and State University, Blacksburg, VA, USA. His current research includes: pavement management systems, non-destructive evaluation, pavement and bridge rehabilitation, and asphaltic mixtures.

Concrete 2000. Edited by Ravindra K. Dhir and M. Roderick Jones.
© 1993 Published by E & FN Spon. ISBN 0 419 18120 2.

INTRODUCTION

Chloride induced corrosion of reinforced concrete is a monumental problem in efforts to maintain the transportation infrastructure in the United States. Standard methods used to rehabilitate decks include the patching of deteriorated areas and overlaying with either a preformed membrane bituminous concrete system, latex modified concrete, low slump dense concrete, or micro-silica concrete.

For substructures and superstructures, the deteriorated areas are removed and patched with either cast-in-place or shotcrete. These methods retard the corrosion process but not significantly.

This research was aimed at developing a durable repair and rehabilitation technique using corrosion inhibitors which will extend the service life of treated structures well into the 21st century. The task of developing repair and rehabilitation techniques using corrosion inhibitors for reinforced concrete structures was accomplished in three phases:

  I) Evaluation of Corrosion Inhibitors
  II) Evaluation of the Durability of Inhibitor Modified Concrete
  III) Development of Field Treatment Specifications

Initial corrosion inhibitor evaluations were carried out on 305 x 305 mm reinforced concrete specimens. Thirty-six specimens with varied ranges of corrosion activity were treated. Specimens were cast containing 1 or 2 triad(s) of reinforcing steel (rebar). After initial curing the specimens were alternately ponded with a 6% by weight salt water solution and allowed to air dry to induce corrosion.

Half-cell measurements were initially used to monitor the specimens corrosion activity. Once a drop in the corrosion potential indicated the initiation of corrosion activity, an unguarded linear polarization device, the 3LP, was used to monitor the corrosion rate. Chloride measurements were taken at the bar level prior to treatment.

Collins [1] identified 5 potential inhibitors, 3 commercial and 2 experimental materials used in four separate treatment methods, two of the inhibitors are used in combination. The inhibitors were applied in a 3 step treatment process. First, the chloride contaminated cover concrete was removed to the bar level. Next, an inhibitor was surface ponded on the specimen. A series of specimens were dried to 82° C at a depth of 13 mm below the bar level prior to inhibitor ponding. Finally, a 2" modified overlay was applied. The overlay concrete was tested for slump, air content, and compressive strength in accordance with the American Society for Testing and Materials (ASTM) specifications. Control specimens were also prepared for comparison purposes.

Once the treated specimens had cured, salt water ponding and corrosion rate measurements resumed. Corrosion rate measurements were used to determine which treatments would continue to be studied in Phase II.

Overlay bond strength tests were performed on 11 well cured small scale specimens prior to the treatment of the large deck specimens. Due to the bond reduction effects of 2 inhibitors, additional specimens were treated in an attempt to identify a procedure which would provide an acceptable bond between the original concrete and the overlay.

Freeze-Thaw durability tests were performed on the modified overlay concrete used in Phase II. Concrete samples were evaluated by ASTM C-666-84, "Resistance of Concrete to Rapid Freezing and Thawing," Procedure A.

The large scale specimens treated in Phase III were salvaged from a bridge deck removal project on Interstate 80 in Pennsylvania, USA. Three combinations of inhibitors and modified overlays were applied.   Both the 3LP and a linear polarization device with a guard ring electrode (Gecor Device) were used to monitor the corrosion rate of these specimens.

EVALUATION OF CORROSION INHIBITORS

Small Scale Specimen Design

Small scale specimens, 305x305x133 mm, were cast with both one and two triads of reinforcement steel. Each triad consisted of three electrically connected pieces of reinforcement steel, one placed at the specified cover depth, acted as the anode, and two acted as the cathode placed 44 mm below the anode. A typical configuration is shown in Figure 1.

ASTM grade 60 #4 bar with a nominal 13 mm diameter was used as reinforcing steel. The bars were cleaned with hexane and oven dried to remove any manufacturing latencies. The ends of the bar were covered with electroplating tape to provide a known length of corrodible steel, approximately 184 mm.

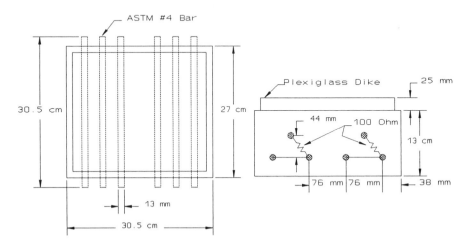

Figure 1 Two Triad Specimens

The specimens were cast in an inverted position from ready-mix concrete supplied to meet Virginia A4AE Bridge Deck Air Entrained concrete specifications. The cover depth of the specimens was varied from 25-52 mm along with the casting dates in order to vary the time to initiation of corrosion. The sides of the specimens were coated with epoxy to reduce the diffusion of oxygen and water-vapor simulating the boundary conditions on an actual bridge component.

After a three day moist curing period, plexiglass dikes 254x254x52 mm were attached to the top of each specimen to contain a salt water solution. The specimens were ponded with 400 ml of a 6% by weight NaCl solution on a weekly basis. The specimens were exposed to a 3 day wet/4 day air dry cycle to initiate corrosion.

The initiation of corrosion was identified with half-cell potentials in accordance with ASTM C-876-87 [2]. Once the initiation of corrosion was observed, corrosion current density (i_{corr}) measurements were made with the 3LP Device. The i_{corr} measurement is proportional to the corrosion rate through Faraday's Law. The device is based on the linear polarization resistance technique with changes in cathodic polarization currents measured at changes in potentials of 0, 4, 8, and 12 millivolts. The value of the Tafel slope constant, B, is 40.76 millivolts.

Further research by Clear correlated the i_{corr} measurement with the time to expected damage of the concrete. These guidelines were used to group the corrosion activity of the specimens prior to treatment as shown in Table 1 [3].

Corrosion Inhibitors

In previous research conducted by Collins [1], 7 corrosion inhibitors and 2 sealers were evaluated to determine their effectiveness in reducing corrosion rates in reinforced concrete specimens. The following 5 corrosion inhibitors were identified as showing promising results and recommended for further study:

1.   Alox 901 (proprietary oxygenated hydrocarbon produced by the partial oxidation of an aliphatic hydrocarbon): An organic inhibitor which is thought to form a protective film by conversion to a metallic soap [4].

2.   Cortec VCI-1337 [MCI-2020] (a proprietary blend of surfactants and amine salts in a water carrier): A secondary electrolyte layer inhibitor with appreciable vapor pressure under

Table 1 i_{corr} correlated to time to expected damage

i_{corr} $\mu A/cm^2$	TIME TO EXPECTED DAMAGE
$i_{corr} < 0.22$	None Expected
$0.22 < i_{corr} < 1.1$	Possible in 10-15 years
$1.1 < i_{corr} < 11$	2-10 years
$i_{corr} > 11$	< 2 years

atmospheric pressure or 'volatile corrosion inhibitor' (VCI) [5]. The product is designed to migrate in a vapor phase and adsorb on a metallic surface forming a mono-molecular film at both anodic and cathodic sites.

3.   Cortec VCI-1609 [MCI-2000] (proprietary alkanolamines): This product is designed to migrate and inhibit in a manner similar to VCI-1337 with the exception that it is a concrete admixture.

4.   DCI (calcium nitrite, $Ca(NO_2)_2$): The nitrite ions in this inhibitor compete with the chloride ions for the ferrous ions at the anode. The nitrite and ferrous ions react as follows:

$$2Fe^{++}+2OH^-+2NO_2 \rightarrow 2NO\uparrow +Fe_2O_3+H_2O$$

This reaction forms a stable passive layer on the reinforcement steel [6].

5.   Sodium borate ($Na_2B_4O_7$): An experimental inhibitor which forms a protective layer on metal surface through the reaction of borate and oxygen. This reaction appears to be highly dependent on the pH of the pore solution [7].

Treatment Procedure

The corrosion inhibitors were divided into four cells of surface ponding agents and concrete admixtures. The application concentrations were based on previous research by Collins [1]. An untreated latex modified overlay was included as a control in each cell combination. The treatments were applied to specimens with the chloride contaminated cover concrete removed to the rebar level. Table 2 presents the inhibitor combinations and application concentrations.

Three methods of application were used to apply the ponding agents. These include: 1 day ponding, 2 day ponding, and 1 day ponding of specimens dried to 82° C at 13 mm below the top reinforcement.

Additionally, 3 overlay systems were applied to specimens for which the chloride contaminated cover concrete was <u>not</u> removed. These systems were: 25 mm Latex Modified Concrete (LMC) overlay, 64 mm Hot Mix Asphalt (HMA) overlay with a waterproof membrane, and a thin polymer overlay.

Table 2 Treatment combinations

SURFACE PONDING AGENTS	OVERLAY ADMIXTURES
0.1M Alox 901 in Denatured Ethyl Alcohol	Dow Latex, 116 kg / m³
Cortec VCI-1337	Cortec VCI-1609, 0.6 kg / m³
0.1M DCI (Calcium Nitrite) in Water	DCI, 30 l / m³
0.1M Sodium Borate in Water	0.1M Sodium Borate in Mix Water
None	Dow Latex, 116 kg / m³

In order to investigate the effectiveness of the treatments on varying corrosion rates, the corroding specimens were divided into 3 categories based on time to expected damage as correlated to i_{corr} (see Table 1). A matrix was designed to incorporate the effect of different treatment procedures and materials on the range of corrosion rates.

Six cells within the matrix were investigated: 1 day ponding of specimens for which damage was expected in 10-15 and 2-10 years (based on pretreatment i_{corr}), 2 day ponding of specimens for which damage was expected in 10-15 years, 1 day ponding of specimens dried to 82° C at a depth of 13 mm below the bar level for which damage was expected in 10-15, 2-10 and < 2 years. The industry standard overlays were applied to specimens for which damage was expected in 10-15 years.

EVALUATION OF CORROSION INHIBITORS

Pre-treatment Corrosion Rate Measurements

Three methods were used to indicate corrosion activity prior to treatment: CSE half-cell potentials, 3LP linear polarization corrosion current density measurements, and chloride ion measurements taken at the level of the reinforcing steel.

Chloride measurements were taken as a function of depth in 13 mm increments starting at a depth of 6 mm. The chloride ion concentration of the powdered sample was measured using the specific ion probe method developed at Virginia Tech [8]. The method uses an acid based solution to digest 3 grams of the sample.

The average i_{corr} values, CSE potentials and chloride concentrations at the bar level are shown in Table 3 for each treatment cell. The measurements were taken immediately prior to treatment. The corrosion rate, as measured by the 3LP was greater than 0.22 $\mu A/cm^2$ for all of the specimens prior to treatment. Some of the CSE corrosion potentials were numerically larger (more noble) than -350 mV, the threshold established in ASTM 876 for a 90% probability if active corrosion [3]. However, all but 3 of the specimens had corrosion potentials more negative than -240 mV [9]. The chloride ion content of all of the specimens was greater than 0.71 kg/m^3.

Analysis of Inhibitor Effectiveness

Two objectives were identified for the evaluation of the corrosion inhibitors, the first was to determine which, if any, of the inhibitors would be successful in the chemical abatement of corrosion. The second was to determine the most effective method of application.

The effectiveness of the inhibitor treatments was primarily based on i_{corr} measurements obtained from the 3LP. In the case of the two triad specimens the i_{corr} measurements shown are the average value for the two top bars.

The post-treatment i_{corr} values for the control overlays are shown in Figure 2. The control overlays represent typical treatment methods used in current practice. Since the impermeable nature of the HMA overlay with a waterproof membrane, and the thin polymer overlay would

Table 3   Average pre-treatment i_{corr}, CSE potential and chloride ion content at the level of the reinforcing steel for each treatment cell

TREATMENT CELL	i_{corr} $\mu A/cm^2$		CSE POTENTIAL -mV		Cl⁻ CONTENT kg/m^3	
	Mean	σ_x	Mean	σ_x	Mean	σ_x
Low Initial i_{corr}, Controls	1.84	0.82	310	49	2.0	0.5
High Initial i_{corr}, Dried Specimens	17.16[1]	11.65	475	17	26.1	1.8
ML Initial i_{corr},1 Day Ponding	1.76	0.45	271	42	1.9	0.3
ML Initial i_{corr},2 Day Ponding	1.72	0.63	290	54	1.7	0.4
Medium Initial i_{corr}, 1 Day Ponding	6.56	1.62	550	16	14.8	1.6
ML Initial i_{corr}, Dried Specimens	1.24	0.14	398	22	2.3	1.0
Low Initial i_{corr}, Dried Specimens	0.36	0.05	233	50	2.6	1.9

[1] The unusually high i_{corr} (40.33 $\mu A/cm^2$) measured for specimen 1H-1D-AX may have been the result of a micro-crack above the bar which may have allowed a direct circuit to form between the probe and the reinforcing steel. An i_{corr} of 11.76 $\mu A/cm^2$ was estimated for the specimen based on a linear regression using the chloride concentration as a predictor variable for i_{corr}.

prevent i_{corr} measurements from being taken, the measurements were taken from the bottom of the specimen with the resistor(s) connecting the upper and lower mats of steel disconnected immediately prior to the measurement.

Both the 25 mm LMC overlay (2M-LMC), where the chloride contaminated concrete was left in place, and the 51 mm LMC overlay where the chloride contaminated concrete was removed to the bar level (2L-0-LMC), show an increase in i_{corr} immediately after treatment as shown in Figure 2. However, later measurements indicated a reduction in corrosion rate. Both the specimens treated with the HMA overlay (2L-BC) and the thin polymer overlay (2L-TP) exhibit a greater than 50% decrease in i_{corr} after treatment. However, at no time did the corrosion rate of either specimen drop below 0.22 $\mu A/cm^2$ indicating that corrosion had not ceased.

The reduction in corrosion rate exhibited by all of the control specimens was probably the result of a decreased moisture content due to the impermeable and low-permeable overlays. It must be noted that all of the control overlays were applied to specimens with relatively low initial corrosion rates, field performance indicates that these overlays are often not effective in the long term.

A specimen identification code was developed for remainder of the small scale specimens based on the specimen configuration, initial corrosion activity, and applied treatment. For example,

Code: 1H-1D-DCI

1H   →   A specimen containing one triad of reinforcing steel, with a high initial corrosion rate as defined by Table 1.

1D   →   The specimen was dried to 82 °C. at a depth of 13 mm below the reinforcing steel, and ponded with the corrosion inhibitor for 1-day.

DCI →   The corrosion inhibitor applied to the specimen according to Table 2.

Figures 3-5 present the post-treatment performance of select cells. Two inhibitors Alox and Cortec, demonstrated their ability to reduce corrosion, regardless of the pre-treatment i_{corr}. Alox seemed to perform better than Cortec if the specimens were not dried prior to ponding. This is probably due to the ethyl alcohol, used as a solvent, displacing some of the capillary water and allowing more of the inhibitor to be absorbed.

In Figure 3, the specimens treated with Alox and Cortec (1H-1D-AX and 1H-1D-COR) showed dramatic decreases in corrosion rate immediately after treatment. Since the control specimen did not decrease as rapidly, this decrease must be the result of the reaction of the corrosion inhibitors with the corrosion cell. The corrosion activity of the specimen treated with Cortec virtually ceased based on its corrosion rate ($< 0.22 \, \mu A/cm^2$) for the period between 56 and 229 days after treatment. At the end of observation period, both specimens had stabilized at an average corrosion rate of 1.9 $\mu A/cm^2$. Similar trends are seen in Figures 4-5. In Figure 4, the specimen treated with Alox demonstrated a mean i_{corr} of 0.10 $\mu A/cm^2$ from 89 days after treatment till the end of the survey. These measurements indicate the cessation of corrosion.

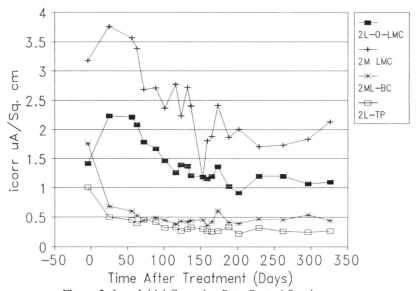

Figure 2 Low Initial Corrosion Rate Control Specimens.

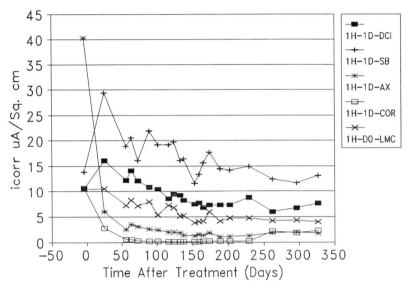

Figure 3 High Initial Corrosion Rate, Dried Specimens

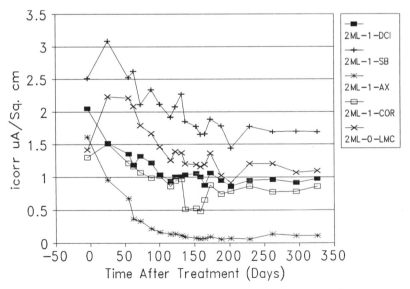

Figure 4 Medium-Low Initial Corrosion Rates, 1 Day Ponding

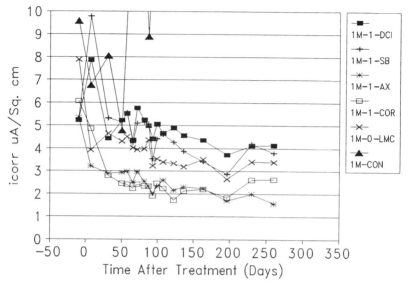

Figure 5 Medium Initial Corrosion Rate, 1 Day Ponding

The LMC controls demonstrated the next best overall performance. Removing the chloride contaminated concrete above the rebar reduced the driving potential for the corrosion reaction. In addition, the fresh concrete helped to reestablish the high pH normally found in uncontaminated concrete.

DCI proved to be an effective treatment when applied to specimens with low initial corrosion rates. Its lack of performance at higher i_{corr} rates may be concentration dependent. Research conducted by Berke *et al* [6], concluded that for inhibition to occur, the chloride:nitrite ratio must be less than two. The concentration used for surface application on the small scale specimens was 0.1 M as recommended in research performed by Dressman *et al* [10]. The concentration used in a similar study on U.S 460 [11] was 15% solids by weight which is 11.4 times more concentrated than 0.1 M. Therefore, an effort was made to estimate the nitrite content at the bar level for each of the specimens treated with DCI [12]. By comparing these estimated values with the pretreatment chloride ion contents chloride:nitrite ratios were determined. All of the specimens with chloride:nitrite ratios less than two (2ML-1-DCI, 2ML-2-DCI, and 1L-D1-DCI) performed better than the LMC controls in their corresponding cells, see Figure 4.

Though some specimens treated with sodium borate showed improvement, in no case did the inhibitor perform as well as the LMC controls. An examination of early research on sodium borate indicates that its inhibitive action may be highly pH dependent, making it unsuitable for this application [13].

No increased inhibitive effect could be discerned for non-dried specimens with similar i_{corr}

values ponded for 2 days as compared to specimens ponded for only 1 day. The capillaries of the non-dried specimens used in the comparison were probably filled with water, allowing a finite amount of absorption independent of ponding time. The effectiveness of drying appears to be dependent on the type of inhibitor used.

DURABILITY OF INHIBITOR MODIFIED CONCRETE

Phase II of the inhibitor evaluation included measuring the effects of the inhibitors used as admixtures on the properties of the fresh and hardened concrete. The effect of the surface applied inhibitors on the bond between the overlay and substrate concrete was also examined. Alox 901, the Cortec products and DCI were included in this phase of the evaluation. Sodium Borate was not included since it had not proved effective in corrosion abatement.

Properties of Fresh and Hardened Concrete

The modified overlays for the small scale specimens were based on Virginia Class A4AE Bridge Deck Air Entrained Concrete specifications. The mix design used type I cement for all mixes with a ratio of cement to fine aggregate to coarse aggregate of (1.00:1.75:3.00). The fine aggregate was a natural sand and the coarse aggregate was a 10 mm crushed limestone. A design water cement ratio of 0.45 was used for all mixes. The high percentage of the 10 mm coarse aggregate used in the initial mixes often produced a harsh concrete. The latex modified concrete was produced by adding 116 kg/m^3 of latex to the standard mix and reducing the water content by 104 kg/m^3. Calcium nitrite is a strong set accelerator. Therefore, a high range water reducer and a retarder were added to the DCI mixes according to the manufacturer's recommendations.

The average properties of the fresh and hardened corrosion inhibitor modified concrete are presented in Table 4. Both Cortec 1609 and DCI tended to reduce the amount of entrained air in the plastic concrete. This deficiency was easily mediated by increasing the dose of the air entrainment agent.

Concrete Resistance to Rapid Freeze-Thaw Cycles

Concrete beams cast from concrete used for the large scale specimens (Phase III) were tested in accordance with ASTM C-666, Procedure A, "Resistance of Concrete to Rapid Freezing and Thawing." The specimens are supported in water and cycled between 22.2 and -17.8° C (40-0° F) in a period of approximately 4 hours. In addition, beams were cast from a normal concrete mix without any inhibitors added for comparison. The air content of the plastic concrete, number of cycles of exposure, and durability factor are presented in Table 5. The calculated durability factor is the average of 2 beams with the exception of the LMC beam. Two sets of Cortec modified beams were tested, Cortec 1609 was added to the first set at the rate of 0.6 kg/m^3 and 1.2 kg/m^3 for the second. The only inhibitor which exhibited any detrimental effects on freeze-thaw durability was DCI. However, the DCI set also had a lower plastic air content than the other specimens.

Table 4   Average properties of fresh and hardened inhibitor modified concrete

ADMIXTURE	SLUMP mm	AIR CONTENT %	28 DAY STRENGTH MPa
Cortec 1609	33	5.4	34
DCI (Calcium Nitrite)	31	5.3	48
Latex	165[1]	10.0	33

[1] Measured 5 minute after mixing.

Evaluation of Bond Strength

The bond strength between the modified overlay and base concrete was measured for 11 specimens 160 days after treatment to determine the effects of the corrosion inhibitors. A poor bond strength would indicate that the overlay would probably delaminate and spall under traffic loadings and freeze-thaw cycles. The bond strength was measured using a method described in American Concrete Institute 503R. A 51 mm core is drilled through the overlay into the substrate concrete. A device is affixed to the surface of the core using a quick set epoxy grout. A dynamometer is used to measure the tensile force required to pull out the core. A tensile force of 1112 N at failure was selected as the minimum acceptable bond strength [13]. The mean bond strength values are presented in Table 6.

Both Alox and Cortec demonstrated detrimental effects on bond strength. Therefore, attempts were made to find measures which would improve the bond strength. Light sandblasting proved effective for both the Alox and Cortec treatments. Average bond strengths for 3 tests were obtained of 4061 and 3781 N for Alox and Cortec respectively.

DEVELOPMENT OF FIELD SPECIFICATIONS

The large scale specimens were treated in order to develop field application specifications. They were salvaged from a bridge deck replacement project on Interstate 80 in

Table 5   Durability factors for inhibitor modified concrete

MIX DESIGN	PLASTIC AIR CONTENT	NUMBER OF CYCLES OF EXPOSURE	DURABILITY FACTOR
DCI-1	5.3%	240	91
Cortec-1	6.5%	315	100
Cortec-2	6.4%	315	100
Normal-1	6.8%	265	100
Latex-1	10.5%	215	100

Table 6 Mean bond strength values for inhibitor modified concrete overlays

TREATMENT	NUMBER OF OBSERVATIONS	MEAN BOND STRENGTH N	σ_{n-1} N
Alox 901/Latex	9	445	543
Cortec 1337/1609	9	534	792
DCI/DCI	9	3959	792
LMC Overlay	6	4137	1099

Pennsylvania. The 203 mm thick, large scale specimens ranged in size from 1.25-2.11 m^2 Prior to treatment a corrosion survey was conducted on the slabs. In addition to the evaluation methods used on the small scale specimens the Geocisa Gecor Device, a linear polarization device with a guard ring electrode, was used to measure corrosion current densities.

The surface ponding technique used for the small scale specimens would be difficult and expensive under field conditions. Therefore, the surface applied corrosion inhibitors were sprayed on the slabs using a 1.9 l (½ gal) polyethylene garden sprayer. Three equal applications were applied to the slab, the second application was applied ½ hour and the third 12 hours after the initial spraying. The spraying rates for a single application are shown in Table 7. The application rates were determined by spraying the surface until it appeared to be uniformly saturated, and then dividing the area of the slab by the volume of inhibitor used. The overlays placed on the large scale specimens were based on the mix designs used for the small scale specimens. After curing, the slabs were placed in an outdoor exposure area.

Due to the amount of time necessary to take i_{corr} readings on the slabs using both the 3LP and the Geocisa device, measurements were taken simultaneously on different slabs. Therefore, measurements were taken on the same date and not the same number of days before or after treatment. For this reason only trends may be compared.

A comparison between pre- and post- 3LP i_{corr} readings is shown in Table 8. The slabs treated with both Alox and DCI show an increase in i_{corr} as measured by the 3LP after treatment. This may be due in part to the overlay concrete increasing moisture content of the treated slab thereby allowing a greater area of polarization and/or decreasing the concrete's resistance at the rebar level and thus increasing the corrosion rate. The second set of readings

Table 7 Spray application rates

SURFACE APPLIED INHIBITOR	APPLICATION RATE m^2/l
Alox 901	1.7
Cortec VCI-1337	5.5
DCI (Calcium Nitrite)	3.7

on the Alox slab demonstrate a decreasing trend in 3LP i_{corr}. However, the mean value is still greater than the pre-treatment values.

The deck section treated with Cortec shows a 17% decrease in corrosion rate after treatment. All of the slabs will require additional monitoring to assess the effectiveness of the corrosion treatments. It must be noted that the objective of this phase of the study was to develop field application techniques.

Theoretically, the guard-ring electrode on the Geocisa device should confine the area of polarization and provide a better estimate of the corrosion activity after treatment. The mean pre- and post-treatment Geocisa i_{corr} measurements are shown in Table 9.

The slab treated with Alox demonstrated a 21% initial decrease in i_{corr}. The mean i_{corr} for the second set of readings was equal to pretreatment values. Cortec was shown to be very effective with a 77% decrease in i_{corr} from the mean pre-treatment readings. This reduction corresponds to the trend indicated by both the CSE potential and the 3LP i_{corr} measurements.

The deck section treated with DCI showed a 96% increase in corrosion rate between its

Table 8   Pre- and post-treatment mean 3LP i_{corr} readings ($\mu A/cm^2$) for the inhibitor modified slabs

TREATMENT	PRE-TREATMENT				POST-TREATMENT			
	Days Prior	i_{corr}	Days Prior	i_{corr}	Days After	i_{corr}	Days After	i_{corr}
Alox 901	77	1.28	50	1.16	34	2.94	52	2.29
Cortec	70	1.31	44	1.34	40	1.10	58	1.20
DCI	46	2.34	20	2.25	36	4.08	65	4.46

Table 9   Pre- and post-treatment mean geocisa i_{corr} readings ($\mu A/cm^2$) for the inhibitor modified slabs

TREATMENT	PRE-TREATMENT				POST-TREATMENT			
	Days Prior	i_{corr}	Days Prior	i_{corr}	Days After	i_{corr}	Days After	i_{corr}
Alox 901	77	.071	50	.073	34	.057	52	.074
Cortec	70	.132	44	.168	40	.035	58	.052
DCI	46	.107	20	.164	36	.315	65	.329

highest pre-treatment average (.164 $\mu A/cm^2$) and the mean of its post-treatment average. This indicates an increase in corrosion activity after treatment even though the slab was sprayed with the manufacturers recommended concentration of DCI. Though this research indicates DCI may not be successful at corrosion abatement, long term data is needed to draw a firm conclusion.

CONCLUSIONS

The use of corrosion inhibitors in combination with removing the chloride contaminated concrete to the level of the reinforcing steel can be used to significantly extend the service life of repair to reinforced concrete structures subject to chloride induced corrosion. This technique is more cost effective than replacement and will provide a long term durable repair.

ACKNOWLEDGEMENTS

The Research described herein was supported by the Strategic Highway Research Program (SHRP). This paper represents the views of the authors only, and is not necessarily reflective of the views of the National Research Council, the views of SHRP, or SHRP's sponsor. The results reported here are not necessarily in agreement with the results of other SHRP research activities. They are reported to stimulate review and discussion within the research community.

REFERENCES

1. Collins, W. D., "Chemical Treatment of Corroding Steel Reinforcement After Removal of Chloride Contaminated Concrete," M.S. thesis, Virginia Polytechnic Institute and State University, Blacksburg, VA, 1991, 168 pp.

2. "Standard Test Method for Half-Cell Potentials of Uncoated Reinforcing Steel in Concrete," C-876-87, Annual Book of ASTM Standards, ASTM, Philadelphia, PA, 1987, pp. 563-570.

3. KCC Inc. 3LP Package: Test Procedures, Data Analysis, and General Information, July 1990.

4. "Chemical Intermediates Oxygenated Hydrocarbons," Technical Data Sheet, Alox Corporation, Niagara Falls, NY, 1990, 2 pp.

5. Miksic, B.A., "Use of Vapor Phase Inhibitors for Corrosion Protection of Metal Products," Corrosion 83, No. 308, NACE, Houston, TX, 1983, 14 pp.

6. Berke, N.S. and A. Rosenberg, "Technical Review of Calcium Nitrite Corrosion Inhibitor in Concrete," Transportation Research Record, No. 1211, 1991, pp. 18-27.

7. Dillard, J.G., J.O. Glanville, T. Osiriff, and R.E. Weyers. "Surface Characterization of Reinforcing Steel and the Interaction of Steel with Inhibitors in Pore Solution," Transportation Research Record 1304, TRB National Research Council, Washington, D.C., 1991, pp. 122-128.

8.   Henry, M. B., <u>Rapid Analysis of Chloride Content of Contaminated Concrete</u>, M.S. thesis, Virginia Polytechnic Institute and State University, Blacksburg, VA, 1992, 160 pp.

9.   "Protective Systems for New Prestressed and Substructure Concrete," <u>Report No. FHWA/RD-86/193</u>, U.S Department of Transportation, Federal Highway Administration, April 1987, 126 pp.

10.   Dressman, S., T. Osiriff, J.G. Dillard, J.O. Glanville, and R.E. Weyers. "A Screening Test for Rebar Corrosion Inhibitors," <u>Transportation Research Record</u> 1340, TRB National Research Council, Washington, D.C., 1991, pp. 135-139.

11.   Berke, N.S., M.P. Dallaire, R.E. Weyers, M.B. Henry, J.E. Peterson, and B.D. Prowell, "Impregnation of Concrete with Corrosion Inhibitors", <u>Corrosion Forms and Control for Infrastructure</u>, <u>ASTM STP 1137</u>, Victor Chaker, Ed., American Society for Testing and Materials, Philadelphia, 1992, pp. 300-327.

12.   Prowell, B. D., <u>Evaluation of Corrosion Inhibitors for the Repair and Rehabilitation of Reinforced Concrete Bridge Components</u>, M.S. Thesis, Virginia Polytechnic Institute and State University, Blacksburg, VA, August 1992, 216 pp.

13.   Webster, L.A., T. Osiroff, J.G. Dillard, J.O. Glanville, and R.E. Weyers. "Electromechanical Studies of Rebar Corrosion and Inhibition in Simulated Pore Solution," <u>Transportation Research Record</u> 1304, TRB National Research Council, Washington, D.C., 1991, pp. 167-176.

14.   Personal Communication with M. Sprinkel, Virginia Transportation Research Council, Virginia State Department of Transportation, January, 1992.

CORROSION CONTROL
USING COATED REINFORCEMENT

J Theophilus

N Woodman

Allied Bar Coaters

United Kingdom

ABSTRACT. Achieving adequately durable reinforced concrete by control of concrete quality and cover alone is subject to diminishing returns and may not be practical. Holistic solutions using complimentary systems such as corrosion protected reinforcement are more reliable and cost effective. The function, manufacture and quality assurance of epoxy coated and galvanised reinforcements are discussed, together with their respective corrosion protection mechanisms. The holistic approach to reinforced concrete design is illustrated by real examples which are perhaps a lesson for the future.

Keywords. Corrosion, reinforced concrete, holistic design, epoxy coated reinforcement, galvanised reinforcement, lifetime costing.

John Theophilus. At the time of writing this paper, John Theophilus was Development Manager with Allied Bar Coaters, moving in early 1993 to assume new technical responsibilities for construction industry projects at ASW Construction Systems. His previous experience includes, consultancy with Harry Stanger where he developed expertise in cement and concrete testing, including the chairmanship of BSI Committees.

Nick Woodman. Director/General Manager has been with Allied Bar Coaters since its launch of EBAR in 1988. Publishing numerous technical papers on Fusion Bonded Epoxy Coated Reinforcement and contributing to the publication of BS7295 in 1990. Currently, the Chairman of the European Trade Association of fusion bonded epoxy coated reinforcement manufacturers.

Concrete 2000. Edited by Ravindra K. Dhir and M. Roderick Jones.
© 1993 Published by E & FN Spon. ISBN 0 419 18120 2.

INTRODUCTION

The cost of structural problems caused by reinforcement corrosion is well known and does not require rehearsal. Similarly the basic principals underlying reinforcement corrosion are well known and can be summarised into the basic statement: "Concrete provides a high alkalinity environment which completely inhibits steel corrosion. When carbon dioxide and/or aggressive salts penetrate the concrete they destroy this protective environment and the reinforcement corrodes".

The phenomenon of reinforcement corrosion has been extensively investigated, for example by Tutti(1). He developed a helpful model to describe the process, a commonly seen illustration of which is shown in Figure 1.

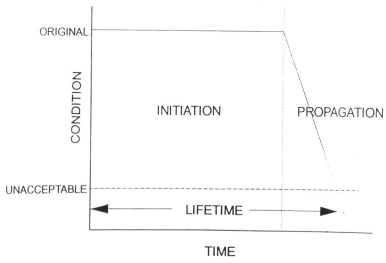

Figure 1: Schematic durability model for reinforced concrete

The initiation period is the time during which aggressive agents are penetrating the concrete but have not reached the reinforcement. Propagation illustrates the deterioration associated with the corrosion process.

The time to initiation is dependant upon the rate at which aggressive agents penetrate the concrete cover, this in turn is dependant on its permeability and thickness. Because the transport through the concrete is via diffusion type mechanism the protection afforded by the cover is proportional to its thickness squared, thus 35m of cover provides half the protection of 50m of cover.

When considering the overall performance of a structure it is important to bear in mind that the important issue is not its average behaviour but the worst case. Corrosion related failure is statistically controlled, it could be described as a possibilistic process, reinforcement will corrode if it is possible for it to do so.

It only requires rather a small percentage of all the reinforcement in a structure to corrode to produce a very unsightly and potentially dangerous situation. This will occur where the cover is lowest, concrete is poorest and local environment most sever. It falls outside the realms of statistics to explain why these circumstances always coincide in a place which is most inconvenient.

It is possible to improve durability by reducing the permeability of the concrete, and/or by increasing cover, although this latter option is limited, as too great a thickness of unreinforced concrete, negating the benefits.

It is obvious that the protection afforded by cover and concrete quality are interdependent. Control of cover can be negated by poor localised concrete quality (honeycombing, poor compaction etc) and visa versa. Thus the law of diminishing returns applies to this situation, there is a practical financial limitation to the degree to which cover and concrete quality can be controlled over the whole of a structure.

HOLISTIC SOLUTION

It is against this background that the use of corrosion protected reinforcement as part of a systematic holistic approach to durable reinforced concrete should be considered.

Two classes of corrosion resistant reinforcement exist, those which are inherently uncorrosive in a concrete environment such as stainless steel, nonmetalics etc and those which control the rate at which corrosion occurs namely galvanised and epoxy coated reinforcement.

The noncorrodible systems do not draw any corrosion resistance from the concrete medium (except perhaps resistance to abrasion or UV degradation) and are not affected by cover or concrete quality. They are, however very substantially more expensive than conventional or corrosion protection reinforcement.

The coated reinforcements, galvanised and epoxy coated effectively reduce the rate at which corrosion occurs at the end of the initiation period. Their behaviour can be illustrated as a modification of the corrosion model described previously (Figure 2).

The coating on reinforcements firstly acts as a barrier between the steel and corrosive environment and secondly reduces the rate at which corrosion occurs, by one or two order of magnitudes should the coating become damaged. This is discussed in a more detail under 'types of coating'.

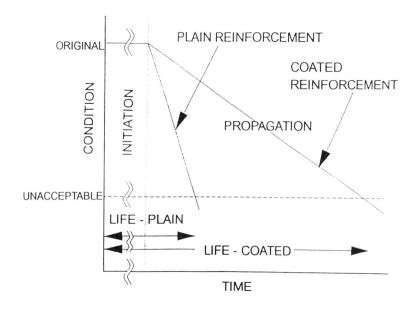

Figure 2. Durability model - coated v uncoated reinforcement

It is important to note that any steel exposed at damage sites in the coating remains passive, in the same way as uncoated steel, during the initiation period of the process.

There is in fact a good argument to be made that, all else being equal, the initiation period for coated reinforcement will be longer than for uncoated reinforcement. This is because before corrosion can start the conditions causing loss of passivity must coincide with a damage site in the coating.

To gain an appreciation of the magnitude of this effect, consider the situation of 16mm rebar with 35mm cover. The time it takes for aggressive conditions to just reach the reinforcement is the same as the time it subsequently takes for these conditions to penetrate to the full thickness of the reinforcement.

This simple calculation is based upon the premise that aggressive agents penetrate concrete on an even front. This is not, in fact, the case. Point to point variation in carbonation depth, for example has been reported to be in the order of 20%(2).

It is very difficult to accurately quantify the overall magnitude of this effect, which varies with the geometry of the reinforcement but it is obviously significant.

What is more interesting is the additive effect of corrosion protected reinforcement to the benefits of good cover control and concrete quality. Reconsidering the possibilistic argument advanced previously we can say that corrosion will occur at the coincidence of lowest cover, poorest concrete quality, most aggressive environment **and** reinforcement coating damage. When these circumstances arise, as noted above, the rate of deterioration will be reduced by an order of magnitude from that which would occur with uncoated reinforcement.

Because reinforcement coating acts as a separate, complimentary, protection mechanism to good cover and concrete quality control their roles may be seen as synergistic. There are, in fact, many synergistic links between the systems, for example, the concrete provides protection for the coatings from UV degradation and mechanical damage. Similarly lowering the permeability of concrete using PFA or GBFS substantially increases its electrical resistance, which in turn increases the effectiveness of the mechanisms by which epoxy coatings reduce corrosion rates.

Adding coated reinforcement to the more usually considered variables of cover and concrete quality enables engineers to design durable structures more effectively by minimising the risk of localised failure.

A good example of the type of systematic approach to achieving durability which we are advocating is the revision of bridge design strategy undertaken by Ontario in 1986(3). They included in this revision; increasing cover in areas of particular risk, concrete quality issues and the inclusion of epoxy coated reinforcement. These measures taken together will increase the useful lifetimes to structures by up to 40 times, ie in practical terms beyond the likely functional lifetime of such structures.

TYPES OF COATED REINFORCEMENT

There are two types of coated reinforcement in common usage, zinc coated (galvanised) and fusion bonded epoxy coated reinforcement (FBECR),

As noted above, the primary function of these coatings is to act as a barrier to aggressive agents. It is in the nature of construction however, that some damage to these coatings occurs and the secondary function of the coating is to reduce the rate of corrosion at these damage sites.

In the case of galvanised reinforcement exposed steel is protected galvanically by sacrificial dissolution of the coatings. Obviously this process is limited by the amount of coating available. This is adequate for normal circumstances however inadvertent electrical connection to uncoated reinforcement can rapidly exhaust the available zinc.

In a carbonated environment galvanised reinforcement has an excellent track record of successful use. There is some disparity in the track record in chloride contaminated concrete. Zinc is passive at the pH found in fresh and carbonated concrete but is depassivated at chloride levels only a little higher than those required to depassivate steel in concrete and so self corrodes in this environment. In many studies (4 and 5) galvanised reinforcement has been shown to provide only modest protection against chloride ingress. Despite this there are many examples of structures containing galvanised reinforcement exposed to chloride environments which appear to be functioning satisfactorily.

With FBECR the corrosion rate at damaged sites is controlled by isolating the active anode (metal dissolution) from cathodes (oxygen reduction) as illustrated in Figure 3. Because the efficiency of the anode reaction is one or two orders at magnitude higher than that of the cathode reaction at approximately 10-100 fold reduction in corrosion rate would be expected to result, compared to uncoated reinforcement. This expectation is borne out of practical measurements (6 and 7).

Because the coating is acting as an inert barrier it is not directly affected by chloride levels although the rate at which corrosion occurs will rise pro-rata with the rate for uncoated steel with rising chloride levels.

As with galvanised reinforcements electrical connections between FBECR and uncoated bar are undesirable as the uncoated steel can act as a new macrocathode tending to negate the benefits of the coating. In practice even when FBE coated and uncoated bars are connected anodes and cathodes are separated and reduction in corrosion rates occurs due to resistance effects.

A reasonable rule of thumb when considering mixing coated and uncoated reinforcement is to continue the coated reinforcement at least 1m past the boundary of the "at risk" concrete it is intended to give added protection to.

It is worth noting that although stainless steel is essentially unaffected by corrosive environments it is more electronegative than plain carbon steel and thus if connected to steel electrically it will cause that reinforcement to corrode galvanically.

MANUFACTURE, SPECIFICATIONS, QUALITY CONTROL

Galvanised reinforcement is normally zinc coated by the hot dip galvanising process. This entails cleaning the steel by acid pickling and dipping it into molten zinc. Usually the reinforcement is cut and bent to fine dimensions before galvanising. Sometimes it is more convenient to galvanise straight lengths and fabricate them subsequently.

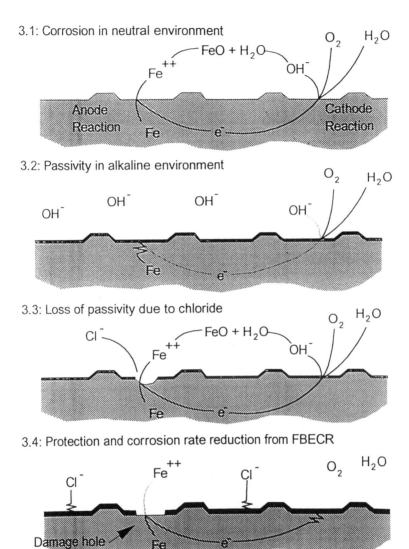

3.1: Corrosion in neutral environment

3.2: Passivity in alkaline environment

3.3: Loss of passivity due to chloride

3.4: Protection and corrosion rate reduction from FBECR

However, the degree of bending of galvanised reinforcement must be limited to avoid cracking and flaking the coating. The Zinc Development Association recommend minimum bending radius for 90° bends of 5 bar diameters up to 16mm and 8 bar diameters for greater than 16mm. (Compared with the industry norm of 180° bends of 3 bar diameters radius up to 25mm and 4 bar diameters radius over 25mm for uncoated reinforcement).

The British Standard for galvanised products in general is BS729:1971(8) which requires a minimum mass of coating of $610g/m^2$, equivalent to 85 microns thickness.

A number of hot dip galvanisers operate quality assurance schemes to BS5750 Part 2 and BS run a Quality Assurance sector scheme to which they may apply for accreditation.

FBECR is manufactured by a specialist factory process in which straight lengths of rebar are prepared by blast cleaning to near white metal (Sa $2^{1/2}$), than heated to 230°c before the application of epoxy coating by electrostatic powder spraying. The epoxy powder melts and fuses on to the surface of the preheated rebar then reacts chemically to form a tough thermoset coating.

FBECR is cut and bent after coating, the cut ends being repaired with a compatible two pack epoxy paint. Provided it is correctly formulated and applied the epoxy coating does not restrict in any way the design of reinforcement, meeting all the requirements of existing British Standards. BS4449(9) which specifies the bond requirements for deformed reinforcement and BS4466(10) which defines the standard details for the design and fabrication of reinforcement.

The British Standard for FBECR is BS7295:1990(11).   This standard is the toughest in the world and was developed in the UK in response to concerns that existing specifications, particularly ASTM A775(12) was too lax and did not guarantee reliable performance from FBECR(13).   BS7295 was designed to integrate with the Quality Assurance requirements of BS5750 and QA schemes for FBECR are now well established.

THE FUTURE

The UK currently lags behind the rest of the world in taking advantage of the available options to improve the durability provided by corrosion protected reinforcement, for example in North America up to 10% of the reinforcement used is epoxy coated, this compares with less than 1% in the UK.

The extra costs of incorporating coated reinforcement into a structure are typically 2 - 4% of the project value. It is to be hoped that as the disproportionate cost of repairing structures which fail before they become redundant will lead to a wider adoption of whole life costing.

For example: The 11 viaducts stretching over 21km which comprise of the Midland Links were originally built in 1972 at a cost of £28 million. Repair cost in the first 17 years of the structures life cost £45 million and it is estimated that in the following 15 years repair costs will exceed £120 million(14).

In the context of whole life costing, holistic approaches towards durability issues become fundamental, seeking to gain optimum value for money by combining the benefits of good design, concrete technology and secondary corrosion protection systems. The Storebaelt tunnel in Denmark is a classic example of how this approach can be applied in practice(15).

The design of the reinforced concrete segments for the Storebaelt tunnel considered a wide variety of options to enhance segment durability, concrete additives, concrete coatings, stainless steel reinforcement and cathodic protection to name but four. The chosen solution was to use fusion bonded epoxy coating but not before it had been integrated into the overall design:

-       The reinforcing steel cage was designed to provide structural integrity whilst being suitable for epoxy coating by fluidised bed dipping.

-       The scale of the project (60,000 segments) was such that the fluidised bed coating process could be specifically designed.

-       Epoxy coating powders were likewise developed to meet the specific requirements of the system, and method of coating application.

-       Finally the concrete mix design incorporated the requirements of physical strength, workability whilst offering optimum impermeability.

Perhaps the design philosophy from the Storebaelt Tunnel is an approach to achieving durability which will be used increasingly in the future. An approach in which this paper has illustrated the value of incorporating corrosion protected reinforcement.

REFERENCES

1.   TUTTI, K. Corrosion Of Steel In Concrete. Swedish Foundation For Concrete. Research Fo4, 1982.

2.   THEOPHILUS, J. AND BAILEY, M. The Significance Of Carbonation Tests And Chloride Level Determination In Assessing. The Durability Of Reinforced Concrete. 3rd International Conference On Durability of Building Materials and Components. Technical Research Centre Of Finland 1984.

3.   MANNING, D.G. A Rational Approach To Corrosion Protection Of The Concrete Components Of Highway Bridges. ME-86-06. Ontario Ministry Of Transportation and Communications. 1987.

4.   TREADWAY, K.W.J., COX, R.N. AND DAVIES, H. Corrosion Protected And Corrosion Resistant Reinforcement In Concrete. IP 14/88. Building Research Establishment. 1988.

5.   EDGELL, T.W. AND RIEMENSCHNEIDER, J.A.   Epoxy Coated Reinforcing Steel Performance In Marine Exposure, A Nine Year Observation.   Conducted by 3M and Florida Department Of Transport Published by 3M, Austin Centre, Texas. 1989.

6.   SAGUES, A. Corrosion Of Epoxy Coated Reinforcing Steel, Final Report. FL/DOT/SMO/89419. National Technical Information Service. 1989.

7.   VIRMANI, Y.P, CLEAR, K.C., PASKO, T.J.   Time To Corrosion Of Reinforcing Steel In Concrete Slabs. Vol 5: Calcium Nitrate Admixture Of Epoxy Coated Reinforcing Bars As Corrosion Protection Systems. FHWA/RD-83/012. National Technical Information Service 1982.

8.   BSI. Specification For Hot Dip Galvanised Coatings On Iron And Steel Articles BS729:1971. British Standards Institute.

9.   BSI. Specification For Carbon Steel Bars For The Reinforcement Of Concrete. BS4449:1988. British Standards Institute.

10.   BSI. Specification For Scheduling, Dimensioning, Bending And Cutting Of Steel Reinforcement For Concrete. BS4466:1989. British Standards Institute.

11.   BSI.   Fusion Bonded Epoxy Coated Carbon Steel Bars For The Reinforcement Of Concrete. BS7295: Parts 1 and 2: 1990. British Standards Institute.

12.   ASTM. Standard Specification For Epoxy Coated Reinforcing Steel Bars. ASTM. A775M:1991.

13.   REED, J.A. FBECR. The Need For Correct Specification And Quality Control.   Proc. Conf. Fusion Bonded Epoxy Coated Reinforcement. Sheffield University.   1989.

14.   NEW CIVIL ENGINEER. 28th February 1989.

15.   ECOB. C.R., KING. E.S., ROSTAM. S, VINCENTSEN. L.J. Epoxy Coated Reinforcement Cages In Precast Concrete Segmental Tunnel Linings, Preliminary Testing and Specification. Sheffield University. 17th May 1989.

CORROSION INHIBITION IN CRACKED CONCRETE: AN ADMIXTURE SOLUTION

G Bobrowski

D J Youn

Master Builders Inc

United States of America

ABSTRACT. Corrosion inhibition in steel reinforced concrete is a major concern to specification engineers. Of several solutions to this problem, utilization of corrosion inhibiting admixtures have become a popular choice. The advent of corrosion inhibiting admixtures is relatively recent and consequently not thoroughly understood. A test method for determining the efficacy of these admixtures has not been normalized. There are many proposed methodologies but no single one has been universally recognized as a standard. A test method proposed to the ASTM committee may become a widely accepted normalized procedure. The mechanics and the relevance of this test method is theoretically discussed and experimentally confirmed.

Keywords: Corrosion, Chloride, Cracking, Inhibition, Durability

Greg Bobrowski is the Vice President of Research and Development at *Master Builders, Incorporated*, Cleveland, Ohio, USA. He and his associates are dedicated to the advancement of concrete admixtures, cementitious repair mortars, grouts and polymer construction materials technologies.

Dr. Dennis J. Youn is a Senior Materials Scientist and Admixture Research Coordinator at *Master Builders, Incorporated*, Cleveland, Ohio, USA. His research interests are focused on admixture technology in concrete applications. Admixture technologies of interest include corrosion inhibition, superplasticizers, accelerators, retarders, and innovative materials.

Concrete 2000. Edited by Ravindra K. Dhir and M. Roderick Jones.
© 1993 Published by E & FN Spon. ISBN 0 419 18120 2.

INTRODUCTION

The prevention of chloride permeation is the key to preventing reinforcement steel corrosion. Civil engineers world-wide have recognized the process by which aqueous chloride ions lead to the destruction of entire reinforced structures through the irreparable corrosion damage to the reinforcement steel.   Minimization of this phenomenon has become a major concern. The battle against chloride attack is further complicated by the presence of stress cracking in concrete. Cracks facilitate chloride permeability and therefore render most chloride screening mechanisms of corrosion inhibition ineffective.

In this investigation, an innovative formulation approach has been documented. The use of oil in water emulsion based admixtures offers an alternative to the presently available ionic salt based admixtures.   The investigation describes performance evaluations of corrosion inhibiting admixtures in an apparatus specifically designed to simulate cracked concrete structures that contain reinforcing steel.

The key to protecting reinforcement steel under cracked concrete situations is to prevent iron atoms in the zero oxidation state from reacting with chloride at the location where the cracks have exposed steel to the exterior environment. The logical way to do this is to mimic or reinforce the natural protection that occurs at the steel surface. With the elevated pH conditions present in concrete, the tendency to form water insoluble ferric oxide from zero state iron is great. Chloride will circumvent this natural barrier since the chemical potential for ferrous chloride formation is also great. Iron in the ferrous state is soluble in water and is the responsible for mass loss from the bar. Logically, if the weak points in the ferric oxide protective layer can be reinforced at the molecular level, the reinforcement bar becomes less susceptible to corrosion even when chloride is allowed free access to the bar.

A strong reinforcement of the passive layer would require a chelation of the zero oxidation state iron by electron rich functional groups that have hydrophobic properties. Iron that is in the zero oxidation state has empty d_{z^2} orbitals and readily accepts electron donating ligands.   One of the most powerful ligands under this capacity is chloride. In order to prevent this particular reaction from occurring, an alternative ligand capable of chelating the iron must be introduced to the surface of the steel.   Zero state iron is accessible at weak spots in the naturally occurring protective layer.

Corrosion research has indicated that chelating functional groups that form 5 to 6 member rings with surface metal atoms are the most stable of all chemicals used in this capacity. **Figure 5-C** illustrates how such a chelant forms a very stable ligand bond with an surface iron atom. Resonance stabilization of this type of structure results in enhanced stability of the chelation.   The long hydrophilic tail which is attached to the ring forming functional groups keep all water soluble ions including chloride away from the site of chelation. This repulsion of chloride ions can lead to an effective protection of the weak spots on the steel surface, consequently inhibiting corrosion when existing cracks allow aqueous chloride ions easy access to the steel.

Innovative admixture formulations were directly assessed in concrete samples that were configured to form electrochemical macro cells. **Figure 1** sparsely illustrates the sample configuration utilized. The test method was derived from the ASTM G-109 corrosion cell test that also utilizes this exact configuration. In the G-109 test, the electrical potential, that is created by oxidation of iron at the anode combined with the reduction of hydroxide at the cathode, is measured as a potential across the resistor. The corrosion activity of the macro cell is determined by the calculated corrosion current.

In this series of experiments, the G-109 based samples were loaded to induce a stress crack in the middle of the beams. This artificially creates a cracked concrete situation which simulates cracks occurring in structures. The crack allows the subsequently applied chloride solution to penetrate directly to the level of the reinforcement. This accelerates a natural process by introducing a series of harsh conditions, that are normally spread out over long periods of time, into a relatively short time frame.

The reason why this method was chosen over other more conventional methods of monitoring corrosion is that this particular inhibition mechanism is very interactive with the cement matrix at the interface of the steel. Consequently, extensive sample preparation procedures or liberal use of externally applied forces will not produce data that correlates to actual performance in structures. This modified G-109 procedure reproduces realistic situations so that less approximations are needed. What is compromised is scientific resolution of quantitative measurable parameters that characterizes the mechanism. Although this test method has met some skeptical opposition, it was still instrumental because it has demonstrated admixture performance in "worst-case" scenarios.

EXPERIMENTAL DETAILS

There are many ways one can artificially accelerate the natural corrosion process under laboratory conditions. The impetus for doing this is to learn details of the specific reinforced concrete systems and to assess the performance of corrosion inhibitors used in admixture form. When fast results are needed, test specimens can be placed under very severe conditions where corrosion occurs very quickly. The effectiveness of a corrosion inhibiting admixture formulation can be assessed quickly so that improvements can be made. The difficulties arise when one tries to extrapolate the actual performance in a reinforced structure from data obtained under such artificially created test environments. The relevance of accelerated test results in general is an issue always under debate. For these reasons, the following test procedure was chosen from the many that are available.

Figure 1

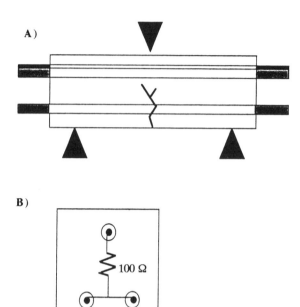

A)

B)

100 Ω

Figure 1.   A) The beams were loaded upside down until the length of the crack had surpassed the level of the single top bar. B) The three bars are wired together as follows. A high percision 100 Ohm resistor is included as shown.

The test is referred to as the *cracked beam   corrosion test.*   The test is consistent with the ASTM proposed procedure submitted by Neal Berke of W. R. Grace on June 23, 1992 to the G1.14 subcommittee.[1] This proposal subsequently became the ASTM G-109 test procedure. Although slight differences in details exist because our experiments were conducted before the proposal was submitted, the basic concepts are identical.

Before the beams were cast, the reinforcement steel was prepared by cutting #3 nominal grade rebar with inter crossing surface patterns and sandblasting the existing layer of surface oxide. This procedure ensures that a fresh surface of iron atoms, predominantly in the zero oxidation state are exposed. One end was drilled, tapped and fitted with a machine screw so that subsequent electrical connections could be made easily. The 1.5 " of both ends of each bar was covered with cement paste composed of w/c = 0.5 with *Medusa* Type I cement. Subsequently, epoxy resin was used to cover the cement paste. The paste ensures that the rebar is uniformly in contact with cement paste so that edge effects are minimized.

The beam design and dimensions were as follows. Please refer to **figure 1** for the illustration. The beams were cast with plywood molds with the reinforcement bars placed into pre-drilled holes in the ends of the prism shaped mold. The holes maintained the reinforcing bars in the designated triangular configuration. The distances were calculated by proportionally scaling down with the original Wiss-Janey-Elstner design dimensions and modified to only three bars instead of six.

The concrete mix design was similar to the one depicted in the G-109 procedure. The order of addition for ingredients was as follows; water, admixture (if any), coarse aggregate, cement, stone. The concrete was mixed for a four minute continues cycle in a commercial 2 cubic-foot capacity rotating drum style mixer. Concrete was poured into the awaiting molds and vibrated in layers for 10 seconds per layer. The top surface was hand finished with a steel trowel. Slump and air content were measured and recorded. Also, compressive strength cylinders were cast for each mix.

The filled molds were covered with plastic for 24 hours and concrete allowed to set. After 24 hours, the molds were removed and the beams were placed in a moist environment for 28 days. After the 28 day period had elapsed, the specimens were removed and allowed to dry at room temperature for 24 hours.

Next the cracks were induced by loading the underside of the beams with a SATEC compressive strength testing machine. The load was increased until a visible crack propagated past the level of the top reinforcement bar but had not reached the level of the bottom bars. **Figure 1** illustrates the procedure. The actual required load depended upon the strength of the concrete so manual regulation of the controls with visual feedback was the only method that was reliable.

Wooden reservoirs were constructed and mounted on the top surface so that the cracked area is well enclosed by the reservoir. Silicone caulk and epoxy resin were used to finalize the reservoir mounting. Wires were attached to the ends of the bars at the pre-installed screws. A 100 Ohm resistor was placed into the circuit.

All the samples were then connected to a data acquisition interface which was controlled by a Hewlett-Packard 9000 computer. The acquisition software was written by *Master Builders, Inc.* Each sample was allotted a single channel on the acquisition input ports. The computer software was programmed to collect data points every five minutes and to calculate the current through the resistor using Ohm's Law. The current through the resistor was considered as the corrosion current which was directly proportional to the amount of corrosion activity.

Once all the hardware was secured and the software initialized, the acquisition program was started and a 6% by weight solution of NaCl was placed into the reservoirs. The reservoirs were covered with plastic sheets to prevent evaporation of water from the reservoirs.

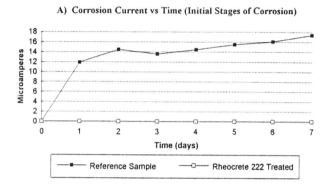

A) Corrosion Current vs Time (Initial Stages of Corrosion)

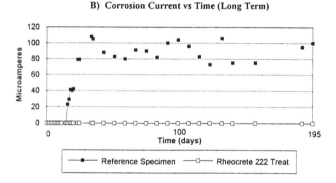

B) Corrosion Current vs Time (Long Term)

Figure 2. A) The initiation of corrosion is monitored by the current through the resistor. After 7 days, the beams were destroyed and the bars retrieved. B) The corrosion current was monitored for 195 days. Both curves represent the average of 3 specimens each. The bars were retrieved after 195 days.

There were two experiments of interest. The first is the evaluation of the test procedure itself. The purpose was to establish the connection between the electrical measurements and the existence of visible corrosion on the steel bars. Electrical measurements were acquired for approximately 7 days in which time, the initial development of voltage across the 100 Ohm resistor had appeared. After 7 days had elapsed, the samples were destroyed and the reinforcement steel bars visually examined. The data is plotted on **figure 2-A** and the photographs of the retrieved bars are shown in **figure 3**.

A)

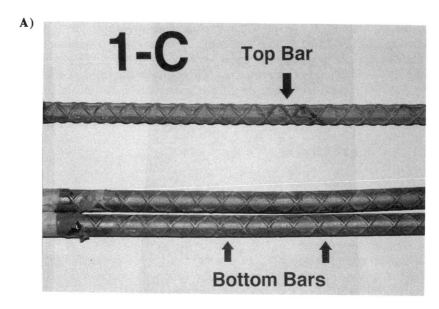

B)

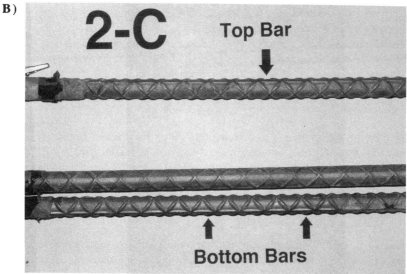

Figure 3. A) The picture of the reinforcement bars retrieved from the untreated sample shows a mass of orange-brown corrosion product. The color of the corrosion indicates a high ferrous oxide content which is the considered bad oxidation. B) The picture of the bars from the Rheocrete 222 treated sample shows no corrosion activity at all. This supports the current readings shown in figure 2-A.

The second experiment was intended to show the corrosion inhibition abilities of the chelant based admixture, *Rheocrete 222*, in a test procedure that simulates a cracked structure exposed to de-icing salts. The prepared specimens were ponded for 5 days with 6% chloride solution and then allowed to dry for 2 days. This cycle was repeated for the duration of the experiment. The corrosion current was monitored for 195 days. At the end of this time period, the beams were destroyed and the steel bars were visually examined for corrosion that had occurred. The data is plotted in **figure 2-B** photographs of the retrieved steel bars are shown in **figure 4**.

RESULTS AND DISCUSSION

Cracked Concrete Test Procedure

The results are presented on **figure 2-A**. The first objective is to see the correlation between current values and actual visible corrosion on the top reinforcement bar. The photos showing the condition of the reinforcement steel are shown in **figure 3.** Generally speaking, there seems to be a good correlation between the voltage readings and visible corrosion. For example, the sample 1-C indicated a reading of 17.4 micro-amperes at 7 days and the visual inspection confirms a noticeable amount of orange-brown corrosion developing on the top bar.   At the other extreme, sample 2-C indicated that the current through the 100 Ohm resistor to be essentially zero. Visual inspection of the reinforcement indicates that no corrosion is occurring on any of the reinforcement bars. Upon further inspection of the whole data set, one can safely conclude that the current values calculated from voltage readings across the resistor gives an indication of when the corrosion process begins. The magnitude of the current values also seem to reflect the magnitude of the visible corrosion that had formed on the top reinforcement bar.

The objective of this study was to determine whether this cracked beam test method was truly indicative of the actual corrosion at the reinforcement surface. The results were very consistent with the current values in determining the actual commencement of the corrosion process.   This asserts that current values through the resistor wired in the specified configuration is reliable method by which one may determine the commencement of corrosion.

A debatable point is whether these current values can be used to quantitatively determine the actual amount of corrosion present in the test samples.   This may be possible with the use of Faraday's Law which can be used to equate the amount of current flow to the number of iron atoms oxidized.   The number of iron atoms oxidized can be further developed to determine the amount of reinforcement mass lost due to corrosion.

This method does have a drawback, however, that prevents this corrosion beam test from being the indisputable method to asses absolute inhibitor performance.   The

A)

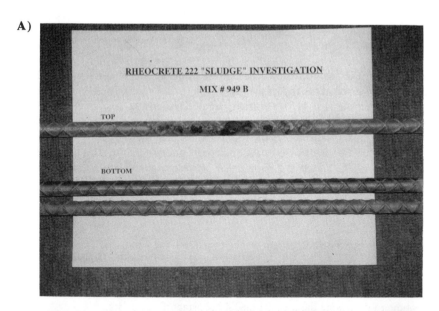

B)

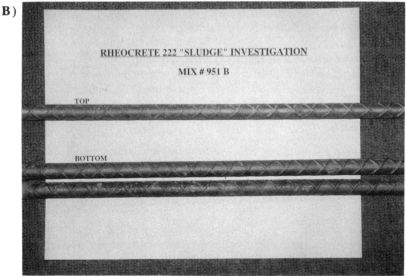

Figure 4. A) The picture of reinforcement bars retrieved from the untreated sample shows that a mass of corrosion has developed on the single anodic bar. B) The picture of the Rheocrete 222 treated sample shows no corrosion activity at all. This is consistent with the current readings shown in figure 2-B.

relationship between the electrical measurements and the absolute amount of steel mass loss only holds true if *all of the corrosion actually occurring is being accounted for in the electrical measurements.* This is only partially true.

Figure 5 illustrates the corrosion mechanisms available to the system. The chloride solution is introduced at the top of the beam. Normally, the chloride concentration at the top bar exceeds that at the bottom bars. This creates a gradient in chloride concentration which increases the probability of corrosion at the top bar significantly over the bottom bars. This forces the top bar to become the anode where Cl^- and O_2 are reduced while Fe^0 is oxidized. Also, the configuration of the steel bars within the beam is designed to create a differential in surface area. There is twice as much effective surface area at the designated cathodes, the bottom bars, than at the anode, the top bar. The result is a macroscopic corrosion cell, or macro-cell which is effectively a battery voltage source.

Since only the macro-cell corrosion can be measured, the micro-cell corrosion , illustrated in **figure 5-B,** is not being directly accounted for in the assessment of corrosion activity. It was assumed that the overall corrosion activity is directly proportional to the amount of macro-cell corrosion activity. There is no clear method at this time to determine the proportionallity constant if one exists.

Evaluation of Organic Chelant Based Admixture

The other point of discussion is the actual active chelation mechanism that is being studied. The most stable forms of chelation configurations are those organic species that form 5 or 6 member rings with surface metal atoms.[2,3] **Figure 5-C** illustrates how resonance stabilized rings that include the metal atom in the ring structure are formed.

These chelants have shown to be effective corrosion inhibitors in traditional uses such as boiler applications. The proprietary admixture, *Rheocrete 222,* that was created based on these types of surface active chelants has been examined in this study. In **figure 2-B,** the extended accelerated testing results are shown.

The cycled periods of drying and 6% chloride solution ponding is estimated to simulate a very harsh environment that a concrete structure would experience in a northern geographical location where the use of de-icing salts is commonplace. The results clearly show that the initiation of corrosion was delayed for at least 6 months even under these extremely exaggerated corrosive conditions. This is evident because the half-cell voltage readings and the corrosion currents are essentially zero during this time period. During the same time period, the plain untreated concrete samples

A) **Macro-cell Corrosion**

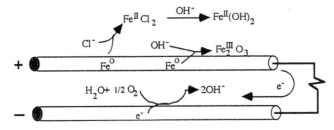

B) **Micro-cell Corrosion**

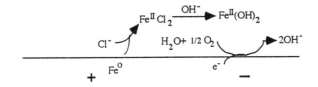

C) **Organic Chelation**

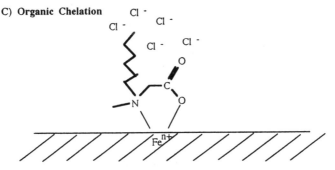

Figure 5. A) Macro-cell corrosion is illustrated. The current produced can be calculated from the voltage across the resistor. B) Micro-cell corrosion is illustrated [4]. This corrosion potential cannot be accurately measured externally. C) Chelation mechanism of ring forming chelants. The hydrophobic tail, which varies in length, keeps water and chloride from easily approaching the metal surface. [2,3]

showed significant amounts of voltage and current. This particular experiment was truncated at 6 months because the specimens were destroyed in order to visually examine the steel bars. Subsequent testing has shown that the delay of the corrosion process be maintained longer than 6 months. Also, other similar studies have shown that once the treated samples do begin to display some corrosion activity, the rate of increase in the current values was much slower than that of the untreated samples.

CONCLUSIONS

This study has shown two points. First, the accelerated test procedure described is a good indicator of overall corrosion activity that is occurring inside the concrete mass of the specimens. The concept is simple so that the results can be easily understood by those who are not corrosion experts. Second, the potential use of an organic chelant based admixture has been shown to be an effective way to inhibit corrosion in a cracked concrete application. The test procedure allowed chlorides to more readily access the steel bars. In the plain untreated specimens, this situation resulted in accelerated development of corrosion within 2 weeks. The corrosion inhibiting admixture had prevented corrosion activity from occurring for over 6 months under the same conditions that produced corrosion so quickly in the untreated samples.

The reason for the added corrosion inhibiting activity could be attributed to the chelating of the mentioned organic species to the steel surface. It should be noted however, that this is not the only source of corrosion inhibition. This study focuses upon just one aspect of a more sophisticated formulation.

A contributing element of the corrosion inhibiting formulation to its function is the presence of anti-wetting agents in the list of ingredients. The overall capillary action is reduced by certain components. This has a pronounced effect on the corrosion inhibition properties of the product, even in the presence of moderate cracks. This mechanism is certainly a large contributor to the overall performance of the formulation.

Although evidence does indicate a protective organic layer is formed, it has not been determined whether it is the solely dominant effect. How much this chelation protection is essential to the overall corrosion inhibiting abilities has been a hotly debated topic.   This question should be addressed shortly in subsequent investigations.

The actual corrosion process in concrete structures is a complex issue. Simulations in small scale experiments such as this one attempt to model years of structure service life by accelerating the exposure rate to the hostile elements. Many other factors could influence the results of any accelerated test. Care was exercised to minimize error from the inability to completely isolate certain phenomenon for observation.

However, physical limitations of present technology allow some uncertainty in assessing quantitative characterizations and predictions.

REFERENCES

1. Berk, Neal; ASTM G01.14 Subcommittee Ballot, 6/23/92.

2. Weisstuch, A.; Carter, D. A.; Nathan, C.C.; *Chelation Compounds as Cooling Water Corrosion Inhibitors*; **Materials Protection and Performance,** Vol 10, Number 4, 4/71.

3. Zecher, David C.; *Corrosion Inhibition by Surface-Active Chelants*; **Materials Performance**, April, 1976.

4. Verbeck, George J.; ACI: *Corrosion of Metals in Concrete* ; Publication SP-49; **Mechanism of Corrosion of Steel in Concrete.**

MONITORING OF CORROSION RISK
FOR NEW CONCRETE STRUCTURES

M Raupach

Technical University of Aachen

Germany

ABSTRACT. To monitor the corrosion risk for the reinforcement in concrete structures due to chlorides penetrating from the outside into the concrete or due to carbonation of the concrete a special sensor has been developed. It consists of several pieces of different metals (anodes and cathodes) which are embedded in the actual concrete at defined positions. The corrosion risk can be determined depending on the concrete depth related to the concrete surface and the age of the structure by measuring the electrical current flow between the anodes and cathodes. The theoretical background and the practical experience from installations and measurements at three reinforced concrete bridges are presented and discussed.

Keywords: Concrete, Steel, Reinforcement, Chlorides, Carbonation, Monitoring, Sensor, Concrete Cover, Galvanic Cell, Potential, Current, Corrosion Risk.

Dr.-Ing. Michael Raupach is a Research Engineer at the Institute for Building Materials Research at the Technical University of Aachen. He has a Ph.D. in Civil Engineering and he has been involved in numerous research projects in the field of corrosion of steel in concrete and corrosion protection. Besides his research work, he is active as a consulting engineer for corrosion problems including diagnosis and repair of reinforced concrete structures. One of his main working areas is the electrochemical monitoring of corrosion of steel in concrete.

Concrete 2000. Edited by Ravindra K. Dhir and M. Roderick Jones.
© 1993 Published by E & FN Spon. ISBN 0 419 18120 2.

INTRODUCTION

During the last few years, corrosion of the reinforcement induced by chlorides, carbonation of the concrete or low quality of the concrete cover have caused several serious damages to concrete structures all over the world. In Europe many bridges and parking structures have been damaged by the use of deicing salts so heavily that lots of them have to be repaired or replaced.

To prevent such corrosion problems at new concrete structures exposed to deicing salts or other aggressive environments, the design codes for reinforced structures in Germany have been improved. Depending on the environmental conditions more restrictive minimum cover thicknesses and maximum values for the water/cement ratio are now defined to ensure a sufficiently high quality of the concrete cover resulting in a high resistance of the structures against corrosion due to chlorides or carbonation. These regulations will ensure a better durability for new concrete structures over the whole design service life.

But special cases remain, especially under extremely aggressive environments, in which additional protection measures are necessary to ensure a sufficiently long service life. In such cases a corrosion protection strategy is required to prevent damages induced by corrosion of the reinforcement, e. g. to use stainless steel or epoxicoated reinforcement or to apply a coating onto the concrete surface and to observe the condition of the structure by intensive maintenance in regular intervals. Besides a lot of different possibilities one corrosion protection strategy is to ensure a high quality of the concrete cover and to monitor the corrosion risk for the reinforcement permanently by installing a suitable warning system.

If the warning system shows no actual corrosion risk over the whole service life of the structure, no additional protection measures are required. On the other hand, if the monitoring system indicates a high corrosion risk for the reinforcement after a certain period of use, protection measures can be taken before corrosion starts and any cracks and spalls occur on the concrete surface. Normally the expenditure for such protection measures, e. g. coating of the concrete surface or installation of a cathodic protection system is very low compared to the costs for the repair of the structure after cracks and spalls have occurred.

For this purpose a corrosion monitoring system has been developed by the Institute for Building Materials Research at TH Aachen, ibac (sensors) and the Company for Sensors and Prestressing Techniques in Cologne, SICOM (electronic equipment for measuring and software for analysis of the data).

The newly developed corrosion monitoring system has already been installed into four concrete structures:

- Bridge "Schießbergstraße" near Cologne, Germany

- Bridge near Nötsch, Austria

- Eastern Railway Tunnel of the Great Belt Link, Denmark,

- West Bridge of the Great Belt Link, Denmark.

DESCRIPTION OF THE CORROSION SENSORS

General

The development of the corrosion sensors is based on an extensive research program on the main factors influencing chloride induced macrocell corrosion of steel in concrete /1-5/. These investigations have been carried out using macrocell current measurements between anodically and cathodically acting steel surface areas. It was shown that the corrosion rate of the reinforcement can easily be monitored continuously by these electrical current measurements.

Operation of the Corrosion Sensors

The operation of a macrocell consisting of pieces of black steel (anodes) and of a noble metal (cathodes) is shown in Figure 1. In chloride free and non carbonated concrete, both electrodes are protected against corrosion due to the alkalinity of the pore solution of the concrete (passive state). The electrical current between both electrodes is negligibly low under such conditions. If, however, a critical chloride content is reached, or if the pH-value of the concrete decreases due to carbonation, the steel surface of the anode is no longer protected against corrosion. Provided that the cathode material is corrosion resistant in chloride contaminated or carbonated concrete (e. g. stainless steel, platinum), and sufficient moisture and oxygen are available, oxygen reduction takes place at the surface of the cathode. The local separation of anodically and cathodically acting areas leads to an electron flow between the black steel and the cathode, which can easily be measured at the external cable connection using a low resistance amperemeter.

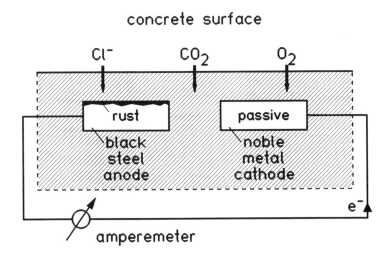

Figure 1   Macrocell consisting of a black steel anode and noble metal cathode

Figure 2 shows the result of electrical current measurements between a black steel anode and a stainless steel cathode in two concretes with different w/c-ratios. The macrocells were embedded with a concrete cover of only 5 mm to initiate corrosion by applying a chloride solution on the concrete surface within a short period of time. The results of the macrocell current measurements show that the critical chloride content reached a depth of 5 mm at the specimen with w/c = 0.7 about 80 days after placement of the concrete, causing a significant increase of the macrocell current while the specimen with lower w/c-ratio and higher resistance against chloride diffusion remained passive.

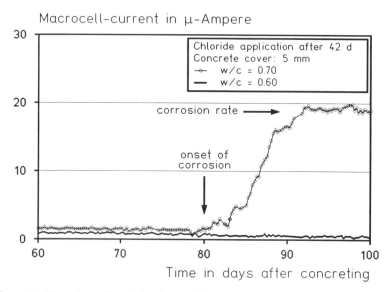

Figure 2   Time-dependent behaviour of the electrical currents between anode and cathode

Arrangement of the Corrosion Sensors

To monitor the corrosion risk for the reinforcement depending on the distance from the concrete surface, several anodes can be placed in the actual concrete structure at defined cover depths. The cathodes should be positioned at locations which are near the anodes and which are not water saturated because oxygen is consumed at the cathodically acting metal surface.

Figure 3 shows exemplarily two possible types of arrangements of anodes and cathodes. The Type-A-Sensors consist of four couples of anodes and cathodes which can be monitored by an external cable connection. As mentioned above the cathodes should be positioned at another location near a ventilated concrete surface if the concrete near the anodes is water saturated. Therefore the Type-B-Sensors with locally separated anodes and cathodes have been developed being additionally more economic because only one cathode is installed for all six anodes. In this case the single anodes are coupled against the cathode one after the other for the measurements. The switching between the anodes can be carried out using the selector switch within the hand device or automatically using the computer controlled measurement system.

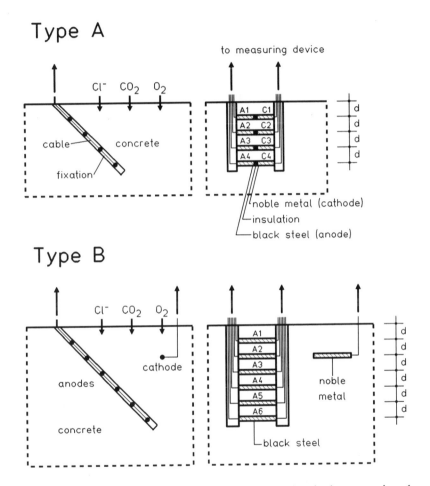

Figure 3   Possibilities for the arrangement of the anodes and cathodes to monitor the corrosion risk for the reinforcement (schematically)

Design of the Corrosion Sensors

The design of a set of six anodes (Type B) is schematically shown in Figure 4. Each of the six black steel anodes is positioned 50 mm from the next one to prevent interactions between the anodes.

Figure 4 shows also that the cables are lead through a stainless steel fixture to the measuring device. The cable shaft is filled with epoxy resin which acts as mechanical protection for the wires and a PT 100 temperature sensor that can be additionally in-stalled. Two wires are connected with each single electrode to get a redundant system. This allows to check the cables and cable connections after the installation by resistance measurements.

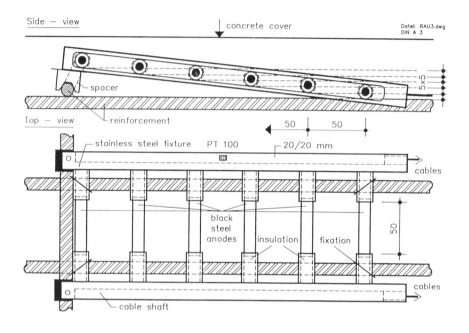

Figure 4   Design of a set of six anodes (Type B)

The fixture is separated from the anodes by an insulation. This geometrical design of the sensor ensures that the concrete cover above every single anode is not affected by parts of the sensor, and that the penetration of chlorides into the concrete and the carbonation process are also not influenced.

The set of six anodes and the cables are fixed to the reinforcement with plastic strips which are easy to handle and sufficiently robust under the conditions on site. A spacer at one side of the stainless steel fixture ensures the correct inclination of the sensor against the reinforcement which can be variably adjusted. The correct positions of the sensors after concreting can easily be checked using a covermeter.

All cables are lead to a junction box at an accessible concrete surface to connect them later with an automatic data collection system or to enable manual electrical current and other readings at regular intervals.

All materials used for the sensor and the cables are resistant against alkalies and chloride attack to ensure a sufficiently high longterm stability of the monitoring system. As stainless steel an austhenitic CrNiMo-steel (Type 316) is used which is resistant against chloride attack in concrete even under extremely strong conditions.

Measurements

The corrosion risk for the reinforcement is monitored by electrical current measurements between anodes and cathodes. To get some additional information about the corrosion rates which can be expected after the onset of corrosion at the existing reinforcement the electrochemical potential, temperature and electrolytic resistance of the concrete (AC-resistances between two anodes) can also be measured /6/.

All measurements can be carried out automatically by computer control or by hand in regular intervals (e. g. one to four times a year). As long as the critical chloride content and the carbonation depth have not reached the surface of the first anode A1 (see Figure 3), all the electrical currents are negligibly small. At the time, when the steel surface of the first anode A1 is depassivated due to the action of chlorides or carbonation, the electrical current between A1 and the cathode increases significantly whereas the currents of the other electrodes remain zero.

In the course of time the other anodes may also be depassivated one after the other. By measuring the electrical currents continuously or in regular intervals, the relationship between the depth of the critical chloride content or carbonation and time can be determined depending on the actual concrete properties and environmental conditions. The time to corrosion of the existing reinforcement can be estimated approximately by extrapolation of this relationship. If the reinforcement is expected to be depassivated during the service life of the structure and if the electrical currents and optionally the additional measurements show that the corrosion rate of the reinforcement is expected not to be negligibly low, corrosion protection measures (e. g. coating of the concrete surface, cathodic protection) can be carried out in time without removing any concrete.

The danger of cracking and spalling of the concrete due to the corrosion of the anodes positioned with low concrete cover depths can be eliminated by cathodic protection using a piece of inert metal as anode which is embedded near the anodes. The electrical currents between the inert anode and the corroding anodes are impressed over the existing cable connections by an external battery which is located in the junction box.

FIRST INSTALLATIONS

General

As mentioned in chapter 1 the corrosion monitoring system has been installed into four concrete structures. About 200 Type-B-anodes have been installed into the Eastern Railway Tunnel of the Great Belt Link in Denmark to monitor the corrosion risk due to the chloride containing soil around the tunnel under the eastern sea. The instrumentation of the West Bridge of the Great Belt Link in Denmark is not finished until now. To show the installation of the sensors under practical conditions the instrumentation and the first measurements of the Bridge Schießbergstraße are explained examplarily in the following chapters.

Design of the Monitoring System

The Bridge Schießbergstraße is a three span bridge with a whole length of 53 m. It was constructed between 1990 and 1992. As warning system for the risk of reinforcement corrosion the monitoring system which was described above has been installed into the bridge.

Generally the first step of the design of the permanent warning system is to define the critical locations of the structure. These critical locations are areas, where the corrosive attack can be expected to be most severe (e. g. spray or splash water zones) or weak points related to the execution of the construction (e. g. joints, low marks). In the case of the Bridge "Schießbergstraße" the most critical locations were

-   the uncoated bridge caps (parapets) which are exposed to deicing salts and

-   the bottom side of the superstructure of the bridge which is exposed to chloride containing spray water from the traffic under the bridge.

To monitor the corrosion risk for the reinforcement in the bridge caps due to deicing salts, eight sets of six anodes (Type-B) have been installed. Additionally, four sets of anodes and cathodes (Type-A) have been installed at the bottom of the superstructure and one set in the wall of the abutment to monitor the corrosion risk due to spray water. As cathodes for the Type-B-Sensors platinum coated titanium bars have been used to get a high driving voltage between anodes and cathodes resulting in high current signals. The cathodes of the Type-A-Sensors are made of stainless CrNiMo-steel (Type 316).

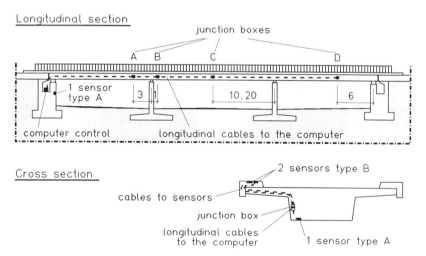

Figure 5   Arrangement of the corrosion monitoring equipment in the bridge "Schießbergstraße"

The arrangement of the corrosion monitoring system in the Bridge Schießbergstraße consisting of the corrosion sensors, cable connections and junction boxes is schematically shown in Figure 5. The positions A and B have been chosen to monitor the area near a support, position C in the field between the supports and position D about 40 meters away from the chamber in the abutment where the measurements are collected.

Installation of the Monitoring System

A few hours before placement of the concrete the sensors (anode ladders and cathodes) have been fixed to the reinforcement. Figure 6 shows two corrosion sensors before laying of the cables. The cathodes of the Type-B-sensors are placed under the anode ladders to ensure a low distance between anodes and cathodes. All cables of the sensors are directly lead into the junction boxes A-D to avoid cable connections being placed in the concrete. From all sensors photographs have been taken before casting of the concrete.

Figure 6   Corrosion sensors in the bridge cap before laying the cables

After placement of the concrete, the cables are extended from the junction boxes to the abutment by leading the longitudinal cables through plastic pipes which have been embedded into the concrete (see Figure 7). In this way all the readings can be carried out in the chamber of the abutment.

To check the correct installation of the sensors and the cable system including the junction boxes short-circuit tests have been carried out. It was shown that no cables have been distroyed by the placement of the concrete. Additionally the correct positions of the sensors have been checked using a covermeter with high accuracy.

Figure 7   Arrangement of junction box and cables in the bridge "Schießbergstraße"

Results of the First Measurements

As expected, the first measurements showed no significant currents between anodes and cathodes. This result indicates no actual corrosion risk for the reinforcement at a concrete cover lower than 10 mm. The additional measurements of the voltages between anodes and cathodes (potentials) indicate also no corrosion risk.

Further readings will be taken at intervals of approximately two times a year to monitor the ingress of aggressive (depassivating) substances.

FURTHER OUTLOOK

A monitoring system for the corrosion risk of the reinforcement of concrete structures has been developed and installed into four concrete structures. The first results show that the system is suitable for the use under practical conditions on site.

Further results from the corrosion monitoring systems and from further installations will be presented during the next years.

REFERENCES

1. SCHIEßL, P AND RAUPACH, M. Macrocell steel corrosion in concrete caused by chlorides. Second CANMET/ACI International Conference on Durability of Concrete, Montreal, 1991, pp 565-583

2. SCHIEßL, P AND RAUPACH, M. Chloride-induced corrosion of steel in concrete-Investigations with a concrete corrosion cell. The Life of Structures : The Role of Physical Testing, International Seminar, Brighton, April 1989, London : Butterworths, 1989, pp 226-233

3. SCHIEßL, P AND RAUPACH, M. Influence of blending agents on the rate of corrosion of steel in concrete. Durability of Concrete; Aspects of Admixtures and Industrial By-Products; 2nd International Seminar, June 1989, Stockholm : Swedish Council for Building Research, 1989, Publ.Nr. D9:89, pp 205-214

4. SCHIEßL, P AND RAUPACH, M. Influence of concrete composition and microclimate on the critical chloride content in concrete. Corrosion of Reinforcement in Concrete, International Symposium Wishaw, Warwickshire, UK, May 1990, London : Elsevier, 1990, pp 49-58

5. SCHIEßL, P AND RAUPACH, M. Influence of the type of cement on the corrosion behaviour of steel in concrete. 9th International Congress on the Chemistry of Cement, New Delhi, November 1992, New Delhi : National Council for Cement and Building Materials, Vol 5, pp 296-301

6. SCHIEßL, P AND RAUPACH, M. Monitoring of the corrosion risk for the reinforcement of bridges. Third International Workshop on Bridge Rehabilitation, Darmstadt, June 1992, 12 pages

COMPUTER MODELLING OF CORROSION AND CORROSION PROTECTION OF STEEL IN CONCRETE

A A Sagüés

S C Kranc

B G Washington

University of South Florida

United States of America

ABSTRACT. A method for modeling of the distribution of corrosion of steel in concrete is presented by means of an example of corrosion computation for marine bridge substructures with cathodic protection. The behavior of the system is modeled by formulating and numerically solving the Poisson equations for the electric potential and for the oxygen concentration in the concrete along with the appropriate boundary conditions for the polarization on the surface of the steel.

Keywords: Corrosion, computation, steel, concrete, marine, substructure, Poisson, oxygen, potential, polarization, cathodic protection.

Professor Alberto A Sagüés, Ph.D., P.E., is on the faculty of the Department of Civil Engineering and Mechanics, University of South Florida, Tampa, FL, U.S.A. He specializes in corrosion mechanisms of reinforcing steel in concrete, behavior of epoxy-coated rebar, electrochemical techniques for corrosion measurement, and modeling of corrosion phenomena. Professor Sagüés has published numerous articles in the present area and in the performance of engineering alloys in energy systems.

Professor SC Kranc, Ph.D., P.E., is on the faculty of the Department of Civil Engineering and Mechanics, University of South Florida. He specializes in transport processes, numerical methods and modelling.

Barbara G Washington is a research and teaching assistant in the Department of Civil Engineering and Mechanics, University of South Florida. Her primary interest is in structural design.

Concrete 2000. Edited by Ravindra K. Dhir and M. Roderick Jones.
© 1993 Published by E & FN Spon. ISBN 0 419 18120 2.

INTRODUCTION

Substructure members and pilings supporting marine bridges are frequently constructed using steel reinforced concrete. In typical installations, the columns are partially submerged in seawater, so that a region of high chloride ion concentration builds up in the splash zone just above the high water line. Passivity breakdown at the surface of the steel embedded in this region and below water results, with subsequent active corrosion of the steel, shortening the useful life of the element.

In several previous papers [1-4], the authors have developed a series of computational models to assist in understanding the corrosion of concrete substructure members in the marine environment. This understanding is essential to develop future design criteria to be based on a quantitative approach to reinforced concrete durability. Models of the type presented here are expected to be the forerunners of the next generation of corrosion control practices, which are to take advantage of increasing computational power for integrated design. In the previous work, as in the model presented here, nonlinear boundary conditions at the reinforcing and oxygen transport have been included. The principal result of that work has been to identify the likely regions of strong corrosion. The purpose of this paper is to illustrate how these advanced methods of corrosion modeling can be applied to the complex problem of computing three dimensional polarization conditions before and after cathodic protection is applied as a means of extending the useful life of the structure.

NOMENCLATURE

i_a	Current density of the iron oxidation reaction.
i_c	Current density of the oxygen reduction reaction.
i_{oa}	Exchange current density for the $Fe/Fe^{++}+2e$ system.
i_{oc}	Exchange current density for the OH^-/O_2+2H_2O+4e system.
I_{CORR}	Corrosion current.
I_w	Total current flowing from rebar assembly to water.
i	Current density.
E	Potential at a point of the electrolyte (through an idealized reference electrode) with respect to the body of the metal. Note that this convention, used throughout this paper, is the opposite of the common usage of referring potentials with respect to a reference electrode placed in the electrolyte.
E_o	Redox potential for the $Fe/Fe^{++}+2e$ system.
E_{O2}	Redox potential for the $4OH^-/O_2+2H_2O+4e$ system.
ECP	Electrode potential applied for cathodic protection.
b_a	Activation Tafel slope for the anodic reaction.
b_c	Activation Tafel slope for the cathodic reaction.
ρ	Concrete resistivity.
ρ_H, ρ_L	Highest and lowest values of ρ.
σ	Concrete conductivity ($\sigma = 1/\rho$)
n	Direction normal to a surface, pointing away from the surface.
C	Oxygen concentration.
C_s	Oxygen concentration at the steel surface.
C_o	Oxygen concentration at the external concrete surface.
D	Oxygen diffusion coefficient.
D_H, D_L	Highest and lowest values of D.

APPROACH

The configuration of the computational model is shown in Figure 1, consisting of a column with a total length of 243.8 centimeters, submerged to a depth of 61 centimeters. The active zone extended to 61 centimeters above the waterline. The column side dimension was 12.7 cm., whereas the concrete cover over the rebar was 2.54 cm. These values were chosen for future comparisons to laboratory experiments with model columns. The diffusion coefficient of oxygen varied along the column from a value $D_L = 10^{-5}$ cm^2/sec to a value $D_H = 10^{-3}$ cm^2/sec. Figure 1 shows the assumed pattern of variation of D along the column. Above water, the log of D was taken to vary linearly with height, to represent the expected rapid variation of D with moisture content [5]. The concrete resistivity was taken to vary from 2kΩ-cm to 40kΩ-cm with linear variation above the waterline. The values of the diffusivity and resistivity correspond to reasonable estimates of actual field conditions. The polarization parameters are typical of those encountered in similar systems. The following assumptions are made

1. The element is assumed to be a vertical, square section reinforced concrete column, with its lower part immersed in seawater.

2. The reinforcement consists of two steel bars placed as shown in Figure 1. Four points are used to approximate round bars (#4 bars, 1.27 cm. in diameter).

3. The concrete is treated as a homogeneous conducting electrolyte with variable conductivity and oxygen diffusivity along the column axis. The effective oxygen concentration is assumed constant along the outer surface of the column (local air-water equilibrium, with D adjusted accordingly [4]) and transport through the ends of the column is assumed to be negligible.

4. Simplified potential-concentration electrode kinetics are assumed to govern reactions at the steel surface in both active and passive regions.

5. In the computations presented here, it is assumed that chloride contamination has reached the threshold for active corrosion for rebar in the region below water and extending into the splash zone. The rest of the rebar is treated as a passive surface.

GOVERNING EQUATIONS

With the assumptions listed above, the equations governing the system are as follows:

The potential and the concentration of oxygen in the bulk of the concrete are determined by charge and mass conservation:

$$\nabla(\sigma \nabla E) = 0 \tag{1}$$

$$\nabla(D \nabla C) = 0 \tag{2}$$

At passive surfaces, only the oxygen reduction reaction is assumed to occur:

$$i_c = i_{0c} \frac{C_s}{C_0} e^{\frac{2.3}{b_a}(E-E_{O_2})}$$

(3)

while the passive anodic current is considered to be negligible:

$$i_a = 0$$

(4)

At active surfaces both oxygen reduction and iron dissolution are considered finite so that the total current is the sum of:

$$i_c = i_{0c} \frac{C_s}{C_0} e^{\frac{2.3}{b_c}(E-E_{O_2})}$$

(5)

$$i_a = i_{0a} e^{\frac{2.3}{b_a}(E_0-E)}$$

(6)

Everywhere on the steel surface the oxygen flow is related to the cathodic current by Faraday's law:

$$i_c = 4FD\frac{dC}{dn}$$

(7)

On the outer, vertical surfaces of the concrete, as indicated earlier:

$$C = C_0$$

(8)

At column ends flow is considered to be negligible

$$\frac{dC}{dn} = 0$$

(9)

Below the water line the potential is assumed to be constant on the concrete surface since the conductivity of seawater is much greater than that of concrete:

$$E = constant$$

(10)

Above the waterline the current flow through the outer concrete surface is zero (except when cathodic protection currents are impressed)

$$\frac{\partial E}{\partial n} = 0$$

(11)

To evaluate the potential and concentration everywhere in the column, the volume was divided into a rectangular grid coincident with the boundaries and the rebar. The horizontal plane was divided into 21 by 21 nodes and the vertical dimension into 25 nodes (Figure 1). The governing equations were reformulated as finite difference equations and solved by a Gauss-Seidel method as explained in Refs. [1-4]. The principal advantage of the present model over previous work is the ability to treat individual reinforcing steel bars.

The system examined here corresponds to an isolated column, so the net electric current between the steel and the seawater, I_w, is zero. This condition was achieved by computing I_w for various values of the potential assigned to the water in Eq. (10), until I_w became zero. This operating point was verified by establishing that the total macrocell current (integrated current flowing from anodic to cathodic regions) was also zero, and that the total consumption of oxygen at the rebar surfaces was equal to the total flow of oxygen entering the column walls.

A baseline case was treated initially, to determine the corrosion state when no cathodic protection was applied. To investigate cathodic protection, a nonpolarizable anode was incorporated in the computations. The anode was placed around the column at a height of 20.3 cm. above the waterline and extending to the top of the active zone as shown in Figure 1. Cathodic protection was achieved by applying the desired potential to the anode. For all cases the reaction kinetic constants and boundary oxygen values have been taken to be comparable to those in previous investigations [1-4]:

$$i_{oa} = 3 \ 10^{-8} \ \text{A/cm}^2 \qquad b_a = 60 \ \text{mV}$$
$$i_{oc} = 1 \ 10^{-9} \ \text{A/cm}^2 \qquad b_c = 100 \ \text{mV}$$
$$E_o = 780 \ \text{mV} \qquad C_O = 3 \ 10^{-7} \ \text{Mol/cm}^3$$
$$E_{O2} = -160 \ \text{mV}$$

RESULTS AND DISCUSSION

Figure 2 reproduces the potential distributions and the corresponding rates of iron dissolution at the surface of the steel along the column for all the conditions examined. The solid line in both graphs displays the results for the baseline case. The below-water portion of the column is governed by a diffusion-limited supply of oxygen, and iron dissolution takes place there at a very active potential but at a low corrosion rate. These results agree with calculations presented elsewhere for comparable systems [4] (note that the potential sign convention used here assigns more positive numbers to less noble conditions). Above water, the oxygen reduction reaction becomes activation limited as the transport of oxygen improves. The rate of iron dissolution increases substantially in the splash zone.

Cathodic protection computations proceeded much like the base case except that the net macrocell current balanced with the impressed current through the anode. Figure 2A shows the result of applying various cathodic protection potentials, ECP (as measured in the "power-on" condition at the reference electrode) on the potential at points immediately next to the rebar surface. Figure 2B shows the effect of the cathodic protection on the corrosion rate along the bars. As the magnitude of the applied potential increases, the corrosion current density decreases dramatically in the above-water region, where corrosion was formerly the greatest. The corrosion rate below water is also strongly affected although to a lesser degree. The maximum effect coincides, as expected, with the position of the anode. The results showed that to achieve a corrosion reduction of about 90% below water, it is necessary to use a driving potential (approximately 1.0 V) greater than that needed to achieve a similar level of protection in the above water region (approximately 0.85 V). Other calculations showed that the corrosion current without protection is approximately 1.5 mA but it decreased, as expected, by one order of magnitude when the total applied cathodic current was about 1.8 mA.

The detailed computation ability of the model is illustrated in Figure 3. The potential and oxygen concentration distribution on a transversal cross-section of the column is shown in 3A for the baseline case, at the same elevation as the reference electrode. The potential deviates by less than 2 mV from the average of the column cross-section, reflecting the small magnitude of the transversal currents. The potential variation is also slight around the rebar perimeter. The oxygen concentration drops markedly from the value at the external surface (source) to near zero at the bar perimeter (sink). This shows that this portion of the rebar assembly is at near diffusion-limited oxygen supply conditions. Upon application of cathodic protection at the level of 1.0 V at the reference electrode (3B), the potential distribution changes reflecting the rebar role as a current sink. There is a potential drop of about 35 mV between the external surface and the rebars. The oxygen distribution is hardly changed by the application of the protective current, except for an even smaller oxygen concentration at the rebar level. This is not surprising, since the system was already closer to limiting behavior in the unprotected state, and the protective current could therefore not induce additional oxygen consumption.

The model presented above supports the treatment of spatially detailed combinations of active-passive steel behavior and the use of complicated rebar geometries. Applications suitable for examination include the development of optimal cathodic anode positioning, selection of concrete surface treatments, behavior of coated rebar and relative corrosion performance of various concrete formulations. Since the model does not rely on local polarization curves, the complex issues resulting from variations in oxygen concentration through the concrete can be handled directly. Improvements of the model underway include time-dependent solutions, and effect of electrolyte availability on the extent of reactions on the rebar surface. As machines with teraflop/second processing speeds become available, development and application of this class of models and related approaches [6] is expected to be an integral part of the design of durable reinforced concrete structures in the next century.

CONCLUSIONS

1. Full three-dimensional modeling of rebar corrosion, including solution of potential and oxygen concentration distributions was demonstrated for a model system.

2. The model provides quantitative expression to corrosion current distribution in a partially submerged structure, modeling trends that agree with qualitative expectations of corrosion behavior in the system.

3. A cathodic protection application was addressed, illustrating the capabilities of the modeling approach for detailed examination of polarization and mass transport conditions in the system before and after protection. The modeling does not rely on local polarization curves.

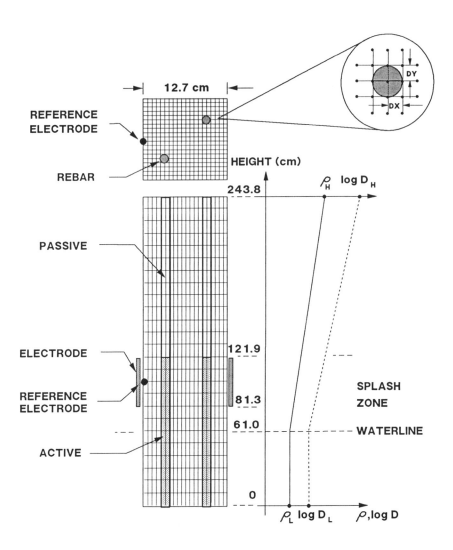

Figure 1.   Idealized, partially submerged reinforced concrete column model.

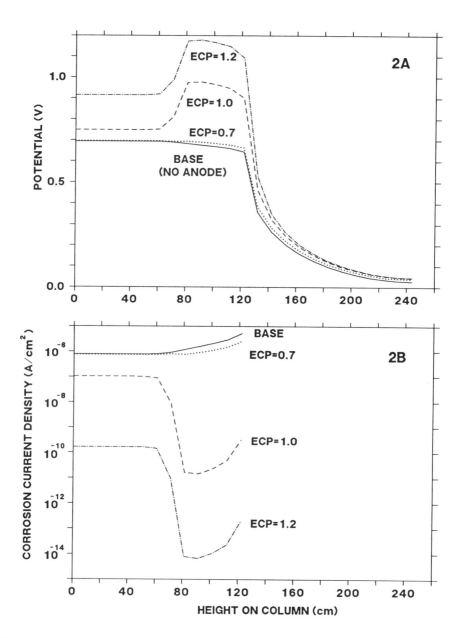

Figure 2.   Potential and corrosion current along the rebar cage surface for the
base case and selected protected conditions.

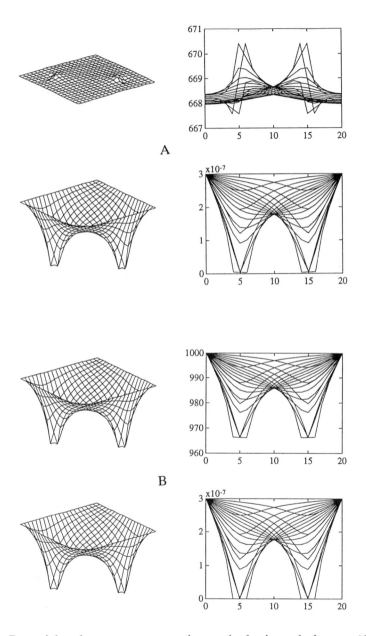

Figure 3.   Potential and oxygen concentration at the horizontal plane at 101.6 cm. Shown above are the results for the base case and below the results for an applied voltage of 1 volt. For correct visualization, the three dimensional representation of potential for the base case has been plotted to the same scale as the potential for the protected case.

ACKNOWLEDGMENTS

This investigation was supported in part by the Florida Department of Transportation (FDOT) in cooperation with the U.S. Department of Transportation (USDOT), and in part by the University of South Florida Engineering Computing Services. The opinions, findings and conclusions expressed in this document are those of the authors and not necessarily those of the FDOT or USDOT.

REFERENCES

1. KRANC, SC AND SAGÜÉS, AA. "Computation of Corrosion Macrocell Current Distribution and Electrochemical Impedance of Reinforcing Steel in Concrete", in Computer Modeling in Corrosion, ASTM STP 1154, R.S. Munn, Ed., ASTM, Philadelphia, 1992, p 95.

2. KRANC, SC AND SAGÜÉS, AA. "Calculation of Extended Counter Electrode Polarization Effects on the Electrochemical Impedance Response of Steel in Concrete", in Electrochemical Impedance: Interpretation and Analysis, ASTM STP 1188, Eds. DC Silverman, JR Scully and MW Kendig, ASTM, Philadelphia, 1993.

3. SAGÜÉS, AA AND KRANC, SC. Corrosion, Vol 48, 1992, p 624.

4. KRANC, SC, AND SAGÜÉS, AA. "Computation of Reinforcing Steel Corrosion Distribution in Concrete Marine Bridge Substructures", Paper No. 327, Corrosion/93, Nat. Assoc. of Corrosion Engineers, Houston, Texas, 1993 (also to appear in Corrosion, Vol 49, 1993).

5. TUUTTI, K. Corrosion of Steel in Concrete, Swedish Cement and Concrete Research Institute, 1982.

6. NAISH, C, HARKER, A AND CARNEY, R. "Concrete Inspection: Interpretion of Potential and Resistivity Measurements", in Corrosion of Reinforcement in Concrete, Eds. C Page, K Treadaway and P Bamforth, Elsevier Appl. Sci., London-New York, 1990, p 314.

RESEARCH, DEVELOPMENT AND EDUCATION

Chairmen

Mr G S Adam
Chairman, The Concrete Society, Scotland

Dr R D Browne
Taywood Engineering Ltd, United Kingdom

Dr H C Chan
University of Hong Kong, Hong Kong

Mr J F Lamond
Joseph F Lamond P.E., United States of America

Professor D M F Orr
University College, Eire

Professor H B Sun
Zhejiang University of Technology,
People's Republic of China

EFFECT OF CEMENT TYPE
AND DIFFERENT ADDITIONS ON SERVICE LIFE

K Tuutti

Cementa AB

Sweden

ABSTRACT. The service life of concrete due to reinforcement corrosion have been discussed intensively the last twenty years. Initiation of the process of corrosion by carbonation is relatively predictable today by the use of simple diffusion theories. The other main initiation mechanism, chloride ion penetration, is more difficult to predict. The main problem is the lack of quantitative figures on threshold values for corrosion initiation. Our investigations indicate that there is not a fixed threshold value. The limit chloride concentration will vary due to the electrochemical inhomogeneity around the steel surface. Although it is possible to make lifetime calculations if we compare our practical experience with corrosion theories. The results indicate that different pure Portland cements are not comparable even if the type is the same. Use of additions will sometimes decrease the service life. On the other hand a small amount of additions often increase the service life. This report will more precisely discuss the most important parameters with the aim to find a comparison method for different concrete mixes.

Keywords: Chloride, Diffusion, Threshold values, Corrosion, Pulverized–fuel ash, Silica fume, Ordinary Portland cement, Lifetime predictions.

Dr Kyösti Tuutti is Manager of the Research and Development section in the Swedish cement company Cementa AB. He specialises in the concrete durability problems and environmental technologies as solidification of waste materials. Dr Tuutti is today active in the harmonization procedure of EEC codes and active in several international research projects.

Concrete 2000. Edited by Ravindra K. Dhir and M. Roderick Jones.
© 1993 Published by E & FN Spon. ISBN 0 419 18120 2.

INTRODUCTION

It is well known that a certain chloride concentration in the pore water in concrete will cause corrosion. Chloride ions are able to penetrate concrete from the environment which is surrounding the structure. The competition between diffferent binders as ordinary Portland cement (OPC), mixed products containing OPC, slag, pulverized fly–ash (PFA) etc have increased research activity into the durability of concrete. The main field of this research have been the comparison of diffusion coefficients and the binding capacity of chlorides in the cement matrix. A linear relationship between the measured chloride penetration and the lifetime have normally been reported. Unfortunately it is not sufficient to simply determine the chloride penetration because such values do not indicate the service life of the structure. It is also necessary to know the chloride content at the initiation moment. Furthermore, the environment, or the type of chemicals and the moisture content in the surroundings, will also affect on the rate of penetration.

Theoretical calculations and modelling of the time of initiation in a chloride rich environment demonstrate the lack of knowledge for the important parameter, the threshold value of chloride ion concentration, which changes the passive stage to an active corrosion stage. A demonstration of this can be seen in Figure 1. Normally the reader believes that the sample with the lowest chloride concentration is preferable. Figure 1 demonstrates that the situation can be the opposite.

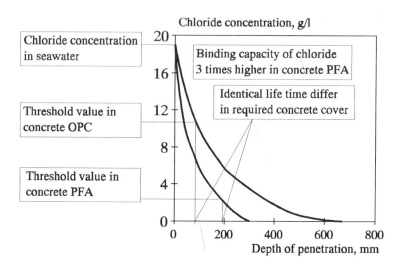

Figure 1   Schematic sketch of the time of initiation for two different concretes as a function of depth.

Furthermore, we are nowardays often discussing the effect of the most incredible products which the industry would like to use in a concrete mix. Normally those products are characterized as more or less waste materials. The owner of such a material will naturally try to increase the value by selling it to the concrete industry. Therefore the normal procedure is, some comparison tests, in a laboratory, or a few of the parameters which appear to produce good behaviour for only specific properties. This report will demonstrate that a laboratory comparison procedure which is not calibrated to a long term field exposure could not be used in service life prediction. Only the corrosion initiation procedure will be discussed in this report.

PARAMETERS IN THE CORROSION INITIATION MODEL

The length of the initiation period is determined by how rapidly the concrete cover is depassified as a result of the fact that chloride ions penetrate to the steel, and by the concentration which is required to start the corrosion process. The penetration sequence is here described as a diffusion process. In practice, the transport is not always quite so clearcut but is rather a combination of capillary suction and diffusion. One example of this is the fact that partly dried–out concrete absorbs a chloride solution through capillary suction. On the other hand such a rapid chloride penetration can not be acceptable for the main part of the concrete cover if we are expecting a service life longer than 30 years. Therefore the diffusion model can be used with some modifications.

In constant wet environments as below the ground and sea water level the diffusion model describe the chloride penetration.

In varying environmental conditions such as the splash zone, concrete near deiced roads etc the moisture conditions are varying by time. In drying periods water will evaporate from the concrete and the salts are remained in the pore water which is still in the pores. The concentration of different salt solutions are then increasing in the pore water as a function of evaporated water. In wet periods water is quickly absorbed through capillary suction which will increase the total amount of salts in the concrete if the water contains such substances. Structures which are not sheltered from rain will also be washed out of chloride ions when the rain water is flowing over the surface.

The chloride concentration will therefore be fluctuating in a surface zone, the convective zone, and reach a limit maximum value inside the concrete. The diffusion process will describe the chloride penetration behind this convective zone, see Figure 2.

Mass transport as a result of diffusion gives the following parameters when studying the initiation period.
 – concentration difference, the ambient concentration minus the
 initial concentration of chloride ions
 – transport distance, the thickness of concrete cover
 – the permeability of the concrete against chloride ions
 – the capacity of the concrete for binding chloride ions

– the threshold value which is required for initiation of the process of corrosion

The depth of the convective zone depends on the
- wetting and drying time
- time of capillary suction during wetting
- permeability of the concrete against water
- difference in wapor pressure

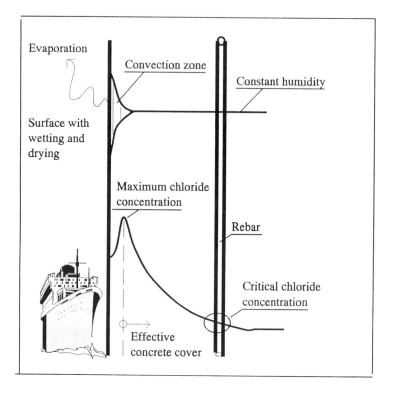

Figure 2   Schematic sketch of the moisture and the chloride variation in concrete in the splash zone, Sandberg [1].

A numerical calculation method of this convective zone, based on a material study, have been developed by Arfvidsson and Hedenblad [2] . The prediction method will also account the effect of a capillary suction in the wetting procedure. Demonstration of the effect of the primary parameters will give one more piece in the corrosion puzzle, see Figure 3. Small concrete covers and/or high permeable concrete will decrease the internal environmental homogeneity of the oxygen concentrations, ion concentrations and moisture conditions. These variations will primary influence on the chloride threshold value in the initiation procedure.

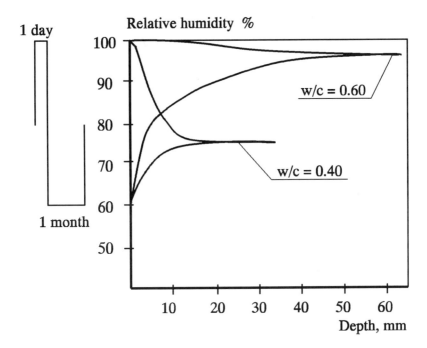

Figure 3. Demonstration of the moisture variation in two different concretes, W/C 0.40 respective 0.60, with an environmental cycling of 1 day capillary suction and 1 month drying in RH = 60%, Arfvidsson and Hedenblad [2].

CHLORIDE BINDING CAPACITY FOR OPC CONCRETE

The concrete codes in several countries are classifying the binding capacity for cement types with regard to the amount of C_3A in the cement. A lot of published results have shown that it is not only the C_3A content which will have an effect on the chloride binding, Kjaer [3]. Swedish measurements on the chloride binding capacity for different binders can be seen in Figure 4.

Degerhamn OPC with a very low C_3A amount is much better in binding chlorides than Slite OPC with four times more C_3A. Also the effect of mineral additives such as slag and PFA will be important. We know that the chemistry varies from coal to coal, which naturally will also change the binding capacity for chlorides.

Designers are often confused by the environment "seawater", where a low C_3A content is favoroable, due to the sulphate attack and in the other way a low C_3A content is negative due to the chloride binding. Therefore new theories which delete the old C_3A concept must be of great interest.

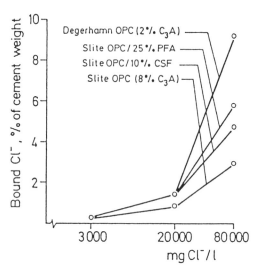

Figure 4   Measured amount bound chloride for different binders, Kajsa Byfors [4].

A calculation of the total amount of C_3A + C_4AF in the two Swedish cement types Degerhamn and Slite gave 16% and 13% respectively. Strictly the amount of hydrated aluminium oxides would probably give a better correlation with the binding capacity of chloride ions.

Chloride ions will also be physically bound in the pore structure which will have an influence on the penetration process. Normal additions will not change the pore structure as much that it will have an influence in the binding capacity.

THE VALUE OF DIFFUSION TESTS IN A SODIUM CHLORIDE SOLUTION

Alot of laboratory experiments have been carried out with the aim of detecting the chloride resistivity for different concrete mixes. These results indicate a very short penetration time to reach the critical chloride concentration for a normal concrete in a chloride environment. An explanation for the bad correlation of these laboratory results to a normal service life for a concrete structure, which also is cracked, is missing. There is today a need of more field investigations instead of small laboratory tests. Structures in service are ageing naturally and if we are not able to predict the service life with our models, we have to find new models, instead of the reliance to the old ones.

With the aim of detecting all missing parameters in the chloride initiated corrosion process an exposure site was set up in Sweden in 1991. About 40 different concrete mixes are in the study, with W/C from 0.25 to 0.75, with PFA and silica fume additions, etc. Large concrete batches have been mixed for the production of both laboratory test specimens and small concrete walls for the field exposure site. The samples in the natural environment are exposed to both the constant wet chloride rich seawater at the Swedish west coast and the splash zone.

All possible corrosion influencing parameters will be detected as:
- different negative and positive ions in the pore water
- binding capacity of chloride ions
- chloride threshold values
- chloride profile
- effective diffusion coefficient for different ions
- the RH profile in the concrete cover
- the rate of the process of corrosion after initiation
- pore structure
- frost resistance

Comparison with old structures will also be an important part of this project. The examination will be made on drilled out cores from existing structures with a known concrete mix.

The research institutes which are involved in this project are
- The Swedish National Testing and Research Institute
- The Cement and Concrete Research Institute
- The University in Lund
- The University in Gothenburg, Chalmers
- The Euroc Research Laboratory
- AEC Danish Concrete Engineer Consultants
and technical advice from
- The Swedish National Road Authority
- Cementa AB
- Technical specialists working in Swedish and Danish companies

Test results are already published in internal working documents, Sandberg [1]. Refering to these reports some interesting results are presented in table 1.

General tendences observed in table 1 are:
- the C_3A content is not a primary chloride binding parameter.
- the laboratory results give higher diffusion coefficients for OPC concrete, than in practice, compared with blended binder mixes.
- a sealing effect is shown for OPC concrete which will decrease the D value.
- OPC concrete mixes have higher threshold values compared with blended binder mixes

The results above indicate that a lot of investigations which have been carried out in laboratories could give missleading results due to the time dependent diffusion constant for OPC concrete. The results also indicate OPC concrete with a small amount of silica fume may be the most optimum binder mix in chloride rich seawater environments. It must however be noted that the presented results are the first from the Swedish project and future results could give other relationships.

Table 1 Measured chloride threshold value and measured effective diffusioncoefficients for laboratory specimens and field exposed specimens. The C_3A content in the first 6 mixes are about 2% and about 5% for the last 3 mixes. The third mix (*) is a concrete core drilled out from a bridge column with an age of 4 years.

Type of binder	W/C	Threshold value (Cl⁻/C)	D in lab (10 m²/s)	D in field (10 m²/s)
OPC 450 kg	0,35	> 1,4	5,0	3,3
OPC 420 kg	0,40	> 1,4	7,3	4,2
OPC 420 kg*	0,38	>1,4	7,9	0,8/0,3
Total 450 kg (5% silica fume)	0,35	<1,0	3,0	1,8/0,5
Total 420 kg (5% silica fume)	0,40	<1,0	2,1	2,0/0,8
Total 450 kg (5% silica fume+ 10%PFA)	0,35	<1,0	1,5	1,8/0,6
Total 420 kg (5% silica fume)	0,40	<1,0	4,0	4,0/1,0
Total 450 kg (5% silica fume+10% PFA)	0,35	0,6	1,2	2,3/0,5
Total 420 kg (4,5% silica fume+17% PFA)	0,40	0,5	0,5	1,4/0,3

Concrete structures exposed to deicing salts will probably correlate better with laboratory results, where the specimens was exposed to sodium chloride solutions. Therefore these two environments, seawater and deicing salts, will have different effects on concrete structures and different optimum binder combinations.

CHLORIDE THRESHOLD VALUES

The chloride threshold level depends on so many parameters that we are today a little bit disorientated. Many investigations are reporting different critical chloride concentrations with a lowest values of around 0.2 – 0.4 % by weight of the cement content. Also several of national codes are using those low values as the allowable amount of chloride in concrete. On the other hand many investigations indicate much higher threshold values around 1 – 2 % by weight of the cement content, Lambert, Page and Vassie [5], Pettersson [6], Pettersson and Woltze [7].

Between 1950 and 1960 numerous results were obtained using calcium chloride admixtures as the accelerator. Laboratory and practical experiments showed that we could expect a threshold value of 2 – 3% by the weight of cement. These samples were both small and large, with a very homogeneous concrete surrounding the reinforcement. The climate was with other words constant. Suppose such experiments were made under other climate conditions. Drying and wetting procedures would have increased the chloride concentration close to the steel surface, in an inhomogeneous way, which certainly would have changed the reported results. In the same manner thick concrete covers will increase the homogeneity around the embedded steel.

This difference indicates the problems we are dealing with. The most important parameter which will give such variable results, as mentioned above, is the transportation or the exchange of water, oxygen, corrosion inhibiting ions and corrosive ions. Therefore such variations must be taken into account in all comparison tests and life time predictions.

Chloride concentrations in the surrounding environment could be high or low. An increase of the chloride concentration in the environment will give the same effect as a reduction of the threshold value. All chloride concentration profiles are related to the concentration at the surface. The threshold value is on the other hand relatively constant, which will drop the relative position of the threshold line in the figures when the surface concentration is increased.

Recent results by Pettersson and Woltze [7] indicate that all binder combinations will have different threshold values. The moisture situation will also complicate the exact prediction of the threshold value on structures in service. However, structures have to be designed in such a way that the concrete quality combined with the effect of the concrete cover will raise a minimum of moisture variations close to the steel surface. If these design roules is used, it is also possible to predict the service life of a concrete structure.

All effects of different parameters discussed in this paper is summarized in Figure 5. The porosity or the permeability of the concrete cover which have not been discussed in detail has of course major influence on the rate of chloride penetration. A change of the diffusion coefficient with a factor of 10 will change the depth of penetration for a specific concentration by a factor of the square root of 10. Binding of chloride ions have only minor effect on the rate of penetration. The threshold value have a great influence on the time of initiation specially if the threshold value is near the surface concentration. According to this discussion the choice of a high threshold value is more favourable than a high chloride binding capacity.

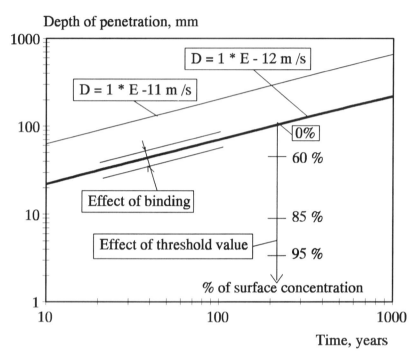

Figure 5   Calculated penetration depths of the chloride front for different diffusion coefficients, binding capacities and threshold values. It has been assumed that the penetration process will follow the mathematical equation of the moving boundary.

REFERENCES

1.   Sandberg, P. Kloridinitierad armeringskorrosion i betong, University of Lund 1992, Building Materials, TVBM–7032.

2.   Arfvidsson and Hedenblad. Calculation of moisture variation in concrete surfaces, University of Lund 1991, Building Materials & Building Physics.

3.   Kjaer, U. Concrete for the fixed link across the Great Belt – Store Bält, Dansk Beton , No 4, 1990.

4.   Byfors, K. Chloride initiated reinforcement corrosion. Swedish Cement and Concrete Research Institute, Report 1:90, Stockholm 1990.

5.   Lambert, Page and Vassie. Investigations of reinforcement corrosion. 2. Electrochemical monitoring of steel in chloride-contaminated concrete. Materials and Structures, Vol. 24, No. 143, 1991.

6.   Pettersson, K. Corrosion threshold value and corrosion rate in reinforced concrete, CBI Report 2:92, Swedish Cement and Concrete Research Institute, Stockholm 1992..

7   Pettersson and Woltze. Fältförsök beständiga marina betongkonstruktioner, Delrapport 1, Rapport nr 92057, Swedish Cement and Concrete Research Institute, Stockholm 1992.

DEVELOPMENT OF HIGH CALCIUM FLY ASH AND SLAG SAND CONCRETE

S I Pavlenko

Siberian Metallurgical Institute

E A Chayka

Scientific Research Institute

Russia

ABSTRACT. The composition of fine-grained cementless concrete on the basis of high-calcium fly ash slag sand produced by burning brown coals from Kansko-Achinsky deposit,
has been designed by the Siberian Metallurgical Institute.
Concrete consists only of the waste products of thermal power plants and ferro-alloy works (silica fume). It contains
neither natural (gravel, rubble, sand) nor artificial porous aggregates (claydite, aggloporite, foam polystyrene).
It has the compressive strength of 5 to 20 MPa and may be
used both for load-bearing and enclosing structures.
This paper presents data on studies of physico-mechanical
and deformation properties of fine-grained cementless slag
ash concrete over a 1 year period. The results of the studies show that the above concrete may be used for the con-
straction of one, two-storey buildings both precast and
cast in-situ.

Keywords: Fine-grained Cementless Slag-Ash Concrete, High-
Calcium Fly Ash, Slag Sand, Silica Fume, Compressive
Strength, Relative Shrinkage, Initial Modulus of Elastici-
ty, Creep Deformation.

Professor Stanislav I Pavlenko, Civil Engineering Department, Siberian Metallurgical Institute, academic adviser
of the Russian Engineering Academy. He is the author of
more than 100 papers on use of fly ash and slag in concrete.

Dr Evgeny A Chayka is Deputy Director of the Scientific-
Research Institute in Scientific work, MNPO "Resurs",
Moscow, Russia. He is a bachelor of science, the author
of 30 articles and papers on use of fly ash in concrete.

Concrete 2000. Edited by Ravindra K. Dhir and M. Roderick Jones.
© 1993 Published by E & FN Spon. ISBN 0 419 18120 2.

INTRODUCTION

In the papers presented at the Conferences in Sheffield, September 1991 |1| and in Istanbul, May 1992 |2| we have already spoken about the creation of fine-grained cementless slag ash concretes for load-bearing and enclosing structures which contains neither natural nor artificial porous aggregates. It entirely consists of the industrial by-products. But at that time we had no data on physico-mechanical and deformation properties of the concretes over a long period. The more so, as the above concrete with a clinkerless binder (high-calcium fly ash in this case) yields to the irregularity of volume change. In present work we have studied the above mentioned properties of concretes the mixture properties of which are given in Table 1.

Table 1   Mixture proportions of cementless slag ash concretes

APPLICATION	QUANTITIES, Kg/m³					MIX SLUMP, Cm	MIX DENSITY, Kg/m³	COMPRESSIVE STRENGTH AT 28 DAYS, MPa
	Fly ash	Silica fume	Slag sand	Water	Air-entraining admixture			
For load-bearing structures	650	70	720	480	—	8-10	1920	15
For enclosing structures	500	50	500	330	5	6-8	1385	5.2

MATERIALS

Fly Ash

Fly ash from the Novosibirskaya TPP-3 is a fine-dispersed powder of a light brown colour with the average specific surface of 4000 cm^2/g. The positive characteristics of this fly ash are its high contents of bound calcium oxide (30%) and silicon oxide (37.6%), small amounts of potassium and sodium oxides (0.66%), of sulfur (2.53%) and of unburnt particles (2.48%). The fly ash has good binding properties. On the other hand, the ash contains a high amount of magnesium oxide (6.44%) and free calcium oxide (5.51%) affecting the irregularity of concrete volume change |3|.

Slag Sand

The slag sand had a particle size distribution of 0 to 5 mm and fineness modulus of 2.7 mm; its colour varied from dark brown to black and the alumina-silicate glass was mostly in the radioamorphous state. It contained neither unburnt particles nor sulfuric compounds.

Silica Fume

Silica fume is a superdispersed powder of a light grey colour with the average density of 20000 cm^2/g.

Air-Entraining Admixture

The air-entraining admixture used was a synthetic detergent called "Progress", the secondary sodium alkyl sulphate. It is usually supplied as a liquid having a density of 1.084 t/m³.

EXPERIMENTAL PROCEDURE

Test cubes, 10x10x10 cm in size and prisms, 10x10x40 cm in size, were cast for studying physico-mechanical and deformation properties of fine-grained slag ash concrete. Mixtures were prepared in a laboratory positive mixer with water having a temperature of 70-

80°C, subjected to vibration, cured for 4 h at room temperature and then were moist-cured in the laboratory steam-curing chamber at 85-95°C using 3+10+3 h cycle.

Shrinkage and Creep Deformations

Test prisms were used for determining shrinkage and creep deformations of cementless concrete |4|, prism strength and initial modulus of elasticity |5| and the cubes, 10x10x10 cm in size |6| were used for determining compressive strength of concrete. The prisms were cured in air with the relative humidity of 50-70% at 18 to 20°C. The measurements of shrinkage deformation were made by clock indicator device with a scale of 0.001 mm (Fig. 1).

Figure 1. Testing prisms for shrinkage

The measurements were made in the following periods: immediately after cooling the specimens, 30 min later, 2, 4, 12, 24 h later, once a day during the next 6 days, once in 2 days during the following 9 days and twice a week after 15 days. The test results are illustrated in Figures 2 and 3.

RELATIVE SHRINKAGE STRAIN OF DENSE CONCRETE

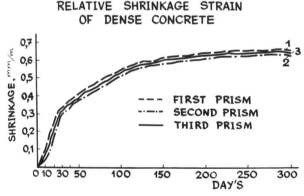

Figure 2. Shrinkage of dense concrete

As can be seen from Figure 2, during the first day after heat treatment, shrinkage of dense concrete is comparetively small and does not exceed 0.3 mm/m, then it increases amounting to 0.6 mm/m at 28 days. At 28 to 180 days shrinkage increases insignificantly ceasing after that period. The maximum shrinkage value of 0.65 mm/m is in accordance with the building code |7| for fine-grained (sand) concretes up to 0.75 mm/m. It should be noted that shrinkage of dense concrete develops smoothly as compared to fine-grained (sand) concrete. Gain in strength is observed. Slower rate of bleeding water from the concrete and higher rate of strength gain as compared to sand concrete result in higher crack resistance.

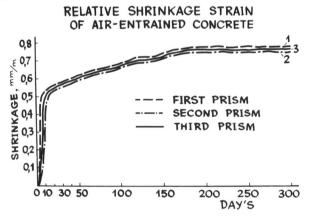

Figure 3. Shrinkage of air-entrained concrete

As seen from Figure 3, the main drying shrinkage of air-entrained lightweight concrete takes place during the heat treatment and cooling at 24 h (0.5 mm/m), after that it increases smothly and insignificantly. At 180 days shrinkage ceases. The maximum shrinkage magnitude of 0.76 mm/m complies with the requirements of the building code for lightweight concretes (up to 1 mm/m). Creep strain tests of cementless fine-grained slag ash concrete were commenced at 28 days at spring devices with clock indicators Figure 4.

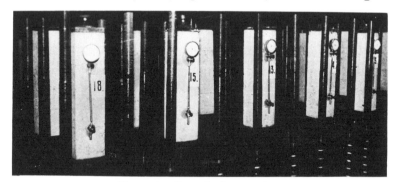

Figure 4. Creep tests on prisms

10x10x40 cm prisms were loaded for a long period, stresses constituting 50% by prism strength (0.5 R prism). After unloading, readings were made in the following periods: 30 min later, 1, 3, 6 and 12 h later during the first 24 h, once a day during the next 6 days, once in a two-day time during the following 9 days and twice a week at an age greater than 15 days.

Data on creep strains are presented in Figures 5 and 6. Figure 5 shows that the relative creep strain of concrete for load-bearing structures increased during the first 20 days (up to 0.8 mm/m, it was insignificant at 20 to 180 days of age (up to 0.94 mm/m) and ceased at the greater age. Creep strain of slag ash concrete for enclosing structures has a longer period of stabilization. The strains of the prisms were: 0.9 mm/m at 20 days, 1.2 mm/m at 20 to 180 days and maximum 1.3 at 240 days. They correspond to the building code |4| requirements for fine-grained and lightweight concretes (1.2 and 1.5 mm/m, respectively, are the norms with 5% loading).

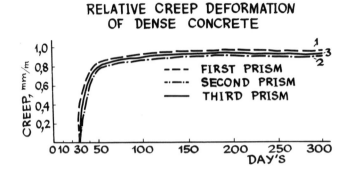

Figure 5.   Creep of dense concrete

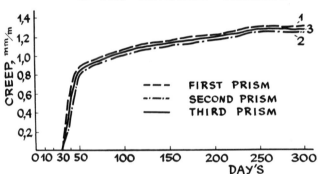

Figure 6.   Creep of air-entrained concrete

Strength characteristics

Compressive strength of 100-mm cubes stored in natural conditions after curing at 24 h, 28, 90, 180 and 365 days was taken as a control strength of fine-grained cementless slag ash concrete. Data are given in Table 2. It is evident from these data that both types of concrete had the gain in strengths. The strength of concrete for load-bearing structures increased by 23% between 28 and 360 days, while that of ordinary concrete increased maximum by 10% over this period. This demonstrates that the reaction of hydrotation of the concrete continues. On the other hand, such rate of strength development may result in destructive processes. That is why, we go on investigating beyond this period. The rate of gain of strength of concrete for enclosing structures is considerably lower (10%), and at 180 days it is even lower than at 90 days. Specimens of lightweight concrete are left for long-term studies.

In order to determine resistance of concrete to axial compression in structures, we determined the so-called prism strength of concrete on test prisms, 10x10x40 |5| and com-

Table 2. Main physico–mechanical characteristics of cementless concrete over 1year
         period

Concrete characteristics	Period of testing, days				
	1	28	90	180	365
1. For load–bearing structures					
Compressive strength of cubes, MPa	10.80	15.20	17.50	18.30	18.00
Prism strength, MPa	8.10	11.86	13.48	14.46	15.00
Prism–to–Cube strength Ratio	0.75	0.78	0.77	0.79	0.79
Initial Modulus of Elasticity, MPa	9.50	12.10	12.50	13.00	17.60
Compressibility, mm/m	0.85	0.87	0.88	0.97	1.04
Extensibility, mm/m	0.09	0.12	0.14	0.15	0.16
2. For enclosing structures					
Compressive strength of cubes, MPa	4.23	5.80	6.30	6.15	6.40
Prism strength, MPa	3.00	4.29	4.73	4.49	4.80
Prism–to–cube strength Ratio	0.71	0.74	0.75	0.73	0.72
Initial Modulus of Elasticity, MPa	6.25	7.15	7.87	8.79	9.20
Compressibility, mm/m	0.90	1.02	1.18	1.26	1.34
Extensibility, mm/m	0.14	0.18	0.20	0.22	0.23
Frost resistance, cycle	—	51	53	56	68
Heat conductivity, W/m°C	0.44	0.36	0.32	0.29	0.26

pared the relationships between prism and cube strengths of the two types of concrete in
accordance with the building code requirements |7|. According to the norms, these rela-
tionships should be no less than 0.7 and 0.65 for load–bearing and enclosing structures,
respectively. As can be seen from Table 2, they correspond to the requirements being
0.75 to 0.79 and 0.71 to 0.75 for load–bearing and enclosing structures, respectively.
The initial modulus of elasticity (E · 10^{-3}) of the concretes was defined by loading
10x10x40 cm prisms with multi–step load according to the NIIZhB method |5|. The data are
given in Table 2. The initial modulus of elasticity of the concretes is in accordance
with the building code requirements |7| (6.5 to 15.5 MPa and 6.0 to 8.8 MPa for classes
B3.5–12.5 fine–grained moist–cured concrete and for classes B2.5–5 lightweight and air-
entrained concrete with the average density of 1200–1400 kg/m^3, respectively).
Compressibility and extensibility of the two types of concretes (Table 2) are 10–12%
higher than the norms. It indicates that crack resistance of the concretes too is higher
than the norms for fine–grained cement concretes .
Frost resistance and waterproofhees of the concretes for load–bearing structures have
not been investigated as the structures planned to be used inside the heated buildings.
Frost resistance and heat conductivity were studied on air–entrained concrete for enclosing structures (external walls). Cubes, 10x10x10 cm in size, were tested for frost resistance in a freezing chamber "Nema" according to the methods developed by NIIZhB. The
data are in Table 2. According to the requirements, frost resistance for external walls
of classes 2 and 3 buildings is 50 and 35 cycles, respectively, with the relative humi-

dity of air exceeding 75%, and 35-25 cycles with the humidity less than 75%. The frost resistance of our concrete after 1 year of testing was 51 to 68 cycles which exceeds the norm by 1.5 to 2 times.

CONCLUSIONS

1. Classes B3.5-15 (5 to 20 MPa) cementless fine-grained concrete for load-bearing and enclosing structures may be produced on the basis of high-calcium ash and slag sand from thermal power plants.

2. The main physico-mechanical and deformation characteristics of this concrete are in accordance and partially surpass the building code requirements for fine-grained concretes. In order to expand the application of concrete, the studies of its characteristics will be continued.

3. Fine-grained cementless concrete on the basis of high-calcium fly ash and slag sand from TPP seems to be a promising material for the 21st century. Excluding the use of natural and artificial energy consuming materials it solves three problems, namely: economic, ecological and social (solution of the problem of housing construction).

REFERENCES

1. PAVLENKO, S.I. Lightweight cementless concrete on the base of high-calcium fly ash and slag sand from TPP. The volume consists of papers presented at the International Conference on Blended Cements in Construction, held at the University of Sheffield, UK, 9-12 September 1991. Edited by R.N.Swamy. Elsiver Applied Science, London and New York, 1991, pp. 95-106.

2. PAVLENKO, S.I. Fine-grained cementless concrete made with high-calcium Fly ash and slag sand from thermal power Plants. Fourth CANMET/ACI International Conference on Fly Ash, Silica Fume, Slag and Natural Pozzolans in Concrete, Supplementary Papers. Istanbul, 1992, pp. 749-763.

3. IGNATOVA, O.A. Study of the homogeneity of high-calcium ashes from Kansko-Achinsky coal and development of standart requirements for use in concretes. Proceedings of the All-Union Conference on Concrete Containing Ash and Slag from TPP and their Use in Construction. Edited by S.I.Pavlenko, Vol. 1, 1990, pp. 146-147.

4. NIIZhB. Methodic recommendations for Investigation of shrinkage and creep of concrete, Moscow, 1976, pp. 10-76.

5. NIIZhB. Methodic recomendations for determination of strength and structure characteristics of concretes under shot-and-long duration loading, Moscow, 1976, pp. 10-76.

6. LESHCHINSKY, M.Yu. Concrete testing, Reference Book, Moscow, Stroyizdat, 1980, pp.71-318.

7. GOSSTROY USSR. Concrete and reinforced concrete structures, SNIP 2.03.01-84, Moscow, 1985, pp. 12-20.

HIGH-CALCIUM FLY ASH GROUTS

I Papayianni

University of Thessaloniki

Greece

ABSTRACT. The paper deals with the use of a high-calcium fly ash in grout production and forms part of a research programme funded by Greek Public Power Corporation in relation to high-calcium fly ash utilization in grouting. The cement which is the main costituent of grouts is partially replaced by this fly ash at different levels 0, 20, 40, 60, 80 and 100% (by weight) for sanded grouts and 0, 30, 60, 80 and 100% for slurries. Some important properties in grouts in fresh state, such as the time of efflux, the bleeding capacity and the water retentivity were measured for all mixes. An adequate number of mortar specimens (40x40x160)mm were constructed for compressive and flexural strength. Dynamic modulus of elasticity was also estimated by measuring ultrasonic pulse velocity through mortar specimens. Based on test results, it could be said that depending on the required strength level of sanded grout or of impregnated soil, the under question fly ash is shown very effective. Especially ground fly ash is possible to replace large quantities of cement.

Keywords: Grout, High-calcium Fly ash, Fluidity, Bleeding, Water retentivity, Compressive, Flexural, Strength, Dynamic modulus of elasticity.

Dr. Ioanna Papayianni is Assoc. Professor at Dept. of Civil Engineering of Aristotle University of Thessaloniki. Her research field is on concrete technology and materials for restoration of monuments and historical buildings. She specialises in the use of fly ashes in concrete as well as durability aspects, rehabilitation and resistance to high temperature of concrete. She also deals with the development of criteria for suitability of building materials for restoration.

Concrete 2000. Edited by Ravindra K. Dhir and M. Roderick Jones.
© 1993 Published by E & FN Spon. ISBN 0 419 18120 2.

INTRODUCTION

The use of low-calcium fly ash as a constituent of grout mixtures is well known in Great Britain [1] and other countries [2] whereby the utilization of fly ash in concrete products is specified by national or European standards. This does not occur in the case of high-calcium fly ashes (HCFA) which are considered as marginal materials. Thus, while (HCFA) may be used in blended cements under the status of relevant regulations, their application in the sector of grouting as a separate constituent of the mixtures is not favoured and therefore cement is literally wasted for such a low strength grade concrete. Prof. T.P. Naik has recently published [3] his experience in using very effectively and economically HCFA in low strength concrete products.

In Greece the fly ash produced by Public Power Corporation (PPC) has a CaO content over 10%. In fact, for the 80% of the fly ash production, the CaO amounts from 25 to 35% including 10% of free lime. The pozzolanicity and hydraulic reactivity of this HCFA has been investigated [4] and its good performance in structural concrete was shown by long-term experimental results [5].

As grouting is involved almost in every Dam construction, PPC who is responsible for these hydraulic projects is directly interested in benefiting from the use of HCFA in grout production. This paper is believed to contribute to this direction.

Among the most known uses of grouts are the curtain walls around or under dams to reduce seepage, the filling of cracks in masonries or in the case of subsidence and the filling and sealing of spaces between tunnel lining and surrounding ground. In this paper two kinds of grouts are studied: sanded grouts for strengthening and slurries made of cementitious materials and water for increasing strength and impermeability of ground. Two parameters are also examined. The HCFA content in the grout mixture and the fineness of it.

EXPERIMENTAL DETAILS

Materials

A blended type Portland cement II 35 and a HCFA from the area of Ptolemaida in Northern Greece were used. The chemical composition and some physical characteristics of them are given in Table 1.

Proportioning

The materials and their mix proportions are shown in Table 2.

Table 1 Chemical composition and some physical properties
of Portland cement and fly ash

Constituents	Portland Cement II 35	Ptolemaida fly ash Mean value
SiO_2	20.10	26.00
Al_2O_3	5.46	10.60
Fe_2O_3	2.74	6.59
CaO	63.90	35.5 (free≈10)
MgO	1.50	1.48
SO_3	2.55	5.57
Na_2O	1.30	0.17
K_2O	0.22	0.80
TiO_2	0.25	0.90
Insoluble residue	15.5	21.50
Loss of ignition	1.37	4.55
Specified gravity	3.17	2.56
Percent retained on		Not ground 12%
4900 mesh sieve	8.0	Classified 4%
Fineness kg/m^2	350-380	380-430

Table 2 Mix proportions of grouts tested

Code No.	Cement	HCFA %(w/w) of cement		Water cementitious ratio	Sand max size 1mm	Betonite	Superplasticiser ‰ (w/w) of cementitious
		raw	ground				
C1	1	-	-	0.62	1	-	-
FA1	0.8	0.2	-	0.64	1	-	3.0
FA2	0.6	0.4	-	0.69	1	-	4.0
FA3	0.4	0.6	-	0.76	1	-	4.5
FA4	0.2	0.8	-	0.83	1	-	6.0
FA5	0.0	1.0	-	1.04	1	-	8.0
C2	1	-	-	0.63	1	-	-
GFA1	0.8	-	0.2	0.64	1	-	3.0
GFA2	0.6	-	0.4	0.71	1	-	5.0
GFA3	0.4	-	0.6	0.84	1	-	6.0
GFA4	0.2	-	0.8	0.97	1	-	8.0
GFA5	0.0	-	1.0	1.03	1	-	10.0
C3	1	-	-	2.0	-	0.25	-
SF1	0.7	-	03	2.0	-	0.25	-
SF2	0.5	-	0.5	2.0	-	0.25	-
SF3	0.8	-	0.2	2.0	-	0.25	-
SF4	0.0	-	1.0	2.0	-	0.25	4.0

Properties of fresh grout mixtures

Flow properties and segregation tendency of grout mixtures are the main factors governing their good appliance on site. For sanded grouts the required water for adequate fluidity was determined by keeping the sinking time (DIN 4227 Teil 5, Seite 5) stable 30min ± 80sec. For other slurries tested, the water: cementitious ratio was kept 2:1. One hour after mixing the time of efflux was measured according to ASTM C 939-81 for all grout mixtures. Water retentivity of the sanded mixtures was measured according to ASTM C 941-81. Volume changes of sanded grouts 24 hours after mixing were measured according to DIN previously mentioned while for the final bleeding of other slurries, ASTM C 940-81 was followed. The values for properties tested in this experimental work are indicated in Table 3.

Table 3 Properties of fresh grouts tested

Code No.	Time of efflux 1h after mixing (sec) (ASTM C 939-81)	Water retentivity (ASTM C 939-81) time: sec	Final bleeding (ASTM C 940-81) 1%	Volume change % 24h after mixing
C1	18	58	0.0	1.51
FA1	24	60	0.0	2.80
FA2	32.5	84	0.0	1.80
FA3	47	80	0.0	2.49
FA4	74	64	0.0	2.82
FA5	64	100	0.0	3.20
C2	19	62	0.0	1.41
GFA1	20	80	0.0	2.10
GFA2	17	138	0.0	1.90
GFA3	42	130	0.0	1.90
GFA4	38	125	0.0	1.70
GFA5	48	120	0.0	3.05
C3	8.5	-	6.03	9.17
SF1	8.0	-	7.15	10.05
SF2	9.5	-	5.24	6.08
SF3	13.5	-	0.0	3.15
SF4	14.8	-	0.0	3.95

Curing

The curing regime of 23°C and 99% RH used for concrete specimens was also followed for all grout specimens after remoulding. Twelve series of sanded grout mixtures were prepared. Six with raw HCFA and six with ground HCFA. Another five series of slurries were also prepared. Twenty four specimens (40x40x160)mm were taken from each series to check compressive, flexural strength and dynamic modulus of elasticity at different ages.

RESULTS AND DISCUSSION

Compressive and flexural strength as well as dynamic modulus of elasticity for sanded grouts with raw and ground HCFA are given in Fig. 1 and 2 respectively. For the same sinking time (this means higher water cementitious ratios when HCFA is added) the strength development for plain HCFA grouts was under 5.0 MPa for raw while for ground HCFA was almost 10.0 MPa. The fly ash percentage of 20 presented the higher strength values while after the 40% replacement of cement by HCFA, grouts showed lower strength than that of the first series with cement only. Flexural and dyn. modulus of elasticity generally do not differ much among mixtures with different percentages of HCFA and they comprise a relatively small portion of compressive strength. The rate of strength development is plotted in Fig. 5 for compressive and flexural strength. It is obvious that ground HCFA is more reactive. At the age of 90 days the values for compressive and flexural strength are 30 MPa and 6.5 MPa for ground HCFA instead of 22.0 MPa and 5.5 MPa, respectively of raw HCFA.

For the slurries (without sand) only ground HCFA was used. Up to the HCFA percentage of 80, compressive strength is higher than this of cement-water slurry. The highest value was noticed for a HCFA percentage of 30 and reached 3.8 MPa at 90 days. The relatively high values for dyn. modulus of elasticity were attributed to high moisture content of the specimens of the series, (Fig. 3 and 4).

Comparing the time of efflux it could be said that it is increased with the percentage of HCFA in the mixtures although a small quantity of superplasticiser-retarder up to 1% by weight of cementitious material was used. However this incresement is lower in ground HCFA mixtures and almost dissappears for the percentages up to 80 in slurries. Water retentivity of sanded grout mixtures is obviously better when HCFA is included and especially ground HCFA. The higher the percentage of HCFA the greater the measured time for the same water: cementitious ratio. In the case of slurries the bleeding tendency is reduced with HCFA addition while for sanded grouts (where the W/C ratio is changed in order to meet sinking time requirement of 30 secs) this is not clear.

CONCLUSIONS

Evaluating the overall effects of HCFA on the properties in fresh state, on the mechanical strengths and on the elastic characteristics of grouts it could be said that ground HCFA behaves better in grout mixtures and it is preferable to be used instead of raw material.

In sanded grouts, ground HCFA may replace up to 40% of cement by weight without any change in strength and other characteristics of grouts in fresh state.

Considering fly ash-water slurries, ground HCFA could replace up to 80% of cement by weight with the advantage of lower final bleeding and loss in volume.

Depending on the required strength level, elastic characteristics and fluidity of the grouts used during the construction of a project, there are many possibilities to incorporate HCFA in the mixtures in an economically effective way, provided that the particularities of these fly ashes have been taken into consideration.

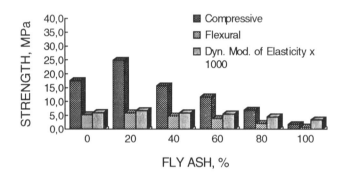

Figure 1   Effect of raw HCFA on mechanical strength of grouts

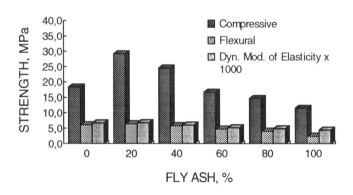

Figure 2   Effect of ground HCFA on mechanical strength of grouts

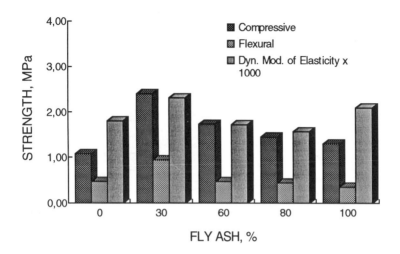

Figure 3 Effect of ground HCFA on strength of slurries ($\frac{water}{cement.} = \frac{2}{1}$) at an age of 28 days

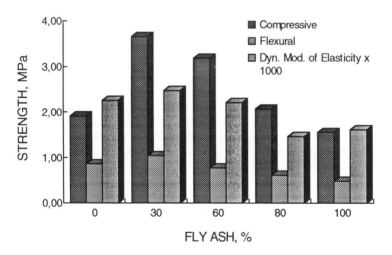

Figure 4 Effect of ground HCFA on strength of slurries ($\frac{water}{cement.} = \frac{2}{1}$) at an age of 90 days

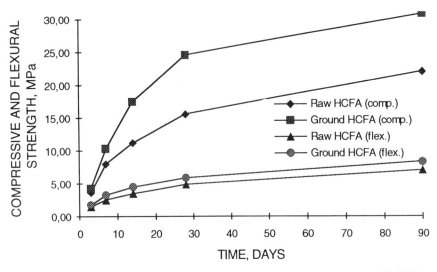

Figure 5 Rate of strength development in grouts with raw and ground HCFA

ACKOWLEDGEMENTS

The author would like to acknowledge Greek Public Power Corporation for their financial support on the research programme "Use of High-calcium fly ash in Grouting".

REFERENCES

1.   CENTRAL ELECTRICITY GENERATING BOARD. PFA Utilization. 1981, pp 35-46.

2.   MANZ, O E , FABER J H, TAGAKI H. Worldwide production of fly ash and utilization in concrete. Proc. of Third CANMET-ACI International Conference on Fly Ash Silica Fume and Natural Pozzolanas in Concrete. Trondheim, Norway 1989, pp 280-294.

3.   NAIK, T P Utilization experience with high-calcium fly ashes in structural grade concrete and other construction materials. A Report of Center for By-Products Utilization, College of Engineering and Applied Science, University of Wisconsin-Milwaukee, 1991, pp 13-23.

4.   PAPAYIANNI, J. An investigation of the pozzolanicity and Hydraulic Reactivity of a high-calcium fly ash. Mag. of Conc. Research, Vol. 39, No 138, March 1987, pp 19-27.

5.   PAPAYIANNI, J. Strength and bond data for Greek high-lime fly ash concrete, ACI SP-91, Editor V.M. Malhotra, Vol. 1, 1986, pp 367-386.

PROPERTIES AND APPLICATIONS
OF NEW CEMENTITIOUS MATERIALS

M Singh
C L Verma

Central Building Research Institute

India

ABSTRACT The paper brings out newer products and processes leading to development of low energy, high performance materials such as reactive belite, alinite, porsal, modified portland and blended cements. The use of mineralizers, additives, grinding aids and slurry thinners, being cost effective parameters for cement industry, has been detailed. Investigations on the formulation of water-resistant gypsum binder based on calcined phosphogypsum, granulated blast furnace slag, flyash, portland cement and additives for use in masonry mortars, plastering and glass fibre reinforcced composites have been discussed. Production of hydraulic binder from the non- conventional materials such as waste lime sludges from acetylene generator, paper and sugar mills and flyash from thermal power plants has been highlighted. Data on the properties of the binders and mortars, concretes and precast stone building blocks made from them are reported.

Keywords : Portland Cement, Cementitious binder, Mineralizers, Grinding aids, Phosphogypsum, Flyash, Slag, Lime sludges, Energy Conservation.

Dr. Manjit Singh is a Senior Scientist working in the area of building materials from industrial by-products. He has published over 45 papers in the National and International journals.

Dr. C.L. Verma is the Scientist Coordinator and Head of the Cement and Lime Products Division. He is working in the area on Building Materials Technologies and pollution abatement.

Concrete 2000. Edited by Ravindra K. Dhir and M. Roderick Jones.
© 1993 Published by E & FN Spon. ISBN 0 419 18120 2.

INTRODUCTION

The socio-economic conditions of the countries worldwide
are beset with complexities of energy crisis, fuel
shortage and environmental pollution. Cement, a prime
building material, is one of the most natural resource
consuming and energy intensive industry, and its contribution to combat the menace of pollution and energy
crunch varies significantly. India is the fourth largest cement producer in the world next to China, Japan
and USA. Its production capacity, presently about 65
million tonnes is estimated to reach 90 million tonnes
by the terminal year of the Eighth 5-year plan (1992-97)
and about 100 million tonnes by the turn of the 21st
century. The requirement of coal is envisaged to be
enormous, about 89 million tonnes [1]. Eversince the
invention of Portland cement about 168 years ago, no
efforts have been reported on the modification of its
compound composition with similar setting, hardening and
water-resisting qualities. With the depletion of fossil
fuel reserves, the situation changed and it is an incum-
bent necessity to think about using energy intensive
materials. A closer look at the economics of the production of portland cement shows that energy inputs
account for 58% of the total cost of production (28% of
power, 30% for fuel). Hence, serious efforts are needed
to thoroughly examine the portland cement composition.

The chemical, metallurgical, coal and other industries
throw out over 100 million tonnes of by-products (chemical gypsum, phosphorous slag, non-ferrous metallurgical
slags, lime sludges, red mud, fly ash, etc.) in India
which have not been sufficiently utilized as yet. Many
of these so-called wastes may be used as starting materials and active mineral admixtures in cement industry.
The utilization of by-products to economise energy
consumption in the cement industry is the crying need of
present time. In the two decades, extensive research
and experimental work was accomplished in India [2] and
elsewhere [3] in the areas such as (i) activators /
accelerators / promoters / modifiers / catalysts with
the objective of improving kinetics of decomposition of
raw materials and improving either quality of cement
clinker or lowering down temperatures of its formation,
(ii) grinding aids, (iii) additives for improved performance, (iv) material conservation and (v) utilization
of industrial by-products resulting in the development
of newer energy efficient cement and cementitious materials.

This paper brings out the development of low energy, high
performance cements such as reactive belite, alinite,

porsal, modified portland and blended cements. The role of mineralizers, additives, grinding aids and slurry thinners in reducing the cost of cement are discussed. Laboratory results of the newly synthesised water-resistant binder from by-product phosphogypsum, and the hydraulic binder based on fly ash and lime sludges have been detailed and discussed herein.

METHODOLOGY

Newer materials of different types are formulated by jumbling of two or more phases with desirable properties to achieve modified and improved materials. The tailor synthesis of materials with optimum properties can be characterised by low energy, low cost and high perform-ance. The use of modifiers for decreasing activation energy of phase transfomation of raw mix and monitoring and control of microstructure and morphology forms the general approach to produce cements with high perform-ance and lower energy inputs. By suitable activators, modifiers/mineralizers high energy processes are trans-formed to low energy forms resulting in its immense saving.

LOW ENERGY CEMENTS

The characteristics of modified portland cements such as belite, alinite, porsal, modified portland cement and blended cements are discussed in this category.

Belite Cement

Belite portland cement mainly contains C_2S in a highly reactive form. This is provided by alkaline sintering of raw materials containing alumina as the main ingredient [4]. In Russia, nephaline ($2Na_2. Al_2Si_2O_8.2H_2O$) has been tried as the main source of alumina. High reactiv-ity in C_2S can be obtained by introducting crystal defects and lattice dislocation by regulating heating and cooling cycles. A C_2S of much higher strength is also developed by pumping a fine mist of $Ca(NO_3)_2$ solu-tion and aqueous colloidal silica into long hot zone at a temperature of 750 to 1050° C [5].

Alinite Cement

The technology for manufacture of alinite clinker is based on the reactive catalytic media (low melting halogen compounds) as a substitute to the normal liquid phase in OPC clinker that is made at high temperature in the process of OPC manufacture. Alinite cement was developed in Russia which uses $CaCl_2$ as mineralizer to effect clinker temperature lowered by 400-500°C. This technology is also called low temperature salt (LTS) technology. The clinker predominantly contains alinite [6] of composition $C_{11}(Si_{0.75}. Al_{0.25})_4.Cl$. It is softer than alite because of the weak Ca-Cl bonds and, therefore, requires less energy for grinding. Alinite cements are notable for greater activity and strength.

Production of alinite clinker has been reported at 1100°C by using indigenous raw materials with halide bearing components from different sources including industrial by-products and processes, the following properties : specific gravity 3.1, mortar compressive strength - 15.0 - 18.0 MPa and 22 - 24 MPa for 3 and 7 days, respectively with slow setting and low autoclave expansion [2].

Porsal Cement

Porsal cement is characterised by the combined proper-ties of portland cement, sulphate resisting cement and high alumina cement. It is normally prepared from limestone, anorthosite, gypsum and mineralizer while firing at 1300-1500°C. This may be prepared by firing a cement raw mix having limestone, clay, bauxite, gypsum and mineralizer (CaF_2).

The chemical analysis and phase composition of porsal cement are given in Table 1. The modulii values were Al_2O_3/SiO_2:1.21, Al_2O_3/Fe_2O_3 2.70 and Al_2O_3/SO_4 : 4.13. The compressive strength of porsal cement with varying Al_2O_3/SiO_2(A/S) modulii are presented in Figure 1. The

Table - 1
Chemical Analysis and Phase Composition of Porsal Cement

Chemical Analysis		Phase Composition	
Constituent	% W/W	Phase	% W/W
CaO	49.71	C_2S	43.0
SiO_2	14.98	C_4A_3S	30.0
Al_2O_3	18.07	CS	1.0
SO_3	4.37	C_4AF	17.0
Fe_2O_3	6.70	CS	9.0
Other oxides	5.80		

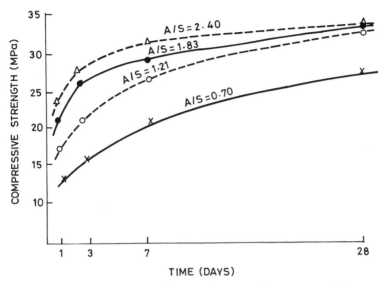

Figure 1 Effect of A/S ratio on the compressive
strength of Porsal cement

porsal cement conforms to IS:269-1989, Specification for
ordinary portland cement, rapid hardening cement and low
heat cement. However, the rate of strength development
is quicker as compared to OPC. The initial setting and
strength development is due to ettringite ($C_3A.3CSH_{32}$)
formation (Figure 2) and its crystallization which takes
place by the interaction of C_4A_3S and $\beta-C_2S$ as follows :

$$C_4A_3S + 2CSH + 31H \rightarrow C_3A\ 3CSH_{32} + 2AH_3$$

As porsal cement is supersaturated with respect to sulphate ions, it is a highly sulphate resistant cement
which is confirmed by negligible potential sulphate
expansion (0.02%) when tested as per ASTM C-452-1973.
Because of low lime composition, saving in energy of the
order of 170 KCal/kg of clinker can be achieved as
compared to OPC. There is a great scope of utilizing
low grade limestones and industrial by-products such as
phosphogypsum, lime sludges, flyash, red mud, etc.

Modified Portland Cement

It is very important to note that 50% of the total heat
is required for the dissociation of $CaCO_3$. Thus the
substitution and lowering of $CaCO_3$ content in cement
raw mix may be considered as one of the ways to save
energy. The lime contents of the four compounds of

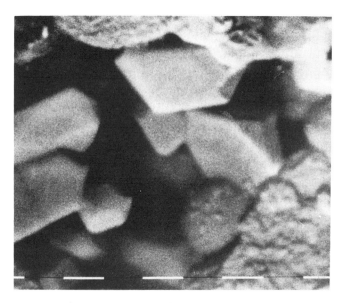

Figure 2 SEM of Porsal Cement
(X2500) showing euhedral hexagonal ettringite

portland cement clinker, namely C_3S, C_2S, C_3A and C_4AF,
are 73.7, 65.1, 62.2 and 46.2 per cent, respectively.
The C_3S and C_3A in portland cement are responsible for
its early setting and hardening properties. Substantial
amount of energy can be saved by partial or full replacement of these phases with the phases requiring less
lime and having similar setting and hardening characteristics. The compounds with low lime contents and carrying such properties were identified by Mehta [3] as
C_4A_3S and CS accounting 36.7 and 41.2 % lime for their
preparation. These compounds are formed at temperatures
between 1000-1300°C.

The chemical analysis and phase composition of modified
portland cements are depicted in Table 2. These are
produced by firing a raw mix containing pure $CaCO_3$,
H_2SiO_3, hydrated alumina, iron oxide and gypsum at
1200°C for about an hour. The energy saving of the order
of 120 KCal/kg compared to OPC was achieved.

Table - 2

Chemical Analysis and Phase Composition of
Modified Portland Cements

Chemical Analysis		Phase Composition	
Constituent	% W/W	Phase	% W/W
CaO	48.03-55.8	C_3S	25-65
SiO_2	8.7 -22.0	C_4A_3S	10-20
Al_2O_3	8.2 -18.4	C_4AF	15-40
Fe_2O_3	5.0 -13.2	CS	10-20
SO_3	7.2-14.4		

Blended Cements

Ordinary portland cement can be mixed with other compatible materials to make blends which can show altered and improved properties. The materials such as granulated blast furnace slags, fly ash and other pozzolanas, finely divided lime based sludges and mineral fines are characterized by a higher intrinsic energy which improves their reactivity towards the constituents of OPC during hydration. These blends are known for low expansion, low heat of hydration, increased late age strength and better resistance to chemically aggressive environments.

Indian Standards Specifications IS:1498-1981 and IS:455-1976 limit the use of 10-25% pozzolana and 20-65 % slag for the manufacture of PPC and PSC. The total saving of fuel and power in portland pozzolana cement (PPC), portland slag cement (PSC) and supersulphated cement (SSC) have been computed as 10-25%, 25-65% and 75-85% (KCal/kg) and 6.5 - 16%, 14-37% & 43-49% (KWH/tonne), respectively as compared to ordinary portland cement (OPC). Average fuel and power consumption for OPC has been assumed as 1100 KCal/kg and 140 KWH/tonne respectively. Extensive work on the PPC, PSC and SSC using a variety of fly ashes, slags, phosphogypsum , fluorogypsum and other industrial by-products has been carried out at the Central Building Research Institute (CBRI), Roorkee [7].

ROLE OF MINERALIZERS

The substances which accelerate the rate of reaction through the modification of solid and liquid state sintering are called mineralizers. Generally fluorides are used as mineralizers. Some of these are NaF, MgF_2, CaF_2, Na_2AlF_6, Na_2SiF_6, $MgSiF_6$ 6 H_2O, H_2SiF_6. The efficacy of mineralizers based on F^- and other mineralizers can be arranged in the order as $Na_2SiF_6 > MgSiF_6 > CaF_2 > ZnO > (CaCl_2 + CaF_2) > CaCl_2$ [8]. It is interesting to record here that F^- bearing compounds are effective at all temperatures.

Effect of CaF_2 in the range 0.5 to 5% on a cement raw meal (LSF - 0.92, SM 2.80 and AM 1.65) has been studied in CBRI at different temperatures [9]. Addition of $CaSO_4.2H_2O$, both natural and by-product forms (fluoro-gypsum and phosphogypsum), also lower the temperature of clinkerization [10].

Addition of chloride ($CaCl_2$) and some oxides such as Cr_2O_3, ZnO, TiO_2, BaO, B_2O_3, P_2O_5, MgO and Li_2O within cement raw mixes has been reported to lower the temperature for liquid phase formation and increase the rate of alite formation. A cement clinker of low grindability conforming to IS:269-1989 has been prepared at 1250°C by using a mineralizer MTM developed at CBRI [9].

USE OF GRINDING AIDS AND SLURRY THINNERS

It is well-known that sintering rate is proportional to the inverse of particle size. Generally, the fineness of raw mix lies in the range 3,000 - 5,000 cm^2/g with 10-25% particles of more than 0.07 - 0.09 mm and 0.5% of over 0.2 mm sizes. For comfortable burning, the particle size of raw mix varies between 0.10 to 0.20 mm for the general purpose portland cement. Use of grinding aids in the range 0.05 - 0.10 % may be helpful in saving the energy to achieve the desired particle size through the rupturing of chemical bonds in the solid mass creating charged particles with enhanced free energy. Some of the commonly employed grinding aids are glycol, organo-silicones, acetates, carbon black, amines, gypsum, etc. Triethanol amine has been found extremely effective as the grinding aid. The increase in the kiln capacity by 1.5 per cent and decrease in the heat requirement by 1 per cent can be achieved during clinker burning by using 0.03-0.06 per cent slurry thinners such as alkali compounds, inorganic and organic polyelectrolytes.

WATER-RESISTANT BINDER FROM PHOSPHOGYPSUM

In order to promote abundant use of gypsum in the exposed damp situations, a water-resistant gypsum binder has been formulated based on the calcined phosphogypsum, granulated slag/fly ash, cement and additives. The physical properties of binder are reported in Table 3. The binder based on unprocessed phosphogypsum shows less retardation of setting time and low development of strength than the one based on the processed phosphogypsum (wet sieved through 300 micron IS sieve and washed). It is attributed largely to removal of impurities (P_2O_5, F, organic matter) in the latter than the former.

Table 3

Physical properties of gypsum binder (GB)

S. No.	Gypsum Binder Designation	Setting time (Minutes) Ini-tial	Final	Compressive Strength (N/mm^2) 1d	3d	7d	28d	Soundness Cold Expn (mm)
1.	GB based on calcined phosphogypsum (PG) and slag							
	- Unprocessed PG	10	40	3.5	11.0	16.2	22.0	3.50
	- Processed PG	70	145	10.1	23.1	29.0	35.0	1.60
2.	GB based on Calcined PG & Fly Ash							
	- Unprocessed PG	45	90	8.0	13.7	19.0	19.6	1.10
	- Processed PG	95	150	13.7	19.0	20.9	21.3	0.88
3.	Plaster of Paris	25		13.3				0.20

DTA, XRD and SEM of binder hydrated for different periods (upto 28 days) have shown formation of ettringite ($C_3A.3CaSO_4.32H_2O$) and tobermorite (CSH). These products fill up voids and pores in the gypsum matrix and improve their stability in water. Durability of gypsum binder studied by immersion in water and by alternate wetting and drying, heating and cooling cycles at 27° to 60° C showed relatively less fall in strength and weight loss than that of the plain plaster of paris [11].

The suitability of the gypsum binder has been examined for masonry mortars, plasters and glass fibre reinforced composites.

In view of low energy consumption in the production of calcined gypsum (1.0544×10^9 Joules/t) which is only one seventh of the energy needed for producing an equivalent amount of portland cement, the saving in cost of gypsum binder may be effected as calcined gypsum forms a lion's share of the binding material.

CEMENT FROM FLY ASH AND WASTE LIME SLUDGES

The production of portland cement clinker using fly ash in the mix was suggested by Rehsi and Garg [13] on the basis of data which showed that use of fly ash, in the raw mix enabled (i) production of high strength cement clinker at about 1350°C instead of 1450°C normally employed, and (ii) Production of cement clinker with MgO content as high as 6 per cent without causing unsoundness in the cement.

Investigations on the production of cement (compressive strength (70 mm cube) 26.7 (7 day) and 43.2 MPa (28 day) and hydraulic binder (compressive strength 7.6 (14 day) and 11.0 MPa (28 day)) using waste lime sludge from acetylene generator, paper and sugar mills as replacement of limestone and fly ash from thermal power plants in place of clay in the raw mix conforming to IS:269-1989 and IS:712-1973 for class A lime are described by Rehsi et al [14].

The hydraulic binder is suitable for masonry mortars (mix proportion 1:4, 28-day C.S. 3.95 MPa, water retentivity 78%) lean concrete (28-day C.S. : 8.4 MPa (1:3:6), 6.9 MPa (1:4:8), 4.5 MPa (1:5:10)) and precast stone building blocks (28-day C.S. : 7.56 MPa (1:2;4)) for use in place of portland cement in flooring and foundation concrete.

CONCLUSIONS

1. Production of low energy high performance cements such as belite, alinite, porsal, blended and others may be undertaken in the light of present day national and international scenarios.

2. Use of mineralizers, grinding aids, additives/modi-
    fiers, etc. can affect the production of improved
    quality clinker in the existing cement plants.

3. Breakthrough in new cements and hydraulic binding
    materials using industrial by-products has been
    achieved.   The production of these low cost low
    energy products should be encouraged.

ACKNOWLEDGEMENT

The work reported in this paper forms an integral part
of the normal research programme being conducted at the
Central Building Research Institute, Roorkee.   It is
being published with the permission of the Director.

REFERENCES

1   CEMENT NEWS, Indian Concrete Journal, 1992, April
    pp 179-180.

2. AHLUWALIA, SC, SHARMA, KM AND LAXMI, S.   New
    product development for energy conservation through
    material science approach. First International
    Seminar, NCB, New Delhi, Vol. III, India, 1987 pp
    VI-11-34.

3. MEHTA, PK. Investigation on energy saving cements.
    World Cement Technology, 1980, May. pp 166-177.

4. BOLDYREV, AS.   Other Cements (Cements with high
    content of active C_2S) and their applications.
    Proc. 7th I.C.C.C., Vol. 1, Paris, 1980, pp V 3/1-
    3/15.

5. ROY, DM AND OYEFESOBI, SO. Preparation of very
    reactive $CaSiO_4$. Am. Ceram. Soc., Vol. 60, 1977. pp
    178-82.

6. BIKBAOU, M. Mineral formation processes and phase
    composition of alinite clinker. Proc. 7th I.C.C.C.,
    Vol. IV, Paris, 1980, Posters V-285.

7. DEB, A, SINGH, MANJIT, SREENATH, SG AND BORAH, UC.
    Building Materials and Components — Technology for
    Developing Countries, Tata McGraw Hill, New Delhi,
    1990. pp 185-226.

8. KLEEN, WA AND JAWED, I. Mineralizers and fluxes in the clinkerization process. III Burnability of synthetic and Industrial raw mixes. Proc. 7th I.C.C.C., Vol. II, Paris, 1980. pp 1-50.

9. MASOOD, I, MEHROTRA, SP AND TEHRI, SP. Economisation of energy in cement manufacture. Indian Ceramics Vol. 29, No. 2, 1986, pp 47-52.

10. MEHTA, PK AND BRADY, JR. Utilization of phosphogypsum in portland cement industry. Cem. and Conc. Res.,Vol. 7, 1977. pp 537-544.

11. SINGH, MANJIT, GARG, MRIDUL AND REHSI, SS. Water-resistant binder from waste phosphogypsum. Int. Congress CIB'89 - Quality for Building Users throughout the World, Vol. II, Theme II, Paris, 1989. pp 339-352.

12. SINGH, MANJIT AND GARG, MRIDUL. Investigation of a durable gypsum binder for building materials. Const. & Building Materials, 1992,Vol. 6, No.1, March pp 52-56.

13. REHSI, SS AND GARG, SK. Production of cement clinker using flyash. Proc. 6th Int. Congress of Chemistry, Moscow, 23-27 Sept. 1974.

14. REHSI, SS, LAL, KISHAN AND GARG, SK. Cement from non- conventional materials. National Seminar on Building Materials - their Science and Technology, New Delhi, Vol. II(A), 1982, 15-16 April. pp 1-5.

PRODUCTION AND BEHAVIOUR OF
A NEW WHITE SULPHATE-RESISTANT CEMENT

M T Blanco-Varela

Instituto Eduardo Torroja

S Gimenez

Reposol-Quimica

A Palomo, F Puertas and T Vazquez

Instituto Eduardo Torroja

Spain

ABSTRACT. The manufacture procedure of a new white cement is now presented. The basic difference between a standard fabrication and the one used for making the new cement is the utilization of CaF_2 and $CaSO_4$ as important components of the raw materials in the case of the new method. It involves the obtention of a product having a different chemical and mineralogical composition of the interstial phase compared with a traditional white cement. After an industrial test (more than 1000 tons of the new cement were fabricated) it has been concluded that the new process involves a reduction of 8-9% of the total cost compared with a traditional method. Besides, an increase of production of arround 10% and a decrease of the pollutans emisssion are achieved. The results obtained when characterizing the new cement, have allowed to show that the quality of this material is at least comparable with the best OPC. Finally, special attention must be paid in the fact of obtaining a sulphate-resistant product.

keywords: production, clinkerization, new white cement, fluxes and mineralizers (CaF_2 and gypsum) behaviour, sulphate-resistant, durability.

Dr.M.T. Blanco-Varela, is senior researcher of CSIC, She specialises in clinkerizacion, hydration, durability of cement pastes and mortars.
Dr. S. Giménez. Her main research interest is the effect of mineralizers and fluxes in the clinkerization process.
Dr. A. Palomo, is senior researcher of CSIC. He has been working in cement production and durability of cement pastes for many years.
Dr. F. Puertas, is senior researcher of CSIC. She is specialized in Clinker Formation and hydration. She is experienced in microestructural studies of concrete.
Professor T. Vázquez is investigator of CSIC. He is wide experienced in concrete technology. For several years, he has been the Director of Technology Transfer Office at CSIC.

Concrete 2000. Edited by Ravindra K. Dhir and M. Roderick Jones.
© 1993 Published by E & FN Spon. ISBN 0 419 18120 2.

INTRODUCTION

The energy crisis of the 70's caused the industrialized countries to rationalize their energy utilization as much as possible. The cement industry, being one of the major consumers of fuel and electricity, etc., has therefore had to reconsiderer its energy requirements. In Spain, for example, most of the cement factories changed their energy sources from oil to coal. The crisis periods may appear again so a greater consciousness of the need to save energy should clearly be retained. It is thus a primary concern both in research and industry to look for economic manufacturing processes and for cement formulations involving saving.

In the present paper the results of a long term project are reported with the principal aim of developing an economic method for cement production to fulfill the following requirements:

-Easy adaptation to the current manufacturing processes.
-Significant energy savings to reduce overall production cost.
-To obtain a product of comparable or better performance than OPC.
-Reduction of the level of environmental pollution with respect to the traditional process.

The new method consists of partially replacing the usual raw materials by other materials containing CaF_2 and $CaSO_4$. Thus a system of energy saving through the use of fluxes and mineralizers is achieved. It is evident that the system is not new. Many investigators have studied the effect of fluxes and mineralizers on the clinkering process (1,4); some have even specifically worked with CaF_2 or $CaSO_4$ to study their respective effects on the above-mentioned process or on the formation of the clinker phases (5,7). Hoewever, despite obtainning promising result (8,9), the combined effect of both compounds, i.e. CaF_2 and $CaSO_4$, has not been thoroughly investigated.

Blanco et al when studying the combined effect of CaF_2 and $CaSO_4$ on compositions of the phase system $CaO-Al_2O_3-SiO_2-Fe_2O_3$, discovered that a melted phase appeared at 1180ºC (10). Later, the composition of that phase was studied and it was verified in the laboratory as a suitable interstitial phase, (totally or partially replacing the ferrite and aluminate phases) to obtain low cost clinker.

The present work extrapolates the laboratory results to an industrial scale. A large scale factory test was carried out to produce 1500 tons of white cement using the method proposed by the authors (11).

In a second stage when the viability of this new procedure was proved, it seemed logical to study the behaviour at long-term of the product obtained when exposed under the action of different aggresive agents (durability). In other words, durability behaviour of the new cement (which has proved to be better than that of the traditional white cement) according to its peculiar intersticial mineralogy has been justified.

EXPERIMENTAL PROCEDURE

Production of Cement

Prior to the industrial test, a short experiment was made in the laboratory using the same raw materials as are usually handled in the factory. The result of this experiment gave the optimum composition for the raw mix using the materials obtained from the factory. This composition was (see Table1):

Gypsum 5%, Fluorspar 2%, Limestone 77%, Kaolin 3%, Sand 13%.

In the factory, 3 silos were filled with the raw mix having the previously established composition. The grinding of the raw materials was carried out in two mills; in the first, limestone, kaolin, gypsum and fluorspar were ground, and the sand was ground in the second. The clinkering process was carried out in a 78 m long and 2.7 m mean diameter kiln with a clinker capacity of 180 t/day. The recorded maximum temperature of clinkerization was about 1350º C. A 2hr periodic sampling of clinker was carried out during the test. The samples were chemically analyzed and studied by XRD,IR spectroscopy and optical microscopy techniques.

Some of the samples were mixed and ground with gypsum (2% and 3% of gypsum addition). Specimens of the resulting cements were submitted to the following test: Specific surface (Blaine), Setting time (Vicat needle), Heat of hydration (ASTM C 186-55), Expansion (le Chatelier needle), Compression and flexural strengths at 1, 3, 7, and 28 days on prisms of 4 x 4 x 16 cm.

Evaluation of Durability

The durability tests have been simultaneously carried out with two white cements with the purpose of having a point of reference for comparison.

The first one is a white cement made using the traditional procedure (White Cement Type I). The second one is the cement obtained through the new fabrication procedure. This studies of durability of both cements when submitted to the attack of aggressive solutions have been evaluated by the Koch-

Steinegger accelerated method. Accordingly, mortar specimens of both cements were prepared with 1 x 1 x 6 cm size, cement/sand = 1/3, water/cement = 1/3. The sand has been of the monogranular type. The specimens were submitted to curing in a 100% humidity chamber for 21 days and then were immersed in the types of aqueous solutions:

   a) Destilled water.
   b) Sea water (prepared according to the ASTM D1141-75
      standard).
   c) 4,4% weight Na_2SO_4 solution.

The specimens of each cement were kept immersed in solutions a) b) and c) during the following periods of time:

   1, 7, 28, 56, 90, 180, 270, 365 and 545 days.

After this periods they were removed and submitted to mechanical fracture (flexural and compressive strengths).

Finally, each cement at every age has been studied by means of several instrumental techniques, such as studied, SEM, XRD, IR spectroscopy, Hg Porosimetry, and so on .. in order to correlate the microstructure of each cement with the types of attack applied by means of aggressive solutions and the development of resistances.

RESULTS AND DISCUSSION

Production of Cement

Whit respect to the general characteristics of the new raw mix it is important to note the close similarity to those of the normal raw mix; particularly in aspects like the paste rheology and the homogeneity of the material in the silos. Table presents some data comparing the new process with the normal process. All the values shown in Table 2 have been statistically treated on a basis of 107 measurements.

Another important aspect also taken into consideration was the condition of the refractory kiln. A general visual examination of the klin refractory was carried out before and after the test. No proof of attack or anomalous erosion was observed at any time and the coating on bricks was what would be normally expected.

The mineralogical constitution of the new clinker was identified by XRD which shows the presence of C_3S_{ss} as the major phase as well as C_2S, CaO, $3(C_2S) \cdot 3(CaSO_4) \cdot CaF_2$, C_3A, C_4A_3S, $C_{11}A_7 \cdot CaF_2$ and occasionally some $CaSO_4$. The residue remaining after treating the new clinker with methanol and salicilic acid shows fluorellestadite as the major phase. C_3A, C_4A_3S and $C_{11}A_7CaF_2$ and occasionally some $CaSO_4$ only appears sometimes and in small proportions.

Table 1 Chemical Composition of the Raw Materials

	SiO_2 %wt	Al_2O_3 %wt	Fe_2O_3 %wt	CaO %wt	MgO %wt	SO_3 %wt	CaF_2 %wt	LOI %wt
Gypsum	1.42	0.44	-	31.9	0.72	45.2	-	20.30
Fluorsp.	35.2	0.56	0.45	5.65	1.04	0.24	41.3	11.07
Limesto.	0.15	0.18	0.03	55.5	0.50	-	-	43.60
Kaolin	48.4	36.2	0.28	0.40	0.14	-	-	12.24
Sand	96.4	2.22	0.05	0.35	0.18	-	-	0.80

Table 2. Technical data of the new and normal process

	New Process	Normal Process
Dust emission	9.69 t/day	3 t/day
Temperature of gases in the chimney	136 ºC	195 ºC
Temperature in the chain zone	535 ºC	750 ºC
Temperature of clinker after being cooled	161.5 ºC	62 ºC
Fuel consumption	1500 l/hour	1750 l/h

Microscopic examination of samples of the new clinker shows that it is highly porous; it has a low amount of interstitial phase and idiomorphic crystals of alite surrounded by the scarce liquid phase.

In spite of this, the alite crystals are not too small. Belitic clusters are also observed but not CaO clusters.

The amount of C_2S in the clinker decreases in the samples as the industrial test progresses.

Finally, in a work like this it is necessary to examine the physico-chemical properties of the cements which determine their final quality. Almost all of the samples of the new clinker taken during the test therefore were grouped into four separate mixes as follows:
Mix A: clinker samples from clinkering the raw mix in silo 1.
Mix B: clinker samples from (silo 1 + silo 2)
Mix C: clinker samples from (silo 2)
Mix D: clinker samples from (silo 3).

A part of each mix was mixed 2% wt of gypsum and the other part with 3% except mix D which was only mixed with 2%.

Table 3 and Figures. 1 and 2 summarize the results obtained after submitting the 7 cements to physical and mechanical test.

2A: Mix A + 2% gypsum   3A: Mix A + 3% gypsum
2B: Mix B + 2% gypsum   3B: Mix B + 3% gypsum
2C: Mix C + 2% gypsum   3C: Mix C + 3% gypsum
2D: Mix D + 2% gypsum

In general, it can be said that raw mixes from which white cement is made are difficult to burn because they have low proportions of fluxes and consequently high silica moduli. When these raw mixes are submitted to the clinkering process, the temperature at which the first melt appears may be around 1450°C. In addition this melt clinker does not have the required physical properties to promote the diffusion of Ca^{2+} and SiO_4^{4-} ions as it hardly has any Fe_2O_3 in its composition. Hence producing white clinker involves very high energy costs.

The raw mix prepared for the industrial test has a very different composition from traditional mixes as its Al_2O_3 content is lower and CaF_2 and $CaSO_4 \cdot 2H_2O$ are also present in significant amounts.

Those compositions of the $CaO-SiO_2-Al_2O_3-Fe_2O_3-SO_3$ system which are richest in CaO, melt at about 1200°C. The melt, which has a fluorsolphatic nature, allows SiO_4^{4-} and Ca^{2+} ions to diffuse through it and the rate of formation of alite is then increased at 1200°C.Furthermore, the increase of the rate of formation of alite is so high that the clinkering reactions in raw mixes such as the one being studied, can be completed at temperatures between 1300°C and 1350°C. There is no free lime after burning periods of about 30 min at this temperature.

An examination of the results shown in Table 2 shows that the process of making cement starting from raw mixes with the above-mentioned composition in not only possible from the technological point of view but it also improves upon traditional process in the following key areas: (i) increase of production, (ii) decrease in emission of dust, (iii) increase in efficiency of the mills and (iv) in the specific case in which the work was carried out, elimination of one of the stages in the production process: i.e. consumption of excess free lime.

Table 3. Some properties of the new cement

Properties	Cement						
	2A	2B	2C	2D	3A	3B	3C
Specific weight (g/cm^3)	3.106	3.106	3.107	3.077	3.076	3.076	3.076
Specific surface (cm^2/g)	4500	4000	4100	3900	4500	3850	4311
Slump(%)	24.4	23.2	24.0	23.6	24.8	24.4	24.0
Heat of hydration (cal/g)							
7d	86	84	82	82	76	77	82
28d	100	101	93	92	90	87	90
Expansion (mm)	1.33	1.83	1.83	1.00	1.17	2.00	1.33
Intial Setting	1h15'	2h10'	2h15'	2h40'	1h20'	2h	1h55'
Final setting	2h4'	3h14'	3h19'	4h24'	1h55'	3h30'	3h

The following data concerning the economics of the process were deduced after the industrial test:

-The cost of the raw mixture is increased by 27%
-The cost of mixing the clinker is decreased by 23%
-The cost of making the cement is decreased by 6%
-An 8-9% reduction in general expenses is achieved.

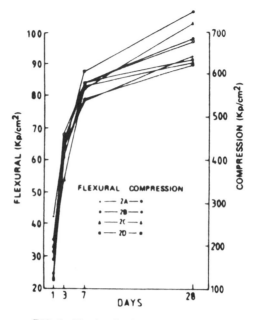

FIG. 1: Mechanical strengths of
cements 2A–D

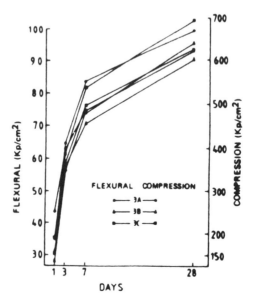

FIG. 2: Mechanical strengths of
cements 3A–D

Evaltuation of Durability

In Table 4 the mineral composition (in %) of the clinkers from which both cements are derived is shown, determined by X-ray Diffraction.

Table 4 Mineral Composition (in % wt) of clinker

	WRC[***]	WNC[****]		WRC	WNC
C_3S	62.9	69.5±4	C_3A	10.8	3±1
C_2S	20.2	6.8±0.7	$C_4A_3\bar{S}$	--	2±0.7
Fl[*]	--	14±0.9	$C_{11}A_7CaF_2$	--	0.5±0.1
CaO	4.2	3±0.1	H[**]	--	0.7±0.1

[*]$Ca_{10}(SiO_4)_3 (SO_4)_3F_2$ [***]White Reference Clinker
[**] $CaSO_4.1/2 H_2O$ [****] White New Clinker

In order to estimate the evolution in time of crystalline compounds in the cement paste of the new procedure (CB), when mortars of the aforement cement are submerged in different solutions, the intensity of the reflections described in the experimental procedure was measured and the value was divided into the fluorellestadite reflection value (2 = 25.64º). It must be pointed out that both I_{Ett}/I_{FL} and $I_{calcite}/I_{FL}$ quotiens remain constant both in time and in all media.

In figure 3 the values of the following quotiens: I_{CH}/I_{FL}, I_{gypsum}/I_{FL} and $I_{Mg(OH)2}/I_{FL}$ are show versus time in the different media.

In figure 4, the flexural strength at different ages showed by mortar prisms of traditional white cement (CBS) and cement mortar obtained by the new procedure (CB) submerged in different media is pointed out.

The usage of a fluorelleestadite reflection as the internal standard is justified by the fact that this compound is a constituent of the clinker and because of its high insolubility, why it does not suffer modification with time.

From figure 3 it is important to emphasize:

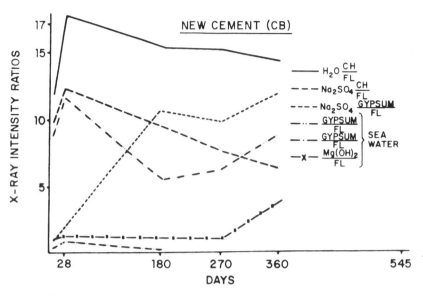

FIG. 3: Mineral evolution with time of new cement pastes (CB) in aggresive media (X-ray results)

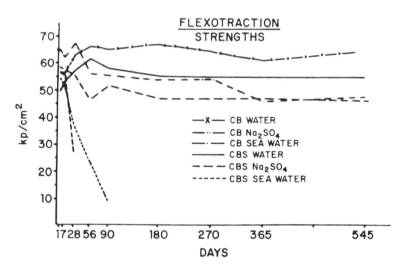

FIG. 4: Comparison of strength evolution with time of cement mortars CB and CBS in aggresive media

a) The content in $Ca(OH)_2$ is at 7 days similar in CB cement pastes in contact with the three media although those from Na_2SO_4 solution and sea water are slightly lower. During the treatment time the content in $Ca(OH)_2$ decreases in the pastes submitted to aggressive media compared to those preserved in water.

b) In the case of mortars obtained using the new cement and preserved in a Na_2O_4 solution it should be observed that simultaneous to the decrease in the quantity of $Ca(OH)_2$ there is also an important increase of the content of gypsum which is the major crystalline phase already at the 180 day stage.

The microstructure of the mortar pastes obtained with CB and CBS cements and preserved in water for a period of 545 days, and examined by S.E.M., is very similar and could be described as essentially composed of C-S-H gel of very dense nature with a C/S ratio > 2 and large $Ca(OH)_2$ crystals. Occasinally in CB cement samples ettringite crystals may be observed. Frequently, in CBS cement pastes, in the C-S-H gel mass, crystals grow in the shape of plaques which according to EDX analysis can be attributed to hydrated aluminates or carboaluminates.

The C-S-H gel of CB cement pastes preserved in sea water for 545 days shows a less dense texture than the one shown by samples preserved in water and C/S ratio 2, while in all cases large content in Mg is observed. Likewise, a large amount of thick $Mg(OH)_2$ crystals has been observed distributed throughout the sample.

Basically, the main difference between the hydrated pastes of both cements is the presence of fluorellesteadite and ettringite in those obtained from CB cement and the almost absence of ettringite in those from CBS cement. The CBS cement aluminates (> 10% C_3A) are found in pastes as hydrated aluminates or carboaluminates, making up plaques that grow in between C-S-H gel or in fissures.

In accordance to S.E.M. observations, C-S-H shows similar morphologies in both cement pastes, being quite dense and with a C/S ratio $\approx$ 2.

The slight improvement in endurance shown by CB cement mortars with regard to those of CBS cement preserved in water could be justified by the greater content in calcium silicates of the first one and/or the absence of ettringite in the second one.

The fast endurance decrease of CBS cement mortars submerged in the two aggressive solutions is due to expansive formation reactions of ettringite and gypsum. These reactions are:

A) $Ca(OH)_2 + Na_2SO_4 + H_2O$ →   Gypsum + NaOH
B) $Ca(OH)_2 + MgSO_4 + H_2O$ →   Gypsum + $Mg(OH)2$
C) Hydrated Aluminates + Gypsum →   Ettringite

The gypsum, obtained from A and B reactions, reacts with hydrated aluminates or with carboaluminates to form ettringite (reaction C).

In samples preserved in Na_2SO_4 solution the gypsum precipitation rate is much greater than the ettringite one, finding in the samples increasing quantities of both compounds up to the 28 day stage after which the destruction of test prisms is absolute.

The lower SO_4^- concentration in sea water produces a lower gypsum formation rate in mortars, which after 90 days has been entirely used in the ettringite expansive formation reaction. This reaction will later cause destruction of the specimens.

The strong behaviour of mortars obtained from CB cement and preserved in Na_2SO_4 solution can be justified by reaction A. Thus, since the 1 day stage gypsum precipitation starts with detriment to $Ca(OH)_2$. This expansive reaction makes, at the beginning, the system to become more dense obtaining an increase of endurance up to the 28 days stage in relation to endurance shown by the same mortar preserved in H_2O. On a long-term basis, the massive gypsum formation implies an endurance decrease.

In addition it is likely that strength decrease is not only due to the expansive process described for reaction A because, as quoted in results, C-S-H gel suffers certain modifications in its microstructure due to a possible crystallization together with gypsum during silicates hydration process.

As a conclusion, the endurance decrease experienced by CB cement mortars preserved in sea water, when increasing treatment time, is mainly due to $Mg(OH)_2$ crystallization. $Mg(OH)_2$ formation seems to be controlled by reaction B during the first stages. Starting from the 90 days stage the gypsum content in samples starts decreasing to end completely after 180 days of treatment. In this period of time an increase in $Mg(OH)_2$ and $Ca(OH)_2$ content is shown.

The gypsum evolution does not seem to be justified by an ettringite increase which, if it happens, is in such a small proportion that its variations (measured by XRD) are part of the measuring error. Some authors quote an increase of gypsum solubility in presence of alkaline (12). If so and because of their concentration in the conservation solution, a gypsum solution in a long-term basis could be justified.

Ca(OH)$_2$ content increase in samples in time, after gypsum has been dissoluted, could be justified by the concentration in Ca^{2+} ions increase released by gypsum in its solution or by a possible C-S-H gel evolution when the pH medium decreases because of Mg(OH)$_2$ precipitation without a simultaneous gypsum precipitation.

These samples, examined by S.E.M., show quite important content in Mg(OH)$_2$ (after 545 days of treatment) which appears well crystallized in thick crystals throughout the sample. Likewise, all the C-S-H gel analyzed has important Mg quantities even though the analysis was carried out in zones where brucite crystals were not evident.

The above-mentioned crystallization could be obtained using reaction B or the following reaction:

D) C-S-H + MgSO$_4$ + H$_2$O → Gypsum + Mg(OH)$_2$ + SiO$_2$

Therefore it is not clear that the strength decrease observed in this sample is due to any of the described process, it seems likely that at the beginning the mechanism described by reaction B occurs, although we can not rule out a possible C-S-H gel alteration (reaction D) along the experiment.

CONCLUSIONS

An industrial test in which 1500 tons of a new white cement was manufactured has demonstrated that:

1) The procedure is both reliable from the technical point of view and preferable to the traditional process, with the following advantages:

   -Estimated total reduction between 8% and 9% of the process cost.
   -Significant increase (> 10%) in the production output.
   -Increase in mill efficiency.
   -Decrease in the emission of polluting agents.

2) The new cement shows high quality characteristics:
   a)Mortars obtained from CB cement and preserved in water reach between 28 and 56 days similar endurance to the one obtained at 545 days.
   b) CB cement mortars submerged in Na$_2$SO$_4$ solution show up to the 28 day stage greater endurance than those mortars kept under H$_2$O, due to gypsum formation (at the expense of Ca(OH)$_2$, that makes the system become more dense.The massive gypsum formation with detriment to Ca(OH)$_2$, because of its expansive nature, brings along an endurance decrease in a long-term basis.

1338   Blanco-Varela et al

In addition it seems probable that C-S-H gel evolution process, in reference to its morphology and qualities, could become altered because of the existence of SO_4^{2-} and Na^+ ions and that the endurance decrease could not only be due to the gypsum expansive formation process.

c) The endurance decrease of CB mortars preserved in sea water in relation to those preserved in water could be partly due to $Mg(OH)_2$ formation at the expense of $Ca(OH)_2$ which would be dissolved (the $Mg(OH)_2$ molar volume is $\approx 1/4$ lower than the $Ca(OH)_2$ one).It seems that in some way the C-S-H gel microstructure is being modified by the aggressive dissolution.

ACKNOWLEDGMENTS

The authors would like to thank the Subdirección General de Promoción de la Investigación for the financing of the PB87-0293 Project without which this paper could not have been possible.

REFERENCES

1) Klemm, W.A., and Skalny, J: Mineralizers and fluxes in the clinkering process. Cements Research Progress 1976, pp. 259-291; Am. Ceram. Soc., Columbus. Ohio. 1977.

2) Odler I., and Abdul Maula, S.: Einfluß von Mineralisatoren auf das Brennen des Portlandzementklinkers. Zement-Kalk-Gips 33 (1980) N₀ 3, pp. 132-136 and 278-282.

3) Toropov, N.A., Luginina, I.G., and Luginin, A. N.: Uber den chemischen Einfluß von Zusätzen auf die der Linkerbildung vorangehenden Prozesse zur Beschleunigung der Klinkerbildung durch Zusatz von Miniralisatoren. Silikattechn. 22 (1971) N₀ 7, pp.220-222.

4) Kumar, S.S., and Kataria, S.S.: Optimization of burning characteristics of raw meal for fuel economy by special mineralizer. World Cement Technol. (1981) July-August, pp. 279-285.

5) Blanco Varela, M.T., Palomo, A., and Vázquez, T.: Effect fluorspar on the formation of clinker phases. Cem. Concr. Res. 14 (1984) pp, 397-406.

6) Klemm, W.A., Jawed, I., and Holub, K.J.: Effects of calcium fluoride mineralization on silicates and melt formation in portland cement clinker. Cem. Concr. Res. 9 (1979) pp. 489-496.

7) Gilioli, C., Massazza, F., and Pezzuoli, M.: Studies on clinker calcium silicates bearing CaF_2 and $CaSO_4$. Cem. Concr. Res 9 (1979) pp. 295-302.

8) Moir, K. G.: Mineralized high alite cements. World Cement Technol. 13 (1982) N. 10, pp. 374-382 and Philos. Trans. R. Soc., London Ser. A, 310 (1511) (1983), pp. 127.

9) Blanco Varela, M. T., Vázquez, T., and Palomo, A.: Utilización de cenizas volantes y mineralizadores como materia prima en la fabricación de cemento. Materiales de Construcción (1983) N. 189, pp. 45-54.

10) Blanco Varela M. T., Vázquez, T., and Palomo, A.: A study of a new liquid phase to obtain low energy cements. Cem. Concr. Res. 16 (1986) pp. 97-104.

11) Blanco Varela, M.T., Vázquez, T., and Palomo, A.: Procedimiento de obtención de clinker con bajo consumo energético utilizando fluorita y sulfatos como componentes del crudo. Spanish Patent. N. 542691 (1985).

12) Van Aardt J.H.P. and Visser. S. Cem. and Concr. Vol. 15 (1985) pp. 485-494.

IMPROVING THE PERFORMANCE
OF OIL-WELL CEMENTS

M Olteanu

University of Bucharest

G Popescu

S Peretz

Institute of Physical Chemistry

Romania

ABSTRACT. This contribution presents the results of studies on some cement pastes intended for BSS type special works. Aluminium powders with 0.03% (against the cement) polyvinyl alcohol (PVA) of different degrees of polymerization (50,90, 120) and hydrolysis (88, 92, 98) were employed as additives. Cement pastes of w/c ratio equal to 0.53 and 0.4 were tested for expansion in time and settling. The influence of the modified expansion additive upon the compression strength of cement stone after 7 and 28 days was determined. The rheological curves, determined by means of a coaxial cylinders viscometer were also obtained for the cement pastes by mixing 10 and 30 minutes. The PVA ($\overline{HG}$ = 88 and $\overline{P}$ = 120) improve the workability of oil-well cement paste (w/c = 0.53) during presettling period because they lower the viscosity, delay the onset of expansion without affecting other characteristics as settling, the final expansion value and compression strength of cement stone.

KEYWORDS: PVA , Expansion additive, Expansion, Settling,Viscosity, Cement paste type G-API, Oil-well.

Professor Mihaela Olteanu, Department of Physical Chemistry, University of Bucharest, Romania. Ph.D. in Physical Chemistry, Classes of Colloidal and Polymer Chemistry. Studies: surfactant solutions, colloidal dispersions, film forming substances.

Georgeta Popescu, Ph.D. in Chemistry. Head of Research Group for Membranes and Membrane Processes. Studies: association colloids, disperse systems, synthetic membrane in separation phenomena.

Sandu Peretz, researcher in Colloidal Chemistry Laboratory,Institute of Physical Chemistry, Bucharest. Studies: disperse systems.

Concrete 2000. Edited by Ravindra K. Dhir and M. Roderick Jones.
© 1993 Published by E & FN Spon. ISBN 0 419 18120 2.

INTRODUCTION

The injectable fresh mixtures must possess certain fluidity, expansivity, settling values and after setting it has to exhibit specified values of mechanical strength in given exploitation conditions [1, 2]. The expanding additives are very important they ensure a new quality of concrete [3-5]. Sometimes in the cementing of oil- wells there are losses in the cement paste circulation between the column and the ground which lowers the safety in exploitation.   The   expanding additive ensures a good cohesion, higher plasticity and controlled expansion of injection mixtures; it also lowers the amount of water in the mixture and prevents the of cement paste. The expander additives are mixtures of expanding and fluidizing agents [6]. This contribution studies the influence of polyvinyl alcohol (PVA) of various degrees of polymerization ($\bar{P}$) and hydrolysis ($\overline{GH}$) upon he behavior of some single cement pastes. The rheological properties, the expansion and settling of cement pastes were studied. The influence of the additive upon the time dependence of the strength of of cement stone was also determined.

EXPERIMENTAL

MATERIALS

BSS   type   cement   similar   to   class   G   special   API   system.   Its physico-mechanical   characteristics   are   listed   in   Table   1.The   additive consisted of 77.5 % quarts sand (average particle size was 63 µm), 18.0 % Na_2Co_3, 3.0 % PVA and 1.5 % metallic aluminium powders (particle size less then 60 µm).PVA (0.03% against the cement) differed by $\bar{P}$ and $\overline{GH}$ according to Table 2.
The expanding agent was added to all samples in a concentration of 1 % with respect to the cement.

METHODS

Cement samples of w/c ratio 0.53 and 0.4 were prepared and different by PVA characteristics (samples I-IV). The rheological curves were plotted by means of a Rhotovisco apparatus equipped with coaxial cylinders, 10 and 30 minutes after preparation of pastes; the expansion was low throughout these time intervals. Free expansion and settling (%) were determined with cylinders whose initial paste volume was 200 cm^3. The compression strength of the concrete stone was determined on 4x4x16 cm prismatic samples; expansion was prevented from occurring. After stripping, samples were preserved six days in water at 20+3°C, then 28 days in atmosphere at the room temperature and 60-65 % humidity.

Table 1 Physico-mechanical characteristics of G-API type cement

PROPERTY		VALUE
Normal water		24.4 %
Beginning of setting		2h 15 min
End of setting		3h 40 min
Tensile strength	- 7 days	6.33 N/mm^2
	- 28 days	7.70 N/mm^2
Compression strength	- 7 days	31.14 N/mm ^{2}
	- 28 days	40.92 N/mm^2

The duration of pumping showed to be within 90-120 minutes.

Table 2 Characteristics of PVA

SAMPLE	$\bar{P}$	$\overline{GH}$
I	120	88
II	90	98
III	50	88
IV	50	92

RESULTS AND DISCUSSION

The experimental data listed in Table 3 evidence the ability of PVA present in the expander of delaying the expansion of cement and lowering the settling compared to cement paste with additive but without PVA.In cement pastes of w/c ratio 0.53 expansion ceases after 2.5 hours in samples I, II and IV but continues in sample III. In samples with w/c ratio equal to 0.4 expansion is slower than in those with w/c = 0.53 and the maximum value of the expansion is reached 3 hours after preparation. In case of injection mixtures of samples without PVA expanding starts practically after preparation and ends after one hour for w/c = 0.53 and 1.5 hour at w/c = 0.4. Therefore the rheological results could not be compared with those obtained with an additivated standard sample yet without PVA owing to the instantaneous evolution of gas bubbles which caused the results to be irreproductibile.

Table 3 Properties of cement type G-API samples as a
function of PVA present in the expander additive

w/c	SAMPLE	EXPANSION (%)		SETTLING (%)	STRENGTH (N/mm²)	
		1h	3h		7 days	28 days
0.53	*	12.5	12.5	7.0	21.8	37.0
0.53	I	4.0	10.0	4.0	12.0	22.0
0.53	II	7.0	10.5	4.5	9.9	17.5
0.53	III	9.0	15.0	3.1	11.6	15.2
0.53	IV	7.5	12.4	4.9	11.0	16.5
0.40	*	11.0	12.3	5.0	31.1	39.9
0.40	I	0.5	10.0	2.5	20.1	38.7
0.40	II	2.1	9.0	2.7	19.0	36.9
0.40	III	2.0	11.0	3.0	17.9	35.4
0.40	IV	1.9	12.0	2.9	17.8	35.5

* without PVA

Examination of expansion 1 hour after preparation of samples reveals the inhibiting effect exerted by the presence of PVA upon H_2 evolution from the reaction:

$$2Al + 3Ca(OH)_2 + 6H_2O \longrightarrow 3CaO \cdot Al_2O_3 \cdot 6H_2O + 3H_2 \quad (1)$$

In case the content of $Ca(OH)_2$ resulted from the hydration of the cement is not sufficient, the optimal advancement of the reaction of hydrogen evolution is ensured by alkalies.The experimental data (Table 3) show that the additive containing PVA with $\bar{P}=120$ and $\bar{G}=88$ (sample I) improve the cement paste for both w/c ratio. The maximum expansion is delayed one hour; the optimal expansion value (10 %) is reached in less than 3 hours; the settling is reduced; the maximum compression strength is reached in 7 hours and the cement stone is formed in 7-28 days. The values of compression strength are lower in case of pastes with PVA additive than in those without PVA but within acceptable limits. The minimum allowable value for the oil-well cement is 15 N/mm². The values of the strength obtained at a ratio w/c = 0.4 suggest the utilization of this additive in civil engineering. Sample III containing PVA of the same $\overline{GH}$ as sample I but having a much smaller $\bar{P}$ exerts a weaker influence on the delaying the expansion of the paste and on the compression strength after 28 days. The behavior of sample III is closer to that of sample IV which evidences the importance of the degree of polymerization of PVA. In oil-well applications the cement paste should be fluid without undergoing separation of water. The influence of expander with PVA upon the rheology of G-API cement pastes is shown in Figs. 1 and 2.

The cement pastes exhibit a plastic flow described by the equation:

$$\tau - \tau_l = \eta \times D^n \qquad (2)$$

where τ_l stands for the limiting share stress, η for the apparent viscosity coefficient, D for the deformation rate and n for a numerical coefficient which is less than unity [7]. The overall value of is given by the contribution of the additive cement paste. All samples exhibited thixotropy. The minimal viscosity values were reached after 4 cycles.One cycle consisted of the increase and then decrease of the deformation rate. The thixotropic properties were evidenced by the reached of equilibrium values of η at a constant rotation rate of viscometer cylinders. The initial torsion momentum α_0 decrease exponentially in time t_o an equilibrium value α_E according to the equation:

$$\alpha = \alpha_E + (\alpha_0 - \alpha_E) \times \exp(-Bt) \qquad (3)$$

where B is the destructuring constant, depends on the shearing rate and the properties of pastes [8].Destructuration reaches equilibrium in 1-2 minutes. Because α_0 is higher than α_E the shape of rheological curves is strongly influenced by the time taken to obtain each value on the rising as well as on the descending curve (decreasing value of the deformation rate. In this respect it is very important to observe the shearing time and duration of each cycle at the obtaining of rheological data [9]. To compare the effect of various PVA samples upon the rheology of cement pastes displayed in Figs. 1 and 2 the experimental data obtained at the first application of the force as well as those after four complete cycles (of about 10 minutes each) were considered. Minimum values of the viscosity coefficients (Table 4) were reached after this treatment. The extending of shear duration after four cycles entailed the increase of viscosity, more so 30 minutes after preparation of pastes.

The experimental rheological data evidence that at a w/c ratio equal to 0.53 the viscosity of additivated samples is lower than that of non-additivated cement pastes. Thirty minutes after preparation, the viscosity of non-additivated pastes increases while that of additivated ones remains practically unchanged. The influence of the characteristics of PVA in the additive is less obvious in laboratory conditions. It seems that the decrease of viscosity should be assigned to the lower degree of hydrolysis ($\overline{GH}$ = 88),samples I and III reach in time the lowest equilibrium values of η . At a w/c ratio of 0.4, 10 min after preparation the rheological behavior is similar to that for w/c = 0.53. The data obtained at first cycle are no longer shown in Fig. 2.a, because they are very close to those obtained after four cycles. The η values are listed in Table 4.

The cement pastes of lower water content show an unusual rheological behavior 30 min. after preparation (Fig. 2.b): the viscosity of additivated pastes is higher than that of non-additivated pastes. With the exception of sample I, the viscosity decreases on shearing (after 4 cycles). In the first series of runs, sample I retains even after 30 min. from paste preparation a lower viscosity.

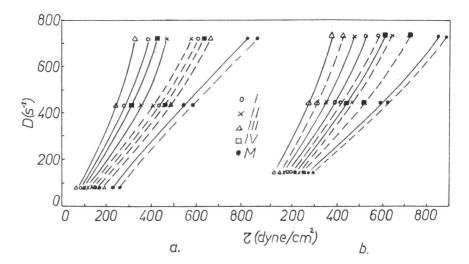

Fig.1. Deformation rate versus shears stress for cement pastes (w/c = 0.53) after 10 min. (a) and 30 min. (b) of mixing. First determination dotted line, after four cycles solid line. M-cement paste without expander additive.

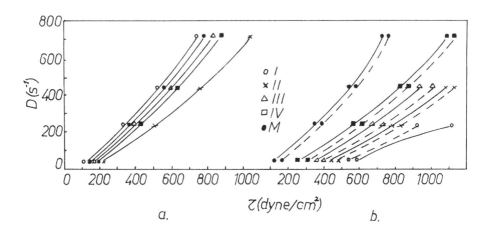

Fig.2. Deformation rate versus shears stress for cement pastes (w/c = 0.40) after 10 min. (a) and 30 min. (b) of mixing. First determination dotted line, after four cycles solid line. M-cement paste without expander additive.

Table 4 Minimal values of apparent viscosity (poise), for
cement pastes with expander additive containing PVA*

w/c	WORKING CONDITIONS	**	I	II	III	IV
0.53	1st cycle-10 min.	120.4	83.5	83.6	64.8	84.1
0.53	1st cycle-30 min.	123.5	81.3	81.3	57.3	96.9
0.53	4th cycle-10 min.	114.0	54.7	64.8	46.6	50.0
0.53	4th cycle-30 min.	126.6	58.1	65.6	51.2	83.6
0.40	1st cycle-10 min.	154.0	114.0	154.0	123.0	148.0
0.40	4th cycle-10 min.	149.0	103.0	151.0	116.0	117.0

* $D = 729 \text{ s}^{-1}$
** without additive

Considering together the rheological data (Figs. 1, 2 and Table 4) and those regarding expansion, settling and compression strength (Table 3) one can conclude that samples with PVA additive of $\bar{P} = 120$ and $\overline{GH} = 88$ may improve the fluidity of cement paste, delay the expansion of cement without any adverse effect on the settling and on the strength of cement stone. These properties are obvious in case of the ratio w/c = 0.53 which is recommended in oil-well cementing. When w/c = 0.4 the additive containing PVA (120/88) is efficient with respect to the delay of expansion, settling and retaining of good compression in time. Pastes with high cement content can be made adequate for surface injection by using both expanding agent and fluidizer.

CONCLUSIONS

1. Utilization of PVA of various degrees of polymerization and hydrolysis as component of expanding additives ensures the improvement of the workability cement paste (type G-API), the delay of expansion and the decrease of settling without changing the final value of expansion, the setting and the strength of cement stone. PVA of chain length 120 and degrees of hydrolysis 88 ensures the best behaviour. The chain length ensures the delaying of expansion and the mechanical properties after setting.
2. The presence of PVA in the expanding additive exerts a thixotropic effect of lowering the viscosity of the paste and maintaining it long enough to facilitate workability, more to for w/c = 0.53. At w/c = 0.40 the viscosity is maintained at shorter time. The decrease of viscosity is more pronounced as PVA degree of hydrolysis decreases.
3. The G-API cement pastes of w/c = 0.53 with expanding additive containing PVA of $\bar{P} = 120$ and $\overline{GH} = 88$ were tested in oil-well cementing in Romania; the reduction of circulation losses ensured an economy of 50 % cement.

REFERENCES

1. RAMACHANDRAN, VS. Cement admixture. Chem. Res. Prog. 1980, pp 119-219.
2. POPESCU, G, OLTEANU, M and PERETZ, S. Influence of calcium gluconate based additives upon the oil-well cement pastes. Il Cemento, Vol. 88, No. 1, 1991, pp 37-44.
3. CZARNESKI, L. Expansive resin concrete. Proceedings of the 3rd Int. Congress on Polymers in Concrete, Koriyama,Fukushima, Japan, 1981, pp 713.
4. AKATSU, K. Cement foaming agent. Japan Pat. 77.119.627/1977.
5. SUGIMA, K. Cement expanding agent. Japan Pat.78.16.007/1978.
6. POPESCU , G. Aditiv expandat pentru paste de ciment.Romanian Pat. 88810/1985.
7. LENK, RS. Plastic Rheology, MacLaren and Sons, London,1968, pp 13.
8. DIMOND, CR,and TATTERSALL, GH. The use of the coaxial cylinders viscometer to measure the rheological properties of cement pastes. Hydraulic Cement Pastes,Publ. 15.121, Cement and Concrete Assoc, England, 1976,
pp 118-133.
9. OLTEANU, M, PERETZ, S, and IANCULESCU, C. Influenta compozitiei aditivilor de expandare asupra fluiditatii pastelor de ciment de sonda, Revista de Constructii, No. 4-5, 1991, pp 84-87.

ROLE OF RESEARCH AND DEVELOPMENT IN THE CONSTRUCTION INDUSTRY

M T Hutchinson

Trafalgar House Technology Ltd

United Kingdom

ABSTRACT. This paper examines the impact of R&D on the Industry from the point of view of a Construction Company. It demonstrates the need to identify a customer who will gain commercial benefit from R&D in order to obtain funding.

It concludes that emphasis on feedback from site and on efficient information dissemination is essential to technological development, to the improvement of Quality and to optimising productivity.

Keywords: Research, Productivity, Quality.

Mr M T Hutchinson is Operations Director of the Research & Development Centre of Trafalgar House Technology, which is responsible for the R&D activities of Trafalgar House Construction. These cover most areas of Building and Civil Engineering and are very much market orientated.

Concrete 2000. Edited by Ravindra K. Dhir and M. Roderick Jones.
© 1993 Published by E & FN Spon. ISBN 0 419 18120 2.

INTRODUCTION

There have been many reports issued over the years (eg.1,2,) which show that the Construction Industry in the UK does not generally value the results of R&D very highly. Comparisons are made with the practice in other countries(3) which demonstrate that the UK Construction Industry makes less investment and has a less effective technology transfer mechanism than for instance the comparable industries in Germany and Japan. It is not proposed to re-iterate here all the facts and arguments which have been put forward in substantiation of this latter statement, but in fact few would argue with it.

We should ask ourselves why this is the case. It is not sufficient to attempt to correct the position by demanding more funding.

The simplistic answer to the question is that the Industry is too fragmented, and thus not able easily to take advantage of new development and there is little doubt that this is a contributory factor.

However, there is another factor which must be considered. This is whether the R&D which is carried out is appropriate to the Industry's needs.

In these days of Quality Assurance, satisfaction of the customer's needs becomes a major objective. If one applies this principle to R&D, then a major concern must be to establish what the "customer's" needs are - and if they are then satisfied, there will be no problem of getting the results of R&D into use.

Indeed, this will result in "pull" from the Industry, rather than "push" from the R&D fraternity, the former being by far the most effective driving force.

Such an approach is used in other industries, where the "customer" might be the end user (as in the Drugs Industry) or another part of the same organisation - such as the Production Engineering Department of a Manufacturer.

In the Construction Industry, the system is not so simple, and the identification of the "customer" for R&D not easy. This Paper attempts to shed some light on this area, and to suggest some possible ways forward, particularly from the point of view of improving quality of construction.

THE PURPOSE OF CONSTRUCTION INDUSTRY R&D

From the point of view of a Construction Company - be it Designer, Constructor, Contractor, Sub-Contractor or Supplier - any R&D which it undertakes must result in benefit to itself. It must:-

- Open up new markets
- Increase market share
- Increase profitability
- Reduce risk
- Reduce tender price

etc

The R&D must therefore give the Company an edge in the market place. From a Materials Supplier's point of view the benefits of R&D are fairly clear and the "customers" well defined, and it should be of no surprise that they are among its biggest supporters in the Industry.

However, if we look at the traditional way in which a building is constructed (see fig 1), the sequential nature of the various stages, and the way in which risk is passed down the chain, means that it is in no one's interest to introduce new ideas. For instance, the sub-contractor ultimately responsible for frame construction would not be consulted before tender stage, so why should he for example, develop a system of frame and floor construction which costs more than conventional methods but which would simplify and cheapen cladding erection, thereby reducing costs overall? This is particularly the case where plant or equipment would have to be purchased requiring a long term strategy in support. Such a development would only be of benefit to him if some financial advantage derived from it - which is unlikely to occur with current tendering systems.

Likewise, a Main Contractor will see little benefit in paying for such a development when he is normally presented with a fully specified design for a proposed building as the basis for his tender, and where he is subsequently mainly concerned with the management of sub-contractors rather than carrying out the work himself. The designer also may not be interested since he will have no financial benefit for using a new system, but just be taking on an extra risk.

In other words without a benefit to the company concerned, funds are unlikely to be forthcoming to sponsor R&D to any extent.

Each individual Company will have its own Technological Strategy - for instance, whether it wishes to be a technological leader in certain areas of its operations, or whether it wishes to be a follower of other's developments. The benefits of R&D may therefore be perceived differently by different companies.

By way of example, the following is extracted from Trafalgar House Technology's R&D Centre Annual Report:-

"The purpose of the R&D Centre is to give an advantage to the

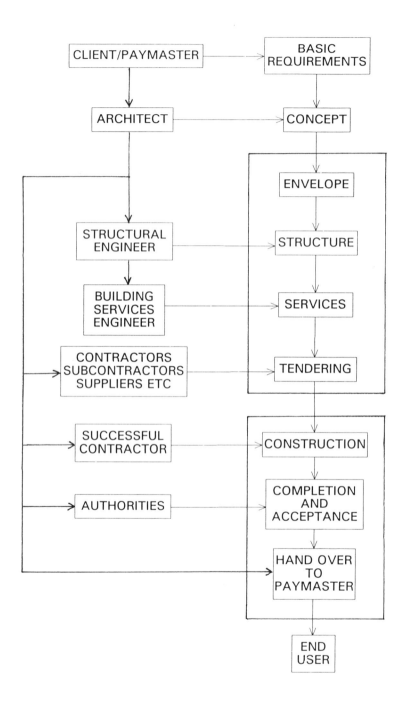

Figure 1:   Traditional Construction Process

Construction Division over its competitors by augmenting and co-ordinating the Division's technical knowledge and expertise. In practice, co-ordination is carried out through the Divisional Technical Development Forum, upon which sit Senior Engineers from the Operating Companies, and which provides for interchange of information between them.

The advantage given to the Construction Division can be of several different kinds. For instance it can be:

a)   Cost advantage

Quicker site operations
Cheaper materials
More economical design
Better performance on site

b)   Commercial advantages

More competitive tenders
Alternative design tenders
Improved Public Relations

c)   Risk reduction

Quantifying risk
Reduction of "factors of ignorance"
Building right first time
Improved Quality Control

This listing is by no means exhaustive. For instance, the advantage may also be by enabling an Operating Company to reduce site costs by introducing innovations, or it may be by enabling effective claims to be supported by high quality technical argument.

These advantages may be achieved in several ways:

d)   Specialist advice at pre-tender stage, contract stage, or in claims.

e)   Development of relevant techniques, materials, processes or procedures.

f)   Problem solving during contracts.

g)   Ensuring availability of up to date information.

h)   Ensuring relevant technical training of site staff.

It is the policy of the R&D Centre to provide a service focused in this way, acting on its own or in conjunction with an Operating Company, and to act as a catalyst to stimulate innovation by others.

To be effective, the R&D Centre must be organised in such a way as to be able to reflect the corporate strategy of the Division, and the place within it taken by technology. For instance, the system required for achieving technological leadership in the market place will be different from that needed for responding rapidly to advances made by others.

In general, our R&D Centre approach is to tend towards the second of these types. The emphasis is on close co-operation with the Engineering Functions within the Operating Companies, rather than generating an entirely independent and separate function. In this way, problems of technology transfer are being addressed, and quick response to technical requests is ensured, with R&D Centre staff taking developments onto site and, if necessary, staying with them during their use in contract work."

There are two features in this extract which is worth emphasising

a)   Definition of R&D

Since every construction can be looked upon as individual, one can include contract - specific technical development in the category of R&D - as would be done in a manufacturing industry, for instance. The Construction Industry in fact does much more of this type of work than is generally known, but as it is not formally reported the results are often lost at the end of the Contract.

b)   Emphasis on technology transfer

One major problem that we have in the Construction Industry is a general lack of impact of technology on site work. This is highlighted in the paper by N P King(4) covering concreting work on site. It is more important in some ways to make use of technical knowledge and understanding which already exists that it is to generate new knowledge, and in any strategy for R&D in our industry the dissemination of knowledge must form a central plank.

As a Contractor we ourselves have to put a major emphasis on getting technology into use on site - otherwise it has very limited impact in construction operations. We also put emphasis on feedback from sites - ie. information transfer in both directions.

CASE HISTORY OF R&D

The emphasis in this case history is on the way that the R&D was approached, rather than in the technical details of what was done. The identification in the early stages of what the client wanted was crucial to the success of the Project.

The Programme considered below is that of the development of the Continuous Flight Auger Piling System.

The system operates in simple terms thus:-

Phase 1   Auger is drilled into the ground to a depth normally pre-determined by site investigation - anything up to 30m.

Phase 2   Concrete is pumped down the hollow stem of the auger while it is withdrawn - sometimes non-rotating, and sometimes with slight forward or reverse rotations. This forms a concrete pile, of nominal diameter that of the flights of the auger, which is normally between 0.4m and 1.0m.

Phase 3   The reinforcement cage is then placed by pushing it through the concrete to the required depth, sometimes using vibrations to assist.

Although it appears simple and straightforward, the method had by the late seventies got a reputation both on the Continent and in the US for unreliability - with large numbers of failures and other disasters. It was not used in the UK to any extent.

This process differs from conventional bored, cast-in-place piling, in several respects, and in particular because:

•   It is not possible to inspect or measure the bore before concreting.

•   The reinforcement is placed after the concrete.

On the other hand it had obvious potential because it was:

•   Quick and thus cheap

•   Quiet

•   Low levels of vibration

Thus, when we first seriously considered the system, the benefits in the market place were already apparent - provided the problems could be overcome.

These problems were discussed at length between the Divisional Piling Company - Cementation Piling & Foundations - and the Research and Development Centre, with technical input from both sides.

As a result a programme of development was put together which focused on the following points:

a)   What were the causes of the failures which others had experienced

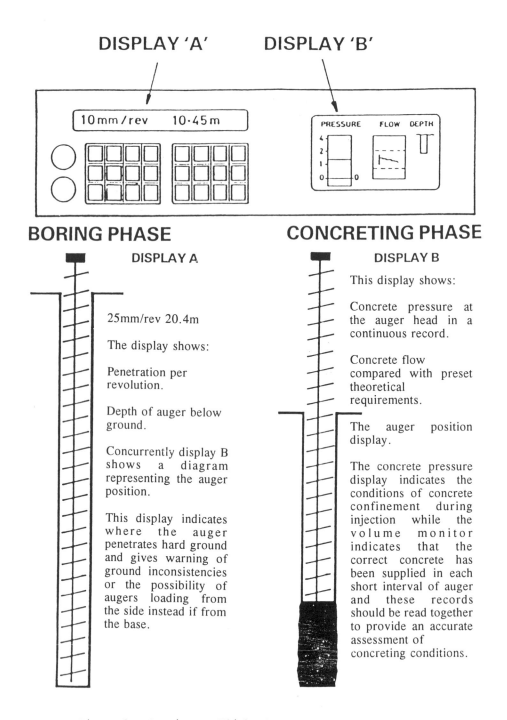

Figure 2:   Continuous Flight Auger Process Monitoring

b)   What process control methods could be devised to avoid such failures.

c)   What simple test method could be applied to piles to establish the integrity of the concrete in them.

d)   What was the concrete mix design which would best facilitate both concrete pumping and reliable placement of reinforcement.

The development of plant was not included in this exercise.

All aspects of this programme have their own elements of Research, and all but the first a strong element of Development.

In the event, the major cause of failures was found to be lack of continuity in the concrete in the pile, and it was also found that TNO in the Netherlands had developed a system suitable for quick pile testing, so that items a) and c) were resolved.

The R&D therefore addressed items b) and d) as a combined Materials and Process development.

Work on the concrete mix design showed that under most circumstances, provided the mix was pumpable it was acceptable.

Subsequent work focused on the development of a system for monitoring the basic factors of:-

•   Auger Depth

•   Concrete Pressure

•   Concrete Flowrate

and to present the information in such a way as to be of assistance to the Operator, and to ensure that sufficient control was excercised to prevent the problems of lack of continuity.

Initially, the development was rather at arm's length with emphasis on push from the R&D Centre.

However, once prototye equipment was operating in the field, it became apparent that it was helpful to the operators and enabled higher production rates to be achieved as well as acting as a quality control. We then saw much more pull from the client and the system eventually became integral to his marketing strategy.

The system now used is shown diagramically in Fig. 2.

All the information is fed onto an on-board data logger, from which it can be extracted and used for a variety of purposes, in addition to monitoring during pile production:-

- Demonstrate to the Piling Company's Client that correct procedures have been followed.

- Indicate where suspect piles may be.

- Used as a management tool - statistical analysis can show a variety of things from operator dependent production rates to site dependent excessive concrete usage.

The benefits of the R&D in commercial terms are now there for all to see:-

- CF Auger Piles are now a considerable success in the market place representing 60% of the Bored Piling Market in 1989. The advantages given above - relatively cheap and quick, quiet, vibration free - are now realised. The latter factors are becoming more and more important in these days when environmental issues are taking on a much higher profile.

- They no longer have the reputation for being unreliable.

- And, because of the accurancy of the logger systems, proper records of piles can easily be computerised for the Client's benefit, for the Piling Companies management's benefit - even for future Researchers' benefit, becuase nothing is perfect and more development will make the system even better.

If we look at the main reasons for the success, they are:-

- Indentification of a "customer" (ie Piling Company) who could benefit directly from the development.

- Focusing on critical issues because of relevance rather than technical interst.

- Proper use of the Scientific Method - ie. making use of the observations of the reported failures and thus completing the R&D "loop".

There are, of course, a number of other important factors which have a bearing on the "possibility" of success. In particular, it could not have been achieved 10 years previously, because suitable instrumentation systems did not exist. The R&D thus involved, not development a suitable flowmeter, but making use of someone else's development in this field.

Finally, it demonstrates that the proper use of quality control measures "on site" can have a beneficial effort on both quality and productivity, which is of benefit to both the contractor "on site" and to his client.

CONSTRUCTION R & D STRATEGY

This paper has so far outlined some of the problems faced by those attempting to inject the results of R&D into the industry.

In an Industry as diverse as ours, it is unlikely that any single strategy to stimulate interest in, and acceptance of, R&D will be effective in all sectors.

There are, however, some points which we would like to put up for discussion which may help to emphasise certain aspects of an overall strategy.

The Process of Technological Development

The Industry consists of a very large number of relatively small companies, partnerships or other concerns and a few very large ones. Focusing on the "Site Construction Process" as the critical part of the operation, it is apparent that the performance of relative small sub-contractors will determine whether the results of R&D are properly made use of. This fact is, of course, well established, and results in the system of Specifications, Codes of Practice and Best Practice Handbooks around which construction revolves.

In fact, the way in which information reaches the industry is outlined simplistically in Fig. 3.

From this simple diagram two problems are immediately apparent.

- How does Technical Development link in to the Industry?

- Information dissemination is critical to success.

The first of these problems is very important. If a development has to be put through the Specification/Code of Practice route, and then when used for a contract it goes through the tendering process, it is difficult to see where funding for the development can come from. If it comes from Industry, they will need a Benefit in the market place; if it is to come from Academia, Near Market Development funding will be required without Industrial contributions, and in the latter case, there is still no benefit to the Developer/Inventor.

In our R&D Centre at present we have just such a problem with Ecopave, a road pavement material developed via BRITE funding and reported on elsewhere in this Conference. The system in the UK does not allow for comparative tendering of different, or "owned" systems. This removes the likelihood of a major Construction Company funding such developments.

The second of the problems is just as important in its own way. There are very many professional, trade and Industry-wide organisations who supply information. Is this information being used

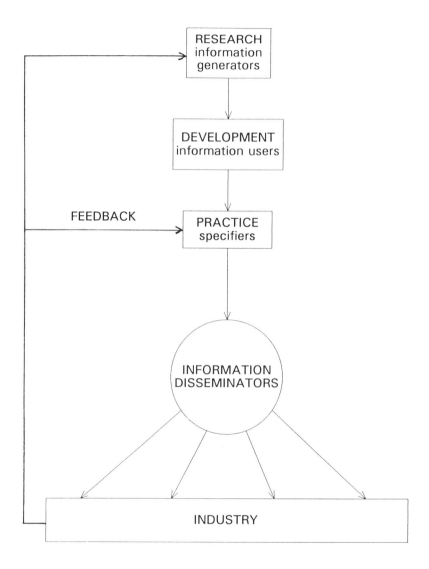

Figure 3:   Technology Development

by Industry?   Does it take account of new information produced by the Generators?   Is there efficient feed-back?   In our experience, in all these cases, efficiency is not high.

Finally, we must ask whether the system is efficient in financial terms. The amount of money spent by the Industry on Professional, Trade and Industry-wide associations must be very high, and because of their number, overlap and repitition is almost unavoidable.   This must bring into question efficiency.

In order to improve the system, the Process needs closely examining to confirm that the assertions made in this Paper are generally correct. Subsequently a much stronger feedback system needs incorporating, which will not only confirm or otherwise that current Research is appropriate to industry's needs, but also check on the efficiency of Codes of Practice and, finally, stimulate new areas for Development.

The Effect of R&D on Quality

The Feedback outlined above has the potential to affect Quality of construction to a very marked extent.

This is because Specifications and Codes of Practice can only control Quality:

- If they are appropriate

- If they are observed

- If they are based on the best available information.

All these factors require site monitoring of

- Site Processes

- Subsequent performance

in order to be achieved.

Such an approach requires a co-ordinated strategy and support from the major players in the Industry - the Professions, the Contractors, the Suppliers and Academia, with the latter playing a major rôle in its implementation.

If we can achieve this, even in some limited areas, then R&D will become central to both Quality and Productivity in the Construction Industry - which is where it should belong.

REFERENCES

1. "Construction Research & Development".   Report by ICE Research Sub-Committee.   December 1986, Thomas Telford, London.

2. "Building Research and Post-Graduate Education", CIOB & CIC, May 1982.

3. "Built by Japan" Fumio Hasegawa, John Wiley & Sons, 1988.

4. "Efficient   Concreting   Practice   and   Review   of   Concreting Procedures" N P King, Concrete 2000, Dundee, 1993.

CONTINUING PROFESSIONAL DEVELOPMENT

C Senior

The Engineering Council

United Kingdom

ABSTRACT. Investment in CPD is recognised increasingly as essential to improve the performance of staff and the competitiveness of employers. Engineers need to be up to date, manage technology and be innovative; in addition they require commercial awareness and management skills.

The Engineering Council has carried out a major study of the key factors that assist CPD. As a result a National System is being established. This sets standards for CPD and encourages action to be taken by the key partners (individuals, employers, professional and academic institutions).

A key aim is for CPD to be high on the agenda of all partners so that CPD is planned and carried out systematically.

The Engineering Council is examining how CPD should be a requirement for engineers who are expected to remain professionally competent throughout their engineering careers.

Mr Chris Senior CEng, is the Senior Executive at The Engineering Council responsible for promoting CPD through employers, and professional and academic institutions. After gaining a degree in Chemical Engineering, Mr Senior worked in several engineering companies establishing training programmes for technical staff. He has recent experience with major national and international projects developing and promoting strategies for education and professional development in a number of industries.

Concrete 2000. Edited by Ravindra K. Dhir and M. Roderick Jones.
© 1993 Published by E & FN Spon. ISBN 0 419 18120 2.

INTRODUCTION

Investment in Continuing Professional Development (CPD) is recognised as an essential factor in improving the performance of engineering staff and the competitiveness of employers. A national system for CPD is being established in the UK aimed at developing engineers and technicians throughout their careers.

The Engineering Council is promoting the term CPD to emphasise:

- the need for development to include a wide range of technical, commercial and management subjects
- the responsibility of engineers for continuous improvement and development to ensure high competence as professionals throughout their careers
- the use of a wide range of structured job-related activities including courses, conferences, distance learning, in-company programmes, projects and professional institution activities

MANAGING CHANGE

The demand for engineers and technologists is growing and this, coupled with demographic trends, is leading to increasing skills shortages. One approach to overcoming these is to widen the access to recruitment and in particular to encourage women to consider engineering and to retain their skills throughout their careers. The number of women taking engineering degree courses is rising and The Engineering Council has taken the lead in encouraging Career Break schemes /1/.

Jobs are more demanding as a result of changes in technology, new systems and increased international competitiveness. As well as technical updating, engineers need to obtain knowledge and skills in such areas as communications, personal effectiveness, commerce and finance. The Engineering Council report 'Management and Business Skills for Engineers' /2/ proposes how engineers can be developed to fill management roles.

CPD is often narrowly defined as the continuing education and training that enables individuals to update their knowledge throughout their careers. Although this is important CPD has a much wider function; it should aim to enhance the potential of all staff by encouraging innovation and enterprise. Engineers must manage technology, be innovative and respond positively to a continuously changing world. Success comes from anticipating needs and recognising opportunities.

The need for greater efforts in continuing education and training was anticipated in 1986 when The Engineering Council published a discussion document 'A Call to Action - Continuing Education' and argued the need for a radical change in attitudes towards continuing education and training and gave recommendations concerning the role and good practice of employers, individuals, engineering institutions, education and training bodies, government and The Engineering Council.

Many factors influence decisions by individuals and employers on taking action on CPD. A pilot study /4/ carried out by The Engineering Council developed and tested a document entitled Career Manager /5/ to assist engineers to structure their CPD. The study showed that the key factors which encourage CPD to take place include:

- recognition of the benefits of CPD
- active commitment by employers to CPD
- ownership of CPD by individual engineers and technicians
- encouragement and support for individuals
- promotion and monitoring of standards for CPD
- marketing and provision of CPD courses, and learning material

PARTNERSHIP IN LEARNING

A fundamental issue in CPD is for individual engineers and technicians to take responsibility for their lifelong learning. Career advancement requires a commitment to continuous improvement and professional development as job requirements and personal interests change.

Although there is greater recognition of the need for CPD, there is less certainty about the action to be taken. CPD is perceived as being demanding in both time and money. Identifying requirements is often difficult. Information is needed on the various options available, their costs and the sources of courses, and other learning opportunities. Small and medium sized companies have particular difficulties in terms of time, staff and information resources. Investment in CPD requires confidence that benefits will result.

The way forward in CPD requires a strategic approach involving effective partnerships where value is added to both individual growth and company performance. To achieve this The Engineering Council is establishing a National System for CPD. A policy document /6/ provides the framework for joint action.

The core partnership is between individual engineers and their employers, as shown in Figure 1.

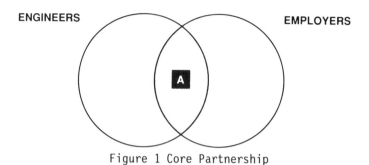

Figure 1 Core Partnership

Action in area A includes identification of needs, and planning and evaluation of CPD action. Individual engineers should draw up personal development plans using an appropriate document. This must be complemented by employers providing a supportive framework of appraisals, coaching and mentoring. Structured CPD activities should complement learning through work experience and be planned so that CPD contributes to both company performance and individual career development.

Professional and academic institutions have key roles in support of the core partnership (see Fig 2).

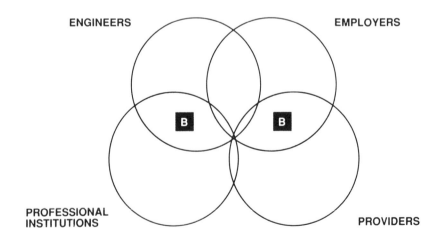

Figure 2 Professional Support

Action in areas B include encouragement of CPD, provision of guidance, information and development of appropriate CPD programmes and learning material. Both employers and individuals require guidance and assistance so that CPD is planned and implemented effectively. Information is needed on technical and commercial developments and the availability of opportunities for CPD.

Qualifications have a valuable role in CPD as motivaters and benchmarks. Work experience, distance learning, projects and courses can be integrated to form qualifications relevant to the needs of both individuals and employers. New modular, flexible work-based qualifications are being established in the UK. These include a masters degree in Technology Management developed by JUPITER (Joint Universities and Polytechnics Industrial Technology Education and Research) and EuroPro, a European Professional Development programme.

The Engineering Council is providing leadership, coordination and support to ensure that the National System operates effectively, Fig 3.

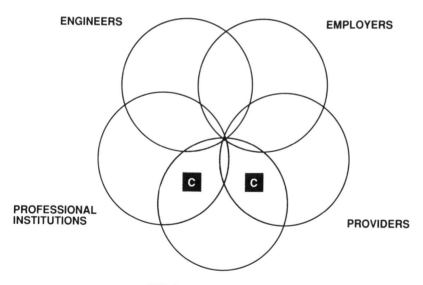

THE ENGINEERING COUNCIL

Figure 3 Leadership

Action in areas C include promoting CPD, providing guidance, setting standards, and accreditation of CPD. A project with funding support from government is underway to establish the National System. Regional CPD advisers have been appointed to give a focus for integrated action by the partners. Workshops to assist employers in progressing CPD have been established. A practical guide /7/ has been published to assist engineers to implement CPD; the need for further support is being examined.

CPD STANDARDS

A key requirement in the UK is for the professional engineering institutions to work together to ensure high standards of CPD amongst their members. A forum of the institutions and The Engineering Council produce a regular newsletter CPD Link /8/ and arrange a National Conference on CPD.

The Engineering Council is responsible for setting standards for professional staff throughout the engineering profession in the UK, and relating these to other national and international standards and qualifications. The charter of The Council requires it to establish the qualifications and corresponding designatory letters Chartered Engineer (CEng), Incorporated Engineer (IEng) and Engineering Technician (EngTech). These designations denote that individual engineers and technicians have acquired appropriate academic qualifications, training and responsible experience.

The existing standards required of engineers relate primarily to initial education and training. A major review of the formation of engineers is underway; this includes establishing the occupational competences and standards which meet the operating needs of industry. One result of this will be a clearer understanding of the requirements of engineers carrying out different roles throughout their careers. The distinction between standards for initial education and training and continuing professional development standards will become blurred. The move is towards total life-long professional development.

The National System for CPD can be considered a framework of quality standards. CPD is a learning partnership; each of the partners has a code of practice for CPD which defines the responsibilities and relationships with other partners. Each code sets out, in measurable terms, the standards required. These standards are based on the key elements of the learning cycle of identification of needs, analysis, planning action, implementation of learning, application and evaluation.

The partners are being encouraged to follow the appropriate code which defines the standard expected. The target is to encourage use of the codes so that they become established practice by engineers, employers, professional institutions and providers of CPD. The principle of self-assessment follows from the principle that CPD must be owned by the partners rather than be imposed from outside.

Professional competence, together with the actions (such as CPD) supporting it, are ultimately the responsibility of the individual professional engineer.

The Engineering Council believes that there may be benefit for CPD to be a requirement for individual engineers and technicians. This should be seen within the context of the profession having a system of quality control for its members who should be required to remain professionally competent throughout their engineering careers. Evidence of commitment to CPD may be required at, for example, registration, upgrading, or in cases where professional negligence or incompetence is examined. The approach being developed focuses on the use of a code of practice rather than one based on prescribing CPD in terms of time or qualifications. Engineers should confirm that they abide by and implement all codes of their profession.

There is demand, particularly from employers for some system of approval or accreditation of providers and their products. Approval of the large number of courses and variety of learning material poses considerable practical difficulties and may only be necessary where they form part of a qualification. A more effective approach may be to accredit the providers through some system of quality assurance e.g ISO 9000. However any accreditation system must take into account the need for flexibility and innovation by providers in meeting the changing requirements of their customers.

Since the focus for much learning lies with employers, possible methods of accreditation of their arrangements for CPD are being examined. In the UK professional institutions increasingly accredit employers' arrangements for initial training and experience. This could be extended into CPD using an appropriate framework or code of practice. Several approaches are being considered including use in the UK of the government-sponsored 'Investors in People' scheme.

PROGRESS AND BENEFITS

Evidence of increasing interest and action on CPD is available from several surveys from The Engineering Council and professional institutions. Over 50% of engineers are participating to the extent of 5-10 days per year in a wide range of activities. The focus is on courses and structured reading in technical updating subjects. However most engineers believe there is a need to improve their CPD, although only a minority currently have a structured approach. Many companies are developing strategies for assisting engineers to plan their career development, within the context of business needs.

Investment in CPD is a central business activity aimed at developing and improving the technical and managerial competences needed for success and enhancing the potential of the enterprise. All partners need to have CPD high on their agendas, develop strategies for action and work together towards effective and innovative approaches.

The benefits of this should be improved performance, job satisfaction and career advancement for individual engineers and technicians. For employers their staff should be innovative and fully capable, both technically and managerially, thus contributing to profitability. The overall aim is high competitive performance for industry, and a positive image for the engineering profession.

REFERENCES

1. Career Breaks for Women Chartered and Technician Engineers and a report of a survey of the Attitudes of Engineering Employers. The Engineering Council, London, 1985

2. Management and Business Skills for Engineers. The Engineering Council, London 1988.

3. A Call to Action: Continuing Education and Training for Engineers and Technicians; with annexes B1 and B2. The Engineering Council, London, 1986

4. Report of A Pilot Study - Continuing Education and Training. The Engineering Council, London 1991

5. Career Manager. The Engineering Council, London, 1989.

6. Continuing Professional Development - A Framework for Action. The Engineering Council, London, 1991.

7. Continuing Professional Development; The Practical Guide to Good Practice. The Engineering Council, London, 1992

8. CPD Link - The CPD Newsletter for the Enginering Forum. The Engineering Council, London, 1992.

DEVELOPMENT OF MULTIFUNCTIONAL
RELEASE AGENTS FOR FORMWORK

K Demura

Y Ohama

Nihon University

Japan

ABSTRACT. The purpose of this study is to develop the techniques for improving the concrete surface layers of reinforced concrete structures by using multifunctional release agents. The multifunctional release agents containing a silicone oil and amino alcohol derivative are prepared, and steel molds and plywood plates for concrete forms are treated with the agents. Mortar specimens are prepared by using the steel molds and the plywood plates as molds, and tested for the penetration depth of the silicone oil, water absorption, chloride ion penetration and carbonation. In conclusion, the multifunctional release agents are useful for improving the concrete surface layers.

Keywords: Multifunctional release agents, Silicone compounds, Amino alcohol derivative, Penetration depth, Water absorption, Chloride ion penetration, Carbonation.

Dr. Katsunori Demura is a lecturer of architecture at the College of Engineering , Nihon University, Koriyama, Fukushima-ken, Japan. He has been involved with research work on concrete-polymer composites, fiber-reinforced concrete and superdurable concrete for about 14 years.

Dr. Yoshihiko Ohama is a professor of architecture at the College of Engineering, Nihon University, Koriyama, Fukushima-ken, Japan. He has actively been involved in the research and development of concrete-polymer composites for over 30 years. He is vice-president of ICPIC and member of RILEM, ACI, ASTM, Architecture Institute of Japan, Japan Technology Transfer Association, Society of Materials Science, Japan and Japan Concrete Institute committees.

Concrete 2000. Edited by Ravindra K. Dhir and M. Roderick Jones.
© 1993 Published by E & FN Spon. ISBN 0 419 18120 2.

INTRODUCTION

For the purpose of inhibiting the wet corrosion of reinforced bars in reinforced concrete structures, it is most important to prevent the penetration of carbon dioxide, oxygen, water and chloride ions into concrete. Therefore, the improvement of the concrete surface layers may strongly raise the durability of the reinforced concrete structures. The additon of alkyl alkoxy silane and amino alcohol derivatives to mortar and concrete results in excellent waterproofness and resistance to chloride ion penetration and carbonation [1].

The purpose of this study is to develop the techniques for improving the concrete surface layers of reinforced concrete structures by using multifunctional release agents. In this study, after examining the penetration depth of three silicone compounds, the multifunctional release agents containing a silicone oil and amino alcohol deriative are prepared, and steel molds and plywood plates for the concrete forms are treated with the agents. Mortar specimens are prepared by using the treated steel molds and plywood plates as molds, and tested for the penetration depth of the silicone oil, water absorption, chloride ion penetration and carbonation. The performance of the multifunctional release agents to improve the durability of the mortar is discussed. The effects of the multifunctional release agents on the setting of the mortar are also discussed.

MATERIALS

Cement and Aggregate

Ordinary portland cement and Toyoura standard sand as specified in JIS (Japanese Industrial Strandard) R 5210 (Portland Cement) and JIS R 5201 (Physical Testing Methods for Cement) respectively are used.

Ingredients for Multifunctional Release Agents

Machine oil ISO VG 150 (Oil) as specified in JIS K 2001 (Viscosity Classification for Industrial Liquid Lubricants), silicone compounds such as a silicone oil (SO), an alkyl alkoxy silane (AAS), an alkyl alkoxy silane emulsion (AS), and an amino alcohol deriative (AM) were employed as ingredients for multifunctional release agents.

TESTING PROCEDURES

Preparation of Specimens

Measurement of Penetration Depth of Silicone Compounds

The cured beam specimens 40x40x160 and 40x28x160mm were split for four blocks, and the split crosssections were sprayed with water. The depth of the rim of each cross-section with water repellency was measured with slide calipers as a silicone compound penetration depth as shown in Figure 1.

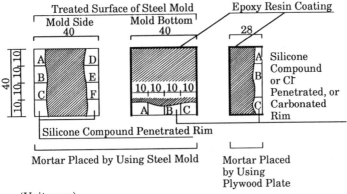

Treated Surface of Steel Mold · Epoxy Resin Coating

Silicone Compound Penetrated Rim

Mortar Placed by Using Steel Mold

Mortar Placed by Using Plywood Plate

A : Silicone Compound or Cl⁻ Penetrated, or Carbonated Rim

(Unit : mm)

Note : A, B, C, D, E and F Measured for Silicone Compound or Cl⁻ Penetration, or Carbonation Depth.

Figure 1 Crosssections of Mortar Specimens after Tests

Water Absorption Test

According to JIS A 6203 (Polymer Dispersions for Cement Modifiers), the cured beam specimens 40x40x160 and 40x28x160mm, whose surfaces untreated with multifunctional release agents, SO, AAS, AS and Oil were coated with an epoxy resin paint, were immersed in water at 20°C for 7 days, and their water absorption was determined.

Chloride Ion Penetration Test

The cured beam specimens 40x40x160 and 40x28x160mm, which were coated with an epoxy resin paint like the beam specimens for water absorption test, were immersed in a 2.5% NaCl solution at 20°C for 7 days for chloride ion penetration. After immersion, the beam specimens were split for four blocks, and the split crosssections were sprayed with 0.1% sodium fluorescein and 0.1N silver nitrate solutions as prescribed in UNI 7928 (Concrete-Determination of the Ion Chloride Penetration). The depth of the rim of each crosssection changed to white color was measured with slide calipers as a chloride ion (Cl⁻) penetration depth as shown in Figure 1.

Accelerated Carbonation Test

The cured beam specimens 40x40x160 and 40x28x160mm, which were coated with an epoxy resin paint like the beam specimens for water absorption test, were placed in a nonpressurizing carbonation test chamber for 7 days, in which temperature, humidity and CO_2 gas concentration were controlled to be 30°C, 60% R.H. and 5.0% respectively.

After accelerated carbonation, the beam specimens were split for four blocks, and the split crosssections were sprayed with a 1% phenolphthalein alcoholic solution. The depth of the rim of each crosssection without color change was measured with slide calipers as a carbonation depth as shown in Figure 1.

Test for Setting Time of Mortars

Mortars with the mix proportions of cement : sand = 1:3 (by weight), water-cement ratio of 76%, multifunctional release agent contents of 0, 3, 5 and 10% (of cement) were mixed in accordance with JIS R 5201, and the Ø 1-mm needle setting time of the mortars was determined according to Japan Concrete Institute (JCI) Standard for Test Methods for Polymer-Modified Mortars, Method of Test for Setting Time of Polymer-Modified Mortars.

TEST RESULTS AND DISCUSSION

Figure 2 shows the penetration depth of silicone compounds of the mortars placed by using the steel molds and plywood plates treated with the silicone compounds at an open time of 0 day. In general, the penetration depth of the silicone compounds is increased with an increase in the coverage rate of the silicone compounds. Larger penetration depth of the silicone compounds is observed for the mortars placed by using the steel molds and plywood plates treated with SO regardless of the type of the molds and coverage rate. It is evident from the test results that the silicone compounds can penetrate into the mortar surface layers at the mortar placing. The penetration depth of silicone compounds is affected by the type of silicone compounds and their coverage rate. It seems that the penetration of the silicone compounds into the mortar surface layers from the steel molds and plywood plates is done by a kind of transcription performance of the silicone compounds.

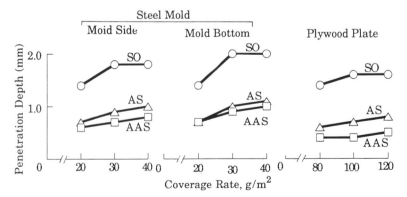

Figure 2   Penetration Depth of Silicone Compounds of Mortars Placed by Using Steel Molds and Plywood Plates Treated with Silicone Compounds at Open Time of 0 Day

A silicone compound, SO is most useful for preparing multifunctional release agetns as compared to AAS and AS.

Figure 3 represents the effect of the number of mortar placing on SO penetration depth of the mortars placed by using the plywood plates treated with SO at an open time of 0 day. At the first mortar placing, SO penetration depths of 1.4 to 1.6mm are observed. A raise in SO penetration depth is observed for the second to fourth placed mortars as compared to the first placed ones regardless of the coverage rate. SO penetration depth of the fouth placed mortars is about two times that of the first placed ones. The reason for this may be due to the prevention of SO absorption into the plywood plates when the plywood plates are recycled because SO penetrated at the previous mortar placings remains in the plywood plates. In general, any treatment for plywood forms may be required to increase the penetration depth of the effective SO in multifunctional release agents into concrete surface layers in the application of the agents for formwork because virgin plywood forms absorb SO in large quantities.

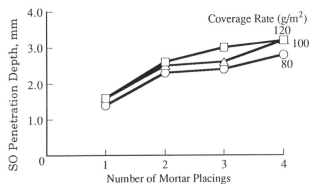

Figure 3 Number of Mortar Placings vs. SO Penetration Depth of
Mortars Placed by Using Plywood Plates Treated with
SO at Open Time of 0 Day

Figure 4 illustrates the effect of open time on SO penetration depth of the mortars placed by using the plywood plates treated with SO at a coverage rate of 100 g/m^2. A remarkable reduction in SO penetration depth is observed for the mortars placed at open times of 1 day or longer as compared to an open time of 0 day. This may be attribured to the absorption of SO into the plywood plates during open time. A difference in SO penetration depth between the first and second placed mortars is hardly recognized except for an open time of 0 day.

Figure 5 indicates the effect of open time on SO penetration depth of the mortars placed by using the steel molds treated with multifunctional release agents at a coverage rate of 30g/m^2. The effect of the open time on SO penetration depth of the mortar surface layers faced to the steel mold bottoms is hardly recognized irrespective of the formulations of the agents. However, SO penetration depth of the surface layers faced to the steel mold sides is decreased with prolonging open time. It appears that the multifunctional release agents may flow down during open time. In the application of multifunctional release agents for formwork, a reduction in the penetration depth of the effective SO in the multifunctional release agents into concrete surface layers due to the flowing down of the agents during open time should be considered when the concrete is placed by using steel forms vertically.

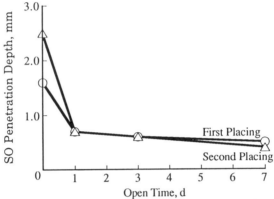

Figure 4 Open Time vs. SO Penetration Depth of Mortars Placed by Using Plywood Plates Treated with SO at Coverage Rate of 100g/m^2

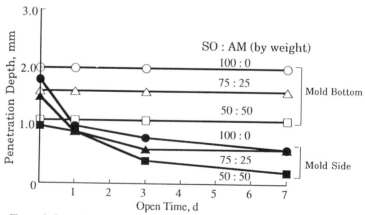

Figure 5 Open Time vs. SO Penetration Depth of Mortars Placed by Using Steel Molds Treated with Multifunctional Release Agents at Coverage Rate of 30g/m^2

Figure 6 represents SO penetration depth of the mortars placed by using the steel molds and plywood plates treated with multifunctional release agents at an open time of 0 day. SO penetration depth of the mortars is 1.0 to 2.0mm. SO penetration depth of the mortars placed by using the steel molds is larger than that of the mortars placed by using plywood plates, though the coverage rate of the multifunctional release agents for the plywood plates is large. This may be explained to be due to the absorption of SO into the plywood plates.

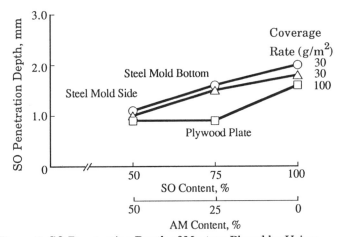

Figure 6 SO Penetration Depth of Mortars Placed by Using
Steel Molds and Plywood Plates Treated with
Multifunctional Release Agents at Open Time of 0 Day.

Figure 7 exhibits the water absorption of the mortars placed by using multifunctional release agents. The water absorption of the mortar placed by using only Oil as a release agent is 9.6%. However, the water absorption of the mortars placed by using the multifunctional release agents is about 1/4 to 1/5 of that of the mortar placed by using Oil regardless of the type of the molds used. The water absorption of the mortars placed by using the steel molds treated with the release agents is slightly increased with prolonging open time. The effect of SO content of the multifunctional release agents on the water absorption of the mortars is hardly recognized in spite of the smaller SO penetration depth when SO content is decreased. It is considered that such a reduction in the water absorption is due to the water repellency of the mortar surface layers with SO.

Figure 8 shows the chloride ion (Cl^-) penetration depth of the mortars placed by using multifunctional release agents. The chloride ion penetration depth of the mortar placed by using only Oil as a release agent is 38 mm. On the other hand, the chloride ion penetration depth of the mortars placed by using the multifunctional release agents is much smaller than that of the mortar placed by using only Oil, and is 3 to 7 mm regardless of the type of the molds used. It is well known that AM can adsorb the chloride ions and carbon dioxide diffused in cement mortar and concrete [1]. However, the effect of AM in the multi-

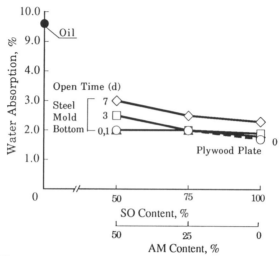

Figure 7   Water Absorption of Mortars Placed by Using
Multifunctional Release Agents

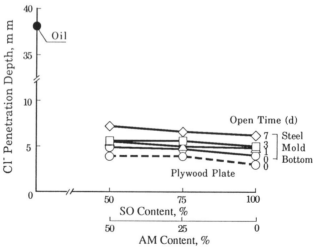

Figure 8 Chloride Ion Penetration Depth of Mortars Placed
by Using Multifunctional Release Agents

functional release agents on the inhibition of the chloride ion penetration into the mortars
is hardly recognized in this study. A reduction in the chloride ion penetration depth of the
mortars is found to be caused by SO which gives the mortar surface layers water
repellency.

Figure 9 illustrates the carbonation depth of the mortars placed by using multifunctional release agents. In general, a silicone compound such as SO does not have any inhibiting effect on the diffusion of carbon dioxide into the mortars because the silicone compound can not fill the micropores or adsorb the carbon dioxide in the mortars. However, the carbonation depth of the mortars placed by using the multifunctional release agents containing AM is smaller than that of the mortars placed by using only SO or Oil. In particular, the carbonation depth of the mortars placed by using the plywood plates treated with the multifunctional release agents containing AM is about a half of that of the mortars placed by using Oil. The addition of AM to the multifunctional release agents is effective to inhibit the carbonation of the mortars because AM can adsorb the carbon dioxide as stated above. It is evident from the above-mentioned test results that AM in the multifunctional release agents can penetrate into the mortar surface layers at the mortar placing like SO. In the mortars placed by using steel molds, a reduction in the carbonation depth with prolonging open time is also recognized irrespective of SO content.

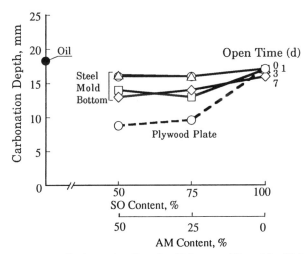

Figure 9 Carbonation Depth of Mortars Placed by Using
Multifunctional Release Agents

Figure 10 represents the setting time of mortars with multifunctional release agents. The Ø 1-mm needle setting time of the mortars is prolonged from 8 to 10 hours with an increase in the content of the multifunctional release agents. However, such a delay in the time within 2 hours may not be any serious problem for the application of the multifunctional release agents for formwork. The effects of the formulations of the multifunctional release agents on the setting time of the mortars are hardly observed.

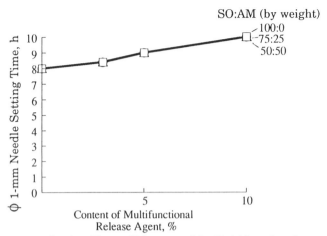

Figure 10 Setting Time of Mortars with Multifunctional Release Agents

CONCLUSIONS

1. Silicone compounds such as a silicone oil, an alkyl alkoxy silane and an alkyl alkoxy silane emulsion, which are sprayed on steel molds and plywood plates for concrete forms, can penetrate into the placed mortar surface layers. Of the silicone compounds, the silicone oil is the most effective to penetrate into the mortar surface layers.

2. The surface layers of the mortars placed by using multifunctional release agents with a silicone oil are improved to inhibit water absorption and chloride ion penetration.

3. An amino alcohol derivative contained in multifunctional release agents can penetrate into the placed mortar surface layers, and inhibit their carbonation.

4. The multifunctional release agents containing a silicone oil and an amino alcohol derivative, developed in this study, are found to be applicable to prevent the deterioration of reinforced concrete structures. However, a reduction in the penetration depth of multifunctional release agents into concrete surface layers due to the flowing down of the agents during open time should be considered when the concrete is placed by using steel forms vertically.

REFERENCE

1. OHAMA, Y., et al., "Development of Admixtures for High Durable Concrete", Proceedings of the Third International Conference on Superplasticizers and Other Chemical Admixtures in Concrete, Publication SP-119, American Concrete Institute, Detrroit, 1989, pp. 321-342.

FINITE ELEMENT MODELLING OF
CORNER JOINTS IN RC FRAMES

Y Hemmaty

Guido De Roeck

L Vandewalle

University of Science & Technology, Iran

Catholic University of Leuven

Belgium

ABSTRACT. The joint should be capable of resisting a bending moment at least as large as the calculated failure moment in the connected members namely beam and column. In this case flexural failure may occur outside the joint, which does not limit the load capacity of the frame. If this requirement is not met, the reinforcement layout should satisfy a second requirement. Then, the joint should have the necessary ductility so that a redistribution of the forces in the structure is possible without brittle failure of the joint. The main objective of this study is to develop fundamental reinforcement principles for corners in reinforced concrete frames, which are mainly acted upon by bending moments. In this study FE Program ANSYS 4.4 has been used for simulation of different reinforcement detailings for corner joints. We have included in our model the bond-slip law of Vandewalle which is modeled using the nonlinear force-deflection element. The bond-slip law of Vandewalle is based on extensive experimental tests carried out in the Department of Civil Engineering of the Catholic University of Leuven. First this law is examined by our FE Model on simple structures such as tension bars in which close agreement with experimental results has been obtained. Later a parametric study has been carried out for several parameters influencing the performance of the joint. Finally the verified FE Model has been used for study of different reinforcement detailings.

Keywords: Reinforced Concrete, Frame, Corner Joint, Finite Element Modelling, Bond-Slip, Diagonal crack failure, Compression failure.

Dr Yahya Hemmaty recently completed his Ph.D at the Department of Civil Engineering, KU Leuven, Belgium. His main research interests are the CAD systems for the design of Reinforced Concrete Structures and nonlinear Finite Element Modelling of Reinforced Concrete.

Professor Dr Guido De Roeck is Professor at the Department of Civil Engineering, KU Leuven, Belgium. His main domains of interest are Structural Dynamics and Advanced Computatinal Mechanics. He is chairman of the National Research Center in Civil Engineering which groups all Belgian Laboratories in this field.

Professor Dr Luci Vandewalle is Assiant Professor at the Department of Civil Engineering, KU Leuven, Belgium. She is mainly interested in Bond-Slip behaviour at low temperatures, use of steel fibers and high strength concrete.

Concrete 2000. Edited by Ravindra K. Dhir and M. Roderick Jones.
© 1993 Published by E & FN Spon. ISBN 0 419 18120 2.

INTRODUCTION

After cracking the stress distribution in a beam-column joint can not be evaluated any longer by the linear elastic theory. The study of the joint up to failure can be carried out either by experiment or by nonlinear FE Methods. The experimental results used in this study date to the early 1980's. At that time nonlinear FE codes were in early developments and the investigators had no choice than experiment.

Experiments show that in certain cases the strength of structural joints are lower than that of the connected members. In order to have a clear insight to the action of forces inside the joint we have used the nonlinear FE program ANSYS [1]. In this model which is described elsewhere [2] three elements has been used.

- Concrete elements
- Steel elements
- Interface elements for simulation of bond-slip behaviour

Concrete is modelled with 3-D solid element. The most important aspect of this element is the treatment of nonlinear material properties. The concrete can undergo cracking (in three orthogonal directions), crushing, plastic deformation and creep. In our model time dependent deformations are not yet considered.

A shear retention factor between 0.0 and 1.0 can be used to account for the aggregate interlock contribution to the shear-flexural capacity of the element. The value 0.0 representing a smooth crack (complete loss of shear transfer). This specification may be made for both the closed and open crack [1]. Later, we will see that how this value has been defined by a parametric study [2,3].

The reinforcing steel bars have been modelled as separate elements. The 3-D spar element is a uniaxial tension-compression element with three degrees of freedom at each node namely translations in the nodal x, y, and z directions. No bending of the element is considered, as in a pin-jointed structure. Plasticity and stress stiffening capabilities are included [1].

To model the bond-slip behaviour between concrete and steel with the law of Wandewalle [4-6], a nonlinear force-deflection element has been used. This is a unidirectional spring element with a nonlinear generalized force-deflection capability that can be used for simulation of the bond-slip law. The element has one degree of freedom at each node. In our model this is a translation in the nodal coordinate direction which can model the slip between the steel bar and the surrounding concrete [1-2].

First, this model was used to study the tension bars in order to show the validity of the FE Results [7,15]. Afterwords, a papametric study has been carried out to investigate the different parameters influencing the performance of the joint. Finally, the calculated results are compared with the experimental ones. Different detailings for joints and the appropriate range of using them for practical applications are proposed.

PARAMETRIC STUDY

A parametric study for some of the parameters that influence the performance of the joint is carried out [3]. In this parametric study two major points are considered.

1) The parameters which have influence on the strength of the joint such as the concrete quality, the percentage of steel, and detailing of the main reinforcement are studied.

2) The parameters which have influence on the validity of the finite element calculations and quality of the results such as the shear retention factor β, the associated or nonassociated flow

rule are examined.

The typical FE Model for a corner joint is shown in Figure 1.

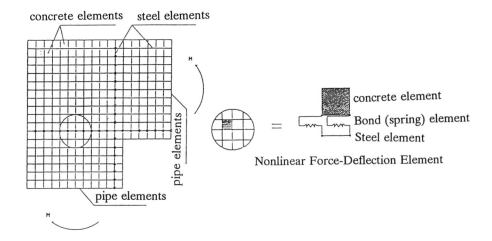

Figure 1 Typical representation of FE Model for a corner joint.

THE INFLUENCE OF DIFFERENT PARAMETERS

To show the influence of the main reinforcement detailing on the efficiency of the joint three specimens as shown in Figure 2 are modelled. The performance of the three specimens are compared in Figure 3. As shown in the figure the specimen with loop reinforcement plus inclined reinforcement shows a higher efficiency than the other two specimens [3]. This is a fact that has been shown by many experiments carried out in the refs. [8-11].

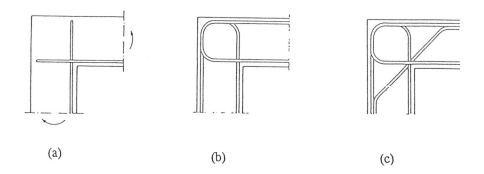

(a)   (b)   (c)

Figure 2 Detailings of main reinforcement for primary investigation.
a) Main reinforcement
b) Loop reinforcement
c) Loop reinforcement + inclined reinforcement

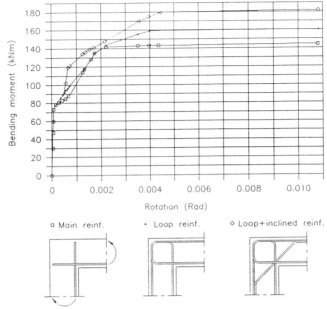

Figure 3 Comparison of the three reinforcement details.

The influence of other parameters are shown by modelling of the traditional detailing as shown in Figure 4. It has been shown in Figure 5a, by increasing the percentage of the main reinforcement the efficiency of the joint is decreasing.

The influence of the concrete quality has been shown in Figure 5b. As can be seen, by increasing concrete quality the efficiency of the joint is increased up to 93 % even for a rather high percentage of steel. This tendency also has been shown by the experiments in refs. [8-11]. It should be mentioned, the efficiency of 100 % refers to a corner joint which is as strong as the connecting members.

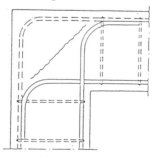

Figure 4 Traditional reinforcement detailing used for parametric study.

Figure 5c shows the influence of β on predicting the failure moment for the traditional detailing subjected to positive bending moment. It can be seen the assumption of $\beta = 0.0$ results in a very low failure moment which is much lower than the expected experimental value, represented by a solid line. The very low value due to the assumption of $\beta = 0.0$ is attributed to the fact that we end up with an illconditional finite element equation system which causes earlier crash of the analysis.

Due to the fact this detailing failed by a diagonal crack as shown by experimental evidence in refs. [8-11], the shear retention factor plays an important role in the analysis and ignoring this effect in a mixed mode failure will result in a very low failure moment estimation. It can be seen that even with introducing a small value of $\beta = 0.01$ the failure moment is considerably increased. From the comparison of the value of β up to 0.2 the influence of β is diminishing. For a value of $\beta = 0.1$ the failure moment shows the closest agreement with the experimental value. In order to see in our study the influence of introducing a dilatancy angle which is smaller than the friction angle specimen J_{11} is modelled. In this specimen the angle of dilatancy is $\phi_d = 30°$ which is smaller than the angle of friction ($\phi = 41.6°$) introduced. The failure moment predicted with the assumption of the nonassociated flow rule in the Drucker-Prager model is quite similar to the result of the specimen J_4 with the associated flow rule (see Figure 5c). In both specimens, a shear retention factor $\beta = 0.1$ is introduced.

To show the influence of the perfect bond assumption we have modelled two identical specimens one with bond-slip relation of Vandewalle as follows:

$$\tau = \tau_u \left(1 - \mu e^{-\lambda\delta} \right)$$

with
$\mu = 0.78$
$\lambda = 9.78$ (mm^{-1}).
τ = the bond stress (N/mm^2)
δ = the slip (mm).

The ultimate bond strength τ_u is a function of the concrete cover on the reinforcement bar (c) and the concrete quality (R_b'). From calculations and tests [4-6] it follows that the mean value of τ_u can be obtained from:

$$\text{If} \quad c/\phi \leq 3 \qquad \frac{\tau_u}{R_b'} = \frac{\sqrt{k}}{2} \left[1 + (1 - k)0.353 \frac{\phi/2 + c}{\phi/2} \right]$$

$$\text{If} \quad c/\phi > 3 \qquad \frac{\tau_u}{R_b'} = \frac{\sqrt{k}}{2} \left[1 + (1 - k)2.473 \right]$$

with

$$k = \frac{R_b}{R_b'}$$

R_b' = mean cylinder compressive strength of concrete (N/mm^2).
R_b = mean uniaxial tensile strength of concrete (N/mm^2).

For comparison, the moment-curvature curves for both of the specimens are shown in Figure 5d. It can be seen that with the assumption of a perfect bond the failure moment of the specimen is overestimated up to 9 %. In many structural applications it may be acceptable up to this accuracy to model the structure with perfect bond assumption.

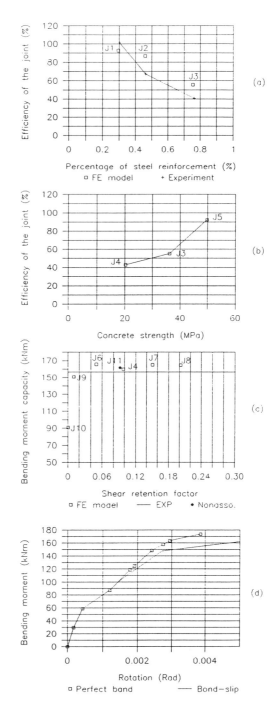

Figure 5 Influence of different parameters on the performance of the joint.

FE STUDY FOR DETAILING OF THE REINFORCEMENT

Corner joints subjected to positive bending moment

To compare the FE Results with experimental evidence we have modelled ten specimens tested in ref. [11]. In our study the same name has been given to the specimens as in the reference. The main objective here is to show the influence of the detailing used for the main reinforcement on the efficiency of the joint. In Table 1 and Figure 6 a summary of the specimens and their detailing is reported. The 1 : 4 scale specimens used in the experimental investigation in comparison to the full scale connections is frequently used in practice. In our study we respected the dimensions and property of the materials from the tests.

The specimens have been chosen in a way that they cover variety of the different details which are possibly usable in practical applications. In some of the specimens where loop reinforcement has been used, the core of the corner joint is confined by the loop. This has a favourable effect on the strength of the core [11-13]. In order to introduce this effect, the strength of the concrete used in this calculation has been increased depending on the confinement ratio.

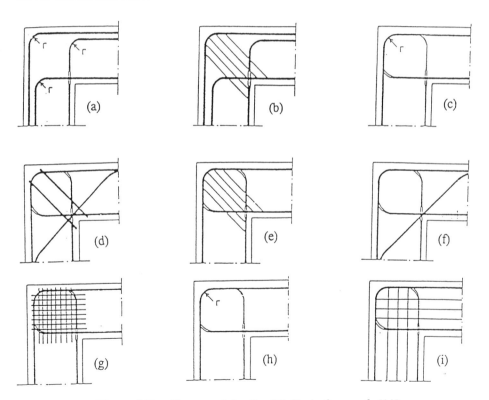

Figure 6 Detailings used for the FE Study from ref. [11]

Table 1 Specimens used for the FE Study of the main reinforcement detailing.

1	2	3	4	5	6	7	8
specimen	dimension mm×mm×mm	reinf. ratio ρ (%)	comp. strength f_c (MPa)	tensile strength f_t (MPa)	bond strength τ_u (MPa)	main reinf. diameter ϕ (mm)	cover from bar center mm
B_{13}	120×120×70	0.74	13.6	1.47	3.91	6	10
B_{14}	120×120×70	0.74	12.9	1.47	3.73	6	10
B_3	120×120×70	0.74	27.3	2.83	8.00	6	10
B_4	120×120×70	0.74	27.2	2.72	7.50	6	10
B_8	120×120×70	0.74	27.2	2.72	7.50	6	10
B_9	120×120×70	0.74	28.2	2.83	7.19	6	10
B_7	120×120×70	0.74	28.2	2.50	6.86	6	10
B_{19}	120×120×70	0.74	17.4	1.70	4.33	6	10
B_{21}	120×120×70	0.74	13.9	1.36	3.61	6	10

Table 1 Specimens used for the FE Study of the main reinforcement detailing.

(continued)

1	9	10	11	12		13		14	15		
specimen	main reinf. f_y (MPa)	E_s (MPa)	E_c (MPa)	Dru.-Prag.		stirrups		detail Fig.6	confined concrete		
				c	ϕ	ratio	f_{yv}		f_{cc}	c_c	ϕ_c
B_{13}	504	210000	18318	3.25	38.9	.0035	286	a	-	-	-
B_{14}	504	210000	17872	3.10	38.7	.0035	286	b	-	-	-
B_3	504	210000	25139	6.25	40.7	.0035	286	c	35.7	7.24	46.4
B_4	504	210000	25099	6.12	41.6	.0035	286	d	35.6	7.02	47.1
B_8	504	210000	25099	6.12	41.6	.0035	286	e	35.6	7.02	47.1
B_9	504	210000	25500	6.34	41.5	.0035	286	f	36.6	7.23	46.9
B_7	504	210000	25500	5.98	44.1	.0035	286	g	36.6	6.81	49.2
B_{19}	504	210000	21647	3.87	42.1	.0035	286	h	25.5	4.67	49.7
B_{21}	504	210000	18510	3.09	42.0	.0035	286	i	21.8	3.87	50.9

To show the performance of different details the failure moment calculated by our FE Model is reported in Table 2 for each specimen.

Table 2: Failure moment predicted by FE Model for different details

1	2	3	4	5	6	7	8	9	10
specimen	concrete strength f_c (MPa)	reinf. ratio ρ (%)	detail Fig. 6	failure moment of joint (FEM) (KNm)		failure moment joint (EXP) (KNm)	failure moment conn.mem. (THEORY) (KNm)	efficiency joint (FEM) (%)	efficiency joint (EXP) (%)
				perf.bond	bond-slip				
B_{13}	13.6	0.74	a	0.75	0.75	0.75	2.46	30	30
B_{14}	12.9	0.74	b	1.50	1.40	1.88	2.44	58	77
B_5	27.3	0.74	c	2.0	2.0	2.7	2.66	75	101
B_8	27.2	0.74	d	2.8	2.8	2.8	2.66	104	104
B_6	27.2	0.74	e	2.8	2.8	2.8	2.66	107	107
B_9	28.2	0.74	f	2.0	2.0	2.78	2.66	75	104
B_{19}	17.4	0.74	h		1.15	1.73	2.54	45	68
B_{21}	13.9	0.74	i		1.35	2.03	2.46	55	82
B_7	28.2	0.74	g	1.90	1.90	2.55	2.66	72	96

Two main objectives are achieved from the comparison of the FE Results with the experimental evidence.
1) To compare the failure moment predicted by the FE Model with the one of the test result;
2) To see the performance of the different details in general by nonlinear FE Method and to propose the best detailing for corners subjected to positive bending moment.
The efficiency of the joint determined by experiment is reported from ref. [11]. The calculated efficiency by FE Method is derived from the division of the failure moment to the theoretical moment of the connecting members as calculated in ref. [11] in order to have the same base for the calculations.
For most of the specimens the FE Results are available with both perfect bond assumption and consideration of bond-slip. As it can be seen from Table 2 similar results are obtained in ultimate state for both cases except for specimen B_{14} in which for the case of imperfect bond the failure moment is slightly less than in the case of perfect bond. The following important results are achieved from the comparison:
As can be seen from Table 2 for specimen B_{13} with traditional reinforcement (as shown in Figure 6a) the FE Calculation shows exact agreement with the experimental one. The efficiency of this detailing is very low for rather high percentages of steel and average concrete qualities. As mentioned for primary investigation even for a high quality of concrete and a very low reinforcement the corner joint cannot reach the 100 % efficiency easily.
To improve the efficiency of this detailing, additional reinforcement as inclined stirrups is used in specimen B_{14}. A considerable improvement in performance is achieved but not acceptable for practical use. The FE Model shows a lower efficiency than the experiment for this detail.

More attention has been paid to the modelling of the specimens with loop reinforcement used for main reinforcement and additional reinforcement such as stirrups and inclined reinforcement for better performance. The rest of the specimens used in this study are those with loop reinforcement only or with including additional reinforcement.

As shown in Table 2 specimen B_5 which has shown the full efficiency in experimental verifications does not show the same high efficiency by FEM for rather high percentages of steel and moderate concrete qualities. The specimen B_{19} with the same reinforcement detailing as B_5 but with a lower concrete quality, shows a much lower efficiency in the test. The strength found by FE Calculation was even lower.

It can be seen that this detailing is much better than the traditional reinforcement of specimen B_{13} but still some improvements are necessary to achieve a better performance to cover all the ranges of concrete quality and reinforcement ratio.

The question remains whether only the loop reinforcement can prevent the diagonal crack failure which is proved by some experimental investigations in refs. [8-11] ? Or this nonlinear FE Model is not capable to model the complete physical phenomena happening inside the loop. It is evident that by improvement in FE Codes and producing more experimental data, the gap between the numerical results and the experimental ones will become smaller. At present, this question is partly answered by improving this detail by adding the additional reinforcement.

Several alternatives for additional reinforcement are proposed in ref. [11] for experimental verifications. These additional reinforcements are modelled in specimens B_6, B_7, B_8, B_9, and B_{21}. Among these five specimens as shown in Table 2 specimens B_6 and B_8 are showing excellent agreement with experimental results and they achieved an efficiency of 107 % and 104 % respectively.

Specimen B_9 which is detailed with loop reinforcement plus inclined reinforcement in the form which is proposed by Nilsson [8-9] for the first time shows satisfactory performance according to the experiment, but FE Results do not show any improvement compared to specimen B_5 which is without inclined reinforcement. Here we can conclude that the FE Analysis shows that loop reinforcement alone does not prevent the diagonal crack failure for high percentages of steel. By additional inclined reinforcement it is necessary to add some stirrups (not so many). At least two stirrups, perpendicular to the direction of the diagonal crack are necessary as is done in the specimens B_6 and B_8. Later these two alternatives will be used to detail reinforced concrete corner joints subjected to positive bending moment for high percentages of reinforcement and will be introduced to the CAD system [14].

Specimen B_7 does not show good performance by lattice form of additional reinforcement by FE Model, also it was not completely succesful by experimental evidence. It should be noted that from the construction point of view this detailing provides congestion of reinforcement in the core and is not suitable. Specimen B_{21}, with a very low concrete strength and additional reinforcement in vertical and horizontal directions as recommended by the CEB model code for seismic design, does not show good performance either by experiment nor by the FE Model. In the next section we will see this detail is suitable for negative bending moment. In this case also stirrups in the direction perpendicular to the diagonal crack would be necessary to take away the tensile splitting forces.

CORNER JOINT SUBJECTED TO NEGATIVE BENDING MOMENT

This model is used to study a corner joint subjected to negative bending moment with detailing of Figure 6i in which efficiency of more than 100 % obtained. The results of our study show that the loop reinforcement can be used for corners subjected to negative bending moment with acceptable performance if we respect the percentage limit for reinforcement which will be mentioned for practical design proposals. The performance of the joint will be increased if we use additional shear reinforcement based on CEB Model code.

PROPOSED DETAILING OF THE CONNECTIONS

Based on the experimental results available and FE Investigations explained in this study the following details are proposed for practical design. These detailings are implemented in a CAD system developed for design of reinforced concrete frames [14].
- corner joints subjected to positive bending moment (Figure 7a-e)
- corner joints subjected to negative bending moment (Figure 7f)

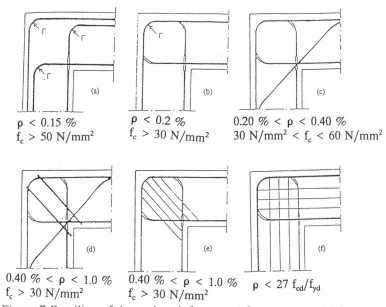

$\rho < 0.15 \%$ $\rho < 0.2 \%$ $0.20 \% < \rho < 0.40 \%$
$f_c > 50 \text{ N/mm}^2$ $f_c > 30 \text{ N/mm}^2$ $30 \text{ N/mm}^2 < f_c < 60 \text{ N/mm}^2$

$0.40 \% < \rho < 1.0 \%$ $0.40 \% < \rho < 1.0 \%$ $\rho < 27 \, f_{cd}/f_{yd}$
$f_c > 30 \text{ N/mm}^2$ $f_c > 30 \text{ N/mm}^2$

Figure 7 Detailing of the main reinforcement for corners and joints subjected to bending moments.

CONCLUSIONS

It has been shown that the proposed FE Model is applicable to study the corner joints in reinforced concrete frames. The primary and parametric study show the same tendency for the influence of different parameters as the experiments. The FE calculations show that the efficiency of the corner joint increases with the concrete quality and decreases with increasing reinforcement percentage in the connecting members beam and column. The value chosen in our model for shear retention factor ($\beta = 0.1$) is in close agreement with the experiments and existing models. Based on our FE calculations and the available experimental results we have proposed a practical range for using different details for corner joints depending on the quality of the concrete and reinforcement ratio in the connecting members. Using nonlinear FE Model for RC applications in combination with a limited number of experiments, can lead to a better understanding of the RC structures. In many cases proposals can be achieved for practical design rules that are of interest for national and international codes.

REFERENCES

1.   ANSYS ENGINEERING ANALYSIS SYSTEM, "Theoretical Manual", Swanson Analysis Systems, Inc., PO Box 65, Houston, Pennsylvania 15342.

2.   HEMMATY Y., "Computer Aided Design of Reinforced Concrete Frames and Nodal Connections", Part II, "Modelling and Design of Joints in Reinforced Concrete Frames", Ph.D dissertation, Catholic University of Leuven, Belgium, 1992.

3.   HEMMATY Y.,DE ROECK G., VANDEWALLE, L. and MORTELMANS F., "Parametric study of RC corner joints subjected to positive bending movement by nonlinear FE Model", ANSYS Conference 1992, 8-12 June, Pittsburgh, Pennsylvania.

4.   VANDEWALLE L., "Hechting tussen wapening met verbeterde hechting en beton bij gewone en cryogene omstandigheden", Ph.D dissertation, Catholic University of Leuven, Belgium, 1988.

5.   VANDEWALLE L., "Cracking behaviour of reinforced concrete members", Asia-Pacific Conference on Structural Engineering and Construction, Chiang Mai, 11-13 January 1989, pp. 384-390.

6.   VANDEWALLE L., "Cracking behaviour of reinforced concrete Tension members at Normal and Cryogenic Temperatures", European Conference on cracking of concrete and durability of construction, Saint-Remy-lés-Chevreuse, August 31st - September 2nd 1988.

7.   HEMMATY Y., DE ROECK G. and VANDEWALLE L., "Finite Element Modelling of Reinforced Concrete taking into consideration Bond-slip", Fifth ANSYS International Conference, 21-24 May 1991, Hilton & Towers, Pittsburgh, Pennsylvania.

8.   NILSSON INGVAR H.E., "Reinforced concrete corner and joints subjected to bending moment - Design of corners and joints in frame structures", Document No D7: National Swedish Institute For Building Research, Stockholm, 1973, 249 pp.

9.   NILSSON INGVAR H.E., "Reinforced concrete corners and joints subjected to bending moment", J. Struct. Engrg. ASCE, Vol. 102, No ST6, June 1976, pp. 1228-1254.

10. STROBAND J. and KOLPA J.J., "The behaviour of Reinforced Concrete column-to-beam joints part 1 - Corner joints subjected to negative moments", Delft University of Technology, Department of Civil Engineering, Report 5-83-9, Research No 2.2.7303, April 1983, 109 pp.

11. STROBAND J. and KOLPA J.J., "The behaviour of Reinforced Concrete column-to-beam joints part 2 - Corner joints subjected to positive moments", Delft University of Technology, Department of Civil Engineering, Report 5-81-5, Research No 2.2.7417, April 1981, 104 pp.

12. MIER J.G.M. VAN, "Examples of nonlinear analysis of reinforced concrete structures with DIANA", Heron. Vol. 32, No 3, 1987.

13. MANDER J.B., PRIESTLY M.J.N. and PARK R., "Theoretical Stress-Strain Model for Confined Concrete", J. Struct. Engrg., ASCE, Vol. 114, No 8, August 1988.

14. HEMMATY Y., DE ROECK G. and MORTELMANS F., "Computer Aided Design of Reinforced Concrete Frame Structures and Nodal Connections", Fifth International Conference on Concrete, Praha, Czechoslovakia, Sept 4-6, 1990.

15. TAERWE L. and LAMBOTTE H., "Studie van het gedrag van beton bij zeer lage temperaturen, Scheurvorming van beton in cryogene omstandigheden", Laboratorium Magnel voor Gewapend Beton, 9710 Gent, 1986.

PREDICTION OF AGGREGATE PERFORMANCE IN STRUCTURES EXPOSED TO FREEZING AND THAWING

Z Rusin

Kielce University of Technology

Poland

P K Mukherjee

Ontario Hydro Research Division

Canada

ABSTRACT. A study was undertaken to develop a rapid technique for the prediction of aggregate performance in concrete structures exposed to freezing and thawing. Seventeen types of crushed coarse aggregates were examined in the laboratory by a new test technique called the RAO-Method. The aggregates were previously used in concrete blocks that were placed in water-filled tubs and subjected to outdoor exposure conditions for many years at the Ontario Hydro Research Division, Toronto. The results of long-term observations of the concrete blocks, as well as those of the RAO-Method and other laboratory standard tests, were compared. An RAO-Index is proposed as a new indicator of the physical quality of coarse aggregates. The index provides improved means for the rapid classification of aggregates for frost-resistant concretes.

Keywords: Aggregates, Concrete Durability, Frost Resistance, Aggregate Performance, Service Life Prediction.

Professor Zbigniew Rusin is the Director of the Materials Section, Kielce University of Technology, Poland. His main research interests include the concrete durability problems with particular reference to diagnostics and classification of coarse aggregates for concretes exposed to freezing and thawing. He is a member of the Science Committee of the Polish Civil Engineers Association.

Mr Pranab K Mukherjee is a Senior Engineer with Ontario Hydro Research Division, Toronto, Canada. He has been the chairman of the Canadian Standards Association (CSA) Technical Committee on Hydraulic Cements and a member of the CSA Technical Committee on Concrete Materials and Testing.

Concrete 2000. Edited by Ravindra K. Dhir and M. Roderick Jones.
© 1993 Published by E & FN Spon. ISBN 0 419 18120 2.

INTRODUCTION

The deterioration of concrete structures due to durability problems is extensive and widespread. The cost of repairing concrete structures in the United States alone, has been estimated to be between one and three trillion dollars over the next twenty years [1]. One of the main problems is caused by poor physical characteristics of aggregates in concrete structures exposed to freezing and thawing. Unintentional use of poor quality aggregates may occur due to the lack of appropriate laboratory tests for their evaluation. A growing shortage in the availability of good quality aggregates accentuates the problem.

A study was undertaken to develop a new, more reliable and rapid laboratory test, called the RAO-Method (RAO in Polish, stands for Roznicowa Analiza Odksztalcen, which means differential analysis of strains), to meet engineers expectations in the area of aggregate classification. This paper describes the test method and discusses the test results obtained on a number of selected samples of aggregates.

BACKGROUND

It is known that certain aggregates show an apparent propensity for quick absorption and retention of water by their pores, while others have pores which cannot be filled at all. Generally, aggregates with a large number of small size pores, showing high adsorption and absorption values, are considered to be of questionable quality for use in concrete. However, laboratory tests, including the determination of properties such as, microporosity, specific surface, water adsorption and absorption, do not always yield satisfactory results for the prediction of performance of aggregates in concrete under field conditions. Therefore, results from laboratory tests are sometimes difficult to correlate with field performance.

An attempt has been made in previous studies [2,3], to address the issues related to laboratory data and field performance, including expounding on Power's hydraulic pressure theory [4]. The proposed RAO-Method assumes that most of the aggregates with fully saturated pores, including those of very low porosity, will damage concrete when exposed to freezing temperatures. Thus, usefulness of aggregate for concrete depends on capacity of aggregate grains to absorb and hold water while confined in cement matrix.

The rationale behind the method is that the character of the process of water crystallization during freezing in fully saturated pores indirectly reflects the characteristics of the pores. The size and the distribution of the pores essentially controls the rate of water absorption prior to freezing. Every aggregate has its own unique pore characteristics and, therefore, has different rates of crystallization of water [2]. The authors believe that a measure of the rate of crystallization of water in an aggregate sample could be used to predict the performance of aggregates in concrete, exposed to freezing and thawing conditions.

RAO-METHOD

The RAO test method has been described elsewhere by the first author [2,3]. The method depends on observations of the relative changes in volume and that of the temperature of aggregate particles during cooling. Measurements are made in two identical dilatometers, as shown in Figure 1. The capacity of the dilatometer is about 250 ml. One of the dilatometers contains aggregate particles saturated in water, while the other dilatometer contains the identical aggregate saturated in carbon tetrachloride (CCl_4). The advantage of

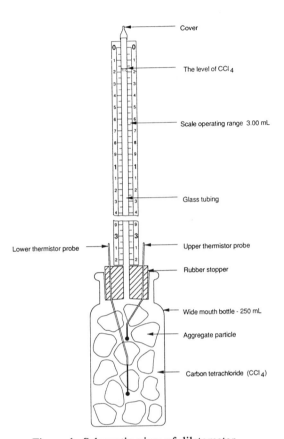

Figure 1 Schematic view of dilatometer

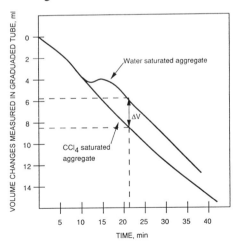

Figure 2 Schematic diagram of measurement of relative volume changes

using CCl_4 is that it neither freezes till -23°C nor mixes with water. Both the dilatometers are filled with CCl_4.

Dilatometers are cooled from approximately +5°C to about -15°C. Volume changes are measured by reading a scale on a glass tube attached to the dilatometers and the values are plotted as shown in Figure 2. The temperature changes are recorded automatically by data logger from thermistor probes placed inside the dilatometers. The difference in volume changes and that of the temperature changes are represented by the following notations:

- Delta V = difference in volume changes as shown in Figure 2
- Delta T = difference in temperature changes.

These two values are termed as RAO parameters and have been used in calculating RAO-Indexes described later. The procedure described above, indirectly measures the rate of crystallization of water in the pores of aggregate particles during freezing. The RAO parameters are precise enough to distinguish small differences in the pore structures of different aggregate samples of low to medium absorption [5].

RESEARCH PROGRAM

A research program was undertaken at the Ontario Hydro Research Division in order to verify the suitability of the RAO-method for classifying aggregates with respect to their performance in concrete exposed to freezing and thawing.

During the last 40 years a large number of coarse aggregate samples have been acquired by the Research Division. These aggregates have been tested for physical properties using appropriate Canadian (CSA) and American (ASTM) test methods.

In addition, concrete blocks 300x300x450 mm in size, and cast with some of the aggregates, have been stored at the outdoor exposure site of the Research Division for over thirty years. The blocks were half immersed in water in rubber troughs. All concretes were made using a standard laboratory procedure having a water to cement ratio of 0.60 by weight and air entrainment of 5 to 6%. Changes in visual condition, length, weight, and ultrasonic pulse velocity were monitored periodically. Also, smaller specimens of the same concrete were tested in a freeze-thaw apparatus following ASTM C 666 (procedure A) method. The findings from these laboratory and field studies have been summarized elsewhere [6].

The results of standard laboratory tests on aggregates provided a data base for comparison with RAO-test results. Also, the tests on concrete blocks provided information on the field performance of the concrete. These were reviewed in the present study. Seventeen aggregate samples were selected for the RAO tests; these samples were crushed aggregates that had been used in the concrete blocks. The only exceptions were samples number 16 and 17; no concrete blocks were made with these two aggregates. However, they were used in two Ontario Hydro structures showing good and poor performances, respectively, under field conditions.

RESULTS AND DISCUSSION

The physical properties of the selected aggregate samples are given in Table 1 and observations made on the corresponding concrete blocks are noted in Table 2.

Table 1 List of crushed aggregates chosen for RAO-Method of examination and their physical properties determined by relevant ASTM tests

Aggregate sample number	Ontario Hydro number of aggregate	Description of aggregate	Results of aggregate tests made from 1960 to 1979(*)			
			Specific gravity, g/cm³	24 h. absorption, %	Sulph. soundness, %	DF, %
1	S-5066	hard, dense, fine grained dolomite	2.67	1.12	0.9	77
2	S-5360	siltstone	2.29	7.54	74.2	13
3	S-5376	weathered, porous chert	2.31	5.58	18.9	1
4	S-5521	hard, dense limestone	2.70	0.68	3.8	74
5	S-5526	hard, dense, fine grained dolomite	2.66	1.28	1.7	70
6	S-5611	weathered limestone with chert nodules	2.64	0.85	7.9	46
7	S-6030	hard, dense limestone	-	0.29	0.8	64
8	S-6203	limestone with minor unleached chert	2.61	2.46	9.5	73
9	S-6345	hard, dense greywacke	2.68	0.24	0.0	63
10	S-6436	hard, dense dolomite/limestone	2.49	6.06	25.3	69
11	S-6562	dense limestone with shaley partings	2.74	0.34	0.4	43
12	S-6650	dense limestone with shaley partings	2.68	0.81	14.9	63
13	S-6790	hard, dense quartzite	2.58	0.85	3.0	43
14	S-7115	dense and shaley limestone	2.64	1.08	7.8	34
15	S-7116	dense and shaley limestone	2.64	1.03	8.2	32
16	S-6400	dense limestone	2.71	1.86	0.8	80
17	S-4744	Iowa limestone	2.70	3.60	-	22

(*) Specific gravity and 24 h. absorption - ASTM C 127
Sulph. soundness - ASTM C 88
DF (Durability Factor) - ASTM C 666-Procedure A

A typical example of the measurements of RAO parameters (Delta V and Delta T) is shown in figures 3 and 4, for sample 1. It may be noted that there is abrupt change in the parameters at about 70 minutes of cooling. This change occurs at the time of crystallization of water in the aggregate pores. The difference between the values of the RAO parameters immediately before and 5 minutes after the beginning of rapid crystallization is indicated by dV5 and dT5 in the figures. These two values are given in Table 3 for all the aggregate samples tested.

In order to compare the various samples, the above values are expressed as a ratio of the theoretical gain of the volume of water during crystallization. The procedure for calculation of the theoretical gain in volume (dVt) is described below.

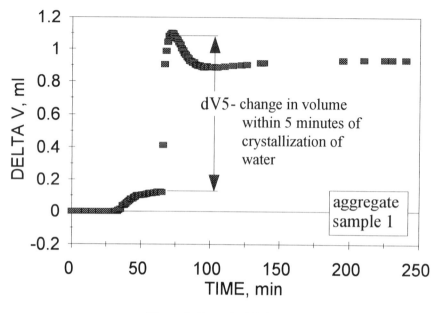

Figure 3 Record of Delta V

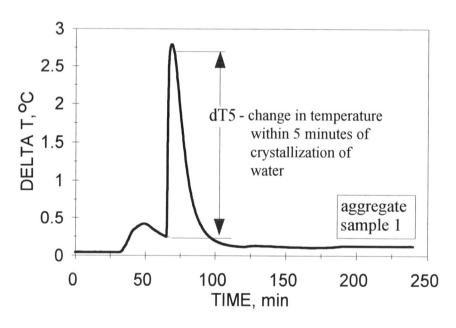

Figure 4 Record of Delta T

Table 2 Visual rating of concrete blocks after exposure to outdoor conditions (half immersed in water)

Aggre-gate sample number	Age* years	Laboratory mix number**	Visual rating ***	Length change**** %
			Concrete blocks	
1	31	10654	0 (very light scaling)	+0.006
2	31	10653	4 (rubble at age of 11 years)	+0.922
3	31	10714	4 (rubble at age of 5 years)	+1.380
4	29	10849	1 (hairline cracks)	+0.092
5	29	10846	0 (excellent)	-0.006
6	29	10847	1 (fine map cracks)	+0.092
7	24	11133	0 (excellent)	+0.018
8	23	11234	1 (mortar scaled at W/L)	+0.006
9	21	11464	0 (excellent)	+0.031
10	21	11486	1 (scaling,popouts,finecracks)	0.000
11	18	11831	0 (excellent)	+0.025
12	17	11996	0 (two hairline cracks)	+0.012
13	15	12498	0 (excellent)	+0.012
14	12	12896	1 (fine map cracks)	+0.012
15	12	12897	1 (fine map cracks)	+0.012
16	no block sample		good field service records	
17	no block sample		poor field service records	

 * The age of the concrete blocks on August 8, 1991 when the visual rating was undertaken.
 ** The Ontario Hydro Laboratory identification numbers of concrete mixes
 *** The description of visual rating:
   0 - no distress
   1 - medium scaling - coarse aggregate exposed or fine surface cracking
   2 - severe scaling - coarse aggregate proud or wide surface cracking
   3 - very severe scaling - coarse aggregate removed or spalling of concrete due to cracking
   4 - disintegration - localized loss of concrete integrity
 **** The results of measurements made at the Ontario Hydro Laboratory in 1989.

It is known that water occupies more space during freezing. In the current study an increase of 9% is assumed due to crystallization of water in the pores. Therefore, the theoretical gain (dVt) during crystallization can be calculated as 9% of the amount of water absorbed (W) during saturation of the samples in water. Therefore:

$$dVt = 0.09 \times W$$

Table 3   RAO test results

Aggregate sample number	Vacuum absorption %	dV5 ml	dT5 °C	dVt ml	RAO - Indexes	
					dV5/dVt	dT5/dVt
1	2.2	0.95	2.57	0.70	1.37	3.69
2	9.0	1.51	3.87	2.44	0.62	1.59
3	6.8	0.88	2.49	1.77	0.50	1.40
4	0.5	0.07	0.35	0.15	0.47	2.27
5	2.7	1.22	3.25	0.82	1.48	3.94
6	1.0	0.17	0.43	0.30	0.57	1.44
7	0.4	0.05	0.14	0.12	0.42	1.19
8	3.3	0.83	2.24	1.01	0.83	2.23
9	0.2	0.06	0.20	0.05	1.15	3.70
10	7.8	1.65	4.23	2.15	0.76	1.96
11	0.5	0.23	0.83	0.15	1.59	5.72
12	0.5	0.10	0.28	0.15	0.70	1.93
13	0.9	0.51	1.70	0.27	1.87	6.25
14	0.9	0.05	0.15	0.26	0.18	0.57
15	0.8	0.07	0.21	0.22	0.31	0.95
16	4.0	1.51	3.97	1.20	1.26	3.30
17	3.6	0.84	2.23	1.10	0.76	2.04

The values of dVt are listed in Table 3. The ratios dV5/dVt, referred to as RAO-Indexes, are also given in the Table 3. These indexes can be used as an idicator of the performance of the aggregates in concrete.

An attempt has been made to compare the RAO-Indexes for the aggregate samples having absorption values in the range of low, intermediate, and high levels. Three pairs of aggregate samples were chosen for comparison, pair I (samples 4 & 11), pair II (samples 13 & 14), and the pair III (samples 16 & 17). The absorptions values of the pairs were 0.5%, 0.9% and 4%, respectively. For comparison, one of the samples in each pair was such that either it indicated good or poor performance in the concrete exposed to the outdoor conditions. Samples 11, 13 and 16 showed good performance and samples 4, 14 and 17 showed poor performance (see Table 2). The RAO parameters, Delta V and Delta T, for each of these pairs are shown in Figures 5, 6 and 7. A significant difference in the RAO-Indexes were noted between the samples of good and poor performances. The RAO-Indexes (dV5/dVt) were 1.59, 1.87, and 1.26 for samples of good performance while those for samples of poor performance were 0.47, 0.18, and 0.76 (see Table 3). A similar difference was noted with the other index (dT5/dVt).

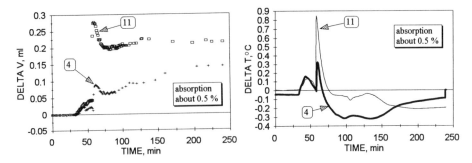

Figure 5   RAO parameters of aggregates with absorption of about 0.5% (sample 11 - good performance, sample 4 - poor performance)

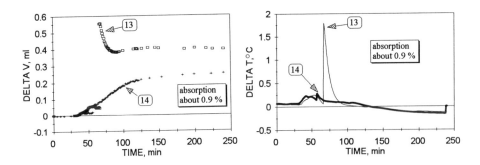

Figure 6   RAO parameters of aggregates with absorption of about 0.9% (sample 13 - good performance, sample 14 - poor performance)

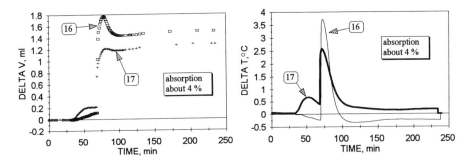

Figure 7   RAO parameters of aggregates with absorption of about 4% (sample 16 - good performance, sample 17 - poor performance)

A low absorption value of an aggregate does not necessarily indicate a good performance in concrete. The RAO-Index, on the other hand, will differentiate between good and the poor quality aggregates.

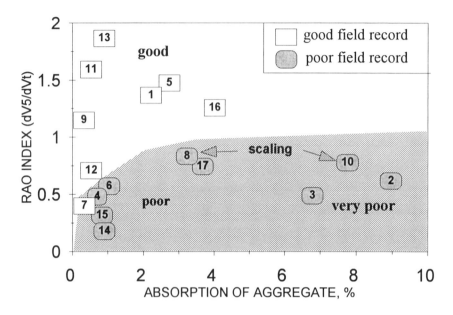

Figure 8   Proposed aggregate classification for concrete structures exposed to freezing and thawing, based on the RAO-Index and absorption

The RAO-Indexes (dV5/dVt) are plotted against absorption values in Figure 8. It may be noted that the aggregates can be classified into broad categories based on the RAO-Indexes. These are shown in the figure as good, poor and very poor.

CONCLUDING REMARKS

1. A rapid technique for the prediction of aggregate performance in concrete exposed to freezing and thawing has been presented. The RAO-Method produces reliable indexes for classifying coarse crushed aggregates which correlate well with field performance of the aggregates in concrete under freezing and thawing conditions. The method is rapid and has increased sensitivity and precision compared with existing laboratory tests.

2. The method is based on theoretical analysis which relates the RAO-Index directly to the mechanism of frost action in aggregate particles, as well as indirectly to the mechanism of water absorption prior to freezing.

3. In this study the RAO-Method of classification has only been evaluated for crushed aggregates. Further evaluation with gravel aggregates are proposed.

4. As carbon tetrachloride (CCl_4) is a hazardous substance, consideration should be given to using alternative substances; it is a prerequisite that candidates are immiscible with water and do not freeze while cooling.

ACKNOWLEDGEMENTS

The authors would like to express their appreciation for the funding and the opportunity provided by the Ontario Hydro Research Division to carry out the research activities presented in this paper.

REFERENCES

1. SKALNY, J. Concrete durability - an issue of national importance. Concrete Durability - Katharine and Bryant Mather International Conference ACI, SP-100-17, Atlanta, 1987, pp 265-279.

2. RUSIN, Z. Physical phenomena in freezing aggregate and their connection with frost resistance of concrete. Kielce University of Technology, Budownictwo 29, 1989, pp 176 (in Polish).

3. RUSIN, Z. A mechanism of expansion of concrete aggregate due to frost action. Cem. and Conc. Res., Vol.21, 1991, pp 614-624.

4. POWERS, TC. Freezing effects in concrete. Durability of Concrete, ACI SP 47-1, 1975, pp 1-11.

5. RUSIN, Z. Prediction of aggregate performance in concrete structures exposed to freezing and thawing. Ontario Hydro Research Division, Report No.91-234-K, Toronto, 1992, pp 130.

6. STURRUP, VR, HOOTON, R, MUKHERJEE, PK AND CARMICHAEL,T. Evaluation and prediction of concrete durability - Ontario Hydro's experience. Concrete Durability - Katharine and Bryant Mather International Conference ACI, SP-100-59, Atlanta, 1987, pp 1121 - 1154.

PORE EFFECTS ON THE
COMPRESSIVE STRENGTH OF CONCRETE

S Akyüz

M A Tasdemir

M Uyan

Istanbul Technical University

Turkey

ABSTRACT : The amount and geometry of pores in hardened cement paste phase, that affect the mechanical behavior of concrete, have been considered in the form of two different parameters: porosity and capillarity coefficient (or water/cement ratio) where the latter represents the geometry of pores in hardened concrete. A mathematical model based on the damage mechanics approach has been developed to relate the compressive strength of concrete to these two parameters. Equations developed in this model have been applied to the values obtained in an experimental work, in which porosities, capillarity coefficients and strengths were measured for 40 different concrete mixtures. Good agreement has been found between experimental and theoretical results.

Keywords : Capillarity Coefficient, Pore Geometry, Amount of Pores, Energy Balance, Damage, Porosity, Compressive Strength.

Professor Saim Akyüz is chairman of the Engineering Materials Division, Faculty of Civil Engineering, Istanbul Technical University (ITU), Turkey. His main research interests include the viscoelastic behavior of engineering materials, consititutive modeling, inclusion mechanics and fracture studies in concrete.

Dr Mehmet A Taşdemir is an associate professor in the Faculty of CE, ITU, Turkey. His research interests include fracture mechanics of concrete, time dependent mechanical behavior and modeling of cement based materials.

Professor Mehmet Uyan is Director of Structural Engineering Laboratories, Faculty of CE, ITU, Turkey. His major research interests are the durability and permeability of concrete, steam curing of concrete at atmospheric pressure and mechanical behavior of fiber reinforced composites.

Concrete 2000. Edited by Ravindra K. Dhir and M. Roderick Jones.
© 1993 Published by E & FN Spon. ISBN 0 419 18120 2.

INTRODUCTION

When quasi-brittle materials such as concrete are loaded in compression, small cracks grow from the pores. Mechanical behavior especillay deformation and fracture generally exhibit most important and complex dependence on the pore structure of concrete. Today's research efforts intent to provide improved strength and more economical and more durable concrete constructions. As a result of the rapid development of new technologies, in the next century, civil engineers will use more sophisticated approaches in desingn of structures. In the last decade, considerable development has occurred in the production of high performance concretes with low water-cement ratio by using strong aggregates, silica fume and superplasticizer. Parallel to the increase in strength of these new materials, durability and permeability are also improved [1-3]. It is believed that the pore structure has a dominant effect on the performance of high strength concrete, thus the main goal of this paper is to study the effect of pore content and geometry on the mechanical behavior of cementitious materials such as concrete by a damage mechanics based model. It is tought that this approach will help to fill the need in bringing the theoretical concepts to implementation for the better understanding of material behavior.

THE ENERGY BALANCE THEORY

Consider a solid body subjected to certain external loads as shown in Figure 1. The cracks in the body grow and propagate under the loads. In most general case, the thermodynamic equilibrium equation of the body can be written as

$$\frac{dU}{dt} = \frac{dV}{dt} + \frac{dT}{dt} + \frac{dD}{dt} \tag{1}$$

where t is the time, U is the work done by the external loads, V is the reversible (elastic) component of the stored energy, T is the kinetic energy, and D is the sum of all the irreversible energies such as surface free energy or fracture energy, plastic

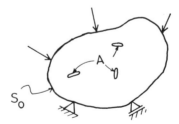

Figure 1 A solid body

work, and viscous dissipation [4]. Since the total dissipative energy is created near the crack [5], the time differential of total irreversible energies dT/dt can be written as:

$$\frac{dD}{dt} = \frac{dD}{dS}\frac{dS}{dt} = \frac{dD}{dA}\frac{dA}{dt} = \gamma_F \frac{dA}{dt} \qquad (2)$$

where $S(t)=S_o+A(t)$ in which, S_o is the total surface area of the body excluding crack surface and $A(t)$ is the crack surface, $dD/dA=\gamma_F$ is the amount of energy required to create a unit area of fracture surface and dA/dt is the rate of fracture surface [4]. It is known that, γ_F is much more greater than the surface energy, approximately $\gamma_F=10^3$ x surface energy.

If the cracks do not propagate when the external loads are kept constant, then the system is quasistatic or quasistable and hence $dT/dt=0$. In this case, Equation (1) may be written as follows:

$$\frac{dU}{dA}\cdot\frac{dA}{dt} = \frac{dV}{dA}\cdot\frac{dA}{dt} + \frac{dD}{dA}\cdot\frac{dA}{dt} \qquad (3)$$

Then, the following equation can be expressed

$$\frac{d}{dA}(U-V) = \gamma_F \qquad (4)$$

and from the integration of Equation (4)

$$U-V=\gamma_F(A-A_o) =\gamma_F A_o(\frac{A}{A_o}-1) \qquad (5)$$

can be derived. In this equation, A_o is the area of crack surface in the solid when $U=V=0$. The close neighbourhood of the crack can be accepted as not being able to carry the load, i.e. in this region the stress is zero. In Figure 2, v_o is the volume which is able to carry load and υ is the total volume of the solid body. $\upsilon-v_o$ and $\upsilon-v=H$ show the dead volume of the solid body under unloaded and loaded conditions respectively. There is a well known relation of geometry between the area of crack surface A and the total dead volume H given as:

$$A^{3/2} =kH = k\ (\mathbf{V}-v) \qquad (6)$$

where k is a constant. When $v=v_o$, A is A_o hence we have

$$\frac{A}{A_o} = (\frac{\mathbf{V}-v}{\mathbf{V}-v_o})^{2/3} \qquad (7)$$

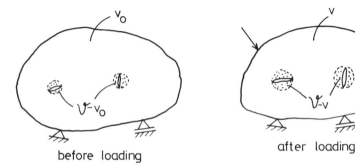

Figure 2 A solid body with flaws

DAMAGE MECHANICS APPROACH

Let us consider the stress-strain curve of concrete under uniaxial compressive loading and if the total volume of the concrete specimen is υ, the work done by the external forces can be written as

$$U = \left\{ \int_o^\epsilon \sigma(\epsilon)\, d\epsilon \right\} \mathbf{V} \tag{8}$$

where σ and ϵ are uniaxial stress and strain respectively. The reversible (elastic) work is

$$V = \frac{1}{2} \cdot \frac{\sigma^2}{E_{ef}} \cdot \mathbf{V} \tag{9}$$

where E_{ef} is the effective modulus of elasticity which is slightly less than the dynamic modulus of elasticity E_d. For the simplicity in calculations, it is assumed that $E_{ef} \approx E_d$. From equations (4),(8) and (9) we have

$$\int_o^\epsilon \sigma(\epsilon)\, d\epsilon - \frac{1}{2}\frac{\sigma^2}{E_d} = \gamma_F \cdot \frac{A_o}{\mathbf{V}} \cdot \left(\frac{A}{A_o} - 1\right) \tag{10}$$

if we take the differential of the both sides, then we have

$$\sigma - \alpha \sigma \sigma' = \beta \frac{d}{d\epsilon} \left(\frac{a}{a_o} - 1 \right) \tag{11}$$

where $a = A/\upsilon$, $a_o = A_o/\upsilon$, $\beta = a_o \gamma_F$ and $\alpha = 1/E$. The damage function can be defined as

$$\psi = \frac{V}{V_o} = \begin{cases} 1, \epsilon = 0 \\ \dfrac{V}{V_o}, 0 < \epsilon < \epsilon_m \\ 0, \epsilon = \epsilon_m \end{cases} \tag{12}$$

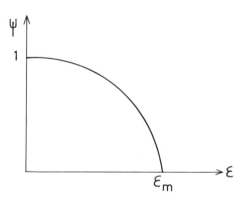

Figure 3 Damage function

As shown in Figure 3, ψ is a decreasing function and as result $\psi' < 0$. From Equation 7, a/a_o can be written as

$$\frac{a}{a_o} = \left(\frac{\dfrac{V}{V_o} - \dfrac{V}{V_o}}{\dfrac{V}{V_o} - 1} \right)^{2/3} = \left(\frac{q - \dfrac{V}{V_o}}{q - 1} \right)^{2/3} \tag{13}$$

Where $q = \upsilon/v_0 > 1$ which is a constant. In this case, the following equation can be expressed

$$\frac{d}{d\epsilon} \left(\frac{a}{a_o} - 1 \right) = -\frac{2}{3} \cdot \frac{1}{(q-1)^{2/3} (q-\psi)^{1/3}} \cdot \frac{d\psi}{d\epsilon} \tag{14}$$

Substitution of Equation (14) into Equation (11), the kinetic equation of damage can be obtained as

$$\psi' = \frac{d\psi}{d\epsilon} = -K(q-\psi)^{1/3} (\sigma - \alpha \sigma \sigma') \tag{15}$$

where $K=(3/2)(q-1)^{2/3}/\beta$. In a quasi-static case, the damage does not increase under a constant stress σ_0 for $\sigma_0<f_c'$, where f_c' is the compressive strength of concrete. It is assumed that, the failure occurs near the peak point under a constant stress $\sigma_0 \approx f_c'$. In this case, the differential equation becomes

$$d\psi/(1-\psi)^{1/3} = -Kf'_c \cdot d\epsilon \qquad (16)$$

Taking integration of Equation (16) with $\psi=1$ at $\epsilon=0$ and $\psi=0$ at $\epsilon=\epsilon_m$, then we have

$$f'_c = \gamma_F \frac{a_o}{\epsilon_m} [\frac{1}{(1-\frac{1}{q})^{2/3}} - 1] \qquad (17)$$

On the other hand, if we take a_m as the maximum area of crack surface per unit volume, then $a_o/a_m=(1-1/q)^{2/3}$. It is known that as the strain at compressive strength (ϵ_m) increases the area of crack surface also increases. From this point of view we assume that $\epsilon_m=a_m\eta$ thus we have

$$f'_c = \frac{\gamma_F}{\eta} [1-(1-\frac{1}{q})^{2/3}] \qquad (18)$$

We assume that G is the volume of concrete excluding the crack. Hence, we can write the inequality of $v_o/\upsilon \le G/\upsilon \le 1$. On the other hand, as shown in Figure 4, when $G/\upsilon=0$, then $v_o/v=0$ and when $G/\upsilon=1$, then $v_o/\upsilon=1$. Thus, v_o/υ can be written as

$$\frac{v_o}{v} = (\frac{G}{v})^m, m\ge 1 \qquad (19)$$

Substitution of v_o/υ given in Equation (19) into Equation (18) the following equation can be obtained:

$$f'_c = M \left\{ 1-[1-(1-p)^m]^{2/3} \right\} \qquad (20)$$

where $M=\gamma_F/\eta$ and $m=1+\Theta C$ in which C is the capillarity coefficient or $m=1+\Theta(w/c-0.23)$ in which w/c is water/cement ratio. In Equation (20), M is the highest compressive strength of the material which corresponds to zero porosity. As shown in Figure 4, m is a parameter which represents pore geometry. In case of spherical pore, there is no region without stress around the pore, thus $k=G/\upsilon=v_o/\upsilon$ and $m=1$. As the sphere type of pore turns in elliptical shape, m takes values greater than one and the stress concentration increases, as a result compressive strength of concrete decreases. Thus, pore geometry can be determined by means of capillary pores as given above. According to the proposed model depending on the equation chosen for m, the compressive strength of concrete (f_c') can be written as

$$f'_c = M_1 \left\{ 1 - [1 - (1-p)^{1+\theta_1 C}]^{2/3} \right\}$$
(21)

or

$$f'_c = M_2 \left\{ 1 - [1 - (1-p)^{1+\theta_2(\frac{W}{C}-0.23)}]^{2/3} \right\}$$
(22)

where M_1 and M_2 are constants which represent the theoretical compressive strength of concrete without porosity (maximum strength), p is the porosity, C is the capillarity coefficient as in Equation (21) and w/c is the water/cement ratio as in Equation (22) and Θ_1 and Θ_2 are the constants of the proposed equations.

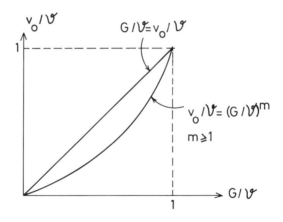

Figure 4 v_0/V versus G/V

Equations developed above was tested on the experimental data obtained from 40 different concrete mixtures. In each mixture the total porosity, the capillarity coefficient and the compressive strength of concrete were measured. In the first 31 different mixtures, porosity took place between 0.11 and 0.15 and its avarage value is 0.13. In the remain of mixtures, the porosity value lay between 0.17 and 0.21 and the avarage was 0.19. The parameters M_i and Θ_i, were calculated using the data given in Ref [7]. The curves obtained by substituting these parameters in Equation (21) and (22) were given in Figures 5, 6 and 7 together with the parameters. Good aggrement obtained between the experimental and theoretical results shows that the amount of porosity as well as the geometry of pores can be related to the compressive strength of concrete.

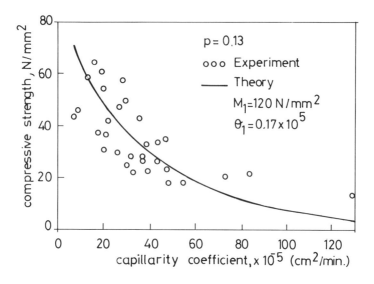

Figure 5 Effect of capillarity coefficient on the compressive strength (p=0.13)

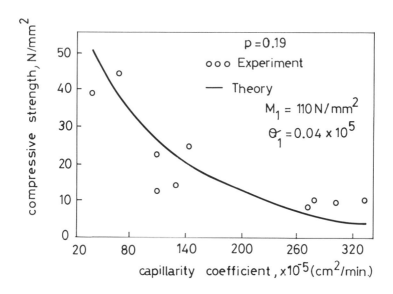

Figure 6 Effect of capillarity coefficient on the compressive strength (p=0.19)

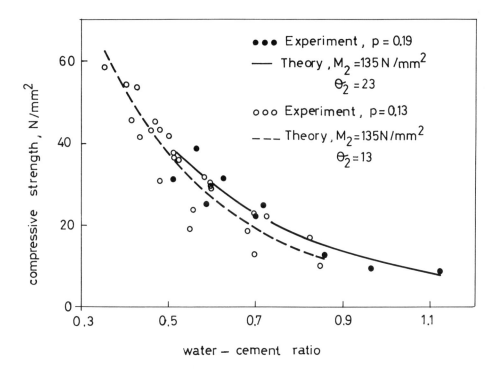

Figure 7 Variation of compressive strength with water/cement ratio

CONCLUSIONS

The dependence of compressive strength on the capillarity coefficient or water/cement ratio successfully represented by the proposed model which based on damage mechanics. The modelling described here not only provides the effect of pore volume, but also the geometry of pores on the compressive strength of concrete. The spherical pores produce low stress concentrations comparing with irregular ones. When pozzolonic additives such as silica fume is used in concrete, especially interface becomes more dense and the refinement in pore structure and homogenity are provided causing increase in strength which is in aggrement with the model presented here.

REFERENCES

1. BENTS D P AND GARBOCZI, E I. Simulation studies of the effects of mineral admixtures on the cement paste-aggregate interfacial zone. ACI Materials Journal, Vol.88, No 5, 1991,pp.518-529.

2. SHAH, S P AND YOUNG, J F. Current research at the NSF Science and Technology Center for Advanced Cement-Based Materials. Ceramic Bulletin, Vol.69, No 8, 1990, pp.1319-1331.

3. JENNIGS, H M AND LANGE D A. Toward high performance cement based materials. New Horizons in Construction Materials, ASCE National Convention, St.Louis, MO/Oct, 26,1988,pp.4-25.

4. ERDOGAN,F. Crack Propagation theories. Fracture, H.Liebowitz, ed., Academic Press, London, Vol.2, 1968,pp.497-590.

5. KNOTT, J F. Fundamental of fracture mechanics. Butterworths, London, 1973.

6. KACHANOV, L V. Introduction to continuum damage mechanics. Martinus Nijhoff Publishers, Dordrecht, 1986, 135 pp.

7. UYAN, M. Capillarity in concrete. PhD thesis, Faculty of Civil Engineering, Istanbul Technical University, 1975, 180 pp. (in Turkish with English summary)

IDENTIFICATION OF COMPLEX MATERIAL PROPERTIES OF MICROCONCRETE

J Vantomme

Belgian Royal Military Academy

J De Visscher

H Sol

W P De Wilde

Vrije Universiteit Brussels

Belgium

ABSTRACT. This paper wants to contribute to the evaluation of the practical usefulness of material damping of concrete in economic design. Attention is focused on the determination of complex material properties, in view of their introduction in numerical calculations of dynamic effects in concrete structures. Advantage is taken from a mixed numerical-experimental technique, based on modal analysis of free vibrating plates. The application is illustrated for the case of microconcrete, the passage towards concrete being straightforward. The obtained values for the complex moduli are discussed, as well as the influencing parameters. It is concluded that material damping appears to be a sensitive parameter for the characterization of microconcrete, and that material damping assessment is not unreachable in structural dynamic problems.

Keywords: Microconcrete, Complex moduli, Material damping, Modal analysis.

Dr. J. Vantomme is assistant-lecturer at the Department of Civil Engineering of the Belgian Royal Military Academy. His main research interests include the use of vibration characteristics for material property determination of concrete, as well as for quality assessment of concrete structures.

J. De Visscher, researcher at the Vrije Universiteit Brussel (VUB) and Professor Dr. H. Sol belong to the Department of Structural Analysis. Their research is focused on the correction of numerical models of structures by means of experimentally measured vibration properties.

Professor Dr. W.P. De Wilde is head of the Department of Structural Analysis of the VUB. He has published widely on numerical analysis problems.

Concrete 2000. Edited by Ravindra K. Dhir and M. Roderick Jones.
© 1993 Published by E & FN Spon. ISBN 0 419 18120 2.

INTRODUCTION

Under normal conditions of use, concrete elements in traditional buildings do generally not show vibration problems, mainly because static design results in a stiff structure with sufficiently high natural frequencies. However, modern economic design is nowadays characterized by the introduction of light-weight materials and larger spans with implicit lower structural resonance frequencies, which increases considerably the risk of unwanted dynamic effects.

From a structural point of view, two types of measures can be taken in order to solve dynamic problems: first, structural design can be modified so that eigenfrequencies do not coincide with the frequency-content of the load, and second, damping of vibration amplitudes may be increased by means of external damping devices. On the other hand, the number of applications of dynamic structural modification, in which the intrinsic damping properties of the construction materials themselves are taken into account, remains very limited. Indeed, the damping capacity of the classical construction materials is rather small and difficult to measure accurately, i.e. isolated from other important sources of damping such as structural or joint damping. Yet, a better knowledge of material damping opens new perspectives in concrete construction: first, the introduction of accurate damping coefficients in numerical analysis may lead to a better prediction of structural dynamic effects; second, a better knowledge of the parameters that determine material damping behaviour of concrete, may lead to a better control of structural damping and consequently structural vibration behaviour.

Undoubtedly, the need for structural dynamic assessment is one of the main parameters in the discussion of how concrete design may develop in future, especially when the economic aspect is emphasized. It would be a waste to continue to neglect the potential damping capacity of reinforced concrete as construction material; however, this can only be realized if reliable methods for material damping prediction are available. So, the paper focuses on the discussion of material damping measurement methods. The application of the methods is illustrated for the particular case of microconcrete; this permits to keep the study on a more controllable laboratory scale, while extrapolation to concrete with normal-size aggregates is straightforward.

DAMPING NOMENCLATURE AND THEORETICAL CONCEPTS OF MATERIAL DAMPING IN MICROCONCRETE

Material damping is defined as the energy dissipation due to inelastic behaviour in a macroscopically uniform material, subjected to cyclic loading. Although the micromechanisms that cause energy dissipation are complicated, the damping phenomenology observed in microconcrete at low stress levels, may be characterized according to the general linear viscoelastic model, in addition to the assumption that microconcrete may be considered as a macroscopically homogeneous, continuous and isotropic material.

A convenient way of describing viscoelastic material behaviour is the complex notation, introducing the concept of complex modulus, which is in general physically explained by considering the phase difference δ between sinusoidally varying stress σ^* and strain ε^* for uniaxial loading [1]:

$$\frac{\sigma^*}{\varepsilon^*} = \frac{\sigma_o e^{i\omega t}}{\varepsilon_o e^{i(\omega t - \delta)}} = \frac{\sigma_o}{\varepsilon_o} e^{i\delta} = K' + iK'' = K^* \tag{1}$$

with: - the real part K' or storage modulus representing the elastic behaviour;
- the imaginary part K" or loss modulus, representing the energy dissipation;
- the angular frequency ω.

According to the linear viscoelastic model (or Kelvin-Voight model), these two moduli can also be related to other damping characteristics:

$$\frac{K''}{K'} = tg\,\delta = \eta = 2\xi = \frac{1}{2\pi}\frac{\Delta W}{W} \tag{2}$$

with: - δ the loss angle;
- η the loss factor;
- ξ the damping ratio;
- ΔW the energy dissipated per unit of volume during the loading cycle;
- W the maximum strain energy stored per unit of volume in the cycle.

The full dynamic identification of microconcrete thus involves the determination of the following properties:

$$\begin{aligned}
E^* &= E' + iE'' = E\,e^{i\delta_E} \\
v^* &= v' + iv'' = v\,e^{i\delta_v} \\
G^* &= G' + iG'' = G\,e^{i\delta_G} \\
k^* &= k' + ik'' = k\,e^{i\delta_k}
\end{aligned} \tag{3}$$

where: - E, v, G, k are respectively the Young modulus, the Poisson coefficient, the shear modulus and the bulk modulus;
- ' and " the real and the imaginary part;
- δ_E, δ_v, δ_G, δ_k represent the loss angles for E, v, G and k respectively.

According to the elastic-viscoelastic correspondence principle, such as formulated in

[2], the material properties in (3) answer to the constitutive equations, written in complex form:

$$G^* = \frac{E^*}{2(1+v^*)}$$
$$k^* = \frac{E^*}{3(1-2v^*)} \qquad (4)$$
$$v^* = \frac{3k^*-E^*}{6k^*}$$

As the complex material properties are interrelated to each other, it would be an ideal situation if all four moduli could be measured independently, which would allow to use the interrelationships as control mechanisms.

EXPERIMENTAL CHARACTERIZATION OF MATERIAL DAMPING IN MICROCONCRETE

Direct measurement of loss moduli

The experimental determination of the complex material properties is unavoidably based on structural dynamic measurements, due to the structure-like nature of test specimens. In order to isolate material damping from other damping mechanisms, experiments are preferably made on specimens with free boundary conditions and in free vibration, for which the passage from modal damping measurements towards material damping characteristics is straightforward. This consequently means that, in a practical way, only two material properties can be determined directly. First, the loss factor associated with the Young modulus can be derived most conveniently from the loss factor associated with the first bending vibration mode of a single beam specimen, which satisfies the Bernoulli-Euler conditions. Second, the loss factor associated with the shear modulus can be determined from the loss factor associated with the first torsional vibration mode of a plate specimen, which satisfies the Love-Kirchoff conditions. In that way, bending invokes a σ-ε damping mechanism, while torsion mainly causes energy dissipation in shear, taking into account a correction for the small contribution of normal stresses.

While experiments to measure η_E and η_G in a direct way are relatively simple to work out, the measurement of η_k and η_ν seems to be much more difficult. According to the strength of materials definition of the bulk modulus, the direct measurement of η_k necessitates the creation of a spherical or hydrostatic stress state. However, the isolation of such a uni-axial state of stress could not be practically realized yet. As to the Poisson coefficient, its definition necessitates the consideration of the relationship between stress-strain combinations in perpendicular directions. Consequently, η_ν and η_k may be determined in a first stage, by means of the experimentally determined η_E

and η_G on beam and plate specimens, in combination with the expressions (4).

A mixed numerical-experimental technique for the determination of the complex material properties

A practical method is developed in [3] to determine the elastic material properties or storage moduli from resonance frequency measurements for the first modes of a free vibrating plate with free boundary conditions. The method has been extended to the determination of complex moduli.

Taking into account the earlier mentioned assumptions concerning the microconcrete material, the test structure is a square plate with free boundary conditions, whose dimensions are chosen in order to satisfy the Love-Kirchoff assumptions, thus involving a plane stress condition. The first three modes of the plate are in order of increasing resonance frequency: the Torsion (T), Saddle (S) and Breath (B) mode; the mode shapes are represented in figure 1.

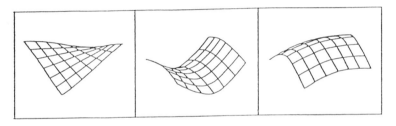

Figure 1   Torsion (T), Saddle (S) and Breath (B) mode shapes

As reported in [4], the modal loss factor may be composed of four terms:

$$\eta_{mode} = \eta_{D_{11}} \frac{W_{11}}{W} + \eta_{D_{22}} \frac{W_{22}}{W} + \eta_{D_{12}} \frac{W_{12}}{W} + \eta_{D_{66}} \frac{W_{66}}{W} \qquad (5)$$

with: - $\eta_{D_{ij}}$ the loss factor associated with the plate rigidity D_{ij};

-    $\dfrac{W_{ij}}{W}$ the fraction of the total strain energy W for the considered

vibration mode, associated with the plate rigidity D_{ij};

-    $\eta_{D_{11}} = \eta_{D_{22}}$ due to the assumption of isotropy.

The fractions of elastic strain energy $\dfrac{W_{ij}}{W}$ may be calculated for the T, S and B mode, by means of a finite element model, while the three modal loss factors η_T, η_S

and η_B can be measured experimentally. Assuming that $\eta_{D_{ij}}$ is independent of frequency and rewriting expression (5) for each mode, turns out to be a system of three equations in three unknowns: $\eta_{D_{11}} = \eta_{D_{22}}$, $\eta_{D_{12}}$ and $\eta_{D_{66}}$. Once determined, these three loss factors are then used to determine the loss factors η_E, η_G and η_ν, according to the scheme presented in figure 2, which is entirely based on the exploitation of the expressions (4). An appropriate correction procedure is needed if damping proves to be frequency dependent.

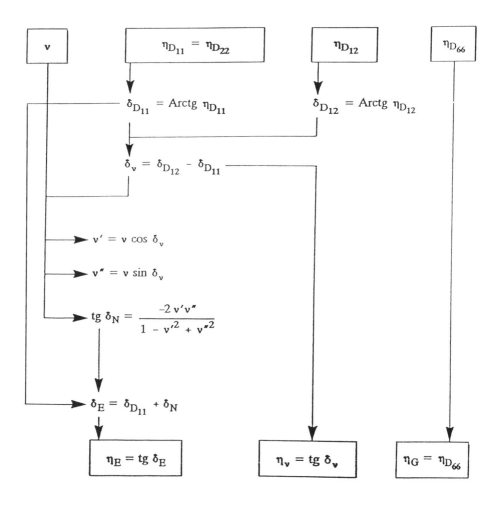

Figure 2   Extraction of η_E, η_ν and η_G out of $\eta_{D_{ij}}$ for isotropic material

Experimental loss factor measurement

A method for modal damping extraction by curve fitting of experimentally measured Frequency Response Functions (FRF) for Single Degree Of Freedom (SDOF) systems, was presented in [4].   FRF measurement methods are characterized by the indispensable excitation technique and excitation signal measurement.   Two main techniques have been studied: hammer or impact-excitation and excitation by means of an electromagnetic shaker.   The latter one is characterized by a flexible tie rod connection between shaker and test structure, which makes an analysis of a test specimen with free boundary conditions impossible.   On the other hand, a short pulse in the time domain corresponds to a uniform distribution of impact energy in the frequency domain.   This often results in poor signal to noise charateristics and leads to bad curve fitting results.

This explains why recent efforts are concentrated on time domain methods for modal parameter extraction, based on the evaluation of the SDOF-Impulse Response Function (IRF), which in practice is obtained by recording the time history of the decaying response of the free vibrating structure, after it was excited by a hammer blow.   It should be noted that the locations of excitation and measurement are carefully chosen in view of the mechanical isolation of the vibration mode that has to be examined. Finally, the damping ratio ξ (and thus the loss factor η) can be determined by a curve fit calculation of an exponential analytical expression to the envelope of the experimentally measured IRF: see figure 3.

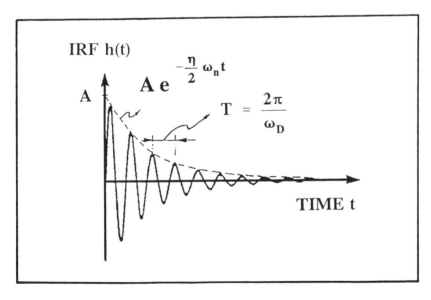

Figure 3   IRF for SDOF system

A CASE STUDY

Description of investigated material

The basic material that is investigated is a mortar made of pozzolanic cement PPz 30 and coarse sand 0.1/5, characterized by a fineness modulus = 3.3 . The selected composition is very traditional: 1 part of cement, 3 parts of sand and 0.5 part of water (parts in mass).

A parametric analysis: results and discussion

After striking of casing after two days, some beam and plate specimens are kept under water at 20 °C (wet specimens), while others are conserved out of the water, at 20 °C and at a relative humidity of 86% (dry specimens). Storage and loss moduli are determined at regularly spaced moments, while bending and compression tests on accompanying prisms are performed. It should be emphasized that the wet specimens are also kept in a water-saturated situation during the vibration measurements. Figure 4 represents in a schematic way the evolution of the compressive strength with time, as well as the evolution of the real part of the Young modulus and of the corresponding loss factor. Results for wet specimens and dry specimens are compared, while some dry specimens are also saturated 24 hours before the last reported measurement.

These results are susceptible to some comments:

- first, the compressive strength increases with time, in accordance with the hardening phenomenon. As expected, the strength increases more quickly for the mortar that is kept under water;
- second, the evolution of the stiffness of the material is very similar to the evolution of the strength: a higher degree of hardening gives a higher modulus. The fact that the test specimens are saturated or not before the vibration measurements, does not influence the values of the storage modulus considerably;
- third, it is observed that damping decreases with a higher degree of hardening, which obviously corresponds to the passage from a viscoelastic material to a material with more and more elastic behaviour;
- fourth, damping measurements seem to be strongly affected by the presence of water in the pores. Indeed, damping is apparently larger for the wet specimens than for the dry specimens. But when the dry specimens are saturated, in order to perform damping measurements for all specimens in the same reference situation, their loss factors become even higher in value than those of the wet specimens. The latter observation certainly suggests the possibility of using loss factor measurements to characterize the porosity and thus the degree of hardening of early age microconcrete.

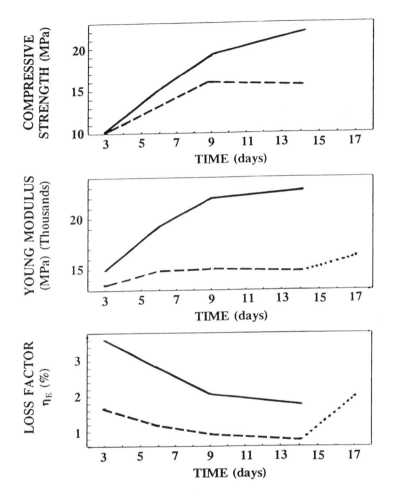

Figure 4   Evolution of compressive strength, E and η_E with time for
the basic mortar with coarse sand;

        ——   is for the wet specimens,
        - - -   is for the dry specimens,
        . . .   is for the dry specimens which are saturated 24 hours
                before the last measurement.

The complex moduli of microconcrete

It may be concluded from the preceding experiments that the presence of water is an
important parameter in damping assessment. In order to determine the complex moduli

of the above mentioned microconcrete, a new series of specimens is produced and conserved under water.   However, in order to get rid of the presence of water as disturbing parameter, the specimens are put into an oven at 105 °C, 24 hours before the loss factor measurements, in order to eliminate the free water in the pores of the hardened mortar, as well as the adsorbed water that is weakly bonded to the surfaces of the hydration products.

Beam and plate specimens of different sizes are investigated, in order to study the frequency dependence of the complex moduli. Figure 5 represents in a schematic way the evolution of the directly measured loss factors η_E and η_G with frequency, as well as the evolution of η_ν which are determined by means of the numerical-experimental model; all loss factors are determined for the previously mentioned microconcrete, at an age of 28 days after manufacturing.   Some results are equally reported for the commercially available shrink-proof mortar "CUGLATON", which is a quick-setting mortar on the basic of an elevated quantity of Portland cement, to which fine quartzsand ($\leq$ 1 mm) is added. In addition, a swelling agent, an adhesive agent and a fluid agent are used, which makes the mortar particularly fluid although the water-cement ratio is reduced to about 0.32 .

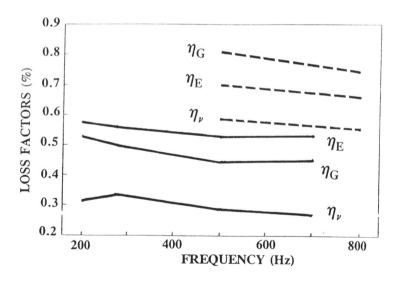

Figure 5   Evolution of loss factors η_E, η_G and η_ν with frequency for
                the basic mortar with coarse sand (—) and for CUGLATON
                (---); all values are determined at the age of 28 days after
                manufacturing.

Some comments may be formulated:
- first, damping appears to be slightly frequency dependent. However, up to now, it is not yet clear if this dependency should be attributed to the material behaviour or to a possible air damping effect. Indeed, according to [5], air damping increases with decreasing frequency;
- second, the variation of the value of η_ν highly depends on the accuracy of vibration measurements, and on the quality of the test plates, i.e. perfect square, flat sides, constant thickness ... The value of η_k may be obtained by exploitation of expression (4), which leads to the order of magnitude of η_k of 0.7 %;
- third, as all complex moduli are now determined, the damping behaviour of microconcrete may be introduced in numerical analyses. It should be noted that the material damping values are not negligible. Yet, attention should be paid to the actual conservation conditions of the (micro)concrete of the real structure, in order to simulate as much as possible the ambient conditions when material properties are determined on laboratory scale specimens. Indeed, it is clearly shown that damping behaviour is highly determined by age (for young concrete), and water content, the latter also being a characteristic of the porosity of the cement-stone, which is in its turn determined by a lot of hardening parameters;
- fourth, the Poisson coefficient appears to be complex valued. It is rather annoying if the idea of the Poisson coefficient being complex must be related to a clear practical explanation in terms of stress-strain phase lags. However, according to the definition of ν, η_ν should be seen in the sense of a phase lag between the stress in one material direction and the strain in the same direction, which is induced by the strain in the perpendicular direction. This formulation consequently confirms that a proper analysis of η_ν should be performed on plate specimens;
- fifth, it is observed that material damping may be a sensitive parameter for the identification of different types of microconcrete. It appears that mortars with a higher cement content give rise to higher damping values. However, further research is needed for the identification of the main contributions to the increase in damping, which may be determined not only by a bigger percentage of cement-stone in the hardened mortar, but also by a different partition of hydration products, or by a modified interface effect.

CONCLUSIONS

This paper wants to study the complex material properties of microconcrete, in view of their introduction in numerical calculations of dynamic effects in concrete structures; this should be seen in the context of the development of economic concrete design rules in future. As the microconcrete is assumed to be a homogeneous, continuous, isotropic and linear viscoelastic material, full identification involves the determination of the complex material properties E^*, G^*, ν^* and k^*. The paper is limited to the determination of the imaginary parts or loss moduli.

The paper discusses material damping measurement methods. While experiments to measure η_E and η_G in a direct way are relatively simple to work out, the experimental determination of η_ν and η_k proves to be much more difficult. Advantage is taken from a mixed numerical-experimental technique to determine η_ν as well as η_E and η_G from the experimental modal analysis of square plates with free boundary conditions. The application of the experimental methods is illustrated for two types of microconcrete.

The presented values for the loss factors associated with the complex moduli reveal that material damping in microconcrete is not negligible; damping even appears to be a sensitive parameter for the identification of different types of microconcrete, but attention should be paid to ambient conditions, as damping behaviour is highly determined by age and water content. Finally, although further research is needed for the identification of the micromechanisms that contribute to the damping phenomenon, it may be concluded that, from a macroscopic point of view, there are no main obstacles left as to concrete material damping assessment in structural dynamic problems.

ACKNOWLEDGEMENTS

I would like to thank

- Mr. GINDO DENGU, for his valued collaboration in the experimental part of the research project;
- The Belgian Fonds voor Kollektief Fundamenteel Onderzoek, for the financial support.

REFERENCES

1. LAZAN, B.J.,   Damping of materials and members in structural mechanics, Pergamon press, 1968, pp 316.
2. HASHIN, Z.,   Complex moduli of viscoelastic composites - I. General theory and application to particulate composites, Int. J. Solids and Structures, 1970, Vol. 6, pp 539-551.
3. SOL, H.,   Identification of anisotropic plate rigidities using free vibration data, PhD thesis, Free University of Brussels VUB, 1986, pp 251.
4. VANTOMME,J.,   Determination of material damping in concrete, Proc. 2nd Int. RILEM/CEB Symposium Quality Control of Concrete Structures, Eds. L. Taerwe and H. Lambotte, E & FN Spon, 1991, pp 215-224.
5. READ, B.E., DEAN, G.D., The determination of dynamic properties of polymers and composites, Adam Hilger Ltd., BRISTOL, 1978, pp 203.

CHLORIDE RESISTANT CONCRETE

M R Jones

M J McCarthy

R K Dhir

University of Dundee

United Kingdom

ABSTRACT. The paper provides an overview of the performance of concrete in chloride containing environments and discusses how this may be improved. Consideration is given to the British Standard documents and the guidance they offer for the design of concrete structures for chloride exposures. Shortcomings are identified in these and an alternative approach to designing service life into concrete structures, based on performance criteria is suggested. From an understanding of the concrete factors influencing chloride ingress a means of producing chloride-resistant concrete is considered. This requires to be fully evaluated, but early indications are, that by careful manipulation of the constituent materials, long-term performance of concrete in chloride environments is possible.

KEYWORDS : Chloride ingress, Concrete microstructure, Chemistry, Environmental conditions, British Standards, Performance specification, Chloride-resistant concrete.

Dr M Roderick Jones is a Lecturer in Concrete Technology, University of Dundee, Scotland, UK. His research interests are concerned with the use of PFA and GGBS in construction. He is particularly interested in the durability of concretes with these materials and also in the use of surface coatings.

Dr Michael J McCarthy is a Research/Teaching Fellow in the Concrete Technology Unit, University of Dundee. His main research interests are concerned with concrete durability; in particular the use of cement replacement materials and reinforcement corrosion due to chlorides and carbonation and in multi-aggressive environments.

Professor Ravindra K Dhir is Director of the Concrete Technology Unit, University of Dundee. He specialises in the use of PFA and GGBS in concrete as well as permeation properties, and the durability and protection of concrete with particular reference to carbonation, chloride ingress and associated corrosive effects, and freeze/thaw. He has published and travelled widely and served on many technical committees.

Concrete 2000. Edited by Ravindra K. Dhir and M. Roderick Jones.
© 1993 Published by E & FN Spon. ISBN 0 419 18120 2.

INTRODUCTION

Reinforced concrete structures that are subject to de-icing salt applications or are located in marine environments are likely, after a certain period of exposure, to exhibit signs of distress due to the ingress of chlorides and the corrosion of reinforcing steel.   This normally becomes apparent with the formation of cracks, frequently accompanied by rust staining and ultimately spalling of concrete.   The period of service, depends on a large number of factors including the type of binder, cover depth, quality of workmanship and the degree of curing.   Unfortunately as things currently stand, it is not possible to quantitatively take account and accommodate these factors as part of the design process. Not surprisingly, therefore, the repair of this type of damage has become a significant part of the work of engineers and this situation is unacceptable for the next century.

The prevention of damage during the service life of structures is therefore of the upmost importance and it is apparent that there are a number of options that will be available.   The use of concrete surface sealants to prevent chloride ingress or coated rebar offer potential solutions, but they are expensive and are not wholly free from difficulties.   Moreover there is a lack of data concerning the reliance of very thin protective coatings over long exposure periods in harsh environments. A potentially more efficient solution is tackle the problem at source, by designing and constructing concrete of a specified durability, which is capable of limiting the transportation of chlorides to the reinforcement.

This paper provides an overview of chloride ingress into concrete structures and examines existing design guidelines. Based on an understanding of the factors influencing the process of chloride ingress, means of producing chloride-resistant concrete, without radically changing existing practice, are discussed.

PAST EXPERIENCE

The use of reinforcement in concrete dates back to the mid-eighteenth century, however, its development and widespread use in construction generally occurred from the early part of the twentieth century.

The occurrence of reinforcement corrosion due to chlorides can also be traced to the early part of this century. In these cases, it was structures containing calcium chloride, as an accelerating admixture[1], a practice which was allowed in the UK until 1977[2], that exhibited damage. In addition, structures located in the marine environment[3] were also found to have similar problems. However, such instances generally occurred in isolation and it was not readily apparent that chlorides represented such a serious threat to RC structures.

Corrosion problems became widespread in the late 1960s. This period also relates to a rapid development of the highway system, with some three-quarters of the UK motorway and trunk road bridges being constructed[4].   Additionally at this time, a number of changes relating to the constituent materials, design of concrete structures and construction procedures occurred[5].   While it is difficult to quantify the effects of these changes in terms of concrete durability, an attitude by engineers of 'pour and forget' concrete was very apparent.

Furthermore, this period saw the widespread use of sodium chloride rock salt as a de-icer for highways. As indicated in Figure 1[6,7], in the UK, 10 times the quantity of salt

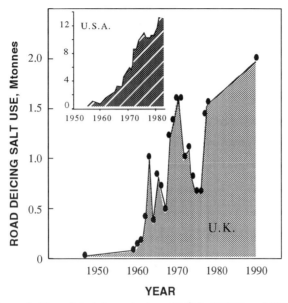

Figure 1   Use of de-icing salt since 1945 in UK[6] and USA[7].

applied to roads in 1960 is currently used, although this, in part, is also due to the expanding highway network over this period. The situation is similar in Europe and in the USA. Not surprisingly deterioration in highway structures has become the most serious corrosion problem faced by engineers.

A recent survey[4] of highway bridges in the UK has indicated that nearly one third of these are in poor condition and are in need of attention. The most common cause of problems was found to be due to chloride corrosion. On the basis of this survey it is expected that the cost of repairs, due to a range of durability problems, of which chloride-induced corrosion represents a significant proportion, for the existing bridge stock, will amount to in excess of £620M over the next 10 years for these structures alone.

REQUIREMENTS FOR DURABILITY

Concrete has traditionally been considered to be a durable material and expectations in this respect are usually high. The main factor that tends to be used to assess this is compressive strength. However it is becoming more widely accepted that concretes of similar strength do not necessarily have the same resistance to a particular environment[8].

Current practice for design and specification of concrete for chloride-containing environments is specified in BS 8110, Structural Use of Concrete[9] and BS 5328, Specification of Concrete[10]. Recently there has been the introduction of equivalent draft European documents as part of the package of standards, harmonized within the member countries of CEN, viz, ENV 1992-1-1, Eurocode 2 (EC2) : Design of Concrete Structures[11] and ENV 206, Concrete Performance, Production, Placing and Compliance

Criteria[12]. Additional standards covering the provision of durable concrete are, BS 5400, Steel, Concrete and Composite Bridges[13] and DTp Specification for Highway works[14]. The main philosophy behind the provision for chloride resistance in these standards is based on the use of a concrete of specified set of characteristics and cover in relation to the environmental conditions.

BS 8110/EC 2

The main requirements covered in BS 8110[9] and the new European document EC2[11] are given in Table 1.

The main philosophy used in BS 8110 for chloride environments considers the provision of adequate concrete cover depth and a concrete of sufficient quality in relation to the environmental conditions. The latter is given in terms of minimum cement content, maximum water/cement ratio and minimum concrete grade. According to this approach it is possible to reduce the cover and increase the concrete quality or vice-versa to achieve the same chloride resistance in a particular environment.

Alternative binders where blends containing pulverized-fuel ash (PFA) and ground granulated blastfurnace slag (GGBS) are used are also covered in BS 8110[9]; the use of these materials is permitted in the more aggressive environments. In these cases equivalent 28 day strength should be achieved. Recommendations are also given in BS8110[9] to the curing periods that should be provided.

EC2 categorises the exposure conditions in a slightly different way to BS 8110 and recommends nominal covers for these. In addition recommendations are also made to allow for tolerances that should be added to these nominal covers for different types of concrete manufacture. Reference is made to ENV 206[12] for material selection.

BS 5328/ENV 206

BS 5328[10] is similar in principle to BS 8110[9] in its specification of concrete against chlorides. This categorises the exposures in a slightly different way to BS 8110[9], but offers similar guidance on the minimum grade, cement content and maximum water/cement ratio that should be used for these. Users are referred to BS 8110[9] for the selection of concrete cover. The use of the recommended figures can be made in the specification of designed or prescribed mixes.

ENV 206[12] is the principle European document for material selection for concrete durability in structures. This is very similar in principle to BS 8110 and BS 5328 and provides guidance on maximum w/c ratio and minimum cement contents for particular environments. In addition a range of minimum concrete grades as a UK annex requirement. In addition no specific reference is made to the use of PFA or GGBS in chloride environments, although it is recommended that the choice of cement type should follow the national standards or regulations valid in the place of use of the concrete. Curing for the less aggressive environments is considered, however it is only suggested that in the more severe exposures, including chloride environments, these times should be substantially increased, with no further guidance.

Table 1 Durability requirements of main codes of practice.

EXPOSURE CONDITION	EC2/ENV 206/BS8110 DURABILITY REQUIREMENTS			
	NOM COVER	MAX W/C	MIN CEMENT CONTENT	MIN GRADE
EC2/ENV 206				
Dry (1)	20	0.65	260	C25/C30+
Humid (2)	35	0.60^{a1}, 0.55^{b1}	280	C30/C37+
De-icing (3)	40	0.5	300	C30/C37+
Seawater (4)	40	0.55^{a1}, 0.50^{b1}	300	C35/C45+
Aggressive (5) Chemicals	35^{a2}, 45^{c1}	0.55^{a2}, 0.45^{c1}	280^{a2}, 300^{c1}	-
BS8110				
Mild	25	0.65	274	C30
	20	0.60	300	C35
Moderate	35	0.60	300	C35
	20	0.45	400	C50
Severe	40	0.55	325	C40
	25	0.45	400	C50
Very Severe*	50	0.55	325	C40
	30	0.45	400	C50
Extreme	60	0.50	350	C45
	50	0.45	400	C50

a1 - without frost   a2 - slightly aggressive/aggressive industrial (gas, liquid or solid)

b1 - with frost   c1 - highly aggressive surface required (gas, liquid or solid)

+ - UK annex requirements

* - De-icing salt/seawater exposure

Considering the widespread nature of the problem and the knowledge gained, the provisions for chloride environments, which are specifically covered in the exposure categories, appear not to have moved significantly from what existed before their introduction.

It is recognised that performance with respect to the environment is important and some attempt is made to quantify the concrete quality by the inclusion of a clause covering concrete impermeability. However this requires compliance with a concrete water absorption test and while this may represent the mechanism by which damage to concrete through chloride-induced corrosion occurs in some instances, it is inappropriate in many situations of chloride ingress.

BS 5400/DOT Specification for highway works

BS 5400[13] again requires that a certain concrete cover and grade be provided in relation to the environment conditions. A similar approach to that of the other documents is used in respect of the cement content and w/c ratio. No coverage however, is given to the use of GGBS or PFA. Curing is reviewed and general recommendations given in relation to construction type and conditions.

It is perhaps surprising with this type of structure, which is known to exhibit problems, that more specific forms of damage prevention are not considered. Recognition of the problem in highway structures and the inadequacy of existing practices to prevent chloride-induced corrosion has been made by the Department of Transport[14] and has lead them to include coating of highway structures with a monomeric silane in their specification of all new works.

In principle the approach adopted by the various codes of practice to concrete durability attempts to provide a low permeation concrete microstructure that should offer resistance to the ingress of chlorides. What is lacking is any guidance on the role of the different binders. Given this engineers may infer that binder type is of little consequence.

While the factors that are considered attempt to provide durability, they are in no way designed to give any quantification of service life. Effectively the engineer is considering individually most of the right factors, but has little idea, collectively of what durability will be achieved, resulting in a 'wait and hope' situation.

WHY IS CONCRETE PERFORMANCE SO VARIABLE ?

The main factors influencing the concrete performance in a chloride environment may be summarized as,

- Microstructure (Permeation properties)

- Chemistry of concrete

- Environmental conditions

Which of the factors plays the dominant role in controlling the rate of chloride ingress varies between different situations. The individual effects of these factors are illustrated in Figure 2.

Microstructure

The quality of the concrete microstructure is influenced both by the quantity and type of binder used and the amount of water in the mix. In general with increasing binder content refinement or densification of the concrete microstructure can be expected. Similarly the use of alternative binders if correctly proportioned can offer some enhancement to the microstructure[15].

Curing of concrete is another factor that can have a significant effect on the concrete microstructure. Table 2, illustrates how curing can effect chloride diffusion. Frequently, however curing is not provided for, particularly on vertical surfaces, where practical difficulties exist and this can significantly influence subsequent concrete performance and potentially can be particularly problematic in bridges.

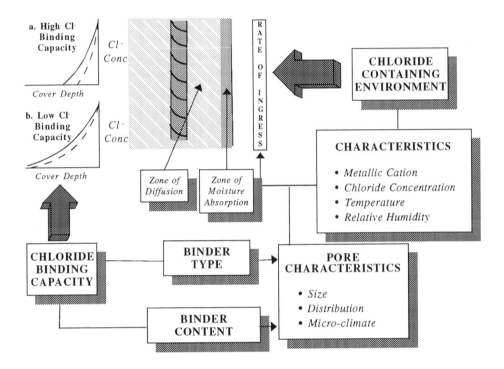

Figure 2 Role of different factors influencing chloride ingress.

Table 2 Comparison of D for differently cured concrete.

CONCRETE GRADE	CHLORIDE DIFFUSION, cm^2/s x 10^{-9}	
	Air	Water
20	110	83
40	48	27
60	20	11

The results shown in Figure 3[16] illustrate the influence of curing on concrete strength and air permeability. These indicate that for equivalent strength, differences are apparent between concretes depending largely on the w/c ratio and curing conditions employed. These therefore highlight the limitation of strength as an indicator of the resistance to the passage of fluids in concrete and the importance of curing to enable the development of concrete resistance to aggressive media. What is also clear from Table 2 and Figure 3 is the improvements in microstructure that can be achieved with the generally used concrete grades and that extending the period of curing and decreasing the w/c ratio alone are unlikely to produce chloride resistant concrete.

Chloride Binding Capacity

Chlorides entering concrete from the environment are considered to exist in one of several forms[17],

- Free

- Weakly Bound (Physi/Chemi-sorbed)

- Strongly Bound (Chemically combined)

Their rate of transport through concrete is influenced by the state of the chloride present. The relative quantities of each depend largely on the characteristics of the cement or binder. As indicated in Figure 4, it is the collective effects of both the cement chemistry or binding ability and the concrete microstructure that control chloride resistance.

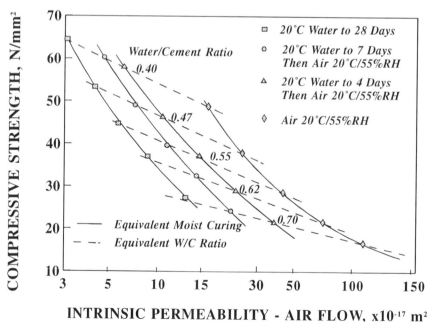

Figure 3   Relationship between compressive strength and permeability of concrete[16].

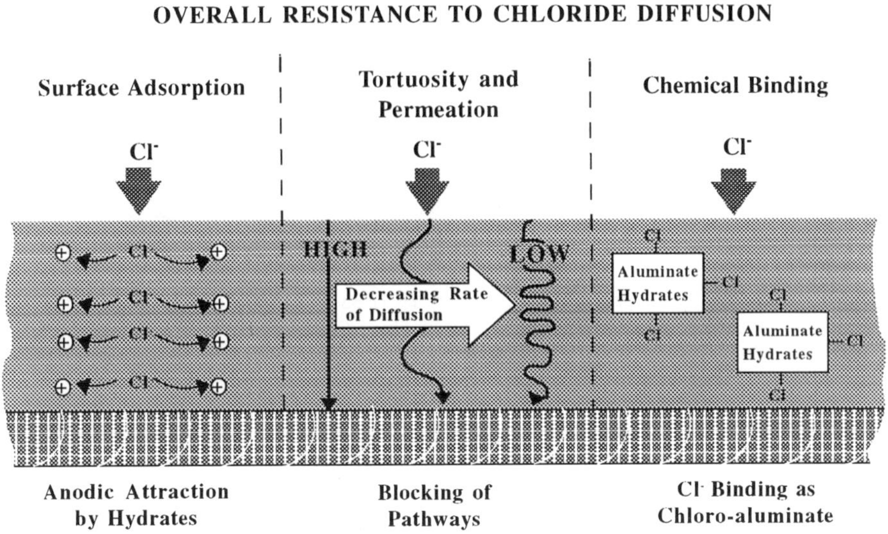

OVERALL RESISTANCE TO CHLORIDE DIFFUSION

Figure 4   Mechanisms controlling chloride ingress in concrete.

Those chlorides existing in the free state are considered to represent the main threat to reinforcement. It is those that are capable of further penetrating into concrete and causing breakdown of the passive film when present in significant quantities at the sites of reinforcement.

The weakly bound chlorides are those that are adsorbed on the pore walls of the cement hydrates[18]. The quantity of adsorbed ions is considered to be mainly dependent on the surface area[19] and nature[20] of the cement hydrates.

Strongly bound chlorides are those combined with the cement compounds. The different phases of cement appear to have different capabilities in relation to taking up and binding chlorides. The silicate phases probably, have very little contribution to chloride binding capacity[21]. The aluminate phases on the other hand are considered to have a major role in the binding of chlorides[22,23].

Work has shown that cements containing a high C_3A[24] level generally offer enhanced chloride resistance compared to sulphate resisting cements. Similarly it has been found that cements containing PFA and GGBS[25,26], which are high in reactive alumina also offer significant benefits in ability to slow down the rate of chloride ingress in concrete. The importance, and potential for producing chloride resistant concrete of high chloride binding capacity is, for example, shown in Figure 5. This Figure suggests that at higher PFA contents it is possible to offset the effects of poor curing.

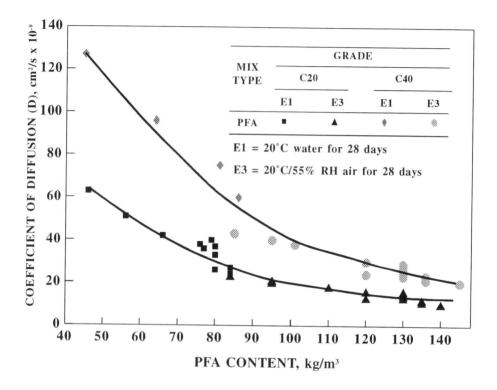

Figure 5 Influence of PFA content on chloride diffusion in concrete[25].

Environmental Conditions

The humidity and temperature of the environment have a significant influence on chloride ingress. If the exposure is subject to periodic wetting and drying, which is the most common type of exposure, then it is likely that chlorides will enter concrete under both absorption (capillary suction) when the concrete is dry, and by diffusion once the pores become filled. Chlorides move faster under the action of absorption[27], although this effect generally only occurs in the outer few millimetres at the concrete surface.

Recent work[28] indicates that temperature also has a very significant effect on the passage of chlorides into concrete. At low temperatures, eg 5°C, the chloride resistance of Portland cement concrete generally increases. However, at higher temperatures, eg 45°C, its resistance drops dramatically. Such effects appear to relate very closely to the nature of the binder as the use of PFA in these situations offers significant advantages in both cases, see Figure 6.

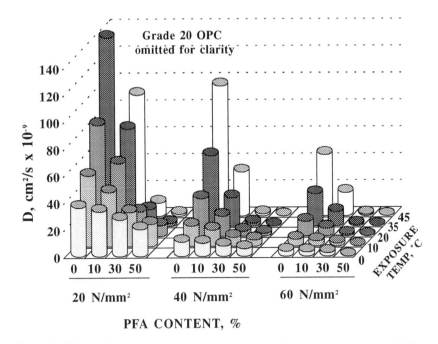

Figure 6   Effect of environment temperature on chloride ingress in concrete[28].

It is clear that little can be done about the environment itself, other than avoid building there. So it is the properties of the concrete itself that have to be considered. This requires that the factors controlling the chemistry and concrete microstructure are clearly understood, such that by careful material selection and manipulation they are collectively maximised. Similarly it is necessary for this to be translated into specifications, where the philosophy should address the provision of a specified durable life. This should free the engineer to balance the performance of available concrete materials with the other main factors ie strength and cover.

DEVELOPING CHLORIDE-RESISTANT CONCRETE

Adequate durability can be better provided for, by specifying concrete in terms of measured performance. Indeed, there is a move in this direction in the development of European codes and harmonised standards. In terms of resistance of structural concrete to chloride attack, the coefficient of chloride diffusion (D) provides the fundamental parameter which can be used for specifying durable life. This parameter collectively takes account of the factors associated with concrete and described above that influence chloride ingress. Figure 7 shows the tripartite relationship that exists between grade, controlled by structural requirements and D, controlled by durability requirements and cover which is influenced by both.

D is best determined using a chloride diffusion half-cell test. This is relatively simple to perform and can be completed within 14 days using a rapid test method[29].

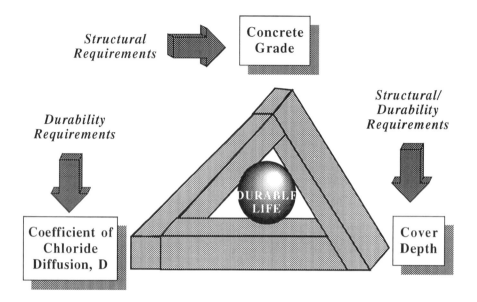

Figure 7 Tripartite relationship between concrete grade, cover and D.

Figure 8 gives a design nomogram[30] which can be used to determine the D that will be required to achieve a specified durable life. The engineer will therefore select a design life and then based on the knowledge of the environment, estimate the likely external chloride concentration. This is followed by the selection of the cover and the permissible extent of contamination acceptable. This can be used to determine the value of D needed to achieve the required period of service.

The effect of cover is taken into account by this nomogram and, for example, illustrates that to obtain 90 years service in a 0.1M chloride environment, with critical water-soluble chloride level of 0.1%, a reduction in cover from 50 to 25 mm will require the D to be reduced from 32 x 10^{-9} cm^2/s to 7 x 10^{-9} cm^2/s. It should be noted that the recommended increase in grade C40 to C50 would not achieve this order of reduction in D as can be interpolated from Table 2. This further reinforces the view that increasing concrete grade is not the route to durability.

What is required is the development of a concrete that can be produced in a conventional way and contain materials that have a large capacity to bind chlorides. In addition, the material should not require any additional treatment and preferably offer reasonable levels of economy. Furthermore, there should be no significant changes to the readily understood characteristics of typical portland concretes, for example handling and placing, early strength development and long-term mechanical and other relevant durability properties.

Studies carried out at Dundee University[8,25,28-32], indicate that both PFA and GGBS have characteristics with the potential to satisfy the criteria given above and point the way forward to the efficient production of chloride-resistant concrete.

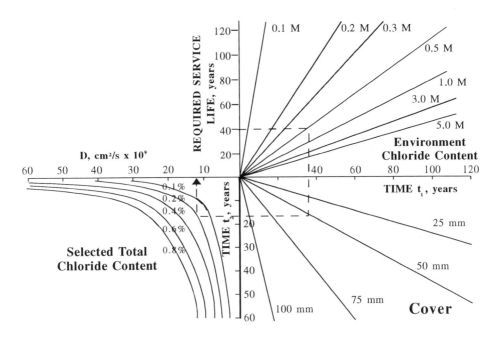

Figure 8   Nomogram for determination of D for particular cover, exposure conditions and acceptable contamination level.

The main beneficial effects of these materials, in this context, can be summarised as,

- High alumina content, which in PFA provides over 6 times the Al_2O_3 content of ordinary Portland cement and for GGBS over 2 times. More importantly, the form of alumina contained is likely to be amorphous with a high degree of chloride binding capacity per unit weight of material.

- Large number of well dispersed fine particles available to adsorb chlorides

- Potential for blocking and increasing tortuosity of pathways in concrete.

Furthermore, these explain the conclusions of a number of studies[25,32], carried out at Dundee University, which indicate that quantity and not quality of PFA or GGBS is the key factor, since this directly leads to increased opportunity for chloride binding.

The inclusion of these materials in high quantities potentially could lead to conflict of performance with both rheology and early strength of concrete. The use of accelerators or activators to initiate reactions at early ages may therefore have to be considered to overcome such effects.

To go beyond this, it is possible to use combinations of PFA, GGBS for the chemical benefits and Microsilica (MS) for its densification of the microstructure. Multiblends of this type have found limited application and it seems likely that with further work and precise quantification of the mechanisms limiting chloride ingress, then their use in the provision of a very high chloride resistant concrete may be possible. In the development of this concrete again it will also be necessary to fully evaluate the material performance with respect to other concrete properties.

In addition to the possible savings in terms of repair costs, it would then be possible to adopt thinner sections and reduced covers for RC construction typically of 25 to 30 mm, thereby offering another significant benefit.

CONCLUDING REMARKS

Chlorides currently represent a serious threat to concrete structures and unless specific consideration is given to preventing the transportation of chlorides to the level of the steel, repairs will continue to be necessary into the next century. National Codes are generally ineffective in their recommendations to provide durable concrete against this form of attack and this appears to be mainly due to a lack of proper consideration of the chemical role of the binder in this process.

The par European code for the first time has introduced a performance based test for durability. While this is the correct direction for specifications, the water absorption test used is unlikely to determine chloride durability, since it takes no account of cement chloride binding capacity.

It is shown that there is little alternative but to use a chloride diffusion test and a rapid method for this has been developed. From the coefficient of chloride diffusion it is possible to make estimations of durability. From this the engineer can be best placed to balance cover depth and concrete resistance to chloride ingress. This can make best use of materials like PFA, GGBS and MS to design for durability and give, for a required service life, a chloride-resistant concrete.

REFERENCES

1.   PULLAR-STRECKER P. Corrosion damaged concrete assessment and repair, Butterworths, 1987, 99pp.

2.   BRITISH STANDARDS INSTITUTION. CP 110 : Part 1, The Structural Use of Concrete, 1972, London.

3.   ENGINEERING NEWS. A British example of electrolytic corrosion in a reinforced concrete structure. Engineering News, 1911.

4.   WALLBANK E J. The performance of concrete bridges: a survey of 200 highway bridges. A report prepared for by G Maunsell and Partners. HMSO, April 1989, 96pp, London.

5.   SOMMERVILLE G. The design life of concrete structures. The Structural Engineer, Vol 64A, No 2, February 1986, pp 60 - 71.

6.   ANON. Heavy snow emphasises de-icing salt deficiencies. New Civil Engineer, 14 February, 1991.

7.   SLATER J E. Corrosion of metals in association with concrete. American society for testing and materials, ASTM STP 818, 1983, 83pp, Philadelphia.

8.   DHIR R K and BYARS E A. PFA concrete : Chloride diffusion rates. Magazine of Concrete Research, Vol 45, No 162, 1993, pp 1 - 9.

9.   BRITISH STANDARDS INSTITUTION. BS 8110 : Part 1, Structural Use of Concrete, 1985, London.

10. BRITISH STANDARDS INSTITUTION. BS 5628 : Parts 1 to 4. Specification of Concrete, 1991, London.

11. BRITISH STANDARDS INSTITUTION. DD ENV 1992-1-1, Eurocode 2 : Design of Concrete Structures, Part 1. General rules and rules for buildings, 1992, London.

12. BRITISH STANDARDS INSTITUTION. DD ENV 206:1992, Concrete Performance, Production, Placing and Compliance Criteria, 1992, London.

13. BRITISH STANDARDS INSTITUTION. BS 5400 : Part 8, Steel, Concrete and Composite Bridges, 1978, London.

14. DEPARTMENT OF TRANSPORT. Notes for Guidance on the Specification of Highway Works, HMSO, 1986.

15. BAKKER R F M. Permeability of blended cement concretes. Proceedings of the first international conference on the use of Fly Ash, Silica Fume, Slag and other mineral by-products in concrete, American Concrete Institute SP 79-30, Vol 1, 1983, pp 415 - 433.

16   DHIR R K, HEWLETT P C and CHAN Y N. Near-surface characteristics of concrete: Intrinsic permeability. Magazine of Concrete Research, Vol 41, No 147, June 1989, pp 87 - 97.

17. BERMAN H A. Determination of chloride in hardened portland cement, mortar and concrete. Journal of Materials, Vol 3, No 7, 1972, pp 330 - 335.

18. RAMACHANDRAN V S. Possible states of chloride in the hydration of thr tricalcium silicate in the presence of calcium chloride. Materials and Constructions, Vol 4, No 19, 1971, pp 3 - 12.

19. BYFORS K. Chloride binding in cement paste. Nordic Concrete Research, No 4, 1986, pp 27 - 38.

20. HANSSON C M and SORENSEN B. The influence of cement fineness on chloride diffusion and chloride binding in hardened cement paste. Nordic Concrete Research Publication No 6, 1987, pp 57 - 72.

21.   LAMBERT P, PAGE C L and SHORT N R. Pore solution chemistry of hydrated system tricalcium silicate/sodium chloride/water. Cement and Concrete Research, Vol 15, No 4, 1985, pp 675 - 680.

22.   ALONSO C and ANDRADE C. Corrosion of steel reinforcement in carbonated mortar containing chlorides. Advances in Cement Research, Vol 1, No 3, 1988, pp155 -163.

23.   MONOFORE G E and VERBECK, G J. Corrosion of prestressed wire in concrete. ACI Journal Proceedings, Vol 57, No 5, 1960, pp 491 - 516.

24.   MEHTA P K. Effect of cement composition on corrosion of steel in concrete. American Society for Testing and Materials, STP 629, 1977, pp 12 - 19, Philadelphia.

25.   DHIR R K, JONES M R and SENEVIRATNE A M G. Diffusion of chlorides into concrete : Influence of PFA quality. Cement and Concrete Research, Vol 21, 1992, pp 1092 - 1102.

26.   HOPE B B AND IP A K C. Corrosion of steel in concrete made with slag cement. American Concrete Institute Materials Journal, Nov-Dec 1987, pp 525 - 531.

27.   SCHIESSL P. Corrosion of reinforcement. CEB RILEM, International Workshop of Concrete, Durability of Concrete, Copenhagen, 18 - 20 May 1983, pp 73 - 93.

28.   DHIR R K, JONES M R and ELGHALY A E. PFA Concrete : Exposure temperature effects on chloride diffusion. Cement and Concrete Research, In press, 1993.

29.   DHIR R K, JONES M R, AHMED H E H and SENEVIRATNE A M G. Rapid estimation of chloride diffusion coefficients in concrete. Magazine of Concrete Research, Vol 42, No 152, 1990, pp 177 - 185.

30.   DHIR R K, JONES M R and AHMED H E H. Concrete durability : Estimation of chloride concentration during design life. Magazine of Concrete Research, Vol 20, 1990, pp 579 - 590.

31.   JONES M R. Chloride environment. Proceedings of National Seminar on Use of GGBS in Concrete Construction, University of Dundee, Ed R K Dhir et al, September 1992, pp 53 - 62.

32.   DHIR R K. GGBS Concrete : Chloride Resistance. Internal Report, University of Dundee, 1993.

CHLORIDE DIFFUSION CHARACTERISTICS
OF CONCRETE

K G Babu
K V Rao

Indian Institute of Technology

India

ABSTRACT . The problem of cracking and spalling of concrete due to the corrosion of steel inside is greatly influenced by the diffusion of environment into the concrete. Diffusion of chlorides in this regard is known to enhance the corrosion by lowering the resistivity of concrete. While the principles of the diffusion process and effects are well understood from the investigations reported earlier it is to be recognised that comprehensive studies on well designed concretes of different grades are scanty, probably due to the fact that these require considerably long exposure periods to achieve any significant results. In the present paper the results of three different concretes exposed to the sea water, both in the laboratory and field, have been presented. The effect of mixing and curing waters on the diffusion characteristics of these concretes were also discussed.

Keywords : Diffusion, Concrete, Chloride Concentration, Ocean Environment, Deterioration, Corrosion of steel.

Dr. K. Ganesh Babu is presently an Associate Professor at the Ocean Engineering Centre of Indian Institute of Technology, Madras. He works in the areas of structures and materials and is also in-charge of the Materials Laboratory. He was earlier a Scientist at the Structural Engineering Research Centre, Madras where he worked primarily in the areas of Polymers in Concrete, Fibre Reinforced Concrete, Ferrocement etc. Dr. Ganesh Babu holds a Doctorate and Masters Degree in Structural Engineering from IIT, Madras.

K. Venkateswara Rao was a former Doctoral student at the Ocean Engineering Centre of IIT, Madras. He is primarily interested in the area of deterioration of concrete in Marine Environment.

Concrete 2000. Edited by Ravindra K. Dhir and M. Roderick Jones.
© 1993 Published by E & FN Spon. ISBN 0 419 18120 2.

INTRODUCTION

The diffusion of salts through concrete affects the long term behaviour in terms of both the deterioration of concrete and the corrosion of steel in concrete, depending on the chemicals diffusing and the characteristics of the concrete. In this context the diffusion of chlorides and sulphates, in general, assume greater significance in the assessment of the performance of concrete. Chlorides generally influence the resistivity of concrete, resulting in a higher corrosion of the embedded reinforcement while the sulphates on the other hand promote the deterioration of concrete itself, which in turn affects the corrosion of steel inside.

Investigations earlier mainly concentrated on the diffusion of chlorides into concrete and have adopted either natural or forced diffusion techniques. In the assessments through natural diffusion, specimens are exposed to a specific environment in the laboratory or field for reasonably long periods to ensure measurable levels of diffusion. Mangat et al [1,2] were one of the earliest to report a systematic study of the chloride diffusion in steel fibre reinforced concrete. In the forced diffusion studies an electric field is applied to force the chloride ions to migrate through concrete and the diffusion is assessed by the amount of charge passing through the cell [3]. Essentially to be brief it was not felt necessary to review all the works that are reported so far on the diffusion characteristics of concrete composites. However, one important factor that should be noted is that the natural diffusion process takes a considerably long period of time and thus many have adopted either electrolytic accelerated [3] or thin section techniques [4] for the evaluation. While these accelerated methods are reasonably fast and adequate for a comparative assessment of the diffusion characteristics of different concretes in the laboratory, it is still felt by many that the natural diffusion in undisturbed samples only can give a clear understanding of the actual diffusion process. There is a lot that can be said on both sides and without going further into these, the present paper reports the results of an investigation on the chloride diffusion characteristics of a few concretes exposed to marine environment in the laboratory and field. The parameters investigated were mainly the concrete strength, the mixing and curing waters apart from the exposure conditions.

MATERIALS AND METHODS

The concretes in the present study were all made using ordinary portland cement. The coarse aggregate used was made up of well graded crushed granite stone chips of maximum size 20 mm, so that the problems related to the aggregate, influencing the diffusion characteristics like alkali aggregate reactivity, aggregate crushing strength, porosity, absorption etc. are avoided completely. Similarly, the fine aggregate used was river sand without any organic impurities and having a fineness modulus of 2.8. The water used for mixing was either tap water or the sea water collected from the shore line at Madras. The sea water essentially consisted of 33.98 ppm dissolved solids with the chlorides and sulphates being 19.30 ppm and 2.39 ppm respectively. The details of mix proportions, mixing and curing waters are explained in Table 1. The table also presents the characteristics of concrete like the slump and compressive strength of the concretes used in the present investigation.

Three mixes with water cement ratios ranging from 0.38 to 0.58 were chosen. Standard 15 cm cubes were used for the assessment of diffusion while the strength characteristics were based on the results obtained from 10 cm cubes. In each of these concretes the mixing and curing conditions have been varied resulting in the three different types - fresh water mixed, fresh water cured (FF); fresh water mixed, sea water cured (FS) and sea water mixed, sea water cured (SS). The curing period was 28 days of immersion in any specific environment like fresh water or sea water. After this period of curing all the specimens were exposed to sea water (immersion) either in the laboratory or in field at Madras Port. The field location was so chosen such that there is no problem of oil floating in the location and there is always fresh sea water available due to the tidal changes.

EXPERIMENTAL INVESTIGATIONS

The diffusion characteristics of these concretes were established by assessing the total chlorides in the concrete specimen at different depths. The samples are obtained by crushing a reasonably large amount of concrete at the various depths from the centre portion of the cube so that the diffusion from the other sides will not affect these values. Samples from the top 1 - 2 mm at the centre of the cube were taken for assessing the surface chloride concentration (C_0) in all concretes. The values of the chloride content at the other depths were calculated by assessing the chloride content in the powdered samples taken from 0 - 25 mm, 25 - 50 mm and 50 - 75 mm. This was essential because of the fact that trial studies indicated some scatter depending on the location and also the calculation of the chloride content as a percentage of cement requires the sample to be representative of the concrete including the aggregates. These values which are the average of the chloride concentrations over the depth studied were seen to be agreeing reasonably well with those at the midlocations of the particular depths. The chloride concentrations in the samples were assessed by using the standard silver nitrate titration method [5]. The procedure adopted for chemical analysis was similar to that reported by Mangat et al [1,2].

RESULTS AND DISCUSSIONS

The mix proportions and the strength characteristics of the concretes were presented in Table 1. The variations of the concentration of chloride with depth for the three different concretes with the different mixing and curing waters were presented in Figs.1 and 2. Fig.1 presents the chloride concentration profiles with depth for all the concretes (fresh water mixed, fresh water cured; fresh water mixed sea water cured

Table 1. Mix proportions and characteristics of concretes investigated

S. No.	Conc.*		w/c ratio	Mix & Curing water	Cement content (kg/m³)	Slump (mm)	Comp.str. (MPa) 28d	360d	Diffusion Constants C_o (%Cem.)	D_c (×10cm/sec)
1.	S2	lab	0.58	FF	320	25	25.9	27.7	0.90	19.13
		field						33.7	0.96	11.77
2.		lab		FS			26.1	29.1	0.92	25.22
		field						34.6	0.96	13.69
3.		lab		SS			25.3	30.0	0.96	22.22
		field						33.2	0.92	21.28
4.	S3	lab	0.45	FF	413	19	32.5	41.3	0.76	30.31
		field						41.2	0.75	18.78
5.		lab		FS			30.5	40.7	0.81	22.53
		field						39.8	0.74	21.11
6.		lab		SS			33.0	39.0	0.74	44.49
		field						39.9	0.74	24.56
7.	S4	lab	0.38	FF	480	11	40.3	55.0	0.67	22.92
		field						54.4	0.65	20.12
8.		lab		FS			41.7	54.3	0.73	24.96
		field						52.8	0.64	21.99
9.		lab		SS			41.2	54.2	0.66	38.53
		field						53.8	0.69	25.00

* Concrete Mix Proportions:- S2 - 1:1.94:3.68; S3 - 1:1.33:2.84; S4 - 1:0.72:2.78.

and sea water mixed sea water cured) immersed in sea water in the laboratory for a period of 12 months after the 28 day curing period. In these experiments care was taken to see that the sea water characteristics do not get altered, due to evaporation or the concrete cured inside, by changing the same at intervals of 15 days in the initial periods and 30 days in the later periods. Fig.2 presents the corresponding chloride concentration profiles with depth for the above concretes after 12 months immersion in field at the Madras Harbour.

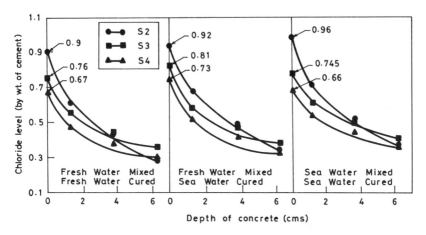

Figure 1 Chloride concentration profiles in concretes (lab - 12 months)

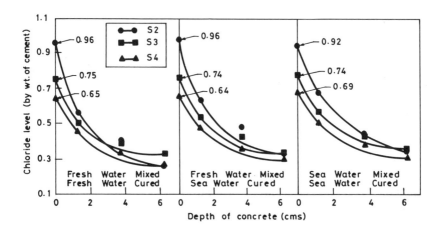

Figure 2 Chloride concentration profiles in concretes (field - 12 months)

This data was used to calculate the chloride diffusion coefficients (D_c) using the Fick's second law for diffusion and the Crank's solution [6]. However, this methodology assumes that the concrete is a porous medium but does not recognise the reactive nature of the same which is also important for a total understanding of diffusion in concrete [7]. The values of the chloride concentration at the surface (C_0) and the chloride diffusion coefficient (D_c) evaluated were also presented in Table 1 as diffusion constants.

The compressive strength values at the end of one year show a higher gain in strength in field environment for the lower strength concrete (S2) with higher water cement ratio. The corresponding age factors for this concrete were in the range of 1.3 for specimens exposed in field, while for the specimens exposed in the laboratory they were about 1.1. However, for the higher strength concretes (S3 & S4) with water cement ratios below 0.45 there was no significant change in the age factors for specimens under the different exposures of field or laboratory and were around 1.3.

The surface chloride concentration for any particular concrete appeared to be the same irrespective of mixing and curing waters at the end of the 12 months exposure period. With the cement contents (which finally would represent the reactive compounds in the system) being 320, 413 and 480 kg/m^3 for the three different concretes, the chloride concentrations on the surface (irrespective of the mixing and curing waters) were around 0.94, 0.76 and 0.67 percent by weight of cement respectively. From this it is apparent that for any concrete the absolute value of the surface chloride concentrations after the 12 months exposure period were nearly the same (about 3 kg/m^3 in all the concretes studied). However, there were significant variations in the diffusion coefficients of the different concretes, with a clear trend not emerging from the present study. Also, one can see that the D_c values of concretes exposed in field were, in general, lower than those for concretes in the laboratory but exposed to the same sea water and were ranging between 55 - 95% of the laboratory values. Furthermore, overall one can see that the D_c values increased due to the use of sea water for curing and more so for concretes with sea water for mixing as well as curing. This can be understood considering the higher porosity at lower ages in case of curing in sea water and the already available chlorides in concretes with sea water for mixing. It is also known that the chlorides in sea water act as accelerators and this could have also influenced the diffusion characteristics reported. Also, there appears to be a marginal increase in the diffusion coefficients with an increase in the grade of concrete.

One should also note that apart from the diffusion coefficients (D_c) a perfect understanding of the surface chloride concentrations (C_0) is essential for evaluating the chloride levels at the different depths, required for specifying the cover over steel from corrosion considerations.

However, it is obvious from this study that much more information is needed for a definite understanding of the diffusion characteristics of concrete, particularly because of the reactive system in which the diffusion is taking place.

CONCLUSIONS

The paper describes the results of an experimental investigation on three concretes with variations in mixing and curing waters. The concrete strengths and the diffusion characteristics of these were evaluated after 12 months submergence in sea water at both the laboratory and field. The primary conclusions may be listed as follows.

1. The age factors for lower grade concretes were higher for the specimens exposed in field compared to the specimens exposed in the laboratory. However, for the two higher grades (with water cement ratios below 0.45) there appeared to be no significant variations in the age factors due to the different exposures.

2. The surface chloride concentrations decreased with an increase in the grade of concrete. Furthermore, in the same grade the variations in mixing and curing waters did not affect the surface chloride concentrations. Also, it is apparent that for all the concretes studied the absolute value of the surface chloride concentrations after the 12 months exposure period were nearly the same (about 3 kg/m^3).

3. The diffusion coefficients evaluated did not give a very clear picture, but for the fact that increased chloride levels incorporated into the concrete by curing in or mixing with sea water showed an increasing trend in the diffusion coefficients. Also, there appears to be a marginal increase in the diffusion coefficients with an increase in the grade of concrete. Furthermore, in general, the diffusion coefficients of concretes exposed in field were lower than those for concretes in the laboratory.

REFERENCES

1. MANGAT, PS AND GURUSAMY, K. Chloride Diffusion in Steel Fibre Reinforced Marine Concrete. Cem. and Concr. Res., Vol.17, 1987, pp.385-396.

2. MANGAT, PS AND GURUSAMY, K. Chloride Diffusion in Steel Fibre Reinforced Concrete Containing PFA. Cem. and Concr. Res., Vol.17, 1987, pp.640-650.

3. WHITING, D. In Situ Measurement of the Permeability of Concrete to Chloride Ions. ACI SP-82, American Concrete Institute, Detroit, 1984, pp.501-524.

4. DHIR, RK, JONES, MR, AHMED, HEH AND SENEVIRATNE, AGM. Rapid Estimation of Chloride Diffusion Coefficient in Concrete. Mag. Concr. Res. 1990, Vol.42, No.152, Sept., pp.177-185.

5. VOGEL, IA. A Textbook of Quantitative Inorganic analysis. Longmans, London, 1961.

6. CRANK, J. The Mathematics of diffusion. Oxford press, London, 1975.

7. ACI COMMITTEE 222. Corrosion of Metals in Concrete. (ACI 222R-85), American Concrete Institute, Detroit, 1985, p.32.

CHLORIDE BINDING AND CORROSION
IN SILICA FUME CONCRETE

A Y Talib

Bahrain Centre for Studies and Research

Bahrain

Rasheeduzzafar

A S Al-Gahtani

King Fahd University of Petroleum and Minerals

Saudia Arabia

ABSTRACT. Accelerated corrosion tests and corrosion rates have been carried out on silica fume blended cement concrete. Pore solution extraction studies carried out on plain and silica fume cement pastes, however, show a significantly higher Cl^-/OH^- ratio for silica fume blended cement pastes in comparison to plain cement pates. In view of this increased aggressivity of the pore solution the improved resisting characteristics of silica fume in terms of corrosion initiation time should be attributed to an interplay of several factors in determining corrosion resistance of cementitious materials. These factors are discussed in this paper in an attempt to develop a better understanding of the complex corrosion mechanism in blended cement.

Keywords: Blended Cements, Corrosion, Durability, Reinforced Concrete, **Silica fume (SF)**.

Abdulla Y. Talib, is a Research Engineer, Building Research Projects, Bahrain Center for Studies and Research, Bahrain. His research interests are in the area of durability of concrete structures. He is an associate member of ACI committee 234, Silica Fume in Concrete.

Rasheeduzzafar, is Professor of Structural Engineering, King Fahd University of Petroleum and Minerals, Dhahran, Saudi Arabia. His research interests are in the area of durability, strength, and behavior of concrete structures. He is a member of ACI Committee 201, Durability of Concrete.

A. S. Al-Gahtani, is Assistant Professor of Structural Engineering, King Fahd University of Petroleum and Minerals. His research interests are in the area of durability of concrete structures and structural design optimization.

Concrete 2000. Edited by Ravindra K. Dhir and M. Roderick Jones.
© 1993 Published by E & FN Spon. ISBN 0 419 18120 2.

INTRODUCTION

Chloride-based corrosion of reinforcement in concrete structures currently constitutes a major concrete durability problem all over the world. Premature corrosion deterioration of concrete structures in the Middle East, bridge deck deterioration due to deicing salts in cold countries, corrosion in coastal marine structures due to sea water and salt spray, and reinforcement corrosion in a large number of structures where chloride-based accelerators have been used, probably constitutes the largest group of concrete structures undergoing deterioration due to a single causal factor.

Chloride has been identified as a unique destroyer of the passivating ferric oxide film around reinforcement which effectively inhibits corrosion in a chloride-free uncarbonated concrete. Chlorides enter concrete either as primary (internal) chlorides at the time of mixing through constituent materials or as secondary (external) chlorides which penetrate concrete subsequently during the service life of structures from a chloride- bearing environment.

Irrespective of their mode of induction, chlorides usually exist in concrete in two forms: either as chemically combined adsorbed by solid cement hydrates or as free chlorides in the pore solution of concrete.

Chlorides chemically bound by cement hydrates are noncorrosive and do not constitute corrosion risk. It is the concentration of free chlorides in the liquid phase of concrete which causes depassivation of steel and its subsequent corrosion. Also, corrosion risk is not measured by the concentration of pore water free chlorides alone; it is measured by a composite parameter Cl^-/OH^- ratio. Whereas Hausmann (1) has recommended a depassivation Cl^-/OH^- threshold value of 0.6 in concrete simulated artificial calcium hydroxide solution of PH = 12.5, more recently Diamond (2), on the basis of Gouda's (3) work has proposed a Cl^-/OH^- threshold value of 0.3 due to the fact that in actual concrete pore solution, the PH is significantly higher than 12.5 and varies from 13.5 to 13.75.

Blended cements have received considerable attention in recent years due to their significantly superior durability performance in aggressive exposure conditions. Silica fume is regarded as a high potential partial cement replacement admixture which imparts to concrete impermeability, sulfate resistance and immunity against expansion and cracking due to alkali-silica reactivity. However, its role in affecting corrosion risk appears to be significantly more complex due to concomitant interplay of several factors, such as improvement in denseness of the physical matrix, chloride binding and the reduction in the alkalinity of the pore solution. In its turn, a reduction in the alkalinity affects the corrosion situation in two conflicting ways: firstly, adversely, by increasing the corrosion risk through a lowering of the OH^- ion concentration, and secondly, beneficially by reduction corrosion risk by causing an increase in the chloride binding capacity in an environment of lowered alkalinity (4).

This paper evaluates the corrosion resistance performance of silica fume blended cement for corrosion situations where primary and secondary chlorides contaminate the concrete. Firstly, pore pressure extrusion technique has been used to evaluate the effect of different levels (5 to 25 %) of cement replacements by silica fume on chloride binding, alkalinity, and corrosion risk when primary chlorides are present in concrete. Secondly, a half cell automatic data acquisition system has been used to develop data on the important practical aspect of evaluating the
effect of different levels of silica fume blending on the corrosion initiation time when concrete is exposed to external chlorides.

EXPERIMENTAL PROGRAM

Materials and Specimen Preparation

ASTM type I cement having Bogue potential C_3A content of 7.5% was used in preparing mortars and concrete specimens. 5, 10, 15, 20, and 25 % by weight silica fume was used on a cement replacement basis to formulate blended cements. Table 1 shows the chemical compositions of the parent cement and silica fume.

For pore solution extrusion tests, cement paste specimens were prepared with a constant water/cement ratio of 0.6 . Four levels of chloride, 0.3, 0.4, 0.6, and 1.2 % by weight of cementitious material, were inducted through initially deionized mix water using sodium chloride source. After mixing in a Hobart mixer using the mixing procedure specified in ASTM C305, the specimens were cast in 49 mm x 75 mm cylindrical impermeable plastic molds, sealed and stored at 20 ∓ 2 ° C.

For the accelerated corrosion testing program, concrete specimens were made with the same parent plain cement (C_3A:7.5%) and the same levels of cement replacement by silica fume (5, 10, 15, 20, 25) as used in the pore solution extrusion tests. The coarse aggregate was 3/8 in (9.5 mm) maximum size crushed limestone, having a bulk specific gravity 2.42 and average absorption 3.8%. The fine aggregate was beach sand of specific gravity 2.7 and average absorption 0.23%. A coarse to fine aggregate ratio of 2.0 by weight was adopted. All mixes were prepared with water/cementitious material ratio of 0.5 and a cement content of 600 lb\cu.yd. After casting, the specimens were covered with wet burlap for one day, then demolded and cured in potable water for 27 days.

Pore Solution Expression and Analysis

After 90 days of curing in sealed containers, specimens were demolded and immediately placed in a 49 mm x 75 mm cylindrical pore solution expression device similar to that described by Longuet et al (5) and Barneyback and Diamond (6). Pressure was gradually increased to 350 MPa (49,000 psi), where it was sustained till a small quantity (3 to 6 ml) of pore fluid was recovered by hypodermic syringe through
the fluid drain located at the base of pore solution expression vessel. The pore fluid was transferred to sealed plastic vials for analysis.

Chloride concentrations in the pore solution were determined by a micro-processor ion-analyzer in conjunction with a solid-state chloride ion activity double junction reference electrode. OH^- concentrations in the pore solution were determined by direct titration against nitric acid using phenolphthalein indicator.   The PH values of the pore solution were calculated from the measured hydroxyl ion concentrations.
Evaporable water on parallel specimens was determined as the loss of weight per 100 g. of unhydrated cement when the specimens were heated to a constant weight at 105° C.

Accelerated Corrosion Monitoring

The accelerated reinforcement corrosion tests were carried out on 2 x 2 x 12 in (5.08 x 5.08 x 30.48 mm) prisms containing a 1/2 in (12.5 mm) bar embedded centrally. The specimens were partially immersed in 5 % NaCl solution in a tank located in a controlled laboratory environment at 24 ∓ 1 ° C.   The concentration of the sodium chloride was monitored and adjusted each week.   The corrosion activity

was monitored by obtaining half cell potentials on a Hewlett
Packard 3054 DL data acquisition system in conjunction with
a saturated calomel electrode. The threshold potential for
corrosion initiation is taken at -270 millivolts (SCE).
Potentials numerically greater (more negative) than this
value   indicate   that   reinforcing   steel   corrosion   is
occurring.   Each value reported is an average of readings
obtained on three specimens.

Corrosion rate measurements of the reinforcing steel in
concrete   specimens   were   carried   out   using   a   linear
polarization technique.

RESULTS

OH Ion Concentration

Fig.1 shows the effect of increasing cement replacement by
silica fume on OH^- concentrations of different chloride
treatment levels. It is seen that for plain cement as well
as for all chloride levels the OH^- concentrations decrease
sharply with increase in silica fume. For plain cement and
low chloride levels up to 0.3%, a sharp reduction in OH^-
concentrations occur with 5% silica fume, and thereafter
with increasing cement replacement up to 25%, the decrease
in OH^- concentration is relatively gradual. For example for
0.3% chloride level, 5% cement replacement by silica fume
reduces the OH^- concentration from 396 Mm to 117 Mm, and
thereafter for each additional 5% silica fume the OH^-
concentration is decreased in the range of 12 to 35 Mm only.
For chloride levels between 0.3% and 0.6%, 10% silica fume
brings down the OH^- concentration from in excess of 400 Mm
to below 100 Mm and thereafter small reductions are caused
for each 5% increase up to 25%.   For 1.2% chloride content
OH^- concentrations reduction is, however, sharp up to 15%
replacement level, after which further increases in silica
fume only causes marginal reductions in OH^- concentrations.

The PH level, as expected, decreases as the silica fume
percentage increases. For example, for 0.6% Cl^- level, the
PH of the plain cement is 13.65, whereas the PH values for
5, 10, 15, 20, and 25% silica fume decrease to 13.39, 12.95,
12.73, and 12.67 respectively. A similar trend is observed
for other chloride levels included in this study. For the
plain as well as 5 and 10% silica fume blended cements, the
PH values are observed to increase with increasing chloride

levels. When the chloride level was increased from 0.3 to
1.2%, the PH of plain cement increased from 13.6 to 13.72,
whereas the PH values of 5 and 10% silica fume replacement
cements increased from 13.07 to 13.52 and from 12.91 to
13.17 respectively. For blended cements with 15, 20, and
25% silica fume, the PH values generally increase with the
chloride level up to 0.6%, but decrease when chloride level
is increased to 1.2%.

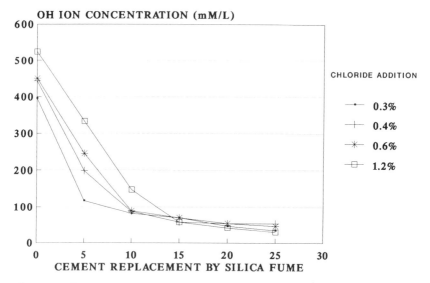

Fig.1 OH⁻ Ion Concentrations in Pore Solutions
of Plain and Silica Fume Blended Cements.

Chloride Ion Concentrations

The concentration of free chloride ions in the pore solution
and the proportion of free chlorides in relation to the
total chlorides, estimated on the basis of evaporable water,
are shown in Table 2. The general pattern of results may be
illustrated by reviewing the data for 0.6% chloride level.
Plain cement has the highest chloride ion concentration; the
concentration decreases as the silica fume percentage
increases up to 10 and 15% corresponding to chloride levels
of 0.3% to 0.6%, and 1.2% respectively. With further
increase in cement replacement by silica fume, the chloride
concentration, however, increases. The unbound chloride
(free chloride) ions in the pore solution, Fig.2, follow a
similar trend as observed for chloride ion concentrations
with respect to silica fume percentages and chloride levels.

Table.1 Chemical Composition of Cement and Silica Fume

Oxides Composition	S_iO_2	Al_2O_3	Fe_2O_3	CaO	MgO	SO_3	K_2O	C	Na_2O
Silica Fume	92.5	0.72	0.96	0.48	1.78		1.84	1.12	0.5
Cement Type I	21.3	5.1	3.56	64.5	2.1	1.89	0.34		0.29
Phase Composition of Cement, % By Weight						C_3S	C_2S	C_3A	C_4AF
						55.9	19.0	7.5	10.83

Table.2 Pore Solution Composition of Plain and Silica Fume Pastes

Cement replaced by silica Fume (% by weight)	CL^- Addition (% by weight of cementitous Material)	Pore Solution Composition						
		CL^- mM/L	OH– mM/L	pH	CL^-/OH^-	CL^- Concentrations in Pore Solution (% of CL^- Concentration in Mix Water)	Evaporable water (% by weight of Cementitous material)	Unbound CL^- (% by weight of CL-Addition)
0	0.3	15	396	13.60	0.04	10.6	36.8	6.52
5	0.3	8.4	117	13.07	0.07	5.9	31.3	3.10
10	0.3	5.6	82	12.91	0.07	4.0	37.4	2.48
15	0.3	7.3	58	12.85	0.13	5.2	35.6	3.07
20	0.3	9.5	47	12.67	0.20	6.8	36.4	4.10
25	0.3	15.2	35	12.54	0.44	10.8	34.7	6.25
0	0.4	26.5	443	13.65	0.06	14.1	38.9	9.16
5	0.4	16.4	198	13.30	0.08	8.7	42.6	6.21
10	0.4	9.6	88	12.85	0.11	5.1	40.5	3.46
15	0.4	12.4	58	12.76	0.21	6.6	42.0	4.62
20	0.4	20.1	54	12.73	0.37	10.7	43.7	7.80
25	0.4	24.6	54	12.73	0.46	13.1	48.5	10.57
0	0.6	67.6	450	13.65	0.15	24.0	40.0	15.98
5	0.6	38.0	245	13.39	0.16	13.5	40.6	7.93
10	0.6	24.0	89	12.95	0.27	8.5	42.1	5.97
15	0.6	27.3	70	12.85	0.39	9.7	41.9	6.76
20	0.6	38.0	54	12.73	0.70	13.5	44.0	9.96
25	0.6	50.6	54	12.67	0.94	18.0	43.6	13.04
0	1.2	286.3	524	13.72	0.55	50.1	37.3	31.6
5	1.2	211.2	333	13.52	0.63	37.5	37.8	23.6
10	1.2	163.0	147	13.17	1.11	28.9	39.1	18.9
15	1.2	136.3	70	12.76	1.95	24.2	38.2	15.4
20	1.2	148.4	56	12.62	2.65	26.3	39.8	17.5
25	1.2	175.0	54	12.48	3.24	31.1	40.4	21.1

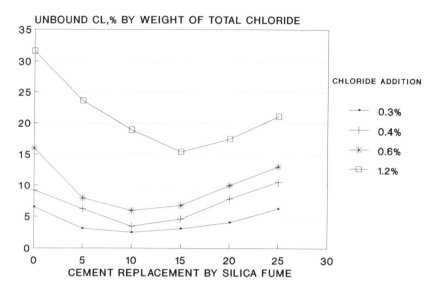

Fig.2 Chloride Remaining Unbound in Pore Solutions Expressed From Plain and Silica Fume Blended Cements.

Cl^-/OH^- Ratios in pore Solution

The Cl^-/OH^- ratios are shown in Table 2, and Fig.3. The presentation of Fig.3 shows that, as silica fume percentage increases, the Cl^-/OH^- ratio also increases. For 10 and 20% silica fume blending and 1.2% chloride level, the Cl^-/OH^- ratios increase respectively 2 and 11 fold compared to Cl^-/OH^- ratio for the plain cement. The trend remains the same for all other chloride levels.

Corrosion of Reinforcing Steel

Half cell potential records for the accelerated corrosion monitoring reinforced concrete specimens are shown in Fig. 4. Fig.5 shows the relationship between time to initiation of corrosion and the percentage of silica fume used for blending. It is seen that the silica fume blended cement concrete performed better than the plain cement concrete in terms of corrosion initiation time. The performance improved with increase in cement replacement by silica fume. A 25% silica fume blended cement concrete performed 2.2 times better than the plain cement.

Corrosion rates for the 1/2 in (12.5mm) reinforcing bar in plain and 5 to 20% silica fume blended cement concretes are

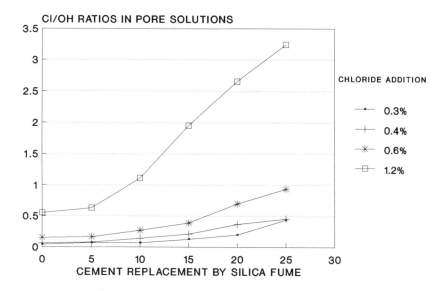

Fig.3   Cl/OH Ratios in Pore Solutions Expressed
From Plain and Silica Fume Blended Cement Pastes.

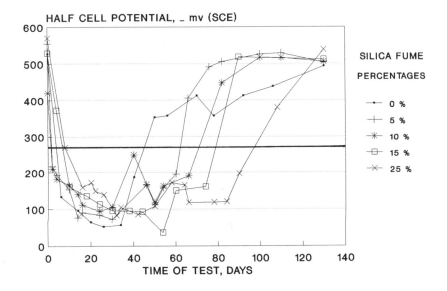

Fig.4 Potential Measurement Record Showing The Effect
of Silica Fume Cement on Corrosion of Reinforcing Steel

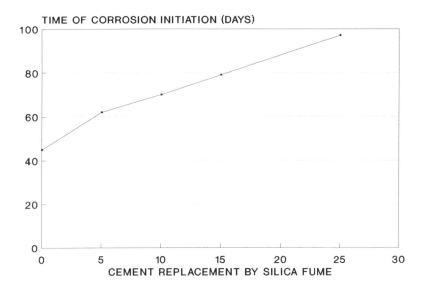

Fig.5 Corrosion Resistance Performance of Plain
and Silica Fume Blended Cements in Term of
Corrosion Initiation Time.

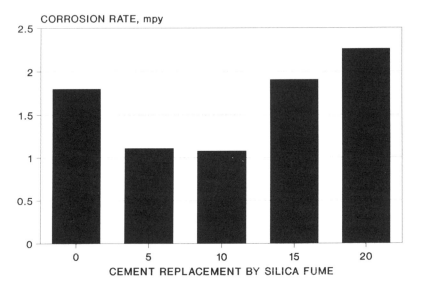

Fig.6 Corrosion Rate of Reinforcing Steel
in Plain and Silica Fume Blended Concrete.

shown in Fig.6. The corrosion rates were measured after 350 days of immersion in 5% NaCl solution, after the half cell potentials had indicated corrosion initiation. The corrosion rate data indicate that the 5 and 10% silica fume blended cement concrete performed better than the plain cement concrete in terms of corrosion rate. However, for 15 and 20% silica fume blended cement concretes the corrosion rates were higher than the plain cement as well as 5% and 10% silica fume blending.

DISCUSSION

The alkalinity of the concrete pore solution is contributed by the sodium cation of the chloride source, alkalies in cement, and the alkaline cement hydrates. The OH^- ion concentration in the pore fluid for various chloride contents and different levels of silica fume blending are therefore affected by the sodium cation content and the pozzolonic reaction between silica fume and calcium hydroxide. As the chloride content decreases, OH^- concentrations are also generally lowered. Also, as silica fume blending increases up to a certain level, pozzolanic reaction causes a sharp reduction in OH^- ion concentration. However, it appears 10% to 15% silica fume reduces OH–concentration 4 to 5 fold, well below 100 ml,
and is adequate for the consumption of $Ca(OH)_2$ available for reaction. Increases in silica fume blending to 20% and 25% do not further reduce OH^- ion concentrations significantly.

Free chloride ion concentrations in the pore solution show a complex behavior which appears to be the result of a concomitant interplay of several factors affecting chloride binding with cement hydrates, specially the hydrates of tricalcium aluminate. Rasheeduzzafar et.al and others (7,8) have observed an inhibiting effect of increased OH^- concentration on chloride binding. A marked reduction in OH^- concentrations and PH values observed up to 10 to 15% silica fume blending, may have facilitated chloride binding resulting in a reduction of chloride concentration up to 10 to 15% silica fume addition, the exact percentage depending on chloride treatment level. However, no significant reduction in OH^- concentrations and PH values are obtainable beyond 10 to 15% silica fume addition thereby eliminating this additional factor in chloride binding. Beyond this level, probably what dominates is the increased solubility or decomposition of Friedel's salt ($3CaO\ Al_2O_3\ Cacl_2.10\ H_2O$) (9), and possibly its ferrite analogue ($3CaO\ Fe_2O_3\ Cacl_2.10\ H_2O$) at reduced PH levels of the pore solution. These two compounds are the products of C_3A hydration and are known for binding chlorides. Increased solubility and decomposition of these compounds would release chloride ions into the pore solution raising their level of concentration.

A consistent increase in the Cl^-/OH^- ratios for all levels of cement replacement by silica fume and for all chloride contents indicate a predominant effect of marked reduction in OH^- concentrations with silica fume addition. This effect is particularly operative up to 10 to 15% silica fume blending. With increase in silica fume addition, an increase in free chloride ion concentrations in the pore solution provide additional support in enhancing Cl^-/OH^- ratios and hence in increasing the corrosion aggressivity of the internal environment of silica fume blended cement concrete.

Corrosion initiation time in corrosion situations involving external chlorides is clearly affected by the speed of chloride ion penetration to the steel-concrete interface. Silica fume addition is known to significantly increase denseness of cement matrix and its impermeability.

As is clearly indicated by the results of accelerated corrosion tests, silica fume blended cement concrete, therefore, provides a significantly better corrosion protection in situations where external chlorides cause corrosion by penetration into the concrete matrix.

Once corrosion is initiated, its propagation is affected by several concomitant factors. Diffusion of oxygen at steel-concrete interface, electrical resistivity of concrete, and the aggressivity of the internal environment measured by Cl^-/OH^- ratio are the relatively more important parameters affecting corrosion rate. It appears that up to 10% silica fume addition, the beneficial effect attributed to a densification of cement matrix dominates over increased corrosion aggressivity of the pore solution. However, with increase in silica fume addition to 15 and 20%, the resulting sharp increase in Cl^-/OH^- ratio more significantly affects corrosion propagation, causing a 25% increase in corrosion rates.

CONCLUSIONS

1. 10 to 15% silica fume blending causes a steep reduction in the OH^- ion concentration of the pore solution in both chloride-free and chloride-bearing cement pastes. Further increase in silica fume addition causes marginal reductions in OH^- ion concentration.

2. 15% cement replacement by silica fume brings down the PH for all chloride levels from an average value of 13.65 to 12.80. With 25% silica fume

replacement in 1.2% chloride treatment paste, the PH decreases below the equilibrium PH of saturated $Ca(OH)_2$ solution (12.5).

3. Free chloride concentration in the pore solution decreases up to 10 to 15% silica fume addition, but increases for 20 and 25% silica fume, although for these silica fume blended cements free chlorides are below the concentration level of plain cement. This behavior is attributable to an interactive effect of increased chloride binding and increased dissolution and decomposition of Friedel's salt in low PH environment.

4. Silica fume addition results in significantly enhanced corrosion aggressivity of the pore solution as measured by the Cl^-/OH^- ratio. For 1.2% chloride level, 10 and 20% silica fume blending raises Cl^-/OH^- ratios by 2 and 11 times the value obtainable for plain cement.

5. Accelerated corrosion monitoring data indicate a significantly superior corrosion protection of reinforcing steel against external chloride induced corrosion. A 20% silica fume blended cement concrete performed two times better than plain cement concrete in terms of time to initiation of corrosion.

6. Once the corrosion is initiated, corrosion propagation is affected by an interplay of several concomitant factors. The corrosion rates are lowered compared to plain cement concrete for 5 and 10% silica fume blended cement concretes. However, corrosion rate increases by 25% when silica fume addition is enhanced to 15, or 20%.

ACKNOWLEDGMENT

The authors gratefully acknowledge the support provided for this research by the Department of Civil Engineering, King Fahd University of Petroleum and Minerals, Dhahran, Saudi Arabia. The authors also wish to thank Mukaram Khan, Research Engineer, for his helpful assistance in carrying out the experimental studies.

REFERENCES

1. Hausamnn, D.A., Materials Protection, Vol.6, No.19, Nov. 1967, pp 19-23.
2. Diamond, S.E., Cement, Concrete and Aggregates, CCAGDP, Vol.8, No.2, Winter 1986, pp. 97-102.
3. Gouda, V. K., British Corrosion Journal, V.5, Sept. 1970, pp. 198-203.
4. Rasheeduzzafar, Hussain, and Saadoun., ACI Materials Journal, Vol.89, No.1, January-February, 1992, pp 3-12.
5. Longuet,P., Burglen, L. and Zelwer, A., Revue des Materiaux et Construction de Travaux Publics, 676,1973, pp. 35-41.
6. Barneyback, R.S.Jr. and Diamond, S. Cement and Concrete Research, Vol.11, No.2, 1981, pp.279-285.
7. Rasheeduzzafar., ACI Materials Journal, Vol.89, No.6, November-December, 1992.
8. Tritthart, J., Cement and Concrete Research, Vol.19. No.5, 1989, pp. 683-691.
9. Page, C.L. and Vennesland, O., Materiaux et Constructions (RILEM), Vol.16, No.91, 1983, pp. 19-25.

REINFORCED CONCRETE SHELLS
OF INTRICATE DESIGN CONFIGURATION

A S Zhiv

B Akimov

O Mubarak

M Al-Nadjar

H Akel

Vladimir Polytechnical Institute

Russia

ABSTRACT. The paper presents an application of the finite element method of evaluation of the stressed-and-strained state of reinforced concrete shells of intricate design configuration. Computation results using a unified series computer are compared to experimental data. Reinforced concrete shells of intricate configuration have been designed for construction in the city of Vladimir and in Sudan.

Keywords: Shell, Transfer surface, Continium systems, Node points displacements, Moment and non-moment theory, Digitization.

A.S.Zhiv is Doctor of Technical Sciences, Professor at Vladimir Polytechnical Institute, Russia. He specialises in the field of experimental investigation and application of spatial structures under static and dynamic load. The structures built according to his designs over the last 20 years have proved to be highly efficient.

V.B.Akimov is Candidate of Technical Sciences, he specialises in computer-based design of shells.

O.Mubarak, M.Al.Nadjar and H.Akel are post-graduates at Vladimir Polytechnical Institute.

Concrete 2000. Edited by Ravindra K. Dhir and M. Roderick Jones.
© 1993 Published by E & FN Spon. ISBN 0 419 18120 2.

INTRODUCTION

Spatial structures have found wide application in current construction practice in Russia. They have been realized in square and rectangular plan reinforced concrete shells. The most widely used are slightly bent reinforced concrete shells of positive Gaussian curvature. In such shells reinforced concrete can be used more advantageously than prestressed concrete. The structures spans may exceed 100 metres. In the case of large spans and high loads the stresses developing in shell sections are relatively small.

Transfer or torsion surfaces are taken as the starting point for the analysis of such structures. The design analysis is done according to the moment theory developed by V.Z.Vlasov [1] . Different Codes and Specifications governing the design procedures in Russia allow designers to find forces and displacements in basic sections comparatively quickly. This theory has been refined at present when specifying particular rigidity of supporting contour structures and actual boundary conditions, and has been successfully used in computations for dynamic, wind and seismic loads.

However, it has been found that when some changes are introduced into the shell design, for example, non-traditional plan or some additional structural elements influencing the strained state of the shell the theory developed by V.Z.Vlasov for the analysis of such structures appears to be unsuitable. This has been proved by the design experience in Moscow (Olympic projects) and in the city of Vladimir (our latest designs).

The finite element method offers great opportunities for designers and it has been used on a large scale in current practice. The analysis involves the design model allowing for application of classical methods of structural mechanics for load-bearing rod systems. It has become evident that the method can be effectively implemented in the evaluation of intricate design spatial systems of optional configuration.

When designing continium two-dimensional structures the region under investigation is divided by the imaginary digitization grid into a certain number of interdependent in node point finite elements. The generalized displacements of the node points are the basic unknown parameters of the problem under investigation as with the classic displacement method. Once the rigidity matrix of separate elements, based on the principle of possible displacements is computed, followed by the matrix of the whole system, the system of linear algebraic equations for unknown point displacements is solved to calculate the stressed-and-strained state of the whole structure.

Recent Russian experience in the application of the finite element method has resulted in the development of a great number of programs. These programs include sets of finite elements being used for approximation of different designs.

The computer-based design program for a unified series computer (EC-1020) for reinforced concrete structures has been successfully used at Vladimir Polytechnical Institute for a number of years. The following examples illustrate the proposed design method for different spatial structures of intricate design configuration. The results of the investigation are compared to the experimental data.

REINFORCED CONCRETE SHELL OF POSITIVE GAUSSIAN CURVATURE FOR A COVERED SWIMMING POOL IN VLADIMIR

The shell measuring 78x78 is a polyhedron on plan, the surface of which is formed by a system of folded-plate vaults inscribed into the initial toroidal surface. The parametres of the initial surface such as rise and camber of supporting arches have been taken as satisfying radius criteria.

The particular design feature of the shell in comparison with classical designs is that large angular openings are necessitated by architectural considerations to provide entrance to the building.

The structure is assembled with 7sm thick flat ribbed slabs with the span up to 6m and monolithic contour supports. The shell is made of concrete with the strength of 30 N/mm^2.

The construction of the swimming pool shell was preceded by computations and testing on the 1/26 scale model. When designing the model the similarity theory was used 2 . However, as the thickness of the shell could not be modelled from technological considerations the test shell structure measuring 3x3m on plan has been made with the thickness of 10mm and without ribs. Reinforcing of the model has been made in accordance with the design requirements for small-size structures when calculating for load acting in the real shell (5.50 kN/m^2). Concrete strength on the test date was 30.5 N/mm^2 and the test shell structure was reinforced with the tied-wire fabric with the rods diameter of 1.5mm and the design strength of 375 N/m^2.

Fig.1 presents the computed and experimental data for the test model with rigid supporting contour and gives the scheme of cracks formation in the shell. As can be seen, large angular cuts in the shell-slab greatly influence its strained-and-stressed state. Great tensile stresses develop along the supporting contours and at the cut zones. The biaxial compression zone has significantly shortened and shifted into the shell-slab causing cracks.

The experiment called for correction of the working drawings including placement of additional reinforcing bars in the reinforced zones of the shell. The amount and section of reinforcement were calculated as for eccentrically tensioned concrete section.

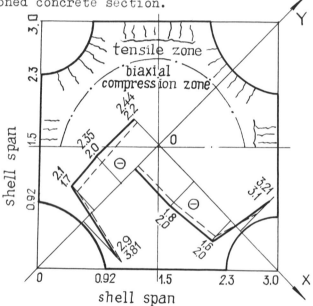

Figure 1 Normal stresses σ_Y (N/mm^2) in different shell sections — computed; --- experimental

CONOIDAL SHELLS FOR SUDAN

Conoidal reinforced concrete shells measuring 18x18 m have been designed and tested on the 1/6 scale model. According to the design the shell is built of precast and cast-in-place concrete, and the model is built of cast in-place reinforced concrete. The shell model was designed according to the similarity theory [2] . From technological considerations the thickness of the shell slab was taken as 12 mm. Reinforcing of the model was made with tied-wire fabric with rods design strength of

375 N/mm2. The test model was calculated for load of
2.5 kN/m2 and the strength of concrete used for making
the model was 45 N/mm2 .

The current approach to the analysis of such shells is
based on the non-moment theory [3] , and the analysis
based on the moment theory has not yet been developed. It
should be noted that experimental investigations of conoidal shells have not been carried out on a large scale
and the design procedure for shells of negative Gaussian
curvature has been assumed the basic one worldwide. The
use of computer helped to solve this problem by the moment theory [1] .

Fig.2 presents the experimental and computed data for the
model at uniformly distributed load of 1.0 KN/m2 applied
to a shell-slab. As can be seen, the design work based on
the non-moment theory does not give acceptable results
and cannot be recommended. The results of experimental
investigations were used in construction practice.

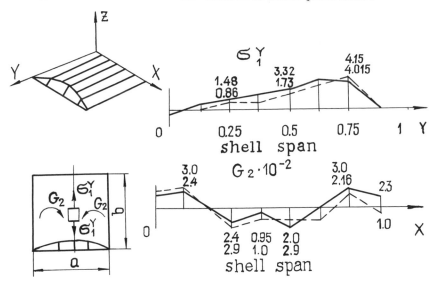

Figure 2   Normal stresses σ_1^Y (N/mm^2) and transverse flexural moments G_2 (kNm) in the middle
sections of the shell ——— computed;   --- experimental

CLOSED SHELL VAULTS

The behaviour of closed shell vaults with flat contour
with the sides of 1.5 m has been under investigation

(Fig.3). The shell-slab was 0.02 m thick, radius of the
middle surface of annular vault elements was 1.1 m and
rise was taken as 0.3 m. Specimen P-2 had a central
opening of 0.70 m in diameter. Specimen P-1 was made continuous. The flat contour was reinforced with rods of
10 mm in diameter (with the yield limit of 390 N/mm2).
The shell-slab was reinforced with fine-structure welded mesh with rods diameter of 1.5 mm. The specimens were
made of fine-graded concrete with axial compression
strength of 20 N/mm2 and initial modulas of elasticity
as 24 N/mm2. Specimen P-1 has been tested for load uniformly distributed over the continuous field and Specimen
P-2 has been tested for load on the border of the central
opening.

According to computations for Specimen P-1 the central
region of the specimen field has experienced biaxial compression in the elastic state and the near-support section of the diagonal has experienced transverse tension.
The compression forces acting along the meridian of the
middle section have been gradually increasing from the
top toward the contour. Forces acting across the meridian
in the near-contour section have resulted in axial tension.

Specimen P-2 has experienced strong diagonal compression
and biaxial tension in the middle section.

The computation and experimental data comparison allowed
to reveal changes in the behaviour of the structure provided with an opening. The tests caused failure of Speciments P-1 and P-2 when two-way reinforcement reached
the yield limit. The space diagram for Specimen P-2 may
appear as spatial rod system where the load from the
opening border is transfered to reinforcing bars of the
supporting contour along four narrow diagonal sections.
Specimen P-2 has been specifically modelled to be tested
for fractures occuring in tent roofs, having been divided
into five discs jointed by the reinforcement of the supporting contour.
The design procedure is based on "Recommended Practice
for the Design of Reinforced Concrete Spatial Structures"
[4] which has been successfully used in Russia over a
number of years.

Thus, for closed shell vaults it is essential that computations be made for angular tensile reinforcement in
diagonal section. Further verification computations for
longitudional compressive forces are reauired for designs
where an opening is provided.

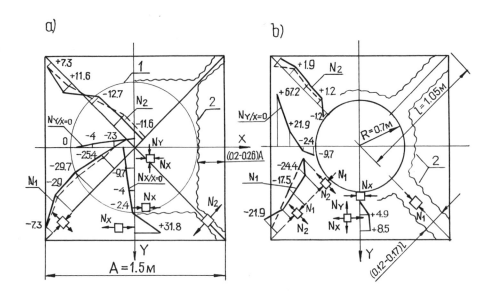

Figure 3   Stressed state of the structure (kN)
a - Shell P-1; b - Shell P-2
1 - boundary of compressed region; 2 - failure scheme
—computed;   --- experimental

CONCLUSION

Computer-aided analysis based on the finite element method using a unified series computer is successfully used
for design computations at Design Institutes in Russia.

Computer-aided design of spatial structures of intricate
design configuration allows to embody reliability in design, and to shorten design time.

The results of the investigation indicate that the finite
element method gives good correlation with experimental
results and is highly efficient in the design practice.

REFERENCES

I. Власов В.З. Избранные труды. Издательство Академии
   наук СССР. Москва 1962, т.I, 528 с.
2. Питлюк Д.А. Расчёт строительных конструкций на основе
   моделирования, Стройиздат, Москва 1965, 152 с.
3. Флюгге В. Статика и динамика оболочек, Стройиздат,
   Москва, 306с.
4. Руководство по проектированию железобетонных прост-
   ранственных покрытий и перекрытий. Стройиздат, Москва,
   1979, 424 с.

SIMPLIFIED ANALYSIS OF PRECAST FRAMED TUBE STRUCTURES FOR TALL BUILDINGS

V N Budiu

Technical University of Cluj-Napoca

Romania

A Pocanschi

University of Stuttgart

Germany

ABSTRACT. Recognizing the generally accepted fact that in framed tube structures, lateral forces are resisted mainly by shear action of the lateral frames and bending action of the tubular structure, a simplified method suitable for computation with desk calculators has been developed. Experimental investigations on precast framed models, in order to evaluate the influence of the precasting on the tubular bending stiffness, were carried out. The results showed a close correlation.

Keywords: Framed tube structure, Tall building, Perforated shearwall structure, Side panel, Normal panel, Equivalent stiffness, Degrees of restraint, Unit degree of restraint, Perfect hinged joint, Reduction coefficient, Monolithism coefficient.

Dr Viorica N Budiu, Reader at the Reinforced Concrete Department of Technical University of Cluj-Napoca, Romania, is a specialist in the domain of Tall Concrete Buildings (Framed Tube Structures and Perforated shearwall Structures) and Thin Shell Structures, member of the Building Engineers Association of Romania, with residence in Cluj-Napoca.

Dr Adrian Pocanschi was Reader at the Reinforced Concrete Department of Technical University of Cluj-Napoca, Romania, in the present he is a researcher at the Department of Structures and Engineering Design of University of Stuttgart, Germany. He is well known in Romania as a specialist in the domain of Thin Shell Structures, Tall Concrete Buildings and Structures in seismic Zones, domains in which he worked. Now he is continuing his research activity in Germany.

Concrete 2000. Edited by Ravindra K. Dhir and M. Roderick Jones.
© 1993 Published by E & FN Spon. ISBN 0 419 18120 2.

INTRODUCTION

The reinforced concrete framed tube structure, widely accepted as economic solutions for tall buildings have proved in recent years their efficiency and economy not only for high rise construction but also as for seismic resistant structures for medium rise buildings.

The problem of calculation of precast framed tube structures under lateral loads is somehow more complex than that of monolithical framed tube because of the influence of the joints on the bending stiffness of the structural members.

A simplified method of analysis that takes into account the real conformation of the framed tube has been developed and presented here. The method requires minimum amount of computing time and gives reasonable assessment of the structural behavior of precast as well as monolithical framed tube structures.

METHOD OF ANALYSIS

It is assumed that the framed tube structure possesses two horizontal axes of symmetry passing through the vertical central axis of the structure, so that the stress system in the side panels, P, are identical and those in the normal panels, N, are equal and opposite, Figs 1 and 2. In accordance with the structural conformation of the frames; i.e., the spandrel-beam-column stiffness ratio and the monolithism coefficient α as defined by Albiges [1] , it appears possible to evaluate the bending stiffness of the side panels, P, taken as "whole structure" by means of the well known relations given in Table 1. In this way the lateral framed panels are replaced by cantilever beams of equivalent stiffness $I_{equiv.}$ For precast structures the equivalent bending stiffness of the side panels may be evaluated using the relations for monolithic structures from Table 1 affected by a reduction coefficient C_r, determined further by experiments. This results a statically indeterminate system composed from lateral beams of equivalent bending stiffness connected at the edges with the frontal frames, N.Cutting the spandrel beams of the frontal frames, the unknown shear forces X_i^k are introduced. Further the force method is used to solve the system.

The unknowns result by solving the matrix equation:

$$[X] \cdot [\delta] = [\triangle] \qquad\qquad (a)$$

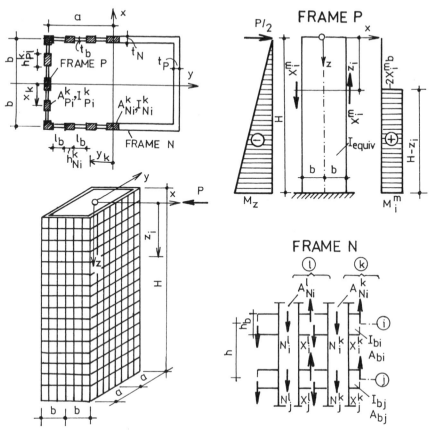

Figure 1 Geometric represen-
          tation of the frame

Figure 2 Equivalent web frame
          and unknown   shear
          forces in flange frame

where:

$[X]$ - redundant vector

$[\delta]$ - matrix of the displacements caused by unit value
          of redundants acting in the statically determi-
          nate system

$[\triangle]$ - vector of displacements produced by the external
          loads in statically determinate system.

Table 2 comprises the expressions of the leading diagonal
displacements of the matrix $[\delta]$ for monolithic structures
and some types of precast structures. The asymmetric terms
δ_{ij} have the following expressions:

Table 1 Equivalent stiffness of the web frame

COUPLED SHEAR WALL	I_{equiv}
1.VERY SLENDER BEAMS	$I_{equiv} = \sum\limits_{k=1}^{m} I_{Pi}^{k}$
2.SLENDER BEAMS	(see below)
3.DEEP BEAMS	$I_{equiv} = \sum\limits_{k=1}^{m} I_{Pi}^{k} + \sum\limits_{k=1}^{m} A_{Pi}^{k} \cdot x_{k}^{2}$

For 2. SLENDER BEAMS:

$$I_{equiv} = \frac{I}{1 + \beta \dfrac{E}{G} \dfrac{I}{H^2 A_{Pi}^k} + \gamma \dfrac{I}{\sum\limits_{k=1}^{m} I_{Pi}^k}}$$

where : $I = \sum\limits_{k=1}^{m} I_{Pi}^{k} + \sum\limits_{k=1}^{m} A_{Pi}^{k} \cdot x_{k}^{2}$ $A_{Pi}^{k} = h_{Pi}^{k} t_P$

$$I_{Pi}^{k} = \frac{(h_{Pi}^{k})^3 \, t_P}{12}$$ $G = 0,4E$

$\beta, \bar{\beta}, \gamma$		TYPE OF LOADING		
		P	P	P
$\bar{\beta} = \beta \dfrac{E}{G}$	$\beta \leftarrow$	5,25	4,70	3,44
	$\bar{\beta} \leftarrow$	12,30	11,10	8,10
γ FOR $\frac{H}{h}$	1	0,734	0,725	0,679
	3	0,266	0,259	0,232
	5	0,129	0,123	0,103
	8	0,061	0,057	0,044
	10	0,041	0,039	0,030
	15	0,020	0,018	0,014
	20	0,011	0,010	0,008

-for unit unknowns acting in the same bay, k :

$$\delta_{ij}^{kk} = \begin{cases} \dfrac{4(H-z_i)}{EA_N} & \text{for current spandrels} \\[2ex] \dfrac{4(H-z_i)}{EA_N} + \dfrac{4b^2(H-z_i)}{EI_{equiv}} & \text{for boundary spandrels} \end{cases}$$

-for unit unknowns acting in different bays: k, l

$$\delta_{ij}^{kl} = \begin{cases} \dfrac{-2(H-z_i)}{EA_N} & \text{for adjacent spandrels} \\[2ex] 0 & \text{for the rest of the spandrels} \end{cases}$$

Table 2 Leading diagonal terms of the matrix $\lfloor \delta \rfloor$

δ_{ii}^{kk} –the displacements corresponding to the curren spandrels , for :

1. CAST IN PLACE STRUCTURE

1.1. Spandrel beam : $I_b = \text{const} \, (h_{bo} = h_{br})$; $\rho_1 = \rho_2 = 1$

$$\delta_{ii}^{kk} = \frac{l_b^3}{6EI_b} + \frac{4(H-z_i)}{EA_N} + \gamma \frac{2l_b}{GA_b} \qquad (1)$$

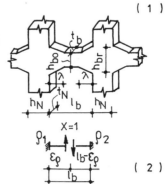

1.2. Spandrel beam : $I_b = \text{var.}\,(h_{bo} \neq h_{br})$; $\rho_1 = \rho_2 = 1$
    expressions : $(4),(5),(6),(7)$, where :

$$\varepsilon_\rho = l_b / 2$$

2. PRECAST STRUCTURE

2.1. Spandrel beam : $I_b = \text{const}\,(h_{bo} = h_{br})$

2.1.1. One end hinged : $\rho_1 = 0$, $\rho_2 = 1$

$$\delta_{ii}^{kk} = \frac{2l_b^3}{3EI_b} + \frac{4(H-z_i)}{EA_N} + \gamma \frac{2l_b}{GA_b} \qquad (2)$$

2.1.2. Partial restrained end : $\rho_1 < 1 , \rho_2 = 1 , \varepsilon_\rho = \dfrac{\rho_1 \cdot l_b}{\rho_1 + 1}$

End partial restraint   : $\rho_1 < 1, \rho_2 \leqslant 1, \varepsilon_\rho = \dfrac{\rho_1 \cdot l_b}{\rho_1 + \rho_2}$

Span field joint   : $\rho_1 = \rho_2 = 1$

$$\delta_{ii}^{kk} = \frac{2\left[\varepsilon_\rho^3 + (l_b - \varepsilon_\rho)^3\right]}{3EI_b} + \frac{4(H-z_i)}{EA_N} + \gamma \frac{2l_b}{GA_b} \qquad (3)$$

2.2. Spandrel beam : $I_b = \text{var.}$ Span field joint

$$\delta_{ii}^{kk} = \frac{2\left[(\varepsilon_\rho - \lambda)^3 + (l_b - \varepsilon_\rho - \lambda)^3\right] + 6\left[\Gamma_\rho + \Gamma'_\rho\right]}{3EI_{bo}} + \frac{4(H-z_i)}{EA_N} + \gamma \frac{2(l_b - 2\lambda) + 4\Phi_\rho}{GA_{bo}} \qquad (4)$$

where : $\Phi_\rho = \dfrac{\lambda h_{bo}}{h_{br} - h_{bo}} \ln \dfrac{h_{br}}{h_{bo}}$ $A_{bo} = h_{bo} \cdot t_b$ $\qquad (5)$

$$\Gamma_\rho = \frac{\lambda^3 h_{bo}^3}{(h_{br} - h_{bo})^3} \ln \frac{h_{br}}{h_{bo}} + \frac{2\lambda^2 h_{bo}^2}{h_{br}(h_{br} - h_{bo})^2}\left[\varepsilon_\rho (h_{br} - h_{bo}) - \lambda h_{br}\right] +$$

$$+ \frac{\lambda^3 h_{bo}^3 (h_{br} + h_{bo})}{2 h_{br}^2 (h_{br} - h_{bo})^2}\left[\varepsilon_\rho (h_{br} - h_{bo}) - \lambda h_{br}\right]^2 \qquad (6)$$

$$\Gamma'_\rho = \frac{\lambda^3 h_{bo}^3}{(h_{br}-h_{bo})^3} \ln \frac{h_{br}}{h_{bo}} -$$

$$- 2 \frac{\lambda^2 h_{bo}^2}{h_{br}(h_{br}-h_{bo})^2} \left[l_b(h_{br}-h_{bo})-\mathcal{E}_\rho(h_{br}-h_{bo})-\lambda h_{br} \right] -$$

$$- \frac{\lambda^3 h_{bo}^3 (h_{br}+h_{bo})}{2 h_{br}^2 (h_{br}-h_{bo})^2} \left[l_b(h_{br}-h_{bo})-\mathcal{E}_\rho(h_{br}-h_{bo})-\lambda h_{br} \right]^2 \qquad (7)$$

δ_{ii}^{mm} – the displacements corresponding to the boundary spandrels, for any types of structures:

$$\delta_{ii}^{mm} = \delta_{ii}^{kk} + \frac{4 b^2 (H-z_i)}{EI_{equiv}} \qquad (8)$$

ρ_1, ρ_2 – the degrees of restraint of the spandrel beams ends
A_N – the cross area of the columns
z_i – the ordonate corresponding to the spandrels of i-storey

Table 3   Terms of the matrix $[\triangle]$

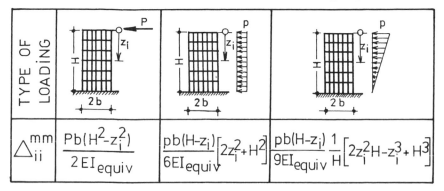

TYPE OF LOADING			
$\triangle_{ii}^{mm}$	$\dfrac{Pb(H^2-z_i^2)}{2 EI_{equiv}}$	$\dfrac{pb(H-z_i)}{6EI_{equiv}}\left[2z_i^2+H^2\right]$	$\dfrac{pb(H-z_i)}{9EI_{equiv}}\dfrac{1}{H}\left[2z_i^2 H-z_i^3+H^3\right]$

Table 4 Stiffness reduction coefficients

MONOLITHIC	PRECAST			
	VARIANT 1 "BIG PANELS"	VARIANT 2 "COLUMNS"	VARIANT 3 "+ UNITS"	VARIANT 4 "T UNITS"
c_r				
1,00	0,90	0,82	0,78	0,70

The expression of the vector $[\triangle]$ components for three types of external loads are given in terms of the storey coordinate, z_i, in Table 3.

Solving equation (a) the axial forces acting in the normal panels columns are determined summing the shear forces from the adjacent spandrel beams:

$$N_i^k = X_i^k - X_i^l$$

Further, the axial forces acting in the side panel columns result from the bending moments of the lateral panels, P, obtained by superposing on the external moments M, the resistant moments of the boundary shear forces X_i^m.

EXPERIMENTAL INVESTIGATIONS

The primary objective of the experimental investigation was to determine at what extent the prefabrication of the perforated shearwall structures influences their stiffness and hence, to obtain data about the values of the reduction coefficient, C_r, used in evaluating the equivalent bending stiffness of the side panels of precast framed tube structures. For this purpose five types of perforated shear wall models made of reinforced microconcrete were tested under horizontal loads.

The controlling parameters of the framed panel models, as defined by Khan and Amin [2] are: stiffness ratio 0,503; stiffness factor 0,306; aspect ratio 1,355. The specimens are directly comparable because they have the same

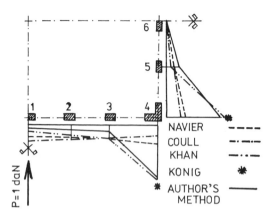

Figure 3 Comparison of values of axial forces in the columns

dimensions and reinforcement, the difference consisting but in the manner of execution. The reference model, denoted model 1, is continuously reinforced and cast insitu as a whole unit while the other four models, summarized in Table 4, consist of precasting variants of it.

To simulate the gravity loads, compression stresses were induced in the columns of the model by tensioning high-tensile wires. The connections among the precast pieces were achieved by splitting the reinforcement and cast insitu joints.

The reduction coefficient of the stiffness results as a ratio between the top lateral deflection under a load of 100 daN recorded on the monolithical model and that recorded on the precast models:

$$C_r = \frac{W_{mon}}{W_{prec}} \leqslant 1$$

Table 4 summarizes the values of C_r determined for the four types of precast models.

COMPARISON WITH OTHER ANALYTICAL METHODS

In order to check the accuracy of the proposed method as compared to other analysis methods, a monolithic framed tube structure has been analysed.

The axial forces in the columns under a unit horizontal

force acting at the top of the structure have been calculated using the Khan and Amin method [2], [3], Coull and Bose simplified analysis [4], [5], König and Liphardt method [6], [7], Navier beam theory and the proposed method. The values of the first story axial forces are summarized in Fig.3.

CONCLUDING REMARKS

A simplified procedure for an analysis of bending action in monolithical as well as in precast reinforced concrete framed tube structures is presented. By replacing the discrete structure of the side panels of the tube by cantilever beams of equivalent bending stiffness, a simplified static indeterminate structure is obtained and then solved using the force method, with minimum amount of computing time.

In order to evaluate the influence of the precasting on the tubular bending stiffness, experimental investigations have been carried out on four types of precast frame panels models.

An example illustrates the accuracy of the method as compared to others more or less simplified method of analysis of frame-tube structures, the results pointing out its reliability.

REFERENCES

1. ALBIGES, M, AND GAULET, I.Contreventement des batiments, Annales de l'I.T.B.T.P.,May 1960, Vol.149, pp 413-500.

2. KHAN, F AND AMIN, N.Analysis and design of framed tube structures for tall concrete buildings. The Structural Engineer, March 1973, No.3, Vol.51, pp 85-92.

3. KHAN, F.R.Tubular structures for tall buildings.Handbook of Concrete Engineering, Van Nostrand, Reinhold Company, New York, 1974.

4. COULL, A AND BOSE, B.Simplified analysis of framed tube structures.Journal of the Structural Division, ST-11, November 1975, pp 2223-2240.

5. COULL, A AND SUBEDI, N.K.Framed-tube structures for high-rise buildings.Journal of the Structural Division, Proceedings, ASCE, Aug.1971, pp 2097-2099.

6. KÖNIG, G AND LIPHARDT, S.Hohlkästen aus rahmen als aussteifung von hochhausern. Beton und Stahlbetonbau, July 1978, Vol.73, pp.157-162.

7. KONIG, G.Perforierter hohlkasten als tragende konstruction eines hochhauses. Der Bauingenieur, No.7/1975, pp 285-286.

8. KONIG, G.Hochhauser aus Stahlbeton, Beton Kalender, Vol.II, 1975, W.Ernst & Sohn, Berlin 1975.

9. FINTEL, M.Multistory structures. Handbook of Concrete Engineering, Van Nostrand, Reinhold Company, New York, 1974.

10. FINTEL, M, KHAN, F.R.Effects of Column Exposure in Tall Structures, ACI Journal, Proceedings V.62, Dec.1965, pp 1533-1556, V.63, Aug.1966,pp 843-863, V.65, Febr. 1968, pp 99-110, V.66, Dec.1968.

11. FINTEL, M, KHAN, F.R.Effect of Creep and Shrinkage in Tall Structures-Prediction of Inelastic Column Shortening, ACI Journal Proceedings, V.66, 1969, pp 957-967.

12. HEIDEBRECHT, AC, AND SMITH, BS.Approximate Analysis of tall wall-frames structures, Journal of the Structural Division, Proceedings ASCE, Febr. 1973.

13. POCANSCHI, A, OLARIU,I.Orthotropic Membrane for Tall Building Analysis, Journal of the Struct.Div., Proceedings ASCE, Dec. 1979, pp 2135-2137.

14. SMITH, B.S, COULL, A.Elastic Analysis of Tall Concrete Buildings, Report nr.1, Technical Committee nr.21, Int.Symp., Missouri, Aug. 1976.

15. STAMATO, M.C, SMITH, B.S.An Approximate Method for the Three - Dimensional Analysis of Tall Buildings, Proceedings the Inst. of Civ.Engng., July 1969.

16. Proceedings of the Conference on Tower Shaped Structures, the Hague 24-26 April 1969, Delft, A.M-Haas-H.van Koten, 1970.

17. ACI Committe 442, Response of Building to Lateral Forces, ACI Journal, Febr. 1971, pp.81-106.

COMPUTER MODELLING OF CONCRETE STRUCTURES BEHAVIOUR UNDER INTENSIVE DYNAMIC LOADING

A V Zabegayev

Moscow Civil Engineering Institute

Russia

ABSTRACT. Two main approaches to the analysis of reinforced concrete structures subjected to accidental explosion and impact loadings are mostly used in design practice: a simplified one, based on rather rugh assumptions and followed by mere but conservative relationships, and a computerized approach, based on numerical methods, which, being considered very accurate, is of little value when complicated dynamic problems are under consideration because of uncertainties in input parameters of both loads and materials.

That is why in these cases advanced computerized engineering methods of analysis, reflecting integrally observed in tests characteristic features of structural behaviour can be recommended for the future decade. The approach is illustrated in the paper by a method of analysis of reinforced concrete beams under accidental impact loading.

Keywords: Reinforced concrete structures, Explosion, Impact, Mechanical models, Simplified Computer Analysis.

Professor Alexander V. Zabegayev is Prorector of the Moscow Civil Engineering Institute, Head of Department of Reinforced Concrete Structures. He is well-known in Russia both as an expert in design of RC structures subjected to intense dynamic loading and as an auther of popular text-books on concrete. He is also Member of the Institution of Civil Engineers and keeps close scienfitic links with the University of Birmingham.

Concrete 2000. Edited by Ravindra K. Dhir and M. Roderick Jones.
© 1993 Published by E & FN Spon. ISBN 0 419 18120 2.

INTRODUCTION

There are two main approaches in design techniqnes nowerdays: a simplified one, developed for practicing civil engineers, and a computer added design, based on numerical methods (FDM, FEM etc.). The first technique is based on simple formuli and usually gives a conservative assessment of structural bearing capacity followed by some extra expenditure of materials and money. Its merits are simplicity and reliability.

The second approach has recently been developed up to sophisticated softwares which can solve any analytic problem if itput data are relevant to the real behaviour of materials and structures. However, this rather expensive techniques can become of little value when such a non-ordinary composite as reinforced concrete is considered.A number of parameters of concrete (shear, behaviour of confined concrete etc.) essential for numerical procedures have not been investigated to a proper extant, especially under instant loadings. An uncertainty in input load's parameters, reducing significantly the accuracy of the numerical results should also be taken into account.

The optimal approach lays, to our opinion, in between the two abovementioned. It is based on advanced mechanical and physical models reflecting all features of structural behariour, observed in tests, included as integral pieces into numerical procedures. This approach seems to be the cheapest and most reliable for the future; it is illustrated below by a method of analysis of reinforced concrete beams under accidental impact.

NOTATION

K_1 = stiffness of the contact zone

Y = beam's deflection

K = kinetic energy

U = potential energy

B_o = flexural stiffness of an uncracked cross-section

B_1 = flexural stiffness of a cracked cross-section

x = coordinate of the impacted cross-section

$\tilde{a}$ = distance between the impacted cross-section and the edge of cracked zone

α = penetration

V_o = impact velocity

M_s = mass of the striker

φ_1 = angle of rotation

$l =$ length of the beam

$m =$ mass of the beam per unit length

$M_{u,d} =$ ultimate bending moment at the impacted cross-section

$C_{up} =$ stiffness of the concrete layer above upper longitudinal reinforcement

$C_1 =$ stiffness of the upper layer within the reinforcement cage

$C_2 =$ the same, of the lower layer

$C_b =$ stiffness of the cantilever "beam"

$C_s =$ stiffness of the dowels

$C_{bc} =$ stiffness of the stirrups in compressions

$C_{wt} =$ stiffness of the stirrups in tension

ASSUMTIONS

Recent investigations have shown [1], that many of accidental impact loadings can be reffered to as hard low-velocity impacts. Strain - rate effect for concrete and reinforcement should be taken into account. That can be done by analogy with [2].

A contact law linking contact force with penetration of the striker should also be known to describe adequately the structural behaviour (corresponding joint study has been undertaken in MCEI and the University of Birmingham (prof. B.P.Hughes)). It has resulted in mechanical models and the contact law for a hard flat-nosed impact.

According to the observed in tests the structural behaviour can be divided into two stages: before and after cracking. At the first stage overall deflections of the structure are negligibly small and a theoretical solution can be derived from the theory of elasticity's problem, regarding penetration of a rigid indentor into an elastic strip, allowing for peculiarities of concrete [2]. For a description of the contact zone behaviour after cracking some models has been proposed, one of them is presented in Figure 1. Its major elements

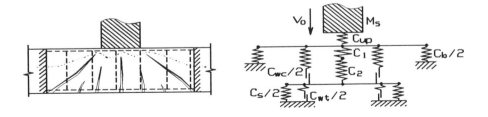

Figure 1. Model of the contact zone

are as follows:

1) concrete layer above upper longitudinal reinforcement;

2) triaxically compressed concrete layer within the reinforcement cage above the neutral axis;

3) cracked concrete layer under the neutral axis;

4) cantilever "beams" outward the contact area above the inclined cracks;

5) dowels formed by the bottom longitudinal reinforcement in the inclined cracks;

6) stirrups in tension crossed by the inclined cracks.

7) stirrups in compression under the indentor.

A total stiffness of the mechanical system can be written as

$$K_1 = \frac{C_{up}\,(K + C_b)}{K + C_b + C_{up}} \qquad (1)$$

$$K = \frac{(C + C_{wc})(C_d + C_{wt})}{C_d + C_{wt} + C + C_{wc}}; \qquad C = \frac{C_1 C_2}{C_1 + C_2} \qquad (2)$$

The study carried out has resulted in a determination of all nessessary parameters in eqs.(1) and (2). For example, contact moduli of plain and confined concrete E''_c and E''_{cc} were proposed as it was shown in [2]. The model allows for the yielding in stirrups both in tension and in compression. It is valid if the contact duration $t > \dfrac{3h}{c}$, $h =$ the cross-sectional depth, $c =$ a velocity of sound waves propagation in concrete, $c = \sqrt{E_c/\rho}$. The last requirement is met the majority of practical cases.

The design diagram for the contact zone behaviour is illustrated by Figure 2. The unloading stage can be described by analogy with the loading one provided E''_c and E''_{cc} substituting by E_c.

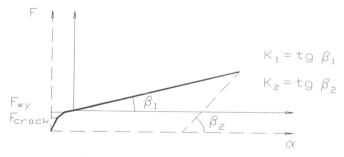

Figure 2. Design diagram " F -   "

A comparison of K_1 values for the first and the second stages has shown that K_1 after cracking is 5 ... 7 times lower as before cracking; at the same time a part of impulse transferred. into the structure during the first stage does not exeed 5% ot the total one, that is why the stage before cracking can be neglected in the practical analysis.

METHOD OF ANALYSIS

According to the observed in tests overall behaviour of the structure can also be divided into two stages:

1) before yielding in the longitudinal reinforcement;

2) after yielding up to ultimate strains in the compressed concrete.

STAGE 1. A comparative analysis of the beam, considering rotational inertia and shear, has shown that these factors usually taken into account in the analysis of structures under local dynamic loadings can be neglected if the interaction between the striker and the contact zone is taken into consideration.

The beams deflection can be expressed as follows:

$$Y = \sum_n T_n X_n \qquad (3)$$

where $X_n = n\text{-}th$ mode of vibration of the beam with cracks:

T_n = a corresponding unknown time function.

Lagrange's procedure is used to obtain the eguations of motion of the system. Kinethic and potential energies will be

$$K = \frac{m}{2} \int_0^1 \dot{Y}^2 dx + \frac{M_s}{2} [\dot{Y}(\bar{x}, t) + \dot{\alpha}]^2 \qquad (4)$$

$$U = \frac{B_0}{2} \int_0^{\bar{x} - \tilde{a}} [\frac{\partial^2 Y}{\partial x^2}]^2 dx + \frac{B_1}{2} \int_{\bar{x} - \tilde{a}}^{\bar{x} + \tilde{a}} [\frac{\partial^2 Y}{\partial x^2}]^2 dx +$$

$$+ \frac{B_0}{2} \int_{\bar{x} + \tilde{a}}^{l} [\frac{\partial^2 Y}{\partial x^2}]^2 + \frac{K_1 \alpha^2}{2} \qquad (5)$$

Subsfituting eq (3) into (4), (5) and then into Lagrange's equations

$$\frac{d}{dt} \frac{\partial K}{\partial \dot{T}_n} - \frac{\partial K}{\partial T_n} - \frac{\partial U}{\partial T_n} = \frac{\partial W}{\partial T_n} \qquad (6)$$

we can obtain the final system

$$|| \ddot{x} || \, (\ddot{T}) + || \dot{\eta} || \, (\dot{T}) + (\Delta) \, \ddot{\alpha} = 0 \tag{7}$$

$$[X_n (\bar{x})] \, (\ddot{T}) + \ddot{\alpha} + w_o^2 \, \alpha = 0$$

where x_{ij}, η_{ij}, W_o^2, Δ_i are constants.

Initial conditions will be

$$t = 0; \quad (T) = (\dot{T}) = \alpha = 0; \quad \dot{\alpha} = \mathcal{V}_o, \tag{8}$$

time derivatives are notified by dots.

Eqs (7) will be valid till a time t_1 when the dynamic yield-point is reached in the longitudinal reinforcement or till a time $\bar{t}$ when the maximum value ot the contact force occers; the later one can be determined from eq. $\dot{\alpha}(\bar{t}) = 0$. If $t > \bar{t}$ the unloading in the contact zone should be allowed for by changing of eq. (5) and initial conditions which now state equality of deflections and its velocities just before and after $\bar{t}$.

If $t > t_1$ the second stage of the beam's behaviour takes place.

STAGE 2. Assuming that the structure is reinforced with a mild steel, its behaviour can be represented by a mechanical model, consisting of rigid blocks jointed by a plastic hinge (zone).

The beam's deflection at this stage can be presented as follows

$$Y = \begin{cases} \varphi_1 \, x & (0 < x < \bar{x}) \\ \varphi_1 \, \bar{x} \, \dfrac{l - x}{l - \bar{x}} & (\bar{x} < x < l) \end{cases} \tag{9}$$

Kinetic and potential energies

$$K = \frac{m}{2} \int_0^{\bar{x}} (\dot{Y}^I)^2 \, dx + \frac{m}{2} \int_{\bar{x}}^l (\dot{Y}^{II})^2 \, dx + \frac{M_s}{2} [\dot{\alpha} + \dot{\varphi}_1 \, \bar{x}]^2; \tag{10}$$

$$U = M_{u,d} \, \frac{l}{l - \bar{x}} \, \varphi_1 + \frac{K_1 \, \alpha^2}{2} \tag{11}$$

and the beam's motion equations will be

$$a_1 \ddot{\varphi} + b_1 \ddot{\alpha} = - M_{u,d}$$

$$\bar{x} \, \ddot{\varphi}_1 + \ddot{\alpha} + \omega_o^2 \alpha = 0 , \qquad (12)$$

where a_1 and b_1 are constant.

Moving the beginning of time counting to the beginning of the second stage we can get initial conditions as follows

$$t = 0 ; \quad \varphi_1 = \varphi_{1o} ; \quad \dot{\varphi} = \dot{\varphi}_{1o} ; \quad \alpha = \alpha_o ; \quad \dot{\alpha} = \dot{\alpha}_o \qquad (13)$$

where the initial rotational velocity is derived from the equality of momentum at the end of Stage 1 and the beginning of Stage 2.

Eqs. (12) will be valid until $t = \bar{t}$. After that time unloading in the contact zone starts. Motions eguations for this case can be represented as

$$a_1 \ddot{\varphi}_1 + b_1 \ddot{\alpha} = - M_{u,d}$$

$$\bar{x} \, \ddot{\varphi}_1 + \ddot{\alpha} + \omega_{o2}^2 \alpha = \Phi , \qquad (14)$$

where $\Phi = \dfrac{(K_2 - K_1) \alpha \ (\bar{t})}{M_s}$

The last system will, in turn, be valid untill the contact between the striker and the structure ends at a time $\bar{\bar{t}}$ which can be determined from

$$\alpha (\bar{\bar{t}}) = \frac{\alpha (\bar{t}) \ (K_2 - K_1)}{K_2} \qquad (15)$$

A further free motion of the beam can be easily considered by analogy with eqs. (14).

The maximum deflection takes place at time t_m and can be obtaind from

$$\dot{\varphi}_1 (t_m) = 0 \qquad (16)$$

Bearing capacity of the structure will be sufficient if the maximum angle of rotation in the plastic hinge does not exceed an ultimate value [3]:

$$\varphi (t_m) < \varphi_u \qquad (17)$$

CONCLUSIONS

Calculations show a very good coincidence of theoretical and experimental results provided that at Stage 1 only 5 ... 7 terms can be left in series (3). The interaction between the striker and the structure also helps to define more precisely design parameters under minimum expenditures ot IBM PC time. Thus, maximum contact force reduces up to 65% and the impulse value can be only about 35 ... 40% of that determined by a traditional engineering approach.

The proposed technigue has been expanded to a wide range of reinforced concrete structures subjected to accidental explosion and impact loadings.

REFERENCES

1. Zabegaev A.V. On the determination of accidental impact loadings in Civil Engineering// Stroitelnaya mechanica i raschhet soorugheny/.-1988, No 1, pp. 5-9.

2. Zabegayev A.V. Experimental study and theoretical analysis of reinforced concrete structures under accidental impact loading //Earthguake, blast and impact; Int. Conf, Manchester, "Elsevier Applied scince" 1991.- p.p 385-394.

3. Popov N.N., Rastorguyev B.S., Zabegayev A.V. Analysis of structures subjected to specific dynamic loadings."Vysshaya schola", Moscow, 1992, 320 p.

COMPUTER MODELLING OF CONCRETE ELEMENTS UNDER HYDROSTATIC PRESSURE EFFECT

N K Subedi

University of Dundee

United Kingdom

Q Zhou

Chengdu University of Science and Technology

People's Republic of China

ABSTRACT. The Understanding of the effects of hydrostatic pressure on the structural behaviour of concrete is of fundamental importance for the safety and design of underwater structures. Offshore concrete gravity structures, underwater storage facilities and habitats are structures which have to operate under longterm exposure to large depths of seawater. Currently, there is very little information, both theoretical and experimental, available on the behaviour of concrete under hydrostatic external pressure and under partial and full saturation conditions. One key question often asked is 'Does concrete lose strength under hydrostatic pressure ?' Current opinions amongst the professional engineers on this question are uncertain, divided and inconsistent. In this paper, a theoretical study carried out on the structural behaviour of concrete elements subjected to hydrostatic pressures simulating various depths of saturation is discussed. The computer model was developed using the nonlinear finite element analysis package ABAQUS. The research highlights the computer model and the structural behaviour of concrete under various combinations of hydrostatic pressure and external load.

Keywords: Concrete, Hydrostatic pressure, Pressure ingress, Strain energy, Hydrostatic strain energy density (HSE), Distortion strain energy density (DSE).

Dr Nutan K Subedi is a Lecturer in Civil Engineering, University of Dundee, UK. His research interests include reinforced concrete deep beams, panel walls, concrete steel plate composite beams, tall buildings, coupled shear walls and concrete elements in hydrostatic pressure environment.

Professor Qi Zhou is an Associate Professor in Hydraulic Engineering, Chengdu University of Science and Technology, Chengdu, PR China. His research interests include analysis and design of concrete dams, hydrostatic pressure effects and numerical analysis.

Concrete 2000. Edited by Ravindra K. Dhir and M. Roderick Jones.
© 1993 Published by E & FN Spon. ISBN 0 419 18120 2.

INTRODUCTION

The structural behaviour of concrete under hydrostatic pressure conditions is a major concern in the design of structures such as concrete dams, offshore gravity structures, underwater storage facilities and habitats. The overall strength, deformation and cracking characteristics of concrete exposed to hydrostatic pressure over a period of time are important aspects of the behaviour from the designers' point of view.

Landbased structures are designed and constructed based on the behaviour of materials in the normal atmospheric environment as studied from experiments also carried out in the normal atmospheric conditions. The behaviour of the materials, concrete included, and the performance of the structures can not be assumed to remain unaltered if these structures are constructed in the oceans unless the behaviour of the material is thoroughly investigated.

The main objectives of this paper are to study (1) the mechanism of pressure ingress in concrete elements (2) the effects of hydrostatic pressure in concrete elements using ABAQUS.

This study forms a part of a major research project currently being investigated at the University of Dundee. In this study the effects of hydrostatic pressure in mature concrete is assumed purely as a physical phenomenon.

MECHANISM OF PRESSURE INGRESS IN CONCRETE

Concrete consists of crushed rock aggregates embedded uniformly in a matrix of cement and sand mortar containing numerous voids either filled with air or water. The microstructure of cement paste which constitutes the region where the moisture movement takes place consists of gel particles, interstitial spaces or gel pores and capillary cavities. Only capillary pores are sufficiently large for water to move freely in them. The gel pores are much smaller, therefore the water molecules do not freely move in them. It is also believed that most of the practical situations in which concrete structures will be required to operate under hydrostatic pressure will only affect the movement of water in the capillary pores. This study is confined to the phenomenon of hydrostatic pressure effect in concrete related to the process of movement of water in the capillary pores and the large voids randomly dispersed in concrete.

Concrete under hydrostatic pressure

In Fig 1(a), a normal concrete element subjected to a hydrostatic pressure, p, is shown. A normal concrete is defined as a concrete which is neither too porous nor impermeable.

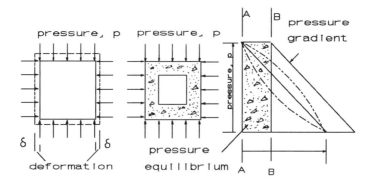

Figure 1 Pressure ingress into concrete

Immediately on pressurisation, *time t_o, Stage 0*, the concrete element will undergo a deformation δ. At this instant the pressure on the external surface is p which also forms the pressure front.

After *time t_1, Stage 1*, a pressure gradient will develop between the surface and distance, d, from the surface. The pressure gradient is partly due to the process of absorption and partly due to intrusion under pressure. The gradient may be either linear or nonlinear. The development of pressure gradient indicates that, in this region, the material is now subjected to a pressure less than the initial pressure, p. This may be due to the process of strain reversal as the pressure in the material builds up.

After *time t_2, Stage 2*, the pressure front will move into the concrete, from AA to BB, as shown in Fig 1(b). In the region, AABB, the pressure in the concrete will be in equilibrium with the external pressure and the strain reversal completed. Whether or not there will be a full recovery of the strain will depend on the initial deformation of the element. The pressure gradient will, at this stage, progress further into the material towards the centre.

At, *time t_3, Stage 3*, as the pressure front reaches the core of the material a state of saturation is reached. The pressure equilibrium and the reversal of strain are completed in all parts of the element. The total time required from *Stage 0* i.e., the application of pressure p to the surface to *Stage 3*, i.e., complete pressure ingress into the concrete element, will depend on (a) the quality of concrete: permeability and porosity (b) the applied hydrostatic head (c) the geometry of the element.

Two extreme examples of pressure ingress into concrete are:

(a) A highly porous element : In a highly porous element as soon as the external pressure starts to build up the pressure ingress occurs with the equilibrium reaching instantly. The material in such case will not undergo deformation and there will be no time lapse to effect the reversal of strain.

(b) An impermeable element : In an impermeable element the time required from *Stage 0* to *Stage 3* will be infinite. Theoretically, the pressure ingress will not take place. The material will undergo the full deformation under the effect of the hydrostatic pressure, but, as the pressure gradient is unlikely to develop across the depth, the reversal of strain will not take place.

All normal concretes for practical application in construction fall within the extremes of highly porous and impermeable concrete.

Fundamental questions

Concrete is basically a nonhomogeneous material with variable mechanical behaviour in tension and compression. Normal concrete has much higher strength in compression than in tension. A number of fundamental questions may be asked.

(a) The first stage under hydrostatic pressure is the build up of pressure on the exposed surface. What is the state of stress in the concrete at this stage ? Can the concrete be weakened or damaged at this stage of pressurisation ?

(b) What are the states of stress in the concrete at subsequent stages of pressure ingress ? These may be investigated under partial and full saturation conditions.

(c) What parameters or characteristics of behaviour can be used to study the phenomenon of pressure ingress in concrete ?

It will be sometime before the answers to all these questions can be found. Here the results of a preliminary study on the subject is discussed.

ANALYSIS

Structural idealisation

The theoretical analysis was carried out using ABAQUS. The structural element selected for the analysis was a concrete cylinder 200 mm in diameter and 400 mm in length. The cylinder was idealised with axisymmetric elements with pore pressure available as CAX8RP from the element library of the software. The idealised structure is shown in Fig 2. Only one-half of the cylinder was modelled for the analysis. Some of the important material details used in the analysis were as follows:

Number of elements	16
Element type	CAX8RP
Concrete properties	

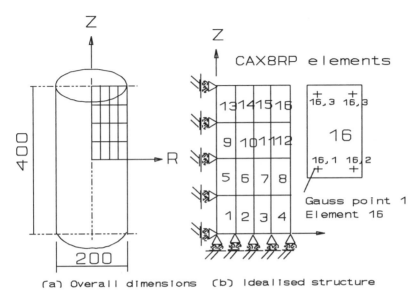

(a) Overall dimensions   (b) Idealised structure

Figure 2 Concrete cylinder for study

Elastic modulus	31 kN/mm^2
Poisson's ratio	0.15
Stress at limit of elas behaviour(compression)	20 N/mm^2
Peak stress at failure(compressive)	40 N/mm^2
Plastic strain at failure	1.05 x 10^{-3}
Ratio of uniaxial tensile/comp failure stress	8.0 x 10^{-2}
Coefficient of permeability	1.0 x 10^{-11} m/s

The analysis was carried out using the nonlinear analysis facility CONCRETE and also the effective stress analysis facility SOILS for fluid filled porous media. The control parameters included the application of full pressure loading in 20 increments, each increment allowing 15 iterations. The tolerance factor for load was 0.01. The pore pressure is specified by the degree of freedom 8. The boundary conditions for the structure are shown in Fig 2.

Loading cases

The structure was analysed for a number of load cases defined under three different loading conditions. The loading conditions are shown in Fig 3.

Loading condition 1 : Hydrostatic pressure : Fig 3(a)

Under Loading condition 1 four stages of pressure were applied (a) hydrostatic pressure on the external surface (b) pressure ingress after seven days calculated using permeability equation (c) pressure ingress after fourteen days (d) full pressure saturation. At each of the four stages the pressure itself was varied from 3 N/mm² (300 m depth) to 40 N/mm² (4000 m depth), Table 1.

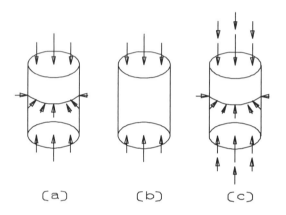

Figure 3   Loading cases (a) hydrostatic pressure (b) external pressure
(c) hydrostatic plus external pressures

Loading condition 2 : External pressure : Fig 3(b)

In this loading condition only external loading was applied with no hydrostatic pressure. The external pressure loading was applied uniaxially and increased from 3 N/mm² to 39.5 N/mm² (assumed f_{cu} for concrete = 40 N/mm²).

Loading condition 3 : Hydrostatic plus external pressures : Fig 3(c)

This was a combined load case in which the specimen was subjected to both hydrostatic and external uniaxial pressures. A number of load combinations were applied. Here the results for only one case of hydrostatic pressure, 5 N/mm², are discussed. The external pressure varied from 5.0 N/mm² to 39.5 N/mm² (see Table 2).

Analysis

It is considered for the study of concrete under hydrostatic pressure the appropriate concept is the consideration of the total strain energy incorporating hydrostatic strain energy, HSE, and distortion strain energy, DSE.

From the theory of elasticity[1] the strain energy per unit volume of a three dimensional element, U, may be expressed in a general form as

$$U = 1/2 \ (\sigma_{ij}\varepsilon_{ij}) \qquad . \qquad . \qquad . \qquad . \qquad . \qquad . \qquad (1)$$

in which σ_{ij} and ε_{ij} represent the stress and strain components. Equation (1) may be expressed in terms of the principal stresses as

$$U = 1/(2E) \ [\sigma_1^2 + \sigma_2^2 + \sigma_3^2 - 2v(\sigma_1\sigma_2 + \sigma_2\sigma_3 + \sigma_3\sigma_1)] \qquad . \qquad (2)$$

Referring to Fig 4, the total strain energy may be expressed as

$$U = U_v + U_d \ . \qquad . \qquad . \qquad . \qquad . \qquad . \qquad . \qquad (3)$$

in which, U_v is the strain energy due to hydrostatic or volumetric effect and U_d is the strain energy due to distortion, given by

$$U_v = 1/(6E) \ [(1-2v)(\sigma_1 + \sigma_2 + \sigma_3)^2] \ . \qquad . \qquad . \qquad . \qquad (4(a))$$

$$U_d = (1+v)/(3E) \ [(\sigma_1 - \sigma_2)^2 + (\sigma_2 - \sigma_3)^2 + (\sigma_3 - \sigma_1)^2] \qquad . \qquad (4(b))$$

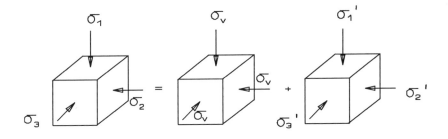

(a) Total stress   (b) Hydrostatic stress   (c) Distortion stress

Figure 4 Hydrostatic and distortion components of a stress system

Using ABAQUS, the total strain energy density, elastic and plastic , at any particular point in the concrete specimen can be computed. However, for the components, hydrostatic and distortion strain energies, a separate subroutine will be necessary.

Critical strain energy densities

Concrete is a brittle material which has inherent defects such as voids and microcracks in its matrix since its early stages. The defects make concrete susceptible to damage sometime even under small applied pressure. Both stresses and strains are important factors in determining the characteristics of the behaviour. The strain energy densities defined by the equations 4(a) and 4(b) which indirectly incorporate the effects of both stress and strain are therefore appropriate parameters for determining the behaviour of the material.

Equation 4(a) represents the strain energy in the system due to volumetric change without distortion. Equation 4(b) represents the strain energy in the system due to distortion or change of shape of the element. An excessive amount of strain energy in the system either due to volume change or due to distortion or both will signal cracking or damage to the material. It is therefore essential to establish the critical values of the volumetric and distortion strain energies for the material in order to assess its behaviour under hydrostatic and/or external loading. Tests reported in the past[2] showed that the fracture of concrete cylinders can occur even if the cylinder is under overall compression. It is believed that the concept of critical strain energy may be used to explain such phenomena.

For the case of specimens subjected to compressive loading, the critical strain energy densities may be determined by calculating the energies for an uniaxial compressive load equivalent to the ultimate strength of the concrete.

RESULTS AND DISCUSSION

In Tables 1 and 2, the critical strain energy densities were calculated from the Loading condition 2.

Loading condition 1 : Hydrostatic pressure

In Fig 5 the applied hydrostatic pressure is plotted against (i) hydrostatic strain energy, HSE, and (ii) distortion strain energy, DSE. Each pair of the plots represents the results for a particular Gauss point on the element. The elements and the appropriate Gauss points are shown in Fig 2. Only selected Gauss points are discussed here.

(a) Every element subjected to a triaxial stress system gives rise to two components of the total strain energy (i) the hydrostatic strain energy accompanied by the volume change (ii) the distortion strain energy accompanied by the distortion or change of shape of the element.

(b) For a cylinder subjected to hydrostatic pressure the HSE increases from the surface towards the centre of the element. The least values of the HSE are found in the elements located around the edges of the structure. For example, compare the maximum HSEs at (4,2), (16,4), (15,3) with (5,3), (1,1) etc.(see Fig 5 and Table 1). The DSE, on the other hand, decreases from the surface towards the centre of the element. The maximum DSEs are found around the free edges of the structure where the elements undergo large distortions.

(c) Generally, as the hydrostatic pressure ingress increases, the total strain energy in the element decreases. At the maximum saturation the total strain energy and the components HSE and DSE are at their lowest. The pressure equilibrium is maintained throughout the structure at every element. In this situation both the HSE and DSE at every point in the structure are considerably reduced as represented by the almost vertical nature of the line in each figure after 14-day saturation. This also indicates that the critical case occurs when the pressure is acting on the exposed surface and that the pressure ingress has not taken place.

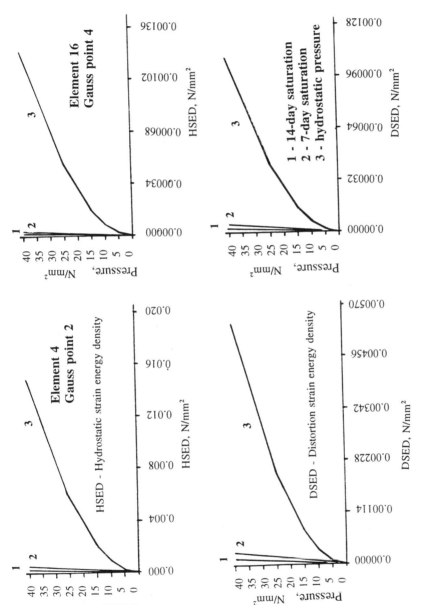

Figure 5(a) Hydrostatic and distortion strain energy plots for hydrostatic pressure(no pressure ingress), 7-day pressure ingress and 14-day pressure ingress

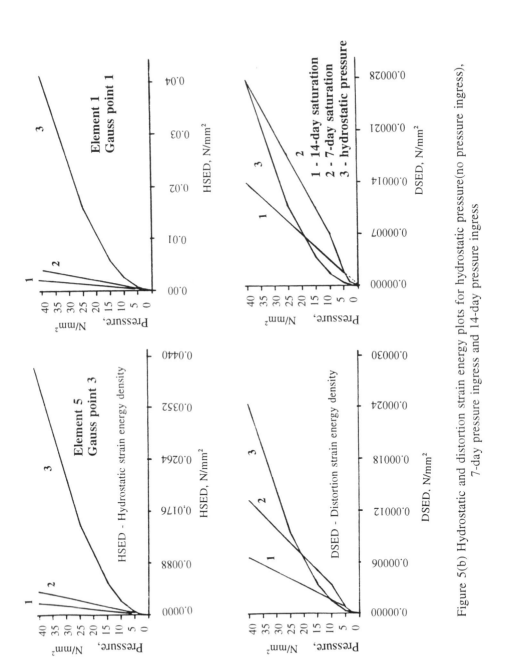

Figure 5(b) Hydrostatic and distortion strain energy plots for hydrostatic pressure(no pressure ingress),
7-day pressure ingress and 14-day pressure ingress

(d) The HSE at each location is directly proportional to the applied hydrostatic head as shown by the similarity of all the HSE plots in Fig 5. In contrast, the DSE at a particular location depends on the applied pressure head, degree of saturation and the geometry of the element. Depending on the intensity of the applied pressure and the degree of saturation, the magnitude and location of the maximum DSE changes from point to point as represented by the intersecting nature of some of the DSE curves in Fig 5.

Table 1 : Load case : Hydrostatic pressure on exposed surface
$E = 31000$ N/mm^2, $f_{cu} = 40$ N/mm^2

Element Gauss point	Applied hydrostatic pressure in N/mm^2						
	3.0	5.0	10.0	15.0	25.0	40.0	

Hydrostatic strain energy density x 10^{-3}

1,1	0.232	0.646	2.585	5.816	16.150	41.350	
3,1	0.234	0.650	2.600	5.851	16.250	41.610	
4,2	0.083	0.231	0.926	2.082	5.785	14.810	Critical
5,3	0.219	0.609	2.434	5.477	15.210	38.960	HSE
6,4	0.224	0.622	2.487	5.596	15.550	39.790	density
8,3	0.187	0.519	2.076	4.671	12.970	33.210	5.872 x 10^{-3}
13,3	0.044	0.121	0.484	1.088	3.023	7.740	
15,1	0.128	0.356	1.425	3.207	8.907	22.800	
15,3	0.034	0.094	0.375	0.844	2.345	6.003	
16,1	0.101	0.281	1.125	2.532	7.036	18.010	
16,4	0.007	0.019	0.076	0.170	0.473	1.211	

Distortion strain energy density x 10^{-3}

1,1	0.002	0.004	0.017	0.039	0.109	0.278	
3,1	0.001	0.003	0.013	0.029	0.082	0.209	
4,2	0.030	0.082	0.329	0.739	2.054	5.259	Critical
5,3	0.001	0.004	0.015	0.034	0.095	0.243	DSE
6,4	0.001	0.004	0.015	0.033	0.093	0.239	density
8,3	0.002	0.006	0.024	0.053	0.149	0.383	19.29 x 10^{-3}
13,3	0.008	0.022	0.089	0.199	0.555	1.421	
15,1	0.004	0.012	0.046	0.104	0.289	0.740	
15,3	0.006	0.017	0.070	0.158	0.438	1.121	
16,1	0.009	0.024	0.097	0.218	0.609	1.556	
16,4	0.006	0.017	0.067	0.152	0.422	1.078	

(e) From Table 1, it also indicates that for the concrete, $f_{cu} = 40$ N/mm^2, the critical hydrostatic density, HSE of 5.872 x 10^{-3} is exceeded at all points except (16,4) at the confining hydrostatic pressure of 40 N/mm^2. The distortion strain energy densities, DSE, are well below the critical values.

(f) The principal stresses for all the elements were found to be compressive. However, with the concept of critical strain energy, it should be possible to locate the possible sites of cracking in the specimen by examining the levels of the strain energies and comparing them with the critical values. It is clear that further research is required in this area.

Loading condition 3 : Hydrostatic plus external pressures

The results for a combined load case in which the applied hydrostatic pressure on exposed surfaces was 5 N/mm^2 is presented in Table 2.

Table 2 : Load case : Hydrostatic plus external uniaxial : E = 31000 N/mm^2

Element Gauss point	Hydrostatic pressure on all exposed surface = 5 N/mm^2 Applied uniaxial pressure in N/mm^2					
	5.0	8.5	11.5	21.5	31.5	39.5
Hydrostatic strain energy density x 10^{-3}						
1,1	0.646	1.0371	1.446	3.297	6.048	8.680
3,2	0.650	1.042	1.452	3.307	6.062	8.705
4,2	0.231	0.484	0.774	2.223	4.112	6.328
5,3	0.609	0.989	1.390	3.213	5.992	8.766 Critical
6,4	0.622	1.007	1.410	3.243	6.015	8.728 HSE
8,3	0.519	0.874	1.252	3.001	5.498	7.975 density
13,3	0.121	0.316	0.557	1.850	3.581	5.693 5.872 x 10^{-3}
15,1	0.356	0.659	0.991	2.590	5.262	7.924
15,3	0.094	0.271	0.497	1.738	3.520	5.632
16,1	0.281	0.555	0.863	2.380	4.719	7.071
16,4	0.189	0.124	2.876	1.323	2.957	4.791
Distortion strain energy density x 10^{-3}						
1,1	0.004	0.105	0.431	3.128	8.460	14.140
3,1	0.003	0.110	0.443	3.161	8.483	14.150
4,2	0.082	0.336	0.794	3.930	9.234	16.240 Critical
5,3	0.004	0.107	0.437	3.144	8.550	14.400 DSE
6,4	0.004	0.108	0.438	3.147	8.524	14.300 density
8,3	0.006	0.161	0.535	3.389	8.670	14.640 19.29 x 10^{-3}
13,3	0.022	0.058	0.329	2.843	8.297	14.230
15,1	0.012	0.175	0.557	3.437	8.682	14.530
15,3	0.017	0.076	0.367	2.945	8.342	14.250
16,1	0.024	0.182	0.558	3.422	8.664	14.590
16,4	0.017	0.143	0.492	3.266	8.589	14.740

The table shows that the critical HSE is exceeded in all points, except (16,4), at the additional external pressure of 39.5 N/mm^2. There are only a few points where this occurs at the lower value of the external pressure of 31.5 N/mm². This indicates that the hydrostatic pressure of 5 N/mm² is not very significant to change the behaviour for this particular specimen.

The levels of DSE are high at most points indicating that when there is a large external pressure applied uniaxially, the element undergoes large distortion. Without the hydrostatic pressure the DSE at these points would have reached the critical value.

CONCLUSIONS

1. The strain energy concept which takes into account both stresses and strains is an appropriate approach to study the structural behaviour of brittle materials such as concrete subjected to hydrostatic pressures.

2. The determination of the critical values for the hydrostatic and distortion strain energies are the key factors for the assessment of the material behaviour.

ACKNOWLEDGEMENT

The work described in this paper was funded by a grant from the Marine Technology Directorate Ltd (MTD Ltd) and the Science and Engineering Research Council (SERC). This is gratefully acknowledged.

REFERENCES

1. Jayatilaka A S, Fracture of engineering brittle materials, Applied Science Publishers Ltd, London, 1979.

2. Clayton N, Strain of concrete cylinders subjected to fluid pressure, Title no. 77-36, ACI Journal, Sept-Oct 1980,332-339.

COMPUTERISED DESIGN OF CONCRETE
FOR REQUISITE PROPERTIES

T Chmielewski
A Świtoński
E Świtońska
Technical University of Opole

Poland

ABSTRACT. The paper deals with theoretical foundations of forming of the structure and concrete strength. The thesis that the concrete strength under normal conditions of mix hardening is the function of activity and the degree of fineness of cement, water/cement ratio and adhesion of cement paste to aggregate, has been formulated. Presenting concrete mix as a configuration of solid phase grains suspended radomly in the aqueous solution, the mathematical model of the structure and concrete strength is given. The application of this model to the computer aided design of concrete provides large possibilities to gain a significant economic benefit. The paper is due to be published in full in the monograph series at the Technical University of Opole in 1993.

Keywords: Structure and concrete strength, Cement paste, Aggregate grains, Mathematical model, Computer aided design of concrete.

Professor Tadeusz Chmielewski is Dean of the Faculty of Civil Engineering, Technical University of Opole, Poland. The specializes in the application of the probability theory and stochastic processes in civil engineering, especially in wind and earthquake engineering and reliability of structures. Professor Chmielewski has published widely and was an active participant of many scientific conferences and symposia in Poland and abroad.

Dr Aleksander Świtoński is a Lecturer at the Faculty of Civil Engineering, Technical University of Opole. He received his Ph.D degree in civil engineering from Technical University of Mińsk in 1978. His research interests include construction engineering, especially building physics and materials engineering. He is an author of many articles and patent solutions in these fields.

Master Eng. Ewelina Świtońska is an Assistant Lecturer at the Faculty of Civil Engineering, Technical University of Opole. She received her M.Sc. degree in 1978. Her research interests include construction engineering and engineering of building materials.

Concrete 2000. Edited by Ravindra K. Dhir and M. Roderick Jones.
© 1993 Published by E & FN Spon. ISBN 0 419 18120 2.

INTRODUCTION

Experiences in the concrete application, especially in the last years, allow to ascertain that concrete in the coming century should have the added resistance to weather factors, better moisture resistance and a more stabilized in time constancy of volume.

Rational forming of concrete structure through the proper selection of components and the consolidation of concrete mix is one of the main factors leading to the improvement of the above mentioned exploitation properties. In reality the process of concrete hardening is not only restricted to phenomena of structure forming at the stage of the components selection and consolidation of concrete mix but it also comprises complex mechanism of kinetics of cement hydration.

The process of cement hydration under normal conditions is the consequence of binder properties and mix structure. Therefore the thesis that the concrete strength is affected by activity and the degree of fineness of cement, water/cement ratio and adhesion of cement paste to aggregate, has been formulated in the paper.

CONCRETE STRENGTH AS A FUNCTION OF STRUCTURE

Tightness of the structure of cement paste is one of the main factors bearing upon concrete strength. In the general case tightness of the cement paste structure is conditioned by many factors. Still it may be assumed that tightness of cement paste is a function of water/cement ratio ω and the degree of fineness of cement in the case of mix hardening under normal conditions.

In laboratory tests the degree of fineness of cement is commonly estimated on the ground of the standard water absorbability of cement ω_n determined by Vicat. Therefore a criterion of concrete durability respecting ratio ω of concrete mix and the standard absorbability of cement ω_n is stated below.

CONDITION OF CONCRETE DURABILITY

It is known that durability of concrete is affected by the structure of cement paste. In literature durability of concrete is defined on the ground of tightness criteria, in which ratio ω is the main factor of forming of cement paste porosity. Therefore in researches [1,2,3] it is shown that the tightness of the cement paste structure is also affected by the standard water absorbability of cement ω_n. The maximum tightness of the binder groins disposal in paste we can obtain at the water content corresponding to the ratio $\omega = \omega_n$.

In order to estimate univocally the effect of the standard absorbability of cement w_n on tightness of cement paste the concept of corrected tightness is introduced in the following form

$$s' = \frac{\rho_{op}}{\rho_{op_{max}}} = \frac{\frac{c+w}{\frac{c}{\rho_c}+\frac{w}{\rho_w}}}{\frac{c+w_n}{\frac{c}{\rho_c}+\frac{w_n}{\rho_w}}} = \frac{c+w}{\frac{c}{\rho_c}+\frac{w}{\rho_w}} \cdot \frac{\frac{c}{\rho_c}+\frac{w_n}{\rho_w}}{c+w_n} = \frac{(1+w)(\rho_w+w_n\rho_c)}{(\rho_w+w\rho_c)(1+w_n)} \qquad (1)$$

where, c = mass of cement

        w = mass of water

        ρ_c, ρ_w = mass density of cement and water, respectively

        $\rho_{op}, \rho_{op_{max}}$ = mass density and max mass density of cement paste

Corrected tightness of cement paste s' is a much more adequate characteristic of the structure quality of hardened paste than the ratio w applied nowadays.

After rearrangements of the expression (1) the following equation determining value of the ratio w resulting from the determined tightness of the cement grains in paste

$$w = \frac{\rho_w + w_n\rho_c - s' - w_n s'}{\rho_c s' + w_n \rho_c s' - w_n \rho_c - \rho_w} \qquad (2)$$

The equation (2) gives large possibilities to define the evaluative function of concrete resistance against weather factors. The conditions concerning the limitations of the value w of concrete mix are derived for the exemplification. It is assumed that the limit values of ratio w of concrete mix determined by the Polish Standard PN-88/B-06250 are adequate in the case of use of cements of the mean standard water absorbability which is equal to 0.275. Then taking into account the above ascertainments the limit values w of concrete mix made of cement at any standard water absorbability may be determined by combining the equations (1) and (2).

Accurate evaluative criteria of concrete weather resistance are presented in Table 1. In order to indicate the effect of the standard water absorbability of cement on tightness of the cement paste structure there are also given the limit values w computed for cements of the standard water absorbability which is equal to 0.23 and 0.32.

The values of the ratio w given in Table 1 show clearly that the corrected tightness s' determined from the equation (1) is a univocal criterion of forming of the cement paste structure in concrete. Consequently, it should be the ground of the rational mix design in the aspect of the assurance of the requisite exploitation properties of concrete.

Table 1 Limit values of mix ratio ω in relation to intensity
of action of weather factors on concrete

| Normal concrete | $\frac{PN-88}{B-06250}$ | The limit values of ω determined by | | |
		the proposed criterion (2)	the criterion (2) $\omega_n = 0.23$	$\omega_n = 0.32$
Shielded from the direct action of the weather factors	0.75	$\frac{\omega_n(\rho_c-0.765\rho_w)+0.235\rho_w}{\rho_c(0.765-0.235\omega_n)-\rho_w}$	0.64	0.86
Directly exposed to the action of weather factors	0.60	$\frac{\omega_n(\rho_c-0.810\rho_w)+0.190\rho_w}{\rho_c(0.810-0.190\omega_n)-\rho_w}$	0.50	0.70
Exposed to the constant access of water (before freezing)	0.55	$\frac{\omega_n(\rho_c-0.830\rho_w)+0.170\rho_w}{\rho_c(0.830-0.170\omega_n)-\rho_w}$	0.47	0.63

GENERAL EQUATION OF CONCRETE STRENGTH

In the above considerations the relationships defining the effect of the ratio ω and ω_n on tightness of the cement paste structure were presented. However, the concrete structure parameters could not be adequately evaluated without taking into account the factors resulting from the internal structure of concrete.

To reach a more fundamental understanding of the space disposal of solid phase elements it is necessary to consider a geometric model of cement paste in which binder forms a suspension of grains randomly disposed in an aqueous solution (Figure 1).

Taking into account an individual dimension and the total number of cement grains, the paste volume V_p may be expressed as

$$V_p = A_c \sum_{i=1}^{N_c}(r_{ci} + \delta_{wi})^3 + \left(\frac{c}{\rho_c} + \frac{w}{\rho_w}\right)j = \frac{c}{\rho_c} + \frac{w}{\rho_w} \qquad (3)$$

where, A_c = coefficient of the shape of the cement grain
j = porosity of the cement grains disposal in paste
r_{ci} = radius of the cement grain
δ_{wi} = thickness of the solution film on the cement grain
N_c = number of the cement grains in paste

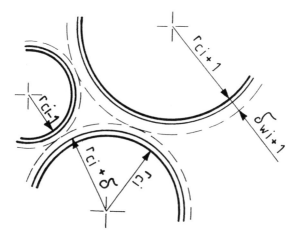

Figure 1 Geometric model of cement paste

Taking into consideration the mean radius $\bar{r}_c$ and the mean number of the grains $\bar{n}_c$ in unit mass of binder, the equation (3) takes the form,

$$\bar{n}_c A_c (\bar{r}_c + \delta_w)^3 = \left(\frac{1}{\rho_c} + \frac{\omega}{\rho_w}\right)(1 - j) \qquad (4)$$

The dependence between the grains number and unit mass of cement may be expressed as

$$\bar{n}_c A_c \bar{r}_c^3 = \frac{1}{\rho_c} \qquad (5)$$

The analysis of the study [4] has stated that the tightness of the disposal of solid phase elements in paste may be defined as

$$s_c = 1 - j = 1 - \frac{0.55\omega_n \rho_c}{\rho_w + \omega_n \rho_c} \qquad (6)$$

The equations (4), (5) and (6) may be solved simultaneously to give the general relationship determining the thickness of the solution film covering the cement grains

$$\delta_w = \bar{r}_c \left[\sqrt[3]{\left(1 + \frac{\omega}{\rho_w}\rho_c\right)\left(1 - \frac{0.55\omega_n \rho_c}{\rho_w + \omega_n \rho_c}\right)} - 1 \right] \qquad (7)$$

Determining a portion of water in which the cement hydration processes are proceeding, the concept of corrected thickness of the solution film on the cement grains δ'_w is introduced. By the aid of the equation (7) the magnitude of the water portion may be computed assuming the value of the tightness of the disposal of the cement grains s_c is equal to 1.

Analyzing the effect of an initial structure on the mechanical properties of cement stone, the thesis that its strength is inversely proportional to the relative thickness of the liquid phase film separating cement grains has been formulated in the form:

$$R_p = R_n \frac{\delta'_n}{\delta'_w} = \frac{R_n}{\Delta} \tag{8}$$

where, R_p, R_n = strength of cement stone at the ratio w that is equal to ω and ω_n, respectively

δ'_n, δ'_w = corrected thickness of the solution film on cement grains at the ratio w that is equal to ω_n and ω, respectively

The value of the relative thickness of the solution film on cement grains Δ is determined from the relation

$$\Delta = \frac{\delta'_w}{\delta'_n} = \frac{\sqrt[3]{1 + \omega \frac{\rho_c}{\rho_w}} - 1}{\sqrt[3]{1 + \omega_n \frac{\rho_c}{\rho_w}} - 1} \tag{9}$$

The function

$$\Delta = a \ exp \ b(\omega - \omega_n) \tag{10}$$

approximates to the relation (9). On the other hand the values of parameters a and b may be determined from the boundary conditions, computing logarithm from the equation (10), on the ground of the relation (9).

There is a close relationship between the strength of cement paste, standard paste and concrete made of the same kind of cement. Yet concrete properties are affected by such parameters as adherence of cement paste to aggregate and the ratio w. Considering the above conditions the following equation of concrete strength is given [5]

$$R_b = \frac{\alpha_k R_{cs}}{exp[2.4(\omega - \omega_n)]} \tag{11}$$

where, α_k = effect of the interaction of aggregate and cement paste in the contact zone

R_{cs} = corrected strength of standard cement paste

Because testing of cement mark is not standardized in the international scale, then the corrected strength of standard paste may be expressed as

$$R_{cs} = R_{cn} exp\left[2.4(\omega - \omega_n)\right] \tag{12}$$

where, R_{cn} is defined as the strength of standard cement paste determined at any value ω.

The values of the function α determining the effect of adherence of cement paste to aggregate are presented in the study [5].

MATHEMATICAL MODEL OF SELECTION OF CONCRETE MIX COMPONENTS

A formation of the concrete structure is conditioned by the rational selection of aggregate components and volume of cement paste. Although many studies deal with this problem, still theoretical approaches to the mechanism of concrete mix consolidation vary in many cases. Taking into account the necessity of introducing methods of the rational mix design, an attempt has been made to elaborate the mathematical model of the selection of concrete mix components. This model may represent the essential factor of forming of the structure and strength of concrete thanks to the application of the computer technique.

Tightness of aggregate grains disposal in concrete mix

In practice the optimum aggregate composition consisting of several fractions is often selected by the method of experimental iteration. Considering the state of knowledge in the range of loose media it may be ascertained that the aggregate composition and its parameters may be analytically estimated on the ground of the determined characteristics of components as well.

In the case of mixing and consolidating of gravel and sand the volume of the aggregate composition may be written as

$$V_k = V_g + V_d - V_g j_g \tag{13}$$

where, V_g = volume of coarse aggregate (gravel)
V_d = volume of fine aggregate (sand)
$V_g j_g$ = volume of sand packing free spaces (pores) between grains of gravel

In reality the tightness of sand in the composition lessens on account of an increase in the primary porosity of sand. It is caused by the phenomenon of the internal effect of the wall (internal friction). Then the volume of the aggregate composition may be expressed as [6]

$$V_k = V_g + V_d - V_g j_g \cdot \varphi_k \tag{14}$$

where, φ_k is defined as the effect of the internal friction on the increase in sand porosity.

Bulk density of the consolidated aggregate mixture may be written as

$$\rho_{nk} = \frac{G + D}{\frac{G}{\rho_{ng}} + \frac{D}{\rho_{nd}} - \frac{G}{\rho_{ng}} \left[1 - \frac{\rho_{ng}}{\rho_g} \right] \varphi_k} = \frac{1 + x_p}{\frac{1 - \varphi_k}{\rho_{ng}} + \frac{x_p}{\rho_{nd}} + \frac{\varphi_k}{\rho_g}} \tag{15}$$

where, x_p = volumetric ratio of sand to gravel
D, G = mass of fine and coarse aggregate
ρ_{nd}, ρ_{ng} = bulk density of fine and coarse aggregate
ρ_g = mass density of coarse aggregate

On the grounds of the experimental evidence the function of the increase in sand volume in the aggregate composition is approximated in the work [6] as

$$\varphi_k = \ln \frac{1 + 1.75 e x_p}{1 + 1.75 x_p} \tag{16}$$

where, e = 2.71...

The volume of pores of this aggregate composition is equal to:

$$V_{jk} = \frac{\rho_{nd} \left[\rho_g + \varphi_k (\rho_{ng} - \rho_g) \right] + x_p \rho_g \rho_{ng}}{(1 + x_p) \rho_g \rho_{ng} \rho_{nd}} - \frac{\rho_d + \rho_g x_p}{\rho_d \rho_g (1 + x_p)} \tag{17}$$

The tightness of the aggregate mixture may be expressed as

$$S_k = \frac{\rho_d + \rho_g x_p}{\rho_g \rho_d \left(\frac{1 - \varphi_k}{\rho_{ng}} + \frac{\varphi_k}{\rho_g} + \frac{x_p}{\rho_{nd}} \right)} \tag{18}$$

The verification of the relationships (15 ÷ 18) presented in the study [6] pointed out the practical usefulness of the above conditions in the selection of the optimum aggregate composition.

In the consolidated concrete mix aggregate grains are stowed tighter than in the composition of dry components. In the process of the vibration aggregate grains are being concentrated as a result of the medium transition into the viscous liquid state. In this case the intergranular spaces between the gravel grains are being filled with sand (the internal effect of the wall does not occur). Then considering the equation (14) the condition of tightness of the aggregate grains disposal in concrete mix may be formulated as

$$S_{kb} = \begin{cases} 1 - [j_g + (j_d - 1)V_d] & for \quad 0 \le V_d \le j_g \\ 1 - [j_g + (1 - j_g)(1 - V_g)]j_d & for \quad j_g \le V_d \le 1 \end{cases} \tag{19}$$

Such tightness of the aggregate grains in concrete is obtained at the following gravel fraction

$$V_G = \begin{cases} 1, & for \quad 0 \le V_d \le j_g \\ 1 - \frac{V_d - j_g}{1 - j_g} & for \quad j_g \le V_d \le 1 \end{cases} \tag{20}$$

When the sand content in the aggregate composition exceeds the volume of pores of coarse aggregate $(V_d > j_g)$, the fine aggregate fraction may be expressed as

$$V_d = j_g + (1 - j_g)(1 - V_g) \tag{21}$$

Mass of fine aggregate D and coarse aggregate G is equal to

$$D = V_d \cdot \rho_{nd} \qquad G = V_g \cdot \rho_{ng} \tag{22}$$

The relative fraction of fine aggregate p_d and coarse aggregate p_g in the aggregate composition may be expressed as

$$p_d = \frac{D}{D + G} = \frac{1}{1 + \frac{V_g \rho_{ng}}{V_d \rho_{nd}}} \qquad p_g = \frac{1}{1 + \frac{V_d \rho_{nd}}{V_g \rho_{ng}}} \tag{23}$$

The grain-size distribution of the aggregate composition can be determined with the aid of the commonly known relationships.

Equation of cement paste volume

The volume of cement paste V_{pm} indispensable for covering the grains and packing the pores in 1 m^3 of aggregate in the consolidated state may be expressed as

$$V_{pm} = A_k \sum_{i=1}^{N_k} \left[\left(\frac{d_{ki}}{2} + \delta_{pi} \right)^3 - \left(\frac{d_{ki}}{2} \right)^3 \right] + j_k m_b \tag{24}$$

where, A_k = coefficient of the shape of the aggregate grain
d_{ki} = diameter of the aggregate grain
δ_{pi} = thickness of the cement paste film on the aggregate grain
m_b = swelling coefficient of the aggregate composition

Taking into account the mean statistic quantities and determining the mean number of the aggregate grains from the tightness definition

$$\bar{N}_k = \frac{8 S_{kb}}{A_k \bar{d}_k^3} \tag{25}$$

the equation (24) may be rearranged to the form

$$V_{pm} = \left[\left(1 + \frac{2\delta_p}{\bar{d}_k} \right)^3 - 1 \right] S_{kb} + j_k m_b = m_b - S_{kb} \tag{26}$$

In relation to unit volume of concrete mix the relationship (26) becomes

$$V_p = 1 - \frac{1}{m_b} S_{kb} \tag{27}$$

Absolute volume of cement paste is defined as

$$V_p = \frac{c}{\rho_c} + \frac{w}{\rho_w} = c \left(\frac{1}{\rho_c} + \frac{w}{\rho_w} \right) \tag{28}$$

If we compare the equations (27) and (28), we get

$$c = \frac{1 - \frac{1}{m_b} S_{kb}}{\frac{1}{\rho_w} \left[\frac{\rho_w}{\rho_c} + w_n + \frac{1}{2.4} \ln \frac{\alpha_k R_{cs}}{R} \right]} \tag{29}$$

which is the cement quality in concrete mix.
The value of the ratio w of paste is determined by the aid of the equation of concrete strength (11).
Hence

$$w = w_n + \frac{1}{2.4} \ln \frac{\alpha_k R_{cs}}{R} \tag{30}$$

On the other hand a coefficient of swelling of concrete mix m_b is mainly conditioned by the consistence of concrete mix.

Criterion of consistence of concrete mix

For the given characteristics of aggregate it may be presupposed that the consistence of concrete mix is mainly dependent on the fluidity and quantity of cement paste. Yet the most essential factor affecting consistence is thickness of the paste film on aggregate grains. Considering the above conditions the effect of ratio $w = w/c$ and thickness of the cement paste film covering the aggregate grains on the consistence of concrete mix are given [6].

Gravel with the maximum grain diameter of 40 mm and sand was applied to concrete mix. The obtained aggregate composition corresponded to the mean graining curve according to the Polish Standard PN-88/B-06250. The tightness of the aggregate composition S_{kb} computed by the aid of the equation (19) was equal to 0.860.

The investigations were carried out with the use of mathematical design of experiments. The effect of fluidity of cement paste is considered as the factor $x_1 = \omega' = \frac{\omega}{\omega_n}$. For the thickness of the paste film ($x_2 = \delta_p$) resulting from the investigation plan the swelling coefficient of concrete mix is

$$m_b = \frac{1}{100}\left[P_d \sum_{i=1}^{n} P_{id}\left(1 + \frac{2\delta_p}{d_{ki}}\right)^3 + P_g \sum_{i=1}^{n} P_{ig}\left(1 + \frac{2\delta_p}{d_{ki}}\right)^3\right] \qquad (31)$$

On the other hand the volumes of paste, cement and aggregate have been determined by the aid of equations (27), (29) and (20).

On the grounds of the obtained mathematical model the course of values δ_p corresponding to consistences of concrete mix is plotted in relation to ω' (Figure 2).

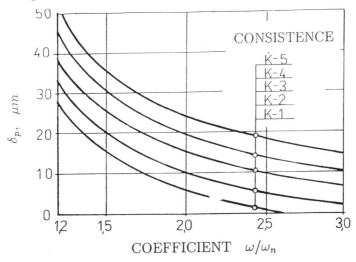

Figure 2 Thickness of cement paste film on aggregate grains δ_p
for mix consistence in relation to $\omega' = \frac{\omega}{\omega_n}$

Dependences presented in Figure 2 provide facilities for forming of the spatial disposal of aggregate grains of concrete mix according to the required consistence.

Granting the practical usefulness of the presented mathematical model of forming of the structure of concrete mix a computer program of mix design has been developed [8].

CONCLUSIONS

The presented relationships state precisely the previous conditions of forming of the structure and strength of concrete. The proposed mathematical model of the determination of concrete mix ratio provides facilities for computer aided mix design with respect to the requisite concrete properties. It may be also useful for the determination of the composition of different composite materials. The application of the proposed model used to form the structure and the exploitation properties of designed concretes may concur with an increase in the operational reliability of buildings and in the reduction of overhaul costs.

REFERENCES

1. ŚWITOŃSKI A. Technological and Structural Factors of Moulded Cement Pastes Strength (in Polish). Scientific Papers of the Institute of Building of the Technical University of Wrocław, No 35, Wrocław, 1981, pp. 135-146.

2. ŚWITOŃSKI A. New Method of Cement Class Estimation (in Polish), Cement, Wapno, Gips, No 1, 1984, pp. 26-28.

3. ŚWITOŃSKI A. Experimental Evaluation of Mix Compacting Parameters as Factors Determining the Physical Properties of Concrete Moulded with Concurrent Vibration (in Polish), Cement, Wapno, Gips, No 2, 1989, pp. 20-24.

4. SEBOK T. A Study of Sorption of Water on the Surface of Grains of Cement in the First Phase of Hydration, Cement and Concrete Research, vol.16, No 4, 1986, pp. 461-471.

5. ŚWITOŃSKI A. An Attempt to Evaluate the Conventional Strength of Concrete as a Function of Selected Technological Factors Responsible for the Structure of Cement Stone (in Polish), Przegląd Budowlany, No 2-3, 1987, pp.. 76-79.

6. ŚWITOŃSKI A. Physical Model of Assortment of Optimum Aggregate Graining in Concrete Design (in Polish). Konferencja Naukowa KILiW, PAN i KN, PZITB, Krynica, 1992, t.3, pp. 91-96.

7. ŚWITOŃSKI A. Basic Conditions of the Concrete Structure Modelling (in Polish), Scientific Papers of the Institute of Building of the Technical University of Wrocław, No 64, Wrocław, 1991, pp. 153-159.

8. ŚWITOŃSKI A., ANTOSZAK W. Concrete Design Computer Program ,,COMIDI" for microcomputer IBM, Catalogue of Computer Programs, Technical University of Opole, 1990.

OPTIMUM DESIGN OF SFRC BASED
ON STRENGTH AND TOUGHNESS

T W Shiah

A S Ezeldin

Stevens Institute of Technology

United States of America

ABSTRACT: During the last decade steel fiber reinforced concrete (SFRC) has been increasingly used as a construction material. Addition of steel fibers to concrete improves its flexural, shear, and torsion strengths, and more significantly its toughness performance. This paper presents an algorithm capable of satisfying the fibrous beam flexural, shear, torsion, and toughness design requirements. In order to obtain an economical design, the algorithm uses an optimization technique to minimize the cost objective function of such beams. The design variables include beam width, beam depth, fiber content, bending reinforcing bars, stirrups size, and stirrups spacing. A sensitivity analysis is performed to evaluate the variables effect on the cost objective function.

Keywords: Beams; Flexural strength; Metal fibers; Microcomputers; Optimization; Reinforced concrete; Shear strength; Torsion strength; Toughness.

Mr. Tai-Woei Shiah is a Ph.D student in the Civil, Environmental, and Coastal Engineering Department of Stevens Institute of Technology, Hoboken, New Jersey, where he received his MS.

Dr.A. Samer Ezeldin is an assistant professor in the Civil, Environmental, and Coastal Engineering Department of Stevens Institute of Technology, Hoboken, New Jersey, His research interests include the development of new construction materials and computer-aided design of structural elements.

Concrete 2000. Edited by Ravindra K. Dhir and M. Roderick Jones.
© 1993 Published by E & FN Spon. ISBN 0 419 18120 2.

INTRODUCTION

Steel fiber reinforced concrete (SFRC) is concrete made of hydraulic cement, aggregates, conventional reinforcing steel bars, and discontinuous discrete steel fibers. Steel fibers have an aspect ratio (ratio of length to diameter) ranging from 20 to 100, and could have several cross-sections (square, circular, or crescent). A large number of studies [1-2] investigated the use of steel fibers to reinforced concrete members with or without conventional reinforcement. These investigations indicated that steel fibers greatly improve the toughness and to a lesser extent increase the bending, shear, and torsion capacities of concrete members. Such improvement in performance depends on the type and volume percentage of fibers. During the last decade, SFRC has been used in many applications, such as airport and highway paving, industrial flooring, bridge deck and floor overlays, rock stabilization, and refractories [3]. In order to achieve saving in materials cost and efficiency in performance, optimization techniques should be used. This paper presents a computer algorithm that, based on a systematic direct search method, analyzes and optimizes the contribution of steel fibers to toughness, torsion, shear, and bending of SFRC beams. Six design variables are considered, namely, concrete dimension (depth and width), fiber content, bending reinforcing area, stirrups size, and stirrups spacing. The algorithm is capable of implementing any specified design requirements and construction constraints, making it suitable for economically designing SFRC beams. A sensitivity analysis is performed to evaluate the effect of variations on the cost objective function.

ANALYTICAL METHOD

Flexural Strength

Several methods have been developed to evaluate the strength of SFRC beams in flexure [2]. In general, these methods predict the extra tensile strength of the fibrous concrete and add it to the strength provided by the reinforcing bars. The method developed by Craig [4] is used in the proposed algorithm. This method is similar to the ACI ultimate strength design method [5]. The nominal strength is represented as:

$$M_n = A_s\, f_y\, \left(d - \frac{a}{2}\right) + \sigma_t\, b\, \left(h - \frac{a}{\beta_1}\right)\left(\frac{h}{2} + \frac{a}{2\beta_1} - \frac{a}{2}\right) \text{ ,(lb-in.)} \tag{1}$$

$$a = \frac{\dfrac{A_s\, f_y}{b} + \sigma_t\, h}{0.85\, f_c' + (\sigma_t/\beta_1)} \quad\text{, (in.)} \tag{2}$$

$$\sigma_t = 1.12\, F_{be}\, (\ell_f/d_f)\, \rho_f \quad\text{, (psi)} \tag{3}$$
$$\quad = 1.12\, F_{be}\, (RI)$$

To ensure ductile failure and to avoid excessive cracking, the amount of area of tension reinforcing bars, As, is limited to:

$$\left[\frac{400}{f_y}\right] bd \leq As \leq \left[0.75 \left[\frac{0.85\ f_c'\ \beta_1 + \sigma_t}{f_y}\right]\ \frac{\epsilon_c}{\epsilon_c + \epsilon_y} - \frac{\sigma_t}{f_y}\frac{h}{d}\right] bd,\ (in^2)\ \ [4]$$

Shear Strength

Research investigations have shown that stirrups and steel reinforcement can be used effectively to increase the shear capacity of SFRC beam [2]. This shear strength increase is attributed to: a) small spacing between randomly distributed fibers, b) increase in the concrete first crack and ultimate tensile strengths, and c) increase the shear-friction strength. Narayanan and Darwish [6] proposed the following equation to predict the ultimate shear strength of mortar fiber reinforced concrete beams:

$$V_{cf} = \left[e\ (\ 0.24\ f_t' + 80\ \rho\ \frac{d}{a}\ ) + 250\ F \right] bd\ \ ,\ (N)\ \ \ \ \ \ [5]$$

where $\frac{d}{a}$ = the effective depth-to-shear-span ratio

$e = 1.0$ when $\frac{d}{a} > 2.8$ and $2.8(\frac{d}{a})$ when $\frac{d}{a} \leq 2.8$

F = fiber factor (RI d) where d = 0.5 for round fibers, 0.75 for crimped fibers, and 1.0 for fibers with deformed end

This equation incorporates the contribution of fiber concrete to the total shear represented in term of the split cylinder strength, the dowel action provided by the amount of tensile strength, and the effect of the shear-span ratio. The shear design approach follows the method of the ACI Code [5]. Essentially, the contribution of stirrups, V_s is added to the concrete resisting force, V_{cf}, to obtain the shear capacity, V_n.

$$V_s = \frac{A_v\ F_y\ d}{s} \qquad\qquad ,\ (lb.) \qquad\qquad [6]$$

$$V_n = V_{cf} + V_s \qquad\qquad ,\ (lb.) \qquad\qquad [7]$$

Torsion Strength

The torsional resistance of SFRC beams is contributed to three sources, namely, the concrete matrix, T_c, the combination of closed stirrups and longitudinal reinforcing bars, T_s, and steel fibers contribution, T_f. Nanni [7] proposed the following equations to estimate the torsional strength of SFRC beams.

$$T_c = \frac{0.8\ \sqrt{f'c}\ \ \ \Sigma\ x^2\ y}{[1 + (0.4\ V_u\ /\ C_t\ T_u)^2]^{0.5}} \qquad\qquad ,\ (lb\text{-}in.) \qquad [8]$$

where $\quad C_t = \dfrac{bw\ d}{\Sigma\ x^2\ y}$

$$T_s = \dfrac{A_t}{s}\ x_1\ y_1\ f_y\ a_t \qquad\qquad ,\ (\text{lb-in.}) \qquad [9]$$

where $\quad a_t = 0.66 + 0.33\ \dfrac{y_1}{x_1} \leq 1.5$

$$T_f = T_{f0} + T_{f1} \qquad\qquad ,\ (\text{lb-in.}) \qquad [10]$$

where $\quad\begin{aligned} T_{f0} &= 0.42\ F\ T_c \\ T_{f1} &= 0.60\ F\ A\ell\ F_y\ x \\ &= 0.0\ (\text{if}\ T_s \neq 0) \\ F &= \dfrac{RI\ F_{be}}{100} \end{aligned}$

Hence,

$$T_n = T_c + T_s + T_f \qquad\qquad ,\ (\text{lb-in.}) \qquad [11]$$

The longitudinal torsional torsional reinforcement can be expressed as:

$$A\ell = 2\ (\tfrac{A_t}{s})\ (x_1 + y_1) \qquad ,\ (\text{in}^2) \qquad [12]$$

Toughness

Toughness is an important characteristic of SFRC beams. Toughness can be estimated using the area under the load-deflection curve, Figure 1. The Toughness Ratio (TR) is defined as the ratio of the toughness of SFRC beams to the toughness of rigid plastic material.

$$TR = \dfrac{AREA(oab)}{AREA(Pmax*\Delta max)} \qquad\qquad [13]$$

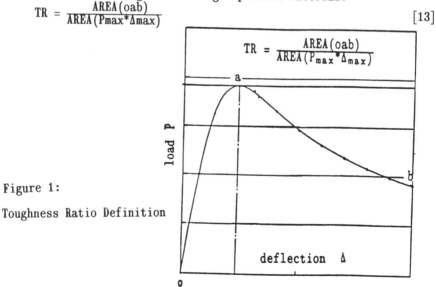

Figure 1:

Toughness Ratio Definition

The relation between (TR) and Reinforcing Index (RI) can be represented as [8,9]:

$$TR = 0.5 \quad \text{(if RI < 40)}$$
$$= 0.005 \; RI + 0.3 \quad \text{(if RI} \geq 40) \tag{14}$$

OPTIMIZATION ALGORITHM

Constraints

The following constraints are considered to control the algorithm.

Dimensions: $b_{min} \leq b \leq b_{max}$ $h_{min} \leq h \leq h_{max}$

Fiber Content: $RI_{min} \leq RI \leq RI_{max}$

Bending: $M_n > M$

Shear: $V_s \leq 4 \; V_{cf}$ (otherwise enlarge section)

$V_n > V$ $V \geq \dfrac{V_{cf}}{2}$ (No shear analysis required)

Torsion: $T_s \leq 4 \; (T_c + T_{cf})$ $Tn > T$

$T > \dfrac{4}{3} \; (f_c')^{0.5} \; \Sigma \; x^2 \; y$ (otherwise no torsion analysis required)

Stirrups spacing: $s_{max} \leq \dfrac{d}{2} < \dfrac{x_1 + y_1}{4} \leq 24$ inches

Toughness: $TR_{required} \geq TR$

Cost Objective Function:

The cost objective function ,Z, to be minimized can be formulated as:

$$Z = C_c (b \; h) + C_s (A_s + A_l) + C_v \; 2(b+h)(A_{vt}/s) + C_u (2h + b) + C_f (RI)(bh) \tag{15}$$

The flow chart of the computer algorithm is presented in Figure 2. Essentially, the program is set to read the required data: the objective function, the design constraints, material properties, and applied loading. The data is provided in an interactive mode or in a data base mode. Then the program searches for a minimum for the objective function in the spaces of the six variables, namely, the reinforcing index RI, beam width b, beam depth h, steel reinforcing bar area A_s, stirrups spacing S, and stirrups area A_v, respectively. A minimum for the objective function is recorded if M_n, V_n, T_n, and, TR are found to be greater than the applied M, V, T, and $(TR)_{required}$, respectively and if that objective function value is smaller than any previously recorded value.

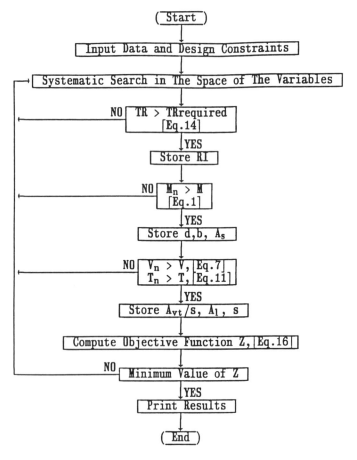

Figure 2:   Computation flow of proposed algorithm.

Results and Sensitivity Analysis:

The proposed algorithm can be used to evaluate the effectiveness of fibers in SFRC beams as well as their economical feasibility. Table 1 presents an example of such evaluations. Assuming the following material costs-concrete: $100/yd^3$; steel: $500/t$; fibers: $0.40/lb$; and labor: $150/ft^2$, Equation [15] becomes

$$Z = \frac{1}{1200} \left[2.4(b\ h) + 2100(A_s + A_l) + 2100\ (b+h)(A_{vt}/s) \right.$$
$$\left. + 1200(2h + b) + 0.01(RI)(bh) \right] \qquad [16]$$

For a cross-section with b = 13 in., d = 16 in., A_s = 2.81 in. and stirrups of #3 spaced at 6 inches, the variations in flexural strength, shear strength, torsional strength, and toughness with the inclusion of steel fibers are indicated in Table 1. The increase in the section properties depends on the RI value (i.e. fiber type and content). This improvement in concrete performance is coupled with a higher cost. The decision-making process on whether this that cost increase is acceptable in return for the additional benefits is made much simpler. To account for local material costs and specific design considerations, the cost objective function and the other constraints can be easily controlled.

Table 1:   Parametric Study results.

RI	b in	d in	A_s in²	A_v in²	s	M_n lb-in	V_n lb	T_n lb-in	TR	Z $	percent of increase				
											M_n	V_n	T_n	TR	Z
0	12	16	3.5	0.2	6	2114978	93536	225057	0.500	57.97	—	—	—	—	—
25	12	16	3.5	0.2	6	2161876	136049	242499	0.500	58.02	2.22	45.45	7.75	—	0.08
50	12	16	3.5	0.2	6	2207851	178562	259941	0.550	58.07	4.39	90.90	15.50	10	0.16
75	12	16	3.5	0.2	6	2252930	221075	277384	0.675	58.11	6.52	136.35	23.25	35	0.24
100	12	16	3.5	0.2	6	2297139	263588	294826	0.800	58.16	8.61	181.80	31.00	60	0.32
125	12	16	3.5	0.2	6	2340501	306101	312269	0.925	58.21	10.66	227.25	38.75	85	0.40

A sensitivity analysis is performed to evaluate the effect of six variables included in the algorithm. For each variable, the optimum value for a given problem is change from -20% up to +20%, the corresponding variations in the cost objective function are shown in Figure 3. The results of the analysis indicate beam depth h is the most sensitivity variable.

Figure 3:

Sensitivity Analysis

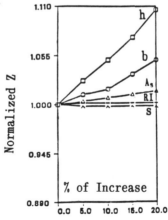

CONCLUSIONS

The proposed computer algorithm, when applied to the SFRC beam, can be used successfully to evaluate the optimum volume of steel fibers. The effect of fibers on flexural strength, shear strength, torsion strength, toughness, and construction costs is evaluated to reach the most suitable decision.

REFERENCES

1. *"Fiber Reinforced Concrete Properties and Applications"*, SP-105, Detroit, 1987.

2. ACI Committee 544, "Design Considerations for Steel Fiber Reinforced Concrete (ACI 544.4R-88)", ACI Structural Journal, Vol.85, No.5, Sept-Oct. 1988, pp.563-580.

3. Balaguru, P.N., and Shah,S.P., *"Fiber-Reinforced Cement Composites"*, McGraw-Hill, Inc., 1992.

4. Craig,R., "Flexural Behavior and Design of Reinforced Fiber Concrete Members", SP-105, American Concrete Institute, Detroit, 1987, pp. 517-563.

5. ACI Committee 318, "Building Code Requirements for Reinforced Concrete and Commentary (ACI 318-89)", American Concrete Institute, Detroit, 1989, 353 pp.

6. Narayanan, R., and Darwish, I. Y. S., "Use of steel fibers as Shear Reinforcement", ACI Structural Journal, (83/4),1986, pp. 624-628.

7. Nanni, A., "Design for Torsion Using Steel Fiber Reinforced Concrete", ACI Materials Journal, (87/6), 1990, pp. 556-563.

8. Ezeldin, A. S., and Balaguru,P.N., "Normal- and High Strength Fiber-Reinforced Concrete Under Compression", ASCE Journal of Materials In Civil Engineering, Vol.4, No.4,Nov. 1992, pp. 415-429.

9. Moens, J., and Nemegeer, D.,"Designing Fiber Reinforced Concrete Based on Toughness Characteristics", Concrete International, Nov. 1991, pp. 38-43.

NOTATION

a = depth of rectangular stress block
A_c = the cross-sectional of beam
$A\ell$ = area of symmetrical longitudinal reinforcing bars in absence of stirrups
A_s = area of tension reinforcement
A_t = the cross section of one stirrup leg
A_v = the area of the cross section of the stirrups
A_{vt} = the total stirrups area combined for torsion and shear
b = width of beam
β_1 = the value of the stress block depth factor
C_c = the unit cost of concrete
C_f = the unit cost of steel fiber
C_s = the unit cost of reinforcement bar

C_u = the unit cost of labor for forming
d = distance from extreme compressive fiber to centroid of
      tension reinforcement
d_f = fiber diameter
D_f = density of steel fiber
D_s = density of reinforcement bars
e = distance from extreme compressive fiber to top of tensile
      stress block of fibrous concrete (Fig.1)
E_s = modulus of elasticity of steel
ϵ_s = tensile strain in steel at theoretical moment strength of
      beam, for bars = F_f/E_s, for fibers = σ_f/E_s based on fiber
      stress developed at pollout
F_{be} = bond efficiency of the fiber which varies from 1.0 to 1.2
      depending on fiber characteristics
f_e = flexural strength
f_f = the flexural strength of steel fiber concrete
f_r = the rupture strength of concrete
,
f_t = splitting tensile strength
f_y = yield strength of reinforcing bar
h = depth of beam
L = span of beam
ℓ_f = fiber length
ℓ_f/d_f = the aspect ratio of steel fiber

M_n = the norminal moment
N = the total number of stirrups
RI = reinforcing index
ρ = percentage of area of tensile steel to area of concrete
ρ_b = the balanced reinforcement ratio

ρ_f = percent by volume of steel fiber

ρ_{min} = the minimum reinforcement ratios = space between two stirrups
T_c = the torsional capacity contributed by concrete
T_f = the torsional capacity contributed by steel fibers
T_{f0} = the increment oft he torsional resistance of matrix
      strength
T_{f1} = the contribution of torsion resistance by the symmetrical
      longitudinal reinforcement when stirrups are not used
T_{max} = the maximum toughness
T_n = the nominal torsion resistance
T_s = the torsional capacity contributed by a combination of
      closed stirrups and longitudinal reinforcement bars
T_u = the factored torsional moment
UW = unit weight of concrete
μ = a constant depending on F_{be}
V_{cf} = shear strength of steel fiber
V_f = volume fraction of fiber
V_m = volume fraction of the matrix
V_{nf} = the nominal shear strength
V_s = shear strength of web reinforcement
V_u = the factored shear strength

W_c = concrete weight
W_f = steel fiber weight
W_s = reinforcement bars weight
x = the shorter side of the rectangular section
y = the longer side of the rectangular section
x_1 = the dimension of the stirrup in the short direction
y_1 = the dimension of the stirrup in the long direction
y_t = the center gravity of beam section

DEVELOPMENT OF FLEXIBLE CONCRETE

S Kakuta

Akashi College of Technology

Japan

R C Joshi

University of Calgary

Canada

A B S T R A C T. This study is an important one in the development of flexible concrete. Improvements were made to the flexibility of a large volume of fly ash mortar by adding a water soluble polymer, Poly Vinyl Alchohol (PVA), to the mixture. This polymer was added to bind the solid particles of cement, fly ash and sand. Replacement levels of high volume fly ash mortar were larger than 50 % by weight to the amount of cementious material. An anti-foamer, a cross-linking agent and a superplasticizer were added as admixtures. A silica fume also added to the mixture of PVA mortar. Flexural, compressive and tensile strengths of mortar were tested respectively. Mortar specimens sized 4 x 4 x 16 cm were used for the flexural and compressive tests and briquet specimens in accordance with ASTM C 190 for the tensile test. Flexural, compressive and tensile strengths of mortar were tested respectively. The deflection and elongation of mortar was also tested. Ductility of the PVA mortar was remarkably improved over short period of time. The rate of deflection at center span of the PVA mortar specimens was about nine times that of the controlled mix at 28 days. This flexible mortar was produced with PVA polymer composing less than 10 % of cementious material.

K e y w o r d s : Flexibility, Elongation, Fly ash, Water soluble polymer, Poly Vinyl Alchohol (PVA), Silica fume, Dissolve in water, Polymer mortar.

D r. S h i n o b u K a k u t a is a professor at The Akashi College of Technology, Akashi Japan. He specializes in the rheology of fresh concrete and in the use of chemical admixtures. Lately, he is interested in the utilization of industrial by-products and usage for water soluble polymers to high workable concrete. He has published many papers on fresh concrete and early age concrete.

D r. R a m e s h C. J o s h i is a professor at The University of Calgary, Calgary, Alberta, Canada. His recent interest is the utilization of industrial waste materials to concrete and soil foundation. He is also interested in the effects on the durability of high volume fly ash concrete in low temperature environments. He has published many papers on fly ash concrete and improvement of soft soils using industrial by-products.

Concrete 2000. Edited by Ravindra K. Dhir and M. Roderick Jones.
© 1993 Published by E & FN Spon. ISBN 0 419 18120 2.

INTRODUCTION

Concrete is generally believed a typical brittle material from both reason of higher modulus of elasticity and the weak tensile strength to compressive strength. Indeed, if cracks occur at tensile zone in a unreinforced section, the concrete member will be seriously damaged. In order to cover this weak point, the strength of concrete is becoming strong although more brittle at the same time. Lately, high compressive strength concrete of more than 100 MPa can be easily produced by adding an ultra-fine particle like a silica fume with a superplasticizer. However, this mix is also becoming more brittle. At the same time, the demands on new performance to concrete are diversifying. Take, flexibility for example. Provided that a flexible concrete is developed, the joint interval of concrete slab will be elongated and the concrete mat slab on soft foundation will follow up the un-uniform settlement without cracks.

This study is the first step in the development of flexible concrete. In this study, the flexible mortars were tested rather than concrete. Poly Vinyl Alchohol (PVA) was used as a binder of solid particles. In order to increase the flexibility, a large volume of fly ash was used. Replacement levels were more than 50 % by weight to the amount of cementious material. Also a mortar composed of commercialized acrylic emulsion [1] was tested to compare with performances of PVA mortars. Mix proportions of mortar were varied with volume of cement, fly ash, sand, PVA and admixtures.

Flexibility of PVA mortars is remarkably improved in the early stages in comparison with the flexibility of traditional cement mortar. This results from the network of PVA film forming in paste matrix. PVA is basically of water soluble polymer so that the PVA mixture dissolves in water. In this study, it was observed that the application of either the silica fume or the cross-linking agent to the PVA mortar has the effect of inhibiting dissolution while maintaining both mortar strength and flexibility.

FLEXIBILITY OF CONCRETE

Both properties of the higher modulus of elasticity and the weaker tensile strength lead concrete to become brittle. The flexibility of concrete will be increased by adding the paste matrix which has a lower modulus of elasticity. It follows that the flexibility of concrete will not be improved, as long as the paste matrix consists mainly of hard cement hydrates. Before the bending member of concrete cracks, the curvature of beam can be calculated by the following equation.

$$\Phi = \frac{M}{E\,I}$$

Where, Φ = curvature
M = bending moment
E = modulus of elasticity
I = moment of inertia

Modulus of elasticity of concrete E is given by the following equation.

$$1/E = V_a/E_a + V_g/E_g + V_h/E_h + V_p/E_p$$

where,   V = volume content

subscripts of a = aggregate
              g = unhydrated cementious grain
              h = hydrate of cementious grain
              p = polymer

This equation indicates that the way to increase flexibility of concrete is by decreasing the modulus of elasticity of cementious matrix. The polymer cement is composed of polymer exhibiting a low modulus of elasticity like a rubberized polymer. As it has been described above, provided that concrete pores are fully saturated with cement hydrates, traditional cement concrete becomes more rigid as it is strengthened. Flexibility of concrete, thus, comes from preparing the polymer which has a low modulus of elasticity and from stopping/reducing hydration speed at very early age. Most of polymer cements or polymer mortars demonstrating flexibility have been composed of a large volume of polymer with a low modulus of elasticity. It is impractical, however, to use such material in field construction because of the of the polymer involved. If a large volume of fly ash were used in lieu of Portland cement, it will contribute to the suppression of hydration speed and the reduction of concrete production costs. Forming the polymer film network in cement matrix during early age should change the properties of concrete and mortar. Figure 1 provides a schematic explanation of this concept. Polymer dispersions gradually absorb cement hydrates with reduction of water content through evaporation and hydration. Polymer films will form by adhering to each polymer dispersion after evaporating free water. Since fly ash hydrates slowly, the process of curing becomes a more important factor. It indicates that the evaporation of water process (dry cure) that allows the polymer film networks to form is required at least once after mixing. Flexibility comes from this polymer network.

a)PVA solution with cement
  and fly ash particles

b)Dry cured

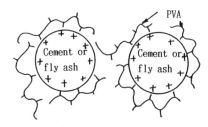
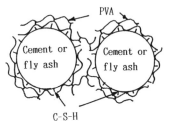

c)Wet cure

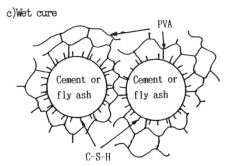

Figure 1 Diagrammatic representation of the production of polymer film

There are two proposed theories for whether materials between polymer and concrete interact or not [2]. Recently, the existence of interaction in polymer cement systems with or without a cross-linking agent between cementious materials and some polymers has been gaining acceptance [2]-[7]. In this study, microanalysis of the interaction between polymers and cement hydrates was also conducted through the X-ray diffraction analysis and Scanning Electron Microscope (SEM) analysis.

EXPERIMENTAL DETAILS

Fly Ash and Cement

Fly ash was used for both reasons of technicality and economy. The ASTM Class C fly ash produced at a coal burning plant in Forestburg Canada was mixed in mortars. The fly ash was classified by ASTM C-618 Specification on gradation and chemical composition. An Ordinary Portland Cement (OPC) classified by ASTM Type I was used. Chemical and physical properties are given in Table 1.

Table 1 Chemical and physical properties of fly ash and cement.

Composition	SiO_2	Al_2O_3	Fe_2O_3	CaO	MgO	K_2O	Na_2O	SO_3
Fly ash	56.3	21.7	4.9	9.0	1.2	1.0	4.2	0.4
OPC	20.8	4.4	2.6	62.7	4.4	0.8	0.2	2.5

L.O.I. (%)	Specific gravity (gr/cm^3)	Specific surface (cm^2/gr)	Pozzolanic activity index
0.4	2.01	3690	93.0
1.1	3.14	4300	——

Aggregate

The river sand source from BURNO and Ottawa silica sand were used for the fine aggregate. The specific gravity of river sand was 2.65 and the fineness modulus was 2.80. The used natural silica sand from Ottawa was graded from 0.3 mm (No.50 sieve) to 0.6 mm (No.30 sieve) and the specific gravity was 2.66.

Polymer

The roles of polymer as a bending aid and a bonding matrix have been described above. The polymer used in this study exhibited following characteristics;
 (1)Appropriate strength,   (2)Ability of the elongation, (3)Adsorption and adhesive
    properties to the cementious materials and aggregate,   (4)Insoluble in water,
 (5)Durable in environment, (6)Improvement of fluidity, (7)Harmless and (8)Economical.

Poly Vinyl Alcohol has been used as a molding assistant in production of MDF cement[8]. There is a report that PVA reacts as a binder at interface of cement hydrates [9]. PVA which satisfied the above conditions was selected as the main polymer. Another polymer, a commercialized acrylic type emulsion in Japan, was prepared for a comparison of characteristics with the developed PVA flexible mortar.

Data for used PVA are shown in Table 2. The acrylic emulsion used[1] was a cationic acrylic polymer type emulsion. A methyl methacrylate 2 ethylhexel acrylate with dimethylaminoethyl acrylate was used as copolymer. The concentration of emulsion is 60%.

Table 2 Data of the used Poly Vinyl Alcohol

PVA	High M.W.	Low M.W.
Molecular Weight	114,000	22,000
Minimum degree of hydrolysis	87 %	98 %
Viscosity of 4 % aqueous solution at 20 C	about 40 cP	about 6 cP
Minimum limit of impurity ash	0.7 %	1 %

Chemical admixtures

Due to an increase in the fluidity of the mortar a superplasticizer (a modified poly-condensation product of melamine and formaldehyde) was used. Most polymers will produce many bubbles at the time of mixing. These bubbles must be eliminated to avoid any reduction in the strength of the concrete. Two types of silicon type antifoaming agents, FS-antifoam 025 as emulsion type and SN defoamer 14-HP as powder type, were tested.

PVA is a water soluble polymer so that mortar containing PVA basically dissolves in water. If the PVA is partially saponificated of -OH radical, it will dissolve better than pure PVA. Therefore either the cross-linking agent or a grafting technique is needed to diminish the dissolution of PVA mortar. This has been a ongoing problem in MDF cement studies. Resistance to dissolution in water can be improved to a limited extent through heat treatment or by adding cross-linking agents [4]. Glycerin was adopted as a lubricant agent and a wetting agent for a rheological aid to increase the mixibility of mortar. Formaldehyde was used as a cross-linking agent of PVA products.

Mix proportions

Mortar mixes were prepared in the same manner as the flexible concrete mix. Tested mortar mix proportions are summarized in Table 3. Specimens were made in accordance with same treatment of ASTM C190 for the tensile test and ASTM C349 for the flexural and the compressive tests. Mortars were mixed by Hobart mixer and the mixing time was three minutes.

Table 3 Mix proportions

Control 1	W/C=45%, S/C=2
Control 2	W/C=45%, S/C=2, F/(C+F)= 0.5 to 0.8
Flexible Mortar	W/(C+F)=0.45 − 0.55, S/(C+F)=1.0 to 4.3, F/(C+F)=0 to 0.8 P/(C+F)=0 to 8%, E/C*=1.0, SP/(C+F)=0 to 3%, AF/(C+F)=1%, HCHO/PVA=3 to 9%, Glycerol/(C+F)=0 to 3%

F:Fly ash, P:Polymer by weight, E:Emulsion by weight, SP:Superplasticizer
AF:Anti-foamer by weight. [Mark * is in case of Acrylic emulsion is used.]

Test procedure

Specimens were cured in a water bath controlled to the constant temperature of 23 C until age 14 days or 28 days after one day fog cure. Tests were conducted in accordance with ASTM C190 and ASTM C349. Deflection of mortars was measured at the centre span of the mortar beam (4 x 4 x 16 cm) by Linear Voltage Differential Transducer (LVDT). The elongation of tensile test specimens were measured by LVDT. Even though this elongation is not an accurate value because it includes measurements attributes to play in the device as well as perforation in the specimens, it might be used for the relative estimation to real deformation.

TEST RESULTS

Strength and deformability

The concrete strength is reduced as replacement levels of fly ash to cement increase especially in early age. The loss of strength is in proportion to replacement levels of fly ash as in shown   Table 4. The strength ratio of flexural to compression however increases when replacement levels reaches 60 % or more. Increase in the fluidity of fresh mortar from addition of fly ash may partially attribute for this. As illustrated in Table 5, the addition of polymer suppressed the reduction in strength through the void filling effect. The eight per cent mix of PVA contributed was 70 % recovery to the control mix on flexural strength. Swelling of mortars was small in comparison with control mixes.

Deformability of mortars was tested to compare with the high volume fly ash mortars. Test results appear in Figures 2 – 4 and Table 6. The deformability of mortar decreased with   age but increased in proportion to the volume content of fly ash in the mix. Subsequently, the effect of polymer content was tested for a high volume of 70 % replaced mortars. Test results in Figure 4 show that mix containing eight per cent of PVA produces   deformability of mortar. Furthermore it indicates that the increase in sand content to cement had no effect on the reduction in the flexibility over time. Effects of admixtures to strength and deformability were tested. Results are shown in Table 5. Use of formaldehyde in PVA mortar had little effects as a cross-linking agent to PVA in this experiment. Measured PH values of solution of PVA mortar were 12.26 at 14 days and 12.33 at 28 days respectively. It may have hindered the reaction between PVA and formaldehyde. However, as evidenced from the rubbing and unit weight tests, the PVA mortars given silicon type antifoamer resisted dissolution in water. Strength and deformability were also improved after a five per cent extra addition of silica fume was added to the PVA mortars.

Table 4 Rate of strength of fly ash mortars to control mixed mortar (%)

Age (days)	Rate	Control	50% replaced	60% replaced	70% replaced	80% replaced
	Flex/Comp	17.6	16.7	20.1	21.0	25.5
14	Comp/Comp'	100	70.0	48.1	26.3	12.8
	Flex/Flex'	100	66.3	55.1	31.4	18.5
	Flex/Comp	13.9	15.8	18.1	21.5	26.4
28	Comp/comp'	100	64.1	47.2	22.5	7.4
	Flex/Flex'	100	79.6	67.0	37.9	15.4

Table 5 Rate of strength of polymer mortar to control mixed mortar (%)[1]

Age (days)	Rate	Control	4 % PVA	6 % PVA	8 % PVA	Acryclic Em. [2]
	Flex/Comp	17.6	31.3	29.9	45.1	62.6
14	Comp/Comp'	100	8.4	21.0	27.6	5.3
	Flex/Flex'	100	14.4	34.3	68.0	19.0
	Flex/Comp	13.9	55.3	29.8	46.0	59.4
28	Comp/comp'	100	3.5	20.4	22.1	6.9
	Flex/Flex'	100	24.9	43.7	72.9	29.6

Comp' and Flex' mean strengths of the control mix.
1)Replacement level of fly ash was constantly 70 % to cementious materials.
2)Two days wet cured and then five days water cured before room cure.

Table 6 Rate of maximum deflection of polymer mortar to control mixed mortar (%)

Age(days)	Control	050*	060	070	080	470	670	870	Acrylic E.
14	100	75.2	76.3	61.5	52.5	211	162	306	289
28	100	120	121	63.9	46.8	284	335	953	691

* 050 means 0 % addition of polymer and 50 % fly ash replaced mortar

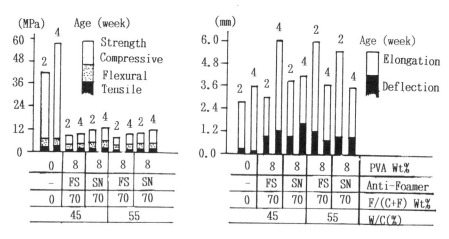

Figure 2 Strength and deformation test results of PVA mortars (S/C=2)

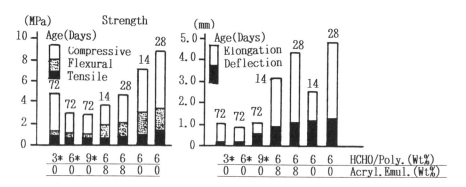

Figure 3 Effects of formaldehyde (PVA=8%, Marked * is a PVA of low M.W., S/C=2)

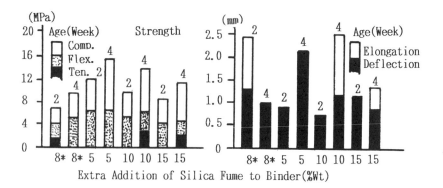

Figure 4 Effects of silica fume (PVA=8%, S/C=2, * is acrylic emulsion composed)

MICROANLYSIS

Microstructure of the flexible mortars were analyzed by a SEM and a X-ray diffraction analyzer. The photograph in Figure 5 shows a co-matrix of cement and PVA film in the flexible mortar. This co-matrix in paste should give flexibility to mortar. However, swelling of the water soluble polymer in water allows the water to migrate from the surface of specimens to the surface of the inner co-matrix. Therefore, the filling effect of micro-grains like silica fume can prevent the swelling and dissolving of PVA in the specimen.

Results from the E-DAX analyzer of X-ray analysis, silicate, aluminum and calcium were observed in polymer film of the co-matrix. Subsequently, existence of calcium acetate ($b-C_6H_6CaO_4$) was determined by X-ray diffraction study of co-matrix (Figure 6). However, there were not satisfactory evidence of reaction between PVA and particles from the X-ray study. Although calcium acetate has the potential to dissolve in water, there was little damage resulting from dissolution test immersing in water.

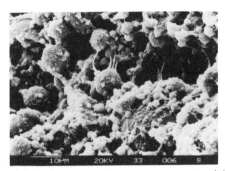 

(a)PVA film network   (b)Condensed co-matrix by silica fume

Figure 5 Co-matrix of cement hydrates and polymer

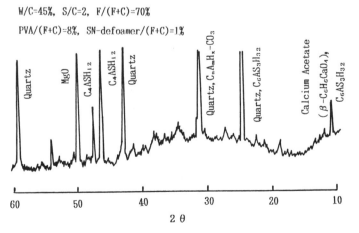

Figure 6 X-ray powder diffraction tracer for high volume fly ash mortar with PVA

CONCLUSIONS

This mortar will be able to apply as a joint mortar and a grout mortar of the after bond method in prestressed concrete. Conclusions are summarized as follows.

1. Flexibility of PVA mortar is remarkably increased in comparison with a traditional cement mortar until 28 days cure. This flexibility is caused by the network of PVA film in the paste matrix. Rate of deflection at center span to traditional cement mortar was about nine times at 28 days.

2. Adding PVA reduces the strength of mortar. However, more than seven percent addition contributes both to the increase of strength and the increase of flexibility.

3. A five percent addition of silica fume to the PVA mortar suppresses reduction in strength while maintaining flexibility.

4. Dissolution of PVA immersed in water can be reduced by using a cross-linking agent.

5. Developed flexible mortar could be composed less than ten percent PVA to cementious materials.

REFERENCES

1. TAMAI, M, YAMASHITA, N AND YOKOE, S. A study on the flexible cement paste and cement mortar containing new acrylic emulsion. Proceedings of 6th International Conference of ICPIC (Tongji University, Shanghai, China), 1990, pp.24–27.

2. CHANDRA, S AND FLODIN, P.   Interactions of polymer and organic admixtures Portland cement hydration. Cem. and Concr. Res., Vol. 17, 1987, pp.875–890.

3. SUGAMA, T, KUKACKA, L. et al. Study of interactions at water–soluble polymer/Ca(OH)$_2$ or gibbsite interfaces by XPS. Cem. and Concr. Res., Vol. 19, 1989, pp.857–869.

4. MONTANARO, L, FESTA, D et al. Influence of added polymer emulsions on the short–term physical characteristics of plastic mortar. Cem. and Concr. Res., Vol. 20, 1990, pp.62–68.

5. RUSSEL, PP, SHUNKWILER, M, BERG, M and YOUNG, JF. Moisture resistance of Macro–Defect–Free cement. Ceramic Transactions, Advances in Cementious Materials, Vol. 16, 1990, pp.501–519.

6. YOUNG, JF. Macro–Defect–Free Cement: A review. Materials Research Society Symposium Proceedings, Vol. 179, 1989, pp.101–121.

7. POON, CS, WASSEL, LE, and GROVES, GW.   Stability of macro–defect–free cement, Materials Science and Technology, Vol. 3, 1987, pp.993–996.

8. BIRCHALL, JD, HAWARD, AJ and KENDAL, K.   Flexural strength and property of cement, Nature, Vol. 289, 1981, pp.338–339.

9 .SINCLAIR, W and GROVES, GW. High strength cement pastes. Journal of Materials Science, Vol. 20, 1985, pp.2846–2852.

DEVELOPMENT OF LOW-HEAT
HIGH-STRENGTH CONCRETE

K Sakai

H Watanabe

Hokkaido Development Bureau

Japan

A B S T R A C T. Recently, high-strength concrete has been the object of active study, and it is no longer difficult to make ultra-high-strength concrete with more than 100 MPa compressive strength. In general, however, the temperature rise of such concrete is significantly greater than that of normal concrete. Today, in the construction of large-size structures concrete with not only high-strength but also low-heat of hydration is required. The purpose of this study is to develop concrete which satisfies that demands. In this paper, the test results with concrete are described for compressive strength, freeze-thaw resistance, adiabatic temperature rise, and carbonation. As the principal materials for low-heat high-strength concrete, moderate-heat portland cement and granulated blast-furnace slag were considered. In addition, the effect of gypsum, limestone powder, and super-plasticizer on the performance of the concrete were also examined. From this study it is concluded that by properly exploiting the potential of materials such as binders and admixtures, it is possible to make low-heat high-strength concrete.

Keywords : High-strength, Low-heat, Concrete, Moderate-heat portland cement, Granulated blast-furnace slag, Compressive strength, Freeze-thaw resistance, Adiabatic temperature rise, Carbonation.

Dr Koji Sakai is head of the Materials Section at the Civil Engineering Research Institute, Hokkaido Development Bureau, Japan. His current research interests are the durability of concrete, low temperature effects on concrete, roller compacted dam concrete, and fiber reinforced concrete.

Hiroshi Watanabe is a senior research engineer in the Materials Section at the Civil Engineering Research Institute, Hokkaido Development Bureau, Japan.

Concrete 2000. Edited by Ravindra K. Dhir and M. Roderick Jones.
© 1993 Published by E & FN Spon. ISBN 0 419 18120 2.

INTRODUCTION

The development of high-performance concrete (HPC) is being actively pursued in its various aspects in many countries (1). The high strength of HPC is regarded as one of its most significant properties. Many studies on high-strength concrete have been carried out (2,3,4,5). As a result, it is no longer difficult to make ultra-high-strength concrete with more than 100 MPa compressive strength.

High-strength concrete is already used in buildings and offshore platforms (6,7,8). Generally, however, the temperature rise of such concrete is significantly greater than that of normal concrete. In case of mass concrete, the high temperature rise can cause cracking due to the thermal stress.

Yet, today, it is necessary to construct mass concrete structures, such as the towers of cable-stayed or suspension bridges, in which both high strength and low heat are taken into consideration. While high strength and low heat would seem to be mutually exclusive requirements, efforts are being made to develop such concrete (9). Various possibilities should be examined.

The purpose of this study is to develop low-heat high-strength concrete. As the principal materials for the concrete, moderate-heat portland cement, granulated blast-furnace slag, and superplasticizer were considered. In addition, the effects of gypsum and limestone powder on performance were also examined. The tests for compressive strength, adiabatic temperature rise, carbonation, and freeze-thaw resistance were carried out.

MATERIALS

Portland Cement

Moderate-heat portland cement manufactured at a plant in Hokkaido was used. The physical properties are shown in Table 1 and the chemical composition in Table 2.

Table 1 Physical properties of moderate-heat portland cement

Fineness, Blaine (m²/kg)	Specific Gravity	Setting Time (hrs.-min)	
		Initial	Final
342	3.21	2-50	4-50

Table 2 Chemical Composition of moderate-heat portland cement (%)

ig. loss	insol	SiO_2	Al_2O_3	Fe_2O_3	CaO	MgO	SO_3	R_2O
0.8	0.1	22.9	4.2	3.5	64.0	1.7	2.1	0.47

Granulated Blast-Furnace Slag

Granulated blast-furnace slag produced at a plant in Muroran was used. The slag fineness and content range from 578m²/kg to 1691 m²/kg and from 50% to 70%, respectively. The physical properties are shown in Table 3 and the chemical composition in Table 4.

Table 3 Physical properties of granulated blast-furnace slag

Notations	Fineness, Blaine (m²/kg)	Specific Gravity
S- 60	578	2.91
S- 80	789	2.90
S-110	1101	2.90
S-170	1691	2.88

Table 4 Chemical composition of granulated blast-furnace slag (%)

ig. loss	insol	SiO₂	Al₂O₃	Fe₂O₃	CaO	MgO	SO₃	TiO₂	MnO	R₂O	Cl⁻
0.5	0.0	33.8	16.0	0.4	41.4	6.6	0.1	0.7	0.4	0.4	0.0

Table 5 Physical properties and chemical composition of limestone powder

Fineness, Blaine (m²/kg)	Specific Gravity	Chemical Composition (%)		
		ig. loss	SiO₂	CaO
234	2.73	41.2	5.3	51.4

Table 6 Chemical composition of gypsum

Combined Water	SiO₂+insol	Al₂O₃	Fe₂O₃	CaO	SO₃
20.4	1.1	0.1	0.1	32.4	45.1

Limestone Powder

The physical properties and chemical composition of limestone powder used are shown in Table 5.

Gypsum

The chemical composition of gypsum used is shown in Table 6.

Aggregates

For coarse aggregates and fine aggregates, crushed stone produced at Otaru and seacoast sand at Tomakomai were used. The maximum size of the coarse aggregate was 25 mm. The physical properties of the aggregate are shown in Table 7.

Table 7 Physical properties of aggregate

Items	Coarse Aggregate	Fine Aggregate
Specific Gravity	2.67	2.60
Absorption (%)	1.66	0.21
Fineness Modulus	7.00	2.78
Weight of Unit Volume (kg/m³)	1540	1560

Table 8 Mixture proportions of concrete

Fine. of Slag (m²/kg)	Slag Cont.	Gypsum (C×%)	Super-plast. (C×%)	Lime. Powder (C×%)	Water	Cement	Fine Agg.	Coarse Agg.	Lime-stone	SP	AEA (mℓ/m³)
578	60		0.9	0	124	310	867	1099	—	2.79	17.1
	60		1.1	15	122	305	825	1105	45.8	3.36	29.0
	70	2	0.9		122	305	872	1103	—	2.75	24.4
789	50		1.2	0	118	295	882	1118	—	3.54	14.8
			1.2		115	288	888	1125	—	3.46	15.8
	60	4	1.2		115	288	888	1125	—	3.46	15.8
			1.4	15	111	278	854	1136	41.7	3.89	25.0
			1.7	45	108	270	778	1145	121.5	4.59	72.9
	70	2	1.2		114	285	890	1128	—	3.42	22.8
1101	60		1.4	0	120	300	877	1111	—	4.20	19.5
1691			2.0		116	290	885	1111	—	5.80	23.2

Admixtures

An aminosulfonate retarding-type superplasticizer and a rosin-based air-entraining admixture were used.

MIXTURE PROPORTIONS

The mixture proportions of concrete are shown in Table 8. The targets of slump and air content were 8±1cm and 5±1%, respectively. The water cement ratio was kept at 40%. The sand-coarse aggregate ratio was 43%. As much superplasticizer as possible was added, to the limit of segregation from the concrete. The limestone powder and superplasticizer content are a percentage to the weight of cement. The limestone powder is regarded as the fine aggregate in the mixture proportions.

EXPERIMENTAL DETAILS

Mixing

For mixing the concrete, a 100-liter forced-mixing type mixer was used. When mixing the concrete, first,dry mixing was done for 30 seconds with the cement and fine aggregates, and then it was mixed for another 10 seconds after adding water. Finally, coarse aggregates were added, and the concrete was mixed for another 180 seconds.

Compressive Strength

The dimensions of specimens for compressive strength tests were $\phi 10 \times 20$cm. The specimens were moist-cured for 24 hours at 20 ℃, demolded and cured in water at 20℃ until the time for testing. The ages at the time of the compressive strength tests were 3,7,28 and 91 days.

Adiabatic Temperature Rise

The dimensions of specimens for adiabatic temperature rise tests were $\phi 44 \times 29$ cm. The test apparatus was air-circulated.

Carbonation

The dimensions of specimens for carbonation tests were $\phi 15 \times 30$cm. The specimens were moist-cured for 48 hours at 20 ℃, demolded and cured in water at 20 ℃ until the testing age of 28 days. The upper and lower end surfaces of the specimens were coated with epoxy resin before the specimens were put inside the accelerated-carbonation test-apparatus. The accelerated carbonation tests were carried out under conditions of carbon dioxide concentration, 10%; relative humidity, 60%; and temperature, 40 ℃. The depth of carbonation was measured using an alcohol solution of 1% phenolpthalein. The depth of carbonation at eight points was averaged.

Freeze-Thaw Resistance

The dimensions of specimens for freeze-thaw tests were $10 \times 10 \times 40$cm. Up to 300 cycles of freeze-thaw tests were carried out for specimens which were cured in water at 20 ℃ until the age of 28 days. The tests were conducted in accordance with Procedure A of ASTM C666.

RESULTS AND DISCUSSION

Compressive Strength

Figure 1 shows the effects of slag fineness, slag content, and limestone powder content on compressive strength and unit water content.

The amount of addable superplasticizer increased as the slag fineness increased. The unit water content decreased with the increase in slag fineness from $578m^2$ /kg to $789m^2$/kg. The reduction rate was 7%. The unit water content with a slag fineness of $1691m^2$/kg was the same as at $789m^2$/kg. Thus, in the case of slag fineness of $1691m^2$/kg, the superplasticizer could be used in large quantities. In other words, the unit water content was kept lower by the utilization of superplasticizer.

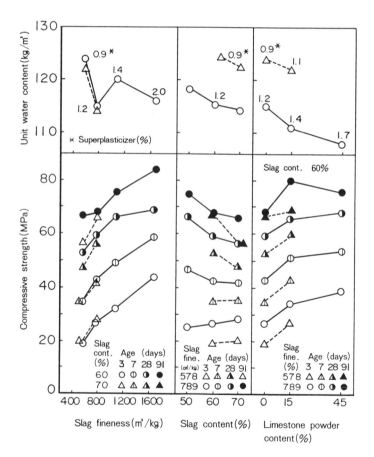

Fig.1 Effect of slag fineness, slag content, and limestone powder content on compressive strength and unit water content

The slag content did not affect the amount of addable superplasticizer. However, the unit water content decreased as the slag content increased. The amount of addable superplasticizer increased with the increase of limestone powder content. As a result, the unit water content decreased.

The effect of slag fineness on compressive strength was marked, even at the age of 91 days. There was some increase in compressive strength at the age of 3 days with an increase in slag content. However, the compressive strength after 7 days decreased as the slag content increased.

The compressive strength of concrete with limestone powder was greater than without limestone powder. In the case of the slag fineness of 578 m^2/kg, the effect of limestone powder was remarkable until the age of 28 days, but small at the age of 91 days.

Thus, it was found that high-strength concrete can be made by the proper combination of superplasticizer, slag fineness, slag content and limestone powder content.

Adiabatic Temperature Rise

When slag fineness was 578, 789, 1101 and 1691m^2/kg with a slag content of 60% and without limestone powder, the maximum adiabatic temperature rises were 38.7, 40.0, 39.0 and 35.5 ℃, respectively. It seems that the relatively low temperature rise in the case of the slag fineness of 1691 m^2/kg came from the use of superplasticizer in large quantities, i.e., 2%.

Figures 2 and 3 show the effect of slag content and gypsum content on adiabatic temperature rise. The adiabatic temperature rise in the case of the slag content

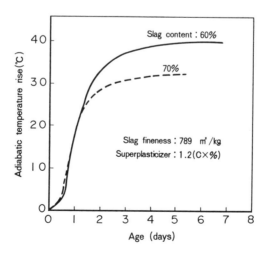

Fig.2   Effect of slag content on adiabatic temperature rise

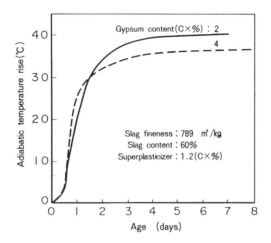

Fig.3   Effect of gypsum content on adiabatic temperature rise

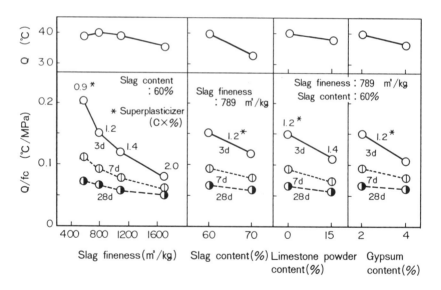

Fig.4   Effect of slag fineness, slag content, limestone powder and gypsum content on the ultimate adiabatic temperature rise (Q) and adiabatic temperature rise per unit compressive strength (Q/fc)

of 70% was approximately 7℃ less than when the content was 60%. When the slag fineness, slag content and superplasticizer content were 789m²/kg, 60% and 1.2%, the maximum adiabatic temperature rise of concrete with a gypsum content of 2% and 4% was 40.0 ℃ and 36.6 ℃.

Figure 4 shows the effect of slag fineness, slag content, limestone powder content and gypsum content on the maximum adiabatic temperature rise (Q) and adiabatic temperature rise per unit compressive strength (Q/f_c). The value of Q/f_c decreased as the slag fineness increased. In general, high-strength concrete causes high temperature rise. However, Figure 4 indicates that the temperature constraint due to the superplasticizer and reduction of cement content, and the high compressive strength due to the increase of slag fineness were successfully attained. In other words, high strength with low heat of hydration was achieved.

The value of Q/f_c also decreased as the slag content increased. Since the increase in slag content caused a reduction in compressive strength, this test result means that the effect of the reduction in Q was considerably great.

As to the effect of limestone powder on the value of Q/f_c, it can be said that the additional strength development due to the addition of 15% limestone powder was significant than the reduction in the heat of hydration.

The value of Q/f_c decreased as the gypsum content increased. Since the compressive strength in cases of 2% and 4% gypsum content was almost same, this result means that the effect of Q was dominative.

The effect of each factor on these general characteristics was remarkable at early ages in concrete. This property is favorable as the low-heat high-strength concrete.

Carbonation

Figures 5, 6, and 7 show the effect of slag fineness, slag content and limestone powder content on the depth of carbonation.

In case of the slag fineness of 789 and 1691m²/kg, the depths of carbonation became the minimum and maximum after 8 weeks, respectively. The test results indicate that the higher fineness of slag caused a greater reduction in calcium hydroxide in the concrete, due to the latent hydraulicity of the slag. The depth of carbonation increased as the slag content increased.

The addition of limestone powder also increased the depth of carbonation. This means that a pozzolanic reaction with the limestone powder occurred. Namely, the calcium hydroxide was consumed in the pozzolanic reaction.

Freeze-Thaw Resistance

The results of the freeze-thaw tests are shown in Table 9. In all mixture proportions, the mass loss was less than 0.5% and the durability factor was greater than 98%.

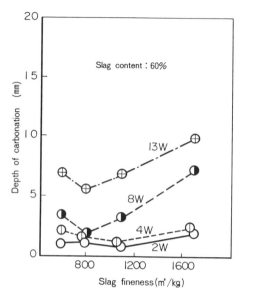

Fig. 5 Effect of slag fineness on the depth of carbonation

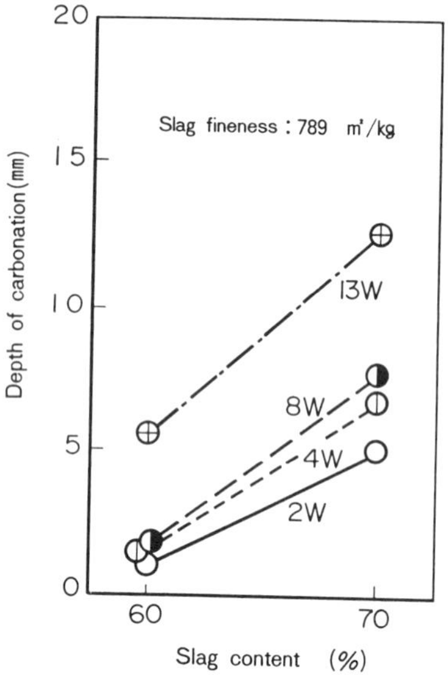

Fig. 6 Effect of slag content on the depth of carbonation

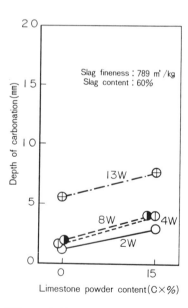

Fig. 7 Effect of limestone powder content on the depth of carbonation

Table 9   Freeze-thaw test results

Slag Fineness (m²/kg)	Slag Content (%)	SP (C×%)	Limestone Powder (C×%)	Mass Loss (%)	Durability Factor (%)
578	60	0.9	0	0.5	100
789	60	1.2	0	0.5	100
		1.4	15	0.2	99
	70	1.2		0.3	98
1101	60	1.2	0	0.1	99
1691		2.0		0.2	98

CONCLUSIONS

1. As the slag fineness increases, the amount of addable superplasticizer increases. The effect of slag fineness on compressive strength is marked. The compressive strength of concrete with limestone powder is greater than without limestone powder.

2. The retarding-type superplasticizer used is effective in reducing the temperature rise. The adiabatic temperature rise per unit compressive strength decreases as the slag fineness, slag content and gypsum content each increase.

3. An increase in slag content and addition of limestone powder increase the depth of carbonation.

4. By properly exploiting the potential of materials such as binders and admixtures, it is possible to make low-heat high-strength concrete with the performance required.

5. The next century will require concrete with multiple properties such as high strength, low heat, low shrinkage, high fluidity, low material segregation, and so on. Such high-performance concrete will improve the usefulness and durability of concrete, and, as a result, reduce the lifetime cost of concrete structures. The challenge of our research ia to develop such concrete.

REFERENCES

1. Carino, N.J. and Clifton, J.R., "High-Performance Concrete:Research Needs to to Enhance its Use," V.13, No.9, Concrete International, ACI, September 1991 pp.70-76.

2. Russell, H.G./Editor, "High Strength Concrete," ACI, SP-87, 1985,278pp.

3. Hwee, Y.S. and Rangan, B.V.,"Studies on Commercial High-Strength concretes," ACI Materials Journal, V.87, No.5, September-October 1990, pp.440-445.

4. Luciano, J.J., Nmai, C.K., and DelGado J.R.,"A Novel Approach to Developing High-Strength Concrete," V.13, No.5, Concrete International, May 1991, pp.25 -29.

5. Giaccio, G., Rocco, C., Violini, D., Zappitelli, J., and Zerbino, R., "High-Strength Concretes Incorporating Different Coarse Aggregates," ACI Materials Journal, V.89, No.3, May-June 1992, pp.242-246.

6. Vaugh, R. and Keneth, F.,"High Strength Concrete for Pacific First Center," Concrete International, V.11, No.4, April 1989, pp.14-16.

7. Moreno,J.,"The State of the Art of High-Strength Concrete in Chicago," Concrete International, V.12, No.1, January 1990, pp.35-39.

8. Ronneberg, H. and Sandvik, M.,"High Strength Concrete for North Sea Platforms," Concrete International, V.12, No.1, January 1990, pp.29-34.

9. Yurugi, M., Mizobuchi, T., and Terauchi, T.,"Utilization of Blast-Furnace Slag and Silica Fume for Controlling Temperature Rise in High-Strength Concrete," American Concrete Institute, SP-132, 1992, pp.1433-1450.

NEW APPLICATIONS - THE FUTURE

Chairmen   **Dr D H Bager**
Aalborg Portland A/S, Denmark

Dr W J Harvey
University of Dundee, United Kingdom

Professor M Kawamura
Kanazawa University, Japan

Professor A A Sagüés
University of South Florida
United States of America

Professor P Spinelli
University of Florence, Italy

Mr M Wiig
AAS-JAKOBSEN A.S., Norway

FRM LINERS FOR NUCLEAR REACTOR BUILDINGS

R H Mills

University of Toronto

Canada

ABSTRACT. Fibre reinforced mortars containing, alternatively, Stainless steel, Alkali-resistant glass, Polypropylene, Aramid and Carbon fibres were compared for leak-tightness and strength under simulated service conditions.

Fibre-reinforced mortar liners were applied to one end of a structural concrete cylinder which had been cracked on a diametral plane. The crack was then opened in increments of about 0.05 mm to 0.25 mm, thus straining the FRM at one end and allowing free opening of the crack at the other. Flow of gas through the strained FRM was a small fraction of free flow through the crack for all crack widths.

Modulus of Rupture beams were exposed to radiation levels of zero, 42 and 142 MRad, equivalent to, respectively, 100 year service life in a nuclear structure, and 100 year service plus a major loss of coolant accident.

In every case, radiation improved the cracking strength but caused excessive embrittlement in specimens reinforced with organic fibres. In the case of steel fibres it also improved the residual strength and fracture toughness.

Keywords: Fibre reinforced, Mortar (FRM), Concrete (FRC), Leak-tightness, Permeability, Gamma radiation, Nuclear reactor building, Flexural strength, Toughness.

Professor Emeritus R.H. Mills, Department of Civil Engineering, University of Toronto, is a consultant for concrete in hydroelectric power generation projects in Uganda and Niagara Falls. Over the past decade he has performed research for the Atomic Energy Control Board and Atomic Energy of Canada Ltd. on aging of concrete in a nuclear environment and on FRM liners respectively. His early research concerned the use of blastfurnace slag and fly ash added at the concrete mixer in partial substitution for Portland cement.

Concrete 2000. Edited by Ravindra K. Dhir and M. Roderick Jones.
© 1993 Published by E & FN Spon. ISBN 0 419 18120 2.

INTRODUCTION

Aging of concrete may affect its performance as a barrier against mass transfer of water, steam, gas and aerosols in Nuclear reactor buildings. Time-dependent changes in concrete include: spontaneous reduction of surface area due to coarsening pore structure, migration of alkalis in solution, micro-cracking due to shrinkage, load-induced microcracking, thermally induced cracking and cracking due to Alkali-aggregate reaction.

Cracks in Fibre reinforced mortar (FRM) are very fine and widely distributed compared with those in concrete. For tensile strains exceeding 10^{-4}, the leakage through an FRM liner should be a small fraction of that through a concrete sub-strate. Structural advantages of FRM may include strain hardening in the post-cracking region and superior fracture toughness compared with normal structural concrete.

This work was designed to assess the value of FRM liners under long-term service in Nuclear reactor buildings.

EXPERIMENTAL DETAILS

Materials and Mix Proportions

Two different volume proportions of each of five different fibres were incorporated in a standard mortar matrix. The fibre characteristics are given in Table 1.

The matrix was proportioned to have initial porosity = 20 per cent and Modulus of Rupture at 28 days ≈ 5 MPa. The concrete sub-strate had initial porosity = 19.7 per cent and 28 day cylinder strength = 35 MPa. The characteristics of these mixes are given in Table 2.

Table 1 Fibre content and characteristics of FRM's

Code	Name	Fibre Material	V_f % A B	Length (mm)	Aspect Ratio
SFRM	Dramix	Steel	1.5, 2.5	30.0	75.0
GFRM	Cem-Fil	AR Glass	1.6, 2.5	25.0	1838.0
PFRM	Monofil	Polypropylene	1.0, 1.5	25.0	125.0
CFRM	Dialead	Carbon	0.5, 1.5	18.0	1059.0
AFRM	Kevlar 49	Aramid	0.75, 1.5	12.5	800.0

Table 2 Mix proportions kg/m³

Material	Concrete Substrate	Fibre Reinforced mortar
OPC	303	773
Water	197	200
Fine aggregate (FM - 2-3)	759	1485
Coarse aggregate (-20 mm)	1136	-
Latex Polymer	-	4
Lomar-D superplasticiser	-	
For SFRM, PFRM and CFRM		5.5
For GFRM and AFRM		25.0

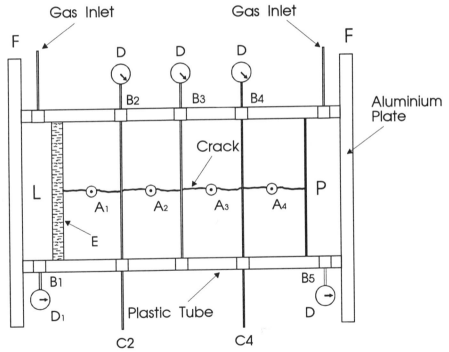

Fig. 1.   Specimens for leakage tests showing: A - 12.5 mm holes for introducing expanding device; B = 7.5 mm instrument ports; C connection to gas burette; D pressure gauges; E 12.5 mm FRM layer, F Aluminium end plates and G 400 mm long concrete. Gas flow through the FRM was measured between L and C_2, and between P and C_4. End plates G are connected with 4 threadbars (not shown).

Leakage Tests [1]

Fig. 1 shows a leakage test specimen consisting of a 250 mm diameter by 400 mm long concrete cylinder cast into a heavy duty PVC tube 500 mm long.   At age = 7 days, the cylinder was split on a diametral plan A_nA_n by pressurising 12.5 mm diameter holes A_1 ... A_4. The pressurising devices were then removed from holes A_1 and A_4, but left in holes A_2 and A_3. The crack width was subsequently controlled by varying the pressure in holes A_2 and A_3. The relationship between Nitrogen gas flow rate, pressure gradient and crack width was established by direct measurement.

Initially the crack width was set at 0.1 mm and a 12.5 mm thick FRM layer was cast over one end and both ends of the plastic tube were sealed with polythene sheet to prevent gain or loss of moisture for 14 days.

The pressure in A_2 and A_3 was then adjusted so as to give flow rates through the plain end corresponding to various crack widths between 0.1 and 0.25 mm. For each value of crack width the corresponding flow through the liner was monitored and compared with the flow through the unlined end.

In the case of a Loss of Coolant Accident (LOCA) in a CANDU 6 reactor, the pressure gradient through the wall is:

$$\frac{\Delta P}{\ell} = \frac{124 \text{ kPa}}{1.07 \text{ m}} = 116 \frac{\text{kN}}{\text{m}^3} ;$$

where ΔP = the accident over pressure = 124 kPa
      ℓ = the wall thickness = 1.07 m.

For each designated crack width, the functional relationship between the rate of gas flow and pressure was determined by linear regression and the characteristic flow Q* inter-polated for the standard value of $\Delta P/\ell$ = 116 kN/m³.

The Effects of Exposure to Radiation [2]

Two levels of radiation were chosen for this study: 42 MRad equivalent to 100 years of service in a CANDU 6 reactor building; and 142 MRad equivalent to 100 years of service plus one major accident. It was decided to evaluate the different FRM's on the basis of a 0.25 mm crack under the standard pressure gradient of 116 kN/m³.

For each of the five fibre types, and for two fibre concentrations, a slab of FRM measuring 1 x 0.3 x 0.025 m³ was cast. After 14 days moist curing these specimens were cut into modulus of rupture beams measuring 300 x 60 x 25 mm. After a further 14 days moist curing the specimens were irradiated at dose rates varying from 1.54 to 1.79 Mrad/hour.

Each slab was saw-cut to provide 9 beams for each fibre and each fibre concentration. These were divided into 3 groups of 3 replicates.   One group was tested after exposures ranging from 42 to 49 Mrad and a second after exposures ranging from 142 to 165 Mrad. The third group was left unexposed to radiation.

The 99 modulus of rupture beams thus included the following variables:

- 5 maximum different fibres in the FRM
- 2 different concentrations of fibres in the FRM
- 3 specimens to be exposed to 42 Mrad   i.e. 30 FRM + 3 plain = 33 in all
- 3 specimens to be exposed to 142 Mrad   i.e. 30 FRM + 3 plain = 33 in all
- 3 specimens to be unexposed i.e. 30 FRM + 3 plain = 33 in all

Before the 66 specimens were dispatched for irradiation, they were moist cured for 28 days. After irradiation the beams were stored at 50% relative humidity until they were tested at 56 days. The control specimens were maintained in an atmosphere of 100 per cent R.H for 56 days until tested.

The specimens were tested in 3-point bending with auto-recording of load and deflection. The effectiveness of the fibre reinforcing, before and after radiation, was assessed according to the following parameters which are also illustrated in Figures 2 and 3.

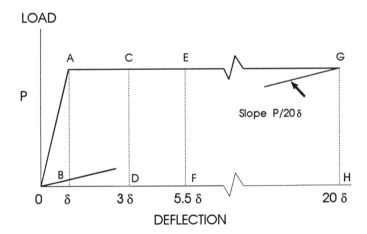

Fig. 2 Linear Elastic - Perfectly Plastic behaviour of a beam in flexure.   The toughness index I_5 = Area OACD divided by Area OAB = 5. Similarly I_{10} = Area OAEF ÷ Area OAB. E/20 = Area OAH ÷ Area OAB. Residual strength over the range CE = $R_{5,10}$ = 20 (I_{10} - I_5) = 100 per cent.

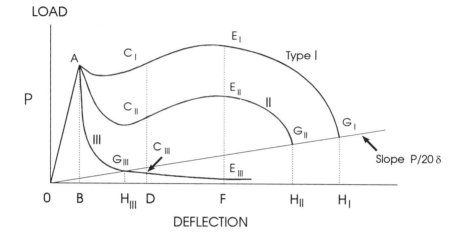

Fig. 3 Typical load-deflection curves for fibre reinforced mortar. Curve I shows quasi strain hardening in the post-cracking region: $I_5 > 5$ and $I_{10} > 10$. The residual strength $R_{5,10} = 20 \, (I_{10} - I_5) > 100\%$. Curve II shows $I_5 < 5$, $I_{10} < 10$ and $R_{5,10} = 20 \, (I_{10} - I_5) < 100\%$. This behaviour shows substantial ductility and good post-cracking characteristics though somewhat inferior to the Linear Elastic-Perfectly Plastic case. Curve III shows totally inadequate post-cracking performance with $I_5 \ll 5$, $I_{10} \ll 10$ and $R_{5,10} \ll 100\%$.

σ_e Flexural strength at the elastic limit also known as First Crack Strength (1).

σ_c Flexural strength at maximum load.

E   Modulus of Elasticity calculated from the linear part of the load-deflection curve (1).

TI   The area under the load-deflection curve up to a specified end point divided by the area under the linear elastic part of the curve.

I_n The end point, corresponding to deflection $= (n + 1)\delta/2$, which gives TI $= n$. In this investigation values I_5 and I_{10} corresponding to deflections 3δ and 5.5δ were adopted for comparison (1).

E/20   The ratio of the area under the load-deflection curve in the post-cracking region divided by the area under the linear elastic curve. In this case the end point was defined by the intersection on the curve of a line drawn from the origin with 1/20 the initial slope.

RESULTS

Leakage Test Results

The results of leakage tests before drying the liner are shown in Table 3. This table lists flows at $\Delta P/\ell$ = 116.2 kN/m^3 for concrete crack widths of 0.1, 0.15 and 0.25 mm and corresponding values for flow through the liner. Generally flow through the liners was not measurable i.e. it was < 1 ml/s until the crack width at the plain end reached 0.25 mm. It is worth noting in this context that the absolute permeability of the uncracked concrete used in this investigation was D_s = 624 x 10E - 18 m^2. This means that the rate of flow under the standard pressure gradient of 116.2 kN/m^3 would have been 2 x 10E -4 ml/s. This is much less than the readability of the apparatus used in this investigation. In this context, the flow through uncracked concrete was effectively zero in all cases. In only one case, that of Carbon fibres, was the flow through the liner appreciable. Table 4 classifies the fibres in order of merit according to fibre concentration. The most striking feature of the mass cured tests is that the performances of FRM's with the lower fibre concentration A were in all cases superior to those with the higher concentration B. Also shown in Table 4 is the dramatic increase in leakage when the liners were dried.

Irradiated Specimens

The results of flexural tests are summarized in Table 5 and typical curves are shown in Figure 4.

It is clear that irradiation caused embrittlement of the 3 FRM's with organic fibres. Only Steel fibres and Glass fibres produced FRMs which had satisfactory post-cracking behaviour after irradiation.

DISCUSSION

Although all the FRMs provided good sealing over a widening crack before drying the performance after drying was unacceptable. Measures are necessary to reduce cracking due to drying shrinkage and removal of pore water. These may include increase in the aggregate:cement ratio and use of shrinkage compensated cement.

The most outstanding feature of the irradiated specimens was the dramatic increase in strength of the unreinforced matrix. This was, of course, mimicked in the FRMs. After exposure to 142 MRad the cracking strengths were lower than the matrix strength for steel FRM as shown in Table 6.

Normally one would expect the cracking strength of FRM to be about the same as the cracking strength of mortar matrix. This is indeed the case except for Steel fibres.

Table 3   Summary of Leakage Test Results after 14 days Mass Curing

The table gives the flow through the unsealed end as X mℓ/s for 3 different crack widths and standard value of pressure gradients $\Delta P/\ell = 1162$ kN/m^3. The flow through the sealed end Y mℓ/s is recorded as a fraction of the flow through the unsealed end x 100 percent. Figures in parenthesis are standard deviations.

Specimen		Flow mℓ/s for crack width		
		0.1 mm	0.15 mm	0.25 mm
Steel A	X flow through unsealed end mℓ/s	13(10)	69(3)	181(11)
	Y flow through sealed end %	0	0	1.1
Steel B	X mℓ/s	34(3)	59(10)	109(25)
	Y %	0	0	2.6
Glass A	X mℓ/s	46(6.5)	79(12.3)	151(17.0)
	Y %	0	0	0.4
Glass B	X mℓ/s	45(6.0)	80(9.1)	150(16.0)
	Y %	< 0.4	<0.4	5.1(5.0)
Carbon A	X mℓ/s	57(17)	88(24)	150(36)
	Y %	0	0	8.7
Carbon B	X mℓ/s	45(11)	78(8)	155(23)
	Y %	< 0.5	< 0.15	31(58)
Kevlar A	X mℓ/s	50(3)	87(8)	160(20)
	Y %	0	0	0.4
Kevlar B	X mℓ/s	44(13)	79(17)	157(37)
	Y %	0	1.0(2.0)	3.8(6.4)
Polypropylene A	X mℓ/s	41(4.2)	71(5.6)	130(8.5)
	Y %	0	0	< 0.1
Polypropylene B	X mℓ/s	36(2)	63(7)	117(19)
	Y %	0	0	8.5(15)

Table 4 Order of Merit

Order of Merit	For mass cured liner				After drying			
	A		B		A		B	
Best	Polypropylene	(<0.1)	Steel	(2.6)	Kevlar	(5.7)	Glass	(10.5)
	Kevlar	(0.4)	Kevlar	(3.8)	Polypropylene		Polypropylene	
	Glass	(0.4)	Glass	(5.1)		(11.5)		(20.0)
	Steel	(1.1)	Polypropylene		Carbon	(12.4)	Kevlar	(22.9)
				(8.5)	Glass	(14.3)	Steel	(22.9)
Worst	Carbon	(8.7)	Carbon	(31.0)	Steel	(62.0)	Carbon	(37.3)

LOAD (KN)

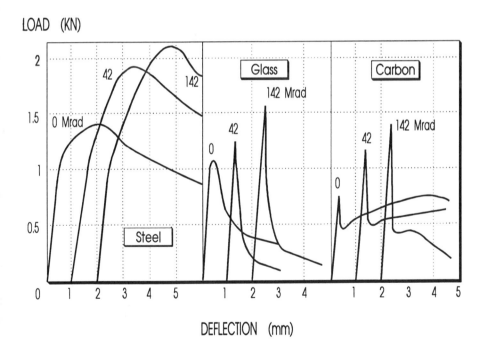

DEFLECTION (mm)

Fig. 4 Typical load-deflection curves for Steel, Glass and Carbon reinforced FRM's. Note that strength increased with the level of radiation. Steel showed satisfactory type I post-cracking behaviour. Carbon showed unsatisfactory type III behaviour while Glass showed Type II behaviour.

Table 5 Summary of Flexural Test Results

			Stresses			Toughness Indices		
		Elastic Limit σ_e (MPa)	Maximum Strength σ_{max} (MPa)	Residual Strength R5,10%	Elastic Modulus E (GPa)	I_5	I_{10}	E/20
Unreinforced	N-0	6.11 (0.05)	6.11 (0.05)	6	8.53 (0.29)	0.82 (0.13)	1.12 (0.33)	0.72 (0.11)
	N-42	10.10 (0.44)	10.10 (0.44)	6	14.10 (1.54)	0.60 (0.06)	0.92 (0.07)	0.45 (0.00)
	N-142	11.84 (0.57)	11.84 (0.57)	7	14.82 (0.73)	0.56 (0.15)	0.92 (0.23)	0.38 (0.18)
Steel	SA-0	8.12 (0.72)	8.50 (0.93)	88	5.48 (2.07)	3.20 (0.67)	7.61 (0.33)	12.04 (3.63)
	SB-0	9.23 (0.16)	11.77 (1.21)	207	10.11 (2.39)	5.87 (0.46)	16.23 (2.74)	37.10 (5.80)
	SA-42	8.25 (0.61)	9.32 (0.87)	154	13.64 (0.41)	5.18 (0.84)	12.87 (2.55)	39.20 (8.20)
	SB-42	7.05 (0.40)	8.93 (0.07)	182	12.31 (0.06)	6.97 (0.47)	16.08 (1.64)	77.29 (15.06)
	SA-142	6.02 (0.16)	8.62 (0.07)	316	9.91 (1.69)	6.16 (0.41)	14.3 (0.8)	54.80 (12.93)
	SB-142	7.87 (0.35)	9.73 (0.52)	152	11.12 (1.86)	6.04 (2.39)	13.62 (5.19)	87.70 (36.6)
Glass	GA-0	5.77 (0.69)	5.92 (1.98)	99	11.93 (0.85)	4.34 (0.95)	9.30 (0.96)	10.04 (1.49)
	GB-0	8.40 (0.24)	8.71 (0.75)	76	6.77 (0.56)	4.24 (1.03)	8.04 (2.50)	9.84 (3.08)
	GA-42	9.82 (0.38)	7.03 (0.75)	58	12.16 (0.57)	3.15 (0.30)	6.03 (0.89)	6.66 (1.16)
	GB-42	11.36 (0.85)	12.26 (1.13)	20	8.32 (1.63)	2.44 (0.36)	3.45 (0.54)	2.93 (0.51)
	GA-142	10.60 (1.93)	6.84 (0.32)	57	12.26 (1.13)	3.31 (1.89)	6.16 (3.64)	7.63 (6.03)
	GB-142	11.82 (0.73)	8.64 (5.64)	30	11.97 (1.73)	2.97 (0.80)	4.45 (1.54)	4.22 (1.90)

		Stresses				Toughness Indices		
		Elastic Limit σ_e (MPa)	Maximum Strength σ_{max} (MPa)	Residual Strength R5,10%	Elastic Modulus E (GPa)	I_5	I_{10}	E/20
Polypropylene	PA-0	5.97 (0.59)	6.28 (0.86)	94	6.91 (1.75)	5.03 (2.55)	9.75 (5.47)	27.13 (11.43)
	PB-0	4.92 (0.59)	6.04 (0.04)	110	10.54 (0.92)	4.38 (0.92)	9.88 (1.83)	63.61 (30.51)
	PA-4.2	7.44 (0.58)	6.69 (1.04)	71	8.95 (0.94)	2.55 (0.15)	6.08 (0.90)	24.89 (15.31)
	PB-4.2	10.23 (0.01)	10.23 (0.01)	48	13.65 (0.11)	1.29 (0.42)	3.68 (0.07)	8.68 (1.61)
	PA-14.2	11.48 (0.38)	11.48 (0.38)	25	13.01 (2.10)	1.36 (0.46)	2.52 (0.46)	2.31 (0.67)
	PB-14.2	11.15 (0.55)	11.15 (0.55)	18	12.85 (0.03)	1.04 (0.19)	1.92 (0.25)	1.47 (0.48)
Kevlar	KA-0	5.73 (0.32)	5.98 (0.03)	16	6.38 (0.73)	1.61 (0.38)	2.42 (0.60)	1.86 (0.58)
	KB-0	5.64 (0.57)	6.16 (0.55)	30	6.63 (1.02)	2.44 (0.42)	3.94 (0.99)	3.66 (1.30)
	KA-4.2	9.48 (0.28)	9.31 (0.07)	11	8.08 (0.70)	1.10 (0.32)	1.63 (0.38)	0.84 (0.16)
	KB-4.2	8.43 (1.82)	7.53 (0.26)	18	7.58 (0.03)	2.73 (0.26)	3.63 (0.33)	3.84 (0.20)
	KA-14.2	9.95 (0.25)	9.95 (0.25)	14	9.56 (1.38)	1.44 (0.20)	2.12 (0.25)	1.55 (0.27)
	KB-14.2	9.27 (0.33)	9.27 (0.33)	13	10.23 (0.25)	1.25 (0.04)	1.89 (0.00)	1.30 (0.07)
Carbon	CA-0	6.82 (0.61)	7.27 (0.67)	30	9.52 (2.07)	2.91 (0.31)	4.40 (0.67)	4.89 (1.34)
	CB-0	6.38 (0.04)	6.80 (0.21)	49	8.86 (1.59)	4.50 (0.60)	6.95 (2.06)	8.05 (3.06)
	CA-4.2	8.94 (0.12)	9.18 (0.29)	17	10.20 (0.74)	1.91 (0.45)	2.74 (0.54)	2.41 (0.67)
	CB-4.2	9.51 (0.31)	9.51 (0.31)	35	10.60 (0.54)	2.21 (0.35)	3.98 (1.32)	3.02 (1.23)
	CA-14.2	10.85 (0.94)	10.85 (0.94)	10	11.80 (1.73)	1.25 (0.10)	1.74 (0.28)	1.35 (0.06)
	CB-14.2	10.37 (0.52)	10.37 (0.52)	13	10.40 (0.22)	1.31 (0.18)	1.96 (0.16)	1.49 (0.04)

Table 6   Cracking Strength of FRM after exposure to 142 MRad - per cent of
                 matrix strength

Steel		Glass		Poly		Kevlar		Carbon	
A	B	A	B	A	B	A	B	A	B
55	72	96	107	105	102	91	85	99	96

The prime function of fibre reinforcement is to impart residual strength and toughness of the FRM after cracking has taken place. After exposure to 142 MRad, only Steel FRM shows an increase in residual strength over initial cracking strength. The three organic fibres: Polypropylene, Kevlar and Carbon, show unacceptably low values of residual strength.

Toughness is a measure of the capacity of the material to absorb mechanical energy after cracking. All fibres show an improvement in this value compared with the unreinforced mortar but the best performers were Steel (about 1500 per cent improvement) and Glass (above 600 per cent improvement).

Exposure to radiation caused embrittlement in all FRMs other than those reinforced with steel.

In view of the superior performance of steel fibre reinforced mortar (SFRM) after exposure to radiation it is clear that additional tests are necessary to improve and optimize its leak tightness.

CONCLUSIONS

Before drying, all of the fibres provided satisfactory sealing against leakage for crack widths ranging from 0.1 to 0.15 mm and all except Carbon were satisfactory in the range 0.15 mm to 0.25 mm.

After drying, the leakage rates at 0.25 mm crack width were unacceptable and further investigation is required to reduce drying shrinkage in the FRMs.

Irradiation caused unacceptable embrittlement in FRMs made with the three organic materials.

Steel fibre reinforced FRM gave superior post cracking behaviour after radiation.

The prognosis for possible use of FRM's in nuclear reactor buildings hinges on hygiene, i.e. the need for easily cleaned, smooth and hard surfaces. The most economical method of application to finished concrete is by shotcreting which is difficult to finish to an acceptable standard. In new construction the problem is easily solved by using FRM for permanent formwork for walls, beams and slabs and by simple addition of fibres to the concrete for flow slabs.

Further investigation of recently developed materials, such as chopped steel ribbon and specially sized alkali-resistant glass is required.

REFERENCES

[1]   MILLS, R.H. and SENI, C.   Designer/Researcher/User Interface for Enhancement of Concrete Durability.   RILEM International Seminar, 45th General Council. Buenos Aires 1991.

[2]   MILLS, R.H. and SENI, C. Mechanical Properties of Fibre Reinforced Mortar Exposed to Gamma Radiation. Fibre Reinforced Cement and Mortar, pp. 775-787 E & FN Spon. ed, R.N. Swamy, Sheffield 1992.

CEMENTS AND CONCRETES
FOR WASTE IMMOBILISATION

F P Glasser

University of Aberdeen

United Kingdom

ABSTRACT.   Cements and concretes have many uses in nuclear waste repositories.   During construction and operational phases, durable constructional concretes will be required as well as special grouts for sealing faults, rock bolting, etc. In shallow repositories, concretes may have a useful physical barrier action: low permeability and resistance to cracking are important in this application.   In deeper repositories with favourable hydrology, the chemical conditioning action of the cementitious material is important: high pH limits the solubility of radionuclides.   In some circumstances high permeability grouts may be advantageous to prevent gas buildup.   An important area of research lies in predicting the behaviour of materials at long ages, $> 10^2$ years.   The decline in chemical potential, as measured by pH, can be modelled as a function of time. The effects of elevated temperature on cement properties are less well understood; research in this area, as well as on the impact of saline waters, is currently underway.   Towards the repository closure phase, performance criteria and formulations for seals and grouts will have to be developed.

Keywords: Cement immobilisation: Nuclear waste: Blended cements: Aqueous chemistry: Durability: Modelling properties.

F.P. Glasser is Professor of Chemistry at the University of Aberdeen.   He is the author of more than 300 professional papers, many on cements and concretes, and is editor in chief of 'Advances in Cement Research'.   Research in his group working on cements for nuclear waste immobilisation is supported by the Commission of the European Communities, the UK Department of the Environment and Nuclear Electric.

Concrete 2000. Edited by Ravindra K. Dhir and M. Roderick Jones.
© 1993 Published by E & FN Spon. ISBN 0 419 18120 2.

INTRODUCTION

Cement and concretes have a wide range of uses in nuclear waste immobilisation which are summarised in Fig. 1. Wastes may be cement grouted into containers, which may themselves be concrete. These may be backfilled in the repository with cementitious grout. Meantime, constructional concrete may be used to maintain the stability of vaults, tunnels and shafts: the local rock may require stabilisation, fissure grouting and/or construction of impermeable barrier walls. It is unlikely that all these applications will be found in any one repository: the diagram is a composite. However the specialised requirements for waste conditioning and immobilisation are often less widely appreciated and are described here.

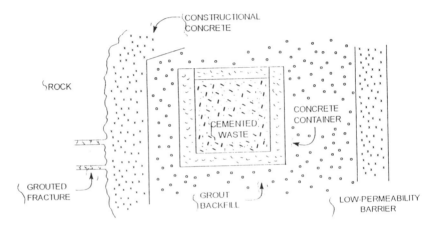

Fig. 1. Schematic drawing showing some uses of cement and concrete in a nuclear waste repository.

Cements may be used to solidify and immobilise low to intermediate level liquids, flocs, sludges, resins and other particulates; also larger metallic and non metallic components as well as miscellaneous wastes including rubber, plastic and paper. The bulk of the waste is likely to consist of materials which, from the radiological standpoint, are inactive. However, certain soluble waste components, including salts, e.g. borates, complexing agents such as EDTA and citrate, and decontaminating agents may physically inhibit the set of cement. Cement-rich formulations are commonly used; sand and aggregates tend unnecessarily to increase the wasteform volume; cement-rich formulations also help overcome the set inhibition arising from waste components. However large cement-rich monoliths may exhibit excessive temperature rise, so high-replacement slag and fly ash-rich combinations have been used to reduce initial heat evolution. Various conditioning processes may also have been used; for example, borates - which inhibit set - may be pretreated with $Ca(OH)_2$ and the resulting sludge mixed into the cement matrix formulation. $Ca(OH)_2$ pretreatment is also useful to neturalise waste acids. The result is that many of the matrix formulations used are unconventional in terms of normal cement practice. Mixes may on occasion have high water contents, low strengths and long set times. Nevertheless, they may be fit for purpose: if transport is required, concrete overpacks or steel drums will provide the strength needed. There are however, two problem areas. One concerns organic ion exchangers (resins) which, when incorporated in cement, imbibe water and calcium, etc. and swell excessively: resin loading may have to be restricted. The other class of materials comprise ions which are not readily insolubilised, e.g. chloride, but which may accelerate steel corrosion or attack concrete.

Organic ion exchangers and other combustible material may be also incinerated prior to cementation. Combustion solves some problems, notably swelling, and undoubtedly reduces waste volume, although the physical and chemical nature of the resulting ash may increase water demand.

The design and construction of containers for interim storage and transportation is a challenging task. Concrete is competitive with steel in this application. The biological shielding provided by concrete may be important, but resistance to accident, including fire, is also required. If the encapsulated wastes are not cement conditioned, but are also wet and acidic, waste components may react with hardened concrete or, if they contain chloride, may rapidly depassivate steel reinforcements. Although the general intention is normally to dispose of conditioned wastes as soon as practicable, instances are known where interim storage may be necessary for decades. Corrosion and container durability in the storage environment are therefore important considerations. Compatibility between the waste components, particularly the non-radioactive matter, may impose design criteria.

The most challenging task is the design and formulation of cement and concrete for nuclear waste repositories. The usual design concept, known as the multibarrier concept, provides multiple barriers to the return of radioactive materials to the biosphere. Figure 1 also suggests these. Geological barriers are also important; ideally, man-made and geological barriers will work in conjunction with each other to prevent the return of wastes to the biosphere until decay has reduced the original radioactivity to acceptable levels.

The overall design philosophy of a nuclear waste repository must also reflect the amount and nature of waste. Low level wastes, containing mainly short-lived radioisotopes, may be suitable for shallow burial whereas longer-lived isotopes, especially in quantity, may require deeper burial and more elaborate barriers. Quantitative models of repository and barrier performance have been and are being developed, for example in the UK by NIREX; also by statutory organisations or their agents in France, Sweden, Switzerland, Germany, USA, Japan, etc.

Table 1 Some Properties of Cement and Concretes in Nuclear Waste Repositories

Materials	Advantages	Disadvantages
1. Physical		
Well-cured slag cement blends	Low permeability, $~10^{-12}ms^{-1}$.	Propensity to crack providing 'short circuit' pathways.
$Ca(OH)_2$-rich formulations	High permeability, to prevent gas build up	Low strength.
2. Chemical		
$Ca(OH)_2$, Portland cement and fly ash blends	High pH: limits solubility of many species, e.g. U, Pu, Np, Am.	Does not limit solubility of Cs, Sr, etc.
Slag blends	Chemical reduction to less soluble forms of some species, e.g. Tc.	Potential for sulfur-based corrosion.
3. Other		
All hydraulic cements, e.g. OPC and blends containing OPC, $Ca(OH)_2$, slag, fly ash, etc.	Availability, cost, proven technology and durable in a range of natural environments: resistant to radiation. Inhibit bacterial action.	Potentially dissolved by aggressive waters. Subject to set interference during initial formulation.

Perhaps the first question which needs to be addressed is: why use cement and concrete? Table 1 gives a survey of the immobilisation properties of cement, including its advantages and disadvantages. The time factor under consideration is long, between 10^2 and 10^6 years. On this scale, even well-made concretes are relatively permeable compared with, say, metallic barriers, so concretes are likely to afford significant long-term physical immobilisation. The answer to the above question lies in the unique chemical conditioning action of cements and the outcome is that cementitious materials are frequently used to provide short term physical confinement but longer term chemical immobilisation, in conjunction with other barriers. In the following sections, some aspects of cement performance are explored in more detail.

CEMENT AND CONCRETE PROPERTIES

Matrix properties. High strength is not normally a primary requirement for cements and concrete matrices intended for conditioning wastes. The matrix may need sufficient strength for handling, but the required composite stiffness and strength may also be attained by steel drums or cannisters. The properties of advanced cementitious materials, e.g. macro defect-free (MDF) cements, have not been exploited by the nuclear industry. It would be difficult to construct large, monolithic barriers of MDF material. A problem with direct MDF encapsulation of waste is that extensive processing is required, with concomitant contamination of machinery, plant and exposure hazards to workers, whose safety must also be considered, whereas conventional materials can be mixed, if required, in remote operations with less contamination of plant and personnel.

Strong concretes may be required for physical construction of the repository: for example, in tunnel linings and roof supports. Conventional civil engineering formulations and practice are probably satisfactory in this respect. It is noteworthy that many repositories, especially deep repositories, could be 5-20 years in the course of construction and subsequently kept open for access for decades while they are gradually filled. Hence adequate attention to durability may be necessary, especially in repositories situated in regions of saline groundwaters. Various special grouts may also be required for fissure sealing, roof bolting, etc., but these lie outside the scope of this review. Nevertheless, these materials must be considered as part of the total cementitious inventory and their impact on repository performance will require assessment.

Permeability. A wide range of permeabilities may be required. For example, some wastes may generate gas. Since pressure buildup is undesirable, high permeability grouts may be used to permit gas to diffuse and minimise pressure rise.   On the other hand, shallow repositories are more likely to employ concrete as a physical barrier to the migration of ground water, or to the movement of radionuclides, or both.   Barrier applications demand low permeability concretes. The design of   low permeability concretes is well-established and it appears that the potential for low permeability will increase, assuming adequate cure, in the order SRPC < OPC < OPC/fly ash < OPC/slag.   The moist or wet conditions necessary to ensure good cure are often encountered, although exceptions may occur, as in potential repository sites in desert climates.   However, generalisations about the permeability functions need to be tempered with caution; relatively little is known about very low permeability ($< 10^{-12} ms^{-1}$) concretes. Much of their residual hydraulic permeability seems to be associated with cracks and more research is needed in this field, especially as laboratory field evidence shows that the origin of cracking may be complex and, moreover that cracks, once formed, may be subject to rehealing.   A simple model of different regimes of crack enlargement or rehealing as a consequence of reactions with CO_2-containing groundwaters has been presented elsewhere (1).   Aggregate in concrete may also be responsible for formation of high-permeability interfacial regions which act as short-circuit paths for migration.   A recent symposium has described the characterisation and properties of these regions (2).

Concrete additives.   Good quality, low permeability concretes are frequently formulated with superplasticisers.   In nuclear applications, the main benefits would be to reduce accidental voidage and ensure low permeability by enabling low w/c ratios to be used.   However, the constitution of these materials, often obtained as by-products from other industrial processes, is poorly understood (3). They certainly undergo complex reactions in cement (4) and in the long term may degrade.   Soluble organic materials are known in certain instances to increase the solubility of actinides, e.g. Pu, and there is concern that degradation products of superplasticisers may complex actinides and thereby enhance their solubility, either as complexes in true solution or as colloids.   Until their role, if any, in transport processes is established, it may be difficult to make a case for the use of water-reducing admixtures in concretes which are in intimate contact with radioactive waste.

Radiation.   Most water-containing materials including set cement are subject to radiolysis.   Ionizing radiation breaks water molecules, resulting in the liberation of H_2 and O_2.   However, experiment has shown that the rate at which radiolysis occurs when cement is used to contain low to medium active wastes is sufficiently low as not to give cause for concern (5).

Alkalinity (pH). It may seem strange that a solid such as cement can be said to have a pH, a property ordinarily associated with aqueous solutions.   But cements ordinarily contain water in excess of that required for hydration, the excess being contained in pores; it is this pore water whose pH function we describe.   Pore water can be expressed for analysis, using a powerful hydraulic press, so its constitution is known.

Typically, cement pH 's are reported to lie in the range 12.5-14.   The pH of a saturated solution of $Ca(OH)_2$ - a component of a set Portland cement - is about 12.4 at $18°C$;   values in excess of 12.4 are maintained by the sodium and potassium contents.   These are effectively present in pore fluid as "NaOH" and "KOH", other potential anions (sulfate, aluminate, silicate) being rather insoluble. Thus alkalis elevate the pH above that of the $Ca(OH)_2$ threshold.   However, pore fluid alkalis are rather easily leached, and the assumption is generally made that they will leach away over the course of time.   During the period where alkalis dominate leachate chemistry, $Ca(OH)_2$ exhibits very low solubility owing to the common ion effect. $Ca(OH)_2$ has a solubility product, Ksp, defined as:

$$Ksp = [Ca][OH]^2$$

where [ ] indicate solution concentrations.   Hydroxide ions, initially from cement alkali but subsequently replenished from solid $Ca(OH)_2$, are the main buffering agent which control pH.   Fig. 2 shows the initial decline in pH which occurs during leaching, in order to maintain Ksp. As the available alkali is leached, the solubility of $Ca(OH)_2$ increases.   This leach behaviour has been related to number of cycles of renewal of leachant or, assuming a water flow rate, to time (6).

Many blended cement formulations are predicted to contain relatively little or no $Ca(OH)_2$. Materials (slag, fly ash) which are more siliceous than Portland cement consume free $Ca(OH)_2$.   In nuclear waste repositories we have little choice but to assume that equilibrium will obtain and that all free $Ca(OH)_2$ may spontaneously react in blends containing significant proportions of slag and, especially, silica-rich class F fly ash.   One of the principal products of reaction of $Ca(OH)_2$ with slag and fly ash is a hydrous calcium silicate gel, designated C-S-H. This C-S-H is itself slightly soluble and, like $Ca(OH)_2$, it buffers a high pH. Whereas $Ca(OH)_2$ has a fixed composition and hence fixed solubility, C-S-H has variable composition and solubility.   The dependence of internal pH on the gel composition is also shown in Fig. 2.   Addition of blast furnace slag and siliceous fly ash change the bulk composition of the paste, generally consuming $Ca(OH)_2$ and lowering the Ca/Si ratio of the paste thereby decreasing the pH of the buffering solids.

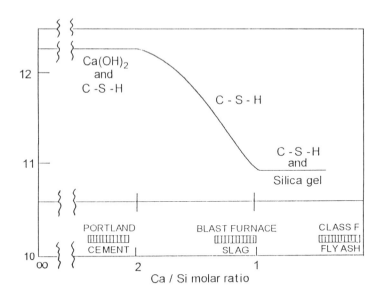

Fig. 2.   The   evolution of pH in a cement system buffered by Ca(OH)$_2$ and/or C-S-H.   Alkalis are assumed absent.   The range of cement and blending agents compositions are shown for reference.

Much attention has been directed towards determining the ability of cements to maintain a high pH in the vicinity of the repository, both now and in the future. Not only does high pH reduce the solubility of many key nuclides, but it also affects other aspects of the repository performance, e.g. corrosion rates of cannisters, inhibition of microbiological activity.   The present state of knowledge appears to be that in a chemically-simple geological site, i.e. one having low-mineral content ground water and low flow rates and not subject to elevated temperatures, it should be possible to condition high local pH for $^{-}10^6$ years (7).

Thermal factors.   Unfortunately, exposure to "warm" conditions may cause C-S-H to crystallise; the nature of the crystalline products obtained depends on temperature and Ca/Si ratio, but will have reduced solubility, and hence condition lower pH, than their amorphous, gel-like precursor.   Reduction of pH arising from thermally-induced crystallisation of the gel component could thus reduce the chemical effectiveness of cement conditioning.

Deeper repositories are often suited to the co-disposal of more active heat-generating wastes. These may elevate repository temperatures well above ambient. The 'ambient' temperature will depend on the local geothermal gradient and depth, but could be 20-25°C, to which must be added the impact of waste heat. The thermal profile of the repository will be complex, depending on the amount and distribution of heat generating wastes as well as the thermal conductivity and diffusivity of the local geology. Thus cements and concretes could be subject to a thermal pulse of 10^2-10^3 years duration in the immediate post-closure phase. If the repository is subject to "warm" conditions, $Ca(OH)_2$ will remain unaffected; its solubility actually decreases with rising temperatures up to ˜180°C but it is always sufficiently soluble to maintain high pH and condition low actinide solubility. Blended cements, on the other hand, will experience a more substantial decrease in solubility as $Ca(OH)_2$ is consumed and C-S-H gel crystallises to jennite, 11 Å tobermorite, etc. In prolonged cures, crystalline products can be obtained from low Ca/Si ratio gels at temperatures as low as 55°C (8). It is probable, but not certain, that the pH of blended cements will remain above 10 to 10.5, the threshold which is commonly assumed adequate to condition low actinide solubility. The decreased solubility of more crystalline cement components does bring a possible benefit: other factors being equal, their lifetime for dissolution will be extended. The advantages and disadvantages of different types of backfill are thus known in broad outline. There are, however, other specific repository-related conditions which might affect a final choice of formulation.

Groundwater interactions. The impact of saline water on cement and backfill conditioning of pH has yet to be assessed fully. Engineers will be familiar with the rapid deterioration and loss of high pH which characterises cement behaviour in sea water. Over a short lifetime, 20-100 years, it may be practicable to prevent diffusion of saline water through barriers and cover concrete, but it is not practicable to obtain impermeability over the longer timescales required for containment of nuclear waste. Therefore it is necessary to assume that intimate contact of paste and groundwater will occur and determine the course and consequences of ensuing reactions. Empirical studies provide some guidance to the nature of the reactions: Table 2 gives a summary. More quantitative calculations, now in progress, should enable the course of reactions and their impact on cement pH to be assessed. Dimensional changes in the paste matrix, which may lead to cracking or increased permeability, must also be calculated.

Oxidation-Reduction (E_h). Aqueous solutions have a characteristic oxidation reduction potential: its scale is measured in E_h units broadly analagous to the pH

Table 2 Reactions of Cements with Saline Water

Component	Nature of reaction
Mg^{2+}	exchanges for Ca^{2+}; conversion of $Ca(OH)_2$ to $Mg(OH)_2$ etc.
$C\ell^-$	formation of chloride AF_m type phases; at higher levels, formation of monochloroaluminate, Friedel's salt.
SO_4^{2-}	formation of ettringite
SO_4^{2-}, CO_3^{2-}	formation of thaumasite,
CO_3^{2-}	conversion of $Ca(OH)_2$ to $CaCO_3$ and of C-S-H to $CaCO_3$ and silica gel.

scale.   Ordinary cements have near neutral E_h values (i.e. are neither strongly oxidising or reducing).   Moreover, they do not contain large quantities of substances which participate readily in oxidation-reduction reactions, other than sulfate and possibly ferric iron.   Fly ash contains potentially reducing substances such as unburnt carbon and iron spinel, with both Fe(II) and Fe(III) but this phase is very inert (9).   Slag, on the other hand, contains abundant sulfide (S^{2-}) ions. The S^{2-}/SO_4^{2-} couple is known to be electrochemically active and, as they mature, slag cements develop a chemically-reducing internal environment (10). Interaction between sulfur species leads to development of other species: polysulfide, S_n^{2-} ($n \geq 2$) and thiosulfate $(S_2O_3)^{2-}$ both of which are somewhat soluble in pore fluid.   The impact of these changes in pore fluid and matrix chemistry on corrosion potential is, as yet largely unknown although there are reports of enhanced corrosion of embedded steel (11).   However, it appears that embedded materials e.g. steel,   will themselves also influence the E_h.   Corroding steel will exhaust the supply of free oxygen in the repository and thereafter, continue to corrode by liberating hydrogen (12).   Thus   the repository will probably develop a low E_h in its post-closure phase.

Special Cements.   In the post-filling closure phase of the repository, borehole and shaft sealing will be necessary.   Specifications have not yet been established for these materials: should permeable materials be used to act as a safety valve for gas release?   Or would a permeable material merely act as a short circuit path for radionuclides? Should sealant materials be expansive, to improve physical contact between seals and country rock?   In general, the closure stage of repository design is still conceptual but will assume greater importance in the decades ahead. The selection of materials will probably reflect the projected scenario for the evolution of the repository and its properties.

Aggregate materials.   It is inevitable that constructional concretes will be used in the repository and desirable that excavated spoil used wherever possible to minimise cost.   Of course shallow repositories in clay will, of necessity, have to use 'imported' aggregates.   There may also be an advantage in using limestone aggregate to help counteract acidity arising form oxidation of sulfur and organic matter in clay.   However deep repositories may be both warm and wet.   It is important that constructional aggregates free from suspicion of alkali-aggregate reaction be used.   Criteria for aggregate selection and progress in understanding the nature of alkali-aggregate reaction have been reviewed (13,14) but may not be entirely applicable to warm repository environments.

SUMMARY

Research on radioactive waste immobilisation has disclosed that multiple barriers to the escape of radionuclides provides higher standards of safety than single barriers.   Cementitious materials play an important role.   Their barrier action depends upon the time scale involved for containment.   For shortlived isotopes, and in shallow repositories physical properties, e.g. impermeability, are important. But for longer lived isotopes, and in deep repositories with significant geological retardation, the chemical conditioning action of cements is the most beneficial aspect of their use.   The high pH conditioned by cementitious materials limits the solubility of many long-lived isotopes.   Cement, in conjunction with other components, e. g. slag, steel, also gives rise to chemically-reducing conditions which help control the solubility of radionuclides with variable oxidation states: typically, these are less soluble in their chemically-reduced forms, e.g. Tc^{4+} is less soluble than Tc^{7+}.   Much research effort has been devoted to calculating the persistence of pH over long time scales, to $^{\sim}10^6$ years, and modelling studies are being extended to cope with cement-saline goundwater interactions and transient thermal pulses.   Many special cement formulations have been developed for nuclear waste encapsulation, but conventional concretes, grouts and sealants will also be required in the construction and closure stages.   It is suggested that the predictive methods being developed are potentially applicable to durability problems encountered in other, more conventional engineered structures.   But more research is required on crack formation, and rehealing, on corrosion mechanisms and rates and durability in warm, saline water.

ACKNOWLEDGEMENT

Much of the experience of cements and concretes for nuclear waste immobilisation has been gained in the course of undertaking contract work for the Commission of the European Communities and the HMIP (UK).

REFERENCES

1. COWIE J. and GLASSER F.P.   The Reaction Between Cement and Natural Waters Containing Dissolved Carbon Dioxide.   Advances in Cement Research (1992) 4 No. 15, pp119-134.
2. MASO J.C. (ed.) Interfaces in Cementitious Composites. E. and F. Spon, London, 1993. pp315 + xvi. ISBN 0 419 18230 6.
3. RAMACHANDRAN V.S.   Cement Admixtures Handbook, Properties Science and Technology.   Noyes Publications, Park Ridge NJ. USA (1984). pp 626 + xxvi. ISBN 0 8155 0981 2.
4. SAGOE-CRENTSIL K.K., YILMAZ V.T. and GLASSER F.P. Impedance Spectroscopy Analysis of the Influence of Superplasticizer in Steel Corrosion in OPC Mortars. Journal of Materials Science. (1992) Vol 27 No. 12, pp3400-3404.
5. ATKINS M. et al.   Medium Active Wasteform Characterisation: the Performance of Cement-Based Systems (1991) pp 164 + vii EUR report 13542 EN ECSC-EEC-EAEC Brussels: Luxembourg. ISBN 92-826-2908-2.
6. SAROTT F.-A., BRADBURY M.H., PANDOLFO P. and SPIELER P. Diffusion and Adsorption Studies on Hardened Cement Paste and the Effect of Carbonation on Diffusion Rates. Cement and Concrete Research 1992 Vol 22, pp439-444.
7   HARRIS, A.W. An Assessment of the pH Buffering Provided by the Cementitious Backfill within a Radioactive waste Repository NIREX UK. Harwell. NSS/B102 (in press).
8. BENNET D., READ D., ATKINS M. and GLASSER F.P.   A Thermodynamic Model for Blended Cements: Cement Hydrate Phases, Thermodynamic Values and Modelling Studies.   Journal of Nuclear Materials (1992) Vol 190, pp315-328.
9. GLASSER F.P. DIAMOND S. and ROY D.M.   Hydration Reactions in Cement Pastes Incorporation Fly Ash and Other Pozzolanic Materials.

(1987) pp 139-158 in "Fly Ash and Coal Conversion By-Products: Characterisation, Utilization and Disposal III" Materials Research Society, Pittsburgh PA Symposium Proceedings Volume 86. ISBN 0-931837-51-0.

10   SPENCE R.D. Chemistry and Microstructure of Solidified Waste Forms. Lewis Publishers, Boca Raton, Florida (1993). Chapter 1, Chemistry of Cement Solidified Waste Forms, pp 1-39. ISBN 0-87371-748-1.

11.   MACPHEE D.E. and CAO H.T. Theoretical Description of the Impact of Blast Furnace Slag (BFS) on Steel Passivation in Concrete (1993). Advances in Cement Research (in press).

12.   REES J.H. and RADWELL W.R. Gas Evolution and Migration in Repositories: Current Status (19880) Nuclear Safety Studies NSS/G104 Nirex UK, Harwell pp 22.

13.   HOBBS D.W. Alkali-Silica Reaction in Concrete. Thomas Telford, London (1988). pp 182. ISBN 0 7277 1317 5.

14.   CONCRETE SOCIETY The 9th International Conference on Alkali-Aggregate Reaction in Concrete. The Concrete Society, Wexham, Slough 1992. pp 129 (2 volumes).

ENVIRONMENTALLY SAFE IMMOBILISATION OF ALKALI METAL RADIOACTIVE WASTE

P V Krivenko

Civil Engineering Institute

J V Skurchinskaya

L V Lavrinenko

Scientific Research Institute of Binders and Materials

Ukraine

ABSTRACT. In the present work the essentially new approach to solving the problem of nuclear waste management by immobilization is disclosed. The works of the scientific school of Pr. V.D. Glukhovsky served as background for this study. The low- energy technology of immobilization of radioactive waste (RAW) from nuclear power installations by means of strong chemical bonding of radionuclides in a composition of a mineral-like cementitious stone resulting in a high rate of filling by an alkaline element (up to 25 mas.%), low rate of leachate (10^{-4} kg/ sq m day),etc. and predicting their reliability for the further long- term containment has been developed. This study summarises long-term experience of investigations and practice in the field of synthesis of the analogs to natural minerals of alkaline aluminosilicate composition and forms part of a governmental programme on liquidation of the after-effects of Chernobyl disaster, dealing with the problems on durability and other physico-mechanical characteristics.

Keywords: Radioactive waste (RAW), Compound, Leachate, Alkali, Zeolite, Radionuclide, Cement, Solidification, Immobilization.

Professor, Dr.Sc.(Eng) Pavel V Krivenko is Vice- Rector , Head of Building Materials Department, Civil Engineering Institute, and Director of the Scientific Research Institute on Binders and Materials named after V.D. Glukhovsky (SRIBM),Kiev, Ukraine. He heads the investigations in the field of synthesis of the binding materials of alkaline and alkaline- alkali- earth aluminosilicate compositions and concretes based on them. Professor Krivenko has published more than 300 works, including 5 monograph books, and serves on Engineering Sciences Academy of Ukraine.

Cand.Sc(Eng) Janna V Skurchinskaya is Chief Researcher in the SRIBM. Her scientific interests include modelling of binding materials of alkaline and alkaline-alkali-earth aluminosilicate compositions.

Engineer Lubov V Lavrinenko is Senior Researcher in the SRIBM. She specialises in the creation of the reinforced materials based on alkaline and alkaline- alkali-earth aluminosilicate binders.

Concrete 2000. Edited by Ravindra K. Dhir and M. Roderick Jones.
© 1993 Published by E & FN Spon. ISBN 0 419 18120 2.

INTRODUCTION

Sharpness of ecological situation caused by great amounts of RAW collected, severity of regulating requirements to environmental problems and specific attitude of the peoples to nuclear energy danger moved forward the problem of environmentally safe localization of the RAW and it appeared to become now a first- aid problem to be solved by official bodies of different countries worldwide. The main aim is a reliable isolation of radionuclides from biosphere through the whole period of their potential danger. It seems to be apparent that the only way to succeed is that radionuclides should be immobilized into chemically bonded mineral-like new formations and disposed in stable geological formations. The works of Glukhovky V.D. and his pupils and associates in the fields of synthesis of alkaline and blended alkaline- alkali-earth aluminosilicate cementitious materials, analogous to natural minerals, have been taken as a theoretical concept for solving this problem (1, 2, 3, 4, 5, 6, 7). The alkali metal compounds being an independant component of a binding system participate in structure-formation and new formation processes. As a result of the reaction an alkaline component forms strong chemical bonds,a mineral-like stone by substantial composition and structure analogous to natural alkaline aluminosilicate minerals of zeolite-, feldspathoid- and feld spar type having the lower solubility as compared to that of OPC new formations, being formed. Thus, the theoretical conception for creation of these binders provides for as an obligatory condition presence in their compositions of alkali metal compounds which are present in the majority of RAW being a necessary component (Table 1).

EXPERIMENTAL DETAILS

Analysis of RAW of different nuclear energy installations showed that the RAW to be immobilizated are characterized by different chemical, radionuclide compositions and physico- chemical properties. The alkaline elements (Na, K, Cs, etc.) of the spent sodium and potassium- sodium carriers and liquid RAW with large content of sodium nitrate being produced at service of nuclear power stations are referred to these waste. Chemical composition of the first is presented by alloy of potassium- sodium metals, radioactivity of which is caused, first of all, by sodium-22 and caesium-137 radionuclides dissolved in them, which refer them to a class of waste with average level of specific activity.

Liquid RAW of nuclear power centres are differed by large variety of chemical and radionuclide composition, all range of fission products and radionuclides of which nuclear fuel consists are present in them. These waste are differed by large content of sodium nitrate. Besides, sodium chlorides, phosphates, tetraborates and other salts as well as organic substances (oils, fats, soaps and synthetic detergents) are present in them. Salt content in waste is 0.3- 0.4 kg/l (8).

Table 1 Solubility of new formations of
the slag-alkaline and portland cement stone

MINERAL	STOICHIOMETRIC FORMULA	SOLUBILITY, KG/CUB M
	SLAG-ALKALINE BINDER	
CSH(B)	$5CaO \ 6SiO_2 \ nH_2O$	0.050
XONOTLITE	$6CaO \ 6SiO_2 \ H_2O$	0.035
RIVERSIDITE	$5CaO \ 6SiO_2 \ 3H_2O$	0.050
PLOMBIERITE	$5CaO \ 6SiO_2 \ 10.5H_2O$	0.050
GYROLITE	$2CaO \ 3SiO_2 \ 2,5H_2O$	0.051
CALCITE	$CaCO_3$	0.014
HYDROGARNET	$3CaO \ Al_2O_3 \ 1,5SiO_2 \ 3H_2O$	0.020
SODIUM-CALCIUM HYDROSILICATE	$(Na,Ca)SiO_4 \ nH_2O$	0.050
THOMSONITE	$(Na,Ca)Al_2O_3 \ Si_2O_5 \ 6H_2O$	0.050
HYDRONEPHELINE	$Na_2O \ Al_2O_3 \ 2SiO_2 \ 2H_2O$	0.020
NATROLITE	$Na_2O \ Al_2O_3 \ 3SiO_2 \ 2H_2O$	0.020
ANALCIME	$Na_2O \ Al_2O_3 \ 4SiO_2 \ 2H_2O$	0.020
	OPC CLINKER	
CALCIUM HYDROXIDE	$Ca(OH)_2$	1.300
C2SH2	$2CaO \ SiO_2 \ nH_2O$	1.400
CSH(B)	$5CaO \ 6SiO_2 \ nH_2O$	0.050
4-CALCIUM HYDROALUMINATE	$4CaO \ Al_2O_3 \ 13H_2O$	1.080
3-CALCIUM HYDROAlUMINATE	$3CaO \ Al_2O_3 \ 6H_2O$	0.560
CALCIUM HYDRO-SULPHOALUMINATE	$3CaO \ Al_2O_3 \ 3CaSO_4 \ 31H_2O$	high

For all varieties of substances present in compositions of RAW are combined by high content of alkaline elements resulting in great difficulties while immobilization in the known-in-the-art compositions.

Taking into account the above, the modelling blends of alkaline compounds by composition imitating the real RAW and natural or synthetic aluminosilicates such as clays of different structural types (kaolinite,montmorillonite) as well as slags of different industrial processes (blast- furnace, steel- making and non-ferrous, etc.) and power station fly ashes in combination with the modifying setting time regulating additives were used as organic bearing cementitious materials. Chemical composition of liquid RAW used is given in Table 2, of a slag- in Table 3.

Resulting from general regularitires of creation of artificial stone in a system Me2O- Me2O3- SiO2- H2O (where Me2O- Na2O, K2O, Li2O, Cs2O; Me2O3- Al2O3, Cr2O3, Fe2O3) with regard to a type of alkaline RAW and aluminosilicate component the quantitative composition of a reactive mix modelling acomposition of the natural alkaline aluminosilicate minerals adjusted such that molar ratio of the oxides involved into reaction (Me2O3/ Me2O) would be less or equal to 1, has been designed.

Table 2 Chemical composition of waste used

CHEMICAL COMPOSITION, MAS.%	NO 1 *	NO 2**
NaNO3	54.5	45
Na2C2O4	8.1	10
NaOH, KOH	8.3	12
Na3PO4	7.1	–
NaCl	1.1	–
SULPHANOL***	3.6	10
Mn2O3	1.2	–
Fe2O3	2.8	–
FILTER PEARLITE	4.5	–
ION EXCHANGER	8.7	–
Na2B4O7	–	12.5
Na2CO3		10

*   waste from a reactor of large power with channels;
** waste from a water- cooled power reactor;*** trade mark..

Table 3 Chemical composition of slag used, mas.%

SiO2	Al2O3	Fe2O3	FeO	MnO2	CaO	MgO	S	TiO2	Na2O+K2O
39.1	8.8	0.7	0.6	0.1	37.8	11.3	0.5	1.0	1.0

Table 4 Mechanical strength of final products   based
on different binders and waste tested

TYPE OF BINDER USED	CDR, MAS.% ****	WATER/ BINDER RATIO	COMPRESSIVE STRENGTH,MPA AFTER 28 DAYS	
			NO 1*	NO 2 **
OPC	10	0.40	0.5	0.7
Ba- CONTAINING OPC	20.0	0.30	78.7	10.2
HIGH ALUMINA CEMENT	20.0	0.40	9.4	11.6
			cracking	
SLAG PORTLAND CEMENT ***	21.0	0.30	17.4	20.0
ALKALINE CEMENT	25.5	0.45	25.0	32.0

* ,** SEE NOTE TO TABLE 2;
*** 20 MAS. % OF CLINKER;.
**** CONTENT OF DRY RESIDUE OF WASTE IN A HARDENED PRODUCT
(here and below" CDR").

Table 5 Influence of salt content in liquid RAW of
reactor of large power with channels on
hardened alkaline cement strength

SALT CONTENT, KG/ L	CDR, MAS.%	WATER/BINDER RATIO	COMPRESSIVE STRENGTH,MPA
0.3	14.25	0.45	22.0
0.6	20.22	0.45	29.2

Table 6 Influence of sodium hydroxide content on strength
of hardened alkaline cement (salt
content in RAW 0.6 kg/l)

NAOH CONTENT IN A MIX, MAS.%	CDR, MAS.%	WATER/BINDER RATIO	COMPRESSIVE STRENGTH,MPA
2.85	20.22	0.45	11.5
4.22	21.84	0.45	23.6
8.01	25.0	0.45	32.0

Owing to multi-purposes of the problems to be solved covering waste of different nuclear energy installations the experiments were carried out in two stages. As to RAW containing sodium and potassium- sodium alloy after their conversion into the explosion and fire resistant compounds (processing is "know- how" (9),their solidification was carried out by means of mixing with an aluminosilicate constituent, placing into the moulds and posterior vibrating for removal of air involved, hardening during 28 days at normal temperature or drying at 250° C during 5 hours. The specimens prepared using the model systems were tested on strength, while the specimens prepared using real waste- on leachate by caesium- 137. The tests showed that the compressive strength of these specimens was within 15- 20 MPa and increased in time to 28- 40 MPa not depending upon curing conditions.

Tests on rate of leachate in accordance with MAGATE's procedure (Figure) testify that the final product has the high water resiatance with rate of leachate less than 10^{-4} kg/ sq m day.

KG/SQ M   DAY

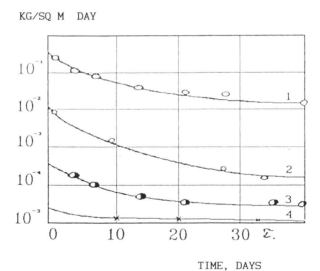

TIME, DAYS

1- from the specimens based on Portland cement,
2- on bitumen,
3,4 on the binders developed.

FIGURE   Rate of CS- 137 leachate

For immobilization   of liquid   nuclear   waste   into a   mineral-   like
artificial stone   the   finely ground slag (specific surface by   Blaine
520 sq   m per kg   ) in a combination   with a clayish additive in   the
ratio: 85 mas.% of slag: 15 mas.% of clay was used as a mineral binder,
technological procedure of producing a reactive blend was " know- how "
(10). The mechanical strength of the   specimens from the   cement   paste
after their hardening at normal temperature during 28 days was taken as
the main   criterion   for   comparison   of the   efficiency   of   the
compositions developed and   known Portland   cement ones.

Rate of   bonding   of   the   alkaline   elements   was   evaluated   by
quantitative X- ray analysis of alkaline aluminosilicate new formations
present   in a   hydration product   composition. Analysis of the   test
results   showed the greater   efficiency of   the use of   the   alkaline
cements modified   with clay,   for immobilization   of   liquid RAW   of
different origin, containing the whole range of alkaline salts. The
last, owing to   large   content secure the   high   values of   pH   of   a
medium,namely: 13-   14, which is   necessary condition for   intensive
hardening   of alkaline   binding systems,   and   flowing   of structure-
formation   processes   with   their   close   participation   as   well,   the
characteristics of   strength   and   dry   residue   content being
essentially   super   to those known-   in   -the-   art.   During
investigations it   was established that   it   seems   to   be possible to
optimize   the strength indexes   and to   increase   the content   of   dry
residue   in   case of   the   use   of   the alkaline cement at   the expense
of   vapourization of   liquid RAW and   increase   in   sodium   hydroxide
concentration as well (Tables 5,6).

RESULTS AND DISCUSSION

Untill nowadays the solidification of   waste with   inorganic   binders
was carried   out   with   the   use of   Portland   cement, modified   with
additives. It   is   known   that sodium   salt   and   alkali   content   in
compositions of Portland cement binders is restricted, as its excess in
a system affects negatively   on cement body properties (11).

The   study suggest to   consider solidification of liquid RAW with   high
salt concentration by cementing   not   as   a   chemical   process   of
water   stable   artificial   stone   formation   but   as   a   physical
immobilization   of   the   alkaline   compounds   into   a   dense   structure
confined them   to larger   or less   degree.

Resulting from   it   a Portland cement   matrix   can not   serve   as   a
reliable barrier   securing long- term stable   immobilization of   RAW
containing   the alkaline compounds.From this standpoint the essentially
new approach to a solution   of a problem of RAW immobilization based on
synthesis of   analogs   to   natural   alkaline   and alkaline- alkali-
earth aluminosilicate   minerals   of   zeolite   type   based   on   alkaline
compounds, contained in these   waste causes chemical bonding   of   these
compounds into   a water- stable mineral- like   stone.

The peculiarity of these structures is that the alkali metal compounds at interaction with an aluminosilicate constituent form atmosphere- and water resistant compounds described by general formulas: $Me_2O \cdot Al_2O_3 \cdot (2-4)SiO_2 \cdot 2H_2O$, where Me- atom of an alkaline element, and creating strong chemical bonds in a system: Me- Al- Si- O of a zeolite structure.

The investigations showed that by analogy with the natural zeolites, the artificial ones have typical for these classes of substances a three- dimentional structure consisiting of MeO_4- tetrahedra (where Me- Si, Al, Ca, P), forming channels and cavities with the rectilinear dimensions between which positive ions Na^+, K^+, Li^+, Ca^{++}, Ba^{++} balancing the negative ions of Al^{3+} in a IV- fold coordination are present.

Chemical and thermal resistance of zeolite structures results from structure and composition of zeolite (12). Owing to a cohesive structure having large energy- saturated cavitites the alkaline elements present in RAW not only form structure of a mineral- like synthetic stone but turned to be "locked" in a three- dimentional network of a zeolite matrix. It should be mentioned that the peculiarities of phase composition of hydration products of alkaline binding systems containing zeolite-like new formations of analcime type result in increased thermal resistance besides high atmosphere- and chemical resistance. It is explained by the fact that the zeolite- like hydration products at thermal treatment at 673- 1273 K undergo the phase conversion step by step expressed in dehydration and followed crystallization of unhydrous alkaline aluminosilicates of feldspathoid (nepheline, leucite) and feld spar types (albite, orthoclase, anorthite),the solid phase reactions occuring without a participation of a liquid phase resulting in the increased crack resistance of a cementitious stone while phase composition being formed- in thermal resistance.

CONCLUSIONS

High physico- mechanical properties of the alkaline binding systems, high early strength, low shrinkage, increased frost resistance, sulphate-, corrosion resistance, thermal stability as well as low rate of leachate predict high durability of an artificial stone based on above systems and possibility to use it as competitive to a natural stone for reliable safe long- term immobilization of RAW of nuclear power stations with different specific activity. A complex of igh physico- mechanical properties of a mineral- like cementitious artificial stone enlarges potential fields of its applications under the conditions where ordinary Portland cement does not work.

These findings suggest a cardinal direction for solution of environmental problems which are of great importance nowadays.

ACKNOWLEDGEMENTS

The authors gratefully appreciate the support of the Physical Power Institute, Obninsk, Russia, and especially Dr.Sc.(Chem) Starkov O.V. and Cand.Sc. (Chem) Konovalov E.E. for the help in the experimental work using real RAW.

REFERENCES

1. GLUKHOVSKY, V D. The Soil Silicates,Gosstroiizdat Publish., Kiev, USSR,1959, pp 127.

2. GLUKHOVSKY, V D The Soil Silicate Articles and Constructions, Budivelnik Publish., Kiev, USSR, 1967, pp 154.

3. GLUKHOVSKY, V D, PETRENKO, I JU, SKURCHINSKAYA, J V. On Crystallization of Carnegieite. Proc. Acad. Sc.of USSR, Ser.B, No.9, 1969, pp 822-823.

4. GLUKHOVSKY, V D, KRIVENKO, P V, STARCHEVSKAYA, E A.Investigations on Silicate-Formation in the Blends of Clay, Quartz Sand and Soda. Ukr. Chem. Jour,Vol. 35, Issue 4, 1969, pp. 433-435.

5. GLUKHOVSKY, V D, PETRENKO, I JU, SKURCHINSKAYA, J V . Physico-Chemical Characteristics of the Artificial Minerals in a System of Na2O-Al2O3-SiO2-H2O. Geological Jour., Vol 34, Issue 2, 1974, pp 133-137.

6. GLUKHOVSKY, V D, KRIVENKO, P V, ors. Slag- Alkaline Concretes Based on Fine Aggregates, Vischa Schkola (Higher School) Publish., Kiev, USSR, 1981, pp 224.

7. KRIVENKO, P V. Special Slag- Alkaline Cements, Budivelnik Publ., Kiev, Ukraine, 1992,-pp. 192.

8. NIKIFOROV, A S, ors. Rendering of Liquid Radioactive Waste Harmless, Energoatomizdat Publish., Moscow, 1985.

9. The USSR Author's Certificate (Patent) No 1471571, 1988 (unpublished).

10. The USSR's Authors Certificate (Patent)No 1625252, 1989 (unpublished).

11. RAMACHANDRAN, V S., ors. Concrete Admixtures Handbook, Properties, Science and Technology, Ed. V. S. Ramachandran, Noyes Publicacations, Park Ridge, New Jersey, USA, 1984.

12. WILLIAMS, X, TERNER, F J, GILBERT, C M. Petrography, Foreign Literature Publish., Moscow, 1957.

POLYMER DISPERSIONS IN CONCRETE:
INFLUENCE OF HAZARDOUS LIQUIDS

P Schiessl

C Alfes

Aachen University of Technology

F Sybertz

Cement Industry Research Institute

Germany

ABSTRACT. Where concrete structures are used as secondary barriers during the transshipment of environmentally hazardous liquids, special requirements are imposed on the impermeability of the concrete. Polymer dispersions can help to enhance concrete impermeability, but in order to exploit the sealing effect, the amount added must be more than 5 % in relation to cement mass. The polymer dispersion is therefore subject to approval as a concrete addition in Germany. Certification testing for an aqueous styrene butadiene dispersion as an organic concrete addition was performed for the first time at the Institute for Building Research (ibac) of the Aachen University of Technology (RWTH Aachen). The tests, which are reported in the paper, were intended to demonstrate suitability for use in structural components, investigating the influence of the dispersion on workability, strength, deformation behaviour and durability of concrete. The sealing effect against environmentally hazardous liquids was likewise tested. Apart from water, nine different organic liquids representing a broad spectrum of water-solubilities and viscosities were used in the tests. Toluene is used as an example to illustrate the way in which the swelling effect of the styrene butadiene dispersion increases impermeability.

Keywords: Concrete, Polymer Dispersion, Curing, Impermeability, Durability, Environmental Compatibility

Professor Dr.-Ing. Peter Schiessl is director of the Institute for Building Research (Institut für Bauforschung, ibac) of the Aachen University of Technology (RWTH Aachen) and holds the chair for inorganic construction materials at that university. Key research topics include concrete technology, utilization of industrial by-products, operational performance and durability of reinforced and prestressed concrete, corrosion, corrosion protection and repair. Professor Schiessl chairs or sits on numerous national and international committees.

Dipl.-Ing. Christoph Alfes is head of the "Cement and Concrete" working group at ibac. Research activities are focused on high-strength concrete, the use of silica fume in concrete and the properties of natural stone in respect to physical mechanics and fracture mechanics.

Dr.-Ing. Franz Sybertz is a former member of the ibac team. Since 1991 he has been at the Cement Industry Research Institute (Forschungsinstitut der Zementindustrie), where he is concerned with questions of cement quality assurance, certification and standardization.

Concrete 2000. Edited by Ravindra K. Dhir and M. Roderick Jones.
© 1993 Published by E & FN Spon. ISBN 0 419 18120 2.

INTRODUCTION

Safety Concept in Germany

In the chemicals industry and in the chemicals processing sector, a number of liquids hazardous to the environment, and especially to groundwater, are produced, stored and transshipped. In Germany, uncoated concrete can be used only as a so-called secondary barrier for moderately water-hazardous liquids, intended to prevent penetration of environmentally hazardous liquids to the groundwater following failure of the primary barrier, e.g. a steel tank. If a leakage occurs in the primary system, the secondary barrier must ensure sealing for a specified time. According to the "Guidelines on Concrete Construction in Relation to Water-Hazardous Materials" [1], impermeability is defined as meaning that, allowing for an additional safety margin, penetration of the medium as a liquid during the wetting period should demonstrably fail to reach the opposite side of the concrete component.

Three checks can be used to assure impermeability according to this definition when dimensioning reinforced concrete structures. In the case of uncracked concrete, concrete tensile stresses must be limited and a sufficient component thickness is required (Check 1 in Fig. 1). In the case of cracked concrete, an adequate compression zone (Check 2 in Fig. 1) or a sufficiently low crack width (Check 3 in Fig. 1) must be confirmed. Check 3 is permissible solely in connection with high-viscosity liquids.

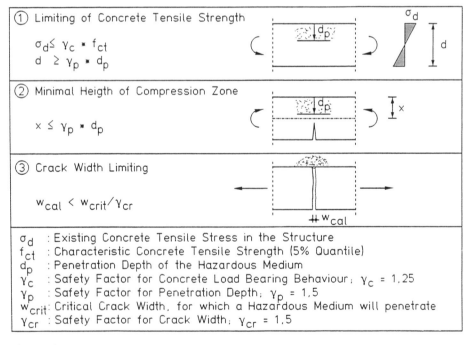

(1) Limiting of Concrete Tensile Strength

$$\sigma_d \leq \gamma_c * f_{ct}$$
$$d \geq \gamma_p * d_p$$

(2) Minimal Heigth of Compression Zone

$$x \leq \gamma_p * d_p$$

(3) Crack Width Limiting

$$w_{cal} < w_{crit} / \gamma_{cr}$$

σ_d	: Existing Concrete Tensile Stress in the Structure
f_{ct}	: Characteristic Concrete Tensile Strength (5% Quantile)
d_p	: Penetration Depth of the Hazardous Medium
γ_c	: Safety Factor for Concrete Load Bearing Behaviour; $\gamma_c = 1,25$
γ_p	: Safety Factor for Penetration Depth; $\gamma_p = 1,5$
w_{crit}	: Critical Crack Width, for which a Hazardous Medium will penetrate
γ_{cr}	: Safety Factor for Crack Width; $\gamma_{cr} = 1,5$

Figure 1 Checks according to [1] to assure adequate impermeability of concrete structures affected by environmentally hazardous liquids

Polymer Dispersions

Polymer dispersions can help to enhance the impermeability of concrete. They have long been in successful use for non-constructional applications, e.g. to increase the workability of repair mortars and improve their adhesion to the substrate. Polymer dispersions are systems of finely-dispersed plastic particles in water. The polymers used are styrene butadienes, pure acrylates and styrene acrylates [2]. Polymer dispersions contain emulsifiers as stabilizers. The particle size of the plastics is between roughly 0.1 and 0.2 μm, i.e. it is comparable with the mean grain size of the inorganic addition "silica fume". Owing to their small particle size, the plastic particles fill the voids between the cement grains, enhancing the impermeability of the solid structure in the concrete. When water is removed by cement hydration and drying, the plastic particles "stick" together, forming a spatially polymerized film in the hardened cement structure. They also swell in contact with organic liquids (Fig. 2, cf. [7]). Both effects increase the impermeability of concrete to penetrating liquids.

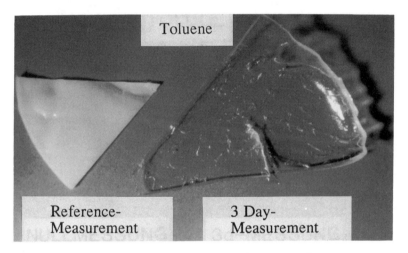

Figure 2 Swelling effect of the styrene butadiene dispersion
Left: Plastic film (after drying of the dispersion)
Right: Plastic film after three-day storage in toluene

There is a particular cost benefit from using polymer addition in concrete if its impermeability-enhancing effect can be exploited to make plastic coating of the concrete or use of a steel liner unnecessary.

In order to utilize their additional sealing effect against water-hazardous liquids in the hardened concrete, polymer dispersions must be used in quantities greater than 5 % in relation to cement mass. According to German concrete standard DIN 1045, they are therefore to be classified as addition and require a testmark of conformity from the Institute for Structural Engineering (Institut für Bautechnik, IfBt) in Berlin. Certification tests were performed for the first time at ibac [4,5], on a polymer dispersion manufactured by Hüls AG as an organic concrete addition [3].

The following descriptions are based on the certification tests carried out at ibac. From the point of view of the supervising authority, checks to establish the harmlessness and uniformity of new construction materials are required before they can be used. In this instance, uniformity checks were unnecessary, as uniformity is implicit in the production parameters of the polymer dispersion manufacturing process. The tests described in the following sections are aimed at confirming the harmlessness or suitability of the polymer dispersion as a concrete addition.

SUITABILITY OF A STYRENE BUTADIENE DISPERSION FOR CONCRETE

Concretes in the Tests

A styrene-butadiene-based polymer dispersion was used in the tests. The polymer may be assigned to the elastomer group [2]. The density of the aqueous dispersion was 1010 kg/m^3, its solids content 47 wt.% and its pH value roughly 7.9. At 0.015 wt.%, chloride content was well below the maximum limit of 0.1 wt.% specified for concrete additions in Germany. According to the manufacturer, the minimum film-forming temperature of the tested styrene butadiene dispersion is 3 °C. The special modification of the dispersion excludes any tendency to saponification.

Fresh concrete properties, strength, deformation behaviour and durability were investigated on concretes with and without polymer dispersion. Table 1 shows the concrete composition. The dispersion content was approximately 50 kg/m^3, with a cement content of the concrete of 300 kg/m^3, i.e. 17 wt.% in relation to the cement. The water content of the dispersion was taken into account for the water content of the concrete in the tests. Tests were carried out using a blast-furnace cement HOZ 35 L (slag content 50 %) and a PZ 45 F portland cement. The water/cement ratio was a constant 0.45 for Mixes 1 to 4 (Table 1). Owing to the powerful liquefying effect of the dispersion, there would be an extreme difference in consistency between concretes with and without the addition under test. For this reason, the reference mixes were made up using 3 % superplasticizer in relation to cement mass. The aggregate was a Rhine gravel with a relatively low sand content and a maximum grain size of 32 mm (grading curve A/B 32 according to DIN 1045).

Since the compressive strength of concretes containing the dispersion was somewhat lower than that of the reference concretes without polymer dispersion, an additional reference concrete with the same 28 d compressive strength (Mix 5) was included in the tests. The w/c ratio of this reference concrete with blast-furnace cement was 0.54 (Table 1).

Hardened concrete properties depend significantly on storage conditions; the fundamental interrelationships for concrete are well known. This is not true in the case of concrete made up with polymer dispersion. In such concretes, two materials reacting very differently to moistening and drying co-exist in the cement matrix. Cement hydration requires an adequate period of moist storage, whereas film formation of the polymer dispersion demands the driest conditions possible. In order to determine the influence of storage conditions, the curing time and storage temperature of the concretes were varied as follows:

D2: 2 days moist, then 20/65 climate (20 °C, 65 % relative humidity)
D7: 7 days immersed in water, then 20/65 climate
W: continuously immersed in water
H7: 7 days immersed in water, then in air at +40 °C

In addition to compressive strength tests on 150 mm cubes, the static modulus of elasticity of concretes stored under the various conditions outlined above was tested according to DIN 1048, using cylinders with a diameter of 150 mm and a height of 300 mm. The upper test stress was 1/3 of the compressive strength.

Table 1 Mix composition and 28 day compressive strength of the concretes in the test for approval tests as an organic concrete addition according to DIN 1045

Mix No	Cement/ Class	$f_{c,cem,28}$ N/mm^2	c kg/m^3	w kg/m^3	p kg/m^3	a [2] dm^3/m^3	$\frac{w}{c}$	$\frac{w+p+a-15}{c}$	$f_{c,con,28}$ N/mm^2
1	BFSC 35	49	302	136	- [3]	8	0,45	0,426	53
2	BFSC 35	49	301	135	24 [1]	15	0,45	0,529	42
3	OPC 45	59	302	136	- [3]	12	0,45	0,440	60
4	OPC 45	59	291	131	23 [1]	27	0,45	0,570	42
5	BFSC 35	49	303	164	-	13	0,54	0,533	42

1) means a dispersion content of 50 and 48.7 kg/m^3 resp.
2) measured values
3) addition of 3 wt-% superplasticizer related to the cement

c: cement content
w: water content
p: polymer dispersion content
a: air content

Fresh Concrete

The styrene butadiene dispersion in the tests exhibited favourable workability properties. Consistency was investigated on Mixes 1 to 5 and in preliminary tests on other mixes. In all cases, the polymer dispersion had a powerful liquefying effect. Concretes with the polymer dispersion had a much softer consistency than concretes with the same cement and water contents but without the dispersion. The cohesion of concretes containing styrene butadiene was extremely good. The liquefying effect of the dispersion in the concrete increased with rising dispersion content [9]. At the permissible value of 17 % added dispersion addition, the polymer dispersion in the tests improves consistency more effectively than many superplasticizers.

Polymer dispersions may lead to an increase in air content. For example, with Mix 2 (Table 1), an air content of 1.6 vol.% was determined after 2.5 minutes and an air content of 2.4 vol.% after 6 minutes mixing time [5]. These values are still within the normal range of air contents for fresh concrete. Since, however, the entrained air content depends on a variety of influencing variables, e.g. on dispersion content, on temperature and on mixing time, air content should be checked as part of the quality assurance procedures where a concrete containing a dispersion addition is used on site.

Compressive Strength

The most important variable influencing concrete compressive strength is known to be the w/c ratio. In Germany, this relationship is generally described by the Walz diagram (e.g. in [6]). Concretes which contain dispersion have substantially lower strength at the same w/c ratio than reference concretes (Table 1) and cannot be described with the aid of the Walz diagram. Strictly speaking, the Walz diagram applies only to concrete which has been compacted almost completely, without air entraining agents. Air contents are then generally about 1.5 vol.%. Any significant deviation of air contents from this value must be taken into account. For practical purposes, the air contents may be assumed to represent the same volume of water. Plastic has a much lower modulus of elasticity than hardened cement, and therefore probably acts as a void when the hardened cement structure is exposed to compressive stress. The quantity of polymer introduced into the concrete via the dispersion is therefore also treated here as if it constituted the same volume of water. This assumption disregards bonding conditions in the hardened cement and should therefore be regarded merely as a rough approximation. The good agreement of the measured values with the Walz curve in Fig. 3 shows, however, that concrete strengths can be predicted in this way. The figure is based on the values given in Table 1.

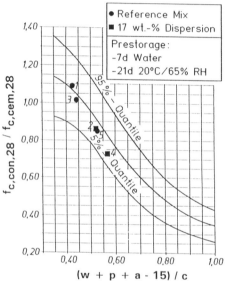

Figure 3 Concrete compressive strength in relation to cement strength at an age of 28 days, as a function of the parameter (w + p + a - 15)/c (index denotes mix number in Table 1)

Modulus of Elasticity

For structural applications, both compressive strength and modulus of elasticity are of importance. The static moduli of elasticity of the concretes in the test are shown as a function of compressive strength in Fig. 4. The graph also shows the calculated values according to DIN 1045. In plotting the calculated values, it was assumed that mean concrete compressive strength is some 8 N/mm² higher than the characteristic strength. It will be readily apparent that the measured moduli of elasticity are relatively close to the calculated values according to DIN 1045. It may be concluded that calculated values for the modulus of elasticity in relation to strength according to DIN 1045 can also be used for concretes containing the polymer dispersion.

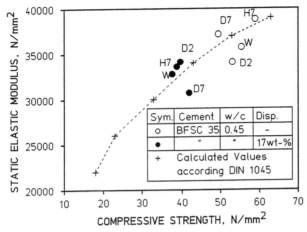

Figure 4 Static elastic modulus as a function of compressive strength

Durability and Curing

Carbonation behaviour and frost resistance were also tested on concrete specimen as part of the certification procedure. Compared to the reference mixes the concretes containing the styrene butadiene dispersion revealed a tendency to a lower carbonation depth and to a smaller scaling in the frost tests.

An additional factor in determining durability is curing sensitivity. It is generally known that polymer dispersions reduce sensitivity to poor curing. The concrete becomes more robust. This is confirmed by the results of the water penetration tests in accordance with DIN 1048 (Fig. 5). The tests were performed on 28-day-old concrete which had been stored according to D2, D7 and W above. Fig. 5 shows that water penetration depth is far less dependent on curing in the concretes with dispersion as

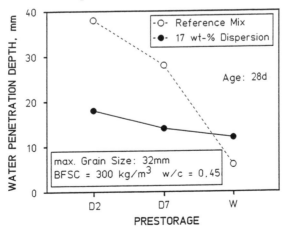

Figure 5 Water penetration depth with various types of prestorage

compared to those without. With storage types D2 and D7, penetration depths were significantly smaller than for the reference concrete; with storage type W somewhat greater. The lower water penetration depth on the air-stored concretes with polymer dispersion as compared to the non-dispersion concretes is probably the film-forming action of the styrene butadiene polymer.

In general, results indicate that the dispersion improves durability in concrete of the same compressive strength.

Further Tests

Tests were also performed on tensile splitting strength, dynamic modulus of elasticity, creep and shrinkage, composite behaviour of steel reinforcement, fire behaviour. None of these revealed any disadvantageous behaviour.

EFFICACY IN CONCRETE

Concretes in the Tests

The only factors of interest to the supervising authority when granting marks of conformity are generally the uniformity and harmlessness of the relevant construction material. As indicated by the above results, harmlessness or suitability as a concrete addition according to DIN 1045 was proved. In view of the possible use of styrene butadiene concretes as secondary barriers (see introduction), the efficacy of the polymer dispersion was also investigated.

Efficacy as a sealing addition against water-hazardous liquids was tested on concretes with 45 kg/m^3 of added dispersion (polymer/cement ratio of 0.07) and on reference mixes without dispersion. The main tests were carried out using a blast-furnace cement HOZ 35 L with 50 % slag. Cement content was 320 kg/m^3 in all cases, the w/c ratio 0.50 and the maximum grain size of the gravelly Rhine sand 16 mm (grading curve A/B 16 according to DIN 1045). A superplasticizer was added to the reference mix to ensure matching consistencies. The test specimens were conditioned according to Storage D7 until wetting tests commenced at an age of 2 months.

Capillary Penetration of Test Liquids

Test set-up, test procedures and test evaluation for the penetration tests were largely in accordance with the Guidelines [1]. Fig. 6 depicts the test set-up. The specimens were drilled cores with a diameter of 80 mm and a height of 120 mm, drilled from a concrete slab at an age of 7 days and then stored for 49 days in a 20/65 climate. Following installation and sealing of the specimens, they were wetted with liquids. The quantity of liquid penetrating over time was determined during the penetration process. In accordance with the Guidelines [1], penetration tests were ended after a wetting time of 72 hours; the specimens were split and the penetration depth measured. The penetration tests were conducted with 10 different test liquids (Table 2) selected by an ad hoc committee of the Institut für Bautechnik, Berlin, on the basis of an expert report by Schönberg [8].

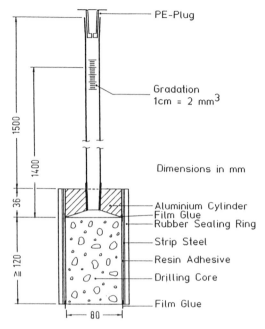

Figure 6 Test set-up for determining the capillary penetration [1, 7]

In general, penetration depth and quantity are proportionate to one another in penetration tests according to the Guidelines [1]. The quantity of toluene penetrating the specimen as a function of wetting time may be taken as an example of penetration test results (Fig. 7). The quantity penetrating the styrene butadiene concrete is substantially less than that penetrating the reference concrete without dispersion. The difference between the concrete with dispersion and the reference concrete is greater with respect to penetration quantity than penetration depth. This phenomenon is probably related to the fact that the preceding toluene gas front is slowed down by the swelling effect of the styrene butadiene (Fig. 2). The greater diffusion resistance of the concretes with styrene butadiene is confirmed in the diffusion tests (see below).

Applying the test results to the dimensioning of concrete components (see introduction), component thickness can be reduced when using a concrete with styrene butadiene, owing to the smaller penetration depth (cf. Fig. 1, Check 1). If a leak occurs, a component produced with concrete containing the dispersion will resist penetration by the liquid longer before allowing it to pass into the groundwater. There will thus be more time for decontamination measures.

Penetration Behaviour of the Gas Phase

Liquid is transported in pore systems not only by means of capillary action but as a gas phase in accordance with diffusion laws. The gaseous penetration front precedes the liquid front [7]. In order to estimate the order of magnitude of the quantity of liquid transported in the gas phase, diffusion coefficients were determined for blast-furnace concretes with and without dispersion, using two selected test liquids.

Table 2   Selected test liquids for the penetration tests (IfBt list)

No.	Test Liquid	Viscosity mPa·s	Boiling Point °C	Miscible with water	Chemical Main Group
1	n-heptane	0.40	98	no	aliphatic and cycloaliphatic hydrocarbons
2	toluene	0.58	111	no	aromatic hydrocarbons
3	n-butanol	2.93	118	no	monovalent and polyvalent alcohols
4	ethyl acetate	0.45	77	no	ester
5	methylene ethyl ketone	0.42	80	no	aldehydes and ketones
6	n-butylamine	0.50	78	yes	aliphatic amines
7	methylene chloride	0.44	40	no	halogenated aliphatic hydrocarbons, without additional functional groups
8	acetic acid, 25%	1.10	118	yes	organic acids (excl. formid acid)
9	chlorobenzene	0.81	132	no	halogenated aromatic hydrocarbons
10	water	1.00	100	-	-

Tests were performed on 2 cm thick concrete discs sawn from cylinders. The concrete discs were bonded to flasks containing the test liquid. A liquid-dependent material concentration collects above the liquid as a gas phase. Owing to the concentration gradient, the liquid diffuses through the concrete. The coefficient of diffusion was determined from gravimetrically-measured liquid losses once a stable state had been attained.

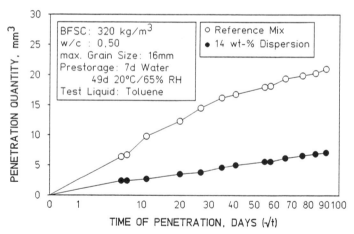

Figure 7   Quantity of toluene penetrating the concrete as a function of penetration time

In concrete with the dispersion, the diffusion coefficient for n-heptane was $1.1*10^{-8}$ m^2/s and that for methylene chloride was $1.2*10^{-8}$ m^2/s. The equivalent values for the reference concrete without the dispersion were $2.7*10^{-8}$ m^2/s and $1.8*10^{-8}$ m^2/s respectively (Fig. 8).

The results show that concretes with polymer dispersion have lower coefficients of diffusion, inhibiting gaseous transport of the liquids to a greater extent. The reason for the lower diffusion coefficients is the swelling effect of the polymer particles in the concrete.

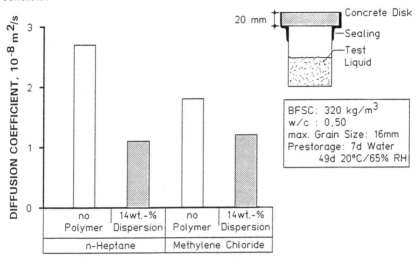

Figure 8 Diffusion resistance of concrete with styrene butadiene as compared to pure cement concrete

SUMMARY AND OUTLOOK

Polymer dispersions can be used to improve penetration resistance where environmentally hazardous materials affect concrete. In Germany, the Institut für Bautechnik has for the first time issued a testmark of conformity for a polymer dispersion as an organic construction material according to DIN 1045. The styrene-butadiene-based dispersion in the tests may thus be used in reinforced concrete according to DIN 1045 and in prestressed concrete with subsequent bonding according to DIN 4227. The permissible quantity is 17 % dispersion in relation to cement mass.

The certification and efficacy tests have yielded the following results:

- Given the same w/c ratios and water contents, concretes with styrene butadiene dispersion have a substantially softer consistency, accompanied by good cohesion behaviour, than reference concretes without polymer dispersion.
- If the entire styrene butadiene dispersion is added to the water content of the concrete and the air content is considered, the usual water/cement ratio laws (Walz diagram) can be used to estimate compressive strength.
- The usual dimensioning methods (DIN 1045, DIN 4227) can be used with respect to deformation behaviour in the case of concrete with styrene butadiene.
- Concretes with styrene butadiene are substantially less sensitive to curing than concretes without polymer dispersion.
- The styrene butadiene dispersion reduces the penetration depths of organic liquids. The check was made using 9 selected organic liquids. The dispersion also increases gas impermeability.

Further research will be carried out into the possible applications and efficacy of the styrene butadiene dispersion in the tests as part of a joint research project on the "Safety of concrete structures in technical plant with environmentally hazardous materials" sponsored by the Federal Research Ministry. The use of polymer dispersions is advantageous if both their enhanced sealing properties and their liquefying action can be exploited. This opens up new prospects for the future. In certain cases, it may be possible to avoid the need for complex coatings by using polymer dispersions in the concrete when erecting concrete structures. This will allow a more economic construction method to be employed.

REFERENCES

1.   DEUTSCHER AUSSCHUSS FÜR STAHLBETON (Ed.). Guideline for Concrete Construction in Relation to using Water Hazardous Materials (in German). Beuth Verlag, Berlin, September 1992

2.   DÖREN, K. Polymer Dispersions for Modifying Cement (in German). VDB-Information 53/1989. Verband Deutscher Betoningenieure e.V., 4100 Duisburg 74, 3 pp

3.   INSTITUT FÜR BAUTECHNIK BERLIN. Organic Addition according to DIN 1045 "Lipaton SB 5850"; Testmark PA VII-21/801, Berlin, Januar 1992 in German)

4.   Certification Tests of the Organic Addition "Lipaton SB 5813" as Addition according to DIN 1045. Part A: Test of the Suitability as Sealing against Water Hazardous Liquids. Part B: Test of the Suitability as Addition. Reports A2100/1 and A2100/6 of the Institut für Bauforschung der RWTH Aachen, April 1990 bzw. March 1991 (in German).

5.   Certification Tests of the Organic Addition "Lipaton SB 5850" as Addition according to DIN 1045. Report A2100/7 of the Institut für Bauforschung der RWTH Aachen, March 1991 (in German).

6.   WESCHE, K. Conctruction Materials as Load Bearing Members, Volume 2: Concrete. 2. Aufl. Bauverlag, Wiesbaden, Berlin, 1981 (in German)

7.   GRUBE, H AND SPANKA, G. Tightness of Concrete against Organic Liquids (in German). Beton 40 (1990), No. 4, pp 148-151, No. 5, pp. 200-203

8.   SCHÖNBERG, M. Expert Report "Test Method for Dividing Chemical Mediums in Main Groups" (in German), Frankfurt/Main, Oktober 1988 (unpublished)

9.   GROCHE, F. Durable, Liquid-Impermeable Concrete Constructions - Concrete Technological Aspects (in German). VGB-Fachtagung "Korrosionsschutz für Stahl und Stahlbeton im Kraftwerksbau", Essen, 14.11.1989, 16 pp.

MACROENCAPSULATION OF INDUSTRIAL WASTE USING HYDRAULIC CEMENTS

A Samarin

Boral Resources (NSW) Pty Ltd

Australia

ABSTRACT. One of the major problems facing industrial countries is to ensure the sustainable development of natural resources, and another is clean-up of soil, water and air pollution, which has resulted from past activities, and unfortunately in some cases still happens at present. Remediation of contaminated land presents a considerable challenge to modern technology and science. A method, suitable for cleaning contaminated sites, which are non-uniformly polluted with relatively high concentrations of hazardous substances, forming "hot spots", and also contain underground fuel storage due for decommissioning, is proposed. It consists of special pre-treatment of contaminated soil (when appropriate), and then using this soil as a part of aggregate in a "high performance" concrete or mortar. The composition of mix is selected to ensure chemical immobilization and physical microencapsulation of pollutants. The mix is then pumped into underground tank, allowing long sitting times of macroencapsulated matrix. Quoting Paracelsus (1493-1541): "All substances are poisons; there is none which is not a poison. The right dose differentiates a poison and a remedy".

Keywords: Clean-up, Remediation, Contaminated Land, Chemical Immobilization, Microencapsulation, Hydraulic Cement, Zeolites, Underground Fuel Storage, Decommissioning, Macroencapsulation, High Performance Concrete.

Professor Alek Samarin is Director of Boral Research and a Professorial Fellow of the Wollongong University, Australia. He has more than thirty years' experience in materials science and engineering; has published widely and taken several patents. He is a Fellow of the Australian Academy of Technological Sciences and Engineering as well as of many Australian and International learned societies. His current interest is in converting waste to value-added raw materials in building and construction.

Concrete 2000. Edited by Ravindra K. Dhir and M. Roderick Jones.
© 1993 Published by E & FN Spon. ISBN 0 419 18120 2.

LEGAL PROBLEMS OF CONTAMINATED LAND CLEAN-UP

The recently released Guidelines for the Assessment and Management of Contaminated Sites of the Australia and New Zealand Environment and Conservation Council (ANZECC) and the National Health and Medical Research Council (NHMRC) define a *contaminated site* as "a site at which hazardous substances occur at concentrations above background or local levels and which are likely to pose an immediate or long-term hazard to human health or the environment".

The definition is sufficiently vague to provide the regulatory authorities with a degree of discretion in the interpretation of the law, and to impose considerable uncertainty on the owner of a contaminated site, as to the extent and the nature of remedial actions which may be required in the clean-up process.

In the United States the problem of contaminated sites goes back to 1980, leading subsequently to the creation of the "superfund" programme, which provides the Federal government with the authority to request remediation of a site defined as contaminated, and to impose a strict, joint and multiple civil liability for the clean-up costs upon an extremely broad class of persons who are perceived to be responsible or even simply connected with a contaminated site.

However, the exact extent of liability remains somewhat unclear, although there was a recent attempt by the US Environment Protection Authority to promulgate a Rule designed to act as a guide, thus reducing the risk to business enterprises. It is not uncommon in the United States to carefully consider legal liability for contaminated sites in all types of transactions, including acquisitions, disposals and prospectus issues.

In Australia, in the latest ANZECC and NHMRC Guidelines, there is now no reference as to who should be responsible for the clean-up of contamination (apart from the polluter), nor is a reference made to the respective liability of owners. Instead, a system of financial incentives providing assistance to owners of contaminated sites in remediation work is advocated.

One can be mistaken to assume that conducting a "benign" operation on a particular site would render this land automatically pollution free.

Virtually the complete spectrum of known industrial and agricultural activities can give rise to contamination of the land in a number of ways.

These may include:-

* accidental spillage,

* leakage of oil,

* use of agricultural products or compost,

* unauthorized disposal of wastes,   and even

* migration of contaminants in the soil or groundwater from neighbouring properties.

The contamination can be due to the activities by the previous owners of the site, particularly if the area has a long history of industrial use.

ASSESSMENT OF ENVIRONMENTAL RISK

It is prudent to regard contaminated soil as a potentially hazardous waste and as such subject it to the comparable controls which should be applied to an industrial waste.

Such controls could relate to the storage, transport and to an ultimate disposal of contaminated soil, when some or all of these actions are appropriate.

In the ANZECC and NHMRC Guidelines the preferred order of options for site management is:-

* onsite treatment by physical, chemical or biological means,

* off-site treatment of excavated contaminated soil which is removed to a waste disposal site or used as landfill,

* removal of contaminated soil for disposal (without treatment) at appropriate disposal facilities,

* dilution of hot spots of contamination,

* containment of contaminated soil with appropriate barriers or caps,   and

* leave contamination on the site and restrict the land use of the site.

It is apparent that the preferred order in some cases may be influenced by the type, the intensity and by the pattern of contamination.

For example, off-site treatment or removal of contaminated soil for disposal is now considered less and less appropriate for a number of reasons. Some of these are:

* potential hazard associated with the transport of badly contaminated soil,

* reduced availability of secure landfilling space in the coastal zones of Australia, where most of the population resides.

The identification of contamination is fundamental in achieving proper remediation of polluted sites.   This must include a clear understanding of the nature and the distribution of contaminants.

The selection of site treatment would be also influenced by the proposed land use, and this in turn can affect the nature and the extent of sampling.

The sampling plan depends on:-

* expected location of contaminants (based on the information arising from the site history and existing condition),

* expected homogeneity of contaminant (ie presence of hot spots from a particular source),

* expected severity of contamination.

The Environmental Site Assessment is a process - not an isolated activity - which can characterise the environmental status of a site, especially in terms of soil and groundwater contamination.

Finally, the Environment Risk Assessment can be considered as the extension of the Environmental Site Assessment.

The Environment Risk is a function of the level of contamination and the probability (including the duration) of exposure.

The main receptors of contaminated soil or water are humans, plants, animals and buildings.

For humans, the exposure to contaminants can be manifested in the following ways:-

* skin contact,

* inhalation of vapours, gases, mists or dust,

* ingestion of contaminated soil,

* uptake of contaminants in food (both plant and animal),

* uptake of contaminated water (surface, groundwater, or storage network).

Perception of risk is an extremely important factor and may alter the types or criteria and the degree of clean-up required for a given site.

The Risk Assessment process should consist of the identification of contaminants, evaluation of toxicity of these contaminants, evaluation of the potential exposure, and an estimation of the potential for adverse health or environmental effects.

METHODOLOGY OF CLEAN-UP OF A TYPICAL INDUSTRIAL SITE

The objective of a site clean-up is to select the most cost effective remediation method, which mitigates environmental threats and provides maximum protection for public health and welfare.

Due to a certain ambiguity in the current government regulations regarding contaminated sites, it may be prudent to err towards the conservative levels of residuals, anticipated to remain on a site after treatment.   The acceptable levels would also depend on the approved end use of the site. For example, the acceptable levels for domestic occupancy are generally lower than those for commercial or industrial use, due to potentially longer (continuous) time of human exposure.

The clean-up strategy thus will depend on the environmental site and risk assessments, on the proposed end use of the site and on the economical aspects of the available remediation techniques.

A typical contaminated site would generally have a long history of agricultural or industrial use and, most likely, as a result of technological progress, will be the subject of different or changing industrial or agricultural activities (or both).

The type, the pattern and the severity of the contamination in such cases is expected to be non-uniform.

There are likely to be local hot spots of contaminated soil resulting from different past and present activities.

For example, the topographical locations of various sources of contaminants are likely to be different for the alternative site utilizations. The soil may be relocated due to the process of denudation and deposition by rain water run-off.

As a result, the spread and the depth of each hot spot will be different in composition, homogeneity and in toxicity of the pollutants present in the soil.

Some of these hot spots may of course overlap.

Another typical feature of an industrial site is the underground fuel storage.

Underground fuel tanks can be made in asphalt-coated steel, double-walled fibreglass, double-walled steel, epoxy-coated steel, fibreglass-coated steel, fibreglass-coated double-walled steel or just in fibreglass.

In Australia, underground storage fuel tanks usually range in size from 10,000 litre to 50,000 litre capacity. Refer to Figure 1: Underground Storage Tank.

These tanks have limited life-cycle, which depends on their construction, on the aggressiveness of soil or ground water in contact with the tank exterior, and on the way and extent of tank usage.

The tank itself, or the pipework may develop leaks, which then become a source of soil contamination. The contamination plume formed by the loss of fuel can grow to a considerable size, without any signs of contamination on the surface. The size and the rate of growth of the plume will depend on the geology of the area and the location of the leak, but some fine grained soils, for example, were reported to contain up to 35,000 litres of petrol in the volume of 100 cubic metres (i.e. 35% saturation).

When an underground tank is out of service a decision must be made as to whether to remove the tank or to leave it in-situ. Large petrol companies such as Mobil, Caltex and Shell, all have the policy that underground fuel tanks should be removed when no longer required.

The decommissioning and removal of underground tanks is both risky and expensive. The atmosphere in the tank may contain fuel vapour and air in the ratio which makes the mixture flammable at normal pressure. For petrol, the flammability range is between 1.4% and 7.6% of fuel vapour by volume of air, and for the diesel the corresponding values are 1.3% and 6.0%.

Prior to the tank's removal, the air in the tank must be either replaced with nitrogen or carbon dioxide, or purged, thus reducing the percentage of vapour below the flammable limit.

The current cost of tank removal is of the order of $6,000 to $7,000.

If the tank and the pipework remained intact up to the time of decommissioning, there is no reason generally, why the tank has to be removed.

The tank nonetheless has to be rendered safe "in situ".

It is not uncommon for some soil contamination to exist surrounding the tank and the pipework free of leaks.

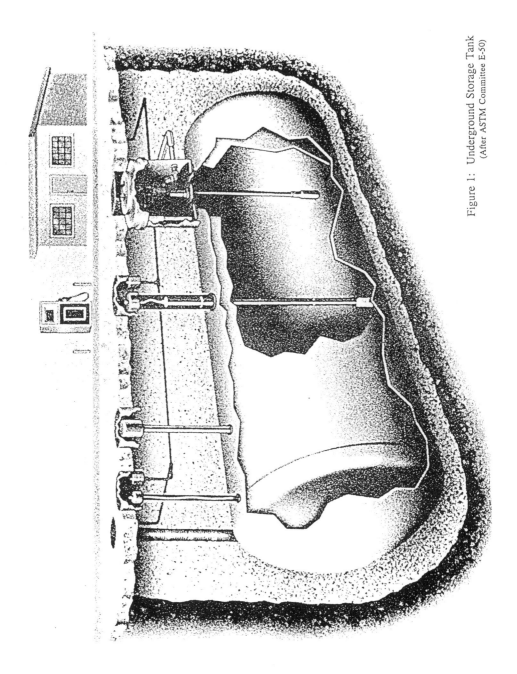

Figure 1: Underground Storage Tank
(After ASTM Committee E-50)

This can result from:-

* overfilling the tank

* spills when filling the tank

* spills when dispensing from the tank

There are currently no specific limits for hydrocarbon contamination of soil, but it is likely that in Australia, the Dutch criteria for groundwater will be adopted, thus:-

Level A $10\mu g/ltr$ - Reference value used in context of clean-up operations.

Level B $40\mu g/ltr$ - Indicative value for further investigation

Level C $150\mu g/ltr$ - Indicative value for cleaning up.

PROPOSED SYSTEM OF MACROENCAPSULATION - SAMARIN'S METHOD

It is apparent that the majority of contaminated industrial sites do not have a single level of a pollutant or pollutants distributed uniformly throughout the entire volume of soil.

It is much more probable that the contaminants have relatively high local concentrations, restricted to comparatively small areas. These hot spots are more likely than not to contain a relatively high level of a single contaminant. By implication, a significant volume of soil outside the hot spots is more likely to have relatively low levels of, possibly, several contaminants.

Indicative costs of removal of contaminated soil to a licensed landfill were quoted recently by Chris Kidd (Ref. 1).

* For a lightly contaminated soil, the cost is $30 to $55 per m³

* For a heavily contaminated soil, it is significantly higher, from $180 to $250/m³

Remedying costs of heavily contaminated soil are quoted as follows:-

* In-place bioremediation of petroleum hydrocarbons: $30 to $50/m³

* Soil washing of petroleum contamination: $80 to $150/m³

* Chemical fixation followed by disposal to a licensed landfill: $200 to $300/m³

Thus, it is the removal or chemical fixation of soil in the hot spots that presents the main problems and expense.

If the site also contains underground fuel tanks, which need removal, the clean-up costs become quite significant.

Hence, the broad philosophy of the proposed Samarin's method of macroencapsulation is as follows:

Step 1   hot spots containing specific pollutant or pollutants are identified, the borders drawn and the concentration levels and the toxicity of contaminants established.

Step 2   A preliminary method of treatment (if necessary) of specific pollutants is evaluated. In many cases, the pre-treatment may not be required.

Step 3   A special high performance concrete or mortar is designed, so that contaminated soil becomes part of the fine aggregate. The high-performance concrete or mortar must be pumpable, with relatively small maximum size aggregate, and be capable of both:- chemical fixation and physical microencapsulation of the hazardous material present in the soil.

Step 4   Using the underground storage tank as a receptacle, the high performance concrete or mortar is pumped into the base inlet of the tank. The top outlet remains open to the atmosphere, thus automatically purging the tank, as the level of the concrete or mortar rises. Instead of implementing the costly process of tank removal, the tank becomes a repository for macroencapsulation of contaminated soil.

Most of the organic and some inorganic pollutants act as set-retarders of concrete or mortar, particularly when their addition levels exceed a critical threshold. Thus, conventional methods of waste microencapsulation in hydraulic cement concrete or mortar are limited to the relatively small per cent of contaminant being immobilized, as highlighted by Samarin (Ref. 2).

Macroencapsulation in the underground storage tank overcomes this problem. High-performance concrete or mortar will not lose its effectiveness in the ability to chemically fix and physically immobilize the contaminants, even if the retardation will last for weeks or even months.

Some particular techniques involved in Samarin's method of macroencapsulation are the subject of a Patent Application, but others, already in the public domain, are described in some detail in this paper.

HOT SPOTS - MOST LIKELY CONTAMINANTS
AND METHODS OF PRE-TREATMENT

Some likely sources of land contamination are listed in Table 1.

Asbestos fibres can also be present on demolition sites containing old buildings or plant.

Areas of capacitor or transformer storage and disposal are likely to be contaminated with polychlorinated biphenyls, (PCB's).

Cooling water discharge areas, scrap metal storage, process wastes and stockpile leachates are likely to contain heavy metals. Lead, mercury, cadmium and chromium are also present in the areas of waste batteries storage.

Chemical plants can be responsible for a wide range of contaminants including dioxins, furans, formaldehydes, phenols, heavy metals and a variety of specific chemicals, depending on the process and the output of a plant.

Agricultural activities such as improved pasture and cattle dips are likely to contain phosphorus and organochlorine pesticides (OCP's).

Old refrigerators, fire extinguishers and some plastic foam materials may be a source of chlorofluorocarbons (CFC's).

It is apparent that pre-treatment, if and when required, will vary considerably, depending on the type and the severity of contamination.

An example of typical pre-treatment of soil contaminated with oil, grease or some heavy metals may be as follows:-

Table 1   Typical activities associated with
land contamination (after ANZEC 1990)

Acid/Alkali Plant and Formulation	Metal Treatment
Agricultural/Horticultural Activities	Mining and Extractive Industries
Asbestos Production	Oil Production, Refining and Storage
Chemicals Manufacture and Formulation	Paint Formulation and Manufacture
Dry Cleaning Establishments	Pesticide Manufacture and Formulation
Electroplating and Heat Treatment Premises	Pharmaceutical Manufacture & Formulation
Explosives Industry	Smelting and Refining
Fertilizer Plants	Tanning and Associated Trades
Iron and Steel Works	Waste Storage and Treatment
Landfill Sites	Wood Preservation

Depending on the grading (proportions of gravel, sand, silt and clay fractions) and the specific nature of the contaminant, the soil is selected to become a pre-determined part of the total raw materials, which will make up a unit volume of high performance concrete or mortar.

This portion of the material, extracted from the hot spot is then pre-mixed in the stationary or transit concrete mixer with the exact quantity of zeolite and added part of the proposed total mixing water.

Zeolites form a group of complex aluminium silicate minerals containing alkali metals and alkali-earth. They have an open, three-dimensional crystal structure, in which water molecules are held in cavities in the lattice. The water can be driven off by heat and the zeolite can then absorb other molecules of suitable size. Zeolites are used for separating mixtures by selective absorption - for this reason they are often called molecular sieves.

Commercially available Australian zeolites contain about 70% of clinoptilolite ($Na/K.AlO_2.5SiO_2.4H_2O$), acting as an ion exchange medium. The material can effectively absorb oil and grease, and, in relatively small additions, remove heavy metals such as lead, cadmium and zinc from solutions.

Phosphates are even more effectively removed in the presence of trivalent cations of iron and aluminium.

The pre-treated material, composing between 100 and 800 kg per cubic metre of high performance concrete or mortar is then mixed with all the other ingredients to produce a rheologically fluid substance, by the addition of high-range water reducers and the balance of mixing water.

The effectiveness of a zeolite is determined from its cation exchange capacity, usually expressed as milliequivalents per one hundred grams (meq/100g).

COMPOSITION OF HIGH PERFORMANCE CONCRETE OR MORTAR

If the contaminant is chemically inert, the process is reduced to physical immobilization only. Microencapsulation of asbestos fibres is a classical example of physical arrest, and will require simply high impermeability and durability of the hydraulic cement matrix. Overall immobilization will also depend on the thermodynamic stability (solubility) and/or on the chemical adsorption of the aggressive species by the encapsulating matrix.

Studies of Portland cement hydration indicate that two types of calcium-silicate-hydrate (C-S-H) products are formed.

The first is formed largely inside the original boundary of cement grain, it is relatively dense and contains no Portlandite. The second, formed mainly between the cement grains, has a needle-like structure, interspaced with ettringite and Portlandite as well as small amounts of other hydrated cement minerals.

The porosity of the outer product is directly dependent of the water-cement ratio of the matrix.

Of all the above phases, the Portlandite is considered to be thermodynamically most stable. Its presence ensures high pH of a system. The stability of a system can also be characterised by its internal redox potential E_h. This is a measure of the electron control that an atom has in a compound, compared to the atom in the pure element, and it is usually expressed in volts.

Reagents with high values of reduction potential are strong oxidizing agents. The internal redox potential E_h, by its value gives the number of electrons over which control has changed and its sign indicates whether the control has increased (negative) or decreased (positive).

Portland cement pastes are generally poorly poised, and their E_h is of the order of +200mV, i.e. only slightly oxidizing.

Addition of fly ash, natural pozzolans (such as zeolites), silica fume and granulated blast-furnace slag would generally have a significant effect on E_h of a cementitious paste.

For example, addition of slag, which usually contains chemically-reduced sulphur, may alter the E_h of the hydraulic cement system to the value of some -400mV.

Addition of electropositive metals would generally lower E_h, and the solubility limiting phase for a wide range of inorganic waste materials will depend on both pH and E_h of the cement matrix.

Depending on the type of the contaminant present, a range of mineral admixtures may be used to ensure improved thermodynamic stability of the concrete or mortar.

The fluidity of fresh mix and very high impermeability of the hardened matrix will be achieved by applying principles of high performance concrete design.

Use of high-range water-reducing admixtures becomes essential, so that the requirements of water-cementitious ratios of about 0.22, and concurrent high fluidity of the fresh concrete or mortar can be satisfied.

Provided the dimensional stability requirements are also met by properly selecting the mineralogy and grading of the aggregate, the impermeability of this matrix will be such that the moisture transport through the concrete or mortar will be by diffusion only.

ADVANTAGE OF MACROENCAPSULATION

As already mentioned, inorganic soil contaminants, such as boric, phosphoric, hydrofluoric, and chromic acids and their respective salts, as well as oxides of lead and zinc are strong retarders of cement hydration, and if present in significant amount, may retard the set of concrete or mortar for days or even weeks.

A number of organic compounds, particularly sugars, but also lignin derivatives, carboxylic acids and their salts, amines and aminoacids (to name just a few) can also act as set retarders.

Microencapsulation of these contaminants with hydraulic cements thus presents a problem of handling finished products, if the levels of contamination or the volume of contaminated soil added to high performance concrete or mortar is large.

Macroencapsulation in underground fuel storage tanks, which are to be decommissioned, as a final stage of the chemical and physical immobilization process of the contaminants, solves this problem.

It is well known that retarded concrete and mortar, provided that they are undisturbed during the hardening stage, not only retain their strength and durability in the solid state, but actually undergo significant improvement of these properties.

It is most unlikely for a high performance concrete or mortar to be shaken or vibrated in an underground storage tank during the solidification, at least to the extent which can adversely affect strength and durability of the encapsulating matrix.

Tanks made of uncoated or unlined steel will be protected from corrosion by the high alkalinity of hardened cement paste, but by the time (which would generally be measured in years or decades) any of the tank's material is likely to decompose, the microencapsulation will be at its optimum effectiveness.

Thus the system ensures the "belt and braces" security:- contaminants (if relevant) are chemically immobilized, physically encapsulated with hydraulic cement or mortar and subsequently macroencapsulated in an underground storage tank.

When macroencapsulation ultimately loses its effectiveness, the undisturbed and protected for all this period microencapsulation will be certain to provide very long term and safe isolation of pollutants from the environment.

From the preliminary calculations on a number of selected contaminated sites, Samarin's method offers considerable economic benefits, when compared with the conventional methods of clean-up or disposal.

As already mentioned, several elements of this method are currently subject to patent applications, and can not be disclosed in any detail.

CONCLUSIONS

There are no clear rules governing clean-up requirements of contaminated industrial sites in Australia and many other developed countries.

The guidelines are generally vague and to minimize the legal risks encourage the owners of contaminated sites to err on the conservative side of the current practice.

Samarin's Method of Macroencapsulation applies to those industrial sites which are non-uniformly polluted by a variety of different industrial or agricultural activities, during the commercial, historical utilization of the land, resulting in a relatively local, but also reasonably high levels or hot spots contamination. The site is also expected to have underground fuel storage facilities, which are due for decommissioning in conjunction with the clean-up.

Soil from the hot spots may be pre-treated, when dealing with certain specific contaminants. In any case, pre-treatment becomes part of the selection of "in-situ" soil as an ingredient of aggregate in the high performance microencapsulating concrete or mortar. This encapsulating matrix is designed not only to chemically immobilize and physically arrest the pollutants, but also to be sufficiently fluid in the fresh state, to pump into the base of the underground storage tank, purging it, as the mixture gradually fills the available space. The tank thus becomes a repository for the microencapsulated contaminants.   Macroencapsulation in the tank ensures optimum setting and hardening of hydraulic cement matrix, which may be retarded to a different degree by the pollutants. The method should have the advantage of additional safety as well as the cost reduction, when compared with the traditional methods applied to comparable site conditions.

REFERENCES

(1) KIDD, C. Environmental Site Contamination Assessment, Waste Management, 1992, February, p.11.

(2) SAMARIN, A.   Encapsulation of Solid Wastes from Industrial By-Products, Proceedings of International Conference: Environmental Management, Geo-Water and Engineering Aspects, editors Chowdhury and Sivakumar, University of Wollongong, A A Balkema/Rotterdam/Brookfield, 1993, February, pp 63-78.

POTENTIAL OF CONCRETE AS A SECONDARY BARRIER AGAINST HAZARDOUS ORGANIC FLUIDS

H W Reinhardt

M Aufrecht

M Sosoro

University of Stuttgart

Germany

ABSTRACT. The study deals with the penetration of organic fluids into concrete and the relevance of this material property with respect to the application of concrete in structures for environmental protection. It is shown how physical parameters like moisture in concrete and viscosity and surface tension of the organic fluid influences the penetration. Mix proportion of the concrete and impregnation of concrete by epoxy and polyurethane have also a distinct effect on the penetration of organic materials. Design and construction recommendations are given for a proper use of concrete in environmental protection.

Keywords: Concrete, Concrete structures, Hazardous fluids, Capillary suction, Organic chemicals, Impregnated concrete

Professor Hans W Reinhardt is Director of the Institute for Building materials of Stuttgart University and of the Research and Testing Laboratory of Baden-Württemberg at Stuttgart, Germany. His main research areas concern physical properties, fracture mechanics and testing of concrete. Professor Reinhardt has published several books and serves on national and international Technical Committees.

Dipl.-Ing. Michael Aufrecht, Research Engineer in the Innovation Research Group of the FMPA BW. The main activities are testing of contamination and decontamination of hazardous organic fluids that are infiltrated in concrete structures. Different testing devices are developed in order to quantify the danger for the environment.

Massimo Sosoro is a physicist and works as junior scientist at the Institute for Building Materials of Stuttgart University, Germany. His main research activities include the testing of fluid transport in concrete and the developement of new testing methods for the detection of fluids in concrete.

Concrete 2000. Edited by Ravindra K. Dhir and M. Roderick Jones.
© 1993 Published by E & FN Spon. ISBN 0 419 18120 2.

INTRODUCTION

The use of concrete is not restricted to structures with load-bearing requirements. Water retaining structures have proven concrete also to be water impervious if precautions in structural design and construction technology are taken. A new area of concrete application may concern structures for environmental protection which need to be impervious for other fluids than water for a certain period of time. Those structures are catching basins, chemical production facilities and structural foundation of deposition devices for chemical and other hazardous residues. Many of those structures have an additional sealing like an epoxy coating or HDPE sheet. However, if the surface of the structures is prone to wear and large temperature variations uncoated concrete may be preferred. This was the motive to start a research project on the penetration behaviour of concrete with respect to organic fluids.

The following deals with experimental results and some theoretical explanations of infiltration tests on concrete.

TESTING METHODS

There are two concrete testing methods in use: the infiltration test with 1.4 m hydraulic head and the capillary suction test. The last one is rather cheap and straight forward while the first one requires additional precaution. It is not suited in a concrete laboratory because the fluids are sometimes dangerous for health which requires chemical exhausts with a rather large free height. It has previously be shown that the two test methods lead to the same results for dense concrete [1]. For rather permeable or cracked concrete the infiltration test yields larger penetration depths [1].

The testing cylinders are coated with dense epoxy on the perimeter while one of the ends is subject either to infiltration or suction. The fluid uptake is measured gravimetically (suction) or volumetrically (infiltration). At the end of the exposure time the cylinder is split and observed visually or by means of an infrared camera. The last procedure is necessary if the fluid is highly evaporable and the wetting front cannot be seen.

PHYSICAL PARAMETERS

Square Root of Time Relation

The capillary absorption of fluids into concrete follows a square root of time relation, if the properties of the specimen do not change with the penetration depth. The absorption of n-decane in concrete specimen with different moisture content is shown in figure 1. The degree of water saturation is given in % of the volume of pores, which are filled with water to the total porosity of the specimen.

Viscosity and Surface Tension

Using the Young and Laplace equation for the pressure difference in Hagen-Poiseulle's law, we get a relation, in which the absorption is proportional to the square root of the ratio of surface tension and dynamic viscosity of the fluids.

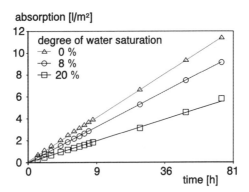

Figure 1   Absorption of n-decane for different degrees of water saturation of the specimen.

Figure 2 shows the absorption coefficients of ethylene glycol, 1-butanol, n-decane,
cyclohexane, n-pentane and water for different degrees of water saturation of the specimen in relation to the square root of the ratio of surface tension and dynamic
viscosity.

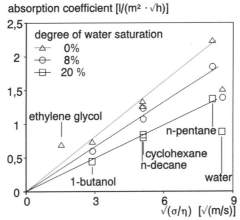

Figure 2   Absorption coefficient as a function of the square root of the
ratio of surface tension σ and dynamic viscosity η, for different
degrees of water saturation of the specimen.

For all investigated fluids, except water and ethylene glycol, which is misceable with
water, the absorption coefficients are on straight lines. So the absorption of any
organic fluid which is immisceable with water can be predicted, if the absorption
coefficient of an other organic fluid is known. For water and some water misceable
fluids this relation is not valid [2].

Moisture Content

With increasing degree of water saturation the absorption of fluids into concrete decreases (see figure 1 and 2). For each investigated fluid the absorption coefficients follow the same relation with changing moisture content. This result is shown in figure 3, where the absorption coefficients of the fluids at different degree of water saturation are related to those of a completely dry concrete.

When the moisture content increases, the small pores will be filled first with water, because the vapour pressure of a fluid in a capillary decreases with decreasing capillary radius [3]. If the small pores had no influence on fluid transport in concrete, the absorption coefficient should decrease linearly with decreasing free pore volume (see broken line in figure 3). The results show that the small pores have an influence on fluid transport in concrete, because the absorption coefficients are smaller.

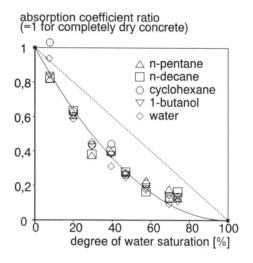

Figure 3   Absorption coefficient ratio: The absorption coefficient follows the same relation for all fluids tested.

CONCRETE COMPOSITION

The last two years, several test series have been carried out investigating the effect of water cement ratio, compressive strength, compaction differences and maximum aggregate size. A few figures will illustrate the findings. As expected a lower water cement ratio leads to higher strength and thus to less penetration (see figure 4).

Core samples taken from a concrete stab were prepared such that the influences of compaction like settlement and bleeding could be studied. 20 mm of the top concrete were removed, or 50 mm were removed, or the core was taken with the skin concrete. Figure 5 shows that the skin concrete takes up more fluid than deeper concrete layers do. It can be also seen from figure 5 that the dried concrete absorbes much more than concrete stored in 65 % relative humidity .

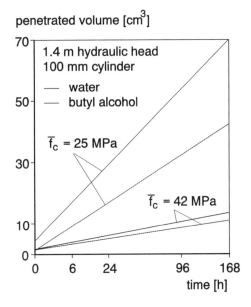

Figure 4 Fluid penetration as influenced by strength

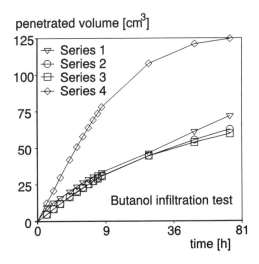

Figure 5 Fluid absorption of concrete with different specimen prepa-
ration, W/C: 0.66, agr.: 1-16 mm.
Series 1: top concrete
Series 2: 20 mm of the top concrete were removed
Series 3: 50 mm of the top concrete were removed
Series 4: 20 mm of the completely dry concrete were removed

A test series aimed at the influence of the maximum aggregate size on the fluid penetration. All mixes had a constant W/C = 0.54 and same workability. The maximum aggregate sizes were 2, 8, 16 and 32 mm respectively with cement contents of 483, 346, 325 and 315 kg/m³, respectively. Figure 6 shows the results of the infiltration tests.

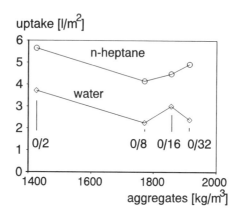

Figure 6   Mean uptake after 72 h as Function of amount of aggregates (infiltration tests)

Since the cement content of the mixes is different, the aggregate content is also different. A smaller grain size means also a smaller aggregate content. As the graph shows the smaller grain size yields a larger uptake. Figure 7 explains partly the result which is due to high concrete porosity. The increasing uptake of the 32 mm grain concrete is attributed to the weak interface between larger grains and the hydrated cement paste.

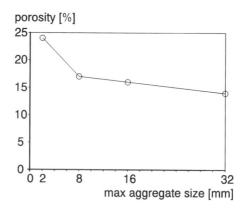

Figure 7   Porosity vs. maximum aggregate size

IMPREGNATED CONCRETE

Scope and Materials

The investigation of the effectiveness of surface protection systems (abbreviated to SPS) with different specifications applied to selected concrete surfaces with different porosities are subject of this chapter. The results are compared with the behaviour of untreated concrete (reference material) concerning tightness. The capillary suction tests were executed with three testing fluids (acetone, n-heptane, water) and nine different, one- or two-component surface protection systems (silicon organic compounds, epoxy, polyurethane). The application of different reaction resins on the surface of a concrete structure as an impregnation has as main goal to increase fluid-tightness within the pores. Vapour diffusion should not be impeded. Sealings or thin coatings (epoxy, polyurethane) needed to be abraded, thus only surface protection systems penetrating the structure remain for testing.

Concrete

The concrete cylinders had the dimensions of 150 mm height and 100 mm diameter. The composition was 320 kg cement per m^3 and $w/c = 0.58$. The total porosity was measured with a helium pycnometer and showed the following results over the height of the samples: At the top of the cast cylinder 18.2 %, in the middle of the cylinder 11.8 % and at the bottom 12.8 %. The significant difference in the porosity close to the surface of the top of the cylinder is result of the production-process of the cylinders. Therefore two different testing series became necessary: for the first testing series the reaction resins were applied to the upper side of the concrete cylinder; the bottom of the cylinder was used for the second testing series.

Testing Fluids

The kind of testing fluid affects the mode of action of the applied surface protection system very much. There are physical changes in transport phenomena (capillary fluid transport and gas diffusion) and there are chemical reactions between the testing fluid, humidity of the specimen, reaction resin and concrete (decomposition, swelling and dissolving [4, 5]).

It is a scientific finding, that the testing fluids acetone and n-heptane penetrate very quickly and deep into uncoated concrete [6, 7, 8]. Viscosity, surface tension and the number of C-atomes (the length of the chain) are the responsible parameters for the penetration process. A differentiation into polar and non-polar fluids leads to the chosen representatives: acetone and n-heptane.

Testing Results: Fluid Uptake

The fluid uptake of all specimens of this testing series follows closely the capillary fluid transport. This effect is independent on testing site, testing fluid and kind of surface protection system. If the abscissa is scaled in the square-root-relation of time, the penetration process is linear. Starting on the assumption, that the reduction of the free porosity in the areas near the concrete surface by appliying a surface protection system results in a strong barrier-effect at least at the beginning of the fluid uptake. The results of the testing series with acetone and n-heptane do not confirm this theory. Independent on the specification of the surface protection system a continuous reduction of the fluid uptake over the whole testing period according to the standard test could be detected. Although some of the pores are completely filled with reaction resin (i.e. sealings), no strong barrier effect was noticed (see table 1).

Epoxy Resins

The testing results of the fluid uptake of SPS 2, that can be classified as impregnation are as follows: The testing of the top side of the cylinders showed for acetone and n-heptane a reduction of the penetrated volume of about 10 % (bottom side 25 %), for water 42 % (bottom side 25 %).

Polyurethane Resins

SPS 5 hardens with a hard layer, has a low viscosity and can be classified as impregnation or sealing.

Silicon-Organic Reaction Resins

The reduction in fluid uptake varies widely: the testing results of n-heptane are on both testing sides within the scatter of the reference experiment. The application of SPS 8 and SPS 9 on the bottom side and the use of acetone as testing fluid showed a significant reduction of fluid uptake of about 25 %. This effect can be explained by the mode of action: Silicon resins consist of polar silanol compounds and unpolar rest compounds (alcyl- or alkoxyl compounds), that reach into the pores of the concrete. The silicon molecule is connected with the concrete by an oxygen compound [5]. All unpolar rest compounds cause a shield impedeing fluid transport of polar media. With an increasing difference in surface tension and polarity between rest compounds and penetrating fluid there is also an increasing effectiveness of this shield against capillary fluid transport. These are the reasons for an excellent barrier-effect for water (surface tension 72.75 mN/m, very polar); the penetrated volume of acetone (surface tension 23.70 mN/m, polar) shows a significant reduction of about 25 %. n-Heptane (surface tension 20.30 mN/m, unpolar) has about the same penetrated fluid quantity as the reference test.

Table 1   Reduction in relative fluid uptake of SPS 5 according to the reference experiment

	Application of SPS 5 on the top side	Application of SPS 5 on the bottom side
Acetone	38 %	29 %
n-Heptane	15 %	30 %
Water	76 %	41 %

CRACKS IN CONCRETE

So far concrete has been considered to be uncracked. However, concrete structures suffer from cracking due to imposed loads and imposed deformations. As impermeability is concerned cracks are potential leakage sources. Therefore cracking should receive due attention. A transverse crack of width w through a slab with width d and with length a the leakage rate is given by

$$q= \frac{p \cdot a \cdot w^3}{\beta \cdot \eta \cdot d}$$

with q = leakage rate in m^3/s, p = pressurehead in Pa, and ß = coefficient which depends on the roughness and tortuousity of the crack. In a smooth crack ß = 12 in a rough crack ß ≈ 100. Comparing the leakage through a tensile crack with uncracked concrete tells that a crack is more permeable by some orders of magnitude. This means that axial cracks (through cracks) should be avoided or confined to such a width that it is acceptable for a certain fluid (with large viscosity).

Flexural cracks, see figure 8, may start at the upper or lower side of the element. In both cases, there is a part b in the cross-section which prevents instantaneous leakage. Finally, surface cracks in an irregular pattern (map cracking) are due to differential shrinkage and thermal movement. The width of these cracks is in the order of a few hundredth of a mm and the depth is about one tenth of the width of the slab. This means that these cracks are of minor importance.

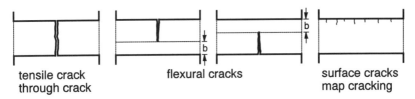

| tensile crack | flexural cracks | surface cracks |
| through crack | | map cracking |

Figure 8 typical cracks in structural concrete

DESIGN RECOMMENDATIONS

The design recommendations refer to the concrete composition, construction phase, and to the structural design of catching basins. As the concrete composition is concerned a water/cement ratio of 0.50 or less is recommended with an appropriate concrete cylinder strength of 35 MPa. Wet curing should be provided at least 7 days immediately after concreting. Both measures will lead to a concrete with little capillary porosity and thus with small capillary suction. If thick members are to be made a cement with low heat production is preferred in order to minimize the chance of cracking due to differential thermal movement during hydration.

The smallest width of a concrete member which can come on contact with the hazardous fluid should be at least two times the mean measured penetration depth by capillary suction. The factor two provides additional safety with respect to the permeation of the fluid through the concrete. The duration of the test should be the same time which is necessary to remove the fluid from the concrete in a hazard. If the infrastructure of the plant is such that the basin is checked every day and that spare tanks are available to transfer the leaking fluid to them within 72 hours, then the test should also last 72 hours. If the basin is controlled once a week (during holidays for instance) then the test has to last one week plus 48 hours. In order to take account of possible surface cracks an increase of the member width is recommended.

If bending cracks may occur, i. e. design according to the cracked state, the remaining compressive zone should be not less than 1.5 times the penetration depth of the fluid. The smaller factor 1.5 is justified since the concrete volume near cracks is small and the chance of the presence of permeable concrete is less. If bending moments in alternate direction can occur the chance of a through crack is large. Therefore alternating moments should be avoided.

If the remaining compressive zone is too small or the chance of through cracks due to alternating moments and imposed deformations is large the structure should be prestressed. The degree of prestressing depends on the type of structure and the loading conditions.

There are a few recommendations with respect to the concreting sequence and the geometry of the structure. The floor slab should be able to move freely. For that reason, two plastic sheets should be put on the prepared surface which should be as smooth and plane as possible. Members of greatly changing width should be avoided since those have always different thermal and shrinkage movement which may lead to cracking. Movements joints should be avoided.

CONCLUSIONS

The scope of concrete application can be extended into new areas if the tightness of concrete with respect to toxic fluids is known. Structures in the chemical industry have proven their appropriateness. Other structures for the protection of the environment are conceiveable. More experiments are necessary and an extended theoretical treatment should support the experimental findings. The RILEM Technical Committee 146-TCF deals with this task. Starting from the experiments on impregnated concrete the chemical industry has a challenge to develop impregnations which retain organic fluids as effectively as water in order to improve the applicability of concrete even more. The joint effort by industry, research, engineering and administration has led to recommendations for the application of concrete to structures for the protection of the environment. These recommendations show that concrete is a suitable material if a few requirements are met:

-     The concrete mix should be such that the capillary suction is small.
-     Concreting should be controlled carefully in order to avoid improper hydration of the concrete skin and cracking during hydration.
-     Cracks are potential areas for leakage; through cracks should be avoided.
-     Special attention has to be paid to imposed deformations due to differential temperature and shrinkage

Although there is experience with concrete structures for environmental protection there are still some areas which need more research. These concern theoretical models for the penetration of all kinds of organic fluids into (wet) concrete and appropriate relations between penetration and other properties of the concrete. Furthermore the quantitative assessment of the leakage rate of small cracks is lacking. Improvement of concrete ductility by admixtures and fibres seems advantageous with respect to impermeable concrete structures.

ACKNOWLEDGEMENT

The investigations were carried out within the framework of the research project entitled "Concrete structures for hazardous materials" which is supported by the German Association for Reinforced Concrete and by the Federal Ministry for Research and Technology (Project no. 13RG90102). Comprehensive publications appear in the Bulletin series of the German Association for Reinforced Concrete (Hefte des Deutschen Ausschusses für Stahlbeton).

The authors are grateful to the members of the working groups for their valuable cooperation. The authors are responsible for the content of this publication.

REFERENCES

1.   REINHARDT, H W. Transport of chemicals through concrete. In "Material Science of Concrete III", ed. J. Skalny, Am. Ceram. Soc. Westerville, Ohio 1992, pp 209-241

2.   WITTKE, H. Lager- und Abfüllanlagen für Gefahrstoffe. VDI-Berichte 1989, No 726, pp 343-375

3.   ADAMSON, A W. Physical Chemistry of Surfaces, 5th ed, John Wiley & Sons, Inc, New York, Chichester, Brisbane, Toronto, Singapore 1990

4.   KLOPFER, H. Anstrichschäden: Strukturen, Verhaltensweisen und Schadensformen von Anstrichen und Kunststoffbeschichtungen. Bauverlag, Wiesbaden 1976

5.   KITTEL, H. Lehrbuch der Lacke und Beschichtungen, Band 1, Teil II, Columb-Verlag, Berlin 1983

6.   FEHLHABER, T and REINHARDT, H W. Transport organischer und anorganischer Flüssigkeiten in Beton. DAfStb, Berlin 1991, Bulletin 416, pp 21-46

7.   AUFRECHT, M and REINHARDT, H W. Concrete as a second surrounding system against hazardous organic fluids. Otto Graf Journal, 1991, Vol 2, pp 37-49

8.   RICHTLINIE FÜR BETONBAU BEIM UMGANG MIT WASSERGEFÄHRDENDEN STOFFEN. Teil 1: Entwurf und Bemessung unbeschichteter Betonbauteile. DAfStb, Sept. 1992

HIGH STRENGTH CONCRETE AS A BY-PRODUCT OF DESIGN FOR LOW PERMEABILITY

R D Hooton

University of Toronto

Canada

ABSTRACT. Typically, engineers have designed for and measured concrete's compressive strength as a measure of its performance. While this is fortuitously true in many cases, high strength concretes can be produced that are neither impermeable nor durable.

The ingress of water or solutions into the pore structure of concrete is responsible for most types of deterioration. Therefore, low-permeability concrete is critical for durability. Low-permeability (and often high-strength as a by-product) is obtained when a discontinuous capillary pore structure is achieved. If and when this discontinuity is achieved depends on the mix water content, W/CM, the type and extent of curing, and is modified by the presence of supplementary cementing materials such as fly ash, slag and silica fume. In addition, good design details and construction practices can affect permeability greatly by minimizing defects in the structure.

Keywords: Permeability, High-Strength, Curing, Supplementary Cementing Materials (SCM).

Professor R. Doug Hooton is Associate Professor in Civil Engineering at the University of Toronto in Canada. He is active in more than twenty CSA, ACI, ASTM and TRB committees including ACI C201 on Durability, and is on the executive of both ASTM C1 on Cements and C9 on Concrete. He chairs the ASTM Task Group on permeability testing and is Vice Chair of CSA A23.5 on Supplementary Cementing Materials. His research has focused on pore structure and permeability of concrete as well as testing for sulphate resistance, alkali-aggregate reactivity and freezing and thawing durability.

Concrete 2000. Edited by Ravindra K. Dhir and M. Roderick Jones.
© 1993 Published by E & FN Spon. ISBN 0 419 18120 2.

BACKGROUND

While the production of high strength concrete is not new, especially in the precast industry, the recent commercial utilization of both superplasticizers and silica fume in ready mixed concrete has made specified strengths of 70, 85 and 100 MPa concrete relatively common and easy to achieve. For example, in Toronto, since 1987, the columns in at least five office towers have been specified at 70 MPa [1] and more recently at 85 MPa. These strengths have only been limited by the local coarse aggregates which seem to limit cylinder strengths to about 120 MPa. In addition, to accommodate, climbing formwork, strengths of 20 to 30 MPa at less than one day have also been required. The permeability of these mixes, as estimated by the rapid chloride ASTM C1202 (also AASHTO T 277) test is very low [1] but, for the relatively benign environment of building columns, permeability has not been a design concern. However, since in some of these structures, similar mixes were used for associated parking decks, exposed to de-icing salts, it was useful that low permeability had accompanied the high strength design.

MIX DESIGN

Water Content Versus W/C

What needs to be recognized is that for so called "high performance" concrete mixtures there is a fundamental difference in design philosophy required to obtain either high-strength or low-permeability. For high strength, all other factors being equal, one needs a low water to cement (W/C) or water to cementing materials ratio (W/CM), but for low permeability a low total water content (to give low initial porosity) is essential. Fortuitously, in many cases these criteria coincide, and with conventional strength (20 to 40 MPa) concretes there is less of a dichotomy. In addition, permeability (and later-age strengths) can be improved by slowing down the rate of hydration during the first day, for example by using retarding admixtures.

While the concept of low water content is not new, there is recent evidence to support it. There is also a need to revisit some of the basics of concrete design in the current rush to utilize high-strength concretes and assume that they will be durable in aggressive environments.

The importance of mix water content on permeability was known by Glanville [2] who in 1926 stated, "It can be taken as a general rule that the least permeable mix is that in which the smallest quantity of mixing water is used which will permit the concrete to be compacted sufficiently to prevent the formulation of visible air pockets." Of course, today with the use of water reducing and superplasticizing admixtures, mix water requirements can be reduced much farther than Glanville envisaged.

In normal mix design without admixtures, the water content is relatively constant and W/C is varied by changing the cement (PC) content.   Therefore, in many experiments, the effect of changing water content on permeability is not observed. When superplasticizers are used in high strength concretes, the water demand is reduced but this effect is masked by the often simultaneous decrease in W/C or W/CM.

To demonstrate the importance of mix water content to permeability, Mills [3] designed a series of concretes maintaining a constant W/C = 0.42 (and therefore approximately constant strength) but varying the cement content from 357 to 695 kg/m^3 (and consequently the water content varied from 150 to 292 kg/m^3), the permeability of concrete to water decreased with the mix water content (ie. initial porosity) by almost three orders of magnitude (from 5.8 x 10^{-11} m/s to 9.7 x 10^{-14} m/s). In another group of mixes, using variable quantities of ground quartz flour, Mills [3] also kept the mix water content constant while varying the W/CM from 0.42 to 0.77. In this series of tests, moist-cured strengths varied dramatically but water permeabilities varied only within one order of magnitude (from 1.6 to 0.2 x 10^{-11} m/s). This is of some concern because of the high cement contents being used in some commercial high strength concretes (eg 600 kg/m^3 PC plus 60 kg/m^3 silica fume) where even at a W/CM = 0.3, the water content will still be about 200 kg/m^3 and the permeability might not be as low as anticipated.

As shown in Table 1, the author (and M. Ben Bassat, unpublished) has also found that when water content was held constant, long-term water permeabilities were not changed significantly by decreasing W/C.

Supplementary Cementing Materials

The relationship between permeability and capillary porosity is altered by the introduction of supplementary cementing materials (SCM). When concretes made with these materials are properly designed and cured, large capillary pores left from the original portland cement matrix become subdivided by secondary or later hydration of the SCM into smaller pores, helping provide discontinuity, and permeability is reduced. As well, the thickness of the porous transition zone around aggregate particles is reduced as calcium hydroxide crystals are used up in the secondary hydration reactions and the permeability of these porous zones is reduced. The reduction of permeability (AASHTO T277) by SCM's can be substantial but effects on strength in many cases are minor as shown in Table 2.

OTHER FACTORS

Obtaining low permeability of concrete involves not only mix proportioning, but also attention to proper consolidation, protection and curing (temperature and moisture). In addition, for a low-permeability concrete structure, the design and detailing must be oriented to minimizing the size and number of defects such as cracks and open joints (due to eg. creep, shrinkage, thermal gradients, loading), or due to large diameter reinforcement.

Table 1   Effect of constant water content of concrete on strength and permeability

PC (kg/m^3)	WATER (kg/m^3)	W/C	28 DAY STRENGTH (MPa)	270 DAY WATER PERMEABILITY (10^{-13} m/s)
250	160	0.64	32.8	1.8
350	160	0.46	63.4	0.4
500	160	0.32	88.6	1.2

Table 2   Effect of curing on strength and permeability of 70 MPa concrete [4]
91 days, W/CM = 0.30, CM = 500 kg/m^3
Note: Air Cured 100 x 200 mm cylinders were saturated one day before test.

	STRENGTH (MPa)		AASHTO T277 (COULOMBS)	
	Moist	Air	Moist	Air
100% PC	74.8	52.2	1870	3390
25% SLAG	77.4	54.2	1040	2360
25% SLAG + 7% SF	70.5	52.7	230	310

The influence of these factors on permeability or penetrability-related durability problems is enormous. While some of these items affect strength, they do so to a much smaller extent.

INFLUENCE OF CURING

Moisture Effects

The effect of moist curing period on permeability is much more pronounced than it is on compressive strength. For example, Glanville [2] found that relative to water immersion at 28 days, air curing only reduced the compressive strength of a 16 MPa mix by 23%; while the water permeability was increased by over 40 times. More recently, as shown in Table 3, Hooton and Bin-Ahmad [4] found that at 91 days of age, water permeability was far more sensitive to the period of moist curing than was strength. For PC mixes, strength reductions of 100 x 200 mm cylinders due to air curing at 23°C were 30 to 34% regardless of W/C, while increases in permeability jumped from 3.7 to 161 times as W/CM was raised from 0.30 to 0.75 and water contents ranged from 150 to 225 kg/m^3.

Table 3 Effect of curing on water permeability and strength of 91 day old concretes, W/CM = 0.45, non-air entrained,constant water content = 225 kg/m^3 [4]
Note: Air cured 100 x 200 mm cylinders were saturated one day before test.

MIX	WATER PERMEABILITY (m/s)			STRENGTH (MPa)	
	Air Cured	Moist Cured	Ratio	Air Cured	Moist cured
100%PC	1.9×10^{-11}	7.7×10^{-13}	24	52.2	74.8
25% slag	2.3×10^{-11}	3.4×10^{-13}	69	54.2	77.4
50% slag	5.0×10^{-11}	1.0×10^{-13}	519	23.3	52.3

Table 4 Variation in strength and water permeability of PC concretes moist cured for various periods [5,6]
Note: Air cured 100 mm cubes were tested in the air dry condition

STRENGTH GRADE	28 DAY CUBE STRENGTH (MPa)			
	Period of Moist Curing (followed by air storage)			
	1 day	3 days	7 days	28 days
C25	25.0	30.5	33.1	32.6
C35	34.2	40.2	44.9	41.9
C45	44.4	45.5	45.7	49.9
	28 Day Water Permeability (m/s)			
C25	10.0×10^{-10}	42.0×10^{-11}	3.9×10^{-11}	2.6×10^{-13}
C35	3.7×10^{-10}	4.9×10^{-11}	3.1×10^{-11}	1.7×10^{-13}
C45	2.2×10^{-10}	6.1×10^{-11}	1.7×10^{-11}	1.1×10^{-13}
	Cement (kg/m^3)	Water (kg/m^3)	W/C	
C25	250	170	0.68	
C35	300	171	0.57	
C45	350	172	0.49	

Thomas and Matthews [5] examined nominal 25, 35 and 45 MPa concretes which were moist cured at 20°C for either 1, 3, 7 and 28 days followed by air storage to 28 days. In Table 4 it is observed that even 1-day moist curing was sufficient to meet the minimum 28 day strength requirements, however, permeability to water was influenced by more than three orders of magnitude. This increase in permeability translated into much higher depths of carbonation [6]. It can also be noted that the three mixtures had a constant water content, thus constant initial porosity, resulting similar permeabilities after 28 days moist curing.

Because of over design to prevent low-strength concrete, due to poor site curing practices, specified strengths are often met. However, permeabilities are orders of magnitude higher than the concrete's potential and durability to aggressive environments are subsequently reduced.

In many cases, to compensate for poor curing practices, a higher strength concrete than is required is ordered, in order that the original design strength will be more easily achieved in the field. This practice may cover a lot of sins, but it will not necessarily provide increased durability. The following example of this has been described by Hansen [9]. At first glance, one might consider any concrete with W/C = 0.40 to be far more durable than one with W/C = 0.70 and because of the consequent higher cement content, one would expect to pay more money to obtain it. However, if the 0.40 concrete is not cured properly and only 50% of the cement hydrates, then using Powers and Brownyard's [7] equations, it would have approximately the same capillary porosity as a well hydrated 0.70 concrete. This is shown in Figure 1 [8]. Therefore, for lack of curing the extra money paid for the 0.40 concrete is wasted as far any improvement to impermeability is concerned. Hansen [9] used this example to show why a large oil terminal jetty in the Mediterranean Sea failed due to corrosion after only 7 years of service. Similar results by the author [4] are shown in Table 5.

Table 5 Strength and water permeabilities of 91 day old concretes [4]

W/C	CURING (at 23°C)	STRENGTH (MPa)	PERMEABILITY (m/s)
0.30	Air (20-40% rh)	52.2	2.3×10^{-12}
0.60	Moist	41.6	2.3×10^{-12}

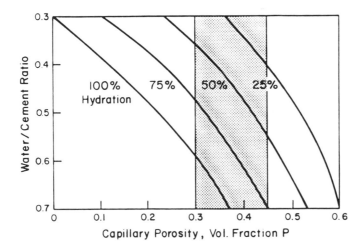

Figure 1 The effect of W/C and degree of hydration on capillary porosity [8]

Because SCM, especially fly ash and slag, react later (after some of the portland cement has hydrated) with the calcium hydroxide by-product of portland cement hydration, they are more susceptible to poor curing. The lack of curing which may have been tolerated previously with portland cement concretes (in terms of strength anyway) can lead to poor quality concrete with supplementary cementing materials because the capillary pores have dried out sufficiently near the surface so that hydration has stopped before the SCM can react. This is especially true in cold weather because the reactivity of supplementary cementing materials is retarded far more at low temperatures than that of portland cement. Ready-mixed concrete companies usually compensate for this by reducing the level of cement replacement in cold weather. In addition, contractors must pay more attention to curing in cold weather. As an example, the concrete slabs under the playing surface of the SkyDome stadium in Toronto were slag concrete (as was the rest of the stadium) and were placed in the winter months when temperatures can drop to -10 to -20°C. To protect the slabs from evaporation and to insulate them from the cold, black plastic bubble mats were laid on top of the deck for several days. This was a relatively economical but effective method of curing in this case.

Plastic Shrinkage Cracks

Recently in Ontario, problems of plastic shrinkage cracking related to inadequate early protection and curing has occurred on new bridge decks. In response to severe chloride related deterioration (due to de-icing salts), since 1978 the Ontario Ministry of Transport (MTO) has required epoxy coated reinforcement in addition to the earlier adoption of larger depths of cover and membrane sealers in new structures [10]. However, standard curing on the projects until 1991 still only consisted of a single coating of a curing compound (machine applied).   In some cases, severe plastic shrinkage cracking resulted within hours penetrating to the top layer of steel and later propagating through the deck.   One deck on a major expressway required expensive epoxy injection of all cracks wider than 0.5 mm within a month of placing and before the membrane sealer was allowed to be applied.   This repair cost $9/m^2 and was not totally effective.   The length of visible surface cracks on a one square meter area of this deck was found by the author to be 4.7 m at approximately 28 days of age.   One solution, used on an adjacent deck section, placed two weeks later, was to double the application rate of curing compound.   But this still resulted in cracking (albeit much reduced) so the remaining deck span was cured with presoaked burlap covered by a white polyethylene sheet for 4 days.   This section of deck had no visible cracks even though the concrete mixes were the same and weather conditions were similar.

Therefore, while strength was largely unaffected, the presence of plastic shrinkage cracks from poor early protection and curing practices dominated the rate of ingress of de-icing salts to the reinforcement.   When so much attention is being paid to corrosion protection, the use of inadequate curing procedures is a false economy. The MTO has since improved its curing specifications.

Curing Compounds

In addition to the previous example, the fact that not all curing compounds are effective was documented by Senbetta and Scholer [11] even though they may pass the requirements of specifications such as ASTM C156 (Figure 2).   Their study led to the recent adoption of an improved test method for evaluation of curing compounds,   ASTM C1151, which is based on a one minute water absorption.   The inadequate nature of some early curing compounds has been documented as far back as 1941 [12].   On the other hand, Mather [13] states that because of the poor application of moist curing on jobs where it is specified, it maybe more effective to use a membrane-forming curing compound even though it is less beneficial than moist curing.   However, the required attention to moist curing of latex overlays, which are commonly used in North America for repair of corroded steel bridge decks, shows that it is possible and necessary to provide effective moist curing when it is understood by all parties that it is essential to the success of the project.

The extra cost associated with the wet burlap and polyethylene sheet curing of bridge decks when added on to existing contracts has been estimated to be $5/m^2 [14].   These costs would be lower, if this type of curing was specified originally. This cost would only add a fraction of one percent to the cost of project but would prevent plastic shrinkage cracks, and probably help prevent de-icer scaling as well as chloride penetration and likely add years to the service life of the structure.

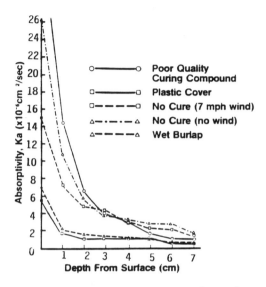

Figure 2   Cover quality as indicated by a one minute absorption test for various types of curing [11]

Temperature Effects

Raising the curing temperature, especially at early ages results in development of a coarser C-S-H and capillary pore structure [15,16]. Therefore, the use of accelerated steam curing, hot weather concreting or high strength (and high heat of hydration) concretes can have at least nominal detrimental effect on long-term strength [17] but also have a major detrimental impact on permeability related properties [18].

For example, Detwiler et al [19] studied the effect of curing temperatures (23, 50 and 70°C) on chloride diffusion rates and AASHTO T277 Rapid Chloride Permeability test results. Only minor differences were noted between concretes cured at 23°C to 50°C, however, large increases in chloride diffusion rates and permeability values were observed when the curing temperature was raised to 70°C. However, at all temperatures, partial cement replacement by either 30% slag or 5% silica fume resulted in reduced chloride diffusions and T 277 test values and were affected to a lesser extent by high temperatures. In fact at 70°C, the chloride diffusion to slag or silica fume mixes were only raised to approximately those of PC mixes cured at 23°C.

Therefore, if in high strength concrete, for use in adverse environmental conditions, care is not taken to keep maximum temperatures as low as possible and to keep temperature gradients to a minimum, the permeability of the concrete material will likely be adversely affected through coarse pore structures as well as due to the possible formation of thermal cracks.

SUMMARY

Because of the sensitivity of in-situ concrete permeability to design details that affect cracking as well as compaction and curing effects, specifying a mix design alone is inadequate for production of a low-permeability concrete for durability concerns. As well, a low W/C mixture does not necessarily translate into low permeability if cement contents are so high as to require high mix water contents and resultant high initial porosities.

However, if one pays attention to the combination of design detailing for minimization of cracks, proper mix design, adequate compaction, and sufficient moist curing, structures with low permeability will result and likely provide relatively high strength as a by-product.

REFERENCES

1. BICKLEY, JA, RYELL, J, ROGERS, C AND HOOTON, RD. "Some Characteristics of High Strength Structural Concrete", Canadian Journal of Civil Engineering, Vol. 18, No. 5, October, 1991, pp. 885-889.

2. GLANVILLE, W H. "The Permeability of Portland Cement Concrete", Building Research Tech. Paper No. 3, DSIR, London, 1926, 50 pp.

3. MILLS, R H. "Mass Transfer of Gas and Water Through Concrete", in Concrete Durability, ACI SP-100, Vol. 1, 1987, pp. 621-644.

4. HOOTON, RD AND BIN-AHMAD, R. "Characterization of Concrete Quality by Absorption and Permeability Tests", Presented at the Engineering Foundation, Potosi, Mo. July 29-Aug. 2, 1991 (also MASc Thesis, 1991).

5. THOMAS, MDA AND MATTHEWS, J. "Durability of PFA Concrete" Building Research Establishment Report, 1993 (to be published).

6. THOMAS, MDA AND MATTHEWS, J. "Carbonation of Fly Ash Concrete", Magazine of Concrete Research, Vol. 44, No. 160, 1992, pp. 217-228.

7. POWERS, TC AND BROWNYARD, TL. "Studies of the Physical Properties of Hardened Portland Cement Paste", PCA Research Bulletin 22, March 1948, 382 pp. (Re-printed from 9 articles in the ACI Journal, Proceedings, Vol. 43, 1947).

8. MEHTA, PK. "Concrete: Structure, Properties and Materials", Prentice-Hall Inc. 1986.

9. HANSEN, TC. "Designed to Fail-Marine Concrete in Hot Climates", in Advances in Cement Manufacture and Use, Engineering Foundation, N.Y., 1989, pp. 189-193.

10. MANNING, DG. "A Rational Approach to Corrosion Protection of the Concrete Components of Concrete Bridges", in Concrete Durability, ACI SP-100, Vol. 2, 1987, pp. 1527-1547.

11. SENBETTA, E AND SCHOLER, CF. "A New Approach for Testing Concrete Curing Efficiency', ACI Journal, Proceedings, Vol. 81, No. 1, Jan-Feb. 1984, pp. 82-86.

12. PARKER, WE. "History of Curing", Hydro-Electric Power Commission of Ontario, Laboratory Report No. LO2812-21, June 4, 1941, 19 pp.

13. MATHER, B. "Curing of Concrete", in Concrete and Concrete Construction, ACI SP104, 1987, pp. 145-159.

14. ROLLINGS, R. Personal Communication, Ontario Ministry of Transportation, March, 1991.

15. GOTO, S AND ROY, DM. "Diffusion of Ions Through Hardened Cement Pastes", Cement and Concrete Research, Vol. 11, 1981, pp. 751-757.

16. KJELLSEN, KO, DETWILER, RJ AND GJØRV, OE. "Pore Structure of Plain Cement Pastes Hydrated at Different Temperatures", Cement and Concrete Research, Vol. 20, No. 6, Nov. 1990, pp. 927-933.

17. VERBECK, GJ AND HELMUTH, RH. "Structures and Physical Properties of Cement Pastes", Proceedings, Fifth International Symposium on the Chemistry of Cement, Tokyo 1968, Vol. 3, pp. 1-32.

18. HIGGINSON, EC. "Effect of Steam Curing on the Important Properties of Concrete", Journal of the ACI, Vol. 58, Sept. 1961, pp. 281-296.

19. DETWILER, RJ, FAPOHUNDA, CA AND NATALE, J. "Use of Supplementary Cementing Materials to Increase the Resistance to Chloride Ion Penetration of Concretes Cured at Elevated Temperatures", ACI Materials Journal (in press).

POSSIBILITIES FOR ELECTRICAL RESISTIVITY TO UNIVERSALLY CHARACTERISE MASS TRANSPORT PROCESSES IN CONCRETE

C Andradé

C Alonso

S Goñi

Institute of Construction Sciences

Spain

ABSTRACT. Being the concrete a porous material whose pores are more or less filled with an aqueous electrolyte, its ability to be permeable could be characterized by its electrical resistivity value. When the concrete is completely saturated of water, the ionic diffusion coefficients can be calculated by means of an appropriate use of Nernst-Einstein equation. In the case the concrete is only partially moist, the resistivity value could be related to its porosity and in consequence can be used to predict gas transport processes.

Carmen Andradé is a research professor at the Institute of Construction Science "Eduardo Torroja", the High Research Council of Spain, Madrid. She has been working in corrosion of reinforcing steel in concrete since 1969, and in 1986 was awarded the Robert L'Hermite RILEM prize. She is the author of about 80 papers on reinforcing steel corrosion.

Mª Cruz Alonso is a researcher at the Institute of Construction Science "Eduardo Torroja", the High Research Council of Spain, Madrid. Her PhD thesis dealt with the corrosion of reinforcing steel in concrete and is the author of about 30 papers on reinforcing steel corrosion.

Sara Goñi is a researcher at the Institute of Construction Science "Eduardo Torroja", the High Research Council of Spain, Madrid. Her PHd Thesis dealt with the reactivity and characterization of Solid State. She actually works on microstructure-property relation ship of cement-based materials, and their main degradation provoked by carbonation, chlorides, sulphates, etc. Dr. Sara Goñi has published about of 30 papers on the Solid State area.

Concrete 2000. Edited by Ravindra K. Dhir and M. Roderick Jones.
© 1993 Published by E & FN Spon. ISBN 0 419 18120 2.

INTRODUCTION

An increasing need is appearing of characterizing concrete in terms of its durability, due to the number of structures that present premature damage of their reinforcements. This need has been identified by different organizations and thus, Rilem has three years ago approved the set up of the Technical Committee TC-116". Performance Criteria for Concrete Durability" chaired at that time by Prof. H.Hilsdorf and at present by Dr. J.Kropp. An other organizations and researchers are also working in this area [1][2][3][4].

Although the term normally used is "durability" it mainly refers to phenomena which may enable corrosion of reinforcement and therefore extensive work is being developped on how to quantify the time needed by an aggressive (either chlorides or carbon dioxide) to reach and depassivate the rebar [2][4][5][6][7]. In addtion to these aggressives, permability of oxygen or water have been also studied [2][7][8][9] due the need of their presence in any corrosion process.

Individual studies of the penetration of these substances (Cl^-, CO_2, O_2 or H_2O) in a particular concrete may be carried out in the laboratory or in cores taken from site and attempts were also made on the development of site tests, which succeed in the case of measuring CO_2, O_2 or water penetration on-site [10-12] in a reasonable short time.

In the case of carbonation there are authors who have related natural exposure in old structures to concrete properties or parameters as w/c ratio, or cement content [13], and papers are published offering prediction formulae [5][7]) in order to calculate the advance of the carbonation front along the time. Other way of research is based on the fact that the CO_2 is a gas and therefore a similitude with O_2 permeability could be produced. Thus carbonation rates based in O_2 permeability coefficients has been established [2].

In the case of Cl^- penetration, the relation to concrete parameters has not been so quantitatively studied and in general, what is measured is the Diffusion Coefficient in paste discs [14][15] or in the concrete cover [6][16][17].

Therefore, the goal of having a fast, easy and cheap test able to be used on site in new structures, and able to characterize concrete "permeability" in general, still remain. The Rilem TC-116 previously mentioned is working on the basis of assuming the O_2 permeability as this possible general test for characterizing concrete durability.

In present paper a contribution to this aim is presented considering concrete Electrical Resistivity, ρ, as a possible general parameter able to characterize mass transport in a porous media as concrete is. This parameter has been selected after a careful observation of its sensitivity to reflect changes in concrete, due to aforementioned four substances considered responsable of the aggressivity: CO_2, Cl^-, O_2, H_2O.

Water content and conversely air availability, are well known [18] to induce dramatic changes in concrete resistivity values when they vary. These changes can therefore be used to predict CO_2 penetration in the same extent that O_2 permeability can predict it, although extensive work is still needed in order to calibrate this possibility. And finally, what seems easier is to calculate Chloride Diffusion Coefficients, from a correct use of Nernst-Einstein equation as will be described later.

However, as in the case of oxygen permeability what Resistivity cannot take itno account is the binding capacity of the concrete which still needs to be characterized by suplementary sources.

The consideration of resistivity as a parameter able to characterize concrete permeation ability has been also deduced from studies of similar parameter in rocks [19][20][21], and from the lecture of papers of Garboczi [22][23][24] who is trying to establish the relationship between resistivity and porosity through the theory of Katz-Thompson and in summary, is trying to find a general expresion of concrete conductance in a very promising and remarkable way.

ELECTRICAL RESISTIVITY OF CONCRETE

Dry concrete is an electrical insulator as was well identified in early papers [25][26], however when it wets becomes a conductor due water fills the pores.

Several interpretations of the complete behaviour have been published [17][27][28] it is not the aim of present paper to discuss the reliability of those interpretations at present time, but to assume only the most simple model of considering concrete as an insulator material in its solid phases (although water remain in the gel pores unless very low relative humidity is reached, this water has more or less the conductive characteristics of the solid phases) and a conductor in its pore solution phase.

Therefore, the solid phase will have a specific value of resistivity ρ_s in function of its structure (composition, constrictivity and tortuosity) which usually is higher than 10^6 ohm·cm [25][26]. The liquid pore solution phase has also a specific conductivity ρ_o in function of its composition, which has been studied from Longuet publications [29] and which ranges between few to about 100 ohm·cm.

In general, in saturate concrete assuming a similar cement and aggregate type and a similar hydration degree, the Resistivity values will be lower as higher is the porosity. That is, a more porous concrete will present a lower resistivity as general trend, although this statement needs calibration for each kind of concrete (cement, aggregate and hydration degree).

A possibility of calibrating this general trend is by submitting a piece of concrete to cycles of wetting and drying or more rigourously, performing water adsorption isotherms and recording the Resistivity changes.

Thus, when a completely dry piece of concrete is increasingly moistened the resistivity value drops dramatically from > 10^6 ohm·cm to values around some hundrends ohm·cm for completely saturated conditions [17][25][26]. As was mentioned this minimum value depends not only on the solid or liquid phase compositions but also on the porosity (amount of liquid phase per total volume of the sample).

Based on this fact an attempt is now presented on the theoretical possibilities of using Resistivity values and its changes with the humidity content of the concrete to characterize the permeability to gases and the remaining concrete humidity content.

GAS PERMEATION PREDICTION

The advance of the carbonation front is mainly a function of concrete water saturation and of the concrete binding capacity (amount of reactants) leaving aside this last parameter the proportion of concrete water saturation can be normalized versus resistivity values based of their symetric changes as figure 1 shows.

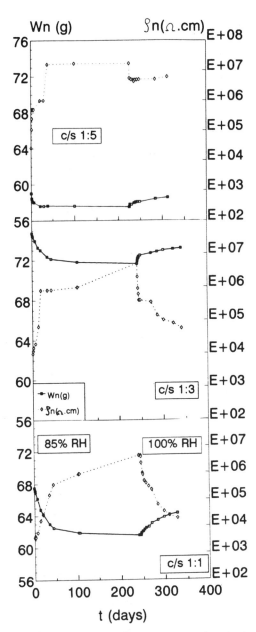

Figure 1. Evolution along time of Resistivity values and
           weight of mortar samples of w/c ratio 0.5 and
           c/s= 1/1, 1/3 and 1/5, when ambient humidity
           varies from 85% - 100%.

In this figure the changes along the time of weight and resistivity of three mortar types (with cement/sand ratios of 1:5, 1:3 and 1:1, being all mixed with a w/c ratio of 0.5) have been represented. It can be observed the "mirror" behaviour of weight changes and resistivity, which enables to deduce the parallel information that can be deduced from both parameters.

Representing now the relative changes of both parameters as is made in figure 2 it can be identified three slopes which are function of the porosity, being the most dense mortar (1:1) which presents the highest negative slope consistent with the fact that this mortar has the highest amount of capillary pores deduced from mercury porosimetry measurements [30] previously published. The addition of NaCl to the mortars does not changes significatively the trend of the slopes.

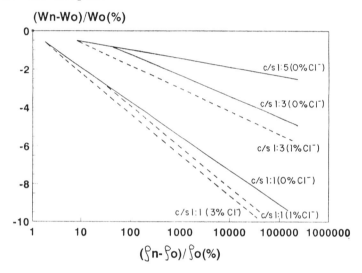

Figure 2. Relative weight change versus relative resistivity changes of previous figure.

Many other examples of the mirror behaviour between weight and resistivity changes could be presented which [17] allows the possibility of using tests as that shown in figure 2 to characterize concrete permeation characteristics. Thus, if resistivity of a concrete sample is measured in saturated conditions and then the sample is held in dry conditions and weight and resistivity are simultaneously recorded, the relative changes could inform on the open porosity for gas penetration. At the same time measurement on-site of the resistivity compared with that of the sample taken as reference could inform on the proportion of water saturation and therefore to indirectly evaluate the relative humidity inside the concrete.

As was stated previously the limitation which remain to be overcome is that, what cannot be obtained from resistivity measurements regarding carbonation risk, is the binding capacity of the concrete which can be of significant importance. However, prediction methods based on measuring O_2 permeation lack of the same information.

CHLORIDE DIFFUSION

The case of chloride diffusion can be more easily characterized from resistivity measurements because the binding capacity is relatively less significant in the penetration rate and because resistivity measurements in water saturated concrete are informative enough for this purpose, as is now presented.

The relation of ion diffusion coefficient and solution resistivity was established by Einstein through what is known as Nernst-Einstein equation [31][32][33].

$$D_{Cl} = (\frac{RT}{nF^2}) \Lambda \qquad (1)$$

where D_{Cl}= chloride diffusion coefficient (cm^2/s)
R= universal gas constant $(cal \cdot mol^{-1} \ ^0K^{-1})$
T= temperature (^0K)
n= number of charges
F= Faraday's number $(coul \cdot eq^{-1})$
Λ= equivalent conductivity $(ohm^{-1} \cdot cm^2 \cdot eq^{-1})$

Attempts were made in the past [3][21] to use this equation to calculate the concrete chloride Diffusion Coefficient from this equation, although the authors concluded without reaching a solution, because what they measured was the total Resistivity and they were not able to calculate the fraction corresponding to the chloride (fixed by the transference number).

The transference number, t_{Cl}, needed for being introduced in equation (1)

$$D_{Cl} = \frac{RT}{nF^2} \Lambda t_{Cl} \qquad (1')$$

can be calculated from the general expression:

$$t_{Cl} = \frac{J_{Cl} n F}{i} \qquad (2)$$

J_a= unidirectional chloride flow (mol/cm²s)
i= intensity recorded or applied (A)

and therefore, equation (1') can be finally expressed as [33]:

$$D_{Cl} = \frac{RT}{nF^2} \cdot \frac{1}{R_{ohm}} \cdot \frac{l}{A} \cdot \frac{1}{C_{Cl} Z} \cdot t_{Cl} \qquad (1'')$$

being R_{ohm}= ohmic resistance of the sample (ohm·cm)
A= cross section area of the sample (cm²)
l= thickness of the sample (cm)
C_{Cl}= bulk activity of the chlorides (mol/cm³)
Z= electrical charge of chloride

In a recent paper [33], part of the authors of present one, have presented the possibilities of using equation (1'') for approximately calculating D_{Cl} in concrete. It can be actually carried out, providing reliable values of chloride flow and intensity flowing are recorded, which will enable the calculation of the transference number for chlorides in particular conditions.

The graphic representation of this equation has been previously published [33] and is depicted by figure 3.

This equation is also used by the researchers in the rock field [19] for the calculation of the Formation Factor [3] represented by the relation of σ_0/σ (σ_0= conductivity of liquid phase, σ= conductivity of the sample), which in fact derives from equation (1) as was mentioned by Wilkins [34], Atkinson [35] or Garboczi [22]:

$$\frac{D_o}{D} = \frac{\sigma_o}{\sigma} = Formation \ Factor \qquad (3)$$

This possibility avoids the need of knowing the transference number if resistivity of the pore solution is measured or calculated.

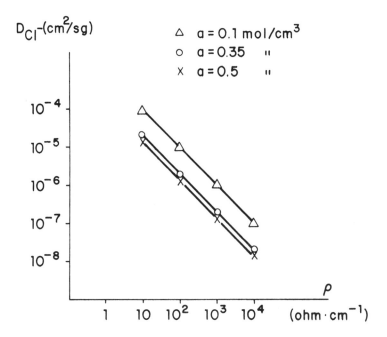

Figure 3. Representation of Nernst-Einstein equation in function of chloride activity values.

As was mentioned the need of introducing the ion transference number appears because what is measured is the total Resistivity. Values of chloride transference number in function of the pore solution composition can be theoretically calculated or measured [33][36] if simultaneous measurements of chloride flow are carried out as is described in the previously mentioned paper. For practical purposes, theoretical values may be assumed.

Its graphic representation is shown in figure 4 in which theoretical values for pore solutions of conductivities 0.05 and 0.1 Siemens are plotted.

Therefore, the ability of a particular concrete to be penetrated by chlorides ions could be characterized by the concrete electrical resistivity, providing pure diffusion is the relevant penetration mechanism.

However in the case of aerial structures the chlorides could ingress by other mechanisms as absorption or pore wall mobilities, and therefore previous deduction would not apply. Further work is needed in this area.

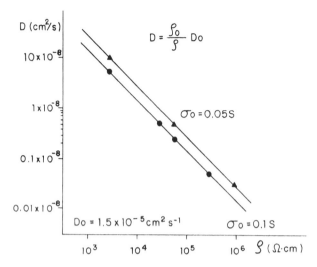

Figure 4. Representation of relative variations of Resistivity and Diffusion coefficients after Nernst-Einstein equation for a D_o of chlorides of 1.5×10^{-5} cm^2/s.

MEASUREMENT OF CONCRETE RESISTIVITY

The main difficulty of using concrete resistivity as a general parameter of characterization of concrete permeation ability, lies in its reliable measurement.

Concrete Resistivity has been measured from many years ago and used to characterize numerous concrete characteristcs: electrical insulating properties [25][26], rate of setting [37], porosity [28] or prediction of corrosion rate [38]. However, in spite of the numerous studies and wide use of this parameter resistivity measurements has not been standarized with the exception of the Wenner method [39].

In the past, controversy was established on the use of A.C. or D.C. to better measure the Resistivity value. Now this discussion has been overcomoe and Resistivity is usually measured at high frequecy using A.C. signals or by the possitive feed-back of the potentiostats [38].

Regarding the geometry of the samples. Resistivity can be measured in two ways:

1)   In cores or specimens of known geometry where the electrodes must be placed externally [17] or through the calibration of a particular electrode disposition with solutions of known resistivities (40). Hope introduced in the same sample geometrie as Hope [40] Suggest.

2) On big structures through the use of Wenner method or
    any other calculation method from Resistance
    measurements [41].

Method 1 seems the most reliable and what can be used in
new structures where specific specimens can be prepared for
these measurements or cores can be taken from the
structure. Several details must be carefully controlled in
order to avoid experimental errors as they are: a)
interface resistances if the electrodes are not well fixed
to the external surface of the concrete samples, b) border
errors if the sample is to big or the relation l/A is not
the adequate (small l and big surface is the most
recommended), c) complicated electrode disposition, in the
case of calibration through resistance measurements in
solutions of known resistivity.

In the case of method 2 the sources of error are several
for the Wenner method due mainly to: a) the presence of
reinforcements near the measurement point and, b)
unhomogeneous distribution of the water with the depth of
concrete, and therefore variation of resistivity values
with depth. When the measurement is made through the use of
an external electrode and the rebar, only an average value
of resistivity of the concrete cover is obtained.

Another alternative for on-site measurement might be the
use of permanent sensors with specific geometries embedded
at several depths, although the introduction of these
sensors could modify the concrete composition between
electrodes from the bulk one, if they are small. In the
case they are big, then, no resistivity values can be
obtained because electrical lines could run long away the
sensor and therefore no defined cross sectional area could
be identifed.

FINAL COMMENTS AND CONCLUSIONS

Concrete durability and more specifically its resistance
against rebar corrosion can be characterized with accuracy
by means of performing specific tests on carbonation,
chloride ingress, oxigen availability and water diffusion
or absorption. Although not standarized in general, the
literature offers a wide variety of tests which can be used
for this purpose.

In spite of this offer of testing methods, the search for
a single one, if possible fast, cheap and easy of
interpretation for quality control, continues. Partial
attempts are presented in the literature on the use of
tests as oxygen permeability, chloride diffusion or

predictions based in the concrete characteristics, which results adequate for either carbonation or chloride rate ingress prediction, but not for both simultaneously.

In present paper it is suggested to use concrete resistivity values for this general purpose as an universal parameter to characterize concrete ability to be permeated. As resistivity is a function of solid phase structure and water filling the pores, this parameter conveniently calibrated or standarized to reference values could give a wide information about the proportion of concrete water saturation and therefore the proportion of pores available for gas penetration or in the case of chlorides, could give the basic information for calculating ionic Diffusion Coefficients. However, the concrete binding capacity cannot be modelled by Resistivity, which only reflects mass transport ability and therefore, this counter parameter needs, at present state, specific treatment.

Extensive experimental work is needed to support this proposal which has already been undertaken by the authors in the case of ionic diffusion. Correlation between resistivity values and carbonation rates are needed to support the same for the ingress of this aggressive.

REFERENCES

1.   CEN TC 104 (Concrete)/WG1 (ENV-206)/TG1 (Durability)

2.   PARROTT, LJ. Design for avoiding damage due to carbonation-induced corrosion - Paper N62 CEN TC 104/WG1/TG1/Panel 1.

3.   BUENFELD, NR, NEWMAN, JB. Materials and Structures 1987, 20, 3,10.

4.   DHIR, RK, HEWLETT, PC, CHAN, YN. Magazine of Concrete Research, 1989, 41, no.147, 87-97.

5.   MARTIN, H, RAUEN, F, SCHIESSL, P. Betonwerk + Fertigteil-Technik, 1975, no.12, 588-590.

6.   PAGE, CL, SHORT, NR, EL TARRAS, A. Cement and Concrete Research 1981, 11, 395-406.

7.   TUUTTI, K. Corrosion of steel in concrete, Swedish Cement and concrete Research Institute, no. 4.82 - Stockholm 1982.

8.   LAWRENCE, CD. 8th Int. Congress of Cement Chemistry. Brasil, 1986, vol.1, 29-34.

9.   FAGERLUND, G. Nordic Concrete Research 1982, vol 1, Oslo.

10. TORRENT, RJ. Materials and Structures 1992, 25, no. 150, 358-365.

11. FIGG, JW. Magazine of Concrete Research, 1973. 25 no.85, 213-219.

12. NIESEL, K. Matèriaux et Constructions, 1973. 6, no.33, 227-231.

13. HO, DWS, LEWIS, RK. Cement and Concrete Research, 1987, 17, 489-504.

14. SERGI, G, YO, SW, PAGE, CL. Magazine of Concrete Research. 1992, 44 no. 158, 63-69.

15. DHIR, RK, JONES, MR, AHMED, HEH. Magazine of Concrete Research 1991, 43, no. 154, 37-44.

16. PAGE, CL, LAMBERT, P, VASSIE, PRW. Materials and Structures 1991, 24, 243-252.

17. GJORV, OE, VENNESLAND, O. Cement and Concrete Research 1979, 9, 229-238.

18. GJORV, OE, VENNESLAND, O, EL-SUSAIDY, AHS. Materials Performance, 1986 Dec, 39-44.

19. DAVID, C, DAROT, M. Proc. of the Symposium "Rocks at Great Depth", Pau, 1989, August.

20. THOMPSON, DH, KATZ, AJ, KROHN, CE. Advances in Physics 1987, 36, no.5, 625-694.

21. BUENFELD, NR, NEWMAN, JB, PAGE, CL. Cement and Concrete Research, 1986, 16, 511-524.

22. GARBOCZI, EJ. Cement and Concrete Research 1990, 20, 591-601.

23. BENTZ, DP, GARBOCZI, EJ. Cement and Concrete Research 1991, 21, 325-344.

24. BENTZ, DP, GINGOLD, DB, GARBOCZI, EJ, LOBB, CJ, JENNINGS, HM. Conference on Advances in Cementitious Materials, Gaithersburg, MD, (American Ceramic Soc., Westerville O.H. 1990).

25. MONFORE, GE. Journal of the PCA. Research and Development laboratories 1986, May, 35-48.

26. HAMMOND, E, ROBSON, TD. The Engineer 1955, Jan, 78-80 and 114-115.

27. HANSSON, ILH, HANSSON, CM. Cement and Concrete Research 1983, 13, 675-683.

28. GJORV, OE, VENNESLAND, O. Offshore Technology Conference. OTC2803, 1977, Houston, Tex, May.

29. LONGUET, P. Silicates Industries 1976, no.7-8, 321-328.

30. GOÑI, S, ALONSO, MC, ANDRADE, C. European Symposium on Corrosion Deterioration of Buildings - CSTB - CEFRACOR, 1990, Nov - París.

31. EINSTEIN, A. Investigation on the Theory of the Brownian Movement-Methmen-London 1926.

32. O'M, J, BOCKRIS, A, REDDY, KN. Modern Electrochemistry Plenum Press. Ed. New York, 1974.

33. ANDRADE, C, SANJUAN, MA, ALONSO, C. NACE. Corrosion 93. New Orleans. March 1993.

34. LAY, P, LAWRENCE, PF, WILKINS, NJM, WILLIAMS, DE. Journal of Applied Electrochemistry 1985, 15, 755-766.

35. ATKINSON, A, NICKERSON, AK. Journal of Materials Science (1984) 19, 3068-3078.

36. MORAGUES, A, GOÑI, S, ANDRADE, C. Advances in Cementitious Materials Ceramic Trausactions 1990, 16, 57-65.

37. CALLEJA, J. Journal of American Concrete Inst. 1953, 25, 249.

38. ALONSO, C, ANDRADE, C, GONZALEZ, JA. Cement and Concrete Research 1988, 18, 687-698.

39. STRATFULL, RF. Materials Proptection, 1968, May, 29-34.

40. HOPE, BB, IP, AK, MANNING, DG. Cement and Concrete Research 1985, 15, 525-534.

41. COCHRAN, J. NACE - Corrosion 82, Paper 169, Houston. Texas, 1982.

IN-PLACE TESTING
PRESENT AND FUTURE

J H Bungey

University of Liverpool

United Kingdom

ABSTRACT. The future of concrete construction relies heavily upon the ability of the industry to provide a durable product which requires minimal maintenance. It is questionable whether reliance upon traditional samples of the material as delivered can adequately monitor the true quality of construction achieved. A move towards performance based specifications has begun, and testing of the in-place concrete has a potentially valuable role to play in this process. In-place testing also has a key role in the field of repairs to concrete structures, to assess both the need for repair and the integrity of the repair that is actually achieved. A large range of test possibilities exist, but the current status of some methods leaves room for improvement. In this paper, the present situation regarding in situ testing is reviewed in this context, and future prospects and avenues for development are identified.

Keywords: Concrete, Testing, In-place, Non-destructive, Strength, Durability, Construction, Repairs.

Dr. John H. Bungey is Senior Lecturer and Head of the Structures group in the Department of Civil Engineering, University of Liverpool. His research interests are concentrated on non-destructive testing of concrete. He has published numerous papers and books on these topics and is a member or chairman of several relevant international and national committees. He has also represented the Institution of Civil Engineers on the British National Committee for N.D.T. since 1985.

Concrete 2000. Edited by Ravindra K. Dhir and M. Roderick Jones.
© 1993 Published by E & FN Spon. ISBN 0 419 18120 2.

INTRODUCTION

The future of concrete construction relies heavily upon the ability of the industry to provide a durable product which requires minimal maintenance. It is questionable whether reliance upon traditional cube specimens can adequately monitor the true quality of concrete achieved in-place, either in terms of strength or durability. It is thus important that those key aspects of construction workmanship are monitored. Both of these factors are heavily dependent upon the efficiency of compaction and curing, whilst correct positioning of reinforcement is a further major concern relating to durability. It is only recently that the shortcomings of traditional methods have achieved any significant degree of recognition and a move towards performance based specifications has now slowly begun. Widespread increase in use of in-place testing during construction has however been constrained by the twin perceived problems of additional costs and limitations of available test methods.

Testing in-place concrete before repairs is essential to determine the cause and extent of deterioration and hence the need for repair and the best method to adopt in a particular case. Tests may relate to the concrete matrix or to embedded reinforcing steel. The need for such testing is widely accepted, as is the need for assessing the integrity of the repair actually achieved. A well established range of tests are available for appraisals prior to repair, although test procedures for repaired concrete are still under development.

TESTS CURRENTLY AVAILABLE

These are wide ranging and generally well documented. The most relevant methods are summarised in Tables 1 and 2 but space does not permit detailed descriptions of individual methods to be given here. The tests have been classified according to their potential for either routine use associated with construction, or for use associated with durability assessment or repair operations. Situations related to non-compliance of control specimens have been included in the latter category. Each method has its particular strengths and shortcomings which will influence applicability to particular situations, but all have the common feature that planning, execution and interpretation are skilled operations. They must be undertaken by appropriately experienced staff if confidence is to be placed upon results.

Most of these test methods are based on well established principles which have been undergoing refinement over many years. A considerable amount of effort has been recently devoted to development of documentation, and some key authoritative sources of information are identified in Tables 1 and 2. Most relevant parts of BS 1881 have been revised and republished since 1986 whilst important reports have also been produced by C.I.R.I.A. [1,2,3], The Concrete Society [4,5] and T.R.R.L.[6]. This work continues within the Concrete Society, with reports on corrosion assessment and the use of radar being currently under preparation, although there is little prospect of

Table 1   Tests during construction

PROPERTY ASSESSED	INSITU TEST	KEY DOCUMENTATION
Steel Location and Cover	Covermeters	BS 1881 Pt.204
Strength	Maturity Temp. Match Curing	CIRIA Rep.73
	Pull-out Break-off Penetration Resist.	BS 1881 Pt.207
Durability/ Quality	Permeability Chemical/ Petrographic	BS 1881 Pt.5 C.S. TR 31,32 BS 1881 Pt.124

Table 2   Tests associated with repairs

STAGE	PROPERTY ASSESSED	INSITU TEST	KEY DOCUMENTATION
Before Repair	Strength (Comparative)	U.P.V. Rebound Hammer	BS 1881 Pt.203 BS 1881 Pt.202
	Strength (Absolute)	Cores (Samples) Pull-out Pull-off Break-off Penetration Resist. Internal Fracture	BS 1881 Pt.120 C.S. TR 11 BS 1881 Pt.207 CIRIA TN 143
	Composition/ Contamination	Chemical/ Petrographic	BS 1881 Pt.124 C.S. TR 32
	Corrosion	Half-Cell Resistivity	TRRL Guide 9 CIRIA TN 143
After Repair	Bond Permeability	Pull-off Surface Absorption	CIRIA TN 139 C.S. TR 31

significant further work in this area by B.S.I. at present.

CURRENT USAGE OF IN-PLACE TESTING

Testing During Construction

Current usage of in-place testing is largely confined to troubleshooting situations following failure of standard specimens to satisfy specification requirements. There are however some circumstances in which more forward-thinking designers and specifiers provide for in-place testing, either as part of quality control procedures or to assist specialised construction operations. It is these relatively rare cases which are considered here.

Cover measurement devices

The use of electromagnetic covermeasuring devices to check the positioning and depth of reinforcing steel immediately after formwork stripping has been suggested for many years. In spite of the widely recognised, and continuing, problems of reinforcement corrosion resulting from lack of adequate cover it is surprising that such usage is still very limited. At least 9 different devices are commercially available within the U.K. at present and, with proper calibration [7], it should easily be possible to estimate cover depth to within $\pm$ 5 mm in new construction where bar sizes and type are known. The available range of equipment includes magnetic and eddy-current devices, and some have audible warning and automatic data storage facilities. Major errors, perhaps resulting from movement of steel during concreting, can thus readily be detected.

In-situ strength testing

Temperature matched curing and maturity techniques are used for monitoring in-situ strength development in situations where this may be critical [1]. Pull-out testing has also been shown to be a useful approach for this purpose which can be performed through openings in shutters and can reliably provide a direct physical measurement of in-place compressive strengths as low as 1.5 N/mm [8]. This, together with other relevant near-to-surface strength testing methods including Windsor Probe and Break-off, is now standardised in BS1881 pt 207 [9]. Ultrasonic pulse velocity tests are also sometimes used for routine monitoring of precast concrete component manufacture.

Pull-out testing has recently been utilised for strength compliance testing as a supplement, or alternative, to traditional standard control specimens. The most notable example of this is the Great Baelt Bridge in Denmark [10] where the approach has been used with considerable success. A great deal of effort has been put into the development of testing specifications and procedures for that project, and these could form the basis of much wider use of this method during construction.

Tests for concrete quality and durability

The correct use and proportioning of constituents of a concrete mix can be checked by chemical and petrographic analysis of samples removed from the in-place concrete. This approach has found particular favour in Scandinavia. Permeability is however probably the most important property relating to future durability perform-performance and this potentially provides a worthwhile property to measure. Several surface zone tests are commercially available for in-situ use, including the Initial Surface Absorbtion, Poroscope, Clam, and B.C.A. methods [3].

Tests which do not require a drilled hole (I.S.A.T. and Clam) avoid uncertainties about the possibility of localised microcracking caused by the drilling operation and consequential effects upon test results. These methods, however, are subject to greater practical difficulties including the formation of a watertight seal around the specified area of concrete surface. The Initial Surface Absorption Test nevertheless has the advantage of simplicity, although the head of water is low, and is favoured by the Author. Classification limits of less than 0.17 mL/m^2/s, $0.17 - 0.35$ mL/m^2/s and greater than 0.35 mL/m^2/s for low, average and high permeability concrete (30 minute values) proposed by the Concrete Society [4] would appear to be adequate although temperature corrections proposed by the Author may be appropriate when testing in hot climates [11]. It has also been found that scatter of results is reduced if measured I.S.A.T. values are integrated over a period of 60 minutes from the start of the text, in which case the classification limits become 657 mL/m^2 and 1328 mL/m^2 respectively. The Clam system can provide a measure of air and water permeability characteristics at pressures up to 1.5 bar and appears to offer considerable potential although procedures have not been formally standardized.

All these permeability tests are greatly influenced by concrete moisture content, although for newly cast concrete this is likely to be reasonably uniform and general classification levels should still be possible in each case. The Initial Surface Absorption method has however been shown to less sensitive to internal moisture content than the Figg method [11]. Some of these tests have been used on a limited scale as part of specifications for prestige projects.

Integrity testing

Testing of this type during construction is generally very limited as a matter of routine. Radiographic surveys of grouted ducts in post-tensioned construction is one of the few examples available, but this is very slow and requires extreme safety precautions.

Testing Before Repairs

In-place assessment of concrete and reinforcement have become an important part of routine maintenance inspections of bridges, whilst they may also be associated with change of ownership or use of buildings. Unfortunately repairs are likely to become necessary for some structures, and when this occurs it is essential that the cause and full extent of deterioration are properly identified. Half-cell potential and resistivity techniques are well established for assessing corrosion risk of buried reinforcing steel and are widely used. These cannot predict corrosion rate, but linear polarisation resistance and other methods are under development which may be able to achieve this in the future. Equipment developments now permit non-damaging 4-probe resistivity measurements, whilst considerable attention has been given to interpretation of these [12] and half-cell results [6]. Particular emphasis is placed on half-cell potential gradients rather than sole consideration of absolute values.

Concrete strength values are not normally critical, unless cubes have failed and compliance or structural adequacy are in question. Ultrasonic pulse velocity tests have however been widely used for comparative strength assessment as well as the location of voids, cracking and similar hidden defects. The author has also demonstrated that this method may be useful when locating and monitoring zones of concrete affected by alkali-silica reaction [13]. More recently, infra-red thermography and sub-surface scanning radar have become established as non-damaging techniques requiring only one exposed surface. These can detect a wide range of defects, including variations in moisture conditions, and in the case of radar may also be useful in assessing element thickness. Sub-surface radar is based on analysis of reflections of pulses of electromagnetic radiation, typically at about 1 GHz frequency, from buried interfaces. This has attracted much interest in the past few years [14], with applications to structural concrete including

- Element thickness estimation (up to about 400 mm)

- Location of reinforcing bars (at depths beyond the range of covermeters)

- Location and identification of major construction features (steelwork, ducts, etc.)

- Location of moisture and salt contaminated zones

- Location of voids/honeycombing/cracking

At present, all such applications must be considered to be comparative, and calibration by trial drilling is usually required.

Dynamic testing is available in a variety of forms ranging from localised impact-echo techniques [15] to large scale vibration of structures or elements. Interpretation is fundamentally comparative, but this may provide useful pointers towards structural integrity and the need for repair, as well as forming a basis for assessment of the effectiveness of repairs by comparison of dynamic signatures before and after the repair.

Testing After Repair

In addition to dynamic testing to assess stiffness changes as described above, localised integrity testing of repairs is important. The pull-off test is becoming established for this purpose [16] and is covered in several overseas Standards. The method is used with partial-coring which passes through the repair into the substrate, and is an excellent way of providing a direct tensile force to the interface of repair and substrate to measure bond. Particular care is needed however to carefully standardise and specify the test configuration, since the Author has recently demonstrated the sensitivity of results to factors such as disk characteristics and depth of partial coring [16]. Standardisation is essential when acceptance limits are to be satisfied.

Monitoring moisture content may be important following some types of remedial work. This is an area which still has many limitations in that surface drilled holes and time are required to achieve reliable results. Chilled mirror dew-point apparatus is now available which may be useful in some situations [3].

FUTURE NEEDS AND PROSPECTS

The increased use of in-place non-destructive testing during construction must be considered as an important contributor to the future production of durable concrete structures. This would enable potential durability problems and other faults to be rectified immediately, thereby reducing the need for costly and disruptive repairs at a later stage and improving the image of concrete as a construction material. One of the most important features of such testing is that it assesses the quality of the critical surface zone concrete which protects both the interior concrete and reinforcement from deterioration. In-place strength tests offer great scope for development as routine methods of compliance assessment which take full account of the critical operations of compaction and curing. The routine use of cover measuring devices during construction has been proposed for many years, and the arguments for this are overwhelming in view of the widely accepted findings that corrosion is the principal source of deterioration of structural concrete.

Developments in testing methodology are urgently required in the areas of assessment of grouting integrity for both newly constructed and existing bonded post-tensioned construction. The identification of corrosion within the prestressing steel in this form of construction is also a matter of major concern, and at present there is no established technique for this purpose. A Concrete Society Working Party has recently reviewed available methods and concluded that there is potential for development of electrical and ultrasonic pulse reflection techniques with measurements along the length pre-stressing steel. Renewed interest in radiography also seems likely.

Whilst it is to be hoped that increased use will be made of in-place strength and quality tests during construction, it seems likely that in the short term attention will be concentrated on testing associated with repairs. The prospects for Linear Polarisation Resistance and Galvanostatic Pulse methods to provide a realistic indication of the corrosion state of reinforcing steel look good. Work is also in hand to develop methods to test the effectiveness of surface treatments and coatings designed to improve durability performance. Current research is being undertaken to further develop radar techniques, pulsed video thermography, laser interferometry, impact-echo and other methods for assessment of integrity and for performance monitoring of concrete structures. Other areas worthy of further attention include increased standardisation of procedures for surface permeability and water absorbtion, coupled with improvements to the measurement capabilities for assessing insitu moisture.

CONCLUSIONS

It is clear that despite the large range of in-place testing methods that are currently available there is considerable scope for increased usage, especially during the construction phase. Whilst minor improvements could perhaps be made to some of the available equipment, this cannot provide a justifiable excuse for not using in-place testing. There can be little doubt that routine use during construction of simple testing, such as cover measurement, would result in major improvements in the durability performance of reinforced concrete structures. As far as concrete quality specification compliance is concerned, the increased use of in-place testing offers many advantages over traditional control specimens.

There are some areas of testing in which further developments of technology are obviously required, and the research community is actively pursuing these at present. Both equipment and understanding are involved, leading to increased interpretative confidence in results. These developments will, in due course, permit Engineers to have greater confidence in the future of their new concrete construction, as well as improving the effectiveness of maintenance and repair procedures for existing concrete.

REFERENCES

1.   HARRISON, TA. Formwork Striking Times - Methods of Assessment, CIRIA Report 73, 2nd Ed., London, 1987, 30 p.

2.   McLEISH, A. Standard Tests for Repair Materials and Coatings for Concrete - Pull-off Testing, CIRIA TN 139, London, 1992, 40p.

3.   BUNGEY, JH. Testing Concrete in Structures - A Guide to Equipment, CIRIA

TN 143, London, 1992, 87p.

4. CONCRETE SOCIETY. Permeability Testing of Site Concrete, Tech Report 31, 1987, 95p.

5. CONCRETE SOCIETY. Analysis of Hardened Concrete, Tech Report 32, 1989, 70p.

6. VASSIE, PR. The Half-Cell Potential Method of Locating Corroding Reinforcement in Concrete Structures, Application Guide 9, Transport and Road Research Laboratory, Crowthorne, 1991, 30p.

7. BS 1881 PART 204 Testing Concrete : Recommendations on the use of electromagnetic cover measuring devices, BSI, London, 1987, 8p.

8. BUNGEY, JH. Monitoring Concrete Early Age Strength Development, Non-Destructive Testing, ed J Boogaard and GM Van Dijk, Elsevier, Amsterdam, 1989, pp 1243-1248.

9. BS 1881 PART 207 Testing Concrete: Recommendations for the assessment of concrete strength by near to surface tests. B.S.I., London, 1992, 13p.

10. PETERSEN, CG AND POULSEN, E. Lok-Test and Capo-Test pullout testing, A/S Storebaeltsforbindelsen, Copenhagen, 1992, 70p.

11. BUNGEY, J.H., MILLARD, S.G. AND GHASSEMI, M.H.. Environmental Effects on Surface Measurements, 3rd Int. Conf. on Concrete in the Gulf, Bahrain Soc. of Engineers, 1989, pp443-457.

12. MILLARD, SG. Reinforced Concrete Resistivity Measurement Techniques, Proc. I.C.E., Part 2, Vol. 91, 1991pp 71-88.

13. BUNGEY, JH. Ultrasonic Testing to Identify Alkali-Silica Reaction in Concrete. British Journal of N.D.T., Vol. 33, No.5, 1991, pp 227-231.

14. BUNGEY, JH AND MILLARD SG. Radar Testing of Structures, Proc. I.C.E. Structures & Buildings Journal, May 1993 (in the press).

15. CARINO, NJ AND SANSALONE, M. Detection of Voids in Grouted Ducts Using the Impact Echo Method. American Conc. Inst. Materials Journal, Vol. 89, No. 3, May-June 1992, pp 296-303.

16. BUNGEY, JH AND MADANDOUST R. Factors affecting Pull-off Tests on Concrete, Mag. of Conc. Res., Vol. 44, No. 158, March 1992, pp 21-30.

A NEW APPROACH TO TESTING
OF CONCRETE BLEEDING

G F Loedolff

University of Stellenbosch

South Africa

ABSTRACT. Bleeding can have an impact on durability and excellence of construction so that more needs to be known about bleeding and the measurement of bleeding. Bleeding after compaction is discussed as well as the implication of water leaving the concrete. Present methods of measuring bleeding are of little value to the concretor because the bleeding values obtained cannot be interpreted into easy usable terms. With this new approach to the problem the amount of water used to make a concrete, is compared with the amount that can be retained in the concrete by adsorption and in small voids. When the amount used is more than can be retained, the concrete can bleed potentially by the difference in these amounts. Low potential bleeding is associated with low binder (cement and additives or extenders) contents, low water requirements and smaller slumps (workabilities).

Keywords: Bleeding, bleeding measurements, cement extenders, bleeding capacity, packing of solids.

Professor **G.F. Loedolff** Pr.Eng, PhD, is a retired professor of the University of Stellenbosch. He specialised in Concrete Technology with particular interest in mix design, packing of the solid ingredients of concrete and bleeding. He attended and participated in several international conferences and published several papers in South Africa.

Concrete 2000. Edited by Ravindra K. Dhir and M. Roderick Jones.
© 1993 Published by E & FN Spon. ISBN 0 419 18120 2.

INTRODUCTION

Economic durable concrete can only be obtained by using durable materials and good sound concrete and concreting practice. This implies well placed and well compacted, dense concrete which will stand up to aggressive environments. Certain admixtures can enhance concrete's resistance against aggressive agents, but the best starting point is no doubt to produce a good, dense concrete with as little and as few capillaries and voids as possible.

Bleeding is one of the factors that can be responsible for capillaries and cavities. Not all bleeding water will appear on the surface of the concrete or drain out through leaking formwork. Loose water may be trapped inside concrete which will bleed and this trapped water may lead to cavities in the concrete when the water has evaporated. When water is trapped underneath reinforcing bars, the bond between concrete and steel will be reduced. Bleeding water will also collect underneath inclined and horizontal formwork and when released spoil the concrete surfaces with sand streaks and other blemishes. It is therefore most desirable to account for all water which may become loose or potentially loose after compaction.

The present measuring devices and specifications to determine bleeding are grossly inadequate and unable to give a full account of what can occur in a concrete. Their best achievements and even this can be disputed, are to disclose that this concrete may bleed more than that concrete, but not much more. When bleeding figures are found, what do they really mean and how should they be interpreted?

Since bleeding and especially internal bleeding cannot be ignored when excellence of and durable concrete is required, a more realistic way of assessing bleeding had to be found. Water which has left the concrete by bleeding cannot affect the concrete itself apart from damaging the surface with sand streaks and wash-outs. What really matters is the way in which the water leaves the concrete and how much is trapped inside underneath coarse aggregates and reinforcing bars. The amount of loose or potentially loose water is therefore of prime concern when concrete excellence and durability is required.

A viable method of evaluating bleeding will be described in the following paragraphs, but before this can be done it is necessary to understand the bleeding process.

BLEEDING

Bleeding is the separation of water from concrete and is generally perceived as water appearing on the surface of the concrete or leaking out through formwork joints.

To obtain dense concrete, the finer particles in the mix must move in between coarser particles to eventually fill all voids. The particles of different sizes must therefore receive some mobility either by vibration or any other means of compaction. Dry particles will not move easily and need some lubrication to encourage movement. The normal lubricant in concrete is water and often cement paste (water plus cement). Water as well as cement pastes are poor lubricants so that a thick film of water is required to cover each particle. This can only be achieved by churning and stirring the concrete with continuous mixing. When the particles become stationary after placing and compaction, the film of water around each particle is not strong enough to support the particle so that a general settlement of all particles will follow. Since the movement is vertically downwards a system of stacking of particles with water columns in between developes. When this stacking is disturbed by vibration or re-compaction, another period of settlement and hence more bleeding will follow. Bleeding will only cease when stacking is completed or when the cement hydrate intervenes and restricts further movement. Retarders will therefore extend the bleeding process in thicker and deeper sections.

The wall effects of containers are very prominent in this stacking process so that the size of the containers should take account of the maximum particle sizes. Larger aggregate sizes require larger diameter containers. The Pipette method (ASTM C232) and even the Valore, Bowling and Blaine method (ASTM C243) use similar containers for concretes with different maximum size aggregates. This can add another element to the intricacy of interpreting the results into a usable form. The disturbances of the concrete by tilting to draw off water with a pipette add another uncontrollable human factor. The major problem concerning these tests, is to interpret and to apply the results apart from just comparing two concretes for their bleeding capabilities. Neither of these methods can predict or evaluate the amount of internal bleeding or of water trapped within the concrete underneath coarse aggregates or reinforcing steel bars.

The method of Powers when meticulously executed with containers of adequate sizes, measuring subsidence of the surface of the concrete by means of a float and mast, can supply valuable information, but once more the problem of interpretation of the results remains. This method is, however, the only means by which the bleeding of cement paste and the expansion of a grout with a swelling agent can be properly evaluated.

A NEW METHOD TO DETERMINE BLEEDING

In this method the amount of water which can be held in a concrete by means of adsorption and filled voids, is compared with the amount of water used to make the concrete. If the water used to make the concrete is more than the amount which can be retained by adsorption and filled voids, the difference can be regarded as water that will be free and which can bleed, if not externally then internally. The amount of loose or potentially loose water is, therefore, of prime concern when concrete excellence and durability is involved.

The method is quite simple and requires only a 0,600 mm standard sieve (200 mm diameter), a scale with accuracy of ±0,5 g, an oven and 24 h time. The test procedure can be described as follows:

> Add extra water to the concrete to obtain a soft mix which can easily be compacted by hand. Place approximately 2 kg of this soft concrete on a standard 0,600 mm sieve and compact the concrete thoroughly. Support the rim of the sieve on 3 support blocks of approximately 50 mm high for approximately 15-20 min. Remove one of the blocks after 15-20 min. so that the sieve adopts a skew or slanting position. This procedure allows all free water to leave the concrete. As soon as the free water has left the concrete, generally after 30-40 min., the last free water is wiped off and the contents of the sieve placed in a wide, shallow container. Weigh the sample and the container to an accuracy of ±0,5 g. Break the sample up and spread it in the container. Dry the sample for approximately 24 h at 100-105°C until the dried contents reaches a constant weight. Cool as quickly as possible in a dry atmosphere. A desiccator is quite useful, but not essential. The loss of weight can now be expressed as a percentage of the dry mass remaining in the container.

> If the original mass of water used to make the concrete is known, the dry mass will be known and the amount of water adsorbed and held in the concrete can be determined. Call this quantity A kg.

This quantity, A, can serve as a good practical approach, but if the initial loose water is to be found, this figure should be modified. As soon as water reaches the cement, hydration will commence. During the 24 h drying period and with sufficient heat available, it can be expected that hydration could bind more water than that which had been adsorbed initially. This amount of combined water can be determined by using a known quantity of cement mixed with water to a water/cement (W/C) ratio of approximately 0,4 and finding the increased weight after 24 h drying. The increase in weight will reflect the amount of combined water. Acceptable increases of weight for OPC, can be between 3,5 to 4,5% of the dry mass of the cement. A figure of 4% was used in table 1. Other cements and cements with extenders can be treated in the same way. It must, however, be remembered that hydration will stop as soon as the relative humidity (RH) in the sample drops below 80%. The cement will therefore not hydrate over the full 24 h.

TABLE 1

The different quantities water/m³ concrete used for a workability of approximately 50 mm slump, the quantities retained (unmodified) and the quantities adsorbed or potentially loose water (modified quantities). The figures in brackets are for expected workabilities of approximately 25 mm slump.

BINDER	PROPORTIONS OF BINDER TO AGGREGATES											
	10/90			20/80			30/70			40/60		
	Water			Water			Water			Water		
	Used l/m³	Retained l/m³	Adsorbed l/m³	Used l/m³	Retained l/m³	Adsorbed l/m³	Used l/m³	Retained l/m³	Adsorbed l/m³	Used l/m³	Retained l/m³	Adsorbed l/m³
100% cement	166 (156)	170	158	188 (178)	191	170	234 (224)	206	178	269 (259)	236	200
80% cement 20% fly-ash	160 (150)	168	156	186 (176)	189	170	233 (223)	222	198	266 (256)	264	234
70% cement 30% fly-ash	160 (150)	165	155	187 (177)	193	176	230 (220)	221	198	265 (255)	261	233
60% cement 40% fly-ash	159 (149)	164	153	186 (176)	193	177	227 (217)	225	208	265 (255)	255	229
50% cement 50% fly-ash	168 (158)	163	153	205 (195)	190	175	242 (232)	226	207	281 (271)	257	234

Water used = the quantity used/m³ to make the concrete.
Water retained = the quantity/m³ which was retained in the concrete.
Water adsorbed = the quantity/m³ adsorbed, excluding that which was absorbed by the binder and aggregates.

The aggregates will also absorb water if they were not saturated before mixing. When this water bound by the cement and absorbed by the aggregates are considered, it is clear that more water than indicated by A above, will initially be available for bleeding. This refinement may appear to be unnecessary, but it must be remembered that water which became free at very early stages can cause surface blemishes. Once water has collected underneath flaky aggregates and reinforcing bars, no form or type of pressure will force the water back into the concrete. It will only re-enter the concrete when absorbed by hydrating cement. Although the sizes of capillaries and voids formed by bleeding water, may be reduced by the hydration products of cement, the chances are very slim that they will be completely filled by the cement hydrate.

Admixtures such as fly-ash, silica fume and slagment will also absorb water, but they will also react with the lime in the cement so that preference should be given to testing the blended cement rather than testing the cement and admixtures separately as described above.

Water will not only be held by adsorption, but will also be held in the smaller voids between particles. Although the total porosity of a fine medium such as cement or very fine sand and coarse aggregates may be virtually the same, the void sizes can differ largely. If the large voids are drained by the bleeding process the medium with the small voids will retain more water than that with the large voids. Concretes with high cement, binder and filler contents, will therefore retain more water than concretes with less cement or binder. Similarly, if all the solid particles in a concrete packs densely, the porosity will decrease so that less water will be required to fill the voids and to lubricate the particles by just over-filling the voids. Poor packing of the solids will increase porosity and even should the void sizes remain small, more water will be retained. Packing and water retention are therefore closely related as shown in figures 1 and 2.

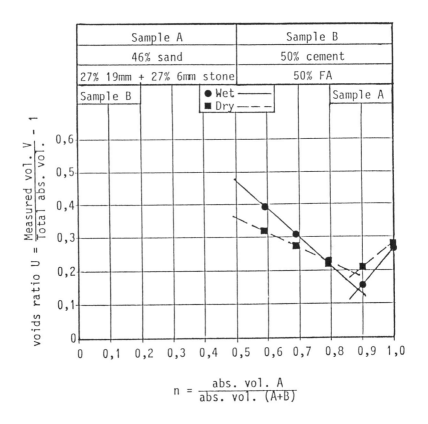

$$n = \frac{\text{abs. vol. A}}{\text{abs. vol. (A+B)}}$$

FIGURE 1
Packing curves for cement blended with 50% FA against aggregates

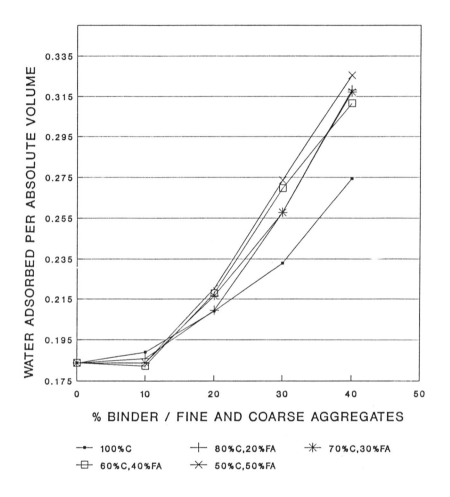

FIGURE 2
Water adsorbed per absolute volume of the solids in the mix for different percentages of binder

INTERPRETATION OF RESULTS

Although the refinements to estimate the exact initial quantity of free water may be essential in some cases, it may in most cases suffice to determine the unmodified excess quantity only. Table 1 is compiled to demonstrate the influence of binder, cement and the

different blends of cement and fly-ash on the water requirement and
the potentially free water or water available for bleeding. A slump
of approximately 50 mm was obtained for each mix.

It is clear that some of the mixes with a 50 mm slump will not bleed
when the water used is compared with the unmodified retainable
quantity, but that most of the 50 mm slump mixes may bleed when the
modified quantities which exclude the water bound by the cement and
absorbed by the aggregates, are considered. The figures in brackets
are for 10 ℓ less water per m³ with an estimated workability of 25 mm.
Again when the water used is compared with the unmodified and
modified quantities some of the mixes will not bleed while some may
still bleed, especially those with high binder contents.

The wet density of concrete includes water. If less water is used,
more solid material will be required for one m³ concrete which can be
related to better packing of the solids. It was found that a good
basis for comparison was the mass water per absolute solid volume of
the solids in a mix. If table 1 is adjusted to include water/absolute
volume of solids and the results plotted on a graph, figure 2 is
obtained. These curves show clearly that the least water retained
coincides with low cement or binder contents and corresponds well
with best packing as shown by the curves in figure 1 which were
compiled for the packing of fine and coarse aggregates versus cement
or binder. Figures 1 and 2 show clearly that optimum conditions can
be achieved with low cement/binder contents of 10-12% binder to
aggregate proportions. In real terms this means cement/binder
contents of approximately 270-310 kg/m³ concrete. Table 1 also
confirms that the least excess or bleeding water is realised with
these low cement/binder contents while the least water is required to
make the concrete.

Figure 2 shows clearly that more water can be retained by increasing
the very fines, cement/binder, content, while the water requirement
as well as excess water increases rapidly as shown in table 1. More
water retained after compaction will increase shrinkage so that there
is little to be gained by adding very fines to curb bleeding when the
cement/binder content is already high. More mixing water required and
more excess water initially available for bleeding makes it much more
important to control bleeding and to know how much water can bleed.
Durability and excellence of concrete construction is therefore
closely associated with bleeding and bleeding potential.

This only emphasises the fact that bleeding should be determined with
much greater care and in a way by which everyone can interpret the
results. If it is found that a concrete will bleed excessively, the
first step to rectify matters, is surely to look at the mix itself
and to consider modifications to improve packing of the solids in
order to reduce the water requirement. Fly-ash (FA) can only reduce
bleeding if it increases the packability of the solids including the
binder. The reduction of water for the same workability often
experienced by the addition of FA can therefore be accounted for by

the better packing achieved by the solids. This is only possible as long as the total binder contents does not exceed the limits for best packing which is associated with low binder contents. FA will therefore only reduce water requirement as well as bleeding with lean cement mixes, but will have a negligent effect of cement rich mixes with more than, say, 320-350 kg cement per m³ concrete.

If the bleeding capacity is found as described above, a vivid picture of the real situation can be formed. When the difference between mixing water and water retainable is 10 ℓ/m³ and only 5 ℓ/m³ bleeds or leaks out visibly, then surely the other 5 ℓ/m³ will stay inside the concrete. When no water bleeds or leaks out, then the total of 10 ℓ/m³ will stay within the concrete with the possibility of forming voids or capillaries which will, when the water has evaporated, leave voids and cause porosity or permeability.

An interesting observation was that when subsidence or settlement was determined with the float method as devised by Powers, the time and bleeding rate compared very favourably with the loss of water from the concrete. The loss of water was determined by compacting the concrete in a sieve suspended from a scale and measuring the loss of weight directly.

CONCLUSIONS

1. Present methods of measuring bleeding are unsatisfactory. Visible bleeding should not be the only method of determining bleeding because it does not display the total character of the concrete.

2. Results obtained from bleeding measurements must be interpretable and applicable.

3. Methods to curb or limit bleeding must be directed towards lower water requirements for making concrete rather than addition of fillers or other fines to decrease visible bleeding. The inherent weaknesses must first be solved.

4. Water requirements can be lowered by improved selection and proportioning of aggregates, improved overall grading and packing of solids, the use of water-reducing agents, plasticisers and superplasticisers and moving towards drier mixes with lower slumps while the concrete is still well compactable in the particular situation where it is used.

5. The proposed new method is viable, easy to apply and to interpret and sheds much light on the characteristics and shortcomings of the concrete. See addendum A for a typical calculation.

REFERENCES

1.   LOEDOLFF, G.F.: Die rol van water in beton (The role of water in concrete) Afrikaans text only. Nasou 1977. pp 319-338.

2.   SOEN, M.: Aanvullende onderzoek na waterafscheiding (bleeding) Vloeibeton verslag No 77/1979 van Mebin kwaliteitsdienste, Holland. pp 1-15.

3.   TAN, S.L. et al.: A consolidation model for bleeding of cement paste, Advances in Cement Research, Vol 1 No 1, October 1987. pp 18-27.

4.   POWERS, C.T.: The properties of fresh concrete, Wiley 1968. pp 533-652.

5.   STEINOUR, H.H.: Rate of sedimentation of non-flocculated suspensions of powders, Industrial and Engineering Chemistry, 1944. pp 618-624, 840-847, 901-907.

6.   POWERS, C.T.: The bleeding of Portland cement paste, mortar and concrete, PCA Bulletin No 2, 1939. pp 1-160.

7.   STEINOUR, H.H.: Further studies of the bleeding of Portland cement pastes, PCA Bulletin No 4. 1945. pp 1-88.

8.   KREIJGER, Ir P.C.: Methodiek voor het bepaling van de bleeding-eigenschappen van cement pasta - TNO-publikasie, 1960. pp 1-15.

9.   NEVILLE, A.M.: Properties of concrete, Pitman 1981. Various pages approximately 30.

10. NEVILLE, A.M. and BROOKS, I.J.: Concrete Technology, Longman Scientific and Technical publication, 1987. pp 81-83.

11. ASTM: Test for bleeding of concrete - C232-71, 1977. pp 826-827.

12. ASTM: Test for bleeding   - C243, 1965. pp 252-256.

13. VALORE, Ir R.C., BOWLING, J.E. and BLAINE, R.L.: The direct and continuous measurement of bleeding of Portland cement mixtures, Proc. ASTM, 49, 1949. pp 891-908.

14. RILEM: Bleeding of Concrete - Draft recommendation, Matériaux et constructions, Vol. 16, No. 91, pp 51-52.

15. LOEDOLFF, G.F.: Kussande van die Wes-Kaap en die benutting van superfyn duinsand in beton - PhD Tesis, Universiteit van Stellenbosch, 1985. pp 120-146.

16. LOEDOLFF, G.F.: Bloei van beton, Concrete/Beton, April 1992. pp 9-13.

ADDENDUM A   -   TYPICAL CALCULATIONS

A description of a typical test to determine the amount retainable water in a concrete mix. The binder was a 50% cement plus 50% fly-ash while a 10% binder with 90% fine and coarse aggregates were used.

1.   More water was added to the concrete sample before the wet concrete sample was compacted on a standard 0,600 mm (200 mm diameter) sieve. After all the water which was free to leave the concrete was drained from the concrete, the drained concrete was placed in a flat container, weighed and subsequently dried in an oven to constant weight.

Weight of the dried concrete (b)   = 1883,4 g
Moisture loss from the drained concrete (a) = 136.4 g

$$\text{Moisture content} = \frac{100 \, a}{b} = 7,242\%$$

2.   If the water per m^3 concrete used to make the concrete is unknown but the constituents of a concrete sample is known, the water requirement for one m^3 concrete can be determined as follows:

Water required to mix 6000 g dry concrete constituents to a slump of 50 mm was 450 g. The concrete was made with cement 300 g, fly-ash (FA) 300 g, fine aggregate (sand) (46%) 248 g and coarse aggregate (54%) 2916 g.

The relative density (RD) of sand was 2,64, of stone 2,77, of cement 3,14 and of FA 2,23.

Absolute volume of water   = 0,450 ℓ

$$\text{Absolute volume of cement} = \frac{0,300}{3,14} = 0,0955 \, ℓ$$

$$\text{Absolute volume of FA} = \frac{0,300}{2,23} = 0,1345 \, ℓ$$

$$\text{Absolute volume of fine aggregate} = \frac{2,484}{2,64} = 0,9409 \, ℓ$$

$$\text{Absolute volume of coarse aggregate} = \frac{2,916}{2,77} = \underline{1,0527}$$

Total = 2,6736 ℓ

$$\text{Water used/m}^3 \;=\; \frac{1000}{2,6736} \text{ x } 0,450 \;=\; 168,3 \approx 168 \; \ell$$

$$\text{Volume density of the concrete was } \frac{1000}{2,6736} \text{ x } 6,450$$

$$=\; 2412,5 \text{ kg/m}^3$$

$$\text{Amount water retained} = (2412,5 - 168) \text{ x } \frac{7,242}{100}$$

$$=\; 162,5 \approx 163 \; \ell/\text{m}^3$$

$$\text{Excess water which can bleed potentially} \;=\; 168 - 163$$

$$=\; 5\ell/\text{m}^3.$$

3.   The amount adsorbed water which was not absorbed by the aggregates and the binder can also be calculated.

A 2000 g mixture was made up with binder (50% cement plus 50% FA) 10% and total aggregates 90%.

	Coarse Aggregate 19 mm	4,8 mm	Fine Aggr.	Fly-Ash	Cement
Relative densities	2,77	2,77	2,64	2,23	3,14
% water absorbed	0,26	0,13	0,14	1,45	*4,00
Weight used	486	486	828	100	100
Water absorbed (g)	1,26	0,63	1,16	1,45	4,00
Absolute volumes (ml)	175,45	175,45	313,64	44,84	31,85

*Assume 4% water was bound by partial hydration.

Generally the water bound by the FA and cement should be determined. Since it is believed that more water will be absorbed by FA than bound by FA, the FA was treated separately.

Weight of dry sample   = 2000 g

Absolute volume   = 741,23 ml

Percentage water absorbed and adsorbed = 7,242 x 2000

                                                        = 144,84 g

Water adsorbed $= 144,84 - 8,50$

$= 136,34$ g

Real percentage adsorbed $= 7,242 - \dfrac{8,50}{2000} \times 100$

$= 6,817\%$

Weight per m³ $= (2412,5 - 168)\, \dfrac{6,817}{100}$

$= 153 \ \ell/m^3$

Weight water/absolute volume $= \dfrac{136,34}{741,23} = 0,184.$

BRIDGING THE GAP BETWEEN MATERIAL SCIENCE AND ENGINEERING PRACTICE

K van Breugel

Delft University of Technology

The Netherlands

ABSTRACT. May be more than ever before it is understood that durability problems in civil engineering practice can be carried back to poor or limited understanding of processes and mechanisms operative in the early lifetime of the concrete and its behaviour under environmental loads. In this papers it is shown how computer-based simulation models can be applied for achieving improvements in this situation in the future. A simulation model is presented called HYMOSTRUC, the acronym for HYdration, MORphology and STRUCtural development, which predicts the hydration of Portland cement-based systems as a function of the particle size distribution and chemical composition of the cement, the water/cement ratio and the actual curing temperature. In the model the development of interparticle contacts, i.e. of microstructural developments, and the effect of microstructural development on the rate of hydration is modelled explicitly. Adiabatic and isothermal hydration curves can be predicted which curves can be used as input curves for numerical analysis of thermal stresses in actual concrete structures. An example of implementation of the proposed materials science oriented simulation model in engineering practice is discussed.

Keywords: Computer simulation, Microstructure, Hydration, Strength, Thermal stresses, Risk of Cracking, Durability

Dr.ir. K. van Breugel is senior lecturer and researcher at the Delft University of Technology in The Netherlands. His main topics are Temperature Effects in Concrete Structures, Early-Age Concrete and Concrete Structures for Environmental Protection. He participates in several task groups of the FIP, RILEM, CEB and CUR and is a member of the Dutch Concrete Society, the International Association for Bridges and Structural Engineering and the American Concrete Institute. At present he is chairman of the FIP-working group "Concrete Structures for Environmental Protection.

Concrete 2000. Edited by Ravindra K. Dhir and M. Roderick Jones.
© 1993 Published by E & FN Spon. ISBN 0 419 18120 2.

INTRODUCTION

If we want to control the quality of concrete, to modify its properties, to produce tailor-made concretes and, last but not least, to control the building process, we need to know the major characterisctis of the material. Many decades of research on cementitious systems has provided us with huge amounts of material data gathered by different disciplines like chemistry, physics, stereology, colloid-chemistry and thermodynamics. It is considered one of the major challenges of coming decades to make all this data accessible and operational in engineering practice. The transfer of knowledge from one research level to another and from one discipline to another, however, has his own characteristic problems and constraints. Each discipline has its own culture, his own language and his own objectives. They look to reality from different standpoints and the way in which they describe and model reality can be substantially different. This is illustrated diagrammatically in Fig. 1. The mutual compatibility of models developed in different disciplines is not seldom rather poor because of having been unable or being unprepared to communicate with representatives of other disciplines.

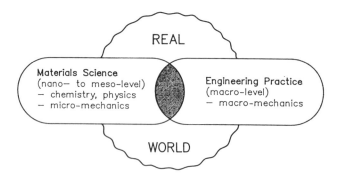

Figure 1   Fundamental models and engineering models as descriptions of the real world.

One possible way to achieve to a successful interdisciplinary transfer of information in the future is the use of computer-based simulation models. A general aim that should be strived at with these models is to increase the mutual compatibility of materials science models and macro- or engineering models. That is, to enlarge the area of the real world covered jointly by these originally different types of models (shaded area in Fig. 1). An example of such a simulation model, with which it is endeavoured to bridge the gap between individual disciplines involved in materials science on the one hand and the practical engineer on the other hand will be discussed in this paper.

MODELLING OF HARDENING PROCESSES IN CEMENT-BASED MATERIALS

Some Aspects Of Hydration And Microstructural Development

Not with the aim to be exhaustive, but just to illustrate the complexity of our subject, a brief survey will be given of some aspects of hydration processes and microstructural development of cement-based materials.

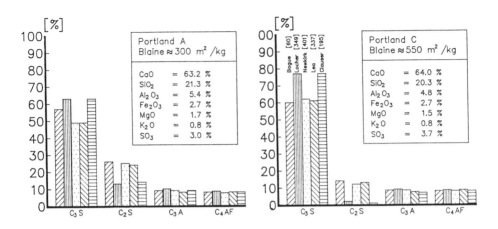

Figure 2 Clinker composition of Portland cement according to different authors [2].

A prerequisite for reliable modelling of any reaction starts with an accurate description of the starting materials. Portland cement is a poly-mineral and poly-size powder. The clinker composition can be determined analytically with the help of adequate formulae or experimentally. The accuracy and reliability that can be achieved with any of these methods is limited (Fig. 2). Since the rate of reaction of individual clinker compounds differs, at least when hydrating separately, it is obvious that the accuracy of any model used to simulate the hydration process will somehow reflect the inaccuracies in the chemical composition of the cement. Additional to the effect of inaccuracies with which the content of major clinker compounds can be determined also minor components, alkalies and gypsum play an important role in the hydration kinetics of a cement-water system.

Another important aspect in view of numerical modelling of microstructural development refers to the question whether hydration occurs *topochemically (Michaelis)* or *through-solution (Le Chatelier)*. According to the first theory the hydration products are formed at the surface of the reactant, whereas in the second theory reaction products are formed in solution and then precipitate at the surface of the solid grain surfaces. According to Shebl et al. [1] hydration of C_3S involves both through-solution reactions and topochemical reactions. The concept of simultaneously operating mechanisms is plausible if we may assume that the *outer product*, i.e. the product which is formed outside the original boundaries of the anhydrous grains, is formed via a through-solution mechanism, while the *inner product*, i.e. the product formed inside the original grain boundaries, is formed topochemically (see also Fig. 3a, upper part). It is noticed that, in a way, the result of both mechanisms is the same as in both cases the original cement grains exhibit an outward growth. Algorithmization of the process of growth of solid particles, including the formation of interparticle contacts, can, to a certain extent, be worked out without knowing exactly which mechanism is predominant.

A third problem of numerical modelling of hydration of poly-mineral materials concerns the question whether the individual clinker components hydrate independently from each other, the so called *independent hydration concept*, or at *equal fractional rates*. The independent hydration concept has been supported by Parrott [3], whereas hydration at equal fractional rates has been considered by Brownmiller [4] and Rexford [5]. The two concepts must be considered as extremes. Individual hydration of different clinker components could be predominant in the early stage of hydration, i.e. the stage in which the *phase-boundary reaction* is the rate controlling mechanism, whereas in the *diffusion controlled* stage hydration would occur at equal fractional rates.

Macro-Level Or Engineering Models

With macro-level or engineering models the development of strength, temperatures and associated thermal stresses and the risk of thermal cracking in early-age concrete is analyzed. With these models the progress of the hydration process as it proceeds on site can be simulated. Based on these simulations well-considered measures can be taken to retard or speed up the hydration process in order to reduce to the risk of early-age thermal cracking or the reduce the stripping times, respectively. With these macro-level programs both the amount of heat of reaction and resulting reaction temperatures are calculated. The development of strength and stiffness can be related to the degree of hydration, the latter quantity assumed to be approximately equal to the percentual amount of liberated heat. It is considered noteworthy that also in recent proposals for *creep* and *relaxation* of early-age concrete the effect of microstructural changes during hydration is considered to play an important role [6,7].

Evaluation And Objectives

The input for most of the macro-level numerical models mentioned in the foregoing exists in, among other things, the *adiabatic* hydration curve of the mix in view. At present these curves must be determined experimentally. Numerical prediction of these curves is the major engineering aim of the development of the simulation model presented in this paper. In this simulation model called HYMOSTRUC, the acronym for HYdration, MORphology and STRUCture development, hydration and microstructural development in hardening concrete are considered as two interrelated phenomena. Major parameters of which the effect of on hardening kinetics are modelled *explicitly* are the *chemical composition* and the *particle size distribution* of the cement, the *water/cement ratio*, the *temperature regime* during hardening and the *mix composition* of the concrete.

Bearing in mind the complexity of the subject the use of advanced computer programs seems to be indispensable. But even with the use of advanced computer hardware it will be necessary to carry through rigorous systematization of the cement itself, of the hydration products and of the mechanisms and processes involved in hydration and microstructural development. In order to be able to insert additional options in the model in later stages without drastic restructuring of the model the structure of the model should be as "open" as possible.

Apart from the required systematizations, simplifications and openness of the model, due attention shall be given to provisions to exclude unjustified use of these advanced programs. This requires due attention for pre- and post-processors, clear help menu's and a well-considered redundancy of the program.

OUTLINE OF THE BASIC STRUCTURE OF THE SIMULATION MODEL

Background Considerations And Assumptions

In the model the development of microstructure is considered as a process of formation of contacts between expanding cement particles. Expansion occurs because the volume of the reaction products exceeds the volume of the dissolving reactant by a factor v, i.e. $v \cong 2.2$. For numerical simulation of the formation of interparticle contacts it is further assumed that [2]:
1. Reaction products are formed in the close vicinity of dissolving cement grains [8];
2. The density of the reaction product (gel) is constant throughout the hydration process and independent of the place where it is formed;
3. Both dissolution and expansion of the cement particles occur concentrically. The rate at which the reaction front proceeds into an anhydrous cement grain is expected to be a function of the chemical composition of the cement.
4. Particles of the same size hydrate at the same rate.
With progress of the hydration process small particles, located in the close vicinity of bigger particles, will gradually become engulfed by and embedded in the outer shell of the latter. The formation of interparticle contacts is considered a basis for simulating microstructural development. For quantification of this interaction process the *stereological aspect* of microstructural development is of paramount importance and compels to consider the *particle size distribution* and the *spatial distribution* of cement particles in the paste.

Stereological Aspects Of Particle Interaction

For the particle size distribution of the cement the well-known Rosin-Ramler distribution

$$G(x) = 1 - \exp(-bx^n) \qquad [g] \qquad (1)$$

has been adopted, with x [μm] the particle diameter and b and n constants which are determined so that $G(x \to \infty) = 1$ g. Although reality is otherwise, the particles are assumed to be spherical.

In the proposed calculation procedure the cement particles are at first assumed to be equally spaced in the paste. An arbitrary particle x is considered to be located in the centre of a "cell", and is called the "central particle". For this homogeneous distribution of the cement particles it is relatively easy to determine the *amount of cement* present in a *fictitious shell* around an arbitrary central particle x. For this purpose a *shell density factor* $\zeta_{sh;x,d}$ has been defined, viz.:

$$\zeta_{sh;x,d} = \frac{\text{amount of cement } [\mu m^3] \text{ in a spherical shell with thickness d}}{\text{total volume } [\mu m^3] \text{ of the shell}} \qquad (2)$$

The course of a shell density factor is shown schematically in the bottom part of Fig. 3a. Going from the periphery of the central particle x in outward direction the shell density gradually increases from zero at the surface of the central particle to the bulk density ζ_{pa} = $[1+\omega_0*\rho_{ce}]^{-1}$, in which ω_0 is the water/cement ratio and ρ_{ce} the specific mass of the cement.

In order the allow, in a way, for the actual randomness of the particle distribution it is assumed in further numerical evaluations that the cement present in a fictitious shell a-round a central particle x consists of particles with diameters < x μm. A consequence of the chosen procedure is that the *number* of particles involved in the interaction process must be counted carefully on penalty of counting them more than once (for details, [2]).

Particle Expansion Mechanism

An arbitrary stage in the hydration process of a central particle x is shown schematically in the upper part of Fig. 3a. At a certain time, say t_j, the degree of hydration of particle x is $\alpha_{x,j}$. For the corresponding *penetration depth* $\delta_{in;x,j}$ of the reaction front it holds:

$$\delta_{in;x,j} = \frac{x}{2} * [1 - \{ 1-\alpha_{x,j}\}^{\frac{1}{3}}] \tag{3}$$

The volume of outer product corresponding with a degree of hydration $\alpha_{x,j}$ follows from:

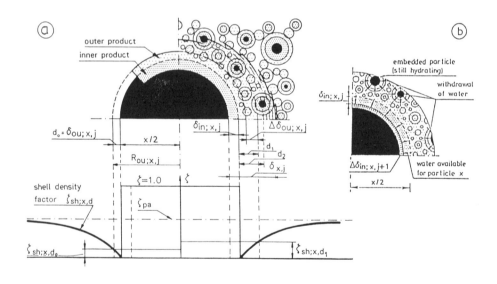

Figure 3   Schematic representation of expansion mechanism and water withdrawal.
a. Upper part - Left: No embedding of particles
   Upper part - Right: Enhanced expansion caused by embedding of neighbour particles
   Bottom part: Shell density curves $\zeta_{sh;x,d}$
b. Water withdrawal mechanism: schematic

$$v_{ou;x,j} = (v-1) * \alpha_{x,j} * v_x \tag{4}$$

with v_x the volume of particle x in its anhydrous state. If no cement would be found in the spherical outer shell which is filled up with outer product of the expanding particle (Fig. 3a, upper-left), the outer radius $R_{ou;x,j}$ of particle x would be:

$$R_{ou;x,j} = [\frac{v_{ou;x,j}}{4\pi/3} + (\frac{x}{2})^3]^{\frac{1}{3}} \tag{5}$$

For the thickness $\delta_{ou;x,j}$ of the outer shell it would follow:

$$\delta_{ou;x,j} = R_{ou;x,j} - \frac{x}{2} \tag{6}$$

In reality a certain amount of cement will be present in the outer shell. The volume of the cement in a shell with thickness $\delta_{ou;x,j}$, called the *directly embedded cement volume* $v_{em;x,j}$, is determined by multiplying the shell volume $v_{ou;x,j}$ with the corresponding shell density factor $\zeta_{ou;x,d_0}$ (with $d_0 = \delta_{ou;x,j}$):

$$v_{em;x,j} = \zeta_{sh;x,d_0} * v_{ou;x,j} \tag{7}$$

The volume of the embedded and partly hydrated cement accounts for an additional expansion $\Delta\delta_{ou;x,j}$ of the outer shell of particle x. This additional expansion, on its turn, results in an increase of the amount of embedded cement. The volume of cement found in the shell with a thickness $\Delta\delta_{ou;x,j}$ is called the *indirectly embedded cement volume*. The total volume of directly and indirectly embedded cement can be calculated analogously to the procedure for the determination of the directly embedded cement (formulae (2) and (7)), albeit that the shell density factor is a little higher now because of the increase of the thickness of the outer shell (Fig. 3a, bottom part: $\zeta_{sh;x,d_1} > \zeta_{sh;x,d_0}$). The increase in the amount of embedded cement, on its turn, causes another additional increase of the outer shell, etc. This expansion mechanism can be written in the form of a geometrical series. Numerical evaluation results in workable expressions for both the thickness of the outer shell of particle x and for the total thickness of the layer of reaction products at time t_j, viz. $\delta_{x,j}$, and the amount of cement embedded in the outer shell of particle x. Adding the amounts of cement embedded in the outer shells of all particles in the system yields the amount of cement involved in the interaction process at time t_j.

Rate Of Penetration Of The Reaction Front

The rate of penetration of the reaction front in an individual cement particle x at time t_j is computed with a *basic rate formula* (in a reduced form):

$$\frac{\Delta\delta_{in;x,j+1}}{\Delta t_{j+1}} = K_0(.)*\Omega_1(.)*\Omega_2(.)*\Omega_3(.)*F_1(.) * [F_2(.) * (\frac{\delta_{tr}(.)}{\delta_{x,j}})^{\beta_1}]^{\lambda} \tag{8}$$

with $\Delta\delta_{in;x,j+1}$ the increase of the penetration depth in time step Δt_{j+1}, $K_0(.)$ the *basic rate factor* [μm/h], $\delta_{tr}(.)$ the *transition thickness* [μm], being the total thickness of the product layer $\delta_{x,j}$ at which the reaction for the particle in view changes from a *boundary reaction* ($\lambda = 0$) into a *diffusion controlled reaction* ($\lambda = 1$). β_1 is an empirical constant. It follows that the first five factors in the right-hand part of eq. (8) are operational during both the boundary reaction and the diffusion controlled stage of the hydration process, whereas the term in straight brackets is only operational in the diffusion controlled stage.

The factors $\Omega_i(.)$ (i=1,2,3) are reduction factors allowing for several effects associated with the state of water in the pore system. The factor $\Omega_1 = \Omega_1(x,\alpha_j)$ accounts for the effect of water withdrawal by embedded and still hydrating particles on the rate of penetration of the reaction front in particle x. The water withdrawal mechanism is schematically shown in Fig. 3b. Examples of values of reduction factors are shown in Fig. 4.
The factor $\Omega_2 = \Omega_2(\alpha_j)$ allows for the distribution of the capillary water in the pore system of the hydrating mass at time t_j and is defined as the ratio of the pore wall area of completely filled pores and the total pore wall area. The reduction factor $\Omega_3 = \Omega_3(\alpha_j)$ allows for the amount of water present in the paste at time t_j. Considerations concerning the effect of the amount of water on the rate of hydration include, in a way, allowance for the chemical composition of the pore water. Assuming a realistic pore size distribution at a certain degree of hydration, thermodynamic considerations enable us to write the relative humidity RH in the pore system as a function of the degree of hydration [2]. This, on its turn, enables to write the combined reduction factor $\Omega_{23} = \Omega_2*\Omega_3$ as function of the relative humidity. An example of a Ω_{23}-RH relationship is shown in Fig. 5, together with reduction factors β_{RH} proposed by Parrott [3] and Jonasson [10].
The effect of temperature on the rate of reaction is accounted for with the function $F_1(.)$. This function is based on the Arrhenius function:

$$F_1\{T,\alpha,C_3S\} = A * e^{-\dfrac{AE\{T,\alpha,C_3S\}}{R*(273+T)}} \tag{9}$$

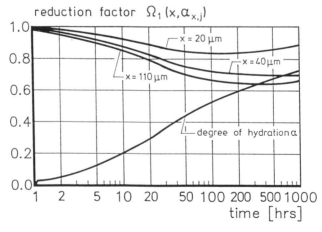

Figure 4   Reduction factor $\Omega_1(x,\alpha_{x,j})$ accounting for water withdrawal by embedded particles (α = overall degree of hydration).

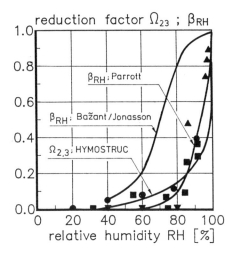

Figure 5   Effect of relative humidity on the rate of hydration. Experimental data indicated with discrete points [2].

in which R is the gas constant (8.31 J/mol°K) and AE the Apparent activation Energy. The latter quantity was found to be function of the actual values of the degree of hydration α, the curing temperature T and the chemical composition, c.q. the C_3S content, of the cement and A a constant [2].

The function $F_2(.)$ is a second temperature function with which the effect of the curing temperature on the morphology of the reaction products is accounted for. What is known about this effect has been interpreted as a densification of the gel when formed at elevated temperatures. This densification goes along with a reduction of the volumetric ratio of the reaction products and the reactant. Hence expansion of particles hydrating at elevated temperatures is less compared with expansion at room temperature. Consequently less interparticle contacts are formed and less gain in strength is to be expected. The function $F_2(.)$ contains a coefficient β_2, which will not be discussed in detail here (for details, see [2]).

Model Parameters

For the determination of the "model parameters" $K_0(.)$, $\delta_{tr}(.)$, β_1 and β_2 an extensive evaluation program has been carried out. In this program over 60 hydration tests were involved, comprising 27 different types of cement with C_3S contents ranging from 15% to 70%. The w/c ratios varied from 0.16 to 0.8, particle size distributions with n-values (eq. (1)) ranging from 0.73 to 3.15 (normally: n $\cong$ 1) and curing temperatures from 4°C up to over 50°C.

The K_0-values could be written as a function of the C_3S content according to:

$$K_0(C_3S) = 0.02 + 6.6 \ 10^{-6} * [C_3S\%]^2 \qquad [\mu m/h] \quad (10)$$

with a standard deviation $\sigma(K_0) = 0.008$ µm/h. It is noticed, that the basic rate factor is the *only* model parameter which influences the rate of the phase-boundary reaction in the early stage of the hydration process. Hence, its value is not affected by the values of the three remaining model parameters $\delta_{tr}(.)$, β_1 and β_2, which become operational no sooner than in the diffusion controlled stage of the process.

The transition thickness $\delta_{tr}(.)$ appeared to be weakly correlated with the C_2S content. Guide values for the transition thickness can be obtained with the expression:

$$\delta_{tr}(C_2S) = -0.02 * [C_2S\%] + 4 \qquad\qquad [µm] \qquad\qquad (11)$$

For the coefficients β_1 and β_2 a value of 2 appeared to be applicable in the majority of cases. Variations in these factors in the range from 1 to 2 could cause variations in the predicted 28-days hydration values of about 5% to 10%. Variations of the same order of magnitude can be ascribed to variations in the gypsum content and the effect of minor compounds [2]. Since the effects of gypsum and minor constituents are not accounted for explicitly in the model yet, attempts to correlate the β-values to the chemical composition of the cement are not warranted. If not indicated otherwise HYMOSTRUC operates with *default values* for the model parameters according to eqns. (10) and (11) and with $\beta_1 = \beta_2 = 2$.

EXAMPLES

Simulation Potential Of The Model

The potential of HYMOSTRUC to simulate the effect of the curing temperature and the w/c ratio on the rate of hydration is illustrated in figures 6 and 7. The experiments are iso-

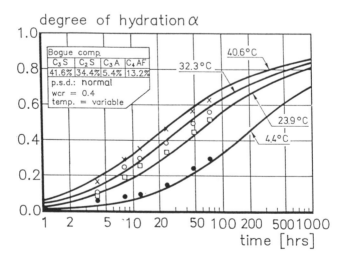

Figure 6 Effect of temperature on the rate of hydration. Experimental data: [9]. Type-II cement. Discrete points: average of four measurements.

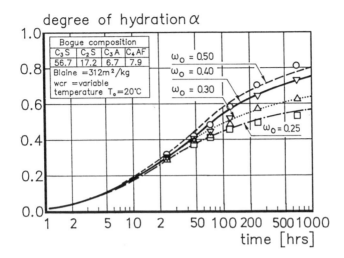

Figure 7 Effect of the w/c ratio on the degree of hydration. Experimental: discrete points [11]. Calculated: solid lines [2].

thermal tests at four different temperatures carried out by Lerch at al. [9] and, again isothermal, tests on pastes with w/c ratios 0.25, 0.3, 0.4 and 0.5 carried out by Danielsson [11], respectively. Test data is given in the insets of the figures. Measured hydration values are indicated with discrete points, whereas the calculated hydration values are given with solid lines.

Predictive Potential Of The Model

The figures 6 and 7 illustrate the potential of HYMOSTRUC to describe the hydration process for different temperatures and w/c ratios, respectively. A real *prediction* of an hydration curve, i.e. a simulation with the *default values* for the model parameters $K_0(C_3S)$, $\delta_{tr}(C_2S)$, β_1 and β_2 is shown in Fig. 8. In the figure two *adiabatic* temperature curves are presented for mixes with $\omega_0 = 0.4$ and $\omega_0 = 0.5$, respectively. The calculated values are indicated with solid lines. For the mix with $\omega_0 = 0.5$ dashed lines indicate the predictions with 5% upper and lower bound values of $K_0(C_3S)$ and values for the transition thickness $\delta_{tr}(C_2S)$ which are 0.5 μm lower and higher than its default values (curves d and c). It can be concluded that the measured adiabatic temperature curves fall within the range bordered by the dashed curves calculated with the upper and lower bound values of the model parameters $K_0(C_3S)$ and $\delta_{tr}(C_2S)$.

Microstructural Development And Strength

The embedded cement volume, i.e. the amount of cement involved in interparticle interactions, is expected to be possible strength parameter. For pastes with w/c ratios $\omega_0 = 0.4$ and $\omega_0 = 0.5$ *absolute* values of the measured compressive strength are presented as a function of the calculated amount of embedded cement per μm³ paste in Fig. 9. It appears that the relationship between strength and embedded cement volume is almost inde-

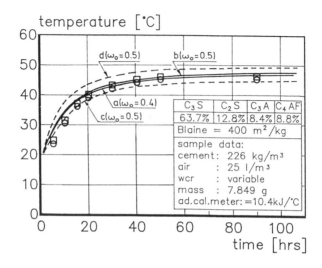

Figure 8   Adiabatic hydration curves: measured and predicted [2].

pendent of the w/c ratio. This information seems to confirm the assumption that strength is correlated with the number of interparticle contacts, provided we may state that the amount of embedded cement is a measure for the number of interparticle contacts.

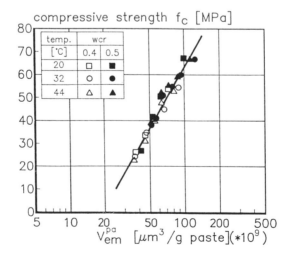

Figure 9   Strength of mortar as a function of the amount of embedded cement v_{em}^{pa} [2].

PRACTICAL APPLICATION

Temperature Predictions In Concrete Structures.

As indicated in the foregoing sections HYMOSTRUC enables to generate adiabatic hydration curves. These curves can be applied as input for computer programs currently in use for analysis of temperature fields in actual concrete structures. Examples of predicted

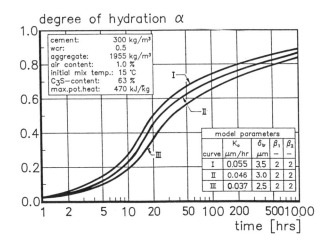

Figure 10 Adiabatic hydration curves illustrating the effect of scatter in the model parameters on the shape of the curves [2].

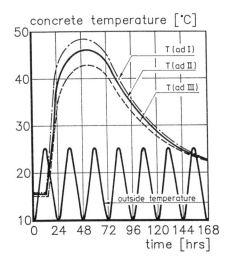

Fig. 11   Temperature fields in a 1 m thick concrete wall for different adiabatic input curves. Calculations carried with computer Code TEMPSPAN [2].

adiabatic input curves and temperature calculations in hardening concrete walls carried out on the basis of these input curves are given in Fig.'s 10 and 11. Mix data is given in the inset of Fig. 10. The adiabatic input curves were determined for three $K_0(C_3S)$-values, viz. the mean value for a C_3S content of 63%, as well as for values corresponding with this mean value minus and plus a (conservative) standard deviation $\sigma(K_0) = 0.009$ μm/h, respectively. Transition thicknesses were chosen so as to simulate - for the cement composition is view -, a more rapid, a moderate and a slow cement. Fig. 11 shows the temperatures in the core of a 1 meter thick concrete wall. The latter calculations were carried out with the computer program TEMPSPAN, a code which calculates the progress of the hydration process and the associated temperatures in hardening concrete structures. It appears that the consequences of the relatively large scatter in the K_0- and δ_{tr}-values results in maximum temperatures from 43°C for the slow cement up to 48°C for the rapid cement.

Probability Of Cracking

With the computer code TEMPSPAN the development of strength and early-age thermal stresses can be represented as a function of time. Strength and stresses being known, the theoretical probability of cracking can be determined, provided that the density functions and standard deviations of both the strength and stresses are known. The calculated probability of cracking is shown in Fig. 12. The calculations refer to a 0.5 m and a 1.0 m thick concrete wall and are carried out for the three adiabatic input curves given in Fig. 10. It appears that the effect of the wall thickness on the risk of cracking dominates the effect of uncertainties in the input curves, i.e. in the scatter of the model parameters for which the adiabatic input curves had been calculated.

From a parametric sensitivity study it could be concluded that the effect of uncertainties in the adiabatic input curves on the calculated probability of cracking are subordinate to

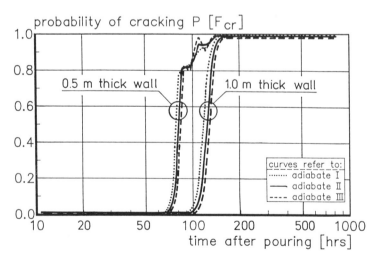

Figure 12   Example of predicted probability of thermal cracking in two hardening concrete walls for the input curves of Fig. 10.

the effect of uncertainties in the modelling of early-age rheological behaviour, c.q. early-age plastic deformations and early-age relaxation. This result greatly enhances the applicability of HYMOSTRUC for executing sensitivity studies concerning the effect of changes in either the mix composition or pouring sequences, insulating schemes, cooling or heating of the concrete and stripping times. It also tells us that further research is required regarding the early-age rheological behaviour of cement-based materials.

DISCUSSION AND PROSPECTS

The potentialities of computer-based models for the simulation of processes and mechanisms involved in hydration and development of microstructure and for macro-level structural analyses can hardly be overestimated [12,13]. In its present form the simulation model model presented in this paper appears to predict adiabatic and isothermal hydration curves for a wide variety of cements, pastes and concretes quite accurately. Sufficiently accurate for adopting them as input curves for macro-level analysis of early-age temperature effects in concrete structures.

An interesting and challenging option of HYMOSTRUC is that it - to a certain extent - bridges the gap between the micro- and meso-level on the one hand, and the macro- or engineering level on the other hand. On both the micro- and macro-level the model can be applied as a powerful research tool for investigations concerning the effects of the chemical composition and the particle size distribution of the cement, the w/c ratio and the initial mix temperature on the macro-level temperature fields in concrete structures.

The particular advantages of computer-based simulation models have not been explained exhaustively in this papers. As most interesting options of them their *openness* and *flexibility* must be mentioned. The step-wise calculation procedures according to which these models operate make it possible to consider a large number of non-linear phenomena and mechanisms from which we would have to refrain if we would stick to a merely analytical approach.

Although most promising results have been obtained already, it is emphasized that the presented model is still in its early stage of development. Further research refers to the potentialities of the model to simulate the effect of extra fines, additives, fly-ashes, the characteristics of the matrix-aggregate interfacial zone and the presence of pressure on the rate of hydration and structure development. There is no doubt, however, that simulation programs as described in this paper will become of increasing importance in the future. This for research on the nano- and micro-level as well as for engineering applications. The development of such programs is a major challenge for the future with, on the one hand, very good prospects but, on the other hand, also the risk of mis-use and misinterpretation of results that have been obtained with advanced programs.

REFERENCES

1. SHEBL, F.A., HELMY, F.M. A new approach on the hydration mechanism of tricalcium silicate. Cem. and Concr. Res., Vol. 15, 1985, pp 747-757.

2. BREUGEL, K. VAN. (1991) Simulation of Hydration and Formation of Structure in Hardening Cement Based Materials. PhD., Delft University of Technology, 1991, 295 pp.

3. PARROTT, L.J., KILLOH, D.C. Prediction of cement hydration. The chemistry and chemically-related properties of cement. Ed. D. Glasser, Univ. of Aberdeen, 1984, pp. 41-53.

4. BROWNMILLER, L.T. The microscopic structure of hydrated Portland cement. Journal of the Am. Concr. Inst., Vol. 14, No. 3, 1943, pp. 193-210.

5. REXFORD, E.P. The microscopic structure of hydrated Portland cement (Disc.). Journal of the Am. Concr. Inst., Vol. 14, No. 6, 1943, pp. 212/1-3.

6. BREUGEL, K. VAN. Development of temperature and properties of concrete as a function of the degree of hydration. RILEM Int. Conf. Concrete at Early Ages, Paris, Proc. Vol. I, 1982, pp. 179-185.

7. BAZANT, Z.P. Solidification theory for aging concrete. Cem. and Concr. Res. Vol. 18, No. 6, 1988, pp. 923-932.

8. TAYLOR, H.F.W., NEWBURY, D. An electron microprobe study of a mature cement paste. Cem. and Concr. Res., Vol. 14, 1984, pp. 565-573.

9. LERCH, W., FORD, C.L. Long-term Study of Cement Performance in Concrete. Journal of the Am. Concr. Inst., 1948, pp. 745-795.

10. BAZANT, Z.P., Ibid. JONASSON, M. Models for calculating times for form-stripping and frost protection. RILEM Int. Conf. Concrete at Early-Ages, Paris, Vol. II, 1982, pp. 213-218

11. DANIELSSON, U. Heat of Hydration of Cement as Affected by Water-Cement Ratio. Proc. 4th. Int. Symposium on Chemistry of Cements, Washington, 1960, pp. 519-526.

12. GARBOCZI, E.J.: Computer-Based Models fo the Microstructure and Properties of Cement-Based Materials. 9th. Int. Conf. Chem. of Cements, New Delhi, 1992.

13. FROHNSDORFF, G, CLIFTON, J., JENNINGS, H., BROWN, P., STRUBLE, L., POMMERSHEIM, J.: Implications of Computer-Based Simulation Models, Expert Systems, Databases and Networks for Cement Research. 8th. Int. Conf. Chem. of Cements, Rio de Janeiro, 1988, pp. 598-602.

PROPORTIONING AND PROPERTIES OF VERY HIGH STRENGTH CONCRETE WITH AND WITHOUT STEEL FIBRES

M Imam

L Vandewalle

F Mortelmans

Catholic University of Leuven

Belgium

ABSTRACT. The methods used to produce concrete with compressive strength exceeding 110 MPa are presented. The data reported in this paper are the results of 23 different trial mixes with and without steel fibres. The role of portland cement, silicafume, superplasticizer, fine and coarse aggregates and their proportioning for use in high-strength concrete are discussed. Special attention is paid to the improvement of splitting strength of high strength concrete by adding steel fibres. The workability of high strength concrete and the problems caused by adding steel fibres are also presented. The validity of the existing equations for measuring the splitting strength of high strength concrete is checked. Some relationships between different strengths of high-strength concrete like compressive strength, and splitting tensile strength are established.

Keywords: High Strength Concrete, Steel Fibre, Splitting Strength, Compressive Strength Development, Mix Proportions, Silicafume, Superplasticizer.

Mahmoud A. IMAM is a Ph.D. candidate in the Civil Engineering Department, Catholic University of Leuven, Belgium. He obtained his BSc (1982) and MSc (1987) in Civil Engineering from Mansoura University, Egypt, where he has worked as an assistant lecturer. His research interests include the areas of fibre reinforced concrete, shear, high strength concrete, and deterioration of concrete by chemical attack.

Professor Lucie VANDEWALLE received her engineering degree in 1981 and Ph.D. in 1988 from the Catholic University of Leuven, Belgium. Her field of research mainly concerns reinforced and prestressed concrete, high strength concrete, fibre reinforced concrete and bond between steel and concrete.

Professor F. MORTELMANS graduated as a civil engineer in 1952, and got his Ph.D. in 1954 at the University of Ghent, Belgium. He worked as a consulting engineer for 15 years and became then a professor at the Catholic University of Leuven (Belgium) in 1969. His main research fields include reinforced and prestressed concrete, fibre reinforced concrete. He has designed several outstanding constructions. Professor Mortelmans is the author of numerous publications concerning concrete.

Concrete 2000. Edited by Ravindra K. Dhir and M. Roderick Jones.
© 1993 Published by E & FN Spon. ISBN 0 419 18120 2.

INTRODUCTION

Currently, it becomes possible to produce concrete with strengths in excess of 110 MPa. However, since not enough information is available on the structural properties of such new material like very high strength concrete, a discussion and much more research concerning construction and design questions are necessary. In this paper the letters (**HSC**) denote Very High Strength Concrete, while Steel Fibre-Very High Strength Concrete is denoted by (**SF-HSC**).

HSC is often called a "brittle material". The failure is sudden and catastrophic, particularly in structures which are subjected to earthquake, blast, or suddenly applied loads. An ideal solution to overcome the serious disadvantage of HSC is to add steel fibres in concrete to convert it into a ductile material and avoid sudden failures. Data reported in this paper is limited to study the improvement of splitting tensile strength of HSC by adding steel fibres. The beneficial value of using steel fibres to improve the ductility of HSC is mentioned elsewhere [6].

The current design codes of practice are mainly based on experimental information obtained from concretes with compressive strength in the range of 21 to 42 MPa. For developing a satisfactory procedure for the design of structures using HSC, additional considerations or modification of existing practice codes may be necessary [15]. Based on the experimental data reported in this paper, some empirical expressions, which could substitute for some of the currently used relationships, have been proposed.

RESEARCH SIGNIFICANCE

The objectives of this investigation are as follows:-

1- To proportion **HSC** mixtures with the desired quality, workability, and strength.
2- To determine whether or not the existing relations between the mechanical properties are valid and applicable for **HSC**.
3- To predict a relationship between compressive strength (f_c) and splitting tensile strength (f_{sp}) for both **HSC** and **SF-HSC**.

EXPERIMENTAL INVESTIGATIONS

Four groups of HSC mixes were examined. Groups P and G were prepared with Porphyry (stone) and Gravel respectively, whereas groups PF and GF were made by adding steel fibres to mixes similar to those in the groups P and G. A general survey of these groups is given in table 1.

Materials:

The cement (**C**) used was portland cement type P50 with compressive strength $\geq$ 50 MPa at 28 days according to European Standard EN 196. The fine aggregate was a 0/5 natural river sand (**S**) with a fineness modulus of 2.6. The coarse aggregates were natural river gravel (**G**) and porphyry stone (**P**). The two sizes 4/14 and 4/16 of gravel, and the three sizes 2/7, 7/10, and 7/14 of porphyry were used.

Table 1. General survey of test program

Group	Number of Mixes	Coarse Aggregate	Steel fibre V_f %	f_c MPa	PZ/(C+SF) % (by weight)	W / (C+SF) (by weight)
P	7	Porphyry	---	95.2 - 111.8	2.5 - 3.5	0.24 - 0.29
G	6	Gravel	---	78.1 - 106.4	2.5 - 3.5	0.24 - 0.29
PF	7	Porphyry	1.0	90.3 - 113.3	3.0	0.30
GF	3	Gravel	1.0	91.6 - 107.2	3.0	0.25 - 0.30

C = Cement   SF = Silicafume   PZ = Superplasticizer   W = Water.

The silicafume (SF) used in this study was ELKEM microsilica, with a specific surface 18.0 m^2/g, and 260 g/l density. To achieve workable mixes with the desired quality and strength, a superplasticizer (PZ) in the form of an aqueous solution was used with a dosage of 2.5 to 3.5 percent by weight of the cement and silicafume. Five types of superplasticizer as a, b, c, d and e from two different manufacturers were used in this experimental program. Hooked steel fibres were used. Fibres were joined together by watersoluble glue to insure good dispersion in the concrete. The volume fraction V_f used was 1.0 %. The fibre length, diameter, and aspect ratio were 50 mm, 0.5 mm, and 100 respectively.

Mix Proportions

The mix proportioning method adopted in this study is based on some facts of designing concrete mixes, as reported elsewhere [3,4,5 and 14]. The concrete composition for mixes without fibre are given in table 2, while table 3 illustrates the composition of steel fibre concrete mixes.

Table 2 Compositions of concrete mixes without fibres (HSC).

MIX	\multicolumn{9} MIX PROPORTIONS "Kg" per cubic meter of concrete									PZ C+SF %	W C+SF
	C	SF	PZ	W	S0/5	G4/16	G4/14	P2/7	P7/10	P7/14		

MIX	C	SF	PZ	W	S0/5	G4/16	G4/14	P2/7	P7/10	P7/14	PZ/C+SF %	W/C+SF
P1	490	---	14.74 (b)*	142.1	458	---	---	458	917	---	3.0	0.29
P2	490	73.6	18.40 (a)	150.9	558	---	---	558	---	558	3.25	0.27
P3	550	82.5	22.14 (a)	151.8	535	---	---	535	---	535	3.5	0.24
P4	550	82.5	15.81 (b)	151.8	540	---	---	540	---	540	2.5	0.24
P5	500	75.0	14.38 (b)	138.0	570	---	---	570	---	570	2.5	0.24
P6	500	75.0	17.25 (b)	143.8	430	---	---	430	860	---	3.0	0.25
P7	500	50.0	16.50 (b)	137.5	442	---	---	442	884	---	3.0	0.25
G1	410	---	12.30 (b)	118.9	588	---	958	---	---	---	3.0	0.29
G2	550	82.5	22.14 (a)	151.8	642	962	---	---	---	---	3.5	0.24
G3	550	82.5	15.81 (b)	151.8	648	---	972	---	---	---	2.5	0.24
G4	500	75.0	14.38 (b)	138.0	683	1026	---	---	---	---	2.5	0.24
G5	500	75.0	17.25 (b)	143.8	654	---	1067	---	---	---	3.0	0.25
G6	500	50.0	16.50 (b)	137.5	672	---	1097	---	---	---	3.0	0.25

C=Cement SF=Silicafume PZ=Superplasticizer W=Water S=Sand G=Gravel P=Porphyry.
* (a) & (b) are two different types of superplasticizer.

Table 3 Compositions of steel fibre concrete mixes (SF-HSC).

| MIX | MIX PROPORTIONS "Kg" per cubic meter of concrete | | | | | | | | | $\dfrac{PZ}{C+SF}$ % | $\dfrac{W}{C+SF}$ |
	C	SF	PZ	W	S0/5	G4/14	P2/7	P7/10	Steel fibre		
PF1	550	82.5	18.98 (b)*	189.8	683	---	835	---	78	3.0	0.30
PF2	500	75.0	17.25 (b)	172.5	485	---	566	566	78	3.0	0.30
PF3	500	50.0	16.50 (b)	165.0	560	---	1120	---	78	3.0	0.30
PF4	500	50.0	16.50 (b)	165.0	420	---	420	840	78	3.0	0.30
PF5	500	50.0	16.50 (c)	165.0	420	---	420	840	78	3.0	0.30
PF6	500	50.0	16.50 (d)	165.0	420	---	420	840	78	3.0	0.30
PF7	500	50.0	16.50 (e)	165.0	420	---	420	840	78	3.0	0.30
GF1	550	82.5	18.98 (b)	189.8	683	835	---	---	78	3.0	0.30
GF2	500	75.0	17.25 (b)	143.8	644	1050	---	---	78	3.0	0.25
GF3	500	50.0	16.50 (b)	154.0	645	1054	---	---	78	3.0	0.28

C=Cement   SF=Silicafume   PZ=Superplasticizer   W=Water   S=Sand   G=Gravel   P=Porphyry.
* (b), (c), (d), and (e) are four different types of superplasticizer.

Experimental Procedure

Concrete mixes were designed, treated, and controlled under similar conditions. The constituents were mixed in dry state for about one minute to ensure the uniformity of the mix. Mixing water and superplasticizer were added gradually and simultaneously during mixing. For mixes without fibres, all contents were mechanically mixed for two minutes, while for fibrous mixes, the contents -except the fibres- were mixed first for one minute, adding the fibres during mixing process, and then mixed for another one minute.

The consistency of fresh concrete for mixes without fibres was measured by the conventional slump test, while both slump and V.B. tests were used for mixes with fibres. Vibrating table was used during placing of concrete to ensure full compaction. To determine the engineering properties of concrete, the following tests and specimen sizes were used:

    - Compressive strength　　: 150 mm plastic cube mould (tested at 7, 28, and 56 days)
    - Splitting tensile strength : 150 * 300 mm iron cylinder mould   (tested at 28 days)
All the test specimens were demolded after 24 hr and then exposed to continuous moist curing until tested (Fog room: 20 ± 2 °C and 95 ± 2 percent relative humidity). For each test the average of three specimens was determined.

TEST RESULTS AND DISCUSSION

Fresh Concrete

The higher surface area of finer particles in HSC mixes adversely affects the workability and makes the concrete more sticky. The use of superplasticizers also affects the period of setting and the rate of slump loss. Thus, the superplasticizer type can be distinguished according to the following effective factors: water-reducing effect, period of required workability, acceptable retardation of set, and price. For ready-mix concrete, a redosage of superplasticizer may be necessary when the automixer reaches the site.

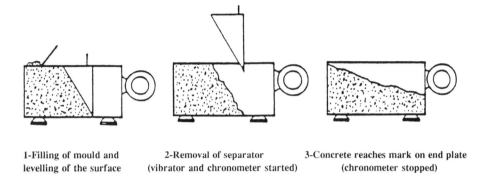

| 1-Filling of mould and | 2-Removal of separator | 3-Concrete reaches mark on end plate |
| levelling of the surface | (vibrator and chronometer started) | (chronometer stopped) |

Fig. 1 Successive stages of the test in the LCL Workabilimeter *(after Rossi P. et al [14])*.

Adding steel fibres to HSC, even in a small amount, leads to a substantial reduction in workability. Improving workability by addition of water leads to a reduction in expected strength and may lead to segregation between fibres and matrix. In the case of HSC, the strength achieved is related to the porosity of the matrix. Adding the fibres in large amounts often tends to entrain air voids in the matrix. This increases the porosity of the matrix, decreases its density, and reduces its strength [10].

As shown in table (4), the mixes made without fibres had slump of 1.0 to 24.0 cm. The slump values of fibre concrete mixes were ranging from 0.0 to 7.0 cm, while the results of the V.B. test for those mixes were 21.0 to 60.0 sec.. It was observed that slump and V.B. measurements can not be related for the same fibre concrete mix. Despite sometimes a low slump (table 4), most of fibre concrete mixes were quite placeable using vibration, consistent with the view that slump is a poor indicator of the workability of steel fibre concrete placed by vibration [7]. V.B. method seems to be better than the slump cone, but they are still not well representative, for measuring the workability of fibre concrete mixes.

In France Lesage [14] developed a device called LCL workabilimeter for measuring the workability of fibre concrete. This method is based on measuring the flow time in the presence of external vibrations. This instrument can test 30 litres of concrete (five times as much as the slump cone or V.B.). The device is an open rectangular mould with an external vibrator and a removable vertical partition that divides it into two parts. One part is filled. The partition is then removed and the vibrator and a chronometer are triggered at the same time. The time the concrete takes to follow to a fixed mark is measured. Fig.1 is a schematic diagram of the test showing the various stages of the procedure used to determine the workability of the concrete. This method seems suitable for measuring workability of steel fibre concrete mixes.

Compressive Strength

The compressive strength (f_c) for ages 7, 28, and 56 days is shown in tables 4 and 5. The strength development of HSC with and without steel fibre expressed as a percentage of 28-day strength is shown in Fig. 2. For non fibre concrete, strengths at 7 and 56 days are 88 and 107 percent of 28-day strength respectively. Whereas for fibre concrete mixes, these percentages were 85 and 104. It can be observed that the strength development of HSC is slightly higher than that of normal strength concrete prepared with the same cement type.

Table 4 Experimental results for concrete mixes without fibre(HSC).

MIX	Slump	f_c MPa	f_c MPa	f_{sp} MPa	f_c MPa	Dry Unit Weight
	Cm	7 days	28 days	28 days	56 days	kg/m³
P1	1.0	86.0	95.2	6.75	102.5	2440
P2	7.6	89.4	105.2	6.64	111.2	2448
P3	11.0	84.0	98.0	6.63	105.7	2442
P4	1.7	85.8	99.7	6.74	104.6	2450
P5	2.0	88.0	98.9	7.71	103.2	2445
P6	16.5	93.9	103.7	7.74	113.2	2462
P7	11.5	100.0	111.8	7.05	119.4	2465
G1	14.0	75.7	78.3	6.74	86.0	2370
G2	19.0	70.5	78.1	5.94	91.2	2374
G3	18.5	83.7	95.7	6.34	99.8	2389
G4	8.0	76.6	87.8	6.07	92.0	2391
G5	24.0	92.6	106.4	6.71	110.0	2401
G6	23.0	84.5	93.5	7.25	101.8	2387

Table 5 Experimental results for fibre concrete mixes(SF-HSC).

MIX	Slump	V.B.	f_c MPa	f_c MPa	f_{sp} MPa	f_c MPa	Dry Unit Weight
	Cm	Sec.	7 days	28 days	28 days	56 days	Kg/m³
PF1	1.0	21.0	80.0	97.2	10.5	101.5	2467
PF2	2.5	23.0	93.8	112.8	12.0	117.0	2478
PF3	0.0	46.0	79.2	90.3	10.77	95.7	2461
PF4	0.0	47.0	92.3	105.3	11.33	109.9	2470
PF5	0.0	55.0	88.5	105.5	10.65	108.5	2474
PF6	0.0	60.0	92.3	108.4	11.23	112.6	2472
PF7	0.0	45.0	98.1	113.3	11.3	115.9	2476
GF1	7.0	26.0	89.3	107.2	11.42	112.5	2418
GF2	0.0	56.0	81.4	94.8	10.23	98.6	2412
GF3	0.0	41.0	80.1	91.6	10.31	94.7	2415

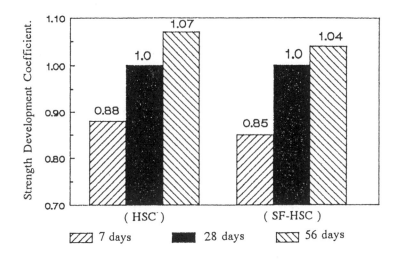

Fig. 2 Compressive strength development of very high strength concrete.

The following observations may be obtained from the results shown in tables 4 and 5:-

1- The mixes prepared with stone exhibited about 12 percent higher in strength than gravel mixes.
2- Silicafume has more significant effect in gravel mixes than stone mixes. The optimum percentage of silicafume in case of stone mixes (P6, P7) seems to be 10%, while this value may raise to 15% in case of gravel mixes (G5, G6).
3- The optimum cement content seems to be 500 kg per cubic meter of concrete. Cement in excess of this maximum value did not produce additional strength (G3, G5) & (PF1, PF3).
4- As shown in tables 4 and 5 - Agree with reference [10] - the compressive strength may increase or slightly decrease (G5, GF2) when fibre are added to concrete. However, it can be generally said that, given the proper fibre and fibre parameters, the strength of fibre reinforced concrete can be made at least equal to that of the concrete without fibres.

Tensile Strength

I- Very High Strength Concrete Without Steel Fibre:

It has been established that the splitting tensile test of the cylindrical specimens gives a more reasonable tensile strength estimation than the direct tensile test or the modulus of rupture test [12]. The relationships between splitting and compressive strength of HSC are rather limited. The few existing relationships are based on data for concrete with a maximum compressive strength of 84 MPa. The validity of these relationships needs to be examined and improved -if necessary- to be representative for concrete with strength up to 115 MPa. An accurate prediction of tensile strength of concrete will help in mitigating cracking problems, improving shear strength prediction, and minimizing failure of concrete in tension. The following is a presentation of some of the existing split-compression relations for high strength concrete (all values of f_c and f_{sp} in MPa):

1- American Concrete Institute (ACI Committee 363) [1]:

$$f_{sp} = 0.59 \times f_c^{0.5} \qquad\qquad 21 < f_c < 83 \;\; MPa \qquad (1)$$

It is reported [1] that the values of splitting strength reach an upper limit for $f_c = 83$ MPa

2- FIP/CEB* [5]:

$$f_{sp} = 0.54 \times f_c^{0.5} \qquad\qquad f_c < 75 \;\; MPa \qquad (2)$$

It is accepted by FIP/CEB [5] that, the tensile strength is not increased for compressive cube strength above 75 MPa.

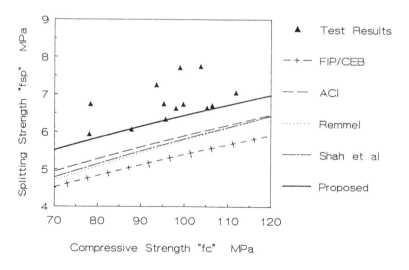

Fig. 3 Splitting Tensile strength of very high strength concrete.

---

* Fédération Internationale de la Précontrainte / Commité Euro-International du Béton.

Table 7   Comparison between the proposed equation and the existing relations for predicting splitting tensile strength of very high strength concrete.

ACI equ.		FIP/CEB equ.		Shah and Shuaib equ.		Remmel equ.		Proposed equ.	
f_{sp} MPa	error %	f_{sp} MPa	error %	f_{sp} MPa	error %	f_{sp} MPa	error %	f_{sp} MPa	error %
5.21	-12.29	4.77	-19.70	5.08	-14.48	5.01	-15.66	5.78	-2.70
5.53	-8.90	5.06	-16.64	5.41	-10.87	5.36	-11.70	6.09	+0.33
5.77	-8.99	5.28	-16.72	5.68	-10.41	5.63	-11.20	6.32	-0.32
5.84	-11.92	5.35	-19.31	5.75	-13.27	5.71	-13.88	6.39	-3.62
6.05	-13.72	5.54	-16.57	5.98	-9.94	5.95	-10.39	6.59	-0.75
6.08	-9.39	5.57	-16.99	6.02	-10.28	5.99	-10.73	6.63	-1.19
5.22	-22.55	4.78	-29.08	5.08	-24.63	5.02	-25.52	5.79	-14.0
5.89	-12.61	5.39	-20.03	5.81	-13.80	5.77	-14.39	6.44	-4.45
5.76	-14.67	5.27	-21.93	5.66	-16.15	5.62	-16.74	6.31	-6.52
6.24	-11.49	5.71	-19.01	6.18	-12.34	6.17	-12.48	6.77	-3.97
5.70	-21.38	5.22	-28.00	5.60	-22.76	5.56	-23.31	6.26	-13.66
5.87	-23.86	5.37	-30.35	5.78	-25.03	5.74	-25.55	6.42	-16.73
6.01	-22.35	5.50	-28.94	5.93	-23.39	5.90	-23.77	6.55	-15.37
	(-14.9)		(-22.0)		(-16.0)		(-16.6)		(-6.4)

Values between parenthesises are the average of error percentages.

3- In Germany, Remmel,G. [13] proposed:

$$f_{sp} = 0.40 \times f_c^{0.58} \qquad\qquad f_c < 80 \ MPa \qquad (3)$$

He [13] also stated that, the splitting strength reaches an upper limit for f_c = 80 MPa.

4- Shah and Shuaib [15] recommended:

$$f_{sp} = 0.462 \times f_c^{0.55} \qquad\qquad f_c < 84 \ MPa \qquad (4)$$

It can be observed, from the previous relations, that it has been accepted by the ACI and FIP/CEB that the splitting strength is proportional to 0.5 power of the compressive strength. Whereas other researchers recommended powers of 0.55 and 0.58. The test results of splitting tensile strength for 13 different HSC mixes are shown in table (4).

The analysis of test results yields the following relations for predicting the design lower bound of splitting tensile strength:

$$f_{sp} = 0.85 \times f_c^{0.44} \qquad\qquad 70 < f_c < 115 \ MPa \qquad (5)$$

In the authors opinion , the tensile strength increases only underproportionally with higher compressive strengths. For example if the compressive strength becomes 200 MPa, perhaps the equation power may be 0.25 instead of 0.44, but there is no upper limit for the splitting tensile strength.

The validity of the existing equations for predicting the splitting strength of concrete with compressive strength up to 115 MPa is checked by extrapolation. Fig. 3 and table 7 compare the test results with the values predicted by both the proposed equation (5) and the existing equations (1 to 4). This comparison shows a better accuracy for the proposed equation. The equations of ACI, Shah and Shuaib, and Remmel are conservative, whereas the equation of FIP/CEB shows underprediction for splitting strength of HSC.

II- Steel Fibre-Very High Strength Concrete:

Steel fibres provide a significant increase of the splitting tensile strength. According to the test results reported in table 5, the splitting strengths of 10 different SF-HSC mixes were ranging from 10.2 to 12.0 MPa. If the results of non fibre mixes (table 4) are compared with those of fibre mixes (table 5), it can be seen that the steel fibre used ($V_f=1\%$) provides an increase of splitting strength of 50 to 70 percent. Predictive relations for splitting strength of SF-HSC are seldomly reported in literature. **Narayanan, R. et al [11]**, proposed a relationship connecting the split cylinder strength (f_{sp}) of steel fibre reinforced concrete with its compressive strength (f_c) as:

$$f_{sp} = \frac{f_c}{a} + b + c \times F^{0.5} \tag{6}$$

where:

a = a nondimensional constant having a value of ($20 - F^{0.5}$).
b = a dimensional constant having a value of 0.7 MPa.
c = a dimensional constant having a value of 1.0 MPa.
F = fibre factor = $(L/D).V_f.d_f$
L/D = fibre aspect ratio, V_f = fibre volume fraction, and d_f = bond factor = 0.5 for round fibres, 0.75 for crimped fibres, and 1.0 for indented fibres.

As mentioned in the same referenc [11], equation 6 has been found to give a quick and safe estimation of split cylinder strength of fibre concrete. Applying this equation to the test results (table 5) to ensure its validity, it results in an underestimation of the splitting strength of SF-HSC.

Table 8 Values of fibre factor I_F in MPa.

V_f L/ϕ f_c MPa	0.2	0.4	0.5	1.0	1.5	2.0
60	1.65	2.55	3.20	3.67	3.98	4.08
70	1.73	2.69	3.38	3.88	4.21	4.31
80	1.83	2.84	3.56	4.09	4.44	4.54
90	1.97	3.05	3.84	4.41	4.78	4.88
100	2.06	3.20	4.02	4.62	5.00	5.12
110	2.16	3.35	4.20	4.83	5.24	5.35
120	2.25	3.49	4.39	5.04	5.46	5.58

Table 9 Experimental and predicted values of splitting tensile strength of SF-HSC.

Test Results		Narayanan et al equ.		Proposed equ.	
f_{sp} MPa	f_c MPa	f_{sp} MPa	error %	f_{sp} MPa	error %
11.30	113.3	7.49	-33.70	11.31	+0.10
12.00	112.8	7.46	-37.82	11.28	-5.93
11.23	108.4	7.23	-35.61	11.08	-1.30
11.42	107.2	7.17	-37.23	11.03	-3.44
10.65	105.5	7.08	-33.52	10.95	+2.80
11.33	105.3	7.07	-37.61	10.94	-3.46
10.50	97.20	6.65	-36.71	10.55	+0.51
10.23	94.80	6.52	-36.26	10.43	+2.03
10.31	91.60	6.35	-38.38	10.28	-0.30
10.77	90.30	6.29	-41.64	10.22	-5.12
			(-36.85)		(-1.40)

Values between parenthesises are the average of error percentages.

On the bases of the strength of a composite material [ref. 8], the efficiency of fibres in concrete [ref. 6, 16], the results of interface bond of fibres [ref. 9], and the obtained test results [table 5], the following relationship for predicting splitting strength of SF-HSC is proposed:

$$f_{sp} = 0.8 \times f_c^{0.44} + \alpha \, I_F \tag{7}$$

where:
  I_F is a dimensional factor depending on the fibre-matrix bond and efficiency of fibres and fibre characteristics (L/ϕ , V$_f$). The values of I_F can be adopted as in table 8.
  α is a nondimensional constant depending on the fibre type as follows:
  $\alpha = 1.0$ for hooked fibres, 0.9 for deformed fibres, 0.5 for smooth fibres.

Table 9 and Fig. 4 show the experimental results as well as a comparison between the values of splitting strength predicted by both equation (6) and the proposed equation (7). It can be seen that the predicted values using the proposed equation give a close agreement with the available test data.

CONCLUSIONS

1- Concrete with compressive strength exceeding 110 MPa can be developed. Maximum Water-Binder ratio of 0.25 is required. Superplasticizer and silicafume are necessary. The dosage of superplasticizer should be determined by trial mixes and can vary from that recommended by the manufacturer (in this study the dosage was doubled without any problems). 10 % of silicafume -by weight of cement- seems to be the optimum percentage in case of stone-concrete, while 15 % in case of gravel-concrete is better.

2- Cement of optimum quality must be utilized. Cement in excess of 500 kg per cubic meter of concrete did not produce any additional strength.

3- The aggregates should be strong enough. Stone-concrete exhibited strength higher than those of gravel-concrete with almost 12 percent.

4- When steel fibres are added to concrete, the compressive strength may increase or slightly decrease, whereas the cylinder splitting strength was increased by 50 to 70 percent.

5- Both V.B. and slump cone are not well representative tests for measuring the workability of SF-HSC. The LCL workabilimeter seems suitable for that work.

6- The compressive strength development of HSC is slightly higher than that of normal strength concrete prepared with the same cement type.

7- The existing equations for measuring the mechanical properties of concrete are valid for concretes with maximum compressive strength of 85 MPa (12325 psi). They give unreliable results for concretes with compressive strength up to 115 MPa (16675 psi). Therefore, some relationships have been developed for such higher strength concretes.

8- The tensile strength increases underproportionally with higher compressive strength, but without any upper limit. The proposed equation (5) shows a better accuracy for predicting the tensile strength of HSC.

9- For (SF-HSC), the predicted values of splitting tensile strength using the proposed equation (7) show a close agreement with the available test data.

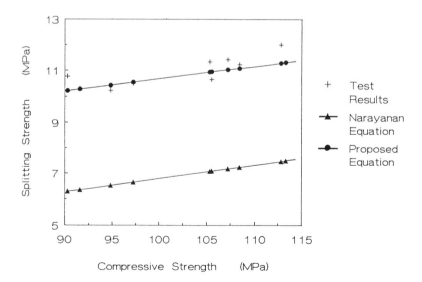

Fig. 4 Splitting tensile strength of steel fibre-very high strength concrete.

ACKNOWLEDGMENTS

The authors are grateful for the help of the assistant staff in Reyntjens laboratory, Leuven. A special thank goes to Bertho Philips for his enthusiasm and assistance. Bekaert international trade, and Addiment have contributed materials to this research, and their contributions are greatly appreciated.

REFERENCES

1. ACI COMMITTEE 363 "State of the Art Report on High Strength Concrete" ACI Journal July-August 1984, pp 364-411.
2. ACI COMMITTEE 544 "Measurement of Properties of Fibre Reinforced Concrete" ACI Materials Journal, November-December 1988, pp 583-593.
3. BLICK R. L. et al "Proportioning and Controlling High Strength Concrete" ACI, SP 46- 9, pp 141-163.
4. DE LARRAD F. "A Method for Proportioning High-Strength Concrete Mixtures" Cement, Concrete, and Aggregates, Vol.12, No. 2, Summer 1990, pp 47-52.
5. FIP/CEB , State of the Art Report "High Strength Concrete" August 1990, 61 pp.
6. IMAM M. et al "The Role of Steel Fibres in Very High Strength Concrete" Under Publication.
7. JOHNSTON C. D. and SKARENDAHL A. " Comparative Flexural Performance Evaluation of Steel Fibre-Reinforced Concrete According to ASTM C1018 Shows Importance of Fibre Parameters" Materials and Structures, 1992, 25 pp 191-200.
8. LIM T. et al "Bending Behavior of Steel-Fibre Concrete Beams" ACI Structural Journal, November-December 1987, pp 524-536.
9. NAAMAN A. and NAJM H. "Bond-Slip Mechanisms of Steel Fibres in Concrete" ACI Materials Journal, March-April 1991, pp 135-145.
10. NAAMAN A. and HOMRICH J. "Properties of High-Strength Fibre Reinforced Concrete" ACI SP 87-13, pp 233-249.
11. NARAYANAN R. and DARWISH Y. "Use of Steel Fibres as Shear Reinforcement" ACI Structural Journal, May-june 1987, pp 216-227.
12. OLUOKUN, f. A. "Prediction of Concrete Tensile Strength from its Compressive Strength : Evaluation of Existing Relations for Normal Weight Concrete" ACI Material Journal, May-June 1991, pp 302-309.
13. REMMEL GERD "Influence of the Tensile Behaviour on the Shear Strength of Longitudinally Reinforced Concrete Members " Proceedings of the first International Conference on Fracture Mechanics of Concrete Structures (FraMCoS1), Colorado, USA, 1-5 June 1992, pp 757-762.
14. ROSSI P. and HARROUCHE N. "Mix Design and Mechanical Behaviour of Some Steel Fibre-Reinforced Concrete Used in Reinforced Concrete Structures" Materials and Structures, 1990, 23, pp 256-266.
15. SHAH S. P. and SHUAIB H. AHMAD " Structural Properties of High Strength Concrete and its Implications for Precast Prestressed Concrete" PCI Journal, November-December, 1985, pp 92-119.
16. VANDEWALLE L. and MORTELMANS F."The Advantage of Long, Thin Steel Fibres " An International Conference on Modern Techniques in Construction 27-28 March 1990 Singapore, pp 630-643.

IMPACT AND TENSILE PROPERTIES OF A THIN CEMENT SHEET REINFORCED WITH GEOTEXTILE MESHES

S Kenai

University of Blida

Algeria

J J Brooks

University of Leeds

United Kingdom

ABSTRACT.Geotextile meshes developed originally for soil stabilisation and reinforcement are inexpensive and highly resistant to chemical attack and such advantages suggested a possible application as reinforcement for thin cement products.Two meshes were used for this investigation: one made of polypropylene and the other was a cellulosic mesh.For comparison purposes two steel meshes were used.The main composite propereties reported are impact strength and direct tension. A falling weight impact test rig and a specially designed gripping device for direct tensile tests were developed and are described.A higher impact dissipated energy, an increase in total crack length and a decrease in their width were observed with increase in the amount of reinforcement. Under direct tensile tests, an increase in reinforcement content leads to an increase in ultimate tensile strength, energy absorption capacity and number of cracks at failure.

Keywords:Geotextile mesh, Impact test, Direct tensile test, Load, Deflection, Dissipated energy, Cracking.

Dr Said Kenai is a Senior Lecturer in construction materials and reinforced concrete, University of Blida, Algeria.His main research interests include fibre reinforced concrete, properties of concrete under dynamic loading, errors and failure in reinforced concrete structures, durability of concrete in hot climates and the use of limestone additions to cement.

Dr J.J.Brooks is a Senior Lecturer in civil engineering materials at the University of Leeds, England.He is the author of numerous papers on creep and shrinkage of concrete, and co-author of text books:"Creep of Plain and Structural Concrete" and "Concrete Technology".He is a full voting member of ACI committee 209, creep and shrinkage of concrete.

Concrete 2000. Edited by Ravindra K. Dhir and M. Roderick Jones.
© 1993 Published by E & FN Spon. ISBN 0 419 18120 2.

INTRODUCTION

Geotextile meshes, developed originally mainly for soil reinforcement and stabilisation, are cheap, lightweight and readily available.They are usually based on polypropylene or polyethylene and hence possess high resistance to corrosion and chemical attack.The use of these polymers in sheet form as reinforcement in cement composites is more advantageous than in fibre form because the mesh can be positioned in the direction of applied stresses.These meshes could favourably be considered as a practical and economical alternative to natural, glass and steel fibres and steel meshes for non-load bearing elements such as roof sheets as those types of fibres could experience some durability problems such as corrosion of steel fibres, rotting and poor dimensional stability for natural fibres and reduction in flexural strength and toughness for glass fibres (1-4).The main mesh used for this investigation is called Lotrak 22/16 and is made of extruded polypropylene tape in the warp direction and extruded polypropylene monofilament in the weft direction.For comparison purposes, a cellulosic mesh called Terram 852c and two steel meshes were also included.Tests in flexure under normal and hot climate curing environments have been reported elsewhere and shown superior performance of these meshes as compared to plain specimens (5). Although, the use of similar meshes in cement has been reported (6-9)with increases in ductility and impact properties due to their viscoelastic characteristics, information on impact behaviour with accurate measuring methods is limited.

This paper presents results on impact and direct tension tests of specimens reinforced with two geotextile meshes.

EXPERIMENTAL DETAILS

Materials and Specimen Fabrication

A 1:1 ordinary Portland cement mortar with a North Notts quartzitic sand (6 00 μ m) and water/cement ratio of 0.5 were used to manufacture all the composite specimens; typical cube strength and modulus of rupture values at 28 days were 59.5 and 3.85 MPa, respectively.The properties of the two geotextile and steel meshes used are shown in Table 1.

To gain insight into the rate sensitivity of the geotextile meshes, tensile tests at different rates of straining were carried out according to ICI guide (10). It was found that the higher the strain rate the higher are the tensile strength and stiffness of the mesh and the smaller the strain at failure.
The composite specimens were small slabs 350x100x15 mm fabricated in purpose-built moulds. The meshes were cut to the right size, a small layer of matrix was placed in the mould and vibrated to remove any voids.Then, a layer of mesh was placed on top of the matrix.After that, another layer of matrix was placed on top of the mesh and worked by hand into the mesh for full impregnation.This procedure was repeated until the required number of layers was embedded.Finally, the top surface was carefully finished with a trowel and covered with polyethylene sheet before being cured in the fog room at 20° C and 98 % R.H until required for testing at an age of 28 days.This manufacture procedure was proved to be successful in obtaining a reasonable distribution of the mesh throughout the thickness of the specimens.

Impact Test Method

A close view of the falling weight assembly and the accelerometer used are shown in Fig.1.The falling weight is a 22N cylindrical piece of steel with a spherical end and the height of drop was 0.5 m. The load is measured by a piezoelectric transducer attached to the falling-weight when it strikes the specimen at mid-span through an impacting pad.The deflection is calculated from the acceleration given by the accelerometer attached to the bottom of the specimen.Tensile and compressive strains were recorded by 60 mm electric strain gauges attached to the bottom and upper faces of the specimen, positioned at 10 mm from the middle to avoid being stripped off. A more detailed description of the rig is given elsewhere(11,12).

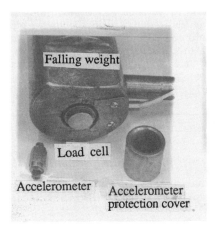

Fig.1 A Close view of the falling weight assembly and the accelerometer used in the impact test rig.

Table 1 Properties of meshes used

Mesh Type	Size lengthxwidth x thickness	Strength	Elongation at break(per cent)
Terram 852c (cellulose)	2x10x0.5	10kN/m	24
Lotrak 22/16 (polypropylene)	0.79x0.79x0.5	22 kN/m(length) 16 kN/m (width)	25
Steel	13x13x0.72	290 MPa	1.2
Steel	25x25x0.85	290 MPa	1.2

ANALYSIS AND DISCUSSION OF IMPACT RESULTS

Typical load, acceleration and compressive strain histories for plain and reinforced specimens are given in Figs. 2 and 3. For plain specimens, the load rises to around 2 kN in approximatively 0.9 msec, followed by a similar period by which the load returns to zero after which the specimen breaks completely and ceases to be in contact with the striker, thus resulting in another contact. For reinforced specimens, the load-time curves show a similar first peak load as with plains pecimens. The load reaches its peak of approximately 2.5 kN at around 0.85 msec. The load shows one or two secondary peaks at a later time and returns to zero in a range of time of 15 to 25 msec.

The acceleration-time curves for both plain and reinforced specimens (Fig.3) rise to a maximum value at about the same time in which the load reaches its peak. The acceleration then continues to oscillate for a much longer period than that of the recorded load. The mid-span deflection of plain specimens increases up to complete failure, whereas for reinforced specimens it reaches a maximum and then starts decreasing. Fig.4 shows that the maximum dynamic deflection is lower the higher the reinforcement content. The time at which maximum deflection occurs is also lower the higher the reinforcement content (Fig.5).

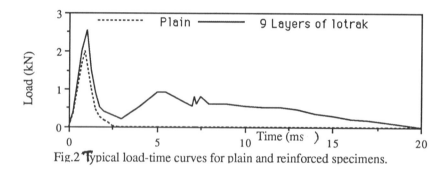

Fig.2 Typical load-time curves for plain and reinforced specimens.

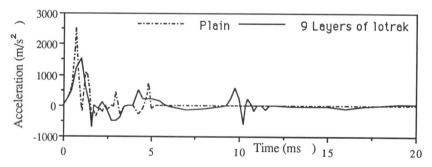

Fig.3 Typical acceleration-time curves for plain and reinforced specimens.

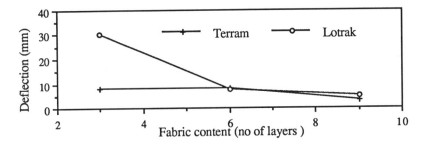

Fig.4 Effect of reinforcement content on maximum dynamic deflection.

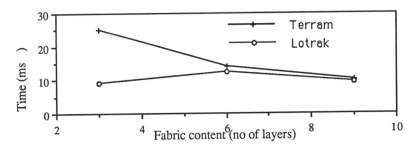

Fig.5 Effect of reinforcement content on time at which maximum deflection occurs.

Dissipated Energy

The potential energy of the falling weight is transformed into elastic, strain, kinetic and applied impact energies.A summary of energy transfer process is given in Table 2.It can be seen that the kinetic energy of plain specimens (around 40% of the applied impact energy)is higher than that of reinforced specimens, whereas the applied energy is less than 40% of that of reinforced specimens.The applied energy ranges from 10 to 30% of the potential energy of he falling weight because of losses at the supports and in the rubber pad. Unlike static energy, impact dissipated energy showed no consistent trend with the type of reinforcement or quantity. Compared with plain mortar, the impact dissipated energy of all reinforced specimens was greater by a factor of 3.2 to 6.8.This is high in comparison with less than 50% increase reported with low volume contents of polypropylene fibres in reference (12).

Cracking Behaviour

At the end of each test, crack pattern, length and maximum residual width were recorded.Obviously, plain specimens produced one single large crack near the mid-span resulting in complete failure and separation of the specimen into two halves. For the reinforced specimens,very fine cracks were produced.The cracks length increases with an increase in reinforcement content but the cracks width decreases (Figs.6 and 7).

Table 2 Influence of reinforcement type and content on the energy process under impact loading; potential (input) energy=10.89 N.m.

Mesh Type	Number of Layers	Impact Energy (N.m)				Static Energy (N.m)*
		Applied	Kinetic	Elastic	Dissipated	
Lotrak 22/16	3	3.18	0.53	0.30	2.35	2.12
	6	2.65	0.00	0.41	2.23	2.18
	9	3.38	0.13	0.45	2.80	2.71
Terram 852c	3	3.22	0.49	0.20	2.53	1.52
	6	2.47	0.14	0.20	2.00	1.93
	9	1.84	0.00	0.20	1.34	1.48
13 mm Steel	1	4.16	2.83	0.08	1.25	1.27
	3	4.22	1.40	0.25	2.57	2.32
25 mm Steel	1	3.52	1.93	0.06	1.53	1.36
	3	4.37	1.21	0.22	2.94	2.22
Plain	0	0.50	0.40	0.24	0.41	0.17

*Calculated from the area of the load-deflection curves under 4 point loading.

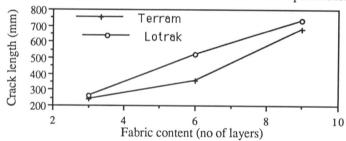

Fig.6 Effect of fabric content on crack length.

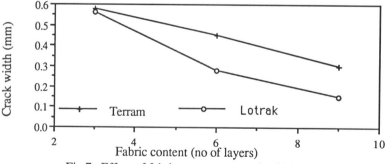

Fig.7   Effect of fabric content on crack width.

Comparison With Steel Meshes

The behaviour of specimens reinforced with steel meshes was similar to that of specimens reinforced with geotextile meshes. The peak loads and impact dissipated energy were comparable. However, the width of cracks for steel mesh reinforced specimens was higher.

DIRECT TENSILE TEST METHOD AND RESULTS

To ensure stable uniaxial loading and avoid problems of stress concentrations near the grips and eccentricities resulting from misalignment in a direct tensile test, the specimen shape of Fig.8 was used.A specially designed gripping device was manufactured .The tests were conducted at the age of 28 days at a constant rate of head displacement of 2mm/min.Typical load-extension curves for plain and composite specimens are shown in Fig.9.From these curves, one can distinguish three stages similar to those observed for ferrrocement and FRC(13-16).

1) *Elastic stage:* in which the load-extension curve is linear as the load is mainly carried by the matrix.

2) *Multiple cracking stage:* which starts after cracking of the matrix and thus load is transmitted to the mesh which elongates under additional load and transfers it back to the matrix by interfacial shear stress so that the matrix will crack again resulting in fluctuation of the load due to the formation of new cracks.

3) *Failure stage*: during this stage the cracks ceased to form but increase in width.The load is mainly carried by the mesh.

An increase in reinforcement content tends to slightly reduce the cracking load of the composite as compared to plain specimens because of the low elastic modulus of the meshes used.However, an increse in reinforcement content increases considerably the ultimate tensile strength.

The energy absorption capacity as measured by the area under load-extension curves also increases with increase in reinforcement content.This is mainly due to the high extension at failure which reached more than 10%.

The crack patterns of specimen under direct tension were similar to those tested in flexure.All cracks run almost perpendicular to the direction of the applied tensile load.Typical crack patterns are shown in Fig.10.It can be clearly seen that an increase in reinforcement content gives an increase in the number of cracks.

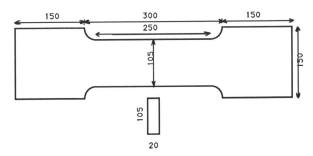

Fig.8 Dimensions (mm) of direct tensile test specimens.

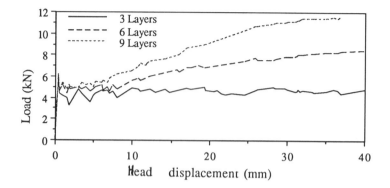

Fig.9 Typical load-displacement for composite specimens reinforced
with lotrak meshes.

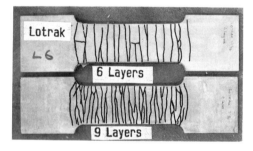

Fig.10 Typical crack patterns.

CONCLUSIONS

1) The geotextile meshes used in this investigation improved the impact dissipated energy of plain specimens by three to seven times.

2) Under impact load, an increase in reinforcement content leads to a decrease in maximum dynamic deflection, an increase in total cracks length and a decrease in cracks width.

3) Under direct tension, the first cracking load decreases with increase in reinforcement content whereas the ultimate tensile strength ,energy absorption capacity and number of cracks increase.

4) These geotextile meshes could be used in roofing elements for low cost housing in developing countries and in other semi-structural elements to replace steel meshes or fibres in severe environments such as that of the middle east where high temperature and corrosive environments are encountered.

REFERENCES

1)KOSA, K, NAAMAN, AE AND HANSEN, W. Durability of fiber reinforced mortar. ACI Materials Journal, May-June 91, pp 310-319.

2)BIJEN, J. Durability of some glass fiber reinforced cement composites. ACI Journal, Proceedings, vol.80, No.4 , July-August 1983, pp 305-311

3)GRAM, HE. Durability of natural fibres in concrete, Report No.5-100 44, Swedish Cement & Concrete Research Institute, Stockholm, 1983.

4)CUSENS,AR. Coorrosion of ferrocement-a review.Journal   of Ferrocement, Vol.5, No.4,1985, pp 365-370.

5)KENAI,S, BROOKS,JJ AND DALTON, DC. Properties of polypropylene-mesh reinforced cement composites, Proceedings of the Fourth Int.Conf.on Polypropylene Fibres, Plastics and Rubber Institute,Nottingham,UK,sep.87, pp 51/1-6.

6)GARDINER, T AND CURRIE, B. Flexural behaviour of composite cement sheets using wooven polypropylene mesh fabrics, Int.Journal of Cement Composites, Vol.5, No.3, August 83, pp 193-97.

7)GARDINER, T, CURRIE, B AND GREEN, H. Flexural behaviour of a cement matrix reinforced with polypropylene mattings, Third Int.Conf.on Polypropylene Fibres & Textiles,Oct.83, York (UK), pp 38/1-8.

8)GARDINER, T, CURRIE, B AND GREEN, H. Performance of civil engineering products made from a cement matrix reinforced with polypropylene mattings, Third Int.Conf.on Polypropylene Fibres & Textiles, Oct.83, York (UK), pp 39/1-7.

9)SWAMY, RN AND HUSSIN, MW. Woven polypropylene fabrics: an alternative to asbestos for thin sheet applications, Proccedings of Int.Conf. on Recent Developments in Fibre Reinforced cements & Concretes, Cardiff (UK), Sep.89, pp 90-101.

10)ICI FIBRES. A guide to test procedures used in the evaluation of civil engineering fabrics, terram publication, UK, Nov.81.

11)BROOKS, JJ AND KENAI, S. Impact properties of polymer grid reinforced cement mortar, The Int.Journal of Cement Composites & Lightweight Concrete, vol.11, No.3, 1989, pp 1-7.

12)KENAI, S. Properties of cement composites reinforced with geotextile meshes, Ph.D Thesis, univ.Leeds (UK), 1988, pp 248.

13)BENTUR, A, MINDESS, S AND SKANLY, J. Reinforcement of normal and high strength concretes with fibrillated polypropylene fibres, proccedings of Int.Conf.on Recent Devp.in FRC&Concretes, Cardiff, Sep.89, pp 229-239.

14)NAAMAN, AE AND SHAH, SP, Tensile tests of ferrocement, ACI Journal, Sep.71, pp 693-98.

15)PROCTOR, BA, OAKLEY, DR AND WIECHERS, W. Tensile stress-strain characteristics of glass fibre reinforced cement, Proceedings of Conf.on Composites, Standard-Testing and Design, 1974, pp 106-7.

16)HUGHES, DC AND HANNANT, DJ. Brittle matrices reinforced with polyalkene films of varying elastic moduli, Journal of Materials Science, Vol.17, 1982, pp 508-16.

17)DESAI, P AND ELKHOLY, SA. Lightweight fibre reinforced ferrocement in tension, Cement and Concrete Composites, Vol.13, 1991, pp 37-48.

EXTERNALLY REINFORCED CONCRETE:
A RETHINK OF STEEL/CONCRETE COMPOSITES

P G Lowe

University of Auckland

New Zealand

Dedicated to the memory of A.L.L. Baker (1905-1986)

ABSTRACT. As we approach the next century we should probably expect that change is likely to accelerate. In some sense change is always with us, and conferences such as this one are encouraging us to think in these terms.

What is being thought of as a possible change here is a radical rethink of the way in which steel and concrete are used in composite in present day reinforced concrete. For around four generations the majority use of steel in composite with concrete has been as steel bar wholly embedded in the concrete.

The proposal examined here is that, instead, the steel be provided as a **thin casing inside** which the concrete is cast. Members of all sorts, beams, columns, other elements can be made in this way. The driving force for such a proposal comes from the prospect such a scheme offers for reducing **costs**. The material has been called **Externally Reinforced Concrete.**

Keywords: Composite, externally reinforced concrete, cost.

Professor Peter G. Lowe, is Professor of Civil Engineering in the University of Auckland, N.Z. and was previously Professor of Structural Engineering at the University of Strathclyde, Glasgow, Scotland. His main research interests are in structural mechanics and particularly, structural innovation in relation to cost reduction of construction.

Concrete 2000. Edited by Ravindra K. Dhir and M. Roderick Jones.
© 1993 Published by E & FN Spon. ISBN 0 419 18120 2.

INTRODUCTION

Reinforced concrete has remained relatively unchanged as a construction material for a long time. Some of the things which have been changing are the cost make-up of the material, aspects of the associated technology such as precasting and the vast amount of related literature which continues to accumulate.

Yet even today there are fundamental aspects of the technology which are crude, such as the continued widespread use of bar lapping as a means of extending bar lengths. And it may happen that the present day technology remains unchanged in many places globally for another generation or more.

But there may also be scope to largely reassess how steel/concrete composites can be achieved, which produce a material with comparable performance but which can produce a finished product for less cost - perhaps substantially less cost. There could also be the prospect of a material with **substantially better performance**, but this aspect will not be pursued here.

The proposal discussed here is to construct the steel and concrete composite not by using bar reinforcement, but by supplying the steel as a casing inside which the concrete is cast. The novelty of the proposal is that it is envisaged that **all** types of structural elements be made in this way. Also the casings which serve the 'best' purpose, 'best' in the sense of achieving cost reduction through mechanisation of handling and all the manufacturing operations, are likely to be very thin, much thinner than current uses of Rolled Hollow Section when concrete filled. The material will be termed **Externally Reinforced Concrete,** and abbreviated to **E.R.C.**.

If the lower cost is to be achieved primary aims should be to ensure that more of the material handling, shaping and erecting can be mechanised. There is good scope to achieve at least some of these with E.R.C., since despite reinforced concrete's long history and the massive amounts of technical and commercial thought which have been applied to the technology, considerable manual manipulation of the materials is still required by present day technology. And clearly, the elimination of temporary formwork requirements is an immediate saving.

Visually such a composite might look like steelwork and some aspects of current steelwork technology could be borrowed, but only about ten percent of the finished member weight would be contributed by the steel.

If such a composite succeeds in meeting technical, economic and aesthetic requirements then the way might be open to draw the presently separate technologies of steelwork and reinforced concrete into a single hybrid technology which would owe something to each current technology. This in turn should produce overall benefits by largely eliminating the present duplication of technologies.

An associated benefit for the civil engineering profession could be, in the fullness of time, a simplification in education and training of the young engineer. Where at present material codes for steelwork are heavy with detail for design against buckling in its various forms, much of this would not be required, since steel used in the proposed new composite, though very thin, is not limited by buckling considerations since it is not required to be load carrying in compression.

Equally, many of the aspects of current concrete technology such as cover requirements, shear strength limits, lapping, cracking, curing etc. are largely taken care of automatically in the new composite.

To recap then, what is proposed is a steel/concrete composite consisting of thin steel cases as the reinforcement inside which the concrete is cast. The material will be termed **Externally Reinforced Concrete** and abbreviated to **E.R.C.**.

FLEXURAL BEHAVIOUR

Any serious building material must produce acceptable behaviour in flexure. The author's research team which has been investigating E.R.C. for the past several years has concentrated on flexural behaviour studies and only after this had been shown to be satisfactory were other aspects investigated, such as the jointing of members in this material.

The data shown in FIGURE 1 relate to a beam in flexure which was about a year old at the time of test. From the experimental plot and the visual observation made at that time, the behaviour was assessed as satisfactory and that is all that is being sought at this time.

The number of beams of various sizes which have now been studied up to failure is more than twenty. Typical features are that the beam strength rarely shows a reduction at large distortion or curvature, probably because, although the compression concrete crushes this is not a signal for subsequent reduction in strength through spalling. The crushed material remains in place and continues to bear load. There is no analogue of the overreinforced situation in conventional reinforced concrete - all E.R.C. beams essentially behave as "under reinforced" and will continue to support increasing load beyond the stage when concrete crushes in compression and on until the steel case fractures in tension.

A suitable theory to explain the experimental observations can be obtained by using the basic concepts set out in the Whitney paper of 1942, Ref.(1). As an approximate procedure, and for the beam proportions shown in FIGURE 1, at ultimate load about **half** the perimeter of the casing can be shown to yield in tension.

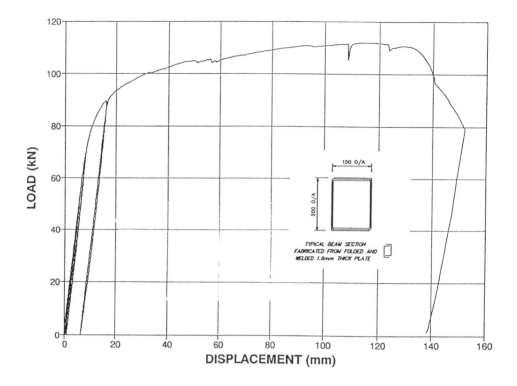

FIGURE 1   Typical Beam Flexure Response

The load-displacement data shown in FIGURE 1 relates to an E.R.C. beam 150 mm wide by 200 mm deep, tested in two point loading with a lever arm of 900 mm. The casing steel was 1.6 mm thick and was shaped into two channel section pieces which were meshed to give 3.2 mm flanges and 1.6 mm webs. It was about a year old at test, and was recycled from the frame described later in this paper. It was originally 4 m long, and had had plastic hinges develop near the ends.

The measured maximum moment of resistance is, from FIGURE 1,

$M_R = \dfrac{112}{2}$ x 0.9 = 50.4 kNm . An estimate, based on a measured ultimate steel

stress of f_u = 440 MPa and f_c = 30 MPa is
$$M_R = 440. 1.6. (2.150.161 + 2.100.111)/10^6$$
$$= 49.7 \text{ kNm}$$
which is adequate agreement.

Final failure in an E.R.C. member, especially a member in flexure, means rupture of the casing. Usually well before this stage is reached, the concrete in compression crushes. This occurred in the beam whose test results are shown in FIGURE 1, but such crushing does not herald loss of current strength, since the crushed material is 'contained' and remains load bearing. It is not easy to detect from the plot in FIGURE 1 when the crushing occurred, and in a sense it is unimportant.

So the characteristic shape of a typical flexural response is of an elastic, followed by a yielding/ductile response. The yielding behaviour will continue, through the phase of compression concrete crushing until finally the casing ruptures. At this stage the member deflections are very large, typically half the member depth.

Compression steel in the casing is likely to buckle but this has little effect on the capacity of the steel casing to retain the crushed compression concrete at ultimate load. The deformation capacity is very impressive.

Means of comparison, especially with conventional reinforced concrete, are probably useful. One suggestion made elsewhere, Ref.(2), is for a Performance Index (P.I.) given by

$$P.I. \equiv \frac{M_R}{C_s}$$

where M_R is the moment of resistance of the beam and C_s is a 'Cost' Quantity which is itself defined by

$$C_s \equiv f . \frac{V_s D}{L}$$

where f is a representative stress, yield or ultimate, V_s is the **volume** of steel in a beam length L and depth D.

This index is non-dimensional and must be less than unity. A value greater than 0.5 is creditable. For the beam data in FIGURE 1 the value is 0.58. But it is quite straight forward to increase the P.I. value of an E.R.C. beam by moving more of the steel into the tension zone.

JOINTING OF E.R.C. MEMBERS

If a building system based on E.R.C. is to be possible, then efficient methods for jointing of beams to columns and other elements will be required.

Several systems have been experimented with and there are improvements possible to all the systems so far tried.

The basic configuration used has been flange plates for the beams which penetrate through the columns, with or without web plates.

Beams with moment capacities from 10 kNm to 400 kNm and depths from 100 mm to 500 mm have been joined in this manner to columns. The requirement sought was a full moment resisting joint, and the general outcome has been adequate strength, but sometimes a need to improve stiffness in specimens where cyclic reversing moments were applied.

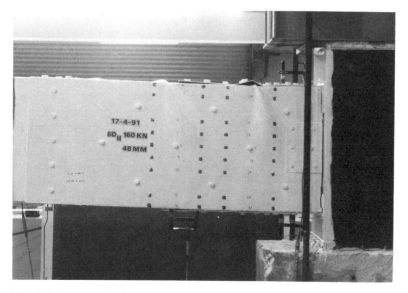

PLATE 1.   Typical Beam/Column Joint.

Typical experimental members are shown in PLATE 1. The full data are reported in Ref.(3).

A COMPLETE STRUCTURE

Based on the experimental results for single member performance, a complete structure has been designed, fabricated, built and tested. See Plate 2.

All the fabrication of cases was contracted out to a sheetmetal fabricator where previously most fabrication had been done in the School of Engineering's own workshop. This was done to check on the practicality of the fabrication, and provide some cost data.

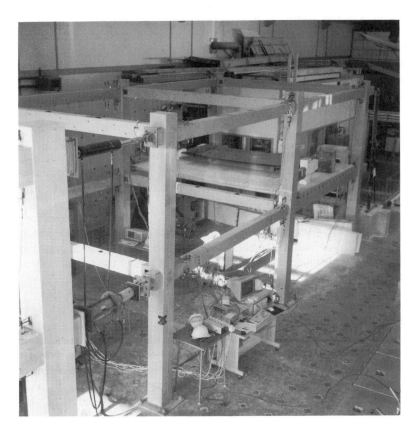

PLATE 2.   Two Storey Frame and Reaction Frame.

The main framework spanned an area 4 m x 8 m and stood 3.78 m high, with six columns and fourteen beams. The empty, but fully assembled, framework weighed about 12 kN. The completed frame when filled weighed about 70 kN. Some of the beams were not filled in order that they could be reused in another application. Plate 2 shows this structure together with a smaller but stronger structure which was used as a reaction frame in the test sequence.

A slab was cast on one bay and one storey of the frame. This can be seen in Plate 2 but will not be discussed further.

The frame pair was tested to destruction by applying beam level horizontal cyclic loads to simulate earthquake forces.   At the ultimate load a state of hinge collapse was produced, with hinges forming at ten sections in each frame.

The member data are: columns 250 x 250 mm x 2.5 mm thick, beams 150 x 200 x 1.6 mm with 3.2 mm flanges (See FIGURE 1). The initial frame stiffness, for horizontal forces kept in the ratio upper storey 1: lower storey 0.75, and the stiffness defined as upper storey force/upper storey (horizontal) displacement, was about 4 kN/mm. Conventional theory applied to these data, and assuming full composite action between steel and concrete, gives a similar figure.

In all about 60 cycles of push/pull load under increasing amplitudes were applied. The hinges formed in turn, beginning at the centre column foot. When the final hinges formed (ten in all/frame) the upper storey force reached 200 kN.

The computed full-plastic moments for the columns of 90 kNm and the beams of 50 kNm, when used in a hinge collapse calculation, confirm the 200 kN figure.

A significant part of the strength demonstrated resulted from the beam hinges forming at approx. 700 mm from the column faces, and the column foot hinges at about 300 mm from the lower ends of the columns. If all these hinges had migrated to the ends of the relevant members then the frame capacity would have been only about three quarters of the observed capacity.

Most of the features designed for were realised in the framework, including beam hinges at approx. 0.7 m from the column faces. The columns at each end of the framework remained essentially straight while hinging about a section in each column approx. 0.3 m from the base, as intended. The end beam/column joints essentially remained rigid, with the hinging in the beam at a section just beyond where the beam flange plates terminated. All site assembly was with regular M16 bolts in groups of six. The tolerances aimed for were for a few mm and were achieved.

The only major short-fall in behaviour was the column-beam junction at the first floor level on the frame centre line. The joint was adequately strong, but the hinging occurred essentially within the column.

DISCUSSION

The main motivation for considering Externally Reinforced Concrete has been to devise a steel/concrete composite which has acceptable strength and stiffness properties, but which also enables all the fabrication of steel components (the cases) to be essentially automated. This in turn should reflect favourably in the cost of the product.

These components provide a totally prefabricated environment and assembly of the empty cases is both a quick and accurate operation. These light-weight components reduce cranage requirements and/or may encourage use of subassemblies, made at ground level and lifted into final position. The filling with concrete can be achieved from just a few points if desired, and would be by pump in most cases. The casings are thus permanent formwork for the in situ concrete. For the frame illustrated, no temporary propping of beams was needed during the filling operation.

Some cost studies have been made and are reported in Ref.(4). But these studies do not reflect savings possible through quantity fabrication, the supply of fabrication data on floppy disc and a number of other factors.

The credibility of the construction in E.R.C. in the long run will depend on the achieved cost, and this will in turn be affected unfavourably if E.R.C. cannot be protected from **FIRE** by less expensive means than are currently available for conventional steelwork.

Some fire tests have been completed, including for members under load and in a fire environment. The trends are that the heat sink capacity of the concrete is significant in slowing the rate of casing heating. But it seems likely that for exposures beyond about 30 minutes specific protection of some sort will be needed.

E.R.C. is more fire affected than conventional reinforced concrete. However, because of the hybrid nature of E.R.C., lying as it does between the current steel and concrete technology, FIRE protection can probably be enhanced by adopting any of a whole variety of measures. Some of these are presently being investigated.

CONCLUSIONS

The research programme which has been investigating E.R.C. as a potential building material has made considerable progress in just a few person-years of effort. The outlook for achieving a measure at least of cost reduction over either current dominant building technology seems promising.

Besides new construction in E.R.C. there is scope to repair damaged structures, especially damaged conventional reinforced concrete structures. Additionally, strengthening understrength structures made from a variety of materials is in context with E.R.C. principles.

Both high and low "tech" E.R.C. can be envisaged. What has been described so far could be termed "high tech" E.R.C.. A "low tech" E.R.C. might be a composite material using any of a variety of tensile-strong materials as a containment, with the filling perhaps a solid waste material.

When it comes to deciding what to do with a structure which has no future purpose, recycling of some or all of the materials is becoming a necessity, and is certainly desirable. E.R.C. can come close to an ideal material in this regard, since the casings can be relatively easily removed and the contents probably broken into reusable blocks comparatively easily.

There may be yet other quite different steel/concrete composites possible. What has been attempted in this paper is to consider one radical departure from current building technologies. We must await the verdict of the future as to the realisable virtues and drawbacks.

ACKNOWLEDGEMENTS

Several graduate students and friends have contributed to the E.R.C. studies, but I especially note the contributions of Choong, K.C., S.M. Dwyer and N.A. Charman. Industry support has been provided by Milburn (NZ) Ltd., McConnell-Dowell Corp. Ltd., Mainzeal Group Ltd and BHP/NZ Steel Ltd. and this has been a very important component in the programme.

REFERENCES

1.   WHITNEY, C.S. Plastic theory of reinforced concrete design.   Trans. A.S.C.E., 1942, Vol 107 pp. 251-282.

2.   LOWE, P.G. and CHOONG, K.C. Externally reinforced concrete. Twelfth Australasian Conf. on Mechanics of Structures and Materials, Brisbane, 1990 pp. 177-182.

3.   CHOONG, K.C. Full size externally reinforced concrete beams under cyclic loading - experimental observations, Internal Report, University of Auckland, 1991.

4.   LOWE, P.G. Externally reinforced concrete - a new steel/concrete composite. Institution of Professional Engineers New Zealand, Annual Conference, Christchurch, 1992 pp. 461-471.

CHEMICALLY PRESTRESSED CONCRETE BEAMS REINFORCED WITH FRP ROD

Y Tsuji

C Hashimoto

Gunma University

Japan

ABSTRACT. The flexural crack widths of beams reinforced with fiber reinforced plastic (FRP) are large compared with RC beams reinforced with reinforcing steel bars due to small tensile rigidities of the FRP. As expected from the strain increment of tensile reinforcement in FRP beams, the deflections of FRP beams are larger than those of RC beams. In order to improve the mechanical behavior of FRP beams, chemically prestressed concrete beams (CPC beam) were introduced by using expansive cement concrete. Based on the flexural test results, it was assured that the effects of chemical prestress on the flexural crack initiation, the flexural crack widths and the deflections, and the shear strength of FRP beams were obtained. The amount of chemical prestress in CPC beam is influenced by the FRP arrangement as well as the amount of expansive admixture. The degree of influence can be evaluated by the concept of "Work Rule" proposed by the authors. Consequently, it is possible to estimate the effects of chemical prestress on the mechanical behavior of FRP beams quantitatively.

Keywords: FRP, Expansive Concrete, Chemical Prestrain, Layered Model, Lattice Spacing, Lattice Intersections, Failure Mode

Yukikazu Tsuji is a professor in the Civil Engineering Department at Gunma University, Gunma, Japan. He received his Doctor of Engineering Degree from the University of Tokyo in 1974. His research interests include behavior of reinforced concrete structures, chemically prestressed concrete, and properties of fresh concrete. He is a member of JSCE, JCI, ACI and IABSE.

Chikanori Hashimoto is an associate professor in the Civil Engineering Department at Gunma University, Gunma, Japan. He received his Doctor of Engineering Degree in 1989 from the University of Tokyo. His current research involves pumpability of fresh concret, flowability of fresh concrete in a concrete pump or a truck agitator and visualization techniques of concrete flow in pipes. He is a member of JSCE and JCI.

Concrete 2000. Edited by Ravindra K. Dhir and M. Roderick Jones.
© 1993 Published by E & FN Spon. ISBN 0 419 18120 2.

INTRODUCTION

Steel is an excellent reinforcing material for concrete and is widely used, but when reinforcing steel in a concrete structure is corroded, the reinforcing effect of the steel is impaired and this becomes the main cause of shortening of the structure's life. In contrast, fiber reinforced plastic (hereinafter referred to as "FRP") is drawing interest as reinforcing material in place of steel due to its excellent corrosion resistance. However, FRP, compared with reinforcing steel, has difference such as lower modulus of elasticity, complete elasticity and low failure strain, and low bond strength with concrete. Consequently, a concrete beam reinforced with FRP (hereinafter referred to as "FRP beam") has the shortcomings that flexural crack width and deformation are larger than for a reinforced concrete beam (hereinafter referred to as "RC beam"), along with which shear yielding strength becomes small. Further, when calculating flexure yielding strength and shear yielding strength, it is thought problematic to use the conventional method for RC beams without modification.

In this report, the results of experiments conducted to improve the mechanical properties of FRP beams by using expansive concrete to induce chemical prestress in concrete and chemical prestrain of initial tensile strain in FRP, respectively, and the results of studies to quantitatively grasp the effects of the above are described.

SPECIMENS AND METHODS OF TEST

The FRP used for these experiments was fabricated in lattice form covering alkali-resistant glass fiber with vinyl ester resin. It was anticipated that bond with concrete could be secured by the intersecting points of lattices. The dimensions of lattices were of the four kinds of $5 \times 10, 10 \times 10, 15 \times 10$, and 20×10cm, and two kinds of FRP, G10 and G13, with tensile strengths corresponding respectively to those of JIS deformed bars, D10 and D13, were used. For comparison purposes RC beams using D10 and D13 reinforcing bars were also made. The mechanical characteristics of the reinforcing materials used are given in Table 1. Photograph 1 shows the FRP rod used for these experiments.

Table 1 Mechnical characterictics of various reinforcing materials

Kind of reinforcing material		F R P		Reinforcing steel(SD35)		
		G10	G13	D10	D13	$\phi 6$
Fiber bundle (number)		30	50	---	---	---
Fiber mixture ratio (%)		42.2	43.3	---	---	---
Apparent cross-sectinal area(mm^2)	Fiber bundle	28.5	47.5	---	---	---
	Resin	39.0	62.1	---	---	---
	Total cross section	67.5	109.6	71.3	126.7	28.3
Tensile yielding strength(kgf/filament)		5574	8935	4137	5448	1562
Tensile or yielding strength (kgf/cm^2)		5258	5152	3970	3750	3450
Elastic modulus (x10^6 kgf/cm^2)		0.333	0.333	2.1	2.1	2.1
Tensile rigidity· (×10^6 kgf)		0.225	0.370	1.498	2.661	0.594

Tensile rigidity·= Total cross-sectional area × Elastic modulus

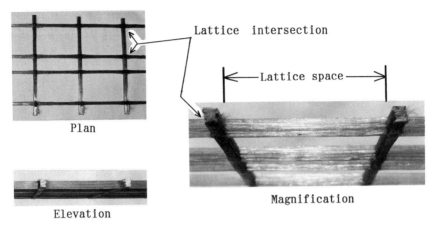

Lattice intersection

Lattice space

Plan

Magnification

Elevation

Photograph 1 The FRP rod used for experiments
(Case of G13, lattice spacing =15cm)

The cement used was ordinary portland cement, the expansive agent an ettringite-base material, and the aggregates Gunma Prefecture Watarase River river sand (specific gravity 2.61, fineness modulus 2.77, absorption 2.49%) and river gravel (specific gravity 2.63, fineness modulus 6.29, absorption 1.50%). The mix proportions were held constant at water-binder ratio 0.50, unit water content 168 kg/m^3, sand-aggregate ratio 46%, slump 8cm, and air content 4%, while the unit expansive agent content (E) was varied at 0,30, and 50kg/m^3.

A total of 15 specimens were made with combinations of various reinforcing materials and mix proportions. Each beam specimen, as shown in Figure 1, was of rectangular cross section 15cm wide and 20cm high, with two reinforcing elements corresponding to D13 arranged at 30mm from the tension fiber, and two corresponding to D10 at 30mm from the compression fiber. Four stirrups of ϕ6 were arranged in each shear span.

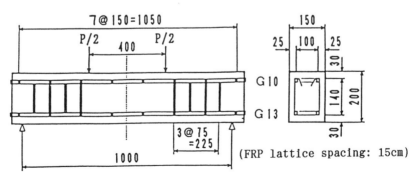

Figure 1 Cross-sectional particulars and loading method

Curing was done in water with flexural strength tests performed at stages when 28-day ages were reached. During this time, the expansive strains of Method A uniaxially restrained specimens and the expansive strains produced in the reinforcements of the various specimens were measured. When performing flexural strength tests, measurements were made of strains of reinforcing materials, strains at compression fibers of concrete, and flexural crack widths.

FLEXURAL ANALYSIS METHOD

In calculations of chemical prestress and chemical prestrain, and in analysis of bending, the layered model as shown in Figure 2, with the cross section of the beam divided into n equal parts parallel to the neutral axis was adopted. Hypothesizing that strains inside the cross section are proportional to distance from the neutral axis, stresses and strains were made to be represented by the centroidal locations of the individual layers. For distributions of expansive strains and chemical prestrains, the method of estimating based on the hypothesis of constant quantity of work that "work done by expansive concrete per unit volume on reinforcing material, the restraining body, is a constant value regardless of the degree of restraint" was adopted[1].

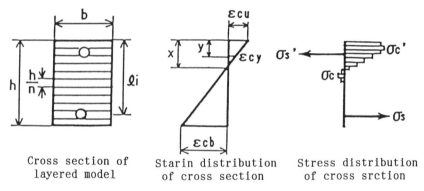

| Cross section of | Starin distribution | Stress distribution |
| layered model | of cross section | of cross srction |

Figure 2 Explanatory diagram of layered model used for flexural analysis

RESULTS AND DISCUSSION

Chemical Prestrain of Reinforcing Material

The experimental values of chemical prestrain, the expansive strain produced in the FRP of beam specimens at 28-day age, and the theoretical values of chemical prestress estimated from the amount of expansion of Method A uniaxially-restrained specimens are shown in Figure 3.

Regarding FRP beams, the lattice spacings of FRP were from 5 to 20cm, while experimental values were less than theoretical values in cases of unit expansive agent content **E** of either 30kg/m^3 or 50kg/m^3. This is thought to have been because the method of restraining expansion of concrete by only the lattice intersections was inadequate and slipping occurred between concrete and reinforcement due to the fact that bond between concrete and FRP equal to the case of an RC beam could not be obtained. Further, the result that chemical prestrain becomes approximately double was obtained when **E** was increased from 30kg/m^3 to 50kg/m^3.

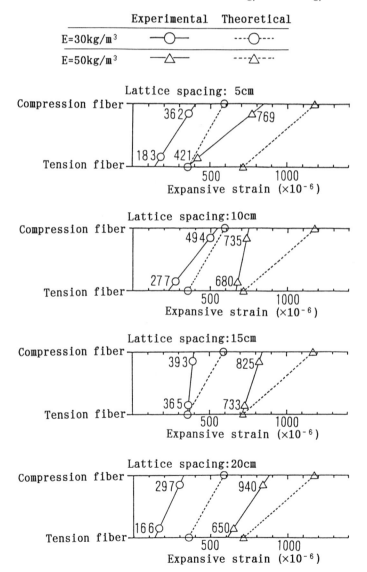

Figure 3 Distribution of expansive strains at 28-day age

Strain of Tensile reinforcement

Examples of the relationship between strain of tensile reinforcement and bending moment are shown for experimental and theoretical values in Figure 4. Although a small amount of scatter can be recognized due to differences in lattice spacings and expansive agent contents E , it may be considered that all theoretical values reflect experimental values well. Compared with the calculated reduction effect of strain of reinforcement due to chemical prestrain, a reduction effect several times greater was obtained in experimental values, but the reasons for this could not be made clear.

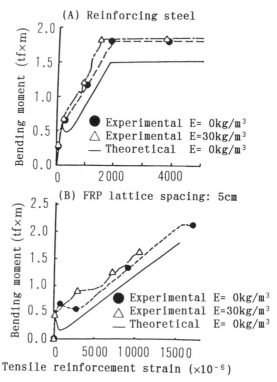

Figure 4 Examples of relationships between
tensile reinforcement and bending moment

Flexural Cracking Moment

The relationships of flexural cracking moments with lattice spacings of FRP reinforcement and unit expansive agent contents are shown in Figure 5. In general, when expansive agent is used, flexural cracking moment increases due to chemical prestress produced at the tension fiber of concrete. This trend is prominent for RC beams, but not distinct for FRP beams.

The reasons for this are that the chemical prestress induced in an FRP beam is small compared with an RC beam, and stress concentrations occur in FRP intersections.

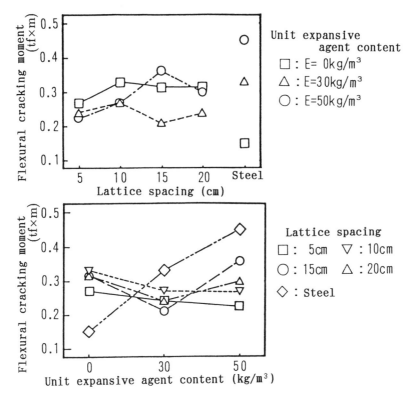

Figure 5 Relationships of flexural cracking moment with
lattice spacing and unit expansive agent content

In case of an RC beam, bond forces between concrete and deformed bars are distributed evenly along the member axis. When this beam is subjected to bending
moment, flexural stresses are also distributed evenly along the member axis, tensile
stresses are transmitted smoothly from reinforcing bars to concrete, hardly any increase in local stress occurs, and flexural cracks are formed when tension fiber strain
reaches the tensile failure strain of concrete. On the other hand, in case of an FRP
beam, the bond force between concrete and FRP reinforcement is smaller than in
case of an RC beam, and when subjected to bending moment, it is thought slip
will occur between concrete and FRP reinforcement under a comparatively small
load. This slipping is stopped by concrete in the vicinity of lattice intersections, and
although FRP reinforcement will not be pulled out from the beam specimen, it is
possible for the tensile stress of FRP reinforcement to be transmitted to only the
concrete near lattice intersections. It is thought that because of this, large stresses
compared with the case of an RC beam are applied to only the concrete in the
vicinities of lattice intersections as bending moment increases, tensile failure strain
of concrete is reached locally, and flexural cracking occurs only in this vicinity. This
is clear from the condition of flexural cracking occurrence shown in Figure 6, and
in case of an FRP beam, flexural cracks are mainly formed in the vicinities of lattice intersections. Hardly any changes were recognized in flexural cracking moments
even when lattice spacings of FRP differed.

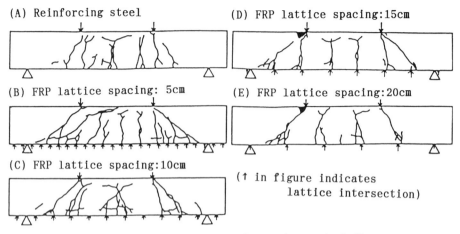

(A) Reinforcing steel

(B) FRP lattice spacing: 5cm

(C) FRP lattice spacing:10cm

(D) FRP lattice spacing:15cm

(E) FRP lattice spacing:20cm

(↑ in figure indicates
     lattice intersection)

Figure 6 Cracking pattern (Case of $\mathbf{E} = 0\,\mathrm{kg/m^3}$)

Even when unit expansive agent content was increased, there was hardly any increase seen in flexural cracking moment of FRP beams. However, when unit expansive agent content was high, tensile reinforcement strain of an FRP beam did not show rapid increase even when flexural cracking occurred, and the rate of increase in strain did not become high up to a load level of about the same degree as flexural cracking load the RC beam.

Diagonal Cracking Moment

The relationship of diagonal cracking moment with lattice spacing of FRP and unit expansive agent content are shown in Figure 7.

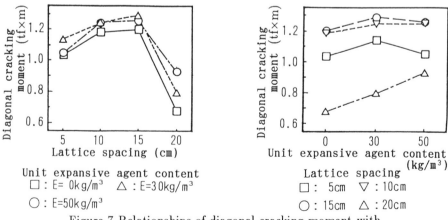

Unit expansive agent content
$\square$: E= 0kg/m³ $\triangle$: E=30kg/m³
$\bigcirc$: E=50kg/m³

Lattice spacing
$\square$: 5cm $\triangledown$: 10cm
$\bigcirc$: 15cm $\triangle$: 20cm

Figure 7 Relationships of diagonal cracking moment with
lattice spacing and unit expansive agent content

Up to the case of FRP lattice spacing of 15cm, there was a trend of diagonal cracking moment increasing with increase in lattice spacing, but when lattice spacing was increased to 20cm, the result was that diagonal cracks were formed with a moment smaller than in other cases. The reasons for this are thought to have been that stresses were concentrated at FRP lattice intersections, that in case of lattice spacing of 20cm there was only one lattice intersection in a shear span, and that the locations of lattice intersections were close to locations where diagonal cracking was liable to occur.

Compared with the case of **E** being 0kg/m^3, the diagonal cracking moments of FRP beams were increased in the cases of **E** being 30kg/m^3 and 50kg/m^3, and this trend was especially prominent in case of lattice spacing 20cm where diagonal cracking moment was small. Further, with regard to an RC beam using steel for reinforcement, distinct diagonal cracks could not be recognized until failure, and the mode of failure was flexural tension failure.

Flexural Crack Width

Figure 8 shows the relationships of average flexural crack width at the same bending moment (0.75tf×m, 5tf in terms of load) with lattice spacing and unit expansive agent content, while Figure 9 shows the relationships of maximum flexural crack width with lattice spacing and unit expansive agent content.

Since the modulus of elasticity of FRP is low compared with reinforcing steel, flexural crack width at identical bending moment is larger for an FRP beam than an RC beam.

At identical lattice spacings, when unit expansive agent content **E** is increased, both average flexural crack width and maximum flexural crack width show trends of decreasing.

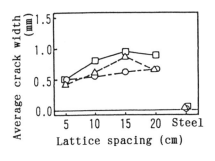

Unit expansive agent content
□ : E= 0kg/m^3 △ : E=30kg/m^3
○ : E=50kg/m^3

Lattice spacing
□ : 5cm   ▽ : 10cm
○ : 15cm   △ : 20cm   ◇ : Steel

Figure 8 Relationships of average crack width with lattice
spacing and unit expansive agent content

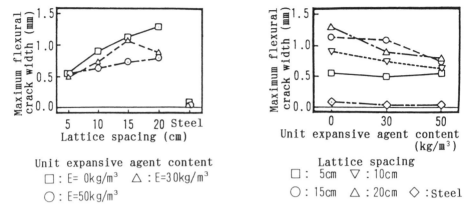

Figure 9 Relationships of maximum flexural crack width with
lattice spacing and unit expansive agent content

Further, the result that flexural crack width becomes large when lattice spacing
is large was obtained. In case of an FRP beam stress concentration occurs at
lattice intersections, and because of this flexural cracks occur at those portions.
When lattice spacing becomes large, the number of lattice intersections in a section
of constant bending moment becomes small, and the number of cracks formed is
decreased. Consequently, the flexural crack width per crack becomes larger as lattice
spacing becomes larger.

In the relationships of reinforcement strain with flexural crack width and maximum
flexural crack width, it was seen that flexural crack width became smaller according
to the degree of reduction in increase of reinforcement tensile strain accompanying
the chemical prestrain induced. As for the relationship between tensile reinforcement
strain and flexural crack width, a trend of distribution in a straight line was seen.
In general, when unit expansive agent content becomes large, there is a trend for
flexural crack width for identical reinforcement tensile strain to become small. It
was possible to confirm this trend in these experiments also.

Flexural Yielding Strength and Shear Yielding Strength

The failure modes of the various specimens determined in the these experiments
and the experimental and theoretical values of failure moments are given in Table
2 and Table 3, respectively. The failure mode shifted from that of shear to flexure
with increase in the unit expansive agent content. This was because chemical prestress was induced not only in the direction of member axis, but also the direction
perpendicular to the member axis through the use of expansive concrete and shear
yielding strength was increased.

In analyses, it was possible to obtain roughly equal yield strengths regardless of
the analysis method used in case of RC beams. In case of FRP beams, in flexural
analyses using layered models, the failure mode became that of flexural compression
failure, and failure loads approximately equal to experimental values were obtained.
However, the failure load according to elasticity calculations obtained hypothesizing
that the compression fiber of the concrete had reached failure strain was conspicu-
ously on the dangerous side.

Table 2 Failure mode

Unit expansive agent content	F R P lattice spacing 5cm	10cm	15cm	20cm	Reinforcing steel
0 kg/m^3	FC	SF	SF	SF	FT
30 kg/m^3	RR	FC	SF	SF	FT
50 kg/m^3	RR	FC	FC	FC	FT

FT:Flexural tension failure
FC:Flexural compression failure
RR:Reinforcement rupture in shear span
SF:Shear failure

Table 3 Failure moment

Unit expansive agent content (kg/m^3)				0	30	50
Experimental value (tf×m)	F R P lattice spacing		5cm	2.16	1.62	2.18
			10cm	1.49	2.37	2.06
			15cm	1.64	1.82	2.12
			20cm	1.76	2.04	2.06
	Reinforcing Steel			1.95	1.95	1.92
Theoreticl value (tf×m)	Flexural failure	Layered model	FRP·	2.10	2.06	1.85
			Steel	1.56	1.50	1.55
		Elasticity	FRP	2.99	2.99	2.97
			Steel	1.55	1.55	1.52
	Shear failure		FRP··	1.53	1.52	1.55
			Steel	1.91	1.86	1.91
Concrete compressive strength(kgf/cm^2)				386	372	315
Method A expansive strain (×10^{-6})				0	169	401

FRP·:Flexural compressive failure
FRP··:Chemical prestress in direction perpendicular to member
  axis not considered.

The shear yielding strength at stirrup yielding determined using the calculation equation of the Standard Specifications for Concrete[2] is given in Table 3. Because specimens used in the experiments had small a/d, the shear yielding strength shared by concrete was calculated as about one half of the whole. At the present point in time, there are problems such as that the improvement effect in shear yielding strength due to use of expansive agent cannot be distinctly reflected. It is necessary for studies to be made of such points in the future.

Since the theoretical value obtained from the layered model was that of flexural compressive failure in case of FRP beams, it is subjected to a great extent to the influence of compressive strength of concrete. On the other hand, the influence can hardly be seen in the experimental values. It is thought that the reason for this is that whereas the compressive strength of concrete used in analysis was a value thought to have been that of the specimen expanding freely to result in strength reduction, the concrete in a beam specimen was subjected to restraint from reinforcement and stirrups so that hardly any strength reduction occurred, hence producing such a difference.

CONCLUSIONS

The following were made clear in the study reported here.

1. Chemical prestrain produced in FRP through the use of expansive concrete was smaller for experimental values than for theoretical values using the concept of work quantity. The reason for this is thought to have been due to slip between concrete and FRP reinforcement caused by the expansive action of concrete since the lattice intersection of FRP was not adequate.

2. Through induction of chemical prestress and chemical prestrain, the increment in strain of FRP beam reinforcement under identical moments is reduced along with which flexural crack width is also reduced.

3. When FRP of lattice form was used as reinforcement, flexural cracks were produced at lattice intersections, and flexural cracking moment showed a trend of decline compared with RC beams. This is thought to have been due to chemical prestress being smaller compared with RC beams, and stresses being concentrated at the lattice intersections of FRP. Hardly any increase in flexural cracking moment was seen even when unit expansive agent content was increased to $50kg/m^3$.

4. Diagonal cracking moment showed a trend of increase since the spacing of flexural crack occurrence became larger the larger the lattice spacing up to a certain limit. It was recognized that there is a slight increase due to use of expansive agent.

ACKNOWLEDGMENT

The authors hereby sincerely thank Nefcom Co.,Ltd. for kindly donating the FRP reinforcing material used in carrying out this study.

REFERENCES

1. TSUJI,Y. Method of Estimating Chemical Prestress and Distribution of Expansion, Concrete Journal,1981,Vol.19,No.6,June,pp.99-105.

2. JAPAN SOCIETY OF CIVIL ENGINEERS (JSCE). Standard Specifications for Concrete, Design Volume,1991 Edition.

A RADICAL NEW APPROACH TO REINSTATEMENT OF INDUSTRIAL FLOOR SURFACES

R S Harbron

L H McCurrich

Fosroc International Ltd

United Kingdom

ABSTRACT. Poor industrial floor surfaces can reduce manufacturing efficiency and can cause expensive damage to internal transport and handling systems. However, traditional floor surfacing techniques such as resin-based systems, thicker-sectioned cement-based screed or total replacement of the floor are often costly, are slow and difficult to install. A quick and cost-effective way to reinstate poor floors is to use pumpable, self smoothing, thin cementitious overlays. However, when applied in thin sections, these require exceptional dimensional stability to combat the stresses caused by drying shrinkage when restrained by the bond to the substrate. This paper describes the advances that have been made to shrinkage control and other physical properties of thin cementitious overlays which allow new techniques of rapid reinstatement of degraded industrial floor surfaces to be achieved. Details are given of restrained and unrestrained shrinkage tests for polymer modified calcium aluminate-based materials and comparisons made with more traditional approaches.

Keywords: Industrial flooring, Pumpable, Self-smoothing, Special cements, Shrinkage, Physical properties, Case histories, Application equipment.

Dr Roland S Harbron is International Technology Manager responsible for cementitious flooring technology for Fosroc International Ltd. He is based at the Fosroc Technology Centre in Aston, Birmingham and is involved with new product development and technical support for Fosroc operations in many parts of the world. He joined Fosroc in 1989 following a PhD at Bristol University and a Research Fellowship at Birmingham University in the field of colloid science.

Mr Laurence McCurrich is Technical Director of Fosroc International Ltd responsible for the operation of the Technology Centre at Aston, Birmingham covering a wide range of formulated construction chemical products. Prior to joining Fosroc in 1974, he worked for 10 years in the Research and Development Division of Taylor Woodrow Construction Ltd.

Concrete 2000. Edited by Ravindra K. Dhir and M. Roderick Jones.
© 1993 Published by E & FN Spon. ISBN 0 419 18120 2.

INTRODUCTION

Increasing emphasis is being placed upon the appearance and performance of industrial floors since damaged flooring gives a generally poor quality image to the environment, is dangerous and can cause expensive damage to internal transport and handling systems. Furthermore, the existing floor may simply require upgrading for change of use. Traditionally a number of techniques have been employed in the reinstatement of existing floors, however, these have either been particularly expensive in terms of length of time that the floor is out of use or are based on costly heavy duty resin systems. Applying cementitious overlays to existing floors has been restricted by the need to cast a new slab with significant thickness (typically 100mm) on top of existing floors or alternatively to break out and replace the existing floor with all the associated costs and problems. One cementitious method for applying thinner flooring has been to use trowel applied polymer modified compounds. These have been proved successful but they tend to need extreme care to avoid problems of shrinkage and tend to be slow to lay.

Recently considerable progress has been made in Europe, particularly in Scandinavia, on the introduction of pumped, self-smoothing underlayments with separate floor finishes applied onto their surface. These were somewhat limited for industrial applications where the separately applied floor finishes were not appropriate and the underlayments were not particularly strong. The latest developments of these ideas is to produce a self-smoothing cementitious floor topping which can be applied in thicknesses as low as 6mm and are abrasion resistant, hard wearing surfaces in their own right. Where appropriate, a dual layer system can be used, with a base layer being employed to fill excessive depths of irregularity in the existing floor. These floors are laid in continuous areas without joints other than following movement joints in the existing floor and this has been made possible by the development of formulated products with extremely low shrinkage and the ability to provide stress accommodation within the flooring products.

The major limitation of all cementitious overlays has been associated with shrinkage and this paper looks at advances that have been made in producing low shrinkage materials.

MATERIALS FOR REINSTATEMENT OVERLAYS

Early attempts at producing self-smoothing overlays were based on ordinary Portland cement modified by the addition of, for example, styrene butadiene or acrylic polymer emulsions. The new materials referred to in this paper, however, are based on calcium aluminate (CA) - calcium sulphate binder system modified with appropriate plasticisers, redispersible polymer powder, shrinkage compensation and other additives.

It is this latter type of flooring powder compound that forms the basis of the new approach outlined in this paper.

SHRINKAGE

In general, most standard shrinkage measurements are done using specimens that are free to change length without restraint.   In the case of cementitious overlays however, the shrinkage of the overlay is restrained by bond to the existing floor and restrained shrinkage measurements may therefore be more appropriate.   Unfortunately, the latter type of test tends to be more difficult to carry out.   It is therefore worth considering results from both types of test.

Unrestrained Shrinkage Testing

Unrestrained drying shrinkage is most commonly measured by casting a standard size of test prism, demoulding 24 hours after casting, and monitoring the length change of the prism stored in standard conditions.   Whilst the principle of this test is straightforward, prism size and standard conditions vary considerably in different parts of the world: USA - ASTM C157-1989, UK - BS1881 Part 5-1970, Germany - DIN 52450-1985.

We find the small 25 x 25 x 285mm specified by ASTM to be the most appropriate for evaluating flooring overlays as the high surface area to volume ratio encourages rapid drying of the specimen and therefore shrinkage.   The curing conditions employed are 20°C and 65% RH.   Typical results using this test specimen are shown in Figure 1.   For these results, specimens have been de-moulded within a few hours, as soon as adequate strength has been obtained so that free movement can be measured from as early a time as possible.   In practice, the slight initial expansion shown will simply cause a small precompression in the floor surface which will then diminish with time.

Restrained Shrinkage Testing

A rough indication of degree of shrinkage can be obtained quickly by carrying out a "plastic cup" test in which the materials to be evaluated are cast into 50mm diameter x 50mm deep clear polystyrene cups.   The results can be evaluated according to the descriptions given in Table 1 and examples are shown in Figure 2.

A somewhat more sophisticated method of measuring performance under restrained conditions is the use of the Coutinho ring (1).   Originally this test was used to monitor the development of stress in a restrained configuration with time by the use of strain gauges.   However, it is more frequently used as a check, with time to cracking being evaluated. Coutinho ring test specimens are shown in Figure 3.

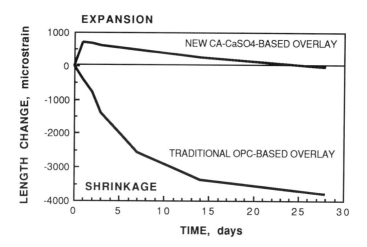

Figure 1 Drying shrinkage of new and traditional cementitious overlays cured at 20°C, 65%RH

Figure 2 Visual assessment of restrained shrinkage by plastic cup test. Left-shrinkage, centre-dimensionally stable, right-disruptive expansion

Table 1 Assessment of Restrained Shrinkage by Plastic Cup Test

CAUSE	EFFECT
Excessive expansion	Cup cracks
Moderate expansion	The clear plastic tends to craze
Slight shrinkage	Shadow appears when viewed through the plastic
Excessive shrinkage	Specimen detaches from surface of plastic and drops outs

Typical results obtained by the Coutinho ring test are shown in Table 2. This test is an appropriate representation of what happens on the floor since it allows for the balance between the development of shrinkage strain and the relaxation with time of the stress that results from this. Cracking then occurs at the point at which this stress exceeds the tensile strength of the material at that given moment.

Figure 3 Assessment of restrained shrinkage by Coutinho ring method. Left - cracks have occurred due to drying shrinkage. Centre - no cracks indicating dimensional stability. Right - surface micro-cracks due to disruptive expansion and loss of contact with steel ring.

Table 2 Coutinho Ring Observations at 20°C, 65% RH

SPECIMEN	OBSERVATION
New CA-CaSO$_4$ - based overlays	No cracks observed
Traditional OPC-based overlays	Shrinkage cracks occur in 2 to 21 days

Another useful test is the measurement of the force required to restore a specimen to its original length (2). Alternative ad hoc methods have been to measure degree of curling in tests utilising the "bimetallic strip" principle, specimens being cast in the form of thin strips or slabs bonded to flexible substrates.

RHEOLOGICAL AND SETTING TIME PROPERTIES

A key property of pumped cementitious overlays is that they should be sufficiently fluid that they are self-smoothing and retain this fluidity for an adequate period of time to allow ease of application. Moreover, the overlay should then set and gain strength rapidly for speed of accepting traffic. Where greater thicknesses are required a dual layer approach is used. In this situation a thicker and less expensive base layer is applied prior to the highly fluid topping. Figure 4 shows the change in fluidity with time of a cementitious overlay as measured by a simple flow spread test. The test involves the measurement of flow spread diameter of material from a standard flow cone (complying with BS6463: Part 3 : 1987) onto a non-absorptive board. Additives can be used to achieve a wide range of workability times depending on temperature conditions.

MECHANICAL PROPERTIES

There are a number of key properties which need to be evaluated: bond strength, abrasion and impact resistance, rate of strength gain, flexural and compressive strength. It should be noted that whilst compressive strength is important, it is not necessarily beneficial for an overlay to have a high compressive strength. For example, although increasing the polymer content of a flooring compound reduces compressive strength, it dramatically improves abrasion and impact resistance, enhances bond strength and increases strain capacity (3). Other benefits of using polymers are that increased deformability makes the floor less tiring to walk on and also makes it less noisy than an ordinary concrete floor. Some typical mechanical properties of the new CA-CaSO$_4$ - based overlays using an acrylic emulsion primer system are given in Table 3.

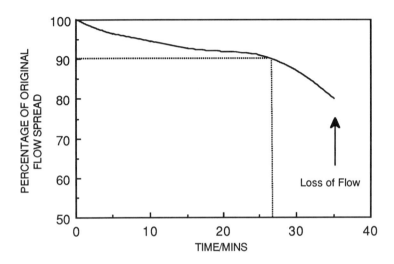

Figure 4 Change in fluidity with time of pumpable cementitious
overlay at 20°C

Table 3 Typical mechanical properties of new flooring overlays
at 28 days

TEST METHOD	MECHANICAL PROPERTY		
Direct Pull-off Strength (4)	>0.8N/mm²		
C & CA Rolling Wheel Accelerated Abrasion Test (5)	Highest Classification "Good"		
BRE Impact Resistance (6)	Highest Classification "Category A"		
Compressive Strength (40mm cubes, 20°C 65% RH)	1 day > 12 7 day > 20 28 day > 30	N/mm² N/mm² N/mm²	
Flexural Strength (BS6319: Part 3 : 1990)	28 day > 8	N/mm²	

EQUIPMENT FOR APPLYING INDUSTRIAL FLOOR OVERLAYS

The development of these new pumped cementitious formulations goes hand in hand with the use of appropriate mixing and pumping equipment. It has been found that the most convenient method of application is to use a combined mixer pump. This involves a continuous mixing process and not batch mixing. An example of such a mixing pump is depicted in Figure 5.

Powder is screw fed into the mixing chamber as water is metered in simultaneously via a flow gauge. The mixed overlay then passes to a worm pump and is pumped through a hose to the point of application. Typically a hose 60m in length and 32mm internal diameter is used. An output of approximately 40l per minute is generally found to be suitable for floor laying and allows an area of approximately 1000m^2 to be reinstated in one day.

CASE HISTORIES

Pumped cementitious overlays have recently been employed throughout the world for the reinstatement/upgrading of existing floors to industrial use. Some typical projects are listed in Table 4 and Figure 6 shows the reinstatement of an industrial floor.

Figure 5 Combined mixer pump for application of industrial overlays

Table 4 Worldwide case histories

COUNTRY	INDUSTRY	APPLICATION
UK	Electrical windings Department store	Assembly hall Retail units
Spain	Plastics Textile	Production area Warehouse
France	Car manufacturer Gas bottling plant	Production area Production area
Holland	Department store Aerospace	Warehouse Workshop
USA	Pharmaceutical	Production area
Singapore	Construction chemicals	Production area

Figure 6 Reinstatement of industrial floor surface of an electrical windings manufacturer

Site experience shows that the potential for floors based on this technology exists both in new construction and in renovation work. The main future application, however, for floors of this type is in renovation, where down time of the floor need only be a week-end compared with many days or weeks if the floor slabs have to be broken out, relaid and cured by conventional techniques. Typically 4 operatives can prepare and lay over 1,000 m^2 of overlay in a week-end period.

CONCLUSIONS

This paper has illustrated the advances that have now been made in shrinkage reduction which enables cementitious overlays as thin as 6mm to be pumped over existing floor slabs to reinstate them to a smooth hardwearing finish. Despite the material having these high flow and low shrinkage characteristics, they also enable rapid reinstatement in that foot traffic can be allowed on the floor after 4 hours and fork lift truck traffic after 36 hours. Excellent early age strength development is achieved together with high abrasion resistance and the paper has illustrated how this technology is being used to provide very suitable industrial floor renovation.

REFERENCES

1.   COUTINHO, A. The influence of the type of cement on its cracking tendency, RILEM Bulletin 5, Dec. 1959, pp 26-40.

2.   MCCURRICH, LH AND KAY, WM. Polyester and epoxy resin concrete. Resins and Concrete Symposium, University of Newcastle upon Tyne, 17 - 18 April 1973.

3.   ALEXANDERSON, J. Self-smoothing floors based on polymer cement concrete, Concrete International, vol. 12, No.1, 1990, pp 49-51.

4.   CIRIA TECHNICAL NOTE 139. Standard tests for repair materials and coatings for concrete-pull-off testing, 1992.

5.   CONCRETE SOCIETY TECHNICAL REPORT NO 34. Concrete Industrial Ground Floors, The Concrete Society, 1988, pp 81-88.

6.   PYE, PW. BRE Screed tester: classification of screeds, sampling and acceptance limits. Building Res Establishment Information Paper, IP 11/84, 1984.

A FUTURE WITH CONCRETE

M A Clarke

L J Parrott

D C Spooner

British Cement Association

United Kingdom

ABSTRACT. The infrastructure of our society and the fabric of the built environment depend fundamentally upon concrete in all its forms. To look to the future we must identify the current pressures for evolution and their likely effects. These includes the appearance of concrete where the visual potential has not always been realised; the economic constraints of time and cost of construction; the environmental issues of energy conservation and waste recycling and the changing needs in education and training.

Keywords: Quality cycle, Visual excellence, Weathering, Durability, European harmonisation, Education and training.

Mr Martin A Clarke is Director of Marketing at BCA responsible for technical marketing in Building and Civil Engineering and for training, information services and publications. He holds a BA degree in Economy and Statistics from Exeter University. He spent eighteen years with the ARC Group, latterly as Business Development Director before joining the BCA in 1990. He is Chairman of the Reinforced Concrete Council, the Ready-Mixed Concrete Bureau and the Structural Precast User Group.

Dr Leslie J Parrott received BSc and PhD degrees in Civil Engineering from London University. He is manager of concrete properties at The British Cement Association. His Research on concrete includes moisture, microstructure, mathematical modelling, deformation, permeation and durability : it has resulted in numerous publications and in membership of several international technical committees.

Dr David C Spooner is Director of Materials and Standards at the British Cement Association and is a physicist who obtained his degree and PhD from London University. He is the author of many papers on the testing and properties of concrete, and also on the thermal performance of concrete in buildings. He is a member of a number of UK and European Standards Committees relating to concrete.

Concrete 2000. Edited by Ravindra K. Dhir and M. Roderick Jones.
© 1993 Published by E & FN Spon. ISBN 0 419 18120 2.

INTRODUCTION

The aim of this paper is to raise some of the critical issues that need to be addressed to encourage and broaden the use of concrete into the 21st Century. This paper represents the views of the BCA and in particular stresses the need to integrate the visual and technical excellence of concrete, with longevity, quality, maintenance needs and economy. The usual limitations of space decree that only a few examples of concrete's potential can be illustrated in the paper and in the accompanying conference presentation. A range of publications are available from the BCA to support the points being addressed. Although concrete is not always visible to the eye, it does play a crucial role in providing economic solutions to a wide variety of building and infrastructure requirements. As we move into the 21st century it is likely that advances in concrete technology will be associated with 'fine tuning' rather than radical changes.

There are many concrete structures that have been and will be candidates for preservation long after the buildings become redundant in terms of their original function. Some were built by architect-engineers such as Freysinnet, Saarinen and Wright, who worked within defined limits that could be achieved, in order to develop and maintain the fluency of their design. Many took advantage of the inherent plasticity of in situ concrete and the mouldability of precast concrete. The subsequent sections of this paper will emphasise the potential benefits of architectural concrete, as well as its structural integrity.

Today, European harmonization is providing an opportunity to consolidate the technical advances of the last decade in the areas of cement and concrete technology, structural design, construction innovation and service performance. Perhaps in the next decade we should attempt to provide an equivalent European stimulus for distilling the architectural and structural advances that have been made with concrete. Education is a natural focal point in considering the future uses of concrete and, in an industry of increasing breadth and complexity, we need to provide such a stimulus to

i)   instil a basic understanding in concrete sciences for future innovation
ii)   explore the aesthetic, technical and economic benefits that concrete offers
iii)   encourage a national syllabus for school, college, university and industrial training.

Quality control has become an essential component of market survival and success. There are numerous, successful quality control schemes within the construction industry that are helping to raise and maintain standards. There may well be a broader need for a 'quality cycle' that more consciously stimulates in-service assessments of concrete, linked with clear feed-back to improve and optimize design. This point will be considered again in the last part of the paper.

VISUAL EXCELLENCE

Advances in structural concrete in the 50s led to a wide range of building technologies and challenging expressions. New structural forms such as thin shells, folded plates, and hyperbolic paraboloids greatly extended and enhanced architectural possibilities and the visual appeal of concrete. The names of Nervi, Candela, Corbusier and Arup, synonymous with structural innovations in both precast and in-situ concrete, had an immediate and inspiring effect on the architectural world.

Alongside these supremely crafted structures, there were many designs that incorporated too much untried innovation and too much for the builder to interpret. With craft skills in short supply, it was inevitable that standards would fall. It was not long before the leaking roof, bowing panels, open joints and spalling concrete would condemn such buildings to early obsolescence.

When finished to a high standard concrete can create pleasing design. In the hands of artists of genius like Giliotti and Calatrava, concrete architecture can be transformed through a complex framework of challenging and invigorating colour and design.

But left to lesser talents, the material can reveal design shortcomings. The rough cast finish of in-situ concrete inspired by Le Corbusier, was also to become a fetish among local authority architects in the 60s, culminating in the Hayward Gallery, National Theatre and Queen Elizabeth Hall that make up the controversial South Bank Complex.

Twenty years on, improvements in the provision and design of visual concrete have brought about renewed architectural and client interest. Other materials have become prominent in the eighties boom, and the technical and aesthetic price is being paid.

There is greater interest in the use of colour. The introduction of synthetic pigments now ensures more uniform grading of particle size and water absorption, leading to better control of concrete colour. Problems associated with loss of colour from carbon black and certain green and blue pigments made from organic compounds that are not alkali stable, have been eliminated.

The inherent problems of plywood absorbency and the special skills and care required in formwork preparation, have been eased with the development of formliners made from plastic, glass fibre and polyurethane. Workmanship has been simplified by improvements in casting methods, the use of neutral non-staining formwork release agents and quality control procedures for placing, compacting and curing concrete.

Aggregate texturing by acid etching, grit blasting and point tooling offers exciting architectural finishes. Such surfaces can be sealed by water repellent coatings, to reduce the risk of surface staining, provided the surface has been profiled to control weathering.

Diligent awareness of the action of weathering on buildings is fundamental to good architecture, as it is to good concrete detailing. The subject of detailing to control weathering must become part of a first degree syllabus in architecture and building technology.

Researches into the effects of changes in materials, water/cement ratio, temperature, formwork surface, compaction, handling and curing regime on the finished colour and surface quality of concrete, should be more thoroughly investigated and reported.

A continuing programme of testing and monitoring of the long term durability of concrete for architectural cladding should be encouraged, to gain more knowledge about the benefits of water repellent admixtures, surface coatings and types of surface finishes.

The quality, range, adaptability and visual excellence of precast concrete as a cladding material is well established. The competitiveness of precast construction has been enhanced by standardisation in production techniques, computer design methods, and faster throughput from factory to site. Confidence has improved by the testing of precast systems prior to finalisation of design and erection, thus minimising the likelihood of poor performance. Engineered tolerance for assembly, and for movement due to changes in temperature and drying shrinkage, also ensures integrity.

Since the days of the Greeks and Romans, various orders of architecture have made use of impediments, carvings, flutings and friezes. Modern earth dry or polymer modified precast concrete mortars, commonly known as reconstituted stone, are used extensively in the restoration and refurbishment of old stonework and masonry. Many of our ancient buildings are maintained in pristine condition by the mouldability and durability of concrete.

It is refreshing to note that the plastic and sculptural versatility of concrete pioneered in the 50s, is once again giving a rejuvenating push for craftsmanship, style, decoration and self-expression in architecture.

The British precast cladding industry is responding to a surge of interest and a number of classic buildings have resulted. Prospects for the future are excellent as the fashion cycle turns against metal and glass.

In the case of Bofill's Taller de Architecture, the ability to mass produce precast panels with such fine detail can be put down to understanding of the mouldability and surface finishing of concrete. The fine detailing of the exterior panels of the SWIFT Headquarters in Belgium, crystallises the success of the technique.

Farrell at Vauxhall Cross turned to concrete for the frame and cladding for this striking ten storey office block, that overlooks the Thames at Vauxhall Bridge. The pigmented precast concrete facade was chosen to give the design solidity and mass and to contrast with the green of the glass curtain walling.

In Outrams case concrete has always been the material of the twentieth century. His design fragments concrete into tiles to create a network of floating colour. The range and stability of synthetic pigments, has given Outram access to a palette of materials and colours from which to precast almost any design.

Whatever the fashion, architecture today is showing an awareness of setting, of place, of scale and form in a way that has not been evident for many a year. In the choice of material options, diversity of building form and visual expression with the recent advances in concrete colour technology there appears to be little to challenge the role and prominence of concrete in architecture in the coming years.

TECHNICAL AND ECONOMIC IMPROVEMENTS

Concrete is a startingly versatile material, providing endless opportunities for those with the imagination to exploit its properties. It is produced in a range of densities from the lowest to the highest, to satisfy exacting thermal or acoustic insulation requirements or the high performance duties of oil platforms, long-span bridges and tall buildings. Exploiting and extending the versatility of concrete depends on continued improvements both in materials and mix design technology, and the production of consistently high quality products. For example, the high strength concretes, routinely possible with modern materials, have enabled space-efficient high rise offices to be built because of reduced column size and better strength to weight ratios. The forty-four storey Pacific First Centre in Seattle has concrete columns with a strength of 115 N/mm^2 increasing lettable space by 30% over normal strength concretes. Modification of other properties of concrete such as its rheological behaviour, setting characteristics, rate of strength gain, heat evolution, durability and cost are commonly achieved using both chemical admixtures and the by-products of other industries such as pfa and blastfurnace slag. Opportunities to imaginatively couple the latest material developments and technical information with novel construction techniques such as controlled permeability formwork, extend the applications and economy of concrete construction.

The question of design for a required service life has become a major factor in the design process. Thus concrete durability has been a subject of major investigations at many research centres, including BCA, over the last fifteen years. As a result of these continuing efforts there is now better understanding of the long-term performance of concrete. Durability is now recognised as a multi-faceted subject which encompasses many processes of potential degradation which do not necessarily have a common solution. Researches to assess the properties of corrosion resistant reinforcement, alternative stressing materials and corrosion inhibiting admixtures could alleviate the present-day problems that can arise.

There are still areas of structural understanding which are incomplete, where empirical solutions prevail. Research leading to more accurate stress analysis, corroborated with confirmatory testing and design predictability, will provide more elegant solutions to structural problems.

Computers and sophisticated software already provide significant time saving in design offices in the areas of reinforced concrete design, detailing and quantities. There are still numerous opportunities to further extend their use in education (for example to include material properties and durability design), in architecture (structural form, sensitivity to environmental and climatic factors) and in training.

EUROPEAN HARMONIZATION

Currently there is an active process of development, assessment and revision to provide the future European codes and standards for cements, concrete, construction and the design of concrete structures. This process gives us an opportunity to consolidate technical knowledge and question some traditional ideas that have their roots more in national habits than in engineering logic. Only sound technical solutions can withstand international scrutiny and take account of the diversity in European climates, materials, methods of construction, and engineering experience. Reliable codes and standards that encourage optimization of design choices will help concrete to improve its market position in the hierarchy of construction materials. Thus for example the designer should be in a position to select, for a given exposure condition, the best combination of reinforcement cover, cement type and concrete mix to optimize for efficiency of construction, service life or some other criteria.

The efficiency of design and construction can be improved if reliable performance tests can be developed. This is the preferred approach in Europe because it avoids over-cautious (and often lengthy) prescriptive rules and permits novel solutions to meet specific requirements. The need for agreed performance tests has highlighted certain deficiencies in concrete test methods, particularly with regard to durability. This is partly due to the scientific complexity of durability and the wide variety of potential deterioration processes to which the designer must give consideration. Even though short-lists for test methods are now being accepted, there is an obvious shortage of information on the in-service behaviour of structures, against which the credibility of performance tests can be checked.

There is clearly an urgent need for internationally co-ordinated research on such topics, preferably with reliable long-term support extending well into the 21st century.

ENVIRONMENT

Environmental concerns, responsibilities and legislation have become one of the pressing issues which face, and will continue to face, the construction industry. A balance is continually being sought between the sophisticated needs of modern society and the potential damage to the environment in satisfying them. Concrete has an enviable position with respect to environmental matters requiring comparatively low energy for its production and offering numerous contributions to environmental well being.

These contributions cover the whole spectrum of the national infrastructure; energy production from hydro-electric schemes, dams, North Sea platforms and wind power, as well as more conventional power stations. Transport applications include roads, railways, airports and local traffic and pedestrianisation schemes.

Concretes contribution to the built environment includes energy conservation by building with insulating blocks and the use of concretes' thermal mass to reduce or eliminate the need for air-conditioning in some building types. Sound insulating properties of concrete are well known to anyone who has lived in a house with solid internal walls and floors. There is considerable scope to fully integrate the thermal and sound performance of concrete into building designs which will be both energy efficient and provide a pleasant environment to work or live in.

Waste disposal schemes are developing rapidly in certain countries and the associated concern with pollution and contamination of ground water and rivers with hazardous or radioactive elements is the subject of intensive world-wide research. Legislation in some countries such as USA, France, Switzerland and The Netherlands has limited the acceptable concentrations of hazardous elements in ground water and has thereby stimulated major programmes of research and development. Cement and concrete are proving to be valuable for immobilizing hazardous elements and for the construction of disposal structures. There are even prospects of using cements to convert thermally treated waste residues into serviceable construction materials. Furthermore, the mounting pressure to conserve the natural environment and our mineral resources will stimulate future recycling of mineral residues from industry and demolition debris, in combination with cement, as a valuable construction material.

EDUCATION AND TRAINING

Education more than any other activity is becoming a central issue for the future, along with the need to encourage our most capable young people into considering and maintaining careers in the construction industry.

Common skill standards, training and higher education needs, must be pursued with the co-operation of those in industry and those who will benefit most from improvements.

Through links with industry and education lead bodies, the BCA will help in the development of training and education programmes, both centralised and regionalised, to turn good practice into best practice, to raise the quality and standard of concrete engineering and construction across the country. Through links with industry and Professional Institutions, the quality of training and education programmes, must be made worthwhile and effective.

In the past the burden of sponsorship for training and education programmes of the BCA has been funded by the cement makers. The benefits of such programmes have advantaged all those companies who make a living from cement and concrete and the cost burden is now going to to have to be shared. Co-operation with other groups in focused market sectors, and shared funding for training will lead to a wider and more effective spread of activities.

The Reinforced Concrete Council (RCC) and Ready-Mixed Concrete Bureau (RCB), in partnership with the BCA, were set up to develop educational and marketing programmes to improve the understanding and usage of concrete in building and civil engineering applications. It is vital that the different sectors of the concrete industry continue to link together to form such partnerships and contribute to this effort.

On the practical and vocational training programmes, the BCA is working closely with the Construction Industry Training Board, the Institute of Concrete Technology and other bodies associated with National Vocational Qualification development to provide more uniform standards for skills and training.

As an industry we have not institutionalised recognised standards for skills and crafts in concrete construction. In the steel industry, welders are a recognised profession, graded and paid according to the level of skill and proficiency. There is as yet no such tag for concrete in UK, though it is coming. Already in some Scandinavian countries there is a long apprenticeship required to qualify and trade as a concretor.

Of equal concern is the drop in apprentices and trainees coming into the industry. Large firms acting as building brokers and managers, do not see themselves requiring this type of training. Small firms taking on the burden of the more difficult building tasks have a need for skills training, but do not have the budget or resources to allow for it, a challenge that the CITB and others must grasp.

The BTEC structure being pursued by Government, in time will help with the skill shortfall, by sponsoring the preliminary training of young persons and mature adults, who wish to enter the industry. However, this initiative may be a little too late, if the industry does not attract sufficient young people to take up such training programmes, in the first place. Therefore, it is vital that the industry through its various educational and promotional initiatives, win the vocational interest of school leavers.

The image of the industry and particularly that of concrete has suffered because of the volatile nature of the industry, a bad press and the visible reminders in our cities of poor building design and bad workmanship. Recognising this, the RCC in 1992 commissioned a series of 20 education packages aimed at providing lecturers on civil and structural engineering degree courses with material on subjects where there has been a shortage of good information. A similar exercise for schools of architecture is now well under way.

Further teaching packages adapted from these could be developed to cater for teaching programmes in schools of Building Technology, Construction Management and The Built Environment.

Training must be directed at the substance of the building process, not narrowed into early specialisations, in order to grasp the subject as a whole. Courses at BCA's Centre for Concrete Training seek to review the whole process of design, construction and supervisory operations. A considerable content of course tutoring covers interpretation of design codes and the benefits of new researches in concrete performance, particularly where the BCA have been involved in developing and managing such work.

BCA wishes to continue to promote advances in concrete technology pioneered from any research group and has welcomed and part-financed the Research Forum established by the Concrete Society. The BCA/Imperial College joint venture CRIC - the Concrete Research and Information Centre - will we believe play its own significant part in driving the industry forward.

Future training and education initiatives should also look to developing programmes for self-teaching through distance learning and for wider access using computer software and knowledge base expert systems.

The next decade is likely to see dramatic changes in the construction industry. There will be a demand for new construction and building forms and new assemblies of construction on site. Improved off-site prefabrication, faster on-site assembly and possibly construction robots are the forerunners of change.

Networking in partnership between professionals in industry and researchers in education should always remain central to education and vocational training programmes, to keep universities and their industrial partners in tune and in touch, with change.

THE DEVELOPMENT CYCLE

The introduction to this paper alluded to a quality cycle for innovation that could lead to the improved and broader use of concrete. Subsequent sections of the paper highlighted topics that, in the very personal opinion of the authors, qualify for special consideration. By way of summarizing the points that have emerged a list is given below of the essential components in a repeated cycle of development:

i)   assess public perception of appearance and function.
ii)   encourage the development and expression of architecture in engineering training.
iii)   provide technical support for achieving better architectural standards in concrete without structural or cost penalties.
iv)   provide technical support for achieving high quality construction and for testing construction quality.
v)   assessment of engineering and architectural performance in service.
vi)   return to i)

The BCA will continue to input into this cycle as much as its resources allow, working in partnership and responsive to user needs. As we move into the next millenium one thing is certain, that concrete will continue to be absolutely fundamental to civilisation. Like the BCA, concrete has much more future than history.

FURTHER READING

1.   STEVENSON J, SPOONER D, CLARKE M, SOMERVILLE G. Concrete in the Environment. BCA. 1993.

2.   FIP/CEB. High Strength Concrete - State of the Art Report. Bulletin d'Information 197, July 1990.

3.   CENTRE FOR STRATEGIC STUDIES IN CONSTRUCTION. Investing in Building 2001. National Contractors Group. September 1989.

4.   PÜTTBACH E. Pigments for Colouring Concrete. Technical information, published by The Bayer Corporation, 1986.

5.   BENNETT D.F.H. Structural Developments - 4 Visual Concrete. Article published in The AJ, 15 May 1991.

LITIGATION AND LAWYER/EXPERT RELATIONSHIPS: PAST, PRESENT AND FUTURE

M Levitt

Laing Technology Group Ltd

United Kingdom

ABSTRACT.- Disputes in the field of construction all too often end up in litigation and the members of the legal profession turn towards the professionals in construction for expert advice and reports. There is a current lack of uniformity in dealing with matters relating to both information and communication. This paper addresses the situation as at the end of 1992 and how it may be improved by innovation.

Keywords : ADR, Arbitration, Claimant, Defendant, Plaintiff, Without prejudice, Privileged, Respondent.

Dr Maurice Levitt is an Associate in the Laing Technology Group where he specialises in dealing with construction problems, development work and litigation. Dr Levitt is one of the original thinkers on the subject of durability of concrete and has published many papers and a book on precast concrete products. He sits on several BSI and Concrete Society Committees as well as the DoE European Joint Advisory Committee.

Concrete 2000. Edited by Ravindra K. Dhir and M. Roderick Jones.
© 1993 Published by E & FN Spon. ISBN 0 419 18120 2.

INTRODUCTION

Types of litigation

When two or more people, companies or organisations are in dispute, they will attempt to resolve their differences in the end by means of litigation. This does not necessarily mean that any one particular party of those above will have tried other and earlier means to solve the issue but some people resort to law alone as if it was the only solution.

Construction contracts normally invoke an arbitration clause wherein the two parties to the contract agree that, failing all other means, their dispute will be heard in arbitration. The Arbitrator would be a mutually-agreed person or failing this, one selected by the President of one of the professional institutions such as the RIBA, ICE or ISE. Although the Arbitration Act does not specify the Arbitrator's qualifications it is clearly sensible to have an experienced person in this role. At the same time the two parties can agree on the venue for the arbitration which would be held as an event not open to the public. Generally, only the two parties are involved, the Claimant and the Respondent, but another party may be "joined", albeit rarely, if there is agreement between all three parties. Arbitration cases may be held contemporaneously with the contract works or at a time when the works have been finished.

Other civil cases such as alleged negligence, fraudulent concealment or other breaches or disputes may be held in the High Court in front of an Official Referee (a Judge experienced in the relevant subject), a County Court Resident or Circuit Judge. Cases such as alleged infringement of Patent would be heard in a Patents Court in front of an experience Patents Judge. Although there is, generally speaking, only one Plaintiff there may be several Defendants. Only barristers may undertake pleading in High Court but, in some other Courts and in arbitration, anyone may plead although barristers would normally undertake this task.

Arguments about the relative costs/merits of Court -v- Arbitration abound and from the writer's own experience there is little in the statistics to give an indication of relative merit. In arbitration, the Arbitrator has to be paid for and, probably, rental of the accommodation etc. The 1992 average cost per day of running a case in either instance is about £7000. This sum ignores all the preliminary works in preparing the cases, reports, searches etc.

Recently, this matter has been partially addressed by the introduction of the Alternative Dispute Resolution (ADR) where part or whole of a dispute may be "sub-contracted" to a mutually agreed third party, usually a barrister, whose opinion would not be binding on the parties concerned.

Sources of expert

The expert will be an expert in a particular discipline or disciplines which would cover, in the construction field, one or more of the following :-

Engineering
Design
Architecture
Materials Science
Quantum

The first persons normally to get involved in a dispute, after the parties in question, are solicitors, and they will seek experts from one or more (depending upon the number of disciplines requiring the use of an expert) sources. At the time of the preparation of this paper (late 1992) the situation was somewhat fragmented but examples can be given on how, in the writer's experience, the five disciplines listed above are currently being addressed.

Engineering. Personal Knowledge. ICE. ISE. CIArb. Journals. BAE.

Design. Personal Knowledge. ICE. ISE. CIArb. Journals. BAE.

Architecture. RIBA. CIArb. Journals

Materials Science. Personal Knowledge. Soc.Chem. Inst.Phys. Concrete Society. British Masonry Society. Building Research Establishment. Journals, BAE.

Quantum, Personal Knowledge. RICS. CIOB. Journals. BAE. CIArb.

The writer's view is that the Solicitors' Journal and/or the British Academy of Experts it would, in conjunction with the professional bodies, be the best be the best vehicles for a 'yellow pages'.

DOCUMENTS

Claim and ensuing papers

Putting all the legal wording aside the expert witness is mainly interested in the specifics which are normally listed under the "Particulars of Claims". The kingpin or workhorse in all the matters is the expert's client's solicitors and, once an action is entered and, subsequently, an expert engaged, the expert will only correspond with the solicitor. Such communications remain under the heading of 'Privileged' and cannot be called up in a case unless the solicitor and the expert are in agreement on the disclosure.

Where many experts are handicapped is by the solicitor giving the expert only part of the story. In order to be honest, and to give a fair opinion, the expert should not only have copies of all papers relative to the terms of his or her discipline but could also be usefully called in to advise on wording before the submission of documents such as :-

(a)   Statement of Claim
(b)   Defence to Claim
(c)   Request for Further & Better Particulars
(d)   Counterclaim
(e)   Reply to one or more of the above documents and so on.

At some time, by order of a judge or an arbitrator, Directions will be given which will lay down dates for the action timetable and, invariably, give a date for exchange of experts' reports.

Reports

The expert will probably have had discussions with his client's solicitor and/or counsel at the times of preparation and submission of his or her draft report. It needs to be borne in mind quite emphatically that the expert must give a full opinion of the case relevant to the contents of the report. At the time of the trial, arbitration or alternative dispute resolution, he or she will be thoroughly questioned and weak points, if not covered in the report, will probably become score points for the other side. If an expert is asked to change, delete or add to the report a warning should be given that the specifics may be raised in cross-questionning.

Reports submitted by other experts or those referenced in reports by others should also be studied by the expert in order to "prime" the counsel with questions at the trial. Other documents will possibly be passed to the expert by the client's solicitor.

The expert's report should be succinct as possible and is probably best divided into sections as follows :-

(a)   Terms of reference
(b)   Expert's CV with emphasis on that experience relevant to the case
(c)   A list of documents (Unprivileged) relevant to the case including the Statement of Claim etc.
(d)   Particulars of claim
(e)   Discussion on each of these points and opinion with use of references to experience by others where relevant
(f)   Conclusions summarising each of these points and adding others where relevant.

Correspondence

The first type of correspondence is that between the expert and the client's solicitor and has been discussed earlier. The second type of correspondence is that they may have occurred earlier between your client and other parties or between other parties. One's client's solicitor needs to lay down at an early stage (and certainly before preparation of ones's report) which of these documents are privileged and which are not. Non-priviliged documents are exemplified by such as the Claim, the Specification, Variation Orders and Site Meeting Minutes. Letters between parties require separate identification. This second type of correspondence is referred to earlier.

Trade Literature

Reference to manufacturers' data sheets, specifications are often involved in the case and is unique to contracts containing a proprietary specification. Many court and arbitration cases take place many years after the works in question have been completed and it is extremely important that the correct literature is in one's reference. The literature that applies is that which was contemporaneous at the time the contract was made for tender. Manufacturers may have updated their literature in the interim period and so one must be careful to select documents that were relevant to the contract.

Two additional hurdles may confront one. The first is that some literature is not dated by the manufacturer. The second and sometimes insurmountable hurdle is that the company that supplied the product in question went out of business in the interim.

Whichever of these problems the expert encounters he or she should undertake some detective work as it is important to try and obtain the documents in question. Even if these efforts result in failure the expert can fall back on the general construction experience in that only about 15% of problems that occur are based solely on a fault in the product. It is the way the product is used that gives rise to problems.

Microfile and Screen Readers

Modern technology can make litigation far more effective in the use of microfiche and/or word process tapes instead of cumbersome paperwork. It is not uncommon in court or arbitration to have 4 or 5 ring binders in quintuplicate sets to which all parties refer to throughout the proceedings. Provided that the opposing parties agree to the documents, drawings etc. to be in the papers then all the data could be entered, for instance, into a DataBase-type system. Each of the, say, five copies of the tape could be made under supervision of the representatives of the parties concerned and the tape 'windows' immediately removed to prevent changes.   An example of the amount of paperwork that can be involved are courts in London with a lift access to the courts on the higher floors.   The commissioner will only allow one person with a sack barrow full of papers in a lift at a time in a 4 person (300kg) lift.   Packed papers nearly have the same density as water and the barrow and its papers can weight nearly 200kg.   All these courts are equipped for modern technology but only one of them uses screens for information.

Looking into the future at, possibly, a very early stage, the construction field could be dealing with a tender and contract situation where all correspondence will be on computer/word processor with support from facsimile machines and modems. Information in this form would be readily transcribable onto a master disc.   Official Referees operate on computers using 'Wordperfect 5.1' and there is much sense in using common software in the legal and associated professions.

INNOVATIONS

Specialism in lawyers

The innovation of the use of computer technology does not necessarily mean that lawyers are privileged from becoming computer-listed in some form.   What needs to be borne in mind by the client is that his company's or his personal solicitor might not be the best person to deal with the case.   Whether the solicitor's office contains 50 professionals or just the one is a largely irrelevant matter.   What is important is the track record and expertise of the solicitor.   This expertise not only applies to the type of the case, but also into the engagement of a barrister who will also, ideally, have the same leaning.

As barristers, like solicitors, advertise (eg. Chambers Directory), a golden opportunity arises for the whole lawyer fraternity to consider a master data bank or banks where the expertise, names and addresses could be listed on a data base.   The writer knows that most chambers of barristers have brochures listing dates of being called to the bar and, where relevant, dates when silk was taken coupled with the individuals expertises.

Expert Data Banks

The earlier section dealt with the disciplines of experts and the many sources from which lawyers can make their selections.   The current situation is time-consuming and the time is not far away from the possible production of a master data bank of experts covering all the disciplines concerned.   An independent organisation such as the British Academy of Experts could deal with this.   A databank for Law Society or the lawyers could be prepared just as easily.

This could be the first step in setting up a quality assurance service to BS 5750 Part 1 either as a lawyer or as an expert. Selection of the lawyer by the client and selection of the expert by the lawyer would be the last steps in a programme which could loosely be defined as "selection of the sub-contractor". The criteria by which each of these selections would be adjudged remain to be laid down. Track histories of experts, as with lawyers, would be at least one of the criteria.

Expert Split Reports

Based upon the writer's own experience, great difficulty has been experienced in most cases in trying to analyse reports by others where, seldom, has a logical Reports partitioning been operated. Criticism might be levelled at items (a) - (f) of the Reports section and the writer does not claim that it is ideal. It is based upon :-

(a)   What one had been asked to do
(b)   What one's capability is
(c)   What 'tools' one has to work with
(d)   What one thinks about the whole thing and one's evidence to support these thoughts.

The pitfall that many experts encounter is in (d) as (a) - (c) are basically mechanics. In (d), wording in experts reports such as "it is well-known" without references and "was possibly caused by" without supportive evidence are examples of lack of professionalism.

It would make for easier work for experts and lawyers if the format of all expert's reports could be formalised and that unfounded opinions and vague wordings be banned. This action would make for easier comparison of the various experts' reports. It would also allow the expert to transfer, by word processing, large parts of one of his or her expert reports to a report for another case and this could be a dangerous thing.

Pre-hearing Sortations

Very often, prior to cases being heard, experts from all the parties concerned meet at a mutually convenient place for a "Without prejudice" meeting. The purpose of the meeting is mainly to discuss the issues of the case, sort out which ones have general agreement, which are at a slight variance and which constitute complete disagreement. Solicitors do not have to attend these meetings but, if they do not, the expert must submit a written report.

The phrase 'without prejudice' means that whatever is said or displayed cannot be called up in evidence unless the documents concerned are already a part of the agreed evidence. Experience by the writer at these meetings is that the discussions that occur are generally extremely prejudiced. One of the main reasons for this is that experts all too often want to 'sugar the pill' for their client and tend to denigrate evidence they do not want to hear. On no account should one be drawn into a repetitive argument situation. If disagreement is reached on a particular issue one should agree to disagree and move onto the next business.

The expert's task at these meetings is to help in decreasing the potential trial time by a sortation of the issues, especially in obtaining a pre-trial agreement on as many issues as possible.

EURO LAW

Effect of Directives

Herein a rather inconclusive state of affairs exists as there are several Directives that are relevant to construction and to concrete in particular. The European Commission of Ministers (the Commission) issue Regulations & Directives and has a number of Standing and other Committees serving it and giving it advice and drawing up drafts. Regulations are immediately effective from the date of publication whereas Directives, which require national legislation, are given a gestation period before becoming full law in the Community.

The main Directive affecting concrete and construction is the Construction Products Directive. It contains, inter alia essential requirements for products as they affect the works, the CE Mark and Attestation. However, as at the end of 1992 the Commission had not dealt with attestation in a manner which lends itself to implementation of harmonized standards. Import/export of goods that are claimed to comply with a harmonized standard is likely to be fertile ground for future legislation. This will be of special interest to lawyers as claims for non-compliance would be held in the country responsible for the manufacturer or distribution of the product within the Community.

The Product Liability Directive is already UK law in the form of the Consumer Protection Act 1987 and, since health & safety are favourite European specification bases, it may be predicted that experts will become involved in more and more cases.

The Services Liability Draft Directive, as at the end of 1992, excluded the Construction Industry but includes, inter alia, health services, social services inter alia. As one can well imagine, there is a great deal of trepidation in members of these services concerning the insurance premiums likely to be charged to cover this liability.

The field of concrete in the European scene has an "odd man out" and that is ready-mixed concrete. It is not a construction product until it becomes hard so, although one can invoke harmonized standards for cement, aggregates, water for concrete, and admixtures it is not relevant to have a harmonized standard for ready-mixed concrete. Thus, in the UK scene, reliance will have to be placed on the national standard, ie BS 5328. Claims that arise out of things such as alleged non-compliance will come under local, not European law. Experts having the disciplines of concrete technologist or materials scientists have an are being used in many cases of dispute.

Requirements of future Directives

The problems that have been produced by the current Directives are, in the writer's opinion, largely due to a poorly-advised bureaucracy producing legislation without regard to either its effect or for the need of supportive mandates for the people who have to produce or revise standards. Such a complicated situation exists that when European lawyers met in 1991 to assess how European laws would manifest themselves in each of the Member States their 'without prejudice' meeting agreed to disagree on virtually all matters except one. That one was that any dispute concerning the European Laws would be subject to a hearing in the European Court.

This 'closing the stable door after the horse has bolted' would imply that as far as future Directives are concerned lawyers and experts need to contribute to the wording of documents in order to ensure that what is eventually published is workable. The overlap of lawyer/expert disciplines is the bottom line of any activity and each must realise the other's capabilities and limitations.

CONCLUDING REMARKS

Data banks held by independent and well-known organisations would seem to be useful tools in helping to solve the current information/communications problems that exist between the expert witness and the lawyer. However, attention will need to be paid to the Common Market and how the Directives will affect, inter alia, construction law and the registration of expert witnesses (or consultants) and those practising law.

A NEW BUILDING MATERIAL:
THE BIG PORES CONCRETE

A Ionescu

Technical University of Cluj-Napoca

Romania

ABSTRACT. The paper reports on the first experimental reseacrch concerning a new type of construction material, which is the big spherical pores concrete. This new type of concrete can be achieved using a new, special kind of artificial spherical aggregates with thin shells. These aggregates can be made of mortars with different binding materials, they can be variously sized in diameter and shell thickness, consequently displaying a large variety of particular strength properties. The characteristics of the porous concrete to be made depend on these particular strength properties and, according to the variant chosen, either light weight, both resistant and thermoinsulating concrete, or only thermoinsulating one can be obtained. The paper presents the first experimental results obtained in producing this new kind of aggregate and the big spherical pores concrete. Due to the important technical and economical advantages offered by this new type of concrete, it is foreseen to be efficiently used in cast-in-place and prefabricated slabs, in foundations, walls, masonry blocks a.s.o.

Keywords: Big pores concrete (BPC), Artificial spherical aggregates (ASA).

Professor Dr Anton Ionescu is the Dean of the Civil Engineering Faculty within the Technical University of ClujNapoca, Romania, and professor of Reinforced Concrete Structures. He works mainly in the field of prefabricated reinforced concrete structures, especially in demountable ones, and recently in the development of a new, efficient artificial spherical aggregate and of the big pores concrete achieved with this new kind of aggregates.

Concrete 2000. Edited by Ravindra K. Dhir and M. Roderick Jones.
© 1993 Published by E & FN Spon. ISBN 0 419 18120 2.

INTRODUCTION

The known natural aggregates used in light weight concretes, such as: diatomite, pumice stone, volcanic scoria, volcanic ash, tuff and others, as well as the artificial aggregates known so far for these concretes, such as: expanded clay, pearlit, expanded slag and others, all have a series of disadvantages that have prevented them from being widely used, mainly:

- the fact that they are concentrated in certain geographical areas, as referred to world or national scale

- the fact that they require great energy consumption during the expanding process

- the fact that they are highly non-uniform as far as their quality is concerned

- the fact that they have a reduced workability due to their irregular shapes and porosity of their surfaces

The new types of artificial aggregates, conceived for a new sort of concretes - mainly, the big pores concretes - avoid the above mentioned disadvantages by:

- being spherical, which is the optimum shape of aggregates to be used in concretes

- having minimum specific weight, as they are spherically shaped thin shells

- being universal, as they can be achieved anywhere, from mortars with various binding materials, such as: cement, lime, plaster, resins, polymers a.s.o., as well as from different local materials, such as: sand, ashes, slags, dust a.s.o.

- having variable particular strength properties, which depend on the material used, on the external diameter, on the thickness of the shell and on the type of reinforcement.

EXPERIMENTAL RESULTS

As a first step, there have been produced ASA of cement mortar, with the external diameter of 50 mm and 2 mm thick not-reinforced shells (Photo 1).

Figure 1   Artificial spherical aggregates

Figure 2   Internal structure of a BPC cube

Figure 3   View of a BPC cube after rupture test

The density of this kind of aggregate is of 560-620 kg/m^3 and the density in bulk is of 310-340 kg/m^3.

With this type of ASA there have been achieved two kinds of concretes: ordinary BPC (Photo 2), with average densities of 1,300-1,500 kg/m^3 and macro-porous BPC, with average densities of 800-900 kg/m^3.

Preliminary mechanical tests were performed on the ordinary BPC, the rupture strengths obtained, at 1,300-1,500 kg/m^3 densities, being of 15-20 N/mm^2.

CONCLUSIONS

1. The above preliminary physical and mechanical characteristics of BPC make it potentially efficiently usable in cast-in-situ and prefabricated slabs, in foundations, walls, masonry blocks a.s.o.

2. These experimental tests represent only the start in a new direction of research in the field of lightweight concretes, research that aims at making clear all the problems concerning the large number of parameters on which the physical and mechanical characteristics of this new kind of concrete depend on.

REFERENCES

1. LEWICKI, B. Betoane usoare. Editura Tehnica, Bucuresti, 1970.

2. MIHAIL, N. Tehnologia betoanelor usoare. Editura Tehnica, Bucuresti 1982.

3. IONESCU, A. Agregate sferice pentru betoane usoare si procedeu de obtinere a acestora. Brevet de inventie RO 105564 B1, 1991.

APPLICATION OF CALCIUM SULFOALUMINATE CEMENTS IN THE 21ST CENTURY

A D R Brown

Blue Circle Industries plc
United Kingdom

ABSTRACT. A series of special cements based on a new calcium sulfoaluminate clinker has been developed over the last 10 years. This paper covers the development of the clinker, and its differences in relation to traditional Type K clinkers on the one hand and calcium aluminate cements on the other. The production of cements for specific applications by selective blending of the clinker with other components is described, and some applications reviewed. Results for several durability aspects of the cements are presented and areas of further study outlined.

The uses of such cements are numerous but their successful role in construction projects can occasionally require alterations to traditional site practices. This flexibility in usage is discussed in relation to cost benefits and potential future trends.

KEYWORDS: Calcium sulfoaluminate, clinker composition, formulations, applications, durability, future trends.

A. Derek R. Brown is Section Head of Microscopic Services department at Blue Circle Industries PLC Technical Centre at Greenhithe, Kent. He has a varied experience of cement and concrete analysis and testing, in addition to development and technical support expertise in the field of novel cements. Current activities include involvement in NAMAS accredited physical testing of cements, and material evaluations using optical microscopy, scanning electron microscopy, and X-ray diffraction. He has a degree in Geology and Mineralogy, and is a Member of the Institute of Concrete Technology.

Concrete 2000. Edited by Ravindra K. Dhir and M. Roderick Jones.
© 1993 Published by E & FN Spon. ISBN 0 419 18120 2.

INTRODUCTION

A characteristic of calcium sulfoaluminate cements has been their diversity, both in terms of their composition, and in their mode of use or application. The main categories of existing types are Type K, and CSA additives. Type M and S are also closely associated cement types. Reviews are given by Kalousek (1) and Hoff and Mather (2).

This paper describes another patented variant of type K clinker. In addition to describing the clinker composition, a range of cements of which it is a constituent is discussed.

CLINKER DEVELOPMENT

The production of this clinker was initially prompted by the need to develop an improved cement for the production of mining roadway supports. For this purpose, cement slurries are pumped underground to the point of placement References 3 and 4 give more details.

Some existing cements were too alkaline from a safety consideration and required an 'aggregate', usually coal waste, as part of the mix. Such cements were also found to be abrasive to the slurry pumps. Replacements were therefore sought to overcome these shortcomings, and an aggregate free system based on the formation of ettringite ($C_3A.3CaSO_4.32H_2O$) as the sole hydrate was adopted as the most suitable approach.

A sulfoaluminate clinker of high stability, consistent composition and predictable properties was essential, and the other requirement was that the cement slurry could be pumped for a considerable time without setting in the supply pipelines.

Stability was required to avoid variations in performance due to changes on storage, and the clinker was therefore designed to have very low free lime levels, and to be devoid of highly reactive compounds such as $C_{12}A_7$. This also removed the need for expensive retardation of the cement slurry. The composition targeted was free of reactive calcium silicates (C_3S and C_2S) in order to both reduce the alkalinity, and allow the use of high purity aluminous raw materials for product consistency.

The composition finally adopted was one of several investigated, and could be manufactured in a conventional rotary kiln with only slight modifications to the control procedures.

The clinker, and some derived cements, are marketed under the trade name of Rockfast, while the mining system is designated as Hydropack.

ROCKFAST TYPE K COMPOSITION

The closest equivalent production clinkers previously made were Type K clinkers of variable composition which are significantly higher in calcium silicates and free lime and lower in Klein's compound ($C_4A_3\overline{S}$). Data for a low silicate Japanese product (Denka CSA) and a conventional calcium aluminate cement are presented in Table 1 for comparison. Since the clinker formulation is deficient in both CaO and SO_3 for ettringite formation , wet slurries of the neat cement can be pumped for up to 24 hours with little detectable hydration. Having the source of CaO and SO_3 external to the sulfoaluminate clinker allows a degree of flexibility for expansive properties in non mining applications.

Table 1. Chemical and Compound Composition of Rockfast Calcium Sulfoaluminate and of Other Clinkers for Comparison

	Rockfast	Type K (I)	Type K (2)	Denka CSA	Calcium Aluminate Cement
SiO_2	3.6	10.7	23.8	1.6	4.5
Al_2O_3	47.4	20.7	5.8	14.1	38.5
Fe_2O_3	1.4	1.7	1.1	0.3	16.0
CaO	38.0	46.9	61.7	51.8	37.9
MgO	0.3	1.1	2.0	1.2	0.6
SO_3	7.5	18.5	3.5	29.6	0.2
TiO_2	2.2	0.3	0.1	0.2	2.5
K_2O	0.16	0.29	0.25	0.06	0.15
LOI	0.3	0.7	0.7	0.6	-
Free Lime	0.3	0.3	8.0	18.1	0.1
Estimated Compound Composition					
$C_4A_3\bar{S}$	57	38	10	28	0
CA	17	0	0	0	43
$C_{12}A_7$	0	0	0	0	9
$C\bar{S}$	0.5	23	4	44	0
C_2AS	17	0	0	0	10
C_4AF	4	5	3	1	29
CT	4	0.5	0.2	0.3	4
C_2S	0	30	61	0	5
C_3S	0	1	10	6	0
CaO	0.3	0.3	8	18	0.1

Reaction is initiated by splash mixing the cement slurry with an activator slurry containing calcium sulfate, and hydralime as its reactive agents. Mixing is done in flexible plastic 'forms', which subsequently become the tunnel roofing supports, following setting.

This low strength dual slurry system, and a foamed derivative, have also been used for cavity filling operations in mining situations.

PROPERTIES OF HYDROPACK ROADWAY SUPPORT SYSTEM

While this paper concentrates on the civil engineering uses of calcium sulfoaluminate cements, the properties of the mining product for which the clinker was initially developed are briefly presented below.

Table 2. Properties of Hydropack Roofing Support System

Method of Use	2 component slurries - cement + 'activator'. Splash mixed in- situ in 1:1 ratio
Useable life of slurries	24 hours, or up to 7 days using a retarder.
Hydration Products	Ettringite ($C_3A.3CaSO_4.32H_2O$) as the only hydrated compound formed
Water:Solids Ratio	12:1 by Volume
Aggregate used	None
Modulus of Elasticity (N/mm^2) cured at 20°C	8 at 2 hours, 420 at 24 hours, 2260 at 7 days
Modulus of Elasticity (N/mm^2) cured at 35°C	2120 at 2 hours, 900 at 24 hours, 730 at 7 days
Compressive Strengths (N/mm^2) cured at 20°C	0.3 at 1 hour, 2.5 at 4 hours, 4.0 at 24 hours

NOVEL CEMENTS AND APPLICATIONS

In addition to the above use of this sulfoaluminate clinker, the properties of rapid setting and strength development, and controlled dimensional properties have been utilised in several more conventional cement applications, using much lower water cement ratios. Cements are produced by grinding the clinker to specific surface areas in excess of 400 m^2/kg **without** introducing further sulfate compounds such as gypsum as in conventional Portland cement production. The range of cement types developed use Rockfast clinker as one component in blended formulations with Ordinary Portland Cements, anhydrite, and at times pozzolanic additions or fibre reinforcing. Formulations are numerous, and are dictated by the target application. This flexibility of approach is further extended by the use of integral admixtures, where appropriate, to provide improvements in such aspects as water reduction, self levelling, or set control. To date no difficulties have been experienced when using normal commercially available admixtures with sulfoaluminate derived blends.

High early strengths and the desired dimensional behaviour are achieved **consistently** as a result of the tightly controlled composition of the sulfoaluminate component, and its relatively inert state prior to the commencement of normal hydration. High early strengths and expansion or shrinkage compensation are achieved by the formation of ettringite ($C_3A.3CaSO_4.32H_2O$) (5,6), the deposition of which is supplemented both concurrently and subsequently by normal hydration products of the Ordinary Portland Cement component. Indeed, the sulfoaluminate and OPC act as mutual accelerators. Scanning electron microscopy has shown that an initial skeletal hydrate structure of ettringite is infilled and densified as the OPC hydration proceeds. (Figure 1).

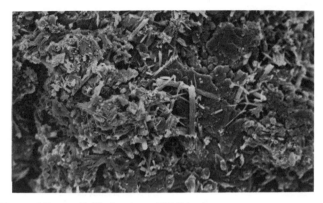

Figure 1 Dense Sulfoaluminate/OPC hydrate structure.   (x 6500).

In contrast with normal OPC hydration, excess CaO in solution is mostly combined in the formation of ettringite leading to the virtual absence of free $Ca(OH)_2$ as a hydration product. This has been confirmed by XRD and SEM studies and has additional benefits in durability terms as discussed later. The following products show the diversity of cement types and uses.

Rockfast PCA - A general purpose cement used primarily where early use of pavement structures is desirable plus reduced shrinkage.
Rockfast 40 - A cement used for ground slab concrete where shrinkage compensation or expansion is required.
Norcrete   - A coated steel pipe joint 'weld' mortar.
Quickrock   - A rapid repair compound which allows very fast use of the repaired concrete to be achieved.
Sprayrock   - A rapid setting, machine applied top coat mortar.
Rockfast RL - A spray applied tunnel lining mortar.
Calcrete   - A cement used in GRC components to allow rapid mould turnaround of precast units, reduced shrinkage, plus a reduction in 'ageing' effects. Calcrete shows significantly less loss of strain with time compared to other GFRC cement products.
Anchor Bolt Grout - A rapid set, high early strength grout where the early introduction of tensional strain or flowing water, or both, is part of the site conditions.

For the concrete applications, mixes of high cement contents have normally been used to augment the Rockfast high early strength properties, and strength development at later ages is significantly greater than with conventional high early strength formulations. As demonstrated in Figure 1, this is due to the ability of the Portland cement to hydrate gradually without retardation due to the initial rapid hydrate formation.

A specification which called for a pumpable mix, 40 N/mm^2 at 28 days and a 0.05% expansion was easily met using Rockfast 40 where the anhydrite to sulfoaluminate ratio is modified to induce expansive behaviour.

Mortar products are numerous and can follow conventional varieties which incorporate fibre reinforcement and can be spray applied. Bonding and moulding is superior due to the reduced shrinkage. Table 3 presents the properties exhibited by the above novel cements.

Table 3. Properties of Calcium Sulfoaluminate Cement Products
Concrete Applications
Rockfast PCA   Cement content 450 kg/m^3 Slump 50 ± 20mm

Working Time	Compressive Strengths (N/mm^2)				Flex Strength (N/mm^2)	Drying Shrinkage ASTM C157
	4hr	1d	7d	28d	28day	
30-60 mins	18.7	35.5	51.2	60.3	4.1	-0.02%

Rockfast 40   Cement content 360 kg/m^3 Slump 100 ± 20mm

Working Time	Compressive Strengths (N/mm^2)			Dimensional Change (Restrained)
	3 day	7 day	28 day	
1-3 hours	28.1	48.9	66.3	+0.08% (ASTM C806-87)

Norcrete   Pipe Weld Concrete 10mm coarse agg. Steel Fibre Reinforced

Working Time	Compressive Strengths (N/mm^2)					Flexural Strengths (N/mm^2)		
	10min	1hr	1d	7d	28d	10mins	1d	7d
5 mins	5	18	37	58	68	1	8	11

Mortar Applications
Quickrock rapid repair mortar

Working Time	Compressive Strength (N/mm^2)			Dimensional Change
	30min	1h	1day	
15 mins	10	24	65	-0.01%

Sprayrock Fibre reinforced render.

Working Time	Compressive Strength (N/mm^2)				Dimensional Change
	1h	6h	1d	7d	
2-3 mins	8	15	27	42	-0.005%

Rockfast RL   Spray applied tunnel lining mortar

Working Time	Comp. Str. (N/mm^2)		Flex. Str.(N/mm^2)	Dimensional Change
	1d	7d		
7-10 mins	33	54	1d - 4.2 7d - MOE 15000 MOR 8 LOP 8	-0.005%

Calcrete for glass fibre reinforced concrete

Working Time	Comp. Str. (N/mm^2)				Flex.Str. (N/mm^2)	Dimensional Change
		1d	7d	28d		
5-30 mins	1:1 sand	43	54	80	LOP	
	1:3 sand	19	26	53	6.4 - 9.3	-0.01%

Grouts
Anchor Bolt Grout

Working Time	Compressive Strength (N/mm^2)			Dimensional Change
	4 hours	1 day	7 days	
65-90 mins	12	40	55	-0.02%

DURABILITY

Durability studies of calcium sulfoaluminate cements are numerous and generally indicate problem areas are limited. The following references are amongst those giving good background information for both general and specific applications (7 - 11).

Studies have been carried out over the last five years at Blue Circle's Technical Centre in a number of areas of durability concern relevant to Rockfast cements. Test specimens were commonly mortar prisms for chemical solution studies but concrete specimens have been used for most other aspects. The incorporation of additions such as ground granulated blastfurnace slag and silica fume have also been explored in relation to strength development and durability.

The simplicity of the hydration system, in particular the virtual absence of $Ca(OH)_2$ and metastable hexagonal calcium aluminate hydrates, means that deleterious ageing effects are absent and strength growth positive. Conditions which may lead to ettringite decomposition are considered later.

Table 1 indicates that the alkali content of the Rockfast clinker is extremely low, and therefore blended formulations have total alkali contents below that of the Portland cement component and thus reduce the risk of alkali silica reaction when using potentially reactive aggregates. Rockfast PCA, for example, has an equivalent Na_2O content of 0.60%, and this can be further reduced for sensitive applications by using a guaranteed low alkali OPC. Pore fluid studies have indicated that the pH values of the pore solutions are 12.8 to 13.5, and therefore still sufficiently alkaline to ensure passivation of steel reinforcement.

Tables 4 to 6, and Figure 2 summarise our findings to date.

Table 4. Rockfast PCA Mechanical and Chemical Stability
Flexural and Compressive Strengths (N/mm^2) of 1:1 PCA:Sand

| | Water Cured | | | | | |
| | 100% PCA | | 60% PCA/40% ggbs | | 85% PCA/15% Si Fume | |
	Flex.	Comp.	Flex.	Comp.	Flex.	Comp.
1 month	7.9	61	6.1	61	4.5	50
3 "	6.6	65	6.3	78	6.8	68
6 "	6.9	68	5.6	80	7.0	68
12 "	7.6	65	5.8	82	6.8	68
	Air Cured (After 24 hours moist curing)					
	100% PCA		60% PCA/40% ggbs		85% PCA/15% Si Fume	
	Flex.	Comp.	Flex.	Comp.	Flex.	Comp.
1 month	9.3	56	6.6	36	3.7	36
3 "	8.3	56	5.6	34	4.1	34
6 "	8.5	59	5.6	33	5.6	30
12 "	9.6	58	7.8	31	7.3	28
Phase composition at 28 days	Unhydrated OPC (25% of original OPC fraction), ettringite, calcium silicate hydrate (C-S-H).					
Phase composition at 5 years	Ettringite, (C-S-H), trace of OPC, and calcite.					

Variable accounts are given regarding the sulfate resistance of sulfoaluminate cements (7,8). This results from the differing ratios of sulfate to aluminate used and consequent variation in potential for the formation of secondary disruptive hydration products in the event of ingress of external sulphates. In a properly designed system it has been demonstrated that the performance of sulfoaluminate cements is as good as that of Sulfate Resisting Portland Cement. Figure 2 shows the results of sulfate resistance and seawater resistance studies using Rockfast PCA.

Under certain conditions such as attack by acidic solutions, leaching of sulfate from sulfoaluminate concrete into surrounding concrete could potentially occur. Testing of this aspect is in progress, but field experience suggest this is avoided due to the impermeability of the sulfoaluminate clinker. Freeze thaw resistance and drying shrinkage results (Table 5) were found to be satisfactory. Air entrainment was not used for these tests which were mainly designed to examine the stability of the hydrate structure under saturated, low temperature conditions

Permeability and chloride ion diffusion data (Table 6) suggest that as expected from the dense microstructure of the hydrated paste, penetrability values for both are low.

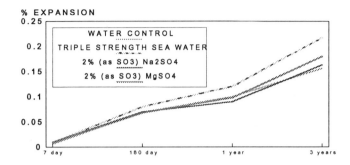

Figure 2.   Sulfate and seawater resistance of Rockfast PCA

The mechanism responsible for the low chloride ion penetration values is probably a combination of low permeability and chemical binding of chloride ions as chloro-aluminate hydrates. This will be the subject of further examination .

Table 5. Freeze Thaw Resistance and Drying Shrinkage

Freeze/Thaw - Mortar Specimens (1:1) 2 cycles of Freeze/Wetting per day

% Expansion

No. of cycles	100% PCA	60% PCA/40% ggbs	85% PCA/15% Si Fume
15	-0.006	+0.041	+0.004
30	-0.003	+0.045	-
100 (1)	+0.004	+0.061	+0.005
145	+0.016	+0.110	-
230	+0.067	+0.120	+0.010

Freeze/Thaw - ASTM C666 Concrete Testing

After 300 cycles there was no visual disintegration and weight less was negligible.

Relative Dynamic Modulus (Durability Factor)

P = 70.1% for prisms cured for 7 days   P = 72.8% for prisms cured for 28 days

Drying Shrinkage

Modified ASTM C157 - concrete prisms.

Maximum shrinkage relative to saturated condition was 0.02% after 16 days, curing at 20°C, 50% relative humidity. No further long term shrinkage detected.

Note (1) An expansion of <0.1% and/or remaining sound at 100 cycles is considered to show adequate durability for this test.

Table 6. Permeability and Chloride Ion Diffusion

Permeability
(Oxygen permeability result were used to calculate **equivalent water permeabilities**.)
3×10^{-18} m^2 or 3×10^{-11} m/s

ISAT Testing - results from a test slab (ml per m^{2}s)

10 mins	30 mins	1 hour	2 hours
0.12	0.04	0.02	0.02

Chloride Ion Diffusion
Accelerated testing . 4.39×10^{-12} m^2/s.

Additionally studies are in progress to test the resistance of Rockfast formulations to carbonation, attack by solutions of varying pH, and reactive chemical reagents such as urea, alcohol, and de-icing salts. Resistance is generally considered adequate, and ettringite has been found to be stable above pH 10.5 (12,13).

Future plans also include a study of the effects of elevated temperatures. Previous studies (14,15) indicated that ettringite will decompose, when dry, above 55°C, and above 95°C when wet. Durability studies therefore indicate few areas of concern, and practical information from usage in potentially aggressive environments has further substantiated this view. It should be appreciated however that many applications are for cement rich mixes which coupled with the dense hydrate structure lead to impermeable, and thus durable concretes.

FUTURE TRENDS

Type K cements, of which Kleins compound ($C_4A_3\overline{S}$), is an essential component, have mainly been used for shrinkage compensating/expansive properties, with the early strength potential largely neglected. Considerable experience in the use of shrinkage compensating and self stressing concretes has been accrued in Japan and the USA, and significant steps taken towards the development of applicable standards (16 - 20). Factory produced cements are employed in the USA while the addition of expansive additives at the mixing stage is more common in Japan. The latter approach has been shown to be prone to accidents where either excessive expansion or increased drying cracking has occurred as a result of incorrect batching. Aeration of cements and unpredictable workability are pitfalls with conventional type K factory produced cements. Various types of structures have benefited from shrinkage compensating concretes, with water retaining structures being the most common. Apart from poorly constructed water stops, drying shrinkage cracks are by far the most common cause of leakage in such structures. The initial compressive force developed in restrained shrinkage compensated concrete is subsequently relieved or released by tensional stress due to drying and cracking can be virtually eliminated. Lightly reinforced pavement slabs, and restrained bridge decks have also shown advantages when shrinkage compensating concrete was used. In addition to reduced cracking, cost benefits are reported due to the ability to use larger pours, fewer water stops and joints, reduced levels of steel reinforcing and thinner members using modifications in design. By contrast, experience in the UK and mainland Europe is more limited, and standards absent. Most experience to date is in the fields of floor screeds and repair compounds as opposed to large scale structural use of concrete. Substantial scope therefore exists if European construction is to gain from the use of such cements, but much practical knowledge and work towards the production of standards is required. We may see specialised contractors offering the required expertise from design through to finishing, and innovation could be required in areas of novel construction practice, for example when workable life of concrete is short.

CONCLUSIONS

Future development in construction will tackle the following areas ; (1) cost effectiveness, (2) production of well designed, defect free, new structures, and (3) subsequent durability.

Initial experience with Type K and Rockfast cements suggests that sufficient performance durability, and reliability exists to enable their use in applications which will benefit from one or more of the following properties :- (1) High early and late strength. (2) Reduced drying shrinkage. (3)Expansion/Self stressing. (4) Non aggressive to GFRC.

ACKNOWLEDGEMENTS

The author would like to thank the Directors of Blue Circle Industries PLC for permission to publish this paper, and Pozament Limited for supplying some test data.

REFERENCES

1. KALOUSEK, GL. Development of expansive cements. Kleins Symp. on Expansive Cement Concrete. ACI Pub. SP-38, 1973, pp.1-20 .

2. HOFF, GC, MATHER, K. A look at Type K shrinkage-compensating cement Production and Specifications. Cedric Willson Symp. on Expansive Cement. ACI Pub. SP-64, 1980, pp.153-180.

3. LONG, GR, LONGMAN, PA, GARTSHORE, GC. Special cements for mining applications. Proc. 9th Int. Conf. Cement Microscopy, Reno, 1987, pp. 236-246.

4. BROOKS, SA, SHARP, JH. Ettringite-based cements. Proc Int. Conf. Calcium Aluminate Cements, Ed. RJ Mangabhai Pub.E & FN Spon, 1990, pp 335-349.

5. MEHTA, PK. Mechanism of expansion associated with ettringite formation. Cement and Concrete. Research. Vol 3 No. 1, 1973, pp.1-6.

6. OKUSHIMA, M, CORDO, R. et al. Development of expansive cement with C_4A_3S clinker.Proc 5th Int.Symp.Chemistry of Cement,TokyoVol. IV, 1968, pp.419-438

7. MEHTA, PK, POLIVKA, M. Sulfate resistance of expansive cement concretes. Durability of Concrete . ACI Pub. SP 47, 1975, pp.367-379.

8. MEHTA,P.K.. Durability of expansive cement concretes. Proc. Conf. Expansive Cement Concretes, Berkeley, California, June 1972.

9. TANAKA, M, UCHIDA, I. Durability of GFRC with Calcium silicate - C_4A_3S Type low alkaline cement. Proc. Durability of GFRC Sym,.1985, pp. 305-314.

10. MOORE, GB. Tidal exposure effects on concrete made with shrinkage compensating cement. Cedric Wilson Symp. on Expansive Cement ACI Pub. SP-64, 1980, pp.115-122.

11. SAKAI, E, KOSUGE, K, TERAMURA, S, NAKAGAWA, K. Carbonation of expansive concrete and change of hydration products. Proc 2nd Int. Conf. Durability of concrete, Montreal. ed. VM Malhotra, 1991, Vol. 2, pp.989-999.

12. GABRISOVA, A, HAVLICA, J, SAHU, S. Stability of calcium sulphoaluminate hydrates in water solutions with various pH values. Cement and Concrete Research, 1991,Vol. 21 No. 6, , pp.1023-1027.

13. GHORAB, HY, KISHAR, EA. The stability of the calcium sulfoaluminate hydrates in aqueous solutions. 8th Int. Cong. Chem. of Cement Rio de Janeiro, 1986 Vol. V. pp.104-109.

14. MEHTA, PK. Stability of ettringite on heating. J. Am Ceram Soc. Vol 55, No. 1, 1972, pp.55-56.

15. SATARA, V. VEPREK, O. Thermal decomposition of ettringite under hydro-thermal conditions. J. Am Ceram Soc. 1975, Vol 58 No. 7-8, pp.357-358 .

16. ACI COMMITTEE 223 Standard practice for the use of shrinkage compensated concretes. ACI Journal, 1976, Vol 73 No. 6, pp.319-339.

17. POLIVKA, M. Properties of shrinkage compensating concretes. Proc. Conf Expansive Cement Concrete, Berkeley, California. June 1972.

18. LILJESTROM, WP, POLIVKA, M. A five year study of the Dimensional stability of shrinkage-compensating lightweight concrete used in post tensioned slabs. Klein Symp. on Expansive Cement Concrete ACI Pub. SP-38, 1973, pp.89-105.

19. WILLIAMS, JV, Hydraulic structures designed with shrinkage-compensating concrete. Cedric Willson. Symp. on Expansive Cement. ACI Pub. SP-64,1980, pp. 7-12.

20. NAGATAKI, S. Expansive cement concretes in Japan. Cedric Willson Symp. on Expansive Cement ACI Pub SP-64, 1980, pp.43-79.

EFFICIENCY OF NEW CONCRETE TYPES

C Bob

I Buchman

E Jebelean

Technical University of Timisoara

Romania

ABSTRACT. An overview on new special concrete types such as
concrete with superplasticizers and silica fume, polymer
impregnated concrete and concrete reinforced with steel
fibers is presented in this paper. Physical and mechanical
characteristics obtained by laboratory teste are also presented. A part of the analysis concerns the economic aspect
of the new special concrete types. It is discussed by calculation of the specific cost of stress and of the specific
cost of strain energy. Some conclusions concerning the
technical and economical efficiency will be given.

Keywords: New concretes, Concrete with fibres, Concrete
with superplasticizers, Concrete with silica fume, Polymer
impregnated concrete, Technical and economical efficiency.

Professor Corneliu Bob is a full-time professor at the
Faculty of Civil Engineering, Technical University,
Timişoara, Romania. He has been most active in concrete
behaviour, new special concrete types, admixtures, assessment of concrete quality and durability of concrete. His
current research work also includes methods of analysis and
design of RC structures. He has published many papers and
some books on various aspects of civil engineering.

DR. Iosif Buchman is Assoc. Professor at the Faculty of
Civil Engineering, Technical University Timişoara, Romania.
He has been primarily involved in research on concrete
structures as well as on new special concrete types as steel
fiber reinforced concrete and concrete with silica fume. He
has published many papers on various aspects of civil eng.

DR. Eugen Jebelean is a Lecturer at the Faculty of Civil
Engineering, Technical University, Timişoara, Romania.
Dr. Jebelean has been principally involved in the research
and development of new special concrete types (concrete
with superplasticizers and with other additives).

Concrete 2000. Edited by Ravindra K. Dhir and M. Roderick Jones.
© 1993 Published by E & FN Spon. ISBN 0 419 18120 2.

INTRODUCTION

New special concrete types were created to satisfy specific applications where conventional concrete has neither good behaviour nor durability. Some of the new concrete types have very good mechanical, physical and chemical characteristics.

The efficiency of classical concretes and of new special concrete types may be analysed only in the role of concreting elements into a structure. One of the above requirements shall be met by the choice of suitable materials; it is possible by analysis of technical and economical efficiency.

HIGH-STRENGTH CONCRETE

High-strength concrete (HSC) presents considerably distinct characteristics compared with ordinary concrete (normal-strength concrete with concrete strengths of less than 60 N/mm^2). In the following, some results concerning the concrete mixtures and the characteristics of HSC will be given. The authors have studied three types of HSC: concrete with superplasticizers, concrete with superplasticizers and silica fume, polymer impregnated concrete.

Concrete with superplasticizer (CS)

Many additives were tested by the authors with the aim of getting a superplasticizer for concrete: it was denoted SP4. This superplasticizer is based on sulfosuccinic polyethylenepolyamides. The effect of superplasticizer SP4 on the workability of concrete was measured by slump test for

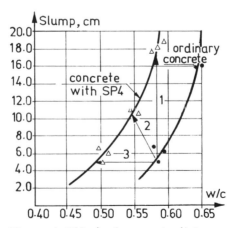

Figure 1 Effect of superplasticizer

different water-cement (w/c) ratio (Fig.1). Three research methods were used: 1-improvement of workability at the same w/c ratio; 2-light improvement of workability at temperate reduction of w/c ratio; 3-high reduction of w/c ratio at the same workability. The effect of superplasticizer SP4 on compressive strength for different w/c ratios is presented in Fig.2 where the following are illustrated: ordinary concrete with low strength (20 N/mm^2) fluid concrete, concrete with reduced w/c ratio, concrete with reduced cement content.

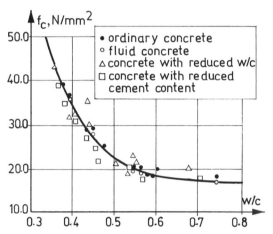

Figure 2 Effect of superplasticizer on
compressive strength

Concrete with superplasticizers and silica fume (CSF)

Using low water-binder ratios, adding silica fume as a new admixture and using superplasticizer, it is no problem to reach high-strength concrete: typical mixtures of HSC are shown in Table 1.

The 7 and 28-day concrete strength, determined on 40x40x160 mm prisms demonstrated that desired concrete strength could be reached either by using French silica fume and superplasticizer or by using Romanian admixtures (Table 2).

Polymer impregnated concrete (PIC)

Polymer impregnated concrete (PIC) is a precast and hydrated cured cement concrete which has been impregnated with a low viscosity monomer and polymerized in-situ. The

Table 1   Typical mixtures of concrete with
superplasticizers and silica fume

Materials		Batch			
		A	B	C	D
Cement P40,	kg/m^3	506	494	494	494
Sand	kg/m^3	1519	1482	1482	1482
Water	$1/m^3$	253	163	171	168.5
Silica fume;Type;	kg/m^3	-	49.4/F	49.4/R	49.4/R
Superplastici-zer; Type;	kg/m^3	-	11.0/NS	5.56/M	5.5/S
W/B - ratio		0.5	0.300	0.315	0.310
Cone penetration, cm		4	2	2	2

Note: Sand is of 0.08/0.16; 0.16/0.5; 0.5/1; 1/2 mm;
      F-French silica fume; NS-French superplasticizer;
      R-Romanian silica fume; M-Mighty superplasticizer;
      S-SP_4

Table 2   The strengths of concrete with
superplasticizers and silica fume

Batch	Strength, N/mm^2			
	f_c-compressive strength		f_{ct}-tensile strength	
	7 d	28 d	7 d	28 d
A	24,93	29.37	6.00	7.35
B	45.80	55.60	7.50	11.23
C	54.59	75.75	10.97	13.38
D	43.12	52.34	7.95	11.12

significant..improvement in structural and durability properties has been obtained with PIC compared with to
ordinary concrete.

The main steps of processing techniques for producing PIC
has been: fabrication of precast concrete specimens in a similar way to conventional concrete; oven-drying for 24 h at
105°; saturation with monomer by immersion in methylmetha-
crylate (MMA) at normal pressure and temperature; in-situ
polymerization by thermal-catalytic techniques at 75°C for
2 h.

Main mechanical and physical properties are given Table 3 for unimpregnated and MMA-impregnated concrete polymerized by thermal-catalytic means.

The efficiency of impregnation on the compressive strength of PIC is defined as the difference between compressive strength of PIC and unimpregnated concrete - Δf_c |3|. It was found |2| |3| that the efficiency of impregnation Δf_c is an exponential relation with the polymer loading p_g (in %), as:

$$\Delta f_c = \alpha \, p_g^{3}/2$$

where α is a numerical parameter ($\alpha_{min}=4; \alpha_{midd}=6; \alpha_{max}==8$). The dependence between the efficiency of impregnation Δf_c and the polymer loading p (in % by volume) is an exponential relation too:

$$\Delta f_c = 2.5 \, p^{3/2}$$

Table 3 Main characteristics of polymer impregnated concrete

Characteristics			Unimpregnated Concrete	Polymer Impregnated Concrete
Compressive strength (f_c)			25.00	68.00
Tensile strength (f_{ct})	$\frac{N}{mm^2}$		2.60	11.50
Flexural strength (f_{cf})			4.42	19.55
Modulus of elasticity (E)			$3.5 \cdot 10^4$	$4.28 \cdot 10^4$
Abrasion loss (U)	mm		1.00	0.48
Water absorption (a_w)	%		3.00	0.40
Density (γ_a)	$\frac{kg}{m^3}$		2400	2416

FIBER REINFORCED CONCRETE

Fiber reinforced concrete is essentially a composite system in which, unlike conventional reinforced concrete, the material as a whole carries the tensile and compressive stresses due to load. In the composite material discussed in this paper, short discrete steel fibers are randomly distributed throughout the concrete mass.

The investigation was made to determine the influence of the randomly oriented fiber on the mechanical properties and ductility of SFRC. Both plain and fiber reinforced concrete were tested. The concrete mixture consisted of: Portland cement (P40; Pa35); regular tap water; sand (0... 10 mm); Romanian additive DISAN (0.3% of cement). The fiber used for the investigations were of 0.28 mm diameter, 30 mm length (aspect ratio is 107) and manufactured from low-carbon steel wire by a chopping process. The concrete specimens were reinforced with 1-1.5% by volume. All mixing was done in a rotary mixer: sand and cement were dry mixed (30 sec.), then the fiberswere added slowly to insure random distribution; the water was then added and all components were mixed (30 sec.).

Main characteristics of SFRC are presented in Table 4. For a wide spectrum of mechanical properties, the improvement imported by fibers is mainly dependent on fiber concentration p (p represents the volume reinforcement coefficient) and aspect ratio L/D (L and D are the length and the diameter of the fiber).

Table 4 Main characteristics of steel fibre reinforced concretes

Characteristics		Plain concrete	Steel fibre reinforced concrete	
			Value of characteristics	p (%)
Flexural strength	N/mm^2	1.98	3.38	2
Impact resistance	N/mm^2	6.9	17.25	1
			19.12	1.5
			16.90	2
Freeze-thaw (200 cycles)	Loss of flexural strength %	18.3	4	1.5
Flexure toughness	Area under load-de-flexion curve	1	14.8-23.5	2

On the basis of the large amount of data for flexural strength analysed in |1|, it was found:

$$r_1 = 1 + 0.57 \, p \, \frac{L}{D} - 0.018 \, (p \, \frac{L}{D})^3$$

where r_1 is the ratio of the flexural strength of SFRC members to that of plain concrete members.

EFFICIENCY OF NEW SPECIAL CONCRETE TYPES

The efficiency of classical concretes and of new special
concrete types may be analysed only in the role of
concreting elements into a structure. A structure shall be
designed and constructed in such a way that it will remain
fit for the use for which it is required, it will sustain
all actions and influences and have adequate durability in
relation to maintenance cost. The above requirements shall
be met by the choice of suitable materials, by appropriate
design and by specifying control procedures for production,
construction and use.

Technical efficiency

The technical efficiency of new special concrete types can
be focussed by calculation of some efficiency coefficients
as in Table 5.

Table 5   Technical efficiency coefficients

Average value of / Type of material		f_{ct}/f_c	$\frac{f_c}{E} \times 10^{-3}$	$\frac{f_c}{\varsigma_a}$ $\frac{KNm}{kg}$	f_c/λ $\frac{MPamk}{W}$	Durability
Ordinary concrete		0.10	0.80	14.60	19.5	poor
Steel		1.00	1.20	3.18	5.7	very poor
High strength Concrete with	superplas-ticizers	0.07	1.25	18.33	31.4	good
	superplas-ticizers and silica fume	0.08	1.28	25.00	40.8	very good
	polymers (PIC)	0.17	1.56	35.40	30.9	very good
Concrete reinforced with	steel fiber	0.15	0.94	20.80	21.4	good
	glass fiber	0.25	1.60	26.30	28.6	good

Technical efficiency coefficients in Table 5 show a
mechanical isotropy (f_{ct}/f_c) which is varied but with
maximum value for concrete reinforced with fibres and for
PIC; deformation property (f_c/E) depends on concrete type
but it can be seen that new concretes are a little more
deformable; the new special concrete types are more
resistant at the same weight (f_c/ς_a) and have better
insulating properties (f_c/λ); the durability is good and

very good for high-strength concrete and good for concrete reinforced with fibres and it is poor and very poor for classical materials.

Economic efficiency

The economic efficiency is calculated by two analysis: ultimate limit states in the case of linear analysis and nonlinear methods of analysis for ultimate limit states.

Linear analysis is used in the case of the ultimate limit state for longitudinal force (Fig.3a-plain concrete and Fig.4a-reinforced concrete) and bending (Fig.3b-plain concrete, Fig.3c-steel, Fig.4a-reinforced concrete and Fig. 4b-steel fiber reinforced concrete). For all cases in Fig.3 and Fig.4 the stress volume V_f is calculated; it is expressed in $(N/mm^2) \times m^3$ or $MPam^3$.

Non-linear analysis takes into account an idealized bilinear diagram which is given in Fig.5. This analysis is used in the case of the ultimate limite states for longitudinal force (Fig.6a) and bending (Fig.6b-elastic stage and Fig.6c-plastic stage). Total strain energy W for elastic stage W_{el} and for plastic stage W_{pl} is calculated in Fig.6; it is expressed in kNm or $MPam^3$.

The economic efficiency of the new special concrete types is analysed, in this paper, by the calculation of the specific cost of stress C_f and of the specific cost of strain energy C_w, which are:

$$C_f = \frac{K_m}{V_f}, \quad \frac{\$}{MPam^3} \quad \text{and} \quad C_w = \frac{K_m}{W}, \quad \frac{\$}{kPam^3}$$

where: K_m is the cost of all materials used, in $\$/m^3$;

V_f - the stress volume; $W = W_{el} + W_{pl}$ - the total strain energy.

In Table 6 is presented the economic efficiency for the materials which were analysed in this paper.

The specific cost analysis presented in Table 6 shows: concrete with superplasticizers (CS) and with superplasticizers and silica fume (CSF) are economicaly to be used for all situations presented in the paper; fiber reinforced concretes are proper to be used for dynamic, cycle and thermal actions because the total strain energy (for tension and bending) is higher than for classical concretes. On the other hand these concretes behaviour are better when faced with shearing, shrinkage, creep, cracks etc.

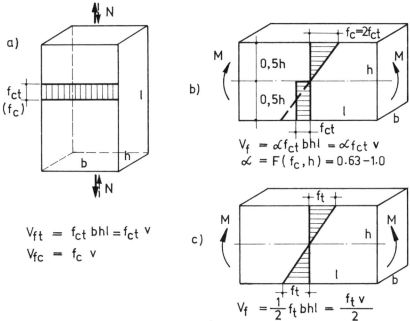

$$V_{ft} = f_{ct}\,bhl = f_{ct}\,v$$
$$V_{fc} = f_c\,v$$

Figure 3 The stress volume for plain concrete and steel

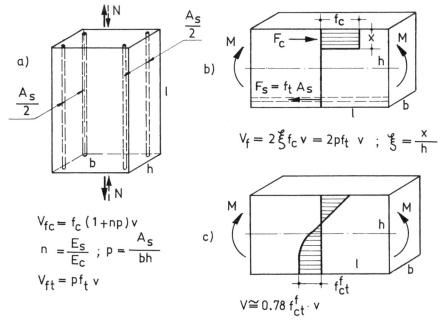

$$V_{fc} = f_c\,(1+np)\,v$$
$$n = \frac{E_s}{E_c}\;;\; p = \frac{A_s}{bh}$$
$$V_{ft} = p\,f_t\,v$$

Figure 4 The stress volume for reinforced concrete

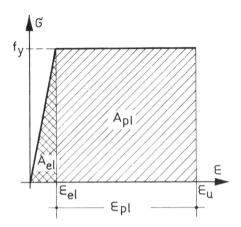

Figure 5 The diagrame $G-E$ for non linear analysis

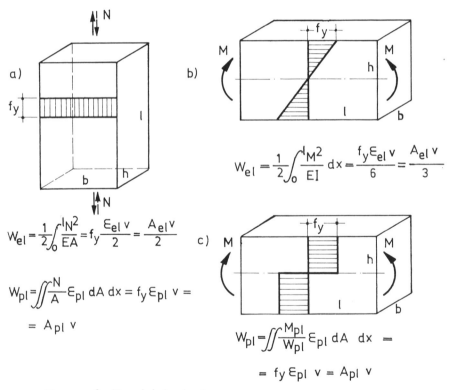

$$W_{el} = \frac{1}{2}\int_0^l \frac{N^2}{EA} = f_y \frac{\mathcal{E}_{el} v}{2} = \frac{A_{el} v}{2}$$

$$W_{pl} = \iint \frac{N}{A} \mathcal{E}_{pl} \, dA \, dx = f_y \mathcal{E}_{pl} \, v =$$

$$= A_{pl} \, v$$

$$W_{el} = \frac{1}{2}\int_0^l \frac{M^2}{EI} \, dx = \frac{f_y \mathcal{E}_{el} \, v}{6} = \frac{A_{el} \, v}{3}$$

$$W_{pl} = \iint \frac{M_{pl}}{W_{pl}} \mathcal{E}_{pl} \, dA \, dx =$$

$$= f_y \mathcal{E}_{pl} \, v = A_{pl} \, v$$

Figure 6 The total strain energy

Table 6   The specific costs for different materials

Type of material		Add. $p^*(p_g)$ %	Cost K_m, $/m^3$	$C_f=K_m/V_f$ for			$C_w=K_m/W$ for	
				T	C	B	C	B
Ordinary concrete		0	15.87	6.10	0.63	7,62	0.23	7.02
Steel		0	2761.5	8.12	8.12	16.24	0.34	0.34
Reinforced concrete		2.0*	80.01	11.76	2.80	5.88	-	-
HSC	CS	0.25	23.77	7.92	0.54	10.28	0.20	-
	CSF	0.25+2.25	25.50	5.10	0.42	6.80	0.17	-
	PIC	4.0	186.96	16.25	2.74	21.95	1.72	-
RC with	steel fiber	1.5*	100.21	22.67	3.34	29.06	0.99	2.24
	glass fiber	1.5*	172.77	17.28	4.31	22.15	1.28	1.27

Note: p^*-volume coefficient, p_g-mass coefficient;
T-tension; C-compression; B-bending.

CONCLUSIONS

1. New special concrete types presented in the paper were
   created and used to satisfy specific applications where
   conventional concrete neither good behaviour nor
   durability.

2. The technical efficiency of new special concrete types
   can be focussed by calculation of some coefficient which
   indicate the area of applications.

3. The economic efficiency can be analysed by calculation
   of the specific cost of stress and of strain energy. In
   such a way it is possible to have the choice of suitable
   materials in accordance with the role of concrete
   elements in a structure.

REFERENCES

1. AVRAM, C and BOB C, New special concrete types (in
   Romanian), Editura Tehnică, Bucureşti, 1980, 336 pp.

2. AVRAM, C, BOB, C and ROSU, M, Some properties of polymer impregnated concrete. ICP/RILEM/IBK International Symposium, Prague, June, pp 627-630.

3. BOB, C and ROSU, M, The efficiency of PIC (in Romanian), Bul. St.şi Tehn. al IPT, Nr.32, Fasc.1,Timişoara, 1975, pp 27-32.

4. BOB, C, BUCHMAN, I, NICOARA, L and IONESCU, N, Steel fiber reinforced concrete. 2nd International Conference on Bearing Capacity of Roads and Airfields,Proceedings, Plymouth, England, September, 1986, pp 185-194.

5. BOB, C, ROSU, M and BUCHMAN, I, Polymer impregnated steel fiber reinforced concrete, IABSE Symposium, Brussels 1990, pp 587-592.

6. ACI Polymers in Concrete, Proceedings of the International Symposium, Publication SP-40, Detroit, 1973, pp 450.

7. ACI Fiber Reinforced Concrete, Proceedings of the International Symposium, Publication SP-44, Detroit, 1974, pp 554.

8. ACI Superplasticizers in concrete, International Symposium, Ottawa, May 1978, pp 801.

HIGH PERFORMANCE CONCRETES INCORPORATING METAKAOLIN: A REVIEW

J A Kostuch

ECC International

V Walters

ECC Quarries

T R Jones

ECC International

United Kingdom

ABSTRACT. It is possible to improve the durability of concrete by careful use of pozzolan-OPC blended cements, and such cements have been in regular use for many years. Metakaolin is a pozzolan of particular interest. It is available in chemically pure form, and it reacts rapidly with calcium hydroxide. The published literature on metakaolin blended cements has grown rapidly since about 1985, and metakaolin blended cements are now being exploited commercially. We review the literature and discuss the properties and future potential for these cements in applications such as mortars, durable concretes and glass fibre reinforced concrete.

Keywords: Calcined clays, Metakaolin, Pozzolanic Reactivity, Alkali-silica reaction (ASR), Chloride, Sulphate, Acid, Durability, Diffusion, Porosity, Ordinary Portland Cement (OPC).

Jacek A. Kostuch has worked in the Research and Development Department of ECC International since 1986 and is currently the Section Leader of the Process Research Group which is involved in process flowsheet development, process optimisation, process equipment development and evaluation. He has been concerned with the development of metakaolins for use in the cement/concrete industry for the last five years.

G. Viv Walters has worked with ECC Quarries since 1965 where he is currently Technical Services Manager. He is a member of several British and European Standards Committees, including B.S.812. Part 123, "Concrete Prism Test Method".

Dr. Thomas R. Jones has worked in the Research and Development Department of ECC International since 1972 and is presently Manager of the Project Development Group specialising in the chemistry and processing of industrial minerals.

Concrete 2000. Edited by Ravindra K. Dhir and M. Roderick Jones.
© 1993 Published by E & FN Spon. ISBN 0 419 18120 2.

INTRODUCTION

Pozzolanic materials have been used for construction since ancient times. Natural pozzolans, or in some cases calcined earths, were blended with lime (calcium hydroxide) and water to make strong cementitious materials. Mehta [1], Malinowski [2], and Mielenz [3] have identified 4000 year old structures made from calcined clay/lime mortars which are still standing today. These include water tanks, walls, aqueducts and bridges. From the beginning of the industrial revolution in Europe, coal ashes and blast furnace slag were used as pozzolanic materials [4].

In the early 19th Century, it was found that certain argillacious limestones could be calcined to give a new and useful cement. It was not necessary to blend pozzolanic material with this so-called Roman cement, and it had the advantages of setting very rapidly - even underwater. During the search for blends of minerals to replace the natural argillacious limestones, Portland cement was discovered in about 1820 [4].

It was later found that Portland cement could be blended with pozzolanic materials. An early review was given by Malquori [5]. In remote areas, where clays are locally plentiful, they are calcined and blended with imported OPC in order to reduce costs. For example in the 1960's about 300,000 tonnes of local calcined clays was blended with OPC for constructing dams in the Amazon basin. It was reported later [6],[7] that the calcined clay had prevented expansion due to ASR, even though highly reactive aggregate was used in the constructions. Calcined clay has also been used, blended with OPC, in China [8].

Concrete made from OPC can suffer from a variety of durability problems, depending on the source of the cement, the type of aggregate, and particularly on environmental factors. Concrete can be cracked as a result of expansive chemical reactions occurring within the structure, for example alkali-silica reaction, sulphate attack, or re-bar corrosion. The cracks allow rapid ingress of water, salts and acids, thus accelerating the degradation process. A common factor in all these deleterious reactions is calcium hydroxide, which is a major constituent of hydrated OPC (approximately 20 wt.% of OPC is converted to portlandite on hydration). Portlandite is relatively soluble, and chemically reactive.

Pozzolanic materials can improve the durability of concrete by reacting with calcium hydroxide being produced by the hydration of OPC. Some of the portlandite is thereby replaced by insoluble cementitious compounds. Pozzolans vary considerably in their purity and reactivity. A number are by-products of other industrial processes: examples are pfa, ggbfs and silica fume, sf, and are therefore of variable composition. They may contain impurities such as alkalis or sulphur compounds which can under certain conditions prove to be deleterious in terms of concrete durability.   The reactivity of these by-product pozzolans is also variable.   Many react slowly with calcium hydroxide, thus delaying the hardening process - ggbfs is better described as a "latent hydraulic material" because of its slow rate of reaction at normal temperatures. Conversely, metakaolin, which is the subject of this review, can be manufactured from pure clays which are calcined under controlled conditions to give rapid reaction rates and maximum pozzolanic reactivity in concrete.

METAKAOLIN

Purity

The pozzolanic reactivity of a metakaolin is determined by the properties of the feed clay [9],[10],[11] and the processing conditions.   The feed clay, kaolin, should be either naturally pure, or refined by standard mineral processing techniques.   Thermal activation (calcination) is the most critical processing stage: the clay is calcined within the temperature range 700-900°C, depending on the mineral source.   Any impurity minerals act as diluents.   Jones et al [9], Murat et al [10] and Ambroise et al [11] all found that with increasing purity of metakaolin, the compressive strength of the concrete increased, and the level of $Ca(OH)_2$ in the hardened matrix decreased.

Pozzolanic reactivity of metakaolin

In ASTM C 618, a pozzolan is defined as a siliceous or siliceous and aluminous material which, in itself, possesses little or no cementitious value but which will, in finely divided form in the presence of moisture, react chemically with calcium hydroxide at ordinary temperature to form compounds possessing cementitious properties.

Metakaolins[1], manufactured as described above, have been found to be highly efficient pozzolanic materials.   Their reactivity was determined using the Chapelle test[2].   The contrasting pozzolanic reactivities of various materials are shown in Table 1.

----

1. Sold by ECCI under the PoleStar tradename.

2. A dilute slurry of the pozzolan is reacted with an excess of calcium hydroxide at 95°C for 18 hours. After this period, the unreacted calcium hydroxide is measured by titrating[12].   It should be noted that the Chapelle test tells us nothing about the *rate* of reaction at ambient temperatures within a concrete matrix.

Table 1 - Pozzolanic Reactivity (Chapelle Test)

Material	Pozzolanic Reactivity mg $Ca(OH)_2$ per g
Bauxite, calcined	534
Microsilica, silica fume	427
Blast furnace slag	300
Pulverised fly ash	875
Polestar 501, metakaolin	1000 (average)

Mechanism of the Pozzolanic Reaction

The reaction mechanism has been discussed by Bredy et al. [13], Turrizani [14], Murat [15] and de Silva and Glasser [16]. When metakaolin (AS_2) reacts with the calcium hydroxide produced during the hydration of OPC new cementitious products are formed, including gehlenite hydrate:

$$\text{Metakaolin + calcium hydroxide} \xrightarrow{\text{water}} \text{calcium alumino silicate hydrates + calcium silicate hydrates}$$

$$AS_2 + CH \xrightarrow{H_2O} C_2ASH_8 + CSH$$

where C:S ratio is in the range 0.8 to 1.5, [14]

Pettifer [17], Larbi and Bijen [18] and our own work [19] (Figure 1) have confirmed that calcium hydroxide (portlandite) is virtually eliminated from the cement matrix if the formulation contains a high purity metakaolin. The petrographic study carried out by Pettifer confirmed the presence of gehlenite hydrate in metakaolin/OPC concrete and also showed that there was more complete hydration of the cement. Possibly this is due to the removal of calcium hydroxide product in the reaction:

$$C_3S, C_2S + H_2O \longrightarrow CSH + CH$$
$$\downarrow$$

Reaction rate enhanced by the removal of CH

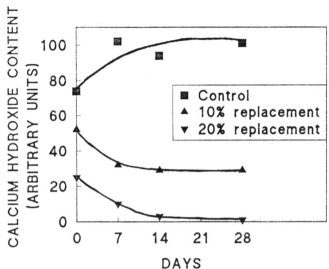

Figure 1 - The effect of replacing part of the OPC by metakaolin on the calcium hydroxide content of concrete as it cures.

THE EFFECT OF ADDED METAKAOLIN ON STANDARD PROPERTIES OF CONCRETE

OPC based concretes are susceptible to degradation. The three main reasons for this are (a) the cement paste is relatively permeable, allowing ingress of water and aggressive chemicals; (b) the cement paste contains high levels of calcium hydroxide, which is both soluble and highly chemically reactive, and (c) the heat evolved during hydration can result in thermal cracking in mass concrete.

Published work shows that metakaolin improves the properties of cured cement paste when it is substituted for part (typically 5-20 wt.%) of the OPC in a concrete or mortar. It decreases porosity of the bulk cement matrix [13],[20]; reduces levels of calcium hydroxide [18],[19],[21] and reduces hydration energy (i.e. there is less heat development on curing [7]).

The effect of metakaolin on the properties of concrete are now reviewed in detail.

Compressive strength

There is no detrimental effect on compressive strength when pure metakaolin replaces some of the OPC in mortars [21],[22] and concrete [7],[22], Figure 2. In many cases strength is slightly enhanced. Larbi and Bijen [22] have shown that in the presence of metakaolin the cement matrix is densified (i.e. becomes less porous) and the thickness of the cement paste-aggregate interfacial zone is decreased. Hence they suggest the aggregate contributes more effectively to the strength of the concrete.

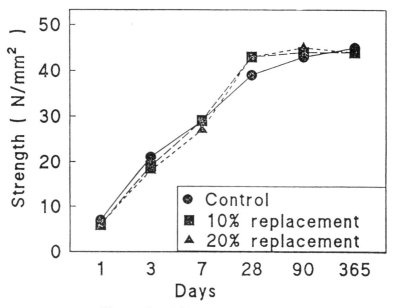

Figure 2 - Effect of metakaolin
on compressive strength of concrete [23]

Pore solution analysis

The pH of the pore solution is slightly reduced in metakaolin
concrete.   Table 2 shows that the effect is small: the pH decreasing
by about 0.4 units, typically from 13.7 to 13.3.   It is generally
accepted that corrosion of re-bars is not significant at pH values
above 12.5.   Therefore it is considered that in concretes containing
up 20 wt.% of a high purity metakaolin, the corrosion rates of
re-bars will not be adversely affected.

Table 2 - Effect of metakaolin on pH of pore solution [23]

OPC			pH of pore solution after 180 days		
Type	Na_2O Wt.%	K_2O Wt.%	% substitution of OPC by metakaolin		
			0	10	20
Low alkali	0.09	0.35	13.5	13.3	13.1
	0.15	0.73	13.8	13.5	13.3
High alkali	0.43	1.10	14.0	13.7	13.5

The alkali metal ion concentration of the pore solution was also
found to be substantially reduced in concretes containing
metakaolin, Table 3.

Table 3 - Effect of metakaolin on Na$^+$/K$^+$
concentration in pore solution [23]

OPC			Na$^+$/K$^+$ concentration in pore solution after 180 days (Molar)	
Type	Na$_2$O Wt.%	K$_2$O Wt.%	% substitution of OPC by metakaolin	
			0	10
Low alkali	0.09	0.35	0.10/0.27	0.06/0.15
	0.15	0.73	0.13/0.50	0.09/0.32
High alkali	0.43	1.10	0.32/0.77	0.21/0.40

Diffusion properties and permeability

Our own work, and that of Bredy et al [13], Larbi et al [20] shows
that the addition of metakaolin to OPC results in a less permeable
concrete matrix.   There is a significant decrease in average pore
size (Figure 3) and a reduction in rate and total quantity of water
absorbed (Tables 5 and 6).   Metakaolin is particularly effective in
reducing the rate of diffusion of Cl$^-$ and Na$^+$ in concrete (Table 7).

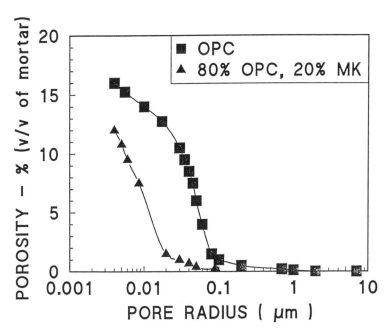

Figure 3 - Effect of metakaolin on the pore size distribution of
mortars   (water/total cement = 0.40; aggregate/total cement =1.0;
age = 100 days) [20]

Table 5 - Water absorptivities of mortars (age = 100 days) [20]

Specimen	Water Absorptivity* $(kg.m^{-2}.s^{-2})$ x 10^{-3}
OPC	1.02
80% OPC + 20% MK	0.45

* Absorptivity is a measure of the rate of adsorption of water.

Table 6 - Water Absorption - Effect of partial substitution of OPC by metakaolin (Authors' results)

Sample	Immersion Time (hrs.)	Water Absorption, (mg water per g sample)		% Sub^n of OPC by MK
		Control (no MK)	OPC + MK	
Mortar bar	160	6.1	4.0	10
Cast stone	24	9.7	7.9	5
Concrete slab	24	24.8	21.5	15
Concrete slab	24	24.8	17.9	25

Table 7 - Coefficient of diffusion of ionic species in portland cement mortars with and without metakaolin [20]

Ionic Species	Diffusion coefficient $(cm^2/s).10^{-9}$	
	OPC	20% replacement of OPC by metakaolin
Cl^-	5.97	0.10
Na^+	1.88	0.03
K^+	2.59	0.07

EFFECT OF METAKAOLIN ON CONCRETE DEGRADATION

Alkali-Silica Reaction, ASR

For ASR to occur and produce a swelling gel, the essential ingredients are soluble Ca^{++} and OH^-, active silica, and water. Soluble alkali metal ions are also necessary, and expansion due to ASR is greatly accelerated if concrete is exposed to concentrated sodium chloride. We have shown [9],[19] that if metakaolin is used to reduce concentrations of calcium hydroxide in the concrete to a sufficiently low level, any ASR gel produced is not expansive, and therefore no cracking occurs. This applies even if highly active aggregate and high alkali cement are used, and if the concrete is immersed in saturated sodium chloride solution.

The world-wide cost of ASR is extremely high [24]. It includes repair costs, and charges for importing aggregates and cement if local supplies are potentially active. For example, the extra cost (per m^3 of concrete) of replacing 10-15 wt.% of OPC by metakaolin is less than 50% of the cost of hauling aggregate and cement an extra 100 km by road (U.K. data).

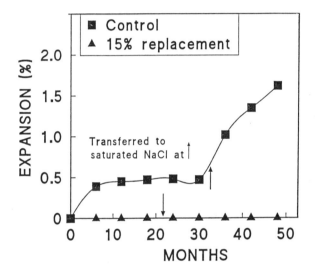

Figure 4 - Effect of metakaolin on expansion due to ASR, after ageing first at 100% relative humidity, and then immersing in saturated NaCl solution

Attack by aggressive solutions

Aggressive solutions enter concrete via the network of fine pores. Sulphate ions can cause expansion and cracking [25]. Chloride ions and carbon dioxide can accelerate the rate of corrosion of re-bars. Organic and inorganic acids dissolve calcium hydroxide and (less rapidly) calcium silicate hydrates. This creates a weakened porous structure that accelerates other degradation processes such as freeze-thaw cracking. Collin-Fevre [21] reports that 10 wt.% replacement of OPC by metakaolin markedly increases the resistance of concrete from attack by mineral and organic acids (Figure 5).

Glass fibre reinforced concrete, GRC

GRC is of considerable academic and commercial interest. It has a high tensile strength, and can be fabricated into thin sheets and complex mouldings which are increasingly used as decorative and functional cladding on public buildings. The durability of GRC exposed to the weather is governed by chemical reactions between calcium hydroxide and the (alkali resistant) glass fibres [26]. These reactions reduce tensile strength and elasticity. It has been found [27],[28] that metakaolin inhibits the crystallisation of calcium hydroxide at the glass surface and improves the durability of GRC. Accelerated tests give estimated lifetimes in excess of 50 years for metakaolin GRC.

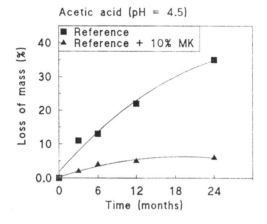

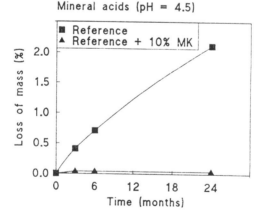

Figure 5 - Effect of metakaolin on resistance of concrete to organic and mineral acids [21]

CONCLUSIONS

Pozzolan-lime cements have a long and successful history. In more recent years pozzolan-OPC cements have been used where supplies of cheap local pozzolans are readily available. The main problem with natural pozzolans, burnt earths and by-product pozzolans is their variable composition, purity and rate of pozzolanic activity. Common impurities, such as clays, alkalis and sulphur compounds, can lead to strength loss and degradation problems, sometimes after a period of many years.

Metakaolin can be manufactured with a high degree of purity and pozzolanic reactivity. The evidence suggests that pure metakaolin combines with approximately its own mass of calcium hydroxide to give stable cementitious compounds, which have no deleterious effect on the strength of concrete. Metakaolin prevents expansion due to ASR, even when reactive aggregates and high alkali cements are used. Concrete incorporating metakaolin is less permeable to water and salts, more resistant to acid, and does not embrittle alkali resistant glass fibre used in GRC. The effect of metakaolin on other durability problems, such as re-bar corrosion, freeze-thaw cycles, sulphate attack etc. is of interest, and is being investigated. There is evidence that metakaolin can reduce the unsightly effects of efflorescence, by inhibiting the migration of calcium hydroxide to the surface of concrete structures.

Concrete is playing an increasing role in infrastructure projects where 50-100 year guarantees of durability are demanded - often in aggressive environments such as sea water or acidic ground water. Metakaolin is now being exploited commercially in specialist areas where durability is of critical importance. The potential application of this technology to larger projects, such as bridges, roads and tunnels, is receiving wide interest.

ACKNOWLEDGEMENTS

The authors wish to express their appreciation to the Building Research Establishment; J.A.Larbi (TNO); J.M.Bijen (Delft/INTRON) and Collin-Fevre (Cerib) whose data has been used along with our own in figures and tables in this paper.

REFERENCES

[1]   MEHTA, P.K. Second Canmet/ACI Int. Conf. Supplementary Cementing materials for concrete, ed. Malhotra,V.M., Ch.1,1991.

[2]   MALINOWSKI, R. "Concrete and mortars in ancient aqueducts"; Concrete International, Jan. 1979, pp.66-76.

[3] MIELENZ, R.C. "Mineral admixtures - History and background";
     Concrete International, Aug.1983, pp.34-42.

[4] Encyclopaedia Brittannica, 9th Edition, 1876, Vol. 4, p.458.

[5] MALQUORI, G., "Portland-Pozzolan Cement", 4th Int. Symp. on
     Chem. of Cement, Washington D.C., 1960, pp983.

[6] ANDRIOLO, F.R. and SGARABOZA, B.C. Proc. 7th Int. Conf. AAR,
     ed. P.E.Grattan-Bellow, 1985, pp.66-70.

[7] SAAD, M.N.A., de ANDRADE, W.P. and PAULON, V.A. "Properties of
     mass concrete containing an active pozzolan made from clay";
     Concrete International, July 1982, pp.59.

[8] XU, H.Y. and CHEN, M. Proc. 7th Int. Conf. AAR, ed.
     P.E.Grattan-Bellew, 1986, pp.253-257.

[9] WALTERS, G.V. and JONES, T.R. 2nd Int. Conf. Durability of
     Concrete, Canada, ed. V.M.Malhotra, 1991, pp.941-953.

[10] MURAT, M., AMBROISE, J. and PERA, J. "Hydration reaction and
     hardening of calcined clays and related minerals."; Cement
     and Concrete Research, v.15, 1985, pp.261-268.

[11] AMBROISE, J., MARTIN-CALLE, S. and PERA, J. 4th Int. Conf.,
     Turkey, ed. V.M.Malhotra, 1992, pp.731-739.

[12] LARGENT, R. Bull. Liasons Lab. Pont Chausees, v.93, 1978,
     pp.63

[13] BREDY, P., CHABANNET, M. and PERA, J. "Microstructure and
     porosity of metakaolin blended cements."; Mat. Res. Soc. Symp.
     Proc., Boston, 1989, v.137, pp.431-436.

[14] TURRIZANI, R., The Chemistry of Cements, v.2, ed.
     H.F.W. Taylor 1964, pp.69-86.

[15] MURAT, M. Cement and Concrete Research, v.13, 1983,
     pp.259-266.

[16] de SILVA, P.S. and GLASSER, F.P. "Hydration of cements based
     on metakaolin: thermochemistry"; Advances in Cement Research,
     v.3, no.12, Oct.1990, pp.167-177.

[17] PETTIFER, K., Private communication, Buiding Research
     Establishment, BRE Contract Report 1991 for ECCI.

[18] LARBI, J.A. and BIJEN, J.M. PhD Thesis, Delft University, Ch.6
     1991.

[19]   JONES, T.R., WALTERS, G.V. and KOSTUCH, J.A.   9th Int. Conf. AAR in Concrete, v.1, 1992, pp.485-496.

[20]   LARBI, J.A. and BIJEN, J.M. ibid.,Ch.8.

[21]   COLLIN-FEVRE, "Use of metakaolinite in the manufacture of concrete products" CIB, Montreal 1992, Poster 479.

[22]   LARBI, J.A. and BIJEN, J.M. ibid.,Ch.9.

[23]   HALLIWELL, M.A. Private Communication. BRE Report TCR 48/92.

[24]   SWAMI, R.N. (Ed.), "The Alkali-Silica Reaction in Concrete", Blackie 1992, p.27.

[25]   LAWRENCE, C.D. "Sulphate attack on concrete" Magazine of Concrete Research, v.42, no.153, Dec. 1990, pp. 249-264.

[26]   YILHAZ, V.T. and GLASSER, F.P., Glass Technology, v.32, no. 4, August 1991, pp.138-147.

[27]   MURAT, M. and AL-CHEIKH, A., Cem. Concr. Res., v.19, no. 1, pp16-24.

[28]   Eur. Pat. Appl. EP 333,584 (1988).

A NEW POLYCARBOXYLATE BASED POLYMER: PHYSICAL PROPERTIES OF CONCRETE

S Okazawa

K Umezawa

Y Tanaka

NMB Ltd

Japan

ABSTRACT : Properties of fresh concrete and hardened concrete of a high strength and a high flowable concrete using a superplasticizer containing a new functional polycarboxylate based polymer (cross–linked polymer) were studied.

Used for high strength concrete with 25–30% water/binding material ratio, this superplasticizer attained high water reduction equivalent to that attained by beta naphthalene sulfonate and melamine sulfonate based superplasticizers. The concrete also exhibits better consistency retention over time than heretofore attained by high range water reducers. This superplasticizer showed significant advantages in consistency, workability, and setting characteristics compared to other superplasticizers.

When used for high flowable concrete, this superplasticizer exhibited not only high strength, but also the durability of hardened concrete.

Key words: Cross–linked polymer, superplasticizer, high strength concrete, high flowable concrete, blast furnace slag micro powder, flyash, chloride ion content, carbonation, pore distribution.

Mr. Satoshi Okazawa is a research staff member of NMB Ltd. He is working on the analysis of the operation mechanisms of chemical admixtures and their properties and studying high performance concrete. He is also a member of major committees of concrete technology in Japan.

Mr. Kenichi Umezawa is a research staff member of NMB Ltd. He is studying the application of various chemical admixtures to concrete, in particular the concrete properties of these admixtures. He is also a member of major committees of concrete technology in Japan and has joined projects overseas as a technician.

Dr. Yoshio Tanaka is a research staff member of NMB Ltd. His research interests include organic chemical synthesis, materials science, and synthesis of polymer dispersing agents and their performance.

Concrete 2000. Edited by Ravindra K. Dhir and M. Roderick Jones.
© 1993 Published by E & FN Spon. ISBN 0 419 18120 2.

INTRODUCTION

Recently, there has been rapid growth and diversification in concrete technology, with concrete structures becoming larger and higher. High strength
concrete has made design of such structures possible, and superplasticizers
have made construction possible.

In Japan, 60–80 N/mm² high strength concrete is already in use for precast
products, PC truss bridges, and RC high rise buildings. Demand is anticipated
to greatly increase in the future.

While construction technology continues to be improved, and concrete structure
diversification progresses, Prof. Okamura et al. of Tokyo University have
proposed and developed non–compaction concrete. This concrete is not influenced by the quality of concrete placement, which improves the reliability and
durability of concrete. (1)

Since then, much research and development relating to this kind of concrete
has been performed, and today it has come into practical use.

This report presents the properties of high strength concrete and high flowable
concrete using a superplasticizer containing a compound of a newly developed
cross–linked polymer and a polycarboxylic acid as the main components
(2),(3),(4).

STABILITY OF HIGH STRENGTH CONCRETE

Experimental details

Table 1 shows the properties of high strength concrete using a cross–linked
polymer based superplasticizer.

Table 1   Study items

Testing	Temp. , °C	Target slump flow, mm	W/B*1 , %	Type of binder	Type of admixture	Study items
Lab testing	20	600±50	35 30 25	OPC *2 OPC+S. F	SP-A SP-B	Setting time Compressive strength
Field testing	30	600±50	30 27	OPC	SP-A	Change in slump flow over time

*1 W/B indicates water/binding material ratio.

*2 OPC stands for ordinary portland cement. S. F. stands for silica fume.
    Silica fume was used only when the W/B was 25%, at a substitution ratio of
    10% by cement weight

Materials

In the lab tests, an ordinary portland cement was used as the binding material, a mixture of land and mountain sand was used as the fine aggregate, and crushed stone (MS: 20mm) of hard sandstone was used as the course aggregate. The silica fume used for the mix-design with a W/B of 25% was a micro powder with specific surface area of 20m²/g.

In the field tests, the materials used by ready mixed concrete plants (ordinary portland cement, a mixture of river and mountain sand, and crushed stone (MS: 20mm) were used.

The admixture used in the lab and field tests was a superplasticizer (SP-A) containing a cross-linked polymer and polycarboxylic ether as the main components. In the lab tests, a superplasticizer (SP-B) containing beta naphthalene sulfonate condensate and a continuous activation polymer as the main components was also studied for comparison.

Concrete mix-design and the properties of fresh concrete

The mix-design of high strength concrete and the properties of fresh concrete in the lab tests are given in Table 2 and in the field tests in Table 3.

Test method

In the lab tests, the concrete was mixed for 3 minutes with a 100 liter pan shaped forced mixing type mixer. In the field tests, the concrete was mixed for 2 minutes with a 3m³ two axis forced mixing type mixer.

The test methods for setting time and compressive strength were based on the JIS standards. The change in slump flow over time in the field tests was measured for the prescribed time using a 5m³ agitator truck.

Table 2 Mix-design of high strength concrete
and the properties of fresh concrete (lab testing)

W/B , %	Admixture		s/a , %	Unit weight , kg/m³			Slump flow , mm	Slump flow rate , mm/sec
	Type	Dosage		W	OPC	S. F*1		
35	SP-A	Bx1.60%	45.4	160	457	–	48.5	–
35	SP-B	1.90%	45.4	160	457	–	47.0	–
30	SP-A	1.80%	43.3	160	533	–	54.5	7.3
30	SP-B	2.20%	43.3	160	533	–	49.5	3.6
25	SP-A	2.20%	40.2	160	640	–	48.5	–
25	SP-A	3.30%	39.4	160	576	64	50.0	–

*1 S.F stands for silica fume.

Table 3   Mix-design of higt strength concrete and
the properties of fresh concrete (field testing)

W/B , %	Admixture		s/a , %	Unit weight, kg/m^3			Slump flow , mm
	Type	Dosage		W	OPC	S. F	
30	SP–A	Cx1. 95%	40. 0	170	567	–	46. 5
27	SP–A	2. 00%	38. 0	170	630	–	51. 5

Lab test results

Table 2 shows the properties of the fresh concrete in the lab tests.

For both admixtures, the admixture dosage to obtain the prescribed slump flow increased with decrease in the water/binding material ratio. When 10% of the cement was replaced with silica fume at the water/binding material ratio of 25%, the dosage of admixture became 1.5 times that of the no silica fume case due to the extremely large surface area of silica fume.

In order to determine the influence of the different components of the admixture on the placability of high strength concrete, the slump flow rate at a water/binding material ratio of 30% was measured. The flow rate of SP–A, containing a cross–linked polymer, was approx. 2 times that of SP–B, containing a naphthalene base as the main component. Therefore, SP–A may reduce the viscosity of high strength concrete (improving workability).

Fig. 1 shows the relationship between the type of admixture and the presence of silica fume with the setting time. At all water/binding material ratios, SP–B retarded more than SP–A.   Concrete containing silica fume showed approx. 2 hour set retardation compared to without silica fume. The cause of this is probably due to the difference in the dosage of the admixture.

Fig 2 shows the relationship between the binding material/water ratio and the compressive strength at various ages. The relationship when SP–A is used shows a very high degree of correlation using a linear regression, even in the range of high strength concrete. The strength development with SP–B used at the water/binding material ratios of 35% and 30% was also studied, and strength equal to the SP–A case was obtained.

Fig. 3 shows the influence of the presence of silica fume at 25% water/binding material ratio on the strength development. The compressive strength when silica fume was replaced was somewhat less at the ages of 3 and 7 days than without silica fume, but the compressive strength at the ages of 28 and 91 days was greatly increased. (by approx. 10% over that without silica fume)

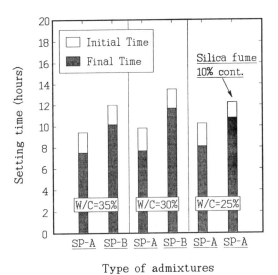

Fig. 1 Relationship between setting time and the type of admixtures

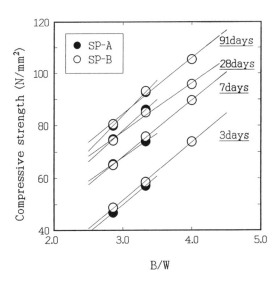

Fig. 2 Relationship between compressive strength and B/W ratio

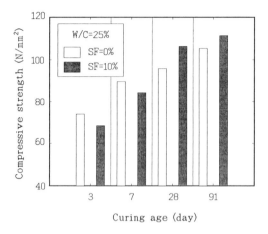

Fig. 3 Influence of the presence of silica fume
on the strength development

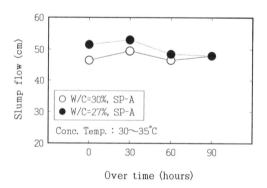

Fig. 4 Change in slump flow over time
(High strength concrete using SP-A)

Field test results

Fig. 4 shows the change in slump flow over time of concrete with
water/binding material ratios of 27% and 30%, which were produced at a
concrete plant. Due to the effect of the cross-linked polymer, the slump flow of
the concrete using SP-A was slightly increased at the age of 30 min, but
remained roughly the same as just after mixing until the age of 90 min. Therefore, excellent placability can be expected.

SUITABILITY FOR USE IN HIGH FLOWABLE CONCRETE (SERIES II)

Filling properties and study items of high flowable concrete

The high flowable concrete discussed here is concrete which exhibits high segregation resistance and flowability and which can fill the space between closely arranged reinforcing steel bars without vibratory compaction. As shown in Fig. 5, the high flowable concrete used in this experiment was mix–designed to obtain excellent fillability in a form in which reinforcing steel bars were closely arranged, without compaction. As shown in Fig. 6, the concrete poured into the form was judged to be excellent: No air voids were seen and the coarse aggregate was observed to be uniform even at the end of the flow.

The properties to relating the strength development and durability of this type of concrete, such as the micro structure of the cement paste, permeability of chloride ions, and carbonation, were compared to ordinary concrete with a water/cement ratio of 55%.

Fig. 5 Fillability of the high flowable concrete

Fig. 6 Uniformity of the hardened high flowable concrete

Table 4 Concrete mix-design

Type of concrete	Type of binder	Target slump flow, mm	W/B , %	s/a , %	Unit weight, kg/m³ *2				Admixture	
					W	OPC	Slag	F.A	Type	Dosage
Higt flowable concrete	2 Component	60±50	0.30	51.0	165	174	372	–	SP-A	Bx1.4%
	2 Component	60±50	0.30	51.0	165	174	372	–	SP-B	2.2%
	3 Component	60±50	0.30	50.0	165	165	165	220	SP-A	1.0%
	3 Component	60±50	0.30	50.0	165	165	165	220	SP-B	1.7%
Ordinary concrete	OPC	(8)*1	0.53	45.0	159	300	–	–	P	250mℓ/
	OPC	(18)	0.55	47.0	176	320	–	–	P	C=100kg

*1 ( ) indicates the slump.
*2 For slag, micro powder of blast furnace slag (relative surface area; 0.6m²/g) was used. F.A. stands for flyash.

Mix designs of high flowable concrete

Two mix-designs for flowable concrete were used in this experiment, a two component type in which blast furnace slag micro powder was mixed with ordinary portland cement, and a 3 component type in which blast furnace slag micro powder and flyash were mixed. The concrete mix-designs are given in Table 4.

Materials

The cement, fine aggregate, coarse aggregate, and admixtures (SP-A and SP-B) used for high flowable concrete were the same as those used for high strength concrete and the admixture used for the ordinary concrete was a standard type AE water reducing agent (P) containing a compound of ligno-sulfonate and polyole as the main components.

Test method

The micro pore size distribution of the cement paste was measured with a mercury pressure porosimeter. Permeation of chloride ion was evaluated based on the permeation depth and volume of specimens cured for 28 days by immersion in a 3% NaCl solution for 3 days, following by drying for 4 days at 20°C and 60% humidity, with this cycle being repeated 4, 12, or 24 cycles . Accelerated carbonation testing was conducted at 20°C and 60% humidity, with a carbonic gas concentration of 5%.

Table 5   Setting time and strength development of high flowable concrete

Type of concrete	Type of binder	Target slump flow, mm	Admixture Type	Admixture Dosage	Setting time, hr-m Ini.	Setting time, hr-m Final	Compressive strength, N/mm^2 3d	7d	28d	6mon.	1yr.
Higt	2 component	60±50	SP-A	Bx1.4%	7-55	11-10	29	46	71	94	95
flowable	2 component	60±50	SP-B	2.2%	31-10	35-35	16	47	73	98	100
concrete	3 component	60±50	SP-A	1.0%	11-45	16-20	17	32	54	79	80
	3 component	60±50	SP-B	1.7%	24-45	28-30	11	30	53	83	89
Ordinary	OPC	(8)*1	P	250mℓ/	6-10	8-30	18	28	42	50	51
concrete	OPC	(18)	P	C=100kg	6-35	8-50	17	27	40	45	48

Test results and considerations

Table 5 shows the setting time and strength development of high flowable concrete. When the dosage of admixture per unit binding material is large, the setting time of high flowable concrete is retarded compared to ordinary concrete. The 3 component type containing flyash is particularly retarded. Since all cases of high flowable concrete containing naphthalene based SP-B were greatly retarded compared to the concrete containing cross-linked polymer based SP-A. SP-A was judged to be more practical.

The compressive strength of high flowable concrete containing 2 component type binding material at all ages was greater than that containing 3 component type binding material. The compressive strength difference due to the difference in the admixture component was larger with SP-A, with its small set retardation, at the early age and with SP-B, with its large retardation, in the long term age.

Fig. 7 shows the micro pore distribution at the ages of 28 days and 6 months. The total volume of the micro pores of high flowable concrete is extremely less than ordinary concrete for both type of admixtures. This is particularly true for the 2 component type, and the hydration products of high flowable concrete form a very dense micro structure.

Fig. 8 shows the relationship between the total micro pore volume at the age of 28 days, when the salt water immersion testing was started, and the amount of chloride ion at 5mm below the concrete surface. Both types of admixtures show excellent correlation between the total micro pore volume and the amount of chloride ion. The density of the structure of the hydration products greatly contributes to reduction of permeation and dispersion of chloride ions.

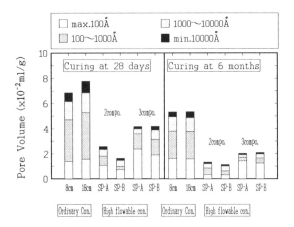

Fig. 7 Micro pore distribution at age of
28 days and 6 months

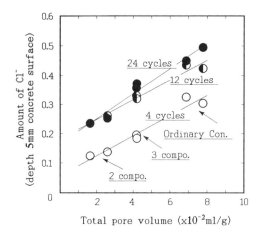

Fig. 8 Relationship between the amount of Cl⁻
and total micro pore volume

Fig. 9 shows the results of accelerated carbonation testing. No difference was seen between SP–A and SP–B in the carbonation of high flowable concrete, but differences due to the binding material composition were observed. While the two component type admixture exhibited no carbonation, the 3 component type exhibited almost the same carbonation depth as ordinary concrete. The cause of this difference may be due to the air permeability of the cement paste and the consumption of calcium hydroxide, but this is unclear at the present stage.

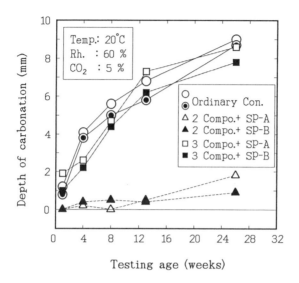

Fig. 9 Results of accelerated carbonation testing

CONCLUSION

The properties of high strength concrete and high flowable concrete were studied using a superplasticizer containing polycarboxylic ether and a cross-linked polymer as the main components. The results are as follows.

1) The placability and the setting time of the high strength concrete are better than the naphthalene based superplasticizers.

2) The slump flow over time of the high strength concrete is unchanged even 90 minutes after mixing at 30–35ºC, which is satisfactory for high strength concrete.

3) The setting time of this superplasticizer was better when used for high flowable concrete than naphthalene based superplasticizers.

4) Since the cement hydration product of high flowable concrete forms a very dense structure similar to the current naphthalene based superplasticizers, the dispersion of the chloride ions and carbonation are suppressed, resulting in higher durability.

REFERENCES

1. Kazumasa Ozawa, Kouichi Maekawa, Hajime Okamura; Development of High Performance Concrete, Concrete Engineering Yearly Anthology, Vol.11 No.1 pp.699-704 1989.6

2. Takao Furusawa, Osamu Nishijo, Kenji Harada, Tadashi Tsuchitani; Rheo-build SP-8 Series Superplasticizer, The NMB Trasactions No.9 pp12-14 1992.7

3. Kenichi Umezawa, Satoshi Okazawa, Katsuyoshi Horibe, Osamu Nakagawa; Study on the Strength and Durability of a High Flowable Concrete, The Concrete Engineering Yearly   Anthology, Vol.14 pp.959-964 1992.6

4. Satoshi Okazawa, Kenichi Umezawa, Takumi Sugamata, Yoshitaka Moriya; Consideration   on the Durability of a High Flowable Concretre using Binding Materials with Different   Types of Component, Civil Engineering Yearly Academic Congress Lecture Outlines pp. 348-349 1992.9

SUPERFINE FLY ASH IN
HIGH STRENGTH CONCRETE

W B Butler

Rocla

Australia

ABSTRACT. This report presents the results of an investigation into the suitability of a superfine Australian fly ash for use in conjunction with a high-range water-reducing admixture in commercial high strength concrete in Melbourne, Australia.

Strength and chloride permeability tests at ages up to 90 days indicate that the combination of materials achieves the desired objectives of high strength and low permeability from a relatively simple mixture.

Keywords: Chloride Permeability, Fly Ash, Superfine Fly Ash, Silica Fume, Supplementary Cementitious Materials, High-range Water-reducing Admixture, High Strength Concrete, Superplasticizer.

W.B. Butler is Manager, Quality & Technical Development for Rocla, Australia and Director of Research for Monex Resources Inc., Texas. He has a degree in chemistry and 40 years experience in concrete materials. He is a Fellow of the American Concrete Institute, a member of the Institute of Concrete Technologists, the Concrete Society and the Concrete Institute of Australia. He is active on Standards Association of Australia , ACI and ASTM committees dealing with fly ash, chemical admixtures and durability, and is currently chairman of ACI Committee 201, Durability of Concrete. He also chaired the organising committee for Concrete for the Nineties held in Australia in 1990.

Concrete 2000. Edited by Ravindra K. Dhir and M. Roderick Jones.
© 1993 Published by E & FN Spon. ISBN 0 419 18120 2.

INTRODUCTION

For several years now, condensed silica fume has been proposed as the appropriate supplementary cementitious material for use in concrete where high strength or low permeability are the prime requirements. Due to the extreme fineness of the silica fume, it is common to use it in concrete in conjunction with a high-range water-reducing admixture and often with supplementary fly ash or ground granulated blastfurnace slag to improve the handling properties of the fresh concrete and enhance the strength development. These additional materials are seldom reported. The combined benefits of all the admixtures used tend to be ascribed to the silica fume.

Ellis et. al. [1] set about examining the validity of choosing silica fume for achieving low chloride permeability (AASHTO T-277) as compared to other supplementary cementitious materials used in conjunction with sulphonated naphthalene formaldehyde superplasicizer. Fifteen concrete mixes were evaluated varying cement content with and without supplementary cementitious materials. All of the mixtures were practical, workable concrete containing Mighty 150 superplasicizer at 750 mL per 100 kg of cement. This addition rate is low in relation to many of the references cited. Eleven of the mixes recorded chloride permeability values (ASTM C1202) below 1000 coulombs. The effectiveness of silica fume, used in conjunction with fly ash and superplasticizer, was confirmed. A permeability value of 171 coulombs was recorded for a mixture containing 300 kg of portland cement, 90 kg of fly ash and 30 kg of silica fume per cubic metre. A similar mixture without the fly ash required extra mixing water to achieve slump and recorded permeability of 408 coulombs. Using the same fly ash at 180 kg/m³ with 255 kg of portland cement but no silica fume, average permeability was 169 coulombs. These results provided a fair indication that low permeability (and high strength) are achievable economically with good quality commercial U.S. fly ash without recourse to addition of an extra pozzolanic ingredient in the form of silica fume.

Gopalan and Haque [2] have recently reported work on high strength fly ash concrete using commercial Australian materials. Strengths achieved were generally in the range 60 to 90 N/mm². The contribution of superplasticizer (added at the rate of 1 litre per 100 kg of total cementitious material) was shown to be highly significant, accounting for strength increases as high as 50 percent above similar untreated fly ash blend concretes. These strength enhancements were shown to exceed the "theoretical" values base on water cement ratio by 20 to 30 percent at 91 days (ignoring extreme values). Mixes in the optimum range seemed to produce the largest improvements.

It is worthy of note that in investigations such as those reported above, the major contributor to concrete strength after portland cement is commonly the high-range water-reducing admixture and yet it receives scant recognition in the reporting.

The current work was instigated to evaluate the potential of a special fine Australian fly ash for use in commercial high strength concrete in Melbourne. A preliminary series of exploratory trials was run using Sydney aggregates.

The second series of trials incorporated Victorian natural sand and crushed Basalt. For this series, chloride permeability tests were included on specimens after 28 days of standard curing. With the exception of the fly ash, all materials used were normal commercial concrete materials. Concrete was mixed in a tumbling drum mixer to simulate truck mixing.

Normally when silica fume is used in concrete its performance is enhanced by the variable superplasticiser addition used to control water demand. Series 3 was designed to assess the relative performance of superfine fly ash directly against silica fume when binder proportions, superplasticiser addition and slump were held constant. Silica fumes E and G were compacted materials from Scandinavia and the United States. Silica fume M was from an Australian source.

Normal commercial fly ash was also incorporated in all mixes to improve workability.

MATERIALS

Full details of the material properties are shown in Tables 1 & 2.

Table 1   Properties of Aggregates

Percent Passing Sieve	10 mm Gravel	14 mm Basalt	River Sand	Glacial Sand
13.2 mm	100	97		
9.5	95	62		
6.7	50	31		
4.75	15	17	99	100
2.36		3	87	98
1.18		1	75	87
600 um		1	53	74
300		1	18	44
150			4	1
75			2	
Absorption %	1.2	0.45	2.0	1.0
Density (S.S.D.) kg/m^3	2650	2880	2590	2590

Table 2   Properties of Cementitious Materials

Superfine Fly Ash

Median Size um*	4.6
Surface Area cm^2/cm^3*	35,880
Specific Gravity	2.3

* Horiba

Portland Cement

	Series 1	Series 2
Fineness Index	355 m^2/kg	380 m^2/kg
C_3A	6%	6%
C_4AF	11%	11%
C_3S	57%	53%
C_2S	17%	20%

In Series 1 and 3 the aggregates were natural sand and crushed gravel from the Nepean River. In Series 2, 14 mm crushed Kilmore basalt was used with washed glacial sand. The portland cement was equivalent to ASTM Type I. Cement from the same source was used in both series. For comparison purposes, one batch was prepared using Temco Silica Fume in place of fly ash.

The high-range water-reducing admixture, Relcrete SP2, is produced from sulphonated naphthalene formaldehyde concentrate and has a solids content of 40%. This equates to admixture solids of 0.8% by weight of portland cement in Series 2.

DISCUSSION OF RESULTS

Results reported in Series 1 (Table 3a) were part of a broader exploratory study of alternatives to silica fume for use in high strength concrete. Strengths at ages up to 7 days were found to be strongly influenced by portland cement content, while strength as later ages were not. Trial 337, containing 149 kg of fly ash with 348 kg of portland cement was more workable with significantly less water than trial 330 with 48 kg of silica fume and 437 kg of cement. At ages of 28 days and beyond, this fly ash concrete was stronger than the silica fume mixture.

Indications from Series 1 were that high additions of the superplasticizing admixture in conjunction with low unit water content

Table 3a   Concrete Proportions and Properties

		SERIES 1			SERIES 2		
TRIAL No.		329	330	337	900	901	902
Cement	kg	393	437	348	400	400	400
Fly Ash	kg	98		149	125	150	150
Silica Fume	kg		48				
Relcrete SP2	L	3.9	6.0	5.0	8.0	8.0	8.0
14mm Basalt	kg				1131	1131	1194
10mm Crushed Gravel	kg	911	899	896			
River Sand	kg	783	777	770			
Glacial Sand	kg				761	729	654
Free Water	L	173	186	143	117	125	118
Unit Mass	kg/m^3	2370	2360	2380	2520	2520	2550
Air Content	%	1.2	0.6	0.2	1.2	1.0	1.4
Slump	mm	100	160	Flowing. 170 at 1 h	600*	675*	600*

* Diameter of flowing pat

Compressive Strength N/mm^2						
7 days	52.0	61.0	50.5	69.0	73.0	75.0
28 days	73.0	78.5	82.0	94.0	100.5	97.5
56 days	77.0	86.0	93.0	97.0	106.0	102.0
90 days	87.0	88.0	96.5	89.0	99.5	104.0

Chloride Permeability Coulombs						
28 days				305	275	120

produced a distinctive "slow motion" flowing concrete which is far more cohesive than is normally the case. The relatively high proportion of fine material in the mixtures no doubt contributes to this effect.

Trial 337, which was flowing concrete at time of mixing, was retested for slump up to 1 hour from the time of mixing, when a slump of 170 mm was recorded.

Trials in Series 2 were curtailed by shortage of materials. Hence, cement content and admixture addition were fixed. Trials 900 and 901 were both highly workable concrete which appeared oversanded. Trial 902 corrected this deficiency. However, the reduction in unit water content realised was not reflected in compressive strength gains. Despite this, permeability was reduced to a very low level.

The compressive strengths at 90 days show signs of regression. The reasons here are not clear and could be artifacts of testing such high strength concrete. Of course, more serious factors such as self-desiccation as has been reported by Hooton [3] for silica fume concrete are equally possible.

Incorporation of supplementary cementitious materials in concrete is commonly accompanied by low strength at ages up to at least seven days. However, when silica fume or superfine fly ash is used in conjunction with a substantial dose of a high-range water-reducing admixture,

Table 3b   Concrete Proportions and Properties

SERIES 3

TRIAL No.		1414	1415	1420	1417
Silica Fume		M	E	G	–
Cement	kg	350	350	350	350
Fly Ash	kg	50	50	50	50
Silica Fume	kg	35	35	35	–
Superfine Fly Ash	kg				35
Relcrete SP2	L	6	6	6	6
20mm Gravel	kg	762	762	762	762
10mm Gravel	kg	390	385	299	385
River Sand	kg	667	653	511	653
Free Water	L	186	187	168	144
Unit Mass	kg/m^3	2400	2380	2400	2450
Air Content	%	1.4	2.0	–	2.1
Slump	mm	175	180	180	205
Compressive Strength N/mm^2					
1 day *		52.0	44.5	45.0	57.3
3 days		34.5	32.5	34.0	49.0
7 days		48.0	45.0	46.0	58.0
28 days		69.0	63.0	65.0	68.0
Water Absorption	%	1.0	1.2	1.1	0.8
Chloride Permeability Coulombs					
at 52 to 56 days		390	750	500	860

* AS 1012.19 Method 1

strength at seven days can be held in the range 70 to 80 percent of the 28 day strength. Strength development at later ages is relatively low for pozzolanic concrete. This may be explained by a combination of high pozzolanic reaction at early ages and by a strength ceiling influence for the materials around the 100 N/mm^2 level.

In Series 3 (Table 3b), because other factors were held constant, a direct comparison is possible between the influence of superfine fly ash and the influence of the various silica fumes on strength development and other properties. Under these conditions, the fly ash out-performed silica fume in early strength development and water absorption. At the proportions evaluated, chloride permeability of the fly ash mix was slightly higher than for silica fume. However, Series 2 demonstrates that very low results are possible with fly ash.

PRACTICAL IMPLICATIONS

These days when concrete is required to have very high strength or resistance to salt penetration or both, the common solution to the problem is to use silica fume. The material is usually expansive, relatively hard to handle and increases the water requirement of the concrete. To offset this water demand it is virtually standard practice to incorporate a high-range water-reducing admixture. Where facilities permit, it can be beneficial and economical to also include fly ash or ground granulated blastfurnace slag to the mixture.

It is difficult to discuss raw material costs in terms which are applicable world-wide. However, in most areas, silica fume is more expensive than cement, often twice to three times the price. Superfine fly ash is becoming available certainly in Australia, at about or less than the price of cement. From the test results (Series 3) it is clear that enhanced impermeability and strength can be achieved more economically with superfine fly ash than with silica fume. The results from Series 2 demonstrate that strengths of around 100 MPa can be achieved with normal concrete aggregates and that rapid chloride permeabilities typical of silica fume concrete are attainable. What is less obvious is the significant part played by the high-range, water-reducing admixture.

CONCLUSIONS

Concrete of high compressive strength and extremely low chloride permeability can be produced with superfine low-calcium fly ash in conjunction with a high-range water-reducing admixture. Such concrete is relatively economical, uses by-product resources and is potentially highly durable.

Indications are that properly designed mixes incorporation superfine fly ash can be at least as durable as similar mixes containing silica fume.

Whereas regular superplasticized concrete tends to segregate at high admixture dose rate, mixes with low water content and relatively high fines content remain cohesive and flowing with 1% admixture active matter by weight of cement.

Such mixes develop a higher proportion of strength in the first 28 days than normal concrete. With the current materials, this is ascribed to the early strength contribution from the chemical admixture and enhanced pozzolanic reaction due to the relatively high surface area of the fly ash used.

REFERENCES

1.   ELLIS, JR. WE, RIGGS, EH AND BUTLER, WB. Comparative results of utilization of fly ash, silica fume and G.G.B.F.S. in reducing the chloride permeability of concrete. ACI SP 126-23, Editor Malhotra, VM. Montreal, Canada, 1991, pp 443-458.

2.   GOPALAN, MK AND HAQUE, MN. Fly ash in high-strength concrete. ACI SP121-17, Editor Hester, WT. Berkeley, California, 1990, pp 331-349.

3.   HOOTON, RD AND McGRATH, P. Influence of self-dessication of non-air-entrained silica fume mortars on resistance to freezing and thawing. CANMET/ACI International Workshop on the Use of Silica Fume in Concrete, CANMET, Ottawa, Canada, 1991, pp 241-254.

PROPERTIES OF CONCRETES CONTAINING HAC AND HIGH VOLUMES OF FLY ASH

F Gomà

Polytechnic University of Barcelona

J M Costa

University of Barcelona

J Artigas

Polytechnic University of Barcelona

Spain

ABSTRACT. This report presents the preliminary results of an investigation forming part of a long term study of concrete incorporating low quantities of High Alumina Cement and high volumes of fly ash high in sulphate (ASTM Class C). This is a new material that has no antecedents. DTA analysis of pastes and concretes and hydrate phases found are given. 150X300mm. concrete cylinders with different mixtures and 590 kgsm3 of total binder, control, 60% and 0.30% replacement a constant workability of 70 mm.,were made. The influence of the type of aggregate calcareous or quartz in loss of strength due to conversion were reported. Electrochemical measurements of the corrosion current were done. From the results obtained, some specific applications of these new materials are suggested.

Keywords: concretes; fly ash; durability; corrosion; aluminous cement; conversion.

Professor Ferran Gomà G., is Director of the Laboratory of chemistry Research in Architectural Construction Department at the Polytechnic University of Barcelona. He specialises in the durability of concrete and materials, analytical chemistry, and has been associated with the research of the manufacturing of Portland cement (Asland assoc. Blue Circle).

Professor J.Ma Costa T., is Director of Physical-Chemistry Research Laboratory of Barcelona University. He specialises in electrochemistry and is Member of the Working Party on Physical-Chemistry Methods of the Corrosion Testing (European Federation of Corrosion).

Concrete 2000. Edited by Ravindra K. Dhir and M. Roderick Jones.
© 1993 Published by E & FN Spon. ISBN 0 419 18120 2.

INTRODUCTION

Research work on structural Portland cement concrete incorporating high volumes of low-calcium (ASTM Class F) fly ash been developed since 1987 at CANMET. The cement content is kept at a relatively low value, typically in the order of 150 kg/m^3 in this concrete, and the proportion of fly ash in the total cementitious materials is about 60 per cent. The W /(C+F) ratio of these concretes are about 0.3 and the workability of the concrete is achieved through the use of a superplasticizer.

It has been demonstrated (1), (2), that this type of concrete has high unit weight, satisfactory early-age strength, high modulus of elasticity, and high later-age strength.

In addition, when the content of the sulphate of the ash used is as high as 5 per cent, no expansion is produced and strength increases (3).

Its good behaviour makes it possible to improve the new concept of "supplementary cementitious materials".

The authors have studied the incorporation of high volumes of fly ash into aluminous cement concretes looking for a new material which is better at resisting sulphate than present existing ones. Though it is well known that concrete of aluminous cement has a serious limitation due to CAH10 conversion (4), the present work and report is justified for the following reasons:

Firstly, because according to the established criterion: aluminous cement concrete resists sulphate, when the w/c ratio is low (<0.4), better than Portland cement concrete, and especially when the filler aggregates are calcareous (5).

Secondly, taking into account that this type of aggregate with limestone filler (6) (7), reacts with calcium hydrate aluminates and the main part of the loss of mechanical strength, which is due to conversion of the metastable calcium hydrate aluminate into more stable compounds, may be reduced.

This report presents the results of preliminary research at early ages up to 10 months on a set of concretes, each incorporating a Class C fly ash with high sulphate content (5%), and A-55 UNE type of aluminous cement.

This new material does not appear in the bibliographies and consequently does not seem to have been made or studied before.

EXPERIMENTAL DETAILS

Scope of investigation

Ten concrete mixtures, namely, two control concretes and seven concretes incorporating high volumes of fly ashes $F/(C+F)= 0.6$), and one with usual addition $F/(C+F)= 0.3$ were made. Two batches from the control concretes and eight batches from fly ash concretes, were prepared. The size of each batch was $0.07 \ m^3$. The water-to-cementitious materials ratio was kept constant at around 0.3. All concrete mixtures were superplasticized with no more than 0.5 % weight of cementitious material and the properties of the fresh concrete were determined.

From all concretes, specimens were subjected to the determination of the compressive strength and densities. In addition, another set of all the concrete mixtures were cast and their behaviour in aggressive solutions was also carried out.

Other complementary tests for electrochemical measurements such as corrosion potential and corrosion intensities were done.

Materials

The concrete mixtures were made in the Research Laboratory of the Architectural Construction Department using the following materials. Their physical properties and chemical analyses are given in Table 1.

Cement. Aluminous cement A-55, UNE type, was used.

Fly Ash. Fly ash of variety (ASTM Type C), but containing a high level of sulphate and were obtained from sources in Cercs Catalonia Spain.

Silica Fume. The Norwegian silica fume was incorporated to decrease its permeability to chloride ions.

Aggregates. The fine and coarse aggregates were local natural calcareous sand and minus 19-mm crushed limestone, respectively. The grading and the physical properties of both aggregates are given in Tables 2 . From these values the standard grading curve was calculated according to the FAURY (8) method to obtain the optimum mixture with compensated "wall effect".

Table 1 Chemical analysis and physical properties of binders

	ALUMINOUS CEMENT SPAIN A-55 UNE	FLY ASH (SPAIN) CERCS CATALONIA	SILICA FUME NORWAY
TiO_2	1.8	–	–
SiO_2	2.1	49.8	94.02
Al_2O_3	41.3	17.3	0.05
FeO	6.1	–	–
Fe_2O_3	8.7	–	–
Fe_2O_3 Total	15.0	8.7	0.04
CaO	39.7	24.9	0.45
MgO	0.2	1.9	1.11
Na_2O Total	0.02	0.3	0.12
K_2O Total	0.03	1.7	0.40
SO_3	0.1	4.3	0.50
CaO Free	0.1	11.4	–
L.O.I. 950º	0.2	2.4	3.2
Insoluble Residue(*)	0.8	41.5	–
Na_2O Soluble	0.02	0.06	–
K_2O Soluble	0.03	0.25	–
Fineness			
>88 μm	0.4	2.4	–
>63 μm	3.2	2.7	–
>45 μm	9.2	26.7	–
>32 μm	24.4	–	–

(*) Soluble in 10% HCl when cold.

Table 2   Grading of aggregates and specific gravity

	SIEVE SIZE IN mm.									SPECIFIC GRAVITY
	19.0	12.7	9.5	4.7	2.36	1.18	0.60	0.30	0.15	
COARSE AGGREGATE CALCAREOUS	0.0	38.5	64.3	93.0						2.67
FINE AGGREGATE CALCAREOUS				0.0	15.8	63.5	70.1	82.3	90.8	2.70
FINE AGGREGATE QUARTZ				0.0	7.0	41.4	74.8	90.2	99.5	2.65

(*) Cumulative retained %

Superplasticizer. (High-Range Water-Reducing Admixture). A sulphonated naphthalene and condensated with formaldeyde was used. This superplasticizer is available as a dark brown 39% solids aqueous solution, having a density of 1.190 kg/m³. The dose was less than 0.5 % to (C+F) content.

Air-entraining admixture. Air entraining agents were not used, nor were other organic additives such as set retardants nor accelerating agents to avoid any other interferences.

Mix Proportions

Concrete mixture proportions are given in Table 3. For all mixtures, the graded coarse and fine aggregates were weighed in room-dry conditions. The true water content of each mixture, when the equilibrium was reached, was determined by dehydration at constant weight. The different 0.07 m³ concrete mixtures were made in a laboratory counter-current mixer with fly ash added as a separate ingredient. The sulphonate hydrocarbon type admixture was used in both the control and fly ash concretes.

Table 3   Mixture proportions

kgs/m³	U CONTROL	V CONTROL	A F.A.	P F.A.	P' F.A.	Q F.A.	R F.A.	X F.A.	S F.A.	T F.A.
Batch no.	1	2	3	4	5	6	7	8	9	10
W/C+F	0.34	0.36	0.51	0.43	0.35	0.39	0.33	0.33	0.30	0.32
F/C+F	-	-	0.60	0.60	0.60	0.60	0.60	0.60	0.60	0.30
F/C	0.10	0.01	0.11	0.09	0.08	0.00	0.25	0.25	0.25	0.14
Σ(C+F)	590	590	420	490	490	490	490	590	590	590
Water	202	211	214	211	176	211	162	198	177	192
Cement	590	590	168	196	196	196	196	236	236	413
Fly Ash	-	-	252	295	295	295	295	354	354	177
C.A. Ca.	1.092	1.092	1.202	1.141	1.141	1.141	1.141	1.092	1.092	1.092
F.A. Ca.	-	757	764	707	754	726	-	-	-	-
F.A. Q.	546	-	-	-	-	-	691	645	645	645
Filer Ca.	59.0	6.4	19.0	18.0	16.4	-	49.0	59.0	59.0	59.0
S. Fume	34.1	34.1	-	-	-	13.6	13.7	17.0	17.0	17.0
S. Plastic.	3.4	3.4	1.7	3.4	3.4	3.4	3.4	3.4	3.4	3.4

(*) F.A.=Fly Ash, CNT=Control, Ca.=Calcareous, Q.=Quartz,

Properties of Fresh Concretes

The properties of freshly-mixed concrete, i.e., slump and unit weight measurements are given in Table 4.

After casting, all the moulded specimens were covered with water-saturated burlap and left in the casting room at 22 ± 1.5 oC and 95% relative humidity. After 24 h, the specimens were demoulded, weighed, and transferred into the lime-saturated water at 22 ± 1.5 oC until required for the test.

Properties of Fresh Concretes

The properties of freshly-mixed concrete, i.e., slump and unit weight measurements are given in Table 4.

Table 4   Properties of fresh concrete

Batch No.		Temperature ºC	Slump m/m	Unit Weight kgs/m³
U Control	1	25	50	2.562
V Control	2	25	50	2.591
A F.A.	3	24	40	2.414
P F.A.	4	23	110	2.481
P'F.A.	5	26	180	2.426
Q F.A.	6	26	70	2.511
R F.A.	7	26	68	2.450
X F.A.	8	25	65	2.408
S F.A.	9	25	65	2.397
T F.A.	10	25	75	2.512

(*)   Bleeding cm³/cm², no water accumulated on the surface when tested according ASTM 232.

Test Results

Table 5   Physical parameters of hardened concrete

MIXTURE	BATCH NO.	BULK DENSITY g/cm³ (*)	APPARENT DENSITY g/cm³	POROSITY % IN VOL.	WATER % ABSORPTION
U Control	1	2.39	2.65	9.7	4.1
V	2	2.36	2.67	11.6	4.9
A Fly Ash	3	2.20	2.64	16.5	7.5
P	4	2.27	2.66	14.6	6.4
P'	5	2.28	2.65	14.1	6.2
Q	6	2.30	2.66	13.4	5.8
R	7	2.26	2.65	14.4	6.4
X	8	2.25	2.64	14.8	6.6
S	9	2.22	2.63	15.5	7.0
T	10	2.32	2.66	12.5	5.3

(*) In vacuum in cold conditions.

For all series the densities were determined at ages up to
28 days of immersion cured concretes. These determinations
were done under vacuum and in cold conditions. The results
are given in Table 5.
The compressive strengths, test results from all batches of
concrete are given in Table 8 for ages up to 56 days,
including results after conversion by temperature treatment.
The average of the three results was given for each test.

Ten days before reaching 56 days ages, cylinders 150x300
mm., of each concrete were put into a heat curing chamber in
immersion at 76 oC for ten days. At the end of this
treatment they were tested to measure the remaining strength
after conversion.

Table 6   Strengths of test results
            Compressive strength in N/mm²

MIXTURE	BATCH NO.	BEFORE CONVERSION			AFTER CONVERSION(*)
		7	28	56	56
U	1 control	24.3	44.7	48.8	45.2
V	2 control	31.9	60.3	48.4	43.8
A	3 Fly Ash	8.0	16.0	18.0	13.4
P	4 "	19.2	25.0	26.0	23.7
P'	5 "	18.0	31.7	32.6	24.8
Q	6 "	9.5	20.6	23.8	20.2
R	7 "	13.2	26.7	31.8	29.5
X	8 "	20.0	28.0	31.8	28.6
S	9 "	14.5	34.0	38.0	33.5
T	10 "	22.0	47.3	48.1	41.7

(*) Ten days in immersion at 76 ºC

The content of Ca(OH)2 was determined by selective
extraction method with ethylene-glycol (3) and the results
shown in the Table 7.

Table 7   Test results of Ca(OH)$_2$ % content of concretes

MIXTURE	BATCH NO.	28 DAYS
U	1 Control	1.0
V	2 "	1.2
A	3 FLY ASH	0.3
P	4 "	0.7
P'	5 "	0.6
Q	6 "	0.6
R	7 "	0.7
X	8 "	0.6
S	9 "	0.8
T	10 "	0.9

New cylinders 100x100 mm., were made from both the
composition control mixtures (series U and V) and also from
the concretes which were considered to represent the most
divergent concrete compositions (A and X). The were cast with
two electrodes in them, for electrochemical measurements.
For the electrochemical measurements, two sets of the samples
were stored in different conditions: immersion in lime-
saturated water, and moist curing room. The results are given
in Table 8.

Table 8   Electrochemical measurements

MIXT.	BATCH NO.	CURED	90 DAYS AGED			125 DAYS AGED		
			E_{CORR} mV	J_{CORR} $\mu A/cm^2$	E FREE mV	E_{CORR} mV	J_{CORR} $\mu A/cm^2$	E FREE mV
U	1	immersion	-97	0.19	-78	-207	0.17	-176
V	2	"	-75	0.11	-58	-205	0.11	-178
A	1	"	-515	0.46	-516	-535	0.36	-516
A	2	"	-430	0.67	-412	-525	0.83	-497
A	3	"	-597	0.68	-550	-530	1.28	-502
X	7	"	-592	2.06	-589	-490	1.09	-490
X	7	air	-630	1.85	-610	-554	1.28	-554

The electrochemical measurements were done when the stability
of the free corrosion potential was achieved after three
months. Measurements   after 48 h. in immersion for all
specimens were taken. The results are shown in Table 6.

D.T.A. Information
The phases of the hydrated compounds were studied with DTA
technique from samples of the pastes and concretes. Fig. 1
shows the diagrams. Netzsch, DTA, 10 °C/min., 100 μV.

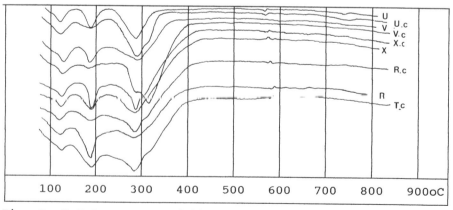

Fig. 1 D.T.A. curves of the relevants concretes

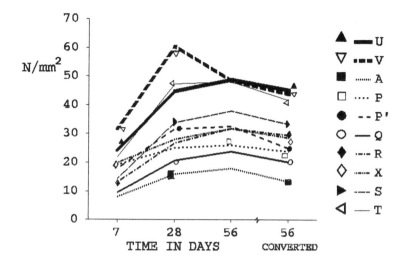

STRENGTH OF CONCRETES IMMERSION CURED AT < 26 oC
Fig. 2 Effect with and without immersion thermal
treatment at 76 oC.

RESULTS AND DISCUSSION

Compressive Strength

The results of compressive strengths of concrete control specimens, with 590 kg/m3 of aluminous cement, incorporated calcareous filler and without fly ash, showed that their strengths before conversion by temperature treatment were no less than 48 N/mm². These were the highest strengths.

Observing the results of strength values of the control concrete V, it showed lower values at 56 days than at 28 days. The fact that the strengths have already notably decreased "before conversions by heat treatment" indicates that other factors are involved. We believe it could well be the morphology of the phase of AH3 which may effects these strength losses. Further research must be carried out in this direction.

After the aluminates conversion, done by keeping at 76 °C for ten days in immersion conditions, the control concretes maintained their strength values at no less than 43 N/mm². The reducing effect on conversion due the presence of the calcareous filler has already been observed (6),(7).

Further research must be carried out in this direction.

Under the same conditions and with the same W/(C+F) ratio, but with calcareous filler, specimen U had a much smaller degree of strength loss. As the calcareous filler leads to the formation of carboaluminates thereby reducing the C_3AH_6 content as is shown in the DTA diagrams Fig. 1.

Samples with a fly ash addition and calcareous filler shown a fall in strength which is not sharp as normal concrete with aluminous cement and the residual strengths after conversion are higher. Therefore both filler and fly ash, with high calcium content, create favourable conditions, especially by introducing Portlandita in these concretes.

The concretes with the incorporated high volumes of fly ash with substitution degree of 0.6 and calcareous filler with F/C ratio = 0.25, made it possible to obtain residual strengths after conversion of over 28 N/mm², up to two months ages concrete under immersion-cured conditions until required for compression test.

DTA phases information on filler and SCH effects

At 28 days, the principal phases present were CAH_{10}, (SCH), AH3, and C_3ACcH_{11}

The concrete control V without fly ash and calcareous filler, F/C ratio 0.01, showed that the C3AH6 was a principal phase in the hydration products after conversion. The conversion degree obtained in these samples after thermal treatment was very high.

In samples with a fly ash substitution degree of 0.6 and a calcareous filler, F/C ratio of more than 0.14, C_3AH_6 was very little found to be one of the products of hydration after conversion by temperature treatment.

Durability Properties

Density of Test Specimens. Bulk density and porosity of test specimens obtained are suitable conditions for durability properties, and it is probably due to the filler effect of the fly ash particles, filling the voids in the mortar matrix.

Corrosion Current   The control concrete has the lowest corrosion current jcorr. The high volumes of fly ash concretes have a high potential corrosion, but the corrosion intensity remains very low.

The soluble alkalies content of the concretes with fly ash is higher than the control concrete. These alkalies come from the fly ash and this may explain the higher corrosion potential, because the chloride ions content in these concretes were tested by VOLHARD method and found 0.03 % in weight of concrete.

On the other hand, the calcium hydroxide introduced in concrete comes from the fly ash itself, augments the OH-concentration. This increases the pH and keeps the current corrosion intensity (jcorr) low as can be seen in the results. Therefore, the passivation effect increases as compensating effect in this materials. In control concretes, the low alkali content in aluminous cement explains why the corrosion potential, as well as the current corrosion intensity is so low.

Sulphate resistance. In accordance with to WOJCIECH (5), whose work has demonstrated that the sulphate expansion is markedly reduced by the effect of the addition of the calcareous filler we expect a good resistance to sulphate of these composites at later ages. In addition, the silica fume incorporated, as is well known, makes it possible to reduce the ions permeability.

These values and the reduced C_3AH_6 content make it possible to hope a good behaviour in aggressively attack tests, whose are pending results at long term. Specimens of exactly the same composition are also being tested at low and normal temperatures for their resistance to sulphate attack, although at the moment we only have early ages results.

Alkaline hydrolysis. When this materials are used as a coating for structural Portland concretes with less resistance to attack of aggressively substances, to avoid transferring the alkali ions from the Portland to HAC concretes to prevent the alkaline hydrolysis, the asphaltic materials or polymer substances must be interposed between their contacts.

In connection with the effect of the alkalies content in concretes which comes from the fly ash itself, it ought to be verified that storage in immersion at later ages with free CO2 does not produce alkaline hydrolysis.

CONCLUSIONS

From the results, it is concluded that the conversion of hexagonal aluminates does not explain completely the reason for strength losses. Therefore, there must be some other contributing factors.

Fly ash with a high calcium oxide content give concretes of aluminous cement a residual content of Portlandita. This considerably favours the cathodical protection of the embedded bars by helping to keep the corrosion current low.

These new materials with optimum conditions in resisting attack from sulphate and acidic substances are hoped to give good results after long term tests.

With the materials we have chosen in the work, seem to be the that we can obtain 2 different interesting new materials:

1. **Materials with a high volumes of fly ash.**

   W/(C+F)=0.3
   Superplasticizer 0.5 % in weight of (C+F)
   Total binder 590 kgs/m3 (C+F)
   Fly ash replacement level F/(C+F)=0.6
   Calcareous aggregate and calcareous filler 30 kgs/m3
   Silica fume 1.3 % in weight of concrete
   Strength after conversion 33 N/mm^2

2. **Materials with expecting high level of resistance to attack of aggressively substances.**

   W/(C+F)=0.3
   Superplasticizer 0.5 in weight of (C+F)
   Total binder 590 kgs/m3
   Fly ash replacement level F/(C+F)=0.3
   Calcareous aggregate and calcareous filler 30 kgs/m3
   Silica fume 2.5 - 5.0 % in weight of (C+F)
   Strength after conversion 41 N/mm^2

These materials have special interest in use as "a coating" for structural Portland cement concretes. Especially when used in environmentally aggressive situations such as constructions on chalky soils, (Triassic), phreatic sea levels, etc.

The fly ash concretes have a higher resistance to the weak acidic substances (10) ionization constants about(10-3 to 10-5) and is for reason that they are interesting and its suggested, to study their use to "encapsulate" waste materials.

The economic benefit may be gained when in this way the durability of Portland concrete structures in these specials environments increases.

REFERENCES

1.   V.SIVASUNDARAM, G.G CARETTE, AND V.M.MALHOTRA.Properties of concrete Low Quality of Cement and High volumes of

Low-Calcium Fly Ash. Proceedings Third International Conference Trondheim, Norway, 1989. SP114-2, pp 45-71

2.   LANGLEY,W.S.,CARETTE, G.G.AND MALHOTRA W.M. "Structural Concrete Incorporating High Volumes of ASTM Class F Fly Ash,MSL Division Report MSL 88-43 (OP&J), January 88.

3.   GOMA, F. G., "Concrete Incorporating High Volumes of Fly Ash of ASTM Class C with High Sulfate Content", Proceedings Fourth International Conference Istambul, Turkey, May 1992. p. 403-418.

4.   NEVILLE, A.M. "High Alumina cement Concrete" The Construction Press Ltd. Lunesdale House.   Hornby. Lancaster La28NB, 1975.

5.   WOJCIECH G. PIASTA, "The Effects of Limestone Fillers on Sulfate Resistance of High Alumina Cement Composites", Proceedings of the International Symposium University of London July 1990, c 18

6.   L. CUSSINO, AND A. NEGRO, "Hydration of Aluminous Cement in the Presence of Silicic and Calcareous Aggregate ", 7 th International Congress on Chemistry of Cement Vol. III V 62-70. Paris 1980.

7.   BHASKARA RAO, P. and VISWANATHAN, V.N. "Chemistry of arresting strength retrogression in structural high alumina cements" 7 th International Congress on Chemistry of Cement Vol. III 51-56. Paris 1980.

8.   FAURY "le béton" DOUNOD; Paris, 1958.

9.   STERN, M., GEARY, A.L., "Electrochemical Polarization, I.A Theoretical Analysis of the Shape Polarization Curves", Jour. of the Electrochemical Society, Vol. 104, pp.56-63.

10. BAYOUX, J.P., and Al, "Acid Corrosion of High Alumina Cement", Proceedings of the International Symposium University of London July 1990, c 17.

ADDITIONAL PAPERS

DESIGNING CONCRETE BEAMS WITH FRP REBARS

H V S Granga Rao

S S Faza

West Virginia University

United States of America

J Anderson

International Composites Ltd

United Kingdom

ABSTRACT. The load-deflection behaviour of concrete beams reinforced with fibre-reinforced plastic (FRP) rebars is investigated extending the current methods used for steel reinforced beams. In addition, certain recommendations to compute post-cracking deflections in beams reinforced with FRP rebars are presented.

Keywords: Chloride, Corrosion, Cracking, Deflection, Bond, Bending, Fibre Reinforced Plastic Reinforcement Bar (FRP Rebar), Design Criteria.

Professor H V S Granga Rao is Director of Construction Engineering Facilities at West Virginia University, Morgantown, West Virginia, USA.

Dr S S Faza has recently been appointed Lecturer in Concrete Technology, Construction Engineering Facilities, West Virginia, Morgantown, West Virginia, USA.

Mr John Anderson is Managing Director of International Composites Ltd (ICL), Falkirk, Scotland. ICL specialise in diverless underwater construction methods and the manufacture and fabrication of fibre composite products and structures for Civil and Marine Construction projects.

Concrete 2000. Edited by Ravindra K. Dhir and M. Roderick Jones.
© 1993 Published by E & FN Spon. ISBN 0 419 18120 2.

INTRODUCTION

Concrete reinforced with mild steel rebars is commonly used in the construction of bridge decks, parking garages, and numerous other constructed facilities. The extensive use of de-icing chemicals is reducing the service life of these facilities. In addition, concrete structures exposed to highly corrosive environments, such as coastal and marine structures, chemical plants, water and wastewater treatment facilities, have been experiencing drastically reduced service life and causing user inconvenience.

The gradual intrusion of chloride ions into concrete leads to corrosion of steel reinforced concrete structures and concrete cracking; which may be due to shrinkage, creep, thermal variations or some unexpected design inadequacies due to external loads (Nawy, 1990). A corrosion protection system that would extend the performance of our constructed facilities would have a payoff in billions of dollars, since the replacement runs twice the original construction cost (America's Highways, 1984).

Several recommendation have been adopted in the design of concrete structures to prevent the corrosion of steel reinforcement such as use of waterproofing admixtures in concrete, impermeable membranes, epoxy-coated steel rebars, and others without a complete success.

Therefore, use of noncorrosive fibre reinforced plastic (FRP) rebars in place of mild steel has been researched as an alternative to improve the longevity of structures.

RESEARCH SIGNIFICANCE

The performance of FRP rebars embedded in concrete is not fully understood, even though FRP rebars have been used in structural applications for over ten years (Nawy, 1977). The current mathematical models and design equations of concrete beams reinforced with mild steel cannot be applied directly to beams reinforced with FRP rebars without fully understanding the following issues:

1. Lower modulus of elasticity of FRP than steel

2. Bond behaviour

3. Long term degradation

4. Post-cracking behaviour of the concrete beams with FRP rebars.

The primary focus of the research conducted at the Constructed Facilities Centre, West Virginia University is to study the behaviour of reinforcing beams and bridge decks with FRP rebars. The main objectives of this paper include two aspects of the behaviour of FRP rebars used as reinforcement in concrete:

(1) Investigation of the pre- and post cracking deflection behaviour under bending of concrete beams reinforced with FRP rebars;

(2) Development of post-cracking deflection design equations for FRP reinforced concrete, which are practical and simple to use for structural design applications.

TEST PROGRAM

Fibre-Reinforced Plastic Rebar Characteristics

Since the 1950s, glass has been considered a good substitute to steel for reinforcing or prestressing concrete structures. For example, a typical E-glass fibre reinforced plastic rebar has minimum 55% glass volume fraction embedded in a matrix of vinylester and an appropriate coating to prevent alkaline reaction (Rubinski, 1954).

In order to develop good bond strength between FRP rebars and concrete, different surface conditions for rebar were developed. Among them, 45 degree angular wrapping or helical ribs produce a deformed surface on the rebar. Coating FRP rebars with epoxy and rolling them in a bed of sand creates a roughened surface and is one of the alternatives that will improve bond strength.

Experimental results indicate that the average tensile stiffness depends on the fibre type and volume fraction and is virtually independent of manufacture, bar size, bar type (with or without ribs), test procedure, and type of resin. A mean tensile stiffness of 48.26 GPa for 55% fibre volume fraction was reported by Wu (1991). However, ultimate tensile strength is sensitive to bar diameter, quality control in manufacturing, matrix system, fibre type, and gripping mechanism. The ultimate tensile strength of continuous glass fibre reinforced rebars with vinylester resin decreases rapidly with an increase in bar diameter (Table 1).

Considering the fact that FRP rebars do not exhibit a yield plateau as steel, it is necessary to assume a 20% reduction in effective yield strength of the rebar for reasons of safety; hence minimum of six rebars have to be tested to obtain an average ultimate rebar strength, f_{ult}.

The reduction factor was arrived at after testing samples from a variety of manufacturers (Wu, 1991, Faza, 1992). If testing of rebar samples is not possible, the following results outline in Table 1 can be used as the effective yield strength, f_{yf} of FRP rebars.

Table 1 Effective Yield Strength of FRP Rebars (MPa)

REBAR SIZE	#3	#4	#5	#6	#7	#8
f_{ult}*	897.4	738.6	655.8	621.3	586.8	552.2
f_{yf}	717.9	590.9	524.6	497.0	469.4	441.8

* Based on test data on Kodiak Rebars

Concrete Properties

In order to take advantage of the high tensile strength of the FRP rebars, concrete strength of 34.5 - 69.0 MPa was used in the testing program. Class K concrete from a local mixing plant was used in all the specimens. For each batch of concrete delivered, eight 101.6 x 203 mm (4 x 8 in.) cylinders were cast, cured and tested with the specimens.

Beam Specimens

Twenty five rectangular beams, 152.4 x 304.8 mm by 3048 (6"x12"x10 feet) were tested under pure bending (as simply supported under four point bending), using different configurations of FRP reinforcement and concrete strength. The variables are:

a)   Rebar size (#3, #4, #7, #8)

b)   Type of rebar (smooth, ribbed, sand coated)

c)   Type of stirrups (steel, smooth FRP, ribbed FRP)

d)   Reinforcement distribution (3#4 versus 5#3)

e)   Concrete compressive strength, 29-69 MPa (f_c^1 = 4.2,5.0,6.5,7.5 and 10ksi).

Experimental Results

The major emphasis of the test program was to investigate the FRP reinforced concrete beam behaviour and compare with the steel reinforced beam, in terms of:

-    Pre- and Post-Cracking Behaviour

-    Load-Deflection and Stress-Strain Variations

-    Elastic and Ultimate Load Carrying Capacities

-    Crack Patterns (spacing, width, propagations)

-    Modes of failure

The simply supported rectangular beams were tested under pure bending using different configurations of FRP reinforcements. In order to take advantage of the high tensile strengths of FRP rebars, beams with higher strength concrete (f_c^1 = 34.5 - 69 MPa) were tested for the purpose of maximising the bending resistance of the beams. In this paper, the pre- and post-cracking deflection behaviour are emphasized.

Pre- and Post-Cracking Behaviour

The precracking segments of load deflection curves in all specimens are essentially straight lines indicating the full elastic behaviour. The maximum tensile stress in concrete beams in this region is less than the tensile strength of concrete. The flexural stiffness E I of the beams can be estimated using Young's modulus E_c of concrete and the moment of inertia of the uncracked reinforced concrete cross section. The load-deflection behaviour before cracking is dependent on the stress-strain relationship of concrete. When flexural cracking develops, contribution of concrete in the tension zone is neglected. Thus the slope of a load-deflection (or stiffness) curve is less steep than in the precracking stage. The stiffness continues to decrease with increasing load, reaching a lower limit that corresponds to the moment of inertia of the cracked section, I_{cr}.

The post-cracking experimental deflection of FRP reinforced beams (Beam #B & #H1) were about four times larger than the beam reinforced with steel rebars (Beam #11) as shown in Fig.1. The larger post-cracking deflections were expected due to the low modulus of elasticity of FRP rebars, which is about 4.83 GPa. The deflection behaviour was vastly improved when sand coated rebars were used as shown in Fig. 1. This behaviour is attributed to the reduction in crack widths, and the improvements in the distribution and propagation of the cracks when sand coated rebars are used (Faza, 1992).

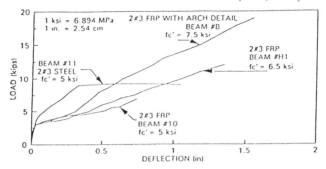

Figure 1 Experimental Load vs Deflection

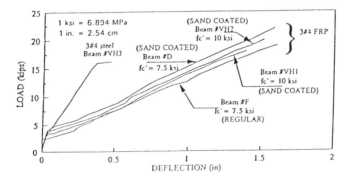

Figure 2 Load vs Deflection (using sand coated FRP bars)

Theoretical Correlation of Experimental Deflections

The theoretical correlation of the experimental deflections utilizes, as a first step, the current mathematical models and design equations for concrete reinforced with mild steel rods. The results from these equations are checked with the experimental deflections and modified as necessary to accommodate FRP reinforcement.

Various methods have been considered by researchers in an attempt to calculate post cracking deflections of concrete beams reinforced with steel (Nawy, 1990). The differences among the various methods consists mainly of the ways to compute the modulus of elasticity, E, and the moment of inertia, I. Both quantities are difficult to define in a steel reinforced concrete member. Considering that cracking behaviour of concrete beams reinforced with FRP bars is different from that of steel reinforced concrete beams, the effective cracked moment of inertia I, would be different from that of conventional steel reinforced beams. Such difference can be attributed mainly to the extent of cracking, which is a function of the bond between concrete and rebar.

Precracking Stage

The precracking segments of load-deflection curves in all specimens were essentially straight lines indicating the full elastic behaviour. The load deflection behaviour before cracking is dependent on EI of the beams and the stress-strain relationship of concrete from which the value of E_c can be calculated either using the ACI 318 code expression

$E_c = 57,000 \sqrt{f_c^1}$ where E_c & f_c^1 (psi, 1psi = 6.903 KPa)   (1)

or ACI 363R committee recommendation

$E = 40,000 \sqrt{f_c^1} + 1 \times 10^6$ where E_c & f_c^1 (psi, 1psi = 6.903 KPa) (2)

An accurate estimate of the moment of inertia I necessitates the consideration of FRP reinforcement area A_F in the computations. This can be done by replacing FRP rebar area by an equivalent concrete area $E_F/E_c) A_F$. However, the use of gross moment of inertia resulted in acceptable results in the precracking stage with the uncracked section and neglecting additional stiffness contribution from the FRP reinforcement.

The precracking stage stops at the initiation of the first flexural crack when concrete reaches its modulus of rupture, f_c, which is typically 7.5 $\sqrt{f_c^1}$, (f_c^1(psi). The ACI 363R recommends a value of 11.7 $\sqrt{f_c^1}$ for normal weight concretes with strengths in the range of 3000 to 12,000 psi (1 psi = 6.903 KPa). For curing conditions such as seven day moist curing followed by air drying, a value of 7.5 $\sqrt{f_c^1}$ is closer to the full strength range.

Postcracking Stage

When flexural cracking develops, tensile strength of concrete is neglected. The slope of a load-deflection (or stiffness) curve is less steep than in the precracking stage as shown in load-deflection curves in Fig 3 and 4. The stiffness continues to decrease with increasing load, reaching a lower limit and corresponds to the moment of inertia of the cracked section, I_{cr}. The moment of inertia of a cracked section can be obtained by computing the moment of inertia of the cracked section about the neutral axis resulting in the following relationship after neglecting the concrete section below the neutral axis:

$I_{cr} = \frac{b\,c}{3} + n A_F (d - c)^2$

where   n = Modular ratio, (E_F/E_c)

          c = Distance from top fibre to the neutral axis

In actual cases, only a portion of a beam along its length is cracked. The uncracked segments below the neutral axis possess some degree of stiffness which contributes to the overall beam rigidity. The actual stiffness of the beam lies between $E_c I_G$ and $E_c I_{cr}$. As the load approaches the ultimate value, beam stiffness approaches $E_c I_{cr}$. The major factors that influence the beam stiffness are:

1)   Extent of cracking

2)   Contribution of concrete below the neutral axis.

The ACI 318 code specifies that deflection shall be computed with an effective moment of inertia, I_G.

$$I_e = (M_{cr}/M_a)^3 \, I_G + [1 - (M_{cr}/M_a)^3] I_{cr}.$$

where $M_{cr} = \dfrac{f_r I_G}{Y_t}$, M_a = Applied Moment, and $Y_t = h/2$

The effective moment of inertia adopted by the ACI 318-89 is considered sufficiently accurate for use in control of deflection of beams reinforced with steel. I_e was developed to provide transitional moments of inertia between I_G and I_{cr} and it is a function of $(M_{cr}/M_a)^3$.

By investigating the experimental versus theoretical load-deflection curves using I as prescribed by eq. (4), a large discrepancy is found in deflections after the first crack as shown in Fig. 3 and 4.

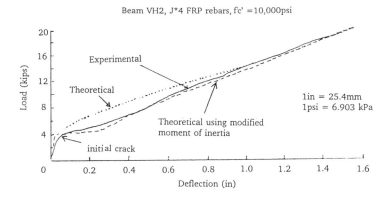

Figure 3 Load vs deflection (theoretical vs experimental)

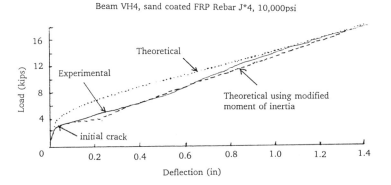

Figure 4 Load vs deflection (theoretical vs experimental)

The equation for deflection of a simply supported beam of span L, loaded with twoconcentrated loads P (Fig.5), in kips, at a distance a from each end is written as:

$$\Delta_{max} = \frac{P\,a}{24E_c I_e}(3L^2 - 4a^2), \text{ (in, 1 in = 25.4 mm)} \tag{5}$$

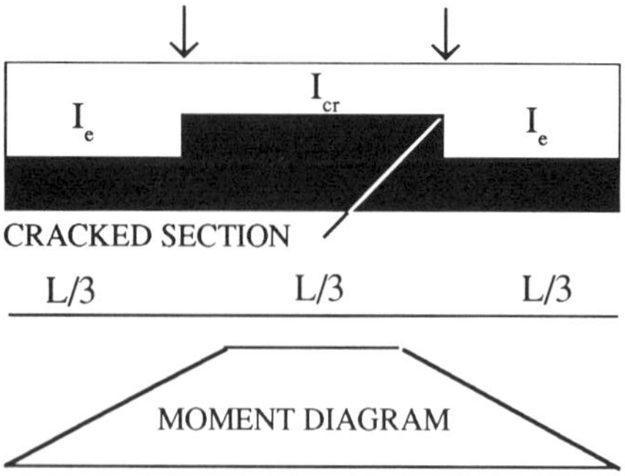

Figure 5 Load, Moment and Cracking Section of Loaded Beam

for a = L/3 $\Delta_{max} = \dfrac{23\,P\,L^3}{648\,E_c I_e}$ (6)

in which, E_c = Concrete modulus of elasticity (experimental values, psi)

I_e = Effective moment of inertia (in⁴)

L = 108 in., the deflection expression can be written as

$$\Delta_{max} = \frac{44712\,P}{E_c I_e} \text{ (in, 1 in = 25.4 mm)} \tag{7}$$

For evaluating I_e, the experimental cracking moment M_{cr}, observed from the tests was used.

It is seen from the load-deflection curves, Fig 3 and 4, that deflection by Eq. (6) overestimates the moment of inertia of the beam after the first crack. Thus, the calculated deflection values from Eq. (8) are lower than the observed values.

A better estimate of the moment of inertia is needed. In the following subsection, a new expression for the effective moment of inertia has been proposed by the researchers.

Modified Moment of Inertia

Due to the nature of crack pattern and propagation and the height of the neutral axis which is very small for FRP reinforced concrete beams, a new method in calculating the effective modulus of elasticity is introduced for FRP reinforced concrete beams. The new expression is based on the assumption that concrete section between the point loads is assumed to be fully cracked, while the end sections are assumed to be partially cracked (Fig. 5).

Therefore, expression for I_{cr} is used in the middle third section, and I_e is used in the end sections.

Using the moment area approach or other methods to calculate the maximum deflection at the centre of the beam, as shown in Fig. 5, would result in an expression for maximum deflection that incorporates both I_e and I_G, as shown in Equation (8).

$$\Delta_{max} = \frac{8P\,L^3 E\,I_{cr} + 15\,P\,L^3 E\,I_e}{648\;E\,I_{cr}E\,I_e}, \text{in. } (1 \text{ in.} = 25.4) \tag{8}$$

$$\Delta_{max} = \frac{8P\,L^3\,I_{cr} + 15\,P\,L^3 I_e}{648\;E\,I_{cr}E\,I_e} \tag{9}$$

Rewriting the deflection expression in equation (9)

$$\Delta_{max} = \frac{23P\,L^3}{648\;E_c\,I_m} \text{ (in)} \tag{10}$$

in which,

$$I_m = \frac{23\,I_{cr}\,I_e}{8\,I_{cr} + 15\,I_e} \tag{11}$$

The resulting deflection equation (10) and the modified moment of inertia (11) which is valid for two concentrated point loads that are applied at the third points on the beams are plotted as shown in Fig. 3 and 4.

Using the same approach as in the case of two concentrated point loads, expressions for maximum deflection and modified moment of inertia are derived for a concentrated point load and for a uniform distributed load. However, no experimental information is available to check their validity. For a concentrated point load applied at the centre of the beam the maximum deflection expression can be written as:

$$\Delta_{max} = \frac{P\,L^3}{48\;E_c\,I_m} \text{ (in) where, } I_m = \frac{54\,I_{cr}\,I_e}{23\,I_{cr} + 45\,I_e} \tag{12}$$

For a uniform distributed load applied on the beam, the maximum deflection expression can be written as:

$$\Delta_{max} = \frac{5\,W\,L^4}{384\;E_c\,I_m} \text{ (in) where, } I = \frac{240\,I_{cr}\,I_e}{45\,I_{cr} + 202\,I_e} \tag{13}$$

SUMMARY AND CONCLUSIONS

Based on the mechanical properties of FRP rebars obtained by Wu (1991), twenty five concrete beams were designed and tested under bending.

Test variables included concrete strengths (29-69 GPa), type of FRP rebar (smooth, ribbed, sand coated), and rebar size. The response of concrete beams reinforced with FRP rebars were investigated in terms of pre- and post-cracking load-deflection behaviour. The use of sand coated FRP rebars in addition to high strength concretes improved the overall behaviour of concrete beams in terms of the ultimate moment capacity, crack width and propagation, thus improving the load-deflection behaviour.

Theoretical correlations with experimental deflections were conducted using current provisions. The current design methodology for steel reinforced concrete beams cannot be applied directly to FRP reinforced concrete beams. New design equations for deflections similar to the ACI 318-89 building code provisions were established based on the experimental results outlined. Theoretical equations were established to compute modified moment of inertia.

Due to the nature of crack formation and propagation in FRP reinforced concrete beams and the low modulus of elasticity of FRP rebars, a modified effective moment of inertia equation is proposed herein to estimate deflection. The modified effective moment of inertia incorporates both the cracked moment of inertia as well as the current ACI code equation, and is valid for sand coated FRP rebars which exhibit a bond strength of at least 1500 psi [eq.(11)].

REFERENCES

ACI Building Code Requirements for Reinforced Concrete (ACI 318-89), American Concrete Institute, Detroit, MI, 1989.

America's Highway, Accelerating the Search for Innovation, Transportation Research Board.

Faza, S.S., PhD Dissertation, West Virginia University, Morgantown, West Virginia, 1991, "Bending and Bond Behaviour and Design of Concrete Beams Reinforced with Fibre Reinforced Plastic Rebars".

Faza, S.S. and GangaRae, H.V.S., Advanced Composites Materials, ASCE, Edited by Iyer S.L., 1991, pp 262, "Bending Response of BEams Reinforced with FRP Rebars for varying Concrete Strengths".

Nawy, E.G. and Neuwerth E.G., ASCE Journal of the Structural Division, Vol. 103, No. ST2, Feb. 1977.

Nawy, E.G., Reinforced Concrete, A Fundamental Approach, 2nd edition, Prentice Hall International, 1990.

Rubinski I. and Rubinski, A., Magazine of Concrete Research, (6), 71-78, 1954.

Wu, W.P., "Thermomechanical Properties of Fibre Reinforced Plastic Bars," Ph D Dissertation, West Virginia University, 1991.

CALCIUM ALUMINATES AND THEIR DERIVATIVES: NEW APPLICATIONS AND NEW TECHNOLOGIES

R G J Montgomery
S Rashid
A Campas
W B Woolley
Lafarge Special Cements
United Kingdom

ABSTRACT. Traditional uses and traditional views on Calcium Aluminate Cements (HAC) are challenged by a new understanding of the chemistry of these materials. New applications are being developed based on this new understanding of blends including industrially available product such as slags and PFA. Applications based on Calcium Sulpho Aluminates are also examined as well as extensions of more usual applications in response to increasing performance specifications.

Keywords : (CAC) Calcium Aluminate Cement, (PFA) Pulverised Fuel Ash, (FS) Fume Silica, (CSA) Calcium Sulpho Aluminates, Corrosion, Rheology, Conversion,

Ronald G.J. Montgomery: is a Senior Scientist based at Lafarge Coppee's new research centre at Isle d'Abeau near Lyon, France. He has over 25 years experience of research and development of calcium aluminate cements.

Shahwana Rashid: is a Development Scientist at Lafarge Special Cements U.K. She is also a Ph.D student working with Dr. Paul Barnes of Birkbeck College on early hydration of calcium aluminate cements using synchrotron radiation.

W. Bernard Woolley: is Commercial & Marketing Director of Lafarge Special Cements U.K. He has almost 25 years experience of the use and applications of CAC.

Alain Capmas: is Lafarge Fondu International's Group Research Manager. He has authored numerous papers on calcium aluminate cements particularly on its mineralogy.

Concrete 2000. Edited by Ravindra K. Dhir and M. Roderick Jones.
© 1993 Published by E & FN Spon. ISBN 0 419 18120 2.

INTRODUCTION

Calcium Aluminate Cement (or High Alumina Cement) as it has previously been named) is an old and established material. It was conceived in the latter part of the 19th century by a number of workers spanning the period from 1848 to 1888. [1-11] After this rather long period, a patent for a suitable method of commercial manufacture of Calcium Aluminate Cement was finally granted to Societe A & J. Pavin de Lafarge in 1908 [12]. Following extensive tests by Lafarge and French government laboratories, it became commercially available from 1918.

Although originally researched for its sulphate resisting properties, Calcium Aluminate Cement (CAC), was soon discovered to have extremely rapid hardening properties and was therefore used to build gun emplacements and shelters during the first World War.
As is the case with many new products, CAC has had a rather chequered career. The rapid hardening properties of CAC concretes were to lead to their extensive use in the manufacture of precast, prestressed beams during the 1950's & 60's, however, there were some fundamental misconceptions and some collapses occurred in the 1970's!

It is a matter of record that these failures were not entirely due to strength losses. [13] Had the relevant Codes of Practice, concerning the upper limit for water/cement ratios been strictly followed, these failures would probably never have occurred. [14] Nevertheless CAC (or HAC as it was then known) was removed from the British Code of Practice CP 116, effectively banning its use in structural applications.
Rather ironically, the banning of CAC in the UK in the mid 1970's, was followed by the lifting of restrictions, that had been imposed in France since 1943, by the publication in 1979 of an official circular. [15] This circular allowed its use under strictly controlled conditions of water/cement ratio and cement content.

During the period from 1975 to 1980 several important papers concerning the hydration and durability of CAC were published.[16-19] At a meeting of the Institute of Structural Engineers in 1981 the concensus was that a new revision of the code of practice on the use of high alumina cement should be undertaken. This has still not been done, however at a more recent debate on the future use of CAC (World of Concrete 1992) the guarded but optimistic concensus was that the current situation with regard to the structural use of CAC concretes should be reviewed following further research into its properties.

In fact much research has already been done on CAC's. In July of 1990, a three day international symposium was held in London, devoted solely to these materials. The proceedings of this symposium were published in a book edited by Mangabhai. [20]

In the last decade of the 20th century, Calcium Aluminate Cement has reached its maturity. We now understand fully its hydration and long term behaviour, we have proof of its durability, its qualities and uses as a cement are unquestionable. However, if this is not enough to take us into the 21st century, this paper will try to review the current research which is underway to further the understanding of the potential of Calcium Aluminates in blended cements, building chemistry, mining and civil engineering applications.

Although many publications and books have dealt thoroughly with the nature and properties of CAC's, it might be useful just to cover the major points in order to set the scene for this paper.
(For a complete account of the properties of CAC's the reader is advised to refer to the books on the subject. e.g. Ref.[21,22]

THE MANUFACTURE AND MINERALOGY OF CALCIUM ALUMINATE CEMENTS

Manufacture

Calcium aluminates are manufactured in many countries, either by fusion or sintering of bauxite and calcereous raw materials. [14] The purity and calcium aluminate content of the finished product, depends in particular on the purity of the bauxites used, those containing significant quantities of iron oxides and silica leading to complex cements such as Ciment Fondu Lafarge and those containing little or none of these oxides, leading to the pure calcium aluminate cements such as Secar 71 or Secar 80. The latter are in fact highly refractory and are used mainly for their high temperature resistance, although some of the intermediate grades do find applications in other industries such as building chemistry.

Mineralogy

The mineralogy of CAC's differs from that of Portland cements, which are based on calcium silicates, rather than calcium aluminates. The series of calcium aluminate compounds using cement chemistry notation
$C = CaO$, $A = Al_2O_3$, $S = SiO_2$, $F = Fe_2O_3$, $f = FeO$, $T = TiO_2$ and in order of A/C ratios are:

$$C_3A \quad C_{12}A_7 \quad CA \quad CA_2 \quad and \quad CA_6$$

Of these the hydraulically active compounds found in CAC's are, $C_{12}A_7$, CA and CA_2. C_3A is also hydraulic and is found as a minor phase in Portland cement clinkers. It is extremely reactive and gypsum additions are necessary to control the flash setting otherwise caused by this compound. For the same reason (i.e. flash setting) C_3A cannot be tolerated in CAC's since it is too reactive to be considered as a viable cement. The last of the calcium aluminate series CA_6, is not hydraulically active and is not found in cements.

Of the three calcium aluminates which constitute CAC's, mono-calcium aluminate is by far the major phase present - 50% or more by weight. The cements which contain significant quantities of iron oxides, silica and titania also contain minor phases such as C_2AS, C_2S, C_4AF and CT. $C_{12}A_7$ is a minor phase but its presence activates the hydraulicity of CA. [21] CA_2 which is only found in high purity cements is practically inactive.

PROPERTIES OF CALCIUM ALUMINATE CEMENTS

Rapid Hardening

CAC's are slow setting (i.e. about the same as Portland cements) but very rapid hardening. Strengths equivalent to the long term design strength are reached within a few hours (typically 40 MPa after about 6 hours). This strength is temporarily exceeded for a period of some months to several years, dependant mainly on temperature, (14,21) until the long term design strength is finally stabilised.

Low Temperature Concreting

The rapid hydration of CAC is accompanied by a release of the heat, which, although of the same order of magnitude as Portland cement, is released within hours and not days. This leads to a substantial increase in the temperature of the concrete, which may be turned to advantage for concreting in extremely cold conditions.

The combined properties of rapid hardening and heat of hydration allow applications in the most severe conditions. Grouting in permafrost soils in Northern Canada at soil temperatures of -10^oC has been possible. Figure 1 shows the temperatures of a Ciment Fondu Lafarge mortar accelerated with Li_2CO_3 cast in frozen sand at -10^oC. This mortar achieved a strength of 20 MPa within hours. Figure 2 shows hydrated Ciment Fondu Lafarge grout from site tests. Note the effects of freezing, followed by thawing and then hydration, on the outside of the specimen.

Resistance to Chemical Attack

The chemistry of CAC's is fundamentally different from that of Portland cements. No portlandite $Ca(OH)_2$, is formed during hydration which means that concretes made from CAC resist attack by many substances which are aggressive to ordinary portland cements e.g. sewage (sulphuric acid), dilute inorganic and organic acids (23), sulphates (24), chlorides (25), sea water (26), oils, fats etc.

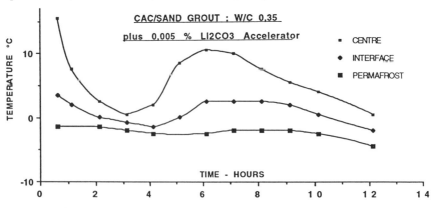

Figure 1   Temperature rise in mortar specimens at 10°C

Figure 2   Hydrated Ciment Fondu Lafarge grout

Figure 3. (ref.23) gives an example of the resistance of Ciment Fondu Lafarge to various acids. This shows the importance of the nature of the acid rather than a given pH value.

It should be noted that Gibbsite (AH_3) which is formed during the hydration of CAC is attacked by caustic alkalis such as NaOH and KOH. The use of CAC concrete should be avoided if these chemicals are likely to be present. However, CAC's are resistant to non-caustic alkalis such as ammonia.

High Temperature Resistance

CAC's are also widely used in refractory concretes for their high temperature resistance, up to $2000^{\circ}C$. The refractory properties of CAC's will not be discussed in this paper. However, it is worth mentioning an example of what is termed "Peri-refractory" concrete. These are usually used for heavy duty heat and abrasion resistant industrial floors in the metallurgical industries.

Rapid Setting Mixes

It is well known that flash setting may occur when CAC is mixed with Portland cements. This is due to the destabilisation of the sulphate/CA_3 balance in Portland cement. Although the use of such mixes is proscribed for making conventional concretes, it can be used to advantage for small repairs, fixings, making good etc. In France this is normal practice for masons who make the mix themselves as required. In the U.K. and other countries proprietary mixes are available.

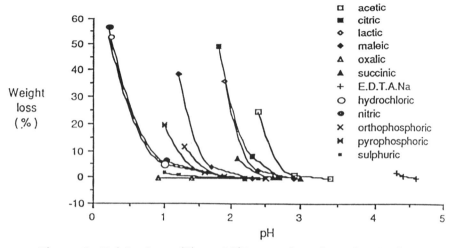

Figure 3   Weight loss (%) at 20°C as a function of solutions pH after 8 renewals

These mixtures of CAC with Portland cement and Calcium Sulphate, together with additives fillers and polymers, are the basis of many building chemistry products.

Conversion of CAC

A much researched and publicised property of CAC concretes is the phenomenon known as conversion. When the major phase of CAC, mono-calcium aluminate (CA), hydrates at low temperatures (<20°C), the hydrates formed are CAH_{10} with AH_x gel. The presence of $C_{12}A_7$ in industrial products also leads to the formation of some C_2AH_8. Both CAH_{10} and C_2AH_8 transform spontaneously to the stable, cubic hydrate C_3AH_6, with the formation of further AH_3 and the liberation of water.

$$3CAH_{10} \longrightarrow C_3AH_6 + 2AH_3 + 18H \qquad (i)$$

$$3C_2AH_8 \longrightarrow 2C_3AH_6 + AH_3 + 11H \qquad (ii)$$

This reaction, which is inevitable, is very rapid at higher temperatures (30°C - 100°C)[27]. In a recent publication [28], using Synchrotron Radiation-Energy Dispersive Diffraction (SR-ED) techniques, it has been shown that reaction (i) does not occur directly but passes via C_2AH_8. At various temperatures between 50-90°C the appearance of the C_2AH_8 hydrate during the hydration of pure CA and the conversion of CAH_{10} was revealed. Figures 4 & 5 shows the conversion of CAH_{10} at 70°C passing via C_2AH_8 and finally to C_3AH_6.

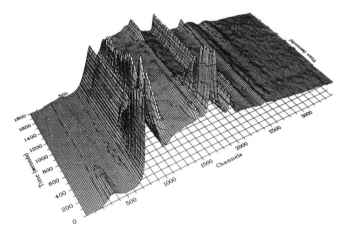

Figure 4   Conversion of CAH_{10} at 70°C to C_3AH_8

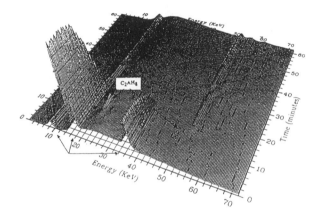

Figure 5   Conversion of C_2AH_8 at 70°C to C_3AH_6

The transformation of the meta-stable hydrates CAH_{10} and C_2AH_8 to stable C_3AH_6 is the process which is commonly known as CONVERSION. This process is fully understood and well documented in the literature, [14,21,28]. Conversion is accompanied by the release of bound water, which increases the porosity of the concrete and causes a certain loss of strength. The increase in porosity and hence the decease of strength are governed mainly by the water/cement ratio of the concrete and is therefore limited and quantifiable. [16,17,18.29]. Figure 6.

The failures of CAC prestressed concrete roof beams in the 1970's attributed at least in part to conversion, understandably lead to much public concern.

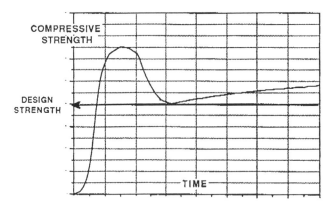

Figure 6   Rationalised strength development of calcium aluminate
cement concrete

The future of CAC was put in question and the uses of the product were seen as being limited to a few specialist applications only. In fact the markets for CAC continued to grow. Today it is certainly a specialist product but its applications are far from limited.

ACID CORROSION/BACTERIALOGICAL RESISTANCE

It has been known for some time that CAC's show very high resistance to sulphuric acid attack even in high ambient temperature sewers.However, these results had so far not been reproduced in the laboratory even though the resistance of CAC's had been shown to be higher than traditional cements : [43].

Recent on site investigations in Cairo [44] have again reconfirmed the good resistance to sulphuric acid attack particularly biogenic sulphuric acid.

Recent work [45] at Hamburg, in simulated sewer pipe conditions using sulphuric acid produced by bacterial action, has now demonstrated that observed field performance can be reproduced in the laboratory. This confirms the good potential performance of calcium aluminates compared to other materials and the test can be used as a more reliable method of evaluating materials. Using special mortars based on synthetic calcium aluminate aggregate even better results have been achieved [46].

CAC AND CALCIUM SULPHATE

CAC'S react with many inorganic salts, with sulphates they may form calcium aluminomonosulphate $C_4A\bar{S}_{12}$ ($\bar{S}$ is the cement notation for sulphate) which has been studied extensively particularly in Russia. Lately $C_4A\bar{S}H_{12}$ has been produced in the USA and Japan by direct combination to produce the expansive agent in the so called shrinkage compensated cements. CAC and $C\bar{S}$ may also be blended together in the correct proportions to manufacture ettringite $C_3A\bar{S}_3H_{32}$ for use in mine support systems. Ettringite with its large number of bound water molecules in the crystal structure and its interlocking growth habit produces relatively strong materials with an extremely high water content up to 90% by volume [41]. The use of CAC and $C\bar{S}$ has also been developed in modern self levelling compounds, again the type of $C\bar{S}$ used plays an important part in determining the properties [42] even when other hydraulically active materials are present.

MIXTURES OF CAC AND PORTLAND CEMENT

CAC as an accelerator for Portland cement has been used on site in building mortars for many years, chiefly for renderings and temporary fixings. In the last few years many new technical mortars have been developed based on these mixtures, however predicting the reaction may be difficult. As already stated the CAC appears to play some role in preventing the $C\bar{S}$ reacting with the C_3A in the portland cement to form a coating of ettringite thus slowing the reaction down somewhat. It also appears that CAC's accelerate low C_3A cements [40]. The nature of the $C\bar{S}$ used is known to have a marked affect on the rate of reaction. Cements containing hemi-hydrate show the most marked acceleration. Manufacturing parameters have also some affect particularly on the state of the $C\bar{S}$ and the resultant reactivity.

Modern industrial formulations often use fatty acids or their sodium salts to enable the reaction to be controlled more effectively. In blends where CAC's are the dominant binder the stable hydrate C_3AH_6 is formed preferentially.

CALCIUM ALUMINATE BLENDED CEMENTS

In recent years a number of blended cements have been developed using various fillers with CAC's. Among these are limestone, pulversised fuel ash, ground granulated blast furnace slag, and fume silica.

Calcareous Fillers

Fillers such as ground limestone lead to the formation of the mono-carbo hydrate $C_3A(CaCO_3)H_{11}$.

This hydrate was thought to be stable and hence eliminated conversion [30], however, although more thermodynamically stable than CAH_{10}, it is not stable at temperatures above 50^oC [31], and probably transforms to stable C_3AH_6 over long periods of time. Figure 7 show the strength development of various blends of Ciment Fondu/Limestone filler at different temperatures. It is clear that the system is not stable at high curing temperatures.

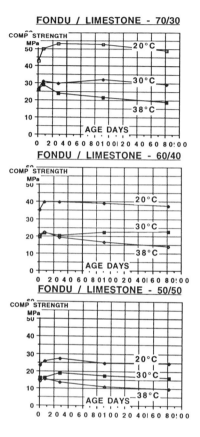

Figure 7   Strength development of various Ciment Fondu/Limestone
filler blends at different temperatures

Slags and Pulverised Fuel Ash

Fillers which release soluble silica, such as Ground Granulated Blast Furnace Slag (GGBFS) lead to hydration into stratlingite C_2ASH_8, which is reported to be completely stable (32-33). The strength stability of CAC/GGBFS blends was confirmed by curing at 38°C which would normally provoke rapid loss of strength see Figure 8. Furthermore exceptionally good results have also been obtained concerning resistance to attack by sulphates and sea water, see Figure 9. In accelerated tests (2x2x10cm prisms semi-immersed in aggressive solutions), CAC/GGBFS blended cements were intact after 2 years semi-immersion, showing a performance equivalent to sulphate resisting portland and even better than pure CAC though at a very high water/cement ratio (0.60) which has not been recommended for many years.

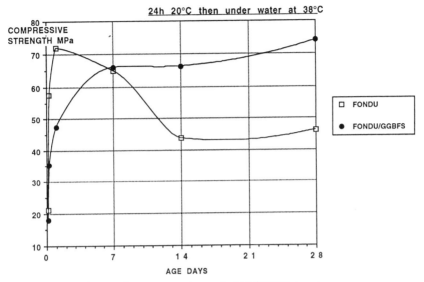

Figure 8   Conversion of CAC/GGBFS mortars

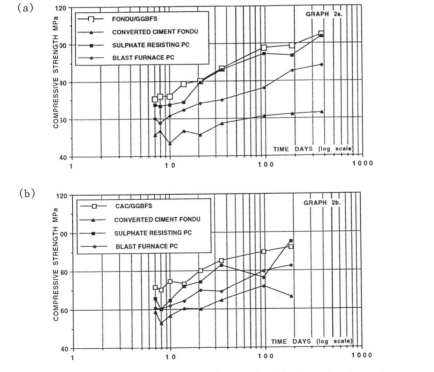

Figure 9   Immersion at 20°C (W/C 0.40) (a) in solution of CaSO$_4$
(b) in reconstituted sea water

Blends of CAC/PFA (Pulverised Fuel Ash) are not as successful as GGBFS in maintaining the strengths. The strength development at 38°C shows the classic loss of strength. However, there is evidence of some hydraulic reaction, since the strengths obtained are better than with an equivalent volume of inert filler (ground silica sand) see Figure 10.

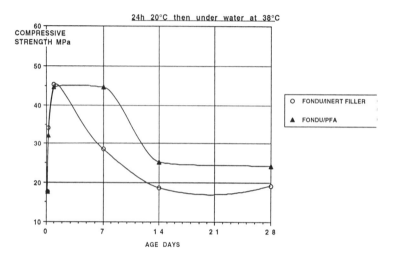

Figure 10   Conversion of CAC/PFA mortars

Fume Silica

Fume silica also seems to be particularly successful in blended systems. Strengths well in excess of 100 MPa have been reported [34]. Figure 11. shows the strength of a 1-3 mortar containing 86% CAC and 14% Fume Silica (FS) cured at 38°C or at 20°C then 50°C. This would normally provoke conversion and a marked loss of strength, however a continued increase in strength is observed. In fact the 50°C treatment increases the strength above that of the normal levels obtained at 20°C.

These exceptionally high strengths are explained by two phenomena. Firstly the presence of excess soluble silica in the system effectively blocks the conversion of CAH_{10} to C_3AH_6 and secondly the formation of C_2ASH_8, which is itself stable and adds to the strengths of the CAH_{10}.

The stability of the systems depends on two parameters - the fume silica content and the addition of the defloculent Sodium Tripoly-Phosphate (TPP). Figures 12 and 13. show the development of the hydrates CAH_{10} and C_2ASH_8 after curing at 20°C for 28 days followed by 28 days at 50°C, against the percentage Fume Silica in the blend.

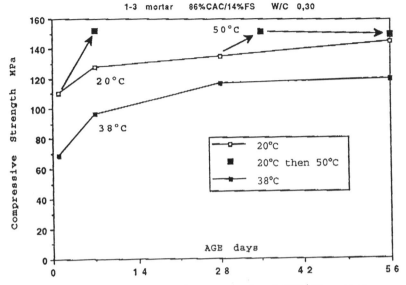

Figure 11   Compressive strength of CAC/FS mortar

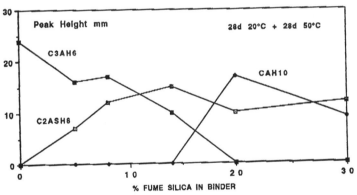

Figure 12   Evolution of hydrates in CAC/FS systems

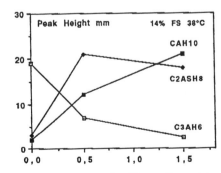

Figure 13   Effect of TPP on formation of hydrates

This shows clearly that with blends containing less than 14% FS the CAH_{10} regresses and C_3AH_6 is formed (i.e. conversion occurs) at 14-30% FS the CAH_{10} is stabilised, the C_3AH_6 decreases and then no longer appears. For all levels of FS there is a progressive formation of C_2ASH_8 which increases with FS content.

The importence of TPP to the system has been shown by the results obtained with various additions from 0 to 1.5% by weight of combined binder (CAC + FS). Without TPP, C_3AH_6 is formed in preference to C_2ASH_8. The introduction of TPP progressively reduces the C_3AH_6 and promotes the formation of C_2ASH_8. It is probable that this effect is due solely to the progressive deflocuation of the FS which when fully dispersed becomes more active, stabilising the CAH_{10} and favouring the formation of C_2ASH_8.

It is very often necessary to use two or more admixtures which have complementary effects. For example Lithium salts are very effective set accelerators of CAC [37][38]. Again when used alone they are extremely sensitive to dose rate, but when used in tandem with fluidifying retarders the control of rheology , setting and hardening is possible.

Admixtures and Fillers

Fillers also have an effect on rheology, fume silica is well known for its water reducing and densifying properties by filling interstitial porosity otherwise filled with water. However, a defloculant such as Tri-poly Phosphate is usually necessary [39]. Using ultra-fine fillers such as fume silica, and micronised alumina has led to a new generation of high performance refractory concretes known as "low cement castables" ("low water castables" in the USA).

The complete control of the rheology of CAC systems by additives and fillers has also led to the development of new products with unusual characteristics. A commercial product was developed originally as a repair system for bomb damaged runways. The basis of the system is percollation of a slurry of controlled rheology, setting and hardening characteristics into a cavity (bomb crater) which had been filled with large gravel (20-40mm). The slurry infiltrates the gravel and hardens rapidly (15min) to give a usable concrete surface. A civil engineering version has been developed for rapid temporary road laying on large building sites, or even for more permanent repairs.

The recent legislation regarding the utilities and the obligation to make permanent repairs to trenches, in some cases so that the trench can be reinstated and black topped within 4-5 hours, has also led to the development of regulated rheology and hardening products. These are mixtures of CAC or CAC/Portland Cement, together with foaming agents to produce foamed concretes. The specification for this material is somewhat unusual, a flowing self levelling material, the strength of which is required to reach a plateau early on so that it may be dug out easily again if necessary. Obviously the rheological properties are again of major importance. Figure 14.

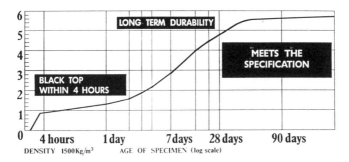

Figure 14 Rapid strength development

RHEOLOGY OF CAC'S

The rheology of any concrete or mortar is one of its most critical properties. If the rheology is incorrect, this will lead to poor compaction or the use of excessive amounts of water. In either case the performance of the product will be impaired.
CAC's have had the reputation of being difficult to handle due to the rapid loss of workability. This may well have been the case in the past but today the situation has radically changed. The two reasons for this area - the improved control of the manufacturing process and the use of admixtures and/or fillers which modify the rheology.

The mineralogy and particularly the morphology of the various phases in CAC have a very marked effect on the rheology of the final product.

If we look closely at the area of the RANKIN diagram which includes Calcium Aluminates and Calcium-Silico Aluminates, we find that the zone is bisected by the line CA-C_2S. This line is of major importence with regard to the hydraulicity of Calcium Aluminate Cements. Cements whose composition fall below this line i.e. in the CA zone, will be composed mainly of CA plus $C_{12}A_7$. These cements are more reactive and will have the tendency to stiffen rapidly after mixing. Cements with compositions above the CA-C_2S line i.e. in the C_2AS zone will be composed of CA plus C_2AS. These cements will be less reactive have a fluid rheology and longer working times. This is of course an over simplification since the C-A-S Rankin diagram does not take account of the iron rich phases in low purity CAC's and many more parameters such as fusion conditions, cooling rates etc. have an affect on morphology and hence on rheology.

Over the last 4-5 years research by Lafarge into this aspect of CAC has led to the possibility of controlling the rheological properties of the final product at a very early stage in its manufacture. It is possible now to manufacture at will products which have a reactivity and rheology suited to different applications. Furthermore the strict use of Statistical Process Control means that the hydraulic properties of CAC's are constant.

The control of the rheology of the pure cement is not the only factor, rheology of mortars and cements must also be controlled. The use of proprietary brand water reducers and plasticisers is now commonplace. However, most proprietary admixtures are developed for use with Portland cements and whilst many of these do work with CAC there are some notable exceptions, especially in the family of so called "super plasticisers". For this reason it is often preferred to use standard chemicals for use with CAC's. Chemicals such as citrates (35) and gluconates (36) have been shown have marked effects on the rheology of CAC concretes. However, used alone they can severely extend the setting time and hence the early strength development may be lost.

POLYMER CEMENT INTERACTION

The use of polymers with hydraulic cements is by no means new. CAC is no exception to this and is often used in systems containing polymers, either as the principle hydraulic binder or more frequently combined with calcium sulphates (gypsum, plasters or anhydrite) and/or portland cement.

Cements as binders for mortars and concretes are generally considered as brittle and weak in tension. Organic polymers are excellent binders with good tensile properties, ductile and generally resistant to most of the agents which can deteriorate conventional concretes. They are however, considerably more expensive than cements. The complementarity between hydraulic cements and organic polymers in terms of cost and performance has led to a large and growing industry of composite materials in which cements and polymers are used.

When polymer latexes are incorporated in mortar or concrete the flow characteristics are often greatly enhanced which usually allows the water content to be reduced with improvement of subsequent properties. The volume proportion of polymer in a binder matrix is typically 20% or so, this at a totally different level to that is traditional admixtures which are typically less than 1%.

In addition to a reduction in brittleness, other advatanges of polymer additions are :

- reduction in micro cracking
- improved workability
- decreased permeability
- improved flexural strength and strain capacity
- better resistance to abrasion, corrosion and freeze thaw
- increased bond strength

all of which leads to a marked improvement in DURABILITY.

The widest use of polymer latexes with CAC is for floor screeds where a combination of super fluidity in the fresh state, rapid hardening and a smooth, flexible, abrasion resistant finish in the hardened state is essential. They are also extensively used in repair mortars, tile adhesives and rapid setting mortars, many of which contain CAC in combination with Portland Cement or calcium sulphates.

The addition of calcium sulphates to CAC systems as described above, largely eliminates the problems of shrinkage associated with cements, this is a major advantage compared to portland cement systems [47]. Active fillers such as ground limestone, PFA, ground slags and fume silica may also be used in conjunction with the more traditional fine quartz sands.

A typical ternary system may be represented as shown on Figure 15

The physio-chemistry of cement-polymer systems is obviously complex and in the case of CAC is currently being studied in Japan and USA. A generalised explanation of the interaction between cement and polymers is illustrated in Figure 16.

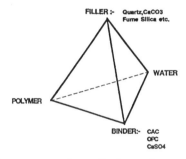

Figure 15   Representation of the polymer-cement-water system

When cement hydrates in the presence of polymer latex, a co-matrix consisting of an interpenetrating 3 dimensional hydrate/polymer film structure develops.

Latexes are typically a 50% emulsions of polymer/solvent droplets in water. The emulsion is stabilised (deflocculated) with surfactants and these can absorb onto the surface of cement grains and assist their deflocculation hence the water demand of the cement paste is considerably lowered.

During hydration of the cement, water is combined and the latex emulsion becomes increasingly concentrated. Surface evaporation may intensify this effect. As a result the emulsion droplets eventually coagulate until a polymer film network is formed. Figure 17.

The applications of cement polymer products, including those based on or containing CAC are found in a recent market survey in Japan. Table 1. The same markets exist in most developed and developing countries of the world. Certainly in Europe the industry is already very large and growing. In a recent publication [48] the use of self levelling floor screeds in Sweden alone was estimated at 4.5 million M^2.

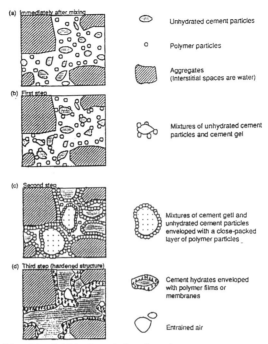

Figure 16   Simplified model of polymer-cement comatrix formation

Some typical properties of such systems are shown in Figure 18. The improvement of strain capacity and abrasion resistance is strongly related to the polymer content as is the indentation resistance. The latter also shows the advantage in hardening characteristics of CAC based systems.

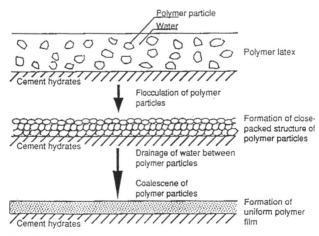

Figure 17   Simplified model of process of polymer film formation on cement hydrates

Table 1 Applications of polymer modified mortar (or paste) in Japan

APPLICATION	LOCATION OF WORK
Flooring & pavings	Floors for houses, warehouses, schools, hospitals, offices, shops, toilets, passages, stairs, gymnasiums and factories, garages, railway platforms, roads, airport runways etc.
Integral waterproofings	Concrete roof-decks, mortar walls, concrete block walls, water tanks, swimming pools, septic tanks, silos, etc.
Adhesives	Tile adhesives, adhesives for floorings, walling materials and heat-insulating materials, adhesives for joining new cement concrete or mortar to old cement concrete or mortar, etc.
Decorative coatings (including surface - preparing materials)	Wall coatings, lightweight aggregate coating materials, cement filling compounds and self levelling cements for surface preparation etc.
Repair Materials	Grouts for repairing cracks and delaminations of concrete structures, patching materials for damaged concrete structures, protective coatings for corroded reinforcing bars etc.
Anti-corrosive linings	Effluent drains, chemical or machinery plant floors, grouts for acid-proof tiles, floors for chemical laboratories and pharmaceuticals warehouses, septic tanks, hot springs baths etc.
Deck coverings	Internal and external ship-decks, bridge decks, footbridge decks, train floors, etc.

CONCLUDING REMARKS

The above review of the current developments and research focusing on Calcium Aluminate Cements, shows that this material clearly has a future in the 21st Century. despite the setbacks sustained in the mid 70's when many considered the cement to be dead, apart from refractory applications, the markets and applications have continued to grow and diversify. It is this diversity which sustains the market growth. The chemistry and hydration of CAC's are unique. When used alone, good results can be achieved when used in complex systems of mixed binders, fillers, polymers etc. CAC becomes a key ingredient to

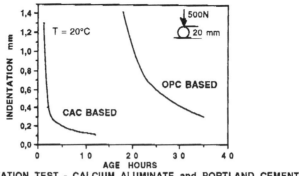

INDENTATION TEST - CALCIUM ALUMINATE and PORTLAND CEMENTS

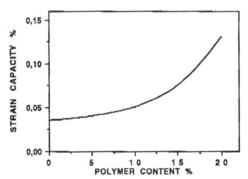

INFLUENCE OF POLYMER CONTENT ON STRAIN CAPACITY

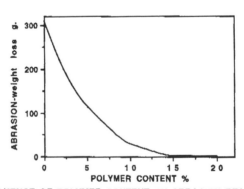

INFLUENCE OF POLYMER CONTENT ON ABRASION RESISTANCE

Figure 18 Typical properties of cement-polymer systems

the excellent performance of many building products, already established and still being developed. A number of markets remain closed to CAC's due to past misuse and misunderstanding of the properties. The misunderstandings have long since been eradicated, past misuse is not a valid reason to not use a valuable and reliable product.

A type of Calcium Aluminate Cement is currently being studied by NASA for use in Lunar Base construction, this if nothing else demonstrates that the future of these materials is assured.

REFERENCES

1. EBELMAN, Ann.Chim (Phys.) 1848 22 (3), 227
2. SAINTE-CLAIRE DEVILLE, H, Ann.Phys.Chem., 1856,46,(3),196
3. WINKLER, J, .Pract.Chim., 1856.67.(444).455
4. FREMY, E, Compt.Rend., 1865.60.993
5. MICHAELS, W, Hydraulic, Mortel, Leipzig, 1869,35
6. SCOTT, D, Doct. Thesis, Heidelberg, 1906 :
   Rev. Metall, 1908,5 (11), 363
7. LE CHATELIER, H, Compt. Rend., 1883, 1056
8. DUFAU, E, Compt.Rend., 1900,131, 54
9. SHEPHERD, ES, RANKIN, GA, & WRIGHT, FE, Ame, J.Sci., 1909
   RANKIN, GA, WRIGHT, FE, Amer J. Soc., 1915.39,(4),1
10. ROTH, L, German Patent, 1882 19800
11. SNELUS, GJ, GIBB, T, SWAN, JC, SMITH, H, JAMMOND, HH,
    British Patent, 1888, 10312
12. BIED, J, Recherches Industrielles sur les Chaux, Ciments et Mortier, Duned, Paris, 1926,224
13. MIDGLEY, HG, High Alumina Cement in Construction - a future based on experience. Ref 20 1-13,1990
14. GEOR GE, CM, Manufacture and Performance of Aluminous Cement: a new perspective. 181-207 Ref 20 1990
15. Circular No. 79-34 27 March 1979. Ministre de l'Environment, France.
16. GEORGE, CM, Revue des materiaux de Construction 1974 4.201-209 The Structural use of High Alumina Cement 1974. Lafarge Fondu International, France
17. MIDGLEY, HG, MIDGLEY, A , The Conversion of High Alumina Cement 1975, Mag. Conc.Res.27, 59-77
18. TEYCHENNE DC, Long term Research into the Characteristics of High Alumina Cement 1975. Mag. Conc. Res. 27, 78-102
19. BATE, SCC, High Alumina Cement Concrete in Existing Buildings 1980. BRE Special report. PD 101/80
20. MANG ABHAI, RJ , ed. Calcium Aluminate Cements Pub. E&F.N. Spon 1990
21. GEORGE, CM, Industrial Aluminous Cements, Chapt. 9 415-470. BARNES, P, ed. Structure and Performance of Cements, Applied Science Publishers. 1983
22. ROBSON, TD, High Alumina Cements and Concretes, Contractors Record Ltd., London
23. BAYOUX, JP, LETOURNEUX, JP, MARCDARGENT, S, VERSCHAEVE, M, Acidic Corrosion of High Alumina Cement 230-240 1990 Ref20.

24. CRAMMOND, NJ, Long term Performance of High Alumina Cement Concrete in Sulphate Bearing Environments 208-221, 1990, Ref20.

25   KUDOWSKI, W, TACZAK, L, TRYBALSKA, B, Behaviour of High Alumina Cement in Chloride Solutions 222-229, 1990, Ref20.

26. GEORGE, CM, Long Term and Accelerated Tests of Resistances of Cements to Sea Water, with special reference to Aluminous Cement. Amer. Concr. Inst. sp-65, 327-349 1980.

27. FRENCH, PJ, MONTGOMERY, RGJ, ROBSON, TD, High Concrete Strength Within the Hour. Concrete Aug. 1971 3-8

28. RASHID, S, BARNES, P, TURRILLAS, X, Rapid Conversion of Calcium Aluminate Cement Hydrates, as revealed by Synchrotron Energy-Dispersive Diffraction. Adv. Cemn-Res. 1991-1992 K. No.14. 61-67

29. COLLINS, RJ, GUTT, W, Research on Long term Properties of High Alumina cement Concrete. Mag.Conc. Res. Vol. 40 No.145 195-208 1988

30. CUSSINO, L, NEGRO, A, Hydration du Ciment Alumineux en Presence d'Agregat Siliceux et Calcaire. 7th International Congress Chem. Cem., Paris PP V62-67 1980

31. FENTIMAN, CH, Hydration of Carbo-Aluminous cement at Different temperatures. Cem.Conc.Res. Vol15pp622-630 1985

32. EDMONDS, RN, MAJUNDAR, AJ, The Hydration of Mixtures of Monocalcium Aluminate and Blastfurnace Slag, European Patent Application 0312323 (1989).

33. MAJUNDAR, AJ, EDMONDS, RN, SINGH, B, Hydration of Calcium Aluminates in presence of Granulated Blastfurnace Slag. 259-271. Ref 20 1990

34. MARCDARGENT, S, TESTUD, M, BAYOUX, JP, MATHIEU, A, Hydration and Strength of Blends of Calcium Aluminate Cement, Fume Silica and the Stability of Hydrates. IX Internat. (Chem) Cem, Delhi 1992 pp 651-657

35. BAYOUX, JP, SORRENTINO, D, FALASCHI, JP, CAPMAS, A, A Study of Calcium Aluminate Cement Admixtures. IX Internat. Cong. Chem.Cen, Delhi 1992 pp 707-711

36   SORRENTINO, D, BAYOUX, JP, MONTGOMERY, RGJ, MATHIEU, A, CAPMAS, A, The Effects of Sodium Gluconate and Lithium Carbonate on the Properties of Calcium Aluminate Cements., pp375-377 UNITECR Concgress 1991

37. RODGER, SA, DOUBLE, DD, The Chemistry of High Alumina Cement in the presence of Accelerating and Retarding Admixtures, Cem. Concr. Res. 14 1984 pp 73-82

38. MATUSINOVIC, T, VROBES, N, Alkali Metal Salts as Set Accelerators fgor High Alumina cement. Cem. Concr. Res. 23 1993 pp 177-186

39   BAYOUX, JP, GEORGE, CM, LETOURNEUX, JP, Theory and Practice of Fume Silica/Aluminous Cement Interaction : Part I UNTECR Los Angeles 1989. part II A.C.C. Dallas 1990, Part III A.C.C. Cincinatti

40. COTTIN, B, Hydration des melanges silicates aluminates de calcium 7th International Congress on the Chemictry of Cement Paris 1980 v PP113-118

41. BROOKS, SA, and SHARPE, JH, Ettringite-Based Cements See Ref 20 pp 335-349

42.   BAYOUX, JP, BONIN, A, MARCARGENT, S, AND VERSCHAEVE, M, Study of the Hydration Properties of Aluminous Cement and Calcium Sulphate Mixes. Ref. 20 pp 320 - 334

43.   WIERIG, HJ, Final report from the Hamburg research project : building materials. In: Biogene Schwefelsaurekorrosion in teilgefullten Abwasserkanalen, R. Bielecki und H. Schremmer (eds.), LeichtweiBinstitut de TU Braunschweig, Braunschweig, Germany, 33-49.(1987)

44.   DUMAS, T, Calcium aluminate mortars and concrete: an application to sewer pipes in harsh environments, Proceedings of the International Conference on the Implications of Ground Chemistry and Microbiology for Construction, University of Bristol, Great Britain. (1992)

45.   SAND, W, BOCK, E, Biodeterioration of mineral materials by microorganisms - biogenic sulfuric and nitric acid corrosion of concrete and natural stone.
Geomicrobiol. J. 9, 129-138. (1992)

46.   SAND, W, DUMAS, T, AND MARCDARGENT, S, Tests for biogenic sulfuric acid corrosion in a simulation chamber confirm the on site performance of calcium aluminate based in sewage applications. ASTM International Symposium on
Microbiologically Influenced Corrosion (MIC) Testing, November 1992.

47.   ALEXANDERSON, T, Self smoothing floors based on polymer cement concrete. Concrete International Vol 12 No.1 49-51 1990.

48.   OHAMA, Y, Principle of Latex Modification and some Typical Properties of Latex Modified Mortars and Concretes. ACI Materials Journal V,184 No 6 511-518 1987

CONCEPTION OF PRECAST, PRESTRESSED CONCRETE STRUCTURES

I Gosav

A Mihul

Polytechnical Institute of Iaşi

Romania

ABSTRACT. The paper presents three way to conceive the structure for stored industrial buildings, entire precasting, achieved from prestressed member, ansambling by prestressing. The precast member is so conceived that the materials (high rezistent reinforcement and concrete) and the initial streasses will be directed in accordance with the stresses in the structure in the exploitation stage. The prestressed reinforcement which made the assembling, takes also the stresses in the exploitation stage. The three examples for the conceiving of precast prestress structures assambling by prestressing are presented, taking into scount that in the future, the developing of the construction must not be connected with the developing and improvement of materials and technologies only but also with their way of conceiving.

Keywords: conceiving, precast, prestressed, division, assambling, material and stress distribution.

Associate Professor Ionel Gosav, Polytechnical Institute of Iaşi, Civil Engineering Faculty, Materials, Concrete and Technology Departement. Specialised on durability and rehabilitation of buildings, designing and experimentation of new solution for industrial buildings.

Professor Anatolie Mihul, Polytechnical Institute of Iaşi, Civil Engineering. Faculty, Materials, Concrete and Technology Departement. He designed and performed more unique building in our country after original solution, with concern in the durability and rehabilitation of constructions.

Concrete 2000. Edited by Ravindra K. Dhir and M. Roderick Jones.
© 1993 Published by E & FN Spon. ISBN 0 419 18120 2.

INTRODUCTION

In our opinion, in the future, the concrete constructions
will be durable and economical if there will be obtained
high qualities for:

(i) materials (for example, high performance concrete,
concrete with admixture and corrosion rezistance reinforcement, etc.).

(ii) construction member (for example: the concrete com-
pactness, the execution accurancy, etc.).

Technologically this qualities can be obtained if use:

1.**the prestressing**: through the association of high resistance concrete and reinforcement it diminishes the size of
the members, it grows the safety of the buildings, it can
introduce initial tensions, it can realise the assembling
of the precast member on the site.

2.**the precasting**: the execution in the factory of the
building members is adequate to obtain the precision and
the imposed quality, it permits to achieve rational forms
and the using of the prestressed deflected reinforcement.

In the future, the development of the constructions must
not be connected only with the development of **materials**
and technologies but at first with a rational way to conceive the structures, a way which the advanced materials
and technologies will allow us to apply it.

A structure is rationally conceived if it has a much more
statically indeterminated degree (fig.1.a) and the materials ant the initial stresses are distributed in the elements in accordance with the stresses in the assembling
and exploiting stages.

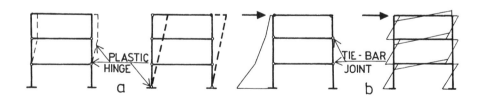

Figure 1. The structures with statically indetermination
degree are more safety. In consequence, the joint are making reinstained, the columns from one piece and the plas-
tice hinge are directed in the beams.

If the structure is composed of precast members the division and the assembling must be made in the minimum stress
areas and/or with keeping the continuity, at least, of
one member in the joint (preferably the column, so that
the plastic hinge will be directed in the beam, fig.1.b).

So, we consider that in the future, a durably and economical building must be conceived in the following way:

1.from precast members, executed in factory with high quality, prestressed, with rational form (fig.2) and prestressed deflected reinforcement (fig.3).

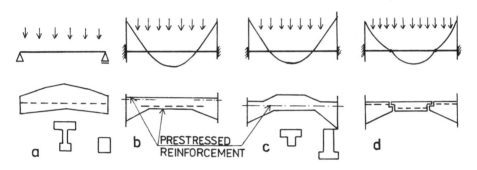

Figure 2. The **rational** distribution of materials and direc-
ting of initial stresses at beams in function of the
stresses in the service stage.

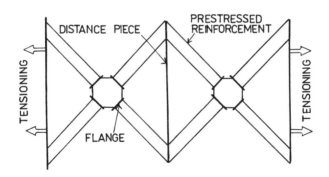

Figure 3.The deflection of prestressed reinforcement by
tensioning in unit.

2.in the construction members, the materials (concrete and
reinforcement) must be distributed in rational forms
(fig.2) both in longitudinal profile and cross section.

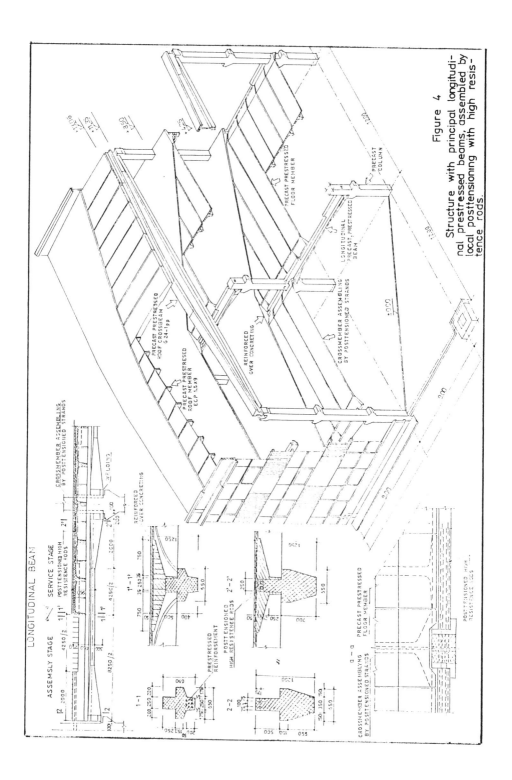

Figure 4

Structure with principal longitudinal prestressed beams, assembled by local posttensioning with high resistence rods.

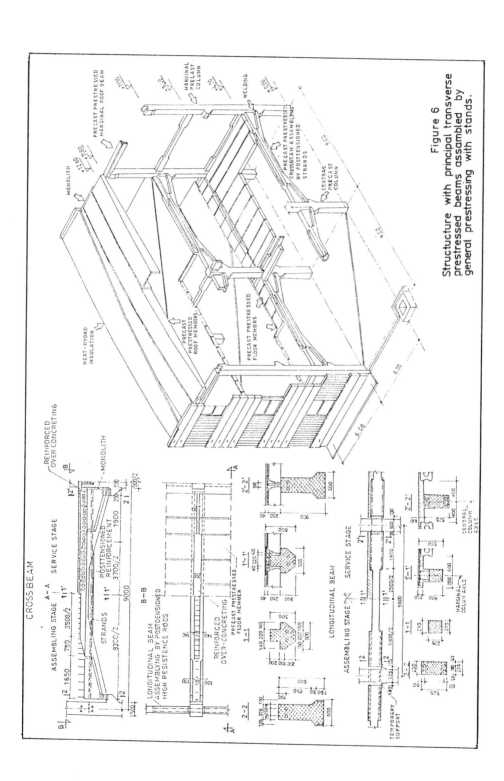

Figure 6

Structure with principal transverse prestressed beams assembled by general prestressing with stands.

3.in the construction members and on the entire structure,
the initial stresses must be directed in accordance with
the stresses in the assembling and exploiting stages.

4.at the assembling of the precast members there must be
provided the stability to the erection (by adequate
joints), the continuity of joints and the wet processes
being achieved after the erection of the entire structure.

In succession, there are presented three types of structures conceived on the ground of the above mentioned
principles.

STRUCTURE WITH PRINCIPAL LONGITUDINAL PRESTRESSED BEAMS ASSEMBLED BY LOCAL POSTTENSIONING WITH HIGH RESISTENCE RODS

The structure is made up (fig.4) of one piece columne on
the entire height of building with cantilevers for the
bearing of the principal longitudinal beams at the floors
and a "pitchfork" for the bearing of the principal transverse beam at the roof.

The principal longitudinal beam, with haunches, is prestressed with prestressed reinforcement and cut up in the
central area, this preventing the cracking at the transfer and permiting the locating of the assembling high resistance rods (fig.5).

Figure 5.Experimental member   Figure 7.Experimental member
for the structure from   for the structure from
figure 4.   figure 5.

This assembling high resistance rods take over the bending
moments on the leaning too (look to the fig.2.b).

The other members (roof and floor elements, the principal
roof beam, fig.2.a) are prestressed. The assembling of
the transverse floor elements among the columns takes on

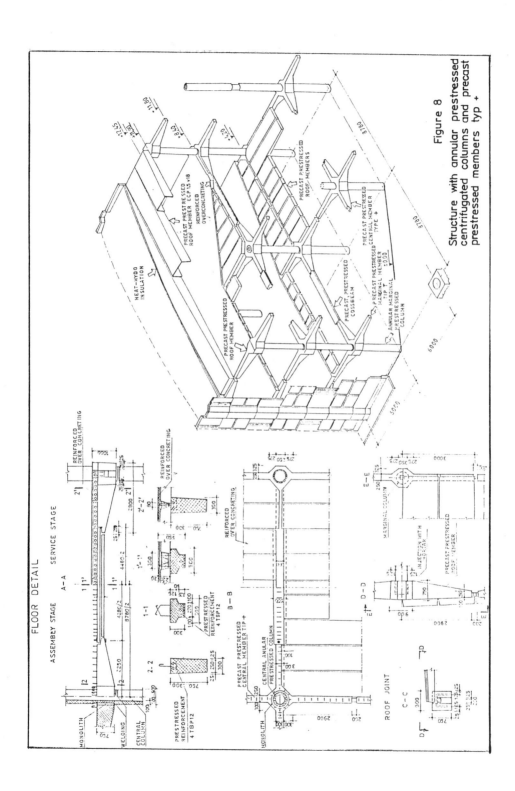

Figure 8

Structure with annular prestressed centrifugated columns and precast prestressed members typ +

with posttensioned strands.

STRUCTURE WITH PRINCIPAL TRANSVERSE PRESTRESSED BEAMS ASSEMBLED BY GENERAL PRESTRESSING WITH STRANDS

The structure is achieved (fig.6) with precast columns like the precedent one, with principal beams displayed on the transverse at the floors and principal longitudinal beam at the roof.

The principal transverse beams have a longitudinal profile with variable height (fig.7) to permit the adoption of the right line of the strands, which achieved bothm the general assambling among beams and columns, and the taking over to the bending momente in the filed and bearing in the exploiting stage (fig.2.c). The cross sections have a variable form in the lenght of the beam, in accordance with the stresses in the exploiting stage and increase thought the overconcreting in the central area.

All the other members from the structure are precasting and prestressing.

STRUCTURES WITH ANNULAR PRESTRESSED CENTRIFUGATED COLUMNS AND PRECAST PRESTRESSED MEMBERS TYPE +

The structure (fig.8) is made up of columns with annular cross section, performed by centrifuging and reinforced with prestressed shrink ring (fig.9). The elements type + are prestresse at the upper fibre with prestressed deflected reinforcement (look at fig.2.d and 3) and are introduced on the columns. On the transverse direction, the junction between the element type + it is achieved by a precast prestressed beam wich increases the height through overconcreting. The other elements of structure are from prestressed concrete.

Fig.9.The testing of annular centrifugated columns (a) and the joining column-beam (b).

OPTIMISATION OF CONCRETE PROPERTIES BY NEURAL NETWORKS

F H Wittmann

G Martinola

Swiss Federal Institute of Technology

Switzerland

ABSTRACT. Properties of concrete can be tailored for specific applications. This specific flexibility of concrete has not always been fully exploited. Most of the time, concrete is characterized by its compressive strength only. For many practical applications, however, ductility is more important and there are other properties such as shrinkage or damping which can play a decisive role for the performance of building elements and structures. In this contribution it is shwon that the method of neural networks can be applied to simulate different influences on concrete properties. Optimisation is carried out in three steps. First, the composition of the fresh concrete is considered. Second, curing conditions and compaction are additionally taken into account and third, parameters influencing durability are introduced. In this way, concrete properties can be optimized for a given application. Results of an experimental and numerical study are presented and discussed.

Keywords: High performance concrete, Fracture energy, Charactersitic length, Ductility, Neural networks.

Professor Dr. Folker H. Wittmann is head of the Laboratory for Building Materials at Swiss Federal Institute of Technology (ETH) in Zurich. He mainly works on durability and fracture mechanics of concrete. He has published more than 200 papers and edited a series of bookson on specific aspects of concrete. He chaired RILEM Technical Committee 50 FMC (fracture mechanics of concrete) and 78 MCA (Model Code for autoclaved areated concrete) and is vice-chairman of RILEM at this moment.

Dipl.Werkstoffing.ETH Giovanni Martinola has just finished his studies of Material Science at Swiss Federal Institute of Technology (ETH) in Zurich. He will continue his studies as PhD-student in the Laboratory for Building Materials at ETH Zurich.

Concrete 2000. Edited by Ravindra K. Dhir and M. Roderick Jones.
© 1993 Published by E & FN Spon. ISBN 0 419 18120 2.

INTRODUCTION

In most cases, concrete properties are optimised in a purely empirical way. This phenomenological approach was probably adequate and sufficient as long as compressive strength was the only required material parameter.

In recent years, mineral and chemical admixtures have been used more and more in order to obtain higher strength. High strength concrete can now be considered to be a standard material. But modern concrete technology allows us to achieve other improved properties than compressive strength only. High ductility, high fracture energy, optimal strain softening and improved durability are just a few examples. As most of these properties are strongly interdependent a traditional approach of trial and error cannot be applied.

In this contribution, it will be shown that neural networks [1, 2] can be applied in order to optimise properties of composite materials such as concrete. Of course, required material properties can be tailored within fixed boundaries in a systematic way.

NEURAL NETWORKS

An advanced technique of numerical simulation has been developed recently, i.e. the neural networks. The elements of this approach have been described in detail (see for example [1,2]). Similar to a human brain, neural networks can be trained to learn from given examples. If the neural network is trained it is possible to predict the behaviour of a system within the given limits. So far, neural networks have been applied in such diverging disciplines, such as image recognition, biochemistry or materials science. As far as we know, however, neural networks have not yet been applied in the field of concrete technology.

In a simplified way, neural networks can be characterised as systems with m inputs and n outputs. Between the input and output there are usually an input layer, sometimes one or several hidden layers, and an output layer. Each layer consists of a number of neurons which are interconnected to form a neural network. This is shown schematically in Figure 1 and Figure 2.

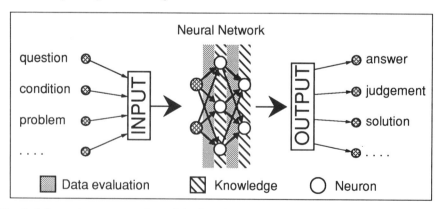

Fig. 1 Schematic representation of the functioning of neural networks

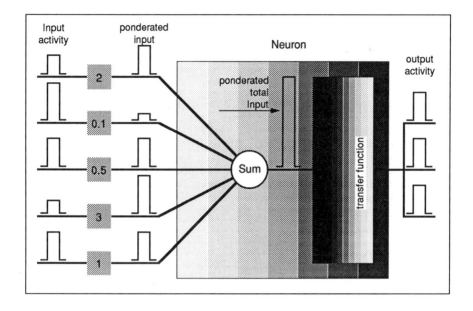

Fig. 2 Idealized representation of the basic functions of a neuron

Each neuron operates according to the principle shown in Figure 3. The result of all neurons is composed and finally gives the output.

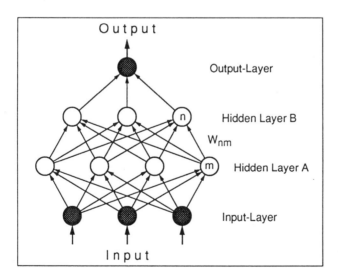

Fig. 3 Simplified structure of a nural network

The neural network can be trained by introducing a sufficiently large set of data where both the input and the output are known. To obtain these data sets, either well documented results described in the literature or results of specially designed test series can be used. In order to demonstrate the potential of the method, we applied both ways in this project.

A CONCEPT TO OPTIMIZE CONCRETE PROPERTIES

Concrete properties depend on the mix proportions, the placing, the compacting and the curing conditions. Further, the evolution of properties in time depend essentially on the environmental and loading conditions. In order to take these different influences into consideration, a system of neural networks in three stages has been developed. This is shown schematically in Figure 4. In the first stage (module 1), the composition of concrete is used as input and properties of fresh concrete are obtained. In the second stage placing compacting and curing are also considered in order to be able to

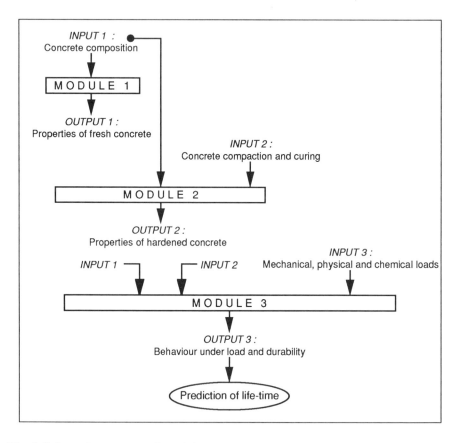

Fig. 4 Schematic representation of the concept to optimize properties of concrete

forecast the properties of hardened concrete. Finally, in the third stage, mechanical, physical and chemical loads are taken into consideration to predict the evolution of concrete properties in time. This last stage may be used for a realistic prediction of the lifetime of concrete elements or structures under arbitrarily chosen conditions.

Details of the input parameters for stage 1, 2 and 3 are given in Figure 5, Figure 6, and Figure 7, respectively.

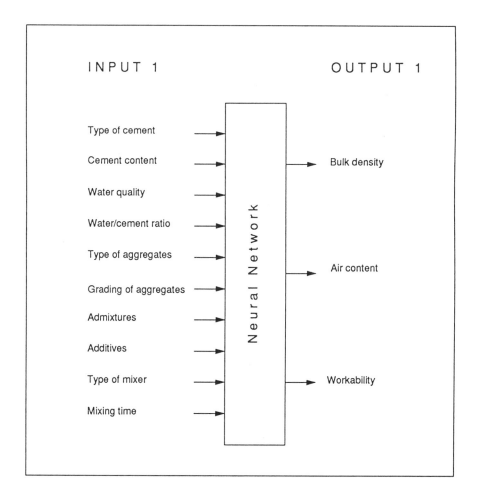

Fig. 5 Input and output parameters for stage 1 of the three stage systems of neural networks. The most important input and output parameters are indicated only.

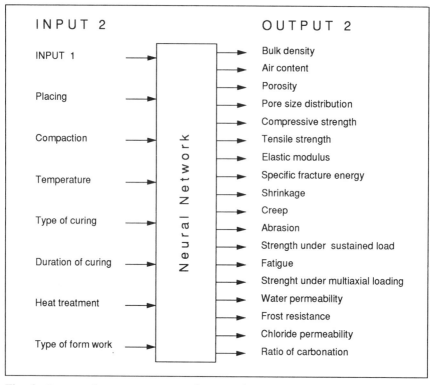

Fig. 6   Input and output parameters for stage 2

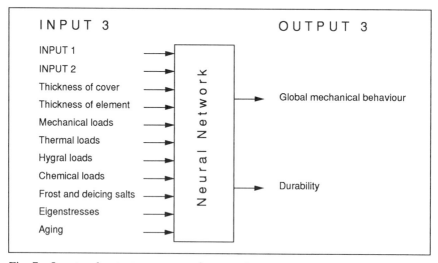

Fig. 7   Input and output parameters for stage 3

SOME CHARACTERISTIC RESULTS

The composition of high performance concretes has been varied in a systematic way. Details of all test series are described elsewhere [3]. A computer programme originally developed by Grolimund and Häutle [4] has been modified and adapted to the situation of concrete technology. It has been shown that the neural network describes well the influences of the various parameters on concrete properties [3]. The different modules can be trained in using eperimental results. The each module predicts well the influence of varying parameters on the corresponding properties.

Here we can select two examples only, and we have chosen compressive strength and characteristic length to demonstrate the potential of the new approach.

Concrete has been prepared with different water/cement ratios. Results are given in Figure 8. It can be seen that concrete strength increases with decreasing water/cement ratio up to a maximum value. If the water/cement ratio is further lowered strength decreases abruptly because of insufficient workability. If a plasticiser is added the maximum value is shifted to lower water/cement ratios and that obviously means to higher strength values. The experimental data as well as the prediction of the neural network are shown in Fig. 8. A fair agreement can be observed. Results shown in Figure 8 allow us to optimise concrete composition for a required value of compressive strength. This also means that it is possible to select a concrete composition which is least sensitive to minor errors in the concrete composition.

Too often, compressive strength is the only requirement in practice and we know that in may cases sufficient ductility may be more important. For this reason, we have determined fracture energy G_f with the wedge splitting technique [5]. Then the characteristic length l_{ch} of concrete defined as follows:

$$l_{ch} = \frac{EG_f}{f_t^2} \tag{1}$$

can be considered as a measure of ductility. In this equation, E stands for the elastic modulus and f_t for the tensile strength of the material.

All these parameters have been determined experimentally [3]. In applying equation (1), the characteristic length as shown in Figure 9 is obtained. Again, we find a reasonable agreement between the experimental values and the prediction of the neural network. Figure 9 enables us to select a concrete composition with a maximum ductility for a given strength.

CONCLUSIONS

It has been shown that neural networks provide us with a new and powerful tool to optimize concrete properties.

Concrete properties other than compressive strength can be optimised in particular.

Durability under arbitrarily chosen conditions can be predicted in a realistic way.

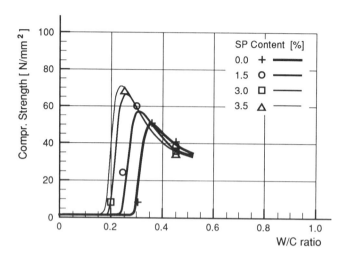

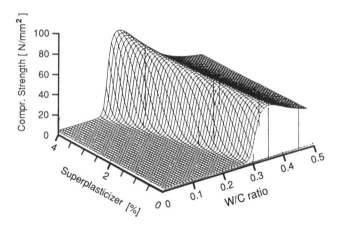

Fig. 8 Compressive strength as function of water/cement ratio. The content of superplasticiser (SP) has been varied between 0% and 3.5% of the cement content and is indicated as a parameter.

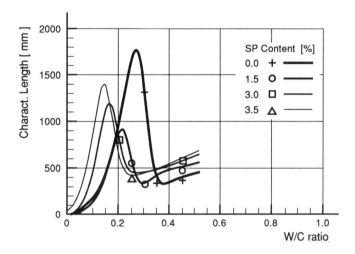

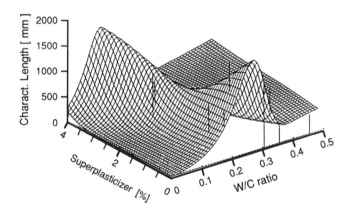

Fig. 9 Characteristic length of concrete as determined with equ. (1) as function of water/cement ratio. The content of superplasticiser (SP) has been varied between 0% and 3.5% of the cement content and is indicated as a parameter.

REFERENCES

1. SHÖNENBURG, E., HANSEN, N., GAWELCZYK, A.: Neuronale Netzwerke. Markt & Technik Verlag, München 1990.

2. KRATZER, K.P.: Neuronale Netze. Karl Hanser Verlag, München 1990.

3. MARTINOLA, G.: Anwendung der neuronalen Netzwerke zur Charakterisierung der Einflüsse auf ausgewählte Eigenschaften hochfester Betone. Diploma Thesis, Institute for Building Materials, ETH Zürich, 1992.

4. GROLIMUND, L.H. and HÄUTLE, H.: Optimierung der Dotierung von Zn-O Varistoren mit Hilfe von neuronalen Netzwerken. Diploma Thesis, Institut für Signal- und Informationsverarbeitung, ETH Zürich, 1990/1991.

5. BRÜHWILER, E. and WITTMANN F.H.: The Wedge Splitting Test, a new method of performing stable Fracture Mechanics tests. Engineering Fracture Mechancis, Vol. 35, 117 - 125, 1990

NEW GENERATION OF ADMIXTURES
FOR WETSHOTCRETING

J F Drs

Master Builders Technologies

Austria

S Valenti

Master Builders Technologies

Switzerland

ABSTRACT. The key parameters of the wet shotcreting process are considered to be: hydration control, slump, slump retention, cohesiveness of the concrete, pumpability, sprayability, compatibility with fibres, rebound, waste material, setting time and strength development. A new generation of admixtures have been developed which permit a very high control of all the above mentioned parameters. This new admixture generation represents a significant contribution to the wet process in shotcrete technology.

Keywords: shotcrete, wet mix process, hydration control, Delvocrete, concrete rheology, rebound.

Josef F DRS is a chemist and head of the Research and Development Laboratory at MBT Austria, which belongs to the Technology Centre of MBT Europe in Schlieren/CH. His research work concentrates on shotcrete and tunnelling products.

Salvatore Valenti is a chemist and head of the Technology Centre of MBT Europe in Schlieren/CH, Switzerland. His research work concentrates on new products, systems and technologies in the construction field.

Concrete 2000. Edited by Ravindra K. Dhir and M. Roderick Jones.
© 1993 Published by E & FN Spon. ISBN 0 419 18120 2.

INTRODUCTION

Shotcrete is concrete projected into place at high velocity and compacted by its own momentum. There are two types of shotcreting system. Dry mix shotcrete is shotcrete based on a dry mix. The dry mix is conveyed by compressed air to a nozzle where the water is added. Wet mix shotcrete is shotcrete based on a wet mix. The wet mixed concrete is pumped to the nozzle where high velocity air is used to propel the mix into position. Dry mixes in general consist of binder and either naturally moist or dry aggregate. Wet mixes consist of binder, aggregate, water and admixtures. Thin concrete flow is the pneumatic conveying of the pre-mix concrete to the point of placement; the loose dry mix is conveyed through the delivery line by a compressed air stream. Dense concrete flow is the way the wet mix is pumped to the nozzle without being loosened.

The nozzle through which the mix is discharged from the delivery line, consists of a pipe with a mixing unit into which liquid and/or air is injected. With the dry process, water and liquid admixtures are added, with the wet process liquid admixtures and the so called propellant air are added. Rebound is a characteristic waste product resulting from the shotcreting process. It is the material passing the nozzle, which does not adhere to the surface on which the shotcrete is being applied. Rebound primarily consists of aggregate and, to a lesser extent, of binder and water. The quantities of rebound are between 20 and 30% of the premix for dry mix shotcreting and 10 to 20% for wet mix shotcreting.

PARAMETERS

Influencing Factors

The hydration process of the cement when shotcreting depends on the wet process and the rheology of the concrete.

Hydration Control

Wet mix shotcrete consists of a ready mixed concrete at a pumpable consistency. It is pumped in a dense concrete flow, to a nozzle where a liquid accelerator and a so-called propellant (high pressurised) air are added before the concrete stream hits the substrate with high velocity.

The equipment used for this method requires a concrete mix which can be easily pumped. The pumps and hoses require a pumpable mixture of fluid consistency (slump 150 - 200 mm). These requirements for high workability concrete require the use of large quantities of setting accelerators, which lead to a loss of strength in the final product.

The useful life of the fresh concrete is also very limited (usually about 40 - 120 mins), which means that the concrete has to be sprayed very quickly after it has been mixed. Should there by any interruptions, as frequently occurs in tunnel operations, you might have a mixer full of concrete, together with the concrete in the pumps and pump lines, which must then be thrown away. This can also be a problem with repair work because this type of work might take a long time to carry out and as hydration is continuously taking place, it might be necessary to throw away 50% of the concrete or more.

In traditional wet mix shotcrete, it is necessary to work with a compromise between high slump, low W/C ratio, long potlife, fast setting and high early strength. This situation is a headache for ready mix producers, applicators and owners. It causes large amounts of wasted material, its production flexibility is very limited, it has limited distances for transportation, it creates overtime, it requires work in the batching plant, and it is costly due to the waiting time for trucks etc. Inevitably, this leads to an increase in costs to everyone involved in the project.

The Delvocrete System offers all kinds of flexibility when using set shotcrete mixes. Lengthy transportation or long storage times do not lead to any loss in the quality. The mixes are always fresh, because hydration only starts when the DELVO^R Activator S is added to the stabilised concrete. The concrete can even be left for 5-6 hours in the pumps and hoses, without being cleaned.

General Description and Use of Delvocrete

Delvocrete is a two-component, nonchloride chemical system which allows control of the dynamics of cement hydration. Delvocrete means DELVO^R technology for shotcrete. The original DELVO^R technology was developed by Master Builders USA and has been in use for several years for ordinary concrete.

Returned plastic concrete treated with DELVO^R Stabiliser can be kept in a plastic state in the drum of a ready-mix truck, or in a central holding vessel for a few hours, overnight or even over a weekend. On the same day, the next day or after a weekend, the stabilised concrete can be activated (if necessary) and combined with freshly manufactured concrete and sent to a job site.

The DELVO^R Stabiliser, when dispensed into plastic concrete, stops cement hydration by forming a protective barrier around cementitious particles. This barrier prevents Portland cement, microsilica, fly ash and granulated slag from achieving initial set. The DELVO^R Activator, when dispensed into stabilised concrete, breaks down the protective barrier around cementitous particles, and permits normal cement hydration to proceed.

Concrete treatment with DELVO^R will result in concrete performance equal or superior to reference concrete manufactured conventionally. There are numerous applications for ready-mix producers including:

- overnight/weekend stabilization of concrete wash water from truck drums.
- same day stabilization of returned plastic concrete.
- same day stabilization of conventionally manufactured concrete for long hauls.
- same day stabilization of returned plastic concrete/conventionally manufactured concrete during truck breakdowns.
- overnight/weekend stabilization of concrete wash water for central mixers.
- same day/overnight stabilization of left over concrete from pump lines in the concrete-hopper.
- overnight/weekend stabilization of retuned plastic concrete.

The recommended dosage range of DELVO^R Stabilizer for the same day, overnight and weekend stabilization of concrete is 0.6 - 2.0% of cement weight. Activation of such stabilized concrete is achieved by adding DELVO^R ActivatorS.

For shotcrete applications, a special DELVO^R Activator S was developed, which not only reactivates but also accelerates the setting of shotcrete. It is a liquid admixture which can be added like a conventional setting accelerator at the nozzle. Normal dosage is between 3 - 8% of cement weight.

Delvocrete in practice: The Flurlinger Tunnel

The Flurlinger tunnel, at the border of the city Schaffhausen in Switzerland, is part of the highway N4. The total length of the tunnel is 1400m, from which 1100m was constructed by drilling and blasting and the rest by cut and cover. Total shotcrete volume: ca. 16.000 m^3.

Tunnel construction started in 1988. The underground part was constructed from two ends. For shotcreting both methods were used at the beginning. The wet-mix process in the North end, the dry-mix in the South end.

In the North, a batching plant was installed on the site to produce the concrete. Due to the close residential area, production was only allowed between 7 am and 10 pm. But the time schedule required a change to a 24 hour day. Therefore the problem of producing the shotcrete mixes for the nightshift, without using the batching plant after 10 pm, had to be solved.

Delvocrete was a simple and very effective solution for the contractor. All the wet mixes for the night shotcrete application could be produced with DELVO^R Stabilizer during the day and stored in 2-3 truck mixers. During the night the shotcrete mix was always available in the right consistency and it could be sprayed in the ordinary way, adding DELVO^R Activator S and liquid admixtures in the nozzle.

Used mix design (per m^3):

- Cement	425 Kg
- Aggregate	0-16 mm
- Rheobuild 1000	0.8%
- DELVO^R Stabilizer	0.6%
- DELVO^R Activator S	5.0%
- W/C ratio	0.45

Concrete flow:	immediately after mixing:	60 cm
		after 4 hours: 58 cm
		after 8 hours: 56 cm

Required compressive strength after 28 days was 25 N/mm^2. With Delvocrete 33.4 N/mm^2 was achieved on average.

The shotcrete was applied with a piston pump for spraying a MEYCO^R Robojet was used. Delvocrete improved the working efficiency significantly:

- Rebound was reduced from 18 to 8-10%
- Optimal slump and consistency, even after several hours, therefore higher throughput of the spraying machine
- No waiting time, shotcrete always available
- No wasted shotcrete
- No cleaning due to interruptions
- No staff needed for the batching plant during the night shift

Delvocrete was only planned, in the beginning, for night application. Due to the very positive experiences and the improved quality and efficiency, it was decided to use the new admixture system also during the day (with a reduced DELVO^3 Stabilizer dosage of 0.4%). In addition the shotcrete method was changed in the South end of the Flurlinger Tunnel, from the dry to the wet-mix process, using identical equipment and the same mix-design as in the North end.

Summary

Delvocrete sets new standards in the world of shotcrete. The Delvocrete system overcomes traditional drawbacks of shotcrete by providing total flexibility, from batching, delivery, storage, to application in both the wet and dry-mixes. With the wet-mix method, cleaning the machinery, due to continuous working interruptions, is no longer necessary. Delvocrete is the new high technical tool for both repair and rock support application.

Rheology of wet shotcrete-mixes

Shotcrete is one of many ways to cast concrete. During the application, wet shotcreting has to deal with the following requirements:

(1)   Good pumpability, with low w/c - ratio
(2)   Be thixotropic when it hits the substrate (must get thixotropic behaviour within seconds, from time it leaves the nozzle till it hits the substrate) in order to be able to build thicker layers without trickling)

In order to be able to fulfil these requirements and needs, higher amounts of different types of admixtures have to be used. Only a few years ago, the major requirements for shotcrete were fast setting and high early strengths. This can quite easily be obtained by using setting accelerators based on aluminate. But this will not gain the quality and longterm durability of the shotcrete because of the large decrease in final strength and quality.

Today shotcrete is used in many different ways, not only as temporary rock support, but also more and more often as a permanent support and final lining in underground construction, in slope protection, repair work for concrete and it is also used for new buildings and new constructions.

This leads to new demands and requirements for wet shotcreting:

- Minimal decrease of final strength of the sprayed concrete compared to plain fresh concrete
- Good compaction - high density
- Homogeneous concrete
- Waterproofed
- Minimal rebound
- Chemical resistance to sulphate, etc
- Low dosage of activators and accelerators

Slumpkilling System

The Slumpkilling system is a two component, chloride free system. The Slumpkilling process is based on the interaction of the two components, resulting in a sharp loss of slump at the moment of their mixing.

Slumpkilling in itself does not influence the setting of the concrete. However a rapid (fast) setting and high early strength can be achieved if desired by adding an accelerator to the slumpkiller component.

Slumpkilling is a process which occurs when two components are mixed together:

- One of the components is added to the concrete during mixing, combined with a superplasticiser. It can also be added directly into the truck mixer.

- The second component is added into the concrete through the shotcrete nozzle in the same way as a traditional accelerator or activator.

There are two different systems of Slumpkilling for wet shotcreting:

- One for Rock Support

- One for Repair, Final lining without requirements of fast setting and early strength

Slumpkilling for Rock Support - Wet Shotcreting:

The Slumpkilling System for Rock Support for wet shotcrete consists of the following components:

- XA 3520 - added into the concrete during mixing, at the batching plant or into the truck mixer.

- Activator XA 65 - added in the nozzle during spraying.

The System gives the following advantages:

● It causes a reduction of rebound and in particular a dramatic reduction of fibre rebound, because the fibres have a better orientation in plastic concrete. Practical experience shows that the fibre rebound can be reduced by up to 50%, compared to the use of normal accelerators.

- Fibre rebound is a typical problem with use of long fibres (more and more in use), and a big loss of fibres causes a reduction in the toughness value. Practical experience has also shown that the toughness index of I^{30} has increased by more than 25% with the use of the Slumpkilling System.

- Improved pumpability, especially with coarse aggregates, with a lack of fineness or with steelfibre concrete.

- Better slump retention than normal superplasticisers.

- More homogeneous concrete, allows you to work with very flowable concrete without any risk of segregation.

Slumpkilling for Repair and Final Lining:

The Slumpkilling system for LC Repair consists of the following components:

XA 3520 - added into the concrete during mixing, at the batching plant or in the truck mixer.

Activator XA90 - added in the nozzle during spraying

The System gives the following advantages:

- You can spray thicker layers vertically and overhead without tricking and problems with the bonding.
- No influence on the cement's setting time, give you a longer open time for surface finish (like trowelling, etc).
- No decrease in the final strength.
- Improves pumpability.
- More homogeneous concrete, allows you to work with very flowable concrete without any risk of segregation.
- Better slump retention and a longer open time on the fresh concrete than normal superplasticisers.

PRODUCTS

XA3520

XA3520 is based on a new polymer technology which has not been used on the market before and gives benefits to the concrete properties, especially the pumpability. In particular at lower contents of cement and by lack of fineness in the aggregates. This makes workability independent of the grading of the sand, primarily due to the thickening and stabilizing on the mix.

XA3520 is supplied as a liquid superplasticiser. Dosage range in wet shotcrete: 1-1.8% c.w.

It is possible to obtain a Rheoplastic concrete with a slump of 200-240 mm and a no slump concrete but very fluid and not segregating at all. The peculiarity of this product is better answered in the workability and pumpability of concrete with low content or lack of fineness, low cement content, concrete containing fibres or deficient grading.

Additionally XA 3520 has a good slump retention compared to normal traditional superplasticisers.

XA3520 will, like Silica concrete, produce a thixotropic characteristic and increase the cohesiveness, this is easily broken when the concrete is moved during pouring, pumping or during external or internal vibration. Experience shows that this small decrease of slump does not cause any problems and can be avoided or eliminated by using a higher dosage of XA 3520. Never add more water!!

XA3520 is also suitable for all situations where a low slump loss is required: long transportation time, massive pouring, hot climates and for pumping.

XA65 - Activator for Rock Support

XA 65 is the second component in the Slumpkilling system for rock support.

XA65 can also be used in combination with Delvo Stabilizer and works as an activator. Dosage: 2-5% of the cement weight.

An important property and a difference between XA 65 and ordinary accelerator is, that the concrete is more plastic when it hits the substrate (delays setting by a few seconds). The concrete has only lost the slump and has received the thixotropic characteristics, so it is possible to achieve bonding and avoid trickling.

XA 90 Activator for Repair/Final Lining

XA 90 is the second component in the Slumpkilling system for Repair/Final Lining, where there are no requirements for fast setting or early strength. It is a liquid admixture. XA 90 does not have any influence on the cements setting time and you achieve a long open time for finishing the surface. XA 90 is added into the nozzle as a normal activator. It replaces the use of traditional accelerators.

If you require fast setting and early strength you must switch to XA 65. When XA 90 is added to the concrete it kills the slump immediately and forms a thixotropic concrete which can adhere in thicker layers vertically and overhead without trickling and no problems with bonding.

Dosage: 2-5 l per m^3 Normal dosing equipment can be used but XA 90 is very sensitive to dosage. Therefore, always use a needle valve to finely tune to the right dosage.

Examples of the practical use of the Slumpkiller system

Rock Support:

- Kiruna mines, Sweden
- Wet shortcreting - 16.000 m^3 per year
- Combined with the Delvorcrete system
- Robot Type: AMV 6400

Problems:

- Coarse sand, with a lack of fineness. Problem with pumpability
- Long transport and problem with slump loss

Requirements: 32 MPa, 28 days

Normal Mix:

- Cement   450 kg
- Silica   30 kg
- Sand   1480 kg
- Pozzolith 322   5 kg
- W/C + S   0.48
- Slump   16-18

New Slumpkilling mix:

- Cement   390 kg
- Silica   25 kg
- Sand   1480 kg
- Delvo Stabilizer   0.6% C.W.
- XA 3520   3 kg
- Pozzolith 322 N   1 kg
- W/C + S   0.5
- Slump   25 cm
- Activator: XA 65   53% C.W.

Result:

- Higher early strength (within 2 hours)
- Reduced rebound
- Better pumpability - reduced pump pressure
- Decreased activator consumption (50% reduction to approx. 3% cW.)
- Long open time - measured slump 26 cm after 1½ hours.

Due to the results it has been decided to change to slumpkiller system during afternoon/night and weekend, combined with Delvocrete.

CONCLUSION

Systems and products like Delvocrete and Slumpkilling, open up new possibilities and areas for the use of shotcrete. The Systems are the new and future generation of shotcrete admixtures, which also contribute to improved quality, increased production and decreased waste material and therefore reduce the final costs per m^3 applied shotcrete.

CLOSING ADDRESS

Dr Tom A Harrison
Technical Director
British Ready Mixed Concrete Association
United Kingdom

Chairman

Professor P C Hewlett
British Board of Agrément
United Kingdom

INDEX OF AUTHORS

SUBJECT INDEX

This index has been compiled from the keywords assigned to the papers, edited and extended as appropriate. The page references are to the first page of the relevant paper. Volume One – pages 1–928. Volume Two – pages 929–1907.

Protection of Concrete

Proceedings of the International Conference, University of Dundee, September 1990

Edited by **Dr Ravindra K Dhir**, Director Concrete Technology Unit, Department of Civil Engineering, University of Dundee, Scotland, UK and **Jeffrey W Green**, Industrial consultant in concrete technology, University of Dundee, Scotland, UK

Concrete is arguably the major construction material used worldwide. It has generally served well, yet too often it has failed to achieve the required performance. Although developments in materials and practice have widened the scope for the use of concrete, they have also had effects on its performance. This book presents current thinking and future developments on means of protecting concrete and ensuring its adequate performance in the required application.

Contents: Preface. Concrete - the construction material. Methods of protecting concrete - coatings and linings. Protection of structural concrete. Protection through design. Protection through construction. Impact on current practice of the integrated European market. Index.

September 1990: 234x156: 1136pp
Hardback: 0-419-15490-6: £94.00

E & F N Spon
An imprint of Chapman & Hall

Structural Lightweight Aggregate Concrete

Edited by **J L Clarke,** Senior Engineer, Special Structures Dept., Sir William Halcrow & Partners, London, UK, formerly of British Cement Assocation, UK

Lightweight aggregate concrete is undergoing something of a renaissance. Although this material has been available for many years, only now is it being used more widely. The volume of structural aggregate concrete used each year is increasing dramatically. Lower structural weight, better fire resistence, use of waste for aggregate, lower costs for aggregate: all these factors are contributing to the rapid increase in the use of acceptance of structural lightweight aggregate concrete. This book provides a comprehensive review of this growing field from an international perspective.

Contents: Lightweight aggregates for structural concrete - *P L Owens.*
Properties of structural lightweight aggregate concrete - *J B Newman.*
Design requirements - *J L Clarke.* Construction - *R N W Pankhurst.*
Lightweight concrete in buildings - *D Lazarus.* Lightweight concrete in bridges - *J H J Manhoudt.* Lightweight concrete for special structures - *B K Bardhan-Roy.* Appendices. Index.

"This volume provides a comprehensive review of the subject from an international perspective." - *British Bookseller*

July 1993: 234x156: 256pp, 80 line illus, 20 halftone illus
Hardback: 0-7514-0006-8: £65.00

Blackie Academic & Professional

An imprint of Chapman & Hall

Fracture and Damage of Concrete and Rock - FDCR-2

Edited by **H P Rossmanith**, Institute of Mechanics, Technical University Vienna, Austria

This book forms the Proceedings of the International Conference held in Vienna in November 1992 dealing with ageing, fatigue and fracture of concrete and concrete structures. Special sections cover demolition and recycling, and anchorage engineering. As well as selected international contributions, five specially invited plenary papers are included from Austria, Spain, Japan, Denmark and Sweden.

Selected Contents: **Part 1: Fracture modelling:** modelling cracking, microcracks in toughening, plasticity softening model, micromechanics and localization, softening curves, flexural strength of sfrc, fractal geometry and size effect, simulation of concrete cracking, environmental factors for post-tensioning, high strength concrete, sigma-w relation **Part 2: Mixed mode fracture and damage:** acoustic emission & mixed-mode loading, mixed-mode fracture propagation, granular microcracked models, acoustic emission & crack identification, multi-domain BEM, BEM for inhomogeneous materials. **Part 3: Fatigue:** concrete & fatigue damage, cyclic loading & FE analysis, cyclic behaviour of beams, damage due to temperature changes, progressive fracture of rock. **Part 4: Demolition and recycling:** recycling of concrete and masonry: goals & barriers, recycled aggregates with fly-ash, demolition & recycling of an RC bridge, anti-bacterial ability of concrete. **Part 5: Fracture and damage of rock:** microdefected materials, multi-scale microcracking, damage model for interacting microcracks, damage propagation of jointed rock, damage of interfaces in layered rock, branching under compressive loading, sliding mode cracks in rock, destruction of rock, informational model of rock destruction, local rock fracture under shock, nonlinear theory of vibrations, dilatant fracturing of geomaterials, loading rates & fracture toughness of rock. **Part 6: Applications:** hydraulic fracturing, cavitation damage in concrete, crack propagation, buckling of shells, seismic loading, 3-D analysis of slab-column connection, slender RC beams, thermal cracks in mass concrete. **Part 7: Anchorage engineering:** bonded anchors, numerical simulation, FE models and pull-out test, FE analysis of anchor bolt pull-out, pull-out of steel anchors, load-bearing capacity of anchor bolts, anchor bolts in plane stress, numerical analysis of bolts in concrete plates, anchorage of strands in precast concrete, glass fiber materials, AE analysis, concrete fatigue fracture, plate anchors in sands. **Part 8: Austrian innovative construction:** Austrian innovative construction. Index.

E & F N Spon: April 1993: 234x156: 700 pp: 150 line illus, 29 halftone illus: Hardback: 0-419-18470-8

For more information or to order your copy, please contact: **The Promotion Dept.**, E & F N SPON, 2-6 Boundary Row, London SE1 8HN Tel: 071 865 0066 Fax: 071 522 9623

Durability of Concrete Structures

Investigation, repair, protection

Edited by **Dr G C Mays,** Head of Civil Engineering Group, School of Mechanical, Materials and Civil Engineering, Royal Military College of Science (Cranfield), Shrivenham, UK

In the rapid expansion of the construction industry during the 1960s basic advice regarding cover to reinforcement and impermeability of concrete to moisture for subsequent durability often went unheeded. Today the UK is seeing the result - a £500 million per annum programme of concrete repair - and similar effects are being observed worldwide. The book draws together experts from the fields of concrete durability, repair and protection to provide a state-of-the-art review on current thinking, materials and techniques. The basic deterioration mechanisms and methods for the site investigation of distressed concrete structures are initially considered. Materials and techniques for repair are critically reviewed and relatively novel ideas for protection are discussed. The second part of the book is presented as a series of case studies for various structure types. They are written by those who have immediate experience of both the technical and financial difficulties of concrete repair and maintenance programmes.

November 1991: 234x156: 288pp, 49 photographs, 40 line diagrams
Hardback: 0-419-15620-8: £32.00

E & F N Spon
An imprint of Chapman & Hall